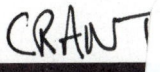

SPSS-X User's Guide

3rd Edition

SPSS Inc.
444 N. Michigan Avenue
Chicago, Illinois 60611
312.329.3500

SPSS International B.V
P.O. Box 115
4200 AC Gorinchem
The Netherlands
Tel. +31.1830.36711
Twx.: 21019 (SPSS NL)

For more information about SPSS-X™ and other software produced and distributed by SPSS Inc., please write or call

Marketing Department
SPSS Inc.
444 North Michigan Avenue
Chicago, IL 60611
312/329-3500

In Europe and the Middle East, please write or call

SPSS International B.V.
P.O. Box 115
4200 AC Gorinchem
The Netherlands
+31.1830.36711
Twx: 21019 (SPSS nl)
Fax: +31.1830.35839

SPSS-X™ User's Guide, 3rd ed.
Copyright © 1988 by SPSS Inc.
All rights reserved.
Printed in the United States of America.
No part of this publication may be reproduced, stored in a retrieval system, or transmitted, in any form or by any means, electronic, mechanical, photocopying, recording, or otherwise, without the prior written permission of the publisher.

6 7 8 9 0   91 90

ISBN 0-918469-51-1

Library of Congress Catalog Card Number: 87-062349

Preface

This third edition of *SPSS-X User's Guide* documents the SPSS-X™ Data Analysis System, Release 3.0. For users of SPSS-X releases through 2.2, the second edition remains in print. Users of Release 2.2 should also consult the additional information available via the INFO command.

SPSS-X is a comprehensive, integrated system for managing, analyzing, and displaying data. For an overview of its capabilities, see the Overviews to the three major parts of this manual and the sample job in Chapter 1. SPSS-X has been substantially extended in Release 3. Some of the new features are:

- Interactive execution, providing immediate evaluation of commands and a substantial online help system.

- A macro language that makes it possible to build new commands from combinations of existing ones, execute procedures repeatedly with slight variations in specifications, assign and use group names for lists of variables, and generally exploit new flexibility in creating SPSS-X commands.

- Nonlinear regression: two procedures to provide the best method for handling constrained and unconstrained models.

- Keyword control of options to all procedures, replacing the OPTIONS and STATISTICS commands (which remain functional for compatibility).

- Additional control over REPORT, plus a new automatic format that reduces the number of specifications needed to obtain attractive reports.

- European number and currency formats.

In addition, several options are available to extend the capabilities of SPSS-X in special areas. SPSS-X Tables, a powerful table builder offering high quality output, contains new facilities in Release 3. New with Release 3 is SPSS-X Trends, an extensive set of procedures for analyzing time series data. SPSS-X Capture provides direct access to database files. Versions are available for several popular database systems, and more are under development. SPSS-X Track gives system managers the tools to analyze the performance of VAX/VMS systems.

Using This Manual. This manual is both a reference to SPSS-X facilities and a guide to their use. To help with access to information, it is divided into three major parts:

- Part A introduces the system and its language. The sample job in Chapter 1 illustrates how the command structure works to perform an analysis. Chapter 2 formally introduces the SPSS-X language, and Chapter 3 shows how to run a job, both interactively and in batch mode. Chapter 4 documents the utilities available to help you control the way SPSS-X operates.

- Part B documents all of the commands for defining, transforming, and managing data.

- Part C documents SPSS-X procedures. It is arranged alphabetically for quick use as a reference. The Overview to this part summarizes the procedures according to the type of analysis they perform.

Several additional features of this manual are provided to help you find the information you need with a minimum of searching:

- Use the thumb index, with its guide inside the back cover, to quickly locate the information you need.

- Consult the outline at the beginning of each chapter for an overview of the topics that are discussed.

- Use the syntax summary at the beginning of each chapter as an overview of the commands discussed in the chapter and as a quick reference to command specifications.
- Use the full index, at the back of the manual, to locate specific information.
- Look for annotated examples set off on separate, shaded pages in each chapter. These examples put the facility being discussed into the context of a complete SPSS-X job.
- If you are familiar with earlier versions of SPSS, turn to Appendix H, "Help for Old Friends," for a discussion of changes.
- Tear out the reference card at the back of the manual, and use it for quick checks on syntax requirements.

Additional Documentation. SPSS-X is supported by other manuals that supplement this document in the areas of statistics and applications. The following manuals are available:

SPSS-X Basics
SPSS Inc.

This manual introduces the SPSS-X system through a series of progressively broadening tasks.

The SPSS Guide to Data Analysis
Marija J. Norusis, Rush-Presbyterian-St. Luke's Medical Center

An introduction to statistics and data analysis, this textbook begins with a discussion of how data are collected and coded and proceeds with a simple, systematic presentation of statistics, the underlying assumptions of data analysis, and the use of SPSS-X to get results.

SPSS-X Introductory Statistics Guide
Marija J. Norusis, Rush-Presbyterian-St. Luke's Medical Center

This text features introductions to statistics with instructions for performing sample analyses with SPSS-X. It is intended as a supplementary guide for teaching and for personal use. It carries the reader from basic statistics through multiple regression.

SPSS-X Advanced Statistics Guide
Marija J. Norusis, Rush-Presbyterian-St. Luke's Medical Center

Designed for researchers and for use in the multivariate statistics course, this text covers regression, discriminant, factor, and cluster analysis; multivariate and repeated measures analysis of variance; and log-linear models. It includes a reference section on SPSS-X commands and a brief introduction to data definition and management.

SPSS-X TABLES
SPSS Inc.

The TABLES procedure, an optional enhancement to the SPSS-X system, produces presentation-quality stub-and-banner tables. The manual includes both a reference section and a user's guide illustrating how to build and combine tables; handle multiple response data; extract percentages based on rows, columns, or subtables; and so on.

SPSS-X Trends
SPSS Inc.

Another optional enhancement to SPSS-X, Trends includes many facilities for handling time series data—from basic curve fitting and exponential smoothing through sophisticated ARIMA models. Its features are documented in this manual, along with examples illustrating various approaches to time series analysis.

SPSS Inc. Reports

The following reports provide additional information about more specialized topics:

SPSS Statistical Algorithms. A complete guide to the computational algorithms used by SPSS-X procedures. (Current through SPSS-X 2.2.)

USERPROC LISREL: Using LISREL VI within SPSS-X. LISREL VI, a program that analyzes linear structural relations, is available as an SPSS-X option. The report on LISREL VI contains a command summary and information on using LISREL within SPSS-X. The report supplements the LISREL VI user's manual available from Scientific Software, Inc.

SPSS-X User Code: Adding User Programs to SPSS-X. The user code facilities allow users to add programs to SPSS-X to define and analyze data. These facilities can be used to build links between SPSS-X and data-base management systems. Separate editions are available for IBM (CMS and MVS) and for Digital VAX/VMS.

SPSS-X Processing of U.S. Census Data.

SPSS-X Capture. Versions are available for VAX/DATATRIEVE, IBM SQL/DS, and HP3000.

SPSS-X Track for VAX/VMS.

Programmer's Guide to SPSS-X Data File Formats. Available in separate editions for IBM, DECSYSTEM 20, VAX, and Prime.

SPSS-X is constantly undergoing enhancements. For information about additional documentation and updates to the system itself, use the INFO command, documented in Chapter 2. If you want to keep up to date with SPSS-X (and related products and services from SPSS Inc.), fill out the return card enclosed in this manual, or contact SPSS Inc. at the address or phone number given below. We will send you a copy of our newsletter and let you know about SPSS Inc. activities in your area.

Marketing Department
SPSS Inc.
444 North Michigan Avenue
Chicago, IL 60611
(312) 329-3500

In Europe, contact

SPSS International B.V.
Avelingen West 80
P.O. Box 115
4200 AC Gorinchem
The Netherlands
Tel. +31.1830.36711
Twx. 21019
Fax +31.1830.35839

Contents

Part I
An Introduction to the System 1

Chapter **1** A Sample SPSS-X Job 3

2 The SPSS-X Language 8

3 Running SPSS-X 16

CLEAR TRANSFORMATIONS
EDIT
EXECUTE
HELP
HOST
INCLUDE
INFO
NEW FILE

4 Controlling the Environment 28

COMMENT
FINISH
NUMBERED/UNNUMBERED
SET
SHOW
SUBTITLE
TITLE

Part II
Data Definition and Management 47

Chapter **5** Defining Data 54

ADD VALUE LABELS
BEGIN DATA/END DATA
DATA LIST
FILE HANDLE
MISSING VALUES
VALUE LABELS
VARIABLE LABELS

6 SPSS-X System Files 88

DISPLAY
DOCUMENT
DROP DOCUMENTS
FILE LABEL
GET
SAVE
XSAVE

7 Numeric Transformations 108

COMPUTE
COUNT
DO REPEAT/END REPEAT
LEAVE
NUMERIC
RECODE
TEMPORARY

8 String Transformations 140

RECODE
STRING

9 Conditional Transformations 154

IF
DO IF/ELSE IF/END IF

Chapter **10**   Printing and Writing Cases   168

FORMATS
PRINT
PRINT EJECT
PRINT FORMATS
PRINT SPACE
WRITE
WRITE FORMATS

11   Selecting, Sampling, and Weighting Cases   182

N OF CASES
SAMPLE
SELECT IF
WEIGHT

12   Defining Complex File Structures   192

FILE TYPE/END FILE TYPE
RECORD TYPE
REPEATING DATA

13   Defining Matrices   218

MATRIX DATA
MCONVERT

14   Input Programs   246

BREAK
END CASE
END FILE
INPUT PROGRAM/END INPUT PROGRAM
LOOP/END LOOP
REREAD
VECTOR

Chapter **15**   Sorting and Splitting Files   268

SORT
SPLIT FILE

16   Combining System Files   276

ADD FILES
MATCH FILES
UPDATE

17   File Interfaces   302

EXPORT
GET BMDP
GET OSIRIS
GET SAS
GET SCSS
IMPORT
SAVE SCSS

Part III
Data Analysis and Reporting   323

Chapter **18**   AGGREGATE   328

19   ALSCAL   338

20   ANOVA   364

21   AUTORECODE   378

22   BOX-JENKINS   384

23   CLUSTER   404

24   CORRELATIONS   418

25   CROSSTABS   428

26   DESCRIPTIVES   446

27   DISCRIMINANT   454

28   FACTOR   480

Chapter **29** FREQUENCIES   500

30 HILOGLINEAR   514

31 LIST   530

32 LOGLINEAR   536

33 MANOVA   568

34 MEANS   642

35 MULT RESPONSE   656

36 Nonlinear Regression   676

CNLR
NLR

37 NONPAR CORR   722

38 NPAR TESTS   732

39 ONEWAY   758

40 PARTIAL CORR   774

41 PLOT   788

42 PROBIT   804

43 PROXIMITIES   822

44 QUICK CLUSTER   840

45 REGRESSION   848

46 RELIABILITY   872

47 REPORT   890

48 SURVIVAL   954

49 T-TEST   968

Appendixes

A The Macro Facility   978

DEFINE
!ENDDEFINE
!DO/!DOEND
!BREAK
!IF/!THEN/!ELSE/!IFEND
PRESERVE
RESTORE

B Command Order   994

C IMPORT/EXPORT Character Sets   999

D Writing User Programs   1003

E Reading Direct Access and Keyed Files   1005
KEYED DATA LIST
POINT

F VAX Data Types   1017

G Portable Files from SAS   1023
TOSPSS

H Help for Old Friends   1027
REFORMAT

References   1045

Index   1049

Part 1: An Introduction to the System

Part I: An Introduction to the System

The SPSS-X™ system is a comprehensive tool for managing, analyzing, and displaying information. It can take data from almost any type of file (or combine several files) and turn them into meaningful information: tabulated reports, plots of distributions and trends, and results of a wide variety of statistical procedures. It brings together data management, report writing, and statistical analysis in one comprehensive system with a single language.

The quickest way to begin an acquaintance with the way SPSS-X works is to examine a sample job. Chapter 1 provides such a job to illustrate how individual SPSS-X commands work together to define, manage, and analyze data. Chapter 2 then sets out the general rules for creating SPSS-X commands, and Chapter 3 follows with information about submitting commands and obtaining output, both in batch mode and the new interactive mode. Chapter 3 also tells you how to test jobs with EDIT runs before committing yourself to an expensive reading of a large data file without knowing that your analysis commands are syntactically correct.

SPSS-X is set up by SPSS Inc., and then often revised by individual sites, with a number of preset values for such things as page width and length, whether variable and value labels should be in upper and lower case, how blanks in the input file should be handled, how many times a loop may be executed, and how many errors should be tolerated before processing ends. Chapter 4 tells how to display these values with the SHOW command and change them with SET. Chapter 4 also documents other utilities for annotating your commands and placing titles on your output. Chapter 4 is the place to consult whenever you want to change some of the basic ways SPSS-X operates.

SPSS-X contains extensive facilities for getting data into the system from various types of data files, managing and storing data files, and manipulating data with functions that modify current variables and create new ones. For an overview of these facilities, plus important information on how SPSS-X uses files, see the Overview to Part II.

Most SPSS-X jobs employ at least one of the statistical and reporting procedures available in the system. These procedures are presented alphabetically in Part III. The Overview to Part III outlines the procedures available for different types of reports and analyses.

With Release 3, SPSS-X contains a macro facility that allows you to alter considerably the way the system appears to operate. Macros generate SPSS-X commands according to rules you set up. You can include a few macros in a job, perhaps to convey a variable list to several different procedures or to automatically change the title of a report to include the month under consideration. Or you can build a complex macro that governs an entire job. This facility is documented in Appendix A.

SPSS-X runs on a wide variety of computers and operating systems. Each of these requires some additional documentation for things that are specific to that version of SPSS-X, such as file- naming conventions. This information, as well as information about features that might have been added since publication of this manual, is available from within SPSS-X by means of the INFO command described in Chapter 3. Also check the Appendixes to this manual for special topics that may be of interest to you.

Chapter 1   A Sample SPSS-X Job

An SPSS-X job consists of a number of commands, from a few to many hundreds, arranged in a logical order to carry out a set of functions. Figure 1.1a illustrates a typical sequence of commands. You could enter these commands interactively one at a time or place them all in a file and enter them all at once in a batch job. The process of entering commands is described in Chapter 3. For now, the way you enter the commands is not important. What is important is how the commands fit together to carry out the desired job. The commands fall into three main steps:

- Bring in some data to create an active file. If the data come from anything other than an SPSS-X system file or one of the other self-defining files that SPSS-X reads, the specifications will have to include names for the variables to be read and the way the values for each variable are recorded in the file.
- Perform any transformations necessary to get the data in shape for analysis. This may involve changing the coding system or creating a new variable based on the values of existing variables.
- Perform one of the procedures that list, tabulate, or analyze the data in the active file.

Each of these steps can be repeated any number of times. To minimize processing time, SPSS-X doesn't actually read the data and create the active file or perform transformations until it needs the data to carry out a procedure. Then it performs all of those operations at once.

1.1
A SAMPLE JOB

In the job in Figure 1.1a, a small amount of data is defined, entered along with the SPSS-X commands, and then used to update an older file containing information about the employment history of a middle-sized company. The variable of interest, average salary increase, isn't included in this file, but it is easily created using beginning and current salaries and the date each employee joined the firm. A listing of a few cases is requested as a way of making sure that the transformation specifications are correct, and then the entire updated file is saved for future use. As SPSS-X saves the file, it also carries out the MEANS analysis requested in the last line of the job. The specific role of each command in this job is discussed below. The output is shown in Figures 1.1b through 1.1d.

SET sets a maximum width of 80 columns for the display file. Width is one of many parameters that can be specified on SET to control the appearance of the output and other functions within SPSS-X operations. (See Chapter 4.)

DATA LIST describes the new data enclosed between the **BEGIN DATA** and **END DATA** commands. The data are in freefield format (with blanks separating values) and contain the two variables ID and SALNOW. ID is the employee identification number, and SALNOW represents salary adjustments made since the last update of the employee file. Once defined, these variables constitute the SPSS-X active file. (See Chapter 5.)

3

Figure 1.1a Input for an SPSS-X job

```
SET WIDTH 80

DATA LIST FREE / ID SALNOW

BEGIN DATA
629 12800
886 7150
962 12667
1112 14300
1129 9600
END DATA

UPDATE FILE=EMPDATA1 / FILE=* / BY ID / MAP

COMPUTE AVGRAISE = (SALNOW-SALBEG)
                    /TRUNC(CTIME.DAYS($TIME-BEGDATE)/365.25)
VARIABLE LABELS   AVGRAISE 'AVERAGE ANNUAL RAISE'
PRINT FORMATS   AVGRAISE (DOLLAR9.2)

LIST VARIABLES = ID BEGDATE SALNOW AVGRAISE
    /CASES = FROM 1 TO 50 BY 5

XSAVE OUTFILE = EMPDATA2

MEANS TABLES = AVGRAISE BY MINORITY BY SEX
```

UPDATE brings in a previously saved SPSS-X system file, EMPDATA1, and uses the current active file (represented as *) to update the salary variable. The cases in the two files are matched by variable ID. Where the IDs match, the new value for SALNOW replaces the value on EMPDATA1. (In this example, it's assumed that EMPDATA1 has a file type, file extension, or other identifying information that corresponds to the defaults established for your particular computer and operating system. See Chapter 5.) The MAP subcommand asks for a record of the variables involved in the updating process. (See Chapter 16.)

COMPUTE creates a new variable, AVGRAISE, the average annual raise. To do this, we subtract beginning salary (SALBEG) from current salary (SALNOW) and divide this number by the number of complete years the employee has worked for the company. To get the number of years, we subtract the beginning date (BEGDATE) from the current date ($TIME, a value supplied by SPSS-X), convert that number to days (the CTIME.DAYS function), divide by 365.25, and finally truncate it to an integer. (See Chapter 7.)

Truncating years in this computation assumes that raises are given at the end of each year of service. For employees with less than a year's service, this function results in an arithmetically impossible division by zero. In this case, SPSS-X issues a warning and assigns a system-missing value, which causes the individual to be excluded from the analysis of average salary increase below.

VARIABLE LABELS supplies the label "AVERAGE ANNUAL RAISE" for AVGRAISE. This label will be used in output from SPSS-X procedures. (See Chapter 5.)

PRINT FORMATS specifies that AVGRAISE be printed in dollar format (with a dollar sign and commas) in a nine-character field including two decimal places. (See Chapter 10.)

LIST simply lists the values of specified variables for the specified cases. (See Chapter 31.)

XSAVE creates a new system file named EMPDATA2. SPSS-X doesn't immediately read the data and create this file; rather, it creates the system file while processing the data to perform the following MEANS. (See Chapter 6.)

MEANS provides means and other descriptive statistics for AVGRAISE within subgroups defined by the categories of MINORITY and SEX within MINORITY. (See Chapter 34.)

Figures 1.1b through 1.1d show the display file created by the sample job. The heading page, which identifies the system and provides some information about the current release, is not shown; nor are the headings at the tops of pages.

As you can see in Figure 1.1b, the SPSS-X display file includes a printback of the commands in the job, along with diagnostic messages and the tabular results of procedures. Thus we learn that the first task, reading in the update file, took .02 CPU seconds. Following the UPDATE command in line 7, SPSS-X prints the requested map of the variables involved, starting with the BY variables used to match cases between files.

We can see in the map of the result file that all of the variables in the result file were present in the old file (INPUT1), while ID and SALNOW were also on the active file INPUT2 (the file that was active before the update process). For ID and SALNOW, values from the active file will take the place of values from EMPDATA1 in the result file.

Figure 1.1b   Command printback and map of the UPDATE result file

```
  1   0            SET WIDTH 80
  2
  3   DATA LIST FREE / ID SALNOW
  4
  5   BEGIN DATA
  6

PRECEDING TASK REQUIRED        0.02 SECONDS CPU TIME;        0.04 SECONDS ELAPSED.

  7   UPDATE FILE=EMPDATA1 / FILE=* / BY ID / MAP
  8

FILE EMPDATA1 SPSSXFIL A1
  LABEL:
    CREATED 14-AUG-87 14:00:45        12 VARIABLES

MAP OF BY VARIABLES

RESULT    INPUT1   INPUT2
------    ------   ------
ID        ID       ID

MAP OF THE RESULT FILE

RESULT    INPUT1   INPUT2      RESULT     INPUT1     INPUT2
------    ------   ------      ------     ------     ------
ID        ID       ID          EDLEVEL    EDLEVEL
SALBEG    SALBEG               WORK       WORK
SEX       SEX                  JOBCAT     JOBCAT
TIME      TIME                 MINORITY   MINORITY
AGE       AGE                  SEXRACE    SEXRACE
SALNOW    SALNOW   SALNOW      BEGDATE    BEGDATE
```

As shown in Figure 1.1c, SPSS-X continues to read commands until it encounters the second command that calls for output—LIST. The values of AVGRAISE are given for every fifth case through case 50. These values are consistent with expected levels of salary increase, so the transformation is probably correct. As noted, SPSS-X reads only the first 50 cases of the file, taking .24 CPU seconds to do so.

Figure 1.1d shows the remainder of the display file, starting with the XSAVE command. Upon encountering XSAVE, SPSS-X reports on the number of variables to be saved and the number of bytes required for each case in an uncompressed file. But note that the report on the number of cases saved follows the MEANS table. That's because SPSS-X writes out the new file as it processes the data for MEANS—saving an extra pass through the data file.

Figure 1.1c Command printback and LIST output

```
 9  COMPUTE AVGRAISE = (SALNOW-SALBEG)
10                     /TRUNC(CTIME.DAYS($TIME-BEGDATE)/365.25)
11  VARIABLE LABELS  AVGRAISE 'AVERAGE ANNUAL RAISE'
12  PRINT FORMATS  AVGRAISE (DOLLAR9.2)
13
14  LIST VARIABLES = ID BEGDATE SALNOW AVGRAISE
15      /CASES = FROM 1 TO 50 BY 5
16

There are 220896 bytes of memory available.
The largest contiguous area has 220896 bytes.

    268 BYTES OF MEMORY REQUIRED FOR LIST PROCEDURE.
    136 BYTES HAVE ALREADY BEEN ACQUIRED.
    132 BYTES REMAIN TO BE ACQUIRED.


 ID     BEGDATE SALNOW  AVGRAISE

 626 13-JUN-1984  10680 $1,760.00
 632 17-JUL-1983  21960 $2,940.00
 637 14-MAR-1985  27250 $7,127.00
 642 17-JUL-1982  10620   $984.00
 652 20-MAR-1961  12300   $230.77
 658 17-AUG-1975  22800 $1,000.00
 664 15-FEB-1980   8040   $394.29
 671 13-SEP-1980  10380   $580.00
 679 19-SEP-1956   9000   $100.00
 688 16-MAY-1981   9600   $860.00


NUMBER OF CASES READ =      50    NUMBER OF CASES LISTED =      10

PRECEDING TASK REQUIRED       0.24 SECONDS CPU TIME;      3.28 SECONDS ELAPSED.
```

In the output from MEANS, AVGRAISE is identified by the label "AVER-AGE ANNUAL RAISE" assigned in the sample job. MINORITY and SEX have labels that were assigned previously and saved in the original file. When the updated file is used later, the label for AVGRAISE will be there.

At the end of the job, SPSS-X reports overall statistics for the run and a normal end-of-job message. Had the job contained errors, error messages would have been included in the printed output at the point where the error was detected. SPSS-X error handling and messages are discussed in Chapter 3.

Figure 1.1d Command printback and MEANS output

```
17  XSAVE OUTFILE = EMPDATA2
18

26-AUG-87 15:31:41      13 VARIABLES,    104 BYTES PER CASE BEFORE COMPRESSION
19  MEANS TABLES = AVGRAISE BY MINORITY BY SEX

There are 239120 bytes of memory available.
The largest contiguous area has 239120 bytes.

***** GIVEN WORKSPACE ALLOWS FOR  5434 CELLS WITH  2 DIMENSIONS FOR BREAKDOWN.

        D E S C R I P T I O N   O F   S U B P O P U L A T I O N S

Criterion Variable    AVGRAISE    AVERAGE ANNUAL RAISE
   Broken Down by     MINORITY    MINORITY CLASSIFICATION
            by        SEX         SEX OF EMPLOYEE


Variable       Value  Label                      Mean     Std Dev    Cases

For Entire Population                         2221.0198  3322.6981     380

MINORITY         0    WHITE                    2622.1633  3692.1118     288
   SEX           0    MALES                    2960.2626  4107.9951     181
   SEX           1    FEMALES                  2050.2382  2779.6308     107

MINORITY         1    NONWHITE                  965.2664   940.9329      92
   SEX           0    MALES                    1054.7018   978.8123      61
   SEX           1    FEMALES                   789.2804   849.2122      31

   Total Cases = 380


THERE WERE  1 XSAVE COMMANDS PROCESSED
      380 CASES WERE WRITTEN TO EMPDATA2 SPSSXFIL A1

PRECEDING TASK REQUIRED       0.24 SECONDS CPU TIME;      1.36 SECONDS ELAPSED.


    22 COMMAND LINES READ.
     0 ERRORS DETECTED.
     0 WARNINGS ISSUED.
     1 SECONDS CPU TIME.
    10 SECONDS ELAPSED TIME.
       END OF JOB.
```

Contents

2.1 PREPARING SPSS-X COMMANDS

2.2 Commands and Specifications

2.3 Variable Names

2.4 The TO Convention

2.5 Keywords

2.6 Truncation

2.7 Numbers and Strings

2.8 Arithmetic Operators and Delimiters

2.9 Notation Used to Describe SPSS-X Commands

2.10 THE ORDER OF SPSS-X COMMANDS

Chapter 2   The SPSS-X Language

To use SPSS-X, you need to become familiar with its language. For the most part, this is easily done, since every attempt has been made to keep the language natural and straightforward. This chapter describes the general characteristics, or *syntax,* of the SPSS-X language; the specific format of each command is explained in the following chapters.

Within this manual and in the enclosed reference card, certain conventions have been adopted for setting out the generalized format of commands. Section 2.9 lists these conventions.

2.1
PREPARING SPSS-X COMMANDS

SPSS-X commands can be entered in either batch-processing or interactive mode (see Chapter 3). Commands entered in batch mode must begin in column 1 and continue on as many lines as needed. Continuation lines must be indented at least one column. You can have a period or some other termination character at the end of a batch-processed command, but it is not required.

Commands entered interactively can begin in any column and require a period, a null (blank) line, or some other specified termination character for SPSS-X to know it is completed. (See the SET command in Chapter 4 for more information on the termination character and null line.) To continue interactive commands on extra lines, simply hit the ENTER key without giving a termination character. Thus, in interactive mode, continuation lines do not need to be indented.

In both batch and interactive mode, you can add space or break lines at any point where a single blank is allowed, including around special delimiters such as a slash, parenthesis, or equals sign. However, you cannot break lines within strings (see Section 2.7). The maximum length of an input line is usually 80 characters but may vary by type of computer and operating system.

Enter commands in any case you wish. SPSS-X preserves upper and lower case within labels and strings but translates keywords and names to upper case before processing. You can use the SET command to control translation of labels and messages to upper case on output (see Chapter 4). Some installations may not recognize lower case and will automatically translate all input to upper case. For information on how your installation handles case translation consult the local documentation available via the INFO command (see Chapter 3).

2.2
Commands and Specifications

Each command begins with a *command keyword* (which may contain more than one word). A few commands, such as EDIT and BEGIN DATA, are complete in themselves, but most require specifications. *Specifications* are made up of names, keywords, numbers, strings, arithmetic operators, special delimiters, and spacing as needed to separate these elements. Many specifications include *subcommands,* such as the FILE, RENAME, DROP, KEEP, and MAP subcommands on the SAVE command, many of which require additional specifications.

2

Specifications begin at least one space after the command and continue for as many lines as necessary. Continuation lines can be indented as much as you want. For example, the command

```
VALUE LABELS
    SEX     0  'MALES'
            1  'FEMALES'  /
    JOBCAT  1  'CLERICAL'
            2  'OFFICE TRAINEE'
            3  'SECURITY OFFICER'
            4  'COLLEGE TRAINEE'
            5  'EXEMPT EMPLOYEE'
            6  'MBA TRAINEE'
            7  'TECHNICAL'  /
```

is equivalent to

```
VALUE LABELS SEX 0 'MALES' 1 'FEMALES'
 /JOBCAT 1 'CLERICAL' 2 'OFFICE TRAINEE' 3 'SECURITY OFFICER'
 4 'COLLEGE TRAINEE' 5 'EXEMPT EMPLOYEE' 6 'MBA TRAINEE' 7 'TECHNICAL'/
```

If you want to indent commands during batch processing to indicate level of control (or for any other reason), place a plus sign (+), dash (−) or period (.) in column 1 and then indent the command as much as you want, as in:

```
DO IF (REGION EQ 8)
+    IF (SEX = 1) WT = .8
+    IF (SEX = 2) WT = 1.2
END IF
```

In interactive mode, you can indent commands as much as you want without using any special symbols in column 1.

2.3
Variable Names

When you define data and create variables using COMPUTE, IF, RECODE, COUNT, and other transformation commands, you assign *names* to your variables. These names must be no longer than eight characters. They must begin with a letter of the alphabet A–Z or with the symbol @, #, or $. See the following paragraphs about variable names beginning with # or $. The remaining characters in the name can be any letter, any digit, a period, @, #, $, or an underscore (_). Some keywords are reserved by SPSS-X and cannot be used as variable names (see Section 2.5). The following are all valid variable names: LOCATION, LOC#5, @2.5, X.1, A#######, OVER$500, and #32 (but see the following paragraphs before using variables that contain #).

If you *begin* a variable name with the character #, SPSS-X understands that this is a *scratch variable* to be used only for convenience in defining the file or in transforming the data. Scratch variables are not available in procedures and are not saved on system files. You might, for example, want to read in a string variable as a scratch variable in preparation for recoding that variable into a new, numeric variable. The string variable disappears when the active file is created.

SPSS-X provides several *system variables* that you can use in transformation commands. They allow you to refer to the current date, page dimensions, the system-missing value, or the sequence number of the current case. System variable names begin with a dollar sign, as in $CASENUM. See Chapter 7 for more information on system variables.

SPSS-X contains a facility that allows you to define and name macros. Macro names are similar to variable names but there are some differences. For example, an exclamation point is valid in a macro name but not in a variable name. See Appendix A for more information on macro names.

2.4
The TO Convention   You can both create and refer to a set of variable names by using keyword TO.

Generating Variable Names. When you are assigning new names, as in DATA LIST specifications, ITEM1 TO ITEM5 is equivalent to five names: ITEM1, ITEM2, ITEM3, ITEM4, and ITEM5. The prefix can be any valid name and the numbers can be any integers, so long as the first number is smaller than the second and the full variable name, including the number, does not exceed eight characters. Note that the number is a part of the variable name, not a subscript. If you include leading zeros in the number, they are preserved in the variable name. X1 TO X100 and X001 TO X100 both generate 100 variable names, but the first 99 names are not the same in the two lists. X01 TO X9 is not valid.

Referring to Variables. When you are referring to variables, as in a list of variables to be analyzed by a procedure, VARA TO VARD refers to VARA, VARD, and any variables that fall between VARA and VARD on the active file. If the active file contains the variables SCORE3, AGE, SEX, SCORE1, SCORE2, SCORE4, the variable list AGE TO SCORE4 includes AGE, SEX, SCORE1, SCORE2, and SCORE4 but not SCORE3. You can use TO in variable lists everywhere except where explicitly stated in this manual.

The order of the variables on the active file is the order in which the variables are defined by the DATA LIST, STRING, and NUMERIC commands or created by the COMPUTE, IF, RECODE, and COUNT commands. If you want to place variables on the active file in a particular order and you can't define or create them in the order you want, you can use the STRING and NUMERIC commands to declare the variables before you name them on a DATA LIST or transformation command (see Chapter 14). When dealing with system files, you can use the KEEP subcommand on the SAVE, GET, MATCH FILES, and ADD FILES commands to reorder the variables (see Chapters 6 and 16).

2.5
Keywords   Keywords have special meaning in SPSS-X. Besides the keywords that identify commands and subcommands, almost every command and subcommand has associated keywords that may be included in its specifications. For example, the SPLIT FILE command, which divides a file into two or more separate files for analysis, uses keyword OFF to return to processing the file as a whole:

```
SPLIT FILE OFF
```

For the most part, the SPSS-X language is structured so that keywords cannot be confused with user-defined variable names or file handles. Therefore, you don't have to worry about whether you use one of these keywords as one of your variable names or file handles. For example, the SPLIT FILE command requires keyword BY before a variable name, so you could have a variable named OFF and use that variable on the SPLIT FILE command.

Some keywords, however, can occur where a name also can be used, such as ALL in:

```
FREQUENCIES VARIABLES=ALL
```

Such keywords are *reserved keywords* and cannot be used as variable names or file handles. Table 2.5 lists the reserved keywords.

Table 2.5   SPSS-X reserved keywords

ALL	AND	BY	EQ	GE	GT	LE
LT	NE	NOT	OR	TO	WITH	

2

2.6
Truncation

The first word of every command keyword can be abbreviated to the minimum number of characters needed to eliminate ambiguity, down to an absolute minimum of the first three characters. For most commands, the first four characters suffice in distinguishing them from one another. All subsequent keywords that make up the command and most other keywords can be truncated to a minimum of three characters. The exceptions are the reserved keyword WITH, the END DATA command, data format keywords (COMMA, DOLLAR, etc.), and all specifications to the INFO command.

2.7
Numbers and Strings

Numbers and strings are common components of specifications. They may refer to the values of variables, or they may serve other purposes such as constants in numeric transformations or strings in string functions.

Numbers can be entered either as integers or decimal numbers, with or without leading zeros, as in:

```
SELECT IF (AMOUNT GT 0.05)
```

The SELECT IF command tests each case to see if numeric variable AMOUNT is greater than 0.05. The zero before the decimal point is optional.

Strings are enclosed within apostrophes, as in:

```
SELECT IF (STATE EQ 'IL')
```

This command tests each case to see if the string variable STATE is equal to the string IL. If you need to break a string across input lines, enclose the first line of the string in apostrophes, end the first line with a plus sign, and begin the second line of the string with an apostrophe, as in this TITLE subcommand to REPORT:

```
TITLE='SELLINGSWORTH COUNTY COMMISSION FOR EMERGENCY PREPAREDNESS'+
    ' AND DISASTER SERVICES'/
```

You can enclose strings in quotation marks instead of apostrophes, as long as you do not begin with one and end with the other. Within a string demarcated by quotation marks, apostrophes are valid characters. Within a string demarcated by apostrophes, quotation marks are valid characters. Within a string demarcated by quotation marks, two quotation marks entered without separation are interpreted as a single, valid quotation mark. Similarly, within a string demarcated by apostrophes, two consecutive apostrophes are interpreted as a single, valid apostrophe. The following are equivalent specifications on TITLE:

```
TITLE='Murphy''s Sports Shop' '1982 Sales by Division'/
TITLE="Murphy's Sports Shop" "1982 Sales by Division"/
TITLE="Murphy's Sports Shop"'1982 Sales by Division'/
```

The space between the two lines of the title is required in the first two examples but optional in the third. See Chapter 8 for more information on strings and string variables.

2.8
Arithmetic Operators and Delimiters

Five arithmetic operators occur in SPSS-X specifications: addition ($+$), subtraction ($-$), multiplication ($*$), division ($/$), and exponentiation ($**$). The equals sign ($=$) is also used to show equivalence in many expressions. These operators are self-delimiting; you can insert space around them if you wish, but none is required. VARA+VARB is equivalent to VARA   +   VARB.

Special delimiters in SPSS-X include parentheses, apostrophes, quotation marks, the slash, and the equals sign. These characters set apart certain elements in specifications, as shown in the general syntax for each command (see Section 2.9). You can insert blanks before and after special delimiters, but none are required.

- **Parentheses** enclose arguments to functions, value ranges in some procedures, keywords that could otherwise be confused with variable names, and certain expressions such as (value list = value) in RECODE specifications and RENAME = (old variable list = new variable list) in GET and SAVE specifications.
- **Apostrophes** and **quotation marks** set off strings. See Section 2.7 for a discussion of strings.
- The **slash** is used primarily to separate subcommands. Although slashes are sometimes optional, entering them as shown in the syntax diagrams is good practice.
- The **equals sign** is used between a subcommand and its specifications, as in FILE=handle, and to show equivalence, as in (old variable list = new variable list). Equals signs following subcommands are frequently optional, but it is best to enter them.

For all commands, both the slash and the equals sign are required where ambiguity is possible. To avoid potential ambiguities, you should always use the equals signs and slashes as shown in the syntax diagrams that precede each chapter in this manual.

Where no arithmetic operator or special delimiter is required between elements within a specification, use either one or more blanks or one or more commas or a combination of the two. In arguments to functions described in Chapters 7 and 8, single commas are required and a blank is not a valid substitute.

2.9
Notation Used to Describe SPSS-X Commands

The following rules apply to the syntax charts shown throughout this manual:

- Elements in capital letters are keywords. Enter them exactly as they appear, or truncate them as discussed in Section 2.6. In Figure 2.9, OUTFILE, MISSING, COLUMNWISE, PRESORTED, and BREAK are keywords. AGGREGATE is the command keyword and can be truncated to AGG.
- Elements in lower case describe specifications you should provide. For example, in Figure 2.9, replace *varlist* with a list of variables.
- Enter special delimiters as they appear, and use blanks or commas to separate keywords, names, labels, and numbers from each other. In Figure 2.9, the slashes between subcommands are required.
- Elements enclosed in square brackets [ ] are optional. In Figure 2.9, subcommands MISSING and PRESORTED are optional. Where brackets might confuse the format, they are omitted and the accompanying text explains what specifications are required or optional.
- Braces { } indicate a choice between the elements they enclose. For the OUTFILE in Figure 2.9, you have a choice between specifying an asterisk (*), which refers to the active file, and a file, which writes the aggregated file to a disk or tape.
- Default elements are shown in boldface. Defaults are instructions understood by SPSS-X if you don't explicitly specify them. For example, the boldface **A** in Figure 2.9 is a default. Many defaults are in effect when you don't specify a subcommand at all. These are indicated by two asterisks next to the specification.

Figure 2.9 General format for procedure AGGREGATE

```
AGGREGATE  OUTFILE={file}  [/MISSING=COLUMNWISE]  [/PRESORTED]

           /BREAK = varlist[({A})][varlist...]
                           {D}

           /aggvar ['label'] aggvar ['label'] ... = function (arguments)
           [/aggvar ...]
```

2

2.10
THE ORDER OF
SPSS-X COMMANDS

There is little formal precedence order for SPSS-X commands. Most ordering of commands will come from your understanding of how SPSS-X works so you can instruct it in the right order. There is a required order for some commands. For example, a variable must be defined before it or its values can be labeled.

Besides formal precedence order, you must keep in mind the logical outcome of the order in which your commands are processed. Although data definitions and transformations are not carried out until a procedure command (including a SAVE command) causes the data to be read, the result is as though the commands were executed when encountered. Thus you can control the logic of calculations by the sequence of commands.

Finally, there are some commands that can appear only in an *input program* where the cases are being created and other commands that operate only in the *transformation program* after the cases have been created. For example, commands REREAD and END CASE are used only to read data records and create cases, and the SELECT IF command works only after the cases are created. On the other hand, the COMPUTE command is used both to create and to transform cases and can appear in either program. For a discussion of these *program states* and command order, see Appendix B.

Syntax

CLEAR TRANSFORMATIONS

```
CLEAR TRANSFORMATIONS
```

EDIT

```
EDIT
```

EXECUTE

```
EXECUTE
```

HELP

```
{HELP} [ {topic   [subtopic  ] }] [SYNTAX]
{ ?  }   {command [subcommand] }
```

HOST

```
HOST [system command]
```

INCLUDE

```
INCLUDE FILE=file
```

INFO

```
INFO [OUTFILE = file]
     [OVERVIEW]
     [LOCAL]
     [ERRORS]
     [FACILITIES]
     [PROCEDURES]
     [ALL]
     [procedure name] [/procedure name...]
     [SINCE release number]
```

NEW FILE

```
NEW FILE
```

Contents

3.1   PROCESSING MODE
3.2   Batch Processing
3.3   EDIT Command
3.4   Interactive Processing
3.5   CLEAR TRANSFORMATIONS and NEW FILE Commands
3.6   HOST Command
3.7   The Journal File
3.8   OPTIONS and STATISTICS Commands

3.9   INCLUDE COMMAND

3.10 EXECUTE COMMAND

3.11 ONLINE ASSISTANCE
3.12   INFO Command
3.13   Selecting the Type of Information
3.14   Specifying Releases
3.15   Writing Information to an External File
3.16   Truncation
3.17   HELP Command
3.18   Other Online Information

3.19 NOTES, WARNINGS, AND ERROR MESSAGES
3.20   Notes
3.21   Warnings
3.22   Errors

16

Chapter 3   Running SPSS-X

SPSS-X runs on a wide variety of operating systems. To get specific information on how to operate SPSS-X at your site, use the INFO LOCAL command explained in Sections 3.12 through 3.16. This chapter describes some general rules, information, and commands that will be helpful to SPSS-X users on all systems.

3.1
PROCESSING MODE

You can run SPSS-X in either batch mode, where you submit a file of SPSS-X commands for execution, or in interactive mode, where you submit commands one at a time for immediate execution. Sections 3.2 through 3.8 describe these two modes of operation.

3.2
Batch Processing

In batch mode, you first assemble your SPSS-X commands in a file using your operating-system editor. The commands are created following the rules discussed in Chapter 2. After assembling this *command file,* you submit it for execution to your operating system. The way this is done differs from system to system, but for many systems, like IBM CMS and VAX VMS, it involves some variant of the command

```
SPSSX filename
```

where *filename* is the name of the command file. On some systems, additional parameters can also be specified on this command. The SPSS-X system is accessed at this point, and your "batch" of SPSS-X commands is processed. Output is directed to the specified device or to the default device at your site.

Batch processing might be the preferred way to run SPSS-X for a number of reasons. It can be a very efficient way to do the same analysis over and over on a regular basis, like for a weekly report. Batch processing can also be less tedious and error prone when you are doing long analyses involving commands with many specifications.

3.3
EDIT Command

At times you may want to have SPSS-X check the syntax of the commands in a command file without actually reading and processing the data. If the job contains a syntax error, this will allow you to correct the error before running a costly job or incurring mounting charges for data files on tape or other off-line media. This also allows you to do your checking in a quick, high-priority job while you wait and then submit a lower-priority job to process a large data file.

The EDIT command causes SPSS-X to evaluate your batch job without reading the data file. EDIT can appear anywhere in your command file and its format is simply:

```
EDIT
```

3

EDIT is not allowed in interactive mode. Commands following the EDIT command are checked for syntax, and variable names are checked against the DATA LIST and other commands that create variables to ensure that they have been defined. Note, however, that some SPSS-X procedures create variables such as standard scores and residuals and add them to the active file. The EDIT facility does not know about these variables and issues error messages when it encounters them in later commands.

Since EDIT checks variable names, if you are using a system file in your job you will have to make it available so that SPSS-X can read the dictionary. Alternatively, you can replace the GET command with a DATA LIST or with NUMERIC and STRING commands within INPUT PROGRAM and END INPUT PROGRAM for the EDIT job. The DATA LIST does not need to correspond exactly to the data, though it must name all the variables to be used in the remainder of the job in the same order as on the system file and with the same format type.

If you're running a batch job that contains inline data, you must at least have the BEGIN DATA and END DATA commands in the appropriate spots. If you leave the data in it is bypassed. If you remove the data it has no effect.

The EDIT facility does not detect every possible error. For example, if you name a defined variable, but the wrong one, in a COMPUTE command, the system will not recognize that the computation is impossible or not what you intend. It will, however, report on a string variable used where a numeric variable is required and vice versa. It will not know if your DATA LIST defines your data correctly, only whether it obeys the syntax rules.

3.4
Interactive Processing

In interactive mode, each command is executed as soon as you've finished entering it. The command for beginning an interactive session is different across systems. On an IBM CMS system, the command is:

SPSSX *

For VAX/VMS systems, the command is simply:

SPSSX

After entering this initial command and hitting the return key, you receive the prompt

SPSS-X>

which means SPSS-X is ready for the first line of a command. If a command takes more than one line, hit the return key at the end of the line and you'll get the prompt:

CONTINUE>

Interactive SPSS-X will repeatedly give you the CONTINUE> prompt when you hit the return key until you enter a command terminator. The default command terminator is a period or a blank line. See SET ENDCMD in Chapter 4 for information on how you can specify a different command terminator.

If you are entering data inline, you get the prompt

DATA>

after you enter the BEGIN DATA command. The system goes back to giving you the SPSS-X> prompt after you enter the END DATA command. More information on the BEGIN DATA and END DATA commands is available in Chapter 5.

You terminate an interactive session by entering the FINISH command. The command terminator is not required after FINISH. You will receive summary messages about how much time you've used and the number of commands, errors, and warnings issued during the session before being returned to your operating system.

Interactive processing can have several advantages over batch processing. Some types of data analyses are inherently interactive; feedback from initial analyses is required before proceeding with further analyses, which in turn might be followed by more analyses. An interactive computing system is more efficient in helping researchers with these kinds of iterative analyses. For users with microcomputer experience, another advantage is that it feels more familiar because of its similarity to SPSS/PC+ and other interactive microcomputer software.

3.5
CLEAR TRANSFORMATION
Command

Use the CLEAR TRANSFORMATIONS command in interactive SPSS-X to discard previous transformations on the active file. CLEAR TRANSFORMATIONS discards all transformation commands that have accumulated since the last procedure. This might be helpful during an interactive session if, after using many transformation commands, you are concerned that you may have made mistakes and are no longer selecting the right cases, creating variables correctly, or making valid transformations. The command is simply:

CLEAR TRANSFORMATIONS.

CLEAR TRANSFORMATIONS has no effect in a command file. If journaling is on during an interactive session and you use CLEAR TRANSFORMATIONS, be sure to delete CLEAR TRANSFORMATIONS and the unwanted transformation commands from the session's journal file. Otherwise the unwanted transformations will cause problems when the journal file is used as a command file.

3.6
HOST Command

The HOST command, available only in interactive mode, enables you to issue commands to your host system during an interactive session. After the command HOST, specify an operating-system command. The system command should be specified in upper case and cannot be continued onto another line. Your system command is immediately executed after you hit ENTER. On an IBM CMS system, for example, the command:

HOST LISTFILE.

displays the usual list of files. After completion of the system command, you are returned to the SPSS-X> prompt. If your host system command requires a terminator which is the same as the one you're using with your SPSS-X commands, specify the terminator twice.

Different operating systems might also allow you to enter HOST without a system command, with different results depending on the system. IBM CMS, for example, puts you into CMS subset from which you can enter most CMS commands (a few, like executing other programs, might be disruptive) and returns you to the interactive session when you type RETURN. Use the INFO LOCAL command (see Section 3.12) or consult your SPSS-X coordinator for specific information on how HOST is implemented on your system.

3.7
The Journal File

In addition to the listing file containing your display output, a journal file is also created when you use interactive mode. This file contains a log of your commands as you entered them into SPSS-X along with any error or warning messages the commands generated. The name of this file depends on the file-naming conventions at your site. See SET JOURNAL in Chapter 4 for information on renaming or closing the journal file.

You can

3

• Edit this file using the editor on your operating system.

• Rename it if you don't want it erased the next time you run SPSS-X.

• Resubmit it or a modified version of it as an SPSS-X batch job or as an INCLUDE file (see Section 3.9).

To facilitate the use of a journal file in batch mode, anything entered at a CONTINUE> prompt during the interactive session is entered into the journal file starting in column 2, to conform with the batch mode rule for continuation lines. In addition, command terminators, which are required in interactive mode and are entered into the journal file, are allowed in the batch mode. Note that error and warning messages and the commands that caused them have to be deleted or changed before resubmitting the file in batch or interactive mode.

　　When the HOST command (Section 3.6) is issued, the journal file and the listing file are closed. They are reopened after returning to the SPSS-X> prompt, and subsequent commands and output are added as usual. If you rename or erase these files through HOST, a new journal file and listing file are created for any subsequent commands and output produced after returning to SPSS-X>.

3.8
OPTIONS and STATISTICS Commands

Previous versions of SPSS-X used OPTIONS and STATISTICS commands to control the actions of some procedures. These commands continue to work in batch mode, but you cannot use these commands in interactive mode. Instead, you should use the new equivalent subcommands available. These subcommands are described in each procedure's chapter. See Appendix H for more information on equivalencies between these subcommands and the old OPTIONS and STATISTICS commands.

3.9
INCLUDE COMMAND

The INCLUDE command allows you to include a file of SPSS-X commands in an SPSS-X batch job or interactive SPSS-X session. This command is especially useful for including a long series of data definition statements or transformations. Another use for INCLUDE is to set up a library of commonly used commands and include them in jobs as you need them. You can nest INCLUDE commands so that one set of included commands includes another set of commands. This "nesting" can go to five levels.

　　By using INCLUDE during an interactive session, you can have the advantages of both interactive and batch processing. Complex or repetitive commands can be stored in a file that you include, while other, simpler commands or commands unique to the current analysis are entered interactively before and after the included file.

　　The following example includes the file GSSLABS:

```
INCLUDE FILE=GSSLABS
```

The FILE subcommand identifies the file containing SPSS-X commands or inline data and is required. When INCLUDE is executed, the commands in file GSSLABS are processed. For example, if the following data definition statement was stored in file GSSLABS, it would be processed and the variables added to the active file immediately after the above INCLUDE command:

```
DATA LIST FILE=DATA52
   / RELIGION 5 OCCUPAT 7 SES 12 ETHNIC 15
     PARTY 19 VOTE48 33 VOTE52 41
```

Commands in an included file must follow the rules described in Chapter 2 on preparing SPSS-X commands *for batch processing,* even if you intend to use the file in an interactive session. In particular, continuation lines within the file *must* have a blank in column 1. Command terminators are optional in included files. You can include a file of raw data, if the first line of the included file contains the

BEGIN DATA command, and the last line contains the END DATA command. However, raw data files cannot be included directly after a procedure.

You can enter as many INCLUDE commands in a batch job or during an interactive session as you want. Recursive INCLUDE commands, however, are not allowed. That is, you cannot include a file that is still open from a previous step.

The NUMBERED or UNNUMBERED (Chapter 4) setting in effect before the INCLUDE command is restored at the end of the included file. The original printback status is also restored when the end of the included file is reached. If an included file contains a FINISH command, the SPSS-X job or session ends and no further commands are processed.

3.10
EXECUTE COMMAND

Facilities such as ADD FILES, MATCH FILES, UPDATE, PRINT, and WRITE do not read the data and are not executed unless followed by a data-reading procedure. For this reason, SPSS-X has a special procedure, EXECUTE, which does nothing but force the reading of the data file. The EXECUTE command contains no subcommands or specifications. For example,

```
TITLE   'A Simple EXECUTE Example'
DATA LIST   FILE=RAWDATA/1 LNAME 1-13 (A) FNAME 15-24 (A)
            MMAIDENL 40-55
VAR LABELS   MMAIDENL 'MOTHER''S MAIDEN NAME'
DO IF (MMAIDENL EQ 'Smith')
WRITE OUTFILE=SMITHS/LNAME FNAME
END IF
EXECUTE
FINISH
```

writes the last and first names of all people whose mother's maiden name was Smith to the file referenced by SMITHS. The EXECUTE command reads the data and executes all of the preceding transformation commands.

3.11
ONLINE ASSISTANCE

There are several ways to get online information about the SPSS-X system, SPSS-X procedures and facilities, the status of your current environment settings, and your files. These ways are the INFO, HELP, DISPLAY, and SHOW commands.

3.12
INFO Command

The INFO command makes available or tells you how to obtain two kinds of documentation not included in this manual: local and update.

Local documentation concerns the environment in which you are running SPSS-X:

- Commands or job control language for running SPSS-X. Of course, you will need some basic instructions before you can obtain documentation from the INFO command.

- Conventions for specifying files. These are especially important since they tell you how your computer's operating system accesses or creates a particular file.

- Conventions for handling tapes and other input/output devices.

- Data formats. The formats that SPSS-X reads and writes may differ from one computer and operating system to another (see Chapter 5).

- Default values for parameters controlled by the SET command (see Chapter 4). Parameters such as translation to upper case or compression of scratch files can be set at your installation. You can use the SHOW command (Chapter 4) to see what values are in effect on a given run; local documentation may contain more information on why you should prefer a particular setting.

- Other information specific to your computer and operating system or to your individual installation.

3

Update documentation includes changes to existing procedures and facilities made after publication of this manual, new procedures and facilities, and corrections to this manual. Specifications to the INFO command allow you to choose update documentation for facilities (all SPSS-X commands except procedures), for all procedures, or for individual procedures. You can also request documentation produced since a particular release of SPSS-X.

While the INFO command provides a handy mechanism for obtaining local and update information, SPSS-X requires more computer resources than most printing utilities. Your installation may provide an alternative method for printing INFO documentation. In that case, the INFO command may simply give you instructions for using the preferred documentation facility.

3.13
Selecting the Type of Information

To select the type of information you want, specify one or more of the following keywords on INFO:

OVERVIEW
Overview of available documentation. This overview includes a table of contents for the documentation available via the INFO command, along with information about documentation available in print.

LOCAL
Local documentation, as described in Section 3.12.

ERRORS
List of known unfixed errors. This documentation lists the known unfixed errors in the current release of SPSS-X. Since ERRORS applies only to the current release, the SINCE keyword, described in Section 3.14, will have no effect on it.

FACILITIES
Update information for SPSS-X facilities. This documentation covers all differences, except in procedures, between the system as documented in this manual and the system as installed on your computer—whether those differences result from updates to the system, revisions required for conversions to particular operating systems, or errors in this manual. However, unless you use keyword SINCE to specify the SPSS-X release documented in this manual, you will receive updates only for the most current release (see Section 3.14).

PROCEDURES
Update information for procedures. This includes full documentation for procedures new in the current release and update information for procedures that existed prior to the current release.

procedure(s)
Documentation for the procedures named. This is the same information as that printed by the PROCEDURES keyword, but limited to the procedure named. Follow every procedure name with a slash.

ALL
All available documentation. ALL is equivalent to OVERVIEW, LOCAL, ERRORS, FACILITIES, and PROCEDURES.

You can enter as many of these keywords as you wish. If you specify overlapping sets of information, only one copy is printed. The order of specifications is not important and does not affect the order in which the documentation is printed.

The following commands produce an overview and documentation for any changes made to system facilities and to the FREQUENCIES and CROSSTABS procedures:

```
INFO  OVERVIEW FACILITIES FREQUENCIES / CROSSTABS
```

Because of possible conflict with procedure names, all keywords on the INFO command must be spelled out in full.

3.14
Specifying Releases

Releases of SPSS-X are numbered by integers, with decimal digits indicating maintenance releases between major releases. For example, Release 1.1 is a maintenance release with few changes from Release 1. The release number appears in the heading to each SPSS-X job. Each SPSS-X manual is identified in the preface by the number of the release it documents. This manual documents Release 3.0.

By default, the INFO command produces update information only for the current release. Documentation for earlier releases may also be available, and that fact will be indicated in the INFO overview. To obtain information for earlier releases or to limit the information to maintenance releases since the last major release, use keyword SINCE followed by a release number.

SINCE n   *Print documentation for all releases since Release* n.

The following command prints documentation for all changes to system facilities and procedures FREQUENCIES and CROSSTABS since Release 3.0 (the release documented in this manual):

```
INFO  OVERVIEW FACILITIES FREQUENCIES / CROSSTABS SINCE 3
```

SINCE is not inclusive—SINCE 3.0 does not include changes made to the system in Release 3.0. To identify a maintenance release, enter the exact number, with decimal, as in 3.1. INFO contains only information since the latest published manual.

3.15
Writing Information to an External File

By default, the output from the INFO command is included in the display file. If you prefer to send the output to another file, use the OUTFILE subcommand, naming the file you want to create. This is particularly useful in interactive mode, where the display is usually sent to the terminal screen. You will probably not want to see all of the information supplied by an INFO command on your terminal screen.

The following command creates a file of text that includes an overview, local documentation, changes, and new procedures since Release 3:

```
INFO  OUTFILE=SPSSXDOC ALL SINCE 3
```

The characteristics of the output file produced by the INFO command may vary by computer type. As implemented at SPSS Inc., the file includes carriage control, with the maximum length of a page determined by the LENGTH subcommand on the SET command (see Chapter 4). A printer width of 132 characters is assumed for some examples, though the text is generally much narrower.

3.16
Truncation

Three-character truncation does *not* apply to INFO command specifications. Spell all keywords out in full. For procedure names, spell the first word out in full and subsequent words through at least the first three characters.

3.17
HELP Command

In interactive mode, you also have an extensive help system available to you. If you specify HELP or ? and a command name or topic at the SPSS-X> prompt and hit return, your screen displays information on that command or topic. The question mark can also be used at the CONTINUE> and DATA> prompts. Many of these command and topic screens have subcommand and subtopic screens, and some of the subcommand screens have even another level of help, the keyword screens, under them. The help screens are arranged as follows:

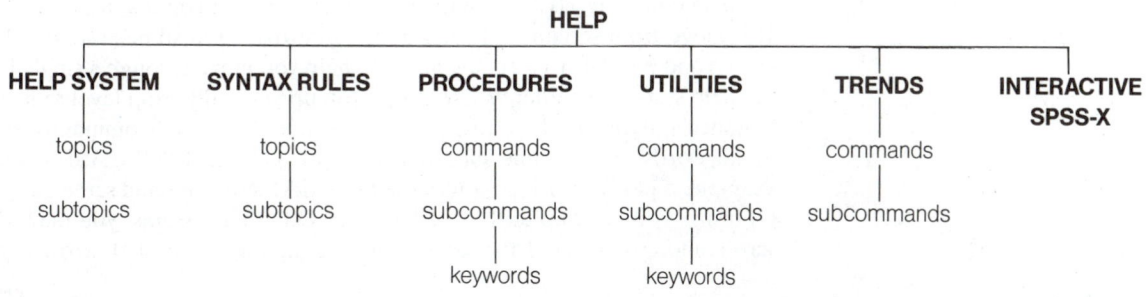

If a command or topic has subcommands or subtopics, a numbered list for you to choose from is provided. You obtain additional help on these commands or topics by typing the number to the left of the subcommand or subtopic at the HELP> prompt provided and hitting the return key. If you want to go directly to a subcommand or subtopic from the command prompt, you can enter "? command subcommand" or "? topic subtopic".

For example, to get information on LIST when at the SPSSX> prompt, type

? LIST.

and hit return. The following screen pops up:

```
***************************************************************************
                                  LIST
LIST can be used to list the values of specified variables for
specified cases.
_____
|LIST VARIABLES=MOHIRED YRHIRED DEPT82 NAME                                 |
|      /CASES=FROM 100 TO 200 BY 5 /FORMAT=SINGLE NUMBERED.                 |
_____

To list all variables for all cases in the file, use no
specifications after the LIST command.  The default format is
  1) to not number lines, and,
  2) to wrap listings if the page is not wide enough.

To specify a subset of variables, a subset of cases, or a format other
than the default, use the optional subcommands.

0 SYNTAX     Syntax chart.
1 VARIABLES  Specifies variables to be listed.
2 CASES      Limits listings to a subset of cases.
3 FORMAT     Controls line wrapping and numbering.
HELP>
***************************************************************************
```

After reading this screen, if you want to see the help screen for the CASES subcommand, at the HELP> prompt type:

2

and hit return. (Remember this is just the "2" key, not the "PF2" key if you have programmable function keys on your keyboard.) The following screen appears:

```
***************************************************************************
                              LIST CASES

The CASES subcommand limits listings to a subset of specified cases.
_____
|          LIST CASES FROM 100 TO 200 BY 5.                                 |
_____

Optional.  Default is to list all cases in the file.

CASES must be followed by at least one of three keywords:

  FROM n    Start listing cases from sequential case number n.
  TO n      List cases up to and including sequential case number n.
  BY n      List cases using an increment of n.

HELP\
***************************************************************************
```

The same screen could have been obtained directly at the SPSS-X> prompt by typing:

? LIST CASES.

In addition to entering subcommand numbers from a command-level screen or typing a complete HELP command sequence from a command prompt, you can also move from screen to screen using keystrokes. On some systems, the minus key (-) and plus key (+) are available to help you move through a single branch of the help system. The minus key moves you up vertically from level to level within a branch and the plus key moves you horizontally across subcommands, subtopics, or keywords at the same hierarchical level. On the LIST CASES screen, for example, a plus (+) brings you to the FORMAT subcommand screen and a minus (-) brings you back up to the LIST screen. On other systems, you may be able to scroll among screens of the same branch using the directional arrow keys.

Each procedure also has an online syntax chart. After the command name, just type keyword SYNTAX, as in:

```
? REGRESSION SYNTAX.
```

This command produces only the syntax chart for the REGRESSION command without the help text.

To get out of the HELP system and back to the SPSS-X prompt just hit the return key at any HELP> prompt.

You can begin exploring the HELP system by issuing the command ? for a list of HELP topics. If you already know a command you're interested in, type ? and the name of the command.

3.18
Other Online Information

Two other commands for getting online information are DISPLAY and SHOW. DISPLAY is used for obtaining information about a system file and is discussed in Chapter 5. The SHOW command, which displays the current settings of your SPSS-X environment and additional information, is explained in Chapter 4.

3.19
NOTES, WARNINGS, AND ERROR MESSAGES

When SPSS-X encounters a peculiarity or error in your job, it issues a message to the display and journal files and takes some action appropriate to the kind of problem. The message immediately follows the place where the error was detected and always indicates what action the system is taking. SPSS-X uses as many lines as necessary to identify the error as fully as possible and to suggest some solutions to the most common causes of the error.

These messages and actions can be organized into five categories. The first three apply to both batch and interactive processing. The last two apply to only batch processing:

- Notes, which call attention to peculiarities in the job that have no effect on output.
- Warnings, which indicate problems that do affect the output but that are probably not serious.
- Errors that cause a command to be skipped but allow processing to continue.
- Errors that cause processing to cease but allow continued scanning of batch commands for syntax errors.
- Errors that cause immediate termination of the batch job.

There are limits to the number of errors and to the combined number of errors and warnings that are permitted before a batch job is terminated (see the MXERRS and MXWARNS subcommands to the SET command in Chapter 4). These limits are ignored in interactive sessions. In interactive SPSS-X, the number of messages is still counted and reported, but your session is not terminated no matter how many you receive.

3.20
Notes

Typical of the kind of information provided by notes is the message issued when SORT CASES is specified and the file contains only one case:

```
    8 SORT CASES PCTGROW

>NOTE    5802
>SORT CASES was not executed because the file has fewer than 2 cases.
```

Notes do not count toward the total number of warnings or errors that cause a job to terminate.

3.21
Warnings

Misspelling a variable name on the VARIABLE LABELS command causes just the label for that variable to be skipped, with a warning such as:

```
  6 VARIABLE LABELS POP70 'Population in 1970'
  7                 POP89 'Population in 1980'

>WARNING  4461 LINE   7, COLUMN 17, TEXT: POP89
>An unknown variable name was specified on the VAR LABELS command.  The name
>and the label will be ignored.
```

Warnings often result from "undefined" data: values encountered in the input data that do not conform to the type of variable defined, such as alphanumeric characters in data defined as numeric. In this case, SPSS-X changes the code to the system-missing value and issues a warning message:

```
>WARNING   652
>An invalid numeric field has been found.  The result has been set to the
>system-missing value.

COMMAND LINE:     2  CURRENT CASE:      4  CURRENT SPLITFILE GROUP:   1
FIELD CONTENTS: 'Albuquerque'
RECORD NUMBER:      4  STARTING COLUMN:   4  RECORD LENGTH:    80
```

You can suppress the warning message for undefined data with the UNDEFINED subcommand on the SET command (Chapter 4), but each occurrence of an undefined value will count toward the maximum number of warnings permitted in a batch job.

A similar warning message can be issued when SPSS-X assigns the system-missing value because of missing data records in a grouped or nested file (Chapter 12) or because of domain errors in computations (Chapter 7).

3.22
Errors

Some errors force SPSS-X to skip an entire command but allow processing to continue for subsequent commands. Frequently this involves a procedure command, such as an error in the variable list for the BREAKDOWN procedure:

```
  5  0        BREAKDOWN TABLES=SALBEG SALNOW AVERAISE BY MINORITY BY SEX

>ERROR    701 LINE   5, COLUMN 32, TEXT: AVERAISE
>An undefined variable name, or a scratch or system variable was specified in a
>variable list which accepts only standard variables.  Check spelling, and
>verify the existence of this variable.
>THIS COMMAND NOT EXECUTED.
```

Errors that are likely to affect the results of later commands force SPSS-X to cease processing in the batch mode. For example, an error on the COMPUTE command causes SPSS-X to assume that later processing would most likely be meaningless. Thus processing ends, though the system continues to check for other errors that might be caught in the same job:

```
 10 COMPUTE PCTGROW = RND((POP80-POP70)/POP70)*100)

>ERROR    4020  LINE  10, COLUMN 47, TEXT: )
>An expression contains unbalanced parentheses.  Check the expression for
>omitted or extra operands, operators, and parentheses.
>NO FURTHER COMMANDS WILL BE EXECUTED.  ERROR SCAN CONTINUES.
```

In interactive mode, SPSS-X does not execute the command causing this type of error, but allows you to continue your interactive session since you can immediately reenter the command on which you made a mistake.

Occasionally SPSS-X is forced to terminate a batch job immediately. This typically happens when the MXERRS or MXWARNS limit is exceeded or when errors occur in accessing files, as in:

```
120S INPUT  ERROR 003 ON BANKDATA.

>ERROR    334
>An I/O error has occurred.  The causes could include a damaged medium such as
>a tape, an improper DCB specification, an attempt to read a file which was
>never written, an attempt to read a BCD file as an SPSS system file, etc.
>THIS IS A CATASTROPHIC ERROR FROM WHICH SPSSX CANNOT RECOVER.
>SPSSX CANNOT CONTINUE.
```

No further error checking is done when this type of error is encountered in a batch job.

This type of error doesn't occur during an interactive session since the MXERRS and MXWARN limits don't apply and an error in accessing a file means you simply need to reenter the command correctly.

Syntax

COMMENT

```
COMMENT text
```

FINISH

```
FINISH
```

NUMBERED, UNNUMBERED

```
{NUMBERED  }
{UNNUMBERED}
```

SET

```
SET [BLANKS={SYSMIS}]  [BOX={'-I+[+++++++]'}]  [CASE={UPPER}]
            {value }         {X'hexstring  '}         {UPLOW}

    [CCA={'-,,,'      }]  [CCB={'-,,,'      }]  [CCC={'-,,,'      }]
         {'format-spec'}       {'format-spec'}       {'format-spec'}

    [CCD={'-,,,'      }]  [CCE={'-,,,'      }]
         {'format-spec'}       {'format-spec'}

    [COMPRESSION={ON }]  [ENDCMD={'.'   }]  [FORMAT={F8.2}]
                 {OFF}           {'string'}         {Fw.d}

    [HEADER={YES}]  [JOURNAL=[{ON }] [file]]  [LENGTH={59  }]
            {NO }             {OFF}                   {n   }
                                                     {NONE}

    [MEXPAND={ON }]  [MITERATE={1000}]  [MNEST={50}]  [MPRINT={ON }]
             {OFF}             {n   }           {n }           {OFF}

    [MXERRS={40}]   [MXLOOPS={40}]   [MXWARNS={80 }]
            {n }             {n }             {n  }

    [NULLINE={YES}]    [PRINTBACK={YES}]
             {NO }                {NO }

    [SCRIPTTAB={'@'      }]  [SEED={2000000}]
               {'character'}        {n      }

    [TBFONT={'1234'     }]  [TB1={'-I[+++++++]'}]  [TB2={'          '}]
            {X'hexstring'}        {X'hexstring' }        {X'hexstring'}

    [UNDEFINED={WARN  }]  [WIDTH={132}]  [XSORT={YES}]
               {NOWARN}           {n  }          {OFF}
```

Defaults may differ by installation.

SHOW

```
SHOW [ALL] [BLANKS] [BLKSIZE] [BOX] [BUFNO] [CASE]

     [CCA] [CCB] [CCC] [CCD] [CCE] [COMPRESSION]

     [ENDCMD] [FORMAT] [HEADER] [JOURNAL] [LENGTH]

     [MEXPAND] [MITERATE] [MNEST] [MPRINT]

     [MXERRS] [MXLOOPS] [MXWARNS] [N] [NULLINE]

     [NUMBERED] [PRINTBACK] [SCOMPRESSION] [SCRIPTTAB]

     [SEED] [SYSMIS] [TBFONTS] [TB1] [TB2] [UNDEFINED]

     [WEIGHT] [WIDTH] [XSORT] [$VARS]
```

SUBTITLE

```
SUBTITLE [']text[']
```

TITLE

```
TITLE [']text[']
```

Contents

4.1 TITLES AND SUBTITLES

4.2 COMMENTS IN SPSS-X COMMANDS

4.3 FINISH COMMAND

4.4 NUMBERED AND UNNUMBERED COMMAND LINES

4.5 SET AND SHOW COMMANDS

4.6 Summary of SET and SHOW Commands

4.7 Blanks and Undefined Input Data

4.8 Maximum Errors and Loops

4.9 Output

4.10 Custom Currency Formats

4.11 Samples and Random Numbers

4.12 Sorting Data

4.13 Scratch File Compression

4.14 Command Terminators and Journal Files

4.15 Macro Displays

4.16 SET and the TABLES Procedure

4.17 Additional Information from SHOW

4

Chapter 4   Controlling the Environment

This chapter describes a set of SPSS-X commands that allow you to control some of the general characteristics of your output and of the environment under which your job is processed. You can use TITLE and SUBTITLE (Section 4.1) to label the pages of your output. To insert comments into your command file, you can choose between the COMMENT command, an asterisk (*), and comments enclosed between the symbols /* and */ (Section 4.2). The FINISH command (Section 4.3) is useful for signaling the end of a job or terminating interactive processing. NUMBERED and UNNUMBERED (Section 4.4) tell SPSS-X whether or not your command file includes line numbers.

With the SET command (Sections 4.5 through 4.16) you can establish the way SPSS-X treats blanks and undefined values in your input data, the starting values for random sampling, the maximum executions of a loop, and the number of errors or warnings to be accepted before a batch job is terminated. You can also set the maximum length and width of the printed output page as well as the default print and write formats for numeric variables created by transformation commands. In addition, you can specify whether you want labels and error messages to print in upper case only or in upper and lower case. You can customize currency formats for your own applications, and you can also specify the characters used to draw grids in procedures like CROSSTABS, MULT RESPONSE, and TABLES. Finally, you can define the characters used for line drawing and those used to define font codes on the TABLES procedure. The SHOW command (Sections 4.5, 4.6, and 4.17) allows you to display the current settings of all SET parameters and several others.

4.1
TITLES AND
SUBTITLES

SPSS-X places a heading that includes the date, a title, and the page number at the top of each page in the display file. At the start of the job, the title is assigned by SPSS-X and indicates the version of the system being used.

To specify your own title, use the TITLE command, as in:

```
TITLE "Running Shoe Study from Runner's World Data"
```

Note that the HEADER subcommand on the SET command (Section 4.9) determines whether any heading (default or specified) prints. Be sure HEADER =YES (the default) when you specify a title.

The title can be up to 60 characters long and can contain any characters valid on your computer. The usual SPSS-X rules for specifying strings apply (Chapter 2). If you enclose the title in apostrophes, double apostrophes within the string will print as single apostrophes and quotation marks are valid characters; if you enclose the title in quotation marks, double quotation marks will print as single quotation marks and apostrophes are valid characters. The following title is equivalent to the one above:

```
TITLE 'Running Shoe Study from Runner''s World Data'
```

You can insert as many TITLE commands as you wish, as long as you do not place them between a procedure command and BEGIN DATA when data are inline, or within the data records. Each command overrides the previous one and takes effect on the next page in the display file (the command does not cause a page eject). Only the title portion of the heading is changed. The date and page number remain.

The SUBTITLE command specifies a subtitle, which prints on the line immediately under the title. The default subtitle contains the installation name and information about the hardware and operating system. SUBTITLE follows the same rules as the TITLE command. For example,

```
SUBTITLE 'Training Shoes Only'
```

along with the title specified above produces the heading shown in Figure 4.1.

Figure 4.1 Output from TITLE and SUBTITLE commands

```
05 APR 85 Running Shoe Study from Runner's World Data           PAGE   2
11:37:29  Training Shoes Only
```

TITLE and SUBTITLE are independent; you can change one without changing the other. To specify a blank title or subtitle, enclose a blank between apostrophes, as in:

```
SUBTITLE ' '
```

4.2 COMMENTS IN SPSS-X COMMANDS

Comments can help you and others review what you intend to accomplish with individual commands and blocks of commands within an SPSS-X job. You can insert comments by using the COMMENT command or an asterisk (*), or by enclosing the comment within the symbols /* and */ in any command line. Comments are included in the command printback on the display file. They do not become part of the information saved on a system file. To include commentary in the dictionary of a system file, use the DOCUMENT command (see Chapter 6).

The COMMENT command takes as its specification any message you want, as in:

```
COMMENT Create uniform distribution for testing computations
```

Instead of the command word COMMENT you can use an asterisk, as in:

```
* Create uniform distribution for testing computations
```

As with specifications to other SPSS-X commands, the message can be continued on as many lines as necessary, as long as you leave the first character of each line blank.

Alternatively, you can use /* and */ wherever a blank is valid (except within strings) to set off comments within a command (leaving the blank in place before the comment). A comment demarcated by /* and */ cannot be continued on the next line. The most reasonable place for the comment is at the end of the line, in which case the closing */ is optional, as in:

```
IF (RACE EQ 1 AND SEX EQ 1) SEXRACE = 1 /*WHITE MALES
```

4.3 FINISH COMMAND

The FINISH command terminates an SPSS-X job. FINISH takes no additional specifications. Its format is simply:

```
FINISH
```

Batch Mode. FINISH is optional in batch mode. Its primary use is to mark the end of a job. Its appearance on the printback of commands on the display file indicates that the job has been completed. FINISH causes SPSS-X to stop reading commands, so anything following it in the command file is ignored. Placing it within a DO IF structure to end a job conditionally doesn't work: FINISH is not subject to DO IF and will end the job unconditionally.

Interactive Mode. FINISH is required in interactive mode (Chapter 3) to terminate the interactive session. Because FINISH is an SPSS-X command, you can only use it after the SPSS-X> prompt, which expects a procedure name. You cannot use FINISH to end an interactive session from a DATA>, CONTINUE>, or HELP> prompt. The FINISH command does not require a command terminator in interactive mode.

4.4
NUMBERED AND UNNUMBERED COMMAND LINES

It is common practice to reserve columns 73–80 of each input line for line numbers. If you or your computer system numbers lines this way, SPSS-X includes the line numbers on the printback of commands on the display file (see Chapter 2). The NUMBERED command instructs SPSS-X to check just the first 72 columns for command specifications. UNNUMBERED instructs SPSS-X to check all 80 columns. Neither command takes any specifications, so their format is simply

NUMBERED

or

UNNUMBERED

The default may vary by installation. You can use the SHOW command (Section 4.17) to ascertain what is in effect or check local documentation available with the INFO command (see Chapter 2).

The status of NUMBERED or UNNUMBERED affects the way data are read if they are inline. If numbered is in effect and your inline data extend beyond column 72, you will receive the following warning:

```
>WARNING     650
>A data element conversion on the indicated command will go past the end of the
>record.  Check the data list and the data file.  The result has been set to
>the system-missing value.

COMMAND LINE:     5  CURRENT CASE:       1  CURRENT SPLITFILE GROUP:   1
RECORD NUMBER:    1  STARTING COLUMN:   73  RECORD LENGTH:    72
```

To instruct SPSS-X to read data beyond column 72, use the UNNUMBERED command.

4.5
SET AND SHOW COMMANDS

The SET command allows you to control a variety of settings that affect some basic ways SPSS-X operates. The SHOW command displays the current settings of those options as well as additional information.

4.6
Summary of SET and SHOW Commands

Specifications for SET are subcommands of the form

SET subcommand = value / subcommand = value / ...

as in:

SET BLANKS=0 / UNDEFINED=NOWARN / MXWARNS=200

The slashes between subcommands are optional, but if you omit them, leave at least one blank.

4

Specifications for SHOW have the form

SHOW subcommand / subcommand / ...

as in:

```
SHOW BLANKS/UNDEFINED/MXWARNS
```

The slashes between subcommands are optional.

The following alphabetical list gives the subcommands available for SET and SHOW along with acceptable arguments.

BLANKS   *Value to which blanks read in numeric format should be translated.* The default is the system-missing value. (See Section 4.7.)

BLKSIZE   *Default block length used for scratch data files and SPSS-X system files.* The setting may vary by installation. Can be specified for SHOW only. (See Section 4.17.)

BOX   *Characters used to draw boxes.* Both character and hexadecimal representations are given when SHOW is specified. The default is set by the installation. (See Section 4.9.)

BUFFNO   *The default number of buffers used for all files managed by the SPSS-X I/O subsystem.* The setting may vary by installation. Can be specified for SHOW only. (See Section 4.17.)

CASE   *Case for display of labels and error messages.* Specifications are UPPER (the default) and UPLOW. The default may vary by installation. (See Section 4.9.)

CC   *Custom currency formats.* Five subcommands enable you to customize currency formats for your own applications. These subcommands are CCA, CCB, CCC, CCD, and CCE. (See Section 4.10.)

COMPRESSION   *Compression of scratch files.* The specification is either ON or OFF (alias YES or NO). The default is set by the installation. (See Section 4.13.)

ENDCMD   *Command terminator for interactive mode.* The specification can be any single character. The default is a period (.). (See Section 4.14.)

FORMAT   *Default print and write formats for numeric variables created by transformations.* The specification can be any F format. The initial setting is F8.2. (See Section 4.9.)

HEADER   *Headings for output.* The specification is either YES or NO (alias ON or OFF). The default is YES. (See Section 4.9.)

JOURNAL   *Journal file during interactive processing.* The specification is either ON or OFF (alias YES or NO). Use SHOW to see the default at your installation. This determines whether the journal file keeps a log of your commands during interactive processing. You can also specify the name of the file. (See Section 4.14.)

LENGTH   *Page length for output.* The specification can be any integer in the range 40 through 999,999 inclusive or NONE to suppress page ejects altogether. The default is 59. (See Section 4.9.)

MEXPAND   *Macro expansion.* The specification is either ON or OFF (alias YES or NO). The default is ON.

MITERATE   *Maximum loop traversals permitted in macro expansions.* The specification is a positive integer. The default is 1000. (See Section 4.15.)

MNEST   *Maximum nesting level for macros.* The specification is a positive integer. The default is 50. (See Section 4.15.)

MPRINT   *Inclusion of macro expansion command list in the display file.* The specification is either ON and OFF (alias YES or NO). OFF is the default. (See Section 4.15.)

MXERRS	*Maximum number of errors permitted before job is terminated.* The default is 40. This setting is ignored when you run SPSS-X in interactive mode. (See Section 4.8.)
MXLOOPS	*Maximum executions of a loop on a single case.* The default is 40. (See Section 4.8.)
MXWARNS	*Maximum number of warnings and errors permitted, collectively, before job is terminated.* The default is 80. This setting is ignored when you run SPSS-X in interactive mode. (See Section 4.8.)
N	*Unweighted number of cases on the active file.* Can be specified for SHOW only. Prints UNKNOWN if no active file has been created yet. (See Section 4.17.)
NULLINE	*Null line command terminator for interactive mode.* The specification is YES or NO (alias ON or OFF). The default is YES. (See Section 4.14.)
NUMBERED	*The current status of the switch set by the NUMBERED and UNNUMBERED commands.* The default may vary by installation. Can be specified for SHOW only. (See Section 4.4.)
PRINTBACK	*Printback of SPSS-X commands in the display file.* The specification is either YES (the default) or NO. ON and OFF are aliases for YES and NO. (See Section 4.9.)
SCOMPRESSION	*Default setting for compression of SPSS-X system files.* This setting can be overridden by the COMPRESSED or UNCOMPRESSED subcommands on the SAVE or XSAVE commands. The default setting may vary by installation. Can be specified for SHOW only. (See Chapter 6 for a complete discussion.)
SEED	*Seed for the random-number generator.* The specification is a large integer. The default is 2,000,000 but may vary by machine. (See Section 4.11.)
SYSMIS	*The system-missing value.* Can be specified for SHOW only. (See Section 4.17.)
TBFONTS	*Font characters for the TABLES procedure.* Both character and hexadecimal representations are given when SHOW is specified. The default is set by the installation. (See Section 4.16.)
TB1	*Box characters for the TABLES procedure.* Both character and hexadecimal representations are given when SHOW is specified. The default is set by the installation. (See Section 4.16.)
TB2	*Box overprint characters for the TABLES procedure.* Both character and hexadecimal representations are given when SHOW is specified. The default is set by the installation. (See Section 4.16.)
UNDEFINED	*Warning message for undefined data.* Specifications are WARN (the default) and NOWARN. NOWARN suppresses messages but does not alter the count of warnings toward the MXWARNS total. (See Section 4.7.)
WEIGHT	*The name of the variable used to weight cases.* Can be specified for SHOW only. (See Section 4.17.)
WIDTH	*Maximum page width for the display file.* The specification can be any integer from 80 through 132. The default is 132 columns. (See Section 4.9.)
XSORT	*The sort program used to sort data.* The specification is either YES (alias ON) for *use SPSS-X sort* or NO (alias OFF) for *use another sort program.* The default is set by the individual installation. (See Section 4.12.)
$VARS	*Values of system variables.* Can be specified for SHOW only. (See Section 4.17.)
ALL	*Display all settings.* Can be specified for SHOW only. (See Section 4.17.)

ANNOTATED EXAMPLE FOR RUN UTILITIES

The following job uses most of the general utilities available for controlling an SPSS-X job. It also contains a number of errors to illustrate how SPSS-X handles errors of varying severity. Refer to Chapter 3 for a complete description of errors and warnings.

```
UNNUMBERED
TITLE '1981 U. S. Almanac Data'
SUBTITLE 'Percent Growth for Fifty Largest Cities
COMMENT    DATA ARE ON TECHSVC 192
SET CASE=UPLOW/WIDTH=72/MXWARNS=5
SHOW COMPRESSION
DATA LIST  FILE=CITYDATA  RECORDS=3
  /1 CITY 1-13 STATE 14-33(A) POP70 38-44 POP80 48-54
COMPUTE PCTGROW = RND((POP80-POP70)/POP70)*100)
VAR LABELS POP70 'Population in 1970'
           POP89 'POPULATION IN 1980'
           PCTGROW 'Percent Population Growth 1970-1980'
PRINT FORMATS POP70 POP80(COMMA9.0)/PCTGROW(F3.0)
SORT CASES PCTGROW (D)
PRINT /CITY TO PCTGROW
DESCRIPTIVES POP70 POP89 PCTGROW
SAVE OUTFILE=CITYSF
FINISH
```

- The UNNUMBERED command instructs SPSS-X to interpret any data in columns 73-80 of the command line as part of the command rather than as a line number (see Section 4.4).

- The TITLE and SUBTITLE commands assign titles to each display page. In the display file these titles begin on the second page (see Section 4.1). The closing quotation mark is omitted from the SUBTITLE specification. This error receives a warning. The specifications shown here are for an IBM CMS system.

- The COMMENT command is inserted as a reminder of where the data are stored (see Section 4.2).

- The SET command sets case to upper and lower, so error messages print in upper and lower case, as seen in the display. It also calls for a width of 72 characters—an error, since the minimum is 80 (see Section 4.9). Note in the output that this error causes SPSS-X to cease processing, since it cannot operate according to the specifications. SPSS-X continues to scan the commands for errors, but the data will not be read.

- The SET command also sets the maximum combined number of errors and warnings to 5. The job exceeds that limit and is terminated with the message near the bottom of the display (see Sections 4.8).

- The SHOW command requests information about compression of scratch files, perhaps to decide whether to alter the default in a subsequent job (see Section 4.13).

- The DATA LIST command contains a single error—CITY is an alphanumeric variable but is not specified as such. SPSS-X cannot detect this error since the data are being not read (due to a previous error). However, the DATA LIST table in the printed output shows that CITY will be read in F format. If the data were read, SPSS-X would begin issuing warnings as soon as it discovered non-numeric characters for CITY (see Section 4.7).

- The COMPUTE command is intended to create a new variable for percentage growth of cities but lacks one of three parentheses that should follow RND. The error message flags the final parenthesis as the error, since the syntax is correct up to that point. If the final parenthesis were also omitted, the command would not be in error, though the outcome would not be the desired one. If this error were the first of its severity in the job, a message would be printed to indicate that processing ceases.

- The VARIABLE LABELS command includes a label for POP89 instead of the correct name POP80. As a result, SPSS-X ignores the label and issues a warning.

- The PRINT FORMATS, SORT CASES, and PRINT commands correctly establish a listing of the cities in order from highest growth rate to most rapid decline.

- The DESCRIPTIVES command names POP89 instead of POP80 and is flagged with an error that causes the procedure to be skipped.

- The SAVE command is misspelled. At this point, the limit of five errors and warnings has been exceeded.

- The FINISH command at the end of the job does not appear on the output because the job terminated before it was reached.

Output with warnings and error messages

```
17-Aug-87   SPSS-X RELEASE 3.0A FOR IBM VM/CMS                                        Page   1
17:39:09    SPSS Inc Developmental System       IBM 4381-2   VM/CMS 4.2


For   VM/CMS 4.2       SPSS Inc Developmental System      License Number 8807

Try the new SPSS-X Release 3.0 features:

* Interactive SPSS-X command execution       * Improvements in:
* Online Help                                *   REPORT
* Nonlinear Regression                       *   TABLES
* Time Series and Forecasting                *   Simplified Syntax
*                                            *   Matrix I/O

See INFO for more information on these features.

    1  0          UNNUMBERED
    2  0   TITLE '1981 U. S. Almanac Data'
    3  0   SUBTITLE 'Percent Growth for Fifty Largest Cities

>Warning # 208 on line 3 in column 10.  Text: Percent Growth for F
>A literal is not correctly enclosed in quotation marks on the command line.
>Literals may not be continued across command lines without the use of the
>continuation symbol '+'.

    4  0   COMMENT    DATA ARE ON TECHSVC 192
    5  0   SET CASE=UPLOW/WIDTH=72/MXWARNS=5

>Error # 804 on line 5 in column 22.  Text: 72
>The WIDTH subcommand of the SET command specified an invalid page width.  The
>allowable range is 80 through 132 inclusive.
>No further commands will be executed.  Error scan continues.

    6  0   SHOW COMPRESSION

COMPRESSION = ON  (WORKFILES ARE COMPRESSED)

    7  0   DATA LIST  FILE=CITYDATA  RECORDS=3
    8  0      /1 CITY 1-13 STATE 14-33(A) POP70 38-44 POP80 48-54

THE COMMAND ABOVE READS   3 RECORDS FROM CITYDATA DATA M1

        VARIABLE   REC  START    END       FORMAT  WIDTH  DEC

        CITY        1     1      13        F        13    0
        STATE       1    14      33        A        20
        POP70       1    38      44        F         7    0
        POP80       1    48      54        F         7    0

END OF DATALIST TABLE

    9  0   COMPUTE PCTGROW = RND((POP80-POP70)/POP70)*100)

17-Aug-87   1981 U. S. Almanac Data                                                   Page   2
17:39:11    Percent Growth for Fifty Largest Cities


>Error # 4020 on line 9 in column 47.  Text: )
>An expression contains unbalanced parentheses.  Check the expression for
>omitted or extra operands, operators, and parentheses.

   10  0   VAR LABELS POP70 'Population in 1970'
   11  0              POP89 'POPULATION IN 1980'

>Warning # 4461 on line 11 in column 12.  Text: POP89
>An unknown variable name was specified on the VAR LABELS command.  The name
>and the label will be ignored.

   12  0              PCTGROW 'Percent Population Growth 1970-1980'
   13  0   PRINT FORMATS POP70 POP80(COMMA9.0)/PCTGROW(F3.0)
   14  0   SORT CASES PCTGROW (D)


PRECEDING TASK REQUIRED       0.01 SECONDS CPU TIME;       0.28 SECONDS ELAPSED.

   15  0   PRINT /CITY TO PCTGROW
   16  0   CONDESCRIPTIVE POP70 POP89 PCTGROW

>Error # 701 on line 16 in column 22.  Text: POP89
>An undefined variable name, or a scratch or system variable was specified in a
>variable list which accepts only standard variables.  Check spelling, and
>verify the existence of this variable.



PRECEDING TASK REQUIRED       0.02 SECONDS CPU TIME;       0.47 SECONDS ELAPSED.

   17  0   SAEV OUTFILE=CITYSF

>Error # 1 on line 17.  Command name: SAEV
>Text appearing in the first column is not recognized as a command.  Is it
>spelled correctly?  If it was intended as a continuation of the previous
>command, the first column must be blank.
>The limit of 5 warnings plus errors has been exceeded.
>The SPSS-X run will terminate now.

   17 COMMAND LINES READ.
    4 ERRORS DETECTED.
    2 WARNINGS ISSUED.
    0 SECONDS CPU TIME.
    5 SECONDS ELAPSED TIME.
      END OF JOB.
```

4

4.7
Blanks and Undefined Input Data

As it reads a data file defined by a DATA LIST command or a REPEATING DATA command, SPSS-X usually assigns the system-missing value whenever it encounters a completely blank field for a numeric variable (see Chapter 5 for exceptions). If you want blanks translated to a number, use the BLANKS subcommand, as in:

```
SET BLANKS = 0
```

Since the command applies only to numeric variables (blanks in strings are taken literally), only numbers are valid specifications.

When SPSS-X encounters anything other than a number or a blank as the value for a numeric-format item, it assigns the system-missing value and issues a warning, as in:

```
>WARNING   652
>An invalid numeric field has been found.  The result has been set to the
>system-missing value.

COMMAND LINE:     5  CURRENT CASE:        1  CURRENT SPLITFILE GROUP:   1
FIELD CONTENTS: '*'
RECORD NUMBER:    1  STARTING COLUMN:     4  RECORD LENGTH:    72
```

This message is printed for each conversion of an alphanumeric symbol to the system-missing value. To suppress the message, specify:

```
SET UNDEFINED = NOWARN
```

If you want to reestablish such warning messages later in the job, you can specify SET UNDEFINED = WARN.

Suppressing the warning message does not stop the counting of warnings toward the maximum allowed before job termination. To control the number of conversions of undefined data permitted within a job, use the MXWARNS subcommand, as described in Section 4.8.

SET UNDEFINED does not allow you to recode alphanumeric values to numbers. To accomplish that, define the variable as alphanumeric and then recode it into a numeric variable, as discussed in Chapter 8.

4.8
Maximum Errors and Loops

Certain errors, such as faulty syntax on a procedure command, cause SPSS-X to disregard the command on which the error occurred but to continue processing. By default, the system allows 40 such errors in batch mode before it decides the job is unredeemable and ought to be discontinued. To raise or lower that number, use the MXERRS subcommand, as in:

```
SET MXERRS = 5
```

SPSS-X also keeps track of the number of warnings issued and terminates a batch job when the number exceeds the maximum. Initially, the maximum is set to 80; you can change that number with the MXWARNS subcommand, as in:

```
SET MXWARNS = 200
```

All errors are included with warnings in the count toward the MXWARNS limit. Notes are not. See Chapter 3 for descriptions of error messages, warnings, and notes.

When you run SPSS-X in interactive mode, each command is executed immediately. Any error or message relative to the command prints upon execution. The MXERRS and MXWARNS settings are therefore ignored when you run SPSS-X in interactive mode.

The LOOP and END LOOP commands (Chapter 14) execute a set of transformation and data definition commands repeatedly for a single case or input record. Without an indexing clause, it is possible to set up a loop such that the conditions for ending it are never met. To cut short such infinite loops, SPSS-X counts the number of times a loop is executed on each case and terminates the loop when a limit is reached. That limit is initially 40. To change this limit, use the MXLOOPS subcommand, as in:

```
SET MXLOOPS = 10
```

4.9
Output

The SET command has subcommands that allow you to control the page length and width for the display file and the print and write formats for numeric variables created by transformation commands. It also has subcommands to control whether lower-case letters in labels and error messages are translated to upper case in the display file and whether your commands are printed back along with other output from your SPSS-X job. You can also control the box-drawing characters displayed in procedures like CROSSTABS and MULT RESPONSE. In addition, SET has subcommands that determine whether headings print at the beginning of every page in the display, and whether macro expansion command lines are included in the command printback.

LENGTH. The LENGTH subcommand establishes the maximum page length for output. Initially, the length is set to 59 lines. You can change that to any length from 40 to 999,999 lines with the LENGTH subcommand, as in:

```
SET LENGTH = 50
```

The length includes the lines from the first printed line on the page to the last that can be printed. The printer you use most likely includes a margin at the top; that margin is not included in the length used by SPSS-X. The default 59 lines allows for a ½-inch margin at the top and bottom of an 11-inch page printed with 6 lines per inch or an 8½-inch page printed with 8 lines per inch.

If you specify a long page length, SPSS-X will continue to give page ejects and titles at the start of each procedure and at logical points in the display, such as between crosstabulation tables. If you want to suppress page ejects altogether, use the NONE keyword, as in:

```
SET LENGTH=NONE
```

SPSS-X will then continue to insert titles at logical points in the display, but the display will not jump to the top of the page when a title is inserted.

WIDTH. The WIDTH subcommand allows you to set the maximum width of the display file to any number of characters from 80 through 132, as in:

```
SET WIDTH = 80
```

The specified width does not include the carriage control character. The default width is 132. All procedures can fit the output to an 80-column page.

CASE. SPSS-X accepts variable labels and value labels in upper and lower case and maintains the case distinction on the active file and on system files. However, the system may translate these labels to upper case before sending them to the display file, depending on the default at your installation. To have them printed in the case in which they were entered, use the CASE subcommand:

```
SET CASE = UPLOW
```

You can set the case to all upper case by specifying SET CASE=UPPER. Use the SHOW command to display your installation's default.

Error messages will appear in upper and lower case if CASE=UPLOW is set, otherwise in upper case only.

The printback of commands, however, is not affected by the case established by SET CASE. Commands are printed back in the case in which they were

4

entered. The same is true of titles. The reason for this is that commands and titles must be entered as part of the command file, and it is assumed that they will be entered in the case appropriate for the device that will print the output. Labels, however, may come from a system file, and it is handy to have a mechanism within SPSS-X for translating these before printing.

Lower-case letters within string variables are not translated to upper case. Thus the results of PRINT and WRITE are not translated even if they are directed to the display file.

PRINTBACK. The PRINTBACK subcommand controls whether SPSS-X includes your commands in the display file. The specification on PRINTBACK is either YES or NO (alias ON or OFF). By default, commands are printed (YES). If you know that your commands are syntactically correct and do not want them included in your display, specify:

```
SET PRINTBACK = NO
```

If you also want to suppress the table indicating how SPSS-X is reading your data from a DATA LIST, see the NOTABLE keyword on DATA LIST, as discussed in Chapter 5.

FORMAT. The FORMAT subcommand establishes the default print and write formats for numeric variables created by transformation commands or read in with the default format on a DATA LIST command specifying LIST or FREE formatted data. The specification must be a simple F format, as in:

```
SET FORMAT = F3.0
```

The default is F8.2. The format established by the FORMAT subcommand applies to all numeric variables created by transformation commands and to numeric variables read on a DATA LIST command with LIST or FREE specified, unless the format is specified. You can use the PRINT FORMATS, WRITE FORMATS, and FORMATS commands to specify the print and write formats for individual variables (see Chapter 10). Note that the actual value maintained on the active file and saved in a system file is not affected by the print or write format.

HEADER. The HEADER subcommand on SET allows you to specify whether output includes headings. It is especially useful to turn the headings off when you are running SPSS-X interactively. The HEADER subcommand applies to both default headings and those specified on the TITLE and SUBTITLE commands (Section 4.1).

The specification on HEADER is either YES or NO (alias ON or OFF). YES is the default. To turn off the heading, specify

```
SET HEADER=NO
```

When HEADER=NO, all general SPSS-X headings in the output, including pagination, are replaced by a single blank line. Some procedure-specific headers like those generated by FREQUENCIES, REPORT, and TABLES will still be displayed.

BOX. The BOX subcommand on SET allows you to specify the characters used to draw grids in procedures such as CROSSTABS, MULT RESPONSE, and TABLES. Other procedures, like FACTOR and REGRESSION, may also use these characters in plots and other displays.

The specification is either a 3- or an 11-character quoted string in which the characters represent, respectively:

1 the horizontal line
2 the vertical line
3 middle (cross)
4 lower-left corner
5 upper-left corner
6 lower-right corner
7 upper-right corner
8 left T
9 right T
10 top T
11 bottom T

If the characters are specified as hexadecimal pairs, specify an X before the quoted string. For example, in IBM conversions,

```
SET BOX '—I+++++++++'
```

is equivalent to

```
SET BOX X'60C94E4E4E4E4E4E4E4E4E'
```

and is the default setting for box-drawing characters. The default settings may have been altered by your local installation to take advantage of characters available on your printer, such as the long dash and vertical bar. To see the current settings, use the SHOW command.

Currently, only TABLES uses all eleven characters (see Section 4.16). All other procedures use only the first three characters, where the third character defines all other intersections. Any characters specified in the fourth through eleventh positions will be ignored by all procedures except TABLES. (If you specify only three characters for TABLES, the same character is used for all nine intersections.) For example,

```
SET BOX '—I*'
```

is equivalent to

```
SET BOX '—I*********'
```

Each specification produces output that uses the dash character for horizontal lines, the capital I for vertical lines, and the asterisk for intersections.

4.10
Custom Currency Formats

Five SET subcommands enable you to specify up to five custom currency formats for your own applications. These subcommands are CCA, CCB, CCC, CCD, and CCE. Each subcommand defines one custom format and include four specifications:

• A negative prefix.
• A prefix.
• A suffix.
• A negative suffix.

Each specification is separated by either a period or a comma, whichever you *do not* want SPSS-X to use as a decimal point in the printed format. While the other specifications are optional, your specification must always contain 3 commas or 3 periods. Use blanks in the specification only where you want blanks in the formatted numbers. You cannot exceed 16 characters in the specification (excluding the apostrophes).

For example, a DOLLAR format on CCA would specify a negative prefix and a prefix, and would use commas for separators. It would look as follows:

```
SET CCA='-,$,,'
```

- A minus sign (−) precedes the first comma; therefore, the minus sign is the negative prefix.
- A dollar sign is specified for the prefix.
- There are no suffixes.
- The commas used as separators indicate that SPSS-X should use a period for a decimal point in numbers assigned the CCA format.

The following SET command defines four custom currency formats. The FORMATS command then assigns these formats to specific variables. Table 4.10 summarizes the currency specifications.

```
SET CCA='(,,,-)'  CCB=',,%,'  CCC='(,$,,)' CCD='-/-.Dfl ..-'
FORMATS VARA(CCA9.0)/ VARB(CCB6.1)/ VARC(CCC8.0)/ VARD(CCD14.2)
```

Table 4.10 Custom currency examples

	CCA	CCB	CCC	CCD
negative prefix	(	none	(	−/−
prefix	none	none	$	Dfl
suffix	none	%	none	none
negative suffix	−)	none	)	−
separator	,	,	,	
sample positive number	23,456	13.7%	$352	Dfl 37.419,00
sample negative number	(19,423−)	13.7%	($189)	−/−Dfl 135,19−

You cannot specify a custom currency format on the DATA LIST command. Use them only on output commands such as FORMATS, WRITE FORMATS, PRINT FORMATS, WRITE, and PRINT.

4.11
Samples and Random Numbers

The pseudo-random number generator that SPSS-X uses in selecting random samples or in creating uniform or normal distributions of random numbers begins with a *seed*, a large integer. Starting with the same seed, the system will repeatedly produce the same sequence of numbers and will select the same sample from a given data file. At the start of each job, the seed is set by SPSS-X to a value that may vary or may be fixed, depending on the implementation. You can set the seed yourself via the SEED subcommand on SET, as in:

```
SET SEED = 987654321
```

The argument can be any integer, preferably a large one but less than 2,000,000,000, which approaches the limit on some machines. The command sets the seed for the next time the random number generator is called. Thus you can reset it following each procedure command in a job if you want to repeat the same random distribution. In the absence of the SEED subcommand, SPSS-X will not reset the seed within a job, so all distributions and samples within the same job will be different.

4.12
Sorting Data

The XSORT subcommand allows you to decide which sort program you wish to use: either the one built into SPSS-X, or the default sort program on your system. The specification is either YES or NO (alias ON or OFF). To use the SPSS-X sort program, specify:

```
SET XSORT=YES
```

Use XSORT if your installation doesn't have a sort program that works with SPSS-X. If your installation provides another sort program you want to use instead of XSORT, specify:

```
SET XSORT=NO
```

The default sort program used by SPSS-X jobs is determined by your SPSS-X coordinator. To see whether XSORT is the default at your site, use the SHOW command.

Because XSORT doesn't compress intermediate work files, it may need more scratch disk space than some other sort programs.

4.13
Scratch File Compression

Compressing scratch files saves disk space at some expense in processing resources. The better choice between compressing scratch files or not depends upon which resources are more readily available at your installation and upon the contents of your file: files containing many variables with small integer values will gain more from compression than will files with primarily large integer or noninteger variables. Your installation will have selected whether scratch files should be compressed by default. (You can use the SHOW command, Section 4.17, to determine what has been set.) If you want to override that choice, use the COMPRESSION subcommand, as in:

```
SET COMPRESSION = YES
```

ON is a synonym for YES. To turn compression off, specify NO or OFF. The command takes effect the next time a scratch file is written and stays in effect until SET COMPRESSION is specified again or until the end of the job.

4.14
Command Terminators and Journal Files

When you run SPSS-X in interactive mode (see Chapter 3), you use a termination character to let SPSS-X know your command specification is complete. When SPSS-X encounters that character, it executes the command. The default termination character is a period. For example, in interactive mode, you issue a command as follows:

```
SORT CASES BY SEX.
```

When you hit the return key after the above command, SPSS-X sorts the data immediately, then returns the SPSSX> prompt. If you do not type the command terminator, when you hit the return key, SPSS-X does not execute the command; instead, it returns the CONTINUE> prompt, expecting further specifications.

Three SET subcommands affect interactive mode of operation. ENDCMD and NULLINE control the definition of the command terminator. JOURNAL determines whether your commands are entered into a command log file.

ENDCMD. When you run SPSS-X in interactive mode (see Chapter 3), you use a termination character to let SPSS-X know your command specification is complete. When SPSS-X encounters that character, it executes the command. The default termination character is a period. You can change that default to any other character using ENDCMD on SET. ENDCMD's only specification is the alternative character in apostrophes, as in

```
SET ENDCMD = '&'.
```

which changes the termination character to an ampersand. If you change the character while in interactive mode, you must use the current termination character to execute the SET command. In the above example, you must type the period (.) to execute the SET command. Subsequent commands terminate with the ampersand (&).

The command terminator can be any single character on your keyboard. You can enter the character as a hexadecimal string by specifying a quoted string containing hexadecimal digits preceded by the letter X.

NULLINE. In addition to the command termination character, a null or blank line can serve as a command terminator. You obtain a null line when running SPSS-X in interactive mode by hitting return from a blank CONTINUE> prompt line.

The NULLINE subcommand on SET determines whether SPSS-X interprets the null line as a command terminator. The specification for NULLINE is either YES or NO (alias ON or OFF). YES, the default, means SPSS-X interprets a null line as a command terminator. To change the default, specify keyword NO, as in

```
SET NULLINE = NO.
```

JOURNAL. The JOURNAL subcommand determines whether SPSS-X maintains a log of your commands during interactive processing. The specification for JOURNAL is either ON or OFF (alias YES or NO). For example, the command

```
SET JOURNAL OFF.
```

during an interactive session turns off the command log. You can also selectively copy commands into the log. For example, you might specify the following sequence of commands during an interactive session.

```
GET FILE=HUBDATA.
SET JOURNAL OFF.
LIST.
SET JOURNAL ON.
FREQUENCIES VARIABLES=ALL.
```

Assuming the default is ON when the GET command is issued (you can specify SHOW JOURNAL to see whether the journal file is on or off), the GET command is copied into the journal log. The SET command then turns the journal off. The LIST command is not copied into the log but is executed in the command file. The second SET command turns the journal on again, and the FREQUENCIES command is copied into the journal file.

The default name of the journal file depends on the file-naming convention at your site. You can also specify a file for the journal. The command

```
SET JOURNAL MYLOG.
```

writes the command log to the journal file MYLOG. The actual file specifications depend on your operating system. See Chapter 5 for more information on referring to a file.

4.15
Macro Displays

The SET command includes four subcommands designed to be used with the macro facility. These subcommands can control the process of macro expansion, the maximum number of loop traversals, and nesting levels. They also allow additional display of the variables, commands, and parameters that macro uses. For more information on the macro facility, see Appendix A.

MEXPAND. MEXPAND controls whether macro expansion will occur. The specification is either ON or OFF (alias YES or NO). MEXPAND is ON by default. Specifying SET MEXPAND OFF will prevent macro expansion. Specifying SET MEXPAND ON will reestablish macro expansion.

MITERATE. MITERATE controls the maximum loop traversals permitted in macro expansions. The specification on MITERATE is a positive integer. The default number of traversals is 1000.

MNEST. MNEST controls the maximum nesting level for macros. The specification on MNEST is a positive integer. The default number of levels that can be nested is 50.

MPRINT. The MPRINT subcommand controls whether the display file includes the command list after macro expansion. The specification for MPRINT is either ON or OFF (alias YES or NO). If you specify

```
SET MPRINT= ON
```

the expanded command list is printed. If you do not include MPRINT or if you specify SET MPRINT=OFF, the expanded command list is not printed. The MPRINT command can be used only in conjuction with the MACRO command and is independent of the PRINTBACK command.

4.16
SET and the TABLES Procedure

Three subcommands on SET and SHOW apply only to the TABLES procedure. The TB1 and TB2 subcommands allow you to define the characters used for line drawing. The TBFONT subcommand permits you to define the font codes used by your Xerox 9700 laser printer. These subcommands produce exactly the same results as BOXCHARS and FONTCHARS within the TABLES procedure but allow you to define these parameters only once, rather than each time you invoke the TABLES command.

- The TBFONTS subcommand is used to set the default TABLES font characters. The parameter is either a 4-character string or an 8-digit hexadecimal string beginning with the character X and followed by a quoted string of hexadecimal pairs, in which the characters represent, respectively:

```
1   LIGHT ROMAN used for line drawing and general text
2   LIGHT ITALIC
3   BOLD ROMAN
4   BOLD ITALIC
```

- The TB1 sets the box characters and has the same specifications as the BOX subcommand (Section 4.9): the characters are specified as either a 3- or 11-character string, and correspond, in order, to the horizontal line, the vertical line, and the nine intersections: middle (cross), lower-left corner, upper-left corner, lower-right corner, upper-right corner, left T, right T, top T, and bottom T. You can specify the characters as a quoted string of hexadecimal pairs preceded by the letter X. The third character will be printed for all nine intersections if only three characters are specified.

- The TB2 subcommand allows you to specify characters that overprint the characters defined in SET TB1. This can be especially useful for printers that do not have T characters (where a vertical and horizontal line meet), so that two corners can be overprinted to form a T. The parameters are the same as for TB1. In the following example, SET TB1 defines dashes for horizontal lines and the capital I for vertical lines; SET TB2 specifies a vertical line to overprint the third character in the first string to form a T.

```
SET WIDTH=80
SET TB1 '-I-----II--'
SET TB2 '   I        '
TABLES  PTITLE = 'CENSUS TRACT SUMMARIES FROM STF3A'
        /FTOTAL = T1 'TOTAL'
        /OBSERVATION = T3.1   T6.1   T9.1   T10.1
        /TABLE = T3.1 + T6.1 + T9.1 + T10.1 BY TRACT + T1
        /TTITLE = 'KENWOOD SUMMARIES (SELECTED TRACTS)'
        /STATISTICS = SUM
```

4.17
Additional Information
from SHOW

The SHOW command displays the current settings of options that can be selected by the SET command. SHOW accepts nine additional subcommands: BLKSIZE, BUFFNO, N, NUMBERED, SCOMPRESSION SYSMIS, $VARS, WEIGHT, and ALL.

- SHOW BLKSIZE displays the default block length for scratch data files and SPSS-X system files.

- SHOW BUFFNO displays the default number of buffers used by all files managed by the SPSS-X I/O subsystem.

- SHOW N gives the unweighted number of cases in the active file. If the active file has not yet been created (the data have not been read because no procedure command has been encountered), N is given as UNKNOWN.

- SHOW NUMBERED displays the current status of the switch set by NUMBERED and UNNUMBERED.

- SHOW SCOMPRESSION shows the default setting for the compression of system files.

- SHOW SYSMIS displays the number used for the system-missing value.

- SHOW $VARS displays the values of all system variables such as $CASENUM and $DATE. See Chapter 7 for a discussion of system variables.

- SHOW WEIGHT displays the name of the variable used to weight the cases on the file.

- SHOW ALL displays the current values of all items available to SHOW.

Part 2: Data Definition and Management

Part II: Data Definition and Management

Although the point of most SPSS-X jobs is to obtain a report or statistical analysis, getting to that report or analysis may involve a number of operations to read in your data and get it into a format suitable for analysis. This part of the manual describes the facilities available for these operations:

- *Data definition.* You (or someone) must tell the system how to interpret the numbers and characters it will read in your data file. This might be a simple process, or it might involve describing a highly complex data structure. You will probably want to provide labels, printing formats, and other information to make your output easier to interpret.
- *Data transformation.* You may need to revise the way your data are coded or to create new variables from existing ones. You can manipulate numbers, dates, and character strings—and you can do so for all cases in your file or just for selected cases.
- *File management.* You may need to combine multiple files to get your data in one place or to update them. You may need to change the unit of analysis (combine all counties into states, for example) or sort the file into a particular order. You may also wish to save the results of your data definition, data transformation, and file combination into a permanent SPSS-X system file or into a file you can transport to another type of computer. Or perhaps you just want to print or write out the information in your file.

This overview ends with a summary of the many types of files you can use and create as you work with SPSS-X.

DATA DEFINITION
Data definition means telling SPSS-X how to read and interpret your data. This involves naming the variables you want to analyze, specifying their location in the data file and their format, informing the system of any values that represent missing data, and supplying any labels you want included in your printed output. SPSS-X uses data definition specifications to build a *dictionary* that describes the variables on the active file. SPSS-X looks to this dictionary whenever it needs such information to carry out an operation. For example, if you use a WRITE command to write out the values of a variable and do not specify the output format on WRITE, SPSS-X looks to the dictionary for the write format assigned to that variable.

Cases and Variables
A data file contains the values of certain *variables* measured for a set of *cases*: the names, ages, and test scores of individuals; the populations and average incomes for cities; the energy requirements and vibration levels of electric generators, and so on. The case can be almost any unit of analysis: an individual, a family, or a country; a sale, a customer, a product line, or an industry; a time interval or a geographical area. A variable could be a measurement such as income in dollars, response time in hundredths of a second, or resistance in ohms; or it could be a set of categories such as sex or response to a multiple-choice questionnaire; or it could be a unique identifier for each case, such as an account or social security number. In short, it can be anything for which a value can be assigned.

Although SPSS-X can accept complex data structures as input, its statistical and tabulation procedures operate on a *rectangular* data file—one in which each case contains one and only one value for each variable and in which the case is the same unit of analysis throughout the entire file.

If the data you want to analyze are already in a rectangular file, you can probably define it with one DATA LIST command, on which you give the names, locations, and formats of every variable you want SPSS-X to read and include in the active file (see Chapter 5). If your data are matrix data, you can probably define it with one MATRIX DATA command, which is similar to DATA LIST but which reads matrix materials rather than raw data. If your file has a more complex structure or if you want to check for missing or duplicate records, you can use some of the facilities outlined in Chapter 12.

Missing Values

It is often useful to code into your data some values that indicate that a true value for a case is not available. You might use several values to indicate several reasons why the value is missing. However, you don't want these values included in most analyses, so you must tell SPSS-X on a MISSING VALUES command which values for which variables indicate missing data. SPSS-X procedures give you options for handling missing values in an analysis, and you can use the keyword MISSING in data transformations to refer to missing values.

In addition to missing values you declare, SPSS-X maintains a system-missing value that it automatically assigns when your data don't conform to the variable type you defined (a letter *A* as a value for a numeric variable, for instance) or when a transformation results in an unknown or impossible computation. If your data include blanks where numbers are expected, SPSS-X also assigns the system-missing value unless you specify otherwise via the BLANKS subcommand on the SET command. See Chapter 5 for information on defining missing values and Chapter 4 for information about the SET command.

Labels

The VARIABLE LABELS command allows you to assign a label to each variable. The label then appears on your output along with the variable name or, in some cases, in lieu of the variable name. Similarly, the VALUE LABELS command allows you to specify labels for the values of a specified variable or list of variables. ADD VALUE LABELS allows you to modify rather than replace an existing set of value labels. Variable and value labels are discussed in Chapter 5.

Format

The *format* of a variable can be both the way the values of that variable are represented to the computer and the way those values are printed on output. SPSS-X accepts data in a wide variety of machine-readable formats and allows you to control the format of both printed output and machine-readable output.

Data in SPSS-X can be either *string* (often called *alphanumeric* or *character*) or *numeric*. String variables can contain numbers, letters, and special characters and can be up to 255 characters long. SPSS-X further differentiates between long strings and short strings. Long strings can be printed out by some procedures and by the PRINT command, and they can be used as "break" variables to define subgroups in REPORT; but they cannot be tabulated as long strings in procedures such as CROSSTABS and cannot have values declared as missing. Short strings, on the other hand, can be tabulated and can have missing values. The maximum length of a short string depends on the computer and operating system you are using; it is typically 8 characters. See Chapters 5 and 8 for information about defining and manipulating string variables, and see the chapters on SPSS-X procedures for information on how a specific procedure handles long and short strings.

Numeric variables vary in width, number of decimal places, and the way they are represented to the computer. You specify these format items when you define input data, and you can (with certain limitations) change the format SPSS-X uses for a numeric variable in a display file or an output data file. Some of the formats available are comma (for variables coded with commas), dollar (with dollar sign and commas), other currencies, zoned decimal, and others depending upon your computer and operating system. A special set of formats for reading and writing dates and time intervals is also available. For a full list of formats available on most computers, see Chapter 5. For formats available specifically on the VAX/VMS operating system, see Appendix F. And for any system, check the LOCAL documentation available via the INFO command for additions and exceptions.

When you supply the format of a variable on a DATA LIST command, SPSS-X enters both a print format and a write format for that variable in the dictionary of the active file. Variables you create within the transformation language are assigned print and write formats. When SPSS-X needs to print or write the values for a variable, it looks to the dictionary for the format to use. Since the dictionary is saved on system files, format information is always available when you retrieve a system file. You can change the print and write formats for individual variables or lists of variables using the PRINT FORMATS and WRITE FORMATS commands, or you can change both formats at once with the FORMATS command. See Chapter 10 for information about how formats are assigned and how to change them.

Defining Complex Files

SPSS-X can read virtually any file it can get at directly (this excludes database systems whose data are available only through their own software). It has a FILE TYPE command that can handle the most common types of complex files, a REPEATING DATA command for files with multiple cases on each input record, and an INPUT PROGRAM facility by which you can give SPSS-X detailed instructions for reading your data. See Chapter 12 for details on defining complex files with the FILE TYPE and REPEATING DATA commands and Chapter 14 for a description of how to build your own input program.

DATA TRANSFORMATION

Data frequently do not come in the form needed for analysis or display. Age may be recorded in years, but you want a variable that assigns each case to one of three age groups. Several test scores may be recorded for each individual, but you want one variable that contains the average score. Or you might want to compute bonuses for employees based on department, length of service, and current salary. SPSS-X provides facilities for revising existing variables and creating new variables. It allows you to transform both numeric and string variables and to do so for every case or only for cases that meet one or more conditions.

Manipulating Numeric Variables

Data manipulation in SPSS-X begins with three basic commands: RECODE, COMPUTE, and COUNT. RECODE allows you to revise the coding structure of one or more variables. You can use it to collapse a variable such as age or income into categories or, if your file has "Yes" and "No" answers coded differently for different variables, to make them consistent.

COMPUTE creates a new variable from an expression made up of existing variables, constants, and functions. A simple example is computing average salary increase from variables giving employees' salaries at the end of each year. A number of functions are available for computing new variables. These include arithmetic functions, such as rounding, truncating, or taking the square root of a value; statistical functions, such as the sum, mean, or variance of a set of values; functions that test for missing values; functions that generate random numbers with uniform or normal distributions; a set of functions that manipulate dates and times; and many others.

Finally, COUNT creates a variable whose value is the number of times a particular value or group of values occurs across a list of variables. You might, for example, want to create an uncertainty index by counting the number of times each respondent answered "Don't know" to a series of questionnaire items.

See Chapter 7 for a discussion of the RECODE, COMPUTE, and COUNT commands and the functions available for numeric transformations.

Manipulating String Variables

The same commands used for manipulating numeric variables can also be used with string variables. Special functions are available for concatenating strings, padding them on the left or right with your choice of characters, trimming characters from the left or right, and converting strings to numbers or numbers to strings. Other functions allow you to take substrings and to index the locations of substrings within strings. Using these functions, you can, for example, insert hyphens within social security numbers, sort names by last name first but print them with first name first, or identify from a list of drugs all those that end in *-ene*. The facilities for manipulating strings are documented in Chapter 8.

Conditional Transformations

The COMPUTE, COUNT, and RECODE commands operate on every case in the file. If you want a command to affect only certain cases, you can use the IF command or a DO IF—END IF structure. The IF command executes a COMPUTE-like operation only if a case meets a certain condition. That condition could be a simple test on a single variable (if variable AGE is greater than 65) or a complex expression involving functions and multiple conditions joined by AND or OR (if variable AGE is greater than 65 and the sum of three income variables is within the range $10,000–15,000).

Like the IF command, the DO IF command establishes a condition, but it applies that condition to any number of subsequent transformation commands. This can save you time in coding multiple IF commands and the computer's time in evaluating those commands. You can also build multiple conditions by enclosing IF commands or DO IF—END IF structures within DO IF—END IF structures. You can also use ELSE IF and ELSE commands to establish a full range of conditional executions.

Examples of IF commands and DO IF—END IF structures can be found in Chapter 9.

Transformation Utilities

SPSS-X provides a number of utilities to simplify coding and to give you added control over the execution of data transformations. DO REPEAT saves coding by performing the same set of transformations on a set of variables. TEMPORARY makes all transformations between the place it appears in the command file and the first procedure that follows it apply only to that one procedure. And LEAVE retains the values of specified variables from one case to the next, allowing you to build cumulative indexes or spread data across cases (see Chapter 7).

FILE MANAGEMENT

SPSS-X provides commands for combining multiple files into a single analysis file, for splitting the active file into subgroups for processing, sorting, and aggregating, and for saving and retrieving efficient system files.

Combining Files

To combine files, you can use ADD FILES, MATCH FILES, or UPDATE. ADD FILES combines the cases of two or more files, either by simply attaching the cases from one file to the end of the other or by interleaving the cases according to the values of a key variable. MATCH FILES combines the variables of two or more files into one file, keeping the same cases wherever possible. If you specify a key variable or variables, SPSS-X combines the cases with matching keys. You can identify one of the files as a table, in which case SPSS-X adds information from the table to every case with a matching key in the other files. UPDATE replaces the values of variables in a master file with updated values stored in one or more transaction files. The many ways in which you can use ADD FILES, MATCH FILES, and UPDATE are discussed in Chapter 16.

Splitting, Sorting, and Aggregating Files

The SPLIT FILE command allows you to process your file in groups defined by one or more variables (see Chapter 15).

SORT CASES orders the active file according to the values of one or more variables. You can specify ascending or descending order for each of the variables you name as sort keys. You can sort on numeric or string variables, but when sorting string variables you may need to pay attention to the collating sequence on your computer (see Chapter 15).

The AGGREGATE procedure builds a new file containing summary statistics for subgroups within the original file and allows you to choose whether to write this file to an external file or replace the active file. See Chapter 18 for details and examples.

System Files

If you plan to analyze a data file several times, consider saving it as an SPSS-X system file. You can do this with either the SAVE command, which causes SPSS-X to read the data and save the file on the spot, or with the XSAVE command, which saves the file when data are processed for the next procedure (often avoiding an unnecessary pass of the data).

The system file is essentially a copy of the active file. The system file contains the dictionary built from data definition commands, so no further definition is required when you retrieve a system file with a GET command. You can use the DOCUMENT command to store any information you choose along with the system file—for example, to keep a record of how the information in the file was gathered, how variables were measured, and so on. You can retrieve this information, as well as dictionary information such as the names, positions, labels, and formats of variables, with the DISPLAY command. Finally, because the system file is stored in a more efficient format than most input data files, using this facility can save considerably on computer resources. You will find it very easy to save and retrieve system files when you need them within a single SPSS-X job. In addition, system files are required as input to ADD FILES, MATCH FILES, and UPDATE. See Chapter 6 for a discussion of system files.

If you want to use an SPSS-X file on a different type of computer, use EXPORT and IMPORT in place of SAVE and GET. These commands create a portable file that can be transferred between computers. The portable file can also be used by SPSS/PC+ on the IBM PC/XT/AT, PS/2, and many compatibles. SPSS-X also has GET SAS, GET BMDP, and GET OSIRIS commands for reading SAS, BMDP, and OSIRIS files (see Chapter 17).

Procedure Output

In addition to tabular or graphical display, SPSS-X procedures create a variety of output data: Z scores; residuals, predicted values, and other values from regression; correlation matrices; aggregated files; and so on. In general, when scores are calculated for each case in the active file, these are simply added to the current active file. Thus, when you use DESCRIPTIVES to calculate standardized scores for one or more variables, the scores are simply added as new variables on your active file. To save them on a permanent file, you must use SAVE or XSAVE to include them in a system file or WRITE to place them in an output data file. The same is true of residuals, predicted values, and other scores from REGRESSION.

On the other hand, when a procedure generates a matrix or new file structure, the current active file is not affected, and a new output file is created. SPSS-X Release 3 uses an entirely new structure for saving and retrieving matrix files. See Chapter 13.

Printing and Writing Cases

Although SPSS-X contains procedures that provide case listings, it also provides the PRINT command that functions as a transformation. That is, it prints out information while it reads the cases for the next procedure (doing both jobs while reading the data only once), and it obeys DO IF and other control structures.

The WRITE command is very similar to the PRINT command, except that it is designed to write out a machine-readable file. It uses a *write format,* which might be quite different from the *print format* used by PRINT. For details about using the PRINT and WRITE commands and the commands for establishing formats, see Chapter 10.

SUMMARY OF FILES USED IN SPSS-X

Operating SPSS-X means dealing with files. Depending on the complexity of your job, you may read or write a variety of files:

• *Command file* (one per job): Contains your SPSS-X commands. The rules for creating these commands are discussed in Chapter 2.

• *Journal file:* Contains a log of commands entered in interactive mode, along with any error or warning messages the commands generated. The journal file and interactive mode are discussed in Chapter 3.

• *Input data file:* Contains your data in almost any format. This file can be imbedded within your SPSS-X command file, or it can be a separate file on tape or disk.

• *Display file:* Contains the tabular output from the SPSS-X procedures you have requested, diagnostic information about your job, and output from any PRINT or WRITE commands for which you have not specified a separate output file. This file is formatted for listing at a terminal or on a line printer.

• *Active file:* Serves as the main input to transformations and procedures. It is created by DATA LIST, GET, IMPORT, MATRIX DATA, or an input program and is modified by transformations and some procedures. It exists only for the duration of the SPSS-X job but can be saved as a system file or exported as a portable file.

• *Output file:* Contains data formatted for reading by a computer. Some procedures create output files containing matrix or other materials, and the WRITE command produces a data file to your specifications.

• *System file:* A file specifically formatted for use by SPSS-X, containing both data and the *dictionary* that defines the data to the system. System files speed processing and are required as input for combining files.

• *Portable file:* A system file created by the EXPORT command and formatted for portability to computers other than the one on which it was created.

Conventions for naming, printing, deleting, or permanently saving files, and for submitting command files for processing differ considerably from one computer and operating system to another. Use the INFO command and look for other documentation at your site for information about handling files outside SPSS-X.

Multiple Files and the Active File

When you submit an SPSS-X job, you tell your system where to find your command file. The procedure that executes SPSS-X at your site then assigns a display file and also allocates scratch files that SPSS-X may need to hold your active file between procedures. The rest of the files are up to you. You must name each file, and you may need to supply additional information, depending on your computer and operating system. For more information on referring to files in SPSS-X, refer to Chapter 5 and the documentation available from the INFO LOCAL command (see Chapter 3).

Data to be used in an SPSS-X job must be defined—that is, it must have names for the variables, formats for reading and printing values, and optionally some labels and missing-value specifications. The essential information can be provided on a DATA LIST command or on one of the other commands that define more complex files. A system file, portable file, SAS data set, or OSIRIS file already contains the necessary definitions. Once this information is available, SPSS-X can build an *active file,* which is then modified by transformation commands and analyzed by procedure commands.

The active file is not actually created until SPSS-X encounters a procedure command—one that causes it to read the data. This allows the data to be read and transformed and the first procedure processed with only one pass through the original file. It also ensures that the system will not use computer resources to read data and perform transformations before it has received syntactically correct instructions to produce some kind of output.

When the system does encounter a procedure command, it executes all of the preceding data definition and transformation commands and performs whatever action the procedure calls for. The active file is then available for further transformations and procedures, and it remains available until the end of the job or until it is specifically replaced. In addition, some procedures are able to add variables to the active file, or, in the case of AGGREGATE, to replace the active file altogether.

Syntax

ADD VALUE LABELS

```
ADD VALUE LABELS varlist value 'label' value 'label'... [/varlist...]
```

BEGIN DATA—END DATA

```
BEGIN DATA
lines of data
END DATA
```

DATA LIST

```
DATA LIST [FILE=file] [{FIXED}] [RECORDS={1}] [{TABLE  }]
                       {FREE }            {n}   {NOTABLE}
                       {LIST }

          [END=varname]
   /{1    } varlist {col location [(format)]  } [varlist ...]
    {rec #}         {(FORTRAN-like format list}
[/{2    } ...] [/ ...]
  {rec #}
```

Numeric and string formats:

Format	FORTRAN-like format	Data type
(d)	Fw.d	Numeric (default)
(N)	Nw	Restricted numeric
(E,d)	Ew.d	Scientific notation
(COMMA,d)	COMMAw.d	Numeric with commas
(DOT,d)	DOTw.d	Numeric with dots
(DOLLAR,d)	DOLLARw.d	Numeric with commas and dollar sign
(PCT,d)	PCTw.d	Numeric with percent sign
(Z,d)	Zw.d	Zoned decimal
(A)	Aw	String
(AHEX)	AHEXw	Hexadecimal character
(IB,d)	IBw.d	Integer binary
(P,d)	Pw.d	Packed decimal
(PIB,d)	PIBw.d	Unsigned integer binary
(PIBHEX)	PIBHEXw	Hexadecimal unsigned integer binary
(PK,d)	PKw.d	Unsigned packed decimal
(RB)	RBw	Floating point binary
(RBHEX)	RBHEXw	Hexadecimal floating point binary

Some formats may not be available on all implementations of SPSS^X.

Date and time input formats:

Format	FORTRAN-like format	Data Input	Type
(DATE)	DATEw	dd/mmm/yyyy	International date
(ADATE)	ADATEw	mmm/dd/yyyy	American date
(JDATE)	JDATEw	yyddd	Julian date
(QYR)	QYRw	qQyyyy	Quarter and year
(MOYR)	MOYRw	mm/yyyy	Month and year
(WKYR)	WKYRw	wkWKyyyy	Week and year
(DATETIME)	DATETIMEw	dd-mmm-yyyy hh:mm:ss.ss	Date and time
(TIME)	TIMEw	hh:mm:ss.ss	Time
(DTIME)	DTIMEw	ddd hh:mm:ss.ss	Days and time
(WKDAY)	WKDAYw	string	Day of the week
(MONTH)	MONTHw	string	Month

*Column binary and unaligned positive integer binary specifications:**

```
startcolumn:startrow [-endrow]
startcolumn:startrow-endcolumn:endrow
startbyte:startbit [-endbit]
startbyte:startbit-endbyte:endbit
```

* Column binary files can be read only if MODE=MULTIPUNCH is specified on the FILE HANDLE command.

FILE HANDLE

```
FILE HANDLE handle / [MODE=MULTIPUNCH] file specifications
```

Specifications differ by implementation of SPSS^X.

MISSING VALUES

```
MISSING VALUES {varlist(value list) [[/]varlist ...]}
               {ALL(value)                          }
```

Keywords for numeric value lists:
LO, LOWEST, HI, HIGHEST, THRU

RENAME VARIABLES

```
RENAME VARIABLES {(varname=varname)  [(varname ...)]}
                 {(varlist=varlist)                 }
```

VALUE LABELS

```
VALUE LABELS varlist value 'label' value 'label'... [/varlist...]
```

VARIABLE LABELS

```
VARIABLE LABELS varname 'label' [/varname...]
```

Contents

5.1	INTRODUCTION TO DATA DEFINITION
5.2	REFERRING TO A FILE IN SPSS-X
5.3	FILE HANDLE Command
5.4	FILE DEFINITION ON DATA LIST
5.5	FILE Subcommand
5.6	FIXED, FREE, and LIST Keywords
5.7	RECORDS Subcommand
5.8	TABLE and NOTABLE Subcommands
5.9	VARIABLE DEFINITION ON DATA LIST
5.10	The Active File
5.11	Specifying the Record Number
5.12	Naming the Variables
5.13	Indicating Column Locations
5.14	Specifying Multiple Records
5.15	Specifying Multiple Variables
5.16	Indicating Decimal Places
5.17	Specifying the Format Type
5.18	N and E Format Types
5.19	Alphanumeric (A) Format Type
5.20	Other Format Types
5.21	FREE and LIST Variable Definition
5.22	Format Types with FREE and LIST
5.23	Undefined Data Values
5.24	Printing and Writing Formats
5.25	MISSING VALUES
5.26	MISSING VALUES Command
5.27	Referencing Several Variables
5.28	Specifying Ranges of Missing Values
5.29	Missing Values for String Variables
5.30	Redefining Missing Values
5.31	VARIABLE AND VALUE LABELS
5.32	VARIABLE LABELS Command
5.33	VALUE LABELS Command
5.34	ADD VALUE LABELS Command
5.35	RENAME VARIABLES Command
5.36	INLINE DATA IN THE COMMAND FILE
5.37	BEGIN DATA and END DATA Commands
5.38	FORTRAN-LIKE FORMAT SPECIFICATIONS ON DATA LIST
5.39	Format Elements
5.40	Printable Numeric Formats
5.41	Nonprintable Numeric Input Formats
5.42	String Formats
5.43	Date and Time Input Formats
5.44	T and X Format Elements
5.45	Format Lists
5.46	Mixing Styles
5.47	Skipping Records
5.48	COLUMN BINARY FORMAT
5.49	Column Binary Data and the FILE HANDLE Command
5.50	Variable Definition on DATA LIST
5.51	Using Non-Column Binary Formats
5.52	Column Binary Data on Tape or Disk
5.53	Limitations
5.54	UNALIGNED POSITIVE INTEGER BINARY FORMAT
5.55	Variable Definition on DATA LIST
5.56	UPIB versus Column Binary Format
5.57	Limitations

5

Chapter 5   Defining Data

SPSS-X consists of a set of commands for defining, displaying and analyzing data. SPSS-X procedures can deal with data in only one form: a rectangular file. Such a file is composed of rows and columns with each row containing one entry for each column. In SPSS-X, each row is called a *case*. Cases do not have names but are identified by the system variable $CASENUM (see Chapter 7). Each case generally corresponds to one of the units under examination (such as a person, a purchase order, or a test answer sheet). The columns in a rectangular file represent *variables*. Each variable has a name and a code that measures or describes some attribute of each case (such as a person's age, the amount of a purchase, or the date written on a test answer sheet).

This chapter explains the commands you need to define and process your data for use with SPSS-X. The chapter assumes that the raw data file is arranged so that for every case, a value is recorded for every variable, and the order of these values is the same from case to case. Chapters 12 and 14 explain how to process raw data files with more complicated structures. Chapter 6 explains how to use system files, files written by SPSS-X that contain both data and descriptive information. Chapter 17 explains how to use other self-describing files. Appendix E describes how to use sequential and random access files. Appendix E also describes IBM-specific files and data types that are available. Appendix F describes VAX-specific files and data types that are available.

5.1 INTRODUCTION TO DATA DEFINITION

SPSS-X data definition requires two parts: *file definition* provides basic information about the data file, and *variable definition* provides specific information about the location, structure, and meaning of the data on the file. You specify the file on the FILE subcommand on the DATA LIST command and use additional DATA LIST subcommands and keywords to further define it for SPSS-X (see Sections 5.4 through 5.8). You define variables beginning on the DATA LIST command and continuing on optional variable definition commands, such as VARIABLE LABELS, MISSING VALUES, and so forth.

For example, the commands

```
DATA LIST  FILE=BALLOONS/ COLOR 1
VARIABLE LABELS  COLOR 'COLOR OF BALLOON'
VALUE LABELS COLOR 1 'BLUE' 2 'RED' 3 'GREEN' 4 'YELLOW' 5 'ORANGE'
                8 'POPPED' 9 'DEFLATED'
MISSING VALUES COLOR (8,9)
```

specify the file BALLOONS on the DATA LIST command, implicitly telling SPSS-X that the file is a simple fixed-format file with one record per case. The variable definition portion of the DATA LIST command begins with a slash and names variable COLOR to be read from column 1 of each record on file BALLOONS. Variable COLOR is implicitly understood to be numeric without decimal places.

55

Once a variable is identified on a DATA LIST command, you can use optional variable definition commands for assigning labels (the VARIABLE LABELS and VALUE LABELS commands) and for declaring specific values representing missing information (the MISSING VALUES command). Information provided via data definition commands is stored in a dictionary and can be saved along with the data values in an SPSS-X system file, which can be retrieved on subsequent SPSS-X jobs without repeating data definitions (see Chapter 6).

5.2
REFERRING TO A FILE IN SPSS-X

SPSS-X can read and write more than one file in a single job. The files include data files, system files, and special files of statistical results.

Subcommands that refer to files in SPSS-X are the FILE, OUTFILE, MATRIX, and WRITE subcommands on various procedures. There are basically three ways in which a file can be referenced on these subcommands:

- You can reference the file by name directly on the subcommand by enclosing the name in quotes.
- You can define a handle for the file on a FILE HANDLE command and then reference the handle on the subcommand. This mechanism permits you to specify other characteristics of the file in addition to its name, for example, the fact that it contains multipunched data.
- You can define a handle outside SPSS-X with a host system command such as FILEDEF or DD and then reference the handle on the subcommand. This mechanism may permit the specification of still more information about the file such as the name of the tape containing the file. It also makes it easier to run the same SPSS-X job with different data.

For example, to refer to the file identified by the file handle BALLOONS on the DATA LIST command, simply specify BALLOONS on the FILE subcommand, as in

```
DATA LIST  FILE=BALLOONS/ COLOR 1
```

When you refer to a file directly, the specification depends on the computer and operating system on which you run SPSS-X. (For details, refer to the documentation available with keyword LOCAL on the INFO command.) For example, the VAX/VMS version of SPSS-X uses a full VAX file specification, which supplies the device, directory, filename, filetype, and version number of the file. The IBM CMS version uses a file specification that supplies the filename, filetype, and optional filemode:

```
DATA LIST FILE='BALLOONS DATA A'/ COLOR 1
```

Throughout this manual, examples of the FILE, OUTFILE, MATRIX, and WRITE subcommands refer to a file by its handle. On the syntax chart for each command, the file handle is abbreviated to the general term *file*.

Not all implementations of SPSS-X offer all three methods of referring to a file. Some implementations require both host system commands and the use of the FILE HANDLE command within SPSS-X. Others offer extensions to the ability to reference the file directly on a FILE, OUTFILE, MATRIX, or WRITE subcommand. For instance, some implementations permit the specification of just a portion of a file name and supply defaults for the other portions.

In the IBM OS version of SPSS-X, a FILE HANDLE command (see Section 5.3) is used when the data set contains column-binary data (see Sections 5.3 and 5.49) or when you are reading VSAM files (see Appendix E). Otherwise, a JCL DD statement provides operating-system-specific information such as the file name, its record length, blocksize, storage location, and so forth. For example, the specification

```
DATA LIST  FILE=BALLOONS/ COLOR 1
```

tells SPSS-X to look for the JCL command

```
//BALLOONS DD DSN= ...
```

which provides operating-system information about the file. For more about writing JCL commands, see the documentation available with the keyword LOCAL on the INFO command (see Chapter 3).

5.3
FILE HANDLE Command

The FILE HANDLE command enables you to assign a unique *file handle* to a file. A file handle is used only during an SPSS-X job. The handle is never saved as part of an SPSS-X system file.

The first specification on the FILE HANDLE command is the file handle. A file handle cannot exceed eight characters and must begin with an alphabetic character (A–Z) or a $, #, or @. It can also contain numeric digits (0–9). It cannot contain imbedded blanks.

The actual file specifications depend on the type of computer and operating system on which you run SPSS-X. For details on writing the file specifications, refer to the documentation available with the keyword LOCAL on the INFO command (see Chapter 3).

For data files that contain multipunch (column binary) data (see Sections 5.48 through 5.53), the FILE HANDLE command naming the MODE= MULTIPUNCH subcommand is required. For example, the command

```
FILE HANDLE ELE48 / MODE=MULTIPUNCH file specifications
```

names ELE48 as the file handle for a column binary data set. Once the handle is assigned on FILE HANDLE, you specify the handle on the FILE subcommand of DATA LIST (see Section 5.5), as in

```
FILE HANDLE ELE48 / MODE=MULTIPUNCH file specifications
DATA LIST FILE=ELE48
```

The FILE HANDLE command is also required for reading IBM VSAM data sets. For more information, see Appendix E.

5.4
FILE DEFINITION ON DATA LIST

The file definition portion of the DATA LIST command points SPSS-X to the data file and indicates the format of the file and the number of records SPSS-X should read per case from fixed-format data files. You can specify five pieces of information describing the data file on the DATA LIST command:

FILE Subcommand. FILE specifies the file described by the DATA LIST command. (See Sections 5.2 and 5.5.)

FIXED, FREE, and LIST Keywords. FIXED, the default, indicates that the data are recorded in fixed format. FREE indicates that the data are recorded in freefield format, and LIST indicates that the data are in freefield format with one case recorded on each record. (See Section 5.6.)

RECORDS Subcommand. RECORDS indicates the number of records per case for fixed-format files. (See Section 5.7.)

END Subcommand. END indicates a variable that is set to a value of 0 until the end of file is encountered. At the end of the file, this variable is set to 1. See Chapter 14 for a more detailed discussion.

TABLE and NOTABLE Subcommands. TABLE, the default for fixed-format files, prints a summary table describing file and variable definitions. NOTABLE suppresses the summary table. (See Section 5.8.)

For example, the command

```
DATA LIST  FILE=BALLOONS,FIXED RECORDS=1 TABLE/ COLOR 1 COUNT 2–5
```

specifies the file BALLOONS, indicates fixed-format data, tells SPSS-X to expect one record per case, and requests a summary table describing the DATA LIST specifications.

- Equals signs after the FILE and RECORDS subcommands are optional.
- FILE, FIXED, RECORDS, and TABLE specifications are separated by at least one blank or comma.
- FILE, FIXED, RECORDS, and TABLE specifications can appear in any order.

5.5
FILE Subcommand

Use the FILE subcommand to specify the file containing the data described by the DATA LIST command. The specification

```
DATA LIST   FILE=HUBDATA RECORDS=3
  /1 YRHIRED 14-15 DEPT82 19 SEX 20
```

indicates that file HUBDATA is being described. For information on referencing files in SPSS-X, see Sections 5.2 and 5.3.

You can omit the FILE subcommand only when the data are included as lines in your SPSS-X command file. Inline data must be entered between the BEGIN DATA and END DATA commands (see Section Section 5.36).

5.6
FIXED, FREE, and LIST Keywords

Use one of the following keywords on DATA LIST to indicate the format of the data:

FIXED *Fixed-format data.* Each variable is recorded in the same location on the same record for each case in the data. FIXED is the default.

FREE *Freefield-format data.* The variables are recorded in the same order for each case, but not necessarily in the same locations. You can enter more than one case on the same record. Values are separated by blanks or commas.

LIST *Freefield data with one case on each record.* The variables are recorded in freefield format as described for keyword FREE except the variables for each case must be recorded on one record.

For example, to indicate explicitly that the HUBDATA file is in fixed format, specify:

```
DATA LIST FILE=HUBDATA FIXED RECORDS=3
  /1 YRHIRED 14-15 DEPT82 19 SEX 20
```

Sections 5.7 and 5.8 describe two other file definition specifications on the DATA LIST command, the RECORDS, TABLE, and NOTABLE subcommands, which can be used only with fixed-format data. The variable definition specifications for fixed-format data are described in Sections 5.11 through 5.20. The variable definition specifications for FREE and LIST format data are described in Sections 5.21 and 5.22.

5.7
RECORDS Subcommand

Use the RECORDS subcommand with fixed-format data to specify the number of records per case. The specification

```
DATA LIST   FILE=HUBDATA RECORDS=3
  /1 YRHIRED 14-15 DEPT82 19 SEX 20
```

tells SPSS-X to expect three records per case in file HUBDATA.

By default, SPSS-X assumes one record per case for fixed-format data. Therefore, you must use the RECORDS subcommand if there are more. You should not use the RECORDS subcommand with freefield data (keywords LIST and FREE).

5.8
TABLE and NOTABLE
Subcommands

By default for fixed-format data, SPSS-X displays a table that summarizes your variable definitions immediately following your DATA LIST command (see Figure 5.8). The table includes the number of records per case along with the following information on each variable: the variable name, the record number, the starting and ending columns, the format, the width, and the number of decimal places.

To suppress this table, specify subcommand NOTABLE, as in:

```
DATA LIST  FILE=TESTDATA NOTABLE / X 1-2
```

Figure 5.8   DATA LIST summary table

```
    1   0            DATA LIST  FILE=TESTDATA / X 1-2
THE ABOVE DATA LIST STATEMENT WILL READ   1 RECORDS FROM FILE TESTDATA.
              VARIABLE  REC    START     END       FORMAT  WIDTH  DEC
                 X         1      1        2          F        2    0
END OF DATALIST TABLE.
```

You can request explicitly the default summary table with the TABLE subcommand. Summary tables are not available with freefield data.

5.9
VARIABLE
DEFINITION ON DATA
LIST

Use the variable definition portion of the DATA LIST command to assign a name to each variable you intend to analyze and, depending on the format of your file, to provide information about the location and format of the individual variables. For fixed-format data, specify the record number, name, column location, and type of each variable (Sections 5.11 through 5.20). For FREE or LIST format data, specify the name and type of each variable (Sections 5.21 and 5.22).

5.10
The Active File

The DATA LIST command does not read the data; it gives SPSS-X information on the location and format of the data. Data are read when a procedure or other data-reading command is executed (see Chapter 3).

Once SPSS-X reads your data according to the DATA LIST command, it creates an *active file* which consists of the data and a *dictionary* containing variable definitions such as variable names, labels, printing and writing formats, and missing-value flags. The active file is the file that you modify using the transformation language (Chapters 7, 8, and 9), that you analyze using any of the procedures, and that you save as an SPSS-X system file (Chapter 6). You can refer to the active file with an asterisk (*) on the file specification on commands other than DATA LIST. The file specified on the FILE subcommand on the DATA LIST command must refer to the original input data file.

5.11
Specifying the Record
Number

Variable definition on the DATA LIST command begins with a slash. Following this slash, specify the sequence number of the first record from which you are defining variables. The specification

```
DATA LIST  FILE=HUBDATA RECORDS=3
 /1 YRHIRED 14-15 DEPT82 19 SEX 20
```

indicates that the variables being defined are located on the first of the three records for each case. If you do not specify the record number, SPSS-X assumes that you are defining variables on the first (or only) record of each case.

You can omit the sequence number of the record and use the slash alone to define the record location. Each slash means "skip to the next record." In the above example, the record sequence number is not needed because variables defined after the first slash are located on the first record. Variables defined after a second slash would be located on the second record, and so forth. See Section 5.47 for additional discussion of using slashes to skip records.

5.12
Naming the Variables

Assign a *variable name* to each variable that you describe. The specification

```
DATA LIST  FILE=HUBDATA RECORDS=3
 /1 YRHIRED 14-15 DEPT82 19 SEX 20
```

defines three variables: year hired, department in 1982, and sex for each case on the file.

Variable names are used on all other SPSS-X commands to refer to the data values. Variable names can contain up to eight characters, the first of which must be an alphabetic letter or the characters @, #, or $. You can use an underscore within the variable name, as long as the underscore is not the first character.

A # character in the first position of a variable name defines a scratch variable. A $ in the first position indicates the variable is a system variable. Scratch variables can be defined on the DATA LIST and used on the transformation commands but cannot be used by procedure commands or saved permanently on a system file. System variables cannot be named on the DATA LIST command and are not available for procedures. See Chapter 7 for a description of the use of scratch and system variables. All other rules and conventions for constructing names must be followed for variable names (see Chapter 2).

The name you give to a variable cannot duplicate that of any other variable named on the same DATA LIST command. You should select variable names that reflect the nature of the variables being named. For example, suppose that your data file contains information for individuals on income, occupation, and age. You could use the variable names INCOME, OCCUP, and AGE for these variables. Note that OCCUPATION cannot be used as a variable name since it is longer than eight characters.

The order in which variable names are mentioned on the DATA LIST command determines their order in the active file. If you save your active file as a system file, the variables will be saved in this order unless you explicitly reorder them (see Chapter 6).

5.13
Indicating Column Locations

Follow the name of the variable with its column location. If the variable is one column wide, specify the number of the column. If the variable is two or more columns wide, specify the number of the first column followed by a dash (–) and the number of the last column, as in:

```
DATA LIST  FILE=HUBDATA RECORDS=3
 /1 YRHIRED 14-15 DEPT82 19 SEX 20
```

This command defines three variables on the first record of a data file with three records per case: variable YRHIRED is found in columns 14 and 15, DEPT82 in column 19, and SEX in column 20.

You do not need to define all of the variables in the data file—only those that you intend to use. SPSS-X ignores the data in columns and on records that you do not mention.

5.14
Specifying Multiple Records

Once you've specified variables from one record, enter a slash, followed by the record number of the next record to be read and the variable definitions for that record.

```
DATA LIST  FILE=HUBDATA RECORDS=3
 /1 YRHIRED 14-15 DEPT82 19 SEX 20
 /2 SALARY82 21-25
```

Three variables, YRHIRED, DEPT82, and SEX, are located on the first record of the data file. One variable, SALARY82, will be read from columns 21 through 25 on the second record. The total number of records per case is specified as three, even though no variables are defined on the third record. The third record will simply be skipped.

Define all variables you want to read from a given record before you proceed to the next record. Within a record, variables do not need to be defined in the same sequence as they are recorded on the file, and you can define the same columns for two different variables, as in:

```
DATA LIST  FILE=HUBDATA RECORDS=3
 /1 DEPT82 19 SEX 20 YRHIRED 14-15 MOHIRED 12-13 HIRED 12-15
 /2 SALARY82 21-25
```

The first two defined variables are DEPT82 and SEX, located in columns 19 and 20 on record 1. The next three variables, YRHIRED, MOHIRED, and HIRED, are also located on the first record. YRHIRED will be read from columns 14 and 15, MOHIRED from columns 12 and 13, and HIRED from columns 12 through 15. The HIRED variable is a four-column variable with the first two columns representing the month when an employee was hired (the same as the MOHIRED variable) and the last two columns representing the year of employment (the same as YRHIRED). The order of the variables in the dictionary is the order in which they are defined on the DATA LIST command, not their sequence on the input data file.

5.15
Specifying Multiple Variables

If several variables are recorded in adjacent columns of the same record and have the same width and format type, they can be defined on the DATA LIST in an abbreviated format. List all of the variable names followed by the beginning column location of the first variable in the list, a dash, and the ending column location of the last variable in the list, as in

```
DATA LIST  FILE=HUBDATA RECORDS=3
 /1 DEPT82 19 SEX 20 MOHIRED YRHIRED 12-15
 /2 SALARY82 21-25
```

where MOHIRED and YRHIRED form a list of variables followed by the column specification for both. The DATA LIST command divides the total number of columns specified equally among the variables in the list. If the total number of columns is not an even multiple of the number of variables listed, SPSS-X prints an error message and continues scanning the commands that follow DATA LIST for syntax errors but does not read the data file.

The list of variable names can include both specific variable names and a sequence of variable names using the keyword TO. For example, ITEM1 TO ITEM5 is equivalent to five names: ITEM1, ITEM2, ITEM3, ITEM4, and ITEM5. The prefix can be any valid name and the numbers can be any integers, so long as the first number is smaller than the second and the full variable name, including the number, does not exceed eight characters. Note that the number is a part of the variable name, not a subscript. If you include leading zeros in the number, they are preserved in the variable name. X1 TO X100 and X001 TO X100 both generate 100 variable names, but the first 99 names are not the same in the two lists. X01 TO X9 is not valid.

You can include both individual variable names and inclusive lists of variable names on a single DATA LIST command, as in:

```
DATA LIST  FILE=HUBDATA RECORDS=3
 /1 MOHIRED YRHIRED 12-15 DEPT79 TO DEPT82 SEX 16-20
 /2 SALARY79 TO SALARY82 6-25
```

DEPT79, DEPT80, DEPT81, DEPT82, and SEX are defined as single-column variables located in columns 16 through 20 on the first record. SALARY79, SALARY80, SALARY81, and SALARY82 are defined as five-column variables located in columns 6 through 25 on the second record.

5.16
Indicating Decimal Places

By default, DATA LIST assumes that the data are whole numbers or that decimal points have been recorded on the data file. To indicate noninteger values when the decimal point is not actually coded in the data, specify the number of *implied* decimal places in parentheses following the column specification. The specification

```
DATA LIST  FILE=HUBDATA RECORDS=3
  /1 MOHIRED YRHIRED 12-15 DEPT79 TO DEPT82 SEX 16-20
  /2 SALARY79 TO SALARY82 6-25 HOURLY81 HOURLY82 42-53(2)
```

locates the variables that record the hourly wage of an employee for 1981 and 1982 in columns 42 through 47 and 48 through 53 on record two. The last two digits of both HOURLY81 and HOURLY82 will be stored as decimal places. Any coded decimal point found in the data overrides the number of implied places defined on the DATA LIST command.

5.17
Specifying the Format Type

When you use the column-style specification shown up to this point in this chapter (as opposed to the FORTRAN style shown in Sections 5.38 through 5.47), the default format is F. You can specify any of the other format types enclosed in parentheses following the column specification. In the following example, the Z format is specified:

```
DATA LIST FILE=TESTDATA/ ZTEST 3-6 (Z,2)
```

The 2 following the Z format type is the number of implied decimal places.

Only numbers can be read with the default variable format type. The numbers can be either signed or unsigned and either integer or noninteger. All alphabetic characters and punctuation characters, except the decimal point and leading plus and minus signs, are considered undefined, and SPSS-X assigns the system-missing value when one of these characters is encountered (see Chapter 2). Blanks to the left or right of a number are ignored; imbedded blanks are errors. By default, SPSS-X assigns the system-missing value to a completely blank field. You can change the value assigned to blank fields by specifying the subcommand BLANKS on the SET command (see Chapter 4).

Table 5.17 illustrates how values are interpreted for a four-column variable defined as the default format type (integer) and as the default format type with two decimal places defined.

Table 5.17 Default format type: values read by SPSS-X

Values in the data file	Integer (default)	Two decimal places
2001	2001	20.01
201	201	2.01
−201	−201	−2.01
2	2	0.02
20	20	0.20
2.2	2.2	2.2
0.201	0.201	0.201
2 01	Undefined	Undefined

5.18
N and E Format Types

Two additional numeric formats that are commonly used are the N and E formats. The N, or restricted numeric, format reads unsigned integers. This format is useful for reading and checking values that you know can be only integers with leading zeros. Leading, trailing, and imbedded blanks are not allowed. Decimal points coded in the data are not allowed. Implied decimal places are allowed, but you must change the print format to F for the decimal places to appear. (See Chapter 10 for changing print and write formats.)

The E, or scientific notation, format reads all forms of scientific notation numbers. E or D preceding the exponent is not necessary if a sign ($+$ or $-$) is coded before the exponent. For example, the value $1-1$ is read under E format as $1.0E-1$. You cannot code decimal points in the exponent portion of the number. However, decimal points can be coded in the number preceding the exponent. You can also specify implied decimal points.

5.19
Alphanumeric (A) Format Type

Another type of variable found in many data files is the *string variable*, also known as the alphanumeric or character variable. The format type specification for a string variable is the letter A enclosed in parentheses following the column specification, as in:

```
DATA LIST   FILE=HUBDATA RECORDS=3
  /1 MOHIRED YRHIRED 12-15 DEPT79 TO DEPT82 SEX 16-20
  /2 SALARY79 TO SALARY82 6-25 HOURLY81 HOURLY82 42-53(2)
  /3 NAME 25-48 (A) NAMEFOUR 25-28 (A)
```

Two string variables are defined on the third record: NAME is the 24-character name of the employee, and NAMEFOUR is only the first four characters of the name. On all computers, NAME would be considered a *long string variable* and NAMEFOUR a *short string variable*.

String variables can be up to 255 characters long. String variables shorter than a certain length can be used in some places where longer ones cannot. Short string variables can have missing values defined and can be counted in procedure FREQUENCIES. The maximum length for a short string variable depends on which type of computer you are using. The maximum length is the number of characters that fill as much computer memory as SPSS-X uses to store a number. On IBM, DEC VAX, and many other types of machines, the maximum length of a short string is 8 characters. On a DEC 10 or DEC 20 computer, the maximum length is 10. Any string variable longer than the maximum length allowed for short strings is considered a long string variable. The maximum length of a long string variable is 255 characters for most implementations of SPSS-X.

5.20
Other Format Types

Table 5.39 lists the most commonly used format types (shown in FORTRAN-like style). All of these format types are implemented on the IBM and IBM systems. Additional format types that are available only for specific operating systems are described in supplemental documentation available through keyword LOCAL on the INFO command (see Chapter 3). See Appendix F for VAX VMS machine-specific data formats.

The custom currency formats available on the SET command (see Chapter 4) cannot be specified on DATA LIST.

5.21
FREE and LIST Variable Definition

If you specify FREE or LIST in the file definition portion of your DATA LIST command, SPSS-X expects freefield-format data. Therefore, you do not specify the location of the variables on the variable definition portion of DATA LIST. Rather SPSS-X reads the values sequentially in the order that the variables are named on the DATA LIST command. The values must be separated in your data by at least one blank or comma.

Use the keyword FREE to read freefield-format data with multiple cases recorded on one record or with one case recorded on more than one record. Use the keyword LIST to read data with one case recorded on each record. If all of the values in your data are numeric, simply list the variable names in the order that the values are recorded, as in:

```
DATA LIST FILE=WINS FREE/POSTPOS NWINS
```

Figure 5.21a shows the data in file WINS. All of the data are recorded on one record. The first two values build the first case in the active file. The value 2 is assigned to variable POSTPOS, and the value 19 to NWINS. The second case is built from the next two values in the data, and so forth. Eight cases are built on the active file.

Figure 5.21a   Data in FREE format

```
2 19 7 5 10 25 5 17 8 11 3 18 6 8 1 29
```

In FREE format, the end of a data record is the same as a blank or comma. That is, a value cannot be split across records. However, multiple blank columns at the end of a record are interpreted as one delimiter between values.

Figure 5.21b shows the same data recorded in LIST format. Each case is recorded on a separate record. To read this data, specify the keyword LIST, as in:

```
DATA LIST FILE=WINSL LIST/POSTPOS NWINS
```

Figure 5.21b   Data in LIST format

```
2  19
7  5
10  25
5  17
8  11
3  18
6  8
1  29
```

The LIST format requires more records in your data file than the FREE format. However, it is less prone to errors in data entry. Since FREE format reads the data as one long series of numbers, if you leave out a value in the data, the values after the missing value are assigned to the incorrect variable for all remaining cases. Since LIST format reads a case from each record, the missing value will affect only the one case.

You cannot use a blank value to indicate missing information in FREE or LIST formatted data. Rather you must assign a value to the missing information and declare the value missing with the MISSING VALUES command (see Section 5.26).

5.22
Format Types with FREE and LIST

With FREE and LIST you can use any of the FORTRAN-like format specifications described in Section 5.39 that are available on your implementation of SPSS-X (except the date and time formats with the free-format option).

A format specification applies only to the immediately preceding variable. However, with keywords FREE and LIST, if you specify a format type for any variable, you must specify an asterisk for all variables preceding it in the list that you want read with the default format type. The asterisk applies to all variables preceding it. Variables at the end of a list that are not given a format are assigned the default format. For example, to explicitly specify the default format for variables POSTPOS and NWINS, specify:

```
DATA LIST FILE=WINS FREE/POSTPOS NWINS *
```

To specify a string variable, you must specify the format type A and the maximum length occurring in your data enclosed in parentheses after the name of the string variable, as in:

```
DATA LIST FILE=WINS FREE/POSTPOS NWINS * POSNAME (A24)
```

The variable POSNAME is specified as a 24-character string. The asterisk preceding POSNAME is required to specify that variables POSTPOS and NWINS are to be read with the default format type. Only one asterisk is required; it applies to all the variables preceding it, unlike other format specifications, which apply only to the preceding variable. For example, if both NWINS and POSNAME are alphanumeric, each would require its own format specification, as in

```
DATA LIST FILE=WINS FREE/POSTPOS * NWINS (A5) POSNAME (A24)
```

If the string in your data is longer than the specified length, the string is truncated and a warning message is printed. If the string in your data is shorter, it is right-padded with blanks, and no warning message is printed. You must enclose the string in your data in apostrophes or quotation marks if the string contains a blank or a comma. Otherwise, the blank or comma is treated as a delimiter between values. You can include apostrophes in a string enclosed in quotation marks, or quotation marks in a string enclosed in apostrophes.

5.23
Undefined Data Values

When SPSS-X encounters a value that it cannot read according to the format type specified, it must consider the value undefined and must assign the system-missing value. SPSS-X prints a warning message when an undefined value is encountered and continues reading the file. The default limit for a batch job is 80 undefined values per job. However, you can use the MXWARNS subcommand on the SET command to change this limit for batch jobs and the UNDEFINED subcommand to suppress the warning messages (see Chapter 4).

5.24
Printing and Writing Formats

For every permanent variable in your file, SPSS-X stores formats in the variable dictionary that are then used to print and write out the values. SPSS-X assigns default print and write formats based on the type of variable (see Table 5.39). These assigned formats allow you to examine values directly in data display procedures such as LIST and REPORT.

If you use the default numeric format on FREE or LIST, the print and write format is set to F8.2 or the format indicated by the FORMAT subcommand on the SET command (see Chapter 4). If you have decimal points coded in your data, you may need to change the dictionary formats depending on the format that you used to read the variable. Use the PRINT FORMATS command to change the printing format, the WRITE FORMATS command to change the writing format, and the FORMATS command to change both (see Chapter 10).

5.25
MISSING VALUES

Very often, your data file lacks complete information on some cases for some variables. Monitoring equipment can malfunction, interviewers can forget to ask a question or record an answer, respondents can refuse to answer, data can be entered incorrectly, and so forth. *Missing* does not always mean the same as unknown or absent. In order to distinguish why information is missing, you can instruct SPSS-X to consider more than one value missing for each variable. For example, if you code the value 9 for "Refused to answer" and the value 0 for "No answer reported," you might want to specify both of these values as missing.

The MISSING VALUES command declares the missing values for certain variables in your file. The values defined as missing are never changed on the data; they are simply flagged in the dictionary of the active file and, if the active file is saved as a system file, in the dictionary of the system file. The SPSS-X statistical procedures and transformation commands recognize this flag, and those cases that contain a user-defined missing value are handled specially. Although all SPSS-X statistical procedures provide options for handling cases with missing values, the exact nature of the options depends on the statistical procedure.

User-missing values defined on the MISSING VALUES command are distinguished from the *system-missing value*. SPSS-X assigns the system-missing value when a value in your data is undefined according to the format type that you have specified (Section 5.23), when a numeric field is blank for the default format type (Section 5.17), or when a value resulting from a transformation command like COMPUTE is undefined (Chapter 7).

5.26
MISSING VALUES
Command

The specification on MISSING VALUES consists of a variable name or variable list and the specified missing value or values, as in:

```
DATA LIST  FILE=BALLOONS/ COLOR 1 COUNT 2-5
MISSING VALUES COUNT(9999) COLOR(8,9)
```

This command names 9999 as the missing value for variable COUNT and 8 and 9 for variable COLOR.

- You can specify missing values for any variable previously defined on a DATA LIST command or a transformation command, except long strings (Section 5.19) and scratch variables (Chapter 7).
- You can specify a maximum of three *individual* values for each variable. (See below for specifying a range of values.)
- Enclose the values that you want to define as missing for a variable in parentheses and separate the values from each other by a comma or blank.
- Missing-value specifications for a variable previously named on a MISSING VALUE command replace all missing values defined for that variable (see Section 5.30).

For example, if you conduct a survey and ask the respondents to report their income level, some respondents may refuse to answer the question, others may indicate that they do not know, and some respondents may simply neglect to fill in an answer. In this instance, you might code 9 for "Refused to answer," 8 for "Don't know," and 0 for "No answer." To declare all of these values as missing data for the variable INCOME, specify:

```
MISSING VALUES  INCOME (0,8,9)
```

To declare a large number of values as missing, you can either specify a range as shown in Section 5.28 or use the transformation language to change the values to a single value and declare that value missing, as in:

```
RECODE X(LO THRU 0=0)
MISSING VALUES X (0)
```

The RECODE command recodes negative values to 0 (Chapter 7) and the MISSING VALUES command declares 0 missing.

5.27
Referencing Several
Variables

You can define missing values for more than one variable on a MISSING VALUES command either by specifying a variable list when the missing values are the same for all variables in the list or by specifying several sets of variable names and missing-value specifications when the values are different.

To define the same missing values for several variables, list all of the variables and follow them with the missing-value specification. You can use the keyword TO to refer to consecutive variables on your active file (the order of the variables corresponds to their listing order on the DATA LIST command). For example, to declare the value 0 as missing for all the variables defined on the DATA LIST beginning with DEPT79 through SALARY82 and for the variable AGE, specify:

```
DATA LIST  FILE=HUBDATA RECORDS=3
 /1 MOHIRED YRHIRED 12-15 DEPT79 TO DEPT82 SEX 16-20
 /2 SALARY79 TO SALARY82 6-25 HOURLY81 HOURLY82 42-53(2)
    AGE 54-55 RAISE82 66-70
 /3 JOBCAT 6
MISSING VALUES  DEPT79 TO SALARY82, AGE (0)
```

To define different missing values for other variables in your file, specify the
additional variables and their missing-value specifications, as in:

```
DATA LIST  FILE=HUBDATA RECORDS=3
 /1 MOHIRED YRHIRED 12-15 DEPT79 TO DEPT82 SEX 16-20
 /2 SALARY79 TO SALARY82 6-25 HOURLY81 HOURLY82 42-53(2)
    AGE 54-55 RAISE82 66-70
 /3 JOBCAT 6
MISSING VALUES  DEPT79 TO SALARY82, AGE (0)
   HOURLY81, HOURLY82, RAISE82 (-999) JOBCAT (9)
```

You can continue this process of specifying variables and missing values on one or
more MISSING VALUES commands.

To declare the same missing values for all of the variables on your active file,
specify the keyword ALL followed by the missing-value specification, as in:

```
MISSING VALUES  ALL (0)
```

Note that all your variables must be numeric or all must be string; otherwise
keyword ALL will cause errors since the value specified will inevitably not
correspond to one type or the other.

If you name the same variable on two MISSING VALUES commands, the
second specification overrides the first (see Section 5.30).

5.28
Specifying Ranges of Missing Values

You can specify a range of values as missing for numeric variables but not for
string variables. Use keyword THRU to indicate an inclusive list of values. For
example, 0 THRU 1.5 includes the values 0 through (and including) 1.5. The
values must be separated from THRU by at least one blank space. Use keywords
HIGHEST and LOWEST with THRU to indicate the highest and lowest values of
a variable. The command

```
MISSING VALUES  RAISE82 (LOWEST THRU 0)
```

defines all negative values and 0 as missing for variable RAISE82.

• Keywords HIGHEST and LOWEST can be abbreviated to HI and LO, respectively.
• Only one THRU specification can be used for each variable list.
• The THRU specification can be combined with one individual value in each
  missing-value specification, as in:

```
MISSING VALUES RAISE82 (LO THRU 0, 999)
```

Only three values, including the values on each side of the keyword THRU and
the keywords HIGHEST and LOWEST, can be specified.

5.29
Missing Values for String Variables

You can define missing values for short string variables but not for long strings. To
specify a value of a short string variable, enclose the value in apostrophes or
quotation marks. The command

```
MISSING VALUES  STRING1 ('X','Y')
```

specifies the values X and Y as missing for a single-column string variable
STRING1.

You can also define the same missing values for several string variables,
whether or not the variables are of equal length. For example, the command

```
MISSING VALUES  STRING1 STRING2 STRING3 ('X','Y')
```

specifies the values X and Y as missing for variables STRING1, STRING2, and STRING3.

The exact value of the string, including blanks, must be enclosed in apostrophes or quotation marks. For example, to indicate the value X recorded in the right-most position of a three-column string variable, specify the value as ' X'. If the value specified is shorter than the variable, the specified value is right-padded without warning. If the value specified is longer than the variable, the specified value is truncated without warning. SPSS-X cannot read more characters in the value than have been defined for the string variable (see Section 5.33).

Value ranges cannot be specified for short string variables. You cannot use the keywords THRU, HIGHEST, or LOWEST with missing-value specifications for string variables.

5.30
Redefining Missing Values

After saving a system file that includes missing-value flags for some variables, you may decide that you want to change these definitions for some variables. You can define new missing values or delete the flags for all previously defined missing values using the MISSING VALUES command.

To delete the flags for all previously defined missing values, specify no values in the missing-value specification. For example, to delete all the flags for previously defined missing values for the variables SALARY79 TO SALARY82, specify:

```
MISSING VALUES  SALARY79 TO SALARY82 ()
```

Missing-value specifications for a variable on a MISSING VALUES command replace all of the previously defined missing values for that variable. For example, the command

```
MISSING VALUES ALL(0)
```

declares 0 as the *only* user-missing value for all variables, overriding all previous declarations.

5.31
VARIABLE AND VALUE LABELS

Although you can construct variable names to represent what the variable actually measures, it is sometimes difficult to fully describe a variable in an eight-character name. Likewise, values of variables sometimes have no apparent meaning by themselves. Use one or more VARIABLE LABELS commands to assign labels to variables in your file, and one or more VALUE LABELS commands to assign labels to values of variables. SPSS-X displays these variable and value labels on the output produced by the procedures and saves them in the dictionary of the active file.

Labels in SPSS-X are specified as *strings*. In the command

```
VARIABLE LABELS  SALARY82 'SALARY IN 1982'
```

the label for variable SALARY82 is specified as the string "SALARY IN 1982".

- Enclose strings within apostrophes or quotation marks, using the same symbol to begin and end the string.
- Enter an apostrophe as part of a label by enclosing the string in quotation marks or by entering the apostrophe twice with no separation.

For example, the command

```
VARIABLE LABELS  SALARY82 "EMPLOYEE'S YEARLY SALARY IN 1982"
```

is the same as

```
VARIABLE LABELS  SALARY82 'EMPLOYEE''S YEARLY SALARY IN 1982'
```

Quotation marks are entered in a label in the same manner. A label cannot be continued from one command line to the next as the same string. However, strings can be concatenated using the plus sign, where

```
VARIABLE LABELS  SALARY82 'EMPLOYEE''S YEARLY SALARY IN'
   + ' 1982' YRHIRED 'YEAR OF FIRST HIRING'
```

assigns labels to variables SALARY82 and YRHIRED. The label for the first variable is the result of concatenating two strings with the plus sign. The blank between IN and 1982 must be included in the first or second string to be included in the label.

5.32
VARIABLE LABELS
Command

Use the VARIABLE LABELS command to assign an extended descriptive label to variables. Specify the variable name followed by at least one comma or blank and the associated label enclosed in apostrophes or quotation marks, as in:

```
VARIABLE LABELS  YRHIRED 'YEAR OF FIRST HIRING'
  DEPT82 'DEPARTMENT OF EMPLOYMENT IN 1982'
  SALARY82 'YEARLY SALARY IN 1982'
  JOBCAT 'JOB CATEGORIES'
```

This command assigns variable labels to the variables YRHIRED, DEPT82, SALARY82, and JOBCAT.

- A variable label applies to only one variable.
- The variable must have been previously defined, either on a DATA LIST command or on a transformation command.
- Each variable label can be up to 120 characters long and can include blanks and any character.

Although the maximum length for a variable label is 120 characters, most procedures print fewer than 120 characters for each label.

To maintain compatibility with earlier releases of SPSS, the command VAR LABELS is accepted and the label does not need to be enclosed in apostrophes. If you don't use quotes or apostrophes, the variable name must be separated from the label by at least one blank space or comma, and each variable and its label must be separated from the next variable and its label by a slash. The variable label specified in this manner cannot contain slashes and cannot begin with a quotation mark or an apostrophe.

5.33
VALUE LABELS
Command

Use the VALUE LABELS command to provide descriptive labels for values. The VALUE LABELS command is followed by a variable name, or variable list, and a list of the values with their associated labels. The command

```
VALUE LABELS  DEPT82  0 'NOT REPORTED' 1 'ADMINISTRATIVE'
          2 'PROJECT DIRECTORS' 3 'CHICAGO OPERATIONS'
          4 'ST LOUIS OPERATIONS'/
```

assigns labels to the values 0, 1, 2, 3, and 4 of DEPT82.

- You can assign labels to values of any previously defined variable.
- Enclose each value label in apostrophes or quotation marks.
- Value labels cannot exceed 60 characters and can contain any characters including blanks.

Value labels are automatically displayed on the output from many procedures and are saved in the dictionary of a system file. It is not necessary to enter value labels for all of the variables or values in your file. In some instances, the value itself is completely descriptive, such as the values for SALARY82.

Although the maximum length for a value label is 60 characters, most procedures print fewer characters for each label. See especially the CROSSTABS procedure in Chapter 25.

To assign the same labels to the same values of several variables, list all of the variables followed by the values and associated labels. Also, additional sets of variable names and value labels can be specified on the same command, as in:

```
VALUE LABELS  DEPT79 TO DEPT82  0 'NOT REPORTED' 1 'ADMINISTRATIVE'
              2 'PROJECT DIRECTORS' 3 'CHICAGO OPERATIONS'
              4 'ST LOUIS OPERATIONS'/
     SEX 1 'MALE'  2 'FEMALE'/
     JOBCAT 1 'OFFICIALS & MANAGERS' 2 'PROFESSIONALS' 3 'TECHNICIANS'
              4 'OFFICE AND CLERICAL' 5 'CRAFTSMEN' 6 'SERVICE WORKERS'
```

The slash is required to separate value labels for one variable or variable list from the next variable or variable list.

You can assign value labels to values of short string variables but not long string variables. To specify a value of a short string variable, enclose the value in apostrophes. For example, to assign labels to the values for string variable JOBGRADE, specify:

```
DATA LIST  FILE=CHIGHOME/JOBGRADE 43 (A)
VALUE LABELS JOBGRADE 'X' 'SALES STAFF'    'S' 'SUPERVISORY STAFF'
                      'M' 'MANAGERIAL STAFF'  'C' 'SUPPORT STAFF'
```

The exact alphanumeric value, including blanks, must be enclosed in apostrophes.

If you specify a value that is longer than the format of the associated variable, SPSS-X will be unable to read the full value and may not be able to associate the value labels correctly. For example, the commands

```
DATA LIST / CITY 1-8(A) STATE 10-11(A)
VALUE LABELS STATE 'TEX' "TEXAS" 'TEN' "TENNESSEE" 'MIN' "MINNESOTA"
BEGIN DATA
AUSTIN    TEX
MEMPHIS   TEN
ST. PAUL MIN
END DATA
FREQUENCIES VARIABLES=STATE
```

assign a length of 2 to the string variable STATE, but the values specified on VALUE LABELS have a length of 3 (TEX, TEN, and MIN). The actual values are also longer than the format specified on the DATA LIST command. When this job is run, SPSS-X issues a warning stating a value named on VALUE LABELS has more characters than the string variable it labels. It also warns that the value (TE) is assigned two different labels but will use only the first (TEXAS). Note that this occurs even though the values named on VALUE LABELS and the actual values agree.

If the value specifications for string variables are shorter than the variable being labeled, the value specifications are right-padded without warning. For example, if the variable RESIDE has a width of 8 and you specify

```
VALUE LABELS RESIDE 'URBAN'    "IN THE CITY"
                    'SUBURBAN' "IN A SUBURB"
                    'COUNTRY'  "IN THE COUNTRY"
```

URBAN is right-padded with three blanks, and COUNTRY with one blank. If the actual data values are left-padded with blanks, the value labels will not be properly assigned.

You can assign the same value labels to a set of string variables of *equal* length. For example, if variables STATE and REGION both have a length of 2, the statement

```
VALUE LABELS STATE REGION 'U ' "UNKNOWN"
```

will assign the label UNKNOWN to value 'U ' for both STATE and REGION.

However, if the string variables have *unequal* lengths, say STATE has a length of 8 and REGION a length of 2, you must specify a separate VALUE LABELS command for each variable, as in

VALUE LABELS STATE 'U' "UNKNOWN" / REGION 'U' "UNKNOWN"

In the above example, the value specification U will be right-padded with 7 blanks for STATE and 1 blank for REGION. If you tried to assign the 'U' to both variables at once, SPSS-X will issue a warning and assign the label UNKNOWN to STATE but not to REGION.

If you assign value labels to any variable that already has value labels assigned to it, the new assignment *completely replaces all of the previously assigned labels*. Value label specifications are not additive. See Section 5.34 for adding and modifying value labels.

To maintain compatibility with earlier releases of SPSS, the value can be enclosed in parentheses, and the label does not need to be enclosed in apostrophes. If you use this syntax, the slash separating the sets of value labels is required, and slashes or parentheses cannot be included in the label.

5.34
ADD VALUE LABELS Command

The ADD VALUE LABELS command allows you to add new value labels or alter existing value labels without deleting existing labels. The command

ADD VALUE LABELS JOBGRADE 'P' 'PARTTIME EMPLOYEE' 'C' 'CUSTOMER SUPPORT'

adds or modifies labels assigned to values P and C without affecting other labels previously assigned to the values of JOBGRADE. ADD VALUE LABELS operates under the same rules as VALUE LABELS:

• Labels can be added to any previously defined variable.
• Each value label must be enclosed in apostrophes or quotation marks.
• Value labels cannot exceed 60 characters and can contain any characters including blanks.
• The same labels can be assigned to the values of different variables by specifying a list of variable names. For string variables, the variables must be of equal length.
• Multiple sets of variable names and value labels can be specified on one ADD VALUE LABELS command as long as each set is separated by slashes.

It is not an error to use ADD VALUE LABELS for variables that have no previously assigned value labels.

5.35
RENAME VARIABLES Command

The RENAME VARIABLES command changes the names of variables in the active file while preserving their original order, values, variable labels, value labels, missing values, and print and write formats. It is especially useful for renaming variables that have been generated and named by an SPSS-X statistical procedure, such as the Z-score transformation variables generated by the DESCRIPTIVES command (See Chapter 26).

To rename one variable, specify the old variable name followed by an equals sign and the new variable name. For example, to rename the variable JOBCAT to TITLE, specify:

RENAME VARIABLES (JOBCAT=TITLE)

JOBCAT is the old name; TITLE is the new name. When you specify one variable, the parentheses enclosing the specification are optional.

You can rename more than one variable on a RENAME VARIABLES command either by specifying several sets of individual variable specifications or by specifying a list of variable names and a list of their new names. When you specify individual sets or lists of variables, the specifications must be enclosed in parentheses. For example, to rename the variables MOHIRED and YRHIRED, specify either

```
RENAME VARIABLES (MOHIRED=MOSTART)(YRHIRED=YRSTART)
```

or

```
RENAME VARIABLES (MOHIRED YRHIRED=MOSTART YRSTART)
```

In the second specification, the two variable lists must name or imply the same number of variables. You can use the keyword TO both to refer to consecutive variables to be renamed (on the left side of the equals sign) and to generate new names (on the right side of the equals sign). For example, if the active file contains SALARY79, SALARY80, SALARY81, and SALARY82, in that order, the specification

```
RENAME VARIABLES (SALARY79 TO SALARY82=WAGES79 TO WAGES82)
```

renames SALARY79 to WAGES79, SALARY80 to WAGES80, SALARY81 to WAGES81 and SALARY82 to WAGES82. See Chapter 2 for more information on the distinction between using keyword TO to refer to existing variables and to define new variables.

All the name changes on a single RENAME VARIABLES command are executed in one operation, so you can exchange the names of two variables, as in:

```
RENAME VARIABLES (A=B) (B=A)
```

You cannot use the RENAME VARIABLES command to rename scratch variables or system variables (Chapter 7), nor can you use it to reorder variables. Variables assigned new names with the TO convention are not consecutive on the active file unless they were consecutive before you renamed them. To reorder variables, use the KEEP subcommand on SAVE or GET.

After the RENAME VARIABLES command, you must refer to a renamed variable by its new name.

5.36
INLINE DATA IN THE COMMAND FILE

If your data are included as lines in your SPSS-X command file, you can omit the FILE subcommand on the DATA LIST command or specify the default FILE= INLINE. Two SPSS-X commands are required to separate lines containing data from lines containing SPSS-X commands: BEGIN DATA and END DATA.

5.37
BEGIN DATA and END DATA Commands

The BEGIN DATA command must be entered immediately before the first line of inline data, and the END DATA command must be entered immediately after the last line of data. The END DATA command must always be spelled out in full and must have only one space between the keywords. Figure 5.37a shows a complete SPSS-X command file with the data included in the file.

In Figure 5.37a, the file definition portion of the DATA LIST command is not needed because the data are contained in the default format of one record per case. In this situation, the first specification on the DATA LIST command must be the slash that begins variable definitions.

If SPSS-X procedure commands are included in the job, the BEGIN DATA command followed by the lines of data and the END DATA command should *follow* the first SPSS-X procedure command, as shown in Figure 5.37a. Addition-

Figure 5.37a   Input data in the SPSS-X command file

```
DATA LIST /NTCPRI NTCSAL NTCPUR RENT 5-16 WORLD 18 CONT 20
   NAME 24-37 (A)
VARIABLE LABELS NTCPRI 'NET PRICE LEVEL'
   NTCSAL 'NET SALARY'
   NTCPUR 'NET PURCHASING LEVEL'
   RENT 'NORMAL RENT'
   WORLD 'ECONOMIC CLASS FOR COUNTRY'
   CONT 'CONTINENT'
VALUE LABELS  WORLD 1 '1ST WORLD' 2 'PETROWORLD' 3 '3RD WORLD'/
   CONT 1 'N EUROPE' 2 'S EUROPE' 3 'MEDITERRANEAN'
     4 'MIDEAST' 5 'ASIA' 6 'AFRICA' 7 'AUSTRALIA'
     8 'N AMERICA' 9 'S AMERICA'
MISSING VALUES NTCPRI TO CONT (0)

CROSSTABS WORLD BY CONT
          /CELLS=ROW COLUMN

BEGIN DATA
01  125 46 27403 2 4    ABU DHABI
02   79 68 86 76 1 1    AMSTERDAM
03   78 34 32 97 3 3    ATHENS
04  124 49 29440 2 4    BAHRAIN
 .
 .

 .
44   78 59 75 40 1 1    VIENNA
45 100100100100 1 1     ZURICH
END DATA
```

Figure 5.37b   Display output produced by Figure 5.37a

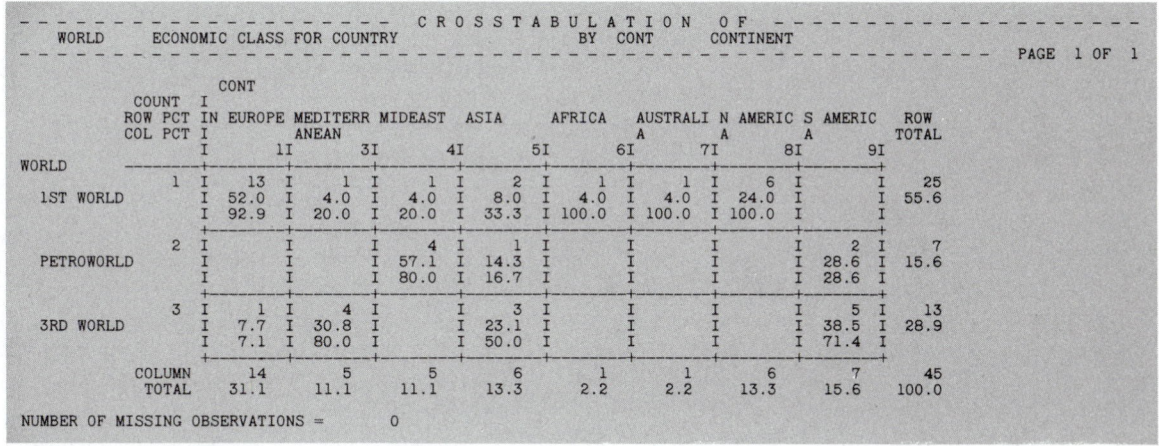

al transformation and procedure commands can follow the END DATA command. If you specify BEGIN DATA, lines of data, and END DATA before a procedure is used (or if no procedure is used), the BEGIN DATA command causes SPSS-X to read the data.

Figure 5.37b shows the display output produced by the CROSSTABS command in the SPSS-X command file in Figure 5.37a. Notice that the variable and value labels assigned to WORLD and CONT are automatically displayed on the table. See Chapter 25 for a detailed description of the CROSSTABS procedure.

ANNOTATED EXAMPLE FOR DATA DEFINITIONS

The following example defines the variables of interest from a personnel file for the fictitious Hubbard Consultants Inc. and produces some basic tables.

```
DATA LIST   FILE=HUBDATA RECORDS=3
  /1 EMPLOYID 1-5 MOHIRED YRHIRED 12-15 DEPT79 TO DEPT82 SEX 16-20
  /2 SALARY79 TO SALARY82 6-25 HOURLY81 HOURLY82 42-53(2) PROMO81 72
     AGE 54-55 RAISE82 66-70
  /3 JOBCAT 6 NAME 25-48 (A)

MISSING VALUES  DEPT79 TO SALARY82, AGE (0)
  HOURLY81, HOURLY82, RAISE82 (-999) JOBCAT (9)

VARIABLE LABELS  YRHIRED 'YEAR OF FIRST HIRING'
  DEPT82 'DEPARTMENT OF EMPLOYMENT IN 1982'
  SALARY82 'YEARLY SALARY IN 1982'
  JOBCAT 'JOB CATEGORIES'

VALUE LABELS  DEPT79 TO DEPT82  0 'NOT REPORTED' 1 'ADMINISTRATIVE'
           2 'PROJECT DIRECTORS' 3 'CHICAGO OPERATIONS'
           4 'ST LOUIS OPERATIONS'/
  SEX 1 'MALE' 2 'FEMALE'/
  JOBCAT 1 'OFFICIALS & MANAGERS' 2 'PROFESSIONALS' 3 'TECHNICIANS'
           4 'OFFICE AND CLERICAL' 5 'CRAFTSMEN' 6 'SERVICE WORKERS'

FREQUENCIES  VARIABLES=DEPT82,SEX,JOBCAT
```

- The FILE subcommand on DATA LIST indicates that the data are contained in the data file HUBDATA.

- The RECORDS subcommand tells SPSS-X to expect three records per employee (see Section 5.7).

- The second line of the DATA LIST command defines variables from the first record (see Section 5.11). The employee identification number is found in the first five columns. Variables MOHIRED and YRHIRED, for month and year of hiring, are found in columns 12 through 15, indicating that that MOHIRED is in columns 12 and 13 and YRHIRED is in columns 14 and 15 (see Section 5.15). Variable DEPT79, implied variables DEPT80 and DEPT81, variable DEPT82, and variable SEX are single-column variables found in columns 16 through 20.

- The DATA LIST command continues with record 2, which names nine variables. First are four salary variables of five columns each. The next two variables, HOURLY81 and HOURLY82 (representing hourly wages), are in columns 42 through 47 and 48 through 53. The last two positions of HOURLY81 and HOURLY82 are to be considered decimal places (see Section 5.16). The final three variables defined on the second record are PROMO81 in column 72, AGE in columns 54 through 55, and RAISE82 in columns 66 through 70.

- The last line of the DATA LIST command defines two variables: a numeric job-category variable in column 6 of record 3, and the employee name, which is in the 24 columns from 25 through 48, and is alphanumeric. The latter is a long string variable in SPSS-X (see Section 5.19).

- The first line of the MISSING VALUES command defines 0 as the missing value for variables defined between AGE, DEPT79, SALARY82, and all the variables between DEPT79 and SALARY82 on the active file (see Sections 5.26 through 5.28). The second line defines −999 as missing for HOURLY81, HOURLY82, and RAISE82, and 9 as missing for job category.

- The VARIABLE LABELS command assigns labels to four variables (see Section 5.32), and the VALUE LABELS command assigns labels to the values of the four department variables, sex, and job category (see Section 5.33).

- The FREQUENCIES command requests tables for three variables (see Chapter 29). These tables are shown in Figure B. The labels assigned for the variables are displayed in the tables. Value 0 for DEPT82 is marked as a missing value.

Figure A shows the first display page from SPSS-X. In particular, notice the summary table produced from the DATA LIST command (see Section 5.8). The F format item indicates the default numeric format.

A Display results from definition commands

```
1  0          DATA LIST   FILE=HUBDATA RECORDS=3
2  0             /1 EMPLOYID 1-5 MOHIRED YRHIRED 12-15 DEPT79 TO DEPT82 SEX 16-20
3  0             /2 SALARY79 TO SALARY82 6-25 HOURLY81 HOURLY82 40-53(2) PROM081 72
4  0                AGE 54-55 RAISE82 66-70
5  0             /3 JOBCAT 6 NAME 25-48 (A)
6  0
```

THE ABOVE DATA LIST STATEMENT WILL READ   3 RECORDS FROM FILE HUBDATA .

VARIABLE	REC	START	END	FORMAT	WIDTH	DEC
EMPLOYID	1	1	5	F	5	0
MOHIRED	1	12	13	F	2	0
YRHIRED	1	14	15	F	2	0
DEPT79	1	16	16	F	1	0
DEPT80	1	17	17	F	1	0
DEPT81	1	18	18	F	1	0
DEPT82	1	19	19	F	1	0
SEX	1	20	20	F	1	0
SALARY79	2	6	10	F	5	0
SALARY80	2	11	15	F	5	0
SALARY81	2	16	20	F	5	0
SALARY82	2	21	25	F	5	0
HOURLY81	2	40	46	F	7	2
HOURLY82	2	47	53	F	7	2
PROM081	2	72	72	F	1	0
AGE	2	54	55	F	2	0
RAISE82	2	66	70	F	5	0
JOBCAT	3	6	6	F	1	0
NAME	3	25	48	A	24	

END OF DATALIST TABLE.

B FREQUENCIES tables

DEPT82   DEPARTMENT OF EMPLOYMENT IN 1982

VALUE LABEL	VALUE	FREQUENCY	PERCENT	VALID PERCENT	CUM PERCENT
ADMINISTRATIVE	1	34	12.4	23.4	23.4
PROJECT DIRECTORS	2	22	8.0	15.2	38.6
CHICAGO OPERATIONS	3	60	21.8	41.4	80.0
ST LOUIS OPERATIONS	4	29	10.5	20.0	100.0
NOT REPORTED	0	130	47.3	MISSING	
	TOTAL	275	100.0	100.0	

VALID CASES   145   MISSING CASES   130

- -

SEX

VALUE LABEL	VALUE	FREQUENCY	PERCENT	VALID PERCENT	CUM PERCENT
MALE	1	83	30.2	30.2	30.2
FEMALE	2	192	69.8	69.8	100.0
	TOTAL	275	100.0	100.0	

VALID CASES   275   MISSING CASES   0

- -

JOBCAT   JOB CATEGORIES

VALUE LABEL	VALUE	FREQUENCY	PERCENT	VALID PERCENT	CUM PERCENT
OFFICIALS & MANAGERS	1	48	17.5	17.5	17.5
PROFESSIONALS	2	62	22.5	22.5	40.0
TECHNICIANS	3	98	35.6	35.6	75.6
OFFICE AND CLERICAL	4	67	24.4	24.4	100.0
	TOTAL	275	100.0	100.0	

VALID CASES   275   MISSING CASES   0

5.38 FORTRAN-LIKE FORMAT SPECIFICATIONS ON DATA LIST

An optional syntax for the variable definition portion of the DATA LIST command uses FORTRAN-like format definitions enclosed in parentheses to describe the format type and location of each variable. The column syntax described in Sections 5.9 through 5.20 is generally more straightforward and easier to use, but the FORTRAN-like formats may be more convenient in some situations.

The variable names are constructed in the same way as described in Section 5.12, and the order of the variable names on the DATA LIST command determines their sequence in the active file. The type and location of each variable are described using FORTRAN-like format elements rather than directly specifying the column location and format type. The number of variables named must equal the number of data format elements.

There are two major differences between SPSS-X format specifications and FORTRAN conventions:

- Whereas FORTRAN interprets blanks as zeros, SPSS-X does not. In SPSS-X, leading and trailing blanks are ignored. FORTRAN interprets blanks as zeros.
- SPSS-X cannot interpret numeric values that contain imbedded blanks. When SPSS-X encounters a field that contains one or more blanks interspersed among the numbers, it issues a warning message and assigns system-missing.

SPSS-X is less tolerant than FORTRAN in accepting data values. For example, standard FORTRAN accepts the value 1-1, as $1.0E-1$. However, SPSS-X accepts this value only if the input format type is for scientific notation. Under standard numeric format (such as F3), SPSS-X issues an error message indicating an imbedded sign and assigns system-missing.

5.39 Format Elements

Each format element defines the type of variable, the input width of the variable, and, if applicable, the number of decimal places. Column style uses column numbers followed by a format type and optional decimal specification enclosed in parentheses. For example,

```
DATA LIST file /VARA 11-14 (Z,2)
```

defines VARA as a four-column zoned decimal field with the two rightmost digits placed after the decimal point. The equivalent FORTRAN-like specification is:

```
DATA LIST file / VARA (T11,Z4.2)
```

Two positioning elements, T and X (available only in FORTRAN-like format specifications), skip columns in the data records and are necessary to describe the location of variables when you do not want to read the entire record. The T and X elements are discussed in Section 5.44.

Most of the FORTRAN-like formats are available for most implementations of SPSS-X. Table 5.39 presents a summary describing the majority of the input formats. Multipunch formats are discussed beginning in Section 5.48. See the supplemental documentation available with the LOCAL subcommand on the INFO command for a description of the formats available and the widths and decimal ranges for your computer (see Chapter 3). Appendix F describes formats interpreted by SPSS-X running on VAX/VMS machines.

Table 5.39   Input data formats

Input format	Min w	Max w	Implied d (max)	Input blank	Default output type	Notes
Printable numerics						
Fw.d	1	40	16	SET	same	
Nw	1	40		SET	F	
Nw.d	1	40	16	SET	F	
Ew.d	1	40	15	SET	same	
Ew	1	40		SET	same	
COMMAw.d	1	40	16	SET	same	
COMMAw	1	40		SET	same	
DOTw.d	1	40	16	SET	same	
DOLLARw.d	1	40	16	SET	same	
DOLLARw	1	40		SET	same	
PCTw.d	1	40	16	SET	same	
PIBHEXw	2	8		SET	F	w must be an even number
PIBHEXw	2	16		SET	F	w must be an even number
RBHEXw	4	16		SET	F	w must be an even number
Zw.d	1	40	16	SET	F	
Zw	1	40		SET	F	
Nonprintable numerics						
IBw.d	1	8	16	value	F	w is in bytes, d is decimal digits
IBw	1	8		value	F	w is in bytes
PIBw.d	1	8	16	value	F	w is in bytes, d is decimal digits
PIBw	1	8		value	F	w is in bytes
Pw.d	1	16	16	SET	F	
Pw	1	16		SET	F	
PKw.d	1	16	16	value	F	
PKw	1	16		value	F	
RBw	2	8		value	F	width must be an even number
Strings						
Aw	1	255		blank	same	
AHEXw	2	254		blank	A	w must be an even number
Date and time					Input form	
DATEw	9	40		SET	same	dd/mmm/yy
ADATEw	8	40		SET	same	mm/dd/yy
JDATEw	5	40		SET	same	yyddd
QYRw	4	40		SET	same	qQyy
MOYRw	6	40		SET	same	mm/yyyy
WKYRw	6	40		SET	same	wkWKyy
TIMEw	5	40		SET	same	hh:mm:ss.ss
DTIMEw	11	40		SET	same	d hh:mm:ss.ss
DATETIMEw	17	40		SET	same	dd/mmm/yy hh:mm:ss.ss
WKDAYw	2	40		SET	same	dd
MONTHw	3	40		SET	same	mmm

5.40
Printable Numeric Formats

The formats described in this section can be printed and then read by people. Generally, each of the printable numeric input formats adhere to the following conventions:

- The format type is named first, then a width, and then an optional specification for the number of implied decimal values.
- The width specification (w) indicates the *total* number of columns used to code the variable.

- The decimal (d) specification indicates how many digits from the right are interpreted as decimal values. SPSS-X "inserts" the decimal point. For example, F2.1 defines a two-column variable with the rightmost digit interpreted as following a decimal point; the value 22 is translated to 2.2. It is useful to specify the number of decimal digits for two reasons: you can indicate where the implied decimal point is placed when decimal points are not coded; and you can provide the desired printing format even when explicit decimal points are present in data values. The default PRINT and WRITE FORMATS include enough space for printing and writing the decimal point (see Chapter 10). If you DISPLAY DICTIONARY, the PRINT and WRITE FORMATS are automatically assigned as F3.1 to allow inclusion of the decimal point. Decimal points coded in the data override the number of places defined by the format statement.

- Blank fields read with any of the printable numeric formats are set to system-missing by default or to the value specified on the BLANK subcommand on the SET command (see Chapter 4).

- By default, SPSS-X translates restricted numeric, hexadecimal numeric, and zoned input formats to output formats of standard numeric (F). All other printable input formats retain the same output format type (see Table 5.39).

Fw.d (Standard Numeric). The F format element is equivalent to the default format type in the column syntax described earlier in this chapter. The syntax for the F element is F$w.d$, where w specifies the total number of columns and d indicates how many positions from the right are interpreted as decimals.

In addition, the F format accepts numbers in scientific notation provided you include E (or D) and the sign and the power of 10 in your data values. For example, the data value, 543E+3, can be read under an F6 format. If a value is coded in scientific notation, the implied decimal specification is ignored.

The default output formats are type F.

Nw.d (Restricted Numeric). The N format is used to specify fields containing unsigned integers. Leading, trailing, and imbedded blanks are not allowed. You can specify the number of digits that follow an implied decimal point. Coded decimal values are not allowed. This format is useful for reading and checking values that you know should be only integers with leading zeros.

For example, N2 defines a two-column variable. The value two must be input as 02; leading blanks are not allowed. A completely blank field is assigned system-missing.

The default output formats are type F.

Ew.d (Scientific Notation). The E format reads all forms of scientific notation numbers. The format assumes that the first digit is an integer followed by up to 15 decimal digits, with an E or D, the sign, and the power of 10. The E or D preceding the exponent is not necessary if a sign is coded before the exponent. You cannot code decimal values in the exponent portion of the number. However, decimal points can be coded in the number preceding the exponent. You can specify implied decimal points for use in output formats. Implied decimals are meaningful on input in the absence of an exponent value. You can use the E input format as a less restrictive form of standard numeric (F) format.

For example, to read 5.432E3, you can use the format E6 and enter the value 5432+3.

The default output formats are type E.

COMMAw.d (Commas in Numbers). The COMMAw.d format reads numeric values containing commas. This format "swallows" commas found in numeric values.

The default output formats are COMMA.

DOTw.d (Dots in Numbers). The DOTw.d format is similar to COMMAw.d format, except that the roles of the comma and the dot (period) are reversed. This is a popular format in many parts of Europe. The DOTw.d format can be used for both input and output. For input, DOTw.d should be used only with keyword FIXED.

The default output formats are DOT.

DOLLARw.d (Dollar Sign and Commas in Numbers). The DOLLARw.d format reads numeric fields containing a leading dollar sign, followed by digits that can contain commas separating groups of three digits preceding the decimal point. You can have only one leading dollar sign, with no imbedded blanks in your values. Commas in the values are swallowed.

The default output formats are DOLLAR.

PCTw.d (Percent Sign after Numbers). PCTw.d format is the percent format. Numbers printed with this format have a trailing percent sign (%), which has to be taken into account when determining field width. The PCTw.d format does not compute percentages, it just adds the percent sign to the value. The result of 1 divided by 2, for example, would be printed as .5% if PCTw.d format is specified. PCTw.d format can be used for both input and output.

The default output formats are PCT.

PIBHEXw (Hexadecimal of PIB). This format interprets a series of hexadecimal characters as an unsigned integer. That is, F0 is interpreted as 250 and FFFF is interpreted as 65,535. The values must be positive, and the width must be an even number. The maximum width specification is 16 columns. You cannot specify implied decimal digits.

The default output formats are an equivalent F format.

RBHEXw (Hexadecimal of RB). This format interprets a series of hexadecimal characters as the memory representation of a floating point number. This representation is highly implementation dependent. If the field width is less than twice the width of a floating point number, padding with binary zeros occurs on the right. The values are real numbers, and the width must be an even number.

The default output formats are an equivalent F format.

Zw.d (Zoned Decimal). This format reads data values that contain zoned decimal data. Such numbers may be generated by COBOL systems using DISPLAY data items, by PL/1 systems using PICTURE data items, or by assembler systems using zoned decimal data items. The general format of a zoned decimal number is one digit per byte. Each byte other than the last contains a hexadecimal "F" in the four leftmost bits and a single digit in the rightmost four bits. The last byte contains a hexadecimal "F" (or "C") in the leftmost four bits for positive numbers or a hexadecimal "D" (or "E") for negative numbers. Leading blanks and coded decimal points are allowed. Zoned decimal is simply a formatted field in which the sign is an overpunch in the rightmost position.

The default output format is an equivalent F format.

**5.41
Nonprintable Numeric Input
Formats**

The formats described in this section apply to data that is readable only by machines. Generally, these formats adhere to the following conventions:

• The format type is named first, followed by a width and an optional specification for the number of implied decimal digits.

• Input blanks are treated as values and are not assigned system-missing.

• Each input format is converted to an equivalent F format for output.

IBw.d (Integer Binary). This format reads fields which contain fixed point binary (integer) data. The data might be generated by COBOL using COMPUTATIONAL data items, by PL/1 using FIXED BINARY data items, by FORTRAN using INTEGER*2 or INTEGER*4, or by assembler systems using fullword and halfword items. The general format of binary items is a binary number of 16 or 32 bits in length using twos-complement notation for negative quantities.

The general format is IBw.d where *w* is the field width in bytes, and *d* is the number of decimal digits to the right of the decimal point. Widths of 2 and 4 represent standard halfword and fullword integers, respectively. Single byte fields are treated as signed. For example, hexadecimal FF is read as –1.

PIBw.d (Positive Integer Binary). This format is essentially the same as IB, except that negative numbers are not allowed. This restriction allows one additional bit of magnitude.

Pw.d (Packed Decimal). This format is used to read fields with packed decimal numbers. Such numbers are generated by COBOL systems using COMPUTATIONAL–3 data items, by PL/1 systems using FIXED DECIMAL data items, and by ASSEMBLER systems using packed decimal data items. The general format of a packed decimal field is two four-bit digits in each byte of the field except the last. The last byte contains a single digit in its four leftmost bits and a four-bit sign in its rightmost bits. The number of digits in a field is (2*w–1) where *w* is the field width in bytes. The sign is X'F' for positive values and X'D' for negative values (C zone equals F and E zone equals D). Remember, when defining a variable under P format, *w* is the number of bytes (not digits) and *d* is the number of digits to the right of the implied decimal point.

PKw.d (Unsigned Packed Decimal). This format is essentially the same as P, except that there is no sign. That is, even the rightmost byte contains two digits, and negative data cannot be represented. One byte under PK format can represent numbers from 0 to 99, while under PIB one byte can represent numbers from 0 through 255.

RBw (Real Binary). The RB format is used to read data values which contain internal format floating point numbers. Such numbers are generated by COBOL systems using COMPUTATIONAL–1 or COMPUTATIONAL–2 data items, by PL/1 systems using FLOATING DECIMAL data items, by FORTRAN systems using REAL or REAL*8 data items, or by assembler systems using floating point data items. On IBM systems, the general format of a floating number is a single-bit sign (1 is negative), a seven-bit hexadecimal exponent with a bias of 64, and a 24– or 56–bit mantissa.

Normally, a width specification of 8 is used to read double precision values, and a width of 4 is used to read single precision values. The width specification must be an even number between 2 and 8.

5.42
String Formats

The string input formats are used to read character data. The values are either alphanumeric characters or the hexadecimal representation of alphanumeric characters. String formats conform to the following rules:

• The field width must supply exactly the number of characters for the string. No truncation or padding is permitted on input or output (but is allowed in string transformations).
• Blank fields are interpreted as valid, not assigned system-missing.
• The default print and write formats are type A.

Aw (Standard Characters). The A format is used to read standard characters.

AHEXw (Hexadecimal Characters). The AHEX format is used to read the hexadecimal representation of standard characters. On input, each set of two characters represents one standard character. The *w* specification must be an even number. By default, the output formats are of type A.

5.43
Date and Time Input Formats

Date and time formats are used to read values representing dates and times or date-time combinations. These formats translate values to "special" internal representations. The internal representation is up to 20 characters indicating the number of seconds from a fixed date (October 14, 1582), the number of seconds in a time interval, or an ordinal number.

Several different formats permit you to read in date and time values. You can use these formats to read in a variety of data values, and you can use DATE and TIME transformations described in Chapter 7 to derive dates and time intervals. You can use the date and time input formats by supplying the column location and format or with FORTRAN-like specifications. You cannot use these formats with free-field input.

There are eleven defined format codes. Each produces either a date, a time interval, or an ordinal number. See Chapters 7 and 10 for transforming and printing values of date and time variables.

DATE. This format reads international dates in the form dd/mmm/yyyy. The following conventions apply:

- Two-digit years are assumed to be prefixed by 19.
- Months may be represented in digits, Roman numerals, three-character abbreviations, or fully spelled out: 10, X, OCT, OCTOBER, or October.
- Dashes, periods, commas, slashes, or blanks can be used as delimiters. For example, the date "December 2, 1984" can be expressed as 02-December-1984, 02.December.84, 02,December,1984, 02/December/1984, or 02 December 1984.
- The width defined on the DATA LIST command must be at least nine characters; however, data values of fewer characters are correctly evaluated.

ADATEw (American Date). The ADATE format reads American format dates of the general form mm/dd/yyyy. As with DATE format, years may be represented as either two or four digits. Acceptable delimiters are blanks, dashes, periods, commas, or slashes. Months may be fully spelled out or represented as digits, Roman numerals, or three-character abbreviations. The width defined on the DATA LIST command must be at least eight characters. However, data values that have fewer characters are correctly evaluated.

JDATEw (Julian Date). The JDATE format reads Julian-formatted dates in the form yyddd. If the number of digits read is five, a two-digit year is assumed, and 1900 will be added. A four-digit year is assumed if the number of digits is seven. The days field can be any number between 001 and 366. Leading zeros are required in the day field. No delimiters are allowed between the year and day fields. For example, the Julian equivalent of September 6, 1954, can be expressed as "1954249" but not as "1954/249".

QYRw (Quarter and Year). The QYR format reads fields containing the quarter and the year in the form qQyyyy. The quarter is expressed as 1, 2, 3, or 4, and the year is represented by two or four digits. If two digits are used, 1900 is added. The quarter and year are separated by the letter Q. Blanks may be used as additional delimiters. The month is $3*(\text{quarter}-1)+1$, and the day is 1. For example, April 1, 1958 is in the second quarter of 1958 and can be represented either as "2 Q 1958" or as "2Q1958".

MOYRw (Month and Year). The MOYR format reads values in the form mm/yyyy. Months can be expressed as digits, Roman numerals, three-character abbreviations (JAN, FEB, and so on), or they may be spelled out. The year is expressed as either two or four digits. If it is two digits, 1900 is added. Blanks, dashes, periods, commas, or slashes can be used as delimiters. The "days" portion of the date is assumed to be 1. The width defined on the DATA LIST command must be at least six characters; however, data values of fewer characters are correctly evaluated.

WKYRw (Week and Year). The WKYR format reads dates in the form wkWKyyyy. A week is expressed as a number from 1 to 53. The year is a two- or four-digit number. Week 1 is assumed to begin on 1 JAN; week 2, on 8 JAN; and so forth. The week and year are separated by the string "WK". Blanks can be used as additional delimiters. For example, you can express the 14th week of 1984 as either "14 WK 1984" or as "14WK1984". The width defined on the DATA LIST command must be at least six characters; however, data values of five characters are correctly evaluated.

TIMEw (Time). The TIME format is used to read a time of day or a time interval into a datum of type time interval. The input field is of the form hh:mm:ss.ss. The following conventions apply:

- Colons, blanks, or periods may be used as delimiters between hours, minutes, and seconds. A period is required to separate seconds from fractional seconds.
- Input fields must contain hours and minutes. Seconds and fractional seconds may be omitted and will default to zeros. Thus, the field "23:59" when read under TIME format will result in "23:59:00".
- Data values can contain a sign.
- Fractional seconds must have the decimal point coded in the data value.
- Hours may be of unlimited magnitude. The maximum for minutes is 59; for seconds, 59.99....

DTIMEw (Days and Time). The DTIME format is used to read a time interval which includes days in the form ddd hh:mm:ss.ss, such as "12 23:44:01.58" or "144 18:40". The number of days is separated from the hours by an acceptable TIME delimiter: a blank, a period, or a colon. A preceding sign (+/−) may be used. The remainder of the field must conform to required specifications for the TIME format. Fractional seconds must have the decimal point coded in the data value.

DATETIMEw (Date and Time). The DATETIME format is used to read values containing a date and a time. The date must be written as an international date (dd-mmm-yyyy) followed by a blank and then a time in the form hh:mm:ss.ss, such as "14-OCT-1977 14:12:51.10". The time conforms to a twenty-four hour clock. Thus the maximum subfields for time are 23 for hours, 59 for minutes, and 59.999... for seconds.

Fractional seconds must have the decimal point coded in the data value. The width defined on the DATA LIST command must be at least 17 characters; however, data values of fewer characters are correctly evaluated.

WKDAYw (Day of the Week). The WKDAY format is used to read the day of the week expressed as a character string. Only the first two characters are significant, and the minimum field width is two. Remaining characters are optional: Sunday could be expressed as "SUNDAY" or as "SU". Result values are integers between 1 and 7, where Sunday equals 1 and Saturday equals 7.

MONTHw (Month). The MONTH format is used to read the month of the year expressed as a character string. Names may be fully spelled out (for example, "OCTOBER") or abbreviated to three characters. For example, OCTOBER could be written as "OCT". The result is an integer between 1 and 12, where January equals 1 and December equals 12.

5.44
T and X Format Elements

Use the T and X format elements to skip columns that you do not want to define. The element T*n* tabs to the column number specified by *n*. The next format element defines the variable to be read beginning in that column. For example, to define a variable MOHIRED located in columns 12 and 13, specify:

```
DATA LIST  FILE=HUBDATA RECORDS=3
  /MOHIRED (T12,F2.0)
```

The element *n*X skips *n* columns. The next format element defines the variable to be read beginning with the column *following* the skip. The above DATA LIST can be specified using the X element, as in:

```
DATA LIST  FILE=HUBDATA RECORDS=3
  /MOHIRED (11X,F2.0)
```

The T format element can be used to move backward and forward within the same record, as in:

```
DATA LIST  FILE=HUBDATA RECORDS=3
  /DEPT82 (T19,F1.0) MOHIRED (T12,F2.0)
```

The first defined variable is DEPT82 located in column 19 on record 1. The second variable is MOHIRED located in columns 12 and 13 on record 1.

5.45
Format Lists

If two or more variables are recorded in adjacent columns of the same record and have the same format type, width, and number of implied decimal places, they can be defined by specifying the number of adjacent variables before the format element. For example, to define 20 adjacent single-column integer variables, specify 20F1.0.

Several format elements can be combined into a *format list* within the same set of parentheses to define a list of variables. The variable list can include individual variable names and variable names defined using the TO keyword (see Section 5.15). The format element or format list enclosed in parentheses follows the variable name or variable list to which it applies. For example, to define the variables MOHIRED, YRHIRED, and DEPT79 through DEPT82, specify:

```
DATA LIST  FILE=HUBDATA RECORDS=3
  /MOHIRED, YRHIRED, DEPT79 TO DEPT82 (T12,2F2.0,4F1.0)
```

All of the defined variables are located on record 1. The T12 format element in the format list positions the next data format element in column 12 (see Section 5.44). The first variable, MOHIRED, is a two-column integer variable located in columns 12 and 13. The second variable, YRHIRED, also a two-column integer variable, is located in columns 14 and 15. The next four variables, DEPT79 through DEPT82, are single-column variables located in columns 16 through 19.

5.46
Mixing Styles

You can mix FORTRAN-like and column format specifications in the same DATA LIST, as in:

```
DATA LIST FILE=HUBDATA RECORDS=3
  /DEPT82 (T19,F1.0) YRHIRED 14-15
```

One style might be convenient for one set of variables and not for another. For example, if you have a repeating pattern that causes you to skip columns, the FORTRAN-like formats may help, as in

```
DATA LIST FILE=TESTDATA
  /SCORE1 TO SCORE5 (T10,5(F2.0,1X))
```

which reads variable SCORE1 from columns 10 and 11, SCORE2 from columns 13 and 14, and so forth, skipping columns 12, 15, and so forth.

5.47
Skipping Records

If your data file has multiple records per case, you can use the slash to skip to the next record, rather than explicitly specifying the record sequence number. For example, to define the variable YRHIRED located on record 1 and the variable NAME located on record 3, specify:

```
DATA LIST  FILE=HUBDATA RECORDS=3
  /YRHIRED 14-15 //NAME 25-48 (A)
```

Format elements can be used with slashes to define these variables, as in:

```
DATA LIST  FILE=HUBDATA RECORDS=3
  /YRHIRED (T14,F2.0)// NAME (T25,A24)
```

Alternatively, the complete format list can follow the list of variables, as in:

```
DATA LIST  FILE=HUBDATA RECORDS=3
  /YRHIRED NAME (T14,F2.0//T25,A24)
```

5.48
COLUMN BINARY FORMAT

The amount of information a computer card or input record can hold varies considerably according to how the information is stored. When stored in the usual manner, with one character per column, the maximum number of data items that can occupy a single card is 80. An alternate way to store data is to allow punches in each of the 12 rows, thereby increasing the maximum number of items by as much as a factor of 12. Data stored in this manner are called *column binary*, or *multipunch*, data.

Column binary format makes it possible to store more than one variable in the same column rather than spanning several columns. This format was especially popular when information was stored almost exclusively on computer cards, making it desirable to compress the data into as small a space as possible. For example, a variable with three possible values could be stored in just two rows of a single column (one punch for each of two values and a zero value if neither row is punched), leaving nine rows for other variables.

SPSS-X only processes multipunch data that have been read by IBM card readers attached to IBM 360-compatible computers. These readers produce a particular representation of the punches. You should look at INFO LOCAL (see Chapter 3) to determine how multipunch data are handled by SPSS-X for your computer.

5.49
Column Binary Data and the FILE HANDLE Command

Although the advantages of the column binary format are obvious, it is often difficult to get at data stored in this manner. To read column binary data, use the keywords MODE=MULTIPUNCH on the FILE HANDLE command (see Section 5.3), as in:

```
FILE HANDLE ELE48 MODE=MULTIPUNCH   file specifications
```

This tells SPSS-X that the file ELE48 contains multiple punches. The FILE HANDLE command is required for reading column binary data. The file handle must match the handle named on the FILE subcommand or the name on the DD statement in the IBM OS environment.

5.50
Variable Definition on DATA LIST

Once a file has been specified as column binary, variables must then be defined in a DATA LIST command, giving starting and ending rows as well as columns. The general format for each variable is

```
varname   starting column:starting row - ending column:ending row
```

The starting column and row are required and must be separated by a colon. The ending row and column are optional if they are the same as the starting row and column. For example, the commands

```
FILE HANDLE  ELE48  MODE=MULTIPUNCH   file specifications
DATA LIST FILE=ELE48
    /1 PARTY    18
       SEX      19:1
       EMPSTAT  20(A)
       SES      48:4-6
       RELIGION 48:7-10
       OCCUPAT  50:11-51:2
```

tell SPSS-X to read SEX in row 1 of column 19; SES in rows 4 through 6 of column 48; RELIGION in rows 7 through 10 of column 48; and OCCUPAT in column 50, row 11 through column 51, row 2. Since columns 18 and 20 were not multipunched, the column numbers alone are sufficient to define the location of PARTY and EMPSTAT.

Each computer card contains 12 rows that are numbered from top to bottom as 1 through 12. This row numbering differs from the way that punch numbers are assigned: a 12 punch goes in the top row; an 11 punch, in the second row; and the third through twelfth rows are reserved for 0 through 9 punches (see Figure 5.50). Thus, row 1 is reserved for a 12 punch; row 2, for an 11 punch; and rows 3 through 12 are used for 0 through 9 punches.

Figure 5.50   Row numbering versus assignment of punches

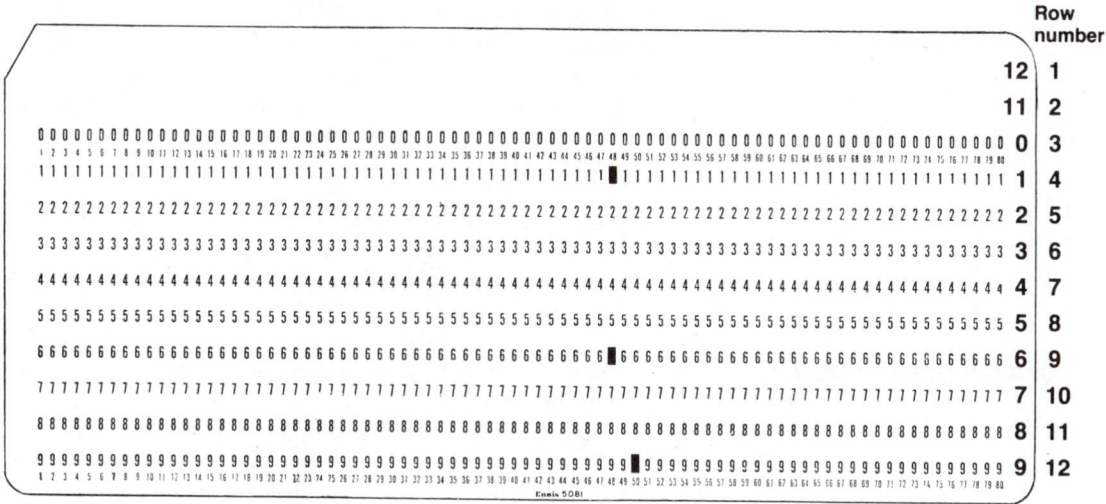

Variables that occupy a single row of one column, such as SEX in the above example, result in a value of 1 if a punch is present, and 0 if a punch is absent. A 12 punch in that instance could indicate a male, and a blank, a female. The variables that take up a series of adjacent rows (SES, RELIGION, and OCCUPAT) are assigned values as follows:

For SES:
1 if row 4 of column 48 is punched
2 if row 5 of column 48 is punched
3 if row 6 of column 48 is punched
0 if there is no punch in rows 4–6 of column 48

For RELIGION:
1 if row 7 of column 48 is punched
2 if row 8 of column 48 is punched
3 if row 9 of column 48 is punched
4 if row 10 of column 48 is punched
0 if there is no punch in rows 7–9 of column 48

For OCCUPAT:
1 if row 11 of column 50 is punched
2 if row 12 of column 50 is punched
3 if row 1 of column 51 is punched
4 if row 2 of column 51 is punched
0 if there is no punch in rows 11–12 of column 50 or in rows 1–2 of column 51

The punches in Figure 5.50 indicate a value of 1 for SES, 3 for RELIGION, and a value of 2 for OCCUPAT.

No more than one punch is allowed in any given field. Any attempt to read fields that contain more than one punch will produce an error, resulting in the system-missing value for the variable. In situations where more than one response is permitted to a question, each response must be coded as a separate variable.

5.51
Using Non-Column Binary Formats

Although multipunch columns can be read only using column binary format, all other formats can be used to read single-punched columns in the same data file. For example, a standard numeric format is used to read the variable PARTY in ELE48 in Section 5.50.

Often, organizations that store data in column binary format use the minus sign (the 11 punch) and the ampersand (the 12 punch in EBCDIC) for "don't know," "no answer," or "non-applicable" responses. When using a non-column binary format, variables containing these values must be read in as string variables. Use the keyword CONVERT on the RECODE command if you want to transform these alphanumeric variables into numeric ones, as in

```
RECODE EMPSTAT (CONVERT) ('-'=11)('&'=12) INTO EMPSTAT2
```

which recodes all numbers in string variable EMPSTAT to numbers for target variable EMPSTAT2 and then changes the minus sign to 11 and the ampersand to 12.

5.52
Column Binary Data on Tape or Disk

Column binary data may have originated on computer cards, but you normally find such data on magnetic tape or disk. On these media, column binary data occur in fixed-length records containing an even number of bytes, normally 160. Each column of the original input card is recorded in two adjacent bytes of a record. Thus, the second column of the original input card is recorded in the third and fourth bytes of the record. The top six rows of the first column of the original card are represented by the rightmost six bits of the first byte, and the bottom six rows of the first column are represented by the rightmost six bits of the second byte. The first two bits (leftmost) of each byte are always set to zero (see Table 5.52). For example, a 2 punch (bit 7 of the first byte) is represented as B'00000010', and a 5 punch (bit 4 of the second byte) is represented as B'00010000'.

Table 5.52 Bit, row, and punch correspondences

	First byte						Second byte					
Bit	3	4	5	6	7	8	3	4	5	6	7	8
Row	1	2	3	4	5	6	7	8	9	10	11	12
Punch	12	11	0	1	2	3	4	5	6	7	8	9

5.53
Limitations

Multipunched files can only be referenced on three commands: DATA LIST, REPEATING DATA, and REREAD. Cases may not be defined via FILE TYPE. For example, you may not specify FILE TYPE MIXED.

5.54
UNALIGNED POSITIVE INTEGER BINARY FORMAT

Unaligned positive integer binary format (known as UPIB) permits you to read positive integer binary (PIB) fields that do not begin and end on byte boundaries. This feature allows you to read individual bits within fields or to read fields that contain a combination of punches as one variable. UPIB also reads multipunched data, with a few important differences from column binary format (see Section 5.56).

5.55
Variable Definition on DATA LIST

Fields are defined according to starting and ending byte and bit locations, as in

```
DATA LIST FILE=FILEIN
  / USERTYPE 1:1-2
    CPUTIME  1:3-4:7
```

USERTYPE is in bits 1 and 2 of byte 1; CPUTIME is defined as a series of bits that begins in bit 3 of byte 1 and ends in bit 7 of byte 4. If multiple adjacent fields containing equal numbers of bits are to be read, the location information follows the list of variable names, as in

```
Vl TO V5 10:3-7
```

In this instance, five single-bit variables will be read from bits 3 through 7 of column 10 of the input record. The contents of each field are read as the positive integer represented in binary by the combination of bits within the field.

The following example illustrates interpreting the IBM machine Program Status Word (EC mode). The protection key is four bits long, the condition code is two bits, and the instruction address is three bytes long. All the other fields are single bits.

```
DATA LIST   FILE=PSWS
  /PERMASK 1:2              /*Program Event Recording Mask
  TRANSMODE                 /*Translation Mode
  IOMASK                    /*Input/Output Mask
  EXTMASK 1:6-8             /*External Mask
  PROTKEY 2:1-4             /*Protection Key
  ECMODE                    /*EC Mode=1
  MCMASK                    /*Machine Check Mask
  WAIT                      /*Wait State
  PROB     2:5-8            /*Problem State
  CC       3:3-4            /*Condition Code
  FXOVMASK                  /*Fixed Point Overflow Mask
  DCOVMASK                  /*Decimal Overflow Mask
  EXUFMASK                  /*Exponent Underflow Mask
  SIGMASK 3:5-8
  ADDRESS 5-8 (PIB)         /*Instruction Address
```

5.56
UPIB versus Column Binary Format

Fields to be read under UPIB format are specified with a syntax identical to that used for column binary. In fact, when used to read single-bit dichotomies, the two formats produce results that are identical. The determination of which type of field the user specified is made by examining the declared data mode of the input field. If the data mode was declared to be MULTIPUNCHED on the FILE HANDLE command, the field is assumed to be column binary. If the data mode was not specifically declared to be multipunched, the field is assumed to be unaligned binary. There are three additional differences between column binary and unaligned positive integer binary:

- The column binary format specifies which rows are to be read from virtual card columns. The UPIB format specifies which bits are to be read from actual bytes.

- The column binary format is restricted to records containing a maximum of 80 virtual card columns. The UPIB format can be used when reading a record of any length supported by SPSS-X.

- For each field, the column binary format expects at most a single punch on a given case and returns the ordinal position of the punch that occurs. The UPIB format accepts any combination of bits and returns the binary integer represented by the bits that are on.

See Appendix F for the value range of bit specifications on VAX/VMS systems.

5.57
Limitations

The following limitations apply to the UPIB format:

- Unaligned binary input field specifications are valid only on DATA LIST, KEYED DATA LIST, and REPEATING DATA.

- The maximum number of bits that can be specified for any single variable is 64. On machines that support OS, DOS, and CMS operating systems, a maximum of 56 significant bits will be retained when reading fields over 56 bits in width.

- Fields to be read as unaligned binary integers are always treated as positive. No parenthesized format type is permitted following the location information. The variables defined are assigned print and write formats of F.

Syntax

DISPLAY

```
DISPLAY [SORTED] [{NAMES**    }] [/VARIABLES=varlist]
                 {INDEX      }
                 {VARIABLES  }
                 {LABELS     }
                 {DICTIONARY }

         [MACROS]
```

DOCUMENT

```
DOCUMENT text
```

DROP DOCUMENTS

```
DROP DOCUMENTS
```

FILE LABEL

```
FILE LABEL label
```

GET

```
GET FILE=file
 [/KEEP={ALL    }] [/DROP=varlist]
        {varlist}
 [/RENAME=(old varlist=new varlist)...]
 [/MAP]
```

SAVE

```
SAVE OUTFILE=file
 [/KEEP={ALL    }] [/DROP=varlist]
        {varlist}
 [/RENAME=(old varlist=new varlist)...]
 [/MAP] [/{COMPRESSED   }]
          {UNCOMPRESSED }
```

XSAVE

```
XSAVE OUTFILE=file
 [/KEEP={ALL    }] [/DROP=varlist]
        {varlist}
 [/RENAME=(old varlist=new varlist)...]
 [/MAP] [/{COMPRESSED   }]
          {UNCOMPRESSED }
```

Contents

6.1   INTRODUCTION TO SYSTEM FILES

6.2   GET COMMAND
6.3   FILE Subcommand
6.4   MAP Subcommand
6.5   RENAME Subcommand
6.6   DROP Subcommand
6.7   KEEP Subcommand
6.8   Reordering Variables
6.9   Multiple Subcommands

6.10 XSAVE COMMAND
6.11   OUTFILE Subcommand
6.12   MAP Subcommand
6.13   RENAME Subcommand
6.14   DROP and KEEP Subcommands
6.15   Reordering Variables
6.16   COMPRESSED and UNCOMPRESSED Subcommands
6.17   XSAVE Messages
6.18   Saving Multiple System Files
6.19   Limitations on XSAVE

6.20 SAVE COMMAND
6.21   SAVE and XSAVE Compared
6.22   SAVE, XSAVE, and TEMPORARY

6.23 SYSTEM FILE UTILITIES
6.24   FILE LABEL Command
6.25   DOCUMENT Command
6.26   DISPLAY Command
6.27   VARIABLES Subcommand
6.28   DROP DOCUMENTS Command

6.29 STRUCTURE OF A SYSTEM FILE
6.30   Binary Storage
6.31   Upper and Lower Case
6.32   Limitations

Chapter 6   SPSS-X System Files

Once you have defined your data file in SPSS-X, you do not need to repeat the data definition process. The data definition information described in Chapter 5 can be permanently saved along with the data on a specially formatted file called the SPSS-X *system file*. Variables created or altered by data transformations and the descriptive information for these variables can also be saved. You can access the system file in subsequent SPSS-X jobs or later in the same job without respecifying variable locations, formats, missing values, or variable and value labels. You can update the system file, altering the descriptive information or modifying the data, and you can save the updated version in a new system file.

6.1
INTRODUCTION TO
SYSTEM FILES

An SPSS-X system file is a self-documented file containing data and descriptive information. The descriptive information is called the *dictionary*. It contains variable names, their printing and writing formats, and optional variable labels, value labels, and missing-value indicators. The dictionary also contains the file label from the FILE LABEL command, the date and time the file was created, and additional documentation supplied on the DOCUMENT command. The FILE LABEL and DOCUMENT commands are described in Sections 6.24 and 6.25.

The data in a system file are stored in binary format, which reduces the time required to read the data. This form of data representation looks quite different from the character form usually used to enter data. You should never list an SPSS-X system file at a terminal or print it on a line printer. You cannot change the information in a system file through another program, package, utility, or text editor; only SPSS-X reads and modifies this file.

You can save a system file with either the XSAVE or SAVE command. XSAVE and SAVE have the same syntax, but SAVE is a procedure command and XSAVE is a transformation command (see Section 6.21). The GET command reads a system file. The only specification required on XSAVE, SAVE, or GET is the subcommand that specifies the name of the system file to be saved or read. The command

```
XSAVE OUTFILE=HUBEMPL
```

saves the active file as a system file designated by the name HUBEMPL. To read the previously saved system file, specify:

```
GET FILE=HUBEMPL
```

Optional subcommands on XSAVE, SAVE, and GET rename variables, select a subset of variables, and reorder the variables. The GET command is discussed in Sections 6.2 through 6.9; the XSAVE command in Sections 6.10 through 6.19; and the SAVE command in Sections 6.20 through 6.22.

Once you read a system file, you can add variables created or altered by transformations and procedures, and you can change descriptive information in the dictionary. Changes are not made directly to a system file. Instead, modifications are made on the active file and are saved on a new system file. You can also display descriptive information from the dictionary using the DISPLAY command (see Section 6.26).

Other facilities in SPSS-X allow you to modify and combine system files by merging two or more system files into one (Chapter 16), by saving aggregated data as a new system file (Chapter 18), and by sorting the cases on any variables in the file (Chapter 15).

6.2
GET COMMAND

The GET command reads a previously created system file. Variable names, labels, and missing-value indicators are retrieved from the system file. The only specification required is the FILE subcommand, which identifies the name of the system file that you want to use (see Section 6.3). Additional subcommands on the GET command are

RENAME Subcommand. Use RENAME to change the names of variables (see Section 6.5).

DROP and KEEP Subcommands. Use DROP and KEEP to save computer resources by accessing only a subset of variables in the system file (see Sections 6.6 and 6.7). KEEP also reorders variables (see Section 6.8).

MAP Subcommand. Use MAP to display the names of the variables in the active file after any renaming, subsetting, or reordering, along with their corresponding names in the system file (see Section 6.4).

Operations are performed as the system file is copied to the active file; the original system file is not changed.

You can use the optional subcommands RENAME, KEEP, DROP, and MAP more than once on a GET command. Separate each subcommand from the other subcommands with a slash. A subcommand acts on the results of all the previous subcommands on the GET command. For example, if you use a KEEP subcommand followed by a RENAME subcommand, you can rename only the variables that you subset with KEEP.

The GET command cannot be used inside the DO IF structure described in Chapter 9 or the LOOP structure described in Chapter 14.

The GET command also retrieves the system file's document text, if any exists (see Section 6.25). If you want to get a system file without its document text, use the DROP DOCUMENTS command (see Section 6.28).

6.3
FILE Subcommand

The FILE subcommand is required and must be the first specification on the GET command. The FILE subcommand specifies the name of the system file. In the example,

`GET FILE=SHOES`

the GET command retrieves all variables and descriptive information from a system file containing the 1980 *Runner's World* rating data on running shoes.

6.4
MAP Subcommand

If you use the RENAME, DROP, or KEEP subcommands to tailor your file, you may find it difficult to keep track of what you have done. To check the results of these subcommands, use the MAP subcommand immediately following the subcommand you want mapped. The command

`GET FILE=SHOES/MAP`

reads the system file dictionary and displays a list of all variables, in this case those containing the 1980 *Runner's World* shoe ratings data. Since no renaming, reordering, or subsetting of variables is specified on the GET command, the resulting variables are identical to the variables from file SHOES. The output displayed by the MAP subcommand is shown in Figure 6.4.

Figure 6.4 Output display of MAP subcommand

```
FILE SHOESX SPSSX M1
   LABEL: 1980 RUNNER'S WORLD SHOE SURVEY DATA
   CREATED 12 APR 82 13:55:22          14 VARIABLES

FILE MAP

RESULT     INPUT1      RESULT     INPUT1
------     ------      ------     ------
RATING79   RATING79    FOREIMP    FOREIMP
RATING80   RATING80    FLEX       FLEX
PREFER     PREFER      SOLEWEAR   SOLEWEAR
TYPE       TYPE        REARCONT   REARCONT
MAKER      MAKER       SOLETRAC   SOLETRAC
QUALITY    QUALITY     WEIGHT     WEIGHT
REARIMP    REARIMP     SHOE       SHOE
```

Usually, you use the MAP subcommand after other subcommands in order to verify the results of complicated sets of subcommands. See the following sections for examples.

6.5
RENAME Subcommand

Use the RENAME subcommand to change the names of variables as they are copied from the system file. Variable names are changed only on the active file, not on the system file. You cannot rename variables to scratch variables. See Chapter 7 for a description of scratch variables.

To rename variables, specify the keyword RENAME followed by an optional equals sign and the rename specification enclosed in parentheses in the form (*old=new*), as in:

```
GET FILE=SHOES
  /RENAME= (RATING79=TOTRAT79)
```

This command changes the name of the variable RATING79 to TOTRAT79. You can omit the parentheses when renaming a single variable.

If you rename more than one variable on a RENAME subcommand, you can specify several sets of individual variable specifications, as in:

```
GET FILE=SHOES
  /RENAME= (RATING79=TOTRAT79) (RATING80=TOTRAT80)
```

Or you can specify a list of variable names and a corresponding list of new names, as in:

```
GET FILE=SHOES
  /RENAME= (RATING79 RATING80=TOTRAT79 TOTRAT80)
```

Both commands rename RATING79 as TOTRAT79 and RATING80 as TOTRAT80.

If you specify lists, both lists must name the same number of variables and the entire specification must be enclosed in parentheses. The first variable listed on the left side of the equals sign is changed to the first name listed on the right side of the equals sign, the second variable listed on the left to the second name on the right, and so forth. You do not need to list the old variable names in the same order as their sequence in the system file.

Name changes take place in one operation for a given RENAME subcommand. Therefore, you can exchange the names of two variables. The command

```
GET FILE=READERS
  /RENAME= (TIME=NEWSWEEK) (NEWSWEEK=TIME)
```

exchanges the names of variables TIME and NEWSWEEK.

You can use keyword TO both to refer to consecutive variables to be renamed (on the left side of the equals sign) or to generate new variable names (on the right side of the equals sign). Keyword TO used in the old variable list refers to consecutive variables in the system file. The command

```
GET FILE=SHOES
  /RENAME= (REARIMP TO FLEX=RIMPACT FIMPACT FLEXIBLE)
```

renames the consecutive variables REARIMP, FOREIMP, and FLEX to RIMACT, FIMPACT, and FLEXIBLE.

To generate new variable names, specify an alphabetic prefix and an inclusive range of associated sequence numbers. This method of defining multiple variable names is discussed in detail in Chapter 2. The variable names implied by the inclusive list are assigned sequentially to the variables referenced in the old variable list. The command

```
GET FILE=SHOES
  /RENAME= (REARIMP TO FLEX=TEST1 TO TEST3) /MAP
```

renames the same variables as in the above example to TEST1, TEST2, and TEST3. Figure 6.5 shows the output displayed by the MAP subcommand. Note the change in names for the three variables specified on the RENAME subcommand.

Figure 6.5 Output display of MAP after RENAME

```
FILE SHOESX SPSSX M1
   LABEL: 1980 RUNNER'S WORLD SHOE SURVEY DATA
   CREATED 12 APR 82 13:55:22          14 VARIABLES

FILE MAP

RESULT     INPUT1      RESULT     INPUT1
-------    -------     -------    -------
RATING79   RATING79    TEST2      FOREIMP
RATING80   RATING80    TEST3      FLEX
PREFER     PREFER      SOLEWEAR   SOLEWEAR
TYPE       TYPE        REARCONT   REARCONT
MAKER      MAKER       SOLETRAC   SOLETRAC
QUALITY    QUALITY     WEIGHT     WEIGHT
TEST1      REARIMP     SHOE       SHOE
```

The RENAME subcommand does not reorder variables. Variables assigned new names created with the TO keyword are not consecutive on the active file unless they were consecutive on the system file or unless you reorder them using the KEEP subcommand.

After the RENAME subcommand, use the new names to refer to the variables.

6.6
DROP Subcommand

When your system file includes variables that you do not want, you can use the DROP subcommand to specify variables you want dropped when SPSS-X creates an active file from the system file. For example, an SPSS-X system file containing all data from the 1980 General Social Survey has 1500 respondents (cases) and 325 variables. The command

```
GET FILE=GSS80
  /DROP=MARITAL TO CUTSPDFG
```

retains only the first seven variables since MARITAL is the eighth variable in the system file GSS80 and CUTSPDFG is the last variable. You would obviously have to know this information ahead of time from a codebook or from a previous job using the DISPLAY command (see Section 6.26).

You do not need to list the variable names on the DROP subcommand in the same order as their sequence in the system file. However, variables retained are always copied in the same sequence as they are in the system file. If you want to reorder the variables, use the KEEP subcommand described in Section 6.8.

After the DROP subcommand, the active file contains only the variables not named on the DROP subcommand.

6.7
KEEP Subcommand

When your system file has many variables and you want to use only a few, use the KEEP subcommand to select a subset of variables, as in:

```
GET FILE=GSS80
    /KEEP=EDUC INCOME AGE CONFINAN TO CONARMY /MAP
```

This command keeps the variables for education, income, age, and the thirteen consecutive variables recording the measure of confidence in people in charge of different institutions. Figure 6.7 shows the map of the resulting active file.

Figure 6.7   Output display of MAP after KEEP

```
FILE GSS80 SPSSX M1
    LABEL: GENERAL SOCIAL SURVEY 1980(N=500)
    CREATED 15 APR 82 16:34:19      322 VARIABLES

FILE MAP

RESULT      INPUT1        RESULT      INPUT1
------      ------        ------      ------
EDUC        EDUC          CONLABOR    CONLABOR
INCOME      INCOME        CONPRESS    CONPRESS
AGE         AGE           CONMEDIC    CONMEDIC
CONFINAN    CONFINAN      CONTV       CONTV
CONBUS      CONBUS        CONJUDGE    CONJUDGE
CONCLERG    CONCLERG      CONSCI      CONSCI
CONEDUC     CONEDUC       CONLEGIS    CONLEGIS
CONFED      CONFED        CONARMY     CONARMY
```

The variables are copied from the system file in the order they are listed on the KEEP subcommand. If you do not want the variables reordered, list the variables in the same order as their sequence on the system file. If you name a variable more than once on the KEEP subcommand, only the first mention of the variable is observed; all subsequent references to the variable are ignored.

After the KEEP subcommand, the active file contains only the variables named on the KEEP subcommand.

6.8
Reordering Variables

On many SPSS-X commands, you can use the TO keyword to specify consecutive variables in your active file. Therefore, you may want to reorder the variables so that you can more conveniently reference them with the TO keyword on subsequent SPSS-X commands. Use the KEEP subcommand to reorder variables in your file. You can either list the names of all the variables in the order that you want them, or you can simply list the names of the variables that you want at the beginning of the file in the desired order, followed by the keyword ALL. Keyword ALL places all the unnamed variables in the same sequence as they appear in the system file. Keyword ALL must be the last specification on the KEEP subcommand, as in:

```
GET FILE=SHOES
    /KEEP=SHOE MAKER TYPE ALL /MAP
```

This command reorders variables in the 1980 *Runner's World* shoe ratings file so that the first three variables are SHOE, MAKER, and TYPE, followed by the remaining variables in the same sequence as in the system file. Figure 6.8 shows the map of the reordered file. Notice the different order of the variables compared with the original order as shown in Figure 6.4.

Figure 6.8   Output display of MAP after KEEP with ALL

```
FILE SHOESX SPSSX M1
  LABEL: 1980 RUNNER'S WORLD SHOE SURVEY DATA
  CREATED 12 APR 82 13:55:22        14 VARIABLES

FILE MAP

RESULT    INPUT1        RESULT    INPUT1
-------   -------       -------   -------
SHOE      SHOE          REARIMP   REARIMP
MAKER     MAKER         FOREIMP   FOREIMP
TYPE      TYPE          FLEX      FLEX
RATING79  RATING79      SOLEWEAR  SOLEWEAR
RATING80  RATING80      REARCONT  REARCONT
PREFER    PREFER        SOLETRAC  SOLETRAC
QUALITY   QUALITY       WEIGHT    WEIGHT
```

6.9
Multiple Subcommands

Use only one FILE subcommand on the GET command, and specify it first. Then use the RENAME, DROP, KEEP, and MAP subcommands in any order and as many times as you wish. Each subcommand refers to the results of previous subcommands. Thus, any variables renamed on the RENAME subcommand must be referred to by their new names on subsequent KEEP or DROP subcommands. Similarly, only variables retained on the active file as the result of KEEP or DROP can be specified on a subsequent RENAME subcommand. If the KEEP subcommand reorders the variables, the keyword TO on subsequent subcommands will refer to the reordered sequence.

For example, to rename the subset of variables selected in Section 6.7, specify:

```
GET FILE=GSS80
  /KEEP=EDUC INCOME AGE CONFINAN TO CONARMY
  /RENAME=(CONFINAN TO CONARMY=CONF1 TO CONF13)  /MAP
```

The map of the resulting active file is shown in Figure 6.9.

Figure 6.9   Output display of MAP after KEEP and RENAME

```
FILE GSS80 SPSSX M1
  LABEL: GENERAL SOCIAL SURVEY 1980(N=500)
  CREATED 15 APR 82 16:34:19        322 VARIABLES

FILE MAP

RESULT    INPUT1        RESULT    INPUT1
-------   -------       -------   -------
EDUC      EDUC          CONF6     CONLABOR
INCOME    INCOME        CONF7     CONPRESS
AGE       AGE           CONF8     CONMEDIC
CONF1     CONFINAN      CONF9     CONTV
CONF2     CONBUS        CONF10    CONJUDGE
CONF3     CONCLERG      CONF11    CONSCI
CONF4     CONEDUC       CONF12    CONLEGIS
CONF5     CONFED        CONF13    CONARMY
```

6.10
XSAVE COMMAND

The XSAVE command saves the active file as a system file. All data-descriptive information is stored in the system file dictionary. Since XSAVE is a transformation command, it must be followed by a procedure for the system file to actually be created.

The placement of XSAVE relative to other commands determines what is saved on the system file. New variables created by transformations and procedures previous to the XSAVE command are included in the new system file, and variables altered by transformations are saved in their modified form. Results of any temporary transformations immediately preceding the XSAVE command are included in the system file; scratch variables are not. See Chapter 7 for a discussion of temporary transformations and scratch variables.

The only specification required on the XSAVE command is the OUTFILE subcommand identifying the name of the system file (see Section 6.11). Additional subcommands on the XSAVE command are

RENAME Subcommand. Use RENAME to change the names of variables (see Section 6.13).

DROP and KEEP Subcommands. Use DROP and KEEP to save a subset of variables (see Section 6.14). You can also use the KEEP subcommand to reorder variables (see Section 6.15).

MAP Subcommand. Use MAP to display the names of the variables saved in the system file after any renaming, subsetting, or reordering, along with their corresponding names in the active file (see Section 6.12).

COMPRESSED and UNCOMPRESSED Subcommands. Use COMPRESSED and UNCOMPRESSED to instruct SPSS-X to save the system file in compressed or uncompressed form (see Section 6.16).

All of these operations are executed as the active file is copied to the system file; the active file is not changed.

After the OUTFILE subcommand, specify the RENAME, DROP, KEEP, and MAP subcommands in any order and as many times as you need, separated by slashes. As with the GET command, if you use multiple subcommands on the XSAVE command, each operation refers to the results of all previous subcommands.

6.11
OUTFILE Subcommand

The OUTFILE subcommand is required and must be the first specification on the XSAVE command. The OUTFILE subcommand specifies the output system file. In the commands

```
XSAVE OUTFILE=HUBEMPL
EXECUTE
```

the XSAVE command followed by the EXECUTE procedure saves the current active file as the system file identified by the HUBEMPL. See the annotated XSAVE example for the complete job.

6.12
MAP Subcommand

If you use the optional subcommands RENAME, DROP, or KEEP, you may want to check the names of the variables that you are saving. Use the MAP subcommand to print a list of the variables on the system file and their corresponding names on the active file, as in:

```
XSAVE OUTFILE=HUBEMPL/MAP
EXECUTE
```

This command displays a list of all variables saved in the system file HUBEMPL. Since no variables were renamed, reordered, or deleted, the variables in the map are identical to those in the active file.

6.13
RENAME Subcommand

The RENAME subcommand changes the names of variables as they are copied into the system file. The command

```
XSAVE OUTFILE=HUBEMPL
  /RENAME=(AGE=AGE80)(JOBCAT=JOBCAT82) /MAP
EXECUTE
```

renames variables AGE and JOBCAT to AGE80 and JOBCAT82. Figure 6.13 shows the output from the MAP subcommand. If you rename only one variable, the parentheses enclosing the specification are optional.

Figure 6.13   MAP of the variables in the system file

```
OUTPUT FILE MAP

RESULT      INPUT1          RESULT      INPUT1
────────    ────────        ────────    ────────
EMPLOYID    EMPLOYID        SALARY81    SALARY81
MOHIRED     MOHIRED         SALARY82    SALARY82
YRHIRED     YRHIRED         HOURLY81    HOURLY81
DEPT79      DEPT79          HOURLY82    HOURLY82
DEPT80      DEPT80          PROMO81     PROMO81
DEPT81      DEPT81          AGE80       AGE
DEPT82      DEPT82          RAISE82     RAISE82
SEX         SEX             JOBCAT82    JOBCAT
SALARY79    SALARY79        NAME        NAME
SALARY80    SALARY80
```

To rename more than one variable, specify several sets of individual variable specifications (as shown above), or specify a list of variable names and a list of new names, as in:

```
XSAVE OUTFILE=HUBEMPL
  /RENAME=(AGE JOBCAT=AGE80 JOBCAT82) /MAP
EXECUTE
```

If you specify variable lists, the same number of variables must be named in both lists, and the entire specification must be enclosed in parentheses. The first variable listed on the left side of the equals sign is changed to the first name on the right side of the equals sign, the second variable listed on the left to the second name on the right, and so forth. You do not need to list the old variable names according to their order on the active file.

Name changes take place in one operation for a given RENAME subcommand. Therefore, you can exchange the names of two variables, as in:

```
XSAVE OUTFILE=MAGS
  /RENAME= (TIME=NEWSWEEK) (NEWSWEEK=TIME)
EXECUTE
```

This command exchanges the names of variables TIME and NEWSWEEK on the new system file.

Keyword TO can be used both to refer to consecutive variables to be renamed (on the left side of the equals sign) and to generate new variable names (on the right side of the equals sign). See Section 6.5 for examples of RENAME subcommands using TO.

6.14
DROP and KEEP
Subcommands

Your active file may contain variables you do not need to save on a system file. To select a subset of variables, use the KEEP subcommand to specify those you want to save or the DROP subcommand to specify those you do not want to save. Depending upon the number of variables you want to save and their sequence, one or the other will probably be easier.

Specify the DROP subcommand followed by an optional equals sign and the list of variables you do not want to save. The variable list can include individual variable names and consecutive variables referenced by the keyword TO.

You can list the variable names on the DROP subcommand in any sequence. However, the variables retained are always saved in the system file in the same sequence as they are in the active file. If you want to reorder the variables, use the KEEP subcommand (see Section 6.15).

Specify the KEEP subcommand followed by an optional equals sign and the list of variables that you want to save. The variable list can include individual variable names and consecutive variables referenced by the keyword TO. The order of the variable names on the KEEP subcommand determines their sequence on the system file. If you name a variable more than once on a KEEP subcommand, only the first mention of the variable is recognized, and the variable is written on the system file in the sequence of the first mention of the name.

For example, assume that you have saved a system file (as shown in the annotated example of the XSAVE command) containing the Hubbard employee data. In your next SPSS-X job, suppose you want to read the system file in order to run a MEANS procedure on the variables RAISE82 by DEPT82 and save a new system file containing only the variables SEX, DEPT79, DEPT80, DEPT81, DEPT82, SALARY79, SALARY80, SALARY81, and SALARY82:

```
GET FILE=HUBEMPL
XSAVE OUTFILE=SUBHUB
     /KEEP=SEX, DEPT79 TO DEPT82, SALARY79 TO SALARY82/MAP
MEANS   RAISE82 BY DEPT82
```

The new system file is saved on a file identified by the name SUBHUB when the data are read for the MEANS procedure. Figure 6.14 shows the map of the new system file. Note that the variables are saved on the new system file SUBHUB in the order that they are listed on the KEEP subcommand. The original system file HUBEMPL is not changed or deleted.

Figure 6.14   MAP of the new system file SUBHUB

```
OUTPUT FILE MAP

RESULT      INPUT1
--------    --------
SEX         SEX
DEPT79      DEPT79
DEPT80      DEPT80
DEPT81      DEPT81
DEPT82      DEPT82
SALARY79    SALARY79
SALARY80    SALARY80
SALARY81    SALARY81
SALARY82    SALARY82
```

6.15
Reordering Variables

If you have created new variables with transformations or procedures, the new variables are added to the end of your active file. To save these variables in a different order in your system file, perhaps so that you can refer to them in subsequent SPSS-X jobs with the TO keyword, use the KEEP subcommand. You can either list variable names in the order you want them saved, or you can list the names of the variables that you want at the beginning of the system file in the desired order, followed by the keyword ALL. Keyword ALL must be the last specification on the KEEP subcommand since it implies all the variables not previously named, as in:

```
GET FILE=HUBEMPL
XSAVE OUTFILE=REORHUB/ KEEP=SEX, AGE, ALL
EXECUTE
```

This command reads the system file containing the Hubbard employee data and saves a new system file with SEX and AGE as the first two variables, followed by the remaining variables in the same sequence as in the original system file.

6.16
COMPRESSED and UNCOMPRESSED Subcommands

Although the binary form of storing data in a system file is efficient in processing time, it sometimes requires a large amount of storage. For example, if your data file contains mostly variables with small integer values, the system file can require significantly more storage space than the original data file. For this type of file, it may be to your advantage to store the system file in *compressed* form. Compression maximizes the number of variables stored in each computer word and thus reduces the storage requirements for files with mostly small integer values (see Sections 6.29 through 6.31 for a discussion of the structure of system files). However, the processing time for saving and retrieving compressed files is greater than for uncompressed files.

Either the COMPRESSED or UNCOMPRESSED keyword can be specified on a XSAVE command. If neither is specified, the default is used. The default will usually be COMPRESSED, but it may be different at your installation. Use the INFO command to check your installation's default (see Chapter 2). However, you can always specify explicitly the form that you want.

If you are saving a very large data file, check with your local coordinator for advice on whether storage and input/output operations are more expensive at your installation than the processing time needed to compress a file.

Once the system file is saved, you need not remember whether it was saved in compressed or uncompressed form. The system file will be accessed automatically in the correct form by the GET command and all other commands that access system files.

6.17
XSAVE Messages

XSAVE processes the dictionary first and tells you how many variables will be saved and how many bytes per case will be required, as in:

```
18 APR 85 09:19:13      19 VARIABLES,     168 BYTES PER CASE BEFORE COMPRESSION
```

Then, once the data are written, XSAVE tells you how many cases were saved, as in

```
THERE WERE  1 XSAVE COMMANDS PROCESSED
      FOR FILE HANDLE: HUBEMPL        275 CASES WERE WRITTEN.
PRECEDING TASK REQUIRED      0.36 SECONDS CPU TIME;      1.68 SECONDS ELAPSED.
```

Both messages include the time and the date. If the second message does not appear, the file was probably not completely written.

Since XSAVE is actually executed by a procedure, the data are not completely written until the procedure is completed. Note also that the CPU time shown in the second message includes the time for both the procedure and XSAVE.

6.18
Saving Multiple System Files

The XSAVE command allows you to selectively send cases to different output system files, as in:

```
GET FILE=GSSIN
COMMENT  CREATE A SEPARATE FILE FOR DIFFERENT SECTIONS OF THE COUNTRY
DO IF  ANY (REGION,1,2,3,4)
 /* NORTH
FILE LABEL  NEW ENGLAND, MIDDLE ATLANTIC, AND NORTH CENTRAL
XSAVE   OUTFILE=OUT1
ELSE IF  ANY (REGION,5,6,7)
 /*SOUTH
FILE LABEL  SOUTH ATLANTIC AND SOUTH CENTRAL
XSAVE   OUTFILE=OUT2
ELSE IF  REGION EQ 8 OR REGION EQ 9
 /*WEST
FILE LABEL  MOUNTAIN AND PACIFIC
XSAVE   OUTFILE=OUT3
END IF
FILE LABEL  ALL REGIONS
FREQUENCIES  VARIABLES=REGION
```

This example uses XSAVE to create a separate system file for each of three geographic regions. The three XSAVE commands are placed within a DO IF structure so that only the appropriate cases are sent to each file. A procedure is necessary to cause the XSAVE commands to be executed. The presence of the XSAVE commands does not affect the active file; all cases are processed by the FREQUENCIES procedure.

XSAVE produces output at two points within the job listing. Immediately following the command, a one-line report of the number of variables saved and the number of bytes per case is displayed (Figure 6.18a). If a MAP subcommand is used, the map also appears here.

Figure 6.18a   First part of XSAVE display

```
    1  0              FILE HANDLE GSSIN/NAME='GSS80 SPSSX'
    2  0              FILE HANDLE OUT1/NAME='XSOUT1 SPSSXFIL'
    3  0              FILE HANDLE OUT2/NAME='XSOUT2 SPSSXFIL'
    4  0              FILE HANDLE OUT3/NAME='XSOUT3 SPSSXFIL'
    5  0              SET WIDTH=80
    6 GET FILE=GSSIN
    7 COMMENT  CREATE A SEPARATE FILE FOR DIFFERENT SECTIONS OF THE COUNTRY

FILE CALLED GSSIN    :
  LABEL: GENERAL SOCIAL SURVEY 1980(N=500)
  CREATED 15 APR 82 16:34:19      322 VARIABLES


    8 DO IF  ANY (REGION,1,2,3,4) /* NORTH
    9 FILE LABEL  NEW ENGLAND, MIDDLE ATLANTIC, AND NORTH CENTRAL
   10 XSAVE  OUTFILE=OUT1

18 APR 85 09:28:14      322 VARIABLES,   2576 BYTES PER CASE BEFORE COMPRESSION
   11 ELSE IF  ANY (REGION,5,6,7) /*SOUTH
   12 FILE LABEL  SOUTH ATLANTIC AND SOUTH CENTRAL
   13 XSAVE  OUTFILE=OUT2

18 APR 85 09:28:16      322 VARIABLES,   2576 BYTES PER CASE BEFORE COMPRESSION
   14 ELSE IF  REGION EQ 8 OR REGION EQ 9 /*WEST
   15 FILE LABEL  MOUNTAIN AND PACIFIC
   16 XSAVE  OUTFILE=OUT3

18 APR 85 09:28:18      322 VARIABLES,   2576 BYTES PER CASE BEFORE COMPRESSION
   17 END IF
   18 FILE LABEL  ALL REGIONS
   19 FREQUENCIES  VARIABLES=REGION
```

Additional XSAVE information is displayed after the output from the procedure in the job. This includes the the number of cases in the file (Figure 6.18b).

Figure 6.18b   XSAVE display after the procedure

```
THERE WERE  3 XSAVE COMMANDS PROCESSED

       FOR FILE HANDLE: OUT1            280 CASES WERE WRITTEN.

       FOR FILE HANDLE: OUT2            127 CASES WERE WRITTEN.

       FOR FILE HANDLE: OUT3             93 CASES WERE WRITTEN.

PRECEDING TASK REQUIRED     1.60 SECONDS CPU TIME;      28.38 SECONDS ELAPSED.
```

6.19
Limitations on XSAVE

The following limitations apply to XSAVE:

• A maximum of 10 XSAVE commands are allowed in a job.
• XSAVE cannot appear with a DO REPEAT-END REPEAT structure.
• Multiple XSAVE commands writing to the same file are not permitted.

6.20
SAVE COMMAND

The SAVE command allows you to save a system file when another procedure is not needed. The subcommands for SAVE are the same as for XSAVE. Both commands will create a system file. The difference is that SAVE is a procedure and will save the active file even if there is no other procedure command in your job. XSAVE is a transformation and requires a procedure to execute it.

6

ANNOTATED EXAMPLE FOR XSAVE

The following job saves an SPSS-X system file from the Hubbard Consultants Inc. employment data. The object is to create a self-documenting file by supplying complete documentary information. The SPSS-X commands are

```
TITLE   SAVE A SYSTEM FILE OF THE HUBBARD EMPLOYEE DATA
DATA LIST    FILE=HUBDATA RECORDS=3
   /1 EMPLOYID 1-5 MOHIRED YRHIRED 12-15 DEPT79 TO DEPT82 SEX 16-20
   /2 SALARY79 TO SALARY82 6-25 HOURLY81 HOURLY82 42-53(2) PROMO81 72
      AGE 54-55 RAISE82 66-70
   /3 JOBCAT 6 NAME 25-48 (A)

MISSING VALUES   DEPT79 TO SALARY82, AGE (0)
   HOURLY82, RAISE82 (-999) JOBCAT (9)

VAR LABELS   YRHIRED 'YEAR OF FIRST HIRING'
   DEPT82 'DEPARTMENT OF EMPLOYMENT IN 1982'
   SALARY82 'YEARLY SALARY IN 1982'
   JOBCAT 'JOB CATEGORIES'

VALUE LABELS   DEPT79 TO DEPT82 1 'ADMINISTRATIVE' 2 'PROJECT DIRECTORS'
   3 'CHICAGO OPERATIONS' 4 'ST LOUIS OPERATIONS' 0 'NOT REPORTED'/
   SEX 1 'MALE' 2 'FEMALE'/
   JOBCAT 1 'OFFICIALS & MANAGERS' 2 'PROFESSIONALS' 3 'TECHNICIANS'
   4 'OFFICE AND CLERICAL' 5 'CRAFTSMEN' 6 'SERVICE WORKERS'

FILE LABEL   HUBBARD INDUSTRIAL CONSULTANTS INC. EMPLOYEE DATA
DOCUMENT   THIS FILE CONTAINS EMPLOYEE RECORDS FOR HUBBARD INDUSTRIAL
   CONSULTANTS, INC.--A CONSULTING FIRM WITH HEADQUARTERS IN CHICAGO
   AND A BRANCH OFFICE IN ST. LOUIS. THE FILE INCLUDES ALL INDIVIDUALS
   EMPLOYED IN 1980 WITH INFORMATION FOR THOSE EMPLOYEES FOR 1979
   THROUGH 1982.
XSAVE   OUTFILE=HUBEMPL/
   RENAME=(AGE=AGE80)(JOBCAT=JOBCAT82)/
   KEEP=EMPLOYID TO MOHIRED SEX AGE80 NAME JOBCAT82 ALL/ MAP

MEANS   RAISE82 BY JOBCAT
```

- The TITLE command provides a title for each page of display output from this job (see Chapter 4).
- The DATA LIST command describes the employment data on the HUBDATA file.
- The MISSING VALUES, VARIABLE LABELS, and VALUE LABELS commands complete definition of the variables (see Chapter 5).
- The FILE LABEL command provides a label that is printed on the display output for this job and, since it is stored on the system file, for any future job from the system file (see Section 6.24).
- The DOCUMENT command saves a block of text on the system file (see Section 6.25). This text can be displayed in a subsequent SPSS-X job via the DISPLAY command (see Section 6.26).
- The XSAVE command saves the employment data and all the definitions, file labels, and documentation in a system file. HUBEMPL is the name for the new system file (see Section 6.10).
- The RENAME subcommand renames two variables (see Section 6.13). The old names remain in effect for the rest of this job, but the variables are saved on the system file with the new names.
- The KEEP subcommand is used here to reorder the variables (see Section 6.15). Keyword ALL tells SPSS-X to keep the rest of the variables in their original order.
- The MAP subcommand provides a record of the variables that were saved, their order in the file, and their names (see Section 6.12).
- The MEANS command asks for a means breakdown of the employees' raises in 1982 by their job categories (see Chapter 34). Since the active file is not affected by the RENAME subcommand on XSAVE, JOBCAT—not JOBCAT82—is specified on MEANS.

In any subsequent job, you would enter the commands

```
GET FILE=HUB
```

to read the system file containing the employment data, variable names, labels, missing-value flags, and the file label and documentation (see Section 6.2).

The MAP display

```
31  0            XSAVE  OUTFILE=HUBEMPL/
32  0               RENAME=(AGE=AGE80)(JOBCAT=JOBCAT82)/
33  0               KEEP=EMPLOYID TO MOHIRED SEX AGE80 NAME JOBCAT82 ALL/ MAP
34  0

OUTPUT FILE MAP

RESULT     INPUT1       RESULT     INPUT1
————       ————         ————       ————
EMPLOYID   EMPLOYID     DEPT82     DEPT82
MOHIRED    MOHIRED      SALARY79   SALARY79
SEX        SEX          SALARY80   SALARY80
AGE80      AGE          SALARY81   SALARY81
NAME       NAME         SALARY82   SALARY82
JOBCAT82   JOBCAT       HOURLY81   HOURLY81
YRHIRED    YRHIRED      HOURLY82   HOURLY82
DEPT79     DEPT79       PROMO81    PROMO81
DEPT80     DEPT80       RAISE82    RAISE82
DEPT81     DEPT81

18 APR 85 09:39:38      19 VARIABLES,    168 BYTES PER CASE BEFORE COMPRESSION
```

6.21
SAVE and XSAVE
Compared

When the SAVE command is used to create an SPSS-X system file, the data are read solely to create the new file. For large files, reading the data can be time-consuming. In most instances, you can achieve the same result at a lower cost by placing the XSAVE command after any permanent transformations and before the first procedure. The system file will be written as the data are read for the procedure, thereby eliminating an extra pass of the data. At the very least, XSAVE followed by the EXECUTE command at the end of the job is equivalent to SAVE as the last command. But whenever SAVE is not the last command, XSAVE can probably save one pass of the data.

6.22
SAVE, XSAVE, and
TEMPORARY

You should pay particular attention to the use and placement of XSAVE or SAVE when you also have a TEMPORARY command in your job. TEMPORARY followed by SAVE turns the temporary transformations off, whereas TEMPORARY followed by XSAVE leaves the temporary transformations in effect for the next procedure. Consider the following job:

```
GET FILE=HUBEMPL
TEMPORARY
RECODE DEPT79 TO DEPT82 (1,2=1) (3,4=2) (ELSE=9)
VALUE LABELS DEPT79 TO DEPT82 1 'MANAGEMENT' 2 'OPERATIONS' 3 'UNKNOWN'
XSAVE OUTFILE=HUBTEMP
CROSSTABS DEPT79 TO DEPT82 BY JOBCAT
```

In this example, both the saved system file and the CROSSTABS output will reflect the temporary recoding and labeling of the department variables. If XSAVE is replaced with SAVE, the data are read twice instead of just once, and the CROSSTABS output does not reflect the recoding.

6.23
SYSTEM FILE
UTILITIES

Two utilities store documentary information on a system file. The FILE LABEL command stores a label that prints automatically whenever the system file is accessed. The DOCUMENT command stores a block of text that can be accessed at any later date via the DISPLAY command (see Section 6.26).

6.24
FILE LABEL Command

Use the FILE LABEL command to provide a descriptive label for your data file. The file label is printed on the first line of each page of output displayed by SPSS-X and is included in the dictionary of the system file. The command

```
FILE LABEL  HUBBARD INDUSTRIAL CONSULTANTS INC. EMPLOYEE DATA
XSAVE OUTFILE=HUBEMPL
  /RENAME=(AGE JOBCAT=AGE80 JOBCAT82) /MAP
EXECUTE
```

assigns a file label to the Hubbard Consultants Inc. employee data saved in the system file.

A file label can be up to 60 characters long. If it is longer, SPSS-X will truncate the label to 60 characters without warning.

6.25
DOCUMENT Command

Use the DOCUMENT command to save a block of text of any length on your system file. The command

```
FILE LABEL  HUBBARD INDUSTRIAL CONSULTANTS INC. EMPLOYEE DATA
DOCUMENT    THIS FILE CONTAINS EMPLOYEE RECORDS FOR HUBBARD INDUSTRIAL
    CONSULTANTS, INC.--A CONSULTING FIRM WITH HEADQUARTERS IN CHICAGO
    AND A BRANCH OFFICE IN ST. LOUIS.  THE FILE INCLUDES ALL INDIVIDUALS
    EMPLOYED IN 1980 WITH INFORMATION FOR THOSE EMPLOYEES FOR 1979
    THROUGH 1982.
XSAVE OUTFILE=HUBEMPL
    /RENAME=(AGE JOBCAT=AGE80 JOBCAT82) /MAP
EXECUTE
```

provides information describing the Hubbard data. This block of text is saved on the system file and is available via the DISPLAY command whenever you or someone else needs to know more about the system file (see Section 6.26).

You can use the DOCUMENT command to add documentation to an existing system file. The new documentation and the date it was entered are saved along with any existing documentation when the new system file is saved.

6.26
DISPLAY Command

The dictionary of a system file is available at any time via the DISPLAY command for exploring an unfamiliar or forgotten system file or for producing a printed archive document. In addition, the DISPLAY utility can be used during any SPSS-X job to display the data definitions that are being applied to the active file, even if a system file is neither being read nor saved.

By default, DISPLAY prints an unsorted list of the variables on the active file. For example, the commands

```
GET FILE=HUB
DISPLAY
```

produce the output shown in Figure 6.26a.

Figure 6.26a   Display of variable names

```
Currently Defined Variables

EMPLOYID  DEPT82    LOCATN81  PAYTYP82  HOSPIN82  SALARY82  RAISE82   MINDIAN
MOBIRTH   SEX       LOCATN82  MARITL79  MEDINS79  HOURLY79  PROMO80   FNEGRO
DABIRTH   RACE      GRADE79   MARITL80  MEDINS80  HOURLY80  PROMO81   FORIENT
YRBIRTH   EE079     GRADE80   MARITL81  MEDINS81  HOURLY81  PROMO82   FLATINO
MOHIRED   EE080     GRADE81   MARITL82  MEDINS82  HOURLY82  JOBCAT    FINDIAN
YRHIRED   EE081     GRADE82   HOSPIN79  SALARY79  AGE       MNEGRO    MALE
DEPT79    EE082     PAYTYP79  HOSPIN80  SALARY80  RAISE80   MORIENT   FEMALE
DEPT80    LOCATN79  PAYTYP80  HOSPIN81  SALARY81  RAISE81   MLATINO   NAME
DEPT81    LOCATN80  PAYTYP81
```

The variables print in compressed format, about 8 names across the page. The names run down each column in the order they appear in the active file. The names are distributed evenly among the 8 columns in order to use the minimum number of lines necessary to display them.

If you specify a keyword, DISPLAY prints only the information you request. For example, to display information from the DOCUMENT command and information supplied on the DATA LIST, VARIABLE LABELS, VALUE LABELS, and MISSING VALUES commands, specify:

```
GET FILE=HUB
DISPLAY DOCUMENTS
DISPLAY DICTIONARY
```

These commands display the documentation and dictionary from the HUB system file. No procedure is needed to read the data from the system file since DISPLAY gets its information from the dictionary alone. Figure 6.26b shows the results of DISPLAY DOCUMENTS.

Figure 6.26b Display of documentary information

```
FILE:      Hubbard Industrial Consultants Inc. employee data

DOCUMENT   This file contains employee records for Hubbard Industrial
   Consultants, Inc.--a consulting firm with headquarters in Chicago
   and a branch office in St. Louis.  The file includes all individuals
   employed in 1980 with information for those employees for 1979
   through 1982.

   (Entered 17-AUG-87)
```

The following keywords can be specified on the DISPLAY command. NAMES is the default:

NAMES *Display variable names.* A list of the variables on the active file is displayed. The names are not sorted and print in a compressed format, about eight names across the page. This is the default.

DOCUMENTS *Display the text provided by the DOCUMENT command.* No error message is issued if there is no documentary information on the system file.

DICTIONARY *Display complete dictionary information for variables.* Information includes the variable names, labels, sequential position of each variable in the file, print and write formats, missing values, and value labels. Up to 60 characters can be displayed for variable and value labels.

INDEX *Display the variable names and positions.*

VARIABLES *Display the variable names, positions, print and write formats, and missing values.*

LABELS *Display the variable names, positions, and variable labels.*

MACROS *Display a list of the currently defined macros.* The variable list is always sorted.

Only one of the above keywords can be specified per DISPLAY command, but you can use as many DISPLAY commands as necessary to obtain the desired information.

In addition, you can use keyword SORTED to display information alphabetically by variable name. SORTED can precede keywords NAMES, DICTIONARY, INDEX, VARIABLES, or LABELS, as in:

```
GET FILE=HUB
DISPLAY DOCUMENTS
DISPLAY SORTED DICTIONARY
```

The first DISPLAY command displays the document information, and the second displays complete dictionary information for variables sorted alphabetically by variable name.

SORTED *Alphabetize the display by variable name.* Use with NAMES, DICTIONARY, INDEX, VARIABLES, or LABELS.

6.27
VARIABLES Subcommand

To limit DISPLAY information to certain variables, follow any specification other than DOCUMENTS or MACROS with a slash, the VARIABLES subcommand, an optional equals sign, and a list of variables, as in:

```
GET FILE=HUB
DISPLAY DOCUMENTS
DISPLAY SORTED DICTIONARY
  /VARIABLES=DEPT82, SALARY82, SEX TO JOBCAT82
```

This specification produces dictionary information only for the variables mentioned (or implied by keyword TO) in the variable list and sorts them alphabetically by variable name. Without keyword SORTED, information is displayed in the order variables are stored on the system file regardless of the order you name them on the VARIABLES subcommand. Compare the results in Figure 6.27 with the information in the job that created the system file in the annotated XSAVE example.

Figure 6.27   Display of dictionary information

```
FILE:       Hubbard Industrial Consultants Inc. employee data
                                           •
            LIST OF VARIABLES ON THE ACTIVE FILE

NAME                                                                 POSITION

AGE                                                                       16
                     PRINT FORMAT: F2
                     WRITE FORMAT: F2
                     MISSING VALUES:  0

DEPT82    Department of employment in 1982                                 7
                     PRINT FORMAT: F1
                     WRITE FORMAT: F1
                     MISSING VALUES:  0

          VALUE    LABEL

            0 M  Not reported
            1    Administrative
            2    Project Directors
            3    Chicago Operations
            4    St Louis Operations

HOURLY81                                                                  13
                     PRINT FORMAT: F8.2
                     WRITE FORMAT: F8.2
                     MISSING VALUES:  -999.00

HOURLY82                                                                  14
                     PRINT FORMAT: F8.2
                     WRITE FORMAT: F8.2
                     MISSING VALUES:  -999.00

JOBCAT82  Job categories                                                  18
                     PRINT FORMAT: F1
                     WRITE FORMAT: F1
                     MISSING VALUES:  9

          VALUE    LABEL

            1    Officials & Managers
            2    Professionals
            3    Technicians
            4    Office and Clerical
            5    Craftsmen
            6    Service Workers

PROMO81                                                                   15
                     PRINT FORMAT: F1
                     WRITE FORMAT: F1


RAISE82                                                                   17
                     PRINT FORMAT: F5
                     WRITE FORMAT: F5
                     MISSING VALUES:  -999

SALARY79                                                                   9
                     PRINT FORMAT: F5
                     WRITE FORMAT: F5
                     MISSING VALUES:  0

SALARY80                                                                  10
                     PRINT FORMAT: F5
                     WRITE FORMAT: F5
                     MISSING VALUES:  0

SALARY81                                                                  11
                     PRINT FORMAT: F5
                     WRITE FORMAT: F5
                     MISSING VALUES:  0

SALARY82  Yearly salary in 1982                                           12
                     PRINT FORMAT: F5
                     WRITE FORMAT: F5
                     MISSING VALUES:  0

SALARY82  Yearly salary in 1982                                           12
                     PRINT FORMAT: F5
                     WRITE FORMAT: F5
                     MISSING VALUES:  0

SEX                                                                        8
                     PRINT FORMAT: F1
                     WRITE FORMAT: F1
                     MISSING VALUES:  0

          VALUE    LABEL

            1    Male
            2    Female
```

6.28
DROP DOCUMENTS
Command

When you retrieve a system file with the GET command, SPSS-X assumes you want the system file's document text, unless you indicate otherwise with the DROP DOCUMENTS command. The DROP DOCUMENTS command enables you to retrieve a system file without its document text. For example, the command

```
GET FILE=HUB
DROP DOCUMENTS
```

retrieves the entire dictionary of HUB, without its document text. The original system file HUB is unchanged. You have the option of adding new document text to the active file with the DOCUMENT command.

6.29
STRUCTURE OF A
SYSTEM FILE

An SPSS-X system file is a fully integrated file containing the data and all descriptive information. The part of the file containing the descriptive information—called the *dictionary*—contains the variable names, their printing and writing formats, and optional extended variable labels, value labels, and missing-value indicators. Descriptive information is supplied on the data definition commands described in Chapter 5. The dictionary also contains the file label from the FILE LABEL command, additional documentation supplied on the DOCUMENT command, and the date and time the file was created. The FILE LABEL and DOCUMENT commands are described in Sections 6.24 and 6.25.

6.30
Binary Storage

When data are initially entered on a machine-readable device, the values are usually recorded in character format. In character format, each character is stored in a single column. Data in a system file are stored in binary format. This form of data representation reduces the time required for SPSS-X to read and interpret the data values. In binary format, each value, regardless of the number of columns it occupies externally, is stored internally in units of storage called *words*. The actual size of a computer word depends on the type of computer. On most computers, SPSS-X stores all values except long string variables in two computer words. Thus, numeric values in SPSS-X are double-precision values. Values of long string variables are stored in as many computer words as are necessary to accurately represent the string.

Many values in a typical data file can be stored in much less than a double word. Therefore, you can instruct SPSS-X to store the system file in *compressed* form (see Section 6.16). Compression reduces the storage requirements for files that contain mostly small integer values.

6.31
Upper and Lower Case

SPSS-X accepts commands in any case but interprets keywords and names as upper case. However, labels, strings, and information from the DOCUMENT command are stored on the active file and system file in the case in which they are entered. SPSS-X prints labels, strings, and DOCUMENT information in mixed case if they are entered in mixed case and if you specify CASE=UPLOW on the SET command. SPSS-X will translate them to upper case if they are entered in mixed case with CASE=UPPER (see Chapter 4). Therefore, if you have access to a printer with upper- and lower-case capabilities, you can specify upper and lower case when using the DISPLAY command, as in:

```
SET CASE=UPLOW
GET FILE=HUBLOW
DISPLAY DICTIONARY
  /VARIABLES=SEX, DEPT82, JOBCAT82
```

These commands display the dictionary information for variables SEX, DEPT82, and JOBCAT82. If this information was originally provided in upper and lower case, DISPLAY will observe the SET command and print in mixed case, as shown in the display output in Figure 6.31.

Figure 6.31   DISPLAY output in mixed case

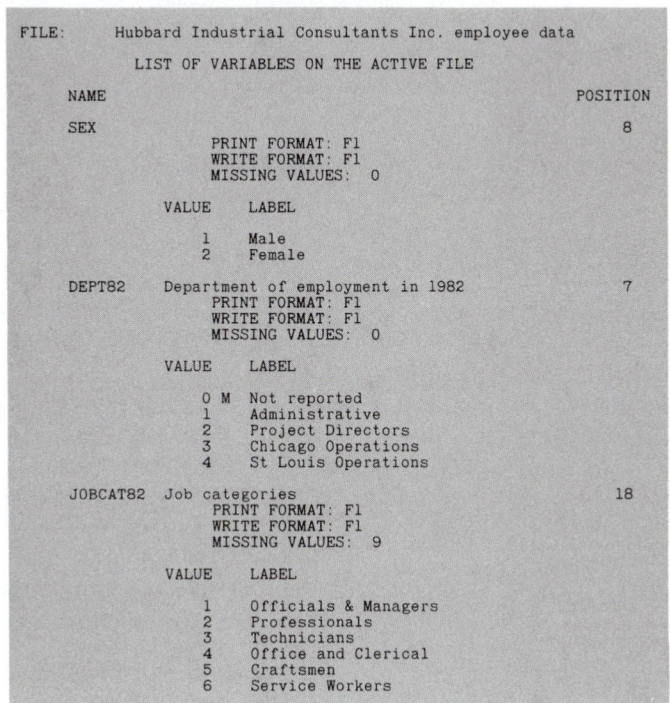

6.32
Limitations

The number of cases or the number of variables that can be saved in an SPSS-X system file is virtually unlimited. Limitations on the size of variables are machine dependent. While there is no fixed limit to the width of a numeric variable, there is a practical limit to the number of digits that can be stored precisely. SPSS-X stores numeric values in double-precision on most computers. For example, the last digit of numbers larger than sixteen digits in the IBM/OS and IBM/CMS environments may be inaccurate. Values of long string variables are limited to 255 characters. The maximum length of a short string variable is defined by the computer you are using and may be as few as eight characters.

Syntax

COMPUTE

```
COMPUTE target variable=expression
```

Arithmetic Operators:

+	Addition	−	Subtraction
*	Multiplication	/	Division
**	Exponentiation		

Arithmetic Functions:

ABS(arg)	Absolute value
RND(arg)	Round
TRUNC(arg)	Truncate
MOD(arg)	Modulus
SQRT(arg)	Square root
EXP(arg)	Exponential
LG10(arg)	Base 10 logarithm
LN(arg)	Natural logarithm
ARSIN(arg)	Arcsin
ARTAN(arg)	Arctangent
SIN(arg)	Sine
COS(arg)	Cosine

Statistical Functions:

SUM[.n](arg list)	Sum of values across argument list
MEAN[.n](arg list)	Mean value across argument list
SD[.n](arg list)	Standard deviation of values across list
VAR[.n](arg list)	Variance of values across list
CFVAR[.n](arg list)	Coefficient of variation of values across list
MIN[.n](arg list)	Minimum value across list
MAX[.n](arg list)	Maximum value across list

Missing Value Functions:

VALUE(varname)	Ignore user-missing
MISSING(varname)	True if missing
SYSMIS(varname)	True if system-missing
NMISS(arg list)	Count number missing values across list
NVALID(arg list)	Number of valid values across list

Cross-case Function:

LAG(varname,n)	Return value of variable n cases before

Logical Functions:

RANGE(varname,range)	True if value of variable is in range
ANY(arg,arg list)	True if value of first arg matches arg list

Other Functions:

UNIFORM(arg)	Uniform pseudo random no. between 0 and n
NORMAL(arg)	Normal pseudo random no. with mean of 0 and std dev of n
CDFNORM(arg)	Return probability random variable falls below n
PROBIT(arg)	Inverse of CDFNORM

The values of "arg" can be numeric values, variables, or expressions.

Date and time aggregation functions:

DATE.DMY(d,m,y)	Read day, month, year and return date
DATE.MDY(m,d,y)	Read month, day, year and return date
DATE.YRDAY(y,d)	Read year, day, number and return date
DATE.QYR(q,y)	Read quarter, year and return quarter start date
DATE.MOYR(m,y)	Read month, year and return month start date
DATE.WKYR(w,y)	Read week, year and return week start date
TIME.HMS(h,m,s)	Read hour, minutes, seconds and return time interval
TIME.DAYS(d)	Read days and return time interval

Date and time conversion functions:

YRMODA(yr,mo,da)	Convert year, month, day to day number
CTIME.DAYS(arg)	Convert time interval to days
CTIME.HOURS(arg)	Convert time interval to hours
CTIME.MINUTES(arg)	Convert time interval to minutes
CTIME.SECONDS(arg)	Convert time interval to seconds

Date and time extraction functions:

XDATE.MDAY(arg)	Return the day of the month
XDATE.MONTH(arg)	Return the month of the year
XDATE.YEAR(arg)	Return the four digit year
XDATE.HOUR(arg)	Return the hour of a day
XDATE.MINUTE(arg)	Return the minute of a hour
XDATE.SECOND(arg)	Return the second of a minute
XDATE.WKDAY(arg)	Return the weekday number
XDATE.JDAY(arg)	Return the day number of a day in a given year
XDATE.QUARTER(arg)	Return the quarter of a date in a given year
XDATE.WEEK(arg)	Return the week number of date in a given year
XDATE.TDAY(arg)	Return the number of days in a time interval
XDATE.TIME(arg)	Return the time portion of a given date and time
XDATE.DATE(arg)	Return integral portion of date

COUNT

```
COUNT varname=varlist(value list) [/varname=...]
```

Numeric value list keywords:

```
LOWEST LO HIGHEST HI THRU  MISSING  SYSMIS
```

DO REPEAT—END REPEAT

```
DO REPEAT stand-in var={varlist    } [/stand-in var=...]
                     {value list}
transformation commands
END REPEAT [PRINT]
```

LEAVE

```
LEAVE varlist
```

NUMERIC

```
NUMERIC varlist[(format)] [/varlist...]
```

RECODE

For numeric variables:

```
RECODE varlist (value list=value)...(value list=value) [INTO varlist]/
       [/varlist...]
```

Input Keywords:

```
LO, LOWEST, HI, HIGHEST, THRU, MISSING, SYSMIS, ELSE
```

Output Keywords:

```
COPY, SYSMIS
```

TEMPORARY

```
TEMPORARY
```

Contents

7.1	INTRODUCTION TO DATA TRANSFORMATIONS
7.2	Printing and Writing Formats
7.3	RECODE COMMAND
7.4	Specifying Numeric Values
7.5	THRU, LOWEST, and HIGHEST Keywords
7.6	ELSE Keyword
7.7	MISSING and SYSMIS Keywords
7.8	Value Ranges
7.9	INTO Keyword
7.10	COPY Keyword
7.11	COMPUTE COMMAND
7.12	Computing Numeric Variables
7.13	Missing Values
7.14	NUMERIC EXPRESSIONS
7.15	Arithmetic Operations
7.16	Numeric Constants
7.17	Order of Operations
7.18	Numeric Functions
7.19	Arithmetic Functions
7.20	Statistical Functions
7.21	Missing-Value Functions
7.22	Across-Case LAG Function
7.23	Logical Functions
7.24	Other Functions
7.25	Using Logical Functions
7.26	Complex Numeric Arguments
7.27	Date and Time Functions
7.28	Aggregation Functions
7.29	Conversion Functions
7.30	YRMODA Function
7.31	Extraction Functions
7.32	Using Date and Time Variables in Procedures
7.33	Logical Expressions
7.34	Missing Values
7.35	Missing Values in Arguments
7.36	Domain Errors
7.37	COUNT COMMAND
7.38	Initialization and Missing Values
7.39	TRANSFORMATION UTILITIES
7.40	LEAVE Command
7.41	Scratch Variables
7.42	TEMPORARY Command
7.43	NUMERIC Command
7.44	DO REPEAT Utility
7.45	Replacement Variable and Value Lists
7.46	PRINT Subcommand
7.47	System Variables
7.48	EXECUTING DATA TRANSFORMATIONS
7.49	Data Definition Commands
7.50	Active File

7

Chapter 7   Numeric Transformations

The ability to transform data before you analyze it or after preliminary analysis is often as important as the analysis itself. You may want to perform simple data-cleaning checks, correct coding errors, or adjust an inconvenient coding scheme. You many want to create new variables from subfields extracted from dates. Or you may want to construct an index from several variables or rescale several variables prior to analysis. The SPSS-X transformation language provides these and many other possibilities.

This chapter describes the major components of the SPSS-X transformation language, with emphasis on manipulating numeric variables. For additional information on string transformations, see Chapter 8. For conditional data transformations, see Chapter 9.

7.1
INTRODUCTION TO DATA TRANSFORMATIONS

Two commands are the core of the transformation language: RECODE and COMPUTE. The RECODE command, documented in Sections 7.3 through 7.10, changes the coding scheme of an existing variable on a value-by-value basis or for ranges of values. For example, to change the coding order for three questionnaire items from 0 for "Agree," 1 for "No opinion," and 2 for "Disagree" to 1, 0, and −1, respectively, specify:

```
RECODE ITEM1,ITEM2,ITEM3 (0=1) (1=0) (2=-1)
VALUE LABELS ITEM1 TO ITEM3 -1 'DISAGREE' 0 'NO OPINION' 1 'AGREE'
```

The three values are recoded as shown for each of the variables in the variable list and labels are provided for the new values.

The COMPUTE command, documented in Sections 7.11 through 7.13, computes a new variable as some combination or transformation of one or more existing variables. For example, to build a simple index averaging the three questionnaire items just recoded, specify:

```
COMPUTE    INDEXQ = (ITEM1 + ITEM2 + ITEM3)/3
VARIABLE LABELS INDEXQ 'SUMMARY INDEX OF QUESTIONS'
```

For each case, the three items are added together, the sum is divided by 3, and the result is stored in new variable INDEXQ, which is then given a label.

You can make execution of data transformations conditional on other information in the data via the IF command or the DO IF—END IF structure, both documented in Chapter 9. For example, to establish a dichotomous (two-valued) variable indicating cities that are classified as poor based on median family income, specify:

```
COMPUTE POOR=0
IF (FAMINC LE 10000) POOR=1
VARIABLE LABELS POOR 'CITIES WITH FAMILY INCOME UNDER $10,000'
```

The COMPUTE command initializes variable POOR to 0 for all cities, and the IF command changes POOR to 1 for cities with values for FAMINC less than or equal to $10,000.

The COUNT command, a specialized version of the COMPUTE command, is documented in Sections 7.37 and 7.38. To create a simple index that counts the number of times a respondent answered "Agree" to the items recoded above, specify:

```
COUNT    AGREE=ITEM1,ITEM2,ITEM3(1)
VARIABLE LABELS AGREE 'NUMBER OF POSITIVE RESPONSES'
```

The COUNT command initializes new variable AGREE to 0 for all cases and changes it to 1 for cases with value 1 for any one of the three items; to 2 for cases with value 1 for any two items; or to 3 for cases with value 1 for all three items.

7.2
Printing and Writing Formats

By default, SPSS-X assigns print and write formats of F8.2 (or the format you specify using the SET command described in Chapter 4) for new numeric variables created by the RECODE, COMPUTE, or COUNT commands. If the default format is not appropriate, use PRINT FORMATS, WRITE FORMATS, or FORMATS to reset it, as in:

```
COMPUTE INCOME=WAGES + BONUS + INTEREST + OTHERINC
COMPUTE PCTWAGES = RND((WAGES/INCOME)*100)
COMPUTE START=DATE.DMY(DAY1,MONTH1,YEAR1)
PRINT FORMATS INCOME (DOLLAR10.2)/ PCTWAGES (F3.0)/START (DATE9)
VARIABLE LABELS INCOME 'INDIVIDUAL INCOME FROM ALL SOURCES'
              /PCTWAGES 'WAGES AS A PERCENTAGE OF TOTAL INCOME'
```

These commands specify a dollar printing format for variable INCOME, a three-digit, no-decimal format for PCTWAGES, and a nine-digit international date format for START. The write format is not changed. See Chapter 10 for a complete discussion of print and write utilities.

7.3
RECODE COMMAND

The most direct data transformation is the RECODE command, which tells SPSS-X to change the code for a variable as the data are being read. The command

```
RECODE X (0=9)
```

instructs SPSS to change all zeros found for variable X to nines.

The variable or variables to be recoded must already exist and must precede the value specifications. You can specify as many value specifications as needed, enclosing each specification within parentheses, as in:

```
RECODE ITEM1 (0=1) (1=0) (2=-1)
```

You can use multiple input values in a single specification but only one output value following the equals sign, as in:

```
RECODE RESPONSE (8,9=1) (4 THRU 7=2) (1,2=3)
```

The RECODE command is evaluated left to right, and the values for a case are recoded only once per RECODE command. For example, if a case has an input value of 0 for variable ITEM1, the command

```
RECODE ITEM1 (0=1) (1=0) (2=-1)
```

recodes ITEM1 to 1 and SPSS-X then moves on to the next specification. The value is *not* recoded back to 0 by the second value specification. Input values not mentioned in the RECODE command are left unchanged.

You can name multiple variables for the same value specifications, as in:

```
RECODE ITEM1 TO ITEM3 (0=1) (1=0) (2=-1)
```

In addition, you can specify different values for different variables on the same RECODE command by separating the recode specifications with a slash, as in:

```
RECODE AGE (0=9)/ ITEM1 TO ITEM3 (0=1) (1=0) (2=-1)
```

These rules apply to both numeric and string variables. See Chapter 8 if your variable is a string or if you want to recode a numeric variable into a string variable.

7.4
Specifying Numeric Values

There are several keyword utilities available for recoding numeric variables. They are

THRU Keyword. Use THRU to specify value ranges, as in 0 THRU 99. (See Section 7.5.)

LOWEST and HIGHEST Keywords. Use LOWEST and HIGHEST to specify the lowest and highest values encountered in a range. (See Section 7.5.)

ELSE Keyword. Use ELSE to recode all values not explicitly mentioned. (See Section 7.6.)

MISSING and SYSMIS Keywords. Use MISSING to reference missing values on input, and SYSMIS to reference missing values on both input and output. (See Section 7.7.)

INTO Keyword. Use INTO to create a new variable as a recoded version of an old one. (See Section 7.9.)

COPY Keyword. Use COPY to copy input values unchanged. (See Section 7.10.) Blank fields for numeric variables are handled according to the BLANKS specification on the SET command (Chapter 4) prior to any recode specifications.

7.5
THRU, LOWEST, and HIGHEST Keywords

To recode ranges of values for numeric variables into a single value, use keyword THRU. Use keyword LO (LOWEST) or HI (HIGHEST) to specify the lowest or highest input value for the variable. For example, to recode all individuals below the United States voting age to 0 and leave all other ages unchanged, specify:

```
RECODE AGE (LO THRU 17=0)
```

You can also use these keywords to collapse variable AGE into gross categories, perhaps for tabular display, as in:

```
RECODE AGE (LO THRU 20=1)(20 THRU 25=2)(25 THRU 30=3)(30 THRU 35=4)
    (35 THRU 40=5)(40 THRU 45=6)(45 THRU 50=7)(50 THRU 55=8)
    (55 THRU 60=9)(60 THRU 65=10)(65 THRU HI=11)

VARIABLE LABELS AGE 'EMPLOYEE AGE CATEGORIES'
VALUE LABELS AGE 1 'Up to 20' 2 '20 to 25' 3 '25 to 30' 4 '30 to 35'
    5 '35 to 40' 6 '40 to 45' 7 '45 to 50' 8 '50 to 55'
    9 '55 to 60' 10 '60 to 65' 11 '65 and older'
```

Keywords LOWEST and HIGHEST do not include the system-missing value. However, user-missing values are included.

7.6
ELSE Keyword

To recode all values not previously mentioned into a single catchall category, use the keyword ELSE. For example, to recode AGE to a dichotomous (two-valued) variable with 0 representing individuals below the voting age and 1 representing potential voters, specify:

```
RECODE AGE (LO THRU 17=0) (ELSE=1)
```

ELSE should be the last specification for the variable. Otherwise all subsequent value specifications for that variable are ignored. Keyword ELSE *does* include the system-missing value.

You can also use keyword ELSE on the RECODE command as a data-cleaning device, as in:

```
RECODE ITEM1 TO ITEM3 (0=1) (1=0) (2=-1) (9=9) (ELSE=SYSMIS)
```

Input values 0, 1, 2, and 9 (user-missing value) are recoded, while remaining values, known to be illegal codes, are recoded to the system-missing value. In this example, it is unnecessary to redeclare 9 as missing for each variable.

**ANNOTATED
EXAMPLE FOR
RECODE**

The job developed in Sections 7.3 through 7.10 is to change all values known to be outside the expected range to system-missing for three ITEM variables and to create a new dichotomous (two-valued) variable from AGE that flags individuals who are eligible to vote in the United States (18 years of age or older). The SPSS-X commands are

```
TITLE   PILOT FOR COLLEGE SURVEY
DATA LIST   FILE=TESTDATA
  /AGE 1-3 ITEM1 TO ITEM3 5-7
VARIABLE LABELS   ITEM1 'OPINION ON LEVEL OF DEFENSE SPENDING'
  ITEM2 'OPINION ON LEVEL OF WELFARE SPENDING'
  ITEM3 'OPINION ON LEVEL OF HEALTH SPENDING'
VALUE LABELS   ITEM1 TO ITEM3 -1 'DISAGREE' 0 'NO OPINION' 1 'AGREE'
MISSING VALUES   AGE(-99,-98) ITEM1 TO ITEM3 (9)

RECODE   ITEM1 TO ITEM3 (0=1) (1=0) (2=-1) (9=9) (ELSE=SYSMIS)

RECODE   AGE (MISSING=9) (18 THRU HI=1) (LO THRU 18=0) INTO VOTER
PRINT /$CASENUM 1-2 AGE 4-6 VOTER 8-10

VARIABLE LABELS   VOTER 'ELIGIBLE TO VOTE'
VALUE LABELS   VOTER 0 'UNDER 18' 1 '18 OR OVER'
MISSING VALUES   VOTER (9)
PRINT FORMATS VOTER(F1.0)
FREQUENCIES VARIABLES=VOTER,ITEM1 TO ITEM3
```

- The TITLE command supplies a title for the top of each page of display from this job (see Chapter 4).

- The DATA LIST command names the input data file and defines the variables (see Chapter 5).

- The VARIABLE LABELS, VALUE LABELS, and MISSING VALUES commands complete the variable definitions (see Chapter 5).

- The first RECODE command recodes input values 0, 1, and 2 to 1, 0, and −1, respectively, for the three ITEM variables and preserves missing value 9 by recoding it to itself. Keyword ELSE can then be used to change all unmentioned values to the system-missing value in order to clean up the coding (see Sections 7.3, 7.6, and 7.7).

- The second RECODE command recodes missing values for AGE (−99 and −98) to 9, values 18 through the highest to 1 (eligible voters), and values less than 18 to 0 (not eligible). The results are stored in new variable VOTER (see Sections 7.5, 7.7, 7.8, and 7.9).

- The PRINT command provides a check on the recoding of AGE by printing the values for AGE and VOTER (see Chapter 10). System variable $CASENUM supplies a case number on the printed results (see Section 7.47). The printed output is shown in Figure A.

- The VARIABLE LABELS, VALUE LABELS, and MISSING VALUES commands complete the definition of new variable VOTER (see Chapter 5).

- The PRINT FORMATS command provides a one-digit printing format with no decimal places for VOTER (see Chapter 10). The default for new variables is F8.2.

- The FREQUENCIES command produces frequency tables as a complete check on the new variable and on the ITEM variables including labels and missing values (see Chapter 29). The output from the FREQUENCIES command is shown in Figure B. Notice that variable ITEM1 has two cases with the system-missing value (denoted with the period), indicating that two cases were miscoded and should probably be corrected.

7

A PRINT values for variables AGE and VOTER

```
 1   22   1
 2    0   9
 3   34   1
 4   17   0
 5   17   0
 6   21   1
 7  -99   9
 8   18   1
 9   18   1
10   19   1
11   16   0
12   21   1
13   20   1
```

B FREQUENCIES for new variable VOTER

```
05 OCT 82 PILOT FOR COLLEGE SURVEY

FILE:

VOTER     ELIGIBLE TO VOTE
```

				VALID	CUM
VALUE LABEL	VALUE	FREQUENCY	PERCENT	PERCENT	PERCENT
UNDER 18	0	3	23.1	27.3	27.3
18 OR OVER	1	8	61.5	72.7	100.0
	9	2	15.4	MISSING	
TOTAL		13	100.0	100.0	

```
VALID CASES    11    MISSING CASES    2
```

- -

```
ITEM1     OPINION ON LEVEL OF DEFENSE SPENDING
```

				VALID	CUM
VALUE LABEL	VALUE	FREQUENCY	PERCENT	PERCENT	PERCENT
DISAGREE	-1	3	23.1	27.3	27.3
NO OPINION	0	5	38.5	45.5	72.7
AGREE	1	3	23.1	27.3	100.0
	.	2	15.4	MISSING	
TOTAL		13	100.0	100.0	

```
VALID CASES    11    MISSING CASES    2
```

ANNOTATED EXAMPLES FOR COMPUTE

The following examples represent most of the applications of the COMPUTE command.

Arithmetic Operations. A complete list of arithmetic operators appears in Section 7.15.

To initialize variable POOR to 0 for all cases (Section 7.1), specify:

```
COMPUTE  POOR=0
```

To compute variable PCTWAGES a percentage of variable INCOME (Section 7.12), specify:

```
COMPUTE  PCTWAGES=(WAGES/INCOME)*100
```

Numeric Functions. A complete list of available numeric functions appears in Sections 7.19 through 7.24. See Section 7.17 for information on the order of operations in complex numeric expressions.

To compute variable PCTWAGES as a percentage of INCOME and round the percentage to an integer (Section 7.26), specify:

```
COMPUTE  PCTWAGES=RND((WAGES/INCOME)*100)
```

To create a scale that is the mean of three variables (Section 7.12), specify:

```
COMPUTE  SCALE=MEAN(Q1,Q2,Q3)
```

To truncate values of a variable with decimal places to integers (Section 7.19), specify:

```
COMPUTE  INCOME=TRUNC(INCOME)
```

To divide the square root of Y1 by the square root of Y2 and then add the square root of Y3 (Section 7.17), specify:

```
COMPUTE  X=SQRT(Y1) / SQRT(Y2) + SQRT(Y3)
```

To find the minimum square root value of variables Q1, Q2, Q3, and Q4 (Section 7.26), specify:

```
COMPUTE  QMINSQRT=SQRT(MIN(Q1,Q2,Q3,Q4))
```

Missing Values. Methods for handling missing values in numeric expressions are described in Sections 7.34 through 7.36.

To compute the sum of three variables only for cases with valid values for all three variables (Section 7.35), specify:

```
COMPUTE  FACTOR=SCORE1 + SCORE2 + SCORE3
```

On the other hand, to compute the sum of three variables for cases with a valid value for any one or more of the three (Section 7.35), specify:

```
COMPUTE  FACTOR=SUM(SCORE1 TO SCORE3)
```

To compute the sum of three variables for cases with valid values for any two or more of the three variables, use the *.n* suffix (Section 7.35), as in:

```
COMPUTE  FACTOR=SUM.2(SCORE1 TO SCORE3)
```

To compute the sum of three variables for cases and include cases with user-defined missing values for any of the three variables (Section 7.35), specify:

```
COMPUTE  FACTOR=VALUE(SCORE1) + VALUE(SCORE2) + VALUE(SCORE3)
```

Logical Operations. Logical functions are described in Sections 7.23 and 7.25. The use of other types of logical expressions with the COMPUTE command is described in Section 7.33.

To create a logical variable WORKERS with value 1 for cases with AGE between 18 and 65 inclusive, value 0 for all other ages, and missing if AGE is missing (Section 7.25), specify:

```
COMPUTE   WORKERS=RANGE(AGE,18,65)
```

To create a logical variable with value 1 when two variables are equal, 0 when they are not, and missing when one or the other is missing (Section 7.25), specify:

```
COMPUTE   QSAME=ANY(Q1,Q2)
```

To create a logical variable with value 1 when AGE is 18 or greater, 0 when AGE is less than 18, and missing when AGE is missing (Section 7.33), specify:

```
COMPUTE   ELIGIBLE=AGE GE 18
```

Across-Case Operations. The across-case LAG function is described in Section 7.22. The LEAVE command is documented in Section 7.40. To set the value of variable RATE4 to the value of RATE for the fourth previous case (Section 7.22), specify:

```
COMPUTE   RATE4=LAG(RATE,4)
```

To accumulate the sum of salaries across cases where TSALARY is the value of SALARY82 for the current case plus the sum of SALARY82 for all cases already read (Section 7.40), specify:

```
COMPUTE   TSALARY=TSALARY+SALARY82
LEAVE   TSALARY
```

7.7
MISSING and SYSMIS Keywords

To recode a variable that may have missing values defined in the system file or resulting from data input errors, computations, or a MISSING VALUES command, use keyword MISSING or SYSMIS. For example, if −98 and −99 were declared missing for variable AGE, the command

```
RECODE AGE (MISSING=9)
```

recodes −98, −99, and any system-missing values (perhaps from input errors) for variable AGE to 9. The command

```
RECODE AGE (MISSING=SYSMIS)
```

recodes all missing values to the system-missing value.

You can use keyword MISSING only as an input value. MISSING references all missing values including the system-missing value. The output value from a MISSING input specification is not automatically missing; use the MISSING VALUES command to declare the new value missing (see Chapter 5). You can use keyword SYSMIS for either input or output. As an input value, SYSMIS references system-missing values. As an output value specification, SYSMIS recodes all values named on the left side of the equals sign to the system-missing value.

Again, the RECODE command evaluates expressions from left to right. You can recode system-missing or all missing values to another value before specifying ELSE. The command

```
RECODE ITEM1 TO ITEM3 (0=1)(2=-1)(MISSING=0)(ELSE=SYSMIS)
```

recodes 0 to 1, 2 to −1, all missing values to 0, and any other values to system-missing.

7.8
Value Ranges

Value ranges include the end points. For variables with noninteger values, values can escape recoding unless you explicitly include them in a range. For instance, you might have calculated variable AGE using a COMPUTE command and the YRMODA function to subtract an individual's birth date from the current date (see Section 7.30). Thus, AGE could be noninteger. If you specify

```
RECODE AGE (MISSING=9) (LO THRU 17=0) (18 THRU HI=1)
```

value 17.01 escapes recoding. (Or worse, unrecoded noninteger values may fall into a catchall ELSE category.) To cover all possibilities, specify the same end point values on two recode specifications, as in:

```
RECODE AGE (MISSING=9) (18 THRU HI=1) (LO THRU 18=0)
```

The specification 18 THRU HI precedes LO THRU 18 so that cases with age exactly equal to 18 are recoded to 1 rather than 0.

7.9
INTO Keyword

To recode the values of one variable and store them in another variable, use the keyword INTO, as in:

```
RECODE AGE (MISSING=9) (18 THRU HI=1) (0 THRU 18=0) INTO VOTER
```

The recoded AGE values are stored in *target variable* VOTER, leaving AGE unchanged.

You can store values for several input variables in one command, as in:

```
RECODE ITEM1 TO ITEM3 (0=1) (1=0) (2=-1) INTO DEFENSE WELFARE HEALTH
```

The number of target variables must equal the number of input variables. Target variables can be existing or new variables. If you use an existing variable, cases with values not mentioned in the recode specification are not changed. If you recode a variable into a new variable, cases with values not specified for recoding are assigned the system-missing value. For example, if a case in the example above has a value less than 0 for variable AGE, new variable VOTER is system-missing. As shown in Section 7.6, you can recode all such wild values using keyword ELSE. The command

```
RECODE AGE (MISSING=9) (18 THRU 110=1) (0 THRU 18=0) (ELSE=8)
    INTO VOTER
```

recodes any case with an AGE value below zero and over 110 to value 8 for variable VOTER.

New numeric variables have default print and write formats of F8.2 (Section 7.2) or the format you specify using the SET command (Chapter 4).

7.10
COPY Keyword

To recode a variable into a new variable or to use keyword ELSE as a cleanup category, you may want to retain a set of input values. The command

```
RECODE ITEM1 TO ITEM3 (0=1) (1=0) (2=-1) (ELSE=COPY)
                INTO DEFENSE WELFARE HEALTH
```

creates three new variables with values 1, 0, and −1. Input values other than 0, 1, or 2 are retained. In other words, if a case has value 9 for variable ITEM1, it will have value 9 for variable DEFENSE, and so forth.

Keyword COPY is an output specification only. Input values to be copied can be a range of values, keywords SYSMIS or MISSING, or keyword ELSE. User-missing values are copied, but their missing-value status is not. In the example above, value 9 should be redeclared missing for new variables DEFENSE, WELFARE, and HEALTH. System-missing is copied as system-missing.

7.11
COMPUTE COMMAND

Often, you want to create a new variable or transform an existing variable using information from other variables on your file. The COMPUTE command generates a variable on your active file that is constructed on a case-by-case basis as an arithmetic or logical transformation of existing variables and constants. For example, the command

```
COMPUTE INCOME=WAGES + BONUS + INTEREST + OTHERINC
```

assigns the sum of four existing variables to variable INCOME for each case on your active file.

To compute a variable, specify the *target variable* on the left of the equals sign and the *expression* on the right. You can compute one target variable per command. The expression must be *numeric* (return a number) if the target variable is numeric and *string* (return a string) if the target is a string variable. Facilities for computing numeric variables are described in Sections 7.12 through 7.36. String variables are described in Chapter 8.

7.12
Computing Numeric Variables

The command

```
COMPUTE X=1
```

assigns the value 1 to variable X for every case. Numeric variable X is the target and 1 is the numeric expression.

The target variable can be an existing variable or a new variable defined by the COMPUTE command itself. If the target variable already exists when SPSS-X encounters the command, the old values are replaced. If the target variable does not exist, it is created by the COMPUTE command. New numeric variables are initialized to the system-missing value unless the LEAVE command is used (Section 7.40) and are assigned a default print and write format of F8.2 (Section 7.2).

Once computed, the variable exists on your active file in its new form and can be labeled, analyzed, and stored on a new system file along with all other variables on your active file. If it is a new variable, it is added to the end of the dictionary on your active file. Scratch variables, described in Section 7.41, are not added to your active file and are not saved on a new system file.

The expression to the right of the equals sign can be composed of existing variables, arithmetic operators such as + and −, arithmetic, statistical, or date and time functions such as SQRT, MEAN, or DATE.DMY, logical functions such as ANY and SYSMIS, system variables, numeric constants, and so forth. For example, the command

```
COMPUTE PCTWAGES=(WAGES/INCOME)*100
```

creates PCTWAGES as a percentage of INCOME through use of the slash for division, the asterisk for multiplication, and the parentheses to clarify the order of operations (see Section 7.17). The command

```
COMPUTE SCALE=MEAN(Q1,Q2,Q3)
```

constructs variable SCALE from three variables using the MEAN function (see Section 7.20). Facilities for handling numeric expressions are documented in Sections 7.14 through 7.36.

7.13
Missing Values

If a case is missing on any of the variables used in an expression when the COMPUTE command is executed, SPSS-X nearly always returns the system-missing value since the operation is indeterminate. For example, in the command

```
COMPUTE PAYHOURS = WORKDAYS * 7.5
```

variable PAYHOURS cannot be computed for any case missing on variable WORKDAYS.

SPSS-X also returns missing values when the expression itself is undefined. In the command

```
COMPUTE PCTWAGES=(WAGES/INCOME)*100
```

variable PCTWAGES is considered indeterminate for a case when the value for INCOME is 0, since division by 0 is not defined (see Section 7.36).

If these rules do not fit your application, you should be able to specify exactly what you want using one or more of the functions described in Section 7.21. A complete discussion of missing values in numeric expressions appears in Sections 7.34 through 7.36.

7.14
NUMERIC EXPRESSIONS

While numeric expressions are commonly used with the COMPUTE command, they can be used as part of a logical expression for commands such as IF, DO IF, LOOP IF, SELECT IF, and so forth (Chapter 9). Arithmetic expressions can also appear in the index portion of a LOOP command (Chapter 14), on the REPEATING DATA command (Chapter 12), and on the PRINT SPACES command (Chapter 10).

Facilities for numeric expressions are

Arithmetic Functions. These functions allow you to round or truncate a variable, take the square root or the log of a variable, and so forth. (See Section 7.19.)

Statistical Functions. Statistical functions allow you to compute statistics such as the mean or variance across variables for each case. (See Section 7.20.)

Missing-Value Functions. Missing-value functions are used to control the propagation of missing values in numeric and logical expressions. In addition, missing-value functions test for the presence of missing values without returning a missing result. (See Section 7.21.)

LAG Function. LAG is a special function that provides access to across-case information. (See Section 7.22.)

Logical Functions. Logical functions check the logic of an expression and yield the result 1 when the expression is true and 0 when it is false. (See Section 7.23.)

Date and Time Functions. Three functions are available for aggregating numeric variables or constants into dates and time intervals, extracting subfields from dates, or changing units of time from seconds to minutes, hours, or days. Earlier releases of SPSS-X contained one function (YRMODA) for handling date values. (See Section 7.27.)

Other Functions. Specialized functions for handling dates, pseudo random numbers, and normal cumulative distributions are also available. (See Section 7.24). Numeric expressions can also be composed of arithmetic operations and numeric constants (see Sections 7.15 and 7.16).

7.15
Arithmetic Operations

Arithmetic operators and their meanings are

+   *Addition.* See also the SUM function described in Section 7.20.
−   *Subtraction.*
*   *Multiplication.*
/   *Division.*
**   *Exponentiation.* See also the SQRT function for taking the square root described in Section 7.19.

No two operators can appear consecutively. You cannot specify VAR1+*VAR2, but VAR1*−VAR2 is valid because the minus sign is also used to represent a negative number. In addition, you cannot imply arithmetic operators. For example, you cannot specify (VAR1)(VAR2) in place of VAR1*VAR2.

The arithmetic operators and the parentheses serve as delimiters. You can insert blanks (not commas) before and after an operator to improve readability, as in:

```
COMPUTE PCTWAGES = (WAGES / INCOME) * 100
```

7.16
Numeric Constants

Constants used in numeric expressions or as arguments to functions can be integer or noninteger, depending on the application or the function. You can specify as many digits in a constant as needed, as long as you understand the precision restrictions of your computer. Numeric constants can be signed (+ or −) but cannot contain any other special characters such as the comma or dollar sign. You can use the alternative exponential format by specifying E and a signed exponent after a number, as in:

```
COMPUTE X = Y * 5.1E+5
```

This command returns the value 510,000.0 for a case with value 1 for variable Y. This is also known as scientific notation. The exponent for a constant in scientific notation used on a transformation command is limited to two digits. For example,

```
COMPUTE X = Y * 5.1E+05
```

would be an acceptable form for your transformation statement, but

```
COMPUTE X = Y * 5.1E+005
```

would be unacceptable. The range of values SPSS-X will allow for exponents in scientific notation is from -99 to +99.

7.17
Order of Operations

You can use variables, constants, and functions with arithmetic operators to form complex expressions. The order in which SPSS-X executes the operations of a COMPUTE command when the data are read and the target variable is constructed is (1) functions; (2) exponentiation; (3) multiplication, division, and unary −; and (4) addition and subtraction. Thus, in the command

```
COMPUTE X = SQRT(Y1) / SQRT(Y2) + SQRT(Y3)
```

the square root operations are executed first, then the division, and then the addition.

You can control the order of operations by enclosing in parentheses the operation you want to execute first. The command

```
COMPUTE X = SQRT(Y1) / (SQRT(Y2) + SQRT(Y3))
```

returns a different value than the previous example since the square roots of Y2 and Y3 are summed before the division takes place.

The order of execution for operations at the same level unspecified by parentheses is left to right. Thus, the command

```
COMPUTE TESTVAR = (X/Y*Z)+1
```

returns 3 for a case with a value of 2 for X, Y, and Z since 2 (variable X) divided by 2 (variable Y) is 1, times 2 (variable Z) is 2, plus 1 is 3. However, the command

```
COMPUTE TESTVAR = (X/(Y*Z))+1
```

returns 1.5 for the same case since the expression $(2/(2*2))$ returns .5 when the parentheses alter the order of execution.

If you are ever unsure of the order of execution, use parentheses to make the order explicit—even if you specify the order SPSS-X would use anyway.

7.18
Numeric Functions

You can use the functions described below in any numeric expression on IF, SELECT IF, DO IF, ELSE IF, LOOP IF, END LOOP IF, and COMPUTE. Numeric functions always return numbers (or the system-missing value whenever the result is indeterminate). The expression to be transformed by a function is called the *argument*. Most functions have a variable name or a list of variable names as arguments. In numeric functions with two or more arguments, each argument must be separated by a comma. You *cannot* use blanks alone to separate each variable name, expression, or constant.

For example, to generate the square root of variable X, specify variable X as the argument to the SQRT function, as in SQRT(X). Enclose arguments in parentheses, as in

```
COMPUTE INCOME = TRUNC(INCOME)
```

where the TRUNC function returns the integer portion of variable INCOME. Separate multiple arguments with commas, as in

```
COMPUTE SCALE=MEAN(Q1,Q2,Q3)
```

where the MEAN function returns the mean of variables Q1, Q2, and Q3.

These functions, their arguments, their applications, and how they handle missing values are discussed in Sections 7.19 through 7.36.

7.19
Arithmetic Functions

ABS(arg)   *Absolute value.* ABS(SCALE) is 4.7 when SCALE equals 4.7 or −4.7.

RND(arg)   *Round the absolute value to an integer and reaffix the sign.* RND(SCALE) is −5 when SCALE equals −4.7.

TRUNC(arg)   *Truncate to an integer.* TRUNC(SCALE) is −4 when SCALE equals −4.7.

MOD(arg,arg)	*Remainder (modulo) of the first argument divided by the second.* MOD(YEAR,100) is 83 when YEAR equals 1983.
SQRT(arg)	*Square root.* SQRT(SIBS) is 1.41 when SIBS equals 2.
EXP(arg)	*Exponential. e is raised to the power of the argument.* EXP(VARA) is 7.39 when VARA equals 2.
LG10(arg)	*Base 10 logarithm.* LG10(VARB) is .48 when VARB equals 3.
LN(arg)	*Natural or Naperian logarithm (base e).* LN(VARC) is 2.30 when VARC equals 10.
ARSIN(arg)	*Arcsine. The result is given in radians (alias ASIN).* ARSIN(ANG) is 1.57 when ANG equals 1.
ARTAN(arg)	*Arctangent. The result is given in radians (alias ATAN).* ARTAN(ANG2) is .79 when ANG2 equals 1.
SIN(arg)	*Sine. The argument must be specified in radians.* SINE(VARC) is .84 when VARC equals 1.
COS(arg)	*Cosine. The argument must be specified in radians.* COS(VARD) is .54 when VARD equals 1.

All arithmetic functions except MOD have single arguments; MOD has two. The arguments to MOD must be separated by a comma. Arguments can be numeric expressions, as in RND(A**2/B).

7.20
Statistical Functions

Each argument to a statistical function (expression, variable name, or constant) must be separated by a comma.

SUM(arg list)	*Sum of the values across the argument list.*
MEAN(arg list)	*Mean of the values across the argument list.*
SD(arg list)	*Standard deviation of the values across the argument list.*
VARIANCE(arg list)	*Variance of the values across the argument list.*
CFVAR(arg list)	*Coefficient of variation of the values across the argument list. The coefficient of variation is the standard deviation divided by the mean.*
MIN(arg list)	*Minimum value across the argument list.*
MAX(arg list)	*Maximum value across the argument list.*

You can use the *.n* suffix described in Section 7.35 with all statistical functions to specify the number of valid arguments you consider acceptable. For example, MEAN.2(A,B,C,D) returns the mean of the valid values for variables A, B, C, and D only if at least two of the variables have valid values. You can also use the TO keyword to reference a set of variables in the argument list.

7.21
Missing-Value Functions

Each argument to a missing-value function (expression, variable name, or constant) must be separated by a comma.

VALUE(arg)	*Ignore user-defined missing values. The argument must be a variable name.* (See Section 7.35.)
MISSING(arg)	*True or 1 if the value is missing, and false or 0 otherwise.* (See Section 7.25.)
SYSMIS(arg)	*True or 1 if the value is system-missing and false or 0 otherwise.* (See Section 7.25.)
NMISS(arg list)	*Count of the number of missing values in the argument list.*
NVALID(arg list)	*Count of the number of valid values in the argument list.*

You can use the keyword TO to reference a set of variables in the argument list for functions NMISS and NVALID. For example,

```
COMPUTE NUMMISS=NMISS( A TO D, OPIN1,OPIN4)
```

returns a count of the number of variables with missing values in the list from A through D plus OPIN1 and OPIN4.

7.22
Across-Case LAG Function

LAG(arg,n) *The value of the variable n cases before.* The argument must be a numeric variable; the second argument, if specified, must be a positive integer constant. PREV4=LAG(GNP,4) returns the value of GNP for the fourth case before the current one. The first (n) cases have system-missing values for the lagged variable.

If you are selecting cases from a file (Chapter 11), LAG returns the value for the *n*th case previously selected.

7.23
Logical Functions

Each argument to a logical function (expression, variable name, or constant) must be separated by a comma.

RANGE(arg,arg list) *Return 1 or true if the value of the first argument is in the inclusive range(s). Otherwise, return 0 or false.* The first argument is usually a variable, and the list usually contains pairs of values. NONWORK=RANGE (AGE,1,17,62,99) returns 1 for ages 1 through 17 and 62 through 99 inclusive. The value of NONWORK is 0 for any other values of AGE.

ANY(arg,arg list) *Return 1 or true if the value of the first argument matches one of the arguments in the list, otherwise, return 0 or false.* The first argument is usually a variable. PARTIC = ANY(PROJECT,3,4, 7,9) returns 1 if the value for variable PROJECT is 3, 4, 7, or 9. PARTIC is 0 for other values of PROJECT.

See the discussion on using logical functions in Section 7.25.

7.24
Other Functions

UNIFORM(arg) *A uniform pseudo random number.* The random number is uniformly distributed with values varying between 0 and the value of the argument. SAMP1 = UNIFORM(150) assigns a value to SAMP1 for each case on the file.

NORMAL(arg) *A normal pseudo random number.* The random number is normally distributed with a mean of 0 and a standard deviation equal to the argument. SAMP2 = NORMAL(2.5) assigns a value to each case for the variable SAMP2.

CDFNORM(arg) *Standard normal cumulative distribution.* This function returns the probability that a random variable with the standard normal distribution (mean of 0 and standard deviation equal to 1) falls below the value of the argument. PROBVAL = CDFNORM(VARA) produces the probability values for PROBVAL based on the values of VARA.

PROBIT(arg) *Inverse of the standard normal cumulative distribution.* The value of the argument must be a probability greater than 0 and less than 1. The function returns the standard normal value having a cumulative probability equal to the argument. IPROBVAL = PROBIT(VARA/ 100) computes probit values in the variable IPROBVAL based on the values of VARA divided by 100.

7.25
Using Logical Functions

Functions MISSING and SYSMIS (Section 7.21) and RANGE and ANY (Section 7.23) are logical functions. Logical functions are useful short cuts to more complicated specifications on the IF, DO IF, and other conditional commands. For example,

```
IF ANY(DEPT82,1,2) BONUS = .16*SALARY82
```

is equivalent to

```
IF  (DEPT82 EQ 1 OR DEPT82 EQ 2)  BONUS = .16*SALARY82
```

To set an individual's bonus to 0 if the department code is missing, specify:

```
IF MISSING(DEPT82) BONUS = 0
```

You can also use logical functions in COMPUTE applications to create *logical variables*, which have values 0, 1, or missing (see Section 7.33). For example, to dichotomize an age variable to indicate those likely to be in the adult work force, you could specify

```
COMPUTE WORKERS = RANGE(AGE,18,65)
```

instead of the commands

```
IF  (AGE GE 18 AND AGE LE 65)  WORKERS = 1
IF  (AGE LT 18 OR AGE GT 65)   WORKERS = 0
```

In both examples, WORKERS is 1 for cases with AGE from 18 to 65, 0 for all other valid values, and system-missing for cases with a missing value for AGE.

Or to create a dichotomous (two-valued) variable that records 1 for individuals who gave the same response to two agree-disagree questions (assuming the same coding scheme), specify

```
COMPUTE QSAME=ANY(Q1,Q2)
```

where QSAME is 1 whenever Q1 equals Q2.

In the RANGE and ANY examples, a missing value for the first argument always returns the system-missing value. However, missing values in the argument list for ANY and RANGE do not always return the system-missing value (see Section 7.35).

Logical functions cannot be used as a number or compared to a number within an expression. For example,

```
DO IF SYSMIS(arg)
```

is a correct statement, but

```
DO IF SYSMIS(arg) EQ 1
```

is incorrect.

7.26
Complex Numeric Arguments

Except where explicitly noted, you can construct complex expressions by nesting functions and arithmetic operators as arguments to functions. For example, to ensure that the result of a numeric expression returns an integer value, specify:

```
COMPUTE PCTWAGES = RND((WAGES/INCOME)*100)
```

Likewise, to determine the minimum square root across a list of variables, specify:

```
COMPUTE QMINSQRT = SQRT(MIN(Q1,Q2,Q3,Q4))
```

SPSS-X evaluates complex numeric arguments in the same order described in Section 7.17. Parentheses can be used to control the order of execution. For example,

```
COMPUTE TESTVAR = TRUNC(SQRT(X/Y)) * .5
```

returns .5 for a case with value 2 for X and Y since 2 divided by 2 (X/Y) is 1, the square root of 1 is 1, truncating 1 returns 1, and 1 times .5 is .5. However,

```
COMPUTE TESTVAR = TRUNC(SQRT(X/Y) * .5)
```

returns 0 since SQRT(X/Y) is 1, 1 times .5 is .5, and truncating .5 returns 0.

7.27
Date and Time Functions

There are three types of date and time functions available in SPSS-X transformations. The functions provide aggregation, conversion, and extraction routines for representing dates and time intervals. Each function transforms an expression consisting of one or more arguments. Arguments can be complex expressions, variable names, or constants. Most of the dates and time intervals are internally stored and expressed as the number of seconds either from a particular date or in a time interval.

Aggregation functions combine arguments expressed as variables and values to produce a date or time interval. For example, you can use an aggregation function to combine variables month, day, and year of birth to produce a variable BIRTHDAY and then display BIRTHDAY using the American or International style for dates.

Conversion functions are used to convert time intervals from one unit to another time unit. For example, you can convert seconds to days, hours, or minutes.

The extraction functions allow you to pull out subfields from dates or time intervals. For example, you might want to examine weekly production over a two-year period. The extraction function XDATE.WEEK allows you to create a variable with values equal to the week number in a given year.

In SPSS-X, a *date* is a floating point number representing the number of seconds (or days for YRMODA) from midnight, October 14, 1582 to a later point in time. Thus, dates represent a particular *point* in time, stored as the number of seconds to that date. A date includes the time of day, which is the time interval past midnight. When time of day is not given, it is taken as 00:00 and the date is an even multiple of 86,400 (the number of seconds in a day).

For example, the function DATE.DMY(DAYVAR,MONTH,YEAR) equals 12,692,764,800 when DAYVAR is 1, MONTH is 1, and, YEAR is 1985. Note that YRMODA(DAYVAR,MONTH,YEAR) with the same three values equals 146,907.

A *time interval* is a floating point number representing the number of seconds in a *time period,* e.g. an hour, minute, or day. For example, the value representing 5.5 days is 475,200; the value representing the time interval 14:08:17 is 50,897.

Both dates and time intervals can be used in arithmetic expressions and produce the following results:

• Date plus or minus date yields a *time interval.*
• Date plus or minus time interval yields a *date.*
• Time interval plus or minus time interval yields a *time interval.*

Each date and time function stores the number of seconds or days on the active file. To print these values as dates or time intervals, use the formats for dates and times described in Chapter 10.

7.28
Aggregation Functions

Aggregation functions generate dates and time intervals from values that are not read by SPSS-X date and time input formats (see Chapter 5). Use the DATE functions to generate dates and the TIME functions to generate time intervals. Both DATE and TIME include subfunctions that correspond to the type of values found in your data. The subfunctions are separated from each function by a period and are followed by a left parenthesis, your argument list, and then a right parenthesis. The arguments to the DATE and TIME functions must be separated by commas and must contain integer values.

DATE.DMY(d,m,y)   *Day, month, year.* Combines a day, month, and year. The value of the argument for day must be expressed as an integer between 1 and 31. The value of the argument for month must be expressed as an integer between 1 and 13 (13 returns January of the following year). Years are expressed in two or four digits. A two-digit specification implies a prefix of 19. For example,

```
COMPUTE BIRTHDAY=DATE.DMY(DAY,MONTH,YEAR)
```

stores the value 1.2E+10 when DAY is 8, MONTH is 11, and YEAR is 57. Procedure LIST prints this value. When followed by a PRINT FORMAT of DATE9, as in

```
PRINT FORMAT BIRTHDAY(DATE9)
```

BIRTHDAY is listed as 08-NOV-57.

DATE.MDY(m,d,y)   *Month, day, year.* Combines a month, a day, and a year. This function follows the same rules as DATE.DMY, except for the order of the arguments. For example,

```
COMPUTE BIRTHD=DATE.MDY(MONTH,DAY,YEAR)
```

stores the same value, 1.2E+10. When supplied with an ADATE print format

```
PRINT FORMAT BIRTHD(DATE9)
```

prints 11/08/57.

DATE.YRDAY(y,d)   *Combines year and day of the year.* The DATE.YRDAY function combines a day of the year and a year. The argument for year can be expressed as either two or four digits. Two-digit years are assumed to have a prefix of 19. The argument for days can be expressed as any number between and including 1 and 366. For example,

```
COMPUTE WHEN=DATE.YRDAY(1688,301)
```

when combined with a DATE print format produces the date 27-OCT-1688.

DATE.QYR(q,y)   *Quarter and year.* Combines a quarter and a year. The argument for quarter must contain digits between and including 1 and 4. The argument for year can contain two or four digits, with two-digit values assumed to have a prefix of 19. For example,

```
COMPUTE QUART=DATE.QYR(QTR,YEAR)
```

using a QDATE print format displays lists 4 Q 57 for a value of 4 for QTR and 57 for YEAR.

Each quarter is assumed to begin on the first day of the first month of the quarter, i.e., the first of January, the first of April, etc. If you provide a DATE print format for the same values, QUART is printed as 01-OCT-57.

DATE.MOYR(m,y)   *Month and year.* Combines a month and a year. The value of the argument for month must be expressed as an integer between and including 1 and 12. The argument for year can be expressed as two or four digits. For example,

```
COMPUTE START=DATE.MOYR(MONTH,YEAR)
```

with the MOYR print format lists NOV 57 for value 11 for MONTH and 57 for YEAR.

DATE.WKYR(w,y)   *Week and year.* Combines a week and a year. The argument for week must contain integer values between and including 1 and 53. The argument for years can be represented by two or four digits. For example,

```
COMPUTE WEEK=DATE.WKYR(WK,YEAR)
```

computes variable WEEK, which with a value of 48 for WK, value 57 for YEAR, and a print format of DATE prints 26-NOV-57.

The DATE.WKYR function computes the date starting the week number for a given year. The first week of each year begins on January 1. By calculating $7*(WEEKvalue-1)+1$ the function produces the date of the start of the week.

TIME.HMS(h,m,s)   *Hour, minute, and second.* Combines an hour, minute, and second into a time interval. You can supply from one to three arguments. Trailing arguments can be omitted and default to 0. For example, you can supply arguments for hours and minutes and omit seconds, as in

```
COMPUTE PERIOD1=TIME.HMS(NUMHRS,NUMMIN)
```

The value of the first nonzero argument can spill over into the next higher argument. For example, you could have values of 0 for HRS and 90 for MIN in the following:

```
COMPUTE PERIOD2=TIME.HMS(HRS,MIN)
```

With a TIME print format, the value would be displayed as 01:30.
The last argument can contain a noninteger value, as in

```
COMPUTE PERIOD3=TIME.HMS(HRS)
```

where the value of HRS is 1.5 (trailing arguments of MINUTES
and SECONDS are assumed to be 0).
Whenever you supply a nonzero argument to a function, each
of the lower-level units must be within the range of -60 to $+60$.

TIME.DAYS(d)   *Days.* Aggregates days into a time interval. The argument can be
expressed as any numeric value. For example,

```
COMPUTE NDAYS=TIME.DAYS(SPELL)
```

with a value of 2.5 for SPELL and a DTIME print format lists the
value 2 12:00.

7.29
Conversion Functions

The conversion functions convert time intervals from one unit of time to another.
Time intervals are stored as the number of seconds in the interval; the conversion
functions provide a means for calculating more appropriate units, e.g., converting
seconds to days.

Each conversion function consists of the CTIME function followed by a
period, the target time unit, and an argument. The argument can be made up of
expressions, variable names, or constants. The argument *must* already be a time
interval (see Section 7.28 or Chapter 5). Time conversions produce noninteger
results, with a default format of F8.2.

CTIME.DAYS(arg)   *Days.* Converts a time interval to the number of days. For
example, the aggregation function TIME.HMS(HR,MIN,SEC)
produces the interval of 45,030 seconds, when HR equals 12,
MIN equals 30, and SEC equals 30. Using the following conversion function

```
COMPUTE NDAYS=CTIME.DAYS(TIME.HMS(HR,MIN,SEC))
```

you obtain a value of .52 for NDAYS for the same values of
HR, MIN, and, SEC.

CTIME.HOURS(arg)   *Hours.* Converts a time interval to the number of hours. For
example, using the same values as above, you could convert
the interval to hours by specifying

```
COMPUTE NHOURS=
        CTIME.HOURS(TIME.HMS(HR,MIN,SEC))
```

This produces a value of 12.51 for NHOURS.

CTIME.MINUTES(arg)   *Minutes.* Converts a time interval to the number of minutes.
Again, given the three variables, HR, MIN, and, SEC, you
can convert the interval from seconds to minutes by specifying

```
COMPUTE NMINS=
        CTIME.MINUTES(TIME.HMS(HR,MIN,SEC))
```

For the values above, this produces a value of 750.50 for
NMINS.

Since time and dates are stored internally as seconds, a function that converts to
seconds is not necessary.

7.30
YRMODA Function

To calculate the number of days between dates, use the YRMODA function to
convert to a day number and subtract. The command

```
COMPUTE AGE=($JDATE − YRMODA(YRBIRTH,MOBIRTH,DABIRTH))/365.25
```

calculates an individual's age by converting birth date to a day number using the
YRMODA function and subtracting that number from the current date using the
$JDATE system variable (see Section 7.47).

The YRMODA function returns the number of days since the first day of the Gregorian calendar, which is October 15, 1582. The expression YRMODA(1582, 10, 15) returns 1, and YRMODA (1800, 1, 1) returns 79337, which means that January 1, 1800, was 79,336 days after the beginning of the Gregorian calendar.

The YRMODA function has three arguments. Arguments can be variables, constants, or any other type of expression, and they must yield integers.

- The first argument can be any year from 1582 to 47516. Or if you specify a number between 00 and 99, SPSS-X will assume 1900 through 1999.
- The second argument is the month from 1 through 13. Month 13 allows the use of Day 0 to refer to the last day of the year, as in YRMODA(YEAR,13,0). Or to indicate the first month of the coming year, specify YRMODA(YEAR,13,DA).
- The final argument is the day from 0 through 31. Day 0 is the last day of the previous month regardless of whether it is 28, 29, 30, or 31. Thus, YRMODA(YEAR, MONTH + 1,0) is the last day of variable MONTH.

You may want to enclose expressions in parentheses for readability, as in YRMODA(YEAR,(MONTH + 1),0).

7.31
Extraction Functions

The extraction functions extract subfields from date or time interval values, targeting the day or a time from a date value. This permits you to classify events by day of the week, season, shift, etc.

Each extraction function consists of the function name followed by a period, the subfunction name (what you want to extract), and an argument. The argument can be an expression, variable name, or constant, provided the argument is already in *date* form (see Section 7.27 or Chapter 5).

XDATE.MDAY(arg)　　*Returns day number in a month.* Returns the day number of the date, expressed as an integer between 1 and 31. The date must have occurred after October 14, 1582.

For example, assume that you have a variable called BIRTHDAY read with a DATE20 format, and the value 05-DEC-1954 5:30:15. You can use the XDATE.MDAY function to extract the day number, as in:

```
COMPUTE DAYNUM=XDATE.MDAY(BIRTHDAY)
```

This yields the value 5 for DAYNUM.

XDATE.MONTH(arg)　　*Returns month number.* Returns the month number from a date, expressed as an integer between 1 and 12. The date must have occurred after October 14, 1582. The command

```
COMPUTE MONTHNUM=XDATE.MONTH(BIRTHDAY)
```

extracts the month number 12 from BIRTHDAY, when BIRTHDAY is read in as DATE20 and contains the value 05-DEC-1954 5:30:15.

In addition you could provide a print format of MONTH12, as in

```
PRINT FORMAT MONTHNUM(MONTH12)
```

to spell out the month of DECEMBER.

XDATE.YEAR(arg)　　*Returns year.* Returns a four-digit year from a date. The date must have occurred after October 14, 1582. The command

```
COMPUTE YEAR=XDATE.YEAR(BIRTHDAY)
```

returns the year 1954 when BIRTHDAY has the same values above.

XDATE.HOUR(arg)　　*Returns hour of the day.* Returns the hour from a date (or time of day), expressed as an integer between 0 and 23. For example,

```
COMPUTE HOUR=XDATE.HOUR(BIRTHDAY)
```

returns 5 for the value of BIRTHDAY described above.

7

XDATE.MINUTE(arg) *Returns minute of the hour.* Returns the minute of the hour from a date (or time of day), expressed as an integer from 0 through 59. For example,

```
COMPUTE MIN=XDATE.MINUTE(BIRTHDAY)
```

returns 30 for the value of BIRTHDAY described above.

XDATE.SECOND(arg) *Returns second of a minute.* Returns the second of minute from a date or time of day. Expressed as an integer or, if there are fractional seconds, with decimals.

```
COMPUTE SEC=XDATE.SECOND(BIRTHDAY)
```

extracts seconds from the value of BIRTHDAY, resulting in a value of 15.00 for the date above.

XDATE.WKDAY(arg) *Returns day number within a week.* Returns the integer number of the day within a week from a date. The date must have occurred after October 14, 1582. The day numbers are from 1 to 7, with Sunday being 1 and Saturday being 7. For example

```
COMPUTE DAYNAME=XDATE.WKDAY(BIRTHDAY)
```

returns the value 1 for the value of BIRTHDAY of 05-DEC-1954 05:30:15. If you provide a format of WKDAY, as in

```
PRINT FORMAT DAYNAME (WKDAY9)
```

you obtain the value SUNDAY for DAYNAME.

XDATE.JDAY(arg) *Returns day number within a year.* Returns the day of the year, expressed as an integer between 1 and 366. The date must have occurred after October 14, 1582. The command

```
COMPUTE DAYNUM=XDATE.JDAY(BIRTHDAY)
```

returns the value 339 for BIRTHDAY for the date described above.

XDATE.QUARTER(arg) *Returns quarter number within a year.* This function returns the quarter number a date falls in, expressed as 1, 2, 3, or 4. The date must have occurred after October 14, 1582. To find out the quarter in which BIRTHDAY occurred, use:

```
COMPUTE Q=XDATE.QUARTER(BIRTHDAY)
```

When BIRTHDAY equals 5-DEC-1954 05:30:15, the value of Q equals 4.

XDATE.WEEK(arg) *Returns week number within a year.* Returns the week number of a date, expressed as an integer between 1 and 53. The date must have occurred after October 14, 1582. The command

```
COMPUTE WEEKNUM=XDATE.WEEK(BIRTHDAY)
```

returns the value 49 for the value of BIRTHDAY described above.

XDATE.TDAY(arg) *Returns number of days in a time interval.* The XDATE.TDAY extraction function returns the number of days in a time period or in the interval from October 15, 1582 to a given date. The value returned is an integer (the fractional portion of a day is ignored). For example,

```
COMPUTE NDAYS=XDATE.TDAY(BIRTHDAY)
```

returns the value 135922, indicating the number of days between October 14, 1582 and December 5, 1954 (the value of BIRTHDAY described above).

XDATE.TIME(arg) *Returns time of day.* This function extracts the time of day from a date, expressed as the number of elapsed seconds since midnight of that date. For example,

```
COMPUTE ELSEC=XDATE.TIME(BIRTHDAY)
```

extracts the value 19815 for the value of BIRTHDAY described above. In addition, you can provide a TIME print format, as in

```
PRINT FORMAT ELSEC(TIME8)
```

to obtain the value 5:30:15 from procedure LIST.

XDATE.DATE(arg)   *Returns the date portion of a date.* The XDATE.DATE extraction function returns the integral date portion of a date or the number of elapsed seconds between midnight October 14, 1582 and midnight of the date in question. The date must have occurred after October 14, 1582. To extract the date from variable BIRTHDAY, use

```
COMPUTE BRTHDATE=XDATE.DATE(BIRTHDAY)
PRINT FORMAT BRTHDATE(ADATE8)
```

These two commands produce the value 12/05/54 for the value of BIRTHDAY described above.

7.32
Using Date and Time Variables in Procedures

Both dates and times are represented internally as seconds. In the case of dates, the numbers are very large, and arithmetic overflows may result. For instance, dates in the 20th century are on the order of 10 to the 10th power (11 digits). For that reason, a few precautions are in order:

• Some machine environments cannot accommodate the computation of higher powers of date and time variables. For example, computations higher than the sixth power may cause overflows on IBM machines.

• The magnitude of the values may cause inaccuracies in some statistical procedures. It is advisable to subtract a fixed date if you want to keep seconds as the unit, or to convert days using the XDATE.TDAYS function. REGRESSION, CORRELATIONS, ANOVA, and ONEWAY procedures use an adaptive centering method, so their accuracy will not be effected.

• LIST, REPORT and TABLES are the only procedures that print values in date and time formats. However, summary variables in REPORT and calculated variables in TABLES print in F format, regardless of the print formats of variables used as arguments.

• All other procedures use the F format in all cases. The default width and number of decimal places is taken from the print format, but the format type is ignored. For example,

```
COMPUTE DATEVAR=DATE.DMY(01,09,57)
PRINT FORMATS DATEVVAR (DATE9)
FREQUENCIES VARIABLES=DATEVAR
```

returns the value 11830147200, not 01-SEP-57.

• Changing the print format in no way alters the values that are stored in SPSS-X. For example, if you assign a print format of DATE9 for a variable read with DATETIME format, the time of day will not print but continues to be part of the value. This means that seemingly identical values can be printed as separate entries within SPSS-X procedures.

7.33
Logical Expressions

As described in Chapter 9, logical expressions can be composed of logical variables, relations comparing two or more values, or a compound expression. Logical expressions are either true, false, or missing. Because SPSS-X actually returns a numeric 1, 0, or system-missing value, logical expressions are numeric expressions and are not limited to commands involving IF expressions. Therefore, you can use logical expressions in a COMPUTE command. For example, the command

```
COMPUTE ELIGIBLE = AGE GE 18
```

returns 1 for cases 18 or over (eligible voters in the United States), 0 for cases under 18, and system-missing if AGE is missing. If you want variable ELIGIBLE to be 1 for those 18 or older who are registered to vote and if you have variable REGISTRD with 1 for "yes" and 0 for "no," specify:

```
COMPUTE ELIGIBLE = AGE GE 18 AND REGISTRD
```

To use REGISTRD in this manner, it must be a *logical variable*, which is a variable with values 0, 1, and missing only. For a logical variable, SPSS-X accepts 1 as true, 0 as false, and system- or user-missing values as missing. All other values cause warning messages and are forced to false. Therefore, REGISTRD EQ 1 would produce the same results as above but would not generate warnings.

You cannot use arithmetic with logical expressions in the computation language. However, you can construct logical variables using arithmetic. For example,

```
COMPUTE X = (A + B EQ C)
```

assigns the value 1 to X whenever (A + B) is equal to C. Zero is assigned otherwise. However, SPSS-X does not evaluate expressions that use arithmetic with logical expressions. For example,

```
COMPUTE X = A + (B EQ C)
```

directs the system to add the logical outcome of B = C (0 or 1) to the value of A. SPSS-X issues an error message when statements like this are encountered.

7.34
Missing Values

Missing values arise in numeric expressions for reasons other than when SPSS-X encounters missing values in variables. Certain arithmetic operations, such as division by zero, produce the system-missing value (see Section 7.36). SPSS-X also returns system-missing for operations that involve functions with arguments that cannot be evaluated (see Section 7.35).

Some arithmetic operations involving 0 produce the same results regardless of what values are used. In these cases, SPSS-X evaluates the operation even when the variables have missing values. These operations are presented in Table 7.34.

Table 7.34   Missing-value exceptions in numeric expressions

Expression	Result
0 * missing	= 0
0 / missing	= 0
missing ** 0	= 1
0 ** missing	= 0
MOD(0,missing)	= 0

7.35
Missing Values in Arguments

SPSS-X tries to evaluate a function using all the information it has and returns the system-missing value only when it doesn't have enough information. Table 7.35 shows when each function returns a system missing value.

Arithmetic functions that take only one argument cannot be evaluated if that argument is missing. The date and time functions cannot be missing on any argument. Otherwise, the result is system-missing. However, statistical functions are evaluated if a sufficient number of arguments are valid. For example, to sum the values of three variables, you could use arithmetic operators, as in:

```
COMPUTE FACTOR = SCORE1 + SCORE2 + SCORE3
```

With this command, variable FACTOR is assigned the system-missing value for any case with a missing value for any one (or more) of the score variables. On the other hand, the SUM function is executed even if only one of the arguments has valid information, as in:

COMPUTE FACTOR = SUM(SCORE1 TO SCORE3)

With this command, a valid value is assigned to FACTOR by summing any two valid score values or by simply assigning the single valid score. FACTOR is missing if all variables are missing.

You can use the *.n* suffix with the statistical functions SUM, MEAN, MIN, MAX, SD, VARIANCE, and CFVAR to specify the number of valid arguments you consider acceptable. For example, to compute FACTOR only if a case has valid information for at least two scores, use the *.n* suffix with the SUM function, as in:

COMPUTE FACTOR = SUM.2(SCORE1 TO SCORE3)

This command instructs SPSS-X to sum any two or more valid scores and to return missing otherwise.

To override the definition for user-missing values, use the VALUE function, as in:

COMPUTE FACTOR = VALUE(SCORE1) + VALUE(SCORE2) + VALUE(SCORE3)

Table 7.35 Missing values in arguments to functions

Function	Returns system-missing if
ABS (x) ARSIN (x) ARTAN (x) CDFNORM (x) COS (x) EXP (x) LG10 (x) LN (x) NORMAL (x) PROBIT (x) RND (x) SIN (x) SQRT (x) TRUNC (x) UNIFORM (x)	x is missing
VALUE (x)	x is system-missing
YRMODA (x1,x2,x3)	any x is missing
MOD (x1,x2)	x1 is missing, or x2 is missing and x1 is not 0
MAX.n (x1,x2,...xk) MEAN.n (x1,x2,...xk) MIN.n (x1,x2,...x1) SUM.n (x1,x2,...xk)	fewer than n arguments are valid (NVALID (x1,x2,...xk) < n) default n is 1
CFVAR.n (x1,x2,...xk) SD.n (x1,x2,...xk) VARIANCE.n (x1,x2,...xk)	fewer than n arguments are valid (NVALID (x1,x2,...xk) < n) default n is 2
LAG (x,n)	x is missing n cases previously (and always for the first n cases)
ANY (x,x1,x2,...xk)	x or all of x1,x2,...xk are missing
RANGE (x,x1,x2,...xk)	x or all of pairs x1,x2, etc. are missing
MISSING (x) NMISS (x1,x2,...xk) NVALID (x1,x2,...xk) SYSMIS (x)	never

This command instructs SPSS-X to treat all user-missing values as valid and to use them in constructing the target variable. (You cannot override system-missing values in this way.) This will produce different results from the SUM command above, which constructs FACTOR when at least one score is valid but does not sum the user-missing values for the other variables.

7.36
Domain Errors

Domain errors occur when numeric expressions are mathematically undefined or are numerically unrepresentable on the computer for reasons other than missing data. Two common examples are division by zero and the square root of a negative number. When SPSS-X detects a domain error in an expression, it issues a warning message and returns the system-missing value for that expression. For example, the command

```
COMPUTE TESTVAR = TRUNC(SQRT(X/Y) * .5)
```

returns system-missing if X or Y is negative or if Y is 0.

The following are domain errors in numeric expressions:

**	A negative number to a noninteger power.
/	A divisor of 0.
MOD	A divisor of 0.
SQRT	A negative argument.
EXP	An argument that produces a result too large to be represented on the computer.
LG10	A negative or 0 argument.
LN	A negative or 0 argument.
ARSIN	An argument whose absolute value exceeds 1.
NORMAL	A negative or 0 argument.
YRMODA	Arguments that do not form a valid date (see Section 7.25).
PROBIT	A negative argument, zero, or an argument 1 or greater.

7.37
COUNT COMMAND

The COUNT command is a special data transformation utility used to create a numeric variable that, for each case, counts the occurrences of the same value (or list of values) across a list of numeric or string variables. For example,

```
COUNT  READER=NEWSWEEK,TIME,USNEWS (2)
```

creates a simple index READER that indicates the number of times the value 2 (those who read each magazine) is recorded for the three variables for a case. Thus, the value of reader will be either 0, 1, 2, or 3. You can enter more than one criterion variable list and more than one criterion value enclosed in parentheses, as in

```
COUNT  READER=NEWSWEEK,TIME,USNEWS (2)
       NYTIMES,WPOST,CHIGTRIB,LATIMES (3,4)
```

which adds four more news sources to the previous index. This time, SPSS-X increases the count for a case by 1 whenever it encounters either value 3 (Sunday only) or 4 (daily plus Sunday) for each newspaper variable.

You can specify a variable more than once in the variable list to increase the count by more than one for that variable, thus giving it more weight. You can also use the TO keyword to list your variables and the THRU, LOWEST, and HIGHEST keywords in the value list. You can also create more than one variable on a COUNT command by separating the specifications with a slash, as in:

```
COUNT  LOWCOUNT = Q1 TO Q10 (LOWEST THRU 5)
       /HICOUNT = Q1 TO Q10 (11 THRU HIGHEST)
```

7.38
Initialization and Missing Values

The COUNT command ignores the missing-value status of user-missing values. In other words, the COUNT command counts a value even if that value has been previously declared as missing. In the command

```
COUNT LOWCOUNT=Q1 TO Q10(LOWEST THRU 5)
```

target variable LOWCOUNT is increased for a case with value 0 for variables Q1, Q2, and so forth, even if 0 was declared user-missing for the Q variables.

COUNT will not propagate missing values automatically. In other words, the target variable will never be system-missing. However, you can use the MISSING VALUES command to declare missing values for the target variable.

You can use keyword MISSING to count all missing values and keyword SYSMIS to count system-missing values. Specify these keywords in parentheses in the value list, as in:

```
COUNT  QMISS = Q1 TO Q10 (MISSING)
       /QSYSMIS= Q1 TO Q10 (SYSMIS)
```

This command creates one variable (QMISS) that counts the number of missing values for the criterion variables and a second variable (QSYSMISS) that counts only system-missing values.

7.39
TRANSFORMATION UTILITIES

SPSS-X provides various utilities to assist in manipulating your data. In general, the basic transformation language without these features can solve your problems. However, your work will be easier if you learn to use scratch variables (Section 7.41), temporary transformations (Section 7.42), the NUMERIC command (Section 7.43), and the DO REPEAT—END REPEAT structure (Section 7.44). The VECTOR command, another utility, is most closely associated with the LOOP structure and is documented in Chapter 14. Finally, the LEAVE command (Section 7.40) is very important since it provides access to information from previous cases and controls how a new variable is initialized.

7.40
LEAVE Command

Normally, SPSS-X reinitializes a numeric or string variable each time it reads a new case. To leave a variable at its value for the previous case as each new case is read, specify the variable on a LEAVE command. Numeric variables named on a LEAVE command are initialized to 0 for the first case and string variables are initialized to blanks. For example, to keep a running total of salaries across all cases, specify

```
COMPUTE TSALARY=TSALARY+SALARY82
LEAVE TSALARY
FORMAT TSALARY (DOLLAR8)/ SALARY82 (DOLLAR7)
PRINT /SALARY82 TSALARY
EXECUTE
```

where SALARY82 is the variable containing the employee's 1982 salary and TSALARY is the new variable containing the cumulative salaries for all previous cases. The results of the PRINT command are shown in Figure 7.40a.

To accumulate a sum across groups of cases (time intervals, departments, and so forth), use the IF command described in Chapter 9, as in:

```
SORT CASES DEPT82
IF DEPT82 NE LAG(DEPT82,1) TSALARY=0/*INITIALIZE FOR NEW DEPT
COMPUTE TSALARY=TSALARY+SALARY82      /*SUM SALARIES
LEAVE TSALARY                         /*PREVENT INITIALIZATION EACH CASE
FORMAT TSALARY (DOLLAR8)/ SALARY82 (DOLLAR7)
PRINT /DEPT82 SALARY82 TSALARY
EXECUTE
```

Figure 7.40a   Accumulating the sum across all variables

```
$10,733   $10,733
 $9,767   $20,500
$11,983   $32,483
$12,888   $45,371
$13,803   $59,174
$24,222   $83,396
$22,111  $105,507
$25,223  $130,730
$27,223  $157,953
$20,100  $178,053
$28,888  $206,941
$21,800  $228,741
$22,338  $251,079
$34,880  $285,959
$28,000  $313,959
$28,888  $342,847
```

The results of this PRINT command are shown in Figure 7.40b. The sum is reset each time the value of DEPT82 changes. This example assumes that the data are sorted in order of DEPT82.

Figure 7.40b   Accumulating sums across groups of variables

```
1 $10,733   $10,733
1  $9,767   $20,500
1 $11,983   $32,483
1 $12,888   $45,371
1 $13,803   $59,174
1 $24,222   $83,396
1 $22,111  $105,507
2 $25,223   $25,223
2 $27,223   $52,446
2 $20,100   $72,546
2 $28,888  $101,434
3 $21,800   $21,800
3 $22,338   $44,138
3 $34,880   $79,018
3 $28,000  $107,018
3 $28,888  $135,906
```

You can name more than one variable on a LEAVE command and can use the TO keyword to reference a list of consecutive variables. The variables named on the LEAVE command must already exist and cannot be scratch variables (see Section 7.41). If you name a variable that is being read from a system file via GET, for example, the LEAVE command has no effect. However, the LEAVE command can be helpful in conjunction with DATA LIST (see Chapters 12 and 14).

7.41
Scratch Variables

To create a *scratch variable*, use the # character as the first character of the numeric or string variable name. Use scratch variables to read or create variables that you want to use in defining files or in other transformations but that you do not want to analyze or to save on a system file. For example, to create a permanent variable that measures an individual's age, you might want to define day, month, and year variables as scratch variables for use with the YRMODA function (Section 7.30), as in:

```
DATA LIST FILE=HUBDATA RECORDS=3
  /1 #MOBIRTH #DABIRTH #YRBIRTH 6-11
COMPUTE   AGE=($JDATE - YRMODA(#YRBIRTH,#MOBIRTH,#DABIRTH))/365.25
VARIABLE LABELS AGE 'EMPLOYEE''S AGE'
```

The #MOBIRTH, #DABIRTH, and #YRBIRTH variables are read from the data file and used as arguments to the YRMODA function. System variable $JDATE is the current date in YRMODA format (see Section 7.47). Division by 365.25 transforms the result from days into years (with an approximate adjustment for leap year).

• Scratch variables are unavailable for procedures and cannot be saved on a system file.

- You cannot assign missing values, variable labels, or value labels for scratch variables.

- Scratch variables are initialized to 0 for numeric variables or blank for string variables for the first case and are "left" across cases (see Section 7.40).

- Scratch variables can be created between procedures but are always discarded as the next procedure begins.

- Once you specify a TEMPORARY command (Section 7.42), the scratch variables are discarded.

- You cannot use the keyword TO to refer to scratch variables and permanent variables at the same time.

- You cannot name scratch variables on a WEIGHT command (see Chapter 11).

7.42
TEMPORARY Command

Use the TEMPORARY command to signal the beginning of temporary transformations that are in effect only for the next procedure. New numeric or string variables created after the TEMPORARY command are *temporary variables*. Any modifications made to existing variables after the TEMPORARY command are also temporary. The commands

```
DATA LIST FILE=HUBDATA RECORDS=3
 /1 #MOBIRTH #DABIRTH #YRBIRTH 6-11 DEPT82 19
COMPUTE    AGE=($JDATE - YRMODA(#YRBIRTH,#MOBIRTH,#DABIRTH))/365.25
VARIABLE LABELS AGE 'EMPLOYEE''S AGE'
         DEPT82 'DEPARTMENT CODE IN 1982'

TEMPORARY
RECODE AGE (LO THRU 20=1)(20 THRU 25=2)(25 THRU 30=3)(30 THRU 35=4)
       (35 THRU 40=5)(40 THRU 45=6)(45 THRU 50=7)(50 THRU 55=8)
       (55 THRU 60=9)(60 THRU 65=10)(65 THRU HI=11)
VARIABLE LABELS AGE 'EMPLOYEE AGE CATEGORIES'
VALUE LABELS AGE 1 'Up to 20' 2 '20 to 25' 3 '25 to 30' 4 '30 to 35'
       5 '35 to 40' 6 '40 to 45' 7 '45 to 50' 8 '50 to 55'
       9 '55 to 60' 10 '60 to 65' 11 '65 and older'

FREQUENCIES VARIABLES=AGE
MEANS AGE BY DEPT82
```

temporarily recode the AGE variable computed in Section 7.41. FREQUENCIES then uses the temporary version of variable AGE with the temporary variable and value labels. MEANS uses the unrecoded values of AGE and the permanent variable label. You can use the following commands after the TEMPORARY command:

- Transformation commands COMPUTE, RECODE, IF, and COUNT, and the DO REPEAT utility.
- The LOOP and DO IF control structures.
- Print and write commands PRINT, PRINT EJECT, PRINT SPACE, and WRITE.
- Format declarations PRINT FORMATS, WRITE FORMATS, and FORMATS.
- Data selection commands SELECT IF, SAMPLE, and WEIGHT.
- Variable declarations NUMERIC, STRING, and VECTOR.
- Labeling commands VARIABLE LABELS and VALUE LABELS, and the MISSING VALUES command.
- SPLITFILE.
- XSAVE.
- All procedure commands.

Once you specify a TEMPORARY command, you cannot refer to previously existing scratch variables. You cannot use SORT CASES, MATCH FILES, or ADD FILES, or COMPUTE with a LAG function, after a TEMPORARY command without an intervening procedure. In addition, you cannot use the TEMPORARY command inside the DO IF—END IF or LOOP—END LOOP structures.

You can use the TEMPORARY command after the first procedure to make additional transformations temporary. Otherwise, transformations between procedures are permanent and cause SPSS-X to rewrite the permanent dictionary.

Since SAVE is a procedure, any temporary transformations between the TEMPORARY and SAVE commands without an intervening procedure are saved on the system file. (See Chapter 4 for a discussion of TEMPORARY and XSAVE.)

7.43
NUMERIC Command

Use the NUMERIC command to declare new numeric variables. While you can also create new numeric variables directly with COMPUTE, IF, RECODE, and COUNT, you may need to refer to a numeric variable in the transformation language before it is created. For example, you might want to add a series of variables to your active file in a fixed order so you can use the TO keyword to reference variables on procedure commands. The specification

```
NUMERIC SCALE79 IMPACT79 SCALE80 IMPACT80 SCALE81 IMPACT81 SCALE82
        IMPACT82
```

declares variables SCALE79 through IMPACT82. Then, regardless of the order in which you actually store values in them, the variables remain in that order on the active file.

The default format for variables named on a NUMERIC command is F8.2 (or whatever you specify using the SET command), but you can declare variables using any simple FORTRAN-like format (Chapter 5) in parentheses following the variable name or names, as in:

```
NUMERIC X(F4.0)/Y(F1.0)
```

Only a single format specification is permitted after each variable name. This format is used as both the PRINT FORMAT and WRITE FORMAT. Permanent or temporary variables are initialized to the system-missing value and scratch variables are initialized to 0.

You can also use the NUMERIC command along with the STRING command to predetermine the order of variables in the dictionary (see Chapter 14).

7.44
DO REPEAT Utility

If you are doing the same basic transformation on a large set of variables, you can reduce the number of commands by using DO REPEAT—END REPEAT. This utility does not reduce the number of commands SPSS-X executes, just the number of commands you enter.

The specification on the DO REPEAT utility is the stand-in variable. The *stand-in variable* stands for a list of numeric variables, string variables, constants, or strings and is used in one or more transformation commands within the DO REPEAT—END REPEAT structure. For example, to initialize a set of five variables to 0 without entering five COMPUTE commands, specify:

```
DO REPEAT R=REGION1 TO REGION5
COMPUTE R=0
END REPEAT
```

The commands between DO REPEAT and END REPEAT are repeated once for each variable in the replacement list. Thus, five COMPUTE commands are generated, one for each REGION variable (see keyword PRINT in Section 7.46).

Stand-in variables (R in this example) do not exist outside of the DO REPEAT—END REPEAT utility. You can use any valid variable name you wish—permanent, temporary, scratch, system, and so forth. The stand-in variable has no effect on any variable with the same name. However, you cannot have two stand-in variables with the same name in the same DO REPEAT structure.

You can use the following commands within the DO REPEAT—END REPEAT structure:

- Data transformations COMPUTE, RECODE, IF, COUNT, and SELECT IF.
- Data declarations VECTOR, STRING, NUMERIC, and LEAVE.
- Data definitions DATA LIST and MISSING VALUES (but not VARIABLE LABELS or VALUE LABELS).
- LOOP structure commands LOOP, END LOOP, and BREAK.
- DO IF structure commands DO IF, ELSE IF, ELSE, and END IF.
- Print and write commands PRINT, PRINT EJECT, PRINT SPACE, and WRITE.
- Format commands PRINT FORMATS, WRITE FORMATS, and FORMATS.

7.45
Replacement Variable and Value Lists

A replacement variable list can be a list of new or existing variable names and can be string or numeric. You can use the TO keyword both to name consecutive existing variables and to create a set of new variables (see Chapter 2). If the new variables are string, they must be declared on a STRING command before being named on the DO REPEAT command (see Chapter 8). All replacement variable and value lists must have the same number of items.

A replacement value list can be a list of strings or numeric values, or it can be of the form n_1 TO n_2, where n_1 is less than n_2 and both are integers. (Note that the keyword is TO, not THRU.) The commands

```
DO REPEAT R=REGION1 TO REGION5/ X=1 TO 5
COMPUTE R=0
IF (REGION EQ X) R=1
END REPEAT
```

create dummy variables REGION1 to REGION5 that measure 1 or 0 for each of 5 regions, perhaps for use in procedure REGRESSION or REPORT (see Chapters 47 and 45).

If you use the PRINT keyword on the END REPEAT command (Section 7.46), SPSS-X prints the commands it generated, as shown in Figure 7.45. The plus signs mark the generated commands.

Figure 7.45   Commands generated by DO REPEAT

```
 2    0          DO REPEAT R=REGION1 TO REGION5/ X=1 TO 5
 3    0          COMPUTE R=0
 4    0          IF (REGION EQ X) R=1
 5    0          END REPEAT PRINT

 6    0          +COMPUTE REGION1=0
 7    0          +IF (REGION EQ 1) REGION1=1
 8    0          +COMPUTE REGION2=0
 9    0          +IF (REGION EQ 2) REGION2=1
10    0          +COMPUTE REGION3=0
11    0          +IF (REGION EQ 3) REGION3=1
12    0          +COMPUTE REGION4=0
13    0          +IF (REGION EQ 4) REGION4=1
14    0          +COMPUTE REGION5=0
15    0          +IF (REGION EQ 5) REGION5=1
```

7.46
PRINT Subcommand

To see the commands that SPSS-X generates from the DO REPEAT utility, use the PRINT subcommand on the END REPEAT command. For example, to initialize one set of variables to 0 and another set to 1, specify:

```
DO REPEAT Q=Q1 TO Q5/ R=R1 TO R5
COMPUTE Q=0
COMPUTE R=1
END REPEAT PRINT
```

The output from the PRINT subcommand on the END REPEAT command is shown in Figure 7.46.

Figure 7.46 Display from the PRINT keyword

```
 2   0           DO REPEAT Q=Q1 TO Q5/ R=R1 TO R5
 3   0           COMPUTE Q=0
 4   0           COMPUTE R=1
 5   0           END REPEAT PRINT

 6   0           +COMPUTE Q1=0
 7   0           +COMPUTE R1=1
 8   0           +COMPUTE Q2=0
 9   0           +COMPUTE R2=1
10   0           +COMPUTE Q3=0
11   0           +COMPUTE R3=1
12   0           +COMPUTE Q4=0
13   0           +COMPUTE R4=1
14   0           +COMPUTE Q5=0
15   0           +COMPUTE R5=1
```

Use the PRINT subcommand to verify the order in which your commands are executed. In this example, notice that the COMPUTE commands are executed such that variables are created in alternating order: Q1, R1, Q2, R2, and so forth. If you plan to use the TO convention to refer to Q1 TO Q5 later, you should use two separate DO REPEAT utilities; otherwise, Q1 TO Q5 will include four of the five R variables. Or you can use the NUMERIC command as explained in Section 7.43 to predetermine the order.

Alternatively, you can specify a series of constants as a stand-in value list and create the Q and R value lists in order, as in:

```
DO REPEAT Q=Q1 TO Q5,R1 TO R5/ N=0,0,0,0,0,1,1,1,1,1
COMPUTE Q=N
END REPEAT PRINT
```

7.47
System Variables

Special *system variables,* such as the number of cases read by the system, the system-missing value, and the current date, can be used in data transformations. The names of these variables begin with a dollar sign. You cannot modify a system variable or alter its print or write format. Except for these restrictions, you can use system variables anywhere a normal variable is used in the transformation language. System variables are not available for procedures.

$CASENUM   *Permanent case sequence number.* For each case, $CASENUM is the number of permanent cases read up to and including that case. The format is F8.0.

$SYSMIS   *System-missing value.* The format is F1.0 so that it will always print as a period (.).

$JDATE   *Current date in YRMODA format.* The format is F6.0. See Section 7.30 for the discussion of the YRMODA function.

$DATE   *Current date.* The format is A9 in the form *dd-mmm-yy.*

$TIME   *Current date and time.* Represents the number of seconds from midnight, October 14, 1582 and the the date and time when the data set is read. The format is F20.

$LENGTH   *The current page length.* The format is F11.0. See the SET command in Chapter 4 for more information.

$WIDTH   *The current page width.* The format is F3.0. See the SET command in Chapter 4 for more information.

7.48
EXECUTING DATA TRANSFORMATIONS

Execution of transformation commands is straightforward. When the data are read, each transformation command is evaluated and executed in order. This means that the order in which you give your transformations to SPSS-X may be important. With the commands

```
RECODE  ITEM1 TO ITEM3 (0=1) (1=0) (2=-1) (9=9) (ELSE=SYSMIS)
COUNT   AGREE=ITEM1 TO ITEM3 (1)
```

the order of execution is critical since the COUNT command assumes that the RECODE has already been executed.

Transformations do not actually take place until the data are read. Unless you use a procedure or other command that instructs SPSS-X to read the data, your transformations are not executed. Likewise, unless you save a system file or write out the data in some other manner, the transformations are in effect only for that single run of SPSS-X.

The major exception is the cross-case function, LAG. You must consider how LAG performs when used with commands that select cases (for example, SELECT IF or SAMPLE). LAG counts cases *after* case selection, even if SELECT IF follows LAG. Therefore, you may need to place a procedure or EXECUTE between LAG and the commands that select cases to achieve the desired result.

7.49
Data Definition Commands

You can use the data definition commands VARIABLE LABELS, VALUE LABELS, MISSING VALUES, and so forth, to fully define any variable created or altered by data transformations. For example, once a new variable is created, you may want to add a complete set of definitions, as in:

```
RECODE    ITEM1 TO ITEM3 (0=1) (1=0) (2=-1) (9=9) (ELSE=SYSMIS)
COUNT     AGREE=ITEM1 TO ITEM3 (1)
FORMATS AGREE (F1)
VARIABLE LABELS AGREE 'LEVEL OF AGREEMENT WITH SPENDING'
VALUE LABELS AGREE 3 'AGREE A LOT' 2 'AGREE' 1 'AGREE A LITTLE'
                   0 'DISAGREE'
```

The only requirement for using data definition commands with transformations is that the variable being defined must already exist on your active file. In other words, the data definitions must follow the transformation commands that create the variable.

7.50
Active File

Data transformations are made to your active file. Unless you submit a command that causes SPSS-X to read the data, there is no active file. Also, unless you save the active file as a new system file, new variables do not exist, altered variables are unchanged in the data, and new data definitions disappear. In the commands

```
DATA LIST  FILE=TESTDATA
  /AGE 1-3 ITEM1 TO ITEM3 5-7
VARIABLE LABELS  ITEM1 'OPINION ON LEVEL OF DEFENSE SPENDING'
  ITEM2 'OPINION ON LEVEL OF WELFARE SPENDING'
  ITEM3 'OPINION ON LEVEL OF HEALTH SPENDING'
VALUE LABELS  ITEM1 TO ITEM3 -1 'DISAGREE' 0 'NO OPINION' 1 'AGREE'
MISSING VALUES  AGE(-99,-98) ITEM1 TO ITEM3 (9)

RECODE  ITEM1,ITEM2,ITEM3 (0=1) (1=0) (2=-1) (9=9) (ELSE=SYSMIS)

RECODE  AGE (MISSING=9) (18 THRU HI=1) (LO THRU 18=0) INTO VOTER
PRINT /$CASENUM 1-2 AGE 4-6 VOTER 8-10

VARIABLE LABELS  VOTER 'ELIGIBLE TO VOTE'
VALUE LABELS  VOTER 0 'UNDER 18' 1 '18 OR OVER'
MISSING VALUES  VOTER (9)
PRINT FORMATS VOTER(F1.0)
FREQUENCIES VARIABLES=VOTER,ITEM1 TO ITEM3

SAVE OUTFILE=NEWDATA
```

the data are read from file TESTDATA when SPSS-X encounters the FRE-QUENCIES command. At that point, SPSS-X applies the transformations and definitions and constructs the frequencies table.

The SAVE FILE command saves a new system file, NEWDATA, that contains the data and dictionary information on the variables read from TESTDATA plus the new variable VOTER.

Syntax

COMPUTE

```
COMPUTE target variable=expression
```

String Functions

Function	Definition
ANY(arg,arg list)	Return 1 if value of arg matches value in arg list
CONCAT(arg list)	Join the arguments into a string
INDEX(a1,a2,a3)	Return number indicating position of first occurence of a2 in a1
LAG(arg,n)	Return value of arg n cases before
LENGTH(arg)	Return length of arg
LOWER(arg list)	Convert upper case letters to lower case
LPAD(a1,a2,a3)	Left pad beginning of a1 to length a2 with character a3
LTRIM(a1,a2)	Trim character a2 from beginning of a1
MAX(arg list)	Return maximum value of arg list
MIN(arg list)	Return minimum value of arg list
NUMBER(arg,format)	Convert argument into number using format
RANGE(arg,arg list)	Return 1 if value of arg is in inclusive range of arg list
RINDEX(a1,a2,a3)	Return number indicating rightmost occurence of a2 in a1
RPAD(a1,a2,a3)	Right pad end of a1 to length a2 with character a3
RTRIM(a1,a2)	Trim character a2 from end of a1
STRING(arg,format)	Convert argument into string using format
SUBSTR(a1,a2,a3)	Return substring of a1 beginning with position a2 for length a3
UPCASE(arg list)	Convert lower case letters to upper case

RECODE

For string variables:

```
RECODE varlist [('string',['string'...]='string')][INTO varlist]
      [/varlist...]
```

Input Keywords:
CONVERT, ELSE

Output Keyword:
COPY

STRING

```
STRING varlist (An) [/varlist...]
```

Contents

8.1   INTRODUCTION TO STRING VARIABLES

8.2   STRING Command

8.3   Strings

8.4   Missing Values

8.5   RECODE COMMAND

8.6   Specifying String Values

8.7   INTO, ELSE, and COPY Keywords

8.8   Changing Variable Types

8.9   CONVERT Keyword

8.10   COMPUTE COMMAND: STRING VARIABLES

8.11   STRING EXPRESSIONS

8.12   Constructing String Expressions

8.13   Logical Expressions

8.14   String Functions

8.15   Padding and Trimming Strings

8.16   Indexing and Substrings

8.17   NUMBER Function

8.18   Comparing Strings

8.19   LAG Function

8.20   Third Argument of INDEX or RINDEX

8

Chapter 8   String Transformations

You can manipulate string variables in SPSS-X using most of the same commands described in Chapter 7 for numeric variables. While you cannot treat strings with a full range of mathematical operations and functions, you can modify strings, split them apart and put them back together, and combine them with constants and other string variables using the RECODE and COMPUTE commands. The RECODE command is specifically discussed in Sections 8.5 through 8.9. A generalized discussion of string expressions is presented in Sections 8.10 through 8.12. Of particular interest are the special string functions described in Section 8.14.

To learn about the complete range of possibilities with string variables, you should also consult Chapter 7 for the following topics:

- String variables can be used in the criterion list of a COUNT command.
- String variables can be named on a LEAVE command.
- Scratch variables can be strings.
- String manipulations specified after a TEMPORARY command follow the same rules given for numeric variables.
- Variables used in the DO REPEAT utility can be string variables and constants can be strings.

8.1
INTRODUCTION TO STRING VARIABLES

The principal difference between string variables and numeric variables in data transformations is that you must always keep track of the length of strings. Only rarely will SPSS-X not allow a requested transformation because one string is longer or shorter than another or because you are referencing a value that is longer or shorter than the length specified for the variable. However, you must keep track of length to be certain that SPSS-X does what you want. In fact, you must know the length of a new string variable before you create it using the required STRING command as shown in Section 8.2.

Another length consideration is the difference between short and long strings. The exact definition of a short string is machine dependent (see Chapter 5). Short strings can have missing values. This has general implications for transformations (see Section 8.4) and specific implications for RECODE (see Section 8.5).

String variables also differ from numeric variables in that there are no range specifications. Keywords LOWEST, HIGHEST, and THRU are not defined for strings in any data transformations.

8.2
STRING Command

A string variable must be declared before it can be used as a target variable in data transformations. If a string variable does not already exist on the active file, you must use the STRING command to declare it. The STRING command keyword is followed by the name of the new variable and its simple format in parentheses, as in:

STRING   SSNUMBER (A11)

• New string variables are initialized as blanks unless the LEAVE command is used (see Chapter 7).

• The length of a string variable is fixed by the format given when it is declared and cannot be changed.

• You cannot use the STRING command to redefine an existing variable.

• String variables cannot have zero length (format A0).

More than one string variable can be declared on a STRING command either by specifying a variable list when the format is the same, as in

```
STRING   ALPHA1 TO ALPHA6 (A8)
```

or by separating the definitions with a slash, as in

```
STRING   ALPHA1 TO ALPHA6 (A8)/ALPHA7,ALPHA10 (A16)
```

All implementations of SPSS-X allow the A format. There may be other valid string formats available on the computer at your installation. Also, the definition of a long string depends on which machine you are using. Use the INFO command to obtain local documentation.

The STRING command can also be used with the NUMERIC command to predetermine the order of variables in the dictionary. See Chapter 14 for a complete discussion.

8.3
Strings

Values of string variables within SPSS-X are called *strings*. In the COMPUTE command, strings can be assigned to string variables or can appear as arguments to functions, depending on the application and the function. In the RECODE command, strings are the old or new values specified for recoding. In the command

```
RECODE STATE ('IO'='IA')
```

values IO and IA are both strings.

• Strings are enclosed within apostrophes or quotation marks. The same symbol must be used to begin and end the string.

• A string must be contained on a single command line; it cannot be continued to the next line, except by concatenation as described below.

• You can concatenate strings using the plus sign, as in

```
RECODE NAME ('Georgianne Baxter Birney' = 'Georgianne Baker'
  +' Baxter')
```

which changes Georgianne Baxter Birney to Georgianne Baker Baxter.

• An apostrophe can be entered as part of a string if the string is enclosed in quotation marks or if the apostrophe is entered twice with no separation. For example,

```
COMPUTE BAR='Harry''s'
```

and

```
COMPUTE BAR="Harry's"
```

both assign Harry's to variable BAR. A quotation mark can be entered in a similar manner, as in

```
COMPUTE  RESPONSE='"Ouch!"'
```

which assigns value "Ouch!" to variable RESPONSE.

Strings must agree in length with the variable to which they are assigned. If not, they are usually trimmed or padded to the correct length, or SPSS-X generates an error. These rules are described for each command.

8.4
Missing Values

The transformation language does not propagate missing values for short string variables (long string variables cannot have missing values). If a string variable for which missing values have been defined appears in an assignment specification for a COMPUTE or IF command, the assignment is made without regard to the missing-value status of any strings. For example,

```
STRING NEWALPHA(A8)
COMPUTE NEWALPHA=ALPHA
```

returns a string of eight blanks for a case with an all-blank value for variable ALPHA, even if a blank string is considered missing for ALPHA. To make a blank string also missing for variable NEWALPHA, use the MISSING VALUES command.

If a string variable for which missing values have been defined appears in a logical expression for an IF, SELECT IF, DO IF, or other conditional command, the comparison is made without regard to the missing-value status of any strings. For example,

```
MISSING VALUES ALPHA ('XA')
SELECT IF ALPHA EQ 'XA' OR ALPHA EQ 'XB'
```

selects cases with ALPHA equal to XA even though XA is a missing value.

Functions MISSING and SYSMIS are not available for string variables.

8.5
RECODE COMMAND

You can use the RECODE command to change one code for a string variable to another as the data are being read. The command

```
RECODE STATE ('IO'='IA')
```

instructs SPSS-X to change all cases coded IO to IA, the correct Postal Service abbreviation for Iowa.

- You can recode both short and long strings.
- Variables to be recoded must be named first and must already exist (see the STRING command in Section 8.2).
- Values must be enclosed in apostrophes.
- You can include as many value specifications as needed, containing each within parentheses.
- You can include multiple input values in a single specification but only one output value after the equals sign, as in:

```
RECODE STATE ('IO','IW'='IA')
```

- The RECODE command is evaluated left to right. If SPSS-X encounters the current case's value in an input value list, that case is recoded and the rest of the recode specifications are ignored. In the command

```
RECODE STATE ('MI'='MN') ('MN'='MI')
```

SPSS-X recodes a case with value MI for variable STATE to MN and then proceeds to the next command. The case is *not* recoded back to MI by the second specification.

- All input values not mentioned on the RECODE command are left unchanged.
- You can name multiple variables for the same value specifications. You can also recode multiple variables differently on the same command by separating the variables with a slash. For example,

```
RECODE STATE ('IO'='IA')/ Q1 TO Q5 ('X'='Y') ('A'='B')
```

recodes STATE and the list of Q variables in the same command.

8.6
Specifying String Values

If you are recoding more than one variable using the same specifications, all variables in the list must have the same length. The rules for specifying values are

- Values must be specified as strings (enclosed in apostrophes or quotation marks).
- Blanks are significant characters in values of string variables.
- If the input or output string is shorter than the variable, the string is right-padded with blanks to the length of the variable being recoded.
- If the input or output string is longer than the variable, it is an error.

Assuming S1 is a two-character string variable, the command

```
RECODE S1 ('M'='MM') (ELSE='X')
```

is not an error, but SPSS-X is actually looking for "M " (M followed by a blank) in the first specification and will change all other values to "X " in the second.

Keywords THRU, HIGHEST, and LOWEST are not available for specifying value ranges for string variables, and keywords MISSING and SYSMIS are not valid.

8.7
INTO, ELSE, and COPY Keywords

You can use keyword INTO to specify a target variable for recoding a string variable, but the variable named must already exist. Usually, you use the STRING command (Section 8.2) to declare a new variable, as in:

```
STRING STATE1 (A2)
RECODE STATE ('IO'='IA') (ELSE=COPY) INTO STATE1
```

In this example, keywords ELSE and COPY are used to copy the other state codes over unchanged. Variables STATE and STATE1 are identical except for cases with original input value IO.

If you are recoding multiple variables with the same specifications, the number of target variables following the INTO keyword must be the same as the number of variables in the input list. All target variables must already exist, and they must all be the same length, although they needn't be the same length as the input variables.

If the original and target variables have different lengths, the criterion for input values is the length of the input variable, and the criterion for output values is the length of the target variable. Otherwise, the same rules apply:

- It is an error if the input string is longer than the input variable or if the output string is longer than the target variable.
- If the input string is shorter than the input variable, the string is right-padded with blanks to the length of the input variable.
- If the output string is shorter than the target variable, the string is right-padded with blanks to the length of the target variable.

8.8
Changing Variable Types

You cannot change a variable from string to numeric or from numeric to string by recoding it into itself. You must use keyword INTO to specify a new variable name (see Section 8.7). The command

```
RECODE SEX ('M'=1) ('F'=2) INTO NSEX
```

recodes variable SEX from a string variable into a numeric variable called NSEX. Any value other than M or F becomes system-missing.

To recode a variable into a string variable, use the STRING command to declare it before naming it with the INTO keyword, as in:

```
STRING SMONTH (A3)
RECODE MONTH(1='JAN')(2='FEB')(3='MAR')(4='APR')(5='MAY')(6='JUN')
       (7='JUL')(8='AUG')(9='SEP')(10='OCT')(11='NOV')(12='DEC')
       INTO SMONTH
```

Since string variables are initialized to blanks, if a case has a value other than 1 through 12 for variable MONTH, it will be blank for variable SMONTH. If you specify an output string longer than the length of the output string variable, it is an error. If you specify a string shorter than the string, it is right-padded with blanks.

8.9
CONVERT Keyword

Use keyword CONVERT to recode the string representation of numbers to their numeric representation. The command

```
RECODE #JOB (CONVERT) ('-'=11) ('&'=12) INTO JOB
```

first recodes all numbers in string variable #JOB (read as a scratch variable) to numbers for target variable JOB and then specifically recodes the minus sign (the "eleven" punch) to 11 and the ampersand (or "twelve" punch in EBCDIC) to 12. Keyword CONVERT is specified first as an efficiency measure to recode cases with numbers immediately.

In the above example, blanks will be recoded to the system-missing value, even if you specifically recode blanks into a value. To recode blanks into a value other than system missing, you must place a recode specification for blanks *before* the keyword CONVERT, as in:

```
RECODE #JOB (' '=-99) (CONVERT) ('-'=11) ('&'=12) INTO JOB
```

The result will be the same as in the above example, except that blanks will be changed to −99 in JOB.

- SPSS-X converts numbers as if the variable were being reread using the F format described in Chapter 5.
- If SPSS-X encounters a field that cannot be converted, it scans the remaining recode specifications.
- If a code cannot be converted and there is no specific recode specification for that code, the target variable will be system missing.

8.10
COMPUTE COMMAND: STRING VARIABLES

Chapter 7 explains how to use the COMPUTE command with numeric variables. You can also use COMPUTE to compute string variables. With strings, the expression on the right of the equals sign in the COMPUTE command must return a string, and the target variable named on the left of the equals sign must be an existing variable. Thus, the target variables must have been defined on a DATA LIST command or exist on the system file as a string variable. Alternatively, you can use the STRING command to declare a new string variable (Section 8.2), as in:

```
STRING  S(A2)
COMPUTE S='NA'
```

The STRING command declares string variable S with a length of two characters and COMPUTE sets S to the string NA for every case.

The length of a string variable is established when it is declared and cannot be altered by data transformations. To change the length, declare a new variable with the desired length.

8.11
STRING EXPRESSIONS

Expressions involving string variables can be used in COMPUTE commands and in logical expressions on commands such as IF, DO IF, LOOP IF, SELECT IF, and so forth. For example, the simplest string expression is a string, as in

```
SELECT IF STATE EQ 'IL'
```

where string variable STATE is compared to the expression IL.

A string expression can be a constant composed of a single string enclosed in apostrophes (Section 8.3), a special string function (Section 8.14), or another string variable.

8.12
Constructing String Expressions

An expression must return a string if the target variable is string. A string expression can simply be a constant, as in:

```
STRING   DRUG (A)
COMPUTE DRUG='A'
```

In this example, the one-character variable DRUG is assigned a value of A for every case, perhaps to initialize it in preparation for further transformations. String expressions can also be complex string operations using the special string functions documented in Section 8.14, as in

```
STRING   SSNUMBER (A11)
COMPUTE  SSNUMBER = CONCAT(SS1,'-',SS2,'-',SS3)
```

where variable SSNUMBER is constructed by concatenating (joining) the three portions of a social security number and separating these portions with hyphens. Presumably, variables SS1, SS2, and SS3 exist and are strings of length 3, 2, and 4, respectively.

The string returned by a string expression does not have to be the same length as the target variable, but no warning messages are issued if the lengths are not the same. If the target variable in a COMPUTE command is shorter, the result is right-trimmed. If the target variable is longer, the result is right-padded. String functions are available for padding (LPAD, RPAD), trimming (LTRIM, RTRIM), and selecting a portion of strings (SUBSTR) so you can control the lengths yourself.

If variables SS1, SS2, and SS3 are numeric instead of string, converting them to a string with the hyphens is more difficult.

8.13
Logical Expressions

String variables, like numeric variables, can be tested in logical expressions. The rules are

- You cannot compare string variables and numeric variables.
- You can compare strings of different lengths using EQ and NE. The shorter string is right-padded with blanks to equal the length of the longer.
- You can compare the "magnitude" of strings using LT, GT, and so forth, but the success or failure of the comparison depends on the sorting sequence of the particular computer. Use with caution.

For example, to check for a particular state code, specify:

```
SELECT IF (STATE EQ 'IL')
```

If variable STATE has an A2 format, the comparison is direct. If for some reason STATE has an A4 format, the comparison is true only for cases with value "IL " for STATE since the constant "IL" is right-padded with blanks for the comparison. It will not be true for cases with value "ILL " or "ILLI." If you want to check only the first two characters, use the SUBSTR function (Section 8.14), as in:

```
SELECT IF (SUBSTR(STATE,1,2) EQ 'IL')
```

You can use the ANY and RANGE functions instead of more complicated specifications on the IF, DO IF, and other conditional commands. For example, the command

```
SELECT IF (REGION EQ 'NW' OR REGION EQ 'NE' OR REGION EQ 'SE')
```

is equivalent to the command

```
SELECT IF ANY(REGION,'NW','NE','SE')
```

8.14
String Functions

Except where otherwise noted, the target variable for each of these functions must be a string and must have already been declared. Multiple arguments in a list must be separated by commas.

ANY(arg,arg list) *Return 1 if the value of the first argument matches one of the arguments in the list, otherwise return 0.* ANY(LNAME,'MARTIN','JONES','EVANS') returns 1 for people whose last names are MARTIN, JONES, or EVANS. The target variable must be numeric. ANY is also available for strings.

CONCAT(arg list) *Concatenate the arguments into a string.* String variables and strings can be intermixed as arguments. CONCAT(A,'**') creates the string ABCD** for a case with value ABCD for string variable A.

INDEX(a_1,a_2,a_3) *Return a number that indicates the position of the first occurrence of a_2 in a_1.* a_1 is the string which will be searched. a_2 is the string variable or string which will be used in the search. If a_3 is not specified, all of a_2 will be used. INDEX(ALPHA6,'**') returns 2 for a case with value X***** for variable ALPHA6. The optional a_3 is the number of characters used to divide a_2 into separate strings to be used for searching (see Section 8.20). a_3 must be a positive integer and must divide evenly into the length of a_2. The target variable must be numeric.

LAG(arg,n) *Return the value of the variable* n *cases before.* LAG(LNAME,2) returns the value of LNAME for the case that is two cases before the current one. *N* must be a positive integer constant. LAG for strings is also available.

LENGTH(arg) *Return the length of the specified string.* The argument can be a string variable or value. LENGTH(LNAME) returns 6 if LNAME has an A6 format. The target variable must be numeric.

LOWER(arg) *Convert upper case to lower case.* All other characters remain unchanged. The argument can be a string variable or value. LOWER(NAME1) returns charles if the value of NAME1 is CHARLES.

LPAD(a_1,a_2,a_3) *Pad left.* Pad the beginning of a_1 up to the length specified by a_2 using the optional single-character a_3 as the pad character. a_2 must be a positive integer from 1 to 255. The default pad character is a blank. LPAD(ALPHA1,10) adds four leading blanks to the target variable if ALPHA1 has an A6 format. a_3 can be any character enclosed in apostrophes or any expression that yields a single character.

LTRIM(a_1,a_2) *Trim left.* Trim the character a_2 from the beginning of a_1. LTRIM(ALPHA3,'0') trims leading zeros from variable ALPHA3. a_2 can be any character enclosed in apostrophes or any expression that yields a single character. The default a_2 is a blank.

MAX(arg list) *Return the maximum value across the argument list.* MAX(LNAME,FNAME) selects the name that comes last in the sort order (see Section 8.18), the first or the last name. MAX for strings is also available.

MIN(arg list) *Return the minimum value across the argument list.* MIN(LNAME,FNAME) selects the name that comes first in the sort order (see Section 8.18), the first or the last name. MIN for strings is also available.

NUMBER(arg,format) *Convert the argument into a number using the format.* The argument is string and the format is a numeric format, but the result is numeric. The string is essentially reread using the format and returned as a number. NUMBER(XALPHA,F3.1) converts the string XALPHA to a number using the F3.1 format.

RANGE(arg,arg list)   *Return 1 if the first argument is in any of the inclusive range(s), otherwise return 0.* The first argument is usually a variable, and the list normally includes pairs of values. String arguments to RANGE should be the same length. RANGE(LNAME,'A','MZZZZZZ') returns 1 for last names which begin with a letter between "A" and "M." The target variable must be numeric. RANGE for strings is also available.

RINDEX(a_1,a_2,a_3)   *Return a number indicating the position of the last occurrence of a_2 in a_1.* a_1 is the string which will be searched. a_2 is the string variable or string which will be used in the search. If a_3 is not specified, all of a_2 will be used. RINDEX(NAME,'N') returns 14 for a case with value STEVEN RACHMAN for variable NAME. The optional a_3 is the number of characters used to divide a_2 into separate strings to be used for searching (see Section 8.20). a_3 must be a positive integer and must divide evenly into the length of a_2. The target variable must be numeric.

RPAD(a_1,a_2,a_3)   *Pad right.* Pad the end of a_1 up to the length of a_2 using the optional single-character a_3 as the pad character. a_2 must be a positive integer from 1 to 255. The default pad character is a blank. RPAD(ALPHA2,8,'*') adds two trailing asterisks to the target variable if ALPHA2 has an A6 format. a_3 can be any character enclosed in apostrophes.

RTRIM(a_1,a_2)   *Trim right.* Trim the character a_2 from the end of a_1. RTRIM(ALPHA4,'*') trims trailing asterisks from variable AL-PHA4. a_2 can be any character enclosed in apostrophes or any expression that yields a single character. The default a_2 is a blank.

STRING(arg,format)   *Convert the argument into a string using the format.* The argument is numeric and the format is a numeric format, but the result is a string. The number is converted from internal representation according to the format and then stored as a string. STRING (INCOME,DOLLAR8) converts the numeric variable INCOME to the dollar format and returns it as a string value. If the result is shorter than the string variable, it is right-justified. If the result is longer than the string variable, it is right-trimmed.

SUBSTR(a_1,a_2,a_3)   *Substring.* Return the substring of a_1 beginning with the position in a_2 and optionally for a length of a_3. a_2 can be a positive integer from 1 to the length of a_1. a_3, when added to a_2, should not exceed the length of a_1. If a_3 is not specified, the substring is returned up to the end of a_1. SUBSTR(ALPHA6,3) returns the last four characters of ALPHA6 if ALPHA6 has an A6 format. SUBSTR (ALPHA6,3,1) returns the third character of ALPHA6. You can also use the SUBSTR function on the left side of the equals sign to replace a substring in a_1 with a string to the right of the equals sign. a_2 is a positive number that specifies the position of the first character to be replaced and a_3 indicates the length of the replacement string (see Section 8.16). If you omit a_3 and the string on the right side of the equals sign is shorter than the length of the substring, the result will be right-padded with blanks to the length of the substring. If you omit a_3, and the string on the right side of the equals sign is longer than the length of the substring, the result will be truncated to the length of the substring.

UPCASE(arg)   *Convert lower case to upper case.* The argument can be a string variable or a string. UPCASE(NAME1) returns CHARLES if the value of NAME1 is Charles.

8.15
Padding and Trimming Strings

Padding and trimming operations can easily be nullified if you don't keep track of the length of the target variable and what SPSS-X is doing. For example, if you use RTRIM to trim trailing blanks from a string and name a target variable the same length as the original string, SPSS-X left-justifies the trimmed string and right-pads it back with the same number of blanks just trimmed. To right-justify a string in a target variable, you can nest functions to instruct SPSS-X to execute the operations simultaneously, as in

```
COMPUTE NAME=LPAD(RTRIM(NAME),24)
```

where all trailing blanks are trimmed from the right of string variable NAME and then the result is left-padded with blanks out to a length of 24. Thus, the string

```
"Georgianne Baker          "
```

becomes

```
"          Georgianne Baker"
```

Variable NAME must have a length of 24 since you cannot alter the length of string variables once they have been declared.

If the length argument (which can be an expression) is illegal or missing, the result is a null string. If the pad or trim is the only operation, the string is then padded to its entire length with blanks. If the operation is nested, the null string is passed to the next nested level.

8.16
Indexing and Substrings

The INDEX, RINDEX, and SUBSTR functions can be used to pull out substrings of varying position and length. For example, if you have recorded people's first name followed by a blank and the last name in a field of length 24, you may want to separate the last name, perhaps for sorting, as in:

```
STRING    LAST (A18)
COMPUTE LAST=SUBSTR(NAME,INDEX(NAME,' ')+1)
```

The expression INDEX(NAME,' ') returns the position of the first blank in variable NAME. For Georgianne Baker, that position is 11. Then, when you add 1 and use it as the second argument to the SUBSTR function, SPSS-X returns everything following the first blank up to the end of the string, which should be the last name. In other words, the command says, "Make LAST equal to the substring of NAME starting with the first character after the first blank through the rest of the string." For Georgianne Baker, it says to take the name starting at the 12th character, which is the *B* in Baker.

If the result of the SUBSTR function is shorter than LAST, the string is left-justified and padded with blanks. Thus, for Georgianne Baker, the value of LAST is:

```
"Baker             "
```

If the result of the operation is longer than LAST, it is right-trimmed to 18 characters.

You can do the same type of operation using RINDEX. RINDEX returns the position of the first occurrence of the specified string moving from right to left. If in the above example middle names were included between the first and last names, the following COMPUTE statement would be used to extract the last name:

```
COMPUTE LAST=SUBSTR(NAME,RINDEX(RTRIM(NAME),' ')+1)
```

In this case the expression RINDEX(RTRIM(NAME),' ') first trims all trailing blanks from the right of NAME and returns the position of the far-right blank in NAME, which is between the middle and last names. Then, when you add 1 and use it as the second argument to the SUBSTR function, SPSS-X returns everything following the last blank up to the end of the trimmed string, which should be the last name. The result is the same as described in the previous example.

You can also use the SUBSTR function to replace a substring on the left side of the equals sign with a string to the right of the equals sign. For example, if you have stored phone numbers in variable PHONE in the form

```
"301 333-8811"
```

you can use the following command to insert a slash between the area code and exchange portions of the phone number:

```
COMPUTE SUBSTR(PHONE,4,1)='/'
```

If a numeric argument to SUBSTR is illegal or missing, the result is a null string. If SUBSTR is the only operation, the string is then padded to its entire length with blanks. If the operation is nested, the null string is passed to the next nested level. If a numeric argument to INDEX or RINDEX is illegal or missing, the result is system-missing.

8.17
NUMBER Function

The NUMBER function is similar to the CONVERT keyword for the RECODE command (see Section 8.9). For example, the command

```
RECODE  STRING1 (CONVERT) INTO X
```

yields the same results for new numeric variable X as the command

```
COMPUTE X=NUMBER(STRING1,F8)
```

In both examples, values that cannot be converted become system-missing.

8.18
Comparing Strings

When you compare two strings in SPSS-X, the case in which they are entered is honored. The LOWER and UPCASE functions are useful for making comparisons of strings regardless of case. For, example, to compare NAME1 with NAME2 if values for NAME1 are in lower case and NAME2 are in upper case, specify:

```
IF (UPCASE(NAME1) EQ NAME2) COMPARE=1
```

The variable COMPARE is set to 1 for all cases where upper-cased NAME1 is equivalent to upper-cased NAME2.

For certain functions (for example, MIN, MAX, ANY, and RANGE), the outcome will be affected by case, whether the string includes numbers or special characters, and the character set used at your installation. For example, with EBCDIC character sets, lower case precedes upper case in the sort order. Therefore, if NAME1 is in lower case and NAME2 is in upper case, MIN(NAME1,NAME2) will invariably return NAME1 as the minimum. The reverse is true with the ASCII character set, which sorts upper before lower case. See Chapter 15 for further discussion of how string variables are sorted.

8.19
LAG Function

One consideration for using the LAG function is that SPSS-X sets undefined lags for string variables to blanks. Thus, if LAG(LNAME,2) is specified, blanks will be returned for the first two cases in the file.

Another consideration is how LAG performs when used with commands that select cases (for example, SELECT IF and SAMPLE). LAG counts cases *after* case selection, even if SELECT IF follows LAG. Therefore, you may need to place a procedure or EXECUTE between LAG and the commands that select cases to achieve the desired result. The second argument of a LAG function must be a positive integer constant.

8.20
Third Argument of INDEX or RINDEX

The third argument of INDEX or RINDEX is helpful when you need to look for more than one character or set of characters in a string. For example, the expression INDEX('MISSISSIPPI','LLSS',2) looks for either LL or SS. If the number of characters in the second string is not evenly divisible by the third argument, an error results. If INDEX finds more than one string, it returns the smallest index value. For example, the function INDEX ('MISSISSIPPI','PPSS',2) returns 3, not 9. On the other hand, if RINDEX finds more than one string, it returns the largest index value. For example, the function RINDEX('JIMMY FERRIS','MMRR',2) returns 9, not 3.

The most useful application of the third argument of INDEX or RINDEX is to look for a single special character among several. For example, if two variables have been recorded in two columns separated by either a blank, a comma, or a semicolon, you could read the two variables as a single string and then separate the string into two numeric variables, as in:

```
DATA LIST  NOTABLE/#VAR (A5)

COMPUTE #DELIM=INDEX(#VAR,' ,;',1)
COMPUTE VAR1=NUMBER(SUBSTR(#VAR,1,#DELIM-1),F2)
COMPUTE VAR2=NUMBER(SUBSTR(#VAR,#DELIM+1),F2)

PRINT /VAR1 VAR2 (F2,1X,F2)
BEGIN DATA
1 3
1,4
3,4
4,3
6;3
10 2
11;4
4 10
END DATA
```

#VAR is a scratch variable (Chapter 7) used to read the first five columns of data as a single alphanumeric variable, and #DELIM is a scratch variable that stores the position of the delimiter character. In the COMPUTE command for variable VAR1, SUBSTR(#VAR,1,#DELIM−1) says, "Return the substring of #VAR starting in the first position and ending one position before a blank, comma, or semicolon." Then SUBSTR(#VAR,#DELIM+1) returns the substring starting one position after any of these characters to the end of the string. The two substrings are converted to numbers using the NUMBER function (see Section 8.17). The PRINT display output is shown in Figure 8.20.

Figure 8.20   PRINT output for the new variables

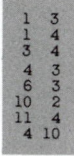

```
 1   3
 1   4
 3   4
 4   3
 6   3
10   2
11   4
 4  10
```

As you develop these transformations, it might be helpful to make several trial runs against a small subset of your data to make certain SPSS-X is generating the desired results. It is also helpful to use the PRINT command to display intermediate results (see Chapter 10).

ANNOTATED EXAMPLE FOR STRING TRANSFORMATIONS

This job corrects known recording errors in the Postal Service's two-letter state abbreviations. The SPSS-X commands are

```
GET FILE=TESTDATA
PRINT /STATE
RECODE STATE ('IO'='IA') ('KA'='KS') ('VE'='VT') ('  '='XX')
MISSING VALUES STATE ('XX')
PRINT /STATE (1X,A2)
SAVE OUTFILE=NEWDATA
```

- The GET command names the input system file (see Chapter 6).
- The first PRINT command provides a check on each case by printing the value of STATE as the cases are being read, before any transformations are performed (see Chapter 10).
- The RECODE command first corrects the abbreviation codes for Iowa, Kansas, and Vermont. Then any codes that are entirely blank are recoded to XX.
- The MISSING VALUES command declares the string XX missing for variable STATE (see Chapter 5).
- The second PRINT command provides a check on the RECODE command by printing the value for STATE after the RECODE command is executed. The recoded value is indented one column to distinguish the results from the first PRINT command.
- The SAVE command saves the active file as the SPSS-X system file NEWDATA (see Chapter 6).

The output from the two PRINT commands prints the value of STATE for each case twice as they are being read, once for each command. The output for the first eight cases is

```
IL
 IL
AZ
 AZ
IO
 IA
NJ
 NJ
IL
 IL

 XX
NY
 NY
UT
 UT
```

The first four lines show the values for the first two cases which are correct and are within the valid range and are therefore copied unchanged. The fifth and sixth lines show that the code for Iowa is changed from IO to IA. The blank code for the sixth case is changed to XX.

Syntax

DO IF, ELSE IF, ELSE, END IF

```
DO IF [(]logical expression[)]
  transformations
[ELSE IF [(]logical expression[)]]
  transformations
[ELSE IF [(]logical expression[)]]

  . . .

[ELSE]
  transformations
END IF
```

IF

```
IF [(]logical expression[)] target variable=expression
```

The following relational operators can be used in logical expressions:

Symbol	Definition	Symbol	Definition
EQ or =	Equal to	NE or a= or <>	Not equal to
LT or <	Less than	LE or <=	Less than or equal to
GT or >	Greater than	GE or >=	Greater than or equal to

The following logical operators can be used in logical expressions:

Symbol	Definition
AND or &	Both relations must be true
OR or |	Either relation can be true
NOT or a	Reverses the outcome of an expression

Contents

9.1   IF COMMAND

9.2   DO IF −END IF STRUCTURE
9.3   DO IF and END IF Commands
9.4   DO IF −END IF Compared with IF
9.5   ELSE Command
9.6   ELSE Compared with IF
9.7   ELSE IF Command
9.8   Multiple ELSE IF Commands
9.9   Missing Values and the DO IF Structure
9.10   Nested DO IF Structures
9.11   Summary

9.12   LOGICAL EXPRESSIONS
9.13   Logical Variables
9.14   Relational Operators
9.15   AND and OR Logical Operators
9.16   NOT Logical Operator
9.17   Order of Evaluation
9.18   Missing Values
9.19   Missing Values and Logical Operators

9

Chapter 9   Conditional Transformations

In certain situations, you may want to construct or alter variables one way for one subset of cases and other ways for other subsets. You can instruct SPSS-X to execute data transformations conditionally via the IF command or the DO IF—END IF structure. The IF command, which executes a single COMPUTE-like assignment based on the truth of a single logical expression, is documented in Section 9.1. The DO IF—END IF structure, which conditionally executes one or more data definitions and transformations based on one or more logical expressions, is documented in Sections 9.2 through 9.11. The use of logical expressions is described in Sections 9.12 through 9.19.

9.1
IF COMMAND

The IF command makes COMPUTE-like transformations contingent upon logical conditions found in the data. The IF command is followed by a *logical expression*, described Sections 9.12 through 9.19, and an *assignment expression,* which has the same syntax described for the COMPUTE command in Chapter 7. For example, the command

```
IF (X EQ 0) Y=1
```

assigns the value 1 to variable Y only for cases with value 0 for variable X. The logical expression is X EQ 0 and the assignment expression is Y=1. The parentheses around the logical expression are optional.

The assignment expression follows all of the rules and possibilities described for the COMPUTE command (see Chapter 7). The assignment is executed only if the logical expression is true. The command

```
IF (DEPT82 EQ 2) BONUS = .14*SALARY82
```

creates variable BONUS (an employee's salary bonus) as 0.14 times salary in 1982 only for cases with value 2 for variable DEPT82 (those in Department 2 as of 1982).

If a logical expression is false or indeterminate because of missing values, the assignment is not made and the target variable remains unchanged from its previous value. If the target variable is being created as a new variable, it retains the initialized system-missing value. If the target variable already exists, it is simply unchanged.

9.2
DO IF—END IF
STRUCTURE

You can execute one or more conditional transformations on the same subset of cases via the the DO IF—END IF structure. The DO IF—END IF structure must begin with the DO IF command and end with the END IF command. For example, the commands

```
DO IF (X EQ 1)
RECODE Y(1=2)(2=1)
RECODE Z(3=4)(4=3)
END IF
```

155

tell SPSS-X to execute the RECODE commands only for cases with value 1 for variable X.

The structure can be further defined with the ELSE (Section 9.5) and ELSE IF commands (Sections 9.7 and 9.8). You can also nest DO IF—END IF structures as long as you include an END IF command for each DO IF command (Section 9.10).

The DO IF—END IF structure transforms data on subsets of cases defined by the logical expressions on the DO IF and ELSE IF commands. You might compare this structure with the LOOP—END LOOP structure described in Chapter 14, which performs repeated transformations on the same case. Like the LOOP—END LOOP structure, the DO IF—END IF structure can encompass transformations such as the DATA LIST, END CASE, END FILE, and REREAD commands, which define complex file structures. See Chapter 14 for examples.

9.3
DO IF and END IF Commands

The DO IF and END IF commands by themselves (without ELSE IF or ELSE) are most frequently used to execute RECODE, COUNT, and multiple COMPUTE transformations conditionally. For example, to reverse the coding order of variable RACE for those individuals hired before 1980, specify:

```
DO IF (YRHIRED LT 80)
RECODE RACE(1=5)(2=4)(4=2)(5=1)
END IF
```

The logical expression on the DO IF command specifies individuals hired before 1980. Thus, the RACE variable for individuals hired in 1980 or later is not recoded.

The DO IF command marks the beginning of the control structure and END IF marks the end. The specification on the DO IF command is a logical expression of the form described in Sections 9.12 through 9.19. The parentheses enclosing the logical expression are optional.

- Commands like MISSING VALUES, VARIABLE LABELS, VALUE LABELS, and so forth specified within a DO IF structure take effect as if they were specified for the entire variable.
- Commands SELECT IF, SAMPLE, and WEIGHT specified within a DO IF structure take effect unconditionally.
- Commands like SET, DISPLAY, SHOW, and so forth specified within a DO IF structure are invoked once when they are encountered in the command file.

9.4
DO IF—END IF Compared with IF

You can express a single conditional COMPUTE command more efficiently with a simple IF command. For example, the commands

```
DO IF (X EQ 0)
COMPUTE Y=1
END IF
```

are equivalent to

```
IF (X EQ 0) Y=1
```

However, you should generally replace multiple IF commands testing the same condition with a DO IF structure in order to reduce processing time. For instance, suppose the day and month of birth on an employee file are recorded in reversed order for individuals hired before 1980. To exchange the values of MOBIRTH and DABIRTH depending on year hired, you might specify

```
IF (YRHIRED LT 80) #HOLD=MOBIRTH
IF (YRHIRED LT 80) MOBIRTH=DABIRTH
IF (YRHIRED LT 80) DABIRTH=#HOLD
```

where scratch variable #HOLD holds the value of month of birth for the exchange. When these IF commands are executed, SPSS-X evaluates logical expressions three times for every case before the complete set of transformations can be accomplished. However, in the commands

```
DO IF (YRHIRED LT 80)
COMPUTE #HOLD=MOBIRTH
COMPUTE MOBIRTH=DABIRTH
COMPUTE DABIRTH=#HOLD
END IF
```

if the logical expression is false, control is passed to the first command after the END IF. Thus, processing of cases with values 80 or greater for YRHIRED is greatly reduced.

<table>
<tr><td>**9.5**
ELSE Command</td><td>Use the ELSE command to execute one or more transformations when the logical expression on the DO IF command is not true, as in:</td></tr>
</table>

```
DO IF (X EQ 0)
COMPUTE Y=1
ELSE
COMPUTE Y=2
END IF
```

In this structure, Y is set to 1 for all cases with value 0 for X, and Y is set to 2 for cases with any other valid value for X. The value of Y is not set to anything by this structure if X is missing (see Section 9.9).

If the logical expression on the DO IF command is true, SPSS-X executes the transformation command or commands immediately following the DO IF up to the next ELSE (or ELSE IF; see Section 9.7). Then control passes to the command following the END IF command. If the result of the logical expression is false, then control passes to ELSE (or ELSE IF).

<table>
<tr><td>**9.6**
ELSE Compared with IF</td><td>With the IF command, SPSS-X executes each transformation for each case regardless of what has been executed before and what will be executed. For example, one IF command can change the value of a variable that was set by a previous IF command. If you specify</td></tr>
</table>

```
IF (DEPT82 EQ 1) BONUS = .12*SALARY82
IF (DEPT82 EQ 2) BONUS = .14*SALARY82
IF (DEPT82 EQ 3) BONUS = .1*SALARY82
IF (DEPT82 EQ 4) BONUS = .08*SALARY82
IF (YRHIRED GT 80) BONUS = 0
```

the BONUS value is set for each case according to the department and then reset for cases with a value greater than 80 for YRHIRED. To prevent these unnecessary operations, you can use the ELSE command, as in:

```
DO IF (YRHIRED GT 80)
COMPUTE          BONUS = 0
ELSE
IF (DEPT82 EQ 1) BONUS = .12*SALARY82
IF (DEPT82 EQ 2) BONUS = .14*SALARY82
IF (DEPT82 EQ 3) BONUS = .1*SALARY82
IF (DEPT82 EQ 4) BONUS = .08*SALARY82
END IF
```

In this structure, if an individual was hired since 1980, the bonus is set to 0 and control passes out of the structure. Otherwise, control passes to the series of IF commands following ELSE.

ANNOTATED EXAMPLE FOR CONDITIONAL TRANSFORMATIONS

The task developed in Sections 9.2 through 9.9 is to compute a company bonus based on an individual's salary, department, and tenure with the company. In addition, this example writes out the computed information onto a file, perhaps for input to a check-writing program, and produces a breakdown analysis of mean bonus by department. The SPSS-X commands are

```
GET FILE=HUBEMPL

DO IF (YRHIRED GT 80)
+ COMPUTE            BONUS = 0
ELSE IF ((DEPT82 EQ 1 OR DEPT82 EQ 2) AND YRHIRED LE 75)
+ COMPUTE            BONUS = .16*SALARY82
ELSE
+ IF (DEPT82 EQ 1) BONUS = .12*SALARY82
+ IF (DEPT82 EQ 2) BONUS = .14*SALARY82
+ IF (DEPT82 EQ 3) BONUS = .1*SALARY82
+ IF (DEPT82 EQ 4) BONUS = .08*SALARY82
END IF

SORT CASES EMPLOYID
FORMAT BONUS(DOLLAR9.2)

DO IF (BONUS NE 0)
WRITE OUTFILE=BONUS /EMPLOYID NAME BONUS
END IF

MEANS BONUS BY DEPT82
```

- The GET command reads the SPSS-X system file containing the personnel data (see Chapter 6).
- The first control structure defined by the DO IF and END IF commands assigns no bonus to individuals hired after 1980 (YRHIRED GT 80) (see Section 9.3). Plus signs are used in column 1 so commands can be indented to improve readability (see Chapter 2).
- The ELSE IF command assigns a special bonus to individuals from Departments 1 and 2 who have been with the company since at least 1975 (see Section 9.7).
- The series of IF commands following the ELSE command set the bonuses for everyone else (see Sections 9.1, 9.5, and 9.6).
- The SORT CASES command sorts the cases according to employee identification number (see Chapter 15). FORMAT provides a printing and writing format for the bonus variable (see Chapter 10).
- The second DO IF—END IF structure limits the WRITE command to those who are eligible for the bonus (see Chapter 10). Figure A shows a listing of the first 20 cases from the file created by the WRITE command.
- The MEANS command asks for a breakdown of the bonus variable by department (see Chapter 34). The output is shown in Figure B.

A Data from the WRITE command

```
1801CONNIE E. JANNSEN         $1,560.00
2211MARY CHAFEE                 $804.00
2690HOLLY C. BRADSHAW         $3,016.00
2821JACKIE HAMILTON            $887.20
3061KARIN HEGEL              $2,275.00
3091CROLE M. BROWN           $1,310.40
3171VERA D. LOGGINS          $1,446.64
3261LUCINDA JACKSON            $984.00
3390ANITA PULASKI            $1,232.80
4381REUBEN D. CROSS          $3,078.40
4981TANI PATEL               $2,215.20
5402PETER D. GAMINO          $4,133.92
5601LUCIA DELMONICO          $2,838.50
6061ROSE C. LANDA            $1,513.80
6151BESSIE D. GRAVES         $1,789.28
6161SUZANNE RADFORD          $2,412.80
6241SEAN D. MCGILLICUDDY     $1,366.40
6251DIANNE HARRINGTON          $816.20
6351BRIAN M. CURTIS          $1,638.56
6402JOANNA C. DRESSLER       $3,120.00
   .
   .
   .
```

B The MEANS results

```
- - - - - - - - - - - - - - -   D E S C R I P T I O N   O F   S U B P O P U L A T I O N S   - - - - - - - - - - - - - - - -

CRITERION VARIABLE     BONUS
     BROKEN DOWN BY    DEPT82     DEPARTMENT CODE IN 1982

- - - - - - - - - - - - - - - - - - - - - - - - - - - - - - - - - - - - - - - - - - - - - - - - - - - - - - - - - - -

VARIABLE          VALUE  LABEL                    MEAN      STD DEV    CASES

FOR ENTIRE POPULATION                          1875.1557  1102.8420    145

DEPT82              1    ADMIN                  2097.8600  1026.4519     34
DEPT82              2    PROJECT DIRECTORS      2551.9136  1536.0324     22
DEPT82              3    CHICAGO OPERATIONS     1733.8267  1011.3238     60
DEPT82              4    ST LOUIS OPERATIONS    1393.0566   620.5001     29

   TOTAL CASES =      275
MISSING CASES =      130 OR  47.3 PCT.
```

9.7
ELSE IF Command

You can further control the flow of execution by using the ELSE IF command. The structure

```
DO IF (X EQ 0)
COMPUTE Y=1
ELSE IF (X LE 9)
COMPUTE Y=9
ELSE
COMPUTE Y=2
END IF
```

sets Y equal to 1 when X equals 0; Y equal to 9 when X is less than 9 but not equal to 0; and Y to 2 for all valid values of X greater than 9. The value of Y is not set at all by this structure if X is missing (see Section 9.9).

Once a case satisfies a logical expression on a DO IF, ELSE IF, or ELSE command, the transformations are made up to the next structure command and control is passed out of the structure. For cases in the example above with value 0 for X, Y is set to 1 and control passes out of the structure. Such cases are not reevaluated by the ELSE IF command, even though 0 is less than 9. However, when the logical expression is false, control passes to the ELSE IF command, where the second COMPUTE is executed only for cases with X less than or equal to 9. Then control passes out of the structure. If the logical expressions on both the DO IF and ELSE IF commands are false, control passes to ELSE, where the third COMPUTE is executed.

For example, to increase the bonuses for individuals in certain departments who have been with the organization for a number of years, specify:

```
DO IF (YRHIRED GT 80)
COMPUTE                BONUS = 0
ELSE IF ((DEPT82 EQ 1 OR DEPT82 EQ 2) AND YRHIRED LE 75)
COMPUTE                BONUS = .16*SALARY82
ELSE
IF (DEPT82 EQ 1) BONUS = .12*SALARY82
IF (DEPT82 EQ 2) BONUS = .14*SALARY82
IF (DEPT82 EQ 3) BONUS = .1*SALARY82
IF (DEPT82 EQ 4) BONUS = .08*SALARY82
END IF
```

If an individual was hired after 1980, the bonus is set to 0 and control passes out of the structure. Otherwise, control passes to ELSE IF, where the second COMPUTE is executed only for those individuals in Departments 1 or 2 who were hired before 1976. Control then passes out of the structure. For all other individuals, control passes to ELSE, where the IF commands are evaluated.

Thus, a number of cases are processed without having to pass through the series of four IF commands following ELSE. Also, a value is set for new variable BONUS only once per case.

9.8
Multiple ELSE IF Commands

In the previous example, cases that do not meet the conditions on the DO IF or ELSE IF commands are evaluated by all four IF commands following ELSE. To pass control out of the structure as soon as the expression on an IF command is true, substitute ELSE IF and COMPUTE commands for each IF command, as in:

```
DO IF (YRHIRED GT 80)
COMPUTE                BONUS = 0
ELSE IF ((DEPT82 EQ 1 OR DEPT82 EQ 2) AND YRHIRED LE 75)
COMPUTE                BONUS = .16*SALARY82
ELSE IF (DEPT82 EQ 3)
COMPUTE                BONUS = .1*SALARY82
ELSE IF (DEPT82 EQ 1)
COMPUTE                BONUS = .12*SALARY82
ELSE IF (DEPT82 EQ 4)
COMPUTE                BONUS = .08*SALARY82
ELSE IF (DEPT82 EQ 2)
COMPUTE                BONUS = .14*SALARY82
END IF
```

As soon as SPSS-X processes a case with value 3 for DEPT82 (and hired before 1980), control passes out of the structure. The other three ELSE commands are not evaluated for that case.

Note that the order of departments differs from previous examples. If Department 3 were the largest, Department 1 the next largest, and so forth, control will pass out of the structure more quickly for many cases. If you have a large number of cases or if your SPSS-X job will be executed frequently, these efficiency considerations can be important.

9.9
Missing Values and the DO IF Structure

If SPSS-X encounters a case with a missing value for the logical expression on the DO IF command, control passes to the first command after END IF. If a case has a missing value for the conditional expression on any subsequent ELSE IF command, control also passes to the first command after END IF. In the structure

```
DO IF (X EQ 0)
COMPUTE Y=1
ELSE IF (Z EQ 0)
COMPUTE Y=2
ELSE
COMPUTE Y=3
END IF
```

the entire structure is skipped (control passes to END IF) for any case with a missing value for X. Even if 0 is a missing value for variable X, Y is never 1. For cases with valid values other than 0 for X, the ELSE IF is evaluated and, if Z is missing, the rest of the structure is skipped.

In the example in Section 9.7, the DO IF—END IF structure is skipped for any case with a missing value for YRHIRED. In the absence of any other transformations, BONUS will remain at the initialized system-missing value. Likewise, if YRHIRED is less than or equal to 80 and DEPT82 is missing, control passes out of the structure and BONUS is system-missing.

9.10
Nested DO IF Structures

To perform transformations involving logical tests on two variables, you can use nested DO IF—END IF structures. For example, to create a single variable that indicates both the sex and minority status of an individual, you might specify:

```
DO IF (RACE EQ 5)            /*DO WHITES
.   DO IF (SEX EQ 2)          /*WHITE FEMALE
.   COMPUTE SEXRACE=3         /*WHITE FEMALE
.   ELSE                      /*WHITE MALE
.   COMPUTE SEXRACE=1         /*WHITE MALE
.   END IF                    /*WHITES DONE
ELSE IF (SEX EQ 2)           /*NONWHITE FEMALE
COMPUTE SEXRACE=4            /*NONWHITE FEMALE
ELSE                         /*NONWHITE MALE
COMPUTE SEXRACE=2            /*NONWHITE MALE
END IF                       /*NONWHITES DONE
```

An optional period (or plus or minus sign) in column one allows you to indent commands to emphasize the nested nature of the structures (see Chapter 2).

9.11
Summary

The DO IF—END IF case control structure, which involves the DO IF, ELSE IF, ELSE, and END IF commands, can be used according to the following rules:

- The DO IF command marks the beginning of the structure and the END IF command marks its end.
- The ELSE IF command is optional and can be repeated as many times as desired within the structure.
- The ELSE command is optional. It can be used only once and must follow any ELSE IF commands.

- The END IF command must follow any ELSE IF or ELSE commands.
- Logical expressions are mandatory on the DO IF and ELSE IF commands. Do not use logical expressions on the ELSE and END IF commands.

The flow of control operates according to the following rules:

- Missing values returned by the logical expression on the DO IF command or on any ELSE IF commands causes control to pass outside of the structure at that point.
- If the logical expression on the DO IF command is true, the commands immediately following the DO IF are executed up to the next ELSE IF or ELSE in the structure. Control then passes to the first statement following the END IF for that structure.
- If the expression on the DO IF command is false, control passes to the first ELSE IF where the logical expression is evaluated. If this expression is true, commands following the ELSE IF are executed up to the next ELSE IF or ELSE command, and control passes to the first statement following the END IF for that structure.
- If the expressions on the DO IF and the first ELSE IF commands are both false, control passes to the next ELSE IF, where that logical expression is evaluated. If none of the expressions are true on any of the ELSE IF commands, commands following the ELSE command are executed and control falls out of the structure.
- If none of the expressions on the DO IF command or the ELSE IF commands are true and there is no ELSE command, then a case falls through the entire structure with no change.

DO IF—END IF control structures can be nested to any level permitted by available memory. Also, DO IF—END IF control structures can be nested within LOOP—END LOOP control structures or LOOP structures within DO IF structures (see Chapter 14).

9.12 LOGICAL EXPRESSIONS

SPSS-X evaluates a logical expression as true or false, or as missing if it is indeterminate. A logical expression returns 1 if the expression is true, 0 if it is false, or system-missing if it is missing. Thus, logical expressions can be any expressions that yield this three-valued logic. The logical expression

```
SELECT IF (X GE 5)
```

is true if X is 5 or greater, false if X is less than 5, and missing if X is missing. The parentheses around the logical expression are optional.

Logical expressions can be simple logical variables or relations, or they can be complex logical tests involving variables, constants, functions, relational operators, logical operators, and nested parentheses to control the order of evaluation.

Logical expressions can appear on the IF, SELECT IF, DO IF, ELSE IF, LOOP, END LOOP, and COMPUTE commands.

IF. A logical expression on an IF command that is true causes the assignment expression to be executed. A logical expression that returns missing has the same effect as one that is false: the value of the target variable is not altered. The command

```
IF (X EQ 5) Y=3
```

sets Y to 3 when the expression is true, but does not set or alter the value of Y when the expression is false or when X is missing. (See Section 9.1.)

DO IF—END IF Structure. If a logical expression on a DO IF command is true, SPSS-X executes the commands immediately following the DO IF up to the next ELSE IF, ELSE, or END IF. A false logical expression on a DO IF command causes SPSS-X to look for the next ELSE IF or ELSE command. A logical expression on a DO IF command that returns missing causes the entire structure to be skipped. The structure

```
DO IF (X GE 5)
RECODE Z (1=2)
ELSE
RECODE Z (0=2)
END IF
```

recodes value 1 for variable Z to 2 when the logical expression is true. When the logical expression is false, value 0 for variable Z is recoded to 2. For cases with missing values for X, variable Z is not changed. (See Sections 9.2 through 9.11.)

SELECT IF. If the logical expression on a SELECT IF command is true, the case is selected. A logical expression that returns missing has the same effect as one that is false: the case is not selected. The command

```
SELECT IF (X GE 5)
```

selects cases when the expression is true and rejects cases when it is false or when X is missing. (See Chapter 11.)

The LOOP—END LOOP Structure. If an IF logical expression on a LOOP command is true, looping begins (or continues). An IF logical expression on a LOOP command that returns missing has the same effect as one that is false: the structure is skipped. On the END LOOP command, if an IF logical expression is *false,* control returns to the LOOP command for that structure and looping continues. If it is true, looping stops and the structure is terminated. An IF command that returns missing has the same effect as one that is true: the structure is terminated. The structure

```
LOOP IF (X GE 5)
COMPUTE Y=Y+1
END LOOP IF (Y GE 10)
```

begins looping and adding 1 to Y only when the expression X GE 5 is true. Looping never begins if X is missing. Looping terminates either when the expression Y GE 10 is true or when Y is missing. (See Chapter 14.)

COMPUTE. A logical expression on a COMPUTE command returns 1 if the expression is true, 0 if it is false, and missing if it is missing. In the command

```
COMPUTE Y=(X GE 5)
```

Y equals 1 if the logical expression is true, 0 if it is false, and missing if X is missing. (See Chapter 7.)

9.13
Logical Variables

The simplest logical expression is a logical variable. A logical variable is any variable that takes on values 1, 0, or system-missing. For example, the expression

```
DO IF PROMO81
```

is true if PROMO81 is 1 (employee promoted in 1981), false if it is 0 (employee not promoted in 1981), or missing if the value of PROMO81 is missing. Any other value for PROMO81 causes a warning message, and SPSS-X evaluates the expression for that case as 0 and false.

Logical variables cannot be strings.

9.14
Relational Operators

A relation is a logical expression that compares two values using a *relational operator*. In the command

```
IF (X EQ 0) Y=1
```

variable X and 0 are expressions that yield the values to be compared by the EQ relational operator. Relational operators are

EQ   *Equal to.* Returns true if the expression on the left is exactly equal to the expression on the right.

NE   *Not equal to.* Returns true if the expression on the left does not equal the expression on the right.

LT   *Less than.* Returns true if the expression on the left is less than the expression on the right.

LE   *Less than or equal to.* Returns true if the expression on the left is less than or equal to the expression on the right.

GT   *Greater than.* Returns true if the expression on the left is greater than the expression on the right.

GE   *Greater than or equal to.* Returns true if the expression on the left is greater than or equal to the expression on the right.

You can specify either the relational operators above or their symbolic equivalents: = (EQ), −= or <> (NE), < (LT), > (GT), <= (LE), and >= (GE).

The expressions in a relation can be variables, constants, or more complicated arithmetic expressions, as in

```
IF (W+Y GT X+Z) NEWX=1
```

which assigns the value 1 to NEWX if the sum of W and Y is greater than the sum of X and Z. Or you can use one or more of the functions described for the COMPUTE command, as in

```
IF MEAN(Ql TO Q5) LE 5 INDEX=1
```

which assigns the value 1 to INDEX if the mean of variables Q1 through Q5 is less than or equal to 5.

You must use blanks (not commas) to separate the relational operator from the expressions, but you are free to introduce more blanks and parentheses in order to make the command more readable, as in:

```
IF (MEAN (Ql TO Q5) LE 5) INDEX=1
```

You cannot compare the result of the logical functions SYSMIS, MISSING, ANY, or RANGE to a number within an expression. For example,

```
DO IF SYSMIS(X)
```

is a correct statement and SPSS-X will execute the transformations following the DO IF statement when variable X is system missing. The command

```
DO IF SYSMIS(X) EQ 1
```

will be flagged as an error.

9.15
AND and OR Logical Operators

You can join two or more relations logically using the *logical operators* AND and OR, as in:

```
IF (X EQ 0 AND Z LT 2) Y=2
```

This command assigns value 2 to variable Y only for cases with X equal to zero and Z less than two. The AND logical operator means that both relations must be true. Logical operators combine relations according to the following rules:

AND   *Both relations must be true.*
OR   *Either relation can be true.*

You can use only one logical operator to combine two relations; AND/OR is invalid. However, you can combine many relations into a complex logical expression. Regardless of the number of relations and logical operators used to build a logical expression, the result is either true, false, or indeterminate because of missing values (see Section 9.18). The command

```
IF (DEPT82 EQ 2 AND YRHIRED LE 75) BONUS = .16*SALARY82
```

assigns the value .16*SALARY82 to BONUS only for those cases where the value of DEPT 82 is 2 and YRHIRED is less than or equal to 75. Similarly,

```
IF (DEPT82 EQ 3 OR YRHIRED GT 80) BONUS = .08*SALARY82
```

assigns the value .08*SALARY82 to BONUS for cases with either 3 for variable DEPT82 or a value greater than 80 for variable YRHIRED.

Operators or expressions cannot be implied. For example, you cannot specify X EQ 1 OR 2 in place of X EQ 1 OR X EQ 2. You can use the ANY and RANGE functions to simplify complex expressions (see Chapters 7 and 8), as in:

```
SELECT IF ANY(X,1,2)
```

The ampersand (&) symbol is a valid substitute for the logical operator AND. The | (vertical bar) or ¦ (broken vertical bar) symbols are valid substitutes for the logical operator OR.

9.16
NOT Logical Operator

The NOT logical operator reverses the true/false outcome of the expression that immediately follows. For example,

```
IF NOT(X EQ 0) Y=3
```

assigns value 3 to Y for all cases with values other than 0 for variable X.

The NOT operator affects only the expression that immediately follows, unless more than one expression is enclosed in parentheses. The expression

```
SELECT IF (NOT X EQ 0 AND Z LT 2)
```

is true for cases where X *is not* 0 and Z *is* less than 2. The expression

```
SELECT IF NOT(X EQ 0 OR Z EQ 2)
```

is equivalent to

```
SELECT IF (X NE 0 AND Z NE 2)
```

because the only way the first logical expression can be true is for the parenthetical expression to be false.

The ¬ symbol is a valid substitute for the NOT keyword.

9.17
Order of Evaluation

When arithmetic operators and functions are used in a logical expression, the order of operations is exactly the same as for the COMPUTE command as described in Chapter 7. Functions and arithmetic operations are evaluated first, then relational operators, then NOT, then AND, and then OR. In the expression NOT VARB/5 GT 10, the value of VARB is divided by 5, the result is compared to 10, and the logical result is reversed by NOT.

When more than one logical operator is used, AND is evaluated before OR. For example, in the command

```
IF (DEPT82 EQ 2 AND YRHIRED GT 80 OR PROMO81 EQ 0)
   BONUS = .08*SALARY82
```

the logical expression is true if a case has either value 2 for DEPT82 and a value greater than 80 for YRHIRED, or if the case has 0 for PROMO81 (the individual was not promoted in 1981) regardless of department or year hired. In other words, the command above is equivalent to the following command using parentheses to clarify the order of evaluation:

```
IF ((DEPT82 EQ 2 AND YRHIRED GT 80) OR PROMO81 EQ 0)
   BONUS = .08*SALARY82
```

You can change the order of evaluation with parentheses. For example, in the command

```
IF (DEPT82 EQ 2 AND (YRHIRED GT 80 OR PROMO81 EQ 0))
   BONUS = .08*SALARY82
```

the expression is true only for cases with value 2 for DEPT82 that also have either a value greater than 80 for YRHIRED or 0 for PROMO81.

9.18
Missing Values

If the logic of an expression is indeterminate because of missing values, the expression returns missing and the command is not executed. In a simple relation, the logic is indeterminate if the expression on either side of the relational operator is missing. For example, in the command

```
IF (X GT Z) Y=Y**2
```

SPSS-X cannot tell whether one variable is greater or less than the other for any case where X and/or Z are missing. In this example, SPSS-X would not evaluate the assignment specification and the case's value for variable Y would not change. Since Y already exists in this example (i.e., it also appears to the right of the equals sign), it retains its previous value. If Y were being defined by this IF command, it would remain at the initialized system-missing value.

9.19
Missing Values and Logical Operators

When two or more relations are joined by logical operators AND and OR, SPSS-X always returns missing if all of the relations in the expression are missing. However, if any one of the relations can be determined, SPSS-X tries to return true or false according to the logical outcomes shown in Table 9.19. The asterisk flags expressions where SPSS-X can evaluate the outcome with incomplete information.

Table 9.19   Logical outcome

Expression	Outcome	Expression	Outcome
true AND true	= true	true OR true	= true
true AND false	= false	true OR false	= true
false AND false	= false	false OR false	= false
true AND missing	= missing	true OR missing	= true*
missing AND missing	= missing	missing OR missing	= missing
false AND missing	= false*	false OR missing	= missing

When two relations are joined with the AND operator, the logical expression can never be true if one of the relations is indeterminate. The expression can, however, be false. Consider the DO IF command in the following structure:

```
DO IF (X EQ 2 AND Y LE 7)
COMPUTE Z=1
ELSE IF (X EQ 0)
COMPUTE Z=2
ELSE
COMPUTE Z=0
END IF
```

For any case with a missing value for both X and Y, the logical expression on the DO IF command is missing and the entire structure is skipped, leaving Z unaltered. Likewise, if X equals 2 but Y is missing, or if Y is less than or equal to 7 but X is missing, the logical expression is missing and the structure is skipped because AND means that both relations must be true.

However, if one of the relations is false and the other is missing, the logical expression is evaluated as false and only the DO IF command is skipped. For example, if X is 0 and Y is missing, SPSS-X does not set Z equal to 1 but evaluates the logical expression on the ELSE IF command. Because X is 0, SPSS-X sets Z equal to 2.

When two relations are joined with the OR operator, the logical expression can never be false if one relation returns missing. In the command

```
IF (DEPT82 EQ 3 OR YRHIRED GT 80) BONUS = .08*SALARY82
```

the logical expression is true if DEPT82 equals 3 or YRHIRED is greater than 80, even if one of these two relations evaluates as missing. In other words, SPSS-X can determine the truth of the expression if it finds a case of someone hired in 1981—even if the case has missing information for department—since the logical expression specifies that only one relation needs to be true.

Syntax

FORMATS

```
FORMATS varlist(format) [varlist...]
```

PRINT

```
PRINT [OUTFILE=file] [RECORDS={1}] [{NOTABLE}]
                              {n}   {TABLE  }
  /{1    } varlist [{col location [(format)]}] [varlist...]
   {rec #}          {(format list)          }
                    {*                       }

  [/{2    }...]
    {rec #}
```

PRINT EJECT

```
PRINT EJECT [OUTFILE=file] [RECORDS={1}] [{NOTABLE }]
                                    {n}   {TABLE   }
  /{1    } varlist [{col location [(format)]}] [varlist...]
   {rec #}          {(format list)          }
                    {*                       }

  [/{2    }...]
    {rec #}
```

PRINT FORMATS

```
PRINT FORMATS varlist(format) [varlist...]
```

PRINT SPACE

```
PRINT SPACE [OUTFILE=file] [numeric expression]
```

WRITE

```
WRITE [OUTFILE=file] [RECORDS={1}] [{NOTABLE}]
                              {n}   {TABLE  }
  /{1    } varlist [{col location [(format)]}] [varlist...]
   {rec #}          {(format list)          }
                    {*                       }

  [/{2    }...]
    {rec #}
```

WRITE FORMATS

```
WRITE FORMATS varlist (format) [varlist...]
```

Contents

10.1   EXAMINING PRINT AND WRITE FORMATS

10.2   PRINT COMMAND

10.3   Variable Specifications

10.4   Specifying Formats

10.5   Printing Multiple Lines per Case

10.6   Using Strings

10.7   Creating Column Headings

10.8   Outfile, Record, and Table Specifications

10.9   Features and Limitations

10.10 PRINT EJECT COMMAND

10.11 PRINT SPACE COMMAND

10.12   Specifying the Number of Blank Lines

10.13 WRITE COMMAND

10.14   Variable Specifications

10.15   File, Record, and Table Specifications

10.16 PRINT AND WRITE FORMAT COMMANDS

10.17   PRINT FORMATS Command

10.18   WRITE FORMATS Command

10.19   FORMATS Command

10

Chapter 10   Printing and Writing Cases

There are occasions when you want to see the actual contents of cases. You may want to see that a DATA LIST command is defining your data as you intend, or you may want to verify results of transformations or examine cases you suspect have coding errors. The PRINT command allows you to display the values of variables for each case in your data file (see Sections 10.2 through 10.9). The LIST command allows you do to the same thing (see Chapter 31).

You may also want to write the values of variables to an output file; for example, to send data to another organization or to use another program to analyze the data. The WRITE command writes values to an output file in nearly any format you wish (see Sections 10.13 through 10.15).

Both PRINT and WRITE are not executed until the data are read. PRINT and WRITE are transformations, executed in order of occurrence as cases are created. You can use any variables—standard, scratch, or system—in PRINT or WRITE commands. SPSS-X stores your specifications and executes them as data are read by a procedure.

By default, the PRINT command uses the associated print formats stored in the dictionary for each variable and WRITE uses the associated write formats. You can specify formats on the PRINT or WRITE commands, or you can change the dictionary formats. You may want to change formats for other reasons, such as to display values in DOLLAR format or to produce dates using one of the DATE formats for procedure REPORT. Three commands allow you to change dictionary formats—PRINT FORMATS, WRITE FORMATS, and FORMATS—described in Sections 10.16 through 10.19.

10.1
EXAMINING PRINT AND WRITE FORMATS

The DISPLAY command with keyword VARIABLES is an economical way to examine current dictionary formats. For example,

```
GET FILE=HUB/KEEP MOHIRED, YRHIRED, DEPT82 SALARY82 NAME
DISPLAY VARIABLES
```

retrieves the dictionary for the specified SPSS-X system file The data are *not* passed; only the dictionary is read. The results of the DISPLAY command are shown in Figure 10.1. See Chapter 6 for more information on the DISPLAY command.

Figure 10.1   DISPLAY VARIABLES output

```
           LIST OF VARIABLES ON THE ACTIVE FILE

NAME        POS  PRINT FMT    WRITE FMT    MISSING VALUES

MOHIRED      1   F2           F2           0
YRHIRED      2   F2           F2           0
DEPT82       3   F1           F1           0
SALARY82     4   F5           F5           0
NAME         5   A24          A24
```

10.2
PRINT COMMAND

The PRINT command is designed to be simple enough for a quick check on reading and transforming data and yet flexible enough for formatting simple reports. As a quick check on data values, the simplest PRINT command begins with a slash followed by the variable list to be printed, as in

```
PRINT   / MOHIRED YRHIRED DEPT82 SALARY82 NAME
FREQUENCIES VARIABLES=DEPT82
```

Values are printed on the display file as the data are read but appear before the output of the first procedure (see Figure 10.2). PRINT uses the dictionary print formats assigned when the variables are defined on a DATA LIST command, on a PRINT FORMATS, or FORMATS command, or assigned when the variables are created with transformation commands. PRINT is executed as the data are being read, once for each case constructed from your data file. Values for each case are displayed with a blank space between each value. Figure 10.2 shows 10 cases of display from the above PRINT command.

Figure 10.2   PRINT results using defaults

```
8 69 3 15600  CONNIE E. JANNSEN
3 80 4 10050  MARY CHAFEE
2 74 1 18850  HOLLY C. BRADSHAW
7 79 2 16250  KARIN HEGEL
6 79 1 10920  CROLE M. BROWN
4 80 4 18083  VERA D. LOGGINS
9 79 3  9840  LUCINDA JACKSON
4 79 3 12328  ANITA PULASKI
1 74 1 19240  REUBEN D. CROSS
7 79 1 18460  TANI PATEL
```

If PRINT is not followed by a procedure command that causes the data to be read, SPSS-X does nothing. To execute the PRINT command anyway, use the EXECUTE command documented in Chapter 3. See the LIST procedure described in Chapter 31 for an alternative.

Because PRINT is a transformation, the results of a PRINT command can be intermixed with casewise procedure output. Procedures that produce individual case listings (REPORT and LIST) should not be used immediately after PRINT. Rather, you should use an intervening EXECUTE command.

10.3
Variable Specifications

Specify the variable names following a slash. The first slash begins definition of the first (and possibly only) line per case of your PRINT output (see Section 10.5). Variables named must already exist, but they can be numeric, string, scratch, temporary, or system variables. You can use the TO convention for naming consecutive variables, as in:

```
PRINT / MOHIRED YRHIRED DEPT82 SALARY79 TO SALARY82 NAME
```

You can use the keyword ALL to print the values of every variable in the active file, as in:

```
PRINT /ALL
```

If you specify more variables than can be printed in 132 columns or within the width you specify using the WIDTH subcommand of SET (Chapter 4), the line will be wrapped starting in the second column of the next line. (The first column of the listing file is reserved for carriage control.) You can override the default dictionary formats by specifying formats in your print command. You can expect lines to wrap whenever you exceed the page widths (see Section 10.5 for an alternative).

10.4
Specifying Formats

You can specify formats for some or all of the *numeric* variables you want printed. For a string variable, a specified format must have a width that is equivalent to that of the dictionary format. Use an asterisk to distinguish those variables that you want printed using dictionary formats from those variables for which you have provided format specifications. Section 10.16 lists all the formats that can be used on the PRINT command. A format specification following a list of variables without formats applies to all variables in the list. There must be one format for each variable in the list, as in

```
PRINT / MOHIRED YRHIRED DEPT82 *
        SALARY79 TO SALARY82 (4(DOLLAR8,1X))
        NAME
EXECUTE
```

When you specify a format, the automatic blank following the variable or variables affected is suppressed. If you want a blank between variables, you must specify it in the format, as shown in the above example. Use a literal, an extra column, or X or T format elements (see Chapter 5) to insert blanks between variables for which you specify formats on the PRINT command.

The asterisk is a special format that tells SPSS-X to use the dictionary format. The automatic blank following the variable is preserved for variables specified with an asterisk format. An asterisk following a variable list with no formats applies to all variables in the list. For example, in the command

```
PRINT  / MOHIRED YRHIRED DEPT82 * SALARY82 (DOLLAR8,1X) NAME *
EXECUTE
```

the asterisk following the first three variables tells SPSS-X to print them using their dictionary print formats, each separated by a single blank. SALARY82 is printed using the DOLLAR format, followed by a blank specified with the 1X format. DOLLAR8 allows the printing of values up to $999,999. Variable NAME is a string variable with a dictionary print format of 24 characters. The asterisk following variable NAME is optional since the default would be to use the dictionary format. See Figure 10.4 for 10 cases of the display from this command.

- Format specifications can be either column-style or FORTRAN-style.
- Printable numeric formats are F, COMMA, DOLLAR, CC, DOT, N, E, PCT, PIBHEX, RBHEX, Z and the date and time formats. Printable string formats are A and AHEX. See Section 10.16 for details.
- Format specifications are in effect only for the output of the PRINT command. They do not change the dictionary print formats.

Figure 10.4 PRINT results specifying a format

```
8 69 3  $15,600  CONNIE E. JANNSEN
3 80 4  $10,050  MARY CHAFEE
2 74 1  $18,850  HOLLY C. BRADSHAW
7 79 2  $16,250  KARIN HEGEL
6 79 1  $10,920  CROLE M. BROWN
4 80 4  $18,083  VERA D. LOGGINS
9 79 3   $9,840  LUCINDA JACKSON
4 79 3  $12,328  ANITA PULASKI
1 74 1  $19,240  REUBEN D. CROSS
7 79 1  $18,460  TANI PATEL
```

10.5
Printing Multiple Lines
per Case

You can use the PRINT command to display variables on more than one line for each case. Specifications for each line of output must begin with a slash. Optionally, an integer can follow the slash, indicating on which line the values are to be printed. For example, to display the values of an individual's department and salary in 1981 on one line, the department and salary in 1982 on the next line, the employee identification number on both lines, followed by a completely blank third line, specify:

```
PRINT  /EMPLOYID DEPT81 SALARY81
       /EMPLOYID DEPT82 SALARY82
       /
EXECUTE
```

The display output for 10 cases in this example is shown in Figure 10.5.

Figure 10.5 PRINT results with three lines per case

```
1801 3 14300
1801 3 15600

2211 4  8840
2211 4 10050

2690 1 16250
2690 1 18850

3061 2 14300
3061 2 16250

3091 1  9750
3091 1 10920

3171 4 16900
3171 4 18083

3261 3  8866
3261 3  9840

3390 3  9750
3390 3 12328

4381 1 16575
4381 1 19240

4981 3 12480
4981 1 18460
```

The command above is equivalent to the following:

```
PRINT /1 EMPLOYID DEPT81 SALARY81 /2 EMPLOYID DEPT82 SALARY82 /3
```

You also can use the RECORDS subcommand to achieve the same result (see Section 10.8).

**10.6
Using Strings**

You can include strings with your variable specifications on the PRINT command. Strings must be enclosed in apostrophes or quotation marks. In the following example, strings are used to label the values being printed and to insert a slash between the month hired (MOHIRED) and the year hired (YRHIRED) to create a composite hiring date.

```
PRINT / NAME * 'HIRED=' MOHIRED(F2) '/' YRHIRED *
         ' SALARY82=' SALARY82 (DOLLAR8)
EXECUTE
```

In this example, the F2 format is supplied for variable MOHIRED in order to suppress the blank that would follow it if the dictionary format were used. The asterisks following variables NAME and YRHIRED are actually optional since formats do not refer back across strings to other variables without formats. That is, a literal string terminates a variable list. Figure 10.6 shows the display with literal strings.

Figure 10.6 PRINT results with strings

```
CONNIE E. JANNSEN     HIRED= 8/69  SALARY82= $15,600
MARY CHAFEE           HIRED= 3/80  SALARY82= $10,050
HOLLY C. BRADSHAW     HIRED= 2/74  SALARY82= $18,850
KARIN HEGEL           HIRED= 7/79  SALARY82= $16,250
CROLE M. BROWN        HIRED= 6/79  SALARY82= $10,920
VERA D. LOGGINS       HIRED= 4/80  SALARY82= $18,083
LUCINDA JACKSON       HIRED= 9/79  SALARY82=  $9,840
ANITA PULASKI         HIRED= 4/79  SALARY82= $12,328
REUBEN D. CROSS       HIRED= 1/74  SALARY82= $19,240
TANI PATEL            HIRED= 7/79  SALARY82= $18,460
```

10.7
Creating Column Headings

You can use strings to include column headings to identify the variables that you are displaying. This can be done using the DO IF—END IF structure discussed in Chapter 9, as in

```
NUMERIC #FIRST
DO IF #FIRST EQ 0
PRINT /'    NAME ' 1 'DEPT' 25 'HIRED' 30 '    SALARY' 35
COMPUTE #FIRST=1
END IF
PRINT / NAME DEPT82 *
        MOHIRED 30-31 '/' YRHIRED *
        SALARY82 35-42(DOLLAR)
EXECUTE
```

The above PRINT commands produce the listing shown in Figure 10.7. The values are printed with column headings that identify the variables. Since PRINT is executed once for each case in your data file, you must enclose the PRINT command that specifies column headings within the DO IF—END IF structure. DO IF #FIRST EQ 0 causes the PRINT command that defines the column heads to be executed only once, as the first case is processed. END IF closes the structure.

The second PRINT command specifies the variables to be printed. It is executed once for each case in your data file. To align the column headings with the list of values, you should specify the format for the printing of the variables rather than relying on the defaults. In this example, the T format element could be used to align the variables and the column headings. For example, specifying MOHIRED (T30,F2) begins the printing of the values for the variable MOHIRED in column 30 in order to line up the composite hiring date under the title HIRED. See Section 10.4 for a discussion of format specifications on the PRINT command.

Figure 10.7   PRINT results with literal strings as column heads

```
    NAME                DEPT HIRED  SALARY
CONNIE E. JANNSEN         3   8/69 $15,600
MARY CHAFEE              4   3/80 $10,050
HOLLY C. BRADSHAW        1   2/74 $18,850
KARIN HEGEL             2   7/79 $16,250
CROLE M. BROWN          1   6/79 $10,920
VERA D. LOGGINS          4   4/80 $18,083
LUCINDA JACKSON          3   9/79  $9,840
ANITA PULASKI           3   4/79 $12,328
REUBEN D. CROSS          1   1/74 $19,240
TANI PATEL              1   7/79 $18,460
```

10.8
Outfile, Record, and Table Specifications

Three specifications are allowed on the PRINT command before the first slash.

OUTFILE Subcommand. OUTFILE specifies the target file for the output from the PRINT command. By default, the PRINT command sends the results to the display file, which is usually what you want.

The RECORDS Subcommand. RECORDS specifies the total number of lines printed per case. You can either use slashes alone (see Section 10.5) or specify a RECORDS subcommand.

TABLE Subcommand. TABLE requests a format table on the display file showing how the variable information is formatted. NOTABLE is the default.

To send output from a PRINT command to a file other than the display file with the number of lines specified and to tell SPSS-X to print a table describing the format of that file, specify:

```
PRINT OUTFILE=PRINTOUT RECORDS=2 TABLE
   /1  EMPLOYID DEPT82 SALARY82 /2  NAME
```

The OUTFILE subcommand names PRINTOUT as the file on which the values specified will be written (see Figure 10.8a). The equals signs after the OUTFILE subcommand is optional. The RECORDS subcommand indicates that each case occupies two lines. EMPLOYID, DEPT82, and SALARY82 print on the first line. The second record contains the values of the variable NAME. TABLE requests a summary table describing the PRINT specifications. The table is printed on the display file (see Figure 10.8b). The file, records, and table specifications can appear in any order and are optional. The output from the PRINT command cannot be longer than 132 characters, even if the external file is defined with a longer record length.

Figure 10.8a PRINT results to an output file

```
 1801 3 15600
CONNIE E. JANNSEN
 2211 4 10050
MARY CHAFEE
 2690 1 18850
HOLLY C. BRADSHAW
 3061 2 16250
KARIN HEGEL
 3091 1 10920
CROLE M. BROWN
 3171 4 18083
VERA D. LOGGINS
 3261 3  9840
LUCINDA JACKSON
 3390 3 12328
ANITA PULASKI
 4381 1 19240
REUBEN D. CROSS
 4981 1 18460
TANI PATEL
```

Figure 10.8b TABLE output

```
THE TABLE FOR THE ABOVE PRINT    COMMAND IS:


       VARIABLE   REC  START     END      FORMAT  WIDTH  DEC

       EMPLOYID    1     1        5        F        5     0
       DEPT82      1     7        7        F        1     0
       SALARY82    1     9       13        F        5     0
       NAME        2     1       24        A       24
```

As shown in Figure 10.8b, the table lists the variable names and the locations of the variables on the output file. REC refers to the number of the record on which the variable is located. START and END give you the first and last positions, respectively, of the variable. FORMAT, WIDTH, and DEC give you the print format type of each variable to be printed, the column width, and the number of decimal places.

10.9
Features and Limitations

• User-defined missing values are printed like any other value for a variable specified on a PRINT command.

System-missing values are represented by a period.

• Lines of output on a PRINT command cannot exceed 132 characters (if WIDTH is set to the maximum). Lines over 132 characters are continued on the next line.

10.10
PRINT EJECT COMMAND

The PRINT EJECT command prints the information requested on the command at the top of a new page of your output or display file each time it is executed. If the PRINT EJECT command is not in a DO IF—END IF structure, it is executed for each case and prints the values each time on a separate page. The syntax for PRINT EJECT is identical to the PRINT command. You can use PRINT EJECT to insert titles and column headings by using the DO IF—END IF structure (see Chapter 9). For example, to force the display output shown in Figure 10.7 to begin on a new page, specify:

```
NUMERIC #FIRST
DO IF #FIRST EQ 0
PRINT EJECT /'   NAME ' 1 'DEPT' 25 'HIRED' 30 '   SALARY' 35
COMPUTE #FIRST=1
END IF
PRINT / NAME DEPT82 *
        MOHIRED(T30,F2) '/' YRHIRED *
        SALARY82 (T35,DOLLAR8)
EXECUTE
```

In this example, the DO IF—END IF structure controls the PRINT EJECT command, allowing it to be executed only once, when the scratch variable #FIRST is equal to 0 (see Chapter 7). Suppose you want to print 50 cases per page, with the headings at the top of each page. You can use the following commands:

```
NUMERIC #LINE
DO IF MOD(#LINE,50) = 0
PRINT EJECT /'   NAME ' 1 'DEPT' 25 'HIRED' 30 '   SALARY' 35
END IF
COMPUTE #LINE=#LINE + 1
PRINT / NAME DEPT82 *
        MOHIRED 30-31 '/' YRHIRED *
        SALARY82 35-42(DOLLAR)
EXECUTE
```

These commands specify that the headings will be printed at the top of the page if the modulo (remainder; see Chapter 7) of #LINE divided by 50 equals 0. The output is essentially the same as that for the previous example except that each page has 50 cases (the default page length is 59 lines), and the headings appear at the top of each page.

10.11 PRINT SPACE COMMAND

The only function of the PRINT SPACE command is to print blank lines. PRINT SPACE with no specifications prints one blank line on the display file. The PRINT SPACE command has two optional specifications, the number of blank lines (the default is 1) and the output file. There are no variable specifications. The command

```
NUMERIC #FIRST
DO IF #FIRST EQ 0
PRINT EJECT /'   NAME ' 1 'DEPT' 25 'HIRED' 30 '   SALARY' 35
PRINT SPACE
COMPUTE #FIRST=1
END IF
PRINT / NAME DEPT82 *
        MOHIRED(T30,F2) '/' YRHIRED *
        SALARY82 (T35,DOLLAR8)
EXECUTE
```

prints a blank line following the headings as shown in Figure 10.11.

Figure 10.11   PRINT SPACE used to set off headings

```
 NAME                DEPT HIRED  SALARY

CONNIE E. JANNSEN      3    8/69 $15,600
MARY CHAFEE           4    3/80 $10,050
HOLLY C. BRADSHAW     1    2/74 $18,850
KARIN HEGEL          2    7/79 $16,250
C. M. BROWN          1    6/79 $10,920
VERA D. LOGGINS      4    4/80 $18,083
LUCINDA JACKSON      3    9/79  $9,840
ANITA PULASKI        3    4/79 $12,328
REUBEN D. CROSS      1    1/74 $19,240
TANI PATEL           1    7/79 $18,460
```

Use an OUTFILE subcommand on a PRINT SPACE command when you want to insert blank lines in the output of a PRINT or WRITE command that is directed to a file other than the display file.

10.12
Specifying the Number of Blank Lines

You can use a numeric expression with the PRINT SPACE command to specify the number of blank lines. The numeric expression can simply be an integer or it can be a more complex expression.

An example of using a complex expression with PRINT SPACE might be when you have a variable number of input records for each name and address that you want printed in a fixed number of lines for mailing labels. The goal is to know when you have printed the last line for each address, how many lines you have printed, and therefore how many blank records to print. Assuming there is already one blank line between each address on input and that you want to print eight lines per label, specify:

```
DATA LIST FILE=ADDRESS/RECORD 1-40 (A)   /*READ A RECORD
COMPUTE #LINES=#LINES+1                   /*BUMP COUNTER AND PRINT
WRITE OUTFILE=LABELS /RECORD

DO IF RECORD EQ ' '                       /*BLANK BETWEEN ADDRESSES?
+  PRINT SPACE OUTFILE=LABELS 8-#LINES    /*PRINT EXTRA BLANK #LINES
+  COMPUTE #LINES=0
END IF

EXECUTE
```

Variable #LINES is the key to this example. #LINES is intialized to 0 as a scratch variable. Then it is incremented for each record written (see Section 10.13 for the WRITE command). When SPSS-X encounters a blank line (RECORD EQ ' '), PRINT SPACE prints a number of blank lines equal to 8 minus the number already printed, and #LINES is then reset to 0. The first three mailing labels from file LABELS are shown in Figure 10.12.

Figure 10.12   PRINT SPACE with a variable number of lines

```
Dr. Theodore Thomson, Superintendent
Central Offices
Northfield School District 29
Room 101-B
525 Sunset Ridge Road
Northfield, IL  60093


Dr. Susan J. Lewis, Superintendent
Dolton School District 149
15141 Dorchester Avenue
Dolton, IL  60419



Mr. Larry A. Bannes, Superintendent
Kenilworth School District 38
Room 596
542 Abbotsford Road
Kenilworth, IL  60043
```

10.13
WRITE COMMAND

The WRITE command is basically the same as the PRINT command except that it is designed for writing data to be read by other software rather than by people. The WRITE command operates the same as the PRINT command with the following exceptions: no blank columns are inserted automatically between variables when you use dictionary formats; there are no carriage-control characters in the output file; the system-missing value is represented by blanks; and you can write lines longer than 132 characters. With WRITE, the dictionary format for a variable is the dictionary write format, not the print format. If WRITE is not followed by a procedure command that causes the data to be read, SPSS-X does nothing. To execute the WRITE command anyway, use the EXECUTE command (see Chapter 3).

10.14
Variable Specifications

You can specify formats for some or all variables you want written, you can write more than one record per case, and you can write out literal strings as well as values of variables. For example, the command

```
WRITE OUTFILE=NEWHUB TABLE
  /EMPLOYID '1' MOHIRED YRHIRED SEX AGE JOBCAT NAME
  /EMPLOYID '2' DEPT79 TO DEPT82 SALARY79 TO SALARY82 *
              HOURLY82(F5.2)
EXECUTE
```

specifies two records per input case, one literal on each record ('1' and '2'), and a format for variable HOURLY82 to override the F7.2 dictionary format.

Formats. Format specifications can be column-style, FORTRAN-style, or the special asterisk symbol that specifies the dictionary format. In addition to the print formats described in Section 10.4, write formats in IBM/OS can be IB, PIB, P, PK, RB and the time and date formats. See Section 10.16 for a complete discussion of formats. Format specifications are in effect only for the output of the WRITE command. They do not change the dictionary write formats.

Multiple Records. You can use the WRITE command to write variables on more than one record for each case. Specifications for each record of output must begin with a slash. Optionally, an integer can follow the slash, indicating on which record the values are to be written. You can specify a RECORDS subcommand to indicate the total number of records per case (see Section 10.15).

Strings. You can include literal strings with your variable specifications on the WRITE command. Strings must be enclosed in apostrophes or quotation marks. In the example above, literal strings are used to assign the constant 1 to record 1 of each case and 2 to record 2 to provide record identifiers in addition to the case identifier EMPLOYID.

If you are writing data, you should consider taking advantage of all of these features of the WRITE command, including the ability to write records longer than 132 characters. Within the same machine environment, some data types are more convenient than others. If you are going across machines, you should take into account that some data types cannot be read on another machine. Seek advice at your local installation.

If long records are less convenient than multiple records per case with shorter record lengths, you can take advantage of the ability to write out a case identifier and to insert a literal as a record identification number. The software at the other end might then be able to check for missing record numbers should something happen to the data in transit.

10.15
File, Record, and Table Specifications

Three specifications are allowed on the WRITE command before the first slash.

OUTFILE Subcommand. The OUTFILE subcommand specifies the target file for the output from the WRITE command. By default, the WRITE command sends the results to the display file, which is usually not what you want (see Chapter 5).

The RECORDS Subcommand. The RECORDS subcommand specifies the total number of records written for each case. The RECORDS specification substitutes for specifying slashes indicating blank lines.

TABLE Subcommand. TABLE requests a format table on the display file showing how the variable information is formatted. NOTABLE is the default.

To write a subset of your data to a file other than the display file and to tell SPSS-X to print a table on the display file describing the format of the external file, specify:

```
WRITE OUTFILE=NEWHUB TABLE
 /EMPLOYID '1' MOHIRED YRHIRED SEX AGE JOBCAT NAME
 /EMPLOYID '2' DEPT79 TO DEPT82 SALARY79 TO SALARY82 * HOURLY82(F5.2)
EXECUTE
```

Ten cases written to the file defined by the NEWHUB file handle are shown in Figure 10.15a.

Figure 10.15a WRITE output

```
18011 8692443CONNIE E. JANNSEN
180123333111801300014300015600 8.00
22111 3802264MARY CHAFEE
221120444    0 8190 884010050 5.15
26901 2742331HOLLY C. BRADSHAW
2690211111371514495162501B850 9.67
30611 7792322KARIN HEGEL
306120222    0101401430016250 8.33
30911 6791251CROLE M. BROWN
309120111    0 8450 975010920 5.60
31711 4802334VERA D. LOGGINS
317120444    0135201690018083 9.27
32611 9792333LUCINDA JACKSON
326120333    0 8060 8866 9840 5.05
33901 4792453ANITA PULASKI
339023333 7605 8255 975012328 6.32
43811 1741491REUBEN D. CROSS
438121111143971527516575l9240 9.87
49811 7792283TANI PATEL
498120331    0101401248018460 9.47
```

The table showing the format of this file is produced only if you specify the TABLE subcommand (see Figure 10.15b). The table lists the variable names and their location on the output file. REC indicates the number of the record on which the variable is located. START and END give you the first and last positions, respectively, of the variable. FORMAT, WIDTH, and DEC give you the format of the variable to be written, the column width, and the number of decimal places.

Figure 10.15b Format table for the data in Figure 10.15a

```
THE TABLE FOR THE ABOVE WRITE    COMMAND IS:
```

VARIABLE	REC	START	END	FORMAT	WIDTH	DEC
EMPLOYID	1	1	5	F	5	0
'1 '	1	6	6			
MOHIRED	1	7	8	F	2	0
YRHIRED	1	9	10	F	2	0
SEX	1	11	11	F	1	0
AGE	1	12	13	F	2	0
JOBCAT	1	14	14	F	1	0
NAME	1	15	38	A	24	
EMPLOYID	2	1	5	F	5	0
'2 '	2	6	6			
DEPT79	2	7	7	F	1	0
DEPT80	2	8	8	F	1	0
DEPT81	2	9	9	F	1	0
DEPT82	2	10	10	F	1	0
SALARY79	2	11	15	F	5	0
SALARY80	2	16	20	F	5	0
SALARY81	2	21	25	F	5	0
SALARY82	2	26	30	F	5	0
HOURLY82	2	31	35	F	5	2

10.16
PRINT AND WRITE FORMAT COMMANDS

SPSS-X stores your data in binary format. However, for most applications you do not want variable values that appear in the results of your SPSS-X job to be displayed or written in this form. So, for each variable defined using SPSS-X there is a print and write format stored on the dictionary associated with your data file. These formats control the form in which values are displayed (when you use a procedure or PRINT command) or written (when you use the WRITE command). These print and write formats are assigned differently depending on how the variables are defined. If you define your variables using a DATA LIST command, the dictionary print and write formats are generally assigned a printable format which includes enough space for punctuation characters (such as a decimal point, commas, or a dollar sign if requested).

If you use a GET command to access variables from a system file, the default print and write formats are those stored on the dictionary of the system file.

When you use the transformation language to create a new numeric variable, the dictionary print and write formats are both F8.2 or the format specified on the FORMAT subcommand of SET. Custom currency formats must be defined on the SET command. Default formats for string variables created using the SPSS-X transformation language are those specified on the STRING command that creates the variable.

Table 10.16 shows all the acceptable SPSS-X output formats. The first column of the table lists the FORTRAN-like specification. The column labeled PRINT indicates whether the format can be used to print values. The columns labeled Min w and Max w refer to the minimum and maximum widths allowed for

Table 10.16   Output data formats

Format type	PRINT	Min w	Max w	Max d	Result form
Numeric					
Fw, Fw.d	yes	1*	40	16	
COMMAw, COMMAw.d	yes	1*	40	16	
DOTw, DOTw.d	yes	1*	40	16	
DOLLARw, DOLLARw.d	yes	2*	40	16	
CCw, CCw.d	yes	2*	40	16	
PCTw, PCTw.d	yes	1*	40	16	
PIBHEXw	yes	2**	16**		
RBHEXw	yes	4**	16**		
Zw, Zw.d	yes	1	40	16	
IBw, IBw.d	no	1	8	16	
PIBw, PIBw.d	no	1	8	16	
Nw	yes	1	40		
Pw, Pw.d	no	1	16	16	
Ew, Ew.d	yes	6	40		
PKw, PKw.d	no	1	16	16	
RBw	no	2	8		
String					
Aw	yes	1	254		
AHEXw	yes	2**	510		
Date and time					
DATEw	yes	9	40		dd-mmm-yy
		11			dd-mmm-yyyy
ADATEw	yes	8	40		mm/dd/yy
		10			mm/dd/yyyy
JDATEw	yes	5	40		yyddd
		7			yyyyddd
QYRw	yes	6	40		q Q yy
		8			q Q yyyy
MOYRw	yes	6	40		mmm yy
		8			mmm yyyy
WKYRw	yes	8	40		ww WK yy
		10			ww WK yyyy
WKDAYw	yes	2+	40		
MONTHw	yes	3+	40		
TIMEw	yes	5++	40		hh:mm
TIMEw.d	yes	10	40	16	hh:mm:ss.s
DTIMEw	yes	8++	40		dd hh:mm
DTIMEw.d	yes	13	40	16	dd hh:mm:ss.s
DATETIMEw	yes	17++	40		dd-mmm-yyyy hh:mm
DATETIMEw.d	yes	22	40	16	dd-mmm-yyyy hh:mm:ss.s

* Add number of decimals plus 1 if number of decimals is more than 1. Total width cannot exceed 40 characters.
** Must be a multiple of 2.
\+ As the field width is expanded, the output string is expanded until the entire name of the day or month is produced.
\+\+ Add 3 to display seconds.

the format type. When specifying the width in PRINT FORMATS, WRITE FORMATS, FORMATS, or in PRINT and WRITE commands, you must allow enough positions to include any punctuation characters such as decimal points, commas, dollar signs, or date and time delimiters. The column labeled Max d in Table 10.16 indicates the maximum number of decimal places allowed.

If a data value exceeds its width specification, SPSS-X makes an attempt to produce some value nevertheless. It takes out punctuation characters, then it tries scientific notation, and only then, if there is still not enough space, it produces asterisks indicating that a value is present which cannot be printed in the assigned width.

10.17 PRINT FORMATS Command

The PRINT FORMATS command changes the print formats for the variables specified on the command. To change print formats, specify the variable name or variable list followed by the new format specification in parentheses, as in

PRINT FORMATS SALARY79 TO SALARY82 (DOLLAR8)

This specification sets a dollar print format with eight positions including the dollar sign and comma when appropriate (the number 11550 is printed as $11,550 for example).

The same command can specify different formats for different variables. Separate the specifications for each variable or variable list with a slash, as in

```
PRINT FORMATS SALARY79 TO SALARY82 (DOLLAR8)
    /HOURLY82 (DOLLAR7.2)
```

The print formats available include the F, COMMA, DOLLAR, DOT, CC, PCT, Z, and A format types. In addition, AHEX, PIBHEX, and RBHEX format types are available on IBM and DEC VAX systems. The hexadecimal format types print in hexadecimal notation. For a complete discussion of format elements see Section 10.16 and Chapter 5.

The formats specified on a PRINT FORMATS command are in effect for the duration of the SPSS-X job. The specified print formats can be saved by using a subsequent SAVE command to create a new system file in which the new print formats become the dictionary formats.

10.18 WRITE FORMATS Command

The WRITE FORMATS command operates exactly like the PRINT FORMATS command except that it changes only the write formats of variables specified on the command. There are also additional format types available for write formats that are not available as print formats. These include various packed decimal and binary formats. For further discussion of these format types see Sections 10.16 and Chapter 5.

10.19 FORMATS Command

The FORMATS command operates exactly like the PRINT FORMATS and WRITE FORMATS commands except that it redefines both the print and the write formats for the variables specified.

Syntax

N OF CASES

```
N OF CASES n
```

SAMPLE

```
SAMPLE {percentage}
       {n FROM m  }
```

SELECT IF

```
SELECT IF [(]logical expression[)]
```

WEIGHT

```
WEIGHT {BY varname}
       {OFF     }
```

Contents

11.1 SELECT IF COMMAND
11.2   Logical Expressions
11.3   Missing Values
11.4   SELECT IF and $CASENUM
11.5   Multiple SELECT IF Commands

11.6 SAMPLE COMMAND
11.7   Multiple SAMPLE Commands

11.8 N OF CASES COMMAND

11.9 WEIGHT COMMAND
11.10   Turning Off or Changing Weights
11.11   How Procedures Use Weights
11.12   Tests of Significance

11.13 PLACEMENT OF SAMPLE, SELECT IF, AND WEIGHT
11.14   Temporary Sampling, Selecting, and Weighting
11.15   SELECT IF, SAMPLE, and Other Transformations
11.16   SAMPLE and SELECT IF with DO IF

11

Chapter 11 Selecting, Sampling, and Weighting Cases

SPSS-X allows you to control the number and groups of cases used in analysis or reporting by selecting, sampling, or differentially weighting cases. Four commands are used to control cases analyzed by procedures. The SELECT IF command selects cases for analysis based upon logical criteria. The SAMPLE command randomly selects cases. With the SAMPLE command, you can specify a proportional or exact-sized sample. The N OF CASES command controls the number of cases built. The WEIGHT command assigns case weights or turns off weighting. Weighting is usually used to compensate for over- or undersampling, or to weight a sample or aggregated file up to population size.

11.1
SELECT IF
COMMAND

The SELECT IF command selects cases based on logical criteria. For example, the command

```
SELECT IF (SEX EQ 'M')
```

selects cases for which variable SEX has the value M. The syntax of the logical expression for the SELECT IF command is the same as for the IF and DO IF commands. The logical expression does not have to be enclosed in parentheses and can be as simple as a logical variable, as in:

```
SELECT IF INVAR
```

This command selects cases for which INVAR is equal to 1 (see Section 11.2). The expression can be as complex as a comparison of arithmetic expressions, as in:

```
SELECT IF ((YRMODA(81,13,0) - YRMODA(STARTYR,STARTMO,STARTDA)) LE 60)
```

This command selects cases dated for the last 60 days in 1981.

11.2
Logical Expressions

The specification field for SELECT IF is a logical expression that can be evaluated as true, false, or missing. See Chapter 9 for a complete discussion of logical expressions. Logical expressions can be any of the following:

A Logical Variable. A logical variable takes on values 0 or 1, where 0 is false and 1 is true. INVAR in Section 11.1 is a logical variable.

A Relation. A relation compares two values using a relational operator. The values can be variables, constants, or arithmetic expressions. Valid relational operators are EQ, NE, LT, LE, GT, and GE (and their symbolic equivalents). SEX EQ 'M' in the example in Section 11.1 is a relation between a variable and a constant. The example using the YRMODA function above is a relation between an arithmetic expression and a constant.

A Compound Expression. A compound expression is composed of two or more relations and/or logical variables joined by logical operators AND and OR. If the expression has more than two relations, AND has precedence over OR. For example, A AND B OR C is evaluated as (A AND B) OR C. However, parentheses can be used to control the order of the evaluation, such as in A AND (B OR C).

If a logical expression is true, the case is selected; if it is false or missing, the case is not selected. There are no programmed restrictions on the complexity of logical expressions used with SELECT IF. Strings can be used according to rules documented in Chapter 8.

11.3
Missing Values

If the logic of the expression is indeterminate because of missing values, the case is not selected. In a simple relational expression, the logic is indeterminate if the expression on either side of the relational operator is missing. For example,

```
SELECT IF (VSAT GT MSAT)
```

selects only cases for which both VSAT and MSAT are valid and VSAT is greater than MSAT. If either VSAT or MSAT is missing, the logic of the expression is indeterminate and the case is not selected.

If you use a compound expression in which relations are joined by the logical operator OR, as in

```
SELECT IF (VSAT GT 600 OR MSAT GT 600)
```

the case is selected if either relation is true, even if the other is missing.

To select cases with missing values for the variables within the expression, use the missing-value functions described in Chapter 7. For example,

```
SELECT IF MISSING(X)
```

selects all cases missing for variable X. The MISSING function returns 1, which is true, if X is missing. To include cases with values that have been declared user-missing along with other cases, use the VALUE function, as in:

```
SELECT IF VALUE(X) GT 100
```

This expression is true if X is greater than 100, even if 999 was defined as missing on the MISSING VALUES command (see Chapter 5). The VALUE function does not include the system-missing value, so the above SELECT IF does not select cases for which X is system-missing.

11.4
SELECT IF and
$CASENUM

System variable $CASENUM is the sequence number of the case in the active file (see Chapter 7). It is established for each case *after* the case has been selected. Although it is syntactically correct to use $CASENUM on SELECT IF, it does not produce the expected results. If you wish to select a set of cases based on their sequence in a file, create your own sequence variable with the transformation language prior to selecting, as in:

```
COMPUTE  #CASESEQ=#CASESEQ+1
SELECT IF (MOD(#CASESEQ,2)=0)
```

This example computes a scratch variable, #CASESEQ, containing the sequence numbers for each case, and it selects every other case beginning with the second. It is important that the sequence number variable (#CASESEQ in this example) be a scratch variable so that it is not reinitialized for every case. (See the LEAVE command described in Chapter 7 for an alternative.)

11.5
Multiple SELECT IF Commands

If you use multiple SELECT IF commands in your job, they must all be true for a case to be selected. For example, the commands

```
SELECT IF (SEX EQ 'M')
SELECT IF RANGE(AGE,18,65)
```

select all males between the ages of 18 and 65.

The SELECT IF command permanently selects cases, unless preceded by the TEMPORARY command (see Section 11.14). Unless you are careful when you use more than one SELECT IF, you might select no cases. For example, consider the following commands:

```
GET  FILE=GSS80/KEEP SEX PRESTIGE SPPRES
SELECT IF (SEX EQ 1)      /*THIS COMMAND SHOULD FOLLOW A TEMPORARY COMMAND
FREQUENCIES  VARIABLES=PRESTIGE SPPRES/FORMAT=CONDENSE/
STATISTICS=MEDIAN
SELECT IF (SEX EQ 2)
FREQUENCIES  VARIABLES=PRESTIGE SPPRES/FORMAT=CONDENSE/
STATISTICS=MEDIAN
```

The second FREQUENCIES command has no cases to analyze since a case cannot have SEX equal to both 1 and 2. As indicated by the comment, a TEMPORARY command should precede the first SELECT IF. The preferred solution in this example is to use SPLIT FILE since the FREQUENCIES specifications are the same for the two groups (see Chapter 15).

11.6
SAMPLE COMMAND

The SAMPLE command selects a random sample of cases. To select an approximate percentage of cases, specify a decimal value between 0 and 1, as in:

```
SAMPLE .25
```

This command samples approximately 25% of the cases in the active file. When you specify a proportional sample, you usually won't obtain the exact proportion specified. If you know exactly how many cases are in the active file, you can obtain an exact-sized random sample by specifying the number of cases to be sampled from the size of the active file, as in:

```
SAMPLE 60 FROM 200
```

In this example, the active file must have exactly 200 cases to obtain a random sample of 60 cases. If the file has fewer than 200 cases, proportionally fewer cases are sampled. If the file has more, the sample is drawn from only the first 200 cases. Note that any SELECT IF commands occurring prior to the SAMPLE command will affect the size of the active file.

The SAMPLE command uses the internal pseudo-random number generator that depends on a seed value established by SPSS-X. The first time a random number series is needed, SPSS-X uses the seed value established by the SEED subcommand of the SET command (see Chapter 4). Since this number defaults to a fixed integer, a SAMPLE command generates the identical sample each time a job is rerun. To generate a different sample each time, use the SET command to reset SEED to a different value for each run.

11.7
Multiple SAMPLE Commands

The SAMPLE command permanently samples the active file unless a TEMPORARY command precedes it (see Section 11.14). Thus, if you use two SAMPLE commands, the second takes a sample of the first, as in:

```
SAMPLE .50
DESCRIPTIVES  SALARY79 TO SALARY82
SAMPLE .50
DESCRIPTIVES  SALARY79 TO SALARY82
```

In this example, the first DESCRIPTIVES command computes statistics for approximately 50% of the cases, and the second DESCRIPTIVES command computes statistics for approximately 50% of those cases, or 25% of the original cases. If you sample by the *n* FROM *m* method and use the TEMPORARY command, successive samples will not be the same because the seed value changes each time a random number series is needed in a job.

11.8
N OF CASES
COMMAND

You can use the N OF CASES command to build the first *n* cases from a file. For example, if you have a data file containing 1,000 cases but want to use only the first 100 cases to test your SPSS-X commands, specify:

```
DATA LIST  FILE=DATA NOTABLE/1 NAME 1-20(A) TOTPOP 21-30 MEDSAL70
                    MEDSAL75 MEDSAL80 31-60
N OF CASES  100
```

The N OF CASES command follows the DATA LIST command. As an alternative to typing the full command, you can use the letter N as an alias.

You can also use the N OF CASES command to control the reading of cases from SPSS-X system files, as in:

```
GET  FILE=CITY
N 40
```

In addition, you can use the N OF CASES command to control the number of cases built when using a FILE TYPE—END FILE TYPE structure to define complex files (see Chapter 12). However, you should bear in mind that N OF CASES controls the building of cases, not the reading of records. For example, when you use FILE TYPE NESTED, cases are built from the lowest level record type defined. The number of cases specified on the N OF CASES command applies to the cases built, not to records read.

If you use SAMPLE or SELECT IF with N OF CASES, SPSS-X reads as many records as required to build the specified *n*. For example, assume each case is built from one record and you have specified a 50% sample. If you specify N OF CASES 100 for a file with 1,000 records, approximately 200 records are read to obtain the 100 cases. It makes no difference whether the N OF CASES precedes or follows the SAMPLE or SELECT IF. Specifying more cases than actually can be built is not an error. Instead, SPSS-X obtains as many cases as possible.

Only one N OF CASES command can be used in a job. It can be placed after a DATA LIST command, after a FILE TYPE or INPUT PROGRAM command, or after a GET command. It can also be placed following a procedure command. In this instance it behaves like a temporary SELECT IF.

11.9
WEIGHT COMMAND

The WEIGHT command is used to weight cases differentially for analysis. For example, if you have a sample from a population for which some substratum has been over- or undersampled, you can apply weights to obtain population estimates. Or you may simply want to weight the sample up to population size for reporting purposes. Or you may want to replicate an example from a table or other aggregated data as shown for the CROSSTABS procedure in Chapter 25. Name the variable following the keyword BY, as in:

```
WEIGHT BY WTFACTOR
```

This command tells SPSS-X to use the value of variable WTFACTOR to weight cases.

• Only one variable can be specified.

• The variable must be numeric and cannot be a scratch or system variable.

• Weight values need not be integers.

• Missing or negative values are treated as if they were 0.

• Weighting is permanent during a job unless TEMPORARY is in effect.

• A file saved when weighting is in effect maintains the weighting.

The variable can be a weighting factor already precoded when the data file was prepared, or it can be computed with the transformation language. For example, assume your file contains a sample of households in which rural households were oversampled by a factor of 2. To compensate for oversampling, you can weight the rural households by one half, as in:

```
COMPUTE WT=1
IF (LOCATE EQ 'RURAL') WT=.5
WEIGHT BY WT
```

Variable WT is initialized to 1 with the COMPUTE command and then changed to .5 with the IF command for cases where the value of LOCATE equals RURAL. Be sure to initialize the weighting variable to 1 when creating it with IF commands. Otherwise, cases not covered by IF commands will be missing and will have a zero weight.

11.10
Turning Off or Changing Weights

Unless you precede the WEIGHT command with a TEMPORARY command, weighting stays in effect. To turn off weighting, simply use a WEIGHT command with the keyword OFF, as in:

```
WEIGHT  OFF
```

To change the weight, use another WEIGHT command specifying a different variable. Weighting is not cumulative. That is, a second weight command changes the weight; it does not weight the weight. For example, in the following job,

```
GET FILE CITY
WEIGHT BY POP81
DESCRIPTIVES  ALL
WEIGHT BY POP82
DESCRIPTIVES  ALL
```

the first DESCRIPTIVES command computes summary statistics based on cases weighted by POP81, and the second DESCRIPTIVES command computes summary statistics based on cases weighted by POP82.

11.11
How Procedures Use Weights

SPSS-X does not physically replicate cases when weighting is in effect. Rather, it arithmetically replicates them. For example, if you use CROSSTABS, the counts in the cells are actually the sums of the case weights. CROSSTABS then rounds cell counts when printing the tables.

Most procedures can handle noninteger weights. Two, NONPAR CORR (Chapter 37) and NPAR TESTS (Chapter 38), cannot. An alternative weighting scheme is used for these procedures. In this scheme, a case is replicated as many times as the integer portion of the weight indicates. The fractional portion of the weight represents the probability that the case will be weighted to the next integer. For example, a case with a weight of 2.3 has a 30% probability of being weighted to 3. To do this, SPSS-X compares a random number generated by SPSS-X for each case with the fractional portion of the weight. If the random number is smaller than the proportion, the case is weighted up. Since, by default, the seed value used to generate the random number is the same across jobs, you can replicate a job. If you specify a different seed value using the SEED subcommand on the SET command (Chapter 4), cases are weighted differently for those procedures requiring integer weights.

ANNOTATED EXAMPLE FOR SELECT IF AND WEIGHT

This job analyzes a file of the fifty largest cities in the United States, based on data from a 1981 almanac. The job contains a frequency distribution of people by region for cities that ranked higher in population in 1980 than in 1970. The SPSS-X commands are

```
GET  FILE=ALMANAC/KEEP REGION RANK70 RANK80 POP80

SELECT IF (RANK80 GT RANK70)
WEIGHT BY POP80

FREQUENCIES  VARIABLES=REGION
```

- The GET command (Chapter 6) defines the data to SPSS-X and retains only the variables of interest.
- The SELECT IF command selects cities that ranked higher in population in 1980 than in 1970.
- The WEIGHT command weights the selected cities by their population in 1980.
- The FREQUENCIES command computes the frequency distribution for regions (see Chapter 29).

Frequencies on a selected and weighted file

```
REGION    REGION OF THE UNITED STATES


                                            VALID     CUM
   VALUE LABEL         VALUE  FREQUENCY  PERCENT  PERCENT  PERCENT
New England              1      562994     5.1      5.1      5.1
Middle Atlantic         2     1111056    10.2     10.2     15.3
East North Central      3     3854272    35.2     35.2     50.6
West North Central      4     1583876    14.5     14.5     65.0
South Atlantic          5     1849448    16.9     16.9     82.0
East South Central      6      582864     5.3      5.3     87.3
West South Central      7      557482     5.1      5.1     92.4
Pacific                 9      833134     7.6      7.6    100.0
                               -------   -----    -----
                        TOTAL 10935126   100.0    100.0

VALID CASES    1E+07   MISSING CASES    0
```

11

11.12
Tests of Significance

Tests of statistical significance usually are based on the weighted sample size. If the weighted number of cases exceeds the sample size, tests of significance are inflated; if it is smaller, they are deflated. See Moser and Kalton (1972) for further information on the use of significance tests with weighted samples.

To avoid inflated or deflated tests of significance, you may consider using a weight factor which, when summed, is the same as the unweighted number of cases. For example, you can use AGGREGATE (Chapter 18) to compute the sum of weights and number of cases. Then, match these numbers back to the file with MATCH FILES (Chapter 16), and use them to adjust the weight factor, as in:

```
COMPUTE   WTFACTOR=1
IF   (LOCATE='RURAL')  WTFACTOR=5
COMPUTE   CONSTANT=1   /* Set up a constant variable for the BREAK

AGGREGATE   OUTFILE=TEMP1/BREAK=CONSTANT/
            MEANWT=MEAN(WTFACTOR)

MATCH FILES   TABLE=TEMP1/FILE=*/BY CONSTANT

COMPUTE   WTFACTOR=WTFACTOR/MEANWT
WEIGHT BY WTFACTOR
```

This set of commands readjusts the weight so that the sum of weights equals the number of cases. AGGREGATE builds one case with two variables, MEANWT and CONSTANT. The aggregated file is written to disk (TEMP1). MATCH FILES then spreads the variables from the aggregated file back to every case in the active file, so that the adjustment to WTFACTOR can be accomplished with the COMPUTE command.

11.13
PLACEMENT OF SAMPLE, SELECT IF, AND WEIGHT

SAMPLE, SELECT IF, and WEIGHT cannot be placed in an input program defined by the FILE TYPE—END FILE TYPE structure or by the INPUT PROGRAM—END INPUT PROGRAM structure. They can be placed nearly anywhere following these commands in a transformation program. See Appendix B for a discussion of the program states in SPSS-X and the placement of commands.

11.14
Temporary Sampling, Selecting, and Weighting

As transformations, SAMPLE, SELECT IF, and WEIGHT are permanent, unless a TEMPORARY command is in effect (see Chapter 7). TEMPORARY operates exactly the same way with these commands as with COMPUTE, IF, RECODE, and so forth. If a SELECT IF, SAMPLE, or WEIGHT command follows a TEMPORARY command, it is in effect only for the next procedure. For example, in the commands

```
TEMPORARY
SAMPLE .25
CORRELATIONS  X1 TO X5
FREQUENCIES   VARIABLES=SCALE1
```

the 25% sample applies only to the CORRELATIONS command. FREQUENCIES uses all the cases in the active file. Since SAVE is a procedure, a temporary SAMPLE or SELECT IF affects the number of cases saved on the file only if the SAVE command is the first procedure following the TEMPORARY command.

11.15
SELECT IF, SAMPLE, and Other Transformations

SELECT IF and SAMPLE operate on realized cases. That is, they operate only on cases that are built from DATA LIST, GET, FILE TYPE, INPUT PROGRAM, and so forth. Use SAMPLE or SELECT IF only in a transformation program (see Chapter 14).

SAMPLE and SELECT IF are executed in the order they occur in a job. If a SAMPLE command follows a SELECT IF command, it samples only cases selected by the SELECT IF. For efficiency considerations, you should place SAMPLE and SELECT IF commands prior to other transformations. For example, if you are going to modify extensively a file that you are sampling, sample first, then modify.

11.16
SAMPLE and SELECT IF with DO IF

You can use SELECT IF and SAMPLE inside a DO IF—END IF control structure. For example, assume you want to select males with prestige scores above 50 and females with prestige scores above 45. You can use one compound SELECT IF, as in:

```
SELECT IF ((SEX EQ 'M' AND PRESTIGE GT 50) OR (SEX EQ 'F' AND
   PRESTIGE GT 45))
```

Or you can use two SELECT IF commands inside a DO IF—END IF, as in:

```
DO IF   SEX EQ 'M'
. SELECT IF PRESTIGE GT 50
ELSE IF   SEX EQ 'F'
. SELECT IF PRESTIGE GT 45
END IF
```

In this example, the optional period in column 1 indents the SELECT IF commands for readability.

Similarly, SAMPLE commands can be placed inside a DO IF—END IF structure to sample substrata differentially. Assume you have a survey of 10,000 people in which 80% of the sample is male, while the known universe is 48% male. To obtain a sample that corresponds to the known universe and that maximizes the size of the sample, 1,846 of the 8,000 (48/52*2000) males and all of females must be sampled. The DO IF is used to restrict the sampling process to the males:

```
DO IF   SEX EQ 'M'
SAMPLE 1846 FROM 8000
END IF
```

11

Syntax

FILE TYPE—END FILE TYPE

For FILE TYPE MIXED

```
FILE TYPE MIXED [FILE=file] RECORD=[varname] col loc [WILD={NOWARN}]
                                                           {WARN  }
```

For FILE TYPE GROUPED

```
FILE TYPE GROUPED [FILE=file] RECORD=[varname] col loc
 CASE=[varname] col loc [WILD={WARN  }] [DUPLICATE= {WARN  }]
                              {NOWARN}              {NOWARN}

[MISSING={WARN  }] [ORDERED={YES}]
         {NOWARN}            {NO }
```

For FILE TYPE NESTED

```
FILE TYPE NESTED [FILE=file] RECORD=[varname] col loc
 [CASE=[varname] col loc ] [WILD={NOWARN}] [DUPLICATE={NOWARN}]
                                 {WARN  }             {WARN  }
                                                      {CASE  }

[MISSING={NOWARN}]
         {WARN  }

END FILE TYPE
```

RECORD TYPE

For FILE TYPE MIXED

```
RECORD TYPE {value list} [SKIP]
            {OTHER     }
```

For FILE TYPE GROUPED

```
RECORD TYPE {value list} [SKIP] [CASE=col loc]
            {OTHER     }
 [DUPLICATE={WARN  }] [MISSING={WARN  } ]
            {NOWARN}           {NOWARN}
```

For FILE TYPE NESTED

```
RECORD TYPE {value list} [SKIP] [CASE=col loc]
            {OTHER     }
 [SPREAD={YES}] [MISSING={WARN  }]
         {NO }           {NOWARN}
```

REPEATING DATA

```
REPEATING DATA [FILE=file] /STARTS=beg pos[-end pos] /OCCURS={value  }
                                                             {varname}

 [/LENGTH={value  }] [/CONTINUED[=beg pos[-end pos]]]
          {varname}

 [/ID={col loc}=varname] [/{TABLE  }]
      {format }           {NOTABLE}
  DATA=data list specifications
```

Contents

12.1 INTRODUCTION TO COMPLEX FILES

12.2 TYPES OF FILES

12.3 FILE TYPE MIXED

12.4 FILE Subcommand

12.5 RECORD Subcommand

12.6 WILD Subcommand

12.7 RECORD TYPE Command for FILE TYPE MIXED

12.8 OTHER Keyword

12.9 SKIP Subcommand

12.10 FILE TYPE GROUPED

12.11 RECORD Subcommand

12.12 CASE Subcommand

12.13 WILD Subcommand

12.14 DUPLICATE Subcommand

12.15 MISSING Subcommand

12.16 ORDERED Subcommand

12.17 RECORD TYPE Command for FILE TYPE GROUPED

12.18 SKIP Subcommand

12.19 CASE Subcommand

12.20 DUPLICATE and MISSING Subcommands

12.21 FILE TYPE NESTED

12.22 RECORD Subcommand

12.23 CASE Subcommand

12.24 WILD Subcommand

12.25 DUPLICATE Subcommand

12.26 MISSING Subcommand

12.27 RECORD TYPE Command for FILE TYPE NESTED

12.28 Keyword OTHER and SKIP Subcommand

12.29 CASE Subcommand

12.30 SPREAD Subcommand

12.31 SUMMARY OF FILE DEFINITIONS

12.32 REPEATING DATA COMMAND

12.33 INPUT PROGRAM|END INPUT PROGRAM Structure

12.34 STARTS Subcommand

12.35 OCCURS Subcommand

12.36 DATA Subcommand

12.37 NOTABLE Subcommand

12.38 FILE Subcommand

12.39 LENGTH Subcommand

12.40 CONTINUED Subcommand

12.41 ID Subcommand

12

Chapter 12 Defining Complex File Structures

Many data files are not organized into the rectangular, case-ordered structure described in Chapter 5. You may have *mixed files*, which contain several types of records that define different types of cases; hierarchical or *nested files*, which contain several types of records with a defined relationship among the record types; or *grouped files*, which contain several records for each case with some records missing or duplicated. Or your data file may contain records with *repeated groups* of information.

SPSS-X has utilities for handling all of these complex types of files. You can define mixed or nested files using FILE TYPE, RECORD TYPE, and END FILE TYPE with the DATA LIST command. Or you can use these commands to read a grouped file with missing records or check for duplicated records. Finally, you can use the REPEATING DATA command to read repeated groups and build cases for each repeated group.

All of these commands and the files they define are documented in this chapter. In addition to the file definition commands discussed here, you can use the data transformation language discussed in Chapter 14 to define complex files.

12.1 INTRODUCTION TO COMPLEX FILES

To define complex files, use the FILE TYPE, RECORD TYPE, and DATA LIST commands. On the FILE TYPE command, specify the type of file, the location of the record type identifier, and optional information on the handling of duplicate, missing, or invalid record types. Include a RECORD TYPE and a DATA LIST command for each type of record that you want to define. At the end of the file definition commands, specify the END FILE TYPE command. The resulting file, the active file, is always a rectangular file.

For example, to define the Hubbard employee data used in Chapter 5 with a FILE TYPE command in order to check for missing or duplicate records, specify:

```
FILE TYPE GROUPED FILE=HUBDATA RECORD=#RECID 80 CASE=ID 1-5
RECORD TYPE 1
DATA LIST    /MOHIRED YRHIRED 12-15 DEPT79 TO DEPT82 SEX 16-20
RECORD TYPE 2
DATA LIST    /SALARY79 TO SALARY82 6-25 HOURLY81 HOURLY82 42-53 (2)
               PROMO81 72   AGE 54-55 RAISE82 66-70
RECORD TYPE 3
DATA LIST    /JOBCAT 6 NAME 25-48 (A)
END FILE TYPE

    Additional Data Definition Commands

SAVE      OUTFILE=HUBEMPL
```

The FILE TYPE command specifies a grouped file type (one record of each type for each case), the record identifier (#RECID) and its location (column 80 of each case), and the case identifier (ID) and its location (columns 1 through 5). All records with the value 1 on #RECID are defined by the DATA LIST command following the RECORD TYPE 1 command. Records with the value 2 on #RECID are defined by the second DATA LIST command, and records with value 3 by the third DATA LIST command. Records with other values on #RECID are reported as errors. If a case has a duplicate record type or if a record type is missing for a case, a warning message is printed. The HUBEMPL file saved as a system file is identical to the file saved in Chapter 6.

12.2
TYPES OF FILES

The file type keyword is the first specification on the FILE TYPE command. This keyword defines the structure of your data file. There are three file type keywords: MIXED, GROUPED, and NESTED. The MIXED file type defines a file in which each record type defines a case. Some information may be the same for all record types but is recorded in different locations. Other information may be recorded only for specific record types. For example, a data file maintained by a hospital may contain a record for each treatment administered to cancer patients, with different data recorded for each type of treatment.

The GROUPED file type defines a file in which cases are defined by grouping together record types with the same identification number. Each case usually has one record of each type. The HUBDATA file in Section 12.1 is a GROUPED data file.

The NESTED file type defines a file in which the record types are related to each other hierarchically. Usually, the last record type defined—the lowest level of the hierarchy—defines a case. For example, in a file containing household records and records for each person living in the household, each person record defines a case. However, information from previous record types may be *spread* to each case. For example, you might want to include a variable from the household record, such as location (CITY), on the person record. The value for CITY for a particular household can be spread to the records for each person in the household.

The specifications on the FILE TYPE and RECORD TYPE commands differ for each file type. Therefore, each file type is discussed in separate sections of this chapter. A summary of the specifications and defaults for all file types are presented in Section 12.31.

12.3
FILE TYPE MIXED

FILE TYPE MIXED builds a file in which each of the record types named on a RECORD TYPE command defines a case. You do not need to define all types of records on the file. In fact, FILE TYPE MIXED is very useful when you are reading only one type of record because SPSS-X can decide whether to execute the DATA LIST for a record by simply reading the variable that identifies the record type. Four types of information are specified on the FILE TYPE command for FILE TYPE MIXED.

MIXED Keyword. Keyword MIXED is required. It indicates that the file being defined is a mixed file type.

FILE Subcommand. FILE lists the name of the file to be defined and is required unless your data are included in the command file (see Section 12.4).

RECORD Subcommand. RECORD names the variable and specifies the column location of the record type identifier. The record type identifier must be located in the same column(s) on all records. The value on this variable determines the type of each record (see Section 12.5).

WILD Subcommand. WILD tells SPSS-X how to handle any undefined record types encountered in your file. By default, SPSS-X skips records that are not defined (see Section 12.6).

12.4
FILE Subcommand

Use the FILE subcommand to specify the name of the file you are defining. For example, the commands

```
FILE TYPE  MIXED FILE=TREATMNT RECORD=RECID 1-2
```

define a mixed file type identified by the handle TREATMNT. The record identifier is recorded in columns 1 and 2 of each record. Figure 12.4 shows the first 10 records of the hospital treatment data stored in the file TREATMNT.

Figure 12.4   Hospital treatment data file

```
21    145010 1
22    257200 2
25    235   250   2
35    167           300       3
24    125150 1
23    272075 1
21    149050 2
25    134   035   3
30    138           300       3
32    229           500       3
```

You must specify the FILE subcommand unless the data are included in the SPSS-X command file.

12.5
RECORD Subcommand

Each record type must be identified by a unique code and the value must be coded in the same location on all records. However, you do not need to sort the records according to type.

Use the RECORD subcommand to define the variable name and the column location of the record identifier. To define the record identifier as variable RECID located in columns 1 and 2 of the hospital treatment data file, specify:

```
FILE TYPE  MIXED FILE=TREATMNT RECORD=RECID 1-2
```

If you do not want to save the record type variable, you can assign a scratch variable name by using the # character as the first character of the variable name. If you do not specify a variable name on the RECORD subcommand, the record identifier is defined as the scratch variable ####RECD.

The FORTRAN-like format specifications listed in Chapter 5 cannot be used on the RECORD subcommand. You can, however, indicate that the record-type variable is a string variable by specifying the letter A in parentheses after the column location, as described in Chapter 5.

12.6
WILD Subcommand

By default, SPSS-X simply skips all record types not mentioned on the RECORD TYPE commands and does not print warning messages. To request the default explicitly, specify WILD=NOWARN. If you want SPSS-X to report as errors all records that are not mentioned, specify:

```
FILE TYPE  MIXED FILE=TREATMNT RECORD=RECID 1-2 WILD=WARN
```

A warning message and the first 80 characters of the record are printed for each record type that is not mentioned on a RECORD TYPE command. Use this specification only when you have explicitly defined all of the possible record types on the RECORD TYPE commands. You cannot use the WARN specification on the WILD subcommand if you use the keyword OTHER on your last RECORD TYPE command to indicate all other record types (see Section 12.8). Use the SKIP subcommand on the RECORD TYPE command to skip specific record types (see Section 12.9).

12.7
RECORD TYPE Command
for FILE TYPE MIXED

The RECORD TYPE command determines the processing for each type of record in the file. You must include a RECORD TYPE command for each type of record that you want to process. The first specification on the RECORD TYPE command is the value of the record type variable defined on the RECORD subcommand of the FILE TYPE command. If the record type variable is a string variable, you must enclose the value in apostrophes or quotation marks. Next, specify a DATA LIST command following the RECORD TYPE command indicating the variables that you want to read.

For example, you might want to read only the records for chemotherapy treatment where Drug A was administered. These records are coded 23 on RECID, the record identifier variable. In addition, you might be interested only in the sex and age of the patients, the dosage of Drug A, and the results. To define this record, specify the FILE TYPE, RECORD TYPE for record type 23, and the DATA LIST command specifying the variables SEX, AGE, DOSAGE, and RESULT from these records, as in:

```
FILE TYPE  MIXED FILE=TREATMNT RECORD=RECID 1-2
.      RECORD TYPE 23
.      DATA LIST    /SEX 5 AGE 6-7 DOSAGE 8-10 RESULT 12
END FILE TYPE
```

By default, SPSS-X skips all other record types on the file. The active file contains only variables SEX, AGE, DOSAGE, and RESULT for all type 23 records.

You can also specify a list of values on the RECORD TYPE command. Separate the values from each other with either a blank or a comma. All record types specified in the value list are defined using the DATA LIST command that follows. For example, to read all of the chemotherapy treatment records, record types 21 through 24, specify:

```
FILE TYPE  MIXED FILE=TREATMNT RECORD=RECID 1-2
.      RECORD TYPE 21,22,23,24
.      DATA LIST    /SEX 5 AGE 6-7 DOSAGE 8-10 RESULT 12
END FILE TYPE
```

All variables defined on the DATA LIST command must be located in the same columns on all record types listed on the RECORD TYPE command.

If the record types have different variables or if they have the same variables recorded in different locations, separate RECORD TYPE and DATA LIST commands are required for each record type. For example, if the DOSAGE and RESULT variables are recorded in different columns on record type 25, separate RECORD TYPE and DATA LIST commands are required for the type 25 records, as in:

```
FILE TYPE  MIXED FILE=TREATMNT RECORD=RECID 1-2
.      RECORD TYPE 21,22,23,24
.      DATA LIST    /SEX 5 AGE 6-7 DOSAGE 8-10 RESULT 12
.      RECORD TYPE 25
.      DATA LIST    /SEX 5 AGE 6-7 DOSAGE 10-12 RESULT 15
END FILE TYPE
```

The variable DOSAGE is read from columns 8–10 on record types 21, 22, 23, and 24 and from columns 10–12 on record type 25. RESULT is read from column 12 on type 21, 22, 23, and 24 records and from column 15 on type 25 records. The active file contains the values for all variables defined on the DATA LIST commands for record types 21 through 25. All other record types are skipped.

If the same variable is defined for more than one record type, the format type and length of the variable should be defined the same on all DATA LIST commands. SPSS-X refers to the *first* DATA LIST command that defines a variable for the print and write formats to be included in the dictionary of the

12

active file. If different variables are defined for different record types, the variables are assigned the system-missing value for those record types on which the variable is not defined.

You cannot define a record type on more than one RECORD TYPE command. If you do, SPSS-X uses the DATA LIST for the first occurrence and ignores all others.

12.8
OTHER Keyword

The keyword OTHER on the RECORD TYPE command specifies all record types that have not been mentioned on previous RECORD TYPE commands. You can specify OTHER only on the last RECORD TYPE command in the file definition. For example, if all other record types on the file are recorded in the same format, specify:

```
FILE TYPE  MIXED FILE=TREATMNT RECORD=RECID 1-2
.       RECORD TYPE 21,22,23,24
.       DATA LIST    /SEX 5 AGE 6-7 DOSAGE 8-10 RESULT 12
.       RECORD TYPE 25
.       DATA LIST    /SEX 5 AGE 6-7 DOSAGE 10-12 RESULT 15
.       RECORD TYPE OTHER
.       DATA LIST    /SEX 5 AGE 6-7 DOSAGE 18-20 RESULT 25
END FILE TYPE
```

If you specify WILD=WARN on the FILE TYPE command, you cannot specify OTHER on the RECORD TYPE command.

12.9
SKIP Subcommand

The SKIP subcommand on the RECORD TYPE command tells SPSS-X to skip all records of the type listed on the command. By default for MIXED file types, SPSS-X skips all records that are not specified on one of the RECORD TYPE commands. To specify explicitly that all other records are to be skipped, you can specify:

```
FILE TYPE  MIXED FILE=TREATMNT RECORD=RECID 1-2
.       RECORD TYPE 21,22,23,24
.       DATA LIST    /SEX 5 AGE 6-7 DOSAGE 8-10 RESULT 12
.       RECORD TYPE 25
.       DATA LIST    /SEX 5 AGE 6-7 DOSAGE 10-12 RESULT 15
.       RECORD TYPE OTHER SKIP
END FILE TYPE
```

If WILD=WARN is specified on the FILE TYPE command, you may want to skip only selected record types. Specify the values for the types that you want to skip followed by the SKIP subcommand, as in:

```
FILE TYPE  MIXED FILE=TREATMNT RECORD=RECID 1-2 WILD=WARN
.       RECORD TYPE 21,22,23,24
.       DATA LIST    /SEX 5 AGE 6-7 DOSAGE 8-10 RESULT 12
.       RECORD TYPE 25
.       DATA LIST    /SEX 5 AGE 6-7 DOSAGE 10-12 RESULT 15
.       RECORD TYPE  30,32 SKIP
END FILE TYPE
```

Record types 21 through 24 are read using the first DATA LIST command, and record type 25 using the second DATA LIST command. Record types 30 and 32 are skipped. The WILD=WARN specification on the FILE TYPE command prints a warning message for all other record types encountered.

12.10
FILE TYPE GROUPED

FILE TYPE GROUPED builds a file in which all record types are grouped together for each case identification number. All records for a single case must be together in your file. By default, SPSS-X assumes that the records are in the same sequence within each case. Use the ORDERED=NO subcommand specification if the records are not in the same sequence within each case (see Section 12.16). Case identification numbers do not have to be in sequence. For example, the following file is sorted in a correct order for a grouped file:

```
CASEID   RECID
 001      1
 001      2
 001      3
 003      1
 003      2
 003      3
 002      1
 002      2
 002      3
```

Four types of information are required on the FILE TYPE command for grouped file types.

GROUPED Keyword. GROUPED indicates that the file being described is a grouped file type.

FILE Subcommand. FILE specifies the name of the file to be defined and is required unless your data are included in the command file.

RECORD Subcommand. RECORD names the variable and specifies the column location of the record type identifier. The record type identifier must be located in the same column(s) on all records. The value on this variable determines the type of each record (see Section 12.11).

CASE Subcommand. CASE names the variable and specifies the column location of the case identifier. Each case must contain a unique value on this variable. The records for each case identification number are grouped together to define a case on the active file (see Section 12.12.).

Optionally, you can specify the following subcommands on the FILE TYPE command.

WILD Subcommand. WILD indicates the action that SPSS-X is to take if an undefined record type is encountered in your file. If this subcommand is not specified, SPSS-X issues a warning message for each undefined record encountered in your file and does not include the record in the active file (see Section 12.13).

DUPLICATE Subcommand. DUPLICATE tells SPSS-X how to handle any duplicate records of the same type encountered within a case. By default, SPSS-X issues a warning message for each duplicate record encountered and builds the case in the active file using the *last* duplicate record (see Section 12.14).

MISSING Subcommand. MISSING tells SPSS-X how to handle missing record types within a case. By default, SPSS-X issues a warning message for each missing record and builds the case in the active file assigning the system-missing value to those variables from the missing record (see Section 12.15).

ORDERED Subcommand. ORDERED specifies whether the records are in the same sequence within all cases. By default, SPSS-X assumes that the records are in the same sequence for all cases and issues a warning message if a record is out of sequence (see Section 12.16).

The example in Section 12.1 shows the file definition commands for the Hubbard employee data file. Only the required subcommands on the FILE TYPE command are included.

12.11
RECORD Subcommand

Each record type must be identified by a unique code, and the value must be coded in the same location on all records. Use the RECORD subcommand to define the variable name and the column location of the record identifier. The specification for the RECORD subcommand is the same as described in Section

12.5. For example, to define the HUBDATA as a grouped file with the record identifier variable #RECID in column 80 of each record, specify:

```
FILE TYPE GROUPED FILE=HUBDATA RECORD=#RECID 80 CASE=ID 1-5
```

If you do not specify a variable name on the RECORD subcommand, SPSS-X assigns the scratch variable name ####RECD to the record identifier variable.

The FORTRAN-like format specifications listed in Chapter 5 cannot be used on the RECORD subcommand. You can, however, indicate that the record-type variable is a string variable by specifying the letter A in parentheses after the column location, as described in Chapter 5.

12.12
CASE Subcommand

The CASE subcommand is required for FILE TYPE GROUPED. It defines the variable name and the column location of the case identifier. The value on the case identification variable defines a case in the active file. For example, to define the variable ID located in columns 1–5 as the case identifier variable, specify:

```
FILE TYPE GROUPED FILE=HUBDATA RECORD=#RECID 80 CASE=ID 1-5
```

If you do not want to save the case identification variable, you can assign a scratch variable name, using the # character as the first character of the variable name. If you specify no variable name on the CASE subcommand, the case identifier is defined as the scratch variable ####CASE.

The FORTRAN-like format specifications listed in Chapter 5 cannot be used on the CASE subcommand. You can, however, indicate that the case identification variable is a string variable by specifying the letter A in parentheses after the column location, as described in Chapter 5.

If the case identification number is not coded in the same columns on all record types, use the CASE subcommand on the RECORD TYPE command (see Section 12.19).

12.13
WILD Subcommand

The specification for the WILD subcommand can be either WARN or NOWARN. The default specification for FILE TYPE GROUPED is WARN. SPSS-X issues a warning message whenever it encounters a record that is not defined as a valid record type on the RECORD TYPE commands. The undefined record is not included in the active file. If you specify WILD=NOWARN, no warning message is issued, but the undefined record is still not included in the active file. For example, if you do not want warning messages issued for undefined records, specify:

```
FILE TYPE GROUPED FILE=HUBDATA RECORD=#RECID 80 CASE=ID 1-5
         WILD=NOWARN
```

You cannot use the keyword OTHER on your last RECORD TYPE command when the default specification WILD=WARN is in effect. To explicitly specify that all other records be skipped, use the specification WILD=NOWARN on the FILE TYPE command and the keywords OTHER and SKIP on the RECORD TYPE command. See Section 12.18 for a discussion of these subcommands.

12.14
DUPLICATE Subcommand

The specification on the DUPLICATE subcommand can be either WARN or NOWARN. The default specification for FILE TYPE GROUPED is WARN. Regardless of whether you specify WARN or NOWARN, only the *last* record from a set of duplicates is included in the active file; other records in the set are skipped. With the default DUPLICATE=WARN, SPSS-X issues a warning message whenever it encounters more than one record of the same type within a case. The first 80 characters of the last record of the duplicate set are also displayed. If you specify keyword NOWARN, no warning message is issued.

For example, suppose that Case 1 of the HUBDATA file contains two type 1 records. If you specify

```
FILE TYPE GROUPED FILE=HUBDATA RECORD=#RECID 80 CASE=ID 1-5
        DUPLICATE=NOWARN
RECORD TYPE 1
DATA LIST    /MOHIRED YRHIRED 12-15 DEPT79 TO DEPT82 SEX 16-20
RECORD TYPE 2
DATA LIST    /SALARY79 TO SALARY82 6-25 HOURLY81 HOURLY82 40-53 (2)
                PROMO81 72 AGE 54-55 RAISE82 66-70
RECORD TYPE 3
DATA LIST    /JOBCAT 6 NAME 25-48 (A)
END FILE TYPE
```

no warning message is issued, and the active file contains only the values from the second type 1 record for Case 1.

12.15
MISSING Subcommand

The specification for the MISSING subcommand can be either WARN or NOWARN. The default specification for FILE TYPE GROUPED is WARN. SPSS-X issues a warning message if a record type is missing within a case identification number and builds the case in the active file with system-missing values for the variables defined on the missing record.

If you do not expect all cases in your file to have each record type, use the keyword NOWARN. If you specify NOWARN, SPSS-X does not issue a warning message but still builds the case assigning system-missing values to the variables defined on the missing record. For example, suppose your data file contains one record for each of four tests administered to a student. However, not all students took all tests. To define this file and allow for missing records for each case, specify:

```
FILE TYPE GROUPED FILE=STUDENTS RECORD=5 CASE=STUDNUM 1-4
        MISSING=NOWARN
RECORD TYPE 1
DATA LIST /IQ 6-9
RECORD TYPE 2
DATA LIST /READING 6-10 (2)
RECORD TYPE 3
DATA LIST /MATH 6-10 (2)
RECORD TYPE 4
DATA LIST /ACT 6-8
END FILE TYPE
```

All students are included in the active file. If a student did not take a test, the record is missing in the input file, and the system-missing value is assigned to the variable for the missing test in the active file. No warning messages are issued for missing records.

12.16
ORDERED Subcommand

The specification for the ORDERED subcommand indicates whether the records are in the same order within each case identification number in your file. The default is YES, indicating that the record order within each case is the same as defined on the RECORD TYPE commands. For example, if the first RECORD TYPE command specifies record type 1, and the second RECORD TYPE command specifies record type 2, SPSS-X expects that the type 1 record is the first record for each case and the type 2 record is the second record.

If the records are not in the same order within each case identification number, specify ORDERED=NO. SPSS-X builds cases on the active file with the records in the same order as defined on the RECORD TYPE commands, regardless of the order of the records on the data file.

12.17
RECORD TYPE Command for FILE TYPE GROUPED

You must include one RECORD TYPE command for each record containing data that you want to include in your active file. The first specification on RECORD TYPE is the value of the record-type variable defined on the RECORD subcommand on the FILE TYPE command. If the record type variable is a string, you must enclose the value in apostrophes or quotation marks. You must also specify a DATA LIST command following the RECORD TYPE command for each record you want to read. For example, the SPSS-X job in Section 12.1 includes three RECORD TYPE commands. The DATA LIST command following each RECORD TYPE command describes the variables to be read from the record type specified on the previous RECORD TYPE command.

For FILE TYPE GROUPED, you can specify a single value or a list of values indicating the record type(s). You can also specify keyword OTHER on the last RECORD TYPE command to include all other record types not described on previous RECORD TYPE commands. The keyword OTHER is usually used with the SKIP subcommand (see Section 12.18).

12.18
SKIP Subcommand

Use the SKIP subcommand on the RECORD TYPE command to skip the record type specified on the command. By default, SPSS-X issues a warning message for all record types not defined on a RECORD TYPE command. For example, to read variables from type 1 records and skip all other types, specify:

```
FILE TYPE GROUPED FILE=HUBDATA RECORD=#RECID 80 CASE=ID 1-5
                                 WILD=NOWARN
RECORD TYPE 1
DATA LIST    /MOHIRED YRHIRED 12-15 DEPT79 TO DEPT82 SEX 16-20
RECORD TYPE OTHER SKIP
END FILE TYPE
```

Keyword OTHER cannot be used when the default WILD=WARN specification is in effect. To suppress the warning messages for undefined record types, use the WILD=NOWARN specification as shown above.

To skip only selected record types, specify the values for the types that you want to skip followed by the SKIP subcommand, as in:

```
FILE TYPE GROUPED FILE=HUBDATA RECORD=#RECID 80 CASE=ID 1-5
RECORD TYPE 1
DATA LIST    /MOHIRED YRHIRED 12-15 DEPT79 TO DEPT82 SEX 16-20
RECORD TYPE 2,3 SKIP
END FILE TYPE
```

Record type 1 is defined for each case, and record types 2 and 3 are skipped. Since WARN is the default specification for the WILD subcommand on the FILE TYPE command for GROUPED files, a warning message is issued for all other record types. Even though record types 2 and 3 are skipped, no warning message is printed for them because they are explicitly specified on a RECORD TYPE command.

12.19
CASE Subcommand

Sometimes, the case identification number defined with the CASE subcommand on the FILE TYPE command is not recorded in the same location on all of the record types. Use the CASE subcommand on the RECORD TYPE command to specify the location of the case identification number for a record type. This specification overrides the location specified on the FILE TYPE command for only that record type. For example, assume that the case identification number is located in columns 1–5 for record types 1 and 2 and in columns 75–79 for record type 3. To indicate this change in location for record type 3, specify:

```
FILE TYPE GROUPED FILE=HUBDATA RECORD=#RECID 80 CASE=ID 1-5
RECORD TYPE 1
DATA LIST    /MOHIRED YRHIRED 12-15 DEPT79 TO DEPT82 SEX 16-20
RECORD TYPE 2
DATA LIST    /SALARY79 TO SALARY82 6-25 HOURLY81 HOURLY82 40-53 (2)
              PROMO81 72  AGE 54-55 RAISE82 66-70
RECORD TYPE 3  CASE=75-79
DATA LIST    /JOBCAT 6 NAME 25-48 (A)
END FILE TYPE
```

The format type of the case identification variable must be the same on all records. That is, if the case identification variable is defined as a string on the FILE TYPE command, you cannot define it as a numeric variable on the RECORD TYPE command, and vice versa.

If the case identification is in the same location on all record types, the CASE subcommand on the RECORD TYPE commands is unnecessary.

12.20
DUPLICATE and MISSING Subcommands

You can also specify the DUPLICATE and MISSING subcommands on the RECORD TYPE command. The specifications for these subcommands are the same as described in Sections 12.14 and 12.15. If specified on a RECORD TYPE command, DUPLICATE and MISSING override the specification or default on the FILE TYPE command for that record type specified on the RECORD TYPE command. For example, you might want SPSS-X to skip missing records for type 3, but to report all missing records for types 1 and 2. The default specification for MISSING is WARN—report all missing record types. To override this default for only record type 3, include the MISSING subcommand on the RECORD TYPE command for record type 3, as in:

```
FILE TYPE GROUPED FILE=HUBDATA RECORD=#RECID 80 CASE=ID 1-5
RECORD TYPE 1
DATA LIST   /MOHIRED YRHIRED 12-15 DEPT79 TO DEPT82 SEX 16-20
RECORD TYPE 2
DATA LIST   /SALARY79 TO SALARY82 6-25 HOURLY81 HOURLY82 40-53 (2)
             PROMO81 72 AGE 54-55 RAISE82 66-70
RECORD TYPE 3 MISSING=NOWARN
DATA LIST   /JOBCAT 6 NAME 25-48 (A)
END FILE TYPE
```

12.21
FILE TYPE NESTED

FILE TYPE NESTED defines a file in which the record types are related to each other hierarchically. The record types are grouped together by a case identification number that identifies the highest level—the first record type—of the hierarchy. The last record type described defines a case on the active file. For example, a data file recording information about automobile accidents contains three types of records related to each other hierarchically. Figure 12.21a shows the structure of this file. The highest level of the hierarchical structure is the accident record. The accident record includes information about the accident, such as weather conditions, location, date, and so forth. For each accident record, there is one vehicle record for each vehicle involved in the accident. The vehicle record contains information about the vehicle, such as type of vehicle, age of vehicle, state of registration, and so forth. The lowest level of the hierarchy is the person record—one record for each person in a vehicle. This record contains information about each person, such as type of injury, hospital costs, position in car, and so forth.

Figure 12.21a Structure of accident file

```
Accident Record  (Type 1)
Vehicle Record   (Type 2)
Person Record    (Type 3)
Person Record
Vehicle Record   (Type 2)
Person Record    (Type 3)

Accident Record  (Type 1)
Vehicle Record   (Type 2)
Person Record    (Type 3)
        .
        .
        .
```

Each record in the file contains a record number identifying the record type and an accident identification number identifying the accident each record relates to. Figure 12.21b shows the set of records for one accident. The accident number is recorded in positions 1 through 4 of each record, and the record identifier in position 6. As the figure shows, the first accident involved three vehicles (three records with the value 2 recorded in position 6). One person was in the first vehicle (one type 3 record), three people in the second, and one person in the third.

Figure 12.21b   Records from accident file

```
0001 1   322 180/ 3/ 3 330
0001 2     1 4IL4 134M
0001 3     1134M1FR 776
0001 2     2 1IL6 322F
0001 3     2122F1FR 463
0001 3     2035M1FR1011
0001 3     2059M1FR 421
0001 2     3 4IL2 146M
0001 3     3146M0FR   0
```

Using FILE TYPE NESTED, you can define an active file with each case representing one person and information from the accident and vehicle records spread to each case.

Three types of information are required on the FILE TYPE command for NESTED file types.

NESTED Keyword. NESTED indicates that the file being defined is a nested or hierarchical file type.

FILE Subcommand. FILE specifies the name of the file to be defined and is required unless your data are included in the command file.

RECORD Subcommand. RECORD names the variable and specifies the column location of the record type identifier. The record type identifier must be located in the same column(s) on all records. The value on this variable determines the type of each record (see Section 12.22).

Optionally, you can specify the following subcommands on the FILE TYPE command.

CASE Subcommand. CASE names the variable and specifies the column location of the case identifier. The case identifier uniquely identifies the highest level of the hierarchy. If you specify the CASE subcommand, SPSS-X issues a warning message for each record with a case identification number not equal to the case identification number on the last highest level record and builds the case using the record with the invalid case number (see Section 12.23).

WILD Subcommand. WILD tells SPSS-X how to handle undefined record types encountered in your file. By default, SPSS-X does not issue a warning message for an undefined record (see Section 12.24).

DUPLICATE Subcommand. DUPLICATE tells SPSS-X how to handle duplicate records of the same type (other than the last defined record) encountered within a case. SPSS-X checks for duplicate records as it builds the case on the active file. By default, SPSS-X does not build a new case on the active file for each duplicate record (see Section 12.25).

MISSING Subcommand. MISSING tells SPSS-X how to handle missing record types within a case defined by the lowest level record of the hierarchy. By default, SPSS-X skips missing record types (see Section 12.26).

ANNOTATED EXAMPLE FOR FILE TYPE NESTED

The job in this example is to crosstabulate type of injury with weather conditions and with type of vehicle, using information from an accident file. The file has three types of records: accident, vehicle, and person. Weather conditions are recorded on the accident record, type of vehicle is recorded on the vehicle record, and injury is recorded on the person record. To create these crosstabulation tables, we must define a rectangular file with one case for each person in the accident, spreading information from all levels of the hierarchy to the appropriate person. The SPSS-X commands to read the accident file in this way and run the crosstabulation tables are

```
FILE TYPE   NESTED FILE=ACCIDENT RECORD=#RECID 6 CASE=ACCID 1-4

.  RECORD TYPE 1            /* ACCIDENT RECORD
.  DATA LIST /WEATHER 12-13

.  RECORD TYPE 2            /* VEHICLE RECORD
.  DATA LIST /STYLE 16

.  RECORD TYPE 3            /* VICTIM RECORD
.  DATA LIST /INJURY 16

END FILE TYPE

VARIABLE LABELS WEATHER 'WEATHER CONDITIONS AT TIME OF ACCIDENT'
                STYLE 'TYPE OF VEHICLE'
                INJURY 'TYPE OF INJURY'

VALUE LABELS  WEATHER 1 'CLEAR' 2 'RAIN' 3 'SLEET'
      4 'LIGHT    SNOW' 5 'HEAVY SNOW' 6 'BLIZZARD'
      /STYLE 1 'SUBCOMPACT' 2 'COMPACT' 3 'MIDSIZE'
      4 'FULLSIZE' 5 'PICKUP' 6 'SMALL TRUCK' 7 'VAN'
      8 'LARGE TRUCK'/
      INJURY 0 'NONE' 1 'MINOR' 2 'MAJOR' 3 'DOA'/

COMMENT   TABULATE TYPE OF INJURY AGAINST WEATHER
          AND STYLE OF VEHICLE

CROSSTABS      INJURY BY WEATHER STYLE
```

- The FILE TYPE command begins the file definition for this hierarchical file and the END FILE TYPE command indicates the end of the definitions. The FILE TYPE command specifies a NESTED file type, indicates that the data are stored in a file identified by the handle ACCIDENT, and defines the variable names and locations for the record identifier and the case identification number.

- The three RECORD TYPE and DATA LIST commands tell SPSS-X which record types and variables to read. The period in column 1 of the RECORD TYPE and DATA LIST commands allows them to be indented to set them off from the other commands in the job.

- The DATA LIST command for record type 1 defines one variable, WEATHER, located in positions 12–13 of the accident record.

- The second RECORD TYPE and DATA LIST commands define the variable STYLE on the vehicle record (record type 2).

- The last set of RECORD TYPE and DATA LIST commands define the variable INJURY on the person record (record type 3). Each person record represents one case in the defined file. Variables WEATHER and STYLE from the accident and vehicle records are spread to the related person record.

- The VARIABLE LABELS and VALUE LABELS commands assign labels to the variables and values.

- The CROSSTABS command requests two two-way crosstabulation tables: type of injury by weather conditions and type of injury by style of vehicle. The following output shows the crosstabulation of type of injury by weather conditions.

12

Table of type of injury by weather conditions

```
- - - - - - - - - - - - - - - - - - - -  C R O S S T A B U L A T I O N   O F  - - - - - - - - - - - - - - - - - - - -
  INJURY   TYPE OF INJURY                             BY  WEATHER   WEATHER CONDITIONS AT TIME OF ACCIDENT
- - - - - - - - - - - - - - - - - - - - - - - - - - - - - - - - - - - - - - - - - - - - - - -  PAGE 1 OF  1

                  WEATHER
          COUNT  I
                 ICLEAR      RAIN      SLEET     LIGHT        ROW
                 I                               SNOW        TOTAL
                 I          1I        2I        3I        4I
INJURY           --------+---------+---------+---------+---------+
             0   I    49 I    29 I    22 I    33 I    133
  NONE           I       I       I       I       I     28.1
                 +-------+---------+---------+---------+---------+
             1   I    66 I    51 I    35 I    46 I    198
  MINOR          I       I       I       I       I     41.8
                 +-------+---------+---------+---------+---------+
             2   I    36 I    27 I    10 I    30 I    103
  MAJOR          I       I       I       I       I     21.7
                 +-------+---------+---------+---------+---------+
             3   I    13 I    11 I     7 I     9 I     40
  DOA            I       I       I       I       I      8.4
                 +-------+---------+---------+---------+---------+
          COLUMN     164       118        74       118       474
          TOTAL     34.6      24.9      15.6      24.9     100.0

NUMBER OF MISSING OBSERVATIONS =          0
```

12.22
RECORD Subcommand

Each record type in a nested file must be identified by a unique code and the value must be coded in the same location on all records. The RECORD subcommand defines the variable name and the column location of the record identifier. The specification for the RECORD subcommand is the same as for MIXED and GROUPED files (see Sections 12.5 and 12.11). For example, to define the ACCIDENT file as a nested file with record identifier variable #RECID in column 6 of each record, specify:

```
FILE TYPE  NESTED FILE=ACCIDENT RECORD=#RECID 6
```

If you do not specify a variable name, the record identifier is defined as the scratch variable ####RECD. The FORTRAN-like format specifications listed in Chapter 5 cannot be used on the RECORD subcommand. You can, however, indicate that the record-type variable is a string variable by specifying the letter A in parentheses after the column location, as described in Chapter 5.

12.23
CASE Subcommand

The CASE subcommand is optional for FILE TYPE NESTED. If used, it specifies the case identifier, which uniquely identifies the highest level record of the hierarchy. SPSS-X issues a warning message for each record with a case identification number not equal to the case identification number on the last highest level record and builds the case using the record with the invalid case number. The specification for the CASE subcommand is the same as for FILE TYPE GROUPED (see Section 12.12). For example, to define the variable ACCID located in columns 1–4 of each record as the case identifier variable, specify:

```
FILE TYPE  NESTED FILE=ACCIDENT RECORD=#RECID 6 CASE=ACCID 1-4
```

As each case is built, the value of the variable ACCID is checked against the value of ACCID on the last highest level record (record type 1). If the values do not match, a warning message is issued. However, the record is used in building the case.

If you do not specify a variable name, the case identifier is defined as the scratch variable ####CASE. The FORTRAN-like format specifications listed in Chapter 5 cannot be used on the CASE subcommand. You can, however, indicate that the case identification variable is a string variable by specifying the letter A in parentheses after the column location, as described in Chapter 5.

If the case identification number is not recorded in the same location on all record types, use the CASE subcommand on the RECORD TYPE command (see Section 12.30).

12.24
WILD Subcommand

The specification for the WILD subcommand can be either WARN or NOWARN. The default specification for FILE TYPE NESTED is NOWARN. SPSS-X does not issue a warning message when it encounters a record type that is not defined on one of the RECORD TYPE commands. However, the undefined record is not included in the active file. If you specify WARN, SPSS-X issues a warning message for each undefined record type encountered. For example, to receive warning messages for all undefined records encountered in the ACCIDENT file, specify:

```
FILE TYPE  NESTED FILE=ACCIDENT RECORD=#RECID 6 CASE=ACCID 1-4
           WILD=WARN
```

12.25
DUPLICATE Subcommand

As a case is built for nested files, SPSS-X checks for consecutive duplicate record types for all levels except the last record type defined. In other words, SPSS-X determines that it has one and only one record of each type for the case that is being built. For example, suppose that the records for an accident included one accident record (type 1), two vehicle records (type 2), followed by three person records (type 3). This series of records is shown in Figure 12.25a.

Figure 12.25a   Accident file with duplicate records

```
0001 1    322 180/ 3/ 3 330
0001 2      1 4IL4 134M
0001 2      2 1IL6 322F
0001 3      2122F1FR 463
0001 3      2035M1FR1011
0001 3      2059M1FR 421
```

If each person record (type 3) defines a case in the active file, the two consecutive type 2 records are considered duplicate records. The DUPLICATE subcommand provides you with three ways to handle this kind of structure.

The specification for DUPLICATE can be NOWARN, WARN, or CASE. The default specification for FILE TYPE NESTED is NOWARN. SPSS-X does not issue a warning message and uses only the *last* record of the duplicate set to build the case; the other record is skipped. Using the default, SPSS-X builds three cases on the active file from the file in Figure 12.25a: one for each type 3 record, using only the information from the second type 2 record, and the information from the type 1 record. The first type 2 record is quietly skipped.

To receive a warning message when a duplicate record is encountered in building a case, specify WARN. SPSS-X issues a warning message whenever duplicate records are encountered and prints the first 80 characters of the last record of the duplicate set. Cases are built in the same way as with the default specification, NOWARN.

To build a case on the active file for the duplicate record, specify CASE. SPSS-X then builds a case on the active file spreading the information from any higher level records and assigning system-missing values to the variables defined on the lower level records. For example, if you specify

```
FILE TYPE NESTED FILE=ACCIDENT RECORD=#RECID 6 CASE=ACCID 1-4
            DUPLICATE=CASE
RECORD TYPE 1
DATA LIST    /WEATHER 12-13
RECORD TYPE 2
DATA LIST /STYLE 16
RECORD TYPE 3
DATA LIST /INJURY 16
END FILE TYPE
```

four cases are built on the active file: one for the first type 2 record, with system-missing for the variable INJURY defined from the type 3 record, and one case for each of the three type 3 records. The cases built on the active file are shown in Figure 12.25b.

Figure 12.25b   Cases built with DUPLICATE=CASE

```
0001 01 4  .
0001 01 6  1
0001 01 6  1
0001 01 6  1
```

12.26
MISSING Subcommand

After a case is built for nested files, SPSS-X verifies that each defined case includes one record of each type. If a record type is missing, SPSS-X assigns system-missing values to the variables defined on the missing record. For example, suppose that the records for an accident included one accident record (type 1), no vehicle records (type 2), and three person records (type 3). These records are shown in Figure 12.26. If a case is defined for each person record, SPSS-X will build three cases with a missing record type 2 for each case.

Figure 12.26   Accident file with missing records

```
0001 1   322 180/ 3/ 3 330
0001 3      2122F1FR 463
0001 3      2035M1FR1011
0001 3      2059M1FR 421
```

The MISSING subcommand has two specifications, NOWARN or WARN. The default for FILE TYPE NESTED is NOWARN. SPSS-X does not issue a warning message if a record type is missing for a defined case and builds the case in the active file assigning system-missing values to the variables defined on the missing record.

To receive a warning message for every case built with a missing record, specify WARN. The cases are built in the same way as with the default specification NOWARN. For example, to request warning messages for the cases with missing records shown in Figure 12.26, specify:

```
FILE TYPE NESTED FILE=ACCIDENT RECORD=#RECID 6 CASE=ACCID 1-4
                 MISSING=WARN
RECORD TYPE 1
DATA LIST    /WEATHER 12-13
RECORD TYPE 2
DATA LIST /STYLE 16
RECORD TYPE 3
DATA LIST /INJURY 16
END FILE TYPE
```

The MISSING=WARN subcommand specification prints the following warning messages:

```
>WARNING   518
>A record is missing from the indicated case.  The variables defined on the
>record have been set to the system missing value.

RECORD IDENTIFIER:  2
CASE IDENTIFIER:     1
CURRENT CASE NUMBER:      1, CURRENT SPLIT FILE NUMBER:      1.


>WARNING   518
>A record is missing from the indicated case.  The variables defined on the
>record have been set to the system missing value.

RECORD IDENTIFIER:  2
CASE IDENTIFIER:     1
CURRENT CASE NUMBER:      2, CURRENT SPLIT FILE NUMBER:      1.


>WARNING   518
>A record is missing from the indicated case.  The variables defined on the
>record have been set to the system missing value.

RECORD IDENTIFIER:  2
CASE IDENTIFIER:     1
CURRENT CASE NUMBER:      3, CURRENT SPLIT FILE NUMBER:      1.
```

and builds the following three cases:

```
0001 01 . 1
0001 01 . 1
0001 01 . 1
```

12.27
RECORD TYPE Command
for FILE TYPE NESTED

You must include a RECORD TYPE command and a DATA LIST command for each record that contains data that you want to include in your active file. The only required specification on RECORD TYPE is the value of the record type variable defined on the RECORD subcommand on the FILE TYPE command. The order of the RECORD TYPE commands defines the hierarchical structure of the file. The first RECORD TYPE command defines the highest level record type, the next RECORD TYPE command the next highest level record, and so forth. The last RECORD TYPE command defines a case in the active file. For example, to build a case for each person record that includes the values of the variable WEATHER from the accident record, the variable STYLE from the vehicle record, and the variable INJURY from the person record, specify:

```
FILE TYPE NESTED FILE=ACCIDENT RECORD=#RECID 6 CASE=ACCID 1-4
RECORD TYPE 1              /*ACCIDENT RECORD
DATA LIST     /WEATHER 12-13
RECORD TYPE 2              /*VEHICLE RECORD
DATA LIST /STYLE 16
RECORD TYPE 3              /*PERSON RECORD
DATA LIST  /INJURY 16
END FILE TYPE
```

You can specify a single value or a list of values indicating the record type(s) to be read by the following DATA LIST command. If the record type variable is defined as a string variable on the RECORD subcommand of the FILE TYPE command, you must enclose each value in apostrophes or quotation marks.

The first record in the file should be the type specified on the first RECORD TYPE command—the highest level record of the hierarchy. If the first record in the file is not the highest level type, SPSS-X skips all records until it encounters a record of the highest level type. If the MISSING or DUPLICATE subcommands have been specified on the FILE TYPE command, these records may produce warning messages but will not be used to build a case on the active file.

12.28
Keyword OTHER and SKIP Subcommand

If FILE TYPE NESTED is specified, the OTHER keyword and the SKIP subcommand on the RECORD TYPE command can be used only in conjunction with each other. Neither can be used separately. By specifying OTHER SKIP, all record types that have not been mentioned on previous RECORD TYPE commands will be skipped. You can specify OTHER SKIP only on the last RECORD TYPE command in the file definition.

For example, to build a file in which the vehicle record defines a case, you would specify:

```
FILE TYPE NESTED FILE=ACCIDENT RECORD=#RECID 6 CASE=ACCID 1-4
RECORD TYPE 1              /*ACCIDENT RECORD
DATA LIST     /WEATHER 12-13
RECORD TYPE 2              /*VEHICLE RECORD
DATA LIST /STYLE 16
RECORD TYPE OTHER SKIP
END FILE TYPE
```

If you specify WILD=WARN on the FILE TYPE command, you cannot specify OTHER SKIP on the RECORD TYPE command.

12.29
CASE Subcommand

You can specify the variable name and column location of a case identification number on the CASE subcommand on the FILE TYPE command (see Section 12.23). However, the case identification number might be recorded in different locations on different record types. To specify the location of the case identification number for a record type, use the CASE subcommand on the RECORD TYPE command. Do not specify the CASE subcommand on RECORD TYPE unless you have specified the CASE subcommand on the FILE TYPE command. The format type of the case identification variable must be the same on all records. That is, if the case identification variable is defined as a string variable on the FILE TYPE command, you cannot define it as a numeric variable on the RECORD TYPE command, and vice versa.

12.30
SPREAD Subcommand

Use the SPREAD subcommand to indicate if the values for variables defined for a record type should be spread to all the built cases related to that record. The default specification for the SPREAD subcommand is the keyword YES—all variables defined for the record type are automatically spread to all cases built from the last record type defined. If you specify the keyword NO, the variables defined on the record type are spread only to the *first* case built from the set of records related to that record type. All other cases built from the same record are assigned the system-missing value for the variables defined on the record type.

For example, suppose that the first person record (type 3) related to each vehicle record (type 2) in the accident file is the driver of the vehicle. To spread the variable STYLE from the vehicle record to only the case built for the driver, specify:

```
FILE TYPE NESTED FILE=ACCIDENT RECORD=#RECID 6 CASE=ACCID 1-4
RECORD TYPE 1                        /*ACCIDENT RECORD
DATA LIST    /WEATHER 12-13
RECORD TYPE 2 SPREAD=NO              /*VEHICLE RECORD
DATA LIST /STYLE 16
RECORD TYPE 3                        /*PERSON RECORD
DATA LIST /INJURY 16
END FILE TYPE
PRINT /ACCID WEATHER STYLE INJURY
EXECUTE
```

Figure 12.30 displays the cases built from the records in the accident file shown in Figure 12.21b. The first vehicle record (type 2) has one related person record (type 3), and the value for STYLE is spread to the case built for the person record. The second vehicle record has three related person records, and the value for STYLE is spread to only the case built from the first person record. The other two persons have the system-missing value for STYLE. The third vehicle record has one related person record, and the value for STYLE is spread to the person.

Figure 12.30   Cases built with SPREAD=NO for record type 2

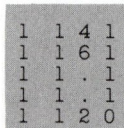

```
1  1  4  1
1  1  6  1
1  1  .  1
1  1  .  1
1  1  2  0
```

12.31
SUMMARY OF FILE DEFINITIONS

Table 12.31 shows the default values for each FILE TYPE subcommand for the three types of files. The notation "Not App." indicates that the subcommand is not available for that type of file. The RECORD subcommand is always required, and the FILE subcommand is required unless your data are included in the command file.

Table 12.31   Summary of defaults for FILE TYPE subcommands

FILE TYPE Subcommand	MIXED	GROUPED	NESTED
FILE	Conditional	Conditional	Conditional
RECORD	Required	Required	Required
CASE	Not App.	Required	Optional
WILD	NOWARN	WARN	NOWARN
DUPLICATE	Not App.	WARN	NOWARN
MISSING	Not App.	WARN	NOWARN
ORDERED	Not App.	YES	Not App.

You can also specify the CASE, DUPLICATE, and MISSING subcommands on the RECORD TYPE command for file type GROUPED. You can specify the CASE and MISSING subcommands on the RECORD TYPE command for file type NESTED. If you specify any of these subcommands on a RECORD TYPE command, the default or specification on the FILE TYPE command is overridden only for the record types listed on that RECORD TYPE command. The default or FILE TYPE specification applies to all other record types.

12.32
REPEATING DATA
COMMAND

Use the REPEATING DATA command to read and generate cases from repeating groups of data from the same input record. Each repeated group contains the same information, and a case is built on the active file for each repeated group. The number of repeated groups often varies for each record. Each input record may also include information that is common to all of the repeated groups that you want *spread* to each case built on the active file. In this respect, a file with a repeating data structure is like a hierarchical file with both levels of information recorded on one record rather than on separate record types.

For example, suppose you have a data file with each record representing a household. Information about the household, such as total number of persons living in the house and number of vehicles owned by the household is recorded on each record. Each record also includes a group of information about each vehicle, such as make of vehicle, model, and number of cylinders. Figure 12.32 shows the first three records from this data file.

Figure 12.32   Vehicle information file

```
1001 02 02 FORD      T8PONTIAC C6
1002 04 01 CHEVY     C4
1003 02 03 CADILAC C8FORD      T6VW       C4
```

The first field of numbers (columns 1–4) for each record is an identification number unique to each record. The next two fields of numbers are number of persons in household and number of vehicles. The remaining portion of the record are the repeated groups—one for each vehicle.

You can use the REPEATING DATA command only within an input program that is explicitly specified with the INPUT PROGRAM and END INPUT PROGRAM commands, or within a FILE TYPE—END FILE TYPE file definition structure for MIXED or NESTED file types. The REPEATING DATA command cannot be used with FILE TYPE GROUPED. See Section 12.33 for a discussion of the INPUT PROGRAM and END INPUT PROGRAM commands.

Because the REPEATING DATA command creates cases, you must define all fixed-format data on a given record before the REPEATING DATA command, even if the fixed-format data follow the repeating data structure. This is not a common construction since most repeating groups are recorded at the end of records rather than within them, but you may encounter the problem in data structures such as IBM SMF and RMF records.

The following three subcommands are required on the REPEATING DATA subcommand.

STARTS Subcommand. STARTS specifies the beginning position of the repeating data segments. Optionally, you can also specify the ending position of the last repeating group. If you do not specify an ending position, SPSS-X scans to the end of the record or to the value on the OCCURS subcommand looking for repeating data groups (see Section 12.34).

OCCURS Subcommand. OCCURS specifies the number of repeating groups on each record. You can specify a number if the number of repeating groups is the same for each record. Otherwise, specify the name of a previously defined variable whose value for each record indicates the number of repeating groups on that record (see Section 12.35).

DATA Subcommand. DATA lists the variable name, location within the repeated group, and the type for each variable to be read from the repeated groups. The specifications for the DATA subcommand are the same as for the variable definition portion of the DATA LIST command (see Chapter 5). The DATA subcommand must be the last subcommand on the REPEATING DATA command (see Section 12.36).

Optionally, you can specify the following subcommands on the REPEATING DATA command.

NOTABLE Subcommand. NOTABLE suppresses the printing of the summary table that lists the variable names, locations, and format types of the variables specified on the DATA subcommand. This table has the same format as the table printed by the DATA LIST command. The default is TABLE (see Section 12.37).

FILE Subcommand. FILE specifies the name of the input data file that you are defining with the REPEATING DATA command. If you do not specify a FILE subcommand, REPEATING DATA defines the file specified on the previous DATA LIST command (see Section 12.38).

LENGTH Subcommand. LENGTH specifies the length of each repeating group on the record. Use the LENGTH subcommand if you do not want to read all variables in each repeating group or if the length of each repeating group varies by record. If you do not specify the LENGTH subcommand, SPSS-X uses the specifications on the DATA subcommand to determine the length of each repeating group (see Section 12.39).

CONTINUED Subcommand. CONTINUED indicates that the repeating groups may be continued on successive records. Optionally, you can specify the beginning position and the ending position of the repeating data groups on the continuation records (see Section 12.40).

ID Subcommand. Use ID with the CONTINUED subcommand only. ID compares the value of an identification variable across records of the same input case. If the values are not equal for all records of an input case, SPSS-X prints an error message and stops reading data (see Section 12.41).

12.33
INPUT PROGRAM—END
INPUT PROGRAM
Structure

When you submit your job for execution, SPSS-X builds the active file dictionary as it encounters commands that create and define variables. At the same time, SPSS-X builds an *input program* that constructs cases and an optional *transformation program* that modifies cases prior to analysis or display. By the time SPSS-X encounters a procedure command that tells it to read the data, the active file dictionary is ready and the programs that construct and modify the active file cases are built. The active file dictionary is described in Chapter 5 and the commands and applications that make up the transformation program are discussed in Chapters 7, 8, 9, and 11.

The input program is usually built from either a single DATA LIST command (Chapter 5) or any of the commands that read or combine system files (the GET command in Chapter 6 or the MATCH FILES and ADD FILES commands in Chapter 16). The input program can also be built from the FILE TYPE—END FILE TYPE structure used to define nested or mixed files (Sections 12.3 through 12.21). The third type of input program is one that you specify yourself using the INPUT PROGRAM and END INPUT PROGRAM commands documented in Chapter 14.

The REPEATING DATA command can appear only in a FILE TYPE—END FILE TYPE structure or in an input program explicitly specified with the INPUT PROGRAM—END INPUT PROGRAM commands. Use a DATA LIST command to define the variables on each record that you want spread to each case built from the repeated groups, and use the REPEATING DATA command to define the variables in each repeating group. You must place the DATA LIST, REPEATING DATA, and any transformation commands used to build the cases between the INPUT PROGRAM and END INPUT PROGRAM commands.

Transformations that apply to the built case, however, should be placed after the END INPUT PROGRAM or END FILE TYPE command.

To read the data shown in Figure 12.32 and build an active file with each case representing one vehicle and the information about the household spread to each of the vehicles, specify:

```
INPUT PROGRAM
DATA LIST FILE=VEHICLE/SEQNUM 2-4 NUMPERS 6-7 NUMVEH 9-10
REPEATING DATA STARTS=12/OCCURS=NUMVEH/
                DATA=MAKE 1-8 (A) MODEL 9 (A) NUMCYL 10
END INPUT PROGRAM
```

The INPUT PROGRAM command indicates the beginning of your data definition commands, DATA LIST reads the variables from the household portion of the record, REPEATING DATA reads the information from the repeating groups and builds the new cases, and END INPUT PROGRAM indicates the end of your data definition program. These commands produce six cases.

The first record shown in Figure 12.32 contains information on two vehicles producing two cases on the active file. One case is built from the second record which contains information on one vehicle, and three cases are built from the third record. The values of the variables defined on the DATA LIST command are spread to every case built on the active file.

12.34
STARTS Subcommand

The STARTS subcommand is required. Use this subcommand to indicate the beginning location of the repeating data segment of each record. The specification on the STARTS subcommand is either a number or a variable name. If the repeating groups begin in the same position on each record, specify the starting location with a number. To indicate that the repeating groups begin in column 12 of each record of the vehicle file, specify:

```
INPUT PROGRAM
DATA LIST FILE=VEHICLE/SEQNUM 2-4 NUMPERS 6-7 NUMVEH 9-10
REPEATING DATA STARTS=12/OCCURS=NUMVEH
                /DATA=MAKE 1-8 (A) MODEL 9 (A) NUMCYL 10
END INPUT PROGRAM
```

If the repeating groups begin in a different location on different records, you can specify the name of a previously defined variable whose value for each record indicates the beginning location of the repeating segment of the record. You can define this variable on the DATA LIST command before the REPEATING DATA command if it is already recorded on each record. Otherwise, you may need to create the variable with transformation commands before the REPEATING DATA command.

For example, suppose that in the vehicle file the repeating groups begin in column 12 for all records with sequence numbers 1 through 100 and in column 15 for all records with sequence numbers greater than 100. To specify the beginning position of the repeating groups for this file, create a new variable that specifies the beginning position for each record and specify the new variable on the STARTS subcommand, as in:

```
INPUT PROGRAM
DATA LIST FILE=VEHICLE/SEQNUM 2-4 NUMPERS 6-7 NUMVEH 9-10
.       DO IF    (SEQNUM LE 100)
.       COMPUTE FIRST=12
.       ELSE IF (SEQNUM GT 100)
.       COMPUTE FIRST=15
.       END IF
REPEATING DATA STARTS=FIRST/OCCURS=NUMVEH
                /DATA=MAKE 1-8 (A) MODEL 9 (A) NUMCYL 10
END INPUT PROGRAM
```

The sequence number is defined as variable SEQNUM on the DATA LIST command for each record. The DO IF—END IF structure and the COMPUTE commands create the variable FIRST with the value 12 for records with sequence numbers through 100 and the value 15 for records with sequence numbers greater than 100. The variable FIRST is specified on the STARTS subcommand. The value for FIRST then indicates the beginning position of the repeating data groups for each record.

If the repeating groups are continued on successive records, you can specify on the STARTS command the ending position of the last possible repeating group on the first record. Separate the beginning position and the ending position specifications by a dash. You can specify the ending position with a number or a variable name. The values of the variable used to define the ending position must be valid values and must be larger than the starting value. If the value of the variable specified as the ending position is undefined or missing, SPSS-X prints a warning message and builds no cases from that record. If the value of the variable specified as the ending position is less than the value specified for the starting position, SPSS-X builds one case from the continuation record but does not print a warning message. You must also use the CONTINUED subcommand (see Section 12.40).

12.35
OCCURS Subcommand

The OCCURS subcommand specifies the number of repeating groups on each record. You can specify a number if the number of groups is the same on all records or a variable if the number of groups varies across records. The variable must be defined on a previous DATA LIST command or created with the transformation commands.

For example, in the vehicle file, some households may own two vehicles, others may own three, and some none. The number of vehicles per household is recorded on each record. To specify the number of repeating groups, first define a variable for the number of vehicles on the DATA LIST command, and then specify this variable on the OCCURS subcommand, as in:

```
INPUT PROGRAM
DATA LIST FILE=VEHICLE/SEQNUM 2-4 NUMPERS 6-7 NUMVEH 9-10
REPEATING DATA STARTS=12/OCCURS=NUMVEH
               /DATA=MAKE 1-8 (A) MODEL 9 (A) NUMCYL 10
END INPUT PROGRAM
```

In this example, the value on variable NUMVEH from columns 9 and 10 indicates the number of repeating groups for each record. A case is built on the active file for each occurrence of a repeating group. For the records shown in Figure 12.32, NUMVEH has the value 2 on the first record, 1 on the second record, and 3 on the third. Thus, six cases are built from these records. If the value of NUMVEH is zero, no cases are built from that record.

If the number of repeating groups is the same for each record or if you want to read the same number of repeating groups from each record, specify the number on the OCCURS subcommand. For example, to read only the first repeating group from each record, specify:

```
INPUT PROGRAM
DATA LIST FILE=VEHICLE/SEQNUM 2-4 NUMPERS 6-7 NUMVEH 9-10
REPEATING DATA STARTS=12/OCCURS=1
               /DATA=MAKE 1-8 (A) MODEL 9 (A) NUMCYL 10
END INPUT PROGRAM
```

One case is built from the first repeating group on each record regardless of the total number of repeating groups actually recorded on the record.

SPSS-X scans to the end of the record or the value specified on the OCCURS subcommand looking for repeating data groups. If the value specified on the OCCURS subcommand is higher than the actual number of repeating groups on the record, SPSS-X will continue to create cases for repeating groups until the end of record is detected. Under these circumstances, some cases generated will include system-missing or other values from your data. If you are in doubt about the accuracy of the value of the variable specified on the OCCURS subcommand, include commands to check the value.

12.36
DATA Subcommand

Use the DATA subcommand to specify the variable names, location within each repeating group, and the format type of all variables you want to read from each repeating group. If the LENGTH subcommand is not specified, the total specifications on the DATA subcommand define the length of each repeating data group. The specifications for the DATA subcommand are the same as for the DATA LIST command (see Chapter 5). The specified location of the variables is their location within each repeating group—*not* the location within the record. The DATA subcommand is required and must be the last subcommand on the REPEATING DATA command. For example, to read all of the variables recorded for each vehicle, specify:

```
INPUT PROGRAM
DATA LIST FILE=VEHICLE/SEQNUM 2-4 NUMPERS 6-7 NUMVEH 9-10
REPEATING DATA STARTS=12/OCCURS=NUMVEH
              /DATA=MAKE 1-8 (A) MODEL 9 (A) NUMCYL 10
END INPUT PROGRAM
PRINT /SEQNUM TO NUMCYL
EXECUTE
```

The variable MAKE is a string variable read from positions 1 through 8 of each repeating group; MODEL is a single-character string variable read from position 9; and NUMCYL is a one-digit numeric variable read from position 10. The DATA subcommand defines a total length of 10 for each repeating group.

The variables SEQNUM, NUMPERS, and NUMVEH defined on the DATA LIST command for each record are spread to each case built from the repeating groups for the record. Figure 12.36 shows the cases built on the active file from the three records shown in Figure 12.32.

Figure 12.36   Cases built with REPEATING DATA

```
1   2   2   FORD       T 8
1   2   2   PONTIAC    C 6
2   4   1   CHEVY      C 4
3   2   3   CADILAC    C 8
3   2   3   FORD       T 6
3   2   3   VW         C 4
```

You can use any of the format types listed in Chapter 5 on the DATA subcommand. You can also use the FORTRAN-like format specifications as well as the column format specifications.

12.37
NOTABLE Subcommand

By default, SPSS-X prints a summary table for all variables defined on the DATA subcommand. The summary table lists the names, locations, and format types of the variables. The format of the summary table is identical to the summary table printed by the DATA LIST command. To suppress the printing of this table, specify the subcommand NOTABLE, as in:

```
INPUT PROGRAM
DATA LIST FILE=VEHICLE/SEQNUM 2-4 NUMPERS 6-7 NUMVEH 9-10
REPEATING DATA STARTS=12/OCCURS=NUMVEH/NOTABLE
              /DATA=MAKE 1-8 (A) MODEL 9 (A) NUMCYL 10
END INPUT PROGRAM
```

To specify the default explicitly, use the subcommand TABLE.

12.38
FILE Subcommand

REPEATING DATA must be used with a DATA LIST, FILE TYPE NESTED, or FILE TYPE MIXED command. The REPEATING DATA command reads the file specified on the previous DATA LIST or FILE TYPE command if the FILE subcommand is not specified. To explicitly specify the name of the file you want to read, use the FILE subcommand on REPEATING DATA, as in:

```
INPUT PROGRAM
DATA LIST FILE=VEHICLE/SEQNUM 2-4 NUMPERS 6-7 NUMVEH 9-10
REPEATING DATA FILE=VEHICLE/STARTS=12/OCCURS=NUMVEH
                /DATA=MAKE 1-8 (A) MODEL 9 (A) NUMCYL 10
END INPUT PROGRAM
```

12.39
LENGTH Subcommand

The LENGTH subcommand specifies the length of each repeating data group. If you do not specify the LENGTH subcommand, the length of each repeating group is determined by the last specification on the DATA subcommand. Use the LENGTH subcommand if the last variable specified on the DATA subcommand is not read from the last position of each repeating group or if the length of the repeating groups varies by record. For example, to read only the variable MAKE for each vehicle, specify:

```
INPUT PROGRAM
DATA LIST FILE=VEHICLE/SEQNUM 2-4 NUMPERS 6-7 NUMVEH 9-10
REPEATING DATA STARTS=12/OCCURS=NUMVEH/LENGTH=10
              /DATA=MAKE 1-8 (A)
END INPUT PROGRAM
```

The LENGTH subcommand indicates that each repeating group is 10 positions long. The DATA subcommand specifies that MAKE is to be read from positions 1 through 8 of each repeating group. Thus, positions 9 and 10 of each repeating group are skipped.

The specification for the LENGTH subcommand can be a number, as above, or the name of a previously defined variable. If the length of the repeating groups varies by record, you need to define a variable on a previous DATA LIST command or create with transformation commands a variable whose value is the length of the repeating groups on the record. Specify the name of this variable on the LENGTH subcommand. If the value of the variable specified on the LENGTH subcommand is an undefined or missing value, SPSS-X prints a warning message and builds one case for that record.

12.40
CONTINUED
Subcommand

If the repeating groups are continued onto more than one record, you must specify the CONTINUED subcommand. Each repeating group must be contained on a single record: in other words, a repeating group cannot be split across records. You can specify on the CONTINUED subcommand the beginning and ending positions of the repeating data groups on the continuation records. If you do not specify the beginning and ending positions, SPSS-X assumes that the repeating groups begin in column 1 of continuation records and scans to the end of the record or to the value specified by the OCCURS subcommand looking for repeating groups.

Figure 12.40 shows the first four records from a mail-order file. The length of each record is defined to the computer as 50 positions long.

Figure 12.40   Records from mail-order file

```
10020 04 45-923-89 001   25.9923-899-56 100 101.99
10020 63-780-32 025   13.9554-756-90 005   56.75
20030 03 45-781-43 010   10.9789-236-54 075 105.95
20030 32-569-38 015   75.00
```

The order number is recorded in columns 1 through 5 of each record. The first two records apply to the same order, and the next pair of records represent a second order. The second field of numbers on the first record for each pair indicates the total number of items ordered. The repeating groups begin in column 10 of the first record and column 7 of the second record. Each repeating data group represents information on one item ordered and contains three variables—the item inventory number, the quantity ordered, and the price of the item—a total of 20 positions for each item.

To define all of the repeating groups on this file, use the CONTINUED subcommand. Since the repeating groups begin in position 7 of the continuation records, you must also specify the beginning position of the repeating groups on the continuation records, as in:

```
INPUT PROGRAM
DATA LIST FILE=ORDERS/ORDERID 1-5 NITEMS 7-8
REPEATING DATA STARTS=10/OCCURS=NITEMS
              /CONTINUED=7
              /DATA=ITEM 1-9 (A) QUANTITY 11-13 PRICE 15-20 (2)
END INPUT PROGRAM
```

The DATA LIST command defines variables ORDERID and NITEMS on the *first record* of each input case. The STARTS subcommand on REPEATING DATA indicates that the repeating groups begin in position 10 of the first record of each input case. OCCURS indicates that the total number of repeating groups for each input case is the value of NITEMS. The CONTINUED subcommand indicates that the repeating groups may be continued onto successive records and that the beginning position of the repeated groups on the continuation records is position 7. The DATA subcommand defines variables ITEM, QUANTITY, and PRICE for each repeating data group.

If each record were defined to the computer as 80 positions long, and the data were actually recorded only in the first 49 positions, the ending column position must be specified on the STARTS subcommand. Otherwise, SPSS-X will read positions 50 through 69 of the first record for each input case as a repeating group and build a case with system-missing values for the variables defined on the DATA subcommand since these columns are blank. For example,

```
INPUT PROGRAM
DATA LIST FILE=ORDERS/ORDERID 1-5 NITEMS 7-8
REPEATING DATA STARTS=10-50/OCCURS=NITEMS/CONTINUED=7
              /DATA=ITEM 1-9 (A) QUANTITY 11-13 PRICE 15-20 (2)
END INPUT PROGRAM
```

indicates that SPSS-X is to scan only the first 50 positions of the first record of each input case looking for repeating data groups. It will scan all columns of subsequent records until the value specified on the OCCURS subcommand is reached.

12.41
ID Subcommand

Use the ID subcommand with the CONTINUED subcommand to compare the value of an identification variable across records of the same input case. If the values are not equal for all records of an input case, SPSS-X prints an error message and stops reading data. The identification variable must be defined on a previous DATA LIST command and must be recorded on all records in the file.

The ID subcommand has two specifications, the location of the variable on the continuation records and the name of the variable defined on the DATA LIST command for the first record of each input case. The specifications must be separated from each other by an equals sign. The format type and length of the variable must be specified the same as for the variable defined on the first record.

For example, in the data shown in Figure 12.40, the order number is recorded in positions 1–5 of each record. To tell SPSS-X to compare the order number for all records in the same input case, specify:

```
INPUT PROGRAM
DATA LIST FILE=ORDERS/ORDERID 1-5 NITEMS 7-8
REPEATING DATA STARTS=10-50/OCCURS=NITEMS/
              CONTINUED=7/ID=1-5=ORDERID
              /DATA=ITEM 1-9 (A) QUANTITY 11-13 PRICE 15-20 (2)
END INPUT PROGRAM
```

In this example, ORDERID is defined on the DATA LIST command as a five-digit integer variable. The first specification on the ID subcommand must therefore specify a five-digit integer variable. Only the location of the identification number can be different on continuation records.

Syntax

MATRIX DATA

```
MATRIX DATA VARIABLES=varlist    [/FILE= {INLINE**}]
                                         {file   }

[/SPLIT= varlist]    [/FACTORS= varlist]

[/CONTENTS= [CORR**] [COV] [MAT] [MSE] [DFE] [MEAN] [SD] [PROX]

    [STDDEV] [N_SCALAR] [N_VECTOR] [N] [N_MATRIX] [COUNT] ]

[/FORMAT= [{LIST**}]  [{LOWER**}]  [{DIAGONAL**}]]
          {FREE  }    {UPPER  }    {NODIAGONAL}
                      {FULL   }

[/CELLS= number of cells]    [/N= sample size]
```

**Default if the subcommand is omitted.

MCONVERT

```
MCONVERT [[/MATRIX=] [IN({*    })]] [OUT({*    })]]
                         {file}          {file}

         [{/REPLACE}]
          {/APPEND }
```

Contents

13.1   MATRIX MATERIALS WRITTEN BY PROCEDURES
13.2   MATRIX Subcommand
13.3   OUT Keyword
13.4   IN Keyword
13.5   Format of the Matrix System File
13.6   Variable Order
13.7   Split Files
13.8   Additional Statistics
13.9   Missing Values
13.10   Matrix File Dictionaries
13.11 MATRIX DATA COMMAND
13.12   Format of the Raw Matrix Data File
13.13   General Syntax
13.14   VARIABLES Subcommand
13.15   VARNAME_ Variable
13.16   ROWTYPE_ Variable
13.17   FILE Subcommand
13.18   FORMAT Subcommand
13.19   Print and Write Formats
13.20   SPLIT Subcommand
13.21   FACTORS Subcommand
13.22   CELLS Subcommand
13.23   CONTENTS Subcommand
13.24   Within-Cells Record Definition
13.25   Optional Specification with ROWTYPE_ Explicit
13.26   N Subcommand
13.27   Subcommand Summary
13.28   MATRIX DATA Examples
13.29   Example 1: MATRIX DATA with Procedure ONEWAY
13.30   Example 2: MATRIX DATA with Procedure REGRESSION
13.31 MCONVERT COMMAND
13.32   General Syntax
13.33   MATRIX Subcommand
13.34   REPLACE Subcommand
13.35   APPEND Subcommand

13

Chapter 13   Defining Matrices

Many procedures in SPSS-X can read raw data and write a representative matrix of the data values to a system file. These matrix system files can be used as input for subsequent analysis. Sections 13.1 through 13.4 discuss the matrix-handling facilities available in the SPSS-X procedures that read and write matrices. Sections 13.11 through 13.30 discuss the MATRIX DATA command, which reads raw matrix values and converts them to a matrix system file that SPSS-X procedures can read. Sections 13.31 through 13.36 discuss the MCONVERT command, which can convert a correlation matrix to a covariance matrix, or a covariance matrix to a correlation matrix.

13.1
MATRIX MATERIALS WRITTEN BY PROCEDURES

Matrix materials in SPSS-X are stored as system files, which means the files use a dictionary to record descriptive information about the matrix data. Table 13.1 shows the types of matrix materials written by SPSS-X procedures. The ROWTYPE_ values of each matrix are also included so you see which procedure matrices are readable by other procedures. If a procedure produces more than one type of matrix, the subcommand required or comments on that matrix are included.

Table 13.1   Types of matrices and their contents

Command	Subcommands/Notes	ROWTYPE_ values*
ALSCAL		PROX
CLUSTER		PROX
CORRELATIONS		MEAN
		STDDEV
		N
		CORR
DISCRIMINANT	/CLASSIFY=POOLED	N (1 per cell)
		COUNT (1 per cell)
		MEAN (1 per cell)
		STDDEV (pooled)
		CORR (pooled)
	/CLASSIFY=SEPARATE, /STATISTICS=BOXM, or /STATISTICS=GCOV	N (1 per cell)
		COUNT (1 per cell)
		MEAN (1 per cell)
		STDDEV (1 per cell)
		CORR (1 per cell)
FACTOR	/MATRIX=OUT(CORR=file) /MATRIX=IN(CORR=file)	CORR
	/MATRIX=OUT(FAC=file) /MATRIX=IN(FAC=file)	FACTOR
MANOVA		N (cell and pooled)
		MEAN (1 per cell)
		STDDEV (pooled)
		CORR (pooled)
NONPAR CORR	/PRINT=SPEARMAN	N
		RHO
	/PRINT=KENDALL	N
		TAUB
ONEWAY	separate variance — can be input and output	MEAN (1 per cell)
		STDDEV (1 per cell)
		N (1 per cell)
	pooled variance — can be input only	MEAN (1 per cell)
		N (1 per cell)
		MSE (pooled)
		DFE (pooled)
PARTIAL CORR		N
		CORR
PROXIMITIES		PROX
REGRESSION		MEAN
		STDDEV
		N
		CORR
RELIABILITY		N
		MEAN
		STDDEV
		CORR

*For any command, if /MISSING=PAIRWISE, all N values of ROWTYPE_ will be a matrix of N's. Otherwise, a single vector of N's is used.

13.2
MATRIX Subcommand

All SPSS-X procedures that handle matrix materials use the MATRIX subcommand. The MATRIX subcommand specifies the file from which the input matrix is read and/or the file to which the output matrix is written. The MATRIX subcommand standardizes the method each procedure uses to read and write matrices.

Though procedures vary in the types of matrix materials they handle, the MATRIX subcommand always uses at least one of two keywords, IN and OUT, to specify the matrix system files. Sections 13.3 through 13.4 discuss the general features of the MATRIX subcommand and the format used by matrix system files in SPSS-X.

13.3
OUT Keyword

All procedures in SPSS-X that read raw data and convert them to representative matrices use the OUT keyword on MATRIX to write matrix materials to a system file. Generally, there are two options:

(file) *Write the matrix materials to a system file.* The output file is specified in parentheses. The file is stored on disk and can be retrieved at any time.

(*) *Replace the active file with the matrix system file.* The matrix materials replace the active file. The matrix is NOT stored on disk. It is resident in the active file.

In the following example, procedure CORRELATIONS reads raw data from the file UNION and writes its representative correlation matrix to the file CORRMTX:

```
GET FILE  UNION/KEEP FOOD RENT PUBTRANS TEACHER COOK ENGINEER SEX
SORT CASES BY SEX
SPLIT FILE BY SEX
CORRELATIONS  FOOD TO ENGINEER
     /MATRIX OUT(CORRMTX)
```

The active file is still the file UNION. Subsequent commands are executed on file UNION.

To write the same matrix, but have it available to subsequent commands, specify an asterisk on keyword OUT. The following commands replace the active file with the matrix materials:

```
GET FILE  UNION/KEEP FOOD RENT PUBTRANS TEACHER COOK ENGINEER SEX
SORT CASES BY SEX
SPLIT FILE BY SEX
CORRELATIONS  FOOD TO ENGINEER
     /MATRIX OUT(*)
LIST
DISPLAY DICTIONARY
```

The active file is replaced with the correlation matrix. The LIST and DISPLAY commands are executed on the matrix file, not on the file UNION (see Figures 13.5a and 13.5b).

13.4
IN Keyword

The IN keyword on MATRIX specifies the file from which the matrix is read. Generally, there are two options:

(file) *Read the matrix materials from an external matrix system file.*

(*) *Read the matrix materials from the active file.* The active file must be an appropriate matrix system file.

MATRIX=IN cannot be used in place of GET or DATA LIST to begin a new SPSS-X command file. MATRIX is a subcommand on procedures that handle matrix materials, and procedures cannot run before an active file is defined. The active file does not need to contain the matrix materials. For example, you can perform a series of analyses on one file and then read matrix materials from another file. MATRIX=IN can be used in that context because there is a defined active file at the time the procedure that specifies the MATRIX subcommand is used.

13

The procedures that read matrix materials can only read them if the matrix file is an appropriate matrix system file. For example, NONPAR CORR writes matrix system files, but REGRESSION cannot read them because REGRESSION reads and writes matrices with Pearson's correlation coefficient and NONPAR CORR writes either Spearman's or Kendall's coefficient.

In addition to compatible coefficients, the missing-value treatment in the procedure that writes a matrix must be analogous to the treatment used by the procedure that reads the matrix. For example, REGRESSION can read a matrix written by CORRELATIONS but only if the missing-value treatment of both procedures is consistent: either both must reference a matrix of N's, or both must reference a single N. For all procedures, pairwise treatment of missing values generates a matrix of N's; any other treatment of missing values generates a single vector of N's. (see Section 13.9). If split-file processing is in effect when a matrix is written, the same split file must be in effect when that matrix is read by any procedure (see Section 13.7).

In the following example, REGRESSION uses matrix input from the CORRELATIONS procedure. Because CORRELATIONS uses listwise deletion to handle missing data, you must specify MISSING=LISTWISE to read the matrix into REGRESSION.

```
GET FILE=RAWDATA/KEEP VAR1 TO VAR7
CORRELATIONS VAR1 TO VAR7
    /MISSING=LISTWISE
    /MATRIX OUT(*)
REGRESSION MATRIX IN(*)
    /VARIABLES=VAR1 TO VAR7
    /MISSING=LISTWISE
    /DEPENDENT=VAR1
    /ENTER VAR2 TO VAR7
```

- The GET command defines the data to SPSS-X and selects the variables needed for the analysis.
- The CORRELATIONS command computes correlations among seven variables. The MISSING subcommand specifies listwise treatment of missing values. The MATRIX subcommand writes out a matrix system file. The OUT(*) specification replaces the active file with the matrix system file.
- The MATRIX IN subcommand on REGRESSION reads the matrix materials CORRELATIONS wrote to the active file.
- The VARIABLES subcommand names the variables to be used in the regression analysis.
- The MISSING subcommand specifies listwise deletion of missing values.
- The DEPENDENT subcommand specifies VAR1 as the dependent variable.
- The METHOD subcommand enters VAR2 to VAR7 with the ENTER method.

13.5
Format of the Matrix System File

The matrix system file shown in Figure 13.5a was produced by procedure CORRELATIONS (the commands are shown in Section 13.3). Figure 13.5b shows the file's dictionary. Because split-file processing is in effect (see Chapter 15), separate matrix materials are generated for each split-file variable. The split-file variable is the first variable in the file (see Section 13.7).

The matrix system file has two special variables created by SPSS-X: ROWTYPE_ and VARNAME_. Variable ROWTYPE_ is a string variable with A8 format having values MEAN, STDDEV, N, and CORR (for Pearson correlation coefficient). The next variable, VARNAME_, is a string variable with A8 format whose values are the names of the variables used to form the correlation matrix. When ROWTYPE_ is CORR, VARNAME_ gives the variable associated with that row of the correlation matrix. The remaining variables in the file are the variables used to form the correlation matrix. Each has an F10.7 format.

All the procedures that write matrices in SPSS-X use a format similar to that shown in Figure 13.5a, and all generate the special matrix variables ROWTYPE_

Figure 13.5a A matrix system file (LIST output)

```
FILE:     MATRIX FILE
SEX:   1   FEMALE

SEX ROWTYPE_ VARNAME_        FOOD        RENT    PUBTRANS     TEACHER        COOK    ENGINEER

  1 MEAN              73.3750000 134.500000  53.5000000  46.8000000  72.4375000  59.8125000
  1 STDDEV            15.4483009 115.534699  25.8173069  19.4209018  29.5746936  21.5196616
  1 N       FOOD      16.0000000  16.0000000  16.0000000  15.0000000  16.0000000  16.0000000
  1 N       RENT      16.0000000  16.0000000  16.0000000  15.0000000  16.0000000  16.0000000
  1 N       PUBTRANS  16.0000000  16.0000000  16.0000000  15.0000000  16.0000000  16.0000000
  1 N       TEACHER   15.0000000  15.0000000  15.0000000  15.0000000  15.0000000  15.0000000
  1 N       COOK      16.0000000  16.0000000  16.0000000  15.0000000  16.0000000  16.0000000
  1 N       ENGINEER  16.0000000  16.0000000  16.0000000  15.0000000  16.0000000  16.0000000
  1 CORR    FOOD       1.0000000    .3658643    .5372333    .1733358    .1378010    .3778351
  1 CORR    RENT        .3658643   1.0000000    .1045105   -.0735708    .2026299    .1237062
  1 CORR    PUBTRANS    .5372333    .1045105   1.0000000    .6097397    .3877995    .6413121
  1 CORR    TEACHER     .1733358   -.0735708    .6097397   1.0000000    .4314755    .7312415
  1 CORR    COOK        .1378010    .2026299    .3877995    .4314755   1.0000000    .7807327
  1 CORR    ENGINEER    .3778351    .1237062    .6413121    .7312415    .7807327   1.0000000

NUMBER OF CASES READ =      14     NUMBER OF CASES LISTED =       14


FILE:     MATRIX FILE
SEX:   2   MALE

SEX ROWTYPE_ VARNAME_        FOOD        RENT    PUBTRANS     TEACHER        COOK    ENGINEER

  2 MEAN              68.8620690 112.137931  45.1379310  33.9310345  60.2142857  60.1785714
  2 STDDEV            20.4148478  81.3430672  24.1819356  26.9588722  30.2952840  28.8752792
  2 N       FOOD      29.0000000  29.0000000  29.0000000  29.0000000  28.0000000  28.0000000
  2 N       RENT      29.0000000  29.0000000  29.0000000  29.0000000  28.0000000  28.0000000
  2 N       PUBTRANS  29.0000000  29.0000000  29.0000000  29.0000000  28.0000000  28.0000000
  2 N       TEACHER   29.0000000  29.0000000  29.0000000  29.0000000  28.0000000  28.0000000
  2 N       COOK      28.0000000  28.0000000  28.0000000  28.0000000  28.0000000  28.0000000
  2 N       ENGINEER  28.0000000  28.0000000  28.0000000  28.0000000  28.0000000  28.0000000
  2 CORR    FOOD       1.0000000    .2012077    .5977491    .6417034    .4898941    .5190702
  2 CORR    RENT        .2012077   1.0000000   -.1405952   -.0540657    .0727153    .3508598
  2 CORR    PUBTRANS    .5977491   -.1405952   1.0000000    .7172945    .7170419    .6580408
  2 CORR    TEACHER     .6417034   -.0540657    .7172945   1.0000000    .6711871    .6650047
  2 CORR    COOK        .4898941    .0727153    .7170419    .6711871   1.0000000    .7688210
  2 CORR    ENGINEER    .5190702    .3508598    .6580408    .6650047    .7688210   1.0000000

NUMBER OF CASES READ =      14     NUMBER OF CASES LISTED =       14
```

Figure 13.5b Dictionary of a matrix system file (DISPLAY output)

```
FILE:     MATRIX FILE

         LIST OF VARIABLES ON THE ACTIVE FILE

NAME                                                              POSITION

SEX                                                                   1
                 PRINT FORMAT: F2
                 WRITE FORMAT: F2

         VALUE     LABEL

           1       FEMALE
           2       MALE

ROWTYPE_                                                              2
                 PRINT FORMAT: A8
                 WRITE FORMAT: A8

VARNAME_                                                              3
                 PRINT FORMAT: A8
                 WRITE FORMAT: A8

FOOD     AVG FOOD PRICES                                              4
                 PRINT FORMAT: F10.7
                 WRITE FORMAT: F10.7

RENT     NORMAL RENT                                                  5
                 PRINT FORMAT: F10.7
                 WRITE FORMAT: F10.7

PUBTRANS PRICE FOR PUBLIC TRANSPORT                                   6
                 PRINT FORMAT: F10.7
                 WRITE FORMAT: F10.7

TEACHER  NET TEACHER'S SALARY                                         7
                 PRINT FORMAT: F10.7
                 WRITE FORMAT: F10.7

COOK     NET COOK'S SALARY                                            8
                 PRINT FORMAT: F10.7
                 WRITE FORMAT: F10.7

ENGINEER NET ENGINEER'S SALARY                                        9
                 PRINT FORMAT: F10.7
                 WRITE FORMAT: F10.7
```

13

and VARNAME_. Procedures like FACTOR or DISCRIMINANT that can use factor or grouping variables in their analyses include values for those variables with the matrix materials. In addition, procedure FACTOR creates matrix variables named ROWTYPE_ and FACTOR_ for FACTOR-format files. See Table 13.1 for the types and contents of the matrices each procedure handles.

13.6
Variable Order

The following variable order is standard for all matrix system files:

1 Split variables, if any. (See Section 13.7.)
2 ROWTYPE_ variable.
3 Factor or grouping variables, if any.
4 VARNAME_ variable (or FACTOR_ variable for FACTOR-format files).
5 Continuous variables used to form the matrix.

13.7
Split Files

When split-file processing is in effect, a full set of matrix materials is written for each split-file group defined by the split variable(s). A split variable cannot have the same variable name as any other variable written to the matrix system file. Not all procedures allow split variables with their matrices.

If split-file processing is in effect when a matrix is written, the same split file must be in effect when that matrix is read by any procedure. For example, the commands

```
GET FILE  UNION/KEEP FOOD RENT PUBTRANS TEACHER COOK ENGINEER SEX
SORT CASES BY SEX
SPLIT FILE BY SEX
CORRELATIONS  FOOD TO ENGINEER
    /MATRIX OUT(CORRMTX)
```

define split-file groups by variable SEX and write the correlation matrix materials to the file named CORRMTX. If you want to read the matrix contained in CORRMTX, the same split-file specification must be in effect, even if the procedure that is reading the matrix is the same procedure that wrote it. For example, if split-file processing is no longer in effect and you want to read file CORRMTX into another CORRELATIONS procedure, you would have to specify SPLIT FILE BY SEX again.

13.8
Additional Statistics

Some procedures include statistics with their matrix materials. For example, CORRELATION matrices always include the mean, standard deviation, and number of cases used to compute each coefficient, as shown in Figure 13.5a. Other procedures, for example PROXIMITIES and FACTOR, include no statistics with their matrices.

See Table 13.1 for a list of the statistics written by each procedure. Refer to the individual procedure chapter to see what each expects to read from a matrix input file.

13.9
Missing Values

Treatment of missing values in a procedure affects the matrix materials written to the system file. With pairwise treatment of missing values, the procedure includes with the materials a matrix of N's used to compute each coefficient. With any other missing-value treatment, the procedure includes the single N used to calculate all coefficients in the matrix. Figure 13.5a shows the matrix of N's written by CORRELATIONS when missing values are excluded pairwise from the analysis. Figure 13.9 shows the single N written by CORRELATIONS when missing values are excluded listwise.

Figure 13.9 Single N in the matrix system file

```
FILE:      MATRIX FILE
SEX:   1   FEMALE

SEX ROWTYPE. VARNAME.     FOOD      RENT    PUBTRANS   TEACHER     COOK    ENGINEER

  1 MEAN                73.4666667 136.800000 54.0000000 46.8000000 73.8666667 60.0000000
  1 STDDEV              15.9860058 119.210019 26.6431444 19.4209018 30.0353760 22.2614337
  1 N                   15.0000000 15.0000000 15.0000000 15.0000000 15.0000000 15.0000000
  1 CORR     FOOD        1.0000000   .3652366   .5371597   .1733358   .1358120   .3773434
  1 CORR     RENT         .3652366  1.0000000   .0989524  -.0735708   .1914448   .1213899
  1 CORR     PUBTRANS     .5371597   .0989524  1.0000000   .6097397   .3811372   .6409265
  1 CORR     TEACHER      .1733358  -.0735708   .6097397  1.0000000   .4314755   .7312415
  1 CORR     COOK         .1358120   .1914448   .3811372   .4314755  1.0000000   .7893533
  1 CORR     ENGINEER     .3773434   .1213899   .6409265   .7312415   .7893533  1.0000000


NUMBER OF CASES READ =      9    NUMBER OF CASES LISTED =       9
                                                                    2                   Page   7

FILE:      MATRIX FILE

SEX:   2   MALE

SEX ROWTYPE. VARNAME.     FOOD      RENT    PUBTRANS   TEACHER     COOK    ENGINEER

  2 MEAN                69.6428571 114.464286 46.1428571 33.7500000 60.2142857 60.1785714
  2 STDDEV              20.3437392 81.8474109 24.0011023 27.4356149 30.2952840 28.8752792
  2 N                   28.0000000 28.0000000 28.0000000 28.0000000 28.0000000 28.0000000
  2 CORR     FOOD        1.0000000   .1752920   .5784136   .6638084   .4898941   .5190702
  2 CORR     RENT         .1752920  1.0000000  -.1817862  -.0491139   .0727153   .3508598
  2 CORR     PUBTRANS     .5784136  -.1817862  1.0000000   .7447511   .7170419   .6580408
  2 CORR     TEACHER      .6638084  -.0491139   .7447511  1.0000000   .6711871   .6650047
  2 CORR     COOK         .4898941   .0727153   .7170419   .6711871  1.0000000   .7688210
  2 CORR     ENGINEER     .5190702   .3508598   .6580408   .6650047   .7688210  1.0000000


NUMBER OF CASES READ =      9    NUMBER OF CASES LISTED =       9
```

13.10
Matrix File Dictionaries

As shown in Figure 13.5b, print and write formats of A8 are assigned to the variables the procedure creates (for example, ROWTYPE_, VARNAME_, and FACTOR_). No labels are assigned to these matrix variables. Print and write formats of F10.7 are assigned to all the continuous variables in the matrix analysis; the names and variable labels defined for these variables in the original data file are retained, but their original values and value labels are dropped because they do not apply to the matrix system file. When split-file processing is in effect, the variable names, variable and value labels, and print and write formats of the split-file variable(s) are read from the dictionary of the original data file.

Procedures read and write square matrices, where each row corresponds to a single case in the matrix system file. For example, the matrix shown in Figure 13.9 has 9 cases. The first three cases, MEAN, STDDEV, and N, have no values for VARNAME_ but do have values for all the variables from FOOD to ENGINEER. The fourth case, CORR, in the matrix generated for split-file 1 (FEMALE) has a value of FOOD for VARNAME_, a value of .3652366 when correlated with variable RENT, a value of .5371597 when correlated with variable PUBTRANS, and so forth.

A matrix system file, therefore, is similar to any SPSS-X system file. It is a self-documented file containing data and descriptive information. The descriptive information, stored in the file dictionary, includes variable names, variable print and write formats, and optional variable and value labels. You can assign or change the names, labels, and formats of the variables in a matrix system file, just as you can in any system file.

13.11
MATRIX DATA COMMAND

The MATRIX DATA command reads raw matrix materials and converts them to a matrix system file that can be read by SPSS-X procedures that handle matrix materials, such as FACTOR, REGRESSION, etc. The data can include various vector statistics (for example, means and standard deviations) as well as matrices.

The MATRIX DATA command is similar to a DATA LIST command: it defines variable names and their order in the raw data file. It can define both inline data that appear between the BEGIN DATA and END DATA commands, and data from an external file. MATRIX DATA can read data in both LIST and FREE format. It clears the current active file to create a new active file.

Unlike DATA LIST, MATRIX DATA defines and writes data in one step. This means you cannot specify data transformations until after the command is executed, and you cannot specify any commands between MATRIX DATA and BEGIN DATA—not even a VARIABLE LABELS or PRINT FORMATS command. In addition, MATRIX DATA can only read data that conform to the general format of SPSS-X matrices. Figure 13.11 shows the typical format for a correlation matrix that MATRIX DATA generates.

Figure 13.11 Typical matrix format

```
ROWTYPE_ VARNAME_     SAVINGS      POP15        POP75       INCOME       GROWTH

MEAN               .        9.6710      35.0896       2.2930    1106.7784       3.7576
STDDEV                      4.4804       9.1517       1.2907     990.8511       2.8698
N                         50.0000      50.0000      50.0000      50.0000      50.0000
CORR     SAVINGS          1.0000       -.4555        .3165        .2203        .3047
CORR     POP15            -.4555       1.0000       -.9084       -.7561       -.0478
CORR     POP75             .3165       -.9084       1.0000        .7869        .0253
CORR     INCOME            .2203       -.7561        .7869       1.0000       -.1294
CORR     GROWTH            .3047       -.0478        .0253       -.1294       1.0000

NUMBER OF CASES READ =        8    NUMBER OF CASES LISTED =        8
```

Like the matrix system files created by procedures, the file that MATRIX DATA defines contains the following variables in the indicated order. If the variables are in a different order in the raw data file, MATRIX DATA rearranges them automatically in the system file.

- Split-file variables. These optional variables define the split files. There can be up to 8 split variables, and they must have numeric values. Split-file variables will appear in the order they are specified on the SPLIT subcommand (see Section 13.20).

- ROWTYPE_. ROWTYPE_ is a string variable with A8 format. Its values define the data type for each record. For example, it might identify a row of values as means, standard deviations, or correlation coefficients. Every matrix in SPSS-X has a ROWTYPE_ variable.

- Factors. There can be any number of factors. They occur only if the data include within-cell information, such as the within-cell means. The factors have the system-missing value on records that define pooled information. Factor variables appear in the order they are specified on the FACTORS subcommand (see Section 13.21).

- VARNAME_. This is a string variable with A8 format. Its values correspond to the variables named on the VARIABLES subcommand. For example, if the data represent a correlation matrix for variables SAVINGS, POP15, and POP75, successive records in the data have VARNAME_ values of SAVINGS, POP15, and POP75. Values for VARNAME_ are blank for records that define vector information, such as the mean and standard deviation. Every matrix in SPSS-X has a VARNAME_ variable. You never enter values for VARNAME_. MATRIX DATA automatically generates VARNAME_ and its values.

- Continuous variables. These are the variables to which the aggregated data pertain. There can be any number of them. Continuous variables appear in the order they are specified on the VARIABLES subcommand (see Section 13.15).

13.12
Format of the Raw Matrix
Data File

By default, MATRIX DATA reads data in LIST format. (MATRIX DATA can also read data entered in FREE format if you specify FREE on the FORMAT subcommand; see Section 13.18.) Like LIST format on DATA LIST, each scalar, vector, or row of a matrix begins on a new record, and the data are entered in freefield format, using blanks and commas as separators. Unlike LIST format with DATA LIST, a vector or row of the matrix can be continued on multiple records.

The continuation records do not have a value for ROWTYPE_. You can enclose ROWTYPE_ values in apostrophes or quotes (see Section 13.16).

The order of the variables in the input data file must match the order in which they are specified on the VARIABLES subcommand (see Section 13.14). However, this order does not have to correspond to the order of variables in the resulting SPSS-X matrix system file (see Sections 13.6 and 13.15).

In the default format, values are entered in the lower triangle of the matrix, including the diagonal values. If MATRIX DATA encounters values in the upper triangle, it issues a series of warnings stating that it will ignore extraneous text on the records. If any matrix rows span records in the data file and you enter values for the upper triangle, MATRIX DATA cannot properly form the matrix. If your data contain values in the upper triangle, use the FORMAT subcommand (see Section 13.18).

The way you enter records for pooled vectors or matrices when factors are present depends upon whether ROWTYPE_ is explicit or implicit on the VARIABLES subcommand (see Section 13.21).

MATRIX DATA recognizes plus and minus signs as field separators when they are not preceded by the letter "D" or the letter "E." This extension allows MATRIX DATA to read scientific notation and to read correlation matrices written by FORTRAN in F10.8 format. For example, values 1, 2, and 3 for two successive records might be entered as follows:

```
1 2 3
+1D+0+.2E+1+.03E+02
```

The plus signs preceded by a "D" or "E" are read as part of the number in scientific notation. The plus signs that are not preceded by a "D" or "E" are interpreted as field separators.

13.13
General Syntax

The minimum syntax for MATRIX DATA is the VARIABLES subcommand and a list of variables, as in

```
MATRIX DATA VARIABLES=varlist
```

You can specify the minimum only if all of the following are true:

- *Data are inline.* If data are not inline, the FILE subcommand is required to specify the file containing the data (see Section 13.17).
- *Data are in lower-triangle format with diagonal values included.* If data are in any other format, the FORMAT subcommand is required (see Section 13.18).
- *Data contain nothing but population coefficients.* If data contain other values, such as the mean and standard deviation, either variable ROWTYPE_ must be specified on the VARIABLES subcommand and ROWTYPE_ values must be included in the data (see Section 13.14), or the CONTENTS subcommand is required to describe the data (see Section 13.23).
- *There are no split-file variables.* If the data include split-file variables, the SPLIT subcommand is required.

When all of the above conditions are met, a list of variables provides MATRIX DATA with the minimum information it needs to define a set of records as CORR coefficients, meaning *Pearson correlation coefficient* records. Because the procedure must infer the information that isn't specified, it issues warning messages to alert you to its major assumptions. For example, MATRIX DATA issues the warning shown in Figure 13.13 when you specify just a list of variables.

The following general syntax rules apply to MATRIX DATA:

- The SPLIT and FACTORS subcommands, when used, must follow the VARIABLES subcommand. The order of the other subcommands is irrelevant, but you cannot duplicate specifications.
- Subcommands should be separated by slashes.

13

Figure 13.13   Typical warning issued by MATRIX DATA

```
>Warning # 16717 on line 4.   Command name: MATRIX DATA
>The MATRIX DATA command does not include a CONTENTS subcommand, and the data
>to be read do not include the variable ROWTYPE_.   CONTENTS=CORR will be
>assumed.
```

13.14
VARIABLES Subcommand

The required VARIABLES subcommand specifies the names of the variables in the data and the order in which they occur. There is no limit to the number of variables you can name, and you can use the TO convention to create consecutive variable names with numeric suffixes, as in:

```
MATRIX DATA VARIABLES=VAR1 TO VAR5
```

specifies variables VAR1, VAR2, VAR3, VAR4, and VAR5.

If you specify only continuous variables on the VARIABLES subcommand, one of two conditions must be met:

1 The data contain only correlation coefficients. There can be no additional information—such as the mean and standard deviation—and no factor information. MATRIX DATA assigns the record type CORR to all records.

2 You specify a CONTENTS subcommand (Section 13.23) to define all record types. The data can then contain information such as the mean and standard deviation, but no factor information. MATRIX DATA assigns the record types defined on the CONTENTS subcommand.

If neither of these two conditions is met in the data, the VARIABLES subcommand requires some combination of the following (in addition to the continuous variables), depending on the nature of your data:

• Variable ROWTYPE_. If ROWTYPE_ is named on the VARIABLES subcommand, the continuous variables must be the last variables specified on the subcommand. (See Section 13.16.)

• Split-file variables. If split-file variables are present, you must also specify them on the SPLIT subcommand. (See Section 13.20.)

• Factor variables. If factor variables are present, you must also specify them on the FACTORS subcommand. (See Section 13.21.)

13.15
VARNAME_ Variable

You cannot name a variable VARNAME_ on the VARIABLES subcommand. VARNAME_ has special meaning in matrix files. The MATRIX DATA command *always* generates variable VARNAME_ automatically. You *never* specify VARNAME_ anywhere on the MATRIX DATA command, and you never specify its values in the data.

13.16
ROWTYPE_ Variable

ROWTYPE_ is a string variable with A8 format. Its values define the data types. All matrices in SPSS-X contain a ROWTYPE_ variable.

Generally, if you specify data inline, you should explicitly name ROWTYPE_ on the VARIABLES subcommand and enter its values in the data. If you don't explicitly name ROWTYPE_ on the VARIABLES subcommand, the MATRIX DATA command must *precisely* define the data. In particular, you must use the CONTENTS subcommand (Section 13.23) to define the order in which the records occur within the file. MATRIX DATA strictly adheres to those specifications. A data entry error, especially skipping a record, can cause the procedure to assign the wrong values to the wrong records.

Explicit Specification. If you name ROWTYPE_ on the VARIABLES subcommand and enter its values in the data, the MATRIX DATA command is primarily used to define the names and order of the variables in the raw data file. For example, the following commands define the matrix shown in Figure 13.11. The ROWTYPE_ variable identifies each record type.

```
MATRIX DATA VARIABLES=ROWTYPE_ SAVINGS POP15 POP75 INCOME GROWTH
BEGIN DATA
MEAN 9.6710 35.0896 2.2930 1106.7784 3.7576
STDDEV 4.4804 9.1517 1.2907 990.8511 2.8699
N 50 50 50 50 50
CORR 1
CORR -.4555 1
CORR .3165 -.9085 1
CORR .2203 -.7562 .7870 1
CORR .3048 -.0478 .0253 -.1295  1
END DATA
```

Note that VARNAME_ is not specified on the VARIABLES subcommand, and its values are not entered in the data (see Section 13.15).

Valid values for the ROWTYPE_ variable include any of the following: CORR, COV, MAT, MSE, DFE, MEAN, STDDEV (or SD), N_VECTOR (or N), N_SCALAR, N_MATRIX, COUNT, or PROX (see Section 13.23 for definitions of these values). You can use three-character abbreviations for these values. You can also enclose the values in quotes or apostrophes. For example, ROWTYPE_ values of mean, standard deviation, N, and Pearson correlation coefficient might be entered as follows:

```
MATRIX DATA VARIABLES=ROWTYPE_ SAVINGS POP15 POP75 INCOME GROWTH
BEGIN DATA
'MEA     ' 9.6710 35.0896 2.2930 1106.7784 3.7576
'SD      ' 4.4804 9.1517 1.2907 990.8511 2.8699
'N       ' 50 50 50 50 50
"COR     " 1
"COR     " -.4555 1
"COR     " .3165 -.9085 1
"COR     " .2203 -.7562 .7870 1
"COR     " .3048 -.0478 .0253 -.1295  1
END DATA
```

Implicit Specification. The following specifications define the matrix shown in Figure 13.11 The ROWTYPE_ specification is implicit.

```
MATRIX DATA VARIABLES=SAVINGS POP15 POP75 INCOME GROWTH
          /CONTENTS=MEAN SD N CORR
BEGIN DATA
9.6710 35.0896 2.2930 1106.7784 3.7576
4.4804 9.1517 1.2907 990.8511 2.8699
50 50 50 50 50
 1
-.4555 1
 .3165 -.9085 1
 .2203 -.7562 .7870 1
 .3048 -.0478 .0253 -.1295 1
END DATA
```

• ROWTYPE_ is not specified on the VARIABLES subcommand, and its values are not included in the data.

• The CONTENTS subcommand is required to define the record types and the order of the records in the file (Section 13.23).

13.17
FILE Subcommand

The FILE subcommand specifies the file containing the data. The default specification for the FILE subcommand is INLINE, which indicates the data are included with the command stream between the BEGIN DATA and END DATA commands.

In the following example, the FILE subcommand indicates data are in the file RAWMTX:

```
MATRIX DATA FILE=RAWMTX /VARIABLES=varlist
```

If you omit the FILE subcommand, the data must be inline.

ANNOTATED EXAMPLE FOR MATRIX DATA

Procedure DISCRIMINANT reads the MEAN, COUNT (unweighted N), and N (weighted N) for each cell in the data, as well as pooled values for STDDEV and CORR. If COUNT=N, only N need be supplied. MATRIX DATA can be used as follows to generate an active file that DISCRIMINANT can read:

```
MATRIX DATA VARIABLES=WORLD ROWTYPE_ FOOD APPL SERVICE RENT
            /FACTOR=WORLD
BEGIN DATA
1 N       25 25 25 25
1 MEAN    76.64 77.32 81.52 101.40
2 N        7 7 7 7
2 MEAN    76.1428571 85.2857143 60.8571429 249.571429
3 N       13 13 13 13
3 MEAN    55.5384615 76 63.4615385 86.3076923
. SD      16.4634139 22.5509310 16.8086768 77.1085326
. COR     1
. COR     .1425366 1
. COR     .5644693 .2762615 1
. COR     .2133413 -.0499003 .0417468 1
END DATA
LIST
DISCRIMINANT GROUPS=WORLD(1,3)/
             VARIABLES=FOOD APPL SERVICE RENT/ METHOD=WILKS/ MATRIX=IN(*)
```

• ROWTYPE_ is explicit on the VARIABLES subcommand to identify record types. Though you could use the CONTENTS and CELLS subcommands to identify record types and distinguish between within-cell data and pooled values, it is usually easier to specify ROWTYPE_ on the VARIABLES subcommands and enter the ROWTYPE_ values in the data.

• Because factors are present in the data, the continuous variables (FOOD, APPL, SERVICE, and RENT) must be specified last on the VARIABLES subcommand and in the data.

• The FACTOR subcommand identifies WORLD as the factor variable.

• The BEGIN DATA command immediately follows the MATRIX DATA command.

• An N and MEAN value for each cell is entered in the data.

• The ROWTYPE_ values for the pooled records are SD and COR. MATRIX DATA assigns the values STDDEV and CORR to the corresponding vectors in the matrix, as shown in Figure A.

• Records with pooled information have the system-missing value (.) for the factors.

• The LIST command displays the matrix materials in the active file, as shown in Figure A.

• Procedure DISCRIMINANT reads the data matrix. An asterisk (*) is specified as the input file on the MATRIX subcommand because the data are in the active file.

A MATRIX DATA with procedure DISCRIMINANT

```
ROWTYPE_ WORLD VARNAME_      FOOD      APPL     SERVICE      RENT

N          1                25.0000   25.0000   25.0000    25.0000
MEAN       1                76.6400   77.3200   81.5200   101.4000
N          2                 7.0000    7.0000    7.0000     7.0000
MEAN       2                76.1429   85.2857   60.8571   249.5714
N          3                13.0000   13.0000   13.0000    13.0000
MEAN       3                55.5385   76.0000   63.4615    86.3077
STDDEV     .                16.4634   22.5509   16.8087    77.1085
CORR       .   FOOD          1.0000     .1425     .5645      .2133
CORR       .   APPL           .1425    1.0000     .2763     -.0499
CORR       .   SERVICE        .5645     .2763    1.0000      .0417
CORR       .   RENT           .2133    -.0499     .0417     1.0000


NUMBER OF CASES READ =     11   NUMBER OF CASES LISTED =     11
```

13.18
FORMAT Subcommand

The FORMAT subcommand indicates how the matrix data are formatted. It applies only to matrix values in the data, not vector values, such as the mean and standard deviation. The format specifications include

- The data entry format for the data. By default, the data are assumed to be in LIST format.
- The matrix shape. By default, the matrix is assumed to be a lower triangle.
- Whether or not the data include diagonal values. By default, the matrix is assumed to include diagonal values.

You can specify up to three keywords on FORMAT: one to specify the data entry format, one to specify matrix shape, and one to specify whether the data include diagonal values. The minimum specification is a single keyword. The other default settings remain in effect unless explicitly overridden.

Data Entry Format. FORMAT has two keywords that specify the data entry format:

LIST   *Each scalar, vector, and matrix row must begin on a new record.* A vector or row of the matrix may be continued on multiple records. This is the defalut.

FREE   *Record boundaries are of no consequence.* Any item can begin in the middle of a record.

Matrix Shape. FORMAT has three keywords that specify the matrix shape. Note that with either of the triangular shapes, no values—not even missing indicators—are entered for the implied values in the matrix.

LOWER   *Read data values from the lower triangle.* This is the default.

UPPER   *Read data values from the upper triangle.*

FULL   *Read the full square matrix of data values.* You cannot specify FULL with NODIAGONAL.

Diagonal Values. FORMAT has two keywords that refer to the diagonal values:

DIAGONAL   *Data include the diagonal values.* This is the default.

NODIAGONAL   *Data do not include diagonal values.* The diagonal value is set to the system-missing value for all matrices except the correlation matrices. For correlation matrices, the diagonal value is set to 1. You cannot specify NODIAGONAL with FULL.

The following command specifies the upper-triangle format with no diagonal values. The resulting matrix is shown in Figure 13.18.

```
MATRIX DATA VARIABLES=ROWTYPE_ V1 TO V3 /FORMAT=UPPER NODIAGONAL
BEGIN DATA
MEAN    5  4  3
SD      3  2  1
N       9  9  9
CORR      .6 .7
CORR         .8
END DATA
LIST
```

Note: Data in the command above and throughout the rest of this chapter are aligned in columns to emphasize the matrix format. You don't have to align the data in your jobs. For example, you could just as easily enter the above data as follows:

```
MATRIX DATA VARIABLES=ROWTYPE_ V1 TO V3 /FORMAT=UPPER NODIAGONAL
BEGIN DATA
MEAN 5 4 3
SD 3 2 1
N 9 9 9
CORR .6 .7
CORR .8
END DATA
LIST
```

Figure 13.18   Matrix data

```
ROWTYPE_ VARNAME_        V1         V2         V3

N                    9.0000     9.0000     9.0000
MEAN                 5.0000     4.0000     3.0000
STDDEV               3.0000     2.0000     1.0000
CORR        V1       1.0000      .6000      .7000
CORR        V2        .6000     1.0000      .8000
CORR        V3        .7000      .8000     1.0000


NUMBER OF CASES READ =        6   NUMBER OF CASES LISTED =        6
```

Table 13.18 shows how the same data might be entered for each combination of FORMAT settings that govern matrix shape and diagonal values. Notice that with UPPER NODIAGONAL and LOWER NODIAGONAL, you *do not* enter the matrix row that has blank values for the continuous variables. If you enter that row, MATRIX DATA cannot properly form the matrix. Each of the data entry format shapes in Table 13.18 produces a matrix similar to that shown in Figure 13.18.

Table 13.18   Various FORMAT settings

FULL				UPPER DIAGONAL				UPPER NODIAGONAL				LOWER DIAGONAL				LOWER NODIAGONAL			
MEAN	5	4	3	MEAN	5	4	3	MEAN	5	4	3	MEAN	5	4	3	MEAN	5	4	3
SD	3	2	1	SD	3	2	1	SD	3	2	1	SD	3	2	1	SD	3	2	1
N	9	9	9	N	9	9	9	N	9	9	9	N	9	9	9	N	9	9	9
CORR	1	.6	.7	CORR	1	.6	.7	CORR		.6	.7	CORR	1			CORR	.6		
CORR	.6	1	.8	CORR		1	.8	CORR			.8	CORR	.6	1		CORR	.7	.8	
CORR	.7	.8	1	CORR			1					CORR	.7	.8	1				

13.19
Print and Write Formats

MATRIX DATA does not allow you to specify print and write formats for the matrix materials. The procedure assigns the formats shown in Table 13.19.

To change data formats (or perform other transformations), execute the MATRIX DATA command and then assign new formats. See Chapter 10 for information on assigning formats.

Table 13.19   Print and write formats for matrix variables

Variable type	Format
ROWTYPE_, VARNAME_	A8
Split-file variables	F4.0
Factors	F4.0
Continuous variables	F10.4

13.20
SPLIT Subcommand

The SPLIT subcommand specifies the variables whose values define the split files. The SPLIT subcommand must follow the VARIABLES subcommand. SPLIT can specify a subset of up to 8 of the variables named on VARIABLES. You can use the TO keyword to imply variables in the order they are named on VARIABLES, as in:

```
MATRIX DATA VARIABLES=ROWTYPE_ SPL1 SPL2 SPL3 VAR1 TO VAR5
        /SPLIT=SPL1 TO SPL3
```

When you specify split variables, enter a separate data matrix for each value of each split variable. The following commands specify two matrices, one for each value of the split variable S1:

```
MATRIX DATA  VARIABLES=S1 ROWTYPE_ D1 TO D3 /SPL=S1
BEGIN DATA
0 MEAN   5  4  3
0 SD     1  2  3
0 N      9  9  9
0 CORR   1
0 CORR   .6  1
0 CORR   .7 .8  1
1 MEAN   9  8  7
1 SD     5  6  7
1 N      9  9  9
1 CORR   1
1 CORR   .4  1
1 CORR   .3 .2  1
END DATA
LIST
```

MATRIX DATA generates a complete set of matrix materials for each value of each split variable, as shown in Figure 13.20a.

Figure 13.20a   Separate matrices for split-file values

```
S1:      0

   S1 ROWTYPE_ VARNAME_        D1          D2          D3

    0 N                     9.0000      9.0000      9.0000
    0 MEAN                  5.0000      4.0000      3.0000
    0 STDDEV                1.0000      2.0000      3.0000
    0 CORR      D1          1.0000       .6000       .7000
    0 CORR      D2           .6000      1.0000       .8000
    0 CORR      D3           .7000       .8000      1.0000


NUMBER OF CASES READ =       6    NUMBER OF CASES LISTED =        6

S1:      1

   S1 ROWTYPE_ VARNAME_        D1          D2          D3

    1 N                     9.0000      9.0000      9.0000
    1 MEAN                  9.0000      8.0000      7.0000
    1 STDDEV                5.0000      6.0000      7.0000
    1 CORR      D1          1.0000       .4000       .3000
    1 CORR      D2           .4000      1.0000       .2000
    1 CORR      D3           .3000       .2000      1.0000


NUMBER OF CASES READ =       6    NUMBER OF CASES LISTED =        6
```

If the data contain neither ROWTYPE_ nor split-file information, SPLIT can specify a single split-file variable that does not appear on the VARIABLES subcommand. MATRIX DATA assigns values 1, 2, 3, etc., to the split variable until end of data is encountered and generates a complete set of matrix materials for each set of matrix data. For example, the following commands specify two matrices in the data:

```
MATRIX DATA VARIABLES=VAR1 TO VAR3 /CONTENTS=MEAN SD N CORR
            /SPLIT=SPL
BEGIN DATA
 5  4  3
 1  2  3
 9  9  9
 1
.6  1
.7 .8  1
 9  8  7
 5  6  7
 9  9  9
 1
.4  1
.3 .2  1
END DATA
LIST
```

MATRIX DATA therefore assigns values 1 and 2 to variable SPL, as shown in Figure 13.20b.

Figure 13.20b   Split-file matrices

```
SPL:     1

  SPL ROWTYPE_ VARNAME_        VAR1        VAR2        VAR3

    1 N                      9.0000      9.0000      9.0000
    1 MEAN                   5.0000      4.0000      3.0000
    1 STDDEV                 1.0000      2.0000      3.0000
    1 CORR       VAR1        1.0000       .6000       .7000
    1 CORR       VAR2         .6000      1.0000       .8000
    1 CORR       VAR3         .7000       .8000      1.0000


NUMBER OF CASES READ =       6    NUMBER OF CASES LISTED =        6

SPL:     2

  SPL ROWTYPE_ VARNAME_        VAR1        VAR2        VAR3

    2 N                      9.0000      9.0000      9.0000
    2 MEAN                   9.0000      8.0000      7.0000
    2 STDDEV                 5.0000      6.0000      7.0000
    2 CORR       VAR1        1.0000       .4000       .3000
    2 CORR       VAR2         .4000      1.0000       .2000
    2 CORR       VAR3         .3000       .2000      1.0000


NUMBER OF CASES READ =       6    NUMBER OF CASES LISTED =        6
```

13.21
FACTORS Subcommand

The FACTORS subcommand specifies the variables whose values define the cells represented by the within-cell data. The FACTORS subcommand must follow the VARIABLES subcommand.

FACTORS must specify a subset of the variables named on the VARIABLES subcommand. You can use the TO keyword to imply variables in the order they are named on VARIABLES, as in:

```
MATRIX DATA VARIABLES=ROWTYPE_ F1 F2 F3 VAR1 TO VAR5
    /FACTORS=F1 TO F3
```

The way you enter pooled information when factors are present depends upon whether ROWTYPE_ is explicit or implicit on the VARIABLES subcommand.

ROWTYPE_ Explicit. If ROWTYPE_ is explicit on VARIABLES and its values are included in the data, MATRIX DATA uses missing values to determine whether the data represent within-cell information or pooled information, since the values of ROWTYPE_ are ambiguous. On records that represent pooled information, you must use decimal points to enter missing values for the factors, as in:

```
MATRIX DATA VARIABLES=ROWTYPE_ F1 F2  VAR1 TO VAR3
    /FACTORS=F1 F2
BEGIN DATA
MEAN 1 1   1   2   3
SD   1 1   5   4   3
N    1 1   9   9   9
MEAN 1 2   4   5   6
SD   1 2   6   5   4
N    1 2   9   9   9
MEAN 2 1   7   8   9
SD   2 1   7   6   5
N    2 1   9   9   9
MEAN 2 2   9   8   7
SD   2 2   8   7   6
N    2 2   9   9   9
CORR . . .1
CORR . . .6  1
CORR . . .7 .8  1
END DATA
```

• ROWTYPE_ is explicitly specified on the VARIABLES subcommand.

• Decimal points represent missing values for the factor CORR values.

ROWTYPE_ Implicit. If ROWTYPE_ is not specified on the VARIABLES subcommand and its values are not in the data, enter data values *only* for the factor records representing within-cell information. Enter nothing for the factor records that represent pooled information. In addition, you must specify the CELLS subcommand indicating the number of within-cells records (Section 13.22) and the CONTENTS subcommand indicating which record types have within-cell data (Section 13.24), as in:

```
MATRIX DATA VARIABLES=F1 F2  VAR1 TO VAR3
            /FACTORS=F1 F2 /CONTENTS=(MEAN SD N) CORR /CELLS=4
BEGIN DATA
1 1  1   2   3
1 1  5   4   3
1 1  9   9   9
1 2  4   5   6
1 2  6   5   4
1 2  9   9   9
2 1  7   8   9
2 1  7   6   5
2 1  9   9   9
2 2  9   8   7
2 2  8   7   6
2 2  9   9   9
    1
     .6  1
     .7 .8 1
END DATA
```

- Nothing is entered for the CORR factor values because the records define pooled information.
- The CELLS subcommand is required because there are factors present without an explicit ROWTYPE_ specification (see Section 13.22).
- The CONTENTS subcommand is required to define the record types and to differentiate between the within-cell and pooled types (see Section 13.24).

13.22
CELLS Subcommand

The CELLS subcommand specifies the number of within-cell records in the data. The only valid specification for CELLS is a single integer, which indicates the number of sets of within-cell information MATRIX DATA must read.

CELLS is required when there are factors in the data but ROWTYPE_ is not explicitly specified on the VARIABLES subcommand. If you use CELLS when ROWTYPE_ is specified on VARIABLES, MATRIX DATA issues a warning and ignores the CELLS subcommand.

For example, in the specification

```
MATRIX DATA VARIABLES=F1 VAR1 TO VAR3 /FACTORS=F1 /CELLS=2
            /CONTENTS=(MEAN SD N) CORR
BEGIN DATA
1   5   4   3
1   3   2   1
1   9   9   9
2   8   7   6
2   6   7   8
2   9   9   9
    1
     .6  1
     .7 .8  1
END DATA
```

CELLS=2 because the factor variable F1 has two values (1 and 2) and there are therefore two sets of within-cell information. If there are two factor variables, F1 and F2, and each has two values, 1 and 2, CELLS would equal 4 to account for the following factor combinations (assuming all 4 combinations are present in the data):

```
F1  F2

 1   1
 1   2
 2   1
 2   2
```

13.23
CONTENTS Subcommand

The CONTENTS subcommand defines the record types when ROWTYPE_ is not included in the data. Each different type of record in the data is indicated by a keyword. The minimum specification is a single keyword. The default keyword is CORR.

The following keywords are available:

CORR *Matrix of correlation coefficients.* This is the default. If ROWTYPE_ is not specified on the VARIABLES subcommand and you omit the CONTENTS subcommand, MATRIX DATA assigns the ROWTYPE_ value CORR to all matrix rows.

COV *Matrix of covariance coefficients.*

MAT *Generic square matrix.*

MSE *Vector of mean squared errors.*

DFE *Vector of degrees of freedom.*

MEAN *Vector of means.*

STDDEV *Vector of standard deviations.* SD is a synonym for STDDEV. If SD is specified, MATRIX DATA assigns the ROWTYPE_ value STDDEV to the record.

N_VECTOR *Vector of counts.* MATRIX DATA assigns ROWTYPE_ value N to the record. N is a synonym for N_VECTOR.

N_SCALAR *Count.* Scalars are a shorthand mechanism for representing vectors in which all elements have the same value. This would be the case for a vector of N's calculated using listwise deletion of missing values. Enter N_SCALAR as the ROWTYPE_ value in the data and then the N_SCALAR value for the first continuous variable, only. MATRIX DATA assigns the ROWTYPE_ value N to the record, and copies the specified N_SCALAR value across all the continuous variables.

N_MATRIX *Square matrix of counts.* Enter N_MATRIX as the ROWTYPE_ value for each row of counts in the data. MATRIX DATA assigns ROWTYPE_ value N to each of those rows.

COUNT *Count vector accepted by procedure DISCRIMINANT.* This contains unweighted N's.

PROX *Matrix produced by PROXIMITIES.* Any proximity matrix that can be used with PROXIMITIES or CLUSTER.

The CONTENTS subcommand is required to define record types and record order whenever ROWTYPE_ is not specified on the VARIABLES subcommand and its values are not in the data. The only exception to this rule is the rare situation in which *all data values represent pooled correlation records and there are no factors.* In this case, MATRIX DATA reads the data values and assigns the default ROWTYPE_ of CORR to all records. For example, the commands

```
MATRIX DATA VARIABLES=VAR1 TO VAR3
BEGIN DATA
 1
.6  1
.7 .8  1
END DATA
LIST
```

generate the matrix shown in Figure 13.23a. MATRIX DATA issues a warning that says both ROWTYPE_ and CONTENTS were omitted from the specifications. The default ROWTYPE_ value CORR is assumed for all records.

The order in which you specify keywords on the CONTENTS subcommand must correspond to the order in which the records appear in the data. For example, assume the matrix records are in the order mean, standard deviation, N, and correlation coefficients. The following commands specify the correct order for the records:

```
MATRIX DATA VARIABLES=V1 TO V3 /CONTENTS=MEAN SD N_SCALAR CORR
BEGIN DATA
 5    4    3
 3    2    1
 9
 1
.6    1
.7   .8    1
END DATA
LIST
```

Notice that the N_SCALAR value is entered only for the first continuous variable. Figure 13.23b shows the matrix generated by MATRIX DATA.

If you specify the keywords on CONTENTS in the wrong order, MATRIX DATA will incorrectly assign values to the records. For example, if you reverse the order of MEAN and SD in the above command, as in

```
MATRIX DATA VARIABLES=V1 TO V3 /CONTENTS=SD MEAN N_SCALAR CORR
```

MATRIX DATA will assign the mean values to the standard deviation and the standard deviation values to the mean.

Figure 13.23a Default CONTENTS setting

```
ROWTYPE_ VARNAME_         VAR1        VAR2        VAR3

CORR      VAR1         1.0000        .6000       .7000
CORR      VAR2          .6000       1.0000       .8000
CORR      VAR3          .7000        .8000      1.0000


NUMBER OF CASES READ =        3    NUMBER OF CASES LISTED =        3
```

Figure 13.23b Order of keywords on CONTENT

```
ROWTYPE_ VARNAME_          V1          V2          V3

N                       9.0000      9.0000      9.0000
MEAN                    5.0000      4.0000      3.0000
STDDEV                  3.0000      2.0000      1.0000
CORR      V1            1.0000       .6000       .7000
CORR      V2             .6000      1.0000       .8000
CORR      V3             .7000       .8000      1.0000


NUMBER OF CASES READ =        6    NUMBER OF CASES LISTED =        6
```

13.24
Within-Cells Record Definition

When factors are present and ROWTYPE_ is not specified, the CONTENTS subcommand distinguishes between keywords that identify within-cell information and keywords that identify pooled information by enclosing the within-cell keywords in parentheses. (See Section 13.21 for information on specifying factors when ROWTYPE_ is explicit.) For example, in the following command MEAN, SD, and N contain within-cells information:

```
MATRIX DATA VARIABLES=F1 VAR1 TO VAR3 /FACTORS=F1 /CELLS=2
             /CONTENTS=(MEAN SD N) CORR
```

CORR is outside the parentheses because it identifies pooled records. The CELLS subcommand (Section 13.22) is required because there is a factor specified and ROWTYPE_ is implicit on VARIABLES.

There are two methods for using the parentheses on CONTENTS, depending on how the data are organized:

1 Enclose multiple cell keywords together within a single set of parentheses if their associated records appear collectively for each set of factor values.

2 Enclose a cell keyword within its own parentheses if its associated records are grouped together across factor values.

For example, the specification

```
MATRIX DATA VARIABLES=Fl VAR1 TO VAR3 /FACTORS=Fl /CELLS=2
              /CONTENTS=(MEAN SD N) CORR
BEGIN DATA
1   5   4   3
1   3   2   1
1   9   9   9
2   4   5   6
2   6   5   4
2   9   9   9
    1
    .6  1
    .7 .8  1
END DATA
```

indicates the data include the mean, the standard deviation, and N for F1 value 1, followed by the mean, standard deviation, and N for F1 value 2. Alternatively, the specification

```
MATRIX DATA VARIABLES=Fl VAR1 TO VAR3 /FACTORS=Fl /CELLS=2
              /CONTENTS=(MEAN) (SD) (N) CORR
BEGIN DATA
1   5   4   3
2   4   5   6
1   3   2   1
2   6   5   4
1   9   9   9
2   9   9   9
    1
    .6  1
    .7 .8  1
END DATA
```

indicates the data include the means for all the cells, followed by the standard deviations for all the cells, followed by the N for all the cells. The specification

```
MATRIX DATA VARIABLES=Fl VAR1 TO VAR3 /FACTORS=Fl /CELLS=2
              /CONTENTS=(MEAN SD) (N) CORR
BEGIN DATA
1   5   4   3
1   3   2   1
2   4   5   6
2   6   5   4
1   9   9   9
2   9   9   9
    1
    .6  1
    .7 .8  1
END DATA
```

indicates the data include the mean and standard deviation for F1 value 1, followed by the mean and standard deviation for F1 value 2, followed by the N values for all the cells.

13.25
Optional Specification with
ROWTYPE_ Explicit

When ROWTYPE_ is explicitly named on the VARIABLES subcommand, MATRIX DATA uses ROWTYPE_ values to determine record types. You can use the CONTENTS subcommand for informational purposes, but the ROWTYPE_ variable will still determine record types. However, if MATRIX DATA reads values for ROWTYPE_ that are not specified on the CONTENTS subcommand, it issues a warning to point out the discrepancy.

For example, the following is a valid specification:

```
MATRIX DATA VARIABLES=ROWTYPE_ Fl F2 VAR1 TO VAR3
              /FACTORS=Fl F2 /CONTENTS=(MEAN SD N) CORR
BEGIN DATA
MEAN 1 1   1   2   3
SD   1 1   5   4   3
N    1 1   9   9   9
MEAN 1 2   4   5   6
SD   1 2   6   5   4
N    1 2   9   9   9
CORR . .   1
CORR . .  .6   1
CORR . .  .7  .8   1
END DATA
```

Note that missing values for the factors must still be entered as decimal points, even though CONTENTS is specified (see Section 13.21).

13.26
N Subcommand

The N subcommand specifies the population N when the data do not include it. The only valid specification is an integer, which indicates the population N. MATRIX DATA generates one record for each split file with a ROWTYPE_ of N, and uses the specified N value for each continuous variable. For example, in the specification

```
MATRIX DATA VARIABLES=VAR1 TO VAR3 /CONTENTS=MEAN SD CORR
             /N=99
BEGIN DATA
  5  4  3
  3  4  5
  1
 .6  1
 .7 .8  1
END DATA
```

MATRIX DATA uses 99 as the N value for all continuous variables, as shown in Figure 13.26.

Figure 13.26   Missing values specified on the N subcommand

```
ROWTYPE_ VARNAME_        VAR1       VAR2       VAR3

N                      99.0000    99.0000    99.0000
MEAN                    5.0000     4.0000     3.0000
STDDEV                  3.0000     4.0000     5.0000
CORR      VAR1          1.0000      .6000      .7000
CORR      VAR2           .6000     1.0000      .8000
CORR      VAR3           .7000      .8000     1.0000


NUMBER OF CASES READ =        6    NUMBER OF CASES LISTED =        6
```

13.27
Subcommand Summary

Table 13.27 summarizes the status of each MATRIX DATA subcommand in relation to the ROWTYPE_ specification.

Table 13.27   Subcommands in relation to ROWTYPE_

Subcommand	ROWTYPE_ implicit on VARIABLES	ROWTYPE_ explicit on VARIABLES
FILE	Defaults to INLINE	Defaults to INLINE
VARIABLES	Required	Required
FORMAT	Defaults to LOWER DIAG	Defaults to LOWER DIAG
SPLIT	Required if split files*	Required if split files
FACTORS	Required if factors	Required if factors
CELLS	Required if factors	Inapplicable
CONTENTS	Defaults to CORR	Optional
N	Optional	Optional

*If the data do not contain values for the split-file variables, this subcommand can specify a single variable that is not specified on the VARIABLES subcommand.

13.28
MATRIX DATA Examples

13.29
Example 1: MATRIX DATA
with Procedure ONEWAY

Following are two examples that illustrate the use of MATRIX DATA with the SPSS-X ONEWAY and REGRESSION procedures.

Procedure ONEWAY reads two types of matrices. The first type includes a vector of frequencies for each factor level, a vector of means for each factor level, and a vector of standard deviations. The second type includes:

• A vector of frequencies for each factor level.
• A vector of means for each factor level.
• A record containing the pooled variance (within-group mean square error).
• The degrees of freedom for the MSE.

MATRIX DATA can be used as follows to generate an active file containing the second type of matrix data for procedure ONEWAY:

```
MATRIX DATA VARIABLES=EDUC ROWTYPE_ WELL /FACTOR=EDUC
BEGIN DATA
1 N 65
2 N 95
3 N 181
4 N 82
5 N 40
6 N 37
1 MEAN 2.6462
2 MEAN 2.7737
3 MEAN 4.1796
4 MEAN 4.5610
5 MEAN 4.6625
6 MEAN 5.2297
. MSE 6.2699
. DFE 494
END DATA
LIST
ONEWAY WELL BY EDUC(1,6)/ MATRIX=IN(*)
```

• ROWTYPE_ is explicit on the VARIABLES subcommand and identifies record types. Though you could use the CONTENTS and CELLS subcommands to identify record types and distinguish between within-cell data and pooled values, it is usually easier to specify ROWTYPE_ on the VARIABLES subcommands and enter the ROWTYPE_ values in the data.

• Because factors are present in the data, the continuous variables (WELL) must be specified last on the VARIABLES subcommand and in the data.

• The FACTOR subcommand identifies EDUC as the factor variable.

• The BEGIN DATA command immediately follows the MATRIX DATA command.

• MSE is entered in the data as the ROWTYPE_ value for the vector of square pooled standard deviations.

• DFE is entered in the data as the ROWTYPE_ value for the vector of degrees of freedom.

• Records with pooled information have the system missing value (.) for the factors.

• The LIST command displays the matrix materials in the active file, as shown in Figure 13.29.

• Procedure ONEWAY reads the data matrix. An asterisk (*) is specified as the input file on the MATRIX subcommand because the data are in the active file. Figure 13.29 shows the results of the ONEWAY analysis.

Figure 13.29 MATRIX DATA with procedure ONEWAY

```
ROWTYPE_ EDUC VARNAME_      WELL

N           1              65.0000
MEAN        1               2.6462
N           2              95.0000
MEAN        2               2.7737
N           3             181.0000
MEAN .      3               4.1796
N           4              82.0000
MEAN        4               4.5610
N           5              40.0000
MEAN        5               4.6625
N           6              37.0000
MEAN        6               5.2297
MSE         .               6.2699
DFE         .             494.0000


NUMBER OF CASES READ =      14   NUMBER OF CASES LISTED =      14
- - - - - - - - - - - - - - - - - - - - - - - - - - - O N E W A Y - - - - - - - - - - - - - - - - - - - - - - - - - - - - - - - - - -


          Variable   WELL
       By Variable   EDUC


Group      Grp 1       Grp 2       Grp 3       Grp 4       Grp 5       Grp 6

COUNT        65.         95.        181.         82.         40.         37.
MEAN       2.6462      2.7737      4.1796      4.5610      4.6625      5.2297

                        ANALYSIS OF VARIANCE

                                SUM OF        MEAN           F       F
           SOURCE      D.F.     SQUARES       SQUARES      RATIO    PROB.

BETWEEN GROUPS           5      361.3150      72.2630     11.5254   .0000

WITHIN GROUPS          494     3097.3306       6.2699

TOTAL                 499     3458.6456
```

13.30
Example 2: MATRIX DATA with Procedure REGRESSION

REGRESSION reads and writes matrices that always contain the mean, standard deviation, N, and Pearson correlation coefficients. Assume your data do not have ROWTYPE_ values, and that the correlation values are from the upper triangle of the matrix without the diagonal values. MATRIX DATA can be used as follows to generate a matrix that REGRESSION can read:

```
MATRIX DATA VARIABLES=SAVINGS POP15 POP75 INCOME GROWTH
            /CONTENTS=MEAN SD N CORR /FORMAT=UPPER NODIAGONAL
BEGIN DATA
9.6710 35.0896 2.2930 1106.7784 3.7576
4.4804 9.1517 1.2908 990.8511 2.8699
50 50 50 50 50
-.4555 .3165 .2203 .3048
-.9085 -.7562 -.0478
.7870 .0253
-.1295
END DATA
LIST
REGRESSION MATRIX=IN(*)/ VARIABLES=SAVINGS TO GROWTH/
           DEP=SAVINGS/ ENTER
```

- ROWTYPE_ is not specified on the VARIABLES subcommand because its values are not included in the data.

- Because there are no ROWTYPE_ values, the CONTENTS subcommand is required to define the record types and also the order of the records in the file.

- By default, MATRIX DATA reads values from the lower triangle of the matrix, including the diagonal values. The FORMAT subcommand is required in this instance to indicate that the data are in the upper triangle and do not include diagonal values.

- The BEGIN DATA command immediately follows the MATRIX DATA command.

- The LIST command displays the matrix materials in the active file, as shown in Figure 13.30a.

13

• Procedure REGRESSION reads the data matrix. An asterisk (*) is specified as the input file on the MATRIX subcommand because the data are in the active file. Since there is a single vector of N's in the data, missing values are handled LISTWISE (the default for REGRESSION). Figure 13.30b shows the results of the REGRESSION analysis.

Figure 13.30a   MATRIX DATA with procedure REGRESSION

```
ROWTYPE_ VARNAME_    SAVINGS      POP15       POP75      INCOME      GROWTH

N                    50.0000     50.0000     50.0000     50.0000     50.0000
MEAN                  9.6710     35.0896      2.2930   1106.7784      3.7576
STDDEV                4.4804      9.1517      1.2908    990.8511      2.8699
CORR     SAVINGS      1.0000      -.4555       .3165       .2203       .3048
CORR     POP15        -.4555      1.0000      -.9085      -.7562      -.0478
CORR     POP75         .3165      -.9085      1.0000       .7870       .0253
CORR     INCOME        .2203      -.7562       .7870      1.0000      -.1295
CORR     GROWTH        .3048      -.0478       .0253      -.1295      1.0000


NUMBER OF CASES READ =        8   NUMBER OF CASES LISTED =        8
```

Figure 13.30b   REGRESSION results

```
                                 * * * *   M U L T I P L E   R E G R E S S I O N   * * * *

Listwise Deletion of Missing Data

Equation Number 1    Dependent Variable..    SAVINGS

Beginning Block Number   1.  Method:  Enter


Variable(s) Entered on Step Number   1..      GROWTH
                                     2..      POP75
                                     3..      INCOME
                                     4..      POP15


Multiple R               .58176     Analysis of Variance
R Square                 .33845                           DF     Sum of Squares     Mean Square
Adjusted R Square        .27964     Regression             4          332.90656        83.22664
Standard Error          3.80269     Residual              45          650.71866        14.46041

                                    F =       5.75548     Signif F =   .0008


------------------ Variables in the Equation ------------------

Variable               B           SE B         Beta          T    Sig T
GROWTH            .409703       .196195      .262433      2.088    .0425
POP75          -1.691585      1.083676     -.487345     -1.561    .1255
INCOME      -3.37392E-04    9.3113E-04     -.074615      -.362    .7188
POP15           -.461240       .144659     -.942132     -3.188    .0026
(Constant)     28.568445      7.355344                   3.884    .0003

End Block Number   1    All requested variables entered.
```

13.31
MCONVERT
COMMAND

The MCONVERT command can perform two types of matrix material conversion:

• It can convert a covariance matrix to a correlation matrix plus a vector of standard deviations.

• It can convert a correlation matrix and vector of standard deviations to a covariance matrix.

MCONVERT can read matrix materials from the active file or from an external matrix system file. It cannot read raw matrix values. If your data are raw values, use the MATRIX DATA command (see Section 13.11) to convert the raw matrix materials to a matrix system file. MCONVERT can write converted matrix materials to the active file or to an external file. MCONVERT can write the converted matrix alone to the output file, or it can append the converted matrix to the end of the original matrix and write both to the output file.

13.32
General Syntax

The minimum syntax on the MCONVERT command is the command name, MCONVERT. Three defaults are in effect when you specify MCONVERT with no further specifications:

- MCONVERT reads matrix materials from the active file. If data are in an external matrix system file, the MATRIX subcommand is required to specify the file (see Section 13.33).
- MCONVERT replaces the original matrix with the converted matrix. The APPEND subcommand is required to append the converted matrix to the end of the original matrix (Section 13.35).
- MCONVERT writes the converted matrix to the active file. Use the MATRIX subcommand to write the matrix materials to an external file.

Split variables (if any) must occur first in the file MCONVERT reads, followed by variable ROWTYPE_, the grouping variables (if any), and variable VARNAME_. All variables following VARNAME_ are the variables for which a matrix will be read and created. See Sections 13.5 through 13.7 for a complete description of the format of matrix system files. The total number of split variables plus grouping variables cannot exceed 8.

In the following example, the MATRIX DATA command reads raw covariance values to create a matrix system file that MCONVERT can read:

```
MATRIX DATA VARIABLES=ROWTYPE_ SAVINGS POP15 POP75 INCOME GROWTH
             /FORMAT=FULL
BEGIN DATA
COV    20.0740459   -18.678638     1.8304990   978.181242  3.9190106
COV   -18.678638     83.7541100  -10.731666  -6856.9888   -1.2561071
COV     1.8304990   -10.731666     1.6660908  1006.52742    .0937992
COV   978.181242   -6856.9888     1006.52742  981785.907  -368.18652
COV     3.9190106    -1.2561071     .0937992  -368.18652   8.2361574
END DATA
LIST
MCONVERT
FACTOR MATRIX IN(COR=*)
```

- The MATRIX DATA command defines the variables in the file and creates an active file of matrix materials.
- Because record type (COV) values are in the data, ROWTYPE_ is specified on the VARIABLES subcommand.
- The FORMAT subcommand indicates that data are in full square format.
- The LIST command lists variables in the active file (see Figure 13.32).
- The MCONVERT command converts the covariance matrix shown in Figure 13.32 to a correlation matrix. By default, the converted matrix is written to the active file.
- The FACTOR command reads the correlation matrix from the active file and performs factor analysis.

Figure 13.32 Covariance matrix

```
ROWTYPE_ VARNAME_   SAVINGS      POP15       POP75      INCOME      GROWTH

COV      SAVINGS     20.0740    -18.6786      1.8305    978.1812      3.9190
COV      POP15      -18.6786     83.7541    -10.7317  -6856.9888     -1.2561
COV      POP75        1.8305    -10.7317      1.6661   1006.5274       .0938
COV      INCOME     978.1812  -6856.9888   1006.5274  981785.907   -368.1865
COV      GROWTH       3.9190     -1.2561       .0938   -368.1865      8.2362

NUMBER OF CASES READ =      5    NUMBER OF CASES LISTED =      5
```

If there are multiple CORR or COV matrices (i.e., one for each factor, or one for each split variable), each will be converted to a separate matrix, preserving the values of any factor or split variables.

If the original matrix is a correlation matrix, data must contain CORR values (Pearson correlation coefficients) and a vector of standard deviations (STDDEV). If the original matrix is a covariance matrix, only COV values are required in the data. Since the diagonal of a covariance matrix is the variance, and the square root of the variance is the standard deviation, COV values alone supply MCONVERT with enough information to calculate a vector of standard deviations for the correlation matrix.

All cases with ROWTYPE_ values other than CORR or COV, such as MEAN, N, and STDDEV, are always copied into the resulting system file. For example, when you convert CORR and STDDEV to COV, the resulting file will have COV and STDDEV (and possibly CORR as well, if APPEND was specified; see Section 13.35).

13.33
MATRIX Subcommand

The MATRIX subcommand specifies the file for the matrix materials and the actual keyword MATRIX is optional. MATRIX has two specifications, IN and OUT, which you use to specify the matrix file in parentheses. Keyword IN specifies the file MCONVERT reads, and keyword OUT specifies the file MCONVERT writes. By default, MATRIX reads the original matrix from the active file, then replaces that matrix with the converted matrix.

Keywords IN and OUT each have two specifications:

(*)   *Active file.* For both keywords IN and OUT, an asterisk refers to the active file. IN(*) instructs MCONVERT to read the matrix from the active file; OUT(*) instructs MCONVERT to write the matrix to the active file. This is the default for both IN and OUT.

(file) *External matrix system file.* For both keywords IN and OUT, you can refer to an external file by specifying the file in parentheses. IN(file) instructs MCONVERT to read the matrix from the specified file; OUT(file) instructs MCONVERT to write the matrix to the specified file. IN and OUT cannot specify the same external file.

Whether the result file is the active file or an external file, MCONVERT replaces the original matrix with the converted matrix, unless you use the APPEND subcommand (Section 13.35).

MATRIX=IN cannot be used in place of GET or DATA LIST to begin a new SPSS^X command file. MATRIX is a subcommand on MCONVERT and MCONVERT cannot run before an active file is defined. To begin a new command file and immediately read a matrix, first GET the matrix file and then specify IN(*) on MATRIX.

In the following example, MCONVERT reads the original matrix from the active file (COVMTX) and writes the converted matrix to file CORMTX.

```
GET FILE=COVMTX
MCONVERT MATRIX=IN(*) OUT(CORMTX)
```

13.34
REPLACE Subcommand

By default, MCONVERT replaces the original matrix with the converted matrix and writes only the converted matrix to the result file. To make the default explicit, use the REPLACE subcommand, as in:

```
MCONVERT REPLACE
```

Again, the REPLACE keyword is the default and is optional.

13.35
APPEND Subcommand

The APPEND subcommand appends the converted matrix to the end of the original matrix. By default, MCONVERT replaces the original matrix with the converted matrix and writes only the converted matrix to the result file. If you want to append the converted matrix to the end of the original matrix and write both to the result file, use the APPEND subcommand, as in

```
MCONVERT APPEND
```

If there are multiple sets of matrix materials in the file MCONVERT reads, each converted matrix is appended to the end of its original matrix in the result file. For example, assume MCONVERT reads a file with two sets of matrices, MTX1 and MTX2. If you specify APPEND, the result file will contain MTX1 followed by its converted matrix, then MTX2 followed by its converted matrix.

13

Syntax

BREAK

```
LOOP ...
DO IF [(] logical expression [)]
BREAK
END IF
END LOOP
```

END CASE

```
END CASE
```

END FILE

```
END FILE
```

INPUT PROGRAM—END INPUT PROGRAM

```
INPUT PROGRAM
commands to create cases
END INPUT PROGRAM
```

LOOP—END LOOP

```
LOOP [varname=n TO m [BY {1**}]] [IF [(]logical expression[)]]
                              {n  }
transformations
END LOOP [IF [(]logical expression[)]]
```
**Default if the subcommand is omitted.

REREAD

```
REREAD [COLUMN=expression]
```

VECTOR

```
VECTOR {vector name=varlist    } [/vector name...]
       {vector name(n) [format] }
```

Contents

14.1   LOOP AND END LOOP COMMANDS
14.2   Indexing Clause for the LOOP Command
14.3   BY Keyword
14.4   IF Clause for the END LOOP Command
14.5   IF Clause for the LOOP Command
14.6   Missing Values and the LOOP Structure
14.7   Nesting LOOP Structures
14.8   BREAK Command

14.9   VECTOR COMMAND
14.10   VECTOR Command Short Form
14.11   Using VECTOR Outside a LOOP Structure

14.12 INPUT PROGRAM AND END INPUT PROGRAM
14.13   Input State
14.14   END CASE Command
14.15   END CASE and Other Commands
14.16   END FILE Command
14.17   END FILE and END CASE
14.18   Creating Data
14.19   End-of-File Processing Using END on DATA LIST
14.20   Concatenating Raw Data Files by Using END
14.21   REREAD Command
14.22   COLUMN Subcommand
14.23   Predetermining Variable Order

14.24 CONTROL STRUCTURES AND DEFINING FILES
14.25   DO IF Structure
14.26   LOOP Structure

14

Chapter 14 Input Programs

SPSS-X builds the active file dictionary as it encounters commands that create and define variables. At the same time, SPSS-X builds an *input program* that will construct the cases and an optional *transformation program* that will modify the cases prior to analysis or display. The internal input program is usually built from either a single DATA LIST command (Chapter 5) or from any of the commands that read or combine system files (described in Chapters 6, 12, 13, 16, and 17). By the time SPSS-X encounters a procedure command that tells it to read the data, the active file dictionary is ready, and the programs that construct and modify the cases in the active file are built. The active file dictionary is described in Chapter 5, and the commands and applications that make up the transformation program are discussed in Chapters 7, 8, 9, and 11.

You can create your own input program with the commands described in this chapter. With an input program, you can perform many different operations on raw data. You can use transformation commands described in Chapters 7, 8, and 9 to build cases. You can read nonrectangular files, concatenate raw data files, and build cases selectively. You can also create an active file without reading any data at all.

The INPUT PROGRAM and END INPUT PROGRAM commands enclose data definition and transformation commands that build cases from input records. These commands establish flow of control with one or more DO IF or LOOP structures and usually include the REPEATING DATA command, multiple DATA LIST commands, the END CASE or END FILE command, or the REREAD command.

The DO IF—END IF structure (Chapter 9) selects subsets of cases on which one or more transformation commands are executed. The LOOP—END LOOP structure discussed in this chapter controls the execution of commands on a single case or on a single input record containing information on multiple cases. In this chapter, the LOOP structure is documented first in general mechanical terms (Sections 14.1 through 14.8) and then in applications for defining files. Applications of LOOP appear throughout the rest of the chapter in conjunction with explanations of other commands (see particularly Section 14.26).

This chapter also documents several utility commands designed primarily for creating input programs. END CASE and END FILE (Sections 14.14 through 14.18) signal that a case or a file is complete. REREAD (Sections 14.21 and 14.22) instructs SPSS-X to read the same record again—usually to define data in light of information gleaned from a previous reading of the record. VECTOR (Sections 14.9 through 14.11) is a shorthand reference to a number of variables. Though the VECTOR command has other uses within the transformation language, its power is most fully exploited in conjunction with LOOP structures.

Input programs are used to create a dictionary and data for an active file; they cannot be used to process SPSS-X system files. To process direct-access and keyed data files, use an input program and the conventions described in Appendix E.

Scratch variables are frequently used in input programs. If you use input program commands interactively on IBM CMS systems, you may have to turn off the line-end character. See Chapter 3 for more information on interactive SPSS-X.

14.1
LOOP
AND END LOOP
COMMANDS

The LOOP command defines the beginning of a LOOP structure and the END LOOP command defines its end. Every LOOP structure must have both a LOOP and an END LOOP command, as in:

```
SET MXLOOPS=10
COMPUTE X=0
LOOP                                /*LOOP WITH NO LIMIT
COMPUTE X=X+1
END LOOP
```

The SET MXLOOPS command limits the number of times the loop is executed to 10. The first COMPUTE command initializes the value of X to 0; otherwise it would be initialized to system-missing (see Chapter 7). The first iteration for the first case sets the value of X to 0 plus 1. Then control returns to the LOOP command and the value of X is set to 1 plus 1. After 10 iterations, as specified in the SET command, control is passed to the first command after the END LOOP command. Thus, the value of X is 10 for every case.

In addition to MXLOOPS, you can control the number of trips SPSS-X makes through the LOOP structure by an optional indexing clause on the LOOP command or by the IF clause on the END LOOP command. You can also terminate a trip before it is complete with the BREAK command (see Section 14.8). Or you can use the IF clause on the LOOP command to control entry into the loop. Without one of these controls, the upper limit on the number of trips is the SPSS-X default limit of 40 iterations (see the MXLOOPS subcommand of the SET command in Chapter 4).

When specified within a LOOP structure, definition commands like MISSING VALUES and VARIABLE LABELS, case selection commands like SELECT IF and SAMPLE, and utility commands like SET and SHOW are invoked once when they are encountered in the command file.

14.2
Indexing Clause for the
LOOP Command

If you know exactly how many times you want to iterate through a LOOP structure, you can include an indexing clause on the LOOP command. The simplest form is

```
COMPUTE X=0
LOOP #I=1 TO 5                      /*LOOP FIVE TIMES
COMPUTE X=X+1
END LOOP
```

where scratch variable #I (the indexing variable) is set to the *initial value* of 1, and increased by 1 each time the loop is executed for a case. The last trip through the loop is when #I reaches or surpasses the *terminal value*, which is 5. Thus, the value of X will be 5 for every case.

• The indexing variable can have any valid variable name.

• Unless you specify a scratch variable, the indexing variable is treated as a permanent variable and is saved on your active file.

14

- If you give the indexing variable the same name as an existing variable, the values of the existing variable are altered by the LOOP structure as it is executed and the original values are lost.
- An indexing clause overrides the maximum number of loops specified by SET MXLOOPS.

The initial and terminal values of the indexing clause can be numeric expressions of the type described in Chapter 7 and can therefore be noninteger and negative. For example, the terminal value is frequently a numeric variable from the data, perhaps the number of records SPSS-X should expect per case (see Section 14.9).

- If the expression for the initial value is greater than the terminal value, no iterations of the loop are executed. #J=X TO Y is a zero-trip loop if X is 0 and Y is −1.
- If the expressions for the initial and terminal values are equal, the loop is executed once. #J=0 TO Y is a one-trip loop when Y is 0.

In the structure

```
COMPUTE X=0
LOOP #I=1 TO Y                      /*LOOP TO THE VALUE OF Y
COMPUTE X=X+1
END LOOP
```

the number of iterations for a case depends on the value of variable Y for the case. For a case with value 0 for variable Y, the loop is not executed and X is 0. For a case with value 1 for variable Y, the loop is executed once and X is 1.

Altering the value of the indexing variable within the structure has no effect on the iterations. At the end of the structure, the indexing variable is restored to its value at the beginning of the iteration before it is incremented again for the next iteration.

14.3
BY Keyword

By default, SPSS-X increases the indexing variable by 1 for each iteration. You can override this increment using keyword BY, as in

```
LOOP #I=2 TO 10 BY 2               /*LOOP FIVE TIMES BY 2'S
COMPUTE X=X+1
END LOOP
```

where #I starts at 2 and increments by 2 for each of 5 iterations until it equals 10 for the last iteration. Order is unimportant: 2 BY 2 TO 10 is equivalent to 2 TO 10 BY 2.

- The *increment value* can be a numeric expression and can therefore be noninteger or negative. Zero causes a warning and results in a zero-trip loop.
- If the initial value is greater than the terminal value and the increment is positive, the loop is never entered. #I=1 TO 0 BY 2 is a zero-trip loop.
- If the initial value is less than the terminal value and the increment is negative, the loop is never entered. #I=1 TO 2 BY −1 is a zero-trip loop.
- If the initial value plus a positive increment value is greater than the terminal value, the loop is entered once. #I=1 TO 5 BY 5 is a one-trip loop since #I becomes 6 after the first trip.
- If the initial value plus a negative increment value is less than the terminal value, the loop is entered once. #I=−1 TO −5 BY −5 is a one-trip loop since #I becomes −6 after the first trip.

In the structure

```
COMPUTE X=0
LOOP #I=1 TO Y BY Z                /*LOOP TO Y INCREMENTING BY Z
COMPUTE X=X+1
END LOOP
```

the loop is executed once for a case with Y equal to 2 and Z equal to 2, because #I is 3 after one loop. The loop is executed twice if Y is 3 and Z is 2.

14.4
IF Clause for the END LOOP Command

Frequently it is more logical to control the iterations using an IF clause on the END LOOP command. The structure

```
COMPUTE X=0
LOOP
COMPUTE X=X+1
END LOOP IF (X EQ 5)          /*LOOP UNTIL X IS 5
```

sets the value of X to 5 for each case. Iterations continue until the logical expression on the END LOOP is true, which for every case is when X equals 5.

14.5
IF Clause for the LOOP Command

You can control the number of trips through a LOOP structure using the IF clause on the LOOP command, as in:

```
COMPUTE X=0
LOOP IF (X LT 5)              /*LOOP UNTIL X IS 5
COMPUTE X=X+1
END LOOP
```

The IF clause is evaluated each trip through the structure, so looping stops once X is 5.

Or if you want to execute transformations within the LOOP structure to be executed only for a subset of cases, specify

```
COMPUTE X=0
LOOP IF (Y GT 10)            /*LOOP ONLY FOR CASES WITH Y GT 10
COMPUTE X=X+1
END LOOP IF (X EQ 5)        /*LOOP UNTIL X IS 5
```

where X will be 5 for cases with values greater than 10 for variable Y. Variable X is 0 for all other cases.

If you need both an indexing and an IF clause on the LOOP command, specify the indexing clause first, as in:

```
COMPUTE X=0
LOOP #I=1 TO 5   IF (Y GT 10)  /*LOOP TO X=5 ONLY FOR CASES Y GT 10
COMPUTE X=X+1
END LOOP
```

This structure produces the same results as the previous structure.

14.6
Missing Values and the LOOP Structure

If SPSS-X encounters a case with a missing value for the initial, terminal, or increment expressions in an indexing clause, or if the conditional expression on the LOOP command returns missing, a zero-trip loop results and control is passed to the first command after the END LOOP command. In the structure

```
COMPUTE X=0
LOOP #I=1 TO Z   IF (Y GT 10)  /*LOOP TO X=Z ONLY FOR CASES Y GT 10
COMPUTE X=X+1
END LOOP
```

the value of X remains at 0 for cases with a missing value for Y or a missing value for Z (or if Z is less than 1; see Section 14.2).

If a case has a missing value for the conditional expression on an END LOOP command, all iterations of the loop are terminated for that case. In the structure

```
MISSING VALUES X(5)
COMPUTE X=0
LOOP
COMPUTE X=X+1
END LOOP IF (X GE 10)        /*LOOP UNTIL X IS AT LEAST 10 OR MISSING
```

looping is terminated when the value of X reaches 5 because 5 is the missing value for X and the logical expression on the END LOOP command returns missing. The value of X is 5 for every case.

14

To prevent cases with missing values on any of the variables used in the LOOP structure from ever entering the loop, use the IF clause on the LOOP command, as in:

```
COMPUTE X=0
LOOP IF NOT MISSING(Y)          /*LOOP ONLY WHEN Y ISN'T MISSING
COMPUTE X=X+Y
END LOOP IF (X GE 10)           /*LOOP UNTIL X IS AT LEAST 10
```

In this structure, X is 0 for cases with a missing value for Y since the loop is never entered.

14.7
Nesting LOOP Structures

LOOP structures can be nested within other LOOP structures or within DO IF structures, and vice versa. The structure

```
COMPUTE X=0
LOOP #I=1 TO 5                   /*LOOP FIVE TIMES
+ LOOP #J=1 TO 5                 /*INNER LOOP FIVE TIMES
+ COMPUTE X=X+1
+ END LOOP
END LOOP
```

sets the value of variable X to 25 for every case. The outer loop executes 5 times and the inner loop executes 5 times, so the result of adding 1 each trip is 25. The optional plus signs (or periods or minus signs) in column one allow indentation of the nested structure so it is easily distinguished.

The indexing variables can be the same for all levels since each structure operates on its own version of the indexing variable. Thus, in the example above, #J could be named #I without affecting the results.

14.8
BREAK Command

If you cannot fully control looping with the IF clauses on the LOOP and END LOOP commands, you may have to resort to the BREAK command inside a DO IF—END IF structure. The expression on the DO IF command specifies the condition in which the BREAK is executed. For example, in the structure

```
COMPUTE X=0
LOOP #I=1 TO 5                   /*LOOP FIVE TIMES
+ LOOP #J=1 TO 5                 /*INNER LOOP FIVE TIMES
+    DO IF (#J EQ 4)             /*BREAK INNER LOOP BEFORE COMPLETE
+    BREAK
+    END IF
+ COMPUTE X=X+1
+ END LOOP
END LOOP
```

the inner loop terminates when the scratch variable #J equals 4.

- You must enclose the BREAK command within a LOOP structure. Otherwise, an error results.
- A BREAK command inside a LOOP structure but not inside a DO IF structure terminates the first iteration of the loop for all cases, since no conditions for the BREAK are specified.

A BREAK command within an inner loop terminates only iterations in that structure, not in any outer loop structures. In the example above, the outer loop always repeats five times, while the inner loop is "broken" when the indexing variable reaches 4. Thus, the value of X in the example is 20 for each case.

14.9
VECTOR COMMAND

The VECTOR command is designed for use with a LOOP structure, though it can be used in data transformations wherever you find an application. The VECTOR command defines a *vector*, which references a list of permanent or temporary variables to be used in other transformations. VECTOR can be used to reference both string and numeric variables. For example, if you want to define a vector as referencing a list of 10 existing variables measuring children's ages, specify:

```
VECTOR AGES=AGEKID26 TO AGEKID35
```

In this command, vector AGES has 10 *elements*, AGES(1), AGES(2), and so forth up to AGES(10), which correspond to AGEKID26, AGEKID27, and so forth up to AGEKID35 from the original variable list.

- Variables specified on a VECTOR command must already exist on your active file.
- Variables specified must be consecutive and must be from the same dictionary, permanent or scratch. Thus, you must specify the variables using the TO convention (see Chapter 2).
- The vector can have the same name as any variable in your active file, but this is not recommended. The vector can also have the name of one of the functions, although you will then lose access to that function.
- You can use vectors in transformations but not in procedures.
- The vector name can never appear without a subscript in parentheses.
- The VECTOR command is in effect only until the first procedure that follows it. The vector must be redeclared to be reused between procedures.

For example, you can use vector AGES to search for teenage children in any of variables AGEKID26, AGEKID27, and so forth. To find the first teenage child in a file on parents, specify

```
VECTOR AGES=AGEKID26 TO AGEKID35

LOOP #I=1 TO KIDS
COMPUTE #TEENAGE=RANGE(AGES(#I),13,19)    /*FIND A TEENAGER
END LOOP IF #TEENAGE                      /*END IF ONE IS FOUND

PRINT /#TEENAGE (F2,2X) AGEKID26 TO AGEKID35
SELECT IF #TEENAGE
```

where KIDS is a variable containing the number of children per case and scratch variable #TEENAGE is used to terminate the loop and then to select only parents of teenagers. As SPSS-X executes the loop, the subscript #I for vector AGES is incremented until either the number of children is reached (the LOOP command) or a teenage child is found (the END LOOP command). That is, the first loop tests AGES(1), the first element of the vector which corresponds to variable AGEKID26. IF the value for AGES(1) is not between 13 and 19, the loop repeats, testing the age of each child until all elements are tested or the loop terminates upon finding an age between 13 and 19. See the display from the PRINT command in Figure 14.9.

Figure 14.9   PRINT variable #TEENAGE and elements of vector AGES

```
1     8 11 15
0     4  8
0     2
0
1    11 12 14 16 20
0     4  4
0    20 22
1    14 21
1    14 14 18
1     4  4  9 11 12 15 17 20 22
```

Multiple vectors can be created on the same command using the slash to separate specifications.

14.10
VECTOR Command Short Form

You can use an alternative form of the VECTOR command to create simultaneously a list of new variables and the vector that refers to them. Simply give a prefix of alphabetic characters followed by the number of variables you want to create in parentheses, as in:

```
VECTOR #WORK(10)
```

SPSS-X creates vector #WORK, which references 10 scratch variables: #WORK1, #WORK2, and so on, through #WORK10. Thus element #WORK(5) of the vector is variable #WORK5.

The new variable names must not conflict with existing variables. They are created according to the rules for scratch variables if the prefix is given a # character, or otherwise according to the rules for permanent and temporary variables.

You can create more than one vector of the same length by naming two or more prefixes before the length specification. The command

```
VECTOR X,Y(5)
```

creates vectors X and Y defining new variables X1 through X5 and Y1 through Y5, respectively.

By default, variables you create with the VECTOR command receive an F8.2 format. You can specify an alternative format for the variables by including the format specification with the the length specification within the parentheses, as in

```
VECTOR X(6A5)
```

which assigns an A5 format to variables X1 through X6, making them string variables with a width of 5. If you create multiple vectors, the assigned format applies to all of them unless you specify otherwise, as in

```
VECTOR X,Y(6A5) Z(3F2)
```

which assigns A5 formats to variables X1 to X6 and Y1 to Y6, and F2 formats to variables Z1 to Z3.

14.11
Using VECTOR Outside a LOOP Structure

The VECTOR command is most commonly associated with the LOOP structure since the index variable for LOOP can be used as the subscript. However, the subscript can come from elsewhere, including from the data. Consider a file of scores on tests recorded in separate cases along with a subject identification number and a test number. To create a single case for each subject, you can use the test number as a subscript to a vector to assign the test score to the right test variable, as in:

```
GET FILE=FILEC
PRINT /ID SCORE TESTNUM

VECTOR RESULT(4)
COMPUTE RESULT(TESTNUM)=SCORE

AGGREGATE OUTFILE=*/BREAK=ID
         /RESULT1 TO RESULT4=MAX(RESULT1 TO RESULT4)

PRINT FORMATS RESULT1 TO RESULT4 (F2.0)
PRINT /ID RESULT1 TO RESULT4
```

Figure 14.11a   PRINT before aggregating

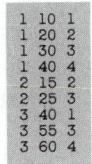

```
1  10  1
1  20  2
1  30  3
1  40  4
2  15  2
2  25  3
3  40  1
3  55  3
3  60  4
```

In this example, there are four possible tests for three subjects. Not all subjects took every test. The first PRINT command shows the data before the new cases are created (see Figure 14.11a). Vector RESULT creates variables RESULT1 through RESULT4, and COMPUTE assigns SCORE values to these variables, depending on the value of TESTNUM. Aggregating by variable ID creates new cases as shown by the results of the second PRINT command (see Figure 14.11b). The MAX function in AGGREGATE returns the maximum value across cases with the same value for ID.

Figure 14.11b   PRINT output after aggregating

```
1  10  20  30  40
2   .  15  25   .
3  40   .  55  60
```

14.12
INPUT PROGRAM AND END INPUT PROGRAM

When a single DATA LIST command does not allow you to define your data and the general file definition facilities described in Chapter 12 are not applicable, you can use one or more DATA LIST commands, transformation commands, and the utility commands documented in this chapter to build your own input program. When you do, you must begin your input program with the INPUT PROGRAM command and end it with the END INPUT PROGRAM command, as illustrated in the examples throughout the remainder of the chapter.

The following utilities are available for use within input programs:

END CASE. Use the END CASE command to write your own end-of-case processing (see Sections 14.14 and 14.15).

END FILE. Use the END FILE command to terminate processing of a data file before the actual end of the file (see Sections 14.16 and 14.17) or to define the end of the file when you are creating data (see Section 14.18).

REREAD. Use the REREAD command to reread the current record using a different DATA LIST (see Sections 14.21 and 14.22).

REPEATING DATA. Use the REPEATING DATA command to read repeating groups of data from the same input record (see Chapter 12).

14.13
Input State

There are four program states in SPSS-X: the *initialization state,* where the active file dictionary is initialized; the *input state,* where cases are created from the input file; the *transformation state,* where cases are transformed; and the *procedure state,* where procedures are executed. While these states are generally of no real importance to you, when specifying either FILE TYPE—END FILE TYPE or INPUT PROGRAM—END INPUT PROGRAM you must pay attention to which commands are allowed within the input state, which commands can appear *only* within the input state, and which are not allowed within the input state. See Appendix B for a discussion of the four program states, command precedence, and a table that describes what happens to each command when it is encountered in each of the four states.

14.14
END CASE Command

Use the END CASE command whenever you change the case structure of your file by building a single case from several cases or by building several cases from a single case. END CASE terminates execution of your SPSS-X commands and delivers a case to the next procedure. For example, consider the following data matrix:

```
2  1  1
3  5  1
```

14

The task is to make each data item into a single case, thereby creating six cases out of two. First, read the three data items into three scratch variables: #X1, #X2, and #X3. Then use a LOOP structure to create a new permanent variable from each scratch variable in turn and an END CASE command to build three new cases from each old one.

```
INPUT PROGRAM
DATA LIST  FILE=TESTDATA /#X1 TO #X3 (3(F1,1X))

VECTOR V=#X1 TO #X3

LOOP #I=1 TO 3
COMPUTE X=V(#I)
END CASE
END LOOP
END INPUT PROGRAM
```

The VECTOR command creates vector V with the original scratch variables as its three elements (see Section 14.9). The indexing expression on the LOOP command increments variable #I three times to control the number of iterations per input case and to provide the index for vector V (see Section 14.2). The COMPUTE command then sets X to each of the scratch variables, and the END CASE command tells SPSS-X to build a case. Thus, the first loop for the first case sets X equal to the first element of vector V. Since V(1) references #X1, and #X1 is 2, the value of X is 2. END CASE then builds the case. The END LOOP returns control to the LOOP command since the indexing is not complete. SPSS-X then sets X to #X2, which is 1, and builds the second case. The third iteration sets X equal to #X3, which is also 1, builds the third case, and terminates the loop. At this point, control is returned to the DATA LIST for the next input case. The six new cases are therefore

```
2
1
1
3
5
1
```

14.15
END CASE and Other Commands

The END CASE command tells SPSS-X that it has built a case and to pass it immediately to the procedure. When you use END CASE in an input program, SPSS-X abandons its default end-of-case processing and gives you total control. In the absence of instructions to the contrary, transformations such as COMPUTE, definitions such as VARIABLE LABELS, and utilities such as PRINT that follow an END CASE inside an input program are executed while a case is being initialized, not when it is complete. For definition commands like VARIABLE LABELS, MISSING VALUES, and PRINT FORMATS, this has no effect since these are merely written into the dictionary. However, for commands that act on the data itself, such as COMPUTE and PRINT, it makes a big difference.

A PRINT command that follows an END CASE command and precedes the END INPUT PROGRAM command prints the cases at initialization using system-missing values for permanent numeric variables, zero for scratch variables, and blanks for string variables. While the printed information is useless, it does not affect the outcome of the variable once the data are read. However, a COMPUTE that is executed at initialization does affect the outcome. For instance, if you specify PRINT and COMPUTE after the END CASE command in Section 14.14, as in

```
INPUT PROGRAM
DATA LIST  FILE=TESTDATA /#X1 TO #X3 (3(F1,1X))

VECTOR V=#X1 TO #X3

LOOP #I=1 TO 3
COMPUTE X=V(#I)
END CASE
END LOOP

COMPUTE Y=X**2
VARIABLE LABELS X 'TEST VARIABLE' Y 'SQUARE OF X'
PRINT FORMATS X Y (F2)
PRINT /X Y
END INPUT PROGRAM

FREQUENCIES VARIABLES=X Y
```

no error or warning is issued, but SPSS-X prints only two lines with two periods each. These periods are the initialized system-missing values of X and Y for the two original cases. After the data are read and the six cases are created, the VARIABLE LABELS and PRINT FORMATS commands have their desired effects, as shown in the FREQUENCIES table in Figure 14.15. However, because Y is computed from the initialized value of X, it is always system-missing.

Figure 14.15   FREQUENCIES output

```
X          TEST VARIABLE

                                                          VALID      CUM
        VALUE LABEL            VALUE  FREQUENCY  PERCENT  PERCENT  PERCENT

                                 1        3        50.0     50.0     50.0
                                 2        1        16.7     16.7     66.7
                                 3        1        16.7     16.7     83.3
                                 5        1        16.7     16.7    100.0
                                       ------    ------   ------
                      TOTAL               6       100.0    100.0

VALID CASES        6     MISSING CASES      0


Y          SQUARE OF X

                                                          VALID      CUM
        VALUE LABEL            VALUE  FREQUENCY  PERCENT  PERCENT  PERCENT

                                          6       100.0   MISSING
                                        ------    ------   ------
                      TOTAL               6       100.0    100.0
```

One solution is to specify PRINT and COMPUTE before the END CASE command. The preferred solution is to specify these commands in the transformation program after the END INPUT PROGRAM command, since they operate on the cases created by the input program.

14.16
END FILE Command

The END FILE command tells SPSS-X to stop reading data before it actually encounters the end of the file. You can also use END FILE to indicate the end of the file when you are generating data (see Section 14.18). Consider a historical study of price increases for a product taken from magazine advertisements in the United States, sorted by date. To instruct SPSS-X to stop reading the file when it first encounters data collected in 1881 (when the product was changed and essentially became a new product), specify:

```
INPUT PROGRAM
DATA LIST FILE=PRICES /YEAR 1-4 QUARTER 6 PRICE 8-12(2)

DO IF (YEAR GE 1881)          /*STOP READING BEFORE 1881
END FILE
END IF
END INPUT PROGRAM

PRINT FORMATS PRICE (DOLLAR7.2)
PRINT /YEAR QUARTER PRICE
```

Figure 14.16 shows the display output from the PRINT command. Notice that the case for 1881 that caused the end of the file is not included.

Figure 14.16   PRINT output for END FILE

```
1867 2   $11.49
1867 4   $11.49
1868 1   $11.49
1869 2   $11.99
1869 3   $12.49
1869 4   $12.99
1870 2   $14.99
1871 2   $15.99
1871 3   $16.99
1872 3   $20.99
1873 1   $27.99
1874 1   $28.99
1874 2   $29.99
1875 1   $31.99
1876 3   $35.49
1877 2   $41.99
1877 3   $43.99
1877 4   $43.99
1878 4   $45.49
1879 2   $52.99
1879 4   $52.99
1880 3   $55.49
```

If you know the exact number of cases you want SPSS-X to create, you can use the N OF CASES command (see Chapter 11). You can also use a SELECT IF (also Chapter 11) to select cases before 1881, but then SPSS-X would unnecessarily read the rest of the file.

**14.17
END FILE and END CASE**

The END FILE command excludes the case it creates to determine the end of the file. If you want SPSS-X to include this case, use the END CASE command, as in:

```
INPUT PROGRAM
DATA LIST FILE=PRICES /YEAR 1-4 QUARTER 6 PRICE 8-12(2)

DO IF (YEAR GE 1881)          /*STOP READING AT 1881
END CASE                      /*CREATE CASE 1881
END FILE

ELSE
END CASE                      /*CREATE CASES
END IF
END INPUT PROGRAM

PRINT FORMATS PRICE (DOLLAR7.2)
PRINT /YEAR QUARTER PRICE
```

Notice that there are *two* END CASE commands. The first END CASE forces SPSS-X to include the last case. Once SPSS-X encounters the END CASE command, it abandons automatic end-of-case processing. Thus, you must include the second END CASE command following the ELSE command to create all cases previous to the first case in 1881.

14.18
Creating Data

To create data without any data input, use a LOOP structure and an END CASE command within an input program, as in:

```
INPUT PROGRAM
LOOP #I=1 TO 20
COMPUTE AMOUNT=RND(UNIFORM(5000))/100
END CASE
END LOOP
END FILE
END INPUT PROGRAM

PRINT FORMATS AMOUNT (DOLLAR6.2)
PRINT /AMOUNT
EXECUTE
```

This example creates 20 cases with a single variable AMOUNT, a uniformly distributed number between 0 and 5000, rounded to a an integer and divided by 100 to provide a variable in dollars and cents (see Figure 14.18).

The END FILE command is required to terminate processing once the LOOP structure is complete.

Figure 14.18 Printing generated cases

```
$32.64
$28.81
$32.22
$13.19
$23.74
$18.63
$11.62
$21.69
$40.58
$39.59
 $7.75
$37.21
$34.61
$11.05
$13.50
$19.33
$38.41
$18.62
$15.08
$23.75
```

14.19
End-of-File Processing Using END on DATA LIST

The END subcommand on DATA LIST gives you control over end-of-file processing. END specifies a variable that is set to a value of 0 until the end of the file is encountered, at which time this variable is set to 1. The values of all variables named on the DATA LIST command are left unchanged. In most instances, variables are initialized to system missing (or blank in the case of strings), so they remain at that value. You can then use the logical variable created with END on DO IF and LOOP to invoke special processing after all the cases from a particular input file have been built.

When you use the END subcommand on DATA LIST, you must make sure that the entire set of commands used to define the cases is enclosed within the INPUT PROGRAM—END INPUT PROGRAM structure. You must also specify the END FILE command to signal the end of case generation. You should be careful to place END FILE so it is not executed before you are finished building cases from the input file. Freefield input is incompatible with the END subcommand, and an error will be generated if either FREE or LIST is used on a DATA LIST that includes an END subcommand.

You can use the END subcommand to direct SPSS-X to do some operation when it comes to the end of the file. For example, you can use the following commands to print case listings and totals for the end of the file:

```
TITLE            'DEMONSTRATE THE USE OF THE END SUBCOMMAND'

INPUT PROGRAM
NUMERIC          TINCOME (DOLLAR8.0)                    /* TOTAL INCOME
LEAVE            TINCOME
DO IF            $CASENUM EQ 1
+   PRINT        EJECT
+   PRINT        / 'NAME          INCOME'/
END IF
DATA LIST        FILE=INCOME END=#EOF NOTABLE/ NAME 1-10(A) INCOME 16-20(F)
DO IF            #EOF
+   PRINT        // 'TOTAL     ', TINCOME
+   END FILE
ELSE
+   PRINT        / NAME, INCOME (A10,COMMA8)
+   COMPUTE      TINCOME = TINCOME+INCOME              /* ACCUMULATE TOTAL
END IF
END INPUT PROGRAM

EXECUTE
```

The data definition commands are enclosed within the INPUT PROGRAM—END INPUT PROGRAM structure.

- The NUMERIC command declares the new numeric value to be created, TINCOME.
- The LEAVE command tells SPSS-X to leave variable TINCOME at its value for the previous case as each new case is read.
- The first DO IF structure, enclosing the PRINT EJECT and PRINT commands, tells SPSS-X to print the headers NAME and INCOME at the top of the display (when $CASENUM equals 1).
- The DATA LIST command defines variables NAME and INCOME, and it specifies the scratch variable #EOF as the END variable.
- The second DO IF accumulates the variable INCOME into TINCOME by passing control to ELSE as long as #EOF is not equal to 1. At the end of the file, EOF equals 1, and the expression on the DO IF is true. The label TOTAL and the value for TINCOME are printed, and control is passed to END FILE.

Figure 14.19 shows the results of the input program.

Figure 14.19   Output from PRINT controlled by an END subcommand

```
NAME        INCOME

JOE         12,345
WILLIE      20,468
MARY        15,000
RONNIE      17,500
VERONICA    22,675

TOTAL       $87,988
```

ANNOTATED EXAMPLE FOR INPUT PROGRAM

Consider a file, each record of which has an invoice number, a series of book codes, and quantities of books ordered. Five example records are

```
1045 182 2 155 1 134 1 153 5
1046 155 3 153 5 163 1
1047 161 5 182 2 163 4 186 6
1048 186 2
1049 155 2 163 2 153 2 074 1 161 1
```

Invoice 1045 is for nine books of four different titles: two copies of book 182, one copy each of 155 and 134, and five copies of book 153. The task is to break each individual book order into a record, preserving the order number on each new case. The SPSS-X commands are

```
INPUT PROGRAM
DATA LIST  FILE=SPORTSBK
  /ORDER 1-4 #X1 TO #X24 (1X,12(F3.0,F2.0,1X))

LEAVE ORDER
VECTOR BOOKS=#X1 TO #X24

LOOP #I=1 TO 24 BY 2
- COMPUTE ISBN=BOOKS(#I)
- COMPUTE QUANTITY=BOOKS(#I+1)
- END CASE
END LOOP IF SYSMIS(BOOKS(#I+2))
END INPUT PROGRAM

SORT CASES ISBN

DO IF $CASENUM EQ 1
- PRINT EJECT /'Order ISBN Quantity'
- PRINT SPACE
END IF

FORMATS ISBN (F3)/ QUANTITY (F2)
PRINT /' ' ORDER ' ' ISBN ' ' QUANTITY

EXECUTE
```

- The INPUT PROGRAM and END INPUT PROGRAM commands begin and end the block of commands that build cases from the input file (see Section 14.12). They are required because the END CASE command is used to create multiple cases from single input records.

- The DATA LIST command names SPORTSBK as the data file, specifies ORDER as a permanent variable, and defines 24 scratch variables to hold the alternating 12 maximum possible book numbers and 12 quantities (see Chapter 5).

- The LEAVE command preserves the value of variable ORDER across the new cases to be generated (see Chapter 7).

- The VECTOR command sets up vector BOOKS such that the first element is #X1, the second is #X2, and so forth (see Section 14.9).

- The LOOP command initiates the LOOP structure that moves through vector BOOKS picking off the book numbers and quantities (see Section 14.1). The indexing clause initiates the indexing variable #I at 1, to be increased by 2 to a maximum of 24 (see Section 14.2).

- The first COMPUTE command sets variable ISBN equal to the element in vector BOOKS indexed by #I, which is the current book number. The second COMPUTE sets variable QUANTITY equal to the next element in vector BOOKS, which is the quantity associated with the book number now stored in variable ISBN (see Chapter 7 for the COMPUTE command).

- The END CASE command tells SPSS-X to write out a case with the current values of ORDER, ISBN, and QUANTITY (see Section 14.14).

- The END LOOP command terminates the loop structure if the next element in vector BOOKS is missing (see Section 14.4). Otherwise, control is returned to the LOOP command where #I is increased by 2 and looping continues (until #I reaches 24).

14

- The SORT CASES command sorts the new cases by book number in preparation for printing (see Chapter 15).
- The DO IF structure encloses a PRINT EJECT command and a PRINT SPACE command to set up titles for the printed output (see Chapter 10).
- The PRINT FORMATS command establishes dictionary print formats for new variables ISBN and QUANTITY. See the output from the PRINT command.
- The EXECUTE command is shown here as the procedure that processes the cases for printing; any procedure will do (see Chapter 3).

PRINT output showing new cases

```
Order ISBN Quantity

1049   74   1
1045  134   1
1045  153   5
1046  153   5
1049  153   2
1045  155   1
1046  155   3
1049  155   2
1047  161   5
1049  161   1
1046  163   1
1047  163   4
1049  163   2
1045  182   2
1047  182   2
1047  186   6
1048  186   2
```

14.20
Concatenating Raw Data
Files by Using END

In addition to the simple example presented in Section 14.19, you can use the END subcommand for a variety of complex applications. For example, you can read several separate data files and create a single SPSS-X system file. The following job reads from three files, two of which contain data in the same format. The third requires a slightly different format for the data items. All three DATA LIST commands are placed within a LOOP structure that is terminated only when all of the records from the three files have been exhausted.

```
TITLE   CONCATENATE THREE FILES BY USING THE END SUBCOMMAND
SET MXLOOPS = 500   /* THE LOOP TO BE USED MAY REQUIRE RESETTING MXLOOPS

INPUT PROGRAM
NUMERIC  #EOFVAR1 TO #EOFVAR3 /*THESE WILL BE USED AS THE END= VARIABLES

LOOP
+    DO IF    #EOFVAR1 NE 1
+     DATA LIST  FILE=ONE END=#EOFVAR1 NOTABLE /1 NAME 1-20(A)
+            AGE 21-22 SEX 24(A)
+        DO IF  #EOFVAR1 EQ 1
+          PRINT //'END OF FILE ONE'/
+        ELSE
+            END CASE
+        END IF
+    ELSE IF    #EOFVAR2 NE 1
+     DATA LIST  FILE=TWO  END=#EOFVAR2 NOTABLE / NAME 1-20(A)
+            AGE 21-22 SEX 24(A)
+        DO IF  #EOFVAR2 EQ 1
+          PRINT  //'END OF FILE TWO'/
+        ELSE
+            END CASE
+        END IF
+    ELSE IF  #EOFVAR3 NE 1
+     DATA LIST   FILE=THREE END=#EOFVAR3 NOTABLE / NAME 1-20(A)
+            AGE 25-26 SEX 29(A)
+        DO IF  #EOFVAR3 EQ 1
+          PRINT  //'END OF FILE THREE'/
+        ELSE
+            END CASE
+        END IF
+    END IF
END LOOP IF #EOFVAR3 EQ 1
PRINT   /'END OF ALL INPUT FILES'
END FILE
END INPUT PROGRAM

PRINT    /NAME AGE SEX
EXECUTE
```

The INPUT PROGRAM contains nested DO IF—ELSE IF—END IF structures within a LOOP.

- This job uses scratch variables on each END subcommand so the value will not be reinitialized to the system-missing value after each case is built.
- The END FILE command is placed outside the LOOP structure so it is executed only after all records from the input file have been read.

The PRINT output from this job appears in Figure 14.20. The lines identifying the end of each file are produced by the PRINT commands within the INPUT PROGRAM—END INPUT PROGRAM section of the command file. The last PRINT command causes the individual name, age, and sex values to be printed.

This application can also be handled by creating three separate system files and using ADD FILES to put them together. The advantage of using the END

14

subcommand is that additional files are not required to store the separate system files prior to performing the ADD FILES.

Figure 14.20   PRINT output

```
WILLIAM              13 M
HARRIET              15 F
PETER                 9 M
ANDREW               11 M
SANDRA               12 F
LEO                  14 M
KATHERINE            10 F
PAULA                12 F
CARL                 15 M
CYNTHIA              11 F

END OF FILE ONE

MARILYN              16 F
PAMELA               13 F
THOMAS               14 M
HERBERT              15 M
SAMUEL               13 M
KAREN                12 F
AMANDA               14 F
TIMOTHY              16 M
RICHARD              15 M
JANET                12 F

END OF FILE TWO

CHARLES              14 M
MARIA                15 F
ELIZABETH            16 F
CAROLINE             13 F
JOHN                 15 M
MATTHEW              17 M
VICTORIA             14 F
FRANK                16 M
PAUL                 13 M
ROBERT               12 M

END OF FILE THREE

END OF ALL INPUT FILES
```

14.21
REREAD Command

Use the REREAD command when you need to obtain information from a record to tell you how to read the remaining portion of the record. Suppose a company that manufactures automobile parts receives orders recorded in different formats for different automobiles. Two of the records may look like the following:

```
111295100FORD
11        CHEVY 295015
```

The name of the automobile appears in columns 10 through 14, but the rest of the information may or may not be in the same place depending on the automobile. In this example, the part number appears in columns 1 and 2 for both types of automobiles, but the price and quantity appear in columns 3 through 9 for the Ford and in columns 15 through 21 for the Chevrolet. To read this file, specify:

```
INPUT PROGRAM
DATA LIST FILE=CARPARTS/KIND 10-14 (A)

DO IF (KIND EQ 'FORD')
REREAD
DATA LIST /PARTNO 1-2 PRICE 3-6 (DOLLAR,2) QUANTITY 7-9
END CASE

ELSE IF (KIND EQ 'CHEVY')
REREAD
DATA LIST /PARTNO 1-2 PRICE 15-18 (DOLLAR,2) QUANTITY 19-21
END CASE
END IF
END INPUT PROGRAM
```

The first DATA LIST defines variable KIND for testing in the DO IF and ELSE IF commands. Since each execution of a DATA LIST command causes a new record to be read, you must use the REREAD command to tell SPSS-X to set the pointer back to the *current* record. The current record is the last record in multiple record DATA LIST specifications. This example is developed in Section 14.25.

14.22
COLUMN Subcommand

Use subcommand COLUMN to specify the beginning column for the REREAD command if the pointer should be placed in a column other than column 1. You can specify a numeric expression for the column, as described in Chapter 7. For example, suppose you do not want to read the part number in the above parts file. Notice that price and quantity for Chevrolets are 12 columns away from price and quantity for Fords. Therefore, you could apply the same DATA LIST to both types of automobiles, as in:

```
INPUT PROGRAM
DATA LIST FILE=CARPARTS/KIND 10-14 (A)
COMPUTE #COL=1
IF (KIND EQ 'CHEVY') #COL=13

DO IF (KIND EQ 'CHEVY' OR KIND EQ 'FORD')
REREAD COLUMN #COL
DATA LIST /PRICE 3-6 (DOLLAR,2) QUANTITY 7-9
END CASE
END IF
END INPUT PROGRAM
```

Scratch variable #COL is set to 13 for Chevrolets and left at 1 for all other automobiles. Thus, for Fords, the DATA LIST begins in column 1 and variable PRICE is read from columns 3 through 6. When the record is a Chevrolet, the DATA LIST begins in column 13, forcing variable PRICE to be read from columns 15 through 18 (15 is 3, 16 is 4, and so forth).

14.23
Predetermining Variable Order

You can use the VECTOR short form or the NUMERIC and STRING commands to establish the dictionary order of a group of variables before they are defined on a DATA LIST command. The VECTOR, NUMERIC, or STRING command and the DATA LIST must be enclosed within INPUT PROGRAM and END INPUT PROGRAM, as in:

```
INPUT PROGRAM
VECTOR X(4)
DATA LIST / X4 X3 X2 X1 1-4
END INPUT PROGRAM

PRINT /X1 TO X4
BEGIN DATA
4321
4321
4321
END DATA
```

This job sets up variables X1, X2, X3, and X4 so they can be referenced using the TO convention even though they are read from the input record in the reverse order.

The ability to predetermine the order of variables is most helpful when you are forced to read variables out of order, such as when they are on different records. The NUMERIC and STRING commands (Chapters 7 and 8) are a more generalized solution to this problem since you can assign any names and formats to the variables, as in:

```
INPUT PROGRAM
STRING CITY (A24)
NUMERIC POP81 TO POP83 (F9) / REV81 TO REV83(F10)
DATA LIST FILE=POPDATA RECORDS=3
    /1 POP81 22-30 REV81 31-40
    /2 POP82 22-30 REV82 31-40
    /3 POP83 22-30 REV83 31-40
    /4 CITY 1-24(A)
END INPUT PROGRAM
```

You should specify the formats you want on the NUMERIC command as shown in this example. Otherwise, SPSS-X will take the default numeric format (F8.2) from the NUMERIC command for the dictionary format, even though it will use the format on the DATA LIST to read the data (that is, the dictionary formats are the first formats SPSS-X encounters).

14.24
CONTROL STRUCTURES AND DEFINING FILES

You may be confronted with data that cannot be handled by the file definition facilities described in Chapter 12. Using combinations of DO IF—END IF and LOOP—END LOOP structures and utilities such as REREAD, VECTOR, END CASE, and LEAVE, you can program your own definitions.

14.25
DO IF Structure

Frequently, defining a complex file structure is simply a matter of imbedding more than one DATA LIST command inside a DO IF structure. Suppose you have a data file that has been collected from various sources. The information from each source is basically the same, but it is simply in different places on the records. For example, suppose an automobile part number always appears in columns 1 and 2, and the automobile manufacturer always appears in columns 10 through 14. Otherwise, the location of other information such as the price and quantity depends on both the part number and the type of automobile. The sample data records are

```
111295100FORD        CHAPMAN AUTO SALES
121199005VW      MIDWEST VOLKSWAGEN SALES
11 395025FORD        BETTER USED CARS
11       CHEVY 195005        HUFFMAN SALES & SERVICE
11       VW    595020        MIDWEST VOLKSWAGEN SALES
11       CHEVY 295015        SAM'S AUTO REPAIR
12       CHEVY 210 20        LONGFELLOW CHEVROLET
 9555032 VW                  HYDE PARK IMPORTS
```

To simplify this example, only the data for Part 11 will be displayed.

Since you must use more than one DATA LIST, you first have to obtain information from each record to determine which DATA LIST applies to which record. Record type 11 has only two formats, one for Fords and one for both Chevrolets and Volkswagens. Thus, three DATA LISTS are required, one to determine which type of record is being read, and one each to reread the two types of records.

```
TITLE   READING DATA FOR PART TYPE 11

INPUT PROGRAM
DATA LIST FILE=CARPARTS/PARTNO 1-2 KIND 10-14 (A)

DO IF  (PARTNO EQ 11 AND KIND EQ 'FORD')
REREAD
DATA LIST /PRICE 3-6 (2) QUANTITY 7-9 BUYER 20-43 (A)
END CASE

ELSE IF  (PARTNO EQ 11 AND (KIND EQ 'CHEVY' OR KIND EQ 'VW'))
REREAD
DATA LIST /PRICE 15-18 (2) QUANTITY 19-21 BUYER 30-53 (A)
END CASE
END IF
END INPUT PROGRAM

PRINT FORMATS PRICE (DOLLAR6.2)
PRINT /PARTNO TO BUYER
WEIGHT BY QUANTITY
DESCRIPTIVES PRICE
```

The first DATA LIST extracts the part number and the type of automobile. Then, depending on the information from the first DATA LIST, the records are reread using one or another format, pulling the price, quantity, and buyer from different places. The two END CASE commands limit the active file to only those cases with Part 11 and automobile type Ford, Chevrolet, or Volkswagen (see Section 14.14). Without the END CASE commands, cases would be created on the active file for other part numbers and automobile types with missing values for price, quantity, and buyer.

The results of the PRINT command are shown in Figure 14.25.

Figure 14.25   Printed information for Part 11

```
11 FORD    $12.95  100  CHAPMAN AUTO SALES
11 FORD     $3.95   25  BETTER USED CARS
11 CHEVY    $1.95    5  HUFFMAN SALES & SERVICE
11 VW       $5.95   20  MIDWEST VOLKSWAGEN SALES
11 CHEVY    $2.95   15  SAM'S AUTO REPAIR
```

14.26
LOOP Structure

You may encounter a file structure that is read by looping on the same DATA LIST command a variable number of times in order to "spread" information from one or more header records to individual records. Suppose you have a header record that tells you how many individual records follow. The information might look like this:

```
1 AC
91
2 CC
35
43
0 XX
1 BA
34
3 BB
42
96
37
```

The 1 in the first column of the first header record (AC), says that only one individual record (91) follows. The 2 in the first column of the second header record (CC) says that two individual records (35 and 43) follow. The next header record has no individual records, indicated by the 0 in column 1, and so on.

To define these cases, read the header record, keep any information you need to spread to multiple individual records, and then loop on reading and creating individual records up to the expected number.

```
INPUT PROGRAM
DATA LIST  /#RECS 1 HEAD1 HEAD2 3-4(A)      /*READ HEADER INFO
LEAVE  HEAD1 HEAD2

LOOP  #I=1 TO #RECS
DATA LIST  /INDIV 1-2(1)                     /*READ INDIVIDUAL INFO
PRINT  /#RECS HEAD1 HEAD2 INDIV
END CASE                                      /*CREATE COMBINED CASE
END LOOP
END INPUT PROGRAM
```

The first DATA LIST reads the expected number of individual records for each header record into temporary variable #RECS. #RECS is then used as the terminal value in the LOOP command to read the correct number of individual records using the second DATA LIST. Variables HEAD1 and HEAD2 are the information in columns 3 and 4, respectively, in the header records. The LEAVE command retains HEAD1 and HEAD2 so that this information can be spread to the individual records. Variable INDIV is the information from the individual record. INDIV is then combined with #RECS, HEAD1, and HEAD2 to create the new case (see Section 14.14). Notice in the output from the PRINT command in Figure 14.26 that no case is created for the header record with 0 as #RECS.

Figure 14.26   Printed information for individual records

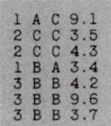

```
1 A C 9.1
2 C C 3.5
2 C C 4.3
1 B A 3.4
3 B B 4.2
3 B B 9.6
3 B B 3.7
```

Syntax

SORT

```
SORT CASES [BY] varlist[({A})] [varlist...]
                       {D}
```

SPLIT FILE

```
SPLIT FILE {BY varlist}
           {OFF     }
```

Contents

15.1   SORT CASES COMMAND

15.2   Ascending or Descending Order

15.3   Multiple Variable Specifications

15.4   String Variables

15.5   SORT CASES with REPORT

15.6   SORT CASES with AGGREGATE

15.7   SORT CASES with ADD FILES

15.8   SORT CASES with MATCH FILES

15.9   SORT CASES with PRINT

15.10 SPLIT FILE COMMAND

15.11 Placement of SPLIT FILE

15.12 SPLIT FILE with AGGREGATE

15.13 SPLIT FILE and Matrices

15

Chapter 15   Sorting and Splitting Files

In managing and analyzing data, you may want to group cases or reorder their sequence in your data file by sorting the cases according to the values of one variable or a set of variables in your file. Sections 15.1 through 15.9 discuss the SORT CASES procedure.

Once your cases are in a desired sequence on the active file, you may want to perform analyses on subgroups of the data. The SPLIT FILE utility allows you to split your file by a specified variable or set of variables. See Sections 15.10 through 15.13 for discussion of the SPLIT FILE command.

15.1
SORT CASES COMMAND

The SORT CASES procedure reorders the sequence of cases in the active file. Reordering is controlled by the variable or variables specified on the SORT CASES command following the optional keyword BY, as in:

```
GET FILE=HUBEMPLX
SORT CASES BY SEX
```

You can name any permanent numeric or string variable as the sort variable (see Section 15.4). You cannot name scratch or temporary variables as sort keys with SORT CASES.

15.2
Ascending or Descending Order

You can sort cases in either ascending or descending order. Ascending sequence —cases with the smallest values for the sort variable or variables at the front of the file—is the default. You can specify the default by following the variable name with (A) or (UP). To sort cases in descending order—cases with the largest values for the sort variable or variables at the front of the file—specify either (D) or (DOWN) after the variable name, as in:

```
GET FILE=HUBEMPLX
SORT CASES BY SEX(D)
```

In this example, if SEX is coded 1 for males and 2 for females, the data for women will sort first, followed by the data for men.

The order of the cases within a sort group remains the same. For example, if the file above is already sorted by age, the cases will be sorted by age within each sex after the SORT CASES command.

15.3
Multiple Variable Specifications

You can specify several variables as sort variables with SORT CASES, as in:

```
GET FILE=HUBEMPLX
SORT CASES BY DEPT82 SEX SALARY82
```

This command sorts by department, by sex within department, and by salary within sex, all in ascending order.

To mix the order, specify the desired order in parentheses after each sort variable, as in:

```
GET FILE=HUBEMPLX
SORT CASES BY DEPT82(D) SEX(A) SALARY82(D)

DO IF YRHIRED GE 80 AND DEPT82 NE 0
PRINT /DEPT82 SEX * SALARY82 (DOLLAR8)
END IF

EXECUTE
```

This command sorts first on department in descending order with Department 4 first, then on sex in ascending order, and then on salary, with the highest salary first within each sex-department grouping. Figure 15.3 shows the results of the PRINT command executed only for those employees hired since 1980 who are still working in the company (a department other than 0). See Chapter 10 for the PRINT command and Chapter 9 for the DO IF structure.

Figure 15.3   Mixed sort order

```
4 1    $9,750
4 2   $18,083
4 2   $15,608
4 2   $15,132
4 2   $12,438
4 2   $11,240
4 2   $10,050
3 1   $17,051
3 2   $39,000
3 2   $19,682
3 2   $13,650
3 2    $9,777
3 2    $9,507
3 2    $8,872
3 2    $8,239
1 1   $35,750
1 1   $17,111
1 1   $13,910
```

An order specification in parentheses applies to all variables to its left that are unspecified. For example, the command

```
GET FILE=HUBEMPLX
SORT CASES BY DEPT82 SEX SALARY82(D)
```

sorts cases in descending order for all three variables.

15.4
String Variables

You can use both short and long string variables as sort keys with SORT CASES, as in:

```
GET FILE=CITIES
SORT CASES BY CITY
PRINT /CITY STATE POP80
EXECUTE
```

In this example, SORT CASES reorders the cases in alphabetical order by CITY, which is a 14-character string variable. Figure 15.4 displays the results of the PRINT command for the first 20 cases.

Figure 15.4   Sorting cases by city name

```
Albuquerque    New Mexico        331,767
Atlanta        Georgia           425,022
Austin         Texas             345,496
Baltimore      Maryland          786,775
Birmingham     Alabama           284,413
Boston         Massachusetts     562,994
Buffalo        New York          357,870
Charlotte      North Carolina    314,447
Chicago        Illinois        3,005,061
Cincinnati     Ohio              385,457
Cleveland      Ohio              573,822
Columbus       Ohio              564,871
Dallas         Texas             904,078
Denver         Colorado          491,396
Detroit        Michigan        1,203,339
El Paso        Texas             425,259
Fort Worth     Texas             385,141
Honolulu       Hawaii            365,048
Houston        Texas           1,594,086
Indianapolis   Indiana           700,807
```

15

The sort sequence of string variables depends on the character set in use at your installation. With EBCDIC character sets, most special characters are sorted first, followed by lower-case alphabetic characters, upper-case alphabetic characters, and, finally, numbers. The order is almost exactly reversed with ASCII character sets. Numbers are sorted first, followed by upper-case alphabetic characters and lower-case alphabetic characters. In addition, special characters are sorted between the other character types. Consult documentation available via the INFO command for information on the character set in use at your installation and the exact sort sequence.

15.5
SORT CASES with REPORT

Since REPORT processes cases in the active file sequentially and reports summary statistics when the value of the break variable or variables changes, the file should be grouped by break variable or variables. The SORT CASES command is the most direct means of reorganizing a file for REPORT. Specify the SORT CASES command before the REPORT command, and list the break variables in the same order on each, as in:

```
SORT CASES BY EDUC SEX
REPORT VARS=SCORE1 TO SCORE5/
       BREAK=EDUC/
       SUMMARY= MEAN/
       BREAK=SEX/
       SUMMARY=MEAN/
```

See Chapter 47 for a discussion of the REPORT command.

15.6
SORT CASES with ADD FILES

You do not have to use SORT CASES prior to running AGGREGATE as the procedure does its own sorting. See Chapter 18 for a discussion of the AGGREGATE command.

15.7
SORT CASES with ADD FILES

You can use SORT CASES in conjunction with the BY keyword in ADD FILES to interleave cases with the same variables but from different files. See Chapter 16 for a discussion of interleaving cases with ADD FILES.

15.8
SORT CASES with MATCH FILES

Cases must be sorted in the same order for all files you combine using MATCH FILES. See Chapter 16 for a discussion of the types of matches that can be done in SPSS-X.

Cases must be sorted in ascending order on the key variable or variables in both the master file and all transaction files. See Chapter 16 for a discussion of updating a master file with UPDATE.

15.9
SORT CASES with PRINT

The PRINT command is not an executable command and must be followed by a procedure or EXECUTE. Thus, to use the PRINT command to check the results of a SORT CASES command, you must specify EXECUTE. See Chapter 10 for a discussion of the PRINT command.

15.10
SPLIT FILE COMMAND

During the analysis of a data file, you may want to perform separate analyses on subgroups of your data. You can use the SPLIT FILE command to split the active file into subgroups that can be analyzed separately by SPSS-X. These subgroups or splits are sets of adjacent cases on the file that have the same values for the split variable or variables.

For example, in analyzing attitudes toward abortion, you may want to perform separate analyses for men and women because you suspect the dimensions are very different for each group. Use the SPLIT FILE command to split the active file into subgroups of men and women. When you split the file, each sex is considered a break group. Cases within a break group must be grouped together on the active file. When a procedure is requested while split-file processing is in effect, the file is processed sequentially. A change or "break" in values on any one of the split variables signals the end of one break group and the beginning of the next. Thus, if you split the file by sex, two splits are created as long as all the cases for men and all the cases for women are grouped together.

If your cases are not grouped together according to the split variable or variables, use SORT CASES to sort them in the proper order before specifying SPLIT FILE. See Sections 15.1 through 15.4 for discussion of the SORT CASES procedure.

BY Keyword. Use the BY keyword followed by a variable list to specify the variable or variables that control split-file processing, as in:

```
SORT CASES BY SEX
SPLIT FILE BY SEX
```

This command splits the file according to the values for each case for the variable SEX. When SPSS-X encounters a command that causes your file to be read, SPLIT FILE creates a new subgroup each time it reads a case with a different value for SEX than on the previous case. Thus, if SEX is coded 1 for males and 2 for females, SPLIT FILE creates two subgroups for your analyses, assuming that your cases are sorted by SEX.

You can specify or imply up to eight variables on a SPLIT FILE command. You can use both temporary transformations and long string variables as break variables. Scratch variables and system variables cannot be used with SPLIT FILE.

15.11
Placement of SPLIT FILE

SPLIT FILE is in effect for all procedures in a job unless you limit it with a TEMPORARY command, turn it off, or override it with a new SPLIT FILE or SORT CASES command. To apply SPLIT FILE to only one procedure, use the TEMPORARY command, as in:

```
SORT CASES BY SEX
TEMPORARY
SPLIT FILE BY SEX
FREQUENCIES VARS=RINCOME/STATISTICS=MEDIAN/
FREQUENCIES VARS=RINCOME/STATISTICS=MEDIAN/
```

With these commands, SPLIT FILE applies to the first procedure only. Thus, the first FREQUENCIES procedure gives you the median income for men and women separately. The second FREQUENCIES procedure gives you the median income for both sexes.

Alternatively, you can specify:

```
SORT CASES BY SEX
SPLIT FILE BY SEX
FREQUENCIES VARS=RINCOME/STATISTICS=MEDIAN/
SPLIT FILE OFF
FREQUENCIES VARS=RINCOME/STATISTICS=MEDIAN/
```

Here, SPLIT FILE applies to the first procedure only because it is turned off after the first FREQUENCIES procedure. This set of commands produces the same results as the example above.

In addition, you can control split-file processing by overriding a SPLIT FILE command with a new SPLIT FILE command, as in:

```
SORT CASES BY SEX RACE
SPLIT FILE BY SEX
FREQUENCIES VARS=RINCOME/STATISTICS=MEDIAN/
SPLIT FILE BY SEX RACE
FREQUENCIES VARS=RINCOME/STATISTICS=MEDIAN/
```

The command SPLIT FILE BY SEX RACE turns off the SPLIT FILE BY SEX command, and the file is now split by sex and race. This split is in effect for the second FREQUENCIES procedure.

The SORT CASES command overrides a *preceding* SPLIT FILE command. For example, in the commands

```
SORT CASES BY SEX
SPLIT FILE BY SEX
FREQUENCIES VAR=JOBCAT
SORT CASES BY JOBCAT
REPORT FORMAT=AUTO /VARS=NAME AGE WAGES /BREAK=JOBCAT /SUM=MEAN
```

the second SORT CASES command overrides the SPLIT FILE command, and REPORT generates a single report, organized by the values of variable JOBCAT.

Alternatively, if variable JOBCAT is specified on the first SORT CASES command, split-file processing remains in effect for the REPORT procedure. In the commands

```
SORT CASES BY SEX JOBCAT
SPLIT FILE BY SEX
FREQUENCIES VAR=JOBCAT
REPORT FORMAT=AUTO /VARS=NAME AGE WAGES /BREAK=JOBCAT /SUM=MEAN
```

the file is sorted by variable SEX, then each subgroup of SEX is sorted by the values of variable JOBCAT. The FREQUENCIES procedure is unaffected by the sort on variable JOBCAT. The REPORT procedure generates two reports, one for each value of SEX. Each report is organized by the values of variable JOBCAT.

15.12
SPLIT FILE with AGGREGATE

AGGREGATE ignores the SPLIT FILE command. To split files using AGGREGATE, name the variable or variables used to split the file as break variables ahead of any other break variables. AGGREGATE still produces one file, but the aggregated cases are in the same order as the splits. See Chapter 18 for a complete discussion of AGGREGATE.

15.13
SPLIT FILE and Matrices

If you use a procedure to write matrices while SPLIT FILE is in effect, SPSS-X writes one set of matrix materials for every split. If you use multiple sets of matrix materials as input to a procedure, the procedure automatically detects the presence of multiple sets. If you use the SPLIT FILE command naming any variable defined by the NUMERIC command, SPSS-X prints page headings indicating the split-file grouping. See Chapter 13 for a discussion of matrix input and output.

ANNOTATED EXAMPLE FOR SORT CASES AND SPLIT FILE

The following job sorts cases in ascending order by sex, splits the file by sex, and produces two bar charts summarizing the distribution of personal income for each sex. The data for this example come from the 1980 General Social Survey. The SPSS-X commands are

```
GET FILE=GSS80/KEEP SEX RINCOME
SORT CASES BY SEX
SPLIT FILE BY SEX
FREQUENCIES VARIABLES=RINCOME/BARCHART PERCENT(45)/STATS=DEFAULTS/
           FORMAT=NOTABLE/
```

- The GET command accesses the data file, keeping only the variables used in this job (see Chapter 6).

- The SORT CASES command sorts the cases in ascending order according to the values of the variable SEX for each case.

- The SPLIT FILE command splits the file into two subgroups according to the values for the variable SEX.

- The FREQUENCIES command requests a bar chart for respondent's personal-income category (RINCOME). The horizontal axis is scaled in percentages with a maximum value of 45%. The frequencies table is suppressed and the default statistics are printed. One bar chart is produced for each split in the file (see Chapter 29).

Bar charts from a sorted and split file

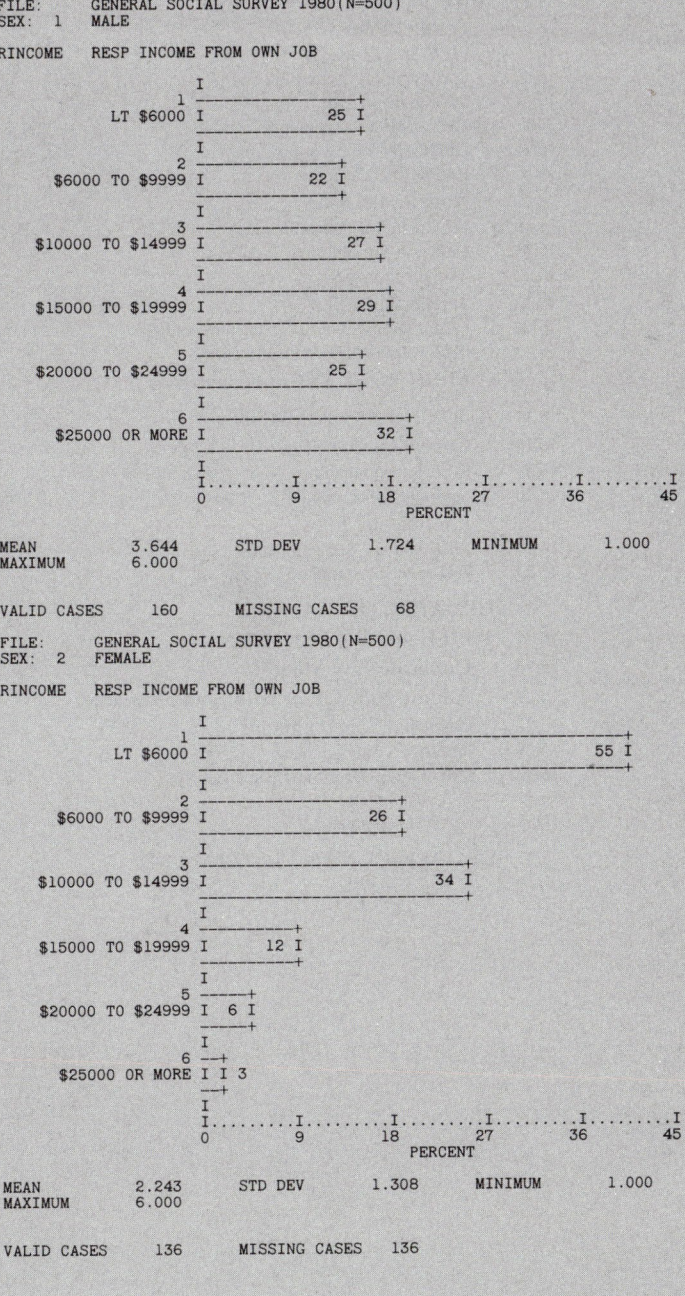

```
FILE:     GENERAL SOCIAL SURVEY 1980(N=500)
SEX:  1   MALE

RINCOME   RESP INCOME FROM OWN JOB

                        I
                   1    ----------------+
         LT $6000  I                 25 I
                        ----------------+
                        I
                   2    --------------+
    $6000 TO $9999  I              22 I
                        --------------+
                        I
                   3    -----------------+
   $10000 TO $14999  I               27 I
                        -----------------+
                        I
                   4    ------------------+
   $15000 TO $19999  I               29 I
                        ------------------+
                        I
                   5    ---------------+
   $20000 TO $24999  I              25 I
                        ---------------+
                        I
                   6    --------------------+
     $25000 OR MORE  I                32 I
                        --------------------+
                        I
                        I........I........I........I........I........I
                        0        9       18       27       36       45
                                          PERCENT

MEAN           3.644     STD DEV    1.724     MINIMUM       1.000
MAXIMUM        6.000


VALID CASES     160     MISSING CASES   68

FILE:     GENERAL SOCIAL SURVEY 1980(N=500)
SEX:  2   FEMALE

RINCOME   RESP INCOME FROM OWN JOB

                        I
                   1    ----------------------------------+
         LT $6000  I                                   55 I
                        ----------------------------------+
                        I
                   2    ----------------+
    $6000 TO $9999  I               26 I
                        ----------------+
                        I
                   3    --------------------+
   $10000 TO $14999  I                   34 I
                        --------------------+
                        I
                   4    -------+
   $15000 TO $19999  I      12 I
                        -------+
                        I
                   5    -----+
   $20000 TO $24999  I   6 I
                        -----+
                        I
                   6    --+
     $25000 OR MORE  I I 3
                        --+
                        I
                        I........I........I........I........I........I
                        0        9       18       27       36       45
                                          PERCENT

MEAN           2.243     STD DEV    1.308     MINIMUM       1.000
MAXIMUM        6.000


VALID CASES     136     MISSING CASES  136
```

Syntax

ADD FILES

```
ADD FILES FILE={file}
               {*   }

[/RENAME=(old varlist=new varlist)...]
[/IN=varname]
[/FILE=...]
[/BY varlist]
[/MAP]
[/KEEP={ALL** }] [/DROP=varlist]
       {varlist}
[/FIRST=varname]  [/LAST=varname]
```
**Default if subcommand is omitted.

MATCH FILES

```
MATCH FILES {FILE  }={file}
            {TABLE }  {*   }
[/RENAME=(old varlist=new varlist)...]
[/IN=varname]
[/{FILE  }=...]
  {TABLE }
[/BY varlist]
[/MAP]
[/KEEP={ALL** }] [/DROP=varlist]
       {varlist}
[/FIRST=varname]  [/LAST=varname]
```
**Default if subcommand is omitted.

UPDATE

```
UPDATE FILE={Master File}
            {*          }

[/RENAME=(old varlist=new varlist)...]
[/IN=varname]
 /FILE={Transaction File1}
       {*                }
[/FILE=Transaction File2]
 /BY Key Variables
[/MAP]
[/KEEP={ALL** }] [/DROP=varlist]
       {varlist}
```
**Default if subcommand is omitted.

Contents

16.1 MATCH FILES COMMAND
16.2   Parallel Files
16.3   FILE Subcommand
16.4   Specifying the Active File
16.5   MAP Subcommand
16.6   RENAME Subcommand
16.7   DROP and KEEP Subcommands
16.8   Reordering Variables
16.9   Nonparallel Files
16.10   FILE and BY Subcommands
16.11   Common Variables
16.12   IN Subcommand
16.13   Tables and Files
16.14   FILE, TABLE, and BY Subcommands
16.15   FIRST and LAST Subcommands
16.16   FIRST and LAST Subcommands on One File

16.17 ADD FILES COMMAND
16.18   Concatenating Files
16.19   FILE Subcommand
16.20   Optional Subcommands
16.21   Interleaving Files
16.22   FILE and BY Subcommands
16.23   Optional Subcommands

16.24 UPDATE COMMAND
16.25   FILE and BY Subcommands
16.26   Duplicate Key Values
16.27   Adding New Observations and Variables
16.28   Optional Subcommands
16.29   RENAME Subcommand
16.30   DROP and KEEP Subcommands
16.31   IN Subcommand
16.32   MAP Subcommand

16.33 DROP DOCUMENTS COMMAND

16

Chapter 16 Combining System Files

The SPSS-X commands MATCH FILES, ADD FILES, and UPDATE allow you to combine information from two or more files into a single active file. The MATCH FILES command combines variables from parallel, nonparallel, and table lookup files into one file. The ADD FILES command combines cases from two or more files by concatenating or interleaving the cases. The UPDATE command replaces values in a master file with updated values in one or more files called transaction files.

The DROP DOCUMENTS command enables you to retrieve system files without duplicating their document text in the active file. Its primary function is to prevent an overabundance of documents when you MATCH, ADD, and UP-DATE system files.

The MATCH FILES, ADD FILES and UPDATE facilities operate much like transformation commands. The data files are not read and the result file is not created when the MATCH FILES, ADD FILES, or UPDATE command is encountered. SPSS-X simply reads the dictionaries of the files and sets up the internal specifications. The result file is built when the data are read by one of the procedure commands or the EXECUTE, SAVE, or SORT CASES commands.

The MATCH FILES command is documented in Sections 16.1 through 16.16; the ADD FILES command is documented in Sections 16.17 through 16.23; the UPDATE command is documented in Sections 16.24 through 16.28; and the DROP DOCUMENTS command is documented in Section 16.33.

16.1
MATCH FILES COMMAND

The MATCH FILES command combines variables from parallel, nonparallel, and table lookup files. In the simplest match, you can combine two *parallel files*, which have the same cases in the same order but different variables (see Sections 16.2 through 16.5). For example, you can combine file TEST1, containing results for a set of subjects from the first testing period, and file TEST2, containing results for the same set of subjects from the second testing period, as in:

```
MATCH FILES  FILE=TEST1/FILE=TEST2
```

Nonparallel files have more or less overlapping sets of cases. For example, a company may maintain separate payroll files for each quarter, where some employees did not work during all quarters and are not recorded on all files. MATCH FILES can perform an unequal match-merge on nonparallel files if there is a key that uniquely identifies each case (see Sections 16.9 through 16.12). A *table lookup file* contains information at one level that can be "spread" across groups of cases on another file. For example, you may have survey information on households recorded on one file that you want spread to individuals within the households recorded on another file. You can spread information from a table lookup file to case files provided the files have key variables (see Sections 16.13 through 16.15).

In all three applications, you specify the file names of all files to be matched and whether the file is to be used as a table lookup file. For nonparallel and table lookup matches, you also specify the key variables. One of the input files can be the active file, but the others must be SPSS-X system files. You can rename variables on the input files, and you can drop or reorder variables in the result file. You can also create special variables that indicate the first and last case within each group defined by the key variable(s) and that indicate which input file or files contributed data to each case.

The result file of the match is the new active file. It contains complete dictionary information copied from the input files, including variable names, labels, print and write formats, and missing-value indicators. The result file also contains the documents from each of the input files, unless you use the DROP DOCUMENTS command (Section 16.33) to drop the document text from the input files before you copy them to the active file.

16.2
Parallel Files

Parallel files have the same cases in the same order but different variables. One file may contain measures across a set of observations for one time period, and another file may contain measures across the same set of observations for another time period. Or one file may contain one type of test results across a set of observations and another file a different set of test results for the same observations.

For a parallel match, a FILE subcommand for each input file is the only required specification on the MATCH FILES command. Four optional subcommands—RENAME, DROP, KEEP, and MAP—can be used with parallel matches.

16.3
FILE Subcommand

FILE is the only subcommand required for matching parallel files. Use one FILE subcommand for each file in the match. For example, suppose one monitoring device at each reporting station measures particulates in the air, and another device measures various gas pollutants, such as ozone and carbon monoxide. Particulate measures for each reporting station are recorded in one SPSS-X system file, and measures of gas pollutants in another. The same reporting stations are included in each file in the same order. The two files are shown in Table 16.3a.

Table 16.3a   Parallel pollution files

Particulate File		Gas File			
STATION	PARTIC	STATION	OZONE	CO	SULFUR
1	15	1	5	2	3
2	1	2	2	1	1
3	4	3	5	3	4
100	8	100	6	3	5

To combine these two files, specify:

```
MATCH FILES  FILE=PARTICLE/FILE=GAS
```

In this example, the resulting active file contains five variables: the station number and the four measures. The PARTICLE file and GAS file are matched case by case. The cases are constructed by first including the variables from the first case in the PARTICLE file (STATION and PARTIC) and then appending the variables for the first case in file GAS. Since STATION is a common variable on both files, only the value from file PARTICLE is included on the result file (see Section 16.11). The process continues until all cases have been read. If the files have unequal numbers of observations, cases are generated from the longer file. System-missing values are assigned for variables unique to the shorter file. Table 16.3b shows the file built from the two files in Table 16.3a.

Table 16.3b   The pollution result file

STATION	PARTIC	OZONE	CO	SULFUR
1	15	5	2	3
2	1	2	1	1
3	4	5	3	4
100	8	6	3	5

You can combine up to 50 SPSS-X system files on one MATCH FILES command. You must specify one FILE subcommand for each file being matched. The specification for the FILE subcommand is the file name of the input system file or an asterisk for the active file (see Section 16.4). Do not include GET commands for the system files that you specify on the FILE subcommands.

RENAME Subcommand. To rename variables on any of the input files before matching, specify the RENAME subcommand. Otherwise, the result file will retain the variable names from the input files. Use RENAME if different variables have the same name on two or more of the input files or if a single variable has several different names (see Section 16.6).

DROP and KEEP Subcommands. Use DROP and KEEP to include only a subset of variables in the result file. By default, all variables from the matched files are included in the result file (see Section 16.7). KEEP also reorders variables in the result file. By default, all variables are included in the result file in their original order, with variables from the first specified file at the beginning of the result file, those from the second file next, and so forth (see Section 16.8).

MAP Subcommand. Use MAP to display the names of the variables in the files being matched and the names of the variables being kept in the result file after any renaming, subsetting, or reordering (see Section 16.5).

**16.4
Specifying the Active File**

If you want to add variables from a data file to an existing system file, use the DATA LIST command to define the data file as the active file and the MATCH FILES command to combine the active file with the system file. In the following example, PARTICLE is a previously saved system file, and GASDATA is the data obtained from the device measuring gases.

```
DATA LIST FILE=GASDATA/1 OZONE 10-12 CO 20-22 SULFUR 30-32

VARIABLE LABELS OZONE 'LEVEL OF OZONE'
   CO 'LEVEL OF CARBON MONOXIDE'
   SULFUR 'LEVEL OF SULFUR DIOXIDE'

MATCH FILES   FILE=PARTICLE/FILE=*

SAVE   OUTFILE=POLLUTE
```

The GASDATA file is defined on the DATA LIST command and variable labels are assigned on the VARIABLE LABELS command. The subcommand FILE=* on the MATCH FILES command specifies the active file, which is now the gas data. FILE=PARTICLE specifies the PARTICLE system file. In this example, the resulting active file is then saved as a system file with the file name POLLUTE.

To match two data files, first use the DATA LIST command to define the first file and then save it temporarily as a system file using the SAVE command (see Chapter 6). Next, use the DATA LIST command to define the second data file as the active file. Finally use MATCH FILES to combine the two.

Do not use the TEMPORARY command with any active file used as an input file with MATCH FILES (see Chapter 7).

16.5
MAP Subcommand

For complicated matches or files containing large numbers of variables, the status of the active file can be difficult to ascertain. To list the names of variables on the active file, their order, and the file from which they were obtained, use the MAP subcommand, as in:

```
MATCH FILES FILE=PARTICLE
 /FILE=GAS/MAP
```

The output displayed by this MAP command is shown in Figure 16.5. Variables are listed in the order they exist in the result file. If variables are renamed, their original names are shown in the source file and the new name appears in the result file. Variables created by IN, FIRST, and LAST are not included in the map since they are automatically attached to end of the file and cannot be dropped (see Sections 16.12 and 16.15).

Figure 16.5 MAP of a simple match

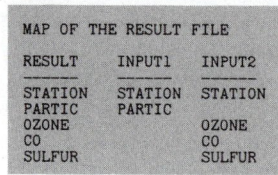

```
MAP OF THE RESULT FILE

RESULT     INPUT1     INPUT2
_____     _____     _____

STATION    STATION    STATION
PARTIC     PARTIC
OZONE                 OZONE
CO                    CO
SULFUR                SULFUR
```

The MAP subcommand has no specification field and must be placed after all FILE and RENAME subcommands. It reports the current status of the active file. If you place the MAP subcommand before a KEEP or DROP subcommand, the results of the KEEP or DROP will not be reflected on the MAP. You cannot obtain a map for a match of more than 12 files; the display page is not wide enough.

If you are not sure what the result of a MATCH FILES will be, you can obtain a map on an SPSS-X EDIT job without actually reading the data and executing the match (see Chapter 4).

Usually, you use the MAP subcommand to verify the results of complicated sets of subcommands. See the following sections for examples.

16.6
RENAME Subcommand

Variables with the same name on two or more of the files being matched are called *common variables*. For parallel matches, MATCH FILES automatically uses the values from the first file named for a common variable. MATCH FILES uses the dictionary information from the first file that has labels or missing-value indicators for the common variable. If the first file named has no such information, MATCH FILES checks the second file, and so forth, searching for dictionary information.

To obtain the values of common variables, use the RENAME subcommand to make all variable names unique across all files being matched. You can also use RENAME to clarify the meaning of variables in the result file even though they are not common variables. The RENAME subcommand must follow the FILE subcommand naming the file that contains the variables you want to rename.

Specify the subcommand RENAME followed by an optional equals sign and the rename specification. To rename one variable, specify the old variable name followed by an equals sign and the new variable name. For example, to rename the variable PARTIC to POLLUTE1, specify:

```
MATCH FILES FILE=PARTICLE
 / RENAME=(PARTIC=POLLUTE1)
  /FILE=GAS
```

PARTIC is the old name; POLLUTE1 is the new name. When you specify one variable, the parentheses enclosing the specification are optional.

You can rename more than one variable on a RENAME subcommand either by specifying a list of variable names and a list of their new names or by specifying several sets of individual variable specifications. For example, to rename the variables OZONE and CO, specify either

```
MATCH FILES FILE=PARTICLE
    /RENAME=(PARTIC=POLLUTE1)
    /FILE=GAS
    /RENAME=(OZONE=POLLUTE2)(CO=POLLUTE3)
```

or

```
MATCH FILES FILE=PARTICLE
    /RENAME=(PARTIC=POLLUTE1)
    /FILE=GAS
    /RENAME=(OZONE CO=POLLUTE2 POLLUTE3)
```

When you specify lists of variables, the specification must be enclosed in parentheses, and the two variable lists must name or imply the same number of variables. You can use the keyword TO both to refer to consecutive variables to be renamed (on the left side of the equals sign) and to generate new names (on the right side of the equals sign). For example, the RENAME subcommand

```
MATCH FILES FILE=PARTICLE
    /RENAME=(PARTIC=POLLUTE1)
    /FILE=GAS
    /RENAME=(OZONE TO SULFUR=POLLUTE2 TO POLLUTE4)/MAP
```

renames OZONE to POLLUTE2, CO to POLLUTE3, and SULFUR to POL-LUTE4 (see Figure 16.6). See Chapter 2 for more information on the distinction between using keyword TO to refer to existing variables and to define new variables.

Figure 16.6   MAP of a match with renamed variables

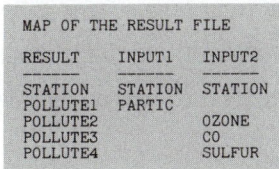

```
MAP OF THE RESULT FILE

RESULT      INPUT1     INPUT2
-------     -------    -------
STATION     STATION    STATION
POLLUTE1    PARTIC
POLLUTE2               OZONE
POLLUTE3               CO
POLLUTE4               SULFUR
```

You can use more than one RENAME subcommand to rename variables on one file. All renaming specifications in one RENAME subcommand are executed in one operation and a variable is renamed only once. Thus, you can switch variable names, as in:

```
RENAME=(A=B) (B=A)
```

You cannot rename variables to scratch variables (see Chapter 7).

After the RENAME subcommand, refer to a renamed variable by its new name.

16.7 DROP and KEEP Subcommands

By default, all variables from the files being matched are included in the result file. MATCH FILES first copies the variables in order from the first file, then the variables in order from the second file, and so on. Use either the KEEP or DROP subcommands to select a subset of variables. These subcommands apply to the result file and must follow all FILE and RENAME subcommands.

Specify the subcommand DROP or KEEP followed by an optional equals sign and a list of variables. KEEP saves the variables named, and DROP saves the variables not named. The variable list can include individual variable names or variables implied by the keyword TO. If you have renamed variables, specify the new names on the DROP and KEEP subcommands. For example, to exclude the renamed variable POLLUTE4 from the result file, specify:

```
MATCH FILES FILE=PARTICLE
    /RENAME=(PARTIC=POLLUTE1)
  /FILE=GAS
    /RENAME=(OZONE TO SULFUR=POLLUTE2 TO POLLUTE4)
    /DROP=POLLUTE4
```

You cannot use the DROP subcommand with variables created by the IN, FIRST, or LAST subcommand (see Sections 16.12 and 16.15). With the KEEP subcommand, variables are kept in the order they are listed on the subcommand. If you name a variable more than once on the KEEP subcommand, only the first mention of the variable is in effect; all subsequent references to that variable name are ignored.

16.8
Reordering Variables

You may want to reorder the variables in the result file so that you can more conveniently refer to them with the TO keyword on subsequent SPSS-X commands. Since KEEP saves variables in the order they are named, it can be used to reorder variables.

To reorder variables, you can either list the names of all the variables in the order that you want them, or simply list the names of the variables that you want at the beginning of the file in the desired order, followed by the keyword ALL. Keyword ALL must be the last specification on the KEEP subcommand, and it implies all the variables not previously named on the KEEP subcommand. You can use KEEP to reorder variables and DROP to delete variables in the same MATCH FILES command, as in:

```
MATCH FILES FILE=PARTICLE
    /RENAME=(PARTIC=POLLUTE1)
  /FILE=GAS
    /RENAME=(OZONE TO SULFUR=POLLUTE2 TO POLLUTE4)
    /DROP=POLLUTE4
    /KEEP=POLLUTE1 POLLUTE2 POLLUTE3 ALL/MAP
```

The map of the result file produced by this MATCH FILE command is shown in Figure 16.8.

Figure 16.8 MAP from a parallel match

```
MAP OF THE RESULT FILE

RESULT      INPUT1     INPUT2
--------    --------   --------
POLLUTE1    PARTIC
POLLUTE2               OZONE
POLLUTE3               CO
STATION     STATION    STATION
```

16.9
Nonparallel Files

There are two reasons why files may not have a parallel one-to-one case structure: cases in one file may be missing from another; or cases may be duplicated in one or the other files. MATCH FILES can handle most of these problems if there is a *key*. The key is a variable or set of variables that identifies the cases. As long as the files are sorted in ascending order on the key, cases can be properly matched.

The two subcommands required for nonparallel MATCH FILES are FILE and BY (see Section 16.10). The following subcommands are optional:

RENAME Subcommand. To rename variables on any of the input files before matching, specify the RENAME subcommand (see Section 16.6).

DROP and KEEP Subcommands. Use DROP and KEEP to include only a subset of variables in the result file (see Section 16.7). KEEP also reorders the variables in the result file (see Section 16.8).

MAP Subcommand. Use MAP to display the names of the variables in the files being matched and in the result file after any renaming, subsetting, or reordering (see Section 16.5).

IN Subcommand. IN creates a logical variable in the result file that flags whether a case was present in the input file. The IN subcommand is associated with the FILE subcommand for each input file (see Section 16.12).

16.10
FILE and BY Subcommands

To properly match cases from nonparallel files, specify one or more variables as keys for the match. Use the BY subcommand to specify the variables to be used as the keys. You can use any type of variable, including long string variables. When BY is used to name the key variables, cases from one file are matched only with cases from other files having the same values for the key variables.

Table 16.10a   Nonparallel employee files

Week 10 file		Week 11 file	
EMPID	HOURS10	EMPID	HOUR11
34	38.5	34	41.5
50	18.5	50	36.5
50	20.5	61	25.0
61	25.0	1015	40.0
1015	35.0	1150	40.0
1150	40.0	4003	15.0
1212	40.0		

For example, consider the two payroll files in Table 16.10a. Each employee has the same identification number in both files. The first file contains hours worked during the tenth week of the quarter. The second file contains hours worked during the eleventh week of the quarter. The employee identification number is the key to the match. Note that Employee 4003 did not work during the tenth week, and Employee 1212 did not work during the eleventh week. In addition, two time cards were submitted for Employee 50 for the tenth week. To combine the files shown in Table 16.10a, specify:

```
MATCH FILES   FILE=WEEK10/FILE=WEEK11/BY=EMPID
```

Table 16.10b shows the combined employee file after matching by EMPID. A period indicates that the system-missing value has been supplied.

Table 16.10b   The combined employee file

EMPID	HOURS10	HOURS11
34	38.5	41.5
50	18.5	36.5
50	20.5	.
61	25.0	25.0
1015	35.0	40.0
1150	40.0	40.0
1212	40.0	.
4003	.	15.0

If a case is missing on one of the files being matched, the variables for that case are set to the system-missing value for numeric variables and to blanks for strings. Employee ID 4003 does not exist in the file for the tenth week, and variable HOURS10 is assigned the system-missing value in the result file for that case.

If several cases in the files have the same value for the key variable(s), they are matched sequentially, and unmatched cases are assigned system-missing values or blanks. For example, the file for the tenth week contains two cases for Employee 50, and the file for the eleventh week contains only one case. Table 16.10b shows that the result file contains two cases for Employee 50, and the second case is assigned a system-missing value for variable HOURS11. In addition, SPSS-X prints a warning when duplicate keys are encountered in one or more of the files being matched.

All files must be sorted in ascending order on the key variables, and the key variables must have the same name on all files. There is no way to tell from the data whether the right matches have been made. The matches are right only if the sequence of cases acts as a correct key. If your files are not already sorted, use the SORT CASES command prior to MATCH FILES (see Chapter 15). You can use the RENAME subcommand on MATCH FILES to rename the variables if they do not have the same name on all of your files (see Section 16.6).

Missing values on the key variables are handled the same as valid values. You can match a case with a missing value for the key variable with a case from another file with the same value (whether or not the value is missing on the second file). The BY subcommand must follow the FILE subcommands and any associated RENAME and IN subcommands.

16.11
Common Variables

Variables with the same name on two or more of the files being matched are called common variables. For the values of common variables, MATCH FILES automatically uses the values from the first file named in which a case exists for that variable. It uses the dictionary information from the first file containing value labels, missing values, or a variable label for the common variable. If the first file has no such information, MATCH FILES checks the second file, and so on, seeking dictionary information. You should be certain that the first file with a common variable contains the appropriate dictionary information; otherwise the value of the common variable can come from one file while the dictionary information can come from another.

Table 16.11a shows two files with the common variable B. To combine the files without renaming the common variable B, specify:

```
MATCH FILES  FILE=FIRST/FILE=SECOND/BY=ID
```

Table 16.11a Files with a common variable

File FIRST			File SECOND		
ID	A	B	ID	B	C
1	5	3	2	3	4
2	1	6	3	2	5
4	4	9	4	1	7
5	2	.	5	9	8

Table 16.11b shows the result file. A period indicates that a system-missing value has been supplied. For case identifiers 1, 2, 4, and 5, the value for variable B comes from the first file since it is named first on the MATCH FILES command. For case identifier 3, the value for variable B comes from the second file since that case does not exist on the first file.

To combine the files in Table 16.11a and retain the values for variable B from both files, use the RENAME subcommand to rename variable B on one of the files, as in:

```
MATCH FILES  FILE=FIRST
  /FILE=SECOND/RENAME=B=BB/BY=ID
```

The result file after renaming is shown in Table 16.11c. The result file contains five variables: A and B from the first file, and BB (the renamed B variable) and C from the second file.

Table 16.11b   Result file from files with a common variable

ID	A	B	C
1	5	3	.
2	1	6	4
3	.	2	5
4	4	9	7
5	2	.	8

Table 16.11c   Result file after renaming

ID	A	B	BB	C
1	5	3	.	.
2	1	6	3	4
3	.	.	2	5
4	4	9	1	7
5	2	.	9	8

16.12
IN Subcommand

When you match nonparallel files, some cases in the result file do not come from all files. For example, in the combined employee file shown in Table 16.10b, the last case is missing on the first file, WEEK10. The system-missing value is supplied on the result file for the variable HOUR10 from that file. Use the IN subcommand to create a new variable on the result file that indicates whether a case was contained on the associated input file. The IN subcommand is optional and applies to the previously named file on the FILE subcommand. The variable created by the IN subcommand has the value 1 for every case where the associated input file contains a case, or the value 0 if no matching case was found on the input file. The IN subcommand has one specification, the name of the flag variable, as in:

```
MATCH FILES  FILE=WEEK10/FILE=WEEK11/IN=INWEEK11/BY=EMPID
```

The IN subcommand creates the variable INWEEK11, which has the value 1 for all cases in the result file that had values in the input file WEEK11 and the value 0 for those cases that were not in file WEEK11.

The variable name for the variable created by the IN subcommand must be different from any other name in the result file, including after renaming, keeping, or dropping variables. When the files are matched, the new variable is added to the result file after all the variables supplied from the input files. The variable created by subcommand IN can be used to screen partially missing cases for subsequent analyses. For example,

```
MATCH FILES  FILE=WEEK10/FILE=WEEK11/IN=INWEEK11/BY=EMPID
SELECT IF  (NOT INWEEK11)
```

selects only the cases in the result file for which there are no matching cases in file WEEK11. Since IN variables have either the value 1 or 0, they can be used as logical expressions where 1=true and 0=false. See Chapter 9 for the use of logical expressions and Chapter 11 for the use of the SELECT IF command.

**ANNOTATED
EXAMPLE FOR
MATCH FILES**

In Chapter 18, the Hubbard Research Company's personnel file was aggregated by department. The job below transfers the information in the aggregated file to the employee file, computes the ratios of each employee's salary and raise to the department averages, and runs a breakdown analysis on these ratios by sex of the employee. The SPSS-X commands are

```
GET FILE  HUBEMPL/KEEP=LOCATN82 DEPT82 HOURLY82 RAISE82 SEX

AGGREGATE  OUTFILE=AGGFILE
  /BREAK=LOCATN82 DEPT82
  /AVGHOUR 'AVERAGE HOURLY WAGE'
   AVGRAISE 'AVERAGE RAISE'=MEAN(HOURLY82 RAISE82)

MATCH FILES  TABLE=AGGFILE
  /FILE=*/BY LOCATN82 DEPT82
  /KEEP AVGHOUR AVGRAISE LOCATN82 DEPT82 SEX HOURLY82 RAISE82/MAP
FILE LABEL COMBINED FILE WITH DEPARTMENT INFORMATION

COMPUTE  HOURDIF=HOURLY82/AVGHOUR
COMPUTE  RAISEDIF=RAISE82/AVGRAISE
MEANS  HOURDIF RAISEDIF BY SEX
```

- The GET command reads the HUBEMPL system file and keeps the variables LOCATN82, DEPT82, HOURLY82, RAISE82, and SEX in the active file (see Chapter 6).

- The AGGREGATE command creates a file aggregated by LOCATN82 and DEPT82 with the two new variables, AVGHOUR and AVGRAISE, indicating the means by location and department for HOURLY82 and RAISE82. The aggregated file is saved as the system file AGGFILE (see Chapter 18).

- The MATCH FILES command specifies a table lookup match with the AGGFILE system file as the table file and the active file (the sorted and subsetted HUBEMPL file) as the case file (see Section 16.14).

- The BY subcommand indicates that the keys for the match are the same variables used for the break variables in procedure AGGREGATE, LOCATN82 and DEPT82 (see Section 16.10).

- The KEEP subcommand specifies the subset and order of variables to be retained on the result file (see Sections 16.7 and 16.8).

- The MAP subcommand provides a listing of the variables in the result file and the two input files (see Section 16.5). The map display is shown in Figure A.

- The FILE LABEL command prints a new label at the top of each page of SPSS-X display output after this command is encountered (see Chapter 6).

- The COMPUTE commands calculate the ratios of each employee's hourly wage and raise to the department averages for wage and raise. The results are stored in the variables HOURDIF and RAISEDIF (see Chapter 7).

- The MEANS command displays a means breakdown of the ratio variables by sex of employee to determine if there are observed differences between men and women (see Chapter 34). The MEANS tables are shown in Figure B.

16

A MAP display from MATCH FILES

```
MAP OF BY VARIABLES

RESULT     INPUT1     INPUT2
------     ------     ------
LOCATN82   LOCATN82   LOCATN82
DEPT82     DEPT82     DEPT82


MAP OF THE RESULT FILE

RESULT     INPUT1     INPUT2
------     ------     ------
AVGHOUR    AVGHOUR
AVGRAISE   AVGRAISE
LOCATN82   LOCATN82   LOCATN82
DEPT82     DEPT82     DEPT82
SEX                   SEX
HOURLY82              HOURLY82
RAISE82               RAISE82
```

B MEANS table display

```
FILE:     COMBINED FILE WITH DEPARTMENT INFORMATION
          D E S C R I P T I O N   O F   S U B P O P U L A T I O N S

Criterion Variable    HOURDIF
     Broken Down by    SEX        EMPLOYEE'S SEX


Variable       Value  Label               Mean     Std Dev    Cases

For Entire Population                     1.0000     .4941      145

SEX              1    MALE               1.1213     .6747       38
SEX              2    FEMALE              .9569     .4070      107

   Total Cases = 275
Missing Cases = 130 or  47.3 Pct

FILE:     COMBINED FILE WITH DEPARTMENT INFORMATION
          D E S C R I P T I O N   O F   S U B P O P U L A T I O N S

Criterion Variable    RAISEDIF
     Broken Down by    SEX        EMPLOYEE'S SEX


Variable       Value  Label               Mean     Std Dev    Cases

For Entire Population                     1.0000    1.6816      138

SEX              1    MALE                .9178    2.7326       38
SEX              2    FEMALE             1.0312    1.0578      100

   Total Cases = 275
Missing Cases = 137 or  49.8 Pct
```

16.13
Tables and Files

Parallel and nonparallel matches combine files with the same kinds of observations or units of analysis. That is, a case in one file corresponds to a case in another. You can also use MATCH FILES to transfer information from a table lookup file to another file with a different unit of analysis. For example, you can match information about households with persons in the household, unit prices with shipping records to produce billing information, schoolwide reading scores with student records, and so on. In all these examples, a key is used to look up information in the table file and transfer it to the case file. In the household example, each individual in the person file has a variable identifying the household to which she or he belongs. This key variable corresponds to a variable identifying each household in the household file. When the files are matched, information on a household is spread to the cases in the person file with the same value for the key variable.

The TABLE, FILE, and BY subcommands are required to specify a table lookup MATCH FILES (see Section 16.14). The following subcommands are optional:

RENAME Subcommand. To rename variables on any of the input files before matching, specify the RENAME subcommand (see Section 16.6).

DROP and KEEP Subcommands. Use DROP and KEEP to include only a subset of variables on the result file (see Section 16.7). KEEP also reorders the variables in the result file (see Section 16.8).

MAP Subcommand. Use MAP to display the names of the variables in the files being matched and in the result file after any renaming, subsetting, or reordering (see Section 16.5).

IN Subcommand. IN creates a logical variable that flags in the result file whether each case was present in a particular input file. The IN subcommand is associated with the FILE subcommand for each input file (see Section 16.12).

FIRST and LAST Subcommands. FIRST and LAST create logical variables that flag the first or last case of a group of cases with the same value on the BY variables (see Section 16.15).

16.14
FILE, TABLE, and BY Subcommands

Two subcommands are used to name input files for table lookup. Use the FILE subcommand to refer to a file containing cases and the TABLE subcommand to refer to a table lookup file containing information to be supplied to the cases on the case file. Each subcommand has one specification, either the file or an asterisk to indicate the active file. You must specify each file to be matched on a separate FILE or TABLE subcommand.

For example, Table 16.14a contains two files. The catalog file contains the supplier name and the unit prices for each product. The orders file contains the number of units shipped. Both files contain the product name, which will be specified as the key in the BY subcommand. The command

```
MATCH FILES  TABLE=CATALOG/FILE=ORDERS/BY=PRODUCT
```

transfers unit price information from the catalog file (the table lookup file) to the order file (the case file). Table 16.14b shows the result file. (Note that both files are sorted in alphabetical order by product name.)

As Table 16.14b demonstrates, MATCH FILES treats table lookup files differently from case files. An entry in a table file not matched with an entry in a case file is ignored. For example, cases for corn oil and cracked wheat are not included in the result file shown in Table 16.14b.

Table 16.14a   A table and case file

Catalog file			Orders file	
Product	Supplier	Price	Product	Qty
Corn Oil	General Products	$1.10	Cottage Cheese	1200
Cottage Cheese	Foods Inc.	$1.95	Cows Milk	4800
Cracked Wheat	ABD Dist.	$2.01	Dried Peas	1440
Dried Peas	ABD Dist.	$1.45	Sunflower Oil	900
Sunflower Oil	General Products	$2.98		

Table 16.14b   A matched shipping order file

Product	Supplier	Price	Qty
Cottage Cheese	Foods Inc.	$1.95	1200
Cows Milk		.	4800
Dried Peas	ABD Dist.	$1.45	1440
Sunflower Oil	General Products	$2.98	900

A table file cannot have duplicate keys. For example, there is only one entry for each product (the key) in the table file displayed in Table 16.14a. Note also that there is no entry for cows milk in the table file. Thus, blanks are used in place of the supplier's name in the result file, and the price is set to system-missing.

16.15 FIRST and LAST Subcommands

You may have files in which several cases have the same values on the key variables. For example, if you are matching individuals with household information (a case file with a table file), more than one individual will usually have the same household identifier. It is sometimes useful to identify either the first or last case in a group sharing a common set of values for the key variables. For example, you may want to do a transformation contingent upon a case being the first case in a group, or you may want to write a specialized report "breaking" on the first or last case in a group.

The FIRST subcommand creates a variable with the value 1 for the first case of each group and the value 0 for all other cases. The LAST subcommand creates a variable with the value 1 for the last case of each group and the value 0 for all other cases. For example, if you are adding household information to a person file, you may want to indicate the first person in each household as the head of the household, as in:

```
MATCH FILES  TABLE=HOUSE/FILE=PERSONS
  /BY=HOUSEID/FIRST=HEAD
```

The variable HEAD contains the value 1 for the first person in each household and the value 0 for all other persons. Assuming that the person file is sorted with the head of household as the first case for each household, variable HEAD identifies the case for the head of household.

The FIRST and LAST subcommands are associated with the result file and must be placed after all FILE and TABLE subcommands and their associated RENAME and IN subcommands. The variable names for the variables created by the FIRST and LAST subcommands must be different from any other names in the result file, including after renaming, keeping, or dropping variables. When the files are matched, the new variables are added to the result file after the variables supplied from the input files and the variables created with IN subcommands.

16.16
FIRST and LAST Subcommands on One File

You may have one file that has several cases with a single value on a key variable(s), and you want to create a variable that flags the first or last case of the group. To create flag variables for a single file, use the FIRST and LAST subcommands on the MATCH FILES command, as in:

```
MATCH FILES  FILE=PERSONS/BY HOUSEID/FIRST=HEAD
SELECT IF  (HEAD EQ 1)
CROSSTABS  JOBCAT BY SEX
```

The MATCH FILES command replaces the GET command and reads the system file PERSONS. The BY and FIRST subcommands identify the key variable (HOUSEID) and create the variable HEAD with the value 1 for the first case in each household and value 0 for all other cases. The SELECT IF command selects only the cases with value 1 for HEAD, and the CROSSTABS procedure is run on these cases.

16.17
ADD FILES COMMAND

The ADD FILES command combines cases from two to fifty SPSS-X system files by concatenating or interleaving the cases. For example, you may maintain a separate file for each of three schools with information on students attending that school. To analyze all students in the school, you can combine the cases by concatenating the school files, as in:

```
ADD FILES  FILE=SCHOOL1/FILE=SCHOOL2/FILE=SCHOOL3
```

If the files have keys, ADD FILES can interleave the cases by the key. For example, you may have four files recording information for each employee for each quarter of the fiscal year. You can combine the cases from these files by interleaving the cases according to employee identification number. See Sections 16.18 through 16.20 for a description of concatenating files, and Sections 16.21 through 16.23 for interleaving files.

The syntax for the ADD FILES command is the same as for the MATCH FILES command except the TABLE subcommand is not allowed. A FILE subcommand is required for each input file. For each input file, you can also rename variables and create a variable that indicates whether the case in the result file came from that file. You can select a subset of variables and reorder variables in the result file. The result file is the new active file, and it contains complete dictionary information, including variable names, labels, print and write formats, and missing-value indicators, copied from the input files. The result file also contains the documents from each of the input files, unless you use the DROP DOCUMENTS command (Section 16.33) to drop the document text from the input files before you copy them to the active file.

16.18
Concatenating Files

To *concatenate* two or more files, that is, add the cases from one file to the end of the other, use the ADD FILES command. A FILE subcommand for each input file to be concatenated is the only required specification on the ADD FILES command (see Section 16.19). Each FILE subcommand specifies the name of the input system file or an asterisk to indicate the active file.

Optional subcommands are the RENAME subcommand, the DROP and KEEP subcommands, the MAP subcommand, and the IN subcommand (see Section 16.20).

16.19
FILE Subcommand

The FILE subcommand is the only required ADD FILES subcommand when you are concatenating files. For example, suppose you have two SPSS-X system files on two schools, each containing test scores for students. These two files are shown in Table 16.19a. To concatenate these files, specify:

```
ADD FILES FILE=SCHOOL1/FILE=SCHOOL2
```

16

The result file contains three variables: the student identification number, reading scores, and math scores. The result file contains all the cases from the SCHOOL1 file followed by all the cases from the SCHOOL2 file. Table 16.19b shows the result file. To save the result file (the new active file) as a permanent system file, you must use a SAVE command (see Chapter 6).

Table 16.19a   School files

School1 File				School2 File			
STUDENT	READ	MATH	GRADE	STUDENT	READ	MATH	GRADE
25	350	425	7	20	250	300	7
27	425	375	8	25	325	225	9
30	475	485	8	27	300	375	9
35	375	400	9				

Table 16.19b   Concatenated school files

STUDENT	READ	MATH	GRADE
25	350	425	7
27	425	375	8
30	475	485	8
35	375	400	9
20	250	300	7
25	325	225	9
27	300	375	9

You can combine up to fifty SPSS-X system files on one ADD FILES command. You must specify one FILE subcommand for each file being added. The specification for the FILE subcommand is the name of the input system file or an asterisk for the active file. Do not include GET commands for the system files that you specify on the FILE subcommand. The TEMPORARY command cannot be used with any active file that is used as input with ADD FILES (see Chapter 7).

If you want to add cases from a data file to an existing system file, use the DATA LIST command to define the data file as the active file and the ADD FILES command to combine the active file with the system file.

16.20
Optional Subcommands

In addition to the required FILE subcommand, you can use optional subcommands to rename variables, save a subset of variables, reorder variables, create a variable indicating whether a case came from a particular input file, or produce a map of the result file and the source files. All of these subcommands are the same as those used on the MATCH FILES command.

RENAME Subcommand. Like MATCH FILES, ADD FILES takes the dictionary information for a common variable from the first file that has labels or missing-value indicators for that variable. The value for the variable always comes from the file where each case resides; however, the dictionary information can come from another file.

Usually, most or all of the variables in the files being combined with ADD FILES will be common variables. However, if the same variable does not have the same name on all input files, or if different variables have the same name, you can use the RENAME subcommand to rename the variables. For example, suppose that the variable measuring reading scores was named VERBAL on the SCHOOL1 file. The command

```
ADD FILES FILE=SCHOOL1/RENAME=(VERBAL=READ)
  /FILE=SCHOOL2
```

renames the variable VERBAL to READ on file SCHOOL1. The result file is the same as the one shown in Table 16.19b. See Section 16.6 for a complete discussion of the syntax for the RENAME subcommand.

DROP and KEEP Subcommands. By default, all variables from the files being combined are included in the result file. If a variable is not common across all files, the cases that do not reside on the file containing the variable are assigned the system-missing value on the variable. You may want to delete those variables that are not common across all files being combined or to select a subset of common variables. Use either the DROP or KEEP subcommand to select a subset of variables to be retained on the result file. DROP and KEEP must follow the FILE and RENAME subcommands on the ADD FILES command. See Section 16.7 for a complete discussion of the DROP and KEEP subcommands.

Reordering Variables. By default, all variables from the files being added are included in the result file in the same order as in the input files. Use the KEEP subcommand to reorder variables on the result file. If variables are not in the same order across files to be concatenated, use KEEP to reorder them (see Section 16.8). For example, if variable MATH was recorded before READ on the SCHOOL2 file, you would specify:

```
ADD FILES FILE=SCHOOL1/RENAME=(VERBAL=READ)
 /FILE=SCHOOL2/KEEP=STUDENT READ MATH GRADE
```

MAP Subcommand. Use the MAP subcommand to describe the result file. The map lists the names of the variables on the result file, their order, their source file, and their original names. For example, to produce a map of the result file for the combined SCHOOL file, specify:

```
ADD FILES FILE=SCHOOL1/RENAME=(VERBAL=READ)
 /FILE=SCHOOL2/KEEP=STUDENT READ MATH GRADE/MAP
```

The map is shown in Figure 16.20.

Figure 16.20   MAP of the concatenated school files

```
MAP OF THE RESULT FILE

RESULT      INPUT1     INPUT2
--------    --------   --------
STUDENT     STUDENT    STUDENT
READ        VERBAL     READ
MATH        MATH       MATH
GRADE       GRADE      GRADE
```

You must place the MAP subcommand after the FILE and RENAME subcommands. If you place it before a KEEP or DROP subcommand, the results of the KEEP or DROP will not be reflected on the MAP. You cannot obtain a map for an ADD FILES of more than 12 files; the display page is not wide enough. You can use the MAP subcommand on an SPSS-X EDIT job to check the result of renaming, reordering, or subsetting before running the job with your data (see Chapter 4).

IN Subcommand. When you combine files using the ADD FILES command, you might want to identify whether a case came from a particular file. Use the IN subcommand to create a variable on the result file that flags whether a case was contained on the associated input file. The IN subcommand applies to the previously named file on the FILE subcommand and creates a variable that has the value 1 for every case that came from the associated input file and the value 0 if the case was not in that file. For example, to create the variable INSCH1 that has the value 1 for all students in SCHOOL1 and the value 0 for all students in SCHOOL2, specify:

```
ADD FILES FILE=SCHOOL1/IN=INSCH1
 /FILE=SCHOOL2/MAP
```

16

The variable name for the variable created by the IN subcommand must be different from any other name in the result file, including after renaming, keeping, or dropping variables. The new variable is added to the result file after variables supplied from the input files.

16.21
Interleaving Files

You may want to combine cases from two or more files by interleaving the cases according to the values of a *key*. The key variable(s) must exist on all files being combined and the cases must be sorted in ascending order on the values of this variable in all files being combined. Two subcommands, FILE and BY, are required to interleave cases from two or more files. Optional subcommands are RENAME, KEEP, DROP, MAP, IN, FIRST, and LAST.

16.22
FILE and BY Subcommands

The two ADD FILES subcommands required for interleaving files are FILE and BY. FILE specifies each file being interleaved, and BY lists the key variables. For example, consider the two files in Table 16.19a. The students in each file are identified by their grade in school and the files are sorted in ascending order on this variable. To interleave the cases in the school files by the grade in school of each student, specify:

```
ADD FILES FILE=SCHOOL1/FILE=SCHOOL2
  /BY  GRADE
```

Table 16.22 shows the combined file using GRADE as the key variable. The cases and variables in the file are the same as in Table 16.19b, the result of concatenating the files. However, when combining the files with the key variable, the cases in the result file are ordered by GRADE. All cases from the first file with a value on the key variable are included on the result file followed by cases from the second file with the same value, then all cases from the first file with the next value on the key variable, and so forth, interleaving the cases from the input files according to the values of the key variable. For example, Student 25 in grade 7 from SCHOOL1 file is the first case in the result file, followed by the first case from the SCHOOL2 file, Student 20 also with the value 7 for GRADE. Then the two students from SCHOOL1 file in grade 8 are included in the result file, followed by the case from SCHOOL1 and the two cases from SCHOOL2 in grade 9.

Table 16.22   Interleaved school files

STUDENT	READ	MATH	GRADE
25	350	425	7
20	250	300	7
27	425	375	8
30	475	485	8
35	375	400	9
25	325	225	9
27	300	375	9

You can specify multiple key variables on the BY subcommand as long as all key variables have the same name on all files being combined, and all input files are sorted in ascending order on the key variables. If your files are not already sorted, use the SORT CASES command prior to ADD FILES (see Chapter 15). You can use the RENAME subcommand on ADD FILES to rename the variables if they do not have the same name on all of your files.

The BY subcommand must follow all FILE subcommands and any associated RENAME and IN subcommands.

16.23
Optional Subcommands

In addition to the required FILE and BY subcommands, you can use the following optional subcommands when interleaving files.

RENAME Subcommand. Usually the files that you are interleaving with ADD FILES will have all or most of the variables as common variables. However, if the same variable is stored under different names on one or more files, use RENAME to rename them to a common variable. For example, suppose that the grade-level variable was named LEVEL in the SCHOOL2 file. You would need to change the name of the variable to GRADE before you can use it as a key variable, as in:

```
ADD FILES FILE=SCHOOL1/FILE=SCHOOL2/RENAME=(LEVEL=GRADE)
 /BY GRADE
```

See Section 16.6 for a complete discussion of RENAME.

DROP and KEEP Subcommands. By default, all variables from the files being combined are included in the result file. If a variable is not common across all files, cases that do not reside on the file containing the variable are assigned the system-missing value on that variable. Use either DROP or KEEP to delete those variables that are not common across all files being interleaved or to select a subset of common variables (see Section 16.7).

Reordering Variables. The KEEP subcommand can also be used to reorder variables on the result file. If variables are not in the same order across files to be interleaved, you can use KEEP on one or more of the files to reorder them (see Section 16.8).

MAP Subcommand. Use the MAP subcommand to describe the result file. The map lists the names of the variables on the result file, their order, the file from which they came, and their original names (see Section 16.5).

IN Subcommand. Use IN to identify whether a case came from a particular file. The IN subcommand applies to the previously named file on the FILE subcommand and creates a variable that has the value 1 for every case that came from the associated input file and the value 0 if the case was not in that file. For example, you might want to create a variable using the IN subcommand that indicates whether a student is enrolled in SCHOOL1 or SCHOOL2 (see Section 16.20).

FIRST and LAST Subcommands. Occasionally, the result file from an ADD FILES using the BY subcommand will have more than one case for each value or combination of values for the key variable(s). For example, the combined school file has two students in grade 7, three students in grade 8, and three students in grade 9 (see Table 16.22).

It is sometimes useful to identify the first or last case of a group sharing a common value for the key variable(s). For example, the first student listed in each grade in the SCHOOL1 file may be the highest scoring student for the entire school district. Use the FIRST or LAST subcommand to create a logical variable that flags, respectively, the first or last case in each group identified by a particular value for the key variable. For example, to create the variable HISCORE in the combined school file, specify:

```
ADD FILES FILE=SCHOOL1/FILE=SCHOOL2
 /BY GRADE/FIRST=HISCORE
```

The new variable HISCORE is added to the result file after all variables from the input files and has the value 1 for the first case in each grade in the result file and the value 0 for all other cases.

The FIRST and LAST subcommands are associated with the result file. They must be placed after all FILE subcommands and any associated RENAME and IN subcommands.

16

ANNOTATED EXAMPLE FOR ADD FILES

The following set of commands adds the cases from the raw data file, SCHOOL2, to the system file, SCHOOL1. The result file is a system file, SCHOOL. The SPSS-X commands are

```
TITLE ADDING SCHOOL2 DATA TO SCHOOL1 SYSTEM FILE
DATA LIST FILE=SCHOOL2/STUDENT 1-2 MATH 7-9 READ 4-6 GRADE 11

ADD FILES FILE=SCHOOL1/RENAME=(VERBAL=READ)
 /FILE=*/KEEP=STUDENT READ MATH GRADE/MAP

SAVE OUTFILE=SCHOOL
```

- The TITLE command prints a title at the top of each page of output.
- The DATA LIST command defines the variables for the raw data file SCHOOL2.
- The ADD FILES command adds the cases from the active file to the system file. The first FILE subcommand refers to the system file SCHOOL1. The RENAME subcommand instructs SPSS-X to rename the variable VERBAL to READ on file SCHOOL1.
- The second FILE subcommand refers to the active file (*) defined by the previous DATA LIST command. The KEEP subcommand requests that the four variables STUDENT, READ, MATH, and GRADE be included in the result file.
- The MAP subcommand requests a map of the result file.
- The SAVE command saves the result file into the system file SCHOOL.

MAP of the result file

```
MAP OF THE RESULT FILE

RESULT     INPUT1    INPUT2
-------    -------   -------
STUDENT    STUDENT   STUDENT
READ       VERBAL    READ
MATH       MATH      MATH
GRADE      GRADE     GRADE
```

16.24
UPDATE
COMMAND

The data contained in a system file sometimes become outdated or contain errors. Rather than updating the file by writing out the raw data, correcting the values, adding new data, and recreating a new system file, you can use the UPDATE command to replace values in a *master file* with updated values recorded in one or more files called *transaction files*. Cases in the master file and transaction file are matched according to a key variable. When the transaction and master files contain a common variable, cases in the new file take on values for that variable from the transaction file. If more than one transaction file is specified on the UPDATE command, the value comes from the last transaction file with a nonmissing value for that variable.

16.25
FILE and BY
Subcommands

The FILE and BY subcommands are the only required subcommands for UPDATE. One FILE subcommand is required for each file to be matched. The master file must be listed first. All subsequent FILE subcommands identify the transaction files. Each FILE subcommand specifies the name of an input system file or an asterisk to indicate the active file. The BY subcommand identifies the key variable(s).

For example, suppose you have one file containing a mailing list of individuals around the country that is out of date and is incomplete (Table 16.25a). Specifically, the street names for Cases 057 and 338 are missing; there is no zip code for Cases 227 and 690; the name Marge Sutter for Case 359 is incorrect because she married and changed her name; and all the information except the name is incorrect for Case 907 because he moved. Table 16.25b contains the corrections and additions.

Table 16.25a   MAILIST file

ID	Name	Address	City	State	Zip
041	Beverly Davis	7200 Acoma	Denver	CO	80222
057	William Jones		Portsmouth	NH	03801
092	Barbara Cohen	624 N. Cedar	New York	NY	10025
116	Louise Jason	1417 Circle Dr	San Diego	CA	92117
227	Timothy Evans	666 Ridge	Boston	MA	
338	Stuart Dubin		Boise	ID	83707
359	Marge Sutter	1110 Oneida St	Denver	CO	80217
690	Kim DePaulo	557 Shannon Ln	Los Angeles	CA	
907	Stanley Klecka	44448 S. Bay	San Francisco	CA	94112

Table 16.25b   NEWLIST file

ID	Name	Address	City	State	Zip
057		775 S. Main			
227					02160
338		1 E. Oaklawn			
359	Marge Sarner				
690					90017
907		1237 W. High	Salt Lake City	UT	84401

The file MAILIST can be updated by NEWLIST with the following commands:

```
UPDATE FILE=MAILIST/FILE=NEWLIST/BY ID
```

In this example, MAILIST is defined as the master file, NEWLIST is the transaction file, and ID is the key variable. The updated file is shown in Table 16.25c.

Table 16.25c   Updated MAILIST file

ID	Name	Address	City	State	Zip
041	Beverly Davis	7200 Acoma	Denver	CO	80222
057	William Jones	775 S. Main	Portsmouth	NH	03801
092	Barbara Cohen	624 N. Cedar	New York	NY	10025
116	Louise Jason	1417 Circle Dr	San Diego	CA	92117
227	Timothy Evans	666 Ridge	Boston	MA	02160
338	Stuart Dubin	1 E. Oaklawn	Boise	ID	83707
359	Marge Sarner	1110 Oneida St	Denver	CO	80217
690	Kim DePaulo	557 Shannon Ln	Los Angeles	CA	90017
907	Stanley Klecka	1237 W. High	Salt Lake City	UT	84401

Observations in the master file and transaction files must be sorted in ascending order on the key variable. If the files have not already been sorted, use the SORT CASES command prior to UPDATE. Duplicate values for the key variables are not permitted in the master file. Only nonblank values of string variables and nonmissing values of numeric variables are used to update values in the master file.

16.26
Duplicate Key Values

While duplicate values on the key variables are not allowed in master files, transaction files can and often do contain cases with duplicate keys. When UPDATE encounters duplicate keys within the same transaction file or over several files, it applies each transaction sequentially to that case to produce one case per key value in the result file. If more than one transaction file is specified on the UPDATE command, the value for a variable comes from the last transaction file with a nonmissing value for that variable.

For example, consider the two files shown in Tables 16.26a and 16.26b. The MASTER file contains closing bank balances for customers on December 7, 1984. The TRANS file contains balances following transactions on December 8. There are two observations in the TRANS file for Paul Scott since he made two withdrawals on December 8—one for $25.00 and another for $45.00. These are both applied to ID 987743 during the updating process. The first transaction changes his balance to $961.22, and the second changes it to $916.22.

Table 16.26a   MASTER file

Account	Name	Date	Balance
411678	Gregory Lee	07-DEC-84	$3,487.86
572589	Francis Davis	07-DEC-84	$114.90
923378	Ethel Reese	07-DEC-84	$88.71
987743	Paul Scott	07-DEC-84	$986.22
1278963	Margaret Pope	07-DEC-84	$1,486.38

Table 16.26b   TRANS file

Account	Name	Date	Balance
411678	Gregory Lee	08-DEC-84	$3,532.63
572589	Francis Davis	08-DEC-84	$94.90
923378	Ethel Reese	08-DEC-84	$58.71
987743	Paul Scott	08-DEC-84	$961.22
987743	Paul Scott	08-DEC-84	$916.22
1278963	Margaret Pope	08-DEC-84	$1,601.38

The following commands produce an updated master file showing the correct closing balance for December 8, 1984:

```
UPDATE FILE=MASTER/FILE=TRANS/BY ACCOUNT
SAVE OUTFILE=NEWMASTR
```

The SAVE specification saves the updated file as a new system file called NEWMASTR. Table 16.26c shows the result file.

Table 16.26c   NEWMASTR file

Account	Name	Date	Balance
411678	Gregory Lee	08-DEC-84	$3,532.63
572589	Francis Davis	08-DEC-84	$94.90
923378	Ethel Reese	08-DEC-84	$58.71
987743	Paul Scott	08-DEC-84	$916.22
1278963	Margaret Pope	08-DEC-84	$1,601.38

16.27
Adding New Observations and Variables

When UPDATE encounters cases or nonmissing variables in the transaction files that are not in the master file, the new cases or variables are added to the master file. The value of the key variable determines where a new case resides in the result file.

For example, to update the NEWMASTR file with a data set containing information on where each customer banks (see Table 16.27a), use the following:

```
SORT CASES BY ACCOUNT
UPDATE FILE=NEWMASTR/FILE=BRANCH/BY ACCOUNT
```

The results are shown in Table 16.27b.

Table 16.27a   BRANCH file

Account	Branch
411678	Downtown
572589	Suburban
923378	Downtown
987743	Downtown
1278963	Downtown

Table 16.27b   Updated NEWMASTR file

Account	Name	Date	Balance	Branch
411678	Gregory Lee	08-DEC-84	$3,532.63	Downtown
572589	Francis Davis	08-DEC-84	$94.90	Suburban
923378	Ethel Reese	08-DEC-84	$58.71	Downtown
987743	Paul Scott	08-DEC-84	$916.22	Downtown
1278963	Margaret Pope	08-DEC-84	$1,601.38	Downtown

16.28
Optional Subcommands

FILE and BY are the only subcommands required on the UPDATE command. Five optional subcommands, RENAME, DROP, KEEP, IN, and MAP, are also available.

16.29
RENAME Subcommand

When UPDATE encounters variables with the same name in two or more files, it automatically uses the dictionary information in the first file containing a variable by that name. Thus, different variables must not share the same name, and a single variable cannot have more than one name in two or more files.

To rename a variable in a master or transaction file, specify the RENAME subcommand followed by a parenthesis, the current variable name, an equals

16

sign, the new name, and a closing parenthesis. RENAME should be specified immediately after the file to which it applies.

For example, suppose that variable ADDRESS in the MAILIST file had been named STREET in the NEWLIST file. While the two variables are the same, only named differently, the updated file would store them as two separate variables. The command

```
UPDATE  FILE=MAILIST/FILE=NEWLIST/RENAME=(STREET=ADDRESS)/BY ID/MAP
```

renames the variable STREET to ADDRESS in the NEWLIST file and assures a proper match. The map of the result file is shown in Figure 16.29.

Figure 16.29   Map of result file with a renamed variable

```
MAP OF THE RESULT FILE

RESULT     INPUT1     INPUT2
-------    -------    -------
ID         ID         ID
NAME       NAME       NAME
ADDRESS    ADDRESS    STREET
CITY       CITY       CITY
STATE      STATE      STATE
ZIP        ZIP        ZIP
```

16.30 DROP and KEEP Subcommands

By default, the UPDATE command stores all the variables from the master and transaction files in their original order. Variables from the master file are placed first, followed by any variables unique to each transaction file in the order the files are named on the UPDATE command. When a variable is unique to a file, cases that are not in that file are assigned the system-missing value for that variable.

To delete some variables, specify the DROP or KEEP subcommands following the FILE and RENAME subcommands. The KEEP subcommand may also be used to reorder the variables in the result file. For example, if you want variable ID at the end of the result file rather than at the beginning, specify:

```
UPDATE FILE=MAILIST/FILE=NEWLIST/RENAME=(STREET=ADDRESS)/BY ID
      /KEEP=NAME ADDRESS CITY STATE ZIP ID
```

16.31 IN Subcommand

Use the IN subcommand to create a new variable in the result file that indicates whether a case was in an associated input file. A variable created by IN applies to the file on the preceding FILE subcommand. Variables created by IN will have the value 1 if the case is in the associated file, and a 0 if the case is not in the file. The variable name for the new variable must be different from any other in the result file.

For example, in the following specification

```
UPDATE FILE=MAILIST/IN=MAILIST1/FILE=NEWLIST/IN=NEWLIST1/BY ID
```

a case that is in file MAILIST but not in NEWLIST has a value of 1 for MAILIST1 and a value of 0 for NEWLIST1. A case in NEWLIST but not in MAILIST has a 1 for NEWLIST1 and a 0 for MAILIST1. If a case is contained in both files, it has a value of 1 for both MAILIST1 and NEWLIST1.

16.32 MAP Subcommand

After renaming, deleting, or reordering variables, you may want to check the results. The MAP subcommand displays the variable names and their order in the master file and all of the transactions files, along with their names and order in the updated version of the file. The MAP subcommand must be placed after the FILE and RENAME subcommands. The map from each MAP subcommand reflects only preceding DROP and KEEP subcommands, not any that follow.

ANNOTATED EXAMPLE FOR UPDATE

The following commands update cases in the master system file MAILIST1 with cases in a raw data file. The result is a system file, MAILIST2.

```
DATA LIST
   / ID 1-3
     NAME 5-17 (A)
     ADDRESS 19-28 (A)
     ZIP 30-34

BEGIN DATA
033              872 ONEIDA
041 BEVERLY JONES
...
078              14 OAK
043                        80618
END DATA

SORT CASES BY ID

UPDATE FILE=MAILIST1/RENAME=(STREET=ADDRESS)/FILE=*/ BY ID/MAP

SAVE OUTFILE=MAILIST2
```

- The DATA LIST command defines variables in the transaction file, which will be used to update values in the master file.
- The BEGIN DATA—END DATA commands indicate lines of data for the variables in the active file. These values will be added to the master file.
- The SORT CASES command sorts cases in the transaction file in ascending order on the key variable, ID. Cases in the master file were previously sorted in this manner.
- The UPDATE command replaces values in the system file with values in the active file. The first FILE subcommand refers to the master file, MAILIST1. The RENAME subcommand instructs SPSS-X to rename the variable STREET to ADDRESS on file MAILIST1.
- The second FILE subcommand refers to the active file (*) defined in the DATA LIST command.
- The BY subcommand indicates that values in MAILIST1 and the active file are to be matched by the key variable, ID.
- The MAP subcommand requests a map of the result file.
- The SAVE command saves the result file into the system file MAILIST2.

MAP of the result file

```
MAP OF THE RESULT FILE

RESULT     INPUT1    INPUT2
-------    ------    ------
ID         ID        ID
NAME       NAME      NAME
ADDRESS    STREET    ADDRESS
CITY       CITY      CITY
STATE      STATE     STATE
```

16.33
DROP DOCUMENTS
COMMAND

The DROP DOCUMENTS command drops the documents from *all* the files you specify with the MATCH, ADD, or UPDATE commands. If you want, you can then add new document text to the active file with the DOCUMENT command.

There are no subcommands with DROP DOCUMENTS. The only requirement is that you fully define the active file before you invoke the command. For example, in the commands

```
UPDATE FILE=MAILIST / FILE=NEWLIST / BY ID
DROP DOCUMENTS
```

the UPDATE command opens and reads the system file and defines variables. It must precede the DROP DOCUMENTS command, which simply drops the document text from both MAILIST and NEWLIST as their data are copied into the active file. The document text within files MAILIST and NEWLIST remains unchanged.

Syntax

EXPORT

```
EXPORT OUTFILE=file
  [/TYPE={COMM**}]
         {TAPE  }
  [/KEEP={ALL** }] [/DROP=varlist]
         {varlist}
  [/RENAME=(old varlist=new varlist)...]
  [/MAP]
  [/DIGITS=number]
```
** Default if the subcommand is omitted.

GET BMDP

```
GET BMDP FILE=file
  [/SCAN={YES }] [/CODE=name]
         {ONLY}
  [/CONTENT=name] [/LABEL=quoted string]
  [/KEEP={ALL** }] [/DROP=varlist]
         {varlist}
  [/RENAME=(old varlist=new varlist)...]
  [/MAP]
```
**Default if subcommand is omitted.

GET OSIRIS

```
GET OSIRIS DICTIONARY=file1 DATA=file2
  [/RENAME=(old varlist=new varlist)...]
  [/KEEP={ALL** }] [/DROP=varlist]
         {varlist}
  [/MAP]
```

GET SAS

```
GET SAS DATA=ddname.membername [SASLIB=ddname]
  [/KEEP={ALL** }] [/DROP=varlist]
         {varlist}
  [/RENAME=(old varlist=new varlist)...]
  [/MAP]
```

GET SCSS

```
GET SCSS MASTERFILE=file [/WORKFILE=file]
              {ALL**                      }
              {varlist                    }
  [/VARIABLES={$varlist                   }]
              {$ALL                       }
              {(old varlist=new varlist)  }
```
**Default if subcommand is omitted.

IMPORT

```
IMPORT FILE=file
  [/TYPE={COMM}]
         {TAPE}
  [/KEEP={ALL** }] [/DROP=varlist]
         {varlist}
  [/RENAME=(old varlist=new varlist)...]
  [/MAP]
  [/DIGITS=number]
```

SAVE SCSS

```
SAVE SCSS OUTFILE=file
  [/KEEP={ALL    }] [/DROP=varlist]
         {varlist}
  [/RENAME=(old varlist=new varlist)...]
```

Contents

17.1 SCSS INTERFACE
17.2   SAVE SCSS Command
17.3   OUTFILE Subcommand
17.4   KEEP and DROP Subcommands
17.5   RENAME Subcommand
17.6   Display Output
17.7   GET SCSS Command
17.8   MASTERFILE Subcommand
17.9   WORKFILE Subcommand
17.10   VARIABLES Subcommand

17.11 TRANSPORTING SPSS-X SYSTEM FILES
17.12   Methods of Transporting Portable Files
17.13   Characteristics of Portable Files
17.14   Character Translation
17.15   Hints for Successful File Transfer
17.16   EXPORT Command
17.17   TYPE Subcommand
17.18   DROP and KEEP Subcommands
17.19   RENAME Subcommand
17.20   MAP Subcommand
17.21   DIGITS Subcommand
17.22   IMPORT Command
17.23   TYPE Subcommand
17.24   DROP and KEEP Subcommands
17.25   RENAME Subcommand
17.26   MAP Subcommand

17.27 READING SAS FILES WITH SPSS-X
17.28   DATA Subcommand
17.29   SASLIB Subcommand
17.30   DROP and KEEP Subcommands
17.31   RENAME Subcommand
17.32   MAP Subcommand
17.33   SAS to SPSS-X Data Conversion

17.34 READING OSIRIS FILES WITH SPSS-X
17.35   GET OSIRIS Command
17.36   DROP and KEEP Subcommands
17.37   RENAME Subcommand
17.38   MAP Subcommand
17.39   OSIRIS to SPSS-X Data Conversion

17.40 READING BMDP FILES WITH SPSS-X
17.41   GET BMDP Command
17.42   KEEP, DROP, and RENAME Subcommands
17.43   MAP Subcommand
17.44   BMDP to SPSS-X Data Conversion

OSIRIS is a system of data-management and statistical analysis programs developed by the Institute for Social Research, University of Michigan, and the Inter-University Consortium for Political Research.

17

Chapter 17   File Interfaces

SPSS-X provides five types of file interfaces. One type let you interface with the SCSS™ Conversational System via the SAVE SCSS and GET SCSS commands. The SAVE SCSS command saves an SPSS-X system file in an SCSS masterfile format (see Sections 17.2 through 17.6). The GET SCSS command reads SCSS masterfiles and workfile/masterfile combinations (see Sections 17.7 through 17.10). A second type of interface lets you write portable files that include all of the information on an SPSS-X system file, including the dictionary and the data. A portable file can be read by SPSS-X on another computer, by SPSS/PC, or by other software using the same portable-file format. The EXPORT command writes portable files (see Sections 17.16 through 17.21), and the IMPORT command reads portable files (see Sections 17.22 through 17.26).

Three additional types of file interfaces enable you to read SAS®, OSIRIS™, and BMDP™ data sets. The GET SAS command (see Sections 17.27 through 17.33), the GET OSIRIS command (see Sections 17.34 through 17.39), and the GET BMDP command (see Section 17.40) convert SAS, OSIRIS, and BMDP data information so it can be stored into SPSS-X system files. You can tailor the files with optional DROP, KEEP, and RENAME subcommands.

17.1
SCSS INTERFACE

The interface between SPSS-X and the SCSS™ Conversational System is entirely through SCSS files written and read by SPSS-X. Use the SAVE SCSS command to create an SCSS masterfile from SPSS-X and the GET SCSS command to read an SCSS masterfile (or workfile and masterfile) into SPSS-X. SCSS neither reads nor writes SPSS-X system files.

The following documentation assumes a knowledge of the SCSS system, including workfiles, masterfiles, variable types, variable masks, and so forth.

17.2
SAVE SCSS Command

You can save an SCSS masterfile at any point after you have created your SPSS-X active file. For example, to save the file defined in Chapter 5 as an SCSS masterfile, specify:

```
DATA LIST   FILE=HUBDATA RECORDS=3
 /1 EMPLOYID 1-5 MOHIRED YRHIRED 12-15 DEPT79 TO DEPT82 SEX 16-20
 /2 SALARY79 TO SALARY82 6-25 HOURLY81 HOURLY82 42-53(2) PROMO81 72
    AGE 54-55 RAISE82 66-70
 /3 JOBCAT 6 NAME 25-48 (A)

MISSING VALUES  DEPT79 TO SALARY82, AGE (0)
  HOURLY81, HOURLY82, RAISE82 (-999) JOBCAT (9)

VARIABLE LABELS  YRHIRED 'YEAR OF FIRST HIRING'
  DEPT82 'DEPARTMENT OF EMPLOYMENT IN 1982'
  SALARY82 'YEARLY SALARY IN 1982'
  JOBCAT 'JOB CATEGORIES'

VALUE LABELS  DEPT79 TO DEPT82  0 'NOT REPORTED' 1 'ADMINISTRATIVE'
             2 'PROJECT DIRECTORS' 3 'CHICAGO OPERATIONS'
             4 'ST LOUIS OPERATIONS'/
  SEX 1 'MALE' 2 'FEMALE'/
  JOBCAT 1 'OFFICIALS & MANAGERS' 2 'PROFESSIONALS' 3 'TECHNICIANS'
             4 'OFFICE AND CLERICAL' 5 'CRAFTSMEN' 6 'SERVICE WORKERS'

FREQUENCIES VARIABLES=SEX

COMPUTE PCTRAISE=RAISE82/SALARY82*100

SAVE SCSS OUTFILE=HUBOUT
```

The OUTFILE subcommand is discussed in Section 17.3. The display output from the SAVE SCSS command, including the DROP and RENAME subcommands discussed in Sections 17.4 and 17.5, is shown in Section 17.6.

Since SAVE SCSS saves the current active file, it saves the dictionary information and the data in their form at the point SAVE SCSS is encountered. This includes all permanent transformations and any temporary transformations made just prior to the SAVE SCSS command.

- SCSS does not support string variables and they are not saved. SPSS-X informs you which variables will not be saved (see Figure 17.6a).
- The system-missing value for numeric variables is recoded to a value at one end of the range (usually the highest value plus one) for each variable. Look in the variable-by-variable listing in your SPSS-X display output for the missing value selected for each variable (see Figure 17.6b).
- In converting from double precision in SPSS-X to single precision in SCSS, numeric values are usually truncated (SPSS-X actually does a mixed mode assignment which may result in rounding in some operating-system environments).
- SCSS has some reserved keywords that are not reserved in SPSS-X, so variables with the names AGAINST, ON, SPSS, and SPSS0001 will not be saved. They can be renamed using the RENAME subcommand (see Section 17.5).

17.3
OUTFILE Subcommand

The OUTFILE subcommand is required and must be first. It specifies the masterfile to be saved.

17.4
KEEP and DROP Subcommands

Following the OUTFILE subcommand, you can specify a list of variables to be kept or dropped before saving your file. For example, to drop a list of variables before saving the masterfile, specify:

```
SAVE SCSS OUTFILE=HUBOUT
 /DROP=DEPT79 TO DEPT81, SALARY79 TO SALARY81, HOURLY81
```

The DROP and KEEP subcommands affect only the file written with the SAVE SCSS command. Variables dropped (or variables not kept) within the SAVE SCSS procedure are still available on the active file. Slashes are required between subcommands.

17

In addition, you can use the KEEP subcommand to control the order in which variables are written onto the SCSS masterfile. If you use a KEEP subcommand, variables are written onto the masterfile in the order named. You can name a subset of the variables followed by the keyword ALL. This will write the variables specifically named in the order specified followed by the rest of the variables in the active file in their order on the active file.

17.5
RENAME Subcommand

To rename variables saved on the SCSS masterfile, use the RENAME subcommand, as in:

```
SAVE SCSS OUTFILE=HUBOUT
 /DROP=DEPT79 TO DEPT81, SALARY79 TO SALARY81, HOURLY81
 /RENAME=(DEPT82,SALARY82,HOURLY82,PROMO81=DEPT,SALARY,HOURLY,PROMO)
```

This subcommand renames DEPT82 to DEPT, SALARY82 to SALARY, and so forth. The format of the RENAME command is *old names = new names* enclosed in parentheses. If you use variable lists the lists on each side of the equals signs must specify the same number of variables. Both lists can employ TO conventions, the old variable list implying a list of consecutive variables from the SCSS file and the new variable list creating a set of names, as in VAR01 TO VAR99.

Alternatively, you can rename variables one at a time, each pair enclosed in optional parentheses, as in:

```
SAVE SCSS OUTFILE=HUBOUT/
 DROP=DEPT79 TO DEPT81, SALARY79 TO SALARY81, HOURLY81/
```

RENAME=(DEPT82=DEPT)(SALARY82=SALARY)(HOURLY82=HOURLY)(PROMO81=PROMO)

Variables that have been renamed retain their variable and value labels. Renaming variables within the SAVE SCSS procedure does not rename them on the active file. However, if you rename a variable and then list it on a subsequent KEEP or DROP subcommand on SAVE SCSS, use the new name. Subcommands must be separated by slashes.

17.6
Display Output

The first piece of information displayed as a result of the SAVE SCSS command shown in Section 17.5 is shown in Figure 17.6a. SPSS-X tells you which string variables are not going to be saved, the number of variables to be saved, and the total number of variables possible given the memory available.

Figure 17.6a   SAVE SCSS messages

```
    27  0          FILE HANDLE HUBOUT/NAME='HUBEMPL SCSSMF'
    28  0          SAVE SCSS OUTFILE=HUBOUT/
    29  0            DROP=DEPT79 TO DEPT81, SALARY79 TO SALARY81, HOURLY81/
    30  0            RENAME=(DEPT82,SALARY82,HOURLY82,PROMO81=DEPT,SALARY,HOURLY,PROMO)

'NAME    ' IS A STRING VARIABLE AND WILL NOT BE SAVED.

WORKSPACE ALLOWS FOR 7380 VARIABLES.    12 VARIABLES ARE TO BE KEPT.
```

SPSS-X then produces a table of variable names that are to be saved, their SCSS type (DISCRETE or CONTINUOUS), the number of cases that can be compressed per word, the valid cases, minimum and maximum values encountered reading the data, and the value selected to replace the SPSS-X system-missing value (see Figure 17.6b).

Figure 17.6b Table of variables

VARIABLE	LABEL	TYPE	CASES /WORD	VALID CASES	MINIMUM	MAXIMUM	SYSMISS RESULT
EMPLOYID		DISCRETE	2	275	1801.00	43902.00	
MOHIRED		DISCRETE	4	275	1.00	12.00	
YRHIRED	YEAR OF FIRST HIRING	DISCRETE	4	275	48.00	81.00	
DEPT	DEPARTMENT OF EMPLOYMENT IN 1982	DISCRETE	4	145	0.0	4.00	
SEX		DISCRETE	4	275	1.00	2.00	
SALARY	YEARLY SALARY IN 1982	DISCRETE	2	145	0.0	50700.00	
HOURLY		CONTINUOUS	1	145	-999.00	26.00	
PROMO		DISCRETE	4	275	0.0	9.00	
AGE		DISCRETE	4	272	0.0	69.00	
RAISE82		DISCRETE	2	138	-5739.00	11700.00	
JOBCAT	JOB CATEGORIES	DISCRETE	4	275	1.00	4.00	
PCTRAISE		CONTINUOUS	1	138	-98.44	50.00	50.00

Finally, SPSS-X tells you if the file was saved and the internal file name (see Figure 17.6c). It also repeats the number of cases and the variable names in alphabetical order (including special SCSS variables SPSS and SPSS0001), and tells you if any additional numeric variables were dropped because alphanumeric or extreme values were encountered when the data were read.

Figure 17.6c File messages

```
SCSS MASTERFILE 'M24APR85' SAVED WITH    275 CASES.


SORTED LIST OF VARIABLES SAVED:

    9 AGE          4 DEPT         1 EMPLOYID      7 HOURLY      11 JOBCAT
    2 MOHIRED     13 PCTRAISE     8 PROMO        10 RAISE82      6 SALARY
    5 SEX          0 SPSS        14 SPSS0001      3 YRHIRED


    0 VARIABLES WITH ALPHA OR EXTREME VALUES WERE DROPPED.
```

17.7
GET SCSS Command

You can read an SCSS masterfile or a workfile/masterfile combination in SPSS-X using the GET SCSS command, as in:

```
GET SCSS MASTERFILE=HUBIN
FREQUENCIES VARIABLES=MOHIRED TO SEX, JOBCAT
```

This set of commands retrieves the SCSS masterfile saved in Sections 17.2 through 17.6. The MASTERFILE subcommand is discussed in Section 17.8. The frequency table for variable SEX from this command is shown in Figure 17.7a.

Figure 17.7a Frequency table from the SCSS masterfile

```
FILE:      FILE BUILT VIA GET SCSS

SEX


                                                     VALID     CUM
    VALUE LABEL           VALUE   FREQUENCY  PERCENT  PERCENT   PERCENT

    MALE                    1        83       30.2    30.2      30.2
    FEMALE                  2       192       69.8    69.8     100.0
                                   -------   ------   ------
                          TOTAL      275     100.0    100.0

VALID CASES     275    MISSING CASES     0
```

SPSS-X can encounter problems with missing values because SPSS-X and SCSS handle missing values differently. First, SCSS allows more than three missing values. In addition, SCSS variables can have missing-value ranges that include valid values. Also, SCSS can use alphabetical ranges to declare missing values. Problem numeric values will be recoded to the system-missing value and problem alphabetical values will be recoded to blanks. Furthermore, in SCSS a value can be missing for some cases (via value revision) and not for other cases. SPSS-X considers such a value missing for all cases when the file is read using GET SCSS. In any case, SPSS-X informs you what has been done, as shown in Figure 17.7b.

Figure 17.7b   Missing-value message

```
          MIS VAL        RESULT
VARIABLE  PROBLEM        VALUE  OBSERVED VALUES

AGE       TOO MANY         .  M    69.00
```

The print and write formats for numeric variables are based on the length of the values. Variables copied with original alphanumeric values have print and write formats of A1, A2, or A4 for variables with three or four characters. (Alphanumeric values cannot occur in a variable in a masterfile created using the SAVE SCSS command in SPSS-X but can occur in a masterfile defined directly in SCSS where the original values are alphanumeric but were revised as the masterfile was created.)

17.8
MASTERFILE Subcommand

The MASTERFILE subcommand specifies the masterfile to be read. If you specify the masterfile alone, only masterfile information is copied. Revisions or additions kept on any of the workfiles that point to that masterfile are not available to SPSS-X unless you also specify a WORKFILE subcommand. See Section 17.9 for the additional specification of a workfile.

17.9
WORKFILE Subcommand

Optionally, you can use the WORKFILE subcommand to specify a workfile associated with the masterfile you are reading, as in:

```
GET SCSS WORKFILE=WHUBIN/ MASTERFILE=MHUBIN
FREQUENCIES VARIABLES=MOHIRED TO SEX, JOBCAT
```

If you specify the workfile in addition to the masterfile, SPSS-X builds the active file to reflect changes recorded on the workfile including labels, revisions to existing variables, and computed variables. For example, variable SEX was revised in SCSS by assigning new labels and by changing the value for females from 2 to 0. Value 0 was labeled WOMEN and value 1 was labeled MEN. Compare the table produced from workfile information (Figure 17.9) with the table produced from the masterfile alone (Figure 17.7a).

Figure 17.9   Frequency table from the SCSS workfile

```
FILE:      FILE BUILT VIA GET SCSS

SEX        SEX OF RESPONDENT


                                                  VALID    CUM
     VALUE LABEL            VALUE  FREQUENCY  PERCENT  PERCENT  PERCENT

WOMEN                          0       192      69.8     69.8     69.8
MEN                            1        83      30.2     30.2    100.0
                                      ----     -----    -----
                          TOTAL       275     100.0    100.0

VALID CASES     275    MISSING CASES      0
```

You can specify the WORKFILE and MASTERFILE subcommands in any order. The slash between these subcommands is optional. If you specify the workfile alone, SPSS-X will try to locate the masterfile but will not always succeed (depending on the completeness of the specification on the workfile and on your operating system).

17.10
VARIABLES Subcommand

To limit the number of variables SPSS-X copies from the SCSS files, use the VARIABLES subcommand, as in:

```
GET SCSS WORKFILE=WHUBIN/ MASTERFILE=MHUBIN/
  VARIABLES=MOHIRED TO SEX, JOBCAT
FREQUENCIES VARIABLES=ALL
```

- Variables are copied in the order specified on the VARIABLES subcommand.
- Variable name THRU is allowed in SCSS but not SPSS-X, so it must be renamed.
- Keywords ALL and $ALL are recognized. Keyword ALL is the default if a workfile is specified. Keyword $ALL specifies the unrevised masterfile version of all of the variables.

If you also want to rename the variables you are reading, use the *old name = new name* format enclosed in optional parentheses, as in:

```
GET SCSS WORKFILE=WHUBIN/ MASTERFILE=MHUBIN/
  VARIABLES=MOHIRED TO SEX ($SEX=SEX$) JOBCAT
FREQUENCIES VARIABLES=ALL
```

This example shows use of the dollar sign to signal to SCSS that you want the unrevised masterfile version of variable SEX. Since variable names beginning with dollar signs are not allowed in SPSS-X, the variable has to be renamed.

If you have a list of variables you want to rename in a single specification, the parentheses are required, as in:

```
VARIABLES=(DEPT,SALARY,HOURLY,PROMO=DEPT82,SALARY82,HOURLY82,PROMO81)
```

Variable DEPT is renamed DEPT82, SALARY is renamed SALARY82, and so forth. The lists must contain the same number of variables. Both lists can employ TO conventions, the old variable list implying a list of consecutive variables from the SCSS file and the new variable list creating a set of names, such as VAR01 TO VAR99.

17.11
TRANSPORTING SPSS-X SYSTEM FILES

SPSS-X allows you to read and write portable data files. A portable file contains all of the data and dictionary information stored in the system file from which it was created. Use portable files if you are transporting files between installations having different conversions of SPSS-X (such as for the PRIME, VAX, or HONEYWELL GCOS computers) or if you are transporting files between SPSS-X, SPSS/PC, or other software using the same portable file format. If you are sending data to an installation having the same machine as your own, send an SPSS-X system file. A system file is cheaper to process than a portable file.

To write portable files, use the EXPORT command (see Sections 17.16 through 17.21). To read portable files, use the IMPORT command (see Sections 17.22 through 17.26).

17.12
Methods of Transporting Portable Files

You can transport portable files either on magnetic tape or by a communications program. Each method involves special considerations, discussed below.

Magnetic Tape. Before you transport files on magnetic tape, make sure the receiving installation can read the tape you are sending. You should know the following tape specifications for the installation before writing the tape:

- Number of tracks—either 7 or 9.
- Tape density—200, 556, 800, 1600, or 6250 bits per inch (BPI).

17

- Parity—even or odd. You need to know this only if you are writing a 7-track tape.
- Tape labeling—labeled or unlabeled. Check whether the site can use tape labels. Also make sure that the site has the ability to read multivolume tape files if the file you are writing uses more than one tape.
- Blocksize—the maximum blocksize the receiving installation can accept.

A tape written with the following characteristics can be read at most installations: 9-track, 1600 BPI, unlabeled, and a blocksize of 3200 characters. However, you have no guarantee that a tape written with these characteristics will be read successfully at a particular receiving installation. The best policy is to know the acceptable characteristics for tapes that a specific receiving installation can read.

Communications Programs. Transmission of a portable file by a communications program may not be possible if the program misinterprets any characters in the file as control characters (for example, as a line feed, carriage return, or end of transmission). You can prevent this problem by specifying TYPE=COMM on the EXPORT command (see Section 17.17). This specification replaces each control character with the character zero. The affected control characters are in positions 0–60 of the IMPORT/EXPORT character set (Appendix C).

The line length that the communications program uses must be set to 80 to match the 80-character record length of portable files. A transmitted file must be inspected with an editor for blank lines or special characters inserted by the communications program. These must be edited out prior to reading the file with the IMPORT command.

17.13
Characteristics of Portable Files

A portable file contains all the information in an SPSS-X system file, including the dictionary and the data. The dictionary contains variable and value labels, missing-value flags, and printing and writing formats for each variable. Also included on the portable file are the file label, the name of the originating installation, the name, release, and version of the originating software, and the date and time the portable file was created.

Portable files are character files, not binary files, and they have 80-character records so they can be transmitted over data links. By dumping the first few records, you can check that a file you receive is an SPSS-X portable file. If you have a copy of a portable file, one of the first few records contains the words *SPSS-X Portable File.*

17.14
Character Translation

A receiving installation may not use the same character set as the installation where a portable file was written. If possible, SPSS-X translates characters in the portable file to the character set of the receiving installation. Depending on the character set in use, some characters in labels and in string data may be lost in the translation. For example, if you transport a file from an installation using a seven-bit ASCII character set to an installation using a six-bit ASCII character set, some characters in the file may have no matching characters in six-bit ASCII. For a character that has no match, SPSS-X generates an appropriate nonprintable character (the null character in most character sets). For a complete display of the character-set translations available with the IMPORT and EXPORT commands, refer to Appendix C. A blank in a column of the appendix means that there is no matching character for that character set, and an appropriate nonprintable character will be generated by SPSS-X when you import a file.

17.15
Hints for Successful File Transfer

The following advice may help you to transfer files successfully by magnetic tape:

• Unless you are sure that the receiving computer can read labels written by the originating computer, prepare an unlabeled tape.

• Make sure that the record length of 80 is not changed.

• Do not use a separate character translation program. (In particular, do not attempt ASCII/EBCDIC translations; EXPORT/IMPORT takes care of that for you.)

• Make sure you use the same blocking factor when writing and reading a tape. A blocksize of 3200 is frequently a good choice.

• If possible, write the portable file directly to tape in your SPSS-X job. This avoids possible interference from some copy programs. Read the file directly from the tape for the same reason.

• Use the INFO LOCAL command to find out about using SPSS-X on your particular computer and operating system. INFO LOCAL generally includes additional information about reading and writing portable files.

If you are communicating a portable file via telephone modem, consider using an error-checking communications system such as Kermit.

17.16
EXPORT Command

Use the EXPORT command to create a portable file. The EXPORT command is very much like the SAVE command. It can occur in the same position in the command file as the SAVE command and saves the current active file. This includes the results of all permanent transformations and any temporary transformations made just prior to the EXPORT command. The active file is unchanged after the EXPORT command.

The OUTFILE subcommand is the only required specification on the EXPORT command, as in:

```
EXPORT OUTFILE=HUBOUT
```

These commands save the active file as a portable file referred as HUBOUT.

In addition, you can use optional subcommands to control the format of portable files, restrict the number of variables saved, to rename variables, to get a map of the variables, and to control the minimum precision to be used in representing numbers. The subcommands must be separated by slashes.

17.17
TYPE Subcommand

You can use the TYPE subcommand to create either a communications- or tape-formatted portable file. Specify TYPE=TAPE if you plan to transport portable files on magnetic tape. The default is TYPE=COMM, which removes all control characters and replaces them with the character zero.

You should always use the COMM option when transmitting portable files by a communications program. For example, to save HUBOUT as a communications-formatted portable file, specify:

```
EXPORT TYPE=COMM/OUTFILE=HUBOUT
```

All portable files from releases earlier than SPSS-X 2.1 are in tape format and may not be suitable for transmission by communications programs.

17.18
DROP and KEEP Subcommands

Use the DROP and KEEP subcommands to save a subset of variables on the exported file. For example, to drop a list of variables before writing the portable file, specify:

```
EXPORT OUTFILE=HUBOUT/
  DROP=DEPT79 TO DEPT81, SALARY79 TO SALARY81, HOURLY81
```

The DROP and KEEP subcommands affect only the portable file created by the EXPORT command. These subcommands do not change the active file.

17.19
RENAME Subcommand

Use the RENAME subcommand to rename variables being written onto the portable file, as in:

```
EXPORT OUTFILE=HUBOUT/
  DROP=DEPT79 TO DEPT81, SALARY79 to SALARY81, HOURLY81/
  RENAME=(DEPT82,SALARY82,HOURLY82,PROMO81=DEPT,SALARY,HOURLY,PROMO)
```

In this example, the RENAME subcommand renames variable DEPT82 to DEPT, variable SALARY82 to SALARY, and so forth. The format of the RENAME subcommand is *old name = new name*, enclosed in parentheses. If you use variable lists, the same number of variables must be specified on both sides of the equals sign. Both lists can employ the TO convention, the old variable list implying a list of consecutive variables on the active file and the new variable list creating a set of names, such as VAR01 TO VAR99, on the portable file.

Alternatively, you can rename variables one at a time, with each pair enclosed in optional parentheses, as in:

```
EXPORT OUTFILE HUBOUT/
  DROP=DEPT79 TO DEPT81, SALARY79 TO SALARY81, HOURLY81/
  RENAME=(DEPT82=DEPT) (SALARY82=SALARY)
  (HOURLY82=HOURLY) (PROMO81=PROMO)
```

Variables that are renamed on the EXPORT command retain any variable and value labels. Using the RENAME subcommand does not rename variables on the active file. However, if you rename a variable and then list it on a subsequent DROP or KEEP subcommand on the EXPORT command, use the new name.

17.20
MAP Subcommand

If you use the RENAME, DROP, or KEEP subcommands to tailor your file, you may find it difficult to keep track of what you have done. To check the results of these subcommands, use the MAP subcommand immediately following the subcommand you want mapped, as in:

```
EXPORT OUTFILE HUBOUT/
  DROP=DEPT79 TO DEPT81, SALARY79 TO SALARY81, HOURLY81/MAP/
```

```
RENAME=(DEPT82=DEPT)(SALARY82=SALARY)(HOURLY82=HOURLY)(PROMO81=PROMO)/MAP
```

In this example, the first MAP subcommand gives you a map of the variables after the DROP subcommand has dropped the specified variables. The second MAP subcommand displays the results following the renaming of a set of variables. Since this is the last subcommand specified, the second map displays the variables that are written onto the portable file.

17.21
DIGITS Subcommand

The EXPORT command encodes a number on the portable file to ensure that the receiving machine sees the same number the sending machine saw. The methods used work perfectly for integers that are not too large and for fractions whose denominators are products of 2, 3, and 5 (meaning all decimals, quarters, eighths, sixteenths, thirds, thirtieths, sixtieths, and so forth.) For other fractions and for integers too large to be represented exactly in the active file (usually more than 9 digits, often 15 or more), the representation used in the active file contains some error already, so no exact way of sending these numbers is possible. SPSS-X sends enough digits to get very close. The number of digits sent in these cases depends on the originating program: on the IBM versions of SPSS-X, it is the equivalent of 15 decimal digits (in integer and fractional parts combined).

If many numbers on a file require this treatment, the file can grow quite large. These numbers take a great deal of space. If you do not need the full precision normally used, you can save some space on the portable file by using the DIGITS subcommand.

The DIGITS subcommand has the general form DIGITS=n, where n is the number of decimal digits of precision you want. Specifying DIGITS=6, for example, means you will be satisfied if 1.23456789087654 is rounded to 1.23457 on the portable file. Since the number base used is not 10, the actual representation used will be different, but the rounding error will not exceed that of a six-decimal-digit representation. The DIGITS subcommand specification is applied to all numbers for which no exact representation in a reasonable number of digits is possible. It cannot be different for different variables, so it should be set according to the requirements of the variable that needs the most precision.

17.22
IMPORT Command

Use the IMPORT command to read SPSS-X portable files created with the EXPORT command. For example, if you are at an IBM installation you can use the IMPORT command to read a portable file created with the EXPORT command at a DIGITAL VAX site. The only required subcommand is the FILE subcommand followed by an optional equals sign and a specified file, as in:

```
IMPORT FILE=HUBIN
```

These commands create an active file of the portable file referred to as file HUBIN.

You can use additional subcommands to define the portable file format, restrict the number of variables brought into the active file from the portable file, to rename variables on the active file, and to get a map of the variables on the active file.

17.23
TYPE Subcommand

You can use the TYPE subcommand to define the format of the portable file as either communications or tape. Specify TYPE=COMM for communications-formatted files and TYPE=TAPE for files in tape format. In the following example, the TYPE subcommand defines HUBIN as a tape-formatted portable file:

```
IMPORT TYPE=TAPE/FILE=HUBIN
```

17.24
DROP and KEEP Subcommands

Use the DROP and KEEP subcommands to retain a subset of variables on the active file. For example, to drop a list of variables read from the portable file, specify:

```
IMPORT FILE=HUBIN/
  DROP=DEPT79 TO DEPT81, SALARY79 TO SALARY81, HOURLY81
```

The DROP and KEEP subcommands affect only the active file created by the IMPORT command. They do not change the portable file.

17.25
RENAME Subcommand

Use the RENAME subcommand to rename variables being read from the portable file, as in:

```
IMPORT FILE=HUBIN/
  DROP=DEPT79 TO DEPT81, SALARY79 to SALARY81, HOURLY81/
    RENAME=(DEPT82,SALARY82,HOURLY82,PROMO81=DEPT,SALARY,HOURLY,PROMO)
```

In this example, the RENAME subcommand renames variable DEPT82 to DEPT, variable SALARY82 to SALARY, and so forth. The format of the RENAME subcommand is *old name = new name*, enclosed in parentheses. If you use variable lists, the same number of variables must be specified on both sides of the equals sign. Both lists on the RENAME subcommand can employ the TO convention, the old variable list implying a list of consecutive variables on the portable file and the new variable list creating a set of names, such as VAR01 TO VAR99.

17

Alternatively, you can rename variables one at a time, with each pair enclosed in optional parentheses, as in:

```
IMPORT FILE HUBIN/
  DROP=DEPT79 TO DEPT81, SALARY79 TO SALARY81, HOURLY81/
    RENAME=(DEPT82=DEPT) (SALARY82=SALARY)
    (HOURLY82=HOURLY) (PROMO81=PROMO)
```

Variables that are renamed on the IMPORT command retain any variable and value labels. If you rename a variable and then list it on a subsequent DROP or KEEP subcommand on the IMPORT command, use the new name.

17.26
MAP Subcommand

If you use the RENAME, DROP, or KEEP subcommands to tailor your file, you may find it difficult to keep track of what you have done. To check the results of these subcommands, use the MAP subcommand immediately following the subcommand you want mapped, as in:

```
IMPORT FILE HUBIN/
 DROP=DEPT79 TO DEPT81, SALARY79 TO SALARY81, HOURLY81/MAP/

RENAME=(DEPT82=DEPT)(SALARY82=SALARY)(HOURLY82=HOURLY)(PROMO81=PROMO)/MAP
```

In this example, the first MAP subcommand gives you a map of the variables after the DROP subcommand has dropped the specified variables. The second MAP subcommand displays the results following the renaming of a set of variables. Since this is the last subcommand specified, the second map displays the variables that are currently on the active file.

17.27
READING SAS FILES WITH SPSS-X

You can read SAS files with the GET SAS command. In most instances, you can retrieve the data and the data definition items—including the file label, variable and value labels, print and write formats, and missing values. You can then store this information in an SPSS-X system file with the SAVE command. Note: GET SAS is available only on IBM CMS and OS systems.

17.28
DATA Subcommand

The GET SAS command must be followed by a DATA subcommand, which names the SAS data set to be used as input. The name consists of two parts separated by a period. The meaning of the parts depends on the operating system being used. In an OS environment, the first part refers to the DDNAME in the JCL, and the second to the member name, or the internal name of the SAS file. If the DDNAME begins with TAPE, the SAS file is assumed to be in tape format. Other DDNAMES refer to SAS files in disk format. For example, the data name in the command

```
GET SAS DATA=ELECT.Y1948
```

refers to a disk-formatted SAS FILE whose DDNAME is ELECT and whose member name is Y1948.

In CMS, the first part of the data set name corresponds to the FILE TYPE and the second part to the FILE NAME. In the above command, ELECT would refer to the FILE TYPE, and Y1948 would refer to the FILE NAME. If the FILE TYPE begins with TAPE, the SAS file is expected to be in tape format. If a file in tape format resides on disk, it must have a FILE MODE of 4, for example, A4. You must issue a FILEDEF command to let SPSS-X know the SAS file is in tape format. Other FILE TYPES correspond to SAS files in disk format.

17.29
SASLIB Subcommand

Use the SASLIB subcommand after the DATA option to specify the DDNAME for the library containing SAS formats, as in:

```
GET SAS DATA=ELECT.Y1948 SASLIB=LABELS
```

These formats may contain value labels for some or all of the variables. The SASLIB statement can be omitted if value labels are not needed; if formats are stored in the STEPLIB, JOBLIB, or link libraries in an OS environment; or if formats are stored as TEXT files in CMS.

17.30
DROP and KEEP Subcommands

Refer to the sections on the GET command in Chapter 6 for further discussion of these subcommands.

By default, SPSS-X stores all variables from the SAS file in their original order. If you need only a subset of these variables, use either the DROP or KEEP subcommand, whichever is most convenient. You can also use the KEEP subcommand to reorder the variables in the result file.

17.31
RENAME Subcommand

Some variables in SAS files may automatically be renamed when you use the GET SAS command (see Section 17.33). To change the names of other variables in the SAS file before storing them into the result file, use the RENAME subcommand. Of course, variable names must conform to SPSS-X naming conventions, which (unlike SAS conventions) do not allow leading underscores.

17.32
MAP Subcommand

After renaming, deleting, or reordering variables, you may want to check the results. The MAP subcommand displays the variable names and their order for both the SAS file and the SPSS-X file. If you specify MAP on the same GET SAS command as DROP or KEEP, MAP should come last; if it does not, the results of DROP and KEEP will not appear in the map of the new file.

17.33
SAS to SPSS-X Data Conversion

The GET SAS command can retrieve most of the information from SAS data sets.

File Label. The file label for the SPSS-X file is obtained from the name specified on the LABEL option of the SAS DATA statement.

Variable Types. Both SAS and SPSS-X allow two types of variables, numeric and character string. During conversion, SAS numeric variables become SPSS-X numeric variables, and SAS character string variables become SPSS-X character string variables of the same length. Values for SAS variables that can be identified in date format are converted to the number of seconds from October 15, 1582, to the given date. Similarly, values for any SAS variables that are clearly in date-time format are changed to the number of seconds from October 15, 1582, to the given date and time.

Missing Values. SAS and SPSS-X treat missing values in basically different ways. In SPSS-X, the user can designate certain numbers or strings in the data as missing. In SAS, special values (like the SPSS-X system-missing value) indicate missing data items, and there is no way to tell what type of information was intended in the missing code and missing values fields. Since SAS has no user-defined missing values, all SAS missing codes are converted to SPSS-X system-missing values.

Print and Write Formats. Formats are present in the SAS data set only if an INFORMAT or a FORMAT statment appeared in the DATA step that created the data set. The FORMAT statment gives the format to use on output, so if there is an equivalent printable format in SPSS-X, it will be used as the print format. Otherwise, an attempt to use the INFORMAT will be made. The INFORMAT, if

17

present, will be preferred for the SPSS-X write format. If an INFORMAT is not present, an attempt will be made to use the format on the FORMAT statement.

If there are no SPSS-X equivalents for SAS formats, or if no format information exists, a default F8.2 format is used for numeric variables and an A format is used for character string variables. The only exceptions are date formats, which default to F14.0, and date-time formats, which have a default of F16.1. Table 17.33 shows the correspondence between SPSS-X and SAS formats.

Table 17.33   Output format correspondence

SPSS-X format	SAS format	Print	Write
Aw	$w	x	x
AHEXw	$HEXw	x	x
COMMAw.d	COMMAw.d	x	x
DOLLARw.d	DOLLARw.d	x	x
Fw.d	w.d	x	x
IBw.d	IBw.d		x
PIBHEXw	HEXw wa=16	x	x
Pw.d	PDw.d		x
PIBw.d	PIBw.d		x
PKw.d,PKw	n/a	n/a	n/a
RBw.d	RBw.d		x
RBHEX16	HEX16	x	x
Zw.d	ZDw.d		x
Ew.d	Ew.d	x	x

Variable Names. Like SPSS-X, SAS allows variable names up to eight characters long, but the SAS naming conventions are somewhat different from those in SPSS-X. A SAS variable name must begin with a letter or an underscore. The underscore can be used within SPSS-X variable names but not at the beginning of a name. All leading underscores in SAS files are therefore changed to @ symbols. If an SPSS-X reserved keyword is used as a SAS variable name, SPSS-X appends the # symbol to the name and issues a warning message. The SPSS-X reserved keywords are ALL, AND, BY, GE, GT, LE, LT, NE, NOT, OR, TO, and WITH. A SAS variable named AND, for example, would be converted to AND#.

Variable Labels. Variables mentioned on a LABEL statement in the SAS DATA step will have the corresponding label in SPSS-X.

Value Labels. Two conditions must be met to obtain value label data from SAS data sets: SAS form value labels must have been stored into a SASLIB via the DDNAME= option on the PROC FORMAT statement; and a FORMAT statment must have appeared on the DATA step to associate the value labels to variables in the data set. If these conditions are met, SPSS-X attempts to read and convert the value labels. To be usable as an SPSS-X value label, a numeric format should have a FUZZ value equal to or smaller than the standard value assigned by SAS.

17.34
READING OSIRIS
FILES WITH SPSS-X

OSIRIS is a package of computer programs designed for the analysis of social science data. It was developed by the Institute for Social Science Research (at the University of Michigan) and the Inter-University Consortium for Political Science. The GET OSIRIS command allows you to use OSIRIS data files as input for SPSS-X programs. This facility lets you access information in the OSIRIS dictionary and avoid having to prepare equivalent specifications in SPSS-X.

17.35
GET OSIRIS Command

The GET OSIRIS command creates appropriate input formats to read the variables in the OSIRIS data set. OSIRIS variable numbers are converted into SPSS-X variable names, so you do not need to supply a DATA LIST. Print formats and write formats are automatically assigned using SPSS-X conventions, though you can override the assigned formats with PRINT FORMAT and WRITE FORMAT commands. Variable label information is read from the OSIRIS dictionary. Type 1 data sets (see below) may include a dictionary-codebook file containing value label information, which GET OSIRIS automatically converts into SPSS-X value labels. Missing-value specifications are read from the OSIRIS data set.

There are three types of OSIRIS data sets: types 1, 3, and 5. SPSS-X can currently read only types 1 and 3. Type 1 data sets are the usual form for distribution; they are only produced by the OSIRIS system and after many edit checks have been made. Type 3 data sets may be produced using ordinary text-editing software (or a card punch). Each data set consists of a fixed-format raw data file and a dictionary file containing data definitions associated with OSIRIS variables.

The GET OSIRIS command converts the OSIRIS dictionary into an SPSS-X active file dictionary and generates an SPSS-X transformation program to read the cases in the OSIRIS data file. The DICTIONARY subcommand on GET OSIRIS assigns a file for the OSIRIS dictionary file; the DATA subcommand assigns the file for the OSIRIS data file, as in

```
GET OSIRIS DICTIONARY=DICT48 DATA=DATA48
```

where DICT48 is the OSIRIS dictionary file, and DATA48 is the OSIRIS data file. You can use optional subcommands to drop, keep, or rename the variables to be stored into an SPSS-X system file.

17.36 DROP and KEEP Subcommands

DROP and KEEP are optional subcommands. Refer to the sections on the GET command in Chapter 6 for further clarification.

By default, SPSS-X stores all the variables from the OSIRIS file in their original order. Use the DROP or the KEEP subcommand if you need only a subset of the variables. You can also use the KEEP subcommand to reorder the variables in the result file.

17.37 RENAME Subcommand

OSIRIS data sets contain both single- and multiple-response questions. The GET OSIRIS command converts a single-response variable with the number n to the SPSS-X variable name Vn, and it converts a multiple-response variable n with k possible responses to k SPSS-X variable names: Mn.1, Mn.2, through Mn.k. To change the names of variables before storing them in the result file, use the RENAME subcommand, as in

```
GET OSIRIS  DICTIONARY=FILE1 DATA=FILE2
  /RENAME=(V1 V2 = OCCUPAT EMPSTAT)
        (M5.1 to M5.3 = CHOICE1 CHOICE2 CHOICE3)
```

where V1 is renamed OCCUPAT, and V2 is renamed EMPSTAT (see Section 17.39).

17.38 MAP Subcommand

The MAP subcommand displays the order of the variables in the SPSS-X result file. The display provides a useful check of what you have done by renaming, deleting, or reordering variables from the original OSIRIS data file. MAP reports on the current status of the SPSS-X file, so if you place the MAP subcommand before the RENAME, DROP, or KEEP subcommands, the results of the changes will not be shown. The MAP subcommand takes no field specifications.

17.39 OSIRIS to SPSS-X Data Conversion

In most instances, the GET OSIRIS command is able to retrieve the information from OSIRIS data files that is to be stored into SPSS-X system files.

Variable Types. Both SPSS-X and OSIRIS recognize two variable types, numeric and string. During the conversion process, OSIRIS numeric variables become

SPSS-X numeric variables, and OSIRIS string variables become SPSS-X string variables of the same length.

Variable Names. OSIRIS variable numbers refer to responses to single- or multiple-response survey questions. As described above, SPSS-X converts a multiple-response variable n with k possible responses to k variables named Mn.1 through Mn.k. An SPSS-X variable name is limited to eight characters. With the form Mn.k, therefore, if n has four digits, k can have no more than two, and if n has five digits, k can have only one. The form Mnk is used, without the decimal point, when n has five digits and k has two.

Variable Labels. In OSIRIS, the term *variable name* has the same sense as the term *variable label* in SPSS-X. OSIRIS variable names are converted to SPSS-X variable labels of the same length.

Missing Values. For missing values, OSIRIS lets you specify single values or size limits. Single values, if specified, are used as missing values for the corresponding variables in SPSS-X. An OSIRIS negative size limit x becomes the SPSS-X missing range (LO THRU x), and a positive size limit y becomes the SPSS-X missing range (y THRU HI). Range missing values are not used for string variables. No missing values are used for long string variables. Warnings are issued if missing values occur in violation of these rules.

Value Labels. The dictionary codebook in an OSIRIS type 1 data set may include value label information. If so, this information will be associated with the corresponding SPSS-X variables using the same values. When converted, labels longer than 60 characters are truncated.

Print and Write Formats. OSIRIS string variables with length l are given an A format with width l for print and write formats. OSIRIS numeric variables are assigned one of three formats corresponding to the three forms of OSIRIS data values: numeric character, fixed-point binary, and floating-point binary. Table 17.39 shows the assignment of numeric print and write formats. The width w and the number of decimal places d are taken from the OSIRIS data set.

Table 17.39   Print and write formats for numeric variables

OSIRIS data format	SPSS-X print format	SPSS-X write format
Numeric character	Fw.d	Fw.d
Fixed-point binary	Fw.d	IBw.d
Floating-point binary	Ew.d	RBw

Limitations. Type 3 OSIRIS data sets may contain multiple logical records per case, and they may contain variable values that span logical records. The GET OSIRIS command can handle type 3 data sets when there is only one logical record per case. It can also handle a logical record length of 80 with no variable values spanning different logical records. Because SPSS-X treats OSIRIS multiple-response variables as separate variables, GET OSIRIS can handle a multiple-response variable that spans different logical records provided that no corresponding individual SPSS-X variable spans different logical records.

17.40
READING BMDP FILES WITH SPSS-X

SPSS-X can create an active file directly from a BMDP *save file*. One or more BMDP save files may exist within a single BMDP data set.

17.41
GET BMDP Command

To read a save file from a BMDP data set, use the GET BMDP command with at least the minimum specification

```
GET BMDP  FILE=file
```

where *file* specifies the data set. This command reads the first save file in the data set with the content field DATA. To read other files, use additional specifications for code, content, and label, as described below.

SPSS-X makes assumptions about the record format and other characteristics of the data set based on the type of computer and operating system. Use the command INFO LOCAL to print this information (see Chapter 4).

Identifying Information. BMDP save files are identified within each data set by code, content, and label fields. Code and label are specified by the user within BMDP; content is supplied by the BMDP program to identify the type of file (data, correlation matrix, and so on). To print these fields and other information about the save files in a data set from within SPSS-X, use GET BMDP with the SCAN subcommand. SCAN=YES prints the information and reads the file. SCAN=ONLY prints the information and stops. The command

```
GET BMDP FILE= BMDPFIL3
 /SCAN ONLY
```

produces the output in Figure 17.41 for a data set containing a single save file.

Figure 17.41   Information from SCAN subcommand

```
SAVE        GROUP
FILE  VARS  INFO?  CODE       CONTENT    LABEL

  1    13   NO     BMDPSAV3   DATA       SAVED BY BMDPP8D
END OF FILE
```

You can use the CODE, CONTENT, and LABEL subcommands to specify a particular save file within a single data set. The specification can be a single word or a string enclosed in apostrophes. If you do not specify content, SPSS-X supplies DATA. If you do not use the CODE or LABEL subcommand, SPSS-X reads the first save file with the content you supply (or DATA by default). If you specify CODE or LABEL, SPSS-X reads the first file that matches all of the information provided. Thus the specifications

```
GET BMDP FILE= BMDPFIL
 /LABEL= 'OLD DATA'
```

read the first save file in data set BMDPFIL with content DATA and label OLD DATA.

Subcommand Order. Subcommands on GET BMDP must be given in the following order:

• FILE must be first.
• If present, SCAN must immediately follow FILE.
• CODE, CONTENT, and LABEL may appear in any order but must follow FILE and SCAN.
• KEEP, DROP, RENAME, and MAP may appear multiple times each and in any order but must follow all other subcommands.

Case Selection. In a BMDP save file, each case includes an automatic variable USE, whose value determines whether the case is included in an analysis. Only cases in which USE has a positive, nonmissing value are included. GET BMDP retains all cases, and it retains the variable USE unless the KEEP or DROP subcommands indicate otherwise. To obtain the same case selection in SPSS-X as in BMDP, use the SELECT IF command, as in

```
SELECT IF USE > 0
```

17

17.42
KEEP, DROP, and RENAME
Subcommands

The KEEP, DROP, and RENAME subcommands operate as they do in GET FILE. Specify the converted SPSS-X names, not the original BMDP names. The following example reads the first save file with content DATA from the data set

BMDPFIL4. This file contains variables named X(1), X(2), X1, and X2 (and some others), in that order. SPSS-X converts the variable names X(1) and X(2) to X1 and X2. Then, because of duplication, it converts X1 and X2 to V1 and V2. Note that the KEEP and RENAME specifications use the SPSS-X names.

```
GET BMDP FILE= BMDPFIL4  /SCAN YES
 /KEEP = X1 X2 V1 V2
 /RENAME = (X1 X2 V1 V2 = X1_A X2_A X1_B X2_B)
 /MAP
```

17.43
MAP Subcommand

The result of the MAP subcommand, as shown in Figure 17.43, includes the original name, the converted SPSS-X name, and the name following the rename action.

Figure 17.43   Variable name conversion in GET BMDP

```
SAVE          GROUP
FILE   VARS   INFO?   CODE        CONTENT     LABEL

  1     29     NO     BMDPSAV4    DATA        LOTS OF BAD VARIABLE NAMES
END OF FILE

  26 VARIABLE NAMES (OUT OF   29) WERE CHANGED TO CONFORM TO SPSS-X CON VENTIONS

RESULT    SPSS VAR   BMPD VAR

X1_A       X1         X(1)
X2_A       X2         X(2)
X1_B       V1         X1
X2_B       V2         X2
```

17.44
BMDP to SPSS-X Data Conversion

In most instances, the GET BMDP command is able to retrieve the information from save files that is to be stored into SPSS-X system files.

Variable Names. SPSS-X makes the following conversions to force BMDP variable names to comply with SPSS-X conventions:

- Initial blanks and special characters are changed to @. $VAR, .VAR, /VAR, and VAR preceded by a blank all become @VAR (but see below about duplicate names).
- Internal blanks and special characters are changed to underscores. VAR ONE and VAR/ONE both become VAR_ONE.
- Parentheses are removed. X(1) becomes X1.
- Hash marks are added to SPSS-X reserved keywords. GT becomes GT#, and ALL becomes ALL#.
- If conversion using these rules produces duplicate names, SPSS-X creates names of the form Vn, where *n* is an integer.

Use the MAP subcommand to get a list of original names and converted names.

Missing Values. All three BMDP missing values (missing, lower than the minimum, and higher than the minimum) are converted to the SPSS-X system-missing value.

Print and Write Formats. GET BMDP supplies print and write formats of F8.2 for all numeric variables and A4 for all string variables. Use FORMATS, PRINT FORMATS, and WRITE FORMATS if these formats are inappropriate. SPSS-X recognizes as string variables only those identified by the LABEL clause of BMDP's VARIABLE paragraph. Other string variables might exist and not be detected. The REFORMAT command, originally designed for conversion of system files from earlier versions of SPSS-X, can be useful in this instance.

Limitations. Although it is possible to read files with content other than DATA, such files are likely to be interpreted incorrectly. Experienced users may find ways of reading and redefining such files.

Information generated by the BMDP GROUPS paragraph is ignored.

Part 3: Data Analysis and Reporting

Part III: Data Analysis and Reporting

SPSS-X procedure commands range from LIST, which provides a simple case listing, to complex multivariate statistical and tabulation procedures. In this overview, the procedures are presented by function; in subsequent chapters they are presented alphabetically for quick reference.

CASE LISTINGS

The LIST procedure is easy to specify—only the command name is required if you want to list all cases for all variables on your active file. It allows you to select variables and to limit the cases to be printed. It automatically labels columns with variable names and optionally numbers the cases (within split-file groups if SPLIT FILE is in effect).

The REPORT procedure lists cases if you specify FORMAT=LIST. Since REPORT is designed to produce aggregate statistics for subgroups within a file, it is particularly useful if you want to combine a case listing with group summaries. REPORT also allows you to specify headings, special formatting, and special labeling.

TABLES AND REPORTS

The FREQUENCIES procedure produces frequency tables for single variables, plus optional bar charts and histograms. The CROSSTABS procedure produces two-way to *n*-way crosstabulations. The MEANS procedure produces tables of means in a choice of three formats. All of these procedures also produce a variety of statistics (see below).

For questionnaire or other data in which each case might have more than one value for a single item (for example, "Which of the following periodicals do you read regularly?"), the MULT RESPONSE procedure produces both univariate tables and crosstabulations with ordinary variables or with other multiple-response items.

The REPORT procedure calculates a wide variety of summary statistics for subgroups defined by one or more variables and prints them in a format you can control. Most of the statistics available in FREQUENCIES are available in REPORT, and you can obtain them for groups defined at multiple levels (for example, grade within school within district within state). You can also obtain composite statistics calculated on group summaries, such as the average of the means for several variables. And you can control almost every part of the report format: dimensions, column widths, spacing, titles, footnotes, labels, and so on.

TABLES, an optional procedure in SPSS-X, produces presentation-quality stub-and-banner tables. It can handle multiple-response variables, combine multiple crosstabulations in a single display, and nest categories of one variable within the categories of another. It provides a full range of counts and descriptive statistics for the cells of the table, and it gives you control over the percentaging—row, column, table, or subtable percents as needed. Consult the *SPSS-X Tables* manual for documentation on TABLES.

STATISTICAL PROCEDURES

The SPSS-X statistical procedures described in the following sections perform a wide range of analyses—from frequency tables to multivariate analyses of variance. Using these procedures properly requires an understanding not only of SPSS-X syntax but also of statistical techniques and of the particular data being analyzed. For further examples of the applications of these procedures, consult the *SPSS-X Introductory Statistics Guide* and the *SPSS-X Advanced Statistics Guide*.

Frequency Distributions and Descriptive Statistics

The FREQUENCIES procedure calculates a variety of descriptive statistics, such as the mean, median, mode, range, variance, measures of skewness and kurtosis, and percentiles. Bar charts and frequency tables of the individual values of a variable can be displayed. Histograms are available for ordered variables that have many distinct values. The DESCRIPTIVES procedure calculates many of the same measures of central tendency and dispersion as does FREQUENCIES. However, since it does not sort the observations, it does not compute the median and mode. DESCRIPTIVES also calculates standardized *(Z)* scores for cases and adds them to your active file for use in other procedures.

Tabular Description of Relationships among Several Variables

The CROSSTABS procedure counts the number of times combinations of values of variables occur. It is useful for studying relationships among variables that have a limited number of distinct values. The observed frequencies in each cell can be expressed as a percentage of the row total, column total, or table total. A variety of statistics that measure the strength of association between the variables, such as lambda, gamma, and Kendall's tau *b*, can be computed. The chi-square test of independence and associated residuals and expected values are also available.

The MEANS procedure calculates descriptive statistics, such as the mean and variance, for subgroups of cases. Subgroups can be defined by combinations of values of up to six categorical variables. A one-way analysis of variance table including a test for linearity is also available.

Correlation Coefficients and Scatterplots

The CORRELATIONS procedure calculates the Pearson product-moment correlation coefficient, a measure of linear association between pairs of variables. The NONPAR CORR procedure computes Spearman and Kendall coefficients, two nonparametric measures of association that are based on the ranks of the observations. The output from these procedures includes the coefficients, sample sizes, and observed significance levels. The correlation matrices can be written on a file and used as input to other procedures.

The PLOT procedure produces line-printer plots. Points on the plot can be identified by the value of a control variable. Several plots can be superimposed. Contour plots and regression statistics can also be obtained.

Multiple Regression Analysis

The REGRESSION procedure can be used to study the relationship between a dependent variable and a set of independent variables. Regression coefficients can be calculated, along with a variety of statistics and plots that evaluate how well the model fits and what each individual variable contributes. Forward-inclusion, backward-elimination, and stepwise-selection algorithms are available for selecting the independent variables to be included in the equation. Extensive facilities for analyzing and plotting residuals and influential cases are included. Residuals and other statistics computed for the cases can be added to the active file for use in other procedures.

Nonlinear Regression Analysis

Two procedures, NLR and CNLR, are available for estimating the parameter values and regression statistics for models that are not linear in their parameters. Both procedures estimate the parameter values and optionally compute and save predicted values, residuals, and derivatives. Final parameter estimates can be saved on a system file and used in subsequent analyses. CNLR(Constrained Nonlinear Regression) uses a sequential quadratic programming algorithm and can be used for both constrained and unconstrained problems. The NLR procedure uses a Levenberg-Marquardt algorithm and can only be used for unconstrained problems. NLR and CNLR are both discussed in Chapter 36.

Factor Analysis

The FACTOR procedure can be used to identify underlying constructs or "factors" that account for the observed correlations in a set of variables. Initial factors can be extracted using principal axis factoring, unweighted or generalized least squares, and maximum likelihood algorithms. Principal components can also be calculated. Several methods for orthogonal and oblique rotations are available. Additional statistics and plots useful for factor analysis are also available. Factor scores can be computed using several methods and added to the active file for subsequent analysis in other procedures.

Discriminant Analysis

The DISCRIMINANT procedure calculates linear combinations of variables that can be used to distinguish among members of different groups. All variables can be included, or a stepwise algorithm using one of several possible entry and removal criteria can be used for variable selection. A classification table containing the number of cases classified correctly using the derived functions is printed. A variety of statistics and plots are available. For each case, discriminant scores and probabilities of group membership can be printed and stored on the active file.

Survival Analysis

The SURVIVAL procedure analyzes the time interval between two events. It produces life tables, graphs of survival functions, and comparisons of the survival distributions for various subgroups. The procedure allows censored observations —cases for which the second event has not occurred. Output from procedure SURVIVAL can be written onto an external file.

Analysis of Additive Scales

A variety of coefficients that evaluate the reliability of additive scales can be calculated using the RELIABILITY procedure. In addition, RELIABILITY calculates basic summary statistics including item means, standard deviations, inter-item covariance and correlation matrices, scale means, and item-to-scale correlations. The procedure can perform a repeated-measures analysis of variance, a two-way factorial analysis of variance with one observation per cell, Tukey's test for additivity, Hotelling's T^2 test for equality of means in repeated-measures designs, and Friedman's two-way analysis of variance on ranks.

Nonparametric Statistics

Many nonparametric tests can be computed using the NPAR TESTS procedure. The tests available include the sign test, the runs test, the Wilcoxon signed-ranks test, McNemar's test, the Kruskal-Wallis one-way analysis of variance, and the Kolmogorov-Smirnov test. Quantile values for the variables are also available.

Univariate and Multivariate Comparisons of Means

The T-TEST procedure calculates a test for the equality of two means for independent or paired samples. The ONEWAY procedure can be used to test the hypothesis of equality of several population means when cases are classified by the values of a single factor. A one-way analysis of variance and a variety of multiple comparison procedures are computed.

The ANOVA procedure tests hypotheses about population means when cases are crossclassified on several factors. Different methods for assessing main effects and interactions are available. A multiple classification analysis (MCA) table can also be printed.

The MANOVA procedure is a generalized multivariate analysis of variance and covariance program that will perform univariate and multivariate linear estimation and tests of hypotheses for any crossed and/or nested design with or without covariates. You have complete control over the model specification. Special features include a variety of graphical displays and the ability to collapse and specify multiple error terms, partition degrees of freedom, and specify contrasts and orthogonal polynomials.

Tests of significance for a multivariate analysis of variance model include hypotheses and error matrices, four multivariate test criteria, dimension reduction analysis, univariate F tests, and step-down analysis. In addition, principal components analysis and discriminant analysis can be requested.

MANOVA enables you to analyze a large class of repeated measures designs. The observation can be either single-valued or vector-valued. Covariates can also appear in the model.

Log-Linear Models

The LOGLINEAR procedure is used for modeling multi-way contingency tables. Hierarchical and nonhierarchical models, logit models, quasi-independence models, and models with structural zeros can be estimated. You can choose from available contrasts or specify your own. The data can be entered as tables or counts, or you can build the table from variables in your SPSS-X file. Output includes parameter estimates, their standard errors, the covariance matrix of the estimates, and the likelihood-ratio chi-square statistic. LOGLINEAR also prints observed and expected counts, residuals, standardized residuals, and adjusted residuals. Normal probability plots of the adjusted residuals, as well as plots against the observed and expected cell counts, are available.

The HILOGLINEAR procedure fits hierarchical log-linear models, provides parameter estimates for saturated models, and performs automatic backward elimination of terms. Models are conveniently specified by generating classes. Since an iterative proportional-fitting algorithm is used, HILOGLINEAR is more efficient for hierarchical models than the LOGLINEAR procedure.

Probit

The PROBIT procedure can be used to estimate the effects of one or more independent variables on a dichotomous dependent variable, such as dead or alive, employed or unemployed, product purchased or not. Both probit and logit transformations of the response variable are available. PROBIT calculates parameter estimates and their covariance matrix, fiducial limits for the predictor variable, and relative median potencies. Goodness-of-fit tests of the parallelism model and homogeneity of the residuals are also calculated.

Cluster Analysis

The CLUSTER procedure performs a hierarchical cluster analysis for a small to moderate number of cases or variables. A variety of distance and similarity measures are available. Several different methods for linking cases to form clusters and clusters to form larger clusters can be used. CLUSTER prints an icicle plot detailing each step of cluster formation. Additional statistics and display options are available. For each case, cluster membership at different cluster levels can be saved on the active file.

The QUICK CLUSTER procedure can be used to cluster efficiently a large number of cases into a fixed number of groups. Initial cluster centers can be supplied by the user or estimated from the data. Cluster centers, distances between them, and values of the variables for the resulting clusters can be printed. Cluster membership and distances between a case and its cluster center can be saved for further analysis.

Multidimensional Scaling

The ALSCAL procedure performs either metric or nonmetric multidimensional scaling or unfolding of objects and/or attributes. ALSCAL reads one or more symmetric, asymmetric, or rectangular matrices of proximities between objects and/or attributes. These values can be used to calculate a coordinate configuration such that similar objects are placed close together and dissimilar objects are placed far apart. You can supply initial values for the configurations and constrain sets of coordinates or weights to fixed values for external unfolding analyses.

With the PROXIMITIES procedure you can compute a variety of distance, dissimilarity, and similarity measures for either continuous, frequency count, or binary data, between cases or variables. Data values can be standardized prior to computation of the measures. The coefficients can be written to a file or saved as the active file for input to other procedures such as ALSCAL or CLUSTER.

Analysis of Time Series Data

The BOX-JENKINS procedure is used to fit and forecast time series data by means of a general class of statistical models. The procedure is designed to provide for easy and flexible model identification, estimation, and forecasting. Several models can be examined in a single invocation of the procedure. Parameter estimates, forecasts, and plots of the autocorrelation function, partial autocorrelation function, and forecasts at different leads can be included in the output.

SPSS-X Trends, an optional procedure in the SPSS-X system, includes a wide variety of procedures for analyzing time series data: curve fitting, exponential smoothing, weighted and two-stage least-squares regression, spectral, and state-of-the-art ARIMA modeling. It also contains a number of supplementary utilities to facilitate the handling and analysis of time series data.

Syntax

AGGREGATE

```
AGGREGATE OUTFILE={file} [/MISSING=COLUMNWISE] [/DOCUMENT]
               {*   }

 [/PRESORTED] /BREAK=varlist[({A})])][varlist...]
                            {D}

  /aggvar['label']aggvar['label']...=function(arguments)[/aggvar ...]
```

The following functions are available:

SUM	Sum	MEAN	Mean
SD	Standard deviation	MAX	Maximum
MIN	Minimum	PGT	% of cases gt value
PLT	% of cases lt value	PIN	% of cases between values
POUT	% of cases not in range	FGT	Fraction gt value
FLT	Fraction lt value	FIN	Fraction between values
FOUT	Fraction not in range	N	Weighted n
NU	Unweighted n	NMISS	Weighted n of missing
NUMISS	Unweighted n of missing	FIRST	First nonmissing
LAST	Last nonmissing		

Contents

18.1   OVERVIEW

18.2   OPERATION

18.3   OUTFILE Subcommand

18.4   BREAK Subcommand

18.5   PRESORTED Subcommand

18.6   DOCUMENT Subcommand

18.7   Creating AGGREGATE Variables

18.8   Labels and Formats

18.9   AGGREGATE Functions

18.10   Function Arguments

18.11   MISSING Subcommand

18.12   Including Missing Values

18.13   Comparing Missing-Value Treatments

18

Chapter 18   AGGREGATE

Procedure AGGREGATE computes summary measures such as sum and mean across groups of cases and produces an SPSS-X system file containing one case for each group. The variables on this *aggregated file* are the summary measures. For example, consider a file of employees in which each employee is assigned to a specific department. You can aggregate the employee file to create a department file containing items such as total wages within the department, number of employees within the department, and percentage of female employees within the department. In the new file, each case is a department with aggregated information on employees.

AGGREGATE often is used in conjunction with the MATCH FILES facility (Chapter 16) to perform many of the operations available in relational or hierarchical data-base systems. For example, you could add state information to a file of counties so that each case contains median family income for both the county and for the state. See the annotated example in Chapter 16 for an example using AGGREGATE with MATCH FILES.

18.1
OVERVIEW

To use the AGGREGATE procedure, you must specify three sets of information: the aggregated file, the variable(s) that define the aggregate groups, and the functions that create the new aggregate variables.

The Aggregated File. AGGREGATE produces a system file or a new active file with variable names, optional variable labels, and printing and writing formats. Once this file is created, you can analyze it with any of the procedures in SPSS-X, perform transformations on it, or combine it with any other file using the MATCH FILES facility. In other words, you can use the aggregated file as you would any system file. For example, if you need nested composite functions that are not provided by procedure REPORT, use AGGREGATE to perform the grouping function of the BREAK subcommand in REPORT, use the transformation language to calculate the variables, and then use the PRINT command (Chapter 10) or the REPORT procedure (Chapter 47) to write your own formatted report.

Break Groups. AGGREGATE summarizes groups of cases. A *break group* is a set of adjacent cases on the file that have the same values for a variable or set of variables. For example, in a file of philanthropic organizations, each case is an organization and includes variables for location, source of funding, and primary purpose, among other attributes. Each of these variables can be used individually or jointly to group the organizations. If you were to aggregate by location, all the New York organizations would constitute one group, all the Chicago organizations another, and so on. If you were to aggregate by location and primary purpose, all the New York organizations providing funding to medical research would be in one group, all the New York organizations providing funding to day-care centers would be in another, all the Chicago organizations providing funding to community action groups would be in another, and so forth. Each set of organizations is a break group.

Each break group defines a case on the new aggregated file. The concept of a break group is integral to the correct operation of AGGREGATE. AGGREGATE processes the file sequentially and a change or "break" in values on any one of the grouping variables signals the end of one break group and the beginning of the next. If your cases are not grouped together according to the grouping variables, you do not have to use SORT CASES prior to running AGGREGATE as it can do its own sorting (see Section 18.4). For a further discussion of the concept of breaks, see Chapter 47 on the REPORT procedure which also depends upon a grouped file and the concept of breaks.

AGGREGATE Functions. An aggregate function summarizes the values of one variable across the cases in a break group. Functions include sum, mean, standard deviation, percentages, and fractions.

Missing Values. AGGREGATE computes statistics across cases. If a case has a missing value for a particular source variable, it is not used to compute the statistic. If all the cases in a group have missing values for a particular source variable (or all but one for some functions such as the standard deviation), the target variable is missing. Two additional options are available. To force the target variable to be missing if any case in the group is missing, use the MISSING subcommand (see Section 18.11). To include missing values in functions, use a special form of the function keyword (see Section 18.12).

18.2
OPERATION

The AGGREGATE procedure is operated via subcommands. The OUTFILE and BREAK subcommands are required. The PRESORTED subcommand is required only if the unaggregated file is sorted in the desired order and you do not specify a new sort order on the BREAK subcommand. The MISSING subcommand is optional.

The OUTFILE subcommand specifies a file for the aggregated output file or an asterisk to specify the active file (see Section 18.3). The BREAK subcommand names the variable or variables that define the aggregate groups (see Section 18.4). The PRESORTED subcommand is used to indicate that the file was sorted prior to running AGGREGATE (see Section 18.5). The MISSING subcommand sets the target aggregate variable to system-missing if any case in the group is missing (see Section 18.11).

Following these subcommands, name the variables being created, their source variables, and the functions being applied to the source variables (see Section 18.7). Function keywords such as SUM or MEAN are specified as if they were subcommands. All subcommands are terminated with a slash.

18.3
OUTFILE Subcommand

The OUTFILE subcommand is required and must be first. It specifies the output aggregated file. There are two possible specifications: the filename or an asterisk. If you want to create and save a system file, specify that file's name on the OUTFILE subcommand. Assume that you are creating an aggregated file from the Hubbard employee file. The sequence of commands is:

```
GET FILE=HUBEMPL
AGGREGATE OUTFILE=AGGEMP
    /BREAK=DEPT82
    /AVGSAL=MEAN(SALARY82)
```

In this example, the new aggregated system file is written to the file defined by AGGEMP, and the active file remains unchanged. To replace the active file with the aggregated file, specify an asterisk in place of the filename on the OUTFILE subcommand, as in:

```
GET FILE=HUBEMPL
AGGREGATE OUTFILE=*
    /BREAK=DEPT82
    /AVGSAL=MEAN(SALARY82)
```

When you specify the asterisk rather than a filename, the file is not permanently saved unless you use the SAVE command or the XSAVE command followed by a procedure or EXECUTE (see Chapter 6).

18.4
BREAK Subcommand

The BREAK subcommand follows the OUTFILE subcommand and names the grouping variables, and optionally specifies the sorting order of the cases in the resulting file. To name variable DEPT82 as the grouping variable, specify

```
GET FILE=HUBEMPL
AGGREGATE OUTFILE=AGGEMP
    /BREAK=DEPT82
    /AVGSAL=MEAN(SALARY82)
```

The variable list can be as long as you want. You can use the keyword TO to reference a set of consecutive variables on the file. Each unique combination of values on the break variables defines a group.

You do not have to use SORT CASES prior to running AGGREGATE as AGGREGATE does its own sorting. By specifying an (A) or (D) following each variable or list of variables on the BREAK subcommand, you can sort the file in ascending or descending order, respectively. The order of sorting determines the order of cases in the resulting file. For example, the commands

```
GET FILE=HUBEMPL
AGGREGATE OUTFILE=AGGEMP
    /BREAK=DEPT82(A)
    /AVGSAL=MEAN(SALARY82)
```

produce an aggregated file sorted in ascending order on DEPT82. You can sort the resulting file on more than one variable. For example

```
    /BREAK=DEPT82(A)  SALARY82(D)
```

sorts the resulting file in ascending order on DEPT82 and then in descending order on SALARY82. If you do not include a sorting specification the default order is ascending.

All break variables specified on the BREAK subcommand are saved on the aggregated file with their existing names and dictionary information. If your break variable is DEPT82, the aggregated file includes the value of DEPT82 for each group.

AGGREGATE ignores split-file processing (see Chapter 15). To achieve the same effect, name the variable or variables used to split the file as break variables before any other break variables. AGGREGATE produces one file, but the aggregated cases are in the same order as the split files.

ANNOTATED EXAMPLE FOR AGGREGATE

In the following example, the Hubbard Consultants Inc. personnel file is aggregated to produce one case for each combination of values of LOCATN82 and DEPT82. The mean and sum of employee salaries and raises in 1982, percent black, and percent white are calculated for each group. The variable RACE on this file has codes 1 and 5, where 1=black and 5=white. The SPSS-X commands are

```
GET FILE=HUBEMPL
        /KEEP=LOCATN82 DEPT82 SALARY82 RAISE82 RACE

AGGREGATE OUTFILE=*
    /BREAK=LOCATN82(A) DEPT82(D)
    /COUNT=N
    /AVGSAL AVGRAISE = MEAN(SALARY82 RAISE82)
    /SUMSAL SUMRAISE = SUM(SALARY82 RAISE82)
    /BLACKPCT 'PERCENTAGE BLACK' = PIN(RACE,1,1)
    /WHITEPCT 'PERCENTAGE WHITE' = PIN(RACE,5,5)

FILE LABEL AGGREGATED HUBBARD EMPLOYEE DATA
VARIABLE LABELS AVGSAL 'AVERAGE 1982 SALARY'/
                AVGRAISE 'AVERAGE 1982 RAISE'/
                SUMSAL  'TOTAL 1982 SALARY'/
                SUMRAISE 'TOTAL 1982 RAISE'

PRINT FORMATS AVGSAL (DOLLAR10.2)/ AVGRAISE (DOLLAR9.2)/
              SUMSAL (DOLLAR13.2)/ SUMRAISE (DOLLAR11.2)

DO IF $CASENUM EQ 1
PRINT /'LOC DEP NUM'1 'AVGSAL'16 'AVGRAISE'25 'SUMSAL'38 'SUMRAISE'50
      '%B'62 '%W'68
END IF
PRINT /LOCATN82 DEPT82 COUNT (3(F3,1X)) AVGSAL TO WHITEPCT
EXECUTE
```

- The GET command reads the system file with the Hubbard employee data keeping only variables needed for this job (see Chapter 6).
- The OUTFILE subcommand on the AGGREGATE command uses the asterisk to indicate that the new file will replace the active file (see Section 18.3).
- The BREAK subcommand names the variables indicating the employee's location and department, the combination of which form the groups for aggregation (see Section 18.4). The result file will be sorted in ascending order on LOCATN82 and descending order on DEPT82.
- The first aggregate function creates a new variable COUNT which is equal to the function N, the number of cases in each group (see Section 18.9).
- The next two aggregate functions create two new variables each: AVGSAL, the group mean for salary; AVGRAISE, the group mean for raise; SUMSAL, the group total for salary; and SUMRAISE, the group total for raise.
- The final two functions create two new variables using the PIN function to create BLACKPCT or the percentage black in each group and WHITEPCT or the percentage white. Since black is coded 1 for variable RACE, the percentage between 1 and 1 inclusive is the percentage black. Labels are assigned to these new variables within procedure AGGREGATE.

The output produced by this job includes the following:

AGGREGATE Messages. AGGREGATE prints the messages shown in Figure A. The aggregated file contains nine variables: LOCATN82, DEPT82, COUNT, AVGSAL, AVGRAISE, SUMSAL, SUMRAISE, BLACKPCT, and WHITEPCT. The message also tells you that the aggregated file replaced the active file.

PRINT Output. Figure B shows the PRINT output. Note that SPSS-X prints periods for the system-missing values for each of the four dollar variables that are missing for all cases in the group represented by 0 for location and 0 for department. Also note that DEPT82 is sorted in descending order (the column labeled "DEP") within LOCATN82 (the column labeled "LOC") which is sorted in ascending order.

A AGGREGATE messages

```
'AGGREGATE' PROBLEM REQUIRES      776 BYTES OF MEMORY.
PLUS        140 BYTES PER CASE IN THE AGGREGATED FILE.

A NEW (AGGREGATED) ACTIVE FILE HAS REPLACED THE EXISTING ACTIVE FILE.
IT CONTAINS   9 VARIABLES AND        6 CASES.
```

B PRINT output of the aggregated file

```
LOC DEP NUM    AVGSAL    AVGRAISE      SUMSAL         SUMRAISE      %B     %W
 0   0 130       .           .            .              .        30.0   63.1
 1   3  60 $17,918.22 $3,218.22 $1,075,093.00  $177,002.00       33.3   65.0
 1   2  17 $18,339.29 $1,450.19   $311,768.00   $23,203.00       11.8   82.4
 1   1  34 $15,257.47 $1,704.24   $518,754.00   $57,944.00       55.9   35.3
 5   4  29 $17,413.21 $2,573.39   $504,983.00   $72,055.00       24.1   65.5
 5   2   5 $15,565.40   $464.20    $77,827.00    $2,321.00        .0  100.0
```

18.5
PRESORTED Subcommand

Use the PRESORTED subcommand if the unaggregated file is already sorted into the desired order and you do not specify a new sort order on the BREAK subcommand. If PRESORTED is used it must come between the OUTFILE subcommand and the BREAK subcommand and you should not specify a new sort order on the BREAK subcommand (see Section 18.4). For example, the commands

```
GET FILE=HUBEMPL
AGGREGATE OUTFILE=AGGEMP
  /PRESORTED
  /BREAK=DEPT82
  /AVGSAL=MEAN(SALARY82)
```

tell SPSS-X that the HUBEMPL system file is already sorted by DEPT82 (the break variable). If the PRESORTED subcommand is used and sort qualifiers are specified on the BREAK subcommand, the aggregated file will be sorted in the order of the original file. A warning will be issued stating that the sort direction(s) specified on the BREAK subcommand will be ignored. If you do not use the PRESORTED subcommand and do not specify a new sort order on the BREAK subcommand, the resulting file will be sorted in ascending order on the break variable(s).

18.6
DOCUMENT Subcommand

Use the DOCUMENT subcommand to save document text on the newly created aggregated file. Documents will, by default, be dropped from the new aggregated file, whether the OUTFILE is the active file or a disk file. The DOCUMENT subcommand will place the existing documents on the aggregated file.

The DOCUMENT subcommand must appear after the OUTFILE subcommand and before the BREAK subcommand. It may appear before or after the optional PRESORTED subcommand.

18.7
Creating AGGREGATE Variables

Each variable on the aggregated file is created by applying an aggregate function to a variable on the active file. The simplest form of subcommand used to create aggregated variables is the *target variable list* followed by an equals sign, the function keyword, and a parenthetical list of *source variables*. For example,

```
GET FILE=HUBEMPL
AGGREGATE OUTFILE=AGGEMP
  /BREAK=DEPT82
  /AVGSAL=MEAN(SALARY82)
```

creates new variable AVGSAL as the mean of variable SALARY82 for each department. The target and source variable lists must be of equal length, as in:

```
GET FILE=HUBEMPL
AGGREGATE OUTFILE=AGGEMP
  /BREAK=DEPT82
  /AVGSAL AVGRAISE=MEAN(SALARY82 RAISE82)
```

You can use the keyword TO in both the target variable list and the source variable list. For example, to create averages for four salary years, specify:

```
GET FILE=HUBEMPL
AGGREGATE OUTFILE=AGGEMP
  /BREAK=DEPT82
  /AVGSAL79 TO AVGSAL82=MEAN(SALARY79 TO SALARY82)
```

Any number of function subcommands can be used to create variables. Separate them with slashes, as in:

```
GET FILE=HUBEMPL
AGGREGATE OUTFILE=AGGEMP
  /BREAK=DEPT82
  /AVGSAL AVGRAISE = MEAN(SALARY82 RAISE82)
  /SUMSAL SUMRAISE = SUM(SALARY82 RAISE82)
```

18.8
Labels and Formats

With the exception of functions MAX, MIN, FIRST, and LAST, which copy complete dictionary information from the source variable, new variables are created by procedure AGGREGATE with no labels and with default dictionary print and write formats described in Section 18.9. To label a new variable, place the label in apostrophes immediately following its name, as in:

```
GET FILE=HUBEMPL
AGGREGATE OUTFILE=AGGEMP
    /BREAK=DEPT82
    /AVGSAL 'AVERAGE SALARY' AVGRAISE 'AVERAGE RAISE' =
            MEAN(SALARY2 RAISE82)/
```

The label applies only to the immediately preceding variable.

If you are specifying the aggregated file as the new active file, you can also use the VARIABLE LABELS command to add labels to your file, as in:

```
GET FILE=HUBEMPL
AGGREGATE OUTFILE=*
    /BREAK=DEPT82
    /AVGSAL AVGRAISE = MEAN(SALARY82 RAISE82)
VARIABLE LABELS AVGSAL 'AVERAGE SALARY'
                AVGRAISE 'AVERAGE RAISE'
```

Use the PRINT FORMATS, WRITE FORMATS, or FORMATS commands to change dictionary formats for an active file created from AGGREGATE, as in:

```
GET FILE=HUBEMPL
AGGREGATE OUTFILE=*
    /BREAK=DEPT82
    /AVGSAL AVGRAISE = MEAN(SALARY82 RAISE82)
VARIABLE LABELS AVGSAL 'AVERAGE SALARY'/
                AVGRAISE 'AVERAGE RAISE'
PRINT FORMATS AVGSAL (DOLLAR10.2)/AVGRAISE (DOLLAR9.2)
```

The printing formats for AVGSAL and AVGRAISE are changed to DOLLAR formats of the appropriate width.

18.9
AGGREGATE Functions

The examples above use functions MEAN and SUM to demonstrate the construction of function subcommands. The following functions are available:

SUM(varlist)	*Sum across cases.* Dictionary formats are F8.2.
MEAN(varlist)	*Mean across cases.* Dictionary formats are F8.2.
SD(varlist)	*Standard deviation across cases.* Dictionary formats are F8.2.
MAX(varlist)	*Maximum value across cases.* Complete dictionary information is copied from the source variables to the target variables.
MIN(varlist)	*Minimum value across cases.* Complete dictionary information is copied from the source variables to the target variables.
PGT(varlist,value)	*Percentage of cases greater than value.* Dictionary formats are F5.1.
PLT(varlist,value)	*Percentage of cases less than value.* Dictionary formats are F5.1.
PIN(varlist,value1,value2)	*Percentage of cases between value1 and value2 inclusive.* Dictionary formats are F5.1.
POUT(varlist,value1,value2)	*Percentage of cases not between value1 and value2 exclusive.* Dictionary formats are F5.1.
FGT(varlist,value)	*Fraction of cases greater than value.* Dictionary formats are F5.3.
FLT(varlist,value)	*Fraction of cases less than value.* Dictionary formats are F5.3.
FIN(varlist,value1,value2)	*Fraction of cases between value1 and value2 inclusive.* Dictionary formats are F5.3.
FOUT(varlist,value1,value2)	*Fraction of cases not between value1 and value2 exclusive.* Dictionary formats are F5.3.
N(varlist)	*Weighted number of cases in break group.* Dictionary formats are F7.0 for unweighted files, F8.2 for weighted files.

NU(varlist)	*Unweighted number of cases in break group.* Dictionary formats are F7.0.
NMISS(varlist)	*Weighted number of missing cases.* Dictionary formats are F7.0 for unweighted files, F8.2 for weighted files.
NUMISS(varlist)	*Unweighted number of missing cases.* Dictionary formats are F7.0.
FIRST(varlist)	*First nonmissing observed value in break group.* Complete dictionary information is copied from the source variables to the target variables.
LAST(varlist)	*Last nonmissing observed value in break group.* Complete dictionary information is copied from the source variables to the target variables.

18.10
Function Arguments

Functions PGT, PLT, PIN, POUT, FGT, FLT, FIN, and FOUT have special numeric arguments. PGT, PLT, FGT, and FLT have one numeric argument; PIN, POUT, FIN, and FOUT have two numeric arguments. For example, the specification

```
LOVAC,LOSICK = PLT (VACDAY SICKDAY,10)
```

assigns the percentage of cases with values less than 10 for VACDAY to LOVAC, and SICKDAY to LOSICK. The specification

```
COLLEGE = FIN(EDUC,13,16)
```

assigns the fraction of cases having 13 to 16 years of education to COLLEGE. The first argument should be lower than the second argument for functions PIN, POUT, FIN, and FOUT. If the first argument is higher, AGGREGATE automatically reverses them and prints a warning message.

The percentage functions return values between 0 and 100 inclusive; the fraction functions return values between 0 and 1 inclusive.

Only numeric variables can be used with SUM, MEAN, and SD. Both short and long string variables can be used with all other functions. To obtain the percentage of females when SEX is coded M and F, specify either

```
PCTFEM = PLT(SEX,'M')
```

or

```
PCTFEM = PIN(SEX,'F','F')
```

Blanks and commas can be used interchangeably to delimit arguments to functions.

The N and NU functions do not require arguments. Without arguments, they return the number of weighted and unweighted cases in a break group. If you supply a variable list, they return the weighted and unweighted number of valid cases for the variables specified.

18.11
MISSING Subcommand

By default, if the source variable used in a function has a missing value for a case, the case is not included in the computation of the function. If all cases in a break group have missing values for a variable, the function returns the system-missing value. You can override this rule by including missing values in calculations (Section 18.12) or by forcing the target variable to missing if any case in a break group has a missing value for the source variable (Section 18.11).

Considerations for missing values do not apply to break variables. Even if a break variable has a system-missing value, cases in that group are processed and the break variable is saved on the file with the system-missing value. Use SELECT IF if you want to eliminate cases with missing values on the break variables.

To force target variables to system-missing if any of the cases in the group are missing on the source variable, use the MISSING subcommand. The MISSING subcommand has one keyword specification, COLUMNWISE.

The MISSING subcommand, when used, follows the OUTFILE subcommand, as in:

```
GET FILE=HUBEMPL
AGGREGATE OUTFILE=AGGEMP
    /MISSING=COLUMNWISE
    /BREAK=DEPT82
    /AVGSAL 'AVERAGE SALARY' AVGRAISE 'AVERAGE RAISE'
    = MEAN(SALARY82 RAISE82)
```

The MISSING subcommand has no effect on the N, NU, NMISS, or NUMISS functions. For example, N(AGE) returns the same result for the default and for columnwise deletion.

18.12
Including Missing Values

To force a function to ignore user-missing values, follow the function name with a period, as in:

```
LOVAC = PLT.(VACDAY,10)
```

This function sets new variable LOVAC to the percentages of cases within the group with values less than 10 for VACDAY even if some of the values are defined as missing.

To obtain the first value of AGE in a break group whether it is missing or not, specify:

```
FIRSTAGE = FIRST.(AGE)
```

If the first case in a break group has a missing value on AGE, FIRSTAGE is set to that value and, since variables created with FIRST have the same dictionary information as their source variables, that value is still treated as missing on the aggregated file.

The period is ignored when used with N, NU, NMISS, and NUMISS if these functions have no argument. On the other hand, NMISS.(AGE) gives the number of cases on which AGE has the system-missing value. The rationale for the special missing treatment for N, NU, NMISS, and NUMISS is illustrated by the following identities:

$$N = N. = N(AGE)+NMISS(AGE) = N.(AGE)+NMISS.(AGE)$$

$$NU = NU. = NU(AGE)+NUMISS(AGE) = NU.(AGE)+NUMISS.(AGE)$$

That is, the function N (the same as N. with no argument) is equal to the sum of cases with valid and with missing values for AGE, which is also equal to the sum of cases with either valid or user-missing values and with system-missing values for AGE. The same identities hold for the NU, NMISS, and NUMISS functions.

18.13
Comparing Missing-Value Treatments

Table 18.13 demonstrates the effects of the MISSING subcommand and of the period missing-value convention. Each entry in the table is the number of cases used to compute the specified function for variable EDUC, which has 10 nonmissing cases, 5 user-missing cases, and 2 system-missing cases for the group. Note that columnwise treatment produces the same results as the default for every function except the MEAN function.

Table 18.13   Alternative missing-value treatments

Function	Default	Columnwise
N	17	17
N.	17	17
N(EDUC)	10	10
N.(EDUC)	15	15
MEAN(EDUC)	10	0
MEAN.(EDUC)	15	0
NMISS(EDUC)	7	7
NMISS.(EDUC)	2	2

Syntax

ALSCAL

```
ALSCAL  VARIABLES=varlist  [/FILE=file]
      [CONFIG  [({INITIAL})])]
               {FIXED  }
      [ROWCONF [({INITIAL})])]
               {FIXED  }
      [COLCONF [({INITIAL})])]
               {FIXED  }
      [SUBJWGHT[({INITIAL})])]
               {FIXED  }
      [STIMWGHT[({INITIAL})])]
               {FIXED  }
  [/INPUT=ROWS ({ALL})])]
               { n }
  [/SHAPE={SYMMETRIC**}]
          {ASYMMETRIC }
          {RECTANGULAR}
  [/LEVEL={ORDINAL**[(([UNTIE] [SIMILAR])])]}]
          {INTERVAL[(({1})]                   }
          {            {d}                     }
          {RATIO[(({1})]                       }
          {         {d}                        }
          {NOMINAL                             }
  [/CONDITION={MATRIX       }]
              {ROW          }
              {UNCONDITIONAL}
  [/MODEL  ={EUCLID**}]
      or    {INDSCAL }
    METHOD  {ASCAL   }
            {AINDS   }
            {GEMSCAL }
  [/CRITERIA=[NEGATIVE] [CUTOFF(({0**})])] [CONVERGE({.001})])]
                               {c }                  {c  }
            [ITER({30})])] [STRESSMIN({.005})])] [NOULB]
                  {ni}                 { s }
            [DIMENS({  2** })])] [DIRECTIONS(r)]
                    {min[,max]}
            [CONSTRAIN]             [TIESTORE(n)]]
  [/PRINT=[DATA] [HEADER] [INTERMED]]
  [/PLOT=[DEFAULT] [ALL]]
  [/OUTFILE=file]
  [/MATRIX=IN({file})])]
             {*   }
```

** Default if the subcommand is omitted.

Contents

19.1   OVERVIEW

19.2   OPERATION

19.3   VARIABLES Subcommand

19.4   INPUT Subcommand

19.5   SHAPE Subcommand

19.6   LEVEL Subcommand

19.7   CONDITION Subcommand

19.8   FILE Subcommand

19.9   MODEL Subcommand

19.10   CRITERIA Subcommand

19.11   Specification of Analyses

19.12   Output

19.13   PRINT Subcommand

19.14   PLOT Subcommand

19.15   OUTFILE Subcommand

19.16   MATRIX Subcommand

19.17   IN Keyword

19.18 LIMITATIONS

ALSCAL was originally designed and programmed by Forrest W. Young, Yoshio Takane, and Rostyslaw J. Lewyckyj of the Psychometric Laboratory, University of North Carolina.

19

Chapter 19   ALSCAL

ALSCAL is a multidimensional scaling and unfolding procedure with options for studying individual differences. ALSCAL reads one or more proximity matrices from an active SPSS-X file. (Procedures PROXIMITIES and CLUSTER can produce these matrices; see Chapters 43 and 23.) For the stimuli represented in the matrix or matrices, ALSCAL uses one of five different models to derive stimulus coordinates and/or weights in a multidimensional space. You can specify many forms of multidimensional scaling and unfolding models with appropriate subcommand options. You can also have ALSCAL display a variety of plots, including those for stimulus coordinates, weights, and transformations.

ALSCAL has applications in disciplines ranging from marketing research, advertising, economics, and product development to behavioral sciences such as psychology, sociology, and political science. For example, you can use ALSCAL to

• Identify attributes that influence consumer preferences for a product.
• Study relations among the items in a questionnaire or test.
• Find sources of individual differences in perceptions of persons or events.

The following discussion assumes some knowledge of the concepts of multidimensional scaling. If you are unfamiliar with these concepts, you should read *Introduction to Multidimensional Scaling* (Schiffman, Reynolds, & Young, 1981). It provides a number of useful examples of how to use scaling, and it includes several chapters that relate ALSCAL to other scaling programs, such as INDSCAL, POLYCON, and MINISSA. A more concise introduction is *Multidimensional Scaling* (Kruskal & Wish, 1978), which presents basic concepts, methods of interpretation, and the relation of scaling to other multivariate techniques. Another useful reference is *Multidimensional Scaling* (Davison, 1983).

19.1
OVERVIEW

ALSCAL uses the alternating least-squares approach proposed by Takane, Young and deLeeuw (1977) and later improved by Young, Takane and Lewyckyj (1978). ALSCAL is an extremely flexible procedure, combining metric and nonmetric, classical, replicated, and weighted multidimensional scaling and unfolding (MDS and MDU) into one program. Currently, it is the only scaling program that incorporates individual differences MDS models with MDU models, non-individual differences MDS models, and external MDS and MDU models. ALSCAL is appropriate for all types of two- or three-way data (a single matrix, for example, or a matrix for each of several subjects). The data may be conditional or unconditional, replicated or unreplicated, and with or without missing values. For ordinal data, tied observations may be left tied or may be untied. ALSCAL analyses can include as many as 32,767 values per data partition in the input matrices, though such large problems may add significantly to computer costs.

Proximity Data. ALSCAL can analyze data matrices that are rectangular or square, symmetric or asymmetric (see Sections 19.4 and 19.5). The data may be at the ordinal, interval, ratio, or nominal level of measurement (see Section 19.6).

Distance Matrices. ALSCAL can analyze distance matrices written by procedures CLUSTER and PROXIMITIES (see Section 19.16).

Initial Configuration and/or Weights. ALSCAL can read a file of coordinates and/or weights to provide initial or fixed values for the scaling process (see Section 19.8).

Models. ALSCAL can perform analyses according to many types of models (see Sections 19.9 and 19.11) with constraints you can specify on the models and on the convergence criteria for the scaling solutions (see Section 19.10).

Output. You can obtain standard and optional printed output (see Section 19.12 and 19.13), plots of stimulus coordinates and weight (see Section 19.14), and system files of coordinate and weight matrices (see Section 19.15).

Procedure ALSCAL uses five types of scaling and unfolding models:

• Euclidean distance model (EUCLID).
• Individual differences (weighted) Euclidean distance model (INDSCAL).
• Asymmetric Euclidean distance model (ASCAL).
• Asymmetric individual differences Euclidean distance model (AINDS).
• Generalized Euclidean metric individual differences model (GEMSCAL).

Subcommand specifications let you perform scaling procedures equivalent to the following types of analyses (among others):

• Torgerson's (1952) classical multidimensional scaling model.
• Shepard's (1962) and Kruskal's (1964) nonmetric multidimensional scaling.
• Coombs' (1964) and Young's (1972) multidimensional unfolding.
• McGee's (1968) and Carroll and Chang's (1970) individual differences multidimensional scaling.
• Carroll's (1972) external multidimensional scaling and unfolding models.
• Carroll and Chang's (1972) individual differences in orientation scaling model.
• Harshman's (1972) parallel-factor model.
• Tucker's (1972) three-mode scaling.
• Young's (1975a) conditional rank-order multidimensional scaling.
• Young's (1975b) asymmetric multidimensional scaling.
• Asymmetric individual differences Euclidean distance model, combining Young's (1975a) asymmetric Euclidean model with Carroll and Chang's (1970) individual differences model.
• Young's (1978, 1979a, 1979b) principle directions scaling model.
• Young, Easterling, and Forsyth's (1983) generalized Euclidean metric individual differences scaling.

19.2
OPERATION

The minimum ALSCAL specification is the ALSCAL command followed by the VARIABLES subcommand, which defines the variables you are scaling, as in

```
ALSCAL VARIABLES = V1 TO V10
```

All other subcommands are optional. By default, ALSCAL produces a two-dimensional nonmetric Euclidean multidimensional scaling solution and assumes you are entering one or more square symmetric matrices with elements at the ordinal level of measurement. Printed output automatically includes: the number of missing values, if any, for each matrix; the improvement in Young's S-STRESS for successive iterations; two measures of fit for each input matrix (Kruskal's STRESS and the squared correlation, RSQ); the derived configuration; and weights when appropriate for specific models.

Various subcommands are available for optional specifications of input, models, and output. You can arrange subcommands in any order following the ALSCAL command. Each subcommand must begin with the subcommand keyword and may be followed by an optional equals sign and specifications. Multiple subcommands must be separated by slashes.

19.3
VARIABLES Subcommand

The VARIABLES subcommand is required. It identifies the variables for the columns of the proximity matrix or matrices that ALSCAL reads from the active file. You can use a DATA LIST command to enter proximity matrices directly, or you can use the PROXIMITIES procedure to compute them. All the matrix variables must be numeric, and each matrix must have at least four rows and four columns. You can use the SHAPE subcommand to specify the form (see Section 19.5).

19.4
INPUT Subcommand

The INPUT subcommand is used when ALSCAL reads inline data and specifies how ALSCAL reads a rectangular matrix (one in which rows refer to a different set of items than columns). You provide rectangular data for multidimensional unfolding. Currently, ALSCAL can read matrices only row by row, with each case in the active file representing a single row in the data matrix. (The VARIABLES subcommand specifies the columns.) If you do not use the INPUT subcommand to read rectangular data, ALSCAL assumes that each case in your file represents one row of a single input matrix.

If you have split-file data (see Chapter 15), the number of rows in the input matrix is the number of cases in each split-file group. All split-file groups must have the same number of rows. At least four rows are required.

If your file contains multiple rectangular input matrices, you must specify the number of rows in each, as in

```
ALSCAL VARIABLES = varlist
 /INPUT = ROWS(8)
 /SHAPE=RECTANGULAR
 /CONDITION=ROW
 /LEVEL=ORDINAL
```

which indicates that there are eight rows per matrix, with each case representing one row. The number of rows per matrix must divide evenly into the total number of observations in the data set.

19.5
SHAPE Subcommand

The SHAPE subcommand specifies the form of the input data matrix or matrices you are scaling. The form may be symmetric, asymmetric, or rectangular.

SYMMETRIC   *Symmetric data matrix or matrices.* This is the default. A matrix is symmetric when the corresponding values in the upper and lower triangles are equal. For example, in a study of automobiles, the similarity of a Ford to a Plymouth might be considered the same as the similarity of a Plymouth to a Ford. ALSCAL only looks at the values below the diagonal, so values on and above the diagonal can be left missing.

ASYMMETRIC   *Asymmetric data matrix or matrices.* The corresponding values in the upper and lower triangles are not all equal. The diagonal is ignored.

RECTANGULAR   *Rectangular data matrix or matrices.* The rows and columns represent different sets of items.

ALSCAL calculates the number of input matrices by dividing the total number of observations in the data set by the number of observations in each matrix. All matrices must contain the same number of observations. This number depends on the SHAPE subcommand and the INPUT subcommand (if used). For example, if you specify SHAPE=SYMMETRIC or SHAPE=ASYMMETRIC, ALSCAL expects square matrix data, and it sets the number of observations in each matrix equal to the number of variables (stimuli being analyzed). If you specify SHAPE=RECTANGULAR, ALSCAL sets the number of column "stimuli" equal to the number of variables in the analysis. The number of row "stimuli" is set equal to the number of rows specified in the INPUT subcommand. If no INPUT subcommand is specified, ALSCAL uses the number of cases in the input file or, with split files, the number of cases in the first split-file group. (All groups must contain the same number of cases.)

19.6
LEVEL Subcommand

The LEVEL subcommand identifies the level of measurement for the values in the data matrix or matrices: ordinal, interval, ratio, or nominal. Optionally, you may specify the degree of a polynomial transformation for interval or ratio measurement. The degree follows LEVEL=INTERVAL or LEVEL=RATIO in parentheses, as in

```
ALSCAL VARIABLES = varlist
 /LEVEL=INTERVAL(2)
```

which specifies the degree as 2, indicating a polynomial transformation with linear and quadratic terms. You can specify a degree with any integer value from 1 to 4. The default value is 1, corresponding to a transformation that is linear. The degree specification may not be used if LEVEL=ORDINAL or LEVEL= NOMINAL.

ORDINAL[([UNTIE] [SIMILAR])]   *Ordinal level data.* This is the default. It treats the data as ordinal, using Kruskal's (1964) least-squares monotonic transformation. The analysis is non-metric. By default, ties in the data remain tied throughout the analysis and ALSCAL treats the data as dissimilarities. If you want to regard ordinal data as continuous, specify the UNTIE option, which allows ties to become untied. If you want ALSCAL to treat the data as similarities, specify the SIMI-LAR option. UNTIE and SIMILAR cannot be used with the other levels of measurement.

INTERVAL[(d)]   *Interval level data.* This specification produces a metric analysis of the data using classical regression techniques.

RATIO[(d)]   *Ratio level data.* Like INTERVAL, this specification produces a metric analysis.

NOMINAL   *Nominal level data.* ALSCAL treats the data as nominal by using Takane, Young, and deLeeuw's (1977) least-squares categorical transformation. You can use this specification for a nonmetric analysis of nominal data. This option can be used only in a few situations: that is, when there are few observed categories, there are many observations in each category, and the order of the categories is not known.

19.7
CONDITION Subcommand

Conditionality refers to ways in which the numbers in a data set are not comparable. For example, the subjects in a study may all use a 7-point rating scale, but the meaning of the rating-scale responses may differ from subject to subject. Different subjects may use the scale in different ways. You may correctly interpret a response of 3 from one subject as less than a 5 from that same subject, but you may not be justified in interpreting the 3 from the first subject as less than a 5 from another subject. In this case, the meaning of the numbers would be *conditional* on the subject.

The CONDITION subcommand lets you identify the conditionality of the data matrix or matrices you are scaling. In the previous example, you would use CONDITION=MATRIX when the data for different subjects are in different matrices.

MATRIX   *The meaning of the numbers is conditional on the subject.* This specification is the default.

ROW   *The meaning of the numbers is conditional on the row.* You can make meaningful comparisons only among numbers within rows of each matrix. This specification is appropriate only for asymmetric or rectangular data and may not be used when MODEL=ASCAL or MODEL=AINDS.

UNCONDITIONAL   *The meaning of the numbers is not conditional.* You can make meaningful comparisons among all values in the input matrix or matrices.

19.8
FILE Subcommand

To perform an analysis, ALSCAL requires proximity data (see Sections 19.3 through 19.7). With the FILE subcommand, ALSCAL can read a file containing additional data: an initial or fixed configuration for the coordinates of the stimuli and/or weights for the matrices being scaled. You can create this configuration/ weights file with an ALSCAL OUTFILE subcommand or with an SPSS-X input program. The FILE subcommand is *not* used to read matrix system files written by PROXIMITIES or CLUSTER. Use the MATRIX subcommand for those files (Section 19.16).

To use the FILE subcommand, you must specify a file handle. You can follow this with optional specifications for the matrices and the types of values in the matrices to be read.

The variables in the configuration/weights file that correspond to successive ALSCAL dimensions must have the names DIM1, DIM2 . . . DIMr, where r is the maximum number of ALSCAL dimensions. The file must also contain the short string variable TYPE_ to identify the types of values in all the rows. Specify stimulus coordinate values as CONFIG; row stimulus coordinates as ROWCONF; column stimulus coordinates as COLCONF; and subject and stimulus weights, respectively, as SUBJWGHT and STIMWGHT. ALSCAL accepts CONFIG and ROWCONF interchangeably. You can spell out CONFIG, ROWCONF, COL-CONF, SUBJWGHT, and STIMWGHT in full or use just the first three letters of each.

The sets of coordinates or weights in the file must appear in the order CON, ROW, COL, SUB, STI. ALSCAL skips unneeded types as long as they appear in the file in their proper order. Generalized weights (GEM) and flattened subject weights (FLA) may not be initialized or fixed and will always be skipped. (These can be output by ALSCAL but not input.)

In the example shown in Figure 19.8, ALSCAL reads variables labeled DIM1, DIM2, and TYPE_ from START. The ROWCONF and COLCONF specifications indicate that the file contains initial row and column stimulus configurations.

Figure 19.8   An example with an initial configuration

```
FILE HANDLE START / file specifications
DATA  LIST / DIM1 1-2 DIM2 4-5 TYPE_ 9-12(A)

SAVE OUTFILE = START

BEGIN DATA
-4   4    ROWCONF
-1   4    ROWCONF
 4   4    ROWCONF
-4   2    ROWCONF
-1   2    ROWCONF
 4   2    ROWCONF
-4  -4    ROWCONF
-1  -4    ROWCONF
 4  -4    ROWCONF
-4   4    COLCONF
 2  -4    COLCONF
 1   2    COLCONF
-2   0    COLCONF
-2  -3    COLCONF
END DATA

DATA  LIST / COL1 TO COL5 1-40
ALSCAL    VARIABLES = COL1 TO COL5
 /LEVEL = INTERVAL
 /SHAPE = RECTANGULAR
 /FILE = START
         ROWCONF(INITIAL)
         COLCONF(INITIAL)
 /INPUT = ROWS(9)
 /PLOT
 /PRINT = HEADER
 /CRITERIA = CONVERGE(0.00000001) ITER(100)

BEGIN DATA
 0.0     10.00000 5.38517 4.47214 7.28011
 3.00000 8.54400 2.82843 4.12311 7.07107
 8.00000 8.24621 3.60555 7.21110 9.21954
 2.00000 8.48528 5.00000 2.82843 5.38517
 3.60555 6.70820 2.00000 2.23607 5.09902
 8.24621 6.32456 3.00000 6.32456 7.81025
 8.00000 6.00000 7.81025 4.47214 2.23607
 8.54400 3.00000 6.32456 4.12311 1.41421
11.31371 2.00000 6.70820 7.21110 6.08276
END DATA
```

You can input initial values (option INITIAL) or fixed values (option FIXED) as in an external unfolding model. INITIAL is the default. The FIXED option lets you define an external or hypothesized structure for stimulus coordinates, subject weights, and/or stimulus weights. This option forces ALSCAL to use the defined structure without modification to calculate the best values for all unfixed portions of the structure. In the following example, ALSCAL reads stimulus coordinates as fixed values and stimulus weights as purely initial values.

```
ALSCAL VARIABLES = varlist
 /SHAPE = ASYMMETRIC
 /LEVEL = ORDINAL
 /MODEL = ASCAL
 /FILE  = FIRST
          CONFIG(FIXED)
          STIMWGHT(INITIAL)
```

In the case of split files, ALSCAL reads initial or fixed configurations for each split-file group. If there is only one initial configuration in the file, ALSCAL rereads these initial or fixed values for successive split-file groups.

If you do not include the input matrix specifications for the configuration/weights file, ALSCAL will read sequentially the TYPE_ values appropriate to the model you specify. For instance, if MODEL=ASCAL and SHAPE=ASYMMETRIC, ALSCAL will automatically check TYPE_ to find rows containing the value CON for stimulus coordinates and the value STI for stimulus weights (see Table 19.8). ALSCAL ignores user-missing values in all variables. The system-missing value is an error in the TYPE_ variable and is converted to zero in the other variables.

The following list summarizes and further explains the optional specifications on the FILE subcommand. Table 19.8 shows the default matrices ALSCAL reads if you use the FILE subcommand without optional specifications.

CONFIG[(type)] *Read stimulus configuration.* The configuration/weights file contains initial stimulus coordinates. Input of this sort is appropriate when SHAPE=SYMMETRIC or SHAPE=ASYMMETRIC or when the number of variables in a matrix equals the number of variables in the ALSCAL command. The value of TYPE_ must be either CON or ROW for all the stimulus coordinates of the configuration.

ROWCONF[(type)] *Read row stimulus configuration.* The configuration/weights file contains initial row stimulus coordinates. This specification is necessary if SHAPE=RECTANGULAR. The number of observations equals the number of rows you specify on the INPUT subcommand or, if you do not include INPUT, the number of cases in the proximity file. The command

```
ALSCAL VARIABLES = varlist
 /SHAPE = RECTANGULAR
 /INPUT = ROWS
 /CONDITION = ROW
 /FILE = OUTSET
          ROWCONF
```

specifies that OUTSET contains row stimulus configurations; that the proximity file is rectangular in shape; that each case in the proximity file represents a single row in the data matrix; and that only within-row values in the matrix may be meaningfully compared. The value of TYPE_ must be either ROW or CON for the set of coordinates for each row.

COLCONF[(type)] *Read column stimulus configuration.* The configuration/weights file contains initial column stimulus coordinates. This kind of file may be input only if SHAPE=RECTANGULAR and if the number of observations in the matrix equals the number of variables in the ALSCAL command. The value of TYPE_ must be COL for the set of coordinates for each column.

SUBJWGHT[(type)] *Read subject (matrix) weights.* The configuration/weights file contains subject weights. The number of observations in a subject-weights matrix must equal the number of matrices in the proximity file. Input of subject weights is permissible only if MODEL=INDSCAL, MODEL=AINDS, or MODEL=GEMSCAL. The value of TYPE_ for each set of weights must be SUB.

STIMWGHT[(type)] *Read stimulus weights.* The configuration/weights file contains stimulus weights. You may use this option only if the number of observations in the configuration/weights file equals the number of matrices in the proximity file. Matrix input of this kind is permissible only if MODEL=AINDS or MODEL=ASCAL. The value of TYPE_ for each set of weights must be STI.

Table 19.8   Default input values for the FILE subcommand

Shape	Model	Default
SYMMETRIC	EUCLID	CONFIG (or ROWCONF)
	INDSCAL	CONFIG (or ROWCONF) SUBJWGHT
	GEMSCAL	CONFIG (or ROWCONF) SUBJWGHT
ASYMMETRIC	EUCLID	CONFIG (or ROWCONF)
	INDSCAL	CONFIG (or ROWCONF)
	GEMSCAL	CONFIG (or ROWCONF) SUBJWGHT
	ASCAL	CONFIG (or ROWCONF) STIMWGHT
	AINDS	CONFIG (or ROWCONF) SUBJWGHT STIMWGHT
RECTANGULAR	EUCLID	ROWCONF (or CONFIG) COLCONF
	INDSCAL	ROWCONF (or CONFIG) COLCONF SUBJWGHT
	GEMSCAL	ROWCONF (or CONFIG) COLCONF SUBJWGHT

19.9
MODEL Subcommand

The MODEL subcommand defines the scaling model for the analysis. (The keyword METHOD may be used instead of MODEL.) You can specify any of five scaling and unfolding model types:

EUCLID   *Euclidean distance model.* This model is the default. It may be used with any type of proximity matrix.

INDSCAL   *Individual differences (weighted) Euclidean distance model.* ALSCAL will scale the data using the weighted individual differences Euclidean distance model, as proposed by Carroll and Chang (1970). You can specify this type of analysis only if you are analyzing more than one data matrix and if you specify more than one dimension on the CRITERIA subcommand (see Section 19.10).

ASCAL   *Asymmetric Euclidean distance model.* You can use this model (Young, 1975b) only if SHAPE=ASYMMETRIC and if the number of dimensions requested on the CRITERIA subcommand is greater than one.

AINDS   *Asymmetric individual differences Euclidean distance model.* This option combines Young's (1975a) asymmetric Euclidean model with the individual differences model as proposed by Carroll and Chang (1970). You may specify MODEL=AINDS only when SHAPE=ASYMMETRIC, you are analyzing more than one data matrix, and the number of dimensions on the CRITERIA subcommand is greater than one.

GEMSCAL   *Generalized Euclidean metric individual differences model.* You can control the number of directions for this model with the DIRECTIONS option on the CRITERIA subcommand. By default, the number of directions is set equal to the number of dimensions in the solution. The number of directions you specify can be equal to but not exceed the group space dimensionality. In the following example, the number of directions in the GEMSCAL model is set to 4:

```
ALSCAL VARIABLES = varlist
 /SHAPE = ASYMMETRIC
 /CONDITION = ROW
 /MODEL = GEMSCAL
 /CRITERIA = DIM(4) DIRECTIONS(4)
```

19.10
CRITERIA Subcommand

The CRITERIA subcommand lets you specify aspects of your scaling model and set convergence criteria for the scaling solution. ALSCAL is an iterative algorithm designed to minimize the goodness-of-fit criterion called S-STRESS. ALSCAL iterates until the amount of improvement in S-STRESS is less than the CONVERGE value, until the number of completed iterations reaches a maximum, or until the value of S-STRESS reaches a minimum.

CONVERGE(c)   *Set CONVERGE to c.* This refers to the criterion for improvement in S-STRESS from one iteration to the next. By default, CONVERGE=.001. To increase the precision of your solution, you can replace this value with a smaller number, for example .0001. To obtain a less precise solution (perhaps to reduce computer time), specify a larger value, for instance .05. Negative values of CONVERGE are not allowed. If CONVERGE=0, the algorithm will iterate 30 times unless you specify a different value with the ITER option.

ITER(ni)   *Set the maximum number of iterations to ni.* The default value is 30. The ITER option lets you set the value higher or lower. A higher value may give you a more precise solution, but it may add substantially to your computer time and costs.

STRESSMIN(s)   *Set the minimum stress value to s.* By default, ALSCAL automatically stops iterating when the value of S-STRESS reaches .005 or less. If you want the iterations to continue beyond this point, you can specify a value smaller than .005, for example .001. A larger value will cause ALSCAL to terminate sooner than usual. You can specify a value for STRESSMIN from 0 to 1.

NEGATIVE   *Allow negative weights in individual differences models.* By default, ALSCAL does not permit weights to take on negative values. To allow negative weights, specify CRITERIA= NEGATIVE. Weighted models include INDSCAL, ASCAL, and AINDS, but not GEMSCAL. The NEGATIVE option will be ignored if MODEL=EUCLID.

CUTOFF(c)   *Set the cutoff value for treating distances as missing to c.* By default, ALSCAL treats all negative similarities (or dissimilarities) as missing, and zero and positive similarities as nonmissing (CUTOFF=0). Changing the CUTOFF value causes ALSCAL to treat similarities greater than or equal to that value as nonmissing. User-specified and SYSMIS values are considered missing regardless of the CUTOFF specification.

NOULB   *Do not estimate upper and lower bounds on missing values.* By default, ALSCAL estimates the upper and lower bounds on missing values in order to compute the initial configuration. Specify CRITERIA=NOULB if you do not want upper and lower bounds to be estimated. This specification has no effect during the iterative process, when missing values are ignored.

DIMENS(min[,max])   *Set the minimum and maximum numbers of dimensions in the scaling solution.* By default, ALSCAL calculates a scaling solution with two dimensions. If you want to allow your solution to have other than two dimensions, specify the minimum number and the maximum number of dimensions in parentheses to the right of DIMENS. The minimum and maximum numbers may be any integer values between 2 and 6. You can also specify a single value inside the parentheses to represent both the minimum and the maximum number of dimensions. Thus, DIMENS(3) is equivalent to DIMENS(3,3). The minimum number of dimensions may be set to 1 only if MODEL=EUCLID.

DIRECTIONS(r)   *Set the number of principal directions in the generalized Euclidean model to r.* This option has no effect for models other than MODEL=GEMSCAL. The number of principal directions can be any positive integer between 1 and the number of dimensions specified on the DIMENS option. By default, ALSCAL will set the number of directions equal to the number of dimensions.

TIESTORE(n) *Set the amount of storage needed for ties to n.* This option estimates the amount of storage needed to deal with ties in ordinal data. By default, the amount of storage is set to 1000 or the number of cells in a matrix, whichever is smaller. Should this be insufficient, ALSCAL terminates with a message that more space is needed.

CONSTRAIN *Constrain multidimensional unfolding solution.* Use the CONSTRAIN option if you want the initial constraints to remain constant throughout the analysis.

19.11
Specification of Analyses

Table 19.11a summarizes the types of analyses that can be performed for the major forms of proximity matrices you can use with ALSCAL. Tables 19.11b and 19.11c list the specifications necessary to produce these analyses using SPSS-X ALSCAL, depending on whether you want a nonmetric or metric type of analysis. You can, of course, include additional specifications to control the precision of your analysis with the CRITERIA subcommand.

Table 19.11a Models for types of matrix input

Matrix mode	Matrix form	Model class	Single matrix	Replications of single matrix	Two or more individual matrices
Object by object	Symmetric	Multi-dimensional scaling	CMDS Classical multidimensional scaling	RMDS Replicated multidimensional scaling	WMDS(INDSCAL) Weighted multidimensional scaling
	Asymmetric single process	Multi-dimensional scaling	CMDS(row conditional) Classical row conditional multidimensional scaling	RMDS(row conditional) Replicated row conditional multidimensional scaling	WMDS(row conditional) Weighted row conditional multidimensional scaling
	Asymmetric multiple process	Internal asymmetric multi-dimensional scaling	CAMDS Classical asymmetric multidimensional scaling	RAMDS Replicated asymmetric multidimensional scaling	WAMDS Weighted asymmetric multidimensional scaling
		External asymmetric multi-dimensional scaling	CAMDS(external) Classical external asymmetric multidimensional scaling	RAMDS(external) Replicated external asymmetric multidimensional scaling	WAMDS(external) Weighted external asymmetric multidimensional scaling
Object by attribute	Rectangular	Internal unfolding	CMDU Classical internal multidimensional unfolding	RMDU Replicated internal multidimensional unfolding	WMDU Weighted internal multidimensional unfolding
		External unfolding	CMDU(external) Classical external multidimensional unfolding	RMDU(external) Replicated external multidimensional unfolding	WMDU(external) Weighted external multidimensional unfolding

Table 19.11b   ALSCAL specifications for nonmetric models

Matrix mode	Matrix form	Model class	Single matrix	Replications of single matrix	Two or more individual matrices
Object by object	Symmetric	Multidimensional scaling	`ALSCAL VAR= varlist.`	`ALSCAL VAR= varlist.`	`ALSCAL VAR= varlist` `/MODEL=INDSCAL.`
	Asymmetric single process	Multidimensional scaling	`ALSCAL VAR= varlist` `/SHAPE=ASYMMETRIC` `/CONDITION=ROW.`	`ALSCAL VAR= varlist` `/SHAPE=ASYMMETRIC` `/CONDITION=ROW.`	`ALSCAL VAR= varlist` `/SHAPE=ASYMMETRIC` `/CONDITION=ROW` `/MODEL=INDSCAL.`
	Asymmetric multiple process	Internal asymmetric multidimensional scaling	`ALSCAL VAR= varlist` `/SHAPE=ASYMMETRIC` `/MODEL=ASCAL.`	`ALSCAL VAR= varlist` `/SHAPE=ASYMMETRIC` `/MODEL=ASCAL.`	`ALSCAL VAR= varlist` `/SHAPE=ASYMMETRIC` `/MODEL=AINDS.`
		External asymmetric multidimensional scaling	`ALSCAL VAR= varlist` `/SHAPE=ASYMMETRIC` `/MODEL=ASCAL` `/FILE=file COLCONF(FIX).`	`ALSCAL VAR= varlist` `/SHAPE=ASYMMETRIC` `/MODEL=ASCAL` `/FILE=file COLCONF(FIX).`	`ALSCAL VAR= varlist` `/SHAPE=ASYMMETRIC` `/MODEL=AINDS` `/FILE=file COLCONF(FIX).`
Object by attribute	Rectangular	Internal unfolding	`ALSCAL VAR= varlist` `/SHAPE=REC` `/INP=ROWS` `/CONDITION=ROW.`	`ALSCAL VAR= varlist` `/SHAPE=REC` `/INP=ROWS` `/CONDITION(ROW).`	`ALSCAL VAR= varlist` `/SHAPE=REC` `/INP=ROWS` `/CONDITION=ROW` `/MODEL=INDSCAL.`
		External unfolding	`ALSCAL VAR= varlist` `/SHAPE=REC` `/INP=ROWS` `/CONDITION=ROW` `/FILE=file ROWCONF(FIX).`	`ALSCAL VAR= varlist` `/SHAPE=REC` `/INP=ROWS` `/CONDITION=ROW` `/FILE=file ROWCONF(FIX).`	`ALSCAL VAR= varlist` `/SHAPE=REC` `/INP=ROWS` `/CONDITION=ROW` `/FILE=file ROWCONF(FIX)` `/MODEL=INDSCAL.`

Table 19.11c   ALSCAL specifications for metric models

Matrix mode	Matrix form	Model class	Single matrix	Replications of single matrix	Two or more individual matrices
Object by object	Symmetric	Multidimensional scaling	`ALSCAL VAR= varlist` `/LEVEL=INT.`	`ALSCAL VAR= varlist` `/LEVEL=INT.`	`ALSCAL VAR= varlist` `/LEVEL=INT` `/MODEL=INDSCAL.`
	Asymmetric single process	Multidimensional scaling	`ALSCAL VAR= varlist` `/SHAPE=ASYMMETRIC` `/CONDITION=ROW` `/LEVEL=INT.`	`ALSCAL VAR= varlist` `/SHAPE=ASYMMETRIC` `/CONDITION=ROW` `/LEVEL=INT.`	`ALSCAL VAR= varlist` `/SHAPE=ASYMMETRIC` `/CONDITION=ROW` `/LEVEL=INT` `/MODEL=INDSCAL.`
	Asymmetric multiple process	Internal asymmetric multidimensional scaling	`ALSCAL VAR= varlist` `/SHAPE=ASYMMETRIC` `/LEVEL=INT` `/MODEL=ASCAL.`	`ALSCAL VAR= varlist` `/SHAPE=ASYMMETRIC` `/LEVEL=INT` `/MODEL=ASCAL.`	`ALSCAL VAR= varlist` `/SHAPE=ASYMMETRIC` `/LEVEL=INT` `/MODEL=AINDS.`
		External asymmetric multidimensional scaling	`ALSCAL VAR= varlist` `/SHAPE=ASYMMETRIC` `/LEVEL=INT` `/MODEL=ASCAL` `/FILE=file COLCONF(FIX).`	`ALSCAL VAR= varlist` `/SHAPE=ASYMMETRIC` `/LEVEL=INT` `/MODEL=ASCAL` `/FILE=file COLCONF(FIX).`	`ALSCAL VAR= varlist` `/SHAPE=ASYMMETRIC` `/LEVEL=INT` `/MODEL=AINDS` `/FILE=file COLCONF(FIX).`
Object by attribute	Rectangular	Internal unfolding	`ALSCAL VAR= varlist` `/SHAPE=REC` `/INP=ROWS` `/CONDITION=ROW` `/LEVEL=INT.`	`ALSCAL VAR= varlist` `/SHAPE=REC` `/INP=ROWS` `/CONDITION=ROW` `/LEVEL=INT.`	`ALSCAL VAR= varlist` `/SHAPE=REC` `/INP=ROWS` `/CONDITION=ROW` `/LEVEL=INT` `/MODEL=INDSCAL.`
		External unfolding	`ALSCAL VAR= varlist` `/SHAPE=REC` `/INP=ROWS` `/CONDITION=ROW` `/LEVEL=INT` `/FILE=file ROWCONF(FIX).`	`ALSCAL VAR= varlist` `/SHAPE=REC` `/INP=ROWS` `/CONDITION=ROW` `/LEVEL=INT` `/FILE=file ROWCONF(FIX).`	`ALSCAL VAR= varlist` `/SHAPE=REC` `/INP=ROWS` `/CONDITION=ROW` `/LEVEL=INT` `/FILE=file ROWCONF(FIX)` `/MODEL=INDSCAL.`

ANNOTATED EXAMPLES FOR ALSCAL

The following examples illustrate two different applications of procedure ALSCAL.

Example 1

This example shows how ALSCAL performs classical nonmetric multidimensional scaling to uncover the dimensions on which Americans perceived 12 major presidential candidates for the 1968 election. Prior to the election, people were asked to rate the presidential hopefuls on a "Feeling Thermometer." The responses were then correlated, and the correlations were used as the input to ALSCAL. (Although distance measures are usually used in multidimensional scaling, correlation can be considered a proximity measure.) Since the input matrix was symmetric, all values above the diagonal were ignored. Data for this example come from the *Survey Research Center 1968 American National Election Study,* made available by the Inter-University Consortium for Political Research. The data have also been analyzed by Weisberg and Rusk (1970). The SPSS-X commands for the present analysis are

```
TITLE PERCEPTIONS OF 1968 PRESIDENTIAL CANDIDATES
SET WIDTH = 80
UNNUMBERED
DATA LIST
 / WALLACE HUMPHREY NIXON MCCARTHY REAGAN ROCKFLLR JOHNSON
   ROMNEY KENNEDY MUSKIE AGNEW LEMAY 1-84
ALSCAL VARIABLES = WALLACE TO LEMAY
 / LEVEL = ORDINAL (SIMILAR)
 / PLOT
 / PRINT = HEADER
 / CRITERIA = CUTOFF(-1.000)
BEGIN DATA
 1.000                                                                   WALLACE
-0.312  1.000                                                            HUMPHREY
-0.038 -0.179  1.000                                                     NIXON
-0.139  0.245  0.077  1.000                                              MCCARTHY
 0.197 -0.192  0.415  0.089  1.000                                       REAGAN
-0.140  0.163  0.122  0.329  0.189  1.000                                ROCKEFELLER
-0.226  0.702 -0.088  0.129 -0.105  0.150  1.000                         JOHNSON
-0.062  0.171  0.239  0.328  0.297  0.322  0.243  1.000                  ROMNEY
-0.219  0.526 -0.130  0.356 -0.108  0.228  0.467  0.259  1.000           KENNEDY
-0.260  0.579 -0.102  0.292 -0.077  0.272  0.459  0.236  0.429  1.000    MUSKIE
 0.122 -0.100  0.598  0.116  0.439  0.126 -0.034  0.336 -0.009 -0.028  1.000       AGNEW
 0.683 -0.206  0.113 -0.033  0.275 -0.040 -0.084  0.096 -0.091 -0.159  0.295  1.000 LEMAY
END DATA
```

- The DATA LIST command reads 12 variables in fixed format. The data are inline. ALSCAL uses only the values in the lower triangle of a symmetric matrix. Therefore, values above the diagonal are not entered.

- The VARIABLES subcommand following the ALSCAL command specifies the variables to be scaled.

- The LEVEL subcommand indicates that the input data are at the ordinal level of measurement. The SIMILAR specification indicates that ALSCAL should treat the input data as similarities rather than dissimilarities.

- The PLOT subcommand requests the default plots, which in this case are a plot of the stimulus coordinates, scatterplots of the linear and nonlinear fits between the data and the model, and a plot of the data transformation.

- The PRINT subcommand specifies that the printed output should include a header, defining the data, model, output, and algorithmic options in effect for the analysis.

- The CUTOFF option on the CRITERIA subcommand indicates that values less than or equal to -1.000 are to be treated as missing.

Figure A lists the ALSCAL procedure options in effect for the analysis.

A ALSCAL header information

```
ALSCAL PROCEDURE OPTIONS

DATA OPTIONS—

NUMBER OF ROWS (OBSERVATIONS/MATRIX).   12
NUMBER OF COLUMNS (VARIABLES) .  .  .   12
NUMBER OF MATRICES  .  .  .  .  .  .    1
MEASUREMENT LEVEL .  .  .  .  .  .  .   ORDINAL
DATA MATRIX SHAPE .  .  .  .  .  .  .   SYMMETRIC
TYPE .  .  .  .  .  .  .  .  .  .  .    SIMILARITY
APPROACH TO TIES .  .  .  .  .  .  .    LEAVE TIED
CONDITIONALITY .  .  .  .  .  .  .  .   MATRIX
DATA CUTOFF AT .  .  .  .  .  .  .  .   -1.000000

MODEL OPTIONS—

MODEL .  .  .  .  .  .  .  .  .  .  .   EUCLID
MAXIMUM DIMENSIONALITY  .  .  .  .  .   2
MINIMUM DIMENSIONALITY  .  .  .  .  .   2
NEGATIVE WEIGHTS .  .  .  .  .  .  .    NOT PERMITTED

OUTPUT OPTIONS—

JOB OPTION HEADER .  .  .  .  .  .  .   PRINTED
DATA MATRICES .  .  .  .  .  .  .  .    NOT PRINTED
CONFIGURATIONS AND TRANSFORMATIONS .   PLOTTED
OUTPUT DATASET .  .  .  .  .  .  .  .   NOT CREATED
INITIAL STIMULUS COORDINATES .  .  .
                                       COMPUTED

ALGORITHMIC OPTIONS—

MAXIMUM ITERATIONS  .  .  .  .  .  .    30
CONVERGENCE CRITERION  .  .  .  .  .    0.00100
MINIMUM S-STRESS .  .  .  .  .  .  .    0.00500
MISSING DATA ESTIMATED BY  .  .  .  .
                                       ULBOUNDS
TIESTORE .  .  .  .  .  .  .  .  .  .   66
```

B Iteration history and goodness-of-fit measures

```
ITERATION HISTORY FOR THE 2 DIMENSIONAL SOLUTION(IN SQUARED DISTANCES)
            YOUNGS S-STRESS FORMULA 1 IS USED.

        ITERATION    S-STRESS      IMPROVEMENT

            1         0.07905
            2         0.05343
                                    0.02562
            3         0.04933
                                    0.00410
            4         0.04775
                                    0.00158
            5         0.04691
                                    0.00085

                ITERATIONS STOPPED BECAUSE
        S-STRESS IMPROVEMENT LESS THAN 0.001000


        STRESS AND SQUARED CORRELATION (RSQ) IN DISTANCES

RSQ VALUES ARE THE PROPORTION OF VARIANCE OF THE SCALED DATA (DISPARITIES)
        IN THE PARTITION (ROW, MATRIX, OR ENTIRE DATA) WHICH
        IS ACCOUNTED FOR BY THEIR  CORRESPONDING DISTANCES.

        STRESS VALUES ARE KRUSKAL'S STRESS FORMULA 1.


        FOR  MATRIX
    STRESS  =  0.063      RSQ = 0.982
```

Figure B shows the iteration history for a two-dimensional solution. After five iterations, the improvement in S-STRESS is so small (.00085) that the analysis stops, printing the message that the amount of improvement is less than the minimum permitted. ALSCAL then prints two goodness-of-fit measures, Kruskal's STRESS formula 1 (.063) and the squared correlation coefficient (RSQ=.982). Results in this case show a nearly perfect fit between the data and the solution.

**Annotated Examples for
ALSCAL** *continued*

Figure C shows the derived configuration in two dimensions in printed form. ALSCAL assigns a stimulus number, stimulus name, plot symbol, and a pair of coordinates to each variable in the analysis.

C Printed configuration

```
        CONFIGURATION DERIVED IN 2 DIMENSIONS


              STIMULUS COORDINATES

                                 DIMENSION
                                  1         2
   STIMULUS   STIMULUS   PLOT
    NUMBER      NAME      SYMBOL

       1      WALLACE      1      1.8188    1.2278
       2      HUMPHREY     2     -1.7022    0.3038
       3      NIXON        3      1.1292   -1.0923
       4      MCCARTHY     4     -0.6070   -0.5644
       5      REAGAN       5      1.3508   -0.4459
       6      ROCKFLLR     6     -0.4069   -0.7834
       7      JOHNSON      7     -1.3193    0.5519
       8      ROMNEY       8     -0.0673   -0.2981
       9      KENNEDY      9     -1.3302    0.3449
      10      MUSKIE       A     -1.4210    0.2142
      11      AGNEW        B      1.0571   -0.2937
      12      LEMAY        C      1.4980    0.8351
```

Figure D is a plot of the derived stimulus coordinates. Labels for the points are the plot symbols listed in Figure C. Investigators are free to interpret the configuration in ways that they find meaningful.

D Plot of the stimulus coordinates

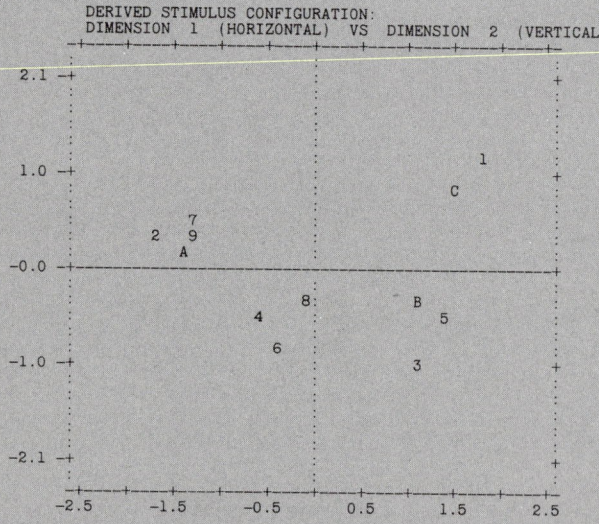

Figure E is a scatterplot of the linear fit between the distances in the stimulus space and the transformed data, or disparities. The plot in this case is nearly a straight line, with little scatter, indicating a close fit between the model and the input data.

E Plot of the linear fit

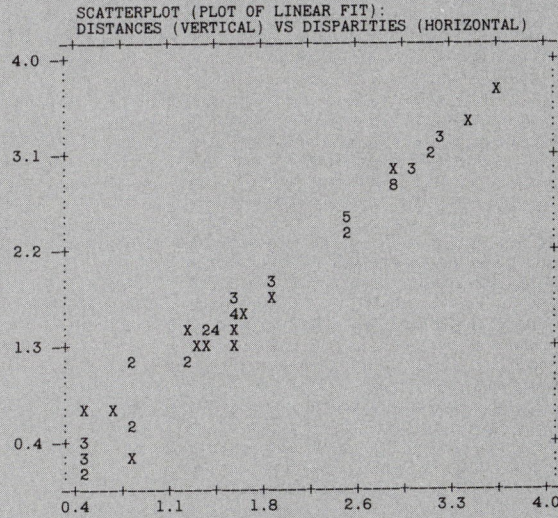

Figure F is a plot of the computed distances versus the actual observations (proximity values). Since the data are similarities, the distances should diminish (and they do) as the degree of similarity increases.

F Plot of the non-linear fit

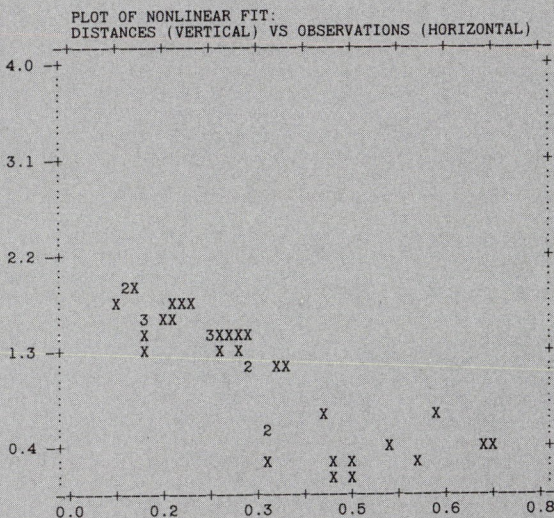

**Annotated Examples for
ALSCAL** *continued*

Figure G shows the relationship between the disparities (using Kruskal's least-squares monotonic transformation) and the actual proximities.

G Plot of the data transformation

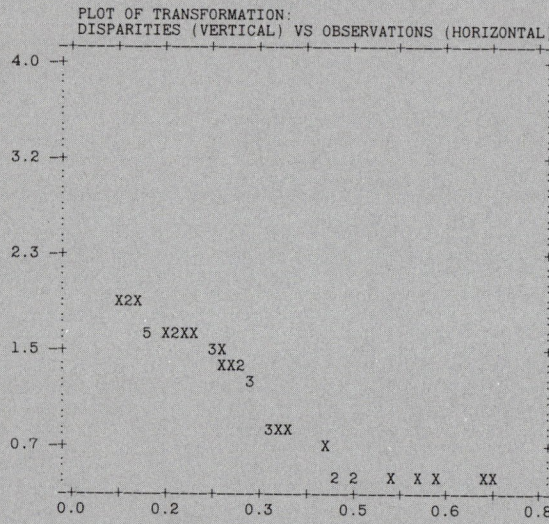

Example 2   This example demonstrates nonmetric external asymmetric scaling using an SPSS-X file containing initial configuration coordinates and weights. In this case, the START file contains stimulus configuration coordinates, subject weights, and stimulus weights. ALSCAL will use only the stimulus coordinates and subject weights. The SPSS-X commands used to produce the results are

```
FILE HANDLE START / file specifications
SET WIDTH=80
DATA LIST / DIM1 1-3 DIM2 4-6 TYPE_ 9-16(A)
SAVE OUTFILE = START

BEGIN DATA
  2   2  CONFIG
  2   1  CONFIG
 -1   2  CONFIG
  1  -2  CONFIG
 -3  -3  CONFIG
  0  -1  CONFIG
  0   0  CONFIG
 .6  .7  SUBJWGHT
 .9  .4  SUBJWGHT
 .7  .7  SUBJWGHT
 .9  .2  SUBJWGHT
1.0  .2  SUBJWGHT
 .6   1  STIMWGHT
 .3  .9  STIMWGHT
 .8  .7  STIMWGHT
 .5  .5  STIMWGHT
 .2  .5  STIMWGHT
 .7  .5  STIMWGHT
 .6  .9  STIMWGHT
END DATA

DATA LIST / A1 TO A7 1-70
ALSCAL VARIABLES = A1 TO A7
 / SHAPE = ASYMMETR
 / LEVEL = ORDINAL
 / MODEL = AINDS
 / FILE = START
          CONFIG(FIXED)
          STIMWGHT(INITIAL)
 / PRINT = HEADER
 / PLOT

BEGIN DATA
      0.000    3.000    5.196   12.083   16.583    9.434    6.633
      2.449    0.000    3.000    7.416   11.000    5.292    3.162
      5.745    5.196    0.000    8.124   10.392    5.196    3.000
      7.071    5.385    5.916    0.000    5.916    2.236    3.742

      . . .

      9.327    9.000    0.000    9.487   11.489    5.745    3.873
      7.348    5.745    7.141    0.000    9.950    3.000    4.243
     12.247   11.091    7.746    7.141    0.000    6.245    7.348
      7.937    6.928    4.583    3.464    9.644    0.000    1.732
END DATA
```

- The FILE HANDLE command identifies the SPSS-X output file to be created with the SAVE command.
- The first DATA LIST command reads in three variables: DIM1, DIM2, and TYPE_. The data are inline. Variables DIM1 and DIM2 correspond to the first two ALSCAL dimensions; TYPE_ identifies the input values as stimulus coordinates (CONFIG), subject weights (SUBJWGHT), and stimulus weights (STIMWGHT).
- The SAVE command stores the configurations in an SPSS-X system file called START.
- The second DATA LIST command defines the column locations of the variables for the proximity matrix. Only part of the proximity data are shown.
- The VARIABLES subcommand following the ALSCAL command specifies seven variables to be scaled.
- The SHAPE subcommand defines the form of the proximity matrix as ASYMMETRIC.

Annotated Examples for ALSCAL *continued*

- The LEVEL subcommand indicates that the proximity data are at the ordinal level of measurement. Since the SIMILAR option is not used, ALSCAL treats the proximity data as dissimilarities.

- The MODEL subcommand specifies the asymmetric individual differences Euclidean distance model (AINDS).

- The FILE subcommand defines the SPSS-X file containing the initial configuration and weights. The CONFIG (FIXED) and SUBJWGHT (INITIAL) options indicate that fixed stimulus coordinates and initial subject weights are to be read from the file with the handle START. ALSCAL will skip over TYPE_ values labeled STIMWGHT.

- The PRINT subcommand specifies that the printed output should include a header, defining the options in effect for the analysis.

- The PLOT subcommand requests default plots. In this case, ALSCAL will produce plots of the derived stimulus configuration, derived stimulus weights, and derived subject weights, as well as a scatterplot of the linear fit between the data and the model.

Figures H through M show portions of the display output. Figure H displays the options in effect for the analysis. The section on output options shows that ALSCAL computed initial subject weights (the default for MODEL=AINDS) and printed stimulus coordinates and stimulus weights.

H ALSCAL header information

```
ALSCAL PROCEDURE OPTIONS

DATA OPTIONS-

NUMBER OF ROWS (OBSERVATIONS/MATRIX).    7
NUMBER OF COLUMNS (VARIABLES) . . .      7
NUMBER OF MATRICES  . . . . . . .        5
MEASUREMENT LEVEL . . . . . . . .        ORDINAL
DATA MATRIX SHAPE . . . . . . . .        ASYMMETRIC
TYPE  . . . . . . . . . . . . .          DISSIMILARITY
APPROACH TO TIES  . . . . . . . .        LEAVE TIED
CONDITIONALITY  . . . . . . . . .        MATRIX
DATA CUTOFF AT  . . . . . . . . .        0.0

MODEL OPTIONS-

MODEL . . . . . . . . . . . . .          AINDS
MAXIMUM DIMENSIONALITY  . . . . .        2
MINIMUM DIMENSIONALITY  . . . . .        2
NEGATIVE WEIGHTS  . . . . . . . .        NOT PERMITTED

OUTPUT OPTIONS-

JOB OPTION HEADER . . . . . . . .        PRINTED
DATA MATRICES . . . . . . . . .          NOT PRINTED
CONFIGURATIONS AND TRANSFORMATIONS . .   PLOTTED
OUTPUT DATASET  . . . . . . . . .        NOT CREATED
INITIAL STIMULUS COORDINATES  . . .
                                         READ, PRINTED AND FIXED
INITIAL SUBJECT WEIGHTS . . . . .
                                         COMPUTED
INITIAL STIMULUS WEIGHTS  . . . . .
                                         READ AND PRINTED

ALGORITHMIC OPTIONS-

MAXIMUM ITERATIONS  . . . . . . .        30
CONVERGENCE CRITERION . . . . .          0.00100
MINIMUM S-STRESS  . . . . . . . .        0.00500
MISSING DATA ESTIMATED BY . . . .
                                         ULBOUNDS
TIESTORE  . . . . . . . . . . .          245
```

Figure I shows the initial stimulus coordinates and initial stimulus weights in two dimensions as read from the START file. The remaining figures show the derived stimulus coordinates, subject weights, stimulus weights, and the flattened subject weights.

I Initial stimulus coordinates and weights

```
ALSCAL will read initial and/or fixed values from file with handle START
  Label:
  Created 24 JAN 85 15:04:54        3 Variables
                INITIAL CONFIGURATION

             INITIAL STIMULUS SPACE

                              DIMENSION
STIMULUS   STIMULUS        1          2

 NUMBER     NAME
    1        A1         2.0000     2.0000
    2        A2         2.0000     1.0000
    3        A3        -1.0000     2.0000
    4        A4         1.0000    -2.0000
    5        A5        -3.0000    -3.0000
    6        A6         0.0       -1.0000
    7        A7         0.0        0.0

             INITIAL STIMULUS WEIGHTS
                              DIMENSION
STIMULUS   NAME           1          2
    1        A1         0.6000     1.0000
    2        A2         0.3000     0.9000
    3        A3         0.8000     0.7000
    4        A4         0.5000     0.5000
    5        A5         0.2000     0.5000
    6        A6         0.7000     0.5000
    7        A7         0.6000     0.9000
```

J Derived stimulus coordinates

```
    CONFIGURATION DERIVED IN 2 DIMENSIONS


             STIMULUS COORDINATES

                              DIMENSION
STIMULUS   STIMULUS  PLOT      1          2
 NUMBER     NAME    SYMBOL

    1        A1        1     1.1315     1.1859
    2        A2        2     1.1315     0.6325
    3        A3        3    -0.6963     1.1859
    4        A4        4     0.5222    -1.0277
    5        A5        5    -1.9149    -1.5811
    6        A6        6    -0.0870    -0.4743
    7        A7        7    -0.0870     0.0791
```

K Subject weights

```
             SUBJECT WEIGHTS

                              DIMENSION
SUBJECT   PLOT   WEIRD-     1          2
NUMBER   SYMBOL   NESS

   1        1    0.4636   0.5316     0.8421
   2        2    0.0612   0.8385     0.5406
   3        3    0.3764   0.5982     0.7966
   4        4    0.4321   0.9460     0.3211
   5        5    0.5476   0.9665     0.2546

OVERALL IMPORTANCE
OF EACH DIMENSION:          0.6345     0.3608
```

L Stimulus weights

```
             STIMULUS WEIGHTS

                              DIMENSION
STIMULUS   STIMULUS  PLOT      1          2
 NUMBER     NAME    SYMBOL

    1        A1        1     0.5970     1.3672
    2        A2        2     0.2890     1.0440
    3        A3        3     0.8208     0.5820
    4        A4        4     0.5134     0.4177
    5        A5        5     0.2964     0.3747
    6        A6        6     0.8455     0.4088
    7        A7        7     0.6480     0.7666
```

M Flattened subject weights

```
         FLATTENED SUBJECT WEIGHTS

                          VARIABLE
SUBJECT    PLOT            1
NUMBER    SYMBOL
   1         1          -1.2614
   2         2           0.0958
   3         3          -1.0041
   4         4           0.9469
   5         5           1.2227
```

19.12
Output

By default, ALSCAL prints

- A list of the number of missing observations, if any.
- The iteration history of improvement in Young's S-STRESS and an explanation of why the iterations terminated.
- Two measures of fit (Kruskal's STRESS and the squared correlation) for the total data set. For certain types of input data, ALSCAL also prints fit measures for each stimulus, for each matrix, and for individual rows of matrices.
- The derived configuration, including the stimulus coordinates and, where appropriate, the stimulus and matrix weights.
- Matrix and flattened subject weights for the INDSCAL, GEMSCAL, and AINDS models; generalized weights for the GEMSCAL model; and stimulus weights for the ASCAL and AINDS models.

Optional output includes

- Listings of the raw and transformed data according to the format implied by the data options you specified.
- The initial configuration you defined in the FILE subcommand.
- Plots of the stimulus coordinates and, for some models, plots of stimulus and matrix weights.
- A scatterplot of the goodness of fit, and in certain cases, scatterplots of the data transformation and the nonlinear fit.

19.13
PRINT Subcommand

You can use the PRINT subcommand to specify output not available by default.

DATA *Print input data.* The printout includes both the raw data and the scaled data for each subject according to the structure you specified on the SHAPE subcommand.

INTERMED *Print intermediate steps in the scaling process.* Intermediate steps leading up to the final scaling solution are not usually of interest. Some of the items the INTERMED option prints are the raw data, the missing-value pattern, the data with missing-value estimates, the normalized data and means, the squared data with additive constant estimated, and the scalar product for each subject. Since this option can produce a great deal of output, you should use it with caution.

HEADER *Print a header page.* This specification prints a listing of the options described below—the data, model, output, and algorithmic options in effect for the analysis.

Data Options. These include the numbers of rows and columns; the number of matrices; the measurement level; the shape of the data matrix; the type of data (similarity or dissimilarity); whether ties were left tied or were untied; the conditionality; and the data cutoff value.

Model Options. These options are the type of model you specified (EUCLID, INDSCAL, ASCAL, AINDS, or GEMSCAL); the minimum and maximum dimensionality; and whether or not negative weights were permitted.

Output Options. The output options section specifies whether the printed output included the job option header and data matrices; whether ALSCAL plotted configurations and transformations; whether it created an output data set; and whether it computed initial stimulus coordinates, initial column stimulus coordinates, initial subject weights, and initial stimulus weights.

Algorithmic Options. For these, ALSCAL lists the maximum number of iterations permitted; the convergence criterion; the maximum S-STRESS value; whether or not missing data were estimated by upper and lower bounds; and the amount of storage allotted for ties in ordinal data.

19.14
PLOT Subcommand

The PLOT subcommand plots the multidimensional scaling results.

DEFAULT   *Produce default plots.* These are plots of the stimulus coordinates, the matrix weights (if MODEL=INDSCAL, MODEL=AINDS, or MODEL= GEMSCAL), and the stimulus weights (if MODEL=AINDS or MODEL= ASCAL). The default also includes a scatterplot of the linear fit between the data and the model and, for certain types of data, scatterplots of the nonlinear fit and of the data transformation. ALSCAL produces d*(d-1)/2 pages of plots for the stimulus space, and, when appropriate, for each of the weight spaces, where d is the number of dimensions in the solution.

ALL   *Plot the stimulus space for each matrix.* You can specify PLOT=ALL to obtain a separate plot of each subject's data transformation (if CONDITION=MATRIX or the data are nominal or ordinal) or a plot for each row (if CONDITION=ROW), and, for weighted models, a separate plot of each subject's weight space. This option can produce thousands of pages of output, especially if CONDITION=ROW.

19.15
OUTFILE Subcommand

The OUTFILE subcommand saves coordinate and weight matrices to an SPSS-X system file whose file handle is specified immediately after the keyword OUT-FILE. This file has a format that the FILE subcommand can use to read initial values. The system file has an alphanumeric (short string) variable named TYPE_ that identifies the kind of values in each row, a numeric variable DIMENS that specifies the number of dimensions, a numeric variable MATNUM that indicates the subject (matrix) to which each set of coordinates corresponds, and variables DIM1, DIM2...DIMr that correspond to the r ALSCAL dimensions in the model. The values of any split-file variables are also included in this file.

The following list indicates the seven different kinds of ALSCAL file output. Only the first three characters of each identifier are written to variable TYPE_ on the system file. For example, CONFIG becomes CON.

CONFIG   *Stimulus configuration coordinates for SHAPE=SYMMETRIC or SHAPE=ASYMMETRIC.*

ROWCONF   *Row stimulus configuration coordinates for SHAPE =RECTANGULAR.*

COLCONF   *Column stimulus configuration coordinates for SHAPE =RECTANGULAR.*

SUBJWGHT   *Subject (matrix) weights for MODEL=INDSCAL, MODEL=AINDS, or MODEL=GEMSCAL.*

FLATWGHT   *Flattened subject (matrix) weights for MODEL=INDSCAL, MODEL =AINDS, or MODEL=GEMSCAL.*

GEMWGHT   *Generalized weights for MODEL=GEMSCAL.*

STIMWGHT   *Stimulus weights for MODEL=ASCAL or MODEL=AINDS.*

Table 19.15 shows the types of values that the OUTFILE subcommand automatically writes according to shape and model. For example, if you specify the OUTFILE subcommand with SHAPE=ASYMMETRIC and MODEL= INDSCAL, ALSCAL writes stimulus coordinates, subject weights, and flat weights to your system file.

Table 19.15   Types of configurations and/or weights in output files

Shape	Model	TYPE
SYMMETRIC	EUCLID	CON
	INDSCAL	CON
		SUB
		FLA
	GEMSCAL	CON
		SUB
		FLA
		GEM
ASYMMETRIC	EUCLID	CON
	INDSCAL	CON
		SUB
		FLA
	GEMSCAL	CON
		SUB
		FLA
		GEM
	ASCAL	CON
		STI
	AINDS	CON
		SUB
		FLA
		STI
RECTANGULAR	EUCLID	ROW
		COL
	INDSCAL	ROW
		COL
		SUB
		FLA
	GEMSCAL	ROW
		COL
		SUB
		FLA
		GEM

19.16
MATRIX Subcommand

Generally, "data" read by ALSCAL are already in matrix form. This matrix can be created in either PROXIMITIES or CLUSTER. You do not need to use the MATRIX subcommand to read this file, simply use the VARIABLES subcommand to indicate the variables (or columns) to be used.

If you use the MATRIX subcommand, the order of rows and columns is unimportant. The MATRIX subcommand has one keyword, IN, which you use to specify the matrix file in parentheses.

19.17
IN Keyword

The IN keyword on MATRIX specifies the file from which the distance matrix is read. There are two options:

(file)   *Read the matrix materials from a matrix system file.*

(*)   *Read the matrix materials from the active file.* The active file must be an appropriate matrix system file.

MATRIX=IN cannot be used in place of GET or DATA LIST to create an active file, since MATRIX is a subcommand on ALSCAL and ALSCAL cannot run before an active file is defined. You can either GET the matrix file and then specify IN(*) on MATRIX or write a matrix to the active file using PROXIMITIES or CLUSTER procedure and then specify IN(*). Or you can specify a file other than the active file on IN as long as an active file already exists.

In the following example, ALSCAL reads a distance matrix written to the active file by PROXIMITIES:

```
GET FILE=CRIME
PROXIMITIES MURDER TO MOTOR
  /ID=CITY
  /MATRIX=OUT(*)

LIST
DISPLAY DICTIONARY

ALSCAL VARIABLES=CASE1 TO CASE8
  /MATRIX=IN(*)
```

- The GET defines the data to SPSS-X.
- The PROXIMITIES command specifies variables for the analysis and reads the raw data from file CRIME. The ID subcommand specifies CITY as the case-identifying variable. The MATRIX subcommand indicates that the resulting matrix is written to the active file.
- The LIST command lists the cases in the matrix system file written by PROXIMITIES (see Figure 19.17).
- The DISPLAY command displays the dictionary of the matrix system file. Results of the DISPLAY command are shown for variable ROWTYPE_ in Figure 19.17.
- The ALSCAL command specifies variables for the ALSCAL analysis. The MATRIX subcommand indicates data are distance matrix materials and are contained on the active file.

Format of the Matrix System File. Figure 19.17 shows the matrix system file written by PROXIMITIES. The file includes two special variables created by SPSS-X: ROWTYPE_ and VARNAME_. Variable ROWTYPE_ is a short string variable with value PROX, for proximity measure. PROX is assigned value labels containing the distance measure used to create the matrix. It is also assigned a similarity/dissimilarity keyword. In this example, the distance measure is EUCLID and the similarity/dissimilarity keyword is DISSIMILARITY, as shown in Figure 19.17.

Figure 19.17 A matrix system file

```
FILE:     MATRIX FILE

ROWTYPE_ CITY                VARNAME_     CASE1      CASE2      CASE3      CASE4      CASE5      CASE6      CASE7      CASE8

PROX     San Francisco       CASE1        .0000   814.0269  1045.9773  1636.8577  2370.1467  1959.1096  2053.4780   950.1677
PROX     Dallas              CASE2     814.0269      .0000  1496.0215  2006.7471  2805.5029  2251.5161  2505.0427  1020.2466
PROX     Baltimore           CASE3    1045.9773  1496.0215      .0000  1133.2859  1840.3933  1705.8193  1387.5959  1006.8323
PROX     Los Angeles         CASE4    1636.8577  2006.7471  1133.2859      .0000   828.1233   729.1794   649.2656  1404.7251
PROX     Detroit             CASE5    2370.1467  2805.5029  1840.3933   828.1233      .0000   890.3674   597.2847  2187.2817
PROX     Houston             CASE6    1959.1096  2251.5161  1705.8193   729.1794   890.3674      .0000   965.4382  1663.0964
PROX     New York            CASE7    2053.4780  2505.0427  1387.5959   649.2656   597.2847   965.4382      .0000  1890.0500
PROX     San Diego           CASE8     950.1677  1020.2466  1006.8323  1404.7251  2187.2817  1663.0964  1890.0500      .0000

NUMBER OF CASES READ =       8    NUMBER OF CASES LISTED =       8

FILE:     MATRIX FILE

       LIST OF VARIABLES ON THE ACTIVE FILE

NAME                                                                 POSITION

ROWTYPE_                                                                    1
                    PRINT FORMAT: A8
                    WRITE FORMAT: A8

           VALUE    LABEL

        PROX        DISSIMILARITY       EUCLID
```

Variable CITY is the case-identifying variable named on the ID subcommand in PROXIMITIES. Up to 20 characters can be displayed for the identifying variable; id variables longer than 20 characters are truncated. The identifying variable is present only when VIEW=CASE (the default) and the ID subcommand have been specified on PROXIMITIES. Since ALSCAL does not support case labeling, it ignores values for the ID variable CITY.

The next variable in the matrix file, variable VARNAME_, is a short string variable whose values are the case numbers of the ID variable. The remaining variables in the matrix file are the distance variables used to form the matrix.

Only 8 cases were included in the analysis that generated Figure 19.17 so that the display would not wrap. With a large number of variables, the display file wraps and the matrix format is less readable. Nonetheless, the matrix values are equally as accurate and just as useful when used as matrix input values for ALSCAL or other procedures.

The order among rows and variables in the input matrix file is unimportant, as long as values for split-file variables precede values for ROWTYPE_. ALSCAL ignores unrecognized ROWTYPE_ values. In addition, it ignores variables present in the matrix file that are not specified on the VARIABLES subcommand in ALSCAL.

When split-file processing is in effect (see Chapter 15), the first variables in the matrix system file will be the split variables, followed by ROWTYPE_, the case-identifier variable (if VIEW=CASE and the ID subcommand is used on PROXIMITIES), VARNAME_, and the distance variable(s). A full set of matrix materials is written for each split-file group defined by the split variable(s). A split variable cannot have the same name as any other variable written to the matrix system file. If split-file processing is in effect when a matrix is written, the same split file must be in effect when that matrix is read by any procedure. (See Chapter 13 for more information on matrix system files.)

Additional Statistics. The proximity matrices ALSCAL reads all have ROWTYPE_ values of PROX. No additional statistics are included with these matrix materials.

19.18
LIMITATIONS

The following limitations apply to procedure ALSCAL:

- You can name a maximum of 100 variables on the VARIABLES subcommand.
- You can scale a maximum of six dimensions.
- You cannot weight data.
- You can have no more than 32,767 values in a partition.

Syntax

ANOVA

```
ANOVA [VARIABLES=] varlist BY varlist(min,max)...
varlist(min,max) WITH varlist
 [/MISSING={EXCLUDE**}]
            {INCLUDE }
 [/FORMAT={LABELS**}]
           {NOLABELS}
 [/MAXORDERS={ALL** }]
             {n     }
             {NONE  }
 [/COVARIATES={FIRST**}]
               {WITH   }
               {AFTER  }
 [/METHOD={EXPERIMENTAL**}]
           {UNIQUE       }
           {HIERARCHICAL }
 [/STATISTICS=[MCA] [REG†] [MEAN] [ALL] [NONE]]
```

**Default if subcommand is omitted.
† REG (table of regression coefficients) is displayed only if the design is relevant.

Contents

20.1   OVERVIEW

20.2   OPERATION

20.3   VARIABLES Subcommand

20.4   Specifying Covariates

20.5   COVARIATES Subcommand

20.6   MAXORDERS Subcommand

20.7   METHOD Subcommand

20.8   Classic Experimental Approach

20.9   Regression Approach

20.10   Hierarchical Approach

20.11   Summary of Analysis Methods

20.12   STATISTICS Subcommand

20.13   Cell Means

20.14   Regression Coefficients for the Covariates

20.15   Multiple Classification Analysis

20.16   MISSING Subcommand

20.17   FORMAT Subcommand

20.18   LIMITATIONS

20

Chapter 20   ANOVA

Procedure ANOVA performs analysis of variance for factorial designs, with the default being the full factorial model. Although you can specify covariates, ANOVA does not permit a full analysis of covariance. You can choose among three methods for decomposing sums of squares, and you have control over the order of entry of covariates and factor main effects. You can also request a multiple-classification analysis table.

ANOVA is not intended for comprehensive analyses of variance or analyses of covariance. For multiple dependent variables, repeated measures designs, factor-by-covariate interactions in the analysis of covariance, or nested or nonfactorial designs, use the MANOVA procedure (see Chapter 33).

For one-way analysis of variance, you might prefer procedure ONEWAY (see Chapter 39). ONEWAY computes contrasts and multiple comparison tests. ONEWAY also provides a test for trends across categories of an interval-level independent variable and several homogeneity-of-variance test statistics. MEANS provides summary statistics and one-way analyses of variance when all independent variables are categorical (see Chapter 34). T-TEST can be used in the two-group situation, especially when a paired comparison is mandated (see Chapter 49).

20.1
OVERVIEW

Analysis of variance tests the hypothesis that the group means of the dependent variable are equal. The dependent variable is interval level, and one or more categorical variables define the groups. These categorical variables are termed *factors*. The ANOVA procedure also allows you to include continuous explanatory variables, termed *covariates*. When there are five or fewer factors, the default model is *full factorial,* meaning that all interaction terms are included. If there are more than five factors, only interaction terms up to order five are included.

Suppressing Interaction Effects. You can suppress the effects of various orders of interaction. (See Section 20.6.)

Specifying Covariates. You can introduce covariates into the model by means of the WITH keyword. (See Section 20.4.)

Order of Entry of Covariates. By default, SPSS-X processes covariates before main effects for factors. You can, however, tell SPSS-X to process covariates with or after main effects for factors. (See Section 20.5.)

Methods for Decomposing Sums of Squares. By default, the program uses what is termed the classic experimental approach. You can request either the regression approach or the hierarchical approach. (See Section 20.7.)

Cell Means. You can request means and counts for each dependent variable for groups defined by each factor and each combination of factors up to the fifth level. (See Section 20.13.)

Regression Coefficients for Covariates. You can request unstandardized regression coefficients for covariates. The coefficients are computed at the point where the covariates are entered into the equation. Thus, their values depend on the type of design you have specified. (See Section 20.14.)

Multiple Classification Analysis. You can request multiple classification analysis (MCA) results. In the MCA table, effects are expressed as deviations from the grand mean. The table includes a listing of unadjusted category effects for each factor, category effects adjusted for other factors, category effects adjusted for all factors and covariates, and eta and beta values. (See Section 20.15.)

Missing Values. By default, cases are deleted if they have missing values on any variable in your entire ANOVA variable list. You can tell SPSS-X to ignore missing-data indicators and to include all cases in the computations. (See Section 20.16.)

Formatting Options. ANOVA prints analysis of variance results using program format defaults. However, you can suppress both variable and value labels. (See Section 20.17.)

20.2
OPERATION

The only required subcommand on ANOVA is the VARIABLES subcommand, which specifies the variable list to be analyzed (see Section 20.3). The actual keyword VARIABLES can be omitted.

Sections 20.5 through 20.17 describe the optional subcommands. You can specify these subcommands in any order; separate them with slashes. You must first specify the variables to be used in the analysis, however, before you can specify any of the optional subcommands. For example, to include user-defined missing values in an analysis, specify

```
ANOVA PRESTIGE BY REGION(1,9)
     /MISSING=INCLUDE
```

20.3
VARIABLES Subcommand

The VARIABLES subcommand names the variable list, and the actual keyword VARIABLES is optional. If you use the VARIABLES keyword, an equals sign must precede the variable list.

The simplest ANOVA command contains one *analysis list* with a *dependent variable list* and a *factor variable list*. In the command

```
ANOVA  VARIABLES=PRESTIGE BY REGION(1,9)
```

PRESTIGE is the dependent variable and REGION is the factor, with minimum and maximum values of 1 and 9.

- A dependent variable list can name up to five dependent variables. If two or more variables are named, they are treated as a series of separate dependent variables, not as joint dependent variables.
- Value ranges are not specified for dependent variables.
- The factor variable list follows the keyword BY. Each analysis list can include only one BY keyword. Up to 10 integer-valued factors can be named, but a maximum of five interaction effects can be produced.
- Every factor variable must have a value range indicating its highest and lowest coded values. The values are separated by a comma and are enclosed in parentheses. If two or more factors have the same value range, the value range can be listed following the last factor to which it applies. Thus, the value range specification can follow each factor, each subset of factors, or the entire factor list.

- The value range specification need not correspond exactly to the actual range of values of a variable or variables in a factor list. Cases outside the specified range are automatically excluded from the analysis (see Section 20.7). However, bounds larger than the actual range needlessly increase the memory required to process the ANOVA command.

- The factor variables must be integers. If a noninteger variable is used as a factor, the values are truncated.

The command

```
ANOVA  VARIABLES=PRESTIGE BY REGION(1,9) SEX(1,2)
```

is a two-way analysis of variance with PRESTIGE as the dependent variable, and REGION and SEX as factors. By default, the model effects are the REGION and SEX main effects and the REGION by SEX interaction. The command

```
ANOVA VARIABLES=PRESTIGE,RINCOME BY REGION(1,9) SEX,RACE(1,2)
```

specifies two three-way analyses of variance: PRESTIGE by REGION, SEX, and RACE; and RINCOME by REGION, SEX, and RACE. Variables SEX and RACE have the same minimum and maximum values.

You can specify more than one design on the same ANOVA command by separating the analysis lists with a slash, as in

```
ANOVA VARIABLES=PRESTIGE BY REGION(1,9) SEX,RACE(1,2)
     /RINCOME BY SEX,RACE(1,2)
```

which specifies a three-way analysis of variance of PRESTIGE by REGION, SEX, and RACE and a two-way analysis of variance of RINCOME by SEX and RACE. The output from the three-way design is shown in Figure 20.3.

Figure 20.3   A full factorial model

```
              * * *  A N A L Y S I S   O F   V A R I A N C E  * * *

                 PRESTIGE RESP'S OCCUPATIONAL PRESTIGE SCORE
            by   REGION      REGION OF INTERVIEW
                 SEX
                 RACE

                                     Sum of                 Mean              Sig
     Source of Variation             Squares      DF        Square      F     of F

     Main Effects                   6700.371      10       670.037    4.007   .000
        REGION                      3569.855       8       446.232    2.669   .007
        SEX                            2.727       1         2.727     .016   .898
        RACE                        2476.838       1      2476.838   14.813   .000

     2-Way Interactions            4473.061       17       263.121    1.574   .068
        REGION    SEX              1365.014        8       170.627    1.020   .420
        REGION    RACE             2785.131        8       348.141    2.082   .036
        SEX       RACE              366.033        1       366.033    2.189   .140

     3-Way Interactions            1535.267        6       255.878    1.530   .167
        REGION    SEX    RACE      1535.267        6       255.878    1.530   .167

     Explained                    12708.698       33       385.112    2.303   .000

     Residual                     70729.394      423       167.209

     Total                        83438.092      456       182.978


     500 cases were processed.
     43 cases (8.6 pct) were missing.
```

20.4
Specifying Covariates

The *covariate list* can name up to 10 variables as covariates. The list follows the keyword WITH, and you do not specify a value range for the covariates. For example, the command

```
ANOVA VARIABLES=PRESTIGE BY REGION(1,9) SEX,RACE(1,2) WITH EDUC
```

produces the output shown in Figure 20.4.

Figure 20.4 A model with a covariate

```
            * * *   A N A L Y S I S   O F   V A R I A N C E   * * *

                PRESTIGE  RESP'S OCCUPATIONAL PRESTIGE SCORE
           by   REGION    REGION OF INTERVIEW
                SEX
                RACE
           with EDUC      HIGHEST YEAR SCHOOL  COMPLETED


                                   Sum of                   Mean                 Sig
    Source of Variation            Squares      DF          Square      F       of F
    Covariates                   23715.522       1        23715.522   191.701   .000
      EDUC                       23715.522       1        23715.522   191.701   .000

    Main Effects                  2708.380      10          270.838     2.189   .018
      REGION                      1202.574       8          150.322     1.215   .288
      SEX                           10.610       1           10.610      .086   .770
      RACE                        1425.415       1         1425.415    11.522   .001

    2-Way Interactions            3144.833      17          184.990     1.495   .092
      REGION   SEX               1349.220        8          168.653     1.363   .211
      REGION   RACE              1138.839        8          142.355     1.151   .328
      SEX      RACE               534.154        1          534.154     4.318   .038

    3-Way Interactions            1663.399       6          277.233     2.241   .039
      REGION   SEX    RACE       1663.399        6          277.233     2.241   .039

    Explained                    31232.135      34          918.592     7.425   .000

    Residual                     52205.957     422          123.711

    Total                        83438.092     456          182.978


    500 cases were processed.
    43 cases (8.6 pct) were missing.
```

20.5 COVARIATES Subcommand

By default, ANOVA assesses the covariates before it assesses the factor main effects.

The COVARIATES subcommand specifies the order for assessing blocks of covariates and factor main effects. The following keywords can be specified on the COVARIATES subcommand:

FIRST *Process covariates before main effects for factors.* This is the default if you omit the COVARIATES subcommand.

WITH *Process covariates concurrently with main effects for factors.*

AFTER *Process covariates after main effects for factors.*

Note that the order of entry is irrelevant when METHOD=UNIQUE (see Section 20.7).

20.6 MAXORDERS Subcommand

By default, ANOVA examines all the interaction effects up to and including the fifth order.

The MAXORDERS subcommand suppresses the effects of various orders of interaction. The following keywords can be specified on the MAXORDERS subcommand:

ALL *Examine all the interaction effects up to and including the fifth order.* This is the default if you omit the MAXORDERS subcommand.

n *Examine all the interaction effects up to and including the n-order effect.* For example, if you specify MAXORDERS=3, ANOVA examines all the interaction effects up to and including the third order. All higher order interaction sums of squares are pooled into the error term.

NONE *Delete all interaction terms from the model.* All interaction sums of squares are pooled into the error sum of squares.

The keyword NONE suppresses all interaction terms so only main effects and covariate effects appear in the ANOVA table, with interaction sums of squares pooled into the error (residual) sum of squares. For example, to suppress all interaction effects, specify

```
ANOVA VARIABLES=PRESTIGE BY REGION(1,9) SEX,RACE(1,2)
      /MAXORDERS=NONE
```

The resulting main effects model is shown in Figure 20.6.

Figure 20.6   A main effects model

```
          * * *   A N A L Y S I S   O F   V A R I A N C E   * * *

              PRESTIGE   RESP'S OCCUPATIONAL PRESTIGE SCORE
        by    REGION     REGION OF INTERVIEW
              SEX
              RACE


                              Sum of                  Mean                 Sig
Source of Variation           Squares      DF         Square        F      of F

Main Effects                 6700.371      10        670.037      3.894    .000
   REGION                    3569.855       8        446.232      2.594    .009
   SEX                          2.727       1          2.727       .016    .900
   RACE                      2476.838       1       2476.838     14.395    .000

Explained                    6700.371      10        670.037      3.894    .000

Residual                    76737.721     446        172.058

Total                       83438.092     456        182.978


500 cases were processed.
43 cases (8.6 pct) were missing.
```

20.7
METHOD Subcommand

By default, ANOVA uses the *classic experimental approach* for decomposing sums of squares. Optionally, you can request the *regression approach* or the *hierarchical approach*.

The METHOD subcommand controls the method for decomposing sums of squares. The following keywords can be specified on the METHOD subcommand:

EXPERIMENTAL   *Classic experimental approach.* This is the default if you omit the METHOD subcommand.

UNIQUE   *Regression approach.* UNIQUE overrides the WITH and AFTER keywords on the COVARIATES subcommand. All effects are assessed for their partial contribution, so order is irrelevant. The MCA and MEAN specifications on the STATISTICS subcommand are not available with the regression approach.

HIERARCHICAL   *Hierarchical approach.*

20.8
Classic Experimental Approach

This is the default if you omit the METHOD subcommand. Each type of effect is assessed separately in the following order (unless you specify WITH or AFTER on the COVARIATES subcommand):

- Effects of covariates.
- Main effects of factors.
- Two-way interaction effects.
- Three-way interaction effects.
- Four-way interaction effects.
- Five-way interaction effects.

The effects within each type are adjusted for all other effects in that type and also for the effects of all prior types (see Table 20.10).

20.9
Regression Approach

All effects are assessed simultaneously, with each effect adjusted for all other effects in the model. Some restrictions apply to the use of the regression approach:

- The lowest specified categories of all the independent variables must have a marginal frequency of at least one, since the lowest specified category is used as the reference category. If this rule is not followed, no ANOVA table is produced, and a message is printed identifying the first offending variable.

- Given an *n*-way crosstabulation of the independent variables, there must be no empty cells defined by the lowest specified category of any of the independent variables. If this restriction is violated, one or more levels of interaction effects are suppressed, and a warning message is issued. However, this constraint does not apply to categories defined for an independent variable which do not occur in the data. For example, given two independent variables, each with categories of 1, 2, and 4, the (1,1), (1,2), (1,4), (2,1), and (4,1) cells must not be empty. The (1,3), (2,3), (3,3), (4,3), (3,1), (3,2), and (3,4) cells are empty by definition, and the (2,2), (2,4), (4,2), and (4,4) cells may be empty, although the degrees of freedom will be reduced accordingly.

To comply with these restrictions, specify precisely the lowest nonempty category of each independent variable. Specifying a value range of (0,9) for a variable that actually has values of 1 through 9 results in an error and no ANOVA table is produced.

20.10
Hierarchical Approach

The hierarchical approach differs from the classic experimental approach only in the way it handles covariate and factor main effects. In the hierarchical approach, the factor main effects and the covariate effects are assessed hierarchically; the factor main effects are adjusted only for the factor main effects already assessed, and the covariate effects are adjusted only for the covariates already assessed. The order in which the factors are listed on the ANOVA command determines the order in which they are assessed.

The command

```
ANOVA VARIABLES=Y BY A,B,C(0,3)
```

specifies three factor variables: A, B, and C. Table 20.10 summarizes the three approaches with respect to this example.

With the *default classic experimental* approach, each main effect is assessed with the two other main effects held constant, and two-way interactions are assessed with all main effects and other two-way interactions held constant. The three-way interaction is assessed with all main effects and two-way interactions held constant.

With the *regression approach,* each factor or interaction is assessed with all other factors and interactions held constant.

With the *hierarchical approach,* the order in which the factors and covariates are listed on the ANOVA command determines the order in which they are assessed in the hierarchical analysis.

Table 20.10   Terms adjusted for under each option

Effect	Experimental	Unique (Regression)	Hierarchical
A	B,C	ALL OTHERS	NONE
B	A,C	ALL OTHERS	A
C	A,B	ALL OTHERS	A,B
AB	A,B,C,AC,BC	ALL OTHERS	A,B,C,AC,BC
AC	A,B,C,AB,BC	ALL OTHERS	A,B,C,AB,BC
BC	A,B,C,AB,AC	ALL OTHERS	A,B,C,AB,AC
ABC	A,B,C,AB,AC,BC	ALL OTHERS	A,B,C,AB,AC,BC

20.11
Summary of Analysis Methods

Methods for decomposing sums of squares are discussed in Section 20.7, and the order of entry of covariates is discussed in Section 20.5. Table 20.11 summarizes what happens when you invoke various exclusive combinations of these options and their defaults.

Table 20.11   Combinations of COVARIATES and METHOD subcommands

	Assessments between types of effects	Assessments within the same type of effect
Default	*Covariates* THEN *Factors* THEN *Interactions*	*Covariates:* adjust for all other covariates *Factors:* adjust for covariates and all other factors *Interactions:* adjust for covariates, factors, and all other interactions of the same and lower orders
COVARIATES=WITH	*Factors* and *Covariates* concurrently THEN *Interactions*	*Covariates:* adjust for factors and all other covariates *Factors:* adjust for covariates and all other factors *Interactions:* adjust for covariates, factors, and all other interactions of the same and lower orders
COVARIATES=AFTER	*Factors* THEN *Covariates* THEN *Interactions*	*Factors:* adjust for all other factors *Covariates:* adjust for factors and all other covariates *Interactions:* adjust for covariates, factors, and all other interactions of the same and lower orders
METHOD=UNIQUE	*Covariates, Factors,* and *Interactions* simultaneously	*Covariates:* adjust for factors, interactions, and all other covariates *Factors:* adjust for covariates, interactions, and all other factors *Interactions:* adjust for covariates, factors, and all other interactions
METHOD=HIERARCHICAL	*Covariates* THEN *Factors* THEN *Interactions*	*Covariates:* adjust for covariates that are preceding in the list *Factors:* adjust for covariates and factors preceding in the list *Interactions:* adjust for covariates, factors, and all other interactions of the same and lower orders
COVARIATES=WITH and METHOD=HIERARCHICAL	*Factors* and *Covariates* concurrently THEN *Interactions*	*Factors:* adjust only for preceding factors *Covariates:* adjust for factors and preceding covariates *Interactions:* adjust for covariates, factors, and all other interactions of the same and lower orders
COVARIATES=AFTER and METHOD=HIERARCHICAL	*Factors* THEN *Covariates* THEN *Interactions*	*Factors:* adjust only for preceding factors *Covariates:* adjust for factors and preceding covariates *Interactions:* adjust for covariates, factors, and all other interactions of the same and lower orders

20.12
STATISTICS Subcommand

By default, ANOVA calculates only the statistics needed for analysis of variance. Optionally, you can request a means and counts table, unstandardized regression coefficients, and multiple classification analysis.

The STATISTICS subcommand requests additional statistics for ANOVA. You can specify the STATISTICS subcommand by itself or with one or more keywords.

If you specify the STATISTICS subcommand with no keywords, ANOVA calculates MEAN and REG (each defined below). If you include a keyword or keywords on the STATISTICS subcommand, ANOVA calculates only the addi-

ANNOTATED EXAMPLE FOR ANOVA

The example illustrating the use of ANOVA is a three-way analysis of variance with one covariate. The data are 500 cases from the 1980 General Social Survey. The variables are

- PRESTIGE—the respondent's occupational prestige scale score. PRESTIGE is the dependent variable.
- EDUC—the respondent's education in years.
- RACE—the respondent's race, coded 1=WHITE, 2=BLACK, and 3=OTHER.
- SEX—the respondent's sex, coded 1=MALE and 2=FEMALE.
- REGION—The respondent's residence, coded as one of nine regions.

The task is twofold: determine the degree to which the American occupational structure differs across race, sex, and region; and measure the effect of the respondent's educational level, since education might prove to be a concomitant influence. The SPSS-X commands are

```
GET    FILE=GSS80/KEEP PRESTIGE EDUC RACE SEX REGION
ANOVA VARIABLES=PRESTIGE BY REGION(1,9) SEX,RACE(1,2) WITH EDUC
      /STATISTICS=REG
      /METHOD=HIERARCHICAL
```

- The GET command defines the data to SPSS-X and selects the variables needed for the analysis (see Chapter 6).
- The ANOVA command names PRESTIGE as the dependent variable; REGION, SEX, and RACE as the factors; and EDUC as the covariate. The minimum and maximum values for REGION are 1 and 9, and the minimum and maximum values for both SEX and RACE are 1 and 2. Since variable RACE actually has values 1, 2, and 3, cases with value 3 are eliminated from the model.
- The STATISTICS subcommand requests the regression coefficient for the covariate EDUC (see Section 20.14).
- The METHOD subcommand requests the hierarchical approach for decomposing sums of squares. The covariate EDUC is assessed first to establish statistical control. Then the effect of REGION is assessed; next, the effect of SEX adjusted for REGION; and next, the effect of RACE adjusted for REGION and SEX. Finally, each of the interaction effects is assessed (see Section 20.7).

The ANOVA output from this job includes the following standard items of information:

Source of Variation. All interactions are printed by default. In this example, the sources of variation are the covariate, the main effects, the three two-way interactions, the three-way interaction, plus the explained, residual, and total variation.

Sum of Squares. The sum of squares associated with each effect is in part a function of the analysis of variance method chosen. In this example, the *hierarchical approach* was requested. Compare this output to the sum of squares shown in Figure 20.4, where the default classical experimental approach was used to analyze the same ANOVA model. See Section 20.7 for a further discussion of analysis of variance approaches available in ANOVA.

Degrees of Freedom (DF). The degrees of freedom associated with each effect.

Mean Square. The sum of squares divided by the degrees of freedom.

F and Significance of F. The F statistic and the significance level of the F statistic for each effect.

Finally, SPSS-X prints the number of cases processed as well as the number of missing cases. By default, cases with missing values on any of the variables named are excluded from the analysis. In the example job, 43 cases (8.6 percent of the data) are excluded due to missing values (Section 20.16) or values out of range (Section 20.3) for the RACE variable.

Analysis of variance output

```
          PRESTIGE  RESP'S OCCUPATIONAL PRESTIGE SCORE
     by   REGION    REGION OF INTERVIEW
          SEX
          RACE
   with EDUC     HIGHEST YEAR SCHOOL  COMPLETED
```

Source of Variation	Sum of Squares	DF	Mean Square	F	Sig of F
Covariates	23715.522	1	23715.522	191.701	.000
EDUC	23715.522	1	23715.522	191.701	.000
Main Effects	2708.380	10	270.838	2.189	.018
REGION	1260.552	8	157.569	1.274	.255
SEX	22.413	1	22.413	.181	.671
RACE	1425.415	1	1425.415	11.522	.001
2-Way Interactions	3144.833	17	184.990	1.495	.092
REGION SEX	1349.220	8	168.653	1.363	.211
REGION RACE	1138.839	8	142.355	1.151	.328
SEX RACE	534.154	1	534.154	4.318	.038
3-Way Interactions	1663.399	6	277.233	2.241	.039
REGION SEX RACE	1663.399	6	277.233	2.241	.039
Explained	31232.135	34	918.592	7.425	.000
Residual	52205.957	422	123.711		
Total	83438.092	456	182.978		

```
Covariate   Raw Regression Coefficient

EDUC          2.331


500 cases were processed.
43 cases (8.6 pct) were missing.
```

tional statistics you request. The following keywords can be specified on the STATISTICS subcommand:

MEAN   *Means and counts table.* This statistic is not available with METHOD= UNIQUE. (See Section 20.13.)

REG   *Unstandardized regression coefficients.* Prints unstandardized regression coefficients for the covariates. (See Section 20.14.)

MCA   *Multiple classification analysis.* The MCA table is not produced when METHOD=UNIQUE. (See Section 20.15.)

ALL   *Means and counts table, unstandardized regression coefficients, and multiple classification analysis.*

NONE   *No additional statistics.* This is the default if you omit the STATISTICS subcommand.

All ANOVA output, except that produced by STATISTICS=MEANS, fits in 80 columns. If you want to limit the width of the means and counts table, use the SET WIDTH command (Chapter 4).

20.13
Cell Means

STATISTICS=MEAN prints the means and counts table. The means and counts of each dependent variable are printed for each cell as defined by the factors and combinations of factors. This statistic is not available with METHOD=UNIQUE. (See Section 20.7). The command

```
ANOVA VARIABLES=PRESTIGE BY REGION(1,9) SEX,RACE(1,2)
     /STATISTICS=MEAN
```

produces the cell means and counts table shown in Figure 20.13 (only the first page of the output is shown).

For each dependent variable, a separate table is printed for each effect, showing the means and cell counts for each combination of values of the factors that define the effect, ignoring all other factors. If you use the MAXORDERS subcommand to suppress higher order interactions, cell means corresponding to suppressed interaction terms are not printed. The means printed are the observed means in each cell, and they are produced only for dependent variables, not for covariates.

Figure 20.13   Part of a means and counts table

```
                        * * *  C E L L   M E A N S  * * *
                     PRESTIGE  RESP'S OCCUPATIONAL PRESTIGE SCORE
                 BY REGION     REGION OF INTERVIEW
                     SEX
                     RACE

TOTAL POPULATION
      39.52
    (   457)

REGION
          1          2          3          4          5          6          7          8          9
      38.13      36.72      39.35      40.26      39.57      28.77      40.72      42.58      45.15
    (   31) (     93) (     97) (     39) (     56) (     13) (     47) (     33) (     48)

SEX
          1          2
      39.81      39.24
    (   223) (    234)

RACE
          1          2
      40.49      32.45
    (   402) (     55)


          SEX
                     1          2
REGION
          1      38.33      38.00
               (   12) (     19)

          2      36.27      37.20
               (   48) (     45)

          3      36.74      41.71
               (   46) (     51)

          4      41.70      38.74
               (   20) (     19)
```

20.14
Regression Coefficients for the Covariates

STATISTICS=REG requests the unstandardized regression coefficients for the covariates. The regression coefficients are computed at the point where the covariates are entered into the equation. Thus, their values depend on the type of design specified or used as a default by the COVARIATES or METHOD subcommands (see Section 20.7 for discussion of the METHOD subcommand). The coefficients are printed immediately below the ANOVA summary table in the output. If REG were requested on the STATISTICS subcommand for the analysis shown in Figure 20.4, the regression coefficient for EDUC, which would follow the ANOVA information, would appear as shown in Figure 20.14.

Figure 20.14 The regression coefficient

```
Covariate    Raw Regression Coefficient

EDUC            2.331


500 cases were processed.
43 cases (8.6 pct) were missing.
```

20.15
Multiple Classification Analysis

STATISTICS=MCA produces MCA output, which consists of the grand mean of the dependent variable and a table of category means for each factor expressed as deviations from the grand mean. The latter are sometimes termed *treatment effects*. The category means expressed as deviations convey the magnitude of the effect of each category within a factor (Andrews, 1973). The command

```
ANOVA VARIABLES=PRESTIGE BY REGION(1,9) SEX,RACE(1,2) WITH EDUC
     /STATISTICS=MCA
```

produces the MCA table shown in Figure 20.15.

Figure 20.15 The MCA table

```
* * *   M U L T I P L E    C L A S S I F I C A T I O N    A N A L Y S I S   * * *

                PRESTIGE RESP'S OCCUPATIONAL PRESTIGE SCORE
         BY     REGION   REGION OF INTERVIEW
                SEX
                RACE
         WITH EDUC       HIGHEST YEAR SCHOOL  COMPLETED


GRAND MEAN =    39.52                                    ADJUSTED FOR
                                                         INDEPENDENTS
                                          UNADJUSTED     + COVARIATES
VARIABLE + CATEGORY              N        DEV'N  ETA     DEV'N  BETA

REGION
   1 NEW ENGLAND                 31       -1.39           1.73
   2 MIDDLE ATLANTIC             93       -2.80          -2.53
   3 E. NOR. CENTRAL             97        -.17           -.53
   4 W. NOR. CENTRAL             39         .74            .55
   5 SOUTH ATLANTIC              56         .05           1.02
   6 E. SOU. CENTRAL             13      -10.75          -2.02
   7 W. SOU. CENTRAL             47        1.20           1.07
   8 MOUNTAIN                    33        3.06            .25
   9 PACIFIC                     48        5.63           2.57
                                                 .22            .12


SEX
   1 MALE                       223         .29            .16
   2 FEMALE                     234        -.28           -.15
                                                 .02            .01


RACE
   1 WHITE                      402         .97            .67
   2 BLACK                       55       -7.06          -4.91
                                                 .19            .13


MULTIPLE R SQUARED                                      .317
MULTIPLE R                                              .563
```

In an MCA table, deviation values are printed in three forms: unadjusted, adjusted for main effects of other factors, and adjusted for main effects of other factors and covariates (if applicable). The adjusted values show the effect of a certain category within a given factor after variation due to other factors—and sometimes other covariates—has been taken into account.

The results of the MCA table are affected by the form you specify for the analysis (or allow ANOVA to run by default). For example, in Figure 20.15, unadjusted values and values adjusted for independents and covariates print in the table. Values adjusted for independents don't print because the COVARIATES subcommand was omitted from the ANOVA specification. ANOVA therefore ran the default order for entering covariates, which is COVARIATES= FIRST. With covariates present in the analysis, you must specify

```
ANOVA VARIABLES=PRESTIGE BY REGION(1,9) SEX,RACE(1,2) WITH EDUC
      /STATISTICS=MCA
      /COVARIATES=AFTER
```

or

```
ANOVA VARIABLES=PRESTIGE BY REGION(1,9) SEX,RACE(1,2) WITH EDUC
      /STATISTICS=MCA
      /COVARIATES=AFTER
      /METHOD=HIERARCHICAL
```

or

```
ANOVA VARIABLES=PRESTIGE BY REGION(1,9) SEX,RACE(1,2) WITH EDUC
      /STATISTICS=MCA
      /COVARIATES=WITH
      /METHOD=HIERARCHICAL
```

to obtain a complete MCA table.

In the above analysis, if you specify a model in which factors are not processed first, effects adjusted only for factors do not appear in the MCA table. If you specify METHOD=UNIQUE, no MCA table is produced. Ordinarily, if the MCA table is of interest, interaction terms should not be statistically significant.

An MCA table contains several measures of association. First, a correlation ratio, the eta statistic, is associated with the set of unadjusted category effects for each factor in the MCA table; the square of eta indicates the proportion of variance explained by a given factor (all categories considered). Beta is a statistic associated with the adjusted category effects for each factor. More specifically, beta is a standardized regression coefficient in the sense used in multiple regression. Finally, multiple R appears at the bottom of the MCA table. Just as in multiple regression, this R can be squared to indicate the variance in the dependent variable "accounted for" by all factors and covariates.

20.16
MISSING Subcommand

By default, a case that is missing for any variable named in the analysis list is deleted for all analyses specified by that list.

Use the MISSING subcommand to ignore missing-data indicators and to include all cases in the computations. Two keywords can be specified on the MISSING subcommand:

EXCLUDE   *Exclude missing data.* This is the default if you omit the MISSING subcommand.

INCLUDE   *Include user-defined missing data.*

20.17
FORMAT Subcommand   By default, ANOVA prints variable or value labels if they have been defined.

Use the FORMAT subcommand to suppress variable and value labels. Two keywords can be specified on the FORMAT subcommand:

LABELS   *Print variable and value labels.* This is the default if you omit the FORMAT subcommand.

NOLABELS   *Suppress variable and value labels.*

20.18
LIMITATIONS   The following limitations apply to procedure ANOVA:

- A maximum of 5 ANOVA analysis lists.
- A maximum of 5 dependent variables per analysis list.
- A maximum of 10 independent variables per analysis list.
- A maximum of 10 covariates per analysis list.
- A maximum of 5 interaction levels.
- A maximum of 25 value labels per variable displayed in the MCA table.
- The combined number of categories for all factors in an analysis list plus the number of covariates must be less than the sample size.

Syntax

AUTORECODE

```
AUTORECODE VARIABLES=varlist
 /INTO new varlist
 [/DESCENDING]
 [/PRINT]
```

Contents

21.1   OVERVIEW
21.2   OPERATION
21.3   VARIABLES Subcommand
21.4   INTO Subcommand
21.5   PRINT Subcommand
21.6   DESCENDING Subcommand
21.7   Missing Values

21

Chapter 21   AUTORECODE

The AUTORECODE procedure recodes the values of both string and numeric variables to consecutive integers and puts the new values into a different variable. It is similar to the RECODE command because it recodes the values of variables (see Chapter 7). However, unlike RECODE, AUTORECODE automatically assigns new target values into which the given values will be recoded. In RECODE, the user must specify these target values. AUTORECODE does force a pass of the active file.

21.1
OVERVIEW

The AUTORECODE command enhances your ability to recode long string variables into numeric variables that then can be incorporated into the SPSS-X TABLES procedure. (See the SPSS-X TABLES manual for more information.) AUTORECODE also makes it easier to recode the values of factor variables to consecutive integers, which is the form required by MANOVA, and which reduces the amount of workspace needed by other statistical procedures like ANOVA.

The values of each variable to be recoded are sorted and then assigned numeric values. The value 1 is assigned to the lowest nonmissing value of the original variable, the value 2 to the second lowest nonmissing value, and so on for each value of the original variable. If DESCENDING is specified, the values of the variable are sorted and AUTORECODE assigns the value 1 to the highest nonmissing value, the value 2 to the second highest nonmissing value, and so on. Because the values of a variable to be recoded are sorted before they are assigned new values, AUTORECODE does *not* necessarily preserve the order of values as they were entered in the command file.

Ordering of Values. By default, the values recoded by AUTORECODE are numbered so the lowest numeric value recoded is assigned the value 1, the second lowest, 2, and so on. Optionally, you can request that the values be numbered in the reverse order, so the value with the highest numeric value is assigned 1. (See Section 21.6.)

Printing the Recoded Variables. You can print the values of the original and recoded variables. (See Section 21.5.)

Missing Values. Missing values are recoded into missing values higher than any nonmissing values, with their order preserved. (See Section 21.7.)

21.2
OPERATION

The minimum specification for AUTORECODE is two subcommands: VARIABLES, which specifies the variables to be recoded; and INTO, which names the target variables where the new values are stored. All subcommands must be separated by slashes.

SPLIT FILES specifications in effect before the AUTORECODE command will be ignored. (See Chapter 15.) However, SELECT IF specifications can precede AUTORECODE. (See Chapter 11.)

21.3
VARIABLES Subcommand

The required VARIABLES subcommand names the variable list to be recoded. The actual keyword VARIABLES is optional. The equals sign is also optional, unless the first name in the variable list begins with the letters *VAR*. For example, in the specification

```
AUTORECODE VARIABLES=VAR1 VAR2 VAR3
        /INTO=NEWVAR1 NEWVAR2 NEWVAR3
```

VARIABLES= is required. If VAR1, VAR2, and VAR3 are consecutive in the active file, and you refer to them with the TO convention, you can omit the keyword VARIABLES=. For example,

```
AUTORECODE VAR1 TO VAR3
        /INTO=NEWVAR1 NEWVAR2 NEWVAR3
```

In this example, note also that the TO convention can be used to refer to consecutive variables on the active file. You can specify the variable list to be recoded from any user-defined variable in the active file. The number of variables named must equal the number of target variables listed on the INTO subcommand. The VARIABLES subcommand must be specified before the INTO subcommand.

AUTORECODE stores values from variables named on the VARIABLES subcommand in target variables listed on the INTO subcommand. The original variables are left untouched. Newly created variables are assigned the same variable labels as the original variables. Use the VARIABLE LABELS command following AUTORECODE if you want to change them. Value labels are automatically generated for each value on the new variable. If the original value had a label, that label will be used for the corresponding new value. If the original value did not have a label, the old value itself is used as the value label for the new value. The old value is formatted according to its defined print format to create the new value label. You cannot recode a variable into itself; more generally, target variable names must not duplicate any variable names already in the file.

21.4
INTO Subcommand

The required INTO subcommand names the target variables—the variables that will store the new values. The number of variables named must equal the number of variables listed on the VARIABLES subcommand. The equals sign on the INTO subcommand is optional.

You can use the TO convention to generate names for target variables. To do so, specify an alphabetic prefix for the new names and a range of associated sequence numbers, as in

```
AUTORECODE VARIABLES=VARA VARB VARC
        /INTO=VAR1 TO VAR3
```

The AUTORECODE command assigns sequentially the names implied by this inclusive list to the variables referenced in the old variable list.

21.5
PRINT Subcommand

The optional PRINT subcommand prints a correspondence table of values for the original value and the new value. The complete value label is also printed.

By default, or if the width is set to less than 132, the table is formatted to print in 80 columns. If the width has been previously set to 132 (by the SET WIDTH command), then the output will be formatted to print in 132 columns.

Only the first 18 characters of the values for the original variable and the first 48 characters of the value labels for the new variable are printed.

21.6
DESCENDING
Subcommand

The optional DESCENDING subcommand assigns the values to new variables in descending order (from highest to lowest) rather than in ascending order, which is the default. The largest value is assigned 1, the second largest, 2, and so on.

21.7
Missing Values

Missing values are recoded into missing values higher than any nonmissing values, with their order preserved. For example, if the original variable has 10 nonmissing values, the value of the first missing value would be recoded to 11. The value 11 would then be a missing value on the new variable.

ANNOTATED EXAMPLES FOR AUTORECODE

Example 1

Because the TABLES procedure truncates string variables to eight characters, AUTORECODE is extremely useful if you want the whole values to appear in your table. For example, consider the string variable COMPANY, which contains the names of various hypothetical cat food companies. First you can use the AUTORECODE command to recode COMPANY into a numeric variable called RCOMPANY. Figure A shows the correspondence table from the PRINT subcommand for the original variable and the new variable. Then you can use the recoded new variable, RCOMPANY, in the TABLES procedure to produce a table of sales figures for each cat food company, similar to the one in Figure B. Here the variable RCOMPANY is used in the banner. Note that the name of each company was not truncated, and that the entire name of each company was used in the TABLE. The commands that produced this table are shown below.

```
DATA LIST / COMPANY 1-21 (a) SALES 24-28
BEGIN DATA
CATFOOD JOY              10000
OLD FASHIONED CATFOOD    11200
BOSTON CATFOOD           20800
RICHARD'S CATFOODS       11500
CHICAGO CATFOODS, INC.   12300
NEW YORK CATFOOD          9700
PRIME CATFOOD            10900
CHOICE CATFOOD           14600
rest of data here
END DATA
AUTORECODE VARIABLES = COMPANY
           /INTO = RCOMPANY
           /PRINT
TABLES     TABLE = SALES BY RCOMPANY
           /TTITLE = 'CATFOOD SALES BY COMPANY'
```

A PRINT subcommand output

```
            COMPANY   RCOMPANY
         Old Value New Value  Value Label

BOSTON CATFOOD              1   BOSTON CATFOOD
CATFOOD JOY                2   CATFOOD JOY
CHICAGO CATFOODS, INC      3   CHICAGO CATFOODS, INC
CHOICE CATFOOD             4   CHOICE CATFOOD
NEW YORK CATFOOD           5   NEW YORK CATFOOD
OLD FASHIONED CATFOOD      6   OLD FASHIONED CATFOOD
PRIME CATFOOD              7   PRIME CATFOOD
RICHARD'S CATFOODS         8   RICHARD'S CATFOODS
```

**Annotated Examples for
AUTORECODE** *continued*

B TABLES output with recoded variable

CATFOOD SALES BY COMPANY

	RCOMPANY							
	BOSTON CATFOOD	CATFOOD JOY	CHICAGO CATFOODS, INC	CHOICE CATFOOD	NEW YORK CATFOOD	OLD FASHIONED CATFOOD	PRIME CATFOOD	RICHARD'S CATFOODS
SALES								
9700					1			
10000		1						
10700					1			
10900							1	
11000		1						
11200						1		
11500								1
11600					1			
12300			1					
12500			1					1
12600				1				
12700							1	
12900							1	
13200						1		
13300			2					
13400								1
13800				1				
14100		1						
14600				1				
14700						1		
15900							1	
16800	2							
17200						1		
17600				1				
18300								1
19100					1			
20800	1							
21300	1							
22500		1						

Example 2

In statistical procedures, empty cells can reduce performance and increase memory requirements. This means that if factor variables contains empty categories, you should recode the variables into consecutive values. For example, if factor REGION only has five nonempty categories, represented by the numeric codes 1, 4, 6, 14 and 20, this problem would require 4429 bytes of memory:

```
ANOVA Y BY REGION (1,20)
```

In contrast, the amount of memory required by ANOVA if the variable is recoded into a new variable called RREGION, with consecutive values 1, 2, 3, 4, and 5, is 449 bytes.

```
ANOVA Y BY RREGION (1,5)
```

Figure C shows the correspondence table between the original variable and the new variable. The command that created this new variable is shown below. The original value labels are preserved with new values.

```
AUTORECODE VARIABLES=region
           /INTO=rregion
           /PRINT
```

C PRINT subcommand output

```
REGION    RREGION
Old Value New Value  Value Label

    1         1      northeast
    4         2      midwest
    6         3      northwest
   14         4      southeast
   20         5      southwest
```

Example 3   Since MANOVA requires consecutive integer values for factor levels, you need to recode noninteger values for factors into consecutive integers. In addition, if you have a wide value range for a factor, and most of the categories are empty, you must recode the variable to consecutive values. The AUTORECODE command allows you to recode these variables automatically, thus avoiding several RE-CODE specifications. For example, you could recode the six-value alphanumeric variable RELIGION, with values 'CATH', 'PROT', 'JEW', 'NONE', 'OTHER', and ' ' to numeric values 1, 2, 3, 4, 5, 6 and store the recoded values into a new variable called NRELIG. This new variable could then be used as a factor in MANOVA, as in:

```
DATA LIST / RELIGION 1-8 (A)
MISSING VALUES RELIGION (' ')
BEGIN DATA
CATHOLIC
PROTEST
JEWISH
NONE
OTHER
END DATA

AUTORECODE VARIABLES=RELIGION
           /INTO=NRELIG
           /PRINT
MANOVA Y BY NRELIG(1,5)
```

Figure D shows the correspondence table from PRINT between the old and new variables. The value ' ' on both RELIGION and NRELIG is marked with an M to indicate it is missing. It is recoded to the largest value, 6, on NRELIG.

D PRINT subcommand output

```
 RELIGION  NRELIGIO
Old Value New Value  Value Label

 CATHOLIC        1   CATHOLIC
 JEWISH          2   JEWISH
 NONE            3   NONE
 OTHER           4   OTHER
 PROTEST         5   PROTESTA
        M       6M
```

Syntax

BOX-JENKINS

```
BOX-JENKINS VARIABLE=varlist
 {IDENTIFY}
/{ESTIMATE}  at least one is required
 {FORECAST}
```

subcommands controlling identification and model specification:

```
   {LOG[={0       }]                        }
   {      {constant}                        }
[/{                                         }]
   {POWER=(power[,{0       }])              }
   {             {constant}                 }

[/DIFFERENCE=m [THRU n [BY {1}]]]
                           {i}

[/SDIFFERENCE=m [THRU n [BY {1}]] /PERIOD={1}]
                            {i}            {n}

[/LAG={25}]       {P }                  [/{MALAG}=n,n, ...]
      {n }  [/{Q }={0          }]          {ARLAG}
           {SP}  {m [THRU n]}
           {SQ}
```

subcommands controlling estimation:

```
[/{CONSTANT }] [/{NCENTER}] [/ITERATE={40}]
  {NCONSTANT}    {CENTER }             {n }
[/FPR={5}] [/BFR={0}] [/{NTEST}]
      {n }        {n }   {TEST }
   {TCON}
[/{PCON}=(n)]    conditional upon CONSTANT
   {ICON}
   {TP }
   {PP }         conditional upon P
   {IP }
   {TQ }
   {PQ }         conditional upon Q
[/{IQ }=(n, ...)]
   {TSP}
   {PSP}         conditional upon SP
   {ISP}
   {TSQ}
   {PSQ}         conditional upon SQ
   {ISQ}
```

subcommands controlling forecasting:

```
[/ORIGIN=m [THRU n]] [/LEAD={12}] [/CIN={95}]
                            {n }         {n }
[/FCON=(n)]              conditional upon CONSTANT
   {FP }                 conditional upon P
   {FQ }                 conditional upon Q
[/{FSP}=(n, ...)]        conditional upon SP
   {FSQ}                 conditional upon SQ
```

subcommands controlling display:

```
[/PRINT=[ACF] [PACF] [ACVF] [SER] [TSER]
        [DSER] [RESID] [RACF]]
[/PLOT=[ACF] [PACF] [SER] [TSER] [FCF] [FLF]
       [CIN] [DSER] [RESID] [RACF]]
```

Contents

22.1	OVERVIEW
22.2	OPERATION
22.3	VARIABLE Subcommand
22.4	Step-of-Analysis Subcommands
22.5	PLOT Subcommand
22.6	Transformation Subcommands
22.7	LOG and POWER Subcommands
22.8	Differencing Subcommands
22.9	DIFFERENCE Subcommand
22.10	SDIFFERENCE and PERIOD Subcommands
22.11	LAG Subcommand
22.12	Parameters Subcommands
22.13	Estimation Subcommands
22.14	CONSTANT and NCONSTANT Keywords
22.15	CENTER and NCENTER Keywords
22.16	ITERATE Subcommand
22.17	BFR Subcommand
22.18	TEST and NTEST Keywords
22.19	FPR Subcommand
22.20	Perturbation Increment Subcommands
22.21	Tolerance Subcommands
22.22	Initial Estimates Subcommands
22.23	Forecast Subcommands
22.24	ORIGIN Subcommand
22.25	LEAD Subcommand
22.26	CIN Subcommand
22.27	Final Estimates Subcommands
22.28	PRINT Subcommand
22.29	PLOT Subcommand

22

Chapter 22   BOX-JENKINS

The BOX-JENKINS procedure can be used to fit and forecast time series data by means of a general class of statistical models (Box & Jenkins, 1976). An observation at a given time is modeled as a function of its past values and/or current and past values of the random shocks, both at nonseasonal and seasonal lags. BOX-JENKINS will model a variable with observations equally spaced in time and no missing values. Sometimes it may be necessary before modeling the series to transform the data by taking the log or power transformation of the series or differencing the series on a seasonal or nonseasonal basis.

22.1
OVERVIEW

The modeling of time series data is usually done in three steps. First, *identify* a tentative model for a series. Second, *estimate* the parameters and examine diagnostic statistics and plots. Third, if the model is deemed acceptable, *forecast* using the model. If the model is inadequate, other models may be examined until an acceptable fit is obtained, at which time forecasts can be computed. Thus, fitting and forecasting of a given time series typically entails several computer runs. For this reason, SPSS-X BOX-JENKINS syntax is designed for flexibility so that you can request sufficient information easily and efficiently.

Specifying the Time Series. The time series data must be organized with each time point coded on a separate case. Specify the variable containing the time series measurement using the VARIABLE subcommand. (See Section 22.3.)

Specifying the Step of Analysis. Three subcommands specify the step of the analysis. At least one of these subcommands is required. (See Section 22.4.)

Transforming the Time Series. You can specify a log or power transformation of your series. (See Sections 22.6 and 22.7.)

Differencing the Series. You can difference the series at different degrees or for a seasonal component at specified periods. (See Sections 22.8 through 22.10.)

Specifying the Parameters. You can specify any number of autoregressive parameters, moving average parameters, seasonal autoregressive parameters, and seasonal moving average parameters to be fit. (See Section 22.12.)

Controlling the Estimation. You can control the number of iterations and the number of backforecasts used for the parameter estimation, the perturbation increments and convergence tolerances for each parameter estimated, and a check against invertibility conditions. You can also enter initial parameter estimates. (See Sections 22.13 through 22.22.)

Specifying the Forecast. You can control the origin of the forecast values, the number of leads desired, and the confidence level for the forecast values. In addition, you can enter the final parameter estimates at the forecast step rather than having BOX-JENKINS estimate the model again. (See Sections 22.23 through 22.27.)

Displaying Results. You can control the amount of printed material that BOX-JENKINS produces. Plots and printed values of the time series, transformed series, autocorrelation function, partial autocorrelation function, residual series, and residual autocorrelation function are available. You can also plot the forecast function, fixed lead-forecasts, and confidence intervals. (See Sections 22.28 and 22.29.)

22.2
OPERATION

Two subcommands are required on BOX-JENKINS: the VARIABLE subcommand (see Section 22.3) and one of the step-of-analysis subcommands (see Section 22.4). Subcommands are separated by slashes, and the equals signs following the subcommand keywords are optional. The subcommand and specification keywords can be abbreviated to the first three characters.

22.3
VARIABLE Subcommand

Specify the variable name of your time series data using the VARIABLE subcommand, as in:

```
BOX-JENKINS  VARIABLE=AIRLINE/IDENTIFY
```

This series consists of monthly totals, in thousands, of international airline passengers from January 1949 to December 1960. The series must be measured at equally spaced intervals with each measurement recorded on a separate case. Missing values in the series are not allowed.

The VARIABLE subcommand is required and must be the first specification. You can list up to 10 variables following the VARIABLE keyword. Univariate time series analysis is performed for each variable listed.

22.4
Step-of-Analysis
Subcommands

The three steps in the analysis of a time series model are specified by three subcommands in BOX-JENKINS.

IDENTIFY *Produce statistics used for model identification.*
ESTIMATE *Produce parameter estimates.*
FORECAST *Produce forecast functions.*

At least one of these keywords is required on a BOX-JENKINS command and must be the last specification on the command, as in

```
BOX-JENKINS  VARIABLE=AIRLINE/IDENTIFY
```

which requests the identification step of analysis on a variable AIRLINE. By default, the autocorrelation function is plotted and summary statistics for the series are printed when IDENTIFY is specified. The autocorrelation function plot is shown in Figure 22.4. The default number of lags for which autocorrelations are plotted is 25. To override this default, use the LAG subcommand (see Section 22.11).

Figure 22.4   Autocorrelation function plot

```
AUTOCORRELATION FUNCTION FOR VARIABLE AIRLINE
AUTOCORRELATIONS *
TWO STANDARD ERROR LIMITS .

      AUTO. STAND.
LAG   CORR. ERR.  -1  -.75  -.5  -.25   0   .25   .5   .75   1
                  :----:----:----:----:----:----:----:----:
  1   0.948 0.082                      . :**.****************
  2   0.876 0.082                      . :**.***************
  3   0.807 0.082                      . :**.**************
  4   0.753 0.081                      . :**.************
  5   0.714 0.081                      . :**.***********
  6   0.682 0.081                      . :**.**********
  7   0.663 0.080                      . :**.**********
  8   0.656 0.080                      . :**.**********
  9   0.671 0.080                      . :**.**********
 10   0.703 0.080                      . :**.**********
 11   0.743 0.079                      . :**.***********
 12   0.760 0.079                      . :**.***********
 13   0.713 0.079                      . :**.***********
 14   0.646 0.078                      . :**.*********
 15   0.586 0.078                      . :**.********
 16   0.538 0.078                      . :**.********
 17   0.500 0.077                      . :**.*******
 18   0.469 0.077                      . :**.******
 19   0.450 0.077                      . :**.******
 20   0.442 0.076                      . :**.******
 21   0.457 0.076                      . :**.******
 22   0.482 0.076                      . :**.*******
 23   0.517 0.076                      . :**.*******
 24   0.532 0.075                      . :**.*******
 25   0.494 0.075                      . :**.*******
```

Autocorrelation plots in BOX-JENKINS display the autocorrelations up to the specified number of lags and two standard error limits. The standard errors are computed on the assumption that the time series is white noise, that is, random. Standard errors are calculated using the method documented in Ling and Roberts (1980), which differs from the method documented in Box and Jenkins (1976).

22.5
PLOT Subcommand

In addition to the autocorrelation function plot that is printed by default with the IDENTIFY subcommand, you can also obtain the series plot to help identify the series. To request a plot of the time series, use the PLOT subcommand and specify the keyword SER, as in:

```
BOX-JENKINS  VARIABLE=AIRLINE/PLOT=SER/IDENTIFY
```

This plot, shown in Figure 22.5, exhibits three noteworthy attributes. There is an upward tendency in series values from 1949 to 1960, and the series exhibits a periodic component consisting of a regular seasonal pattern with peaks occurring in late summer months of each year. Finally, the series values show greater amplitude in recent years than in earlier ones. Thus, the series is nonstationary and heteroscedastic, and both of these characteristics ought to be taken into account in fitting a model to the series.

Figure 22.5   Series plot and summary statistics

```
GRAPHIC DISPLAY OF SERIES FOR VARIABLE AIRLINE
DATA - *
MEAN - .

   OBS      DATA           80.00    280.00    480.00    680.00    880.00
                           ---------:---------:---------:---------:---------:
     1    112.000      :-----------*         .
     2    118.000      :-----------*         .
     3    132.000      :------------*        .
     4    129.000      :------------*        .
     5    121.000      :-----------*         .
     6    135.000      :------------*        .
     7    148.000      :-------------*       .
     8    148.000      :-------------*       .
     9    136.000      :------------*        .
    10    119.000      :-----------*         .
    11    104.000      :----------*          .
    12    118.000      :-----------*         .
    13    115.000      :-----------*         .
    14    126.000      :-----------*         .
    15    141.000      :-------------*       .
    16    135.000      :------------*        .
    17    125.000      :-----------*         .
    18    149.000      :-------------*       .
    19    170.000      :--------------*      .
    20    170.000      :--------------*      .
    21    158.000      :-------------*       .
    22    133.000      :------------*        .
    23    114.000      :----------*          .
    24    140.000      :------------*        .


   120    337.000      --------------------.---*
   121    360.000      :---------------------.---*
   122    342.000      :--------------------.--*
   123    406.000      :---------------------.------*
   124    396.000      :---------------------.-----*
   125    420.000      :----------------------.------*
   126    472.000      :----------------------.--------*
   127    548.000      :----------------------.-----------*
   128    559.000      :----------------------.------------*
   129    463.000      :---------------------.-------*
   130    407.000      :--------------------.------*
   131    362.000      :--------------------.---*
   132    405.000      :---------------------.-----*
   133    417.000      :---------------------.------*
   134    391.000      :--------------------.-----*
   135    419.000      :---------------------.------*
   136    461.000      :----------------------.-------*
   137    472.000      :----------------------.--------*
   138    535.000      :----------------------.----------*
   139    622.000      :----------------------.------------*
   140    606.000      :----------------------.-----------*
   141    508.000      :----------------------.---------*
   142    461.000      :----------------------.-------*
   143    390.000      :--------------------.----*
   144    432.000      :---------------------.------*

MEAN VALUE OF THE PROCESS
  0.28030E+03

STANDARD DEVIATION OF THE PROCESS
  0.11955E+03
```

22.6
Transformation Subcommands

Two types of transformations of the time series, logarithmic and power, are available in BOX-JENKINS. You can take the log or power of the series to induce constant amplitude in the series over time so that residuals from the fitted model will have a constant variance. When a transformation is called for, it is more convenient to transform the series within the procedure than in the data transformation language outside the procedure, since results will be internally back-transformed and expressed in the original units whenever possible. All of the subcommands controlling transformations of the series can be used with all steps of analysis.

22.7
LOG and POWER Subcommands

The varying amplitude (heteroscedasticity) of a series can often be removed by using a logarithmic or power transformation. Use the LOG subcommand to log transform the series, as in:

```
BOX-JENKINS  VARIABLE=AIRLINE/LOG/IDENTIFY
```

The log transform calculates the natural logarithm (base *e*) of the series. Optionally you can specify a constant that you want added to all of the values in the series before the log transformation is calculated in order to prevent taking logs of negative numbers. For example, the following command adds 10 to all of the values of AIRLINE before calculating the log:

```
BOX-JENKINS  VARIABLE=AIRLINE/LOG=10/IDENTIFY
```

Use the POWER subcommand to take the power of the values in the series, as in

```
BOX-JENKINS  VARIABLE=Y/POWER=(2)/IDENTIFY
```

which squares the values of the series Y. Optionally you can specify a constant to be added to the series values before the power transformation is calculated. For example, the following command adds 10 to the series before calculating the third power:

```
BOX-JENKINS  VARIABLE=Y/POWER=(3,10)/IDENTIFY
```

You can specify either the LOG or the POWER subcommand in a given analysis, but not both.

22.8
Differencing Subcommands

Two types of differencing of the series are available in BOX-JENKINS. Nonseasonal differencing is used to convert a nonstationary series to a stationary series with a constant mean and variance. Seasonal differencing is used to model a systematic, periodic variation. The length of the period must be specified for seasonal differencing. If the series has been transformed with the LOG or POWER subcommands, the differencing is done on the transformed series.

22.9
DIFFERENCE Subcommand

Use the DIFFERENCE subcommand to specify a nonseasonal differencing of the series. The specification for the DIFFERENCE subcommand can be a single number indicating the the degree of differencing desired, as in

```
BOX-JENKINS  VARIABLE=AIRLINE/DIFFERENCE=1/IDENTIFY
```

which specifies a single degree of differencing for the AIRLINE series. You can specify a range of differencing degrees on the DIFFERENCE subcommand by using the keyword THRU. The number before the keyword THRU indicates the lowest degree of differencing requested, and the number following THRU indicates the highest degree. For example, the following command requests zero (none), one, and two degrees of nonseasonal differencing:

```
BOX-JENKINS  VARIABLE=AIRLINE/LOG/DIFFERENCE=0 THRU 2
   /IDENTIFY
```

By default, the differencing is done for each degree specified by the range; that is, the default increment is 1. To specify an increment other than 1, use the keyword BY followed by the desired increment. For example, the following command requests differencing of zero, two, and four degrees:

```
BOX-JENKINS  VARIABLE=AIRLINE/LOG/DIFFERENCE=0 THRU 4 BY 2
   /IDENTIFY
```

Ordinarily, no more than two or three degrees of differencing will be required to achieve stationarity and to overdifference, if variate differencing is being done.

22.10
SDIFFERENCE and PERIOD Subcommands

The SDIFFERENCE subcommand specifies seasonal differencing. The specifications for the SDIFFERENCE subcommand are the same as for the DIFFERENCE subcommand. You can specify a single number to indicate the degree of differencing, the keyword THRU to indicate a range of degrees, and the keyword BY to indicate an increment other than one for the range.

If you request seasonal differencing, you must use the PERIOD subcommand to specify the period for differencing. The PERIOD subcommand specifies the number of observations that make up a period. The default value of PERIOD is 1. For example, the following command requests seasonal differencing of degrees zero, one, and two for the period of one year (12 months):

```
BOX-JENKINS  VARIABLE=AIRLINE/LOG/DIFFERENCE=0 THRU 2
   /SDIFFERENCE=0 THRU 2/PERIOD=12/IDENTIFY
```

This command requests three times three, or nine, combinations of seasonal and nonseasonal differencing. Nine separate autocorrelation function plots will be produced. This, in effect, implements the "variate difference" method discussed in Anderson (1976). The variate difference method, when used in conjunction with series plots and autocorrelation function plots, will often prove useful in identifying the appropriate degrees of differencing.

Note that difference ranges, using the keyword THRU on the DIFFERENCE or SDIFFERENCE subcommand, can be specified with the ESTIMATE or FORECAST keywords. However, this results in the calculation of several different models, and can lead to extra expense and voluminous output.

22.11
LAG Subcommand

The LAG subcommand specifies the highest lag to be considered in computing the autocovariance function, the autocorrelation function, the partial autocorrelation function, and the residual autocorrelation function. The default value is 25. For example, the following command requests 49 lags for the functions:

```
BOX-JENKINS  VARIABLE=AIRLINE/LOG/DIFFERENCE=0 THRU 2
   /SDIFFERENCE=0 THRU 2/PERIOD=12/LAG=49/IDENTIFY
```

Figure 22.11 shows the autocorrelation function plot at one degree of seasonal and one degree of nonseasonal differencing. The autocorrelations are calculated for 49 lags.

Figure 22.11   Autocorrelation of series differenced at degree 1 seasonal and nonseasonal

```
VARIABLE - AIRLINE  SERIES LENGTH - 131
DEGREE OF NONSEASONAL DIFFERENCING -  1 DEGREE OF SEASONAL DIFFERENCING -   1

MEAN VALUE OF THE PROCESS
   0.29088E-03

STANDARD DEVIATION OF THE PROCESS
   0.45673E-01

AUTOCORRELATION FUNCTION FOR VARIABLE AIRLINE
AUTOCORRELATIONS *
TWO STANDARD ERROR LIMITS .

       AUTO. STAND.
  LAG  CORR.  ERR.  -1  -.75  -.5 -.25   0   .25   .5   .75    1
                     ----:----:----:----:----:----:----:----:----
    1  -0.341 0.086                      ****.**
    2   0.105 0.086                          . **
    3  -0.202 0.085                      *.**
    4   0.021 0.085                          *
    5   0.056 0.085                          .*
    6   0.031 0.084                          .*
    7  -0.056 0.084                         *.
    8  -0.001 0.084                          *
    9   0.176 0.083                          .**.*
   10  -0.076 0.083                        **.*
   11   0.064 0.083                          .*
   12  -0.387 0.082                     *****.**
   13   0.152 0.082                          .***
   14  -0.058 0.082                         *.
   15   0.150 0.081                          .***
   16  -0.139 0.081                       ***.
   17   0.070 0.081                          .*
   18   0.016 0.080                          *
   19  -0.011 0.080                          *
   20  -0.117 0.079                        **.
   21   0.039 0.079                          .*
   22  -0.091 0.079                        **.
   23   0.223 0.078                          .**.*
   24  -0.018 0.078                          *
   25  -0.100 0.078                        **.
   26   0.049 0.077                          .*
   27  -0.030 0.077                          *.
   28   0.047 0.077                          .*
   29  -0.018 0.076                          *
   30  -0.051 0.076                         *.
   31  -0.054 0.075                         *.
   32   0.196 0.075                          .**.*
   33  -0.122 0.075                        **.
   34   0.078 0.074                          .**
   35  -0.152 0.074                       ***.
   36  -0.010 0.073                          *
   37   0.047 0.073                          .*
   38   0.031 0.073                          .*
   39  -0.015 0.072                          *
   40  -0.034 0.072                          *.
   41  -0.066 0.071                         *.
   42   0.095 0.071                          .**
   43  -0.090 0.071                        **.
   44   0.029 0.070                          .*
   45  -0.037 0.070                          *.
   46  -0.042 0.069                          *.
   47   0.108 0.069                          .**
   48  -0.050 0.069                         *.
   49   0.105 0.068                          .**
```

22.12
Parameters Subcommands

You can fit autoregressive parameters and moving average parameters. The parameters can be fit as nonseasonal or seasonal parameters. You can request single parameters or multiple sequential or nonsequential parameters. The subcommands used to specify the desired parameters can be used with all steps of analysis.

Use the following subcommands to fit single or multiple sequential parameters:

P   *Autoregressive parameters to fit.*
Q   *Moving average parameters to fit.*
SP   *Seasonal autoregressive parameters to fit.*
SQ   *Seasonal moving average parameters to fit.*

On each subcommand, you can specify one number representing the number of parameters to be fit. For example, the following command requests one nonseasonal moving average parameter and one seasonal moving average parameter:

```
BOX-JENKINS  VARIABLE=AIRLINE/LOG/DIFFERENCE=1/PERIOD=12
   /SDIFFERENCE=1/LAG=49/Q=1/SQ=1/IDENTIFY
```

You can use the keyword THRU on any of the parameter subcommands to specify multiple models to be fit, as in

```
BOX-JENKINS  VARIABLE=AIRLINE/LOG/DIFFERENCE=1/PERIOD=12
   /SDIFFERENCE=1/LAG=49/Q=1 THRU 2/SQ=0 THRU 2/IDENTIFY
```

which specifies two times three, or six models to be fit: one model with one nonseasonal moving parameter and no seasonal parameters, one model with one nonseasonal parameter and one seasonal parameter, one model with one nonseasonal parameter and two seasonal parameters, and so forth.

Note that if you use the THRU keyword on any of the parameter subcommands and request ESTIMATE or FORECAST, you will use a great deal of computer time estimating or forecasting the several models and will produce volumes of output. If you specify only IDENTIFY, you will obtain initial parameter estimates for nonseasonal parameters, along with the usual identification output.

You can specify single or multiple nonsequential parameters by using the following subcommands:

ARLAG   *Autoregressive parameters to fit.*
MALAG   *Moving average parameters to fit.* ·

For each subcommand, specify the numbers corresponding to the order or lag that you want fit. Thus, Q=3 and MALAG=1,2,3 are equivalent specifications; SQ=1/PERIOD=12 and MALAG=12 are equivalent; but Q=3 and MALAG=1,3 specify different models. The latter specification fits no moving average parameter at lag 2, whereas the former does.

The MALAG and ARLAG specifications are alternatives to the Q and P subcommands, respectively. The difference is that MALAG and ARLAG specify single or nonsequential parameters and facilitate fitting more generalized models than those specified by the Q and P subcommands. However, the program will accept both P and ARLAG or Q and MALAG subcommands in the same run. If both P and ARLAG are specified, the same number of autoregressive terms as specified by the P subcommand must be given in the ARLAG list. Similarly, the MALAG list must contain the same number of terms as specified in the Q subcommand.

22.13
Estimation Subcommands

You can control several aspects of the estimation step in BOX-JENKINS. Subcommands specify whether a constant term is to be fit or whether the values are to be centered around their mean before estimation is done. Other subcommands control the number of iterations and the number of backforecasts used for the parameter estimation, the perturbation increments and convergence tolerances for each parameter estimated, and a check against invertibility conditions. You can also enter the initial estimates of the parameters derived from the identification of the model in a previous BOX-JENKINS run. All of these subcommands can be used only with the ESTIMATE keyword.

22.14
CONSTANT and NCONSTANT
Keywords

By default, BOX-JENKINS fits a constant during the estimation step. In general, when differencing is used, the level of the series will be approximately zero and the constant can be constrained to equal zero. Use the keyword NCONSTANT to indicate that no constant term is to be fit, as in:

```
BOX-JENKINS  VARIABLE=AIRLINE/LOG/DIFFERENCE=1/PERIOD=12
/SDIFFERENCE=1/LAG=49/Q=1/SQ=1/NCONSTANT/ESTIMATE
```

To explicitly request the default, estimation of a constant term, specify the CONSTANT keyword.

22.15
CENTER and NCENTER
Keywords

The keyword CENTER is used to center values around their mean before estimation is done, as in:

```
BOX-JENKINS  VARIABLE=AIRLINE/LOG/DIFFERENCE=1/PERIOD=12
/SDIFFERENCE=1/LAG=49/Q=1/SQ=1/NCONSTANT/CENTER/ESTIMATE
```

Ordinarily, if CENTER is chosen, the implication is that you do not wish to search on the overall constant during final parameter estimation. The default is NCENTER.

22.16
ITERATE Subcommand

The estimation routine is an iterative search algorithm. The ITERATE subcommand indicates the maximum number of iterations for use by the estimation routine in parameter estimation. The default number of iterations is 40. The following command requests 100 iterations:

```
BOX-JENKINS  VARIABLE=AIRLINE/LOG/DIFFERENCE=1/PERIOD=12
/SDIFFERENCE=1/LAG=49/Q=1/SQ=1/NCONSTANT/ITERATE=100/ESTIMATE
```

It is unlikely that 100 iterations will be required before convergence. The default of 40 iterations will usually be enough for convergence. Failure to converge may indicate model misspecification, and you will need to investigate this possibility. In general, if you want to avoid failure to converge, specify a relatively large number of iterations; if you want to avoid a lot of costly iterations for what may be a misspecified model, then accept the default or specify a number smaller than 40. You can also specify the convergence tolerances for the parameters (see Section 22.21).

22.17
BFR Subcommand

The BFR subcommand specifies the number of backforecasts to be generated for use in the estimation step. The default number is 0. For example, the following command requests 13 backforecasts to be used in estimation:

```
BOX-JENKINS  VARIABLE=AIRLINE/LOG/DIFFERENCE=1/PERIOD=12
/SDIFFERENCE=1/LAG=49/Q=1/SQ=1/NCONSTANT/ITERATE=100/BFR=13
/ESTIMATE
```

In general, a nonzero backforecast specification will be slightly more expensive than zero backforecasts, but it will often lead to a final model with a smaller residual variance. There is no program limit on the maximum number of backforecasts that can be specified.

22.18
TEST and NTEST Keywords

Box and Jenkins (1976) discuss a set of simultaneous inequalities that constitute invertibility conditions for models with up to three moving average parameters. The keyword TEST instructs BOX-JENKINS to check the estimated parameters at each iteration against these invertibility conditions. The default is NTEST.

22.19
FPR Subcommand

The FPR subcommand specifies the interval of iterations for printing current estimated values from iterative estimation. The default is 5, which implies that you will get printed results at every fifth iteration. The following command prints estimated values after every tenth iteration:

```
BOX-JENKINS   VARIABLE=AIRLINE/LOG/DIFFERENCE=1/PERIOD=12
  /SDIFFERENCE=1/LAG=49/Q=1/SQ=1/NCONSTANT/ITERATE=100/BFR=13
  /FPR=10/ESTIMATE
```

22.20
Perturbation Increment Subcommands

You can use the following subcommands to specify perturbation increments that are used by the estimation routine in final parameter estimation:

PCON=(number)　　　*Perturbation increment for the constant term.*

PP=(number,...,number)　*Perturbation increments for autoregressive parameters.*

PQ=(number,...,number)　*Perturbation increments for moving average parameters.*

PSP=(number,...,number)　*Perturbation increments for seasonal autoregressive parameters.*

PSQ=(number,...,number)　*Perturbation increments for seasonal moving average parameters.*

These subcommands must have matching P, Q (or ARLAG, MALAG), SP, and SQ subcommands. If you specify NCONSTANT, you cannot specify the PCON subcommand. You cannot use these subcommands if you have used the THRU keyword to specify a range of models on the matching P, Q (or ARLAG, MALAG), SP, or SQ subcommands. If you do not specify the perturbation increment, BOX-JENKINS will use the default value of 0.1.

If you do not want to search on a particular parameter because it has some known a priori value, declare its value using the relevant initial estimates subcommand (Section 22.22) and set its perturbation increment to zero.

22.21
Tolerance Subcommands

You can use the following subcommands to specify the convergence tolerances used by the search algorithm when estimating parameters:

TCON=(number)　　　*Convergence tolerance for the constant term.*

TP=(number,...,number)　*Convergence tolerances for autoregressive parameters.*

TQ=(number,...,number)　*Convergence tolerances for moving average parameters.*

TSP=(number,...,number)　*Convergence tolerances for seasonal autoregressive parameters.*

TSQ=(number,...,number)　*Convergence tolerances for seasonal moving average parameters.*

These subcommands must have matching P, Q (or ARLAG, MALAG), SP, and SQ subcommands. If you specify NCONSTANT, you cannot specify the TCON subcommand. You cannot use these subcommands if you have used the THRU keyword to specify a range of models on the matching P, Q (or ARLAG, MALAG), SP, or SQ subcommands.

Default convergence tolerances are equal to 0.001. This means that when estimated parameters in two consecutive iterations differ by no more than 0.001, the search algorithm will stop.

22.22
Initial Estimates Subcommands

You can use the following subcommands to set initial parameter estimates for the estimation step of BOX-JENKINS:

ICON=(number)　　　*Initial estimate for the constant term.*

IP=(number,...,number)　*Initial estimates for autoregressive parameters.*

IQ=(number,...,number)　*Initial estimates for moving average parameters.*

ISP=(number,...,number)　*Initial estimates for seasonal autoregressive parameters.*

ISQ=(number,...,number)　*Initial estimates for seasonal moving average parameters.*

You can use the initial estimates from a previous BOX-JENKINS IDENTIFY run or from any other source. These subcommands must have matching P, Q (or ARLAG, MALAG), SP, and SQ subcommands. If you specify NCONSTANT, you cannot specify the ICON subcommand. You cannot use these subcommands if you have used the THRU keyword to specify a range of models on the matching P, Q (or ARLAG, MALAG), SP, or SQ subcommands. By default, the initial values are set to zero for all parameters unless both the IDENTIFY and ESTIMATE keywords are specified.

22.23
Forecast Subcommands

By default, the forecast step of BOX-JENKINS analysis prints a table of forecast values. The forecast origin is the last case in the file, and values are forecast for 12 leads. You can use the ORIGIN subcommand to specify the series values to be used as forecast origins (Section 22.24) and the LEAD subcommand to specify the highest lead desired (Section 22.25). You can also use the CIN subcommand to specify the confidence level that you want used for the forecasted values (Section 22.26) and the final parameter estimate subcommands to set the final estimates derived from a previous BOX-JENKINS ESTIMATE run (Section 22.27).

22.24
ORIGIN Subcommand

Use the ORIGIN subcommand to specify the series values to be used as forecast origins. You can specify a single positive or negative number. A positive number begins counting from the first series value; a negative number counts back from the end of the series. For example, the following command uses the last 24 series values as the forecast origins:

```
BOX-JENKINS  VARIABLE=AIRLINE/LOG/DIFFERENCE=1/PERIOD=12
    /SDIFFERENCE=1/Q=1/SQ=1
    /ORIGIN=-24/FORECAST
```

You can use the keyword THRU to specify a range of series values. You can specify two positive numbers that correspond to sequential case numbers, as in

```
ORIGIN=130 THRU 144
```

which specifies the 130th through the 144th cases as forecast origins. You can use negative numbers to count back from the end of the series, as in

```
ORIGIN=-24 THRU -12
```

which uses the 24th case from the end of the series through the 12th case from the end of the series as the forecast origins. The default forecast origin is the last case in the file.

22.25
LEAD Subcommand

Use the LEAD subcommand to specify the highest lead for the forecasted values. The default lead is 12. The following command requests forecasts for 24 leads:

```
BOX-JENKINS  VARIABLE=AIRLINE/LOG/DIFFERENCE=1/PERIOD=12
    /SDIFFERENCE=1/Q=1/SQ=1
    /ORIGIN=-24/LEAD=24/FORECAST
```

22.26
CIN Subcommand

The CIN subcommand specifies the forecast confidence level expressed as a percentage. The default level is 95. The following command requests a 99% confidence interval for the forecasts:

```
BOX-JENKINS  VARIABLE=AIRLINE/LOG/DIFFERENCE=1/PERIOD=12
    /SDIFFERENCE=1/Q=1/SQ=1
    /ORIGIN=-24/CIN=99/FORECAST
```

22.27
Final Estimates Subcommands

Use the following subcommands to input final parameter estimates into the forecast step of BOX-JENKINS.

FCON=(number) *Final estimate for the constant term.*

FP=(number,...,number) *Final estimates for autoregressive parameters.*

FQ=(number,...,number) *Final estimates for moving average parameters.*

FSP=(number,...,number) *Final estimates for seasonal autoregressive parameters.*

FSQ=(number,...,number) *Final estimates for seasonal moving average parameters.*

You can use the final estimates from a previous BOX-JENKINS ESTIMATE run or from any other source. For example, the following command uses the final estimates shown in Figure D in the annotated example:

```
BOX-JENKINS  VARIABLE=AIRLINE/LOG/DIFFERENCE=1/PERIOD=12
   /SDIFFERENCE=1/Q=1/SQ=1/FQ=(.39531)/FSQ=(.61406)
   /ORIGIN=-24/FORECAST
```

These subcommands must have matching P, Q (or ARLAG, MALAG), SP, and SQ subcommands. If you specify NCONSTANT, you cannot specify the FCON subcommand. You cannot use these subcommands if you have used the THRU keyword to specify a range of models on the matching P, Q (or ARLAG, MALAG), SP, or SQ subcommands.

22.28
PRINT Subcommand

Use the PRINT subcommand to print the values of various functions and series. Table 22.28 shows the keywords available with the PRINT subcommand and the step of analysis when each can be used.

Table 22.28   Keywords for PRINT subcommand

Keyword	Display	Stage
ACF	Autocorrelation function	IDENTIFY
PACF	Partial autocorrelation function	IDENTIFY
ACVF	Autocovariance function	IDENTIFY
SER	Time series	IDENTIFY
TSER	Log- or power-transformed series	IDENTIFY
DSER	Differenced series	IDENTIFY
RESID	Values of the residual series	ESTIMATE
RACF	Residual autocorrelation function	ESTIMATE

By default, the FORECAST step prints forecast results. Thus, no keywords for FORECAST are available on the PRINT subcommand.

22.29
PLOT Subcommand

The PLOT subcommand requests plots of the values of various functions and series. You can specify all the keywords available on the PRINT subcommand except ACVF, the autocovariance function. If you use the PLOT subcommand, the PRINT subcommand is not necessary because printed values are either in the plot or contiguous to it. Three additional PLOT keywords can be used with the FORECAST keyword.

FCF *Forecast function.*

FLF *Fixed lead forecasts.*

CIN *Confidence intervals.*

If the forecast origin is other than the end of the series, then one-step-ahead forecasts are plotted for all series values starting with the forecast origin, and increasing lead forecasts are plotted from the end of the series. If the origin is not specified, one-step-ahead forecasts are plotted from the beginning of the series.

ANNOTATED EXAMPLE FOR BOX-JENKINS

The example illustrating BOX-JENKINS analyzes the Series G time series from Box and Jenkins (1976). This series consists of monthly totals, in thousands, of international airline passengers from January 1949 to December 1960.

Identifying the Model

The first BOX-JENKINS job requests a plot of the series.

```
DATA LIST FILE=SERIESG/AIRLINE 5-7
BOX-JENKINS   VARIABLE=AIRLINE/PLOT=SERIES/IDENTIFY
```

• The DATA LIST command defines the variable AIRLINE containing the total number of airline passengers (see Chapter 5).

• The BOX-JENKINS command requests the IDENTIFY step of analysis on AIRLINE and the PLOT subcommand requests a plot of the series. By default, the autocorrelation function plot and summary statistics for the series are printed when IDENTIFY is specified. The autocorrelation function plot is shown in Figure 22.4 and the series plot in Figure 22.5.

The series plot shows that the series is both nonstationary and heteroscedastic. Nonstationarity of the series is also suggested by the autocorrelation function since the early autocorrelations remain large rather than dying out quickly. A periodicity of 12 is suggested by the autocorrelation of 0.760 at the 12th lag, which is larger than the neighboring lags.

The second BOX-JENKINS job log-transforms the series to correct for the heteroscedasticity and tries several degrees of nonseasonal and seasonal differencing to achieve a stationary series.

```
DATA LIST FILE=SERIESG/AIRLINE 5-7
BOX-JENKINS   VARIABLE=AIRLINE/LOG/DIFFERENCE=0 THRU 2/PERIOD=12
   /SDIFFERENCE=0 THRU 2/LAG=49/PLOT=DSE,PAC/IDENTIFY
```

• The LOG subcommand requests log-transformation of the series (see Section 22.7).

• The DIFFERENCE subcommand requests zero, one, and two degrees of differencing (see Section 22.9).

• The SDIFFERENCE subcommand and the PERIOD subcommands request annual differencing of the series since the series is measured monthly (see Section 22.10).

• The LAG subcommand requests that 49 lags be calculated for the autocorrelation and partial autocorrelation functions (see Section 22.11).

• The PLOT subcommand requests plots of the differenced series and partial autocorrelation function plots for each of the combinations of differencing (see Section 22.29).

Nine separate autocorrelation function plots also are printed for each combination of differencing. The smallest standard deviation is for the series with one degree of seasonal differencing and one degree of nonseasonal differencing. Figure 22.11 shows this autocorrelation function plot. By comparison, other combinations of differencing are not as good. The plot of the series differenced at one degree seasonal and nonseasonal is shown in Figure A. This plot shows that stationarity has been obtained. The autocorrelation and partial autocorrelation function plots (Figure 22.11 and Figure B) suggest fitting a model with one moving average parameter and one seasonal moving average parameter.

A Differenced series plot

```
GRAPHIC DISPLAY OF DIFFERENCED SERIES FOR VARIABLE AIRLINE
DEGREE OF NONSEASONAL DIFFERENCING -  1 DEGREE OF SEASONAL DIFFERENCING -   1
DATA - *
MEAN - .

  OBS     DATA          -0.15     -0.05      0.05      0.15      0.25
                        :---------:---------:---------:---------:---------:
      1  0.391640E-01   :              .---*
      2  0.360685E-03   :              *
      3 -0.204956E-01   :           *-.
      4 -0.129392E-01   :            *.
      5  0.661483E-01   :              .------*
      6  0.399146E-01   :              .---*
      7  0.000000E+00   :              *
      8  0.113540E-01   :              .*
      9 -0.387145E-01   :         *--.
     10 -0.194181E-01   -          *-.
     11  0.791502E-01   :              .-------*
     12  0.608438E-01   :              .-----*
     13 -0.574482E-01   :        *-----.
     14  0.586703E-01   :              .-----*
     15 -0.445482E-01   :         *---.
     16  0.130705       :              .-----------*
     17 -0.141343       :   *-----------.
     18 -0.203309E-01   :           *-.
     19  0.000000E+00   :              *
     20 -0.516566E-02   -             *.
     21  0.449065E-01   :              .---*
     22  0.501610E-01   :              .----*
     23 -0.770628E-01   :       *------.
     24 -0.541555E-02   :             *.


    120 -0.368219E-01   -          *--.
    121 -0.130854E-01   :            *.
    122 -0.102379       :      *--------.
    123  0.120466       :              .-----------*
    124 -0.352596E-01   :      .   *--.
    125  0.856349E-02   :              .*
    126  0.137704E-02   :              *
    127 -0.459343E-01   :         *--.
    128  0.120239E-01   :              .*
    129  0.318305E-01   :              .--*
    130 -0.500823E-01   -         *--.
    131 -0.996401E-02   :             *.

MEAN VALUE OF THE PROCESS
   0.29088E-03

STANDARD DEVIATION OF THE PROCESS
   0.45673E-01
```

**Annotated Example for
BOX-JENKINS** *continued*

B Partial autocorrelation function plot

```
PARTIAL AUTOCORRELATION FUNCTION FOR VARIABLE AIRLINE
PARTIAL AUTOCORRELATIONS *
TWO STANDARD ERROR LIMITS

     PR-AUT STAND.
LAG  CORR.  ERR.  -1  -.75  -.5  -.25   0   .25   .5   .75   1
                  :----:----:----:----:----:----:----:----:
  1  -0.341 0.087               ****.**:      .
  2  -0.013 0.087                       *      .
  3  -0.193 0.087                  *.**:      .
  4  -0.125 0.087                   ***:      .
  5   0.033 0.087                      :*     .
  6   0.035 0.087                      :*     .
  7  -0.060 0.087                     *:      .
  8  -0.020 0.087                      *      .
  9   0.226 0.087                      :**.** .
 10   0.043 0.087                      :*     .
 11   0.047 0.087                      :*     .
 12  -0.339 0.087               ****.**:      .
 13  -0.109 0.087                   .**:      .
 14  -0.077 0.087                    **:      .
 15  -0.022 0.087                      *      .
 16  -0.140 0.087                   ***:      .
 17   0.026 0.087                      :*     .
 18   0.115 0.087                      :**    .
 19  -0.013 0.087                      *      .
 20  -0.167 0.087                   ***:      .
 21   0.132 0.087                      :***   .
 22  -0.072 0.087                    .*:      .
 23   0.143 0.087                      :***   .
 24  -0.067 0.087                     *:      .
 25  -0.103 0.087                   .**:      .
 26  -0.010 0.087                      :*     .
 27   0.044 0.087                      :*     .
 28  -0.090 0.087                   .**:      .
 29   0.047 0.087                      :*     .
 30  -0.005 0.087                      :*     .
 31  -0.096 0.087                   .**:      .
 32  -0.015 0.087                      :*     .
 33   0.012 0.087                      :*     .
 34  -0.019 0.087                      :*     .
 35   0.023 0.087                      :*     .
 36  -0.165 0.087                   ***:      .
 37  -0.034 0.087                      :*     .
 38   0.009 0.087                      :*     .
 39   0.045 0.087                      :*     .
 40  -0.076 0.087                   .**:      .
 41  -0.175 0.087                   ***:      .
 42   0.074 0.087                      :*     .
 43  -0.103 0.087                   .**:      .
 44  -0.061 0.087                     *:      .
 45  -0.027 0.087                      *:     .
 46  -0.123 0.087                   .**:      .
 47  -0.013 0.087                      *:     .
 48  -0.049 0.087                     .*:     .
 49   0.088 0.087                      :**.   .
```

Estimating the Model

The model is estimated with the following BOX-JENKINS command:

```
BOX-JENKINS VARIABLE=AIRLINE/LOG/DIFFERENCE=1/SDIFFERENCE=1
   /PERIOD=12/LAG=49/Q=1/SQ=1/NCONSTANT
   /BFR=13/PLOT=RAC,RES/ESTIMATE
```

- The LOG subcommand requests a log-transformation of the series. The DIFFER-ENCE subcommand requests one degree of nonseasonal differencing, and the SDIFFERENCE and PERIOD subcommands request one degree of seasonal differencing at period 12. The LAG subcommand requests that 49 lags be calculated for the functions.

- The Q and SQ subcommands specify the parameters to be fit; one nonseasonal moving average parameter and one seasonal moving average parameter (see Section 22.12).

- The NCONSTANT keyword indicates that no constant term is to be fit (see Section 22.14).
- The BFR subcommand requests that 13 backforecasts be used in estimation (see Section 22.17).
- The PLOT subcommand requests a plot of the residual series values and a plot of the residual autocorrelation function (see Section 22.29). If the specified model is a good fit, the residual series should be white noise (random) and therefore uncorrelated for all lags. Except for sampling variation, values of the autocorrelations of the residual should not be statistically different from zero. The residual autocorrelation function plot is shown in Figure C.
- The ESTIMATE keyword requests estimation of the model.

The intermediate iteration results include the "Function value," which is the sum of squares function described in Box and Jenkins (1976). For Series G, convergence criteria are met after 19 iterations. Final estimation results are shown in Figure D. The results include

- Estimated final parameter values and their standard errors.
- Residual variance, equal to the mean squared error.
- Variance-covariance matrix of estimated parameters.
- Correlation matrix of estimated parameters. High correlations may indicate model inadequacies such as over-parameterization or insufficient differencing.
- Mean, standard deviation, and variance of the residual series; chi-square statistic associated with the residual autocorrelation function.

C Residual autocorrelation function plot

```
RESIDUAL AUTOCORRELATION FUNCTION FOR VARIABLE AIRLINE
AUTOCORRELATIONS *
TWO STANDARD ERROR LIMITS .

     AUTO. STAND.
LAG  CORR.  ERR.  -1  -.75  -.5  -.25   0   .25   .5   .75   1
                  :----:----:----:----:----:----:----:----:
  1   0.017  0.086                     . *  .
  2   0.019  0.086                     . *  .
  3  -0.126  0.085                  ***:.
  4  -0.142  0.085                  ***:.
  5   0.050  0.085                     .:*  .
  6   0.062  0.084                     . :*  .
  7  -0.073  0.084                     . *:  .
  8  -0.038  0.084                     . *:  .
  9   0.103  0.083                     . :**
 10  -0.078  0.083                    .**:  .
 11   0.024  0.083                     . *  .
 12  -0.011  0.082                     . *  .
 13   0.031  0.082                     . :*  .
 14   0.043  0.082                     . :*  .
 15   0.048  0.081                     .:*  .
 16  -0.156  0.081                  ***:.
 17   0.025  0.081                     . *  .
 18  -0.001  0.080                     . *  .
 19  -0.107  0.080                    .**:  .
 20  -0.102  0.079                    .**:  .
 21  -0.032  0.079                     . *:  .
 22  -0.027  0.079                     . *:  .
 23   0.220  0.078                     . :** *
 24   0.032  0.078                     . :*  .
```

Annotated Example for
BOX-JENKINS *continued*

D Final estimated values

```
FORECASTS FOR VARIABLE AIRLINE  WITH ORIGIN AT  144 AND  95.00% CONFIDENCE LIMITS

        OBS   LOW CONF LIM   FORECAST   UPP CONF LIM
        145      418.08       450.21       484.81
        146      391.16       426.50       465.02
        147      437.28       481.99       531.27
        148      442.18       492.18       547.83
        149      452.54       508.24       570.79
        150      515.04       583.26       660.51
        151      585.38       668.10       762.50
        152      579.11       665.81       765.50
        153      482.53       558.66       646.81
        154      426.08       496.60       578.80
        155      366.70       430.13       504.54
        156      405.02       478.01       564.16

GRAPHIC DISPLAY OF FORECASTS FOR VARIABLE AIRLINE

DEFINITIONS OF SYMBOLS
DATA — *
FORECASTS AT LEAD   1 — +
ESTIMATED 95% CONFIDENCE LIMITS — .
FORECAST FUNCTION — 0
OVERLAP — X

OBS.     DATA            390.00    490.00    590.00    690.00    790.00
                     :————————:————————:————————:————————:————————:
 121    360.000      :       . +* .
 122    342.000      :      . X . .
 123    406.000      :       . + * .
 124    396.000      :       . +* .
 125    420.000      :        . + *.
 126    472.000      :          . * + .
 127    548.000      :             . + * .
 128    559.000      :              . +* .
 129    463.000      :         . *+ .
 130    407.000      —         . X .
 131    362.000      :      . X . .
 132    405.000      :       . X .
 133    417.000      :        . X .
 134    391.000      :      . *+ .
 135    419.000      :        *. +
 136    461.000      :       . + X .
 137    472.000      :         . +*
 138    535.000      :           . *+ .
 139    622.000      :              . +* .
 140    606.000      —             . *+ .
 141    508.000      :           . X . .
 142    461.000      :        . +* .
 143    390.000      :      *+ .
 144    432.000      :       . *+ .
 145    450.209    F :       . 0 .
 146    426.495    F :       . 0 .
 147    481.986    F :         . 0 .
 148    492.181    F :          . 0 .
 149    508.239    F :           . 0 .
 150    583.259    F —             0      . 0 .
 151    668.095    F :                 . 0 .
 152    665.813    F :                 . 0 .
 153    558.663    F :           . 0 .
 154    496.603    F :         . 0 .
 155    430.132    F :      . 0 .
 156    478.011    F :         . 0 .
```

Forecasting the Model

BOX-JENKINS can now be used to forecast the series.

```
BOX-JENKINS VARIABLE=AIRLINE/LOG/DIFFERENCE=1/SDIFFERENCE=1
    /PERIOD=12/Q=1/SQ=1/FQ=(.39631)/FSQ=(.61506)
    /ORIGIN=-24/PLOT=FCF,FLF,CIN/FORECAST
```

- The command syntax through the SQ subcommand is the same as used for the estimation step.
- The FQ and FSQ subcommands input the final values for the nonseasonal and seasonal moving average parameters that were obtained in the ESTIMATE job shown in Figure D (see Section 22.27).

- The ORIGIN subcommand requests that the forecast origin be the observation in the data 24 back from the last series observation (see Section 22.24).
- The PLOT subcommand requests a plot of the forecast function, fixed lead forecasts, and associated confidence intervals.
- The FORECAST keyword requests the forecast step of analysis.

BOX-JENKINS first prints the parameter estimates that it is using. The augmented autoregressive matrix contains information on both differencing and autoregressive parameters, if any, used in the model. In our example, the augmented autoregressive matrix contains information solely on differencing. The forecast error summary table gives the forecast variance and forecast standard error for increasing leads, as well as the impulse response function, which corresponds to Box and Jenkins' psi weights.

The forecast function is summarized in a table that can be read: (1) horizontally, to compare forecasts from past observations with a given series observation; (2) diagonally, to obtain increasing lead forecasts from a given origin; and (3) vertically, to obtain fixed lead forecasts from consecutive observations. The table of forecast functions is displayed in Figure E.

E Summary table of forecast functions

```
FORECASTS AT INCREASING LEAD FOR VARIABLE AIRLINE
STARTING ORIGIN AT  120
```

LEAD TIME OBS	DATA	1	2	3	4	5	6	7	8	9	10	11	12
120	337.000												
121	360.000	350.038											
122	342.000	340.245	334.529										
123	406.000	394.940	393.715	387.101									
124	396.000	390.916	384.452	383.260	376.822								
125	420.000	403.550	400.415	393.794	392.572	385.978							
126	472.000	486.912	475.308	471.615	463.817	462.378	454.611						
127	548.000	534.468	544.599	531.621	527.490	518.768	517.159	508.471					
128	559.000	545.414	537.244	547.427	534.381	530.229	521.462	519.844	511.112				
129	463.000	468.756	461.845	454.926	463.549	452.502	448.986	441.562	440.193	432.798			
130	407.000	407.740	410.793	404.736	398.673	406.230	396.549	393.468	386.962	385.762	379.281		
131	362.000	355.432	355.823	358.486	353.201	347.910	354.504	346.056	343.367	337.690	336.642	330.987	
132	405.000	399.039	394.653	395.086	398.044	392.175	386.301	393.623	384.242	381.257	374.953	373.790	367.510
133	417.000	418.442	414.713	410.155	410.605	413.679	407.580	401.474	409.084	399.335	396.232	389.681	388.472
134	391.000	398.149	398.979	395.424	391.077	391.507	394.437	388.622	382.800	390.056	380.761	377.802	371.555
135	419.000	460.240	465.301	466.272	462.117	457.038	457.539	460.964	454.168	447.365	455.844	444.981	441.524
136	461.000	423.658	448.361	453.291	454.237	450.190	445.241	445.730	449.067	442.446	435.818	444.079	433.496
137	472.000	462.852	439.840	465.487	470.606	471.588	467.386	462.248	462.755	466.220	459.346	452.465	461.041
138	535.000	541.706	535.343	508.727	538.391	544.311	545.447	540.587	534.644	535.231	539.238	531.288	523.329
139	622.000	610.095	614.700	607.479	577.277	610.938	617.657	618.945	613.430	606.687	607.353	611.900	602.878
140	606.000	623.997	616.760	621.415	614.116	583.584	617.612	624.404	625.707	620.131	613.315	613.988	618.584
141	508.000	514.712	523.887	517.810	521.719	515.590	489.957	518.526	524.228	525.322	520.641	514.918	515.483
142	461.000	448.040	451.604	459.654	454.323	457.752	452.375	429.884	454.950	459.954	460.913	456.806	451.785
143	390.000	400.720	393.880	397.014	404.091	399.404	402.418	397.691	377.919	399.956	404.354	405.198	401.587
144	432.000	438.998	446.243	438.627	442.116	449.997	444.777	448.134	442.871	420.852	445.392	450.290	451.230
145		450.209	454.597	462.100	454.213	457.827	465.987	460.582	464.059	458.608	435.807	461.219	466.291
146			426.495	430.653	437.760	430.289	433.712	441.443	436.322	439.616	434.452	412.852	436.925
147				481.986	486.684	494.716	486.273	490.142	498.878	493.092	496.814	492.465	466.568
148					492.181	496.979	505.181	496.559	500.509	509.431	503.522	507.322	501.363
149						508.239	513.193	521.663	512.760	516.839	526.052	519.950	523.874
150							583.259	588.945	598.665	588.447	593.128	603.701	596.698
151								668.095	674.608	685.741	674.037	679.400	691.510
152									665.813	672.303	683.398	671.734	677.079
153										558.663	564.109	573.419	563.632
154											496.603	501.444	509.720
155												430.132	434.325
156													478.011

**Annotated Example for
BOX-JENKINS** *continued*

The final printed table consists of forecasted values from the end of the series along with 95% confidence limits for the forecasts. Unlike some other forecast routines, SPSS-X BOX-JENKINS, when possible, prints forecasts in the original scale of the series instead of in transformed units because internal transformation was used. The plot of the forecast function shows

- Series values (data).
- One-step-ahead forecasts for series values along with confidence bounds on the forecast values.
- Forecasts from the end of the series along with their confidence bounds.

The table of forecasted values and the plot of forecasts for Series G is shown in Figure F.

F Forecasted values and plot

```
FORECASTS FOR VARIABLE AIRLINE  WITH ORIGIN AT  144 AND  95.00% CONFIDENCE LIMITS

        OBS   LOW CONF LIM    FORECAST    UPP CONF LIM
        145     418.08         450.21        484.81
        146     391.16         426.50        465.02
        147     437.28         481.99        531.27
        148     442.18         492.18        547.83
        149     452.54         508.24        570.79
        150     515.04         583.26        660.51
        151     585.38         668.10        762.50
        152     579.11         665.81        765.50
        153     482.53         558.66        646.81
        154     426.08         496.60        578.80
        155     366.70         430.13        504.54
        156     405.02         478.01        564.16

GRAPHIC DISPLAY OF FORECASTS FOR VARIABLE AIRLINE

DEFINITIONS OF SYMBOLS
DATA - *
FORECASTS AT LEAD   1 - +
ESTIMATED 95% CONFIDENCE LIMITS - .
FORECAST FUNCTION - 0
OVERLAP - X
```

Syntax

CLUSTER

```
CLUSTER varlist [/MISSING={LISTWISE**}]
                          {INCLUDE  }

  [/MEASURE={SEUCLID** }] [/METHOD={BAVERAGE**}[(rootname)] [,...]]
           {EUCLID    }            {WAVERAGE  }
           {COSINE    }            {SINGLE    }
           {POWER(p,r)}            {COMPLETE  }
           {BLOCK     }            {CENTROID  }
           {CHEBYCHEV }            {MEDIAN    }
           {DEFAULT   }            {WARD      }

  [/SAVE=CLUSTER({level  })]  [/ID=varname]
                {min,max}

  [/PRINT=[CLUSTER({level  })] [DISTANCE] [SCHEDULE**] [NONE]]
                  {min,max}

  [/PLOT=[VICICLE**[(min[,max[,inc]])]] [DENDROGRAM] [NONE]]
         [HICICLE[(min[,max[,inc]])]]]

  [/MATRIX=[IN({file})] [OUT({file})]]
              {*   }        {*   }
```

** Default if the subcommand is omitted.

Contents

23.1   OVERVIEW

23.2   OPERATION

23.3   Variable Specification

23.4   METHOD Subcommand

23.5   MEASURE Subcommand

23.6   SAVE Subcommand

23.7   ID Subcommand

23.8   PRINT Subcommand

23.9   PLOT Subcommand

23.10   MISSING Subcommand

23.11   MATRIX Subcommand

23.12   OUT Keyword

23.13   IN Keyword

23.14   LIMITATIONS

23

Chapter 23 CLUSTER

CLUSTER is an agglomerative hierarchical clustering procedure. You can use it to cluster a small to moderate number of cases. CLUSTER provides several methods for linking cases in the agglomeration process, and it provides several proximity measures. CLUSTER can read a proximity matrix that you already have. This feature lets you cluster variables if the input matrix is for variables rather than cases, and it lets you use a proximity measure that CLUSTER itself cannot compute (see Chapter 43 for measures available through PROXIMITIES).

By default, CLUSTER describes the clustering method used, prints the agglomeration schedule, and displays a vertical icicle plot. Optionally, you can have CLUSTER display other plots and/or print the proximity matrix and the cluster membership of cases.

23.1
OVERVIEW

CLUSTER uses an agglomerative process having four steps:

- Compute (or input) the proximities between the initial clusters (the individual cases).
- Combine the two nearest clusters to form a new cluster.
- Recompute the proximities between existing clusters and the new cluster.
- Return to the second step until all cases have been combined in one cluster. Then print and plot the results.

This processs yields a hierarchy of cluster solutions, ranging from one overall cluster to as many clusters as there are cases. Clusters at a higher level can contain several lower-level clusters, but within each level, the clusters are disjoint (each item belongs to only one cluster).

Clustering Methods. You can choose among seven methods of clustering: single linkage, complete linkage, between- and within-groups average linkage, and median, centroid, and Ward's methods (see Section 23.4). You can specify several methods in a single CLUSTER command.

Proximity Measures. You can cluster the data using any one of six proximity measures (see Section 23.5).

Saving Cluster Membership. You can save the cluster membership of cases (for any selected cluster levels) as new variables on the active file (see Section 23.6).

Optional Output. You can have CLUSTER print the cluster membership of cases and/or the proximity matrix that it read or computed (see Section 23.8). You can also have it display a horizontal icicle plot, a vertical icicle plot, and/or a dendrogram of the cluster solution (see Section 23.9). To clarify the output, you can specify a string variable that contains an identifier for each case (see Section 23.7).

Missing Values. CLUSTER automatically performs listwise deletion of cases with missing values. You can choose to include or exclude cases with user-missing values (see Section 23.10).

Matrix Materials. You can write a computed proximity matrix to a matrix system file, which allows you to perform additional clustering later without recomputing the matrix (see Section 23.12). You can read a proximity matrix from a matrix input file (see Section 23.13 and Chapter 43).

23.2
OPERATION

The only required specification on a CLUSTER command is a variable list. For example,

```
CLUSTER A B C
```

would cluster cases based on the values of variables A, B, and C. The default analysis would be a between-group average-linkage clustering of squared Euclidean distances. Otherwise, CLUSTER is a subcommand-driven procedure. Following the variable specification, you can specify any of nine optional subcommands in any order. A subcommand must begin with the subcommand keyword and may be followed by an optional equals sign and specifications. Each subcommand must be preceded by a slash and should be used no more than once. You can specify only one kind of proximity measure, but you can specify more than one clustering method.

23.3
Variable Specification

A variable list must appear immediately after the CLUSTER command. This specification has two distinct purposes in CLUSTER. It can identify the variables for computing similarities or distances between cases, and it can identify (provide labels for) the items in a proximity matrix read from a matrix input file.

If your input data are matrix materials you should omit the variable list (see Section 23.13). This is true only for matrix input.

23.4
METHOD Subcommand

You can use the METHOD subcommand to specify the kind(s) of cluster linkage. Seven methods are available, and you can specify more than one on the subcommand. If you want to save cluster memberships for a method (see Section 23.6), you must specify a rootname. CLUSTER uses the rootname to generate names for cluster membership variables. You can specify rootnames for none, any, or all of the methods. For example, the subcommand

```
/METHOD=SINGLE(SINGCLUS), COMPLETE, WARDS
```

specifies three methods of clustering, but only the clusters obtained by single linkage will be saved and will have the rootname SINGCLUS.

BAVERAGE[(rootname)]	*Average linkage between groups (UPGMA, unweighted pair group method average).* This is the default.
WAVERAGE[(rootname)]	*Average linkage within groups.*
SINGLE[(rootname)]	*Single linkage, or nearest neighbor.*
COMPLETE[(rootname)]	*Complete linkage, or furthest neighbor.*
CENTROID[(rootname)]	*Centroid clustering (UPGMC, unweighted pair group method centroid).*
MEDIAN[(rootname)]	*Median clustering (WPGMC, weighted pair group method centroid).*
WARD[(rootname)]	*Ward's method.*

You should use squared Euclidean distance as the measure for centroid clustering, median clustering, and Ward's method (see Section 23.5). With a large number of cases, centroid and median clustering require significantly more CPU time than other methods.

23.5
MEASURE Subcommand

You can use the MEASURE subcommand to select a single proximity measure. Six measures are available:

SEUCLID   *Squared Euclidean distance.* This measure is the default. You can make it explicit with either SEUCLID or DEFAULT on the MEASURE subcommand. You should use this measure whenever you use centroid, median, or Ward's method of clustering. With this measure, the distance between two cases (*x* and *y*) is the sum of the squared differences between the values of the clustering variables.

$$Distance(x,y) = \Sigma_i(x_i - y_i)^2$$

EUCLID   *Euclidean distance.* The distance between two cases is the square root of the sum of the squared differences between the values of the clustering variables.

$$Distance(x,y) = SQRT(\Sigma_i(x_i - y_i)^2)$$

COSINE   *Cosine of vectors of variables.* This is a pattern similarity measure.

$$Similarity(x,y) = \frac{\Sigma_i(x_iy_i)}{SQRT((\Sigma_ix_i^2)(\Sigma_iy_i^2))}$$

CHEBYCHEV   *Chebychev distance metric.* The distance between two cases is the maximum absolute difference between the values of the clustering variables.

$$Distance(x,y) = Maximum_i|x_i - y_i|$$

BLOCK   *City-block, or Manhattan, distance.* The distance between two cases is the sum of the absolute differences between the values of the clustering variables.

$$Distance(x,y) = \Sigma_i|x_i - y_i|$$

POWER(p,r)   *Distance in an absolute power metric.* The distance between two cases is the *r*th root of the sum of the absolute differences to the *p*th power between the values of the clustering variables. Appropriate selection of the integer parameters *p* and *r* yields Euclidean, squared Euclidean, Minkowski, city-block, and many other distance metrics.

$$Distance(x,y) = (\Sigma_i|x_i - y_i|^p)^{1/r}$$

23.6
SAVE Subcommand

You can use the SAVE subcommand to save cluster memberships at specified cluster levels as new variables on the active file. The format for the SAVE specification is CLUSTER(min,max) or CLUSTER(n), where *min* and *max* are the minimum and maximum cluster levels for the memberships you want to save, and *n* is a single level. For each clustering method whose memberships are to be saved, you *must* specify a rootname on the METHOD subcommand (see Section 23.4). For example,

```
CLUSTER A B C
 /METHOD=BAVERAGE(CLUSMEM)
 /SAVE=CLUSTER(3,5)
```

saves each case's cluster memberships for three-, four-, and five-cluster solutions. The new variables saved on the active file would have names derived from the rootname CLUSMEM and would appear on the active file in the order CLUSMEM5, CLUSMEM4, and CLUSMEM3, because that is the order in which three solutions are obtained. The values of the variables would be integers from 1 to the number of clusters at the specified cluster level. CLUSMEM3, for example, would have a value of 1, 2, or 3 to indicate the cluster to which each case belonged. CLUSTER prints the names of the new variables and the corresponding clustering method (see Figure 23.6).

Figure 23.6 Printed output for SAVE

```
* * * * * * H I E R A R C H I C A L   C L U S T E R   A N A L Y S I S * * * * * *

Variables (Cluster Membership) Saved into Active File
    CLUSMEM5 to CLUSMEM3 for Average Linkage (Between Groups)
```

23.7
ID Subcommand

Use the ID subcommand to specify an identifying string variable for cases. You can name any string variable on your file. CLUSTER uses the values of this variable to identify cases in procedure output. By default, CLUSTER identifies cases by case number alone. The form of the ID subcommand is

/ID=varname

23.8
PRINT Subcommand

CLUSTER always prints the number of clustering methods used, the proximity measure (or an identifier for a matrix that was read in), and the number of cases (see Figure 23.8a). For other, specified printed output, you can use the PRINT subcommand with any of the following keywords:

SCHEDULE   *Agglomeration schedule.* This prints by default. The agglomeration schedule shows the stages of clustering and the corresponding proximity values at which items and clusters combined to form new clusters. For example, as shown in Figure 23.8c, items 17 and 22 combined at stage 2, at a proximity value of .261159. For each stage, the schedule also shows the prior cluster levels at which the combining clusters were formed and the next stage at which the cluster combines with another. As shown in Figure 23.8c, the cluster formed by items 4 and 17 combined with item 10 at stage 6. (Zero indicates no prior stage or no subsequent stage.)

CLUSTER(min,max)   *Cluster membership.* This option produces a table showing a cluster number for each case and for each solution of a specified number of clusters (see Figure 23.8b). ID labels appear for the cases (see Section 23.7). The numbers that identify the clusters are successive integers starting from 1. You can specify the minimum and maximum numbers of clusters in the solutions represented in the table; the range must be within the bounds of the cluster hierarchy. For example, if min=3 and max=5, the cluster membership table will show the identifying number of the cluster to which each case belongs in three-, four-, and five-cluster solutions. (You can also specify just a single level rather than a range.)

DISTANCE   *Matrix of distances between items.* This option prints out the data matrix that was read or computed. As in procedure PROXIMITIES (see Chapter 43), this use of the PRINT subcommand produces a large volume of output and uses a significant amount of CPU time when the number of cases is large.

NONE   *No plots.* You can use the keyword NONE with the PRINT subcommand for CLUSTER. The NONE option prints only the unconditional output: the number of clustering methods used, the similarity or distance measure, and the number of cases (see Figure 23.8a). NONE also overrides any other specification on the PRINT subcommand. If you specify other options with NONE, the others will be ignored.

Figure 23.8a   Unconditional printed output

```
* * * * * * H I E R A R C H I C A L   C L U S T E R   A N A L Y S I S * * * * * *

Data Information

        22 unweighted cases accepted.
         3 cases rejected because of missing value.

Squared Euclidean measure used.

1 Agglomeration method specified.
```

Figure 23.8b   Cluster membership of cases

```
* * * * * * H I E R A R C H I C A L   C L U S T E R   A N A L Y S I S * * * * * *

Cluster Membership of Cases using Average Linkage (Between Groups)

                                 Number of Clusters

Label             Case    5    4    3

Baltimore          1      1    1    1
Chicago            2      2    2    2
Cleveland          3      1    1    1
Columbus           4      3    1    1
Dallas             5      4    3    3
Denver             6      4    3    3
Detroit            7      3    1    1
Houston            8      4    3    3
Indianapolis       9      5    4    2
Jacksonville      10      4    3    3
Los Angeles       11      4    3    3
Memphis           12      3    1    1
Nashville         13      1    1    1
New Orleans       14      2    2    2
New York          15      2    2    2
Philadelphia      16      1    1    1
Phoenix           17      4    3    3
San Diego         18      3    1    1
San Francisco     19      3    1    1
San Jose          20      4    3    3
Seattle           21      4    3    3
Washington        22      4    3    3
```

Figure 23.8c   Agglomeration schedule

```
* * * * * * H I E R A R C H I C A L   C L U S T E R   A N A L Y S I S * * * * * *

Agglomeration Schedule using Average Linkage (Between Groups)

           Clusters    Combined                    Stage Cluster 1st Appears    Next
Stage    Cluster 1   Cluster 2   Coefficient       Cluster 1    Cluster 2      Stage

  1          5          20          .213571             0           0            8
  2         17          22          .261159             0           0            6
  3          4          18          .292620             0           0           11
  4          8          21          .656814             0           0            8
  5          3          13         3.067433             0           0           14
  6         10          17         3.173483             0           2           16
  7          1          16         5.655860             0           0           14
  8          5           8         8.083633             1           4           12
  9          7          12        13.270877             0           0           11
 10         14          15        16.843185             0           0           13
 11          4           7        33.221954             3           9           15
 12          5          11        38.605591             8           0           17
 13          2          14        48.604095             0          10           19
 14          1           3        73.268372             7           5           18
 15          4          19        88.134521            11           0           18
 16          6          10        97.164627             0           6           17
 17          5           6       250.892181            12          16           20
 18          1           4       651.010742            14          15           20
 19          2           9      1026.891846            13           0           21
 20          1           5      1710.032959            18          17           21
 21          1           2      5559.281250            20          19            0
```

ANNOTATED EXAMPLE FOR CLUSTER

This example is a hierarchical cluster analysis of 25 cities according to data from the 1982 *Information Please Almanac*. The cities were the most populous in the United States in 1980. The clustering variables are:

- CHURCHES—number of churches.
- PARKS—number of parks. In some instances, a city has a missing-value code of 9999 for this variable because only total acreage rather than number of parks was available.
- PHONES—number of telephones.
- TVS—number of television sets.
- RADIOST—number of radio stations.
- TVST—number of television stations.
- POP80—city population in 1980.
- TAXRATE—property tax rate.

The aim is to cluster the cities into groups that are relatively homogeneous with respect to these variables. However, cities differ on most of the variables simply as a function of population. Therefore, most are rescaled to yield more comparable, per capita values. The SPSS-X commands follow, and printed and plotted output is shown in the figures cited below.

```
SET WIDTH=80

DATA LIST  FILE=CITYDATA  RECORDS=3
   /1 CITY 6-18(A) POP80 53-60
   /2 CHURCHES 10-13 PARKS 14-17 PHONES 18-25 TVS 26-32
      RADIOST 33-35 TVST 36-38 TAXRATE 52-57(2)

MISSING VALUES PARKS (9999)
DO REPEAT X=CHURCHES PARKS PHONES TVS RADIOST TVST
COMPUTE X=X/POP80
END REPEAT

CLUSTER CHURCHES TO TAXRATE
 /METHOD=BAVERAGE(CLUSMEM)
 /ID=CITY
 /PRINT=DISTANCE CLUSTER(3,5) SCHEDULE
 /PLOT=VICICLE HICICLE DENDROGRAM
 /SAVE=CLUSTER(3)
```

- The SET WIDTH command restricts printed output to a maximum of 80 columns.
- The DATA LIST command reads the necessary data.
- The DO REPEAT and COMPUTE commands divide six variables by city population, yielding per capita values for the number of churches, parks, and other measures.

- The CLUSTER variable specification names seven variables with the TO convention.
- The METHOD subcommand specifies the method of average linkage between groups. It also gives the rootname CLUSMEM to cluster membership variables created for this method.
- The ID subcommand specifies that the values of variable CITY will identify the cases.
- The measure for the clustering will be squared Euclidean distance, the default.
- The PRINT subcommand requests the computed distances between the cases (see Section 23.8), the cluster to which each case belongs for the three-, four-, and five-cluster solutions (see Figure 23.8b), and the cluster agglomeration schedule (see Figure 23.8c).
- The PLOT subcommand requests the cluster solution as a vertical icicle plot (see Figure 23.9a), as a horizontal icicle plot (see Figure 23.9b), and as a dendrogram (see Figure 23.9c).
- The SAVE subcommand saves the cluster membership of the individual cases in the three-cluster solution as a new variable on the active file. CLUSTER assigns this variable the name CLUSMEM3, deriving the name from the rootname CLUSMEM specified on the METHOD subcommand and from the three-cluster solution requested.

23.9
PLOT Subcommand

You can use the following keywords on the PLOT subcommand to specify icicle plots and/or a dendrogram of the cluster solution:

VICICLE[(min[,max[,inc]])] *Produce a vertical icicle plot.* This is the default. Figure 23.9a shows a complete plot, including all cluster levels. At the two-cluster level, for example, one cluster includes cases 9, 15, 14, and 2; the other cluster includes the remaining cases. Optionally, you can specify a lowest cluster level, a highest level, and the increment for intermediate levels that will appear in the plot. For example, if min=1, max=9, and inc=2, only levels 1, 3, 5, 7, and 9 will appear.

HICICLE[(min[,max[,inc]])] *Produce a horizontal icicle plot.* The plot can show all cluster levels (see Figure 23.9b) or only the levels that are specified (in the same format as for VICICLE).

DENDROGRAM *Produce a dendrogram.* This option produces a tree diagram for the cluster solution. CLUSTER scales the dendrogram according to rescaled distances where clusters combine (see Figure 23.9c).

NONE *Unconditional output.* The keyword NONE on the PLOT subcommand for CLUSTER specifies that no plots should be printed. This option overrides other specifications on the PLOT subcommand. If you specify other options with NONE, the others will be ignored.

Figure 23.9a A vertical icicle plot

```
* * * * * * H I E R A R C H I C A L   C L U S T E R   A N A L Y S I S * * * * * *

Vertical Icicle Plot using Average Linkage (Between Groups)

(Down) Number of Clusters  (Across) Case Label and number


    I N N C W P J D L S H S D S M D S C N C P B
    n e e h a h a e o e o a a a e e a o a l h a
    d w w i s o c n s a u n l n m t n l s e i l
    i     c h e k v   s a u n l m t n l u h v l t
    a Y O a i n s e A t t J a F h o D m v e a i
    n o r g n i o r n l o o s r i i i b i l d m
    a r l o g x n   g e n s   a s t e u l a e o
    p k e n t   o   n e   s   n   e u l a n l r r
    o   a       i   e   s       c   a   g   n   p e
    l   n       n   l   s       i   s   o   e   h
    i   s       l   e           s       t   d   i
    s               e           c               a
                                o
     1 1   2 1 1   1 2   2   1 1   1   1 1   1
     9 5 4 2 2 7 0 6 1 1 8 0 5 9 2 7 8 4 3 3 6 1
  1 +XXXXXXXXXXXXXXXXXXXXXXXXXXXXXXXXXXXXXXXXXXXXX
  2 +XXXXXXXXX  XXXXXXXXXXXXXXXXXXXXXXXXXXXXXXXXXX
  3 +XXXXXXXXX  XXXXXXXXXXXXXXXXXXXXXXXXXXXXXXXXXX
  4 +X XXXXXX   XXXXXXXXXXXXXXXXX XXXXXXXXXXXXXXXX
  5 +X XXXXXX   XXXXXXXXXXXXXXXXX XXXXXXXXXX XXXXX
  6 +X XXXXXX XXXXXXXXX  XXXXXXXXX XXXXXXXXXX XXXXXXXXXX
  7 +X XXXXXX XXXXXXX X XXXXXXXXXX X XXXXXXXXXX XXXXXXXXXX
  8 +X XXXXXX XXXXXXX X XXXXXXXXXX X X XXXXXXXXXX XXXXXXXXXX
  9 +X XXXXXX XXXXXXX X XXXXXXXXXX X X XXXXXXXXXX XXXX XXXX
 10 +X XXXX X XXXXXXX X X XXXXXXXXX X XXXXXXXXXX XXXX XXXX
 11 +X XXXX X XXXXXXX X X XXXXXXXXX X XXXXXXXXXX XXXX XXXX
 12 +X XXXX X XXXXXXX X X XXXXXXXXX X XXXX XXXX XXXX XXXX
 13 +X X X X XXXXXXX X X XXXXXXXXXX X XXXX XXXX XXXX XXXX
 14 +X X X X XXXXXXX X X XXXXXXXXXX X X X XXXX XXXX XXXX
 15 +X X X X XXXXXXX X X XXXXXXXXXX X X X XXXX XXXX XXXX
 16 +X X X X XXXXXXX X X XXXX XXXX X X X XXXX XXXX X X
 17 +X X X X XXXXXXX X X XXXX XXXX X X X XXXX XXXX X X
 18 +X X X X XXXX X X XXXX XXXX X X X XXXX X X X X
 19 +X X X X XXXX X X X X XXXX X X X XXXX X X X X
 20 +X X X X XXXX X X X X XXXX X X X X X X X X X
 21 +X X X X X X X X X X X XXXX X X X X X X X X X
```

If there is not enough workspace to produce a dendrogram or an icicle plot, CLUSTER performs the cluster analysis, skips the plot, and prints an error message. To obtain the plot, either enlarge the workspace or specify an increment or restricted range for VICICLE or HICICLE. A reduced icicle plot requires significantly less workspace and time. It may also fit better on the page, and it may help you see the clustering of the cases if you are interested in only a restricted range of cluster levels.

Figure 23.9b   A horizontal icicle plot

```
* * * * * * H I E R A R C H I C A L   C L U S T E R   A N A L Y S I S * * * * * *

Horizontal Icicle Plot Using Average Linkage (Between Groups)

                          Number of Clusters

                              111111111122
         C A S E           12345678901234567890
  Label              Seq   ++++++++++++++++++++

  Indianapolis        9    XXXXXXXXXXXXXXXXXXXX
                           XXX
                           XXX
  New York           15    XXXXXXXXXXXXXXXXXXXX
                           XXXXXXXXXXX
                           XXXXXXXXXXX
  New Orleans        14    XXXXXXXXXXXXXXXXXXXX
                           XXXXXXXXX
                           XXXXXXXXX
  Chicago             2    XXXXXXXXXXXXXXXXXXXX
                           X
                           X
  Washington         22    XXXXXXXXXXXXXXXXXXXX
                           XXXXXXXXXXXXXXXXXX
                           XXXXXXXXXXXXXXXXXX
  Phoenix            17    XXXXXXXXXXXXXXXXXXXX
                           XXXXXXXXXXXXXXX
                           XXXXXXXXXXXXXXX
  Jacksonville       10    XXXXXXXXXXXXXXXXXXXX
                           XXXXX
                           XXXXX
  Denver              6    XXXXXXXXXXXXXXXXXXXX
                           XXXXX
                           XXXXX
  Los Angeles        11    XXXXXXXXXXXXXXXXXXXX
                           XXXXXXXXX
                           XXXXXXXXX
  Seattle            21    XXXXXXXXXXXXXXXXXXXX
                           XXXXXXXXXXXXXXXXX
                           XXXXXXXXXXXXXXXXX
  Houston             8    XXXXXXXXXXXXXXXXXXXX
                           XXXXXXXXXXXXXX
                           XXXXXXXXXXXXXX
  San Jose           20    XXXXXXXXXXXXXXXXXXXX
                           XXXXXXXXXXXXXXXXXX
                           XXXXXXXXXXXXXXXXXX
  Dallas              5    XXXXXXXXXXXXXXXXXXXX
                           XX
                           XX
  San Francisco      19    XXXXXXXXXXXXXXXXXXXX
                           XXXXXX
                           XXXXXX
  Memphis            12    XXXXXXXXXXXXXXXXXXXX
                           XXXXXXXXXXXXX
                           XXXXXXXXXXXXX
  Detroit             7    XXXXXXXXXXXXXXXXXXXX
                           XXXXXXXXXX
                           XXXXXXXXXX
  San Diego          18    XXXXXXXXXXXXXXXXXXXX
                           XXXXXXXXXXXXXXXXX
                           XXXXXXXXXXXXXXXXX
  Columbus            4    XXXXXXXXXXXXXXXXXXXX
                           XXXX
                           XXXX
  Nashville          13    XXXXXXXXXXXXXXXXXXXX
                           XXXXXXXXXXXXXXX
                           XXXXXXXXXXXXXXX
  Cleveland           3    XXXXXXXXXXXXXXXXXXXX
                           XXXXXXX
                           XXXXXXX
  Philadelphia       16    XXXXXXXXXXXXXXXXXXXX
                           XXXXXXXXXXXXX
                           XXXXXXXXXXXXX
  Baltimore           1    XXXXXXXXXXXXXXXXXXXX
```

Figure 23.9c A dendrogram

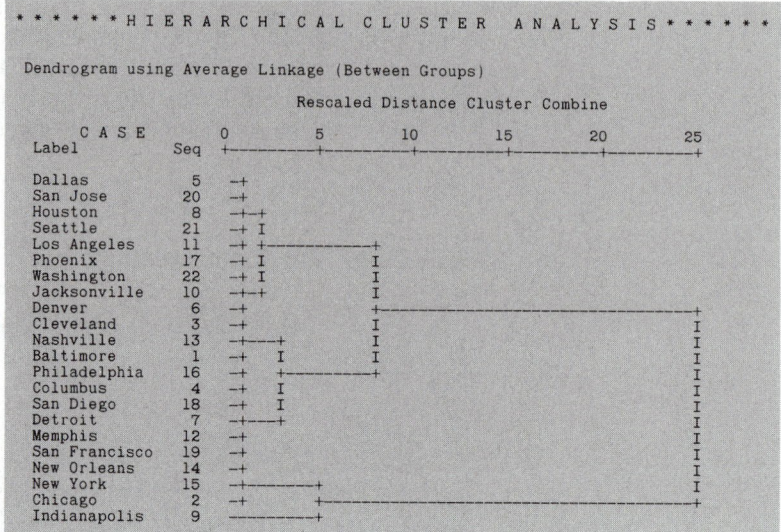

23.10
MISSING Subcommand

To change the treatment of missing values or to make it explicit, you can use the MISSING subcommand with either of the following specifications:

LISTWISE *Perform listwise deletion of cases with missing values.* This is the default. You can make it explicit by specifying either LISTWISE or DEFAULT.

INCLUDE *Include user-missing values as valid.*

23.11
MATRIX Subcommand

CLUSTER can both read and write matrix materials. It writes proximity-type matrices that can be used by subsequent CLUSTER procedures or by procedures PROXIMITIES and ALSCAL (see Chapter 13, Table 13.10).

Use the MATRIX subcommand to read and write matrix materials. The MATRIX subcommand has two keywords, IN and OUT, which you use to specify the matrix file in parentheses. When you use both IN and OUT on the same CLUSTER procedure you can specify each on a separate MATRIX subcommand, or both on the same subcommand. For example,

```
CLUSTER
  /MATRIX=IN(FILEONE)
  /MATRIX=OUT(FILETWO)
```

is the same as

```
CLUSTER
  /MATRIX=IN(FILEONE) OUT(FILETWO)
```

23.12
OUT Keyword

The OUT keyword on MATRIX specifies the file to which the matrix is written. There are two options:

(file) *Write the matrix to a system file.* CLUSTER creates a system file containing the matrix materials. The output file is specified in parentheses. The system file is stored on disk and can be retrieved at any time.

(*)   *Replace the active file with the matrix system file.* The matrix materials replace the active file. The matrix is *not* stored on disk.

Documents from the original file will not be included in the matrix file and will not be present if the matrix file becomes the active file. (For a discussion on documents, see Chapter 6.)

In the following example one set of matrix materials is written to file CLUSMTX:

```
DATA LIST FILE=ALMANAC1 RECORDS=3
   /1 CITY 6-18(A) POP80 53-60
   /2 CHURCHES 10-13 PARKS 14-17 PHONES 18-25 TVS 26-32
     ·RADIOST 33-35 TVST 36-38 TAXRATE 52-57(2)
N OF CASES 8

CLUSTER CHURCHES TO TAXRATE
 /ID=CITY
 /MEASURE=EUCLID
 /MATRIX=OUT(CLUSMTX)
```

The active file is still the file ALMANAC1 defined on DATA LIST. Subsequent commands are executed on ALMANAC1.

To write the same matrix but have it available to subsequent commands, specify the following:

```
DATA LIST FILE=ALMANAC1 RECORDS=3
   /1 CITY 6-18(A) POP80 53-60
   /2 CHURCHES 10-13 PARKS 14-17 PHONES 18-25 TVS 26-32
     RADIOST 33-35 TVST 36-38 TAXRATE 52-57(2)
N OF CASES 8

CLUSTER CHURCHES TO TAXRATE
 /ID=CITY
 /MEASURE=EUCLID
 /MATRIX=OUT(*)
LIST
DISPLAY DICTIONARY
```

The active file is replaced with the matrix system file. The LIST and DISPLAY commands are executed on the matrix file, not on the file ALMANAC1.

Format of the Matrix System File. Figure 23.12 shows the matrix system file produced by the above commands (results of the DISPLAY command are shown only for variable ROWTYPE_). The file includes two special variables created by SPSS-X: ROWTYPE_ and VARNAME_. Variable ROWTYPE_ is a string variable with value PROX, for proximity measure. PROX is assigned value labels containing the distance measure used to create the matrix. It is also assigned a similarity/dissimilarity keyword. In this example, the distance measure is EUCLID and the similarity/dissimilarity keyword is DISSIMILARITY, as shown in Figure 23.12.

Variable CITY is the case-identifying variable named on the ID subcommand. Up to 20 characters can be displayed for the identifying variable; ID variables longer than 20 characters are truncated. The identifying variable is present only when the ID subcommand is used. The next variable in the matrix file, variable VARNAME_, is a string variable whose values are the case numbers of the ID variable. The remaining variables in the matrix file are the distance variables used to form the matrix.

Only 8 cases were included in the analysis that generated Figure 23.12 so that the display would not wrap. With a large number of cases, the display file wraps and the matrix format is less readable. Nonetheless, the matrix values are equally as accurate and just as useful when used as matrix input values.

Figure 23.12   A matrix system file

```
FILE:     MATRIX FILE

ROWTYPE_ CITY          VARNAME_      CASE1       CASE2       CASE3       CASE4       CASE5       CASE6       CASE7       CASE8

PROX      Baltimore    CASE1         .0000  866856.500 2030933.00  550438.313  917515.813  615897.563   83087.5625  555323.813
PROX      Boston       CASE2    866856.500        .0000 2663554.00  490670.375   84965.1875  409640.250  821480.438 1128250.00
PROX      Chicago      CASE3   2030933.00 2663554.00         .0000 2172985.00 2662566.00 2255318.00 2113860.00 1552525.00
PROX      Cleveland    CASE4    550438.313  490670.375 2172985.00         .0000  496106.563   88765.1875  550994.375  644446.250
PROX      Columbus     CASE5    917515.813   84965.1875 2662566.00  496106.563        .0000  409725.375  877483.250 1140197.00
PROX      Dallas       CASE6    615897.563  409640.250 2255318.00   88765.1875  409725.375        .0000  607233.188  732208.688
PROX      Denver       CASE7     83087.5625  821480.438 2113860.00  550994.375  877483.250  607233.188        .0000  632810.250
PROX      Detroit      CASE8    555323.813 1128250.00 1552525.00  644446.250 1140197.00  732208.688  632810.250        .0000

NUMBER OF CASES READ =      8    NUMBER OF CASES LISTED =      8

FILE:     MATRIX FILE

            LIST OF VARIABLES ON THE ACTIVE FILE

NAME                                                                       POSITION

ROWTYPE_                                                                         1
                       PRINT FORMAT: A8
                       WRITE FORMAT: A8

            VALUE     LABEL

            PROX      DISSIMILARITY     EUCLID
```

Variable Order. When split-file processing is in effect (see Chapter 15), the first variables in the matrix system file will be the split variables, followed by ROWTYPE_, the case-identifier variable (if the ID subcommand is used), VARNAME_, and the distance variable(s). A full set of matrix materials is written for each split-file group defined by the split variable(s). A split variable cannot have the same name as any other variable written to the matrix system file. If split-file processing is in effect when a matrix is written, the same split file must be in effect when that matrix is read by any procedure. (See Chapter 13 for more information on matrix system files.)

Additional Statistics. CLUSTER writes a variety of proximity-type matrices. Each has ROWTYPE_ values of PROX. CLUSTER neither reads nor writes additional statistics with its matrix materials.

Missing Values. Missing-value treatment affects the values written to a matrix system file. When reading a matrix system file, be sure to specify a missing-value treatment on CLUSTER that is compatible with the treatment used to generate the matrix materials.

23.13
IN Keyword

The IN keyword on MATRIX specifies the file from which the matrix is read. There are two options:

(file)   *Read the matrix materials from a matrix system file.*

(*)   *Read the matrix materials from the active file.* The active file must be an appropriate matrix system file.

When reading matrix input, you should omit the variable list from the CLUSTER command.

MATRIX=IN cannot be used in place of GET or DATA LIST to create an active file, since MATRIX is a subcommand on CLUSTER and CLUSTER cannot run before an active file is defined. You can either GET the matrix file and then specify IN(*) on MATRIX or create a matrix on the active file and then specify IN(*). Or you can specify a file other than the active file on IN as long as an active file already exists.

In the following example, one set of matrix materials is read from the file named CLUSMTX. This specification assumes the active file is not the file CLUSMTX:

```
CLUSTER
 /ID=CITY
 /MATRIX=IN(CLUSMTX)
```

SPSS-X reads variable names, variable and value labels, and print and write formats from the dictionary of file CLUSMTX. By default, all cases in the matrix system file are used in the analysis.

The order among rows and cases in the input matrix file is unimportant, as long as values for split-file variables precede values for ROWTYPE_. CLUSTER ignores unrecognized ROWTYPE_ values.

CLUSTER can read a matrix written to the active file by a previous CLUSTER procedure or a PROXIMITIES procedure. In the following example, CLUSTER reads a matrix file written to the active file by PROXIMITIES:

```
GET FILE=CRIME
PROXIMITIES MURDER TO MOTOR
 /ID=CITY
 /MEASURE=PH2
 /MATRIX=OUT(*)
CLUSTER
 /MATRIX=IN(*)
```

- The GET command defines the data to SPSS-X.
- The PROXIMITIES command specifies variables for the analysis and reads the raw data from file CRIME. The ID subcommand specifies CITY as the case-identifying variable. The MATRIX subcommand indicates that the resulting matrix is written to the active file.
- MATRIX=IN(*) indicates that the active file contains the matrix. The variable list is omitted on the CLUSTER command. This is recommended because the variables from the PROXIMITIES procedure are now represented by cases in the matrix system file. By default, all cases are used in the analysis. The slash preceding the MATRIX subcommand is required because there is an implied variable list. Without the slash, CLUSTER would attempt to interpret MATRIX as a variable name rather than a subcommand name.

23.14
LIMITATIONS

CLUSTER stores cases and a lower-triangular matrix of proximities in memory. Storage requirements increase rapidly with the number of cases. You should be able to cluster 150 cases using a small number of variables in an 80K workspace.

Syntax

CORRELATIONS

```
CORRELATIONS [VARIABLES=] varlist [WITH varlist] [/varlist...]
  [/MISSING={PAIRWISE**}  [INCLUDE]]
            {LISTWISE }
  [/PRINT={ONETAIL**}  {SIG**}]
          {TWOTAIL }  {NOSIG}
  [/FORMAT={MATRIX**}]
           {SERIAL  }
  [/MATRIX=OUT({*   })]
              {file}
  [/STATISTICS=[DESCRIPTIVES]  [XPROD]  [ALL]]
```

**Default if subcommand is omitted.

Contents

24.1 OVERVIEW

24.2 OPERATION

24.3 VARIABLES Subcommand

24.4 PRINT Subcommand

24.5 STATISTICS Subcommand

24.6 MISSING Subcommand

24.7 FORMAT Subcommand

24.8 MATRIX Subcommand

24.9 LIMITATIONS

24

Chapter 24   CORRELATIONS

Procedure CORRELATIONS (alias PEARSON CORR) produces Pearson product-moment correlations with significance levels and, optionally, univariate statistics, covariances and cross-product deviations. Other procedures that also produce correlation matrices are PARTIAL CORR (Chapter 40), REGRESSION (Chapter 45), DISCRIMINANT (Chapter 27), and FACTOR (Chapter 28).

24.1 OVERVIEW

CORRELATIONS produces one or more matrices of correlation coefficients. For each coefficient, CORRELATIONS prints the number of cases used and the significance level. In addition to the correlation matrix, you can specify methods of handling missing data, control formatting options and significance levels, and request additional statistics. CORRELATIONS also writes matrix materials which can be used by other procedures.

Types of Matrices. You can specify one or more correlation matrices with one CORRELATIONS command. A simple variable list produces a square matrix. You can also request a rectangular matrix of correlations between specific pairs of variables or between variable lists. (See Section 24.3.)

Significance Levels. By default, CORRELATIONS prints Pearson correlation coefficients based on a one-tailed test. Below each coefficient it prints both the number of cases and the significance level. Optionally, you can suppress the number of cases and significance level for each coefficient. You can also request that the significance level be calculated using a two-tailed test. (See Section 24.4.)

Additional Statistics. In addition to the correlation coefficient, number of cases, and significance level, you can obtain the mean, standard deviation, and number of nonmissing cases for each variable, and the cross-product deviations and covariance for each pair of variables. (See Section 24.5.)

Missing Values. By default, CORRELATIONS excludes cases with missing values on an analysis-by-analysis basis. Optionally, you can request that user-missing values be handled as if they were valid or that cases with missing values be deleted listwise. (See Section 24.6.)

Formatting Options. By default, CORRELATIONS includes redundant coefficients in the correlation and prints in matrix format. Optionally, you can include only the nonredundant coefficients and print in serial string format. (See Section 24.7.)

Matrix Output. CORRELATIONS allows you to write matrix materials to a system file. The matrix materials include the mean, standard deviation, number of cases used to compute each coefficient, and Pearson correlation coefficient for each variable. The matrix system file can be read by several other SPSS-X procedures. (See Section 24.8.)

24.2
OPERATION

The only required subcommand on CORRELATIONS is the VARIABLES subcommand, which specifies the variable list to be analyzed (see Section 24.3). The actual keyword VARIABLES variables can be omitted.

Sections 24.4 through 24.8 outline the optional subcommands. You can specify these subcommands in any order; separate them with slashes. You must first specify the variables to be used in the analysis, however, before you can specify any of the optional subcommands. For example, to include user-defined missing values in an analysis, specify

```
CORRELATIONS VARIABLES=FOOD RENT PUBTRANS TEACHER COOK ENGINEER/
    MISSING=INCLUDE
```

24.3
VARIABLES Subcommand

The VARIABLES subcommand names the variable list. The actual keyword VARIABLES is optional. If you explicitly specify keyword VARIABLES, an equals sign must precede the variable list.

CORRELATIONS prints either a square (symmetric) or rectangular (asymmetric) matrix, depending on how you specify the variable list. Both forms of the specification permit the use of the keyword TO to reference consecutive variables. If you provide a simple variable list, CORRELATIONS prints the correlations of each variable with every other variable in the list in a square or lower-triangular matrix. For example, the command

```
CORRELATIONS VARIABLES=FOOD RENT PUBTRANS TEACHER COOK ENGINEER
```

produces the square matrix in Figure 24.3a.

The correlation of a variable with itself is always 1.0000 and can be found on the diagonal of the matrix. Each pair of variables appears twice in the matrix (for example, FOOD with RENT and RENT with FOOD). Since the correlation coefficient is a symmetrical measure, these two values are identical, and the upper and lower triangles of the matrix are mirror images of each other. Use this form of the CORRELATIONS specification when you want to write the correlation matrix for use with another procedure or program (see Section 24.8).

Figure 24.3a Default matrix from a simple variable list

```
- - - - - - - - - - - - - - - P E A R S O N   C O R R E L A T I O N   C O E F F I C I E N T S - - - - - - - - - - - - - - -

              FOOD        RENT      PUBTRANS    TEACHER      COOK      ENGINEER

FOOD         1.0000       .2598       .5798      .5469       .3945      .4823
            (    0)      (   45)     (   45)    (   44)     (   44)    (   44)
            P= .        P= .042     P= .000    P= .000     P= .004    P= .000

RENT          .2598      1.0000      -.0111     -.0249       .1440      .2528
            (   45)      (    0)     (   45)    (   44)     (   44)    (   44)
            P= .042     P= .        P= .471    P= .436     P= .175    P= .049

PUBTRANS      .5798      -.0111      1.0000      .6858       .6058      .6358
            (   45)      (   45)     (    0)    (   44)     (   44)    (   44)
            P= .000     P= .471     P= .        P= .000     P= .000    P= .000

TEACHER       .5469      -.0249       .6858     1.0000       .6215      .6573
            (   44)      (   44)     (   44)    (    0)     (   43)    (   43)
            P= .000     P= .436     P= .000    P= .        P= .000    P= .000

COOK          .3945       .1440       .6058      .6215      1.0000      .7502
            (   44)      (   44)     (   44)    (   43)     (    0)    (   44)
            P= .004     P= .175     P= .000    P= .000     P= .        P= .000

ENGINEER      .4823       .2528       .6358      .6573       .7502     1.0000
            (   44)      (   44)     (   44)    (   43)     (   44)    (    0)
            P= .000     P= .049     P= .000    P= .000     P= .000    P= .

(COEFFICIENT / (CASES) / 1-TAILED SIG)          " . " IS PRINTED IF A COEFFICIENT CANNOT BE COMPUTED
```

To obtain the rectangular matrix, specify two variable lists separated by the keyword WITH. SPSS-X then prints a rectangular matrix of variables in the first list correlated with variables in the second list. For example,

```
CORRELATIONS VARIABLES=MECHANIC BUS WITH PUBTRANS
```

produces two correlations, MECHANIC with PUBTRANS and BUS with PUBTRANS, while

CORRELATIONS VARS=FOOD RENT **WITH** COOK TEACHER MANAGER ENGINEER

produces the eight correlations shown in Figure 24.3b. The variables listed before the keyword WITH define the rows of the matrix and those listed after the keyword WITH define the columns. Unless a variable is in both lists, there are no identity coefficients or redundant coefficients in the matrix. If you want to write the correlation matrix for use with another procedure or program, do not use the keyword WITH (see Section 24.8).

Figure 24.3b   Default matrix from a variable list using WITH

```
– – – – – – – – – – – – P E A R S O N   C O R R E L A T I O N   C O E F F I C I E N T S – – – – – – – – – – –

              COOK      TEACHER     MANAGER     ENGINEER

FOOD         .3945       .5469       .5304       .4823
            (   44)     (   44)     (   44)     (   44)
            P=  .004    P=  .000    P=  .000    P=  .000

RENT         .1440      -.0249       .2069       .2528
            (   44)     (   44)     (   44)     (   44)
            P=  .175    P=  .436    P=  .089    P=  .049


(COEFFICIENT / (CASES) / 1-TAILED SIG)          " . " IS PRINTED IF A COEFFICIENT CANNOT BE COMPUTED
```

You can request more than one matrix on a CORRELATIONS command. Use a slash (/) to separate the specifications for each of the requested matrices. For example,

CORRELATIONS VARS=FOOD RENT WITH COOK TEACHER MANAGER ENGINEER/
    FOOD TO ENGINEER/ PUBTRANS WITH MECHANIC

produces three separate correlation matrices. The first matrix contains eight nonredundant coefficients, the second matrix is a square matrix of all the variables from FOOD to ENGINEER, and the third matrix consists of one coefficient for PUBTRANS and MECHANIC.

You can specify up to 40 variable lists with one CORRELATIONS command and you can name or imply up to 500 variables total. A maximum of 250 individual elements may appear. Each unique occurrence of a variable name, keyword, or special delimiter counts as 1 toward this total. Variables implied by the TO convention do not count toward this total.

A key below each matrix indicates what information is contained in the matrix. The following line

COEFFICIENT / (CASES) / SIGNIFICANCE

appears in the default matrix formats in Figures 24.3a and 24.3b and indicates that each entry in the matrix contains these three pieces of information in the order indicated and that the number of cases is enclosed in parentheses. When other formats are chosen, the key is adjusted accordingly (see Section 24.7).

If all cases have a missing value for a given pair of variables or if they all have the same value for a variable, the coefficient cannot be computed. Since Pearson correlations always have a value in the range -1.00 to $+1.00$, a period is printed if a coefficient cannot be calculated.

24.4
PRINT Subcommand

By default, CORRELATIONS prints a matrix of Pearson correlation coefficients. Below each coefficient, it prints both the number of cases and the significance level, based on a one-tailed test.

The PRINT subcommand switches to a two-tailed test and/or suppresses the display of the number of cases and the significance level. The following keywords can be specified on the PRINT subcommand:

ONETAIL *One-tailed test of significance.* This test is appropriate when the direction of the relationship between a pair of variables can be specified in advance of the analysis. This is the default.

TWOTAIL *Two-tailed test of significance.* This test is appropriate when the direction of the relationship cannot be determined in advance, as is often the case in exploratory data analysis.

SIG *Print the number of cases and significance level.* This is the default for all CORRELATIONS matrices.

NOSIG *Suppress the printing of the number of cases and significance level.* A single asterisk (*) following a coefficient indicates significance at the .01 level or less. Two asterisks (**) following a coefficient indicate significance at the .001 level or less.

Figure 24.4 shows a square matrix with the number of cases and significance level suppressed. The matrix was produced by the following commands:

```
CORRELATIONS VARIABLES=FOOD RENT PUBTRANS TEACHER COOK ENGINEER
  /PRINT=NOSIG
```

If you use the keyword WITH in the variable list, the display will be a rectangular matrix similar to Figure 24.3b, with the number of cases suppressed and asterisks indicating significance levels.

Figure 24.4   Correlation matrix with PRINT=NOSIG

```
- - - - - - - - - - - - - - P E A R S O N   C O R R E L A T I O N   C O E F F I C I E N T S - - - - - - - - - - - - - - - -

             FOOD       RENT      PUBTRANS   TEACHER     COOK      ENGINEER

FOOD        1.0000      .2598      .5798**    .5469**    .3945*     .4823**
RENT         .2598     1.0000     -.0111     -.0249      .1440      .2528
PUBTRANS     .5798**   -.0111     1.0000      .6858**    .6058**    .6358**
TEACHER      .5469**   -.0249      .6858**   1.0000      .6215**    .6573**
COOK         .3945*     .1440      .6058**    .6215**   1.0000      .7502**
ENGINEER     .4823**    .2528      .6358**    .6573**    .7502**   1.0000


* - SIGNIF. LE .01     ** - SIGNIF. LE .001    (1-TAILED, " . " PRINTED IF A COEFFICIENT CANNOT BE COMPUTED)
```

If you specify both FORMAT=SERIAL and PRINT=NOSIG, as in

```
CORRELATIONS VARIABLES=FOOD RENT PUBTRANS TEACHER COOK ENGINEER/
    FORMAT=SERIAL/
    PRINT=NOSIG
```

only FORMAT=SERIAL will be in effect.

24.5
STATISTICS Subcommand

The correlation coefficient, number of cases, and significance level are automatically printed for every combination of variable pairs in the variable list.

The STATISTICS subcommand obtains additional statistics. The statistics for each variable list on the command precedes its corresponding correlation matrix.

The STATISTICS subcommand provides the following additional statistics:

DESCRIPTIVES *Mean, standard deviation, and number of nonmissing cases for each variable.* Missing values are handled on a variable-by-variable basis regardless of the missing-value option in effect for the correlations.

XPROD *Cross-product deviations and covariance for each pair of variables.*

ALL *All additional statistics available in CORRELATIONS.* Includes the mean, standard deviation, and number of nonmissing cases for each variable. Also includes the cross-product deviations and covariance for each pair of variables.

For example, to generate the correlation matrix with the mean, standard deviation, and number of nonmissing cases for each variable, plus the cross-product deviations and covariance for each pair of variables, specify

```
CORRELATIONS VARIABLES=FOOD RENT PUBTRANS TEACHER COOK ENGINEER/
    STATISTICS=ALL
```

Figure 24.5 shows the additional statistics.

Figure 24.5   Additional statistics available with CORRELATIONS

VARIABLE	CASES	MEAN	STD DEV
FOOD	45	70.4667	18.7442
RENT	45	120.0889	94.2250
PUBTRANS	45	48.1111	24.8141
TEACHER	44	38.3182	25.1819
COOK	44	64.6591	30.2785
ENGINEER	44	60.0455	26.1747

VARIABLES		CASES	CROSS-PROD DEV	VARIANCE-COVAR	VARIABLES		CASES	CROSS-PROD DEV	VARIANCE-COVAR
FOOD	RENT	45	20191.1333	458.8894	FOOD	PUBTRANS	45	11865.6667	269.6742
FOOD	TEACHER	44	11227.9545	261.1152	FOOD	COOK	44	9561.0000	222.3488
FOOD	ENGINEER	44	10103.0000	234.9535	RENT	PUBTRANS	45	-1139.4444	-25.8965
RENT	TEACHER	44	-2566.6364	-59.6892	RENT	COOK	44	17747.2500	412.7267
RENT	ENGINEER	44	26927.5000	626.2209	PUBTRANS	TEACHER	44	18637.7727	433.4366
PUBTRANS	COOK	44	19434.2727	451.9598	PUBTRANS	ENGINEER	44	17630.3636	410.0085
TEACHER	COOK	43	20326.3023	483.9596	TEACHER	ENGINEER	43	18627.4884	443.5116
COOK	ENGINEER	44	25566.6818	594.5740					

24.6
MISSING Subcommand

By default, CORRELATIONS deletes cases with missing values on a pair-by-pair basis. A case missing for one or both of the pair of variables for a specific correlation coefficient is not used for that coefficient. Since each coefficient is based on all cases that have valid codes on that particular pair of variables, the maximum information available is used in every calculation. This can also result in a set of coefficients based on a varying number of cases.

The MISSING subcommand controls missing values. The following keywords can be specified on the MISSING subcommand:

PAIRWISE   *Exclude missing values pairwise.* Cases missing for one or both of a pair of variables for a specific correlation coefficient are excluded from the analysis. This is the default if you omit the MISSING subcommand.

LISTWISE   *Exclude missing values listwise.* Each variable listed on a command is evaluated separately. Cases missing on any variable named in a list are excluded from all analyses.

INCLUDE   *Include user-defined missing values.* User-missing values are included in the analysis.

The PAIRWISE and LISTWISE keywords are mutually exclusive; however, each can be specified with INCLUDE. For example, to include user-missing values in an analysis that excludes system-missing values listwise, specify

```
CORRELATIONS VARIABLES=FOOD RENT PUBTRANS TEACHER COOK ENGINEER
    /MISSING=INCLUDE LISTWISE
```

24.7
FORMAT Subcommand

By default, CORRELATIONS includes redundant coefficients in the correlation and prints in matrix format.

The FORMAT subcommand has two keywords that control matrix format:

MATRIX   *Print in matrix format with redundant coefficients.* This is the default if you omit the FORMAT subcommand.

SERIAL   *Print in serial string format with nonredundant coefficients.* Nonredundant coefficients are printed in serial string format with the coefficients from the first row of the matrix printed first, followed by all the unique (in other words, those not already printed) coefficients from the second row and so on for all of the rows in the matrix. Each coefficient is identified with the name of the variable for which it was calculated. The number of cases and significance level are printed below the correlation, just as they are in the matrix form of the output.

Figure 24.7 shows the output from the following example with FORMAT=
SERIAL in effect.

```
CORRELATIONS VARIABLES=FOOD RENT PUBTRANS TEACHER COOK ENGINEER/
    FORMAT=SERIAL
```

Figure 24.7 Correlation matrix with FORMAT=SERIAL

```
- - - - - - - - - - - - - P E A R S O N   C O R R E L A T I O N   C O E F F I C I E N T S - - - - - - - - - - - - - -
VARIABLE            VARIABLE            VARIABLE            VARIABLE            VARIABLE            VARIABLE
PAIR                PAIR                PAIR                PAIR                PAIR                PAIR
_____              _____              _____              _____              _____              _____

FOOD       .2598    FOOD       .5798    FOOD       .5469    FOOD       .3945    FOOD       .4823    RENT      -.0111
WITH    N(   45)    WITH    N(   45)    WITH    N(   44)    WITH    N(   44)    WITH    N(   44)    WITH    N(   45)
RENT    SIG .042    PUBTRANS SIG .000   TEACHER SIG .000    COOK    SIG .004    ENGINEER SIG .000   PUBTRANS SIG .471

RENT      -.0249    RENT       .1440    RENT       .2528    PUBTRANS   .6858    PUBTRANS   .6058    PUBTRANS   .6358
WITH    N(   44)    WITH    N(   44)    WITH    N(   44)    WITH    N(   44)    WITH    N(   44)    WITH    N(   44)
TEACHER SIG .436    COOK    SIG .175    ENGINEER SIG .049   TEACHER SIG .000    COOK    SIG .000    ENGINEER SIG .000

TEACHER    .6215    TEACHER    .6573    COOK       .7502
WITH    N(   43)    WITH    N(   43)    WITH    N(   44)
COOK    SIG .000    ENGINEER SIG .000   ENGINEER SIG .000

SIG IS 1-TAILED, "." IS PRINTED IF A COEFFICIENT CANNOT BE COMPUTED.
```

24.8
MATRIX Subcommand

Use the MATRIX subcommand to write matrix materials to a system file. The matrix materials include the mean, standard deviation, number of cases used to compute each coefficient, and Pearson correlation coefficient for each variable. Several other SPSS-X procedures can read matrix materials produced by COR-RELATIONS, including PARTIAL CORR, REGRESSION, FACTOR, and CLUSTER (see Chapter 13, Table 13.1).

CORRELATIONS can write a correlation matrix for a simple variable list but not for variable lists containing the keyword WITH. If you specify more than one matrix on the CORRELATIONS command, only the last variable list that does not use the keyword WITH is written to the matrix system file. For example, in the commands

```
CORRELATIONS VARIABLES=FOOD RENT COOK TEACHER MANAGER ENGINEER/
    FOOD TO TEACHER/ PUBTRANS WITH MECHANIC/
    MATRIX OUT(*)
```

only the matrix for FOOD TO TEACHER is written to the matrix system file.

OUT Keyword. The OUT keyword on MATRIX specifies the file to which the matrix is written. Specify the matrix file in parentheses. There are two options:

(file) *Write the correlation matrix to a system file.* Assign the file name in the parentheses. CORRELATIONS creates a system file containing the matrix materials. The system file is stored on disk and can be retrieved at any time.

(*) *Replace the active file with the correlation matrix system file.* The matrix materials replace the active file. The correlation matrix is NOT stored on disk. It is resident in the active file.

Documents from the original file will not be included in the matrix file and will not be present if the matrix file becomes the active file. (For a discussion on documents, see Chapter 6.)

In the following example, one set of matrix materials is written to the file named CORRMAT:

```
GET FILE=CITY/KEEP FOOD RENT PUBTRANS TEACHER COOK ENGINEER
CORRELATIONS VARIABLES=FOOD TO ENGINEER/
    MATRIX OUT(CORRMAT)
```

The active file is still the file named CITY. Subsequent commands are executed on file CITY.

To write the same matrix, but have it available to subsequent commands in the active file, specify the following:

```
GET FILE=CITY/KEEP FOOD RENT PUBTRANS TEACHER COOK ENGINEER
CORRELATIONS VARIABLES=FOOD TO ENGINEER/
    MATRIX OUT(*)
LIST
DISPLAY DICTIONARY
```

The active file is replaced with the correlation matrix. The LIST and DISPLAY commands are executed on the matrix file, not on the file named CITY.

Format of the Matrix System File. Figure 24.8 shows the matrix system file produced by the above commands. The file has two special variables created by SPSS-X: ROWTYPE_ and VARNAME_. Variable ROWTYPE_ is a short string variable having values MEAN, STDDEV, N, and CORR (for Pearson correlation coefficient). The next variable, VARNAME_, is a short string variable whose values are the names of the variables used to form the correlation matrix. When ROWTYPE_ is CORR, VARNAME_ gives the variable associated with that row of the correlation matrix. The remaining variables in the file are the variables used to form the correlation matrix.

Figure 24.8   A matrix system file

```
FILE:      MATRIX FILE

ROWTYPE_ VARNAME_       FOOD        RENT     PUBTRANS    TEACHER        COOK     ENGINEER

MEAN                70.4666667 120.088889 48.1111111 38.3181818 64.6590909 60.0454545
STDDEV              18.7442112 94.2250262 24.8140560 25.1819174 30.2785081 26.1746856
N         FOOD      45.0000000 45.0000000 45.0000000 44.0000000 44.0000000 44.0000000
N         RENT      45.0000000 45.0000000 45.0000000 44.0000000 44.0000000 44.0000000
N         PUBTRANS  45.0000000 45.0000000 45.0000000 44.0000000 44.0000000 44.0000000
N         TEACHER   44.0000000 44.0000000 44.0000000 44.0000000 43.0000000 43.0000000
N         COOK      44.0000000 44.0000000 44.0000000 43.0000000 44.0000000 44.0000000
N         ENGINEER  44.0000000 44.0000000 44.0000000 43.0000000 44.0000000 44.0000000
CORR      FOOD       1.0000000   .2598212   .5797951   .5469126   .3945479   .4822806
CORR      RENT        .2598212  1.0000000  -.0110758  -.0248816   .1440218   .2527820
CORR      PUBTRANS    .5797951  -.0110758  1.0000000   .6857778   .6058403   .6357760
CORR      TEACHER     .5469126  -.0248816   .6857778  1.0000000   .6214763   .6573389
CORR      COOK        .3945479   .1440218   .6058403   .6214763  1.0000000   .7502223
CORR      ENGINEER    .4822806   .2527820   .6357760   .6573389   .7502223  1.0000000


NUMBER OF CASES READ =      14     NUMBER OF CASES LISTED =      14
```

When split-file processing is in effect (see Chapter 15), the first variables in the matrix system file will be split variables, followed by ROWTYPE_, VARNAME_, and the variables used to form the correlation matrix. A full set of matrix materials is written for each split-file group defined by the split variable(s). A split variable cannot have the same variable name as any other variable written to the matrix system file. If a split file is in effect when a matrix is written, the same split file must be in effect when that matrix is read by any procedure. (See Chapter 13 for more information on matrix system files.)

Additional Statistics. CORRELATIONS always writes the mean, standard deviation, and number of cases used to compute each coefficient, as shown in Figure 24.8. This information immediately precedes the correlation matrix in your output file.

Missing Values. With PAIRWISE treatment of missing values (the default; see Section 24.6), the matrix of N's used to compute each coefficient is included with the matrix materials. With LISTWISE treatment, a single N used to calculate all coefficients is included with the matrix materials.

24.9
LIMITATIONS

The following limitations apply to CORRELATIONS:

- A maximum of 40 variable lists.
- A maximum of 500 variables total per CORRELATIONS command.
- A maximum of 250 individual elements. Each unique occurrence of a variable name, keyword, or special delimiter counts as 1 toward this total. Variables implied by the TO convention do not count toward this total.

ANNOTATED EXAMPLE FOR CORRELATIONS

This example analyzes 1979 prices and earnings in 45 cities around the world, compiled by the Union Bank of Switzerland. The variables are

- FOOD—the average net cost of 39 different food and beverage items in the city, expressed as a percentage above or below that of Zurich, where Zurich equals 100%.
- RENT—the average gross monthly rent in the city, expressed as a percentage above or below that of Zurich, where Zurich equals 100%.
- SERVICE—the average cost of 28 different goods and services in the city, expressed as a percentage above or below that of Zurich, where Zurich equals 100%.
- PUBTRANS—the average cost of a three-mile taxi ride within city limits, expressed as a percentage above or below that of Zurich, where Zurich equals 100%.
- TEACHER, COOK, ENGINEER, MECHANIC, BUS—the average gross annual earnings of primary-grade teachers in public schools, cooks, electrical engineers, automobile mechanics, and municipal bus drivers, working from 5 to 10 years in their respective occupations. Each of these variables is expressed as a percentage above or below those of Zurich, where Zurich equals 100%.

In this example, we determine the degree to which variation in the costs of goods and services in a city is related to variation in earnings in several occupations. We use CORRELATIONS to compute correlations between the average costs of various goods and services and the average gross earnings in five different occupations. The SPSS-X commands are

```
GET  FILE=CITY
CORRELATIONS VARIABLES=FOOD RENT PUBTRANS TEACHER COOK ENGINEER/
          SERVICE PUBTRANS WITH MECHANIC BUS/
   STATISTICS=ALL/
   FORMAT=SERIAL
FINISH
```

- The GET command defines the data to SPSS-X and selects the variables needed for analysis (see Chapter 6).
- The CORRELATIONS command requests two correlation matrices. The first variable list produces correlation coefficients for each variable with every other variable. However, the redundant coefficients will be suppressed by the FORMAT subcommand. The second variable list produces four coefficients, pairing SERVICE with MECHANIC and BUS, and PUBTRANS with MECHANIC and BUS (see Section 24.3 and Figure B).
- The STATISTICS subcommand requests the mean, standard deviation, and number of nonmissing cases for each variable, and the cross-product deviations and covariance for each pair of variables. The statistics for all the variable lists precede all the correlation matrices (see Section 24.5 and Figure A).
- The FORMAT subcommand suppresses redundant coefficients in both correlation matrices (see Section 24.7).

A Pearson correlation statistics

VARIABLE	CASES	MEAN	STD DEV
FOOD	45	70.4667	18.7442
RENT	45	120.0889	94.2250
PUBTRANS	45	48.1111	24.8141
TEACHER	44	38.3182	25.1819
COOK	44	64.6591	30.2785
ENGINEER	44	60.0455	26.1747
SERVICE	45	73.0889	19.0070
MECHANIC	44	50.7045	30.7462
BUS	43	42.9535	27.3652

VARIABLES		CASES	CROSS-PROD DEV	VARIANCE-COVAR	VARIABLES		CASES	CROSS-PROD DEV	VARIANCE-COVAR
FOOD	RENT	45	20191.1333	458.8894	FOOD	PUBTRANS	45	11865.6667	269.6742
FOOD	TEACHER	44	11227.9545	261.1152	FOOD	COOK	44	9561.0000	222.3488
FOOD	ENGINEER	44	10103.0000	234.9535	RENT	PUBTRANS	45	-1139.4444	-25.8965
RENT	TEACHER	44	-2566.6364	-59.6892	RENT	COOK	44	17747.2500	412.7267
RENT	ENGINEER	44	26927.5000	626.2209	PUBTRANS	TEACHER	44	18637.7727	433.4366
PUBTRANS	COOK	44	19434.2727	451.9598	PUBTRANS	ENGINEER	44	17630.3636	410.0085
TEACHER	COOK	43	20326.3023	483.9596	TEACHER	ENGINEER	43	18627.4884	443.5116
COOK	ENGINEER	44	25566.6818	594.5740					

VARIABLES		CASES	CROSS-PROD DEV	VARIANCE-COVAR	VARIABLES		CASES	CROSS-PROD DEV	VARIANCE-COVAR
SERVICE	MECHANIC	44	12034.8636	279.8805	SERVICE	BUS	43	12806.0233	304.9053
PUBTRANS	MECHANIC	44	23897.6364	555.7590	PUBTRANS	BUS	43	21561.6744	513.3732

B Pearson correlation matrices

VARIABLE PAIR		VARIABLE PAIR		VARIABLE PAIR		VARIABLE PAIR		VARIABLE PAIR		VARIABLE PAIR	
FOOD	.2598	FOOD	.5798	FOOD	.5469	FOOD	.3945	FOOD	.4823	RENT	-.0111
WITH	N(45)	WITH	N(45)	WITH	N(44)	WITH	N(44)	WITH	N(44)	WITH	N(45)
RENT	SIG .042	PUBTRANS	SIG .000	TEACHER	SIG .000	COOK	SIG .004	ENGINEER	SIG .000	PUBTRANS	SIG .471
RENT	-.0249	RENT	.1440	RENT	.2528	PUBTRANS	.6858	PUBTRANS	.6058	PUBTRANS	.6358
WITH	N(44)	WITH	N(44)	WITH	N(44)	WITH	N(44)	WITH	N(44)	WITH	N(44)
TEACHER	SIG .436	COOK	SIG .175	ENGINEER	SIG .049	TEACHER	SIG .000	COOK	SIG .000	ENGINEER	SIG .000
TEACHER	.6215	TEACHER	.6573	COOK	.7502						
WITH	N(43)	WITH	N(43)	WITH	N(44)						
COOK	SIG .000	ENGINEER	SIG .000	ENGINEER	SIG .000						

SIG IS 1-TAILED, "." IS PRINTED IF A COEFFICIENT CANNOT BE COMPUTED.

-------------- P E A R S O N C O R R E L A T I O N C O E F F I C I E N T S --------------

VARIABLE PAIR		VARIABLE PAIR		VARIABLE PAIR		VARIABLE PAIR		VARIABLE PAIR		VARIABLE PAIR	
SERVICE	.4842	SERVICE	.5868	PUBTRANS	.7336	PUBTRANS	.7802				
WITH	N(44)	WITH	N(44)	WITH	N(44)	WITH	N(43)				
MECHANIC	SIG .000	BUS	SIG .000	MECHANIC	SIG .000	BUS	SIG .000				

SIG IS 1-TAILED, "." IS PRINTED IF A COEFFICIENT CANNOT BE COMPUTED.

Syntax

CROSSTABS

General mode:

```
CROSSTABS [TABLES=]varlist BY varlist [BY...] [/varlist...]

[/MISSING={TABLE**}]
          {INCLUDE}
[/FORMAT={LABELS**  }  {AVALUE**}  {NOINDEX**}  {TABLES**}]
         {NOLABELS  }  {DVALUE  }  {INDEX    }  {NOTABLES}
         {NOVALLABS }
[/CELLS={COUNT**}  [ROW   ]  [EXPECTED]  [SRESID ]]
        {NONE   }  [COLUMN]  [RESID   ]  [ASRESID]
                   [TOTAL ]              [ALL    ]
[/WRITE[={NONE** }]]
         {CELLS  }
[/STATISTICS=[CHISQ]  [LAMBDA]  [BTAU]   [GAMMA]  [ETA ]]
             [PHI  ]  [UC    ]  [CTAU]   [D    ]  [CORR]
             [CC   ]  [NONE  ]                    [ALL ]
```

Integer mode:

```
CROSSTABS VARIABLES=varlist(min,max) [varlist...]
/TABLES=varlist BY varlist [BY...] [/varlist...]
[/MISSING={TABLE**}]
          {INCLUDE}
          {REPORT }
[/FORMAT={LABELS**  }  {AVALUE**}  {NOINDEX**}  {TABLES**}]
         {NOLABELS  }  {DVALUE  }  {INDEX    }  {NOTABLES}
         {NOVALLABS }
[/CELLS={COUNT**}  [ROW   ]  [EXPECTED]  [SRESID ]]
        {NONE   }  [COLUMN]  [RESID   ]  [ASRESID]
                   [TOTAL ]              [ALL    ]
[/WRITE[={NONE** }]]
         {CELLS  }
         {ALL    }
[/STATISTICS=[CHISQ]  [LAMBDA]  [BTAU]   [GAMMA]  [ETA ]]
             [PHI  ]  [UC    ]  [CTAU]   [D    ]  [CORR]
             [CC   ]  [NONE  ]                    [ALL ]
```

**Default if the subcommand is omitted.

Contents

25.1   OVERVIEW

25.2   OPERATION

25.3   TABLES Subcommand

25.4   General Mode

25.5   Integer Mode

25.6   VARIABLES Subcommand

25.7   CELLS Subcommand

25.8   STATISTICS Subcommand

25.9   MISSING Subcommand

25.10   FORMAT Subcommand

25.11   WRITE Subcommand

25.12   PROCEDURE OUTPUT Command

25.13   WEIGHT Command

25.14   LIMITATIONS

25

Chapter 25 CROSSTABS

Procedure CROSSTABS produces tables that are the joint distribution of two or more variables that have a limited number of distinct values. The frequency distribution of one variable is subdivided according to the values of one or more variables. The unique combination of values for two variables defines a cell, the basic element of all tables. CROSSTABS can operate in either general or integer mode, similar to FREQUENCIES (Chapter 29) and MEANS (Chapter 34). If you want to analyze contingency tables using a general linear model approach, see procedure LOGLINEAR (Chapter 32).

25.1 OVERVIEW

CROSSTABS produces two-way to *n*-way crosstabulations for variables that have a limited number of numeric or string values. In addition to cell counts, you can obtain cell percentages, expected values, residuals, and optional measures of association. You can also alter the handling of missing values, produce measures of association without printing tables, request an index of tables, and write the cell frequencies to a file.

Methods for Building Tables. CROSSTABS operates in two different modes: *general and integer. General mode* operates via the TABLES subcommand and requires fewer specifications. (See Section 25.4.) *Integer mode* operates via the TABLES and VARIABLES subcommands and requires that you specify the minimum and maximum values for the variables. This mode builds tables more efficiently. (See Section 25.5.)

Cell Contents. By default, CROSSTABS prints only the number of cases in each cell. You can request row, column, and total percentages, expected values, and residuals. (See Section 25.7.)

Summary Statistics. In addition to the tables, you can obtain summary statistics for each subtable. (See Section 25.8.)

Missing Values. By default, CROSSTABS excludes cases with user-missing values on a table-by-table basis. You can request that user-missing values be included in the tables and in the calculation of statistics or only in the tables. (See Section 25.9.)

Formatting Options. You can control the order of values for the row variables and suppress the printing of variable labels, value labels, and the table itself. (See Section 25.10.)

Index of Tables. You can print a list of the tables produced by the CROSSTABS command with the page number where each table begins. (See Section 25.10.)

Writing and Reproducing Tables. CROSSTABS can write cell frequencies to a file and reproduce the original tables. (See Section 25.11.)

25.2
OPERATION

Procedure CROSSTABS operates via a set of subcommands. The specifications for these commands depend on whether you want to use the *general mode* or the *integer mode* to build tables. Each method has advantages and disadvantages in computational efficiency, available statistics, and additional options.

• General mode permits string or noninteger variables. You do not have to specify ranges for variables, which makes general mode more convenient. You can reference any defined SPSS-X variable. The order of the variables in the active file determines the positional order of variables in the tables list. (See Section 25.4.)

• Integer mode builds tables more quickly. However, it requires more space if the table has many empty cells. By specifying the appropriate ranges, you can select a subset of values for processing. You can include missing values in tables while excluding them from the calculation of statistics and percentages. Partial and zero-order gammas are available only in integer mode. The order of the variables on the VARIABLES subcommand determines the positional order of the variables on the TABLES subcommand. (See Section 25.5.)

Sections 25.7 through 25.13 outline the optional subcommands available for CROSSTABS. To specify an optional subcommand, use the appropriate subcommand followed by an optional equals sign and the desired keyword. Separate multiple keywords on a single subcommand with at least one space or comma. Separate subcommands with slashes.

You can specify the subcommands in any order. If TABLES is the first subcommand specified on CROSSTABS, you can omit the keyword TABLES, as in

```
CROSSTABS  FEAR BY SEX
    /MISSING=INCLUDE
```

25.3
TABLES Subcommand

Use the TABLES subcommand in both general and integer modes.

25.4
General Mode

To run CROSSTABS in general mode, use the TABLES subcommand followed by a list of one or more variables, the keyword BY, and another list of one or more variables. For example, the command

```
CROSSTABS  TABLES=FEAR BY SEX
```

produces a bivariate table displayed in Figure 25.4a. The variable FEAR defines the rows of the table and the variable SEX defines the columns. In general mode you can specify numeric and string variables. However, long strings are truncated to short strings for purposes of defining categories (see Chapter 5).

Figure 25.4a   A bivariate crosstabulation using general mode

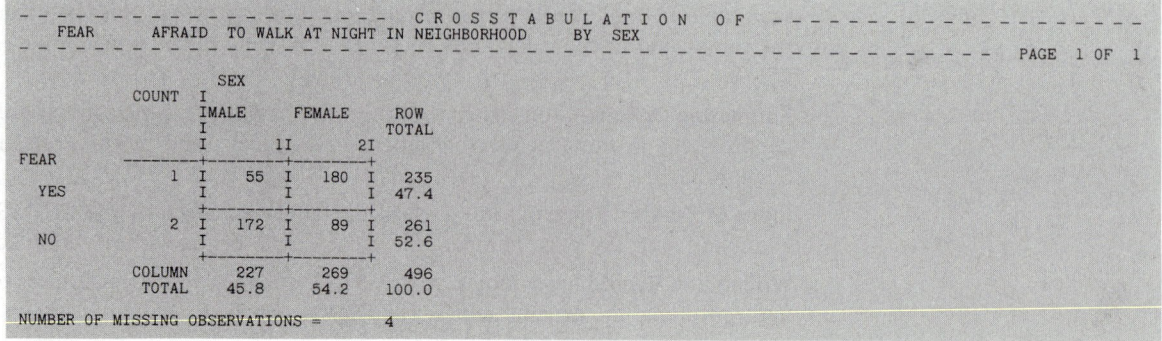

The actual keyword TABLES appears only once in a CROSSTABS command, but it is not required to operate CROSSTABS in general mode. For example, the following commands produce identical displays:

CROSSTABS **TABLES=FEAR BY SEX**

CROSSTABS **FEAR BY SEX**

However, if you use the keyword TABLES for general mode, as shown in the examples in this section, you must also include the equals sign.

A maximum of 10 dimensions can be specified on a tables list in general mode. A list of one or more variables can be specified for each dimension. Separate each list with the keyword BY. The first variable list is the list of *row variables* and the variable list following the first BY keyword is the list of *column variables*. Subsequent variable lists following BY keywords specify orders of *control variables*. For example,

CROSSTABS TABLES=FEAR BY SEX **BY RACE**

crosstabulates FEAR by SEX, controlling for RACE. Figure 25.4b shows the output from this command. In each subtable, FEAR is the row variable and SEX is the column variable. The first subtable crosstabulates FEAR by SEX within the first category of RACE. This category has the value 1 and the label WHITE. The second subtable also crosstabulates FEAR by SEX, but for the next category of RACE, which has the value 2 and the value label NONWHITE. When you use control variables, a subtable is produced for each value of the control variable.

Figure 25.4b   A crosstabulation with two subtables

```
- - - - - - - - - - - - - - - - - - - C R O S S T A B U L A T I O N   O F - - - - - - - - - - - - - - - - - - - -
   FEAR       AFRAID  TO WALK AT NIGHT IN NEIGHBORHOOD      BY  SEX
CONTROLLING FOR..
   RACE                                                      VALUE =          1.  WHITE
- - - - - - - - - - - - - - - - - - - - - - - - - - - - - - - - - - - - - - - - - PAGE  1 OF  1

                    SEX
            COUNT  I
                   IMALE     FEMALE     ROW
                   I                    TOTAL
                   I      1I        2I
FEAR         -------+---------+---------+
              1 I     48  I    149  I    197
   YES          I        I         I    46.5
             -------+---------+---------+
              2 I    153  I     74  I    227
   NO           I        I         I    53.5
             -------+---------+---------+
            COLUMN     201       223       424
            TOTAL     47.4      52.6     100.0


- - - - - - - - - - - - - - - - - - - C R O S S T A B U L A T I O N   O F - - - - - - - - - - - - - - - - - - - -
   FEAR       AFRAID  TO WALK AT NIGHT IN NEIGHBORHOOD      BY  SEX
CONTROLLING FOR..
   RACE                                                      VALUE =          2.  NONWHITE
- - - - - - - - - - - - - - - - - - - - - - - - - - - - - - - - - - - - - - - - - PAGE  1 OF  1

                    SEX
            COUNT  I
                   IMALE     FEMALE     ROW
                   I                    TOTAL
                   I      1I        2I
FEAR         -------+---------+---------+
              1 I      7  I     31  I     38
   YES          I        I         I    52.8
             -------+---------+---------+
              2 I     19  I     15  I     34
   NO           I        I         I    47.2
             -------+---------+---------+
            COLUMN      26        46        72
            TOTAL     36.1      63.9     100.0
NUMBER OF MISSING OBSERVATIONS =         4
```

In CROSSTABS, the value of the first control variable changes most quickly and the value of the last control variable changes most slowly. For example, you might add another order of control to the previous example:

```
CROSSTABS  TABLES=FEAR BY SEX BY RACE BY DEGREE
```

The variable DEGREE has two values: 1=high school or less and 2=college or more. This command produces the four subtables shown in Figure 25.4c. The first subtable crosstabulates FEAR by SEX, controlling for the first value of RACE and the first value of DEGREE; the second subtable controls for the second value of RACE and the first value of DEGREE; the third subtable controls for the first value of RACE and the second value of DEGREE; and the fourth subtable controls for the second value of RACE and the second value of DEGREE.

You can specify more than one variable in each dimension. Use the keyword TO to name a set of adjacent variables in the active file, as in:

```
CROSSTABS  TABLES=CONFINAN TO CONARMY BY SEX TO REGION
```

This command will produce CROSSTABS tables for all the variables between and including CONFINAN and CONARMY by all the variables between and including SEX and REGION. You can use similar variables lists to request higher order CROSSTABS tables. The values of the variables to the right of the last BY keyword change most slowly. Within lists separated by the keyword BY, variables rotate from left to right. For example,

```
CROSSTABS  TABLES=CONFINAN TO CONARMY BY SEX BY RACE,REGION
```

will produce CROSSTABS tables for all the variables between and including CONFINAN and CONARMY by SEX, controlling for RACE, and for all the variables between and including CONFINAN and CONARMY, controlling for REGION. If there are five variables implied by the first variables list, the command produces 10 crosstabulations. The first table is CONFINAN by SEX by RACE and the second table is CONFINAN by SEX by REGION. The last table produced is CONARMY by SEX by REGION. The number of values encountered for the control variables determines the total number of subtables. If RACE has two values and REGION has three values, the output from the command will have a total of 25 subtables.

You can specify up to 20 tables lists on one CROSSTABS command. A maximum of 200 variables can be named or implied by all the tables lists. Use a slash to separate tables lists on one CROSSTABS command. For example,

```
CROSSTABS  TABLES=FEAR BY SEX/RACE BY REGION
```

specifies two bivariate tables, FEAR by SEX and RACE by REGION. If you omit a slash between tables lists, CROSSTABS includes the variables as if one tables list had been supplied. If the preceding command had no slash, as in

```
CROSSTABS  TABLES=FEAR BY SEX RACE BY REGION
```

it would produce two three-dimensional tables, FEAR by SEX by REGION and FEAR by RACE by REGION.

**25.5
Integer Mode**

To run CROSSTABS in integer mode, the values of all the variables must be integers. Two subcommands are required. The VARIABLES subcommand (see Section 25.6) specifies all the variables to be used in the CROSSTABS procedure and the minimum and maximum values for building tables. The TABLES subcommand specifies the tables lists. In integer mode, the equals sign following the VARIABLES and TABLES subcommands is optional. You can use multiple

Figure 25.4c   A crosstabulation with four subtables

```
- - - - - - - - - - - - - - - - - - - - C R O S S T A B U L A T I O N   O F - - - - - - - - - - - - - - - -
    FEAR      AFRAID  TO WALK AT NIGHT IN NEIGHBORHOOD     BY  SEX
CONTROLLING FOR..
    RACE                                                  VALUE =          1.   WHITE
BY  DEGREE    HIGHEST DEGREE,RESP                         VALUE =          1.   LE HS
- - - - - - - - - - - - - - - - - - - - - - - - - - - - - - - - - - - - - - - - - - - - - PAGE  1 OF  1

                    SEX
             COUNT I
                   IMALE    FEMALE    ROW
                   I                  TOTAL
                   I        1I      2I
    FEAR      ---------+--------+--------+
              1 I    39 I   126 I    165
    YES         I      I       I    47.7
              +--------+--------+--------+
              2 I   114 I    67 I    181
    NO          I      I       I    52.3
              +--------+--------+--------+
             COLUMN    153      193       346
             TOTAL    44.2     55.8     100.0


- - - - - - - - - - - - - - - - - - - C R O S S T A B U L A T I O N   O F - - - - - - - - - - - - - - - - -
    FEAR      AFRAID  TO WALK AT NIGHT IN NEIGHBORHOOD     BY  SEX
CONTROLLING FOR..
    RACE                                                  VALUE =          2.   NONWHITE
BY  DEGREE    HIGHEST DEGREE,RESP                         VALUE =          1.   LE HS
- - - - - - - - - - - - - - - - - - - - - - - - - - - - - - - - - - - - - - - - - - - - - PAGE  1 OF  1

                    SEX
             COUNT I
                   IMALE    FEMALE    ROW
                   I                  TOTAL
                   I        1I      2I
    FEAR      ---------+--------+--------+
              1 I     5 I    27 I     32
    YES         I      I       I    50.0
              +--------+--------+--------+
              2 I    17 I    15 I     32
    NO          I      I       I    50.0
              +--------+--------+--------+
             COLUMN     22       42        64
             TOTAL    34.4     65.6     100.0


- - - - - - - - - - - - - - - - - - - C R O S S T A B U L A T I O N   O F - - - - - - - - - - - - - - - - -
    FEAR      AFRAID  TO WALK AT NIGHT IN NEIGHBORHOOD     BY  SEX
CONTROLLING FOR..
    RACE                                                  VALUE =          1.   WHITE
BY  DEGREE    HIGHEST DEGREE,RESP                         VALUE =          2.   COLLEGE
- - - - - - - - - - - - - - - - - - - - - - - - - - - - - - - - - - - - - - - - - - - - - PAGE  1 OF  1

                    SEX
             COUNT I
                   IMALE    FEMALE    ROW
                   I                  TOTAL
                   I        1I      2I
    FEAR      ---------+--------+--------+
              1 I     9 I    23 I     32
    YES         I      I       I    41.0
              +--------+--------+--------+
              2 I    39 I     7 I     46
    NO          I      I       I    59.0
              +--------+--------+--------+
             COLUMN     48       30        78
             TOTAL    61.5     38.5     100.0


- - - - - - - - - - - - - - - - - - - C R O S S T A B U L A T I O N   O F - - - - - - - - - - - - - - - - -
    FEAR      AFRAID  TO WALK AT NIGHT IN NEIGHBORHOOD     BY  SEX
CONTROLLING FOR..
    RACE                                                  VALUE =          2.   NONWHITE
BY  DEGREE    HIGHEST DEGREE,RESP                         VALUE =          2.   COLLEGE
- - - - - - - - - - - - - - - - - - - - - - - - - - - - - - - - - - - - - - - - - - - - - PAGE  1 OF  1

                    SEX
             COUNT I
                   IMALE    FEMALE    ROW
                   I                  TOTAL
                   I        1I      2I
    FEAR      ---------+--------+--------+
              1 I     2 I     4 I      6
    YES         I      I       I    75.0
              +--------+--------+--------+
              2 I     2 I       I      2
    NO          I      I       I    25.0
              +--------+--------+--------+
             COLUMN      4        4         8
             TOTAL    50.0     50.0     100.0

NUMBER OF MISSING OBSERVATIONS =       4
```

VARIABLES and TABLES subcommands, provided a variable referenced on a TABLES subcommand has been defined on a previous VARIABLES subcommand.

Integer mode can produce more tables in a given amount of core storage space than general mode, and the processing is faster. The values supplied as variable ranges do not have to be as wide as the range of the variables; thus, you have control from within CROSSTABS over the tabulated ranges of the variables. Some subcommand and keyword specifications are available only in integer mode.

The TABLES subcommand names the tables list. It has the same syntax as the TABLES subcommand in general mode described in Section 25.4. For example,

```
CROSSTABS  VARIABLES=FEAR (1,2) MOBILE16 (1,3)
    /TABLES=FEAR BY MOBILE16
```

produces the table in Figure 25.5. Variables named on the TABLES subcommand must have been previously named or implied on the VARIABLES subcommand.

You can name multiple tables lists separated by slashes. Like general mode, integer mode can process up to 20 tables lists. However, you can specify only up to 100 tables over all the lists together, and you can name or imply only up to 100 variables on all the tables lists. Also, tables can have a maximum of only eight dimensions in integer mode.

Figure 25.5 A crosstabulation using integer mode

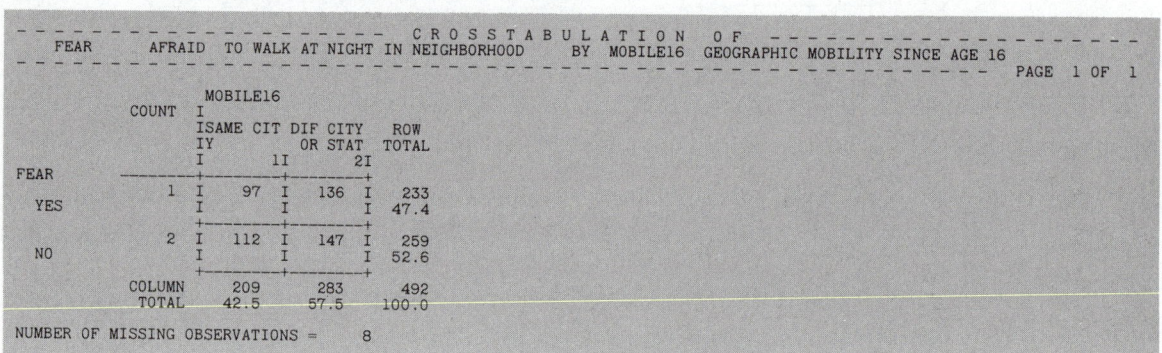

There is one important difference between the tables request in integer mode and the tables request in general mode. In integer mode, the order of the variables implied on the TABLES subcommand is established by the order of the variables named or implied on the VARIABLES subcommand. In general mode, the order of variables implied on the tables lists is established by their order in the active file.

25.6
VARIABLES Subcommand

The VARIABLES subcommand is followed by a list of variables to be used in the crosstabulations. Specify the lowest and highest values in parentheses after each variable. These values must be integers. For example, the command

```
CROSSTABS  VARIABLES=FEAR (1,2) MOBILE16 (1,3)
    /TABLES=FEAR BY MOBILE16
```

produces a table where FEAR has a range from 1 to 2 and MOBILE16 has a range from 1 to 3. Noninteger values are truncated. A maximum of 100 variables can be named or implied by the VARIABLES subcommand.

You must specify a range for each variable to be used in the CROSSTABS procedure and several variables can have the same range. For example,

```
CROSSTABS  VARIABLES=FEAR SEX RACE (1,2) MOBILE16 (1,3)
    /TABLES=FEAR BY SEX MOBILE16 BY RACE
```

defines 1 as the lowest value and 2 as the highest value for FEAR, SEX, and RACE. Variables may appear in any order. However, the order in which you place them on the VARIABLES subcommand affects their implied order on the TABLES subcommand as described in Section 25.3.

CROSSTABS uses the ranges you specify to allocate tables. One cell is allocated for each possible combination of values of the row and column variables for a requested table before the data are read. Therefore, if you specify more generous ranges than the variables actually have, you are wasting some space. If the table is sparse because the variables do not have values falling throughout the range specified, you might consider using the general mode or recoding the variables. If, on the other hand, the values of the variables fall outside the range you specify, cases with these values are considered missing and are not used in the computation of the table.

25.7
CELLS Subcommand

By default, CROSSTABS prints only the number of cases in each cell. The CELLS subcommand prints row, column, or total percentages, and also expected values and residuals. These items are calculated separately for each bivariate table or subtable.

You can specify the CELLS subcommand by itself, or with a keyword or keywords. If you specify the CELLS subcommand by itself, CROSSTABS prints cell counts plus ROW, COLUMN, and TOTAL percentages for each cell. If you specify a keyword or keywords, CROSSTABS prints only the cell information you request.

The following keywords can be specified on the CELLS subcommand:

COUNT   *Print cell counts.* This is the default if you omit the CELLS subcommand.

ROW   *Print row percentages.* Print the number of cases in each cell in a row expressed as a percentage of all cases in that row.

COLUMN   *Print column percentages.* Print the number of cases in each cell in a column expressed as a percentage of all cases in that column.

TOTAL   *Print two-way table total percentages.* Print the number of cases in each cell of a subtable expressed as a percentage of all cases in that subtable.

EXPECTED   *Print expected frequencies.* Print the number of cases expected in each cell if the two variables in the subtable were statistically independent.

RESID   *Print residuals.* Print the value of the observed cell count minus the expected value.

SRESID   *Print standardized residuals.* (Haberman, 1978).

ASRESID   *Print adjusted standardized residuals.* (Haberman, 1978).

ALL   *Print all cell information.* Print cell count; row, column, and total percentages; expected values; residuals; standardized residuals; and adjusted standardized residuals.

NONE   *Print no cell information.* Use NONE to write the tables to a procedure file without printed tables. This has the same effect as specifying FORMAT=NOTABLES.

The following commands print row and column percentages in the cells:

```
CROSSTABS  TABLES=FEAR BY SEX
    /CELLS=ROW COLUMN
```

Figure 25.7 displays this table. The key located at the top left corner of the table describes the information contained in each cell. If you request only percentages and/or cell counts, the percentages are printed without a percent sign and blanks are printed instead of zero values for counts and percents. If you request percentages and any of the expected values or residuals, the percent sign appears next to the percentage and zero values are printed as zeros.

Figure 25.7 Requesting cell percentages

```
- - - - - - - - - - - - - - - - - - - - - - - -   C R O S S T A B U L A T I O N   O F - - - - - - - - - - - - - - - - - - - - - - - -
  FEAR      AFRAID  TO WALK AT NIGHT IN NEIGHBORHOOD      BY  SEX
- - - - - - - - - - - - - - - - - - - - - - - - - - - - - - - - - - - - - - - - - - - - - - - - - - - - - PAGE  1 OF  1
                         SEX
              ROW PCT I
              COL PCT IMALE      FEMALE      ROW
                      I                      TOTAL
                      I        1I        2I
  FEAR        ---------+--------+--------+
              1 I  23.4 I  76.6 I    235
  YES           I  24.2 I  66.9 I   47.4
              ---------+--------+--------+
              2 I  65.9 I  34.1 I    261
  NO            I  75.8 I  33.1 I   52.6
              ---------+--------+--------+
              COLUMN     227       269       496
              TOTAL     45.8      54.2     100.0
NUMBER OF MISSING OBSERVATIONS =      4
```

25.8
STATISTICS Subcommand

CROSSTABS can calculate a number of summary statistics for each subtable. Unless you specify otherwise, it calculates statistical measures of association for the cases with valid values included in the subtable. If you specify a range in integer mode that excludes cases, the excluded cases are *not* used in the calculation of the statistics. If you include user-missing values with the MISSING subcommand, cases with user-defined missing values are included in the tables as well as in the calculation of statistics.

The STATISTICS subcommand requests summary statistics. You can specify the STATISTICS subcommand by itself, or with one or more keywords. If you specify STATISTICS by itself, with no keywords, CROSSTABS calculates CHISQ. If you include a keyword or keywords on the STATISTICS subcommand, CROSSTABS calculates all the statistics you request.

The following keywords can be specified on the STATISTICS subcommand:

CHISQ   *Chi-square.* Fisher's exact test is computed using the rounded values of the cell entries when there are fewer than 20 cases in a 2 × 2 table that does not result from missing rows or columns in a larger table; Yates' corrected chi-square is computed for all other 2 × 2 tables. This is the default if you specify the STATISTICS subcommand by itself, with no keywords.

PHI   *Phi for 2 × 2 tables, Cramer's V for larger tables.*

CC   *Contingency coefficient.*

LAMBDA   *Lambda, symmetric and asymmetric.*

UC   *Uncertainty coefficient, symmetric and asymmetric.*

BTAU   *Kendall's tau-b.*

CTAU   *Kendall's tau-c.*

GAMMA   *Gamma.* Partial and zero-order gammas for 3-way to 8-way tables are available in integer mode only. Zero-order gammas are printed for 2-way tables and conditional gammas are printed for 3-way to 10-way tables in general mode.

D   *Somers' d, symmetric and asymmetric.*

ETA   *Eta.* Available for numeric data only.

CORR   *Pearson's r.* Available for numeric data only.

ALL   *All the statistics available for CROSSTABS.*

NONE   *No summary statistics.* This is the default if you omit the STATISTICS subcommand.

To request all available statistics, use the keyword ALL, as in:

```
CROSSTABS  FEAR BY SEX
    /STATISTICS=ALL
```

Figure 25.8 shows these statistics, which are associated with the crosstabulation in Figure 25.4a. For chi-square, the output shows the degrees of freedom, the significance level, the smallest expected frequency, and the number of cells with an expected frequency less than 5. For lambda, the uncertainty coefficient, Somers' *d*, and eta, SPSS-X prints the symmetric value and both asymmetric values. The remaining statistics display the value of the statistic and the significance level when appropriate.

Figure 25.8 Statistics available with CROSSTABS

```
CHI-SQUARE      D.F.     SIGNIFICANCE        MIN E.F.      CELLS WITH E.F.| 5
----------      ----     ------------        --------      ---------------

   88.26870       1        0.0000            107.550            NONE
   89.97266       1        0.0000          ( BEFORE YATES CORRECTION )

                                                        WITH FEAR        WITH SEX
               STATISTIC               SYMMETRIC        DEPENDENT        DEPENDENT
               ---------               ---------        ---------        ---------

LAMBDA                                  0.37662          0.38723          0.36564
UNCERTAINTY COEFFICIENT                 0.13624          0.13602          0.13646
SOMERS' D                              -0.42591         -0.42685         -0.42496
ETA                                                      0.42591          0.42591

               STATISTIC                 VALUE          SIGNIFICANCE
               ---------                 -----          ------------

PHI                                     0.42591
CONTINGENCY COEFFICIENT                 0.39185
KENDALL'S TAU B                        -0.42591           0.0000
KENDALL'S TAU C                        -0.42379           0.0000
PEARSON'S R                            -0.42591           0.0000
GAMMA                                  -0.72696

NUMBER OF MISSING OBSERVATIONS =        4
```

25.9
MISSING Subcommand

By default, CROSSTABS deletes cases with missing values on a table-by-table basis. A case missing on any of the variables specified for a table is not used either in the printed table or in the calculation of the statistics. When you separate tables requests with a slash, missing values are handled separately for each list. The number of missing cases is always printed at the end of the table, following the last subtable and after any requested statistics.

The MISSING subcommand controls missing values. The following keywords can be specified on the MISSING subcommand:

TABLE   *Delete cases with missing values on a table-by-table basis.* This is the default if you omit the MISSING subcommand.

INCLUDE *Include user-defined missing values.*

REPORT   *Report missing values in the tables.* This option includes missing values in tables but not in the calculation of percentages or statistics. It is available only in integer mode.

If the missing values are not included in the range specifications on the VARIABLES subcommand, they are excluded from the table regardless of the keyword you specify on MISSING.

The following commands produce the table in Figure 25.9a:

```
CROSSTABS  VARIABLES=FEAR (1,8) SEX (1,2)
     /TABLES=FEAR BY SEX
     /STATISTICS=CHISQ
     /MISSING=REPORT
```

Missing rows and columns appear at the bottom and the right of the table. The letter *M* indicates that the cases in these cells are missing. In Figure 25.9a, four cases have the user-defined missing-value code of 8. Only the valid cases appear in the row, column, and total percentages. The statistics also include only the valid cases. For example, the chi-square statistics in Figure 25.9a are identical to those in Figure 25.8, which uses the default treatment for missing values.

Figure 25.9a Missing values with MISSING=REPORT

```
- - - - - - -   - - - - -   - - - - - -  C R O S S T A B U L A T I O N   O F  - - - - - - - - - - - - - - - - -
   FEAR      AFRAID  TO WALK AT NIGHT IN NEIGHBORHOOD      BY  SEX
- - - - - - -  - - - - -  - - - - - - - - - - - - - - - - - - - - - - - - - - - - - -  PAGE  1 OF  1

                      SEX
             COUNT  I
                    IMALE     FEMALE      ROW
                    I                     TOTAL
                    I         1I       2I
   FEAR      -------+--------+--------+
                 1 I    55  I   180  I    235
   YES           I       I       I  I    47.4
                    +--------+--------+
                 2 I   172  I    89  I    261
   NO            I       I       I  I    52.6
                    +--------+--------+
                 8 I    1M  I    3M  I     4M
   DK            I       I       I  I     .0
                    +--------+--------+
             COLUMN    227      269      496
             TOTAL    45.8     54.2    100.0


   CHI-SQUARE    D.F.      SIGNIFICANCE       MIN E.F.      CELLS WITH E.F.| 5
   ----------    ----      ------------       --------      ------------------

    88.26868       1          0.0000          107.550          NONE
    89.97266       1          0.0000        ( BEFORE YATES CORRECTION )

   NUMBER OF MISSING OBSERVATIONS =      4
```

Use the keyword INCLUDE to handle user-missing values as if they were not missing. Cases with values defined as missing are included in the tables as well as the calculation of statistics. For example, the commands

```
CROSSTABS  TABLES=FEAR BY SEX
    /STATISTICS=CHISQ
    /MISSING=INCLUDE
```

produce the crosstabulation in Figure 25.9b of FEAR by SEX which includes missing values in the table and in the statistics. You can use INCLUDE in either general mode or integer mode. Remember, in integer mode, to include the missing values in the range specification on the VARIABLES subcommand.

Figure 25.9b Missing values with MISSING=INCLUDE

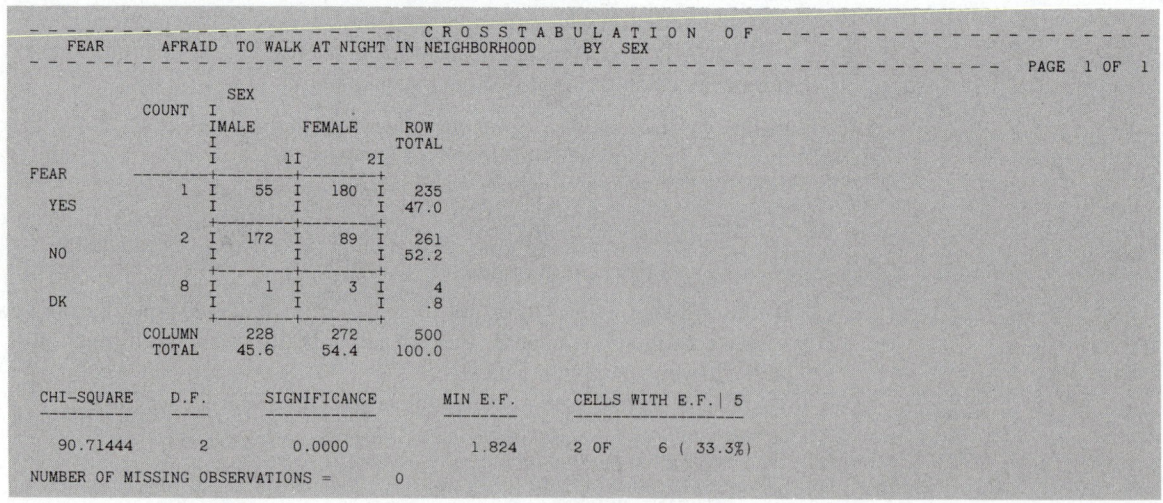

```
- - - - - - - - - - - -   - - - - - - -  C R O S S T A B U L A T I O N   O F  - - - - - - - - - - - -
   FEAR      AFRAID  TO WALK AT NIGHT IN NEIGHBORHOOD      BY  SEX
- - - - - - -  - - - - -  - - - - - - - - - - - - - - - - - - - - - - - - -  PAGE  1 OF  1

                      SEX
             COUNT  I
                    IMALE     FEMALE      ROW
                    I                     TOTAL
                    I         1I       2I
   FEAR      -------+--------+--------+
                 1 I    55  I   180  I    235
   YES           I       I       I  I    47.0
                    +--------+--------+
                 2 I   172  I    89  I    261
   NO            I       I       I  I    52.2
                    +--------+--------+
                 8 I     1  I     3  I      4
   DK            I       I       I  I     .8
                    +--------+--------+
             COLUMN    228      272      500
             TOTAL    45.6     54.4    100.0


   CHI-SQUARE    D.F.      SIGNIFICANCE       MIN E.F.      CELLS WITH E.F.| 5
   ----------    ----      ------------       --------      ------------------

    90.71444       2          0.0000           1.824        2 OF    6 ( 33.3%)

   NUMBER OF MISSING OBSERVATIONS =        0
```

25.10
FORMAT Subcommand By default, CROSSTABS prints tables and subtables with variable labels and value labels when they are available. The values for the row variables print in order from lowest to highest. Although value labels can be up to 60 characters

long in SPSS-X, CROSSTABS uses only the first 16 characters. The value labels for the columns print on two lines with eight characters per line. If the format of the labels is an important consideration in your table, you can redefine the value labels to fit the columns as shown in the annotated example for CROSSTABS.

The FORMAT subcommand modifies the default tables and subtables. The following keywords can be specified on the FORMAT subcommand:

LABELS   *Print both variable and value labels for each table.* This is the default.

NOLABELS   *Suppress variable and value labels.*

NOVALLABS *Suppress value labels, print variable labels.*

AVALUE   *Print row variables ordered from lowest to highest.* This is the default.

DVALUE   *Print row variables ordered from highest to lowest.*

NOINDEX   *Suppress a table index.* This is the default.

INDEX   *Prints an index of tables.* The index lists all tables produced by the CROSSTABS command and the page number where each table begins. The index follows the last page of tables produced by the tables list.

TABLES   *Print the crosstabs tables.* This is the default.

NOTABLES *Suppress printed tables.* If you use the STATISTICS subcommand (see Section 25.8) and specify NOTABLES, only the statistics are printed. If you do not use the STATISTICS subcommand and specify NOTABLES, the CROSSTABS command produces no output. Use NOTABLES to write the tables to a procedure file without printed tables. This has the same effect as specifying CELLS=NONE.

25.11
WRITE Subcommand

CROSSTABS can write cell frequencies to a file for subsequent use by either SPSS-X or some other program. It can also use cell frequencies as input to reproduce tables and compute statistics.

CROSSTABS has two options for producing an output file of cell frequencies. You can write all the cells of the table, or only the nonempty cells. The file contains one record for each cell; each record contains a split-file group number and a table number, which identify the table, and the cell frequency and values, which identify the cell.

The WRITE subcommand writes cell frequencies to a procedure output file. Its only specification is a single keyword. Keyword ALL is available only in integer mode.

NONE   *Do not write the cell counts to the file.* This is the default if you omit the WRITE subcommand.

CELLS   *Write the cell count for nonempty cells to a file.*

ALL   *Write the cell count for all cells to a file.* Available only in integer mode.

If you specify both CELLS and ALL, only CELLS is in effect and only the contents of the nonempty cells are written to a file.

Use keyword CELLS to write only nonempty cells. Combinations of values that include a missing value are not written to the output file. If you include missing values in the tables with keyword INCLUDE on the MISSING subcommand, no values are considered missing and all nonempty cells will be written.

Keyword ALL writes all defined cells and is available only with integer mode. A record for each combination of values defined by the TABLES subcommand is written to the output file. If you include missing values in the tables with either keyword INCLUDE or keyword REPORT on the MISSING subcommand, all defined cells are written whether or not a missing value is involved. If you exclude missing values on a table-by-table basis (the default), no records are written for combinations of values that include a missing value.

When you write tables to a file, you must use the PROCEDURE OUTPUT command (see Section 25.12).

ANNOTATED EXAMPLE FOR CROSSTABS

The example illustrating CROSSTABS analyzes a 500-case sample from the 1980 General Social Survey. The variables are AGE, the respondent's age recoded to four categories, and DRUNK, the response to the question, Did you ever drink too much? This task examines how respondents in different age groups answer a question on alcohol-drinking habits. The following SPSS-X commands produce a crosstabulation of these two numeric variables and print several summary statistics:

```
GET FILE GSS80
TEMPORARY
RECODE  AGE (LOW THRU 29=1) (29 THRU 40=2) (40 THRU 58=3)
    (58 THRU HI=4)/ DRUNK (MISSING=8)
VARIABLE LABELS  AGE 'AGE IN FOUR CATEGORIES'
VALUE LABELS  AGE 1 'YOUNGESTQUARTER' 4 'OLDEST  QUARTER'
    /DRUNK 1 'YES' 2 'NO' 8 "DON'T DRINK/NA"
CROSSTABS  VARIABLES=DRUNK (1,8) AGE (1,4)/ TABLES=DRUNK BY AGE
    /CELLS=COLUMN TOTAL
    /MISSING=REPORT
    /STATISTICS=CHISQ LAMBDA BTAU CTAU GAMMA D
FINISH
```

- The GET command defines the data to SPSS-X (see Chapter 6).

- The TEMPORARY command determines that the transformations are temporary (see Chapter 6).

- The RECODE command redefines the variable AGE into four categories and recodes all missing values for the variable DRUNK to one missing value (see Chapter 7).

- The VARIABLE LABELS command defines a new variable label for AGE and the VALUE LABELS command defines value labels for AGE and DRUNK (see Chapter 5). The value labels for AGE are formatted to print appropriate labels for a column variable. Note that the label YOUNGESTQUARTER has no blanks between the words and the label OLDEST QUARTER has two blanks separating the words (see Section 25.10).

- The CROSSTABS command uses integer mode to set up the table. The VARIABLES subcommand specifies the variables and their minimum and maximum values, including the missing values that will be displayed (see Section 25.6). The TABLES subcommand specifies variable DRUNK as the row variable and AGE as the column variable (see Sections 25.4 and 25.3).

- The CELLS subcommand requests row and column percents (see Section 25.7).

- The MISSING subcommand reports missing values in the table but does not include them in calculating percentages and statistics (see Section 25.9).

- The STATISTICS subcommand requests chi-square, lambda, Kendall's tau-b, Kendall's tau-c, gamma, and Somers' d. Although the table reports missing cases, they are not included in the calculation of statistics (see Section 25.8).

Output from the CROSSTABS command

```
- - - - - - - - - - - - - - - - - - - - -  C R O S S T A B U L A T I O N   O F  - - - - - - - - - - - - - - - - - - - -
    DRUNK    EVER DRINK TOO MUCH                      BY  AGE     AGE IN FOUR CATEGORIES
- - - - - - - - - - - - - - - - - - - - - - - - - - - - - - - - - - - - - - - - - - - -  PAGE  1 OF  1

                       AGE
             COUNT  I
            ROW PCT IYOUNGEST                    OLDEST     ROW
            COL PCT IQUARTER                    QUARTER    TOTAL
                    I        1I        2I        3I        4I
DRUNK               --------+--------+--------+--------+--------+
                 1  I    62  I    33  I    36  I    16  I      147
    YES             I  42.2  I  22.4  I  24.5  I  10.9  I     38.5
                    I  57.9  I  34.7  I  37.9  I  18.8  I
                    +--------+--------+--------+--------+
                 2  I    45  I    62  I    59  I    69  I      235
    NO              I  19.1  I  26.4  I  25.1  I  29.4  I     61.5
                    I  42.1  I  65.3  I  62.1  I  81.2  I
                    +--------+--------+--------+--------+
                 8  I   17M  I   27M  I   31M  I   43M  I      118M
DON'T DRINK/NA      I        I        I        I        I        .0
                    I        I        I        I        I
                    +--------+--------+--------+--------+
           COLUMN       107       95       95       85       382
            TOTAL      28.0     24.9     24.9     22.3     100.0


CHI-SQUARE    D.F.     SIGNIFICANCE        MIN E.F.      CELLS WITH E.F. | 5
---------     ----     ------------        --------      -------------------

 31.57228      3          0.0000           32.709            NONE

                                        WITH DRUNK       WITH AGE
         STATISTIC           SYMMETRIC   DEPENDENT        DEPENDENT
         ---------           ---------  ----------       ---------

LAMBDA                        0.09716    0.11565          0.08727
SOMERS' D                     0.23546    0.19222          0.30381

         STATISTIC           VALUE       SIGNIFICANCE
         ---------           -----       ------------

KENDALL'S TAU B              0.24165      0.0000
KENDALL'S TAU C              0.28768      0.0000
GAMMA                        0.39632

NUMBER OF MISSING OBSERVATIONS =    118
```

25.12
PROCEDURE OUTPUT
Command

When you write tables to a file, you must use a PROCEDURE OUTPUT command to define the output file for the cell records. PROCEDURE OUTPUT uses only only one subcommand, the OUTFILE subcommand, to define the procedure file for the table. Place the PROCEDURE OUTPUT command before the CROSSTABS command. For example,

```
GET FILE  GSS80
PROCEDURE OUTPUT   OUTFILE=CELLDATA
CROSSTABS   VARIABLES=FEAR SEX (1,2)
            /TABLES=FEAR BY SEX
            /WRITE=ALL
```

writes a record for each cell in the table FEAR by SEX to the file CELLDATA. Figure 25.12 shows the contents of the CELLDATA file.

Figure 25.12   Cell output records

```
1    1        55 .       1           1
1    1       172         2           1
1    1       180         1           2
1    1        89         2           2
```

The output record from each cell contains the following information:

Columns	Contents
1–4	Split-file group number, numbered consecutively from 1. Note that this is not the value of the variable or variables used to define the splits.
5–8	Table number. A table is defined by taking one variable from each of the variable lists separated by the keyword BY.
9–16	Cell frequency. The number of times this combination of variable values occurred in the data, or, if case weights are used, the sum of case weights for cases having this combination of values.
17–24	The value of the row variable (the one named before the first BY).
25–32	The value of the column variable (the one named after the first BY).
33–40	The value of the first control variable (the one named after the second BY).
41–48	The value of the second control variable (the one named after the third BY).
49–56	The value of the third control variable (the one named after the fourth BY).
57–64	The value of the fourth control variable (the one named after the fifth BY).
65–72	The value of the fifth control variable (the one named after the sixth BY).
73–80	The value of the sixth control variable (the one named after the seventh BY).

The split-file group number, table number, and frequency are written as integers. If the integer mode of CROSSTABS is used, the values of variables are also written as integers. If the general mode is used, the values are written in accordance with the PRINT FORMAT specified for each variable. Alphanumeric values are written at the left end of any field in which they occur.

Within each table, the records are written in the following order:

the value of the row variable, within
the value of the column variable, within
the value of the first control variable, within

• • •

the value of the fifth control variable

This order implies that the records are written from one column of the table at a time and the value of the last control variable changes most slowly.

If you specify multiple tables, the tables are written in the same order as they are printed. The variable in the row variables list changes the slowest and the variable in the last control variables list change the fastest. For example, the following commands write a set of records for each table to the XTABDATA output file:

```
PROCEDURE OUTPUT   OUTFILE=XTABDATA
CROSSTABS   TABLES=V1 TO V3 BY V4 BY V10 TO V15
            /WRITE=CELLS
```

All of the records for the table V1 BY V4 BY V10 are written first, the records for V1 BY V4 BY V11 second, and the records for V3 BY V4 BY V15 last.

25.13
WEIGHT Command

You can use the file created by the WRITE subcommand in a subsequent SPSS-X job to reproduce a table and compute statistics for it. Each record in the file contains all the information used to build the original table. For example, if you read the CELLDATA file created by the commands in Section 25.13, you can reproduce the table displayed in Figure 25.4a and calculate statistics for it. The following commands read the cell frequency as a weighting factor (WGHT), the value of the row variable (FEAR), and the value of the column variable (SEX):

```
DATA LIST FILE=CELLDATA
         /WGHT 9-16 FEAR 17-24 SEX 25-32
VARIABLE LABELS  FEAR 'AFRAID TO WALK AT NIGHT IN NEIGHBORHOODS'
VALUE LABELS   FEAR 1 'YES' 2 'NO'/ SEX 1 'MALE' 2 'FEMALE'
WEIGHT  BY WGHT
CROSSTABS   TABLES=FEAR BY SEX
            /STATISTICS=ALL
```

The WEIGHT command recreates the sample size by weighting each of the four cases (cells) by the cell frequency (see Chapter 11). You can also use the WEIGHT command to reproduce tables and compute statistics for published tables where you do not have the original data. Each cell in the table becomes a case and each record should include the cell frequency for weighting, the row and column variables, and any control variables. For example, the following commands also reproduce the table in Figure 25.4a:

```
DATA LIST   /FEAR 1 SEX 3 WGHT 5-7
VARIABLE LABELS   FEAR 'AFRAID TO WALK AT NIGHT IN NEIGBORHOOD'
VALUE LABELS   FEAR 1 'YES' 2 'NO'/ SEX 1 'MALE' 2 'FEMALE'
WEIGHT   BY WGHT
CROSSTABS   TABLES=FEAR BY SEX
            /STATISTICS=ALL
BEGIN DATA
1 1   55
2 1  172
1 2  180
2 2   89
END DATA
```

You can define the variables for the cell frequency, row value, and column value in any order.

25.14
LIMITATIONS

The following limitations apply to CROSSTABS in *general mode*:

• A maximum of 200 variables total per CROSSTABS command.
• A maximum of 250 nonempty rows or columns printed for each variable.
• A maximum of 20 tables lists per CROSSTABS command.
• A maximum of 10 dimensions per table.
• A maximum of 250 value labels printed on any single table.

The following limitations apply to CROSSTABS in *integer mode*:

• A maximum of 100 variables named or implied with the VARIABLES subcommand.
• A maximum of 100 variables named or implied with the TABLES subcommand.

- A maximum of 200 nonempty rows or columns printed for each variable.
- A maximum of 200 rows per subtable.
- A maximum of 200 columns per table.
- A maximum of 20 tables lists per CROSSTABS command.
- A maximum of 8 dimensions per table.
- No more than 20 rows or columns of missing values can be printed with MISSING= REPORT.
- The largest range that can be implied on the minimum-maximum range specification on the VARIABLES subcommand is 32,766.

Syntax

DESCRIPTIVES

```
DESCRIPTIVES [VARIABLES=] varname[(zname)] [varname...]
 [/MISSING={VARIABLE**}  [INCLUDE]]
            {LISTWISE  }

 [/FORMAT={LABELS**  }  {NOINDEX**}  {LINE**}]
          {NOLABELS }  {INDEX    }  {SERIAL}

 [/SAVE]

 [/STATISTICS=[DEFAULT**]  [MEAN**]   [MIN**]   [SKEWNESS]]
              [STDDEV** ]  [SEMEAN]   [MAX**]   [KURTOSIS]
              [VARIANCE ]  [SUM   ]   [RANGE]   [ALL]
```

**Default if the subcommand is omitted.

Contents

26.1   OVERVIEW

26.2   OPERATION
26.3   VARIABLES Subcommand
26.4   Z Scores
26.5   SAVE Subcommand
26.6   STATISTICS Subcommand
26.7   MISSING Subcommand
26.8   FORMAT Subcommand

26.9   LIMITATIONS

26

Chapter 26   DESCRIPTIVES

Procedure DESCRIPTIVES (alias CONDESCRIPTIVE) computes univariate summary statistics and standardized variables that are saved on the active file. Although it computes statistics also available in procedure FREQUENCIES (Chapter 29), DESCRIPTIVES computes descriptive statistics for continuous variables more efficiently because it does not sort values into a frequencies table.

26.1
OVERVIEW

DESCRIPTIVES calculates the mean, standard deviation, minimum, and maximum for numeric variables. You can request optional statistics and Z-score transformations. DESCRIPTIVES has alternative formats and methods of handling missing data.

Sections 26.4 through 26.8 outline the subcommands available for DESCRIPTIVES. To specify an option or statistic, use the appropriate subcommand followed by an optional equals sign and the desired keyword. Separate multiple keywords on a single subcommand with at least one space or comma. Separate subcommands with slashes. For example, to include user-defined missing values in an analysis, specify

```
DESCRIPTIVES VARIABLES=NTCPRI TO COOK
    /MISSING=INCLUDE
```

Z Scores. You can request standardized scores for variables named or implied on the DESCRIPTIVES command. These transformed variables are named and stored as new variables on the active file. (See Section 26.4.)

Statistics. In addition to the default statistics, you can obtain the standard error of the mean, variance, kurtosis, skewness, range, and sum. DESCRIPTIVES does not compute the median or mode. (See Section 26.6.)

Missing Values. By default, DESCRIPTIVES excludes cases with user-missing values on a variable-by-variable basis. Optionally, you can request that user-missing values be handled as if they were valid or that cases with missing values be deleted listwise. (See Section 26.7.)

Formatting Options. You can suppress the printing of variable labels, produce reference indexes, print statistics in serial-style format, and restrict the output to an 80-character width. (See Section 26.8.)

26.2
OPERATION

The only required subcommand on DESCRIPTIVES is the VARIABLES sub-command, which specifies the variable list to be analyzed (see Section 26.3). The actual keyword VARIABLES can be omitted.

Sections 26.5 through 26.8 describe the optional subcommands. You can specify these subcommands in any order; separate them with slashes. You must first specify the variables to be used in the analysis, however, before you can specify any of the optional subcommands. For example, to include user-defined missing values in an analysis, specify

```
DESCRIPTIVES VARIABLES=NTCPRI TO COOK
   /MISSING=INCLUDE
```

26.3
VARIABLES Subcommand

The variables subcommand names the variable list. The actual keyword VARIA-BLES is optional. If you explicitly specify keyword VARIABLES, an equals sign must precede the variable list. You can use keyword TO in the list to refer to consecutive variables in the active file. The variables must be numeric.

To request the default summary statistics, specify the VARIABLES subcommand and a simple list of variables, as in:

```
DESCRIPTIVES VARIABLES=NTCPRI FOOD RENT
```

You can also use the keyword ALL to specify all variables in the active file. For example,

```
DESCRIPTIVES VARIABLES=ALL
```

produces the display in Figure 26.3. This output includes the mean, standard deviation, minimum, maximum, number of valid cases, and variable labels. DESCRIPTIVES always displays the number of valid cases that would be available if listwise deletion of missing values had been selected (see Section 26.7).

Figure 26.3 Default statistics

```
NUMBER OF VALID OBSERVATIONS (LISTWISE) =        38.00

VARIABLE      MEAN     STD DEV   MINIMUM    MAXIMUM VALID N   LABEL

NTCPRI      81.378     20.238        46        141      45    NET PRICE LEVEL
NTCSAL      50.341     24.295         8        100      44    NET SALARY LEVEL
NTCPUR      58.705     28.806        10        110      44    NET PURCHASING LEVEL
FOOD        70.467     18.744        40        130      45    AVG FOOD PRICES
WCLOTHES    80.711     30.195        21        174      45    MEDIUM-PRICED WOMEN'S CLOTHES
MCLOTHES    87.044     26.192        22        147      45    MEDIUM-PRICED MEN'S CLOTHES
RENT       120.089     94.225        27        440      45    NORMAL RENT
APPL        78.178     22.255        54        165      45    PRICE FOR APPLIANCES
SERVICE     73.089     19.007        42        113      45    PRICE FOR SERVICES
TEACHER     38.318     25.182         4        108      44    TEACHER'S GROSS SALARY
MECHANIC    50.705     30.746         5        115      44    MECHANIC'S GROSS SALARY
CONSTRUC    64.114     74.722         5        476      44    CONSTRUCTION WORKER'S GROSS SALARY
LATHE       41.814     24.353         4        100      43    LATHE WORKER'S GROSS SALARY
COOK        64.659     30.279        13        137      44    COOK'S GROSS SALARY
MANAGER     53.659     25.074        11        100      44    MANAGER'S GROSS SALARY
ENGINEER    60.045     26.175         8        114      44    ENGINEER'S GROSS SALARY
TELLER      42.636     24.123         7        100      44    TELLER'S GROSS SALARY
SECRET      48.841     22.230         8        100      44    SECRETARY'S GROSS SALARY
FSALES      48.182     27.127         5        100      44    FEMALE SALESWORKER'S GROSS SALARY
FTEX        50.718     31.195         3        111      39    FEMALE TEXTILE WORKER'S GROSS SALARY
CASWGT       1.000       .000    1.0000     1.0000      45
```

You can specify only one variable list with DESCRIPTIVES, but there is no limit to the number of variables named or implied on one command. Variables named more than once will appear in the output more than once. If there is insufficient space to process all the requested variables, DESCRIPTIVES trun-cates the variable list.

26.4
Z Scores

The *Z*-score variable transformation standardizes variables with different ob-served scales to the same scale. DESCRIPTIVES generates new variables, each with a mean of 0 and a standard deviation of 1, and stores them on the active file.

26.5
SAVE Subcommand

Use the SAVE subcommand to obtain one Z-score variable for each variable specified on the DESCRIPTIVES variable list. The SAVE subcommand calculates standardized variables and stores them on the active file. The commands

```
DESCRIPTIVES VARIABLES=ALL
    /SAVE
```

produce the table of old variables and new Z-score variables shown in Figure 26.5.

DESCRIPTIVES automatically supplies variable names and labels for the new variables. The new variable name is created by prefixing the letter Z to a maximum of seven characters of the variable name. For example, ZNTCPRI is the Z-score variable for NTCPRI. When DESCRIPTIVES creates new Z-score variables, it prints a table containing the source variable name, new variable name, its label, and the number of cases for which it is computed.

Figure 26.5 Z-score correspondence table

```
THE FOLLOWING Z-SCORE VARIABLES HAVE BEEN SAVED ON YOUR ACTIVE FILE:

FROM        TO                                              WEIGHTED
VARIABLE    Z-SCORE   LABEL                                 VALID N
--------    -------   -----                                 --------

NTCPRI      ZNTCPRI   ZSCORE:  NET PRICE LEVEL                    45
NTCSAL      ZNTCSAL   ZSCORE:  NET SALARY LEVEL                   44
NTCPUR      ZNTCPUR   ZSCORE:  NET PURCHASING LEVEL               44
FOOD        ZFOOD     ZSCORE:  AVG FOOD PRICES                    45
WCLOTHES    ZWCLOTHE  ZSCORE:  MEDIUM-PRICED WOMEN'S CLOTHES      45
MCLOTHES    ZMCLOTHE  ZSCORE:  MEDIUM-PRICED MEN'S CLOTHES        45
RENT        ZRENT     ZSCORE:  NORMAL RENT                        45
APPL        ZAPPL     ZSCORE:  PRICE FOR APPLIANCES               45
SERVICE     ZSERVICE  ZSCORE:  PRICE FOR SERVICES                 45
TEACHER     ZTEACHER  ZSCORE:  TEACHER'S GROSS SALARY             44
MECHANIC    ZMECHANI  ZSCORE:  MECHANIC'S GROSS SALARY            44
CONSTRUC    ZCONSTRU  ZSCORE:  CONSTRUCTION WORKER'S GROSS SAL     44
LATHE       ZLATHE    ZSCORE:  LATHE WORKER'S GROSS SALARY        43
COOK        ZCOOK     ZSCORE:  COOK'S GROSS SALARY                44
MANAGER     ZMANAGER  ZSCORE:  MANAGER'S GROSS SALARY             44
ENGINEER    ZENGINEE  ZSCORE:  ENGINEER'S GROSS SALARY            44
TELLER      ZTELLER   ZSCORE:  TELLER'S GROSS SALARY              44
SECRET      ZSECRET   ZSCORE:  SECRETARY'S GROSS SALARY           44
FSALES      ZFSALES   ZSCORE:  FEMALE SALESWORKER'S GROSS SALA    44
FTEX        ZFTEX     ZSCORE:  FEMALE TEXTILE WORKER'S GROSS S     39
CASWGT      ZCASWGT   ZSCORE(CASWGT)                               0
```

If you want Z scores for a subset of the variables listed on DESCRIPTIVES, specify the name of the new variable in parentheses following the source variable on the VARIABLES subcommand, and *do not use the SAVE subcommand*. For example,

```
DESCRIPTIVES VARIABLES=NTCSAL NTCPUR (PURCHZ) NTCPRI (PRICEZ)
```

creates Z-score variables for NTCPUR and NTCPRI.

If you specify new names on the VARIABLES subcommand *and* use the SAVE subcommand, DESCRIPTIVES creates one new variable for each variable on the VARIABLES subcommand, using the default names for variables not explicitly assigned names. For example,

```
DESCRIPTIVES VARIABLES=NTCSAL NTCPUR (PURCHZ) NTCPRI (PRICEZ)/
    SAVE
```

creates PURCHZ and PRICEZ and assigns a default name to the Z-score variable for NTCSAL. When you specify the name of the new variable yourself, you can use any acceptable eight-character variable name, including any of the default variable names, that is not already part of the active file.

If DESCRIPTIVES cannot use the default naming convention because it would produce duplicate names, it uses an alternative naming convention: first ZSC001 through ZSC099, then STDZ01 through STDZ09, then ZZZZ01 through ZZZZ09, then ZQZQ01 through ZQZQ09. For example,

```
DESCRIPTIVES VARIABLES=SALARY80 SALARY81 SALARY82
    /SAVE
```

creates ZSALARY8, ZSC001, and ZSC002.

When using the SAVE subcommand, you can name the same variable up to nine times in a variable list. If at any time you want to change any of the variable names, whether those DESCRIPTIVES creates or those you previously assigned, you can do so with the RENAME VARIABLES command (Chapter 5).

DESCRIPTIVES automatically supplies variable labels for the new variables by prefixing *ZSCORE:* to the first 31 characters of the source variable's label. If it uses a name like ZSC001, it prefixes *ZSCORE(varname)* to the first 31 characters of the source variable's label. If the source variable has no label, it uses *ZSCORE(varname)* for the label.

26.6
STATISTICS Subcommand

By default, DESCRIPTIVES prints the mean, standard deviation, minimum, and maximum. If you use the STATISTICS subcommand and any of its keywords, you can specify alternative statistics. If you specify the STATISTICS subcommand with no keywords, DESCRIPTIVES prints the default statistics. When you specify statistics, DESCRIPTIVES prints *only* those statistics you request.

You can use the keyword ALL to obtain all statistics. When requesting the default statistics plus additional statistics, you can specify DEFAULT to obtain the default statistics without having to name MEAN, STDDEV, MIN and MAX.

The following keywords can be specified on the STATISTICS subcommand:

MEAN *Mean.*

SEMEAN *Standard error of the mean.*

STDDEV *Standard deviation.*

VARIANCE *Variance.*

KURTOSIS *Kurtosis.* Also prints standard error.

SKEWNESS *Skewness.* Also prints standard error.

RANGE *Range.*

MIN *Minimum.*

MAX *Maximum.*

SUM *Sum.*

DEFAULT *Mean, standard deviation, minimum, and maximum.* These are the default statistics if you omit the STATISTICS subcommand.

ALL *All the statistics available to DESCRIPTIVES.*

Note that median and mode, which are available in FREQUENCIES, are not available in DESCRIPTIVES. These statistics require that values be sorted, and DESCRIPTIVES does not sort values. If you request a statistic that is not listed above, DESCRIPTIVES issues an error message, and the command is not executed.

The number of columns needed to display the statistics controls the manner in which they are printed. The maximum column width for skewness, kurtosis, and their standard error is 10; the maximum width for mean, standard error of the mean, minimum, maximum, and range is 11; the maximum width for standard deviation is 12; the maximum width for variance is 13; and the maximum width for sum is 14. These widths include a blank between statistics.

DESCRIPTIVES prints all statistics, except for the minimum and maximum values, with three positions to the right of the decimal point if it can fit them into the space allocated within the maximum width. Large numbers are rounded to fit the column width. If the integer portion still exceeds the column width, DESCRIPTIVES uses scientific notation. Extremely small numbers are also printed with scientific notation.

26.7
MISSING Subcommand

By default, DESCRIPTIVES deletes cases with missing values on a variable-by-variable basis. A case missing on a variable will not be included in the summary statistics for that variable, but the case *will* be included for variables where it is not missing.

The MISSING subcommand controls missing values, and three keywords can be specified on it:

VARIABLE   *Exclude missing values on a variable-by-variable basis.* This is the default if you omit the MISSING subcommand.

LISTWISE   *Exclude missing values listwise.* Cases missing on any variable named are excluded from the computation of summary statistics for all variables.

INCLUDE   *Include user-defined missing values.*

The VARIABLE and LISTWISE keywords are mutually exclusive; however, each can be specified with INCLUDE. For example, to include user-missing values in an analysis that excludes missing values listwise, specify

```
DESCRIPTIVES VARIABLES=ALL/
    MISSING=INCLUDE LISTWISE
```

When you use the keyword VARIABLE or the default missing-value treatment, DESCRIPTIVES reports the number of valid cases for each variable. It always displays the number of cases that would be available if listwise deletion of missing values had been selected.

26.8
FORMAT Subcommand

By default, DESCRIPTIVES prints the statistics and a 40-character variable label for each variable on one line, as shown in Figure 26.3.

The FORMAT subcommand controls the formatting options available in DESCRIPTIVES, and the following keywords can be specified on it:

LABELS   *Print variable labels.* This is the default if you omit the FORMAT subcommand.

NOLABELS   *Suppress variable labels.*

INDEX   *Print reference indexes.* INDEX prints a positional and an alphabetic reference index following the statistical display. The index shows the page location in the output of the statistics for each variable. The variables are listed by their position in the active file and alphabetically.

NOINDEX   *Suppress reference indexes.* This is the default if you omit the FORMAT subcommand,

LINE   *Print statistics in line format.* LINE prints statistics on the same line as the variable name. It is the default if you omit the FORMAT subcommand.

SERIAL   *Print statistics in serial format.* SERIAL prints statistics below the variable name, permitting larger field widths and more decimal digits for very large or very small numbers. DESCRIPTIVES automatically forces this format if the number of statistics requested does not fit in the column format.

You can use the SET WIDTH command to restrict DESCRIPTIVES output to 80 columns. The 80-column format is useful if you are examining displays on short-carriage terminals. However, the number of columns for statistics is severely restricted. If you use the NOLABELS keyword to suppress variable labels, more space is available for statistics. Also, specifying a listwise deletion of missing values on the MISSING subcommand suppresses the column for valid number of cases, providing additional space for statistics.

The following commands request reference indexes and print the statistics in serial-style format with an 80-column width:

```
SET WIDTH=80
DESCRIPTIVES VARIABLES=TEACHER FTEX FSALES SECRET
    /STATISTICS=ALL
    /FORMAT=INDEX SERIAL
```

See the display in Figure 26.8.

Figure 26.8 Serial format and reference indexes

```
NUMBER OF VALID OBSERVATIONS (LISTWISE) =        38.00

VARIABLE  TEACHER     TEACHER'S GROSS SALARY

MEAN            38.318              S.E. MEAN          3.796
STD DEV         25.182              VARIANCE         634.129
KURTOSIS         .249               S.E. KURT           .702
SKEWNESS         .727               S.E. SKEW           .357
RANGE          104.000              MINIMUM              4
MAXIMUM         108                 SUM             1686.000

VALID OBSERVATIONS -      44        MISSING OBSERVATIONS -        1

- - - - - - - - - - - - - - - - - - - - - - - - - - - - - - - - - -

VARIABLE  FTEX        FEMALE TEXTILE WORKER'S GROSS SALARY

MEAN            50.718              S.E. MEAN          4.995
STD DEV         31.195              VARIANCE         973.103
KURTOSIS       -1.102               S.E. KURT           .741
SKEWNESS         .218               S.E. SKEW           .378
RANGE          108.000              MINIMUM              3
MAXIMUM         111                 SUM             1978.000

VALID OBSERVATIONS -      39        MISSING OBSERVATIONS -        6

- - - - - - - - - - - - - - - - - - - - - - - - - - - - - - - - - -

VARIABLE  FSALES      FEMALE SALESWORKER'S GROSS SALARY

MEAN            48.182              S.E. MEAN          4.090
STD DEV         27.127              VARIANCE         735.873
KURTOSIS       -1.055               S.E. KURT           .702
SKEWNESS         .185               S.E. SKEW           .357
RANGE           95.000              MINIMUM              5
MAXIMUM         100                 SUM             2120.000

VALID OBSERVATIONS -      44        MISSING OBSERVATIONS -        1

- - - - - - - - - - - - - - - - - - - - - - - - - - - - - - - - - -

VARIABLE  SECRET      SECRETARY'S GROSS SALARY

MEAN            48.841              S.E. MEAN          3.351
STD DEV         22.230              VARIANCE         494.183
KURTOSIS        -.417               S.E. KURT           .702
SKEWNESS         .200               S.E. SKEW           .357
RANGE           92.000              MINIMUM              8
MAXIMUM         100                 SUM             2149.000

VALID OBSERVATIONS -      44        MISSING OBSERVATIONS -        1

POSITIONAL INDEX

VARIABLE  PAGE    VARIABLE  PAGE    VARIABLE  PAGE    VARIABLE  PAGE

TEACHER    3      SECRET     4      FSALES     3      FTEX       3

ALPHABETIC INDEX

VARIABLE  PAGE    VARIABLE  PAGE    VARIABLE  PAGE    VARIABLE  PAGE

FSALES     3      FTEX       3      SECRET     4      TEACHER    3
```

26.9 LIMITATIONS

There are no specific limitations. If there is insufficient workspace to process all the requested variables, DESCRIPTIVES will truncate the variable list.

ANNOTATED EXAMPLE FOR DESCRIPTIVES

This example analyzes 1979 prices and earnings in 45 cities around the world, compiled by the Union Bank of Switzerland. The variables are

- NTCPUR—the city's net purchasing power level, calculated as the ratio of labor expended (measured in number of working hours) to the cost of more than 100 goods and services, weighted by consumer habits. NTCPUR is expressed as a percentage above or below that of Zurich, where Zurich equals 100%.

- FOOD—the average net cost of 39 different food and beverage items in the city, expressed as a percentage above or below that of Zurich, where Zurich equals 100%.

- RENT—the average gross monthly rent in the city, expressed as a percentage above or below that of Zurich, where Zurich equals 100%.

26

- APPL—the average cost of six different household appliances, expressed as a percentage above or below that of Zurich, where Zurich equals 100%.

- SERVICE—the average cost of 28 different goods and services in the city, expressed as a percentage above or below that of Zurich, where Zurich equals 100%.

- WCLOTHES—the cost of medium-priced women's clothes, expressed as a percentage above or below that of Zurich, where Zurich equals 100%.

- MCLOTHES—the cost of medium-priced men's clothes, expressed as a percentage above or below that of Zurich, where Zurich equals 100%.

- CLOTHES—the average cost of medium-priced women's and men's clothes, expressed as a percentage above or below that of Zurich, where Zurich equals 100%.

In this example, we obtain univariate summary statistics about purchasing power and the costs of various goods and services in cities and generate standardized variables for the costs of men's and women's clothes. The SPSS-X commands are

```
GET  FILE=CITY/KEEP NTCPUR TO SERVICE
COMPUTE  CLOTHES=(WCLOTHES + MCLOTHES)/2
VAR LABELS  CLOTHES, AVERAGE COST OF W AND M CLOTHES
DESCRIPTIVES VARIABLES=NTCPUR, FOOD, RENT TO SERVICE, WCLOTHES
  (ZWWEAR), MCLOTHES (ZMWEAR), CLOTHES (ZCLOTHES)
 /STATISTICS=VARIANCE DEFAULT
 /MISSING=LISTWISE
FINISH
```

- The GET command defines the data to SPSS-X and selects the variables needed for analysis (see Chapter 6).

- The COMPUTE command creates the variable CLOTHES by adding the values for WCLOTHES and MCLOTHES and dividing by 2 (see Chapter 7).

- The VAR LABELS command assigns a label to the new variable CLOTHES (see Chapter 5).

- The DESCRIPTIVES command requests statistics for all the variables listed (see Section 26.3) and computes Z scores for variables WCLOTHES, MCLOTHES, and CLOTHES. The new standardized variables are named ZWWEAR, ZMWEAR, and ZCLOTHES (see Section 26.4).

- The STATISTICS subcommand requests the variance plus the default statistics (mean, standard deviation, minimum, and maximum) for each variable (see Section 26.6).

- The MISSING subcommand specifies listwise deletion of user-missing values. A case missing on any variable specified on the DESCRIPTIVES command is excluded from the computation of statistics for all variables (see Section 26.7).

- Since no formatting option is specified, DESCRIPTIVES displays the statistics and variable labels for each variable on one line and can use more than 80 columns (see Section 26.8).

Output from DESCRIPTIVES

```
NUMBER OF VALID OBSERVATIONS (LISTWISE) =      44.00

VARIABLE     MEAN     STD DEV    VARIANCE    MINIMUM   MAXIMUM   LABEL

NTCPUR      58.705    28.806     829.794        10        110   NET PURCHASING LEVEL
FOOD        71.000    18.612     346.419        40        130   AVG FOOD PRICES
RENT       121.750    94.646    8957.773        27        440   NORMAL RENT
APPL        78.705    22.227     494.027        54        165   PRICE FOR APPLIANCES
SERVICE     73.682    18.801     353.478        42        113   PRICE FOR SERVICES
WCLOTHES    81.205    30.360     921.701        21        174   MEDIUM-PRICED WOMEN'S CLOTHES
MCLOTHES    87.864    25.906     671.097        22        147   MEDIUM-PRICED MEN'S CLOTHES
CLOTHES     84.534    26.749     715.505     21.50     160.50   AVERAGE COST OF W AND M CLOTHES

THE FOLLOWING Z-SCORE VARIABLES HAVE BEEN SAVED ON YOUR ACTIVE FILE:

FROM        TO                                            WEIGHTED
VARIABLE    Z-SCORE    LABEL                              VALID N

WCLOTHES    ZWWEAR     ZSCORE:  MEDIUM-PRICED WOMEN'S CLOTHES      44
MCLOTHES    ZMWEAR     ZSCORE:  MEDIUM-PRICED MEN'S CLOTHES        44
CLOTHES     ZCLOTHES   ZSCORE:  AVERAGE COST OF W AND M CLOTHES    44
```

Syntax

DISCRIMINANT

```
DISCRIMINANT GROUPS=varname(min,max) /VARIABLES=varlist
  [/SELECT=varname(value)]
  [/ANALYSIS=varlist(level) [varlist...]]
  [/METHOD={DIRECT**}] [/TOLERANCE={0.001}]
          {WILKS   }                {t    }
          {MAHAL   }
          {MAXMINF }
          {MINRESID}
          {RAO     }
  [/MAXSTEPS={2v}]
            {m }
  [/FIN={1.0}] [/FOUT={1.0}] [/PIN={1.0**}]
        {fi }        {fo }        {pi  }
  [/POUT={1.0**}] [/VIN={0**}]
         {po  }         {vi }
  [/FUNCTIONS={g-1,100.0,1.0**}] [/PRIORS={EQUAL     }]
             {nf , cp ,sig }             {SIZE      }
                                         {value list}
  [/SAVE=[CLASS=varname] [PROBS=rootname]
         [SCORES=rootname]]
  [/ANALYSIS=...]
  [/MISSING={EXCLUDE**}]
           {INCLUDE }
  [/MATRIX=[OUT({*   })] [IN({*   })]]
               {file}       {file}
  [/HISTORY={STEP**}  {END**}  ]
            {NOSTEP}  {NOEND }
  [/ROTATE={NONE**   }]
           {COEFF    }
           {STRUCTURE}
  [/CLASSIFY={NONMISSING  }  {POOLED  }  [MEANSUB]]
            {UNSELECTED  }  {SEPARATE}
            {UNCLASSIFIED}
  [/STATISTICS=[MEAN   ] [COV ]  [FPAIR]  [RAW  ]  [ALL]]
              [STDDEV] [GCOV]  [UNIVF]  [COEFF]
              [CORR  ] [TCOV]  [BOXM ]  [TABLE]
  [/PLOT=[MAP] [SEPARATE] [COMBINED] [CASES] [ALL]]
```
**Default if subcommand is omitted.

Contents

27.1   OVERVIEW

27.2   OPERATION

27.3   Analysis Phase

27.4   GROUPS Subcommand

27.5   VARIABLES Subcommand

27.6   SELECT Subcommand

27.7   ANALYSIS Subcommand

27.8   METHOD Subcommand

27.9   MAXSTEPS Subcommand

27.10   FUNCTIONS Subcommand

27.11   STATISTICS Subcommand

27.12   ROTATION Subcommand

27.13   HISTORY Subcommand

27.14   Classification Phase

27.15   PRIORS Subcommand

27.16   PLOT Subcommand

27.17   CLASSIFY Subcommand

27.18   MISSING Subcommand

27.19   SAVE Subcommand

27.20   MATRIX Subcommand

27.21   OUT Keyword

27.22   IN Keyword

27.23   LIMITATIONS

27

Chapter 27   DISCRIMINANT

Discriminant analysis is a statistical technique in which linear combinations of variables are used to distinguish between two or more categories of cases. The variables "discriminate" between groups of cases and predict into which category or group a case falls, based upon the values of these variables.

The first task of discriminant analysis is to find the linear combination of variables that best discriminates between, or separates, groups. As in regression analysis, there are two approaches to variable selection. The direct-entry method forces a set of variables into the analysis. Alternatively, you can use stepwise methods to find a set of variables that maximizes discriminating power as defined by various criteria. After the discriminant functions have been computed, you can use coefficients to predict group membership.

Frequently, discriminant analysis is used to classify a sample in which actual group membership is unknown. You can do this in two ways with procedure DISCRIMINANT. You can combine two samples, one in which group membership is known and one in which group membership is unknown, into one sample. The cases for which group membership is known are used to compute the discriminant functions. Then, discriminant functions are used to classify all cases or only those cases for which group membership is unknown. Alternatively, you can use DISCRIMINANT to produce the matrix materials required for classification based upon one sample and then use these materials to classify the second sample.

27.1
OVERVIEW

To operate DISCRIMINANT, you must specify a grouping variable, which identifies the group into which each case falls, and a set of discriminating variables. These are the minimum requirements. The GROUPS subcommand described in Section 27.4 defines the grouping variable. Since DISCRIMINANT is capable of performing multiple analyses in which different sets of discriminating variables are used or in which different criteria are used for the entry or removal of variables, two separate subcommands are used to define the variables used in the analysis. The VARIABLES subcommand names the variables to be used in all analyses and is described in Section 27.5. The ANALYSIS subcommand names the variables to be used in the current analysis and is described in Section 27.7.

In addition to the direct-entry method, DISCRIMINANT provides five methods of stepwise variable selection via the METHOD subcommand. (See Section 27.8.) You can also use other optional subcommands to set statistical controls for entry or removal.

Analysis Features. The *analysis phase* of DISCRIMINANT is described in Section 27.3.

Two basic sets of information related to the analysis phase are always printed: statistics for the functions and coefficients for variables used in the functions. In addition, you can obtain classification function coefficients, unstandardized discriminant function coefficients, the structure matrix, univariate F ratios, the matrix of pairwise F ratios after each step, Box's M test, means, standard deviations, and various covariance matrices. (See Section 27.11.) You can use one sample to calculate the statistics required to classify another sample via the SELECT subcommand. (See Section 27.6.)

Classification Features. The *classification phase* of DISCRIMINANT is described in Section 27.14.

Discriminant functions calculated by DISCRIMINANT can be used to classify cases. You can specify prior probabilities for classification purposes via the PRIORS subcommand. (See Section 27.15.) The classification phase produces plots of classified cases, a classification results table, and other statistics to evaluate the classification. By default, DISCRIMINANT uses the pooled within-groups covariance matrix to classify cases. Optionally, it uses separate-group covariance matrices. See Section 27.17 for this and other classification options.

Saving Results. Optionally, DISCRIMINANT saves two types of results for use with other SPSS-X procedures or other programs. Casewise materials, including actual group, predicted group, posterior probabilities, and discriminant scores, may be added to the active file. Matrix materials—including weighted and unweighted number of cases, means, standard deviations, and correlation matrices—are written to a system file. You can use these materials with SPSS-X to classify an entirely different sample. (See Sections 27.19 and 27.20.)

Missing Values. By default, cases are excluded from the computation of functions if they have missing values for any of the variables named on the VARIABLES subcommand. Optionally, you can include user-defined missing values in the analysis. (See Section 27.18.)

27.2
OPERATION

Two subcommands are required in DISCRIMINANT: GROUPS, which specifies the variable used to group cases, and VARIABLES, which specifies the discriminating variables. All other subcommands are optional. All subcommands must be separated by slashes.

The GROUPS, VARIABLES, and SELECT subcommands must precede any other subcommands and may be entered in any order. The ANALYSIS subcommand, which specifies one analysis, must follow. Subcommands METHOD, MAXSTEPS, TOLERANCE, FIN, FOUT, PIN, POUT, VIN, FUNCTIONS, PRIORS, and SAVE may be entered in any order following the ANALYSIS subcommand.

METHOD, MAXSTEPS, TOLERANCE, FIN, FOUT, PIN, POUT, VIN, FUNCTIONS, PRIORS, and SAVE apply only to the previous ANALYSIS subcommand. If any of these subcommands is used more than once for a given ANALYSIS subcommand, the first specification named is in effect for that command.

The following example illustrates syntax rules for DISCRIMINANT:

```
DISCRIMINANT  GROUPS=WORLD(1,3)
 /VARIABLES=FOOD TO FSALES
 /SAVE=CLASS DIRECT SCORES=SCORE
 /ANALYSIS=FOOD TO FSALES
 /PRIORS=SIZE
 /SAVE=CLASS CLASSA
 /ANALYSIS=FOOD TO FSALES
 /METHOD=WILKS
 /PIN=.01
 /SAVE=CLASS WILKS
 /ANALYSIS=FOOD TO FSALES
 /METHOD=WILKS/PIN=.01/PRIORS=SIZE
 /SAVE=CLASS WILKSA
```

This command produces four analyses:

- The first analysis uses the direct-entry method, taking all defaults, and saves the predicted group as variable DIRECT and discriminant scores as SCORE1 and SCORE2.
- The second analysis makes a priors adjustment and saves the predicted group as CLASSA.
- The third analyis is a stepwise analysis using the WILKS method. It sets the probability of *F*-to-enter to .01 and saves the predicted group as WILKS.
- The fourth analysis is the same as the third analysis except that it adjusts for prior probabilities and saves the predicted group as WILKSA.

27.3
Analysis Phase

DISCRIMINANT first calculates the discriminant function(s) that best distinguishes groups you have specified. This process is called the *analysis phase* and is followed by the *classification phase* (see Section 27.14).

27.4
GROUPS Subcommand

The GROUPS subcommand defines the groups. Each case used in the computation of discriminant functions is assigned to a group based on its value on a grouping variable. For example,

```
DISCRIMINANT  GROUPS=WORLD(1,3)
/VARIABLES=APPL TO FSALES
```

assigns each case to one of three groups defined by the variable WORLD. You can specify only one grouping variable, and its values must be integers. The minimum and maximum specifications define the range of values for the group. For example,

```
DISCRIMINANT  GROUPS=TYPE(1,5)/VARIABLES=SYMP1 TO SYMP8
```

specifies a maximum of five groups. Empty groups are ignored and do not affect computations. For example, if no cases have the value 3 for TYPE, then only four groups are present. Cases with values that lie outside the value range are not used during the analysis phase, but they are classified during the classification phase.

27.5
VARIABLES Subcommand

The VARIABLES subcommand names the variables to be used as predictor, or discriminating, variables during the analysis phase. The variable list on the VARIABLES subcommand follows the usual SPSS-X conventions for variable lists. Only numeric variables can be used. For example,

```
DISCRIMINANT  GROUPS=WORLD(1,3)
/VARIABLES=FOOD SERVICE BUS MECHANIC CONSTRUC COOK MANAGER FSALES
```

specifies that variables FOOD through FSALES are to be used during the analysis phase. These commands produce the default DISCRIMINANT output shown in Figures 27.5a, 27.5b, and 27.5c.

The default output includes three sets of information. Figure 27.5a shows the preliminary information, describing the number of cases in each group used in the analysis. DISCRIMINANT excludes cases with missing values for any of the variables named on the VARIABLES or GROUPS subcommands during the analysis phase. See Section 27.18 for alternative missing-value treatments. Figure

27.5b shows the method used to select variables for the analysis and the various statistical criteria in effect. See Section 27.8 for ways to override the default controls. Prior probabilities are printed but are used only for the classification phase. See Section 27.15 for overriding prior probabilities.

Figure 27.5a   Information about the sample

```
- - - - - - - - - - - - - - - - - - - - D I S C R I M I N A N T   A N A L Y S I S - - - - - - - - - - - - - - - - - - - - - - - -
ON GROUPS DEFINED BY WORLD       ECON CLASS FOR COUNTRY


          45 (UNWEIGHTED) CASES WERE PROCESSED.
           2 OF THESE WERE EXCLUDED FROM THE ANALYSIS.
             0 HAD MISSING OR OUT-OF-RANGE GROUP CODES.
             2 HAD AT LEAST ONE MISSING DISCRIMINATING VARIABLE.
          43 (UNWEIGHTED) CASES WILL BE USED IN THE ANALYSIS.



NUMBER OF CASES BY GROUP

                    NUMBER OF CASES
    WORLD      UNWEIGHTED      WEIGHTED    LABEL

         1          25           25.0      1ST WORLD
         2           6            6.0      PETRO WORLD
         3          12           12.0      3RD WORLD

    TOTAL          43           43.0
```

Figure 27.5b   Method specifications

```
- - - - - - - - - - - - - - - - - - - - D I S C R I M I N A N T   A N A L Y S I S - - - - - - - - - - - - - - - - - - - - - - - -
ON GROUPS DEFINED BY WORLD       ECON CLASS FOR COUNTRY


ANALYSIS NUMBER        1

DIRECT METHOD:   ALL VARIABLES PASSING THE TOLERANCE TEST ARE ENTERED.

      MINIMUM TOLERANCE LEVEL.................. 0.00100

CANONICAL DISCRIMINANT FUNCTIONS

      MAXIMUM NUMBER OF FUNCTIONS.............       2
      MINIMUM CUMULATIVE PERCENT OF VARIANCE... 100.00
      MAXIMUM SIGNIFICANCE OF WILKS' LAMBDA....  1.0000


PRIOR PROBABILITY FOR EACH GROUP IS 0.33333
```

Figure 27.5c shows the actual results of the analysis. In this example, two functions are extracted. By default, standardized canonical discriminant function coefficients are printed. To obtain unstandardized canonical discriminant functions and classification function coefficients, you must use the associated STATISTICS subcommand (see Section 27.11). Next, the structure matrix for the analysis is printed. This matrix displays the pooled within-groups correlations between the discriminant functions and the discriminating variables. To facilitate interpretation, the matrix is ordered. Variables are grouped according to the function with which they are most highly correlated. Within each such group, variables are sorted in descending order by the absolute value of the correlation coefficient. If there is more than one function, the largest correlation for each variable is flagged with an asterisk. In addition, you can rotate the structure matrix and the pattern matrix of standardized canonical discriminant functions and variables to facilitate interpretation. Sections 27.12 and 27.13 describe options related to the analysis phase. Finally, the group centroids are reported by default. Centroids are the mean discriminant scores on the functions for each group.

Figure 27.5c Function statistics

```
                            CANONICAL DISCRIMINANT FUNCTIONS


                      PERCENT OF   CUMULATIVE    CANONICAL  :  AFTER
FUNCTION  EIGENVALUE   VARIANCE      PERCENT    CORRELATION :  FUNCTION  WILKS' LAMBDA  CHI-SQUARED   D.F.  SIGNIFICANCE

                                                            :     0       0.2006551       58.625       16     0.0000
    1*     2.25481      80.93        80.93      0.8323237   :     1       0.6530949       15.550        7     0.0296
    2*     0.53117      19.07       100.00      0.5889865   :

     * MARKS THE    2 CANONICAL DISCRIMINANT FUNCTIONS REMAINING IN THE ANALYSIS.


STANDARDIZED CANONICAL DISCRIMINANT FUNCTION COEFFICIENTS

           FUNC  1      FUNC  2

FOOD      -0.11919     1.03495
SERVICE    0.14114    -0.89385
BUS        0.91978    -0.35004
MECHANIC   0.61734     0.29191
CONSTRUC  -0.31667    -0.56073
COOK      -0.46470     0.70515
MANAGER   -0.56156    -0.47097
FSALES     0.32233     0.29270


STRUCTURE MATRIX:

POOLED WITHIN-GROUPS CORRELATIONS BETWEEN DISCRIMINATING VARIABLES
                       AND CANONICAL DISCRIMINANT FUNCTIONS
(VARIABLES ORDERED BY SIZE OF CORRELATION WITHIN FUNCTION)

           FUNC  1      FUNC  2

BUS        0.83191*     0.11195
MECHANIC   0.69362*     0.12815
FSALES     0.66971*     0.13326
MANAGER    0.41159*     0.09707
SERVICE    0.39078*    -0.19472

FOOD       0.29384      0.46681*
COOK       0.31593      0.33120*
CONSTRUC   0.16236     -0.21002*



CANONICAL DISCRIMINANT FUNCTIONS EVALUATED AT GROUP MEANS (GROUP CENTROIDS)

GROUP     FUNC  1     FUNC  2

   1       1.22889    -0.00274
   2      -1.69224     1.54027
   3      -1.71407    -0.76442
```

27.6
SELECT Subcommand

Use the SELECT subcommand to select a subset of cases for computing basic statistics and coefficients. You can then use these coefficients to classify either all the cases or only the unselected cases.

The specification for the SELECT subcommand is a variable name followed by a value in parentheses. Only cases with the specified value on the selection variable are used during the analysis phase. The value must be an integer, as in

```
DISCRIMINANT  GROUPS=TYPE(1,5)/VARIABLES=A TO H
 /SELECT=LASTYEAR(81)
```

which limits the analysis phase to cases containing the value 81 for variable LASTYEAR. The SELECT subcommand must precede the first ANALYSIS subcommand and remains in effect for all analyses.

The following example demonstrates the use of the SELECT subcommand to compute coefficients on a 40% random sample of the cases:

```
COMPUTE   SET=UNIFORM(1) > .4
DISCRIMINANT  GROUPS=WORLD(1,3)
 /VARIABLES=FOOD APPL SERVICE RENT
  /SELECT=SET(0)
  /METHOD=WILKS
```

When you use the SELECT subcommand, DISCRIMINANT by default reports classification statistics separately for selected and unselected cases. To limit classification to unselected cases, use the options described in Section 27.17.

27.7
ANALYSIS Subcommand

You can do several discriminant analyses with one DISCRIMINANT command if the grouping variable is the same across analyses. To perform multiple analyses, name all the variables to be used in the various analyses on the VARIABLES subcommand and then use the ANALYSIS subcommand to specify subsets of variables for individual analyses. The variable list follows the usual SPSS-X conventions for variable lists, except that the sequence of variables implied by the TO keyword refers to their order on the VARIABLES subcommand. For analyses using the direct-entry method, specify:

```
DISCRIMINANT  GROUPS=WORLD(1,3)
 /VARIABLES=FOOD TO FSALES
 /ANALYSIS=FOOD RENT APPL SERVICE WCLOTHES
 /ANALYSIS=FOOD SERVICE BUS MECHANIC CONSTRUC COOK MANAGER FSALES
```

Optionally, you can specify an inclusion level to control the order in which variables are entered or removed in a stepwise analysis (see Section 27.8).

Variable Selection for the Analysis. Several related subcommands control the selection of variables during the analysis phase. The METHOD subcommand specifies the selection criterion. The MAXSTEPS subcommand controls the number of steps in a stepwise analysis. The TOLERANCE, FIN, FOUT, PIN, POUT, and VIN subcommands override default statistical criteria for entering and removing variables. The FUNCTIONS subcommand controls the number of functions extracted. All of these subcommands are optional and are used only to override defaults. These subcommands apply only to the previous ANALYSIS specification and do not reset defaults in subsequent analyses.

27.8
METHOD Subcommand

By default, DISCRIMINANT enters all variables specified on the analysis list (provided that no collinearity problems appear). This method is termed the *direct-entry method*. Optionally, you can specify any one of five different stepwise methods on the METHOD subcommand. These methods enter and remove variables one at time, selecting them on the basis of specific criteria. Different criteria are used for different stepwise methods. In addition, you can control the order in which variables are considered for entry or removal by a given stepwise method (see below).

The METHOD subcommand follows the ANALYSIS subcommand and has one of the following specifications:

DIRECT *All variables are entered simultaneously, provided they satisfy the tolerance criterion. For a discussion of controlling the tolerance criterion, see Section 27.9. DIRECT is the default method.*

WILKS *The variable that minimizes the overall Wilks' lambda is selected.*

MAHAL *The variable that maximizes the Mahalanobis' distance between the two closest groups is selected.*

MAXMINF *The variable that maximizes the smallest F ratio between pairs of groups is selected.*

MINRESID *The variable that minimizes the sum of unexplained variation between groups is selected.*

RAO   *The variable that produces the largest increase in Rao's* V *is selected.* Rao's
V is a generalized measure of the overall separation between groups.

With all methods, all variables must satisfy the tolerance criterion before they can
be entered. With the stepwise methods, all variables must also satisfy the partial F
ratio criterion before they can be entered. Section 27.9 discusses setting the
partial F criterion.

When any of the stepwise methods are used, variables may be removed from
the equation as additional variables are entered. Variables in the equation are
tested for removal on the basis of their partial F values, which must be smaller
than a given value for removal to occur. Section 27.9 also discusses setting the
partial F for removal. Variables are never removed when the DIRECT method
(the default) is used.

Inclusion Levels. When you specify a stepwise method, you can use the ANALY-
SIS subcommand to control the order in which variables are considered for entry.
By default, variables are examined for entry or removal on the basis of their
partial F values. To control the order in which sets of variables are examined,
specify an inclusion level in parentheses following the sets of variables. The
inclusion level can be any integer between 0 and 99. For example,

```
DISCRIMINANT  GROUPS=TYPE(1,5)/VARIABLES=A TO H
 /ANALYSIS=AB C D(4) E F G H(3)
```

sets the inclusion level to 4 for variables A, B, C, and D, and to 3 for variables E,
F, G, and H.

The inclusion level controls the order in which variables are entered, the way
in which they are entered, and whether or not they should be considered for
removal according to the rules outlined below. All variables must still pass the
tolerance criterion to be entered.

- Variables with higher inclusion levels are considered for entry before variables with
  lower levels. Variables do not have to be ordered by their inclusion level on the
  subcommand itself.
- Variables with even inclusion levels are entered together.
- Variables with odd inclusion levels are entered one variable at a time according to
  the stepwise method specified on the METHOD subcommand.
- Only variables with an inclusion level of 1 may be considered for removal. To make a
  variable with a higher inclusion level eligible for removal, name it twice on the
  ANALYSIS subcommand, first specifying the desired inclusion level and then an
  inclusion level of 1.
- An inclusion level of 0 prevents a variable from being entered, although an entry
  criterion is computed and printed.
- The default inclusion level is 1.

In the analysis

```
DISCRIMINANT  GROUPS=WORLD(1,3)
 /VARIABLES=FOOD SERVICE BUS MECHANIC CONSTRUC COOK MANAGER FSALES
 /ANALYSIS=FOOD TO FSALES (2)  FOOD TO FSALES(1)
 /METHOD=WILKS
```

all variables are known to meet the minimum tolerance criterion. The stepping
results are shown in Figure 27.8a. DISCRIMINANT forces all the variables in
first, then removes FSALES, maximizing the overall partial F ratio. The summary
table for the process is shown in Figure 27.8b.

Figure 27.8a Stepwise output

```
------------------ VARIABLES NOT IN THE ANALYSIS AFTER STEP   0 ------------------


                         MINIMUM
VARIABLE  TOLERANCE    TOLERANCE    F TO ENTER    WILKS' LAMBDA

FOOD      1.0000000    1.0000000      6.2086         0.76311
SERVICE   1.0000000    1.0000000      7.2893         0.73289
BUS       1.0000000    1.0000000     31.343          0.38954
MECHANIC  1.0000000    1.0000000     21.871          0.47766
CONSTRUC  1.0000000    1.0000000      1.6574         0.92347
COOK      1.0000000    1.0000000      5.6666         0.77922
MANAGER   1.0000000    1.0000000      7.7398         0.72099
FSALES    1.0000000    1.0000000     20.415          0.49487


* * * * * * * * * * * * * * * * * * * * * * * * * * * * * * * * * * * * * * * * * * *

AT STEP   1, FOOD     WAS INCLUDED IN THE ANALYSIS.
AT STEP   2, SERVICE  WAS INCLUDED IN THE ANALYSIS.
AT STEP   3, BUS      WAS INCLUDED IN THE ANALYSIS.
AT STEP   4, MECHANIC WAS INCLUDED IN THE ANALYSIS.
AT STEP   5, CONSTRUC WAS INCLUDED IN THE ANALYSIS.
AT STEP   6, COOK     WAS INCLUDED IN THE ANALYSIS.
AT STEP   7, MANAGER  WAS INCLUDED IN THE ANALYSIS.
AT STEP   8, FSALES   WAS INCLUDED IN THE ANALYSIS.

                         DEGREES OF FREEDOM  SIGNIF.   BETWEEN GROUPS
WILKS' LAMBDA    0.20066       8     2        40.0
EQUIVALENT F     5.08371            16        66.0   0.0000


------------------ VARIABLES IN THE ANALYSIS AFTER STEP   8 ------------------


VARIABLE  TOLERANCE    F TO REMOVE    WILKS' LAMBDA

FOOD      0.5250845      4.1322         0.25091
SERVICE   0.5534314      3.1670         0.23917
BUS       0.2012584      2.3897         0.22972
MECHANIC  0.2016449      1.0382         0.21328
CONSTRUC  0.6980956      2.3494         0.22923
COOK      0.4511848      2.8056         0.23477
MANAGER   0.3727308      2.0416         0.22548
FSALES    0.3535373       .61534        0.20814


* * * * * * * * * * * * * * * * * * * * * * * * * * * * * * * * * * * * * * * * * * *

AT STEP   9, FSALES   WAS REMOVED FROM THE ANALYSIS.

                         DEGREES OF FREEDOM  SIGNIF.   BETWEEN GROUPS
WILKS' LAMBDA    0.20814       7     2        40.0
EQUIVALENT F     5.78931            14        68.0   0.0000


------------------ VARIABLES IN THE ANALYSIS AFTER STEP   9 ------------------


VARIABLE  TOLERANCE    F TO REMOVE    WILKS' LAMBDA

FOOD      0.5406011      4.8160         0.26710
SERVICE   0.6329976      3.4404         0.25026
BUS       0.2245632      3.7730         0.25433
MECHANIC  0.2017239      1.0750         0.22130
CONSTRUC  0.7419578      1.9998         0.23262
COOK      0.4512511      2.8877         0.24349
MANAGER   0.3757059      1.9673         0.23222


------------------ VARIABLES NOT IN THE ANALYSIS AFTER STEP   9 ------------------

                         MINIMUM
VARIABLE  TOLERANCE    TOLERANCE    F TO ENTER    WILKS' LAMBDA

FSALES    0.3535373    0.2012584      .61534         0.20066

F LEVEL OR TOLERANCE OR VIN INSUFFICIENT FOR FURTHER COMPUTATION.
```

Figure 27.8b Summary table for stepwise analysis

```
                           SUMMARY TABLE

                    ACTION       VARS   WILKS'
     STEP  ENTERED  REMOVED       IN    LAMBDA   SIG.    LABEL

       1   FOOD                    1    .76311  .0045   AVG FOOD PRICES
       2   SERVICE                 2    .57620  .0002   PRICE FOR SERVICES
       3   BUS                     3    .29950  .0000
       4   MECHANIC                4    .29473  .0000   NET MECHANIC' SALARY
       5   CONSTRUC                5    .27390  .0000   NET CONSTRUCTION WORKER'S SALARY
       6   COOK                    6    .23222  .0000   NET COOK'S SALARY
       7   MANAGER                 7    .20814  .0000   NET MANAGER'S SALARY
       8   FSALES                  8    .20066  .0000   NET FEMALE SALESWORKER'S SALARY
       9            FSALES         7    .20814  .0000   NET FEMALE SALESWORKER'S SALARY
```

27.9
MAXSTEPS Subcommand

By default, the maximum number of steps is the number of variables with inclusion levels greater than 1 plus twice the number of variables with an inclusion level of 1. This is the maximum number of steps possible without inclusion loops, in which a variable is repeatedly cycled in and out. Use the MAXSTEPS subcommand to decrease the maximum number of steps.

MAXSTEPS=n   *Controls the number of steps in a stepwise analysis.*

Statistical Controls. You can use several subcommands to override default controls on stepping, such as the tolerance level and *F*-to-enter or *F*-to-remove. These subcommands follow the METHOD subcommand in any order.

TOLERANCE=n *Tolerance level.* The default tolerance level is .001. You can set it to any decimal number between 0 and 1. All variables are tested against this level prior to inclusion for all methods. The tolerance of a variable in the analysis at any given step is the proportion of its within-groups variance not accounted for by other variables in the analysis. The tolerance level also applies to the minimum tolerance level of a variable reported in stepwise methods. The *minimum tolerance* of a variable is the smallest tolerance any variable in the analysis would have if the variable in question were included.

FIN=n *F-to-enter.* The default *F*-to-enter is 1.0. You may set it to any number including 0. If you specify DIRECT on the METHOD subcommand no check is made for *F*-to-enter.

FOUT=n *F-to-remove.* The default *F*-to-remove is 1.0. As additional variables are entered into the equation, the partial *F* value for variables already in the equation changes. If it falls below the *F*-to-remove *and* the variable has an inclusion level of 1, the variable is removed. Variables are not removed with the direct-entry method.

PIN=n *Probability of* F-*to-enter.* There is no default. The *F*-to-enter is used in lieu of the probability of *F*-to-enter in the absence of the PIN subcommand. Since the probability of *F* depends upon the degrees of freedom, this value can change at each step as variables are entered or removed. Use the PIN subcommand to keep the minimum *F*s at a fixed significance level. PIN overrides FIN if both are used.

POUT=n *Probability of* F-*to-remove.* By default, a variable with an inclusion level of 1 is removed from the equation for the stepwise methods if its *F*-to-remove falls below the FOUT specification. The POUT specification is directly analogous to the PIN specification. POUT overrides FOUT if both are used.

VIN=n *Rao's* V-*to-enter.* The default value is 0. If you use the RAO method, variables satisfying the criteria for entry, such as *F*-to-enter, may actually cause a decrease in Rao's *V* for the equation. The default VIN prevents this but does not prevent variables that do not provide any additional separation between groups from being added. The test for VIN applies only when you specify RAO on the METHOD subcommand.

27.10
FUNCTIONS Subcommand

By default, DISCRIMINANT computes the maximum number of functions that are mathematically possible. The maximum number of functions that can be derived for a given analysis is the number of groups minus one or the number of discriminating variables, whichever is less. Use the FUNCTIONS subcommand to set more restrictive criteria for the extraction of functions. The FUNCTIONS subcommand has three parameters:

nf *Maximum number of functions.* The default is the number of groups minus one or the number of discriminating variables, whichever is less.

cp   *Cumulative percentage of eigenvalues*. The default is 100%.

sig   *Significance level of function*. The default is 1.0.

Although you can restrict the number of functions with only one parameter at a time, all three must be specified in the following order: *nf*, *cp*, *sig*. For example, to specify a minimum cumulative percentage, *cp*, you must specify *nf*. Or, to specify a minimum significance level, *sig*, for a five-group analysis, you must also specify *nf* and *cp*, as in:

```
DISCRIMINANT  GROUPS=CLASS(1,5)
 /VARIABLES = SCORE1 TO SCORE20
 /FUNCTIONS=4,100,.80
```

Four functions and a cumulative percentage of eigenvalues of 100 do not restrict the number of functions extracted since they are the default parameters. The number of functions is restricted by the requirement that each function must have a significance level of .80 or less. If more than one nondefault restriction is specified on the FUNCTIONS subcommand, SPSS-X uses the first one encountered.

27.11
STATISTICS Subcommand

The default statistics produced by the analysis phase include

Summary Statistics. Eigenvalues, percent of variance, cumulative percent of variance, canonical correlations, Wilks' lambda, chi-square, degrees of freedom, and significance of chi-square are reported for the functions.

Step Statistics. Wilks' lambda, equivalent *F*, degrees of freedom, and significance of *F* are reported for each step. Tolerance, *F*-to-remove, and the stepping criterion value are reported for each variable in the equation. Tolerance, minimum tolerance, *F*-to-enter, and the stepping criterion value are reported for each variable not in the equation.

Final Statistics. Standardized canonical discriminant function coefficients, the structure matrix of discriminant functions and all variables named in the analysis (whether they entered the equation or not), and functions evaluated at group means, are reported following the last step.

The STATISTICS subcommand requests additional statistics for DISCRIMINANT. You can specify the STATISTICS subcommand by itself or with one or more keywords.

If you specify the STATISTICS subcommand with no keywords, DISCRIMINANT calculates MEAN, STDDEV, and UNIVF (each defined below). If you include a keyword or keywords on the STATISTICS subcommand, DISCRIMINANT calculates only the statistics you request. The following keywords can be specified on the STATISTICS subcommand:

MEAN   *Means*. Prints total and group means for all variables named on the ANALYSIS subcommand. This (along with STDDEV and UNIVF) is the default if you specify the STATISTICS subcommand by itself, with no keywords.

STDDEV   *Standard deviations*. Prints total and group standard deviations for all variables named on the ANALYSIS subcommand. This (along with MEAN and UNIVF) is the default if you specify the STATISTICS subcommand by itself, with no keywords.

UNIVF   *Univariate* F *ratios*. Prints *F* for each variable. This is a one-way analysis of variance test for equality of group means on a single discriminating variable. This (along with MEAN and STDDEV) is the default if you specify the STATISTICS subcommand by itself, with no keywords.

COV	*Pooled within-groups covariance matrix.*
CORR	*Pooled within-groups correlation matrix.*
FPAIR	*Matrix of pairwise* F *ratios.* Prints the *F* ratio for each pair of groups. This *F* is the significance test for the Mahalanobis' distance between groups. This statistic is available only with the stepwise methods.
BOXM	*Box's M test.* This is a test for equality of group covariance matrices.
GCOV	*Group covariance matrices.*
TCOV	*Total covariance matrix.*
RAW	*Unstandardized canonical discriminant functions.*
COEFF	*Classification function coefficients.* Although DISCRIMINANT does not directly use these coefficients to classify cases, you can use them to classify other samples (see Section 27.17).
TABLE	*Classification results table.* If you include a SELECT subcommand in your specifications, two tables are produced, one for selected cases and one for unselected cases.
ALL	*All optional statistics available for DISCRIMINANT.*

27.12
ROTATION Subcommand

The pattern and structure matrices printed during the analysis phase may be rotated to facilitate interpretation of results. To obtain a VARIMAX rotation, use the ROTATION subcommand with one of the following keywords:

COEFF	*Rotate pattern matrix.*
STRUCTURE	*Rotate structure matrix.*

Neither COEFF nor STRUCTURE affects the classification of cases since the rotation is orthogonal.

27.13
HISTORY Subcommand

The HISTORY subcommand controls output display. By default, HISTORY prints both the step-by-step output and the summary table. Its default keywords are STEP and END. Keywords NOSTEP and NOEND enable you to reduce the amount of output produced during stepwise analysis.

STEP	*Print step-by-step output.* This (along with END) is the default.
NOSTEP	*Suppress printing of step-by-step output.*
END	*Print the summary table.* This (along with STEP) is the default.
NOEND	*Suppress printing of the summary table.*

NOSTEP and NOEND only affect printing, not the computation of intermediate results.

27.14
Classification Phase

Once DISCRIMINANT has completed the analysis phase, you can use the results to classify your cases. DISCRIMINANT provides a variety of statistics for evaluating the ability of a particular model to classify cases, along with several subcommands and options to control the classification phase. You can use the SELECT subcommand during the analysis phase to compute the statistics and coefficients used to classify cases on the basis of a subset of cases (see Section 27.6). You can use the PRIORS subcommand to control prior probabilities for classification (see Section 27.15). Section 27.16 describes the various statistics and plots available for the classification phase. Section 27.17 describes the options applying to the classification phase the use of classification coefficients.

ANNOTATED EXAMPLE FOR DISCRIMINANT

This example analyzes 1979 prices and earnings in 45 cities around the world, compiled by the Union Bank of Switzerland. The variables are

- FOOD—the average net cost of 39 different food and beverage items in the city, expressed as a percentage above or below that of Zurich, where Zurich equals 100%.

- SERVICE—the average cost of 28 different goods and services in the city, expressed as a percentage above or below that of Zurich, where Zurich equals 100%.

- BUS, MECHANIC, CONSTRUC, COOK, MANAGER, FSALES—the average gross annual earnings of municipal bus drivers, automobile mechanics, construction workers, cooks, managers, and female sales workers, working from five to ten years in their respective occupations. Each of these variables is expressed as a percentage above or below those of Zurich, where Zurich equals 100%.

- WORLD—economic development status of the country in which the city is located, divided into three groups: economically advanced nations, such as the United States and most European nations; nations that are members of the Organization for Petroleum Exporting Countries (OPEC); and nations that are economically underdeveloped. The groups are labeled 1ST WORLD, PETRO WORLD, and 3RD WORLD, respectively.

There are two objectives to this analysis. First, we discriminate between cities in different categories by examining their wage and price structures. Secondly, we predict a city's economic class category from coefficients calculated using wages and prices as predictors. The SPSS-X commands are

```
GET FILE UNIONBK
DISCRIMINANT GROUPS=WORLD(1,3)
 /VARIABLES=FOOD SERVICE BUS MECHANIC CONSTRUC COOK MANAGER FSALES
 /PRIORS=SIZE/SAVE = CLASS=PRDCLAS SCORES=DISCSCR
 /STATISTICS=RAW TABLE
SAVE OUTFILE=NEWUNION
```

- The GET command defines the data to SPSS-X from the system file UNIONBK (see Chapter 6).

- The DISCRIMINANT command requests a three-group discriminant analysis. The variables FOOD, SERVICE, BUS, MECHANIC, CONSTRUC, COOK, MANAGER, and FSALES are used as discriminating variables during the analysis phase (see Section 27.5). During the classification phase, prior probabilities are equal to the size of the known groups (see Section 27.15 and Figure A). Three variables are saved on the active file: the predicted group for each of the classified cases (variable PRDCLAS) and the two discriminant scores (variables DISCSCR1 and DISCSCR2). The saved variables are shown in Figure B (see Section 27.19).

- The STATISTICS subcommand requests printing of the unstandardized discriminant functions and the classification results table (see Section 27.11 and Figure C).

- The SAVE command saves the SPSS-X system file NEWUNION, which contains the three variables PRDCLAS, DISCSCR1, and DISCSCR2 (see Chapter 6).

A Prior probabilities

```
PRIOR PROBABILITIES

    GROUP    PRIOR     LABEL

       1    0.58140    1ST WORLD
       2    0.13953    PETRO WORLD
       3    0.27907    3RD WORLD

    TOTAL   1.00000
```

B The saved variables

```
FOLLOWING VARIABLES HAVE BEEN CREATED:

    NAME          LABEL

   _____      _____


   PRDCLAS  ---  PREDICTED GROUP FOR ANALYSIS     1

   DISCSCR1 ---  FUNCTION    1 FOR ANALYSIS        1

   DISCSCR2 ---  FUNCTION    2 FOR ANALYSIS        1
```

C Discriminant coefficients and classification results

```
UNSTANDARDIZED CANONICAL DISCRIMINANT FUNCTION COEFFICIENTS

                 FUNC  1        FUNC  2

FOOD         -.7133619D-02    .6194062D-01
SERVICE       .8472984D-02   -.5365943D-01
BUS           .5255502D-01   -.2000084D-01
MECHANIC      .2805062D-01    .1326366D-01
CONSTRUC     -.4256104D-02   -.7536312D-02
COOK         -.1677760D-01    .2545888D-01
MANAGER      -.2570614D-01   -.2155895D-01
FSALES        .1637516D-01    .1486991D-01
(CONSTANT)  -1.852548        -.9620797


CLASSIFICATION RESULTS -

                       NO. OF    PREDICTED GROUP MEMBERSHIP
       ACTUAL GROUP    CASES        1         2         3
   _____ _____   _____   _____   _____


   GROUP       1         25         24         1         0
   1ST WORLD                      96.0%      4.0%      0.0%

   GROUP       2          6          0         5         1
   PETRO WORLD                     0.0%     83.3%     16.7%

   GROUP       3         12          1         0        11
   3RD WORLD                       8.3%      0.0%     91.7%


PERCENT OF "GROUPED" CASES CORRECTLY CLASSIFIED:  93.02%


CLASSIFICATION PROCESSING SUMMARY

       45 CASES WERE PROCESSED.
        0 CASES WERE EXCLUDED FOR MISSING OR OUT-OF-RANGE GROUP CODES.
        2 CASES HAD AT LEAST ONE MISSING DISCRIMINATING VARIABLE.
       43 CASES WERE USED FOR PRINTED OUTPUT.
       45 CASES WERE WRITTEN INTO THE ACTIVE FILE.
```

27.15
PRIORS Subcommand

By default, DISCRIMINANT assumes equal probabilities for group membership when classifying cases. If your model consists of four groups, the prior probability of a case falling into any one group is .25. You can provide different prior probabilities with the PRIORS subcommand. Prior probabilities are not used during the analysis stage. If you do provide unequal prior probabilities, DISCRIMINANT adjusts the classification coefficients to reflect this prior knowledge. Specify one of the following on the PRIORS subcommand:

EQUAL *Equal prior probabilities.* This is the default specification.

SIZE *Proportion of cases actually falling into each group.* If 50% of the cases included in the analysis fall into the first group, 25% in the second, and 25% in the third, the prior probabilities are .5, .25, and .25, respectively. Group size is determined after cases with missing values for the discriminating variables are deleted.

Value list *User-specified prior probabilities.* A list of probabilities summing to 1.0 is specified.

Specifying a list of prior probabilities is often used to produce classification coefficients for samples with known group membership. For example, if you have five groups, the value list might look like the following:

```
DISCRIMINANT  GROUPS=TYPE(1,5)/VARIABLES=A TO H
 /PRIORS = .25 .2 .3 .1 .15
```

If adjacent groups have the same prior probability, you can use a replication factor instead of listing each prior probability individually. For example,

```
DISCRIMINANT  GROUPS=TYPE(1,5)/VARIABLES=A TO H
 /PRIORS = 4*.15,.4
```

establishes prior probabilities of .15 for the first four groups and .4 for the last group in a five-group model. The value list must name or imply as many prior probabilities as groups. You can specify a prior probability of 0. However, no cases falling into a group assigned a prior probability of 0 are classified into that group. If the sum of the prior probabilities is not 1, SPSS-X rescales the probabilities to sum to 1 and issues a warning.

Classification Results Table. The classification results table tells you what proportion of cases are classified correctly and if there is evidence of systematic misclassification of particular cases. To obtain the classification results table, specify TABLE on the associated STATISTICS command, as in:

```
DISCRIMINANT  GROUPS=WORLD(1,3)
 /VARIABLES=FOOD SERVICE BUS MECHANIC CONSTRUC COOK MANAGER FSALES
 /METHOD=WILKS
 /PRIORS=SIZE
 /PLOT=MAP CASES COMBINED
 /STATISTICS=TABLE COEFF
```

As shown in Figure 27.15, the overall classification rate is nearly 91%. (All figures in Sections 27.15 through 27.16 were produced by the above commands.)

TABLE *Classification results table.* If you include a SELECT subcommand in your specifications, two tables are produced, one for selected cases and one for unselected cases. (See Section 27.16.)

The analysis is most successful in classifying cities from Group 1, and least successful in classifying cities from Group 2. These results suggest a greater diversity among cities in Group 2 in terms of the discriminating variables, and that two of these cases resemble Group 3 cases more closely than other Group 2 cases.

Figure 27.15   Classification results table

```
CLASSIFICATION RESULTS -

                            NO. OF     PREDICTED GROUP MEMBERSHIP
        ACTUAL GROUP        CASES          1          2          3
  ──────────────────       ───────    ───────    ───────    ───────

  GROUP       1               25         24          1          0
  1ST WORLD                            96.0%       4.0%       0.0%

  GROUP       2                6          0          4          2
  PETRO WORLD                           0.0%      66.7%      33.3%

  GROUP       3               12          1          0         11
  3RD WORLD                             8.3%       0.0%      91.7%

  PERCENT OF "GROUPED" CASES CORRECTLY CLASSIFIED:   90.70%


  CLASSIFICATION PROCESSING SUMMARY

        45 CASES WERE PROCESSED.
         0 CASES WERE EXCLUDED FOR MISSING OR OUT-OF-RANGE GROUP CODES.
         2 CASES HAD AT LEAST ONE MISSING DISCRIMINATING VARIABLE.
        43 CASES WERE USED FOR PRINTED OUTPUT.
```

27.16
PLOT Subcommand

Classification plots are useful for examining the relationship of groups to each other and graphically depicting misclassification. These plots have two forms, depending on the number of functions produced by your analysis. If your analysis produces more than one discriminant function, two types of scatterplots and a territorial map are available. The separate-groups scatterplot produces a scatterplot for each group. The all-groups scatterplot plots all groups on one scatterplot using different symbols to represent each group. The axes of the scatterplots are the discriminant scores calculated from the first two discriminant functions extracted during analysis. The territorial map can be used with either of these scatterplots. It outlines the general territory for each group and contains registration marks so that if you make a transparency of the scatterplot it can be placed upon the map to identify misclassified cases.

If your analysis produces only one function (you have only two groups or you restrict the number of functions to one), scatterplots are not possible since only one dimension exists in which to plot a case. Instead, DISCRIMINANT produces all-groups and separate-groups histograms of the discriminant scores.

The PLOT subcommand requests classification plots. You can specify the PLOT subcommand by itself or with one or more keywords.

If you specify the PLOT subcommand with no keywords, DISCRIMINANT prints COMBINED and CASES plots (each defined below). If you include a keyword or keywords on the PLOT subcommand, DISCRIMINANT prints only the plots you request. The following keywords can be specified on the PLOT subcommand:

COMBINED   *All-groups plot.* The first two functions define the axes. This statistic produces histograms for one-function analyses. This (along with CASES) is the default if you specify the PLOT subcommand by itself, with no keywords.

CASES   *Discriminant scores and classification information.* This (along with COMBINED) is the default if you specify the PLOT subcommand by itself, with no keywords.

MAP   *Territorial map.* This statistic is ignored for analyses producing only one function.

SEPARATE   *Separate-groups plots*. These are the same types of plots produced by keyword COMBINED. However, each plot contains cases for one group only. If your model has three groups, three scatterplots are produced, unless you restrict the analysis to compute only one function. For one-function analyses, histograms are produced.

ALL   *All plots available for DISCRIMINANT*.

Figure 27.16a shows the territorial map and Figure 27.16b shows the all-groups scatterplot. If you compare the territorial map with the all-groups plot, you can identify the misclassified cases. These are the cases not falling within the outline boundaries on the territorial map.

Figure 27.16a Territorial map

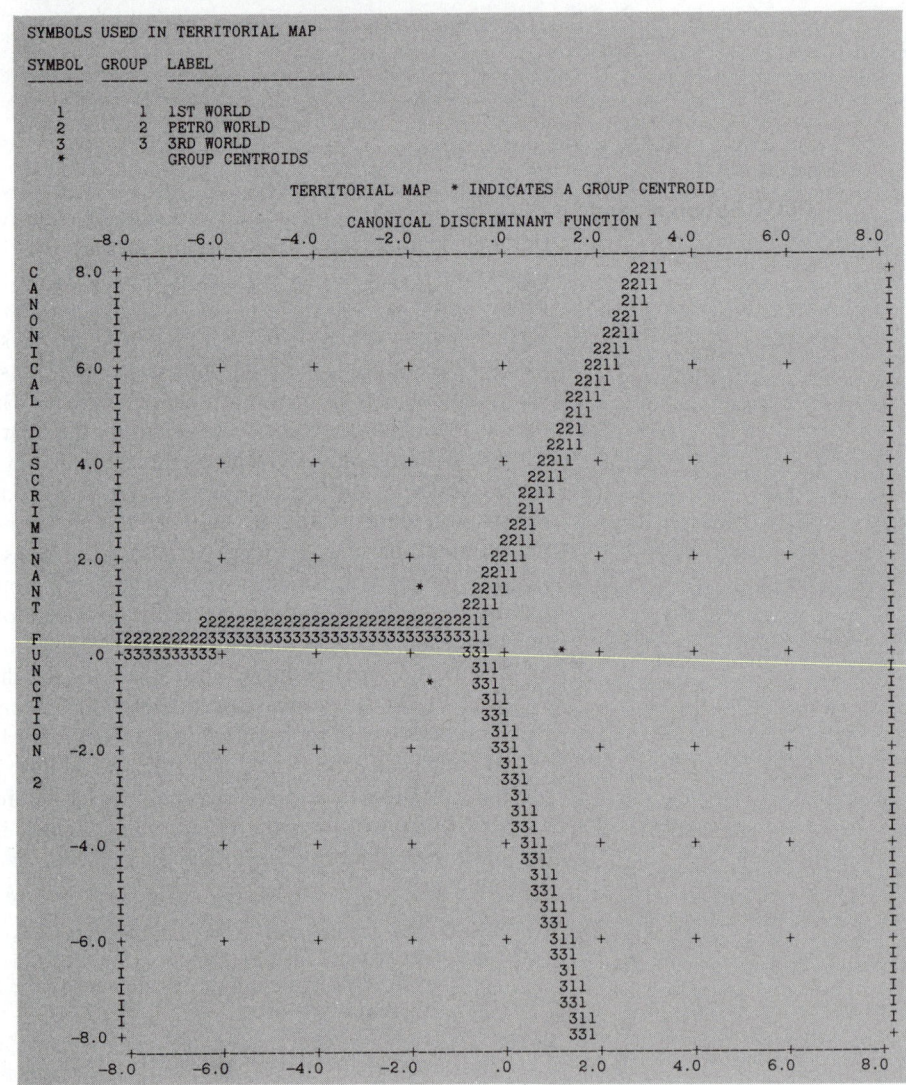

Figure 27.16b   All-groups scatterplot

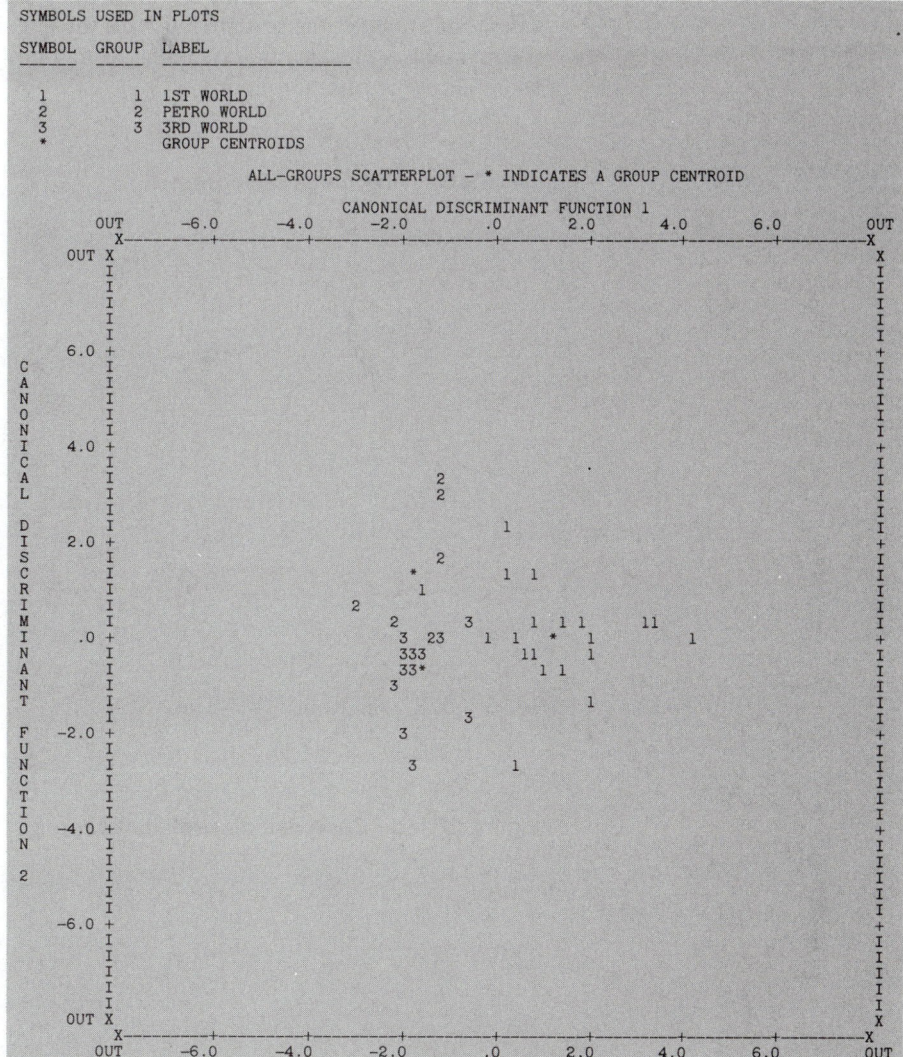

Figure 27.16c is the all-groups histogram produced when you use the FUNCTIONS subcommand to restrict the number of functions to one. This histogram is produced by specifying FUNCTIONS=1 in addition to the specifications in Section 27.16. The horizontal axis is the one discriminant function extracted during the analysis phase. The groups into which cases are classified given their discriminant scores are indicated by the labeling of the horizontal axis. Since no cases are classified into Group 2, the value 2 does not appear on the horizontal axis. No cases are classified into Group 2 because its centroid is extremely close to Group 3 and the cutoff points are very narrow (because of the relatively small prior probability for Group 2).

The histogram is a *stacked* histogram. In a given interval, Group 1 cases are printed first, then the Group 2 cases for that interval, and finally the Group 3 cases. For example, the seventh bar from the left shows four cases in this interval (two symbols represent one case in this histogram). Three cases are from Group 2 and one case is from Group 3.

Figure 27.16c All-groups histogram

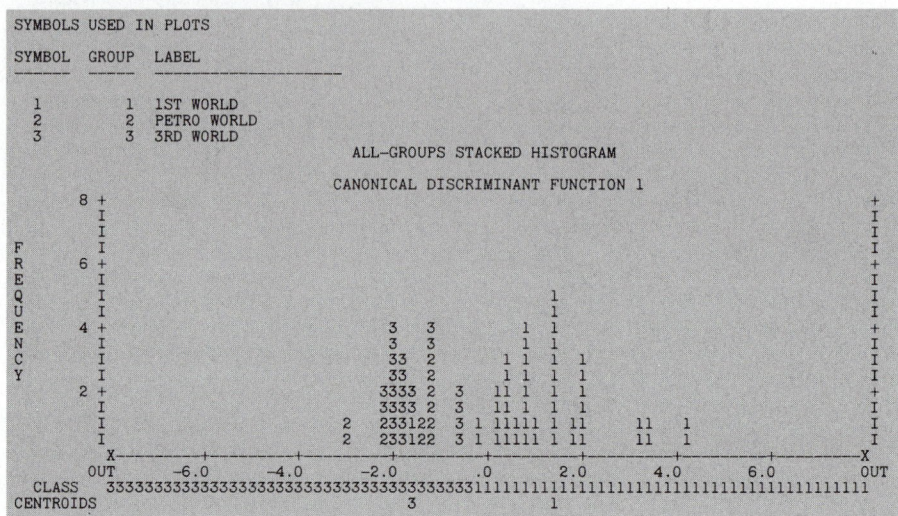

Figure 27.16d Casewise discriminant scores

CASE SEQNUM	MIS VAL	SEL	ACTUAL GROUP	HIGHEST PROBABILITY GROUP P(D/G) P(G/D)	2ND HIGHEST GROUP P(G/D)	DISCRIMINANT SCORES...
1			2	2 0.2237 0.9904	1 0.0060	-1.2634 3.1642
2			1	1 0.7669 0.9952	3 0.0046	1.4846 -0.6631
3			3	3 0.4221 0.7918	1 0.2039	-0.6226 -1.5905
4			2	2 0.3824 0.6049	3 0.3942	-2.9357 0.8136
5			3	3 0.6836 0.7885	2 0.1955	-1.9595 0.0447
6			3	3 0.9738 0.9438	2 0.0424	-1.8694 -0.7051
7			1	1 0.7674 0.9941	3 0.0057	1.4138 -0.6872
8			3	3 0.8412 0.8847	2 0.1026	-1.9899 -0.2915
9			2	2 0.8862 0.8226	3 0.1175	-1.2401 1.5438
10			1	1 0.1033 1.0000	3 0.0000	3.3124 0.3338
11			1	1 0.8410 0.9986	3 0.0011	1.7374 0.2637
12			3	3 0.1722 0.9959	1 0.0036	-1.8354 -2.6363
13			1	1 0.3779 0.9980	3 0.0020	1.9237 -1.1861
14			1	1 0.0129 1.0000	3 0.0000	4.1539 0.1168
15			1	1 0.7484 0.9412	3 0.0491	0.4450 0.0276
16		**	1	2 0.8796 0.6574	3 0.3036	-1.5780 1.0140
17			3	3 0.6765 0.7249	2 0.1461	-1.1817 -0.0190
18		**	2	3 0.7685 0.7910	2 0.1411	-1.4202 -0.0811
20			1	1 0.3590 0.6891	3 0.2738	-0.2152 -0.1588
22			1	1 0.9019 0.9786	3 0.0196	0.8682 -0.2934
23			1	1 0.7512 0.9992	3 0.0007	1.9619 -0.0198
24			1	1 0.7530 0.9989	3 0.0010	1.9151 -0.2442
25		**	3	1 0.2157 0.5147	3 0.3541	-0.5256 0.2731
26			3	3 0.8819 0.9257	2 0.0656	-2.0777 -0.5117
27		**	2	3 0.4244 0.6462	2 0.3471	-2.2848 0.3740
28			1	1 0.7321 0.9377	3 0.0513	0.4183 0.0657
29			1	1 0.7437 0.9846	3 0.0149	1.0907 -0.7506
30			1	1 0.2604 0.8708	2 0.1042	0.2875 1.3693
31			1	1 0.9329 0.9968	3 0.0024	1.4481 0.2938
32			3	3 0.9169 0.8957	2 0.0835	-1.7965 -0.3808
33			1	1 0.9063 0.9765	3 0.0211	0.8175 -0.2038
34			3	3 0.8551 0.9723	2 0.0228	-2.1569 -1.0031
35			1	1 0.4503 0.9745	2 0.0188	0.8308 1.2164
36			3	3 0.4472 0.9944	1 0.0029	-2.0865 -1.9606
37			3	3 0.9525 0.9025	2 0.0697	-1.6762 -0.4594
38			1	1 0.8268 0.9806	3 0.0127	0.8099 0.4829
39			1	1 0.7213 0.9417	3 0.0546	0.5361 -0.4418
40			2	2 0.2182 0.9899	1 0.0066	-1.2320 3.1699
41			1	1 0.0256 0.6523	3 0.3475	0.3369 -2.5546
42			1	1 0.0279 0.5611	2 0.4310	0.2267 2.4998
43			1	1 0.9740 0.9958	3 0.0033	1.3690 0.1718
44			1	1 0.7380 0.9916	3 0.0082	1.3082 -0.7626
45			1	1 0.1159 1.0000	3 0.0000	3.2514 0.3658

Printed Discriminant Scores. In addition to the tables, plots, and histograms described in the previous sections, you can also obtain casewise information, including observed group, classified group, and group membership probabilities. Casewise classification results are useful for examining particular cases. Casewise information is available through keyword CASES on the PLOT subcommand.

CASES *Discriminant scores and classification information.* Prints the following information for each case classified: case sequence number; number of missing values in the case; value on SELECT variable; actual group; highest group classification (G); the probability of a case in group G being that far from the centroid (P(D/G)); the probability of the case being in group G and having a score of D (P(G/D)); second-highest group classification and its P(G/D); and the discriminant scores.

Figure 27.16d shows the printed casewise classification information. Misclassified cases are identified with three asterisks. For example, the 16th case, which is in Group 1, is classified into Group 2.

27.17
CLASSIFY Subcommand

The CLASSIFY subcommand determines how cases are handled during the classification phase of DISCRIMINANT. By default, all non-missing cases are classified, and the pooled within-groups covariance matrix is used to classify cases. The default keywords for CLASSIFY are NONMISSING and POOLED. The following options are available:

NONMISSING *Classify all nonmissing cases.* Two sets of classification results are produced, one for the selected cases (those specified on the SELECT subcommand) and one for the nonselected cases. This is the default.

UNSELECTED *Classify only unselected cases.* The classification phase is suppressed for cases selected via the SELECT subcommand.

UNCLASSIFIED *Classify only unclassified cases.* Cases whose values on the grouping variable fall outside the range specified on the GROUPS subcommand are considered initially unclassified. During classification, these ungrouped cases are classified as a separate entry in the classification results table. UNCLASSIFIED suppresses classification of cases that fall into the range specified on the GROUPS subcommand and classifies only cases falling outside the range.

POOLED *Use the pooled within-groups covariance matrix to classify cases.* This is the default.

SEPARATE *Use separate-group covariance matrices of the discriminant functions for classification.* The separate-group covariance matrices are used for classification. However, since classification is based on the discriminant functions and not the original variables, this option is not equivalent to quadratic discrimination (Tatsuoka, 1971).

MEANSUBSTITUTION *Substitute means for missing values during classification.* Cases with missing values are not used during analysis. During classification, means are substituted for missing values and cases containing missing values are classified.

Using Classification Coefficients. DISCRIMINANT classifies your cases when you specify keyword TABLE on the STATISTICS subcommand (see Section 27.11), the PLOT subcommand (see Section 27.16), or the SAVE subcommand (see Section 27.19). However, DISCRIMINANT is often used on a sample to obtain the materials necessary for classifying a large target sample. Sections 27.21 and 27.22 discuss using matrix materials to classify one sample based on the analysis of another sample.

This section describes how to classify a target sample using the classification coefficients produced by keyword COEFF on the STATISTICS subcommand.

COEFF produces one set of classification coefficients for each group. The equation for one group is

$$C_i = c_{i1}V_1 + c_{i2}V_2 + \ldots + c_{ij}V_j + \ldots + c_{ip}V_p + c_{i0}$$

where C_i is the classification score for group i, the c_{ij}'s are the classification coefficients, c_{i0} is the constant, and the V's are the discriminating variables. A case is classified into the group that produces the highest classification score. If you have three groups, you must compute three linear combinations for each case in the target sample.

For example, assume you have a sample that you want to classify from the classification coefficients produced using the commands in Section 27.15. Figure 27.17 shows the classification coefficients.

Figure 27.17 Classification coefficients

```
CLASSIFICATION FUNCTION COEFFICIENTS
(FISHER'S LINEAR DISCRIMINANT FUNCTIONS)

WORLD  =          1              2              3
               FIRST          PETRO          THIRD
               WORLD          WORLD          WORLD

FOOD          .1833804        .2957176       .1474484
SERVICE       .1959324        .8005063D-01   .1919391
BUS          -.7968080D-01   -.2760144      -.2476949
MECHANIC      .1843633        .1234733       .9310405D-01
CONSTRUC     -.1206325D-01   -.1239856D-01   .3478106D-02
COOK         -.1488994D-01    .7321305D-01   .1464037D-01
MANAGER      -.2942906D-01    .1045250D-01   .5799628D-01
(CONSTANT)  -17.53128       -16.53582      -12.08814
```

To classify the cases in the target sample, use the following transformations:

```
COMPUTE  GRP1 = .1833804*FOOD + .1959324*SERVICE -.07968080*BUS +
               .1843633*MECHANIC - .01206325*CONSTUC - .01488994*COOK -
               .02942906*MANAGER - 17.53128
COMPUTE  GRP2 = .2957176*FOOD + .08005063*SERVICE - .2760144*BUS +
               .1234733*MECHANIC - .01239856*CONSTRUC + .07321305*COOK +
               .1045250*MANAGER - 16.53582
COMPUTE  GRP3 = .1474484*FOOD + .1919391*SERVICE -.2476949*BUS +
               .09310405*MECHANIC + .003478106*CONSTRUC + .01464037*COOK +
               .05799628*MANAGER - 12.08814
IF  (GRP1 > MAX(GRP2,GRP3)) CLASS = 1
IF  (GRP2 > MAX(GRP1,GRP3)) CLASS = 2
IF  (GRP3 > MAX(GRP1,GRP2)) CLASS = 3
```

27.18
MISSING Subcommand

By default, cases missing on any of the variables named on the VARIABLES subcommand and cases out of range or missing on the GROUPS subcommand are not used during the analysis phase. Cases missing or out of range on the GROUPS variable are used during the classification phase. Keyword INCLUDE on the MISSING subcommand enables you to include user-missing values in the analysis.

EXCLUDE *Exclude all missing values.* Both user-missing and system-missing values are excluded from the analysis. This is the default.

INCLUDE *Include user-missing values.* User-missing values are treated as valid values. Only the system-missing value is treated as missing.

27.19
SAVE Subcommand

Much of the casewise information produced by PLOT=CASE can be added to the active file. The SAVE subcommand specifies the type of information to be saved and the variable names assigned to each piece of information. Three different types of variables can be saved using the following keywords:

CLASS   *Save a variable containing the predicted group value.*

PROBS   *Save the probabilities of group membership for each case.* For example, if you have three groups, the first probability is the probability of the case being in Group 1 given its discriminant scores, the second probability is its probability of being in Group 2, and the third probability is its probability of being in Group 3. Since DISCRIMINANT produces more than one probability, a *rootname* is used to create a set of variables of the form alpha1 to alphan. The rootname cannot exceed seven characters.

SCORES   *Save the discriminant scores.* The number of scores equals the number of functions derived. As with the PROBS parameter, the rootname is used to create a set of variables.

Consider the following example:

```
DISCRIMINANT  GROUPS=WORLD(1,3)
 /VARIABLES=FOOD TO FSALES
 /SAVE = CLASS=PRDCLAS  SCORES=SCORE  PROBS=PRB
```

Since the number of groups is 3, DISCRIMINANT writes out 6 variables.

Table 27.19   Saved casewise results

Name	Description
PRDCLAS	Predicted Group
SCORE1	Discriminant score for Function 1
SCORE2	Discriminant score for Function 2
PRB1	Probability of being in Group 1
PRB2	Probability of being in Group 2
PRB3	Probability of being in Group 3

You do not have to request all three types of variables on the SAVE subcommand. Only those specified are saved. You can specify the keywords in any order, but the order in which the variables are added to the file is fixed. The group variable (CLASS) is always written first, followed by discriminant scores (SCORES), and probabilities (PROBS). Variable labels are provided automatically for the newly saved variables. Any value labels defined for the group variable are also saved for the classified-group variable.

The SAVE subcommand applies only to the previous ANALYSIS subcommand. If there are multiple analyses and you want to save casewise materials from each, you must use multiple SAVE subcommands, as in:

```
DISCRIMINANT  GROUPS = WORLD(1,3)
 /VARIABLES = FOOD TO FSALES
 /ANALYSIS = FOOD SERVICE
 /SAVE = CLASS=PRDCLAS SCORES=COSTSCR
 /ANALYSIS = BUS TO FSALES
 /SAVE = CLASS=SALCLAS SCORES=SALSCR
```

27.20
MATRIX Subcommand

DISCRIMINANT can write matrix materials that can be used in subsequent DISCRIMINANT procedures. To read and write matrices in DISCRIMINANT, you use the MATRIX subcommand.

The MATRIX subcommand has two keywords, IN and OUT, which you use to specify the matrix file in parentheses. When you use both IN and OUT on the same DISCRIMINANT procedure you can specify each on a separate MATRIX subcommand, or both on the same subcommand. For example,

```
DISCRIMINANT GROUPS=varname (min,max) /VARIABLES=varlist
 /MATRIX=IN(FILEONE)
 /MATRIX=OUT(FILETWO)
```

is the same as

```
DISCRIMINANT GROUPS=varname (min,max) /VARIABLES=varlist
 /MATRIX=IN(FILEONE) OUT(FILETWO)
```

27.21
OUT Keyword

The OUT keyword on MATRIX specifies the file to which the matrix is written. There are two options:

(**file**)   *Write the correlation matrix to a system file.* DISCRIMINANT creates a system file containing the matrix materials. The file is specified in parentheses. The system file is stored on disk and can be retrieved at any time.

(*)   *Replace the active file with the correlation matrix.* The matrix materials replace the active file. The correlation matrix is *not* stored on disk. It is resident in the active file.

In addition to the Pearson correlation coefficients, the matrix materials include weighted and unweighted numbers of cases, means, and standard deviations. Documents from the original file will not be included in the matrix file and will not be present if the matrix file becomes the active file. (For a discussion on documents, see Chapter 6.)

In the following example, DISCRIMINANT reads raw data from file UNIONBK and writes one set of matrix materials to the file DISCMTX:

```
GET FILE=UNIONBK/KEEP WORLD FOOD SERVICE BUS MECHANIC CONSTRUC COOK
  MANAGER FSALES APPL RENT
DISCRIMINANT  GROUPS=WORLD(1,3)
 /VARIABLES=FOOD SERVICE BUS  MECHANIC CONSTRUC COOK MANAGER FSALES
 /METHOD=WILKS
 /PRIORS=SIZE
 /MATRIX=OUT(DISCMTX)
```

The active file is still the file UNIONBK. Subsequent commands are executed on file UNIONBK.

To write the same matrix to the active file so that it is available to subsequent commands, specify the following:

```
GET FILE=UNIONBK/KEEP WORLD FOOD SERVICE BUS MECHANIC CONSTRUC COOK
  MANAGER FSALES APPL RENT
DISCRIMINANT  GROUPS=WORLD(1,3)
 /VARIABLES=FOOD SERVICE BUS  MECHANIC CONSTRUC COOK MANAGER FSALES
 /METHOD=WILKS
 /PRIORS=SIZE
 /MATRIX=OUT(*)
LIST
```

The active file is replaced with the matrix materials. The LIST command is executed on the matrix file, not on the file UNIONBK.

Format of the Matrix System File. Figure 27.21 shows the matrix system file produced by the above commands. The file has two special variables created by SPSS-X: ROWTYPE_ and VARNAME_. Variable ROWTYPE_ is a short string variable having values N, COUNT, MEAN, STDDEV, and CORR (for Pearson correlation coefficient). Variable VARNAME_ is a short string variable whose values are the names of the variables used to form the correlation matrix. When ROWTYPE_ is CORR, VARNAME_ gives the variable associated with that row of the correlation matrix. Between ROWTYPE_ and VARNAME_ in Figure 27.21 is the group variable WORLD, specified on the GROUPS subcommand of DISCRIMINANT. The remaining variables are the variables used to form the correlation matrix. (See Chapter 13 for more information on matrix system files.)

Variable Order. When split-file processing is in effect, the first variables in the matrix system file will be the split variables, followed by ROWTYPE_, the group variable, VARNAME_, then the variables used to form the correlation matrix. A full set of matrix materials is written for each subgroup defined by the split variable(s). A split variable cannot have the same variable name as any other variable written to the matrix system file. If a split file is in effect when a matrix is written, the same split file must be in effect when that matrix is read into another procedure.

Figure 27.21 A matrix system file

```
FILE:      MATRIX FILE

ROWTYPE_      WORLD VARNAME_     FOOD      SERVICE       BUS   MECHANIC   CONSTRUC       COOK     MANAGER      FSALES

N             1                25.0000000 25.0000000 25.0000000 25.0000000 25.0000000 25.0000000 25.0000000 25.0000000
COUNT         1                25.0000000 25.0000000 25.0000000 25.0000000 25.0000000 25.0000000 25.0000000 25.0000000
MEAN          1                76.6400000 81.5200000 60.8400000 69.2400000 79.4000000 75.2400000 64.1600000 63.9600000
N             2                 6.0000000  6.0000000  6.0000000  6.0000000  6.0000000  6.0000000  6.0000000  6.0000000
COUNT         2                 6.0000000  6.0000000  6.0000000  6.0000000  6.0000000  6.0000000  6.0000000  6.0000000
MEAN          2                74.3333333 57.5000000 21.3333333 29.0000000 20.0000000 63.8333333 41.1666667 29.5000000
N             3                12.0000000 12.0000000 12.0000000 12.0000000 12.0000000 12.0000000 12.0000000 12.0000000
COUNT         3                12.0000000 12.0000000 12.0000000 12.0000000 12.0000000 12.0000000 12.0000000 12.0000000
MEAN          3                56.2500000 64.8333333 16.5000000 22.1666667 55.7500000 42.5000000 36.0833333 23.1666667
STDDEV        .                16.7087876 16.6578860 17.5012095 22.0080818 74.4036709 27.6976503 21.8455430 19.6838301
CORR          . FOOD           1.0000000   .5526813   .4503216   .2130418   .1849338   .2194276   .4060721   .5518620
CORR          . SERVICE         .5526813  1.0000000   .3767222   .2180266   .1198415   .3260503   .2811611   .5639339
CORR          . BUS             .4503216   .3767222  1.0000000   .8189906   .3657804   .6238001   .7403945   .7090058
CORR          . MECHANIC        .2130418   .2180266   .8189906  1.0000000   .4341131   .7172063   .6971960   .5581043
CORR          . CONSTRUC        .1849338   .1198415   .3657804   .4341131  1.0000000   .3285861   .1693849   .3957003
CORR          . COOK            .2194276   .3260503   .6238001   .7172063   .3285861  1.0000000   .5488498   .4855934
CORR          . MANAGER         .4060721   .2811611   .7403945   .6971960   .1693849   .5488498  1.0000000   .5558375
CORR          . FSALES          .5518620   .5639339   .7090058   .5581043   .3957003   .4855934   .5558375  1.0000000


NUMBER OF CASES READ =       18    NUMBER OF CASES LISTED =       18
```

Additional Statistics. DISCRIMINANT always writes the following matrix materials:

- A vector of N's (weighted number of cases) for each cell in the data.
- A vector of COUNT's (unweighted number of cases) for each cell in the data.
- A vector of MEAN's for each cell in the data.
- STDDEV (standard deviation) records and CORR (Pearson correlation coefficient) records. The following paragraph discusses STDDEV and CORR records.

STDDEV and CORR Records. Records written to the matrix file with ROWTYPE_ values STDDEV and CORR are influenced by the specifications made on the STATISTICS and CLASSIFY subcommands. If any of the following specifications are in effect:

STATISTICS=BOXM
STATISTICS=GCOV
CLASSIFY=SEPARATE

then STDDEV and CORR records represent within cell data and receive values for the group variable. If none of the above specifications is in effect, STDDEV and CORR records represent pooled values. When STDDEV and CORR represent pooled values, the STDDEV vector contains the square root of the mean square error for each variable, and STDDEV and CORR records receive the system missing value for the group variable, as shown in Figure 27.21.

Missing Values. Missing value treatment affects the values written to a matrix system file. When reading a matrix system file, be sure to specify a missing value treatment on DISCRIMINANT that is compatible with the treatment used to generate the matrix materials. For example, if user-missing values were included in the analysis that generated the matrix, be sure to specify MISSING= INCLUDE on the DISCRIMINANT procedure that reads the matrix.

**27.22
IN Keyword**

DISCRIMINANT can read correlation matrices written by a previous DISCRIMINANT command or by other procedures. DISCRIMINANT reads only correlation type matrices. If you want to use a covariance type matrix for input in DISCRIMINANT, you must first use the MCONVERT command (see Chapter 13) to change the covariance matrix to a correlation matrix.

The IN keyword on MATRIX specifies the file from which the matrix is read. There are two options:

(file) *Read the correlation matrix from a matrix system file.*

(*) *Read the correlation matrix from the active file.* The active file must be an appropriate matrix system file.

MATRIX=IN cannot be used in place of GET or DATA LIST to begin a new SPSS-X command file. MATRIX is a subcommand on DISCRIMINANT and DISCRIMINANT cannot run before an active file is defined. To begin a new command file and immediately read a matrix, first GET the matrix file, then specify IN(*) on MATRIX.

In the following example, one set of matrix materials is read from the file DISCMTX, which was written by DISCRIMINANT in a previous job:

```
GET FILE=DISCMTX
DISCRIMINANT  GROUPS=WORLD(1,3)
 /VARIABLES=FOOD SERVICE BUS  MECHANIC CONSTRUC COOK MANAGER FSALES
 /METHOD=RAO
 /MATRIX=IN(*)
```

Matrix materials read by DISCRIMINANT must contain records with ROWTYPE_ values MEAN, N or COUNT (or both), STDDEV, and CORR. If records with ROWTYPE_ value COUNT (unweighted number of cases) are not in the data, DISCRIMINANT uses information from records with ROWTYPE_ value N (weighted number of cases). Conversely, if the data do not have N values, DISCRIMINANT uses the COUNT values. These records can appear in any order in the matrix input file, with the following exceptions:

• The order of split file groups cannot be violated.

• All CORR vectors must appear consecutively within each split file group.

Note: If any of the following specifications are in effect when DISCRIMINANT writes a matrix system file

```
STATISTICS=BOXM
STATISTICS=GCOV
CLASSIFY=SEPARATE
```

then STDDEV and CORR records in the matrix materials represent within cell data, and separate covariance matrices are written to the file. This means that when the matrix file is used as input for a subsequent DISCRIMINANT procedure, at least one of the above three specifications must be used on the DISCRIMINANT command that reads the matrix. It doesn't matter which of the three you specify on the DISCRIMINANT command that reads the matrix, and the specification doesn't have to be one that was used on the DISCRIMINANT command that wrote the matrix. BOXM and GCOV on the STATISTICS subcommand and SEPARATE on the CLASSIFY subcommand signal DISCRIMINANT that the matrix materials contain separate covariance matrices.

In the following example, because STATISTICS=BOXM is specified on the DISCRIMINANT command that writes the matrix, at least one of

```
STATISTICS=BOXM
STATISTICS=GCOV
CLASSIFY=SEPARATE
```

must be specified on the DISCRIMINANT that reads the matrix:

```
GET FILE=RAWDATA
DISCRIMINANT GROUPS=variable(min,max) /VAR=varlist
 /CLASSIFY=SEPARATE
 /MATRIX=OUT(*)
DISCRIMINANT GROUPS=variable(min,max) /VAR=varlist
 /STATISTICS=BOXM
 /MATRIX=IN(*)
```

**27.23
LIMITATIONS**   The following limitations apply to procedure DISCRIMINANT:

- Only 1 GROUPS, one SELECT, and one VARIABLES subcommand may be used per DISCRIMINANT command.
- Pairwise deletion of missing data is not available.

Syntax

FACTOR

```
FACTOR VARIABLES=varlist† [/MISSING=[{LISTWISE**}] [INCLUDE]]
                                      {PAIRWISE }
                                      {MEANSUB  }
                                      {DEFAULT  }

   [/WIDTH={132     }]
           {n       }
           {DEFAULT**}
   [/MATRIX=[IN({COR=file})] [OUT({COR=file})]]
               {COR=*   }       {COR=*   }
               {FAC=file}       {FAC=file}
               {FAC=*   }       {FAC=*   }
   [/ANALYSIS=varlist...]
   [/PRINT=[DEFAULT**] [INITIAL**] [EXTRACTION**] [ROTATION**]
           [UNIVARIATE**] [CORRELATION] [DET] [INV] [REPR] [AIC] [KMO]
           [FSCORE] [SIG] [ALL]]
   [/PLOT=[EIGEN] [ROTATION (n1,n2)]]
   [/DIAGONAL={value list}]
             {DEFAULT**  }
   [/FORMAT=[SORT] [BLANK(n)] [DEFAULT**]]
   [/CRITERIA=[FACTORS(n)] [MINEIGEN({1.0**})] [ITERATE({25**})]
                                    {eig  }            {ni  }

              [RCONVERGE({0.0001**})]] [DELTA({0**})] [{KAISER**}]
                        {rl      }           {d  }    {NOKAISER}

              [ECONVERGE({0.001**})]] [DEFAULT**]
                        {el     }
   [/EXTRACTION={PC**   }] [/ROTATION={VARIMAX**}]
                {PAF    }             {EQUAMAX  }
                {ALPHA  }             {QUARTIMAX}
                {IMAGE  }             {OBLIMIN  }
                {ULS    }             {NOROTATE }
                {GLS    }             {DEFAULT  }
                {ML     }
                {PA1    }
                {PA2    }
                {DEFAULT}
   [/SAVE=[{REG    } ({ALL} rootname)]]
          {BART   } {n  }
          {AR     }
          {DEFAULT}
   [/ANALYSIS...]
   [/CRITERIA...]      [/EXTRACTION...]
   [/ROTATION...]      [/SAVE...]
```

** Default if the subcommand is omitted.
† Omit VARIABLES with matrix input.

Contents

28.1   OVERVIEW
28.2   Subcommand Order

28.3   OPERATION

28.4   Global Subcommands
28.5   VARIABLES Subcommand
28.6   MISSING Subcommand
28.7   WIDTH Subcommand

28.8   Analysis-Block Subcommands
28.9   ANALYSIS Subcommand
28.10   PRINT Subcommand
28.11   PLOT Subcommand
28.12   DIAGONAL Subcommand
28.13   FORMAT Subcommand

28.14   Extraction-Block Subcommands
28.15   CRITERIA Subcommand
28.16   EXTRACTION Subcommand

28.17   Rotation-Block Subcommands
28.18   ROTATION Subcommand
28.19   SAVE Subcommand

28.20   MATRIX Subcommand
28.21   OUT Keyword
28.22   IN Keyword

28.23   LIMITATIONS

28

Chapter 28   FACTOR

Procedure FACTOR produces principal components analysis results and factor analysis results. There are no limitations to the number of analyses, the number of variables, the number of extractions, or the number of rotations. You can choose from among six extraction techniques. FACTOR accepts matrix input in the form of correlation matrices or factor loading matrices and also writes these materials to a system file. You can control the number of factors extracted, the number of iterations for extraction and rotation, and other rotation parameters. You can calculate factor scores and save them on the active file.

28.1
OVERVIEW

Factor analysis is logically a three-step process:

1 *Decide on the variables you wish to analyze.* Factor analysis and principal components analysis make no distinction between dependent and independent variables but treat all variables as a dependent set. The basis of the analysis is a correlation matrix built from the variables you name.

2 *Decide on an extraction technique.* In particular, you must decide whether you wish to perform principal components analysis or factor analysis. If you decide on the latter, then you must choose from among the extraction techniques available.

3 *Decide on a rotation technique to aid in interpretation.* FACTOR provides several orthogonal and oblimin rotations. FACTOR calculates factor scores (also called factor scales) using one of three methods. If you want to add these scores to your active file, you can do so with the SAVE subcommand (provided you do not use the MATRIX subcommand to replace the active file with a matrix system file, as discussed in Section 28.21).

FACTOR has three *blocks* of subcommands corresponding to the three steps of factor analysis. Within one invocation of FACTOR, you can perform several different analyses. You can specify multiple ANALYSIS subcommands, multiple EXTRACTION subcommands for each ANALYSIS subcommand, multiple ROTATION subcommands for each EXTRACTION subcommand, and multiple methods of calculating factor scores for each ROTATION subcommand.

28.2
Subcommand Order

FACTOR's standard subcommand order is illustrated in Figure 28.2.

• Subcommands listed in the ANALYSIS block in Figure 28.2 apply to all EXTRACTION and ROTATION blocks within that ANALYSIS block. Subcommands listed in the EXTRACTION block apply to all ROTATION blocks within that EXTRACTION block.

• Each ANALYSIS block can contain multiple EXTRACTION blocks, and each EXTRACTION block can contain multiple ROTATION blocks.

• The CRITERIA and FORMAT subcommands remain in effect until explicitly overridden. Other subcommands affect only the block in which they are contained.

Figure 28.2   Subcommand order for FACTOR

```
FACTOR VARIABLES=...
     / MISSING=...
     / WIDTH=...
     / MATRIX=...
```

Analysis Block(s)

```
/ ANALYSIS=...
/ PRINT=...
/ PLOT=...
/ DIAGONAL=...
/ FORMAT=...
```

Extraction Block(s)

```
/ CRITERIA=(extraction criteria)
/ EXTRACTION=...
```

Rotation Block(s)

```
/ CRITERIA=(rotation criteria)
/ ROTATION=...
/ SAVE=...
```

• The order of subcommands can be different from the order shown in Figure 28.2. However, any analysis can use this order, repeating ROTATION, EXTRACTION, and ANALYSIS blocks as needed. (If MATRIX=IN is specified, VARIABLES should be omitted.)

Because of FACTOR's structured syntax, which allows rotation blocks nested within extraction blocks nested within analysis blocks, you can get unexpected results if you specify commands out of order.

• If you enter any subcommand other than the global subcommands (VARIABLES, MISSING, WIDTH, MATRIX) before the first ANALYSIS subcommand, an implicit analysis block including all variables on the variables subcommand is activated. Factors are extracted and rotated for this implicit block before any explicitly requested analysis block is activated.

• If you enter a SAVE or ROTATION subcommand before the first EXTRACTION in any analysis block, an implicit extraction block using the default method (PC) is activated. Factors are extracted and rotated for this implicit block before any explicitly requested extraction block is activated.

• If you enter CRITERIA *after* an EXTRACTION or ROTATION subcommand, the criteria do not affect that extraction or rotation.

For example, if you specify

```
FACTOR VAR=VAR1 TO VAR12
      /CRITERIA=FACTORS(3)
      /ANALYSIS=VAR1 TO VAR8
      /EXTRACTION=PAF
      /ROTATION=QUARTIMAX
```

the CRITERIA subcommand activates an analysis block of all 12 variables. FACTOR extracts three factors using the default extraction method (principal components) and rotation (varimax) before entering the analysis block with VAR1 to VAR8, where different extraction and rotation methods are requested.

If you specify

```
FACTOR VARIABLES=VAR1 TO VAR12
      /SAVE DEFAULT (ALL,FAC)
      /EXTRACTION=PAF
      /ROTATION=OBLIMIN
```

the SAVE subcommand activates an extraction block using the default extraction method (principal components) and rotation (varimax). These factors are saved on the active file as FAC1, FAC2, and so on. The next extraction block uses principal axis factoring and oblimin rotation but does not contain a SAVE subcommand, so no factor scores for this method are saved in the active file.

If you specify

```
FACTOR VAR1 TO VAR12
      /EXTRACTION PAF
      /CRITERIA FACTORS(5)
```

the CRITERIA subcommand is ignored and default criteria used because the CRITERIA subcommand *follows* the EXTRACTION subcommand. To define an extraction criterion for an analysis, the CRITERIA subcommand must *precede* its corresponding EXTRACTION subcommand.

28.3 OPERATION

The only required subcommand on FACTOR is the VARIABLES subcommand, which specifies the variable list to be analyzed. (See Section 28.5.)

Each FACTOR subcommand begins with a subcommand keyword followed by an optional equals sign and specifications. Subcommands are separated with slashes. Unlike many SPSS-X procedures, subcommand order is very important in FACTOR. (See Figure 28.2.) All keywords can be abbreviated to the first three characters.

A Note on Defaults. FACTOR is an extensive, keyword-driven procedure in which there are many defaults. There are two types of defaults. *Passive defaults* result with no explicit effort on your part. Listwise missing-value deletion is an example of this. (See Section 28.6.) *Active defaults* result when subcommands are specified that invoke features of the program not supplied unless you request them. In the following documentation, two asterisks (**) signify a passive default and one asterisk (*) signifies an active default.

28.4 Global Subcommands

The VARIABLES (Section 28.5), MISSING (Section 28.6), WIDTH (Section 28.7), and MATRIX (Section 28.20) subcommands are *global* because they affect the analysis, extraction, and rotation blocks (see Figure 28.2). The following rules apply to global subcommands:

- The VARIABLES, MISSING, and WIDTH subcommands can be entered in any order.
- If more than one MISSING or WIDTH subcommand is used, the last specified is in effect.

28.5 VARIABLES Subcommand

The VARIABLES subcommand names the variable list. For example,

```
FACTOR  VARIABLES=ABDEFECT TO ABSINGLE
```

produces the default principle components analysis of six abortion scale items. The variable list follows the usual SPSS-X conventions. The keyword TO can be used to reference a consecutive set of variables on the active file, and the keyword ALL can be used to reference all variables on the active file. Variables must be numeric. Only variables named on the VARIABLES subcommand can be referred to in subsequent subcommands. Only one VARIABLES subcommand is permitted. When FACTOR reads a matrix system file, the VARIABLES subcommand should not be used (see Section 28.22).

28.6 MISSING Subcommand

FACTOR builds a correlation matrix of variables named on the VARIABLES subcommand before it produces any factor results. To select the missing-value treatment, specify *one* of the following treatments on the MISSING subcommand:

LISTWISE** *Delete missing values listwise.* If you do not specify a MISSING subcommand, by default, analyses are performed using only cases with nonmissing values on all variables in the VARIABLES subcommand.

PAIRWISE *Delete missing values pairwise.* Each correlation coefficient is computed using cases with complete data on the pair of variables correlated, regardless of whether the cases have missing values on any other variables in the VARIABLES list.

MEANSUB *Replace missing values with the variable mean.* All cases are used in the analyses with the substitutions treated as valid observations. This applies only to the estimation of coefficients. It does not affect the calculation of factor scores.

INCLUDE *Include missing values.* All user-missing values are treated as if they are valid values. System-missing values are always missing.

DEFAULT** *Delete missing values listwise.* Keywords DEFAULT and LISTWISE have the same effect.

For example,

```
FACTOR  VARIABLES=ABDEFECT TO ABSINGLE
   /MISSING=MEANSUB
```

uses mean substitution for missing values. Only one missing-value treatment is in effect for an invocation of FACTOR, and you can use INCLUDE with any of the treatments. If you specify MISSING more than once, the last treatment specified is used.

28.7
WIDTH Subcommand

You can control the width of the output from FACTOR. The default width is 132 characters, but you can specify any width from 72 to 132, as in

```
FACTOR  VARIABLES=ABDEFECT TO ABSINGLE
   /MISSING=MEANSUB
   /WIDTH=100
```

Specify WIDTH once before any of the three blocks.

n *Maximum width in characters of display.*

DEFAULT** *The default width is 132.*

You can make system width declarations for your SPSS-X run by using the SET command. (See Chapter 4.) The following points should be considered in controlling the width of your output.

• A WIDTH subcommmand in FACTOR overrides any system width declarations made using the SET command.

• If you use WIDTH more than once, the last specified is in effect for the procedure.

• If system width is declared but FACTOR width is not declared, FACTOR uses the minimum of the system width declaration and 132.

• Finally, if neither width is declared, FACTOR uses the default width of 132.

28.8
Analysis-Block Subcommands

You can tailor the statistical display for an analysis block to include correlation matrices, reproduced correlation matrices, and other statistics. You can control the order of entries in the factor pattern and structure matrices. You can also request scree plots and plots of the variables in factor space for all analyses within an analysis block.

28.9
ANALYSIS Subcommand

The ANALYSIS subcommand is used to specify a subset of the variables named on the VARIABLES subcommand. For example,

```
FACTOR  VARIABLES=X1 TO X10
   /MISSING=MEANSUB
   /WIDTH=120
   /ANALYSIS=X1 TO X8
```

restricts the analysis to variables X1 to X8. If you omit the ANALYSIS subcommand, FACTOR uses all variables named on the VARIABLES subcommand. The keyword TO refers to the positional ordering of variables as named on the VARIABLES subcommand, and not to their order on the active file. The keyword ALL refers to all variables named on the VARIABLES command.

For correlation matrix input, the ANALYSIS subcommand may specify a subset of the variables in the matrix. For factor matrix input, MATRIX IN reads all the variables in the matrix; it cannot read a subset named on the ANALYSIS subcommand. For either type of matrix input, the ANALYSIS subcommand defaults to the entire set of variables and may be omitted.

Use the ANALYSIS subcommand in two contexts: to subset variables for analysis, as in the above, or to perform different analyses on the same set of variables. You can use more than one ANALYSIS subcommand. For example,

```
FACTOR  VARIABLES=ABDEFECT TO ABSINGLE FEBEAR FEPOL
  /ANALYSIS=ABDEFECT TO FEPOL
  /ANALYSIS=ABDEFECT TO ABSINGLE
```

specifies two complete analyses. When writing matrix materials, only the first analysis block is used.

28.10
PRINT Subcommand

Use the PRINT subcommand and any of the following keyword specifications to print results, many of which are not printed by default.

UNIVARIATE	*Valid n's, means, and standard deviations.* (Not available with matrix input.)
INITIAL**	*Initial communalities, eigenvalues of the correlation matrix, and percent of variance explained.*
CORRELATION	*Correlation matrix.*
SIG	*Significance levels of correlations.*
DET	*The determinant of the correlation matrix.*
INV	*The inverse of the correlation matrix.*
AIC	*The anti-image covariance and correlation matrices* (Kaiser, 1970). The measure of sampling adequacy for the individual variable is printed on the diagonal of the anti-image correlation matrix.
KMO	*The Kaiser-Meyer-Olkin measure of sampling adequacy and Bartletts's test of sphericity.* Tests of significance are not computed with matrix input if an N OF CASES command is not used.
EXTRACTION**	*Communalities, eigenvalues, and unrotated factor loadings.*
REPR	*Reproduced correlations and residual correlations.*
ROTATION**	*Rotated factor pattern and structure matrices, the factor transformation matrix, and the factor correlation matrix.*
FSCORE	*The factor score coefficient matrix.*
ALL	*All available statistics.*
DEFAULT**	*Specifies INITIAL, EXTRACTION, and ROTATION.*

For example,

```
FACTOR  VARIABLES=ABDEFECT TO ABSINGLE
  /MISSING=MEANSUB
  /WIDTH=100
  /PRINT=AIC KMO REPR
  /EXTRACTION=ULS
  /ROTATION=VARIMAX
```

requests the anti-image correlation and covariance matrices, the Kaiser-Meyer-Olkin measure of sampling adequacy, and the reproduced correlation matrix. Note that all symmetric matrices are printed in lower-triangular form. Figure 28.10 is the display produced by this PRINT subcommand.

If you omit the PRINT subcommand, you obtain the defaults. To obtain the defaults plus nondefaults, you must specify them with the DEFAULT keyword or INITIAL, EXTRACTION, and ROTATION.

Figure 28.10 Nondefault display from PRINT subcommand

```
ANALYSIS NUMBER  1  REPLACEMENT OF MISSING VALUES WITH THE MEAN

KAISER-MEYER-OLKIN MEASURE OF SAMPLING ADEQUACY = .81562

BARTLETT TEST OF SPHERICITY = 1346.8207, SIGNIFICANCE =      .00000

THERE ARE    12 (40.0%) OFF-DIAGONAL ELEMENTS OF AIC MATRIX > 0.09

ANTI-IMAGE COVARIANCE MATRIX:

              ABDEFECT     ABNOMORE      ABHLTH       ABPOOR       ABRAPE      ABSINGLE

ABDEFECT        .55012
ABNOMORE       -.02219       .33253
ABHLTH         -.22676       .00421       .64445
ABPOOR         -.02235      -.17065       .00034       .33400
ABRAPE         -.19466      -.01936      -.13492      -.03626       .60240
ABSINGLE       -.01953      -.13193      -.02753      -.12332      -.03027       .39606


ANTI-IMAGE CORRELATION MATRIX:

            ABDEFECT   ABNOMORE      ABHLTH     ABPOOR     ABRAPE    ABSINGLE

ABDEFECT      .80138
ABNOMORE     -.05189     .79197
ABHLTH       -.38085     .00910     .80429
ABPOOR       -.05213    -.51206     .00073     .79898
ABRAPE       -.33815    -.04325    -.21654    -.08083     .85544
ABSINGLE     -.04184    -.36354    -.05449    -.33907    -.06196     .85066


MEASURES OF SAMPLING ADEQUACY (MSA) ARE PRINTED ON THE DIAGONAL.

REPRODUCED CORRELATION MATRIX:

              ABDEFECT     ABNOMORE      ABHLTH       ABPOOR       ABRAPE      ABSINGLE

ABDEFECT       .65233*       .00440       .00004       .00070       .00053      -.00580
ABNOMORE       .37662       .78502*      -.00230      -.00054      -.00301       .00083
ABHLTH         .56003       .28454       .48344*      -.00413      -.00064       .00723
ABPOOR         .38828       .77994       .29536       .77532*       .00381      -.00024
ABRAPE         .56422       .39551       .47961       .40415       .49658*      -.00087
ABSINGLE       .38839       .72900       .29894       .72544       .39798       .68014*


THE LOWER LEFT TRIANGLE CONTAINS THE REPRODUCED CORRELATION MATRIX;  THE
DIAGONAL, COMMUNALITIES; AND THE UPPER RIGHT TRIANGLE, RESIDUALS BETWEEN
THE OBSERVED CORRELATIONS AND THE REPRODUCED CORRELATIONS.

THERE ARE     0 (   .0%) RESIDUALS (ABOVE DIAGONAL) THAT ARE > 0.05
```

28.11
PLOT Subcommand

Use the PLOT subcommand to obtain a scree plot or a plot of the variables in rotated factor space. The scree plot aids in identifying the number of factors needed (Cattell, 1966). It is named for its resemblance to scree, the geological term for an accumulation of stones or rocky debris lying on a slope or at the base of a hill or cliff.

The plot of variables in factor space is a graphic representation of the rotated factor loadings which aids in substantive identification of factors. It is not printed if the ROTATION command is not implicitly or explicitly specified (see Section 28.18).

EIGEN *The scree plot.* Plots the eigenvalues in descending order.

ROTATION(n1 n2) *Plot the variables in factor space.* Specify *n1* and *n2*, which are the numbers to be plotted.

The following FACTOR command requests a scree plot.

```
FACTOR  VARIABLES=ABDEFECT TO ABSINGLE
  /MISSING=MEANSUB
  /WIDTH=100
  /ANALYSIS=ABDEFECT TO ABSINGLE
  /FORMAT=SORT BLANK(.3)
  /PLOT=EIGEN
  /CRITERIA=ITERATE(10)
  /EXTRACTION=ULS
  /ROTATION=VARIMAX
```

Figure 28.11 is the scree plot produced by this example.

Figure 28.11   Scree plot

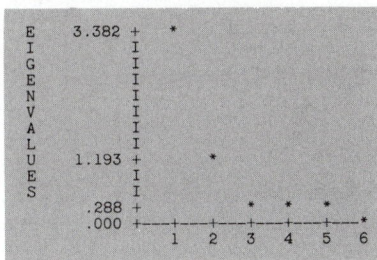

```
E    3.382 +   *
I          I
G          I
E          I
N          I
V          I
A          I
L          I
U    1.193 +   I
E          I
S          I
     .288 +         *    *    *
     .000 +---+---+---+---+---+---*
               1   2   3   4   5   6
```

28.12
DIAGONAL Subcommand

Use the DIAGONAL subcommand to specify initial diagonal values in conjunction with principal axis factoring. Specify one of the following:

valuelist   *Diagonal values.* User-supplied diagonal values are only used for principal axis factoring (EXTRACTION=PAF).

DEFAULT*   *1's on the diagonal for principal components or initial communality estimates on the diagonal for factor methods.*

The following example demonstrates the use of the DIAGONAL subcommand:

```
FACTOR  VARIABLES=ABDEFECT TO ABSINGLE
  /DIAGONAL=.55 .45 .35 .40 .60 .70
  /EXTRACTION=PAF
  /ROTATION=VARIMAX
```

You can use the asterisk operator to indicate replications of the same diagonal value, as in:

```
FACTOR  VARIABLES=ABDEFECT TO ABSINGLE
  /DIAGONAL=.55 .45 3*.40 .70
  /EXTRACTION=PAF
  /ROTATION=VARIMAX
```

28.13
FORMAT Subcommand

The FORMAT subcommand reformats the factor loading and structure matrices to ease interpretability.

SORT   *Order the factor loadings by magnitude.* Aids in identifying clusters of variables.

BLANK(n)   *Suppress coefficients lower in absolute value than threshold* n.

DEFAULT*   *Deactivate blanking and sorting.* Variables appear in the order in which they are named, and all loadings are shown.

For example,

```
FACTOR  VARIABLES=ABDEFECT TO ABSINGLE
  /MISSING=MEANSUB
  /WIDTH=100
  /ANALYSIS=ABDEFECT TO ABSINGLE
  /FORMAT=SORT BLANK(.3)
  /EXTRACTION=ULS
  /ROTATION=VARIMAX
```

specifies that loadings be ordered by magnitude and that loadings smaller in magnitude than 0.3 not be printed. Figure 28.13a is a sorted factor loading matrix with BLANK(.3). Compare it to Figure 28.13b, which is the same matrix unsorted with all loadings printed.

Figure 28.13a   A sorted and blanked factor loading matrix

```
ROTATED FACTOR MATRIX:


                    FACTOR  1      FACTOR  2

ABNOMORE            .85518
ABPOOR              .84428
ABSINGLE            .77944

ABDEFECT                           .77403
ABHLTH                             .67921
ABRAPE                             .64302
```

Figure 28.13b   A default factor loading matrix

```
ROTATED FACTOR MATRIX:


                    FACTOR  1      FACTOR  2

ABDEFECT            .23069         .77403
ABNOMORE            .85518         .23170
ABHLTH              .14870         .67921
ABPOOR              .84428         .25002
ABRAPE              .28827         .64302
ABSINGLE            .77944         .26948
```

28.14
Extraction-Block Subcommands

You can choose among six extraction methods in addition to the default principal components extraction: principal axis factoring, alpha factoring, image factoring, unweighted least squares, generalized least squares, and maximum likelihood. You can supply initial diagonal values for principal axis factoring. You can also select the statistical criteria used in the extraction.

The following rules apply to extraction-block subcommands.

- Multiple extractions can be specified for each ANALYSIS subcommand.
- Multiple CRITERIA subcommands can be specified for each extraction. Previously specified criteria remain in effect for all analyses until explicitly overridden with another CRITERIA subcommand.

28.15
CRITERIA Subcommand

Use the CRITERIA subcommand to override extraction and rotation defaults. You can specify one CRITERIA subcommand for each extraction and each rotation within each extraction. The CRITERIA subcommand must precede the EXTRACTION or ROTATION subcommand or it is ignored for that EXTRACTION or ROTATION.

FACTORS(nf)	*The number of factors extracted.* The default is the number of eigenvalues greater than MINEIGEN.
MINEIGEN(eg)	*Minimum eigenvalue used to control the number of factors.* The default MINEIGEN is 1.
ITERATE(ni)	*The number of iterations for the factor solution.* The default ITERATE is 25.
ECONVERGE(e1)	*The convergence criterion for extraction.* The default ECONVERGE is 0.001.
RCONVERGE(e2)	*The convergence criterion for rotation.* The default RCONVERGE is 0.0001.
KAISER**	*Kaiser normalization.* The default.
NOKAISER	*No Kaiser normalization.*
DELTA(d)	*The value of delta for direct oblimin rotation.* The default DELTA is 0.
DEFAULT**	*Use default values.* Default values are shown with each CRITERIA keyword.

For example, to specify the maximum number of iterations for extraction, use the ITERATE keyword, as in:

```
FACTOR  VARIABLES=ABDEFECT TO ABSINGLE
  /MISSING=MEANSUB
  /WIDTH=100
  /FORMAT=SORT BLANK(.3)
  /ANALYSIS=ABDEFECT TO ABSINGLE
  /PRINT=CORRELATION DET REPR
  /CRITERIA=ITERATE(10)
  /EXTRACTION=ULS
```

The above FACTOR command limits the number of iterations during extraction to 10.

If you use the CRITERIA subcommand to override defaults, they remain in effect for subsequent analyses until explicitly overridden. You can use the keyword DEFAULT to return to FACTOR's defaults for CRITERIA. For example,

```
FACTOR  VARIABLES=ABDEFECT TO ABSINGLE
  /CRITERIA=FACTORS(6)
  /EXTRACTION=PC
  /ANALYSIS=ABDEFECT TO ABSINGLE
  /CRITERIA=DEFAULT
  /EXTRACTION=ML
  /ROTATION=VARIMAX
```

turns off the FACTORS specification for the second analyses.

28.16 EXTRACTION Subcommand

Use one of the following keywords to specify the factor extraction technique to be used.

PC**   *Principal components analysis* (Harman, 1976).

PA1**   *Principal components analysis.* Equivalent to PC.

PAF   *Principal axis factoring* (Harman, 1976).

PA2   *Principal axis factoring.* Equivalent to PAF.

ALPHA   *Alpha factoring* (Kaiser, 1963).

IMAGE   *Image factoring* (Kaiser and Caffry, 1963).

ULS   *Unweighted least squares* (Harman and Jones, 1966).

GLS   *Generalized least squares.*

ML   *Maximum likelihood* (Jöreskog and Lawley, 1968).

DEFAULT** *The default is principal components analysis.*

For example,

```
FACTOR  VARIABLES=ABDEFECT TO ABSINGLE
  /MISSING=MEANSUB
  /WIDTH=100
  /EXTRACTION=ULS
```

specifies unweighted least squares extraction. You can specify more than one extraction method for a given ANALYSIS subcommand. The following example specifies two different extractions:

```
FACTOR  VARIABLES=ABDEFECT TO ABSINGLE
  /MISSING=MEANSUB
  /WIDTH=100
  /EXTRACTION=ULS
  /EXTRACTION=ML
```

28.17 Rotation-Block Subcommands

You can control the criteria for factor roation. You can also choose among three rotation methods (equmax, quartimax, and oblimin) in addition to the default varimax rotation, or you can specify no rotation.

ANNOTATED EXAMPLE FOR FACTOR

For example, six abortion items are used from a 500-case sample of the 1980 General Social Survey. Respondents indicate whether they favor or oppose abortion in the following contexts:

- ABHLTH—if the woman's health is seriously endangered.
- ABRAPE—if the woman is pregnant as a result of rape.
- ABDEFECT—if there is a strong chance of a serious defect in the child.
- ABPOOR—if the woman has a low income and cannot afford more children.
- ABSINGLE—if the woman is not married and doesn't want the child.
- ABNOMORE—if the woman is married and wants no more children.

The SPSS-X commands are

```
TITLE   FACTOR ANALYSIS OF ABORTION ITEMS
GET   FILE GSS80/KEEP ABDEFECT TO ABSINGLE
COMMENT   RECODE THE ITEMS SO THAT 1 IS FAVOR AND 0 IS OPPOSE
RECODE   ABDEFECT TO ABSINGLE(1=1)(2=0)
MISSING VALUES   ABDEFECT TO ABSINGLE(7 THRU 9)
VALUE LABELS   ABDEFECT TO ABSINGLE
  0 'NO' 1 'YES' 7 'NAP' 8 'DK' 9 'NA'
/FACTOR   VARIABLES=ABDEFECT TO ABSINGLE
 /MISSING=MEANSUB
 /WIDTH=100
 /FORMAT=SORT BLANK(.3)
 /PLOT=ROTATION(1 2)
 /EXTRACTION=ML
 /ROTATION=OBLIMIN
 /SAVE REG (ALL FSULS)
```

- The TITLE command puts the title, FACTOR ANALYSIS OF ABORTION ITEMS, at the top of each page of output for this job (see Chapter 4).
- The GET command accesses the data file and keeps only those variables that will be used in this job (see Chapter 6).
- The RECODE, MISSING VALUES, and VALUE LABELS commands redefine the abortion items and label the redefined responses for this job (see Chapters 5 and 7).
- The FACTOR command invokes the FACTOR procedure. The VARIABLES subcommand names all the variables that are used in this FACTOR job (see Section 28.5).
- The MISSING subcommand forces mean substitution for missing data (see Section 28.6).
- The WIDTH subcommand limits the width of the output to 100 columns (see Section 28.7).
- The FORMAT subcommand displays the factor loadings in descending order of magnitude and suppresses the printing of factor loadings less than 0.3 (see Section 35.11 and Figures C and D).
- The EXTRACTION subcommand specifies maximum likelihood as the method of extraction (see Section 28.16).
- The ROTATION subcommand specifies an oblimin rotation (see Section 28.18).
- The SAVE subcommand computes all possible factor scores using the regression method (see Section 28.19).

Portions of the output produced by this set of commands appear in Figures A through E.

Initial Statistics. Figure A contains the initial statistics which are produced by default. Initial statistics are the initial communalities, eigenvalues of the correlation matrix, and percentage of variance explained.

Extraction Statistics. Figure B contains the extraction statistics which are produced by default. Extraction statistics are the communalities, eigenvalues, and unrotated factor loadings. Note the effect of sorting and blanking produced by the FORMAT subcommand.

Rotation Statistics. Figure C contains the rotation statistics which are produced by default if the model is rotated. They are the rotated factor pattern and structure matrices (since this is an oblimin rotation), the factor transformation matrix, and the factor correlation matrix. (The Oblimin rotation will give a Factor correlation matrix, since it is an oblique rotation.)

Factor Plot. Figure D contains the plot of variables in the rotated factor space. Although the rotation is oblimin, the plot axes are orthogonal. Since variable 1 overlaps with variable 3 and variable 2 overlaps with variable 4, they do not appear on the plot.

Saved Factor Scores. Figure E contains the information for the factor scores which are saved as new variables on the active file as a result of the SAVE subcommand.

A Initial statistics

```
ANALYSIS NUMBER  1  REPLACEMENT OF MISSING VALUES WITH THE MEAN


EXTRACTION  1  FOR ANALYSIS  1, MAXIMUM LIKELIHOOD (ML)


INITIAL STATISTICS:
```

VARIABLE	COMMUNALITY	*	FACTOR	EIGENVALUE	PCT OF VAR	CUM PCT
ABDEFECT	.44988	*	1	3.38153	56.4	56.4
ABNOMORE	.66747	*	2	1.19287	19.9	76.2
ABHLTH	.35555	*	3	.50823	8.5	84.7
ABPOOR	.66600	*	4	.40867	6.8	91.5
ABRAPE	.39760	*	5	.28847	4.8	96.3
ABSINGLE	.60394	*	6	.22024	3.7	100.0

B Extraction statistics

```
FACTOR MATRIX:
```

	FACTOR 1	FACTOR 2
ABNOMORE	.86202	
ABPOOR	.86070	
ABSINGLE	.81336	
ABDEFECT	.57319	.56773
ABRAPE	.56086	.42732
ABHLTH	.45491	.52697

```
FINAL STATISTICS:
```

VARIABLE	COMMUNALITY	*	FACTOR	EIGENVALUE	PCT OF VAR	CUM PCT
ABDEFECT	.65086	*	1	2.99548	49.9	49.9
ABNOMORE	.78498	*	2	.87734	14.6	64.5
ABHLTH	.48464	*				
ABPOOR	.77461	*				
ABRAPE	.49717	*				
ABSINGLE	.68057	*				

Annotated Example for
FACTOR *continued*

C Rotation statistics

```
OBLIMIN   ROTATION  1  FOR EXTRACTION  1  IN ANALYSIS  1 – KAISER NORMALIZATION.

   OBLIMIN CONVERGED IN    4 ITERATIONS.

PATTERN MATRIX:

                FACTOR 1    FACTOR 2

ABNOMORE         .89941
ABPOOR           .88066
ABSINGLE         .80192

ABDEFECT                      .80526
ABHLTH                        .72830
ABRAPE                        .63824


STRUCTURE MATRIX:

                FACTOR 1    FACTOR 2

ABNOMORE         .88574      .46625
ABPOOR           .88012      .48004
ABSINGLE         .82426      .47892

ABDEFECT         .44259      .80676
ABRAPE           .45973      .69893
ABHLTH           .33537      .69419


FACTOR CORRELATION MATRIX:

                FACTOR 1    FACTOR 2

FACTOR  1       1.00000
FACTOR  2        .54622     1.00000
```

D Factor plot

```
- - - - - - - - - - - - - - - -  F A C T O R   A N A L Y S I S  - - - - - - - - - - - - - - - -


                    HORIZONTAL FACTOR  1   VERTICAL FACTOR  2
                                      I
                                      I
                                      I
                                      I
                                3     I
                                      I
                                      I   5
                                      I
                                      I
                                      I
                                      I
                                      I
                                      I
                                      I
                                      I
                                      I
                                      I
                                      I
                                      I
                                      I                                  6
- - - - - - - - - - - - - - - - - - - - - - - - - - - +- - - - - - - - - - - - - - - - - - - - - -
                                      I                                  4
                                      I
                                      I
                                      I
                                      I
                                      I
                                      I
                                      I
                                      I
                                      I
                                      I
                                      I
                                      I
                                      I
                                      I
                                      I


SYMBOL VARIABLE    COORDINATES    SYMBOL VARIABLE     COORDINATES

   1    ABDEFECT ( .00274,  .80526)    2    ABNOMORE ( .89941, –.02502)
   3    ABHLTH   (–.06244,  .72830)    4    ABPOOR   ( .88066, –.00099)
   5    ABRAPE   ( .11111,  .63824)    6    ABSINGLE ( .80192,  .04090)
```

E Saved factor scores

```
- - - - - - - - - - - - - - - -  F A C T O R   A N A L Y S I S  - - - - - - - - - - - - - - - -


  2 REGRESSION FACTOR SCORES WILL BE SAVED WITH ROOTNAME: FSULS

FOLLOWING FACTOR SCORES WILL BE ADDED TO THE ACTIVE FILE:

  NAME        LABEL

FSULS1      REGR FACTOR SCORE   1 FOR ANALYSIS    1
FSULS2      REGR FACTOR SCORE   2 FOR ANALYSIS    1
```

28.18
ROTATION Subcommand

If you do not use the EXTRACTION subcommand, the default factor rotation method is VARIMAX. If you use the EXTRACTION subcommand but do not use the ROTATION subcommand, the factor loadings are not rotated, except when there is SAVE subcommand. If you include a SAVE subcommand, a varimax rotation will occur by default, even though you did not use the ROTATION subcommand. If you do not want the rotation to occur use the ROTATE subcommand with keyword NOROTATE. Similarly, if you want the plot of variables in unrotated factor space produced by the PLOT subcommand (Section 28.11), use the ROTATE subcommand with keyword NOROTATE.

VARIMAX**   *Varimax rotation.*

EQUAMAX   *Equamax rotation.*

QUARTIMAX   *Quartimax rotation.*

OBLIMIN   *Direct oblimin rotation.* This is a non-orthogonal rotation; thus, a factor correlation matrix will also be printed.

NOROTATE   *No rotation.*

DEFAULT**   *The default is varimax rotation.*

For example, the command

```
FACTOR  VARIABLES=ABDEFECT TO ABSINGLE
  /MISSING=MEANSUB
  /WIDTH=100
  /ANALYSIS=ABDEFECT TO ABSINGLE
  /PRINT=CORRELATION DET REPR
  /FORMAT=SORT BLANK(.3)
  /CRITERIA=ITERATE(10)
  /PLOT=EIGEN ROTATION(1 2)
  /EXTRACTION=ULS
  /ROTATION
```

specifies varimax rotation.

You can specify more than one rotation for a given extraction. For example,

```
FACTOR  VARIABLES=ABDEFECT TO ABSINGLE
  /EXTRACTION=ML
  /ROTATION=VARIMAX
  /ROTATION=QUARTIMAX
  /ROTATION=OBLIMIN
```

specifies three different rotations for maximum likelihood extraction.

28.19
SAVE Subcommand

Use the SAVE subcommand to compute and save factor scores on the active file. If you are replacing the active file with matrix materials (see Section 28.21), you cannot use the SAVE subcommand.

To use SAVE, indicate the method to be used in calculating factor scores, how many factor scores to calculate, and a *rootname* to be used in naming the factor scores.

First, choose one of the following method keywords:

REG*   *The regression method.*

BART   *The Bartlett method.*

AR   *The Anderson-Rubin method.*

DEFAULT*   *The default is the regression method.*

Second, specify the number of desired factor scores. The maximum number you may specify is equal to the order of the factor solution. You can use the keyword ALL to calculate all possible factor scores.

Third, specify a seven-character-maximum rootname to be used in naming the factor scores. FACTOR names the factor scores sequentially. If you are calculating factor scores for a many-factor solution, make sure that the rootname is short enough to accommodate the number of the highest-order factor score variable. When FACTOR saves the variables on the active file it automatically supplies a variable label with the method used to calculate it, its positional order, and the analysis number (see Figure E in the annotated example).

For example, the following FACTOR command saves factor scores for the abortion items. Note that the parentheses *are* required.

```
FACTOR  VARIABLES=ABDEFECT TO ABSINGLE
  /MISSING=MEANSUB
  /WIDTH=100
  /ANALYSIS=ABDEFECT TO ABSINGLE
  /PRINT=CORRELATION DET REPR
  /FORMAT=SORT BLANK(.3)
  /PLOT=EIGEN ROTATION(1 2)
  /CRITERIA=FACTORS(2)
  /EXTRACTION=ULS
  /ROTATION=VARIMAX
  /SAVE AR (ALL FSULS)
```

FACTOR calculates two factor scores named FSULS1 and FSULS2 using the Anderson-Rubin method and saves them on the active file.

You can use multiple SAVE subcommands for an extraction. For example,

```
FACTOR  VARIABLES=ABDEFECT TO ABSINGLE
  /MISSING=MEANSUB
  /WIDTH=100
  /ANALYSIS=ABDEFECT TO ABSINGLE
  /PRINT=CORRELATION DET REPR
  /FORMAT=SORT BLANK(.3)
  /PLOT=EIGEN ROTATION(1 2)
  /CRITERIA=FACTORS(2)
  /EXTRACTION=ULS
  /ROTATION=VARIMAX
  /SAVE AR (ALL FSULS)
  /SAVE BART (ALL BFAC)
```

saves two sets of factor scores. The first set is computed using the Anderson-Rubin method and the second is computed using the Bartlett method.

28.20
MATRIX Subcommand

FACTOR can write matrix materials built from the raw data it reads. It writes matrix materials in either the form of a correlation matrix or a factor loading matrix, whichever you specify. FACTOR can also read matrix materials written either by a previous FACTOR procedure, or by a procedure that writes matrices with Pearson correlation coefficients (see the table of matrix types on the first page of Chapter 13). To read and write matrices in FACTOR, you use the MATRIX subcommand.

The MATRIX subcommand has two keywords, IN and OUT, which you use to specify the matrix file in parentheses. When you use both IN and OUT on the same FACTOR procedure you can specify each on a separate MATRIX subcommand, or both on the same subcommand. For example,

```
FACTOR MATRIX IN(COR=FILEONE)
       /MATRIX OUT(COR=FILETWO)
```

is the same as

```
FACTOR MATRIX IN(COR=FILEONE) OUT(COR=FILETWO)
```

The MATRIX subcommand must always appear before the analysis block. If you use both MATRIX keywords (IN and OUT), you can specify them in either order.

As part of the specification on both IN and OUT, you must indicate the matrix type. The types are COR for correlation matrix, and FAC for factor loading matrix. Indicate the matrix type within parentheses immediately before you identify the matrix file. For example,

```
FACTOR MATRIX OUT(COR=CORMTX)
```

requests that a correlation matrix be written to the file named CORMTX.

28.21
OUT Keyword

The OUT keyword on MATRIX specifies the file to which the matrix is written. There are four options with OUT:

(COR=file)   *Write the correlation matrix to a system file.* FACTOR creates a system file containing correlation matrix materials. The name of the file is specified in parentheses. The system file is stored on disk and can be retrieved at any time.

(COR=*)   *Replace the active file with the correlation matrix.* The matrix materials replace the active file. The correlation matrix is NOT stored on disk. It is resident in the active file.

(FAC=file)   *Write the factor loading matrix to a system file.* FACTOR creates a system file containing the factor loading matrix. The name of the file is specified in parentheses. The system file is stored on disk and can be retrieved at any time.

(FAC=*)   *Replace the active file with the factor loading matrix.* The matrix materials replace the active file. The factor loading matrix is NOT stored on disk. It is resident in the active file.

FACTOR generates the matrix from the first analysis block and writes one matrix per split file. You cannot write a matrix from subsequent analysis blocks on the same FACTOR subcommand. Documents from the original file will not be included in the matrix file and will not be present if the matrix file becomes the active file. (For a discussion on documents, see Chapter 6.)

In the following example, FACTOR reads data from the file named GSS80 and writes a factor correlation matrix to the file named CORMTX:

```
GET FILE=GSS80/KEEP ABDEFECT TO ABSINGLE
FACTOR VARIABLES=ABDEFECT TO ABSINGLE
       /MATRIX OUT(COR=CORMTX)
```

The active file is still the file named GSS80. Subsequent commands are executed on file GSS80.

To write the same matrix to the active file so that it is available to subsequent commands, specify the following:

```
GET FILE=GSS80/KEEP ABDEFECT TO ABSINGLE
FACTOR VARIABLES=ABDEFECT TO ABSINGLE
       /MATRIX OUT(COR=*)
LIST
```

The active file is replaced with the correlation matrix. The LIST command is executed on the matrix file, not on the file named GSS80.

Format of the Matrix System File. Figure 28.21a shows the matrix system file produced by the above commands. The file has two special variables created by SPSS-X: ROWTYPE_ and VARNAME_. Variable ROWTYPE_ is a short string variable with the value CORR (for Pearson correlation coefficient) for each matrix row. The next variable, VARNAME_, is a short string variable whose values are the names of the variables used to form the correlation matrix. The remaining variables are the variables used to form the matrix. (See Chapter 13 for more information on matrix system files.)

Figure 28.21a   Matrix system file with a correlation matrix

```
FILE:      MATRIX FILE

ROWTYPE_ VARNAME_   ABDEFECT   ABNOMORE    ABHLTH     ABPOOR     ABRAPE    ABSINGLE

CORR      ABDEFECT  1.0000000  .3977723   .5802687   .3892293   .5922749   .3891886
CORR      ABNOMORE   .3977723  1.0000000  .3139752   .8024923   .4153779   .7456214
CORR      ABHLTH     .5802687  .3139752   1.0000000  .3131891   .5174872   .3169778
CORR      ABPOOR     .3892293  .8024923   .3131891   1.0000000  .4299739   .7373698
CORR      ABRAPE     .5922749  .4153779   .5174872   .4299739   1.0000000  .4192810
CORR      ABSINGLE   .3891886  .7456214   .3169778   .7373698   .4192810   1.0000000

NUMBER OF CASES READ =       6    NUMBER OF CASES LISTED =        6
```

For factor loading matrices, SPSS-X generates two special matrix variables named ROWTYPE_ and FACTOR_. The value for ROWTYPE_ is always FACTOR. The values for FACTOR_ are the ordinal numbers of the factors. The following commands generate the factor loading matrix shown in Figure 28.21b:

```
GET FILE=GSS80/KEEP ABDEFECT TO ABSINGLE
FACTOR VARIABLES=ABDEFECT TO ABSINGLE
      /MATRIX OUT(FAC=*)
LIST
```

Figure 28.21b Matrix system file with a factor loading matrix

```
FILE:      MATRIX FILE

ROWTYPE_  FACTOR_   ABDEFECT    ABNOMORE     ABHLTH      ABPOOR      ABRAPE     ABSINGLE

FACTOR         1    .7136521    .8306205    .6332678    .8297869    .7244597    .8134096
FACTOR         2    .4838575   -.4101484    .5663649   -.4057918    .3931885   -.3828545


NUMBER OF CASES READ =         2 .   NUMBER OF CASES LISTED =         2
```

Variable Order. When split-file processing is in effect, the first variables in the matrix system file will be the split variables, followed by ROWTYPE_, VARNAME_ (or FACTOR_), then the variables used to form the matrix. A full set of matrix materials is written for each split-file group defined by the split variable(s). A split variable cannot have the same variable name as any other variable written to the matrix system file. (FACTOR cannot read split file matrices.) If a split file is in effect when a matrix is written, the same split file must be in effect when that matrix is read by any procedure.

Additional Statistics. FACTOR writes only CORR values for correlation matrix materials, and FACTOR values for factor loading matrix materials. It neither reads nor writes additional statistics with its matrix materials. (When FACTOR reads matrix materials, it skips vectors that represent mean, standard deviation, and N values.)

28.22
IN Keyword

The IN keyword on MATRIX specifies the file from which the matrix is read. FACTOR can read both correlation and factor loading matrices (see Chapter 13, Table 13.1).

There are four options with keyword IN:

(COR=file)   *Read the correlation matrix from a matrix system file.*

(COR=*)   *Read the correlation matrix from the active file.* The active file must be an appropriate matrix system file containing a correlation matrix.

(FAC=file)   *Read the factor loading matrix from a matrix system file.*

(FAC=*)   *Read the factor loading matrix from the active file.* The active file must be an appropriate matrix system file containing a factor loading matrix.

MATRIX=IN cannot be used in place of GET or DATA LIST to begin a new SPSS-X command file. MATRIX is a subcommand on FACTOR and FACTOR cannot run before an active file is defined.

The VARIABLES subcommand should not be used with matrix input. If it is used, it must come *after* the MATRIX subcommand, and it is ignored. For correlation matrix input, the ANALYSIS subcommand may specify a subset of the variables in the matrix. For factor matrix input, MATRIX IN reads all the variables in the matrix; it cannot read a subset. For either type of matrix input, the ANALYSIS subcommand defaults to the entire set of variables and may be omitted.

In the following example, one set of correlation matrix materials is read from the file named CORMTX. This specification assumes CORMTX is not the current active file.

```
FACTOR MATRIX IN(COR=CORMTX)
```

SPSS-X reads variable names, variable and value labels, and print and write formats from the dictionary of the matrix system file named CORMTX.

To begin a new command file and immediately read a matrix, first GET the matrix file, then specify IN(COR=*) or IN(FAC=*) on MATRIX. Alternatively, FACTOR can read a matrix written to the active file by another procedure. In the following annotated example, FACTOR uses matrix input from the REGRESSION procedure. When FACTOR reads REGRESSION's matrix materials, it ignores the records containing the means, standard deviations, and N's.

```
GET FILE=COUNTRY/ KEEP SAVINGS POP15 POP75 INCOME GROWTH
REGRESSION MATRIX OUT(*)
           /VARS=SAVINGS TO GROWTH
           /MISS=PAIRWISE
           /DEP=SAVINGS/ENTER
FACTOR MATRIX IN(COR=*) /MISSING=PAIRWISE
```

- The GET command defines the data to SPSS-X and selects the variables needed for the analysis.

- The REGRESSION command computes correlations among five variables with pairwise deletion. The MATRIX=OUT specification writes a matrix system file and replaces the active file with the matrix system file.

- The MATRIX IN(COR=*) specification on FACTOR reads the matrix materials REGRESSION has written to the active file. Notice that FACTOR is using pairwise deletion, since that is how the matrix it read was built.

28.23 LIMITATIONS

The following rules apply to FACTOR subcommands:

- The only required subcommand is VARIABLES (except for matrix input, which does *not* require the VARIABLES subcommand).

- Only 1 MISSING and WIDTH subcommand can be in effect for the FACTOR procedure. If either of these is specified more than once, the last specified is in effect for the entire procedure.

- The MATRIX subcommand must precede the ANALYSIS block. Only 1 IN and 1 OUT keyword can be in effect for the MATRIX subcommand. If either IN or OUT is specified more than once, FACTOR does not execute. VARIABLES is not required for MATRIX=IN and cannot be specified before MATRIX=IN.

- The CRITERIA subcommand must precede the EXTRACTION subcommand or it is ignored.

- If the EXTRACTION subcommand is omitted, ROTATION defaults to VARIMAX; otherwise it defaults to NOROTATE.

- Only 1 PRINT, PLOT, and DIAGONAL subcommand can be in effect for each ANALYSIS subcommand. If any of these is specified more than once in a given extraction block, the last one specified for that extraction block is in effect.

- Specifications on the CRITERIA subcommand carry over from analysis to analysis until explicitly overridden with a subsequent CRITERIA subcommand.

Syntax

FREQUENCIES

```
FREQUENCIES VARIABLES=varlist[(min,max)] [varlist...]
   [/FORMAT=[{CONDENSE}] [{NOTABLE }] [NOLABELS] [WRITE]
            {ONEPAGE }    {LIMIT(n)}
                [{DVALUE}] [DOUBLE] [NEWPAGE] [INDEX]]
                 {AFREQ }
                 {DFREQ }
   [/MISSING=INCLUDE]
   [/BARCHART=[MINIMUM(n)] [MAXIMUM(n)] [{FREQ(n)   }]]
                                        {PERCENT(n)}
   [/HISTOGRAM=[MINIMUM(n)] [MAXIMUM(n)] [{FREQ(n)   }]
                                         {PERCENT(n)}
                [{NONORMAL}] [INCREMENT(n)]]
                 {NORMAL  }
   [/HBAR=same as HISTOGRAM]
   [/NTILES=n]
   [/PERCENTILES=value list]
   [/STATISTICS=[DEFAULT] [MEAN] [STDDEV] [MINIMUM] [MAXIMUM]
                [SEMEAN] [VARIANCE] [SKEWNESS] [SESKEW] [RANGE] [MODE]
                [KURTOSIS] [SEKURT] [MEDIAN] [SUM] [ALL] [NONE]]
```

Contents

29.1   OVERVIEW

29.2   OPERATION

29.3   VARIABLES Subcommand

29.4   General vs. Integer Mode

29.5   FORMAT Subcommand

29.6   Table Formats

29.7   The Order of Values

29.8   Suppressing Tables

29.9   Index of Tables

29.10   Writing Tables to a File

29.11   Bar Charts and Histograms

29.12   BARCHART Subcommand

29.13   HISTOGRAM Subcommand

29.14   HBAR Subcommand

29.15   Percentiles and Ntiles

29.16   PERCENTILES Subcommand

29.17   NTILES Subcommand

29.18   STATISTICS Subcommand

29.19   MISSING Subcommand

29.20 LIMITATIONS

29

Chapter 29 FREQUENCIES

Procedure FREQUENCIES produces a table of frequency counts and percentages for the values of individual variables. Optionally, you can obtain bar charts for discrete variables, histograms for continuous variables, univariate summary statistics, and percentiles. To produce only statistics on interval-level data, you can also use procedure DESCRIPTIVES (see Chapter 26).

29.1
OVERVIEW

FREQUENCIES produces a table of values and the corresponding number of cases for numeric or short string variables. FREQUENCIES operates in two modes: general and integer. General mode can be used with both numeric and short string variables. Integer mode operates on numeric variables only. With integer mode, you must specify the range of values to be tabulated. You can specify all optional subcommands with either mode.

Table Formats. By default, FREQUENCIES prints as many single-spaced tables with complete labeling information as will fit on a page. You can use the FORMAT subcommand to suppress tables or to request double-spaced tables, no value labels, one table per page, or condensed tables. (See Sections 29.6 and 29.8.)

Order of Values. By default, FREQUENCIES orders tables by values in ascending order. You can use the FORMAT subcommand to request tables ordered by values in descending order, by frequencies in ascending order, or by frequencies in descending order. (See Section 29.7.)

Index of Tables. You can use the FORMAT subcommand to request an index of the tables printed by FREQUENCIES. (See Section 29.9.)

Writing Tables to a File. You can use the WRITE keyword on the FORMAT subcommand to write the frequency tables to a separate file on disk or tape. (See Section 29.10.)

Bar Charts and Histograms. You can print a bar chart or histogram for all variables via the BARCHART or HISTOGRAM subcommands, respectively. Or you can request bar charts for variables that fit on one page and histograms for all others via the HBAR subcommand. (See Sections 29.11 through 29.14.)

Percentiles and Ntiles. You can use the PERCENTILES or NTILES subcommand to print percentiles or ntiles for each variable. (See Sections 29.15 through 29.17.)

Statistics. You can use the STATISTICS subcommand to print optional statistics for each variable. Available statistics are mean, median, mode, standard deviation, variance, skewness, kurtosis, sum, and so forth. (See Section 29.18.)

Missing Values. By default, cases with missing values are shown in the frequency table but are deleted from statistics calculations. Use the MISSING subcommand to include user-missing values in statistics calculations. (See Section 29.19.)

29.2
OPERATION

The FREQUENCIES procedure operates via subcommands. Each subcommand begins with a subcommand keyword, followed by an optional equals sign and subcommand specifications. Subcommands can be named in any order and are separated from each other by a slash. With the exception of PERCENTILES and NTILES, each subcommand can be used only once per FREQUENCIES command. The only required subcommand is VARIABLES, which specifies the variables being analyzed. All other subcommands are optional.

29.3
VARIABLES Subcommand

The VARIABLES subcommand names the variables to be analyzed. It is the only required subcommand. The specification on the VARIABLES subcommand depends on whether you want to use the *integer* or *general* mode to build tables. In integer mode, you specify the dimensions of the table, and FREQUENCIES sorts cases into the elements of the table. In general mode, FREQUENCIES dynamically builds the table, setting up one cell for each unique value encountered in the data. You cannot mix integer and general modes on the VARIABLES subcommand.

To use FREQUENCIES in general mode, simply list the variable names on the VARIABLES subcommand, as in:

FREQUENCIES **VARIABLES=POLVIEWS RES16**

Figure 29.3 shows the table for POLVIEWS produced by this command. The variable and value labels are printed, if available, followed by the value and the number of cases that have the value. The percentage is based on all the observations, and the valid and cumulative percentages are based on those cases that have valid values. The number of valid and missing observations is also provided.

Figure 29.3   A default frequency table

```
POLVIEWS   THINK SELF LIBERAL OR CONSERVATIVE


                                                        VALID      CUM
       VALUE LABEL              VALUE   FREQUENCY  PERCENT  PERCENT  PERCENT

   EXTREMELY LIBERAL               1         17       3.4      3.5      3.5
   LIBERAL                         2         38       7.6      7.7     11.2
   SLIGHTLY LIBERAL                3         80      16.0     16.3     27.4
   MODERATE                        4        190      38.0     38.6     66.1
   SLGHTLY CONSERVATIVE            5         88      17.6     17.9     83.9
   CONSERVATIVE                    6         68      13.6     13.8     97.8
   EXTRMLY CONSERVATIVE            7         11       2.2      2.2    100.0
   DK                              8          5       1.0   MISSING
   NA                              9          3        .6   MISSING
                                          ------    ------   ------
                             TOTAL        500     100.0    100.0

   VALID CASES     492     MISSING CASES      8
```

You can use the keyword ALL to name all the variables on the file or the keyword TO to reference a set of consecutive variables on the active file.

General mode tabulates any type of variable, including numeric variables with decimal positions and string variables. However, long strings are truncated to short strings in the tabulation. In other words, only the short-string portion of the variable is actually tabulated. For a discussion of short and long strings, see Chapter 5.

To use FREQUENCIES in integer mode, you must specify in parentheses the value range for each variable following the variable name, as in:

FREQUENCIES VARIABLES=POLVIEWS**(0,9)** RES16**(1,6)**

The value range for POLVIEWS is 0 through 9, and the range for RES16 is 1 through 6. You must specify a value range for every variable listed. If several variables have the same range, you can specify the range once at the end of the variable list, as in:

FREQUENCIES VARIABLES=SEX(1,2) TVHOURS(0,24) **SCALE1 TO SCALE5(1,7)**

In this example, the value range for SCALE1, SCALE2, and so on through SCALE5 is 1 through 7.

Only observations with values within the range are included in the frequency table. Integer mode truncates values with decimal positions when tabulating. For example, 2.46, 2.59, and 2.73 are all counted as value 2. Values outside the range are grouped into an out-of-range category and are considered missing for calculation of percents and statistics. You can specify a more generous range than actually occurs in the data, but this will needlessly increase the amount of memory needed to store the table. If the variables being tabulated are sparsely distributed within the specified range (that is, there are many empty categories), use the general mode or recode the values to consecutive values with the RECODE command (see Chapter 7).

29.4
General vs. Integer Mode

All optional specifications are available with either integer or general mode. However, you should consider the following points when choosing between the two modes.

- Integer mode usually takes less computation time. However, it is impossible to predict savings on time since the amount of time required for general mode depends upon the range of values and the order in which they are read.
- Integer mode requires less memory than does general mode, except when variables are sparsely distributed.
- In integer mode, you can use the value range specification to eliminate extremely low or high values.
- Since integer mode truncates decimal positions, you can obtain grouped frequency tables for continuous variables without having to recode them to integers. On the other hand, general mode tabulates short strings and does not truncate nonintegers.

29.5
FORMAT Subcommand

Several formatting options are available via the FORMAT subcommand. The FORMAT subcommand applies to all variables named on the VARIABLES subcommand. You can control the formatting of tables and the order in which values are sorted within the table, suppress tables, produce an index of the tables, and write the FREQUENCIES display to another file via keywords on the FORMAT subcommand.

You can specify as many formatting options as desired on the FORMAT subcommand. For example,

FREQUENCIES VARIABLES=POLVIEWS PRESTIGE/
     FORMAT=ONEPAGE DVALUE/

specifies conditional condensed formatting of the tables (keyword ONEPAGE) with values sorted in descending order (keyword DVALUE). Keywords on the FORMAT subcommand are described in Sections 29.6 through 29.10.

29.6
Table Formats

The following keywords on the FORMAT subcommand control the formatting of tables:

NOLABELS *Do not print value labels.* By default, FREQUENCIES prints value labels defined by the VALUE LABELS command (see Chapter 5).

DOUBLE *Double-space frequency tables.*

NEWPAGE *Begin each table on a new page.* By default, FREQUENCIES prints as many tables on a page as will fit.

CONDENSE *Condensed format.* This format prints frequency counts in three columns. It does not print value labels and percentages for all cases, and it rounds valid and cumulative percentages to integers.

ONEPAGE   *Conditional condensed format.* Keyword ONEPAGE uses the condensed format for tables that would require more than one page with the default format. All other tables are printed in default format. If you specify both CONDENSE and ONEPAGE, all tables are printed in condensed format.

Specify these keywords following the FORMAT subcommand and an optional equals sign, as in:

```
FREQUENCIES  VARIABLES=PRESTIGE/FORMAT=CONDENSE
```

Figure 29.6 shows the condensed frequency table for PRESTIGE.

Figure 29.6 Condensed frequency table

```
PRESTIGE   RESP'S OCCUPATIONAL PRESTIGE SCORE


                      CUM                      CUM                      CUM
       VALUE  FREQ PCT PCT    VALUE  FREQ PCT PCT    VALUE  FREQ PCT PCT
          12     5   1   1       33    10   2  34       52     1   0  87
          14     2   0   2       34    14   3  37       54     2   0  88
          16     9   2   3       35     3   1  38       55     2   0  88
          17     8   2   5       36    30   7  44       56     7   2  90
          18     7   2   7       37     6   1  45       57    12   3  92
          19     4   1   8       38     4   1  46       58     1   0  93
          20    13   3  10       39     9   2  48       60     8   2  94
          21     1   0  11       40    12   3  51       61     2   0  95
          22     9   2  13       41    15   3  54       62     5   1  96
          23     4   1  13       42     9   2  56       63     4   1  97
          24     1   0  14       43     3   1  57       67     2   0  97
          25    17   4  17       44     4   1  57       68     1   0  97
          26    14   3  20       45    19   4  62       69     2   0  98
          27     5   1  21       46    33   7  69       71     1   0  98
          28     5   1  23       47    14   3  72       72     2   0  98
          29    15   3  26       48    18   4  76       76     4   1  99
          30     2   0  26       49     4   1  77       78     3   1 100
          31     5   1  27       50    39   8  85
          32    20   4  32       51    10   2  87


                          M I S S I N G   D A T A
       VALUE  FREQ             VALUE  FREQ             VALUE  FREQ
          .      39

    VALID CASES     461     MISSING CASES     39
```

29.7
The Order of Values

By default, frequency tables are printed in ascending order of values. You can override this order with one of three sorting options on the FORMAT subcommand. These three cannot be used with the HISTOGRAM option.

AFREQ   *Sort categories in ascending order of frequency.*
DFREQ   *Sort categories in descending order of frequency.*
DVALUE   *Sort categories in descending order of values.*

If you specify more than one sorting option, FREQUENCIES uses the last one specified.

29.8
Suppressing Tables

You might be using FREQUENCIES to obtain univariate statistics not available in other procedures, or to print histograms or bar charts, and thus may not be interested in the frequency tables themselves. Or you might want to suppress tables for variables with a large number of values. Two options are available for suppressing tables.

LIMIT(n)   *Do not print tables with more categories than the specified value.*
NOTABLE   *Suppress all frequency tables.*

If you specify both NOTABLE and LIMIT, NOTABLE overrides LIMIT and no tables are printed. FREQUENCIES displays the number of missing and valid cases for the variable when the table is suppressed.

29.9
Index of Tables

To obtain both a positional index of frequency tables and an index arranged alphabetically by variable name, use the INDEX keyword on the FORMAT subcommand.

INDEX   *Index of tables.*

29.10
Writing Tables to a File

Use the WRITE keyword on the FORMAT subcommand to write the FRE-QUENCIES display to a separate output file. When you write the display to a separate file, you must use a PROCEDURE OUTPUT command before the FREQUENCIES command to specify the name of the output file. The OUTFILE subcommand on PROCEDURE OUTPUT names the file, as shown in the example below. When you use WRITE, no tables, statistics, histograms, or bar charts are printed.

This is a useful option for producing a machine-readable codebook. For example,

```
PROCEDURE OUTPUT  OUTFILE=CODEBOOK
FREQUENCIES  VARIABLES=ALL/
  FORMAT=ONEPAGE WRITE/
```

writes a relatively compact codebook to the file referenced by CODEBOOK.

WRITE   *Direct display to another file.*

29.11
Bar Charts and Histograms

Bar charts and histograms are graphic representations of frequency distributions. Figure 29.11a is an example of a bar chart, and Figure 29.11b is an example of a histogram for the same variable.

Figure 29.11a   A barchart produced by FREQUENCIES

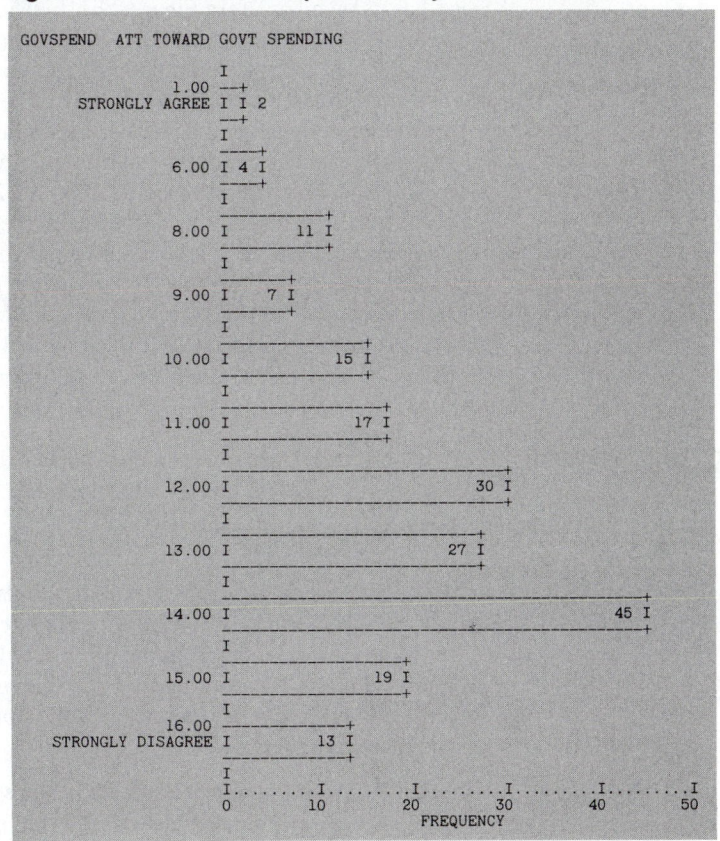

Figure 29.11b   A histogram produced by FREQUENCIES

```
GOVSPEND   ATT TOWARD GOVT SPENDING

    COUNT       VALUE    ONE SYMBOL EQUALS APPROXIMATELY  1.00 OCCURRENCE
        2        1.00    **
        0        2.00
        0        3.00
        0        4.00
        0        5.00
        4        6.00    ****
        0        7.00
       11        8.00    ***********
        7        9.00    *******
       15       10.00    ***************
       17       11.00    *****************
       30       12.00    ******************************
       27       13.00    ***************************
       45       14.00    *********************************************
       19       15.00    *******************
       13       16.00    *************
                         I.........I.........I.........I.........I.........I
                         0        10        20        30        40        50
                                         HISTOGRAM FREQUENCY

VALID CASES      190       MISSING CASES       0
```

Each bar in a bar chart corresponds to a value, and the length of the bar is determined by the number of cases having the value. Each bar is labeled with the value and value label, if a label has been defined. Bars are not displayed for empty categories. In Figure 29.11a, GOVSPEND has no cases with values 2 through 5 and 7. Therefore, the bar for value 1 is next to the bar for value 6. Compare this to the histogram in Figure 29.11b. Since the vertical axis has a scale on the histogram, the missing categories are quite apparent.

A histogram is useful for examining the distribution of a variable with many values. Values are tabulated into intervals of equal width, depending upon the range of values and the number of intervals defined. Each row of asterisks represents the number of cases with values in the interval. If the range of values fits within the default of 21 intervals, the collection process is not used and each value has its own bar, as in Figure 29.11b. The histogram in Figure 29.13 displays a variable with value range of 12 to 78 collapsed into 21 intervals. In a histogram, the vertical axis has a scale, and empty categories within the range implied by the minimum and maximum are identified by the absence of rows of asterisks.

You can request bar charts or histograms on FREQUENCIES. Use the BARCHART subcommand to produce bar charts for all variables named on the VARIABLES subcommand (see Section 29.12) and the HISTOGRAM subcommand to produce histograms for all variables (see Section 29.13). Or use the HBAR subcommand to produce bar charts for variables that fit on one page (11 individual categories for the default page length) and histograms for other variables (see Section 29.14). You can specify only one of these three subcommands on each FREQUENCIES command. If you specify more than one, FREQUENCIES assumes HBAR.

29.12
BARCHART Subcommand

The BARCHART subcommand produces bar charts. No specifications are required for the BARCHART subcommand, as in

```
FREQUENCIES   VARIABLES=POLVIEWS/
              BARCHART/
```

In the default bar chart format, all tabulated values are plotted, and the horizontal axis is scaled in frequencies. The scale is determined by the frequency count of the largest single category plotted. You can specify minimum and maximum bounds for plotting and can request a horizontal scale labeled with percentages or frequency counts via the following optional specifications on subcommand BARCHART:

MIN(n)   *Lower bound.* Values below the specified minimum are not plotted.

MAX(n)   *Upper bound.* Values above the specified maximum are not plotted.

PERCENT(n)   *Horizontal axis scaled in percentages.* The *n* specifies the preferred maximum and is not required. If you do not specify an *n* or your *n* is too small, FREQUENCIES chooses 5, 10, 25, 50 or 100, depending on the percentage for the largest category.

FREQ(n)   *Horizontal axis scaled in frequencies.* While FREQ is the default scaling method, you can use this specification if you want to specify a maximum frequency *(n)* for the scale. If you do not specify an *n* or your *n* is too small, FREQUENCIES chooses 10, 20, 50, 100, 200, 500, 1000, 2000, and so forth, depending on the frequency count for the largest category.

You can enter optional specifications in any order, as in

```
FREQUENCIES   VARIABLES=SIBS/
              BARCHART=PERCENT MAX(10)
```

which requests a bar chart on SIBS with values through 10 plotted and the horizontal axis scaled in percentages.

29.13
HISTOGRAM Subcommand

The HISTOGRAM subcommand produces histograms. No specifications are required for the HISTOGRAM subcommand, as in

```
FREQUENCIES   VARIABLES=PRESTIGE/
              HISTOGRAM/
```

In the default histogram format, all tabulated values are included, and the horizontal axis is scaled by frequencies. The scale is determined by the frequency count of the largest category plotted. The number of intervals plotted is 21 (or fewer if the range of values is less than 21).

Figure 29.13 shows the histogram produced by the previous specification. Since the variable PRESTIGE ranges from 12 to 78, values are collapsed into the 21 bars. The midpoint of each interval is printed.

Figure 29.13   A default histogram with collapsed values

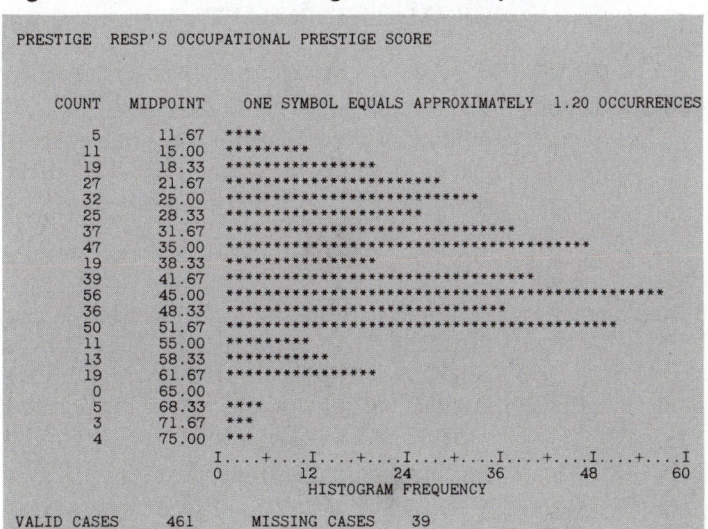

You can use all of the formatting options available with BARCHART on the HISTOGRAM subcommand. In addition, you can specify the interval width and superimpose a normal curve on the histogram. The following specifications are optional on subcommand HISTOGRAM:

MIN(n)   *Lower bound.* Values below the specified minimum are not plotted.
MAX(n)   *Upper bound.* Values above the specified maximum are not plotted.
PERCENT(n)   *Horizontal axis scaled in percentages.* The *n* specifies the preferred maximum and is not required. If you do not specify an *n* or your *n* is too small, FREQUENCIES chooses 5, 10, 25, 50 or 100, depending on the percentage for the largest category.

FREQ(n) *Horizontal axis scaled in frequencies.* While FREQ is the default scaling method, you can use this specification if you want to specify a maximum frequency *(n)* for the scale. If you do not specify an *n* or your *n* is too small, FREQUENCIES chooses 10, 20, 50, 100, 200, 500, 1000, 2000, and so forth, depending on the frequency count for the largest category.

INCREMENT(n) *Interval width.* By default, values are collected into 21 intervals for plotting. You can override the default by specifying the actual interval width. For example, if a variable ranges from 1 to 100 and you specify INCREMENT(2), the width of each interval will be 2, which will produce 50 intervals. If the variable has a range less than 21, a common divisor producing integer multiples of a common difference is used to produce a "nice" interval width.

NORMAL *Superimpose the normal curve.* The normal curve is based on all valid values for the variable and includes values excluded by MIN and MAX. The default is NONORMAL.

You can enter the optional specifications in any order, as in

```
FREQUENCIES  VARIABLES=PRESTIGE/
        HISTOGRAM=NORMAL INCREMENT(4)
```

which produces a histogram of PRESTIGE with a superimposed normal curve and an interval width of four.

29.14
HBAR Subcommand

The HBAR subcommand produces either bar charts or histograms depending upon the number of values encountered in the data. If a bar chart for a variable fits on a page, HBAR produces a bar chart; otherwise, it produces a histogram. For the default page length of 59, a barchart will be displayed for variables with fewer than 12 categories. Histograms will be displayed for all other variables specified on the VARIABLES subcommand. You can use the SET command to change the page length (see Chapter 4). All of the specifications for HISTOGRAM and BARCHART will also work with HBAR.

29.15
Percentiles and Ntiles

You can use either the PERCENTILES or NTILES subcommands to specify the printing of percentiles for all variables specified on the VARIABLES subcommand. If more than one PERCENTILES and NTILES subcommands are specified, FREQUENCIES prints one table with the variable values for all requested percentiles.

29.16
PERCENTILES Subcommand

Percentiles are the values below which a given percentage of cases fall. Use the PERCENTILES subcommand followed by an optional equals sign and a list of percentiles between 0 and 100 to print the variable values for each percentile. For example, to request the values for percentiles 10, 25, 33.3, 66.7, and 75 for variable PRESTIGE, specify:

```
FREQUENCIES VARIABLES=PRESTIGE/
        PERCENTILES=10 25 33.3 66.7 75/
```

The five values of PRESTIGE associated with these percentiles are shown in Figure 29.16.

Figure 29.16   PERCENTILES subcommand output

PERCENTILE	VALUE	PERCENTILE	VALUE	PERCENTILE	VALUE
10.00	20.000	25.00	29.000	33.30	33.000
66.70	46.000	75.00	48.000		
VALID CASES	461	MISSING CASES	39		

29.17
NTILES Subcommand

*N*tiles are the variable values that divide the sample into groups of equal numbers of cases. To print the variable values for each *n*tile, use the NTILES subcommand followed by an optional equals sign and one integer value specifying the number of subgroups. For example, to request quartiles for PRESTIGE, specify:

```
FREQUENCIES VARIABLES=PRESTIGE/NTILES=4/
```

Figure 29.17 shows the printed output from the NTILES subcommand. Note that SPSS-X prints one less percentile than the number specified on the NTILES subcommand. If a requested percentile cannot be calculated, SPSS-X prints a period (.) as the value associated with that percentile.

Figure 29.17   NTILES subcommand output

PERCENTILE	VALUE	PERCENTILE	VALUE	PERCENTILE	VALUE
25.00	29.000	50.00	40.000	75.00	48.000
VALID CASES	461	MISSING CASES	39		

29.18
STATISTICS Subcommand

The STATISTICS subcommand specifies univariate statistics for all variables named on the VARIABLES subcommand. If you are using the integer mode, only cases with values in the specified range are used in the computation of statistics. The available statistics and their keywords are

MEAN	*Mean.*
SEMEAN	*Standard error of the mean.*
MEDIAN	*Median.* The median is defined as the value below which half the cases fall. If there are an even number of cases, the median is the average of the (nth/2) and (nth/2+1) cases when the cases are sorted in ascending order. The median is not available if you specify AFREQ or DFREQ on the FORMAT subcommand.
MODE	*Mode.*
STDDEV	*Standard deviation.*
VARIANCE	*Variance.*
SKEWNESS	*Skewness.*
SESKEW	*Standard error of the skewness statistic.*
KURTOSIS	*Kurtosis.*
SEKURT	*Standard error of the kurtosis statistic.*
RANGE	*Range.*
MINIMUM	*Minimum.*
MAXIMUM	*Maximum.*
SUM	*Sum.*
DEFAULT	*Mean, standard deviation, minimum, and maximum.* You can use DEFAULT jointly with other statistics.
ALL	*All available statistics.*
NONE	*No statistics.*

You can specify as many keywords as you wish on the STATISTICS subcommand. For example,

```
FREQUENCIES   VARIABLES=PRESTIGE POLVIEWS/
              STATISTICS=MEDIAN DEFAULT/
```

prints the median and the default statistics (the mean, standard deviation, minimum, and maximum). The annotated example shows the output produced by this STATISTICS subcommand. If you use the STATISTICS subcommand with no specifications, the default statistics are printed.

ANNOTATED EXAMPLE FOR FREQUENCIES

The following example demonstrates the use of FREQUENCIES to do some preliminary checks on a newly defined file. The file is based on employment data from Hubbard Consultants Inc. Variables include date employee was hired, employee's department, salary, job category, name, age, and sex, as well as salary increases from 1980 to 1982. The SPSS-X commands are

```
FILE TYPE  GROUPED FILE=HUBDATA RECORD=#RECID 80 CASE=ID 1-4

RECORD TYPE 1
DATA LIST    /MOHIRED YRHIRED 12-15 DEPT79 TO DEPT82 SEX 16-20

RECORD TYPE 2
DATA LIST    /SALARY79 TO SALARY82 6-25
                AGE 54-55 RAISE80 TO RAISE82 56-70

RECORD TYPE 3
DATA LIST    /JOBCAT 6 EMPNAME 25-48 (A)

END FILE TYPE

MISSING VALUES  DEPT79 TO SALARY82 AGE (0)
                RAISE80 TO RAISE82 (-999) JOBCAT (9)

VARIABLE LABELS   SALARY79 'SALARY IN 1979'
                  SALARY80 'SALARY IN 1980'
                  SALARY81 'SALARY IN 1981'
                  SALARY82 'SALARY IN 1982'
                  JOBCAT 'JOB CATEGORIES'
VALUE LABELS   SEX 1 'MALE' 2 'FEMALE'/
               JOBCAT 1 'OFFICIALS & MANAGERS' 2 'PROFESSIONALS'
               3 'TECHNICIANS' 4 'OFFICE & CLERICAL' 5 'CRAFTSMEN'
               6 'SERVICE WORKERS'

FREQUENCIES  VARIABLES=SALARY79 TO SALARY82 SEX AGE JOBCAT/
             FORMAT=LIMIT(10)/
             STATISTICS=DEFAULT MEDIAN
FINISH
```

- Since there are three records per case, FILE TYPE GROUPED is used to check for duplicate or missing records (see Chapter 12).
- MISSING VALUES, VARIABLE LABELS, and VALUE LABELS complete the file definition (see Chapter 5).
- FREQUENCIES displays frequency tables for variables having 10 or fewer categories and statistics for all the variables named. The default statistics are the mean, standard deviation, minimum, and maximum.

The FREQUENCIES display produced by this job is on the facing page.

FREQUENCIES display

```
SALARY79  SALARY IN 1979


MEAN      12247.323    MEDIAN     10140.000    STD DEV     6665.182
MINIMUM    6337.000    MAXIMUM    45500.000


VALID CASES    158    MISSING CASES   117

- - - - - - - - - - - - - - - - - - - - - - - - - - - - - - - - - - -

SALARY80  SALARY IN 1980


MEAN      12123.725    MEDIAN     10400.000    STD DEV     6316.356
MINIMUM    5720.000    MAXIMUM    48100.000


VALID CASES    273    MISSING CASES     2

- - - - - - - - - - - - - - - - - - - - - - - - - - - - - - - - - - -

SALARY81  SALARY IN 1981


MEAN      15096.212    MEDIAN     12359.500    STD DEV     8074.387
MINIMUM    7605.000    MAXIMUM    52000.000


VALID CASES    160    MISSING CASES   115

- - - - - - - - - - - - - - - - - - - - - - - - - - - - - - - - - - -

SALARY82  SALARY IN 1982


MEAN      17161.552    MEDIAN     15132.000    STD DEV     8695.734
MINIMUM    5830.000    MAXIMUM    50700.000


VALID CASES    145    MISSING CASES   130

- - - - - - - - - - - - - - - - - - - - - - - - - - - - - - - - - - -

SEX


                                                VALID     CUM
     VALUE LABEL          VALUE  FREQUENCY  PERCENT  PERCENT  PERCENT

MALE                         1       83      30.2     30.2     30.2
FEMALE                       2      192      69.8     69.8    100.0
                                   -----    -----    -----
                          TOTAL     275     100.0    100.0

MEAN       1.698    MEDIAN      2.000    STD DEV      .460
MINIMUM    1.000    MAXIMUM     2.000


VALID CASES    275    MISSING CASES     0

- - - - - - - - - - - - - - - - - - - - - - - - - - - - - - - - - - -

AGE


MEAN      37.158    MEDIAN     34.000    STD DEV    11.335
MINIMUM   20.000    MAXIMUM    69.000


VALID CASES    272    MISSING CASES     3

- - - - - - - - - - - - - - - - - - - - - - - - - - - - - - - - - - -

JOBCAT   JOB CATEGORIES


                                                VALID     CUM
     VALUE LABEL          VALUE  FREQUENCY  PERCENT  PERCENT  PERCENT

OFFICIALS & MANAGERS         1       48      17.5     17.5     17.5
PROFESSIONALS                2       62      22.5     22.5     40.0
TECHNICIANS                  3       98      35.6     35.6     75.6
OFFICE & CLERICAL            4       67      24.4     24.4    100.0
                                   -----    -----    -----
                          TOTAL     275     100.0    100.0

MEAN       2.669    MEDIAN      3.000    STD DEV     1.030
MINIMUM    1.000    MAXIMUM     4.000


VALID CASES    275    MISSING CASES     0
```

29.19
MISSING Subcommand

FREQUENCIES recognizes three types of missing values: user-missing, system-missing, and in integer mode, out-of-range values. Both user- and system-missing values are included in frequency tables. They are labeled as missing and are not included in the valid and cumulative percentages. Missing values are not used in the calculation of descriptive statistics, nor do they appear in bar charts and histograms.

One optional missing-value treatment is available. To include user-missing values as valid values, use the MISSING subcommand, which has one specification, INCLUDE. For example,

```
MISSING VALUES   SATFAM TO HAPPY(8,9)
FREQUENCIES   VARIABLES=SATFAM HAPPY (0,9)/
          BARCHART/
          MISSING=INCLUDE
```

includes values 8 and 9 (which were previously defined as missing with the MISSING VALUES command) in the bar charts.

29.20
LIMITATIONS

The following limitations apply to FREQUENCIES:

• A maximum of 500 variables total per FREQUENCIES command.
• A maximum value range of 32,767 for a variable in integer mode.
• A maximum of 32,767 observed values over all variables.

Syntax

HILOGLINEAR

```
HILOGLINEAR varlist (min,max) [varlist (min,max)...]
 [/MISSING = {LISTWISE}] [INCLUDE]
              {DEFAULT }
 [/CWEIGHT = {varname }]
             {(matrix)}
 [/PRINT = [DEFAULT]  [ASSOCIATION]
           [FREQ]     [RESID]
           [ESTIM]    [ALL]
           [NONE]]
 [/PLOT = [DEFAULT]  [RESID]
          [NORMPROB] [NONE ]]
 [/CRITERIA = [CONVERGE({0.25})] [ITERATE({20})] [P({0.05})]
                       {n   }            {n }      {prob}
                 [DELTA({0.5})] [MAXSTEPS({10})] [DEFAULT]]
                       {d  }             {n }
 [/METHOD [= BACKWARD]]
 [/MAXORDER = k]
 [/DESIGN = effectname effectname*effectname ...]
 [/DESIGN = ... ]
```

Contents

30.1 OVERVIEW

30.2 OPERATION

30.3 Variable Specification

30.4 DESIGN Subcommand

30.5 CWEIGHT Subcommand

30.6 METHOD Subcommand

30.7 MAXORDER Subcommand

30.8 PRINT Subcommand

30.9 PLOT Subcommand

30.10 CRITERIA Subcommand

30.11 MISSING Subcommand

30.12 LIMITATIONS

30

Chapter 30 HILOGLINEAR

The HILOGLINEAR procedure estimates parameters of hierarchical log-linear models for frequency tables. It can also perform automatic backward elimination of terms from such models. HILOGLINEAR is much more efficient for these models than the LOGLINEAR procedure (see Chapter 32) because HILOGLINEAR uses an iterative proportional fitting algorithm.

30.1 OVERVIEW

You have several options for controlling the hierarchical loglinear model, the output, and the operation of the procedure.

Specifying the Model. The DESIGN subcommand specifies a generating class for terms in the model. You can specify more than one DESIGN on a single HILOGLINEAR command. (See Section 30.4.)

Cell Weights. The CWEIGHT subcommand specifies cell weights for the model. It allows you to impose structural zeros on cells that are logically empty. You can also use CWEIGHT to adjust tables to fit new margins. (See Section 30.5.)

Variable Selection Methods. By default, HILOGLINEAR tests the model specified on the DESIGN subcommand and then stops. However, you can specify backward elimination of terms in the model by using the METHOD subcommand. (See Section 30.6.)

Models without Higher-Order Interactions. The MAXORDER subcommand specifies the maximum order of interaction terms in the model. (See Section 30.7.)

Printed Output. HILOGLINEAR prints Pearson and likelihood ratio chi-square goodness-of-fit tests for models. For saturated models, it also provides tests that the k-way effects and the k-way and higher-order effects are zero.

Optional Printed Output. The PRINT subcommand requests statistics and displays that are not produced by default or suppresses unwanted default output. You can request or suppress frequencies and residuals for all cells in a table. For saturated models, you can obtain parameter estimates and measures of partial association. (See Section 30.8.)

Optional Plots. The PLOT subcommand specifies optional plots of residual cell values. (See Section 30.9.)

Criteria for Algorithms. The CRITERIA subcommand specifies values of constants in the iterative proportional fitting and model selection algorithms. (See Section 30.10.)

Missing Values. Use the MISSING subcommand to include cases with user-missing values for variables in the analysis. The default treatment is listwise deletion. (See Section 30.11.)

30.2
OPERATION

You need only a HILOGLINEAR variable specification to run the procedure. (See Sect 30.3.) This specification identifies the variables used by the model. You can also specify any of eight optional subcommands. (See Sections 30.4 through 30.11.) HILOGLINEAR estimates one model for each DESIGN subcommand. Subcommands affecting a given DESIGN subcommand must appear before DESIGN. Otherwise, subcommands can appear in any order. Each subcommand remains in effect until it is explicitly changed.

30.3
Variable Specification

You need to identify the categorical variables used in the model or models you fit. These categorical variables must be numeric and integer. Specify a range in parentheses indicating the minimum and maximum values for each variable. For example,

```
HILOGLINEAR DPREF(2,3) RACE(1,2)
```

builds a 2×2 frequency table for analysis. HILOGLINEAR excludes cases with values for any variable outside the specified ranges. HILOGLINEAR assumes there is a category for every value in the range. Thus, the specification

```
HILOGLINEAR A(1,5) B(8,12)
 /DESIGN
```

means that variable A has values 1, 2, 3, 4, and 5, and variable B has values 8, 9, 10, 11, and 12. Empty categories waste space and can cause computational problems. If variable A has only values of 1 and 5, you can specify

```
TEMPORARY
RECODE A (5=2)
HILOGLINEAR A(1,2) B(8,12)
 /DESIGN
```

The TEMPORARY command restricts the recoding of A values to the HILOGLINEAR procedure.

30.4
DESIGN Subcommand

In a hierarchical model, higher-order interaction terms imply all the lower-order interaction and main effect terms for the same variables. An A by B interaction (A*B) implies main effects for A and B. An A by B by C interaction (A*B*C) implies the two-way interactions A by B, A by C, and B by C plus the main effects A, B, and C. The highest-order terms are the *generating class* for terms in the model.

The DESIGN subcommand specifies the generating class. For example, the subcommand

```
DESIGN = A*B*C D /
```

specifies a hierarchical model with the generating class A*B*C and D. The model with this generating class consists of the effects A, B, C, D, A by B, A by C, B by C and A by B by C.

To fit a saturated model (one with all possible effects), specify:

```
DESIGN /
```

You can use several DESIGN subcommands in a single HILOGLINEAR analysis. If you omit the DESIGN subcommand, SPSS-X issues a warning message and fits a saturated model.

30.5
CWEIGHT Subcommand

The CWEIGHT subcommand specifies cell weights for a model. Do not try to use CWEIGHT to weight aggregated input data (use the SPSS-X WEIGHT command instead). You can use CWEIGHT to impose structural zeros on a model. You can also use CWEIGHT to adjust tables to fit new margins. HILOGLINEAR ignores the CWEIGHT subcommand when you request a saturated model.

You can specify cell weights in two ways. First, you can specify a numeric variable whose values are the cell weights. The specification

```
HILOGLINEAR  AAA(1,2) BBB(1,2) CCC(1,3)
             /CWEIGHT CELLWGT
             /DESIGN
```

weights a cell by the value of the variable CELLWGT when a case for that cell is read. If there are multiple cases for a cell, HILOGLINEAR uses the average value of the CWEIGHT variable.

Alternatively, you can specify a matrix of weights enclosed in parentheses on the CWEIGHT subcommand. Enter cell weights in order so that the value of the last variable varies most rapidly. The specification

```
HILOGLINEAR  DDD(1,3) EEE(1,3)
             /CWEIGHT (0 1 1
                       1 0 1
                       1 1 0)
             /DESIGN
```

is equivalent to

```
HILOGLINEAR  DDD(1,3) EEE(1,3)
             /CWEIGHT (0 3*1 0 3*1 0)
             /DESIGN
```

Both specifications set the diagonal cells in the model to structural zeros.

30.6
METHOD Subcommand

The METHOD subcommand requests a search for the "best" model through backward elimination of terms from the specified model. You can use the subcommand alone or specify METHOD=BACKWARD. The METHOD subcommand affects only the following design. If you omit the METHOD subcommand, HILOGLINEAR tests the model requested on the DESIGN subcommand but does not perform any model selection. Figures 30.6a through 30.6c show output produced by a METHOD=BACKWARD specification.

Figure 30.6a   Display for backward elimination

```
Backward Elimination for DESIGN 1 with generating class

   WATSOFT*BRANDPRF*PREVUSE*TEMP

Likelihood ratio chi square =        .00000   DF = 0  P = 1.000

- - - - - - - - - - - - - - - - - - - - - - - - - - - - - - - - - - -


If Deleted Simple Effect is                 DF   L.R. Chisq Change   Prob   Iter

   WATSOFT*BRANDPRF*PREVUSE*TEMP             2                .738   .6915     3

Step 1

   The best model has generating class

        WATSOFT*BRANDPRF*PREVUSE
        WATSOFT*BRANDPRF*TEMP
        WATSOFT*PREVUSE*TEMP
        BRANDPRF*PREVUSE*TEMP

   Likelihood ratio chi square =        .73767   DF = 2  P =  .692

- - - - - - - - - - - - - - - - - - - - - - - - - - - - - - - - - - -


If Deleted Simple Effect is                 DF   L.R. Chisq Change   Prob   Iter

   WATSOFT*BRANDPRF*PREVUSE                  2              4.571   .1017     3
   WATSOFT*BRANDPRF*TEMP                     2               .162   .9223     3
   WATSOFT*PREVUSE*TEMP                      2              1.377   .5022     3
   BRANDPRF*PREVUSE*TEMP                     1              2.222   .1361     3

Step 2

   The best model has generating class

        WATSOFT*BRANDPRF*PREVUSE
        WATSOFT*PREVUSE*TEMP
        BRANDPRF*PREVUSE*TEMP

   Likelihood ratio chi square =        .89942   DF = 4  P =  .925

- - - - - - - - - - - - - - - - - - - - - - - - - - - - - - - - - - -


If Deleted Simple Effect is                 DF   L.R. Chisq Change   Prob   Iter

   WATSOFT*BRANDPRF*PREVUSE                  2              4.596   .1005     3
   WATSOFT*PREVUSE*TEMP                      2              1.351   .5088     3
   BRANDPRF*PREVUSE*TEMP                     1              2.215   .1367     3


(output for Steps 3 through 7)


Step 8

   The best model has generating class

        WATSOFT*TEMP
        BRANDPRF*TEMP
        BRANDPRF*PREVUSE

   Likelihood ratio chi square =     11.88633   DF = 14  P =  .615

- - - - - - - - - - - - - - - - - - - - - - - - - - - - - - - - - - -


If Deleted Simple Effect is                 DF   L.R. Chisq Change   Prob   Iter

   WATSOFT*TEMP                              2              6.098   .0474     2
   BRANDPRF*TEMP                             1              4.361   .0368     2
   BRANDPRF*PREVUSE                          1             20.578   .0000     2

Step 9

   The best model has generating class

        WATSOFT*TEMP
        BRANDPRF*TEMP
        BRANDPRF*PREVUSE

   Likelihood ratio chi square =     11.88633   DF = 14  P =  .615
```

Figure 30.6b   Generating class of selected model

```
The final model has generating class

     WATSOFT*TEMP
     BRANDPRF*TEMP
     BRANDPRF*PREVUSE

The Iterative Proportional Fit algorithm converged at iteration 0.
The maximum difference between observed and fitted marginal totals is      .000
and the convergence criterion is      .250
```

Figure 30.6c   Goodness-of-fit test for selected model

```
Goodness-of-fit test statistics

     Likelihood ratio chi square =     11.88633     DF = 14   P =   .615
                Pearson chi square =     11.91780     DF = 14   P =   .613
```

30.7
MAXORDER Subcommand

The MAXORDER subcommand specifies the maximum order of terms in the model. If you specify MAXORDER=k, HILOGLINEAR fits a model with all terms of order k or less. Thus, MAXORDER provides an abbreviated way of specifying models.

For five factors, for example, you may be interested in testing a model with only main effects and two-way interactions. The following two specifications for such a model are equivalent:

```
HILOGLINEAR  A B (1,2) C D E (1,3)
 /MAXORDER = 2

HILOGLINEAR  A B (1,2) C D E (1,3)
 /DESIGN = A*B A*C A*D A*E B*C B*D B*E C*D C*E D*E
```

HILOGLINEAR cannot obtain parameter estimates or measures of partial association when MAXORDER is less than the number of factors. It can give you only a goodness-of-fit test and the observed and expected frequencies for that model. You can use MAXORDER with backward elimination to find the best model with terms of a certain order or less. This is computationally much more efficient than eliminating terms from the saturated model.

30.8
PRINT Subcommand

HILOGLINEAR prints Pearson and likelihood ratio chi-square goodness-of-fit tests for models. For saturated models, it also provides tests that the k-way effects and the k-way and higher-order effects are zero.

Both adjusted and unadjusted degrees of freedom are printed for tables with sampling or structural zeros. K-way and higher tests use the unadjusted degrees of freedom.

The unadjusted degrees of freedom is not adjusted for zero cells, and estimates the upper bound of the true degrees of freedom. This is the same degrees of freedom you would get if all cells were filled.

The adjusted degrees of freedom is calculated from the number of non-zero fitted cells minus the number of parameters that would be estimated if all cells were filled (i.e., unadjusted degrees of freedom minus the number of zero fitted cells). This estimate of degrees of freedom may be too low if some parameters do not exist because of zeros.

The PRINT subcommand requests the statistics and the displays not produced by default or suppresses unwanted default output. If you specify PRINT, HILOGLINEAR produces only requested output. You can use the following keywords on the PRINT subcommand:

DEFAULT   *Default displays*. This option includes FREQ and RESID output for nonsaturated models (see Figure 30.8a), and FREQ, RESID, and ESTIM output for saturated models. For saturated models, the observed and expected frequencies are equal, and the residuals are zeros.

FREQ   *Observed and expected cell frequencies.*

RESID   *Raw and standardized residuals.*

ESTIM   *Parameter estimates for a saturated model.* See Figure 30.8b.

ASSOCIATION *Partial associations*. You can request partial associations of effects only when you specify a saturated model. This option is computationally expensive for tables with many factors. (See Figure 30.8c.)

ALL   *All available output.*

NONE   *Design information and goodness-of-fit statistics only.* Use of this option overrides all other specifications on the PRINT subcommand.

Figure 30.8a   Observed and expected frequencies for a selected model

```
Observed, Expected Frequencies and Residuals.

          Factor          Code          OBS count   EXP count   Residual   Std Resid

       WATSOFT         Soft
        BRANDPRF        Brand X
         PREVUSE         Yes
          TEMP            High            19.0        19.5        -.52        -.12
          TEMP            Low             57.0        47.8        9.15        1.32
         PREVUSE         No
          TEMP            High            29.0        28.4         .61         .11
          TEMP            Low             63.0        69.6       -6.58        -.79
        BRANDPRF        Brand M
         PREVUSE         Yes
          TEMP            High            29.0        30.8       -1.85        -.33
          TEMP            Low             49.0        57.5       -8.52       -1.12
         PREVUSE         No
          TEMP            High            27.0        25.2        1.76         .35
          TEMP            Low             53.0        47.1        5.94         .87

       WATSOFT         Medium
        BRANDPRF        Brand X
         PREVUSE         Yes
          TEMP            High            23.0        23.7        -.65        -.13
          TEMP            Low             47.0        47.0         .01         .00
         PREVUSE         No
          TEMP            High            33.0        34.4       -1.40        -.24
          TEMP            Low             66.0        68.3       -2.32        -.28
        BRANDPRF        Brand M
         PREVUSE         Yes
          TEMP            High            47.0        37.4        9.63        1.57
          TEMP            Low             55.0        56.5       -1.48        -.20
         PREVUSE         No
          TEMP            High            23.0        30.6       -7.58       -1.37
          TEMP            Low             50.0        46.2        3.79         .56

       WATSOFT         Hard
        BRANDPRF        Brand X
         PREVUSE         Yes
          TEMP            High            24.0        26.1       -2.09        -.41
          TEMP            Low             37.0        42.9       -5.89        -.90
         PREVUSE         No
          TEMP            High            42.0        37.9        4.06         .66
          TEMP            Low             68.0        62.4        5.63         .71
        BRANDPRF        Brand M
         PREVUSE         Yes
          TEMP            High            43.0        41.2        1.77         .28
          TEMP            Low             52.0        51.6         .44         .06
         PREVUSE         No
          TEMP            High            30.0        33.7       -3.73        -.64
          TEMP            Low             42.0        42.2        -.18        -.03
```

Figure 30.8b   Parameter estimates for a saturated model

```
Estimates for Parameters.

WATSOFT*BRANDPRF*PREVUSE*TEMP

Parameter      Coeff.      Std. Err.      Z-Value Lower 95 CI Upper 95 CI

     1    -.0086293293      .04833        -.17856    -.10335       .08609
     2    -.0296475092      .04734        -.62629    -.12243       .06313

WATSOFT*BRANDPRF*PREVUSE

Parameter      Coeff.      Std. Err.      Z-Value Lower 95 CI Upper 95 CI

     1     .0925171313      .04833        1.91437    -.00221       .18724
     2    -.0318024179      .04734        -.67182    -.12458       .06098

WATSOFT*BRANDPRF*TEMP

Parameter      Coeff.      Std. Err.      Z-Value Lower 95 CI Upper 95 CI

     1    -.0203612840      .04833        -.42132    -.11508       .07436
     2     .0048119005      .04734         .10165    -.08797       .09759

WATSOFT*PREVUSE*TEMP

Parameter      Coeff.      Std. Err.      Z-Value Lower 95 CI Upper 95 CI

     1    -.0474552194      .04833        -.98194    -.14218       .04727
     2     .0488797573      .04734        1.03257    -.04390       .14166

BRANDPRF*PREVUSE*TEMP

Parameter      Coeff.      Std. Err.      Z-Value Lower 95 CI Upper 95 CI

     1    -.0504586672      .03363       -1.50056    -.11637       .01545

WATSOFT*BRANDPRF

Parameter      Coeff.      Std. Err.      Z-Value Lower 95 CI Upper 95 CI

     1     .0118211436      .04833         .24460    -.08290       .10654
     2    -.0139125793      .04734        -.29390    -.10670       .07887

WATSOFT*PREVUSE

Parameter      Coeff.      Std. Err.      Z-Value Lower 95 CI Upper 95 CI

     1    -.0239466773      .04833        -.49551    -.11867       .07078
     2     .0559778278      .04734        1.18251    -.03680       .14876

BRANDPRF*PREVUSE

Parameter      Coeff.      Std. Err.      Z-Value Lower 95 CI Upper 95 CI

     1    -.1570080885      .03363       -4.66916    -.22292      -.09110

WATSOFT*TEMP

Parameter      Coeff.      Std. Err.      Z-Value Lower 95 CI Upper 95 CI

     1    -.0985053522      .04833       -2.03827    -.19323      -.00378
     2    -.0070158821      .04734        -.14821    -.09980       .08577

BRANDPRF*TEMP

Parameter      Coeff.      Std. Err.      Z-Value Lower 95 CI Upper 95 CI

     1    -.0640726747      .03363       -1.90542    -.12998       .00184

PREVUSE*TEMP

Parameter      Coeff.      Std. Err.      Z-Value Lower 95 CI Upper 95 CI

     1     .0258498678      .03363         .76873    -.04006       .09176

WATSOFT

Parameter      Coeff.      Std. Err.      Z-Value Lower 95 CI Upper 95 CI

     1    -.0469971087      .04833        -.97246    -.14172       .04773
     2     .0222074436      .04734         .46913    -.07058       .11499

BRANDPRF

Parameter      Coeff.      Std. Err.      Z-Value Lower 95 CI Upper 95 CI

     1    -.0152366566      .03363        -.45311    -.08114       .05067

PREVUSE

Parameter      Coeff.      Std. Err.      Z-Value Lower 95 CI Upper 95 CI

     1    -.0422974428      .03363       -1.25786    -.10821       .02361

TEMP

Parameter      Coeff.      Std. Err.      Z-Value Lower 95 CI Upper 95 CI

     1    -.2856734854      .03363       -8.49546    -.35158      -.21977
```

Figure 30.8c Partial associations

```
Tests of PARTIAL associations.

Effect Name                                DF  Partial Chisq    Prob   Iter

WATSOFT*BRANDPRF*PREVUSE                     2          4.571   .1017     3
WATSOFT*BRANDPRF*TEMP                        2           .162   .9223     3
WATSOFT*PREVUSE*TEMP                         2          1.377   .5022     3
BRANDPRF*PREVUSE*TEMP                        1          2.222   .1360     3
WATSOFT*BRANDPRF                            2           .215   .8980     3
WATSOFT*PREVUSE                             2          1.004   .6053     3
BRANDPRF*PREVUSE                            1         19.891   .0000     3
WATSOFT*TEMP                                2          6.095   .0475     3
BRANDPRF*TEMP                               1          3.738   .0532     3
PREVUSE*TEMP                                1           .739   .3900     3
WATSOFT                                     2           .502   .7780     2
BRANDPRF                                    1           .064   .7996     2
PREVUSE                                     1          1.922   .1656     2
TEMP                                        1         73.211   .0000     2
```

30.9
PLOT Subcommand

HILOGLINEAR does not produce plots automatically. To obtain plots, specify the PLOT subcommand alone or with any of the following four keywords:

DEFAULT   *Default plots.* Same as RESID and NORMPLOT. These are the plots HILOGLINEAR produces when you specify the subcommand without any keyword specifications.

RESID   *Plots of standardized residuals against observed and expected counts.* (See Figure 30.9a.)

NORMPLOT   *Normal and detrended normal plots of the adjusted residuals.* (See Figure 30.9b.)

NONE   *No plots.* Use this specification to suppress plots requested on a previous PLOT subcommand.

Figure 30.9a Residuals plots

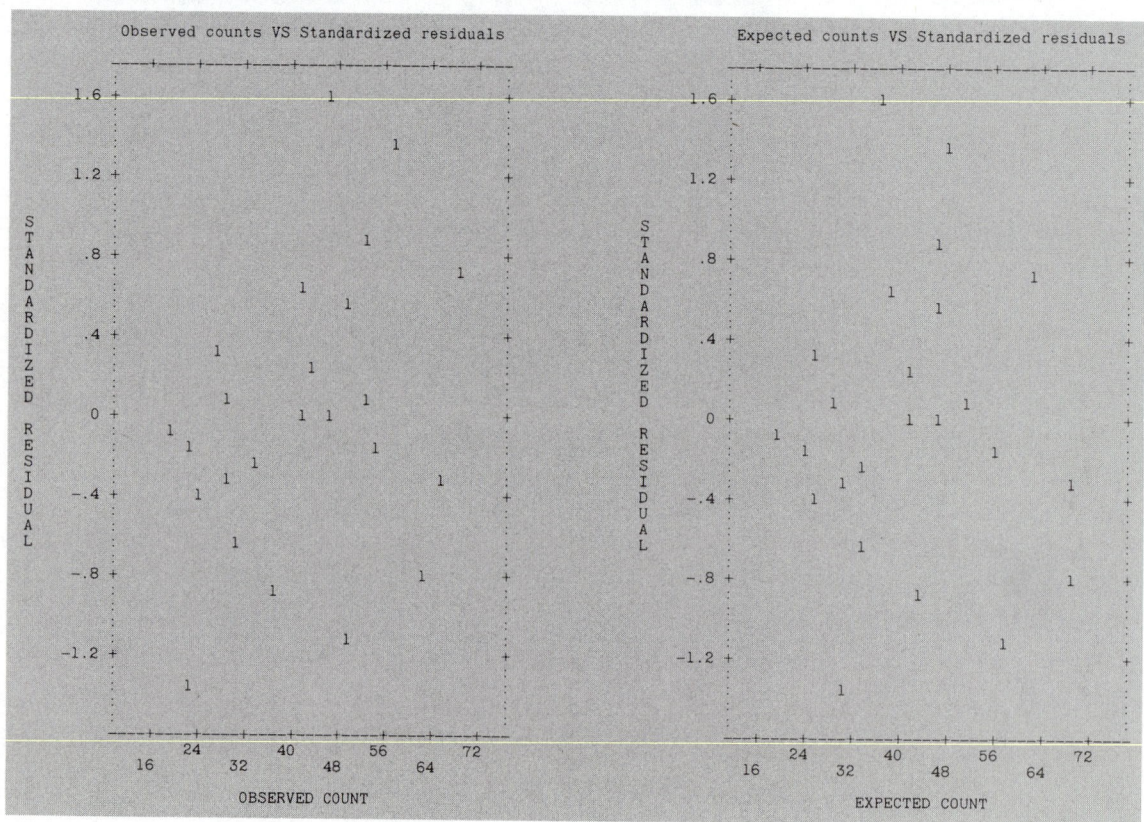

Figure 30.9b   Normal and detrended normal plots

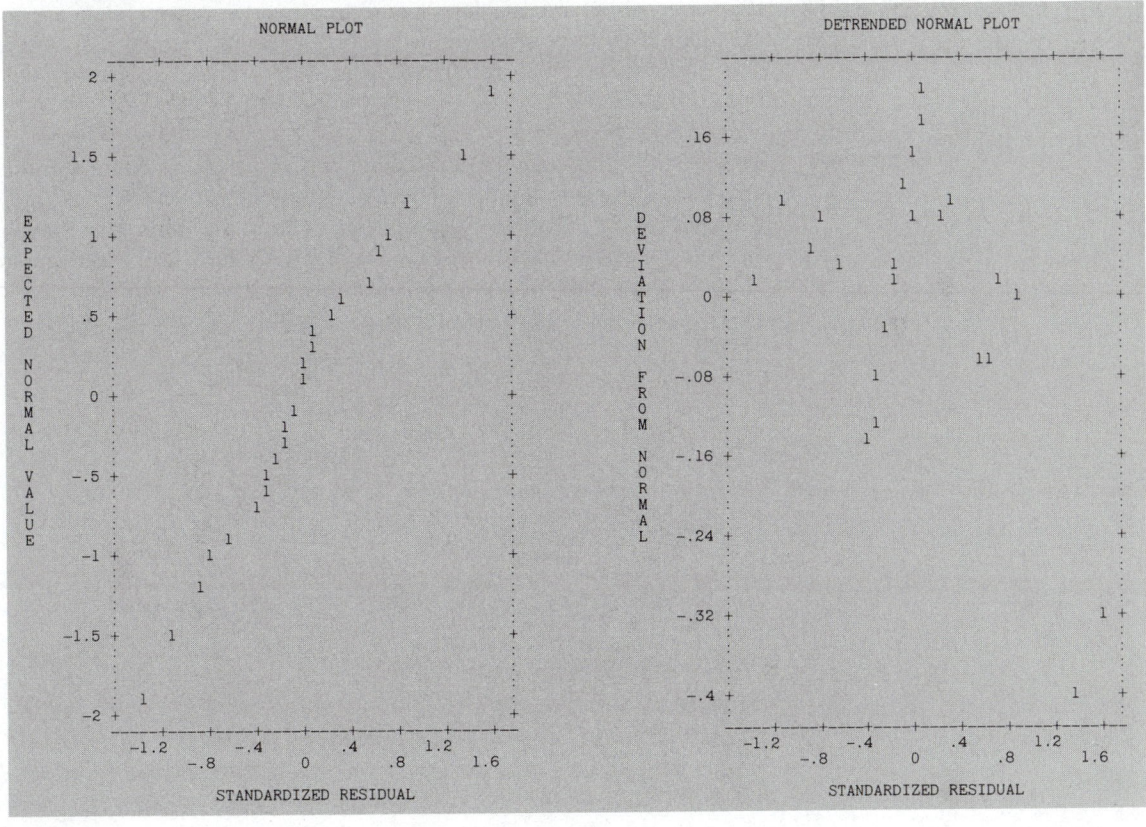

30.10
CRITERIA Subcommand

The CRITERIA subcommand specifies the values of constants in the iterative proportional fitting and model selection routines. You can use any of five keyword specifications with CRITERIA:

DEFAULT — *Reset parameters to their default values.* If you have specified criteria other than the defaults for a design, use this keyword to restore the defaults for a subsequent design.

CONVERGE(n) — *Convergence criterion.* The default is 10^{-3} * the largest cell size, or .25, whichever is larger.

ITERATE(n) — *Maximum number of iterations.* The default is 20.

P(n) — *Probability of chi-square for model.* Specify the significance level indicating an adequate fit of the model. The default is .05.

MAXSTEPS(n) — *Maximum number of steps for model selection.* The default is 10.

DELTA(d) — *Cell delta value.* The value of delta is added to each cell frequency for the first iteration. It is left in the cells for saturated models only. The default value is .5. You can specify any decimal value between 0 and 1 for d. HILOGLINEAR does not print parameter estimates or the covariance matrix of parameter estimates if any zero cells (either structural or sampling) exist in the expected table after DELTA is added.

ANNOTATED EXAMPLES FOR HILOGLINEAR

HILOGLINEAR can efficiently model a variety of complete and incomplete frequency table models. Many hierarchical models for real data are collected as examples in *Discrete Multivariate Analysis* (Bishop, Fienberg, & Holland, 1975). The following two examples from that book illustrate the use of HILOGLINEAR.

Example 1

This example illustrates a saturated model and backward elimination. In a market research study of laundry detergent preferences, consumers prefer either BRAND M or BRAND X detergent. The study considers three additional variables: water softness, previous use of BRAND M, and washing temperature. SPSS-X commands for analyzing the data are:

```
TITLE DETERGENT PREFERENCES (RIES & SMITH, 1963)
SET WIDTH = 80
DATA LIST FREE / WATSOFT BRANDPRF PREVUSE TEMP FREQ
VARIABLE LABELS WATSOFT   'Water Softness'
                BRANDPRF 'Brand Preference'
                PREVUSE  'Previous Use of Brand M'
                TEMP     'Water Temperature'
                FREQ     'Number in Condition'
VALUE LABELS WATSOFT 1 'Soft' 2 'Medium' 3 'Hard'
             /BRANDPRF 1 'Brand X' 2 'Brand M'
             /PREVUSE 1 'Yes' 2 'No'
             /TEMP 1 'High' 2 'Low'
WEIGHT BY FREQ
HILOGLINEAR WATSOFT (1,3) BRANDPRF PREVUSE TEMP (1,2)
            /PRINT = ALL
            /PLOT = DEFAULT
            /METHOD = BACKWARD
            /DESIGN
BEGIN DATA
1 1 1 1 19
1 1 1 2 57
...
3 2 2 1 30
3 2 2 2 42
END DATA
```

- The TITLE command assigns a title, and SET WIDTH limits the page width.
- The DATA LIST command defines five variables, and the VARIABLE LABELS and VALUE LABELS commands assign labels to the variables and values.
- The WEIGHT command weights the observations by FREQ, the variable containing the number of observations for each combination of values.
- HILOGLINEAR specifies four variables. The variable WATSOFT has three levels and each of the other three variables has two.
- The PRINT subcommand requests all available output: observed, expected, and residual values; parameter estimates; and measures of partial association for effects.
- The PLOT subcommand requests the default plots: the normal and detrended normal probability plots and the plots of residuals against observed and expected values.
- The METHOD subcommand requests a search of the "best" model through backward elimination of terms from the specified model.
- The DESIGN subcommand successively eliminates terms from the default saturated model.

The HILOGLINEAR output begins with case and model information (see Figure A). HILOGLINEAR then shows the results of the iterative proportional fitting algorithm (see Figure B). For saturated models, the procedure should converge on the first iteration. If a model fails to converge, HILOGLINEAR prints a message and the values for the parameters at that point.

A Default case and model information

```
DATA   Information

         24 unweighted cases accepted.
          0 cases rejected because of out-of-range factor values.
          0 cases rejected because of missing data.
       1008 weighted cases will be used in the analysis.


FACTOR Information

     Factor   Level   Label
     WATSOFT     3     Water Softness
     BRANDPRF    2     Brand Preference
     PREVUSE     2     Previous Use of Brand M
     TEMP        2     Water Temperature
```

B Results of iterative fit for DESIGN

```
DESIGN 1 has generating class

     WATSOFT*BRANDPRF*PREVUSE*TEMP

The Iterative Proportional Fit algorithm converged at iteration 1.

The maximum difference between observed and fitted marginal totals is      .000
and the convergence criterion is      .250
```

HILOGLINEAR also prints the observed and expected frequencies for the saturated model. Saturated models perfectly account for data in a frequency table. Therefore the observed and expected frequencies are the same, and the residuals are zeros.

Figures C through E show additional default output. Figure 30.8c shows the output produced by the ASSOCIATION keyword (implied by keyword ALL). Figure 30.8b shows the parameter estimates. Figures 30.6a, 30.6b, 30.8a, and 30.6c show the output produced by the METHOD=BACKWARD specification. Finally, Figures 30.9a and 30.9b show the output from the PLOT command.

C Goodness-of-fit test for saturated model

```
Goodness-of-fit test statistics

     Likelihood ratio chi square =      .00000    DF = 0   P = 1.000
               Pearson chi square =      .00000    DF = 0   P = 1.000
```

D Tests for order of saturated model

```
Tests that K-way and higher order effects are zero.

     K    DF    L.R. Chisq    Prob   Pearson Chisq    Prob   Iteration

     4     2         .738    .6916           .738    .6915      NA
     3     9        9.846    .3631          9.871    .3611      NA
     2    18       42.926    .0008         43.902    .0006      NA
     1    23      118.626    .0000        115.714    .0000       0
```

**Annotated Examples for
HILOGLINEAR** *continued*

E Tests for effects of each order

```
Tests that K-way effects are zero.

     K    DF   L.R. Chisq   Prob  Pearson Chisq   Prob   Iteration
     1     5      75.701   .0000        71.812   .0000       0
     2     9      33.079   .0001        34.032   .0001       0
     3     7       9.109   .2449         9.133   .2433       0
     4     2        .738   .6916          .738   .6915       0
```

Example 2
The second example relates two botanical measures of fruits from *Staphylea trifolia* (the American bladdernut). The two measures are locular composition (number of locules in the ovary and odd or even number of ovules) and radial symmetry (standard deviation of numbers of ovules in locules). Certain values of these measures cannot appear in combination, thus producing an incomplete frequency table. HILOGLINEAR tests the quasi-independence of the measures, that is, whether locular composition and radial symmetry are related apart from the mutual exclusivity of certain combinations.

```
TITLE FRUIT OF STAPHYLEA TRIFOLIA  (HARRIS, 1910)
SET WIDTH = 80
DATA LIST FREE / LOCULAR RADIAL FREQ
VARIABLE LABELS LOCULAR  'Locular Composition'
                RADIAL   'Coefficient Radial Asymmetry'
                FREQ     'Number in Condition'
VALUE LABELS LOCULAR 1 '3 Even' 2 '0 Even' 3 '2 Even' 4 '1 Even'
             /RADIAL 1 '0.00' 2 '0.94' 3 '1.63' 4 '1.89'
                     5 '0.47' 6 '0.82' 7 '1.25' 8 '1.41'
                     9 '1.70'
WEIGHT BY FREQ
HILOGLINEAR LOCULAR (1,4) RADIAL (1,9)
            /CWEIGHT = ( 4*1 5*0
                         4*1 5*0
                         4*0 5*1
                         4*0 5*1 )
            /DESIGN LOCULAR RADIAL
BEGIN DATA
1 1 462
1 2 130
...
4 8 8
4 9 5
END DATA
```

- DATA LIST and VARIABLE LABELS define and assign labels to three variables: a measure of locular composition, a measure of radial symmetry, and the number of nuts having that combination of values.

- The WEIGHT command weights the observations by FREQ, the variable containing the number of nuts with each combination of ratings.

- HILOGLINEAR specifies two variables: LOCULAR with four categories, and RADIAL with nine.

- The CWEIGHT subcommand identifies a pattern of cells that are logically empty.

- The DESIGN subcommand specifies main effects only for LOCULAR and RADIAL. Lack of fit for this model indicates an interaction of the two variables.

- Since there is no PRINT or PLOT subcommand, HILOGLINEAR produces default output for an unsaturated model.

Figures F and G show the display output for the quasi-independence model.

F Observed and expected frequencies for incomplete table

Observed, Expected Frequencies and Residuals.

Factor	Code	OBS. count & PCT.	EXP. count & PCT.	Residual	Std. Resid.
LOCULAR	3 Even				
RADIAL	0.00	462.00 (22.05)	458.00 (21.86)	3.996	.187
RADIAL	0.94	130.00 (6.21)	133.75 (6.38)	-3.753	-.325
RADIAL	1.63	2.00 (.10)	2.43 (.12)	-.432	-.277
RADIAL	1.89	1.00 (.05)	.81 (.04)	.189	.210
RADIAL	0.47	.00 (.00)	.00 (.00)	.000	.000
RADIAL	0.82	.00 (.00)	.00 (.00)	.000	.000
RADIAL	1.25	.00 (.00)	.00 (.00)	.000	.000
RADIAL	1.41	.00 (.00)	.00 (.00)	.000	.000
RADIAL	1.70	.00 (.00)	.00 (.00)	.000	.000
LOCULAR	0 Even				
RADIAL	0.00	103.00 (4.92)	107.00 (5.11)	-3.996	-.386
RADIAL	0.94	35.00 (1.67)	31.25 (1.49)	3.753	.671
RADIAL	1.63	1.00 (.05)	.57 (.03)	.432	.573
RADIAL	1.89	.00 (.00)	.19 (.01)	-.189	-.435
RADIAL	0.47	.00 (.00)	.00 (.00)	.000	.000
RADIAL	0.82	.00 (.00)	.00 (.00)	.000	.000
RADIAL	1.25	.00 (.00)	.00 (.00)	.000	.000
RADIAL	1.41	.00 (.00)	.00 (.00)	.000	.000
RADIAL	1.70	.00 (.00)	.00 (.00)	.000	.000
LOCULAR	2 Even				
RADIAL	0.00	.00 (.00)	.00 (.00)	.000	.000
RADIAL	0.94	.00 (.00)	.00 (.00)	.000	.000
RADIAL	1.63	.00 (.00)	.00 (.00)	.000	.000
RADIAL	1.89	.00 (.00)	.00 (.00)	.000	.000
RADIAL	0.47	614.00 (29.31)	611.99 (29.21)	2.012	.081
RADIAL	0.82	138.00 (6.59)	134.90 (6.44)	3.096	.267
RADIAL	1.25	21.00 (1.00)	24.90 (1.19)	-3.896	-.781
RADIAL	1.41	14.00 (.67)	12.74 (.61)	1.262	.354
RADIAL	1.70	1.00 (.05)	3.47 (.17)	-2.474	-1.327
LOCULAR	1 Even				
RADIAL	0.00	.00 (.00)	.00 (.00)	.000	.000
RADIAL	0.94	.00 (.00)	.00 (.00)	.000	.000
RADIAL	1.63	.00 (.00)	.00 (.00)	.000	.000
RADIAL	1.89	.00 (.00)	.00 (.00)	.000	.000
RADIAL	0.47	443.00 (21.15)	445.01 (21.24)	-2.012	-.095
RADIAL	0.82	95.00 (4.53)	98.10 (4.68)	-3.096	-.313
RADIAL	1.25	22.00 (1.05)	18.10 (.86)	3.896	.916
RADIAL	1.41	8.00 (.38)	9.26 (.44)	-1.262	-.415
RADIAL	1.70	5.00 (.24)	2.53 (.12)	2.474	1.557

G Goodness-of-fit test for quasi-independence

Goodness-of-fit test statistics

Likelihood ratio chi square =	7.74676	DF = 6	P =	.257
Pearson chi square =	7.49360	DF = 6	P =	.278

30.11
MISSING Subcommand

Use the MISSING subcommand to change the missing-value treatment or specify the default explicitly. The keywords are:

LISTWISE   *Delete cases with missing values listwise.* This is the default; you can make it explicit by specifying the keyword DEFAULT.

INCLUDE   *Include user-missing values as valid.*

30.12
LIMITATIONS

Procedure HILOGLINEAR cannot estimate all possible frequency models, and it produces limited output for unsaturated models.

- It can estimate only hierarchical log-linear models.
- It treats all table variables as nominal. (You can use LOGLINEAR to fit nonhierarchical models to tables involving variables that are ordinal.)
- It can produce parameter estimates only for saturated models (ones with all possible main effect and interaction terms).
- It can estimate partial associations only for saturated models.
- It can handle tables with no more than 10 factors.

Syntax

LIST

```
LIST [VARIABLES={ALL     }] [/FORMAT=[{WRAP  }] [{UNNUMBERED}]]
                {varlist}            {SINGLE}  {NUMBERED }
     [/CASES=[FROM {1}] [TO {eof}] [BY {1}]]
                   {n}      {n }  .    {n}
```

Contents

31.1   OVERVIEW

31.2   OPERATION

31.3   VARIABLES Subcommand

31.4   CASES Subcommand

31.5   FORMAT Subcommand

31.6   LIST and Case Selection

31

Chapter 31 LIST

The LIST procedure displays the values of variables for each case in the active file in a standard format, which includes column headers using variable names, horizontal spacing, left-justification of string values, and centering of numeric values, depending on the amount of room available. The LIST procedure can also display a subset of all variables or of all cases. Additionally, the format of the list may be altered.

31.1
OVERVIEW

Each execution of LIST begins at the top of a new page. If SPLIT FILE is in effect (see Chapter 15), each split also begins at the top of a new page.

LIST is a procedure that reads data as soon as they are encountered. In contrast, PRINT or WRITE are not procedures and execute data when they are read by another procedure (see Chapter 10).

Limiting the Cases Listed. Use the CASES subcommand to limit the number and pattern of cases listed. (See Section 31.4.)

Wrapping and Numbering. You can accommodate your entire variable list, and you can number the cases being listed with keywords on the FORMAT subcommand. (See Section 31.5.)

Selecting Cases. You can specify the cases you want listed with the SELECT IF command. (See Section 31.6.)

31.2
OPERATION

The minimum specification of the LIST command is the command keyword LIST. All subcommands are optional. When used, subcommands are followed by an optional equals sign (=) and subcommand specifications. Multiple subcommands must be separated with slashes.

The simplest LIST command is the command alone, as in

```
DATA LIST  FILE=HUBDATA RECORDS=3
  /1 MOHIRED YRHIRED 12-15 DEPT82 19
  /2 SALARY79 TO SALARY82 6-25
  /3 NAME 25-48 (A)

LIST
```

Values are printed on the display file when the LIST command is encountered. Listing includes by default every permanent and temporary numeric and string variable in the active file in dictionary order. By default, LIST uses the dictionary print formats assigned when the variables are defined on a DATA LIST, PRINT FORMATS, or FORMATS command, or the formats assigned when the variables are created with transformation commands. You can specify formats on the PRINT or WRITE commands, or you can change the dictionary formats. You must change the dictionary print format to affect LIST. The default LIST specifications are displayed in Figure 31.2.

Figure 31.2   LIST results using defaults

```
MOHIRED YRHIRED DEPT82 SALARY79 SALARY80 SALARY81 SALARY82 NAME

      8      69      3    11180    13000    14300    15600 CONNIE E. JANNSEN
      9      79      0        0     6337        0        0 ESTHER MARX
      3      80      4        0     8190     8840    10050 MARY CHAFEE
      2      74      1    13715    14495    16250    18850 HOLLY C. BRADSHAW
     10      78      3     6370     7410        0     8872 JACKIE HAMILTON
      9      74      0    20150    20800        0        0 RAY J. LUKE
     10      78      0     8450     9880        0        0 ANNETTE JONES
      1      79      0     6987     7410        0        0 EILEEN WOO
      7      79      2        0    10140    14300    16250 KARIN HEGEL
      9      79      0        0    19500        0        0 DOROTHY CAROLE OSBORNE
```

LIST may require more than one line to display each case within the 132-character page width or the width you have established using the SET command (see Chapter 4). (See Figure 31.5a for the wrapped format when the page width will not accommodate the entire variable list.) Values for each case are always displayed with a blank space between the variables. If a long string variable cannot be listed within the entire page width, it is truncated.

31.3
VARIABLES Subcommand

The default specification for the VARIABLES subcommand is keyword ALL. You can limit the listing to specific variables using the VARIABLES subcommand, as in

```
DATA LIST  FILE=HUBDATA RECORDS=3
  /1 EMPLOYID 1-5 MOHIRED YRHIRED 12-15 DEPT79 TO DEPT82 SEX 16-20
  /2 SALARY79 TO SALARY82 6-25 HOURLY81 HOURLY82 40-53(2) PROMO81 72
     AGE 54-55 RAISE82 66-70
  /3 JOBCAT 6 NAME 25-48 (A)
```

LIST **VARIABLES=MOHIRED YRHIRED DEPT82 NAME**

Variables named must already exist. Because LIST is a procedure, variables named cannot be scratch or system variables (see PRINT for an alternative). You can use the TO convention for naming consecutive variables, as in:

LIST VARIABLES=MOHIRED YRHIRED DEPT82 **SALARY79 TO SALARY82** NAME

If you specify more variables than can be printed in 132 columns, or within the width you specify using the WIDTH subcommand of SET (Chapter 4), the line will be wrapped according to the format shown in Figure 31.5a. If all the variables fit on a single line, SPSS-X prints a heading using the variable name and prints a single line per case as shown in Figure 31.2. When the variable name is longer than the print width, SPSS-X centers numeric variables in the column. When all variables fit on a line width, LIST first tries to reserve columns according to the length of the variable name or the print width, whichever requires more space. If this format becomes too wide, LIST then begins reducing column widths by printing variable names vertically.

In addition, if one of the data values cannot be printed in the allotted width, SPSS-X first attempts to print the value by removing punctuation characters, then it tries to use scientific notation, and then, if there is still not enough space, it prints asterisks.

31.4
CASES Subcommand

Use the CASES subcommand to limit the number and pattern of cases listed. Subcommand CASES must be followed by at least one of the keywords FROM, TO, or BY.

FROM n   *The case number of the first case to be listed.* The specification CASES FROM 100 starts listing cases at the 100th sequential case. If LIST is preceded by SAMPLE or SELECT IF, it is the 100th case selected. The default is 1, which means listing begins with the first selected case.

> **TO n** *Upper limit on the cases to be listed.* The specification CASES TO 1000 limits listing to the 1000th selected case or the end of the file, whichever comes first. The default is to list until the end of the file. If LIST encounters the CASE subcommand followed by a single number, TO is assumed. That is, CASES 100 is interpreted as CASES TO 100.
>
> **BY n** *Increment used to choose cases for listing.* The specification CASES BY 5 lists every fifth selected case. The default is 1, which means every case is listed.

You need only specify one of these keywords, but you can specify any two or all three, as in:

```
LIST VARIABLES=MOHIRED YRHIRED DEPT82 SALARY79 TO SALARY82 NAME
  /CASES FROM 50 TO 100 BY 5
```

The output from this command is shown in Figure 31.5c. Note particularly how the LIST numbering (Section 31.5) shows the pattern of cases listed as a result of the CASES specification.

If SPLIT FILE is in effect, case selections specified via the CASE subcommand are restarted for each split.

31.5
FORMAT Subcommand

The default specifications for the FORMAT subcommand are WRAP and UNNUMBERED. If the page width cannot accommodate your entire variable list, keyword WRAP wraps the listing in multiple lines per case as shown in Figure 31.5a, which was generated by the following commands:

```
SET WIDTH=80
DATA LIST   FILE=HUBDATA RECORDS=3
   /1 EMPLOYID 1-5 MOHIRED YRHIRED 12-15 DEPT79 TO DEPT82 SEX 16-20
   /2 SALARY79 TO SALARY82 6-25 HOURLY81 HOURLY82 40-53(2) PROMO81 72
      AGE 54-55 RAISE82 66-70
   /3 JOBCAT 6 NAME 25-48 (A)

LIST
```

Figure 31.5a   LIST in wrapped format

```
EMPLOYID:   1801   8 69 3 3 3 3 2 11180 13000 14300 15600       7.33      8.00 0 44
RAISE82:    1300 3 CONNIE E. JANNSEN

EMPLOYID:   2191   9 79 0 3 0 0 2     0  6337     0     0   -999.00   -999.00 9 20
RAISE82:    -999 3 ESTHER MARX

EMPLOYID:   2211   3 80 0 4 4 4 2     0  8190  8840 10050      4.53      5.15 0 26
RAISE82:    1210 4 MARY CHAFEE

EMPLOYID:   2690   2 74 1 1 1 1 2 13715 14495 16250 18850      8.33      9.67 0 33
RAISE82:    2600 1 HOLLY C. BRADSHAW

EMPLOYID:   2821  10 78 3 3 0 3 2  6370  7410     0  8872   -999.00      4.55 9 53
RAISE82:    -999 3 JACKIE HAMILTON
```

When the list requires more than one line per case, SPSS-X prints the name of the first variable listed in that line. To locate the values of a particular variable, consult the table produced before the listing, as shown in Figure 31.5b.

Figure 31.5b   Variable table

```
THE VARIABLES ARE LISTED IN THE FOLLOWING ORDER:

LINE   1: EMPLOYID MOHIRED YRHIRED DEPT79 DEPT80 DEPT81 DEPT82 SALARY79 SEX
          SALARY80 SALARY81 SALARY82 HOURLY81 HOURLY82 PROMO81 AGE

LINE   2: RAISE82 JOBCAT NAME
```

If there is enough space, keyword WRAP implies one line per case. To tell SPSS-X to use the single-line format only, specify the keyword SINGLE, as in:

```
LIST VARIABLES=MOHIRED YRHIRED DEPT82 SALARY79 TO SALARY82 NAME
  /CASES FROM 50 TO 100 BY 5/ FORMAT=SINGLE
```

If there is not enough room within the line width, SPSS-X issues an error message and does not execute the listing. Therefore, use SINGLE only when you want one line per case or nothing.

If you want LIST to number the cases that are being listed, specify keyword NUMBERED, as in:

```
LIST VARIABLES=MOHIRED YRHIRED DEPT82 SALARY79 TO SALARY82 NAME
  / CASES FROM 50 TO 100 BY 5/ FORMAT=SINGLE,NUMBERED
```

Figure 31.5c shows the output from this command. LIST calculates the width for printing the numbers based on the value you specify using TO on the CASES subcommand. In the above example, LIST chooses a print width of 3 (plus the blank between columns) based on the TO 100 specification. If you specify no TO value, LIST uses a width of 6.

Figure 31.5c   LIST using the CASES subcommand and NUMBERED

```
    MOHIRED YRHIRED DEPT82 SALARY79 SALARY80 SALARY81 SALARY82 NAME

 50      1      79      0    14300    14300    15730        0  EVA ELDER
 55      6      79      0        0    15600        0        0  EDWARD GREEN
 60     12      79      0        0     8840     9503        0  LOVEY E. HUDSON
 65      5      80      0        0    13520        0        0  PATRICIA SMITH
 70      8      79      0        0     8255        0        0  HELEN D. SMITH
 75     10      70      4    14300    18850    21450    26182  MONICA C. RIVERS
 80      1      79      0        0     7442        0        0  THOMAS P. JOHNSON
 85      4      80      3        0    18200    18395    19682  ANN JOHNSON
 90     10      79      0        0     5720        0        0  CHRISTINA P. NORRIS
 95      5      79      0     7670     9490        0        0  M. ELLIOT KRAFT
100      2      70      3    11830    12545    13799    18083  FANNIE SMITH
```

If SPLIT FILE is in effect, numbering restarts at each split. If you want sequential numbering regardless of splits, set a variable equal to the system variable $CASENUM and name that variable as the first variable on your VARIABLES list. Don't forget to override the new variable's print format to whatever you think is appropriate, as in:

```
COMPUTE SEQ=$CASENUM
PRINT FORMATS SEQ (F3)

SORT CASES BY DEPT82
SPLIT FILE BY DEPT82
LIST VARIABLES=SEQ MOHIRED YRHIRED DEPT82 SALARY79 TO SALARY82 NAME
```

31.6
LIST and Case Selection

The automatic numbering in LIST is based on the cases that are seen by LIST. Therefore, the numbering is established for each case *after* the case has been selected. For example, if you want to look at only employees in a particular department, you might specify:

```
DATA LIST  FILE=HUBDATA RECORDS=3
  /1 EMPLOYID 1-5 MOHIRED YRHIRED 12-15 DEPT79 TO DEPT82 SEX 16-20
  /2 SALARY79 TO SALARY82 6-25 HOURLY81 HOURLY82 40-53(2) PROMO81 72
     AGE 54-55 RAISE82 66-70
  /3 JOBCAT 6 NAME 25-48 (A)

SELECT IF DEPT82 EQ 4
LIST VARIABLES=MOHIRED YRHIRED DEPT82 SALARY79 TO SALARY82 NAME/
  FORMAT=NUMBERED
```

In this example, numbering would start with 1 for the first employee with DEPT82 equal to 4. If you want to know the sequential number of the case before selection, you can create a sequence variable with the transformation language prior to selecting, as in:

```
COMPUTE  CASESEQ=CASESEQ+1
LEAVE CASESEQ
PRINT FORMATS CASESEQ (F3)

SELECT IF DEPT82 EQ 4
LIST VARIABLES=CASESEQ MOHIRED YRHIRED DEPT82
   SALARY79 TO SALARY82 NAME/ FORMAT=NUMBERED
```

This example computes a new variable, CASESEQ, containing the sequence number of each case. You must use the LEAVE command (Chapter 7) so CASESEQ is not reinitialized for every case. You should also provide an appropriate print format for LIST to use. The partial listing from this command is shown in Figure 31.6. Compare the automatic numbering with the listing of variable CASESEQ.

Figure 31.6 Using your own sequence variable

	CASESEQ	MOHIRED	YRHIRED	DEPT82	SALARY79	SALARY80	SALARY81	SALARY82	NAME
1	3	3	80	4	0	8190	8840	10050	MARY CHAFEE
2	14	4	80	4	0	13520	16900	18083	VERA D. LOGGINS
3	39	1	79	4	8450	8450	9490	10627	CAROL LAVENDER
4	43	8	79	4	0	8190	9230	10780	MARIA PROVENZA
5	74	7	79	4	0	9490	11050	14309	CLEVELAND SMITH
6	75	10	70	4	14300	18850	21450	26182	MONICA C. RIVERS
7	78	6	80	4	0	12350	12740	15132	ROSE C. SHUMWAY
8	106	7	76	4	12480	13292	14690	16900	CYNTHIA RILEY
9	121	5	72	4	14560	18850	21450	25577	LINDA IVERSON
10	130	11	68	4	15860	19500	21710	25577	SILVIA KUDIRKA
11	132	9	73	4	12220	14950	16640	18599	MARY HAINES
12	133	4	80	4	0	9750	10790	15608	MAUREEN J. WAYNE

Syntax

LOGLINEAR

```
LOGLINEAR varlist(min,max)...[BY] varlist(min,max)
            [WITH covariate varlist]
[/MISSING={LISTWISE**}] [INCLUDE]
         {DEFAULT  }
[/WIDTH={132}]
        { 72}
[/CWEIGHT={varname }] [/CWEIGHT=(matrix)...]
          {(matrix)}
[/GRESID={varlist }]  [/GRESID=...]
         {(matrix)}

[/PRINT={DEFAULT**}] [/NOPRINT={ESTIM** }]
        {FREQ**   }            {COR**   }
        {RESID**  }            {DESIGN**}
        {DESIGN   }            {RESID   }
        {ESTIM    }            {FREQ    }
        {COR      }            {DEFAULT }
        {ALL      }            {ALL     }
        {NONE     }
[/PLOT={DEFAULT }
       {RESID   }
       {NORMPROB}
       {NONE**  }

                    {DEVIATION [(refcat)]   }
                    {DIFFERENCE             }
                    {HELMERT                }
[/CONTRAST (varname)={SIMPLE [(refcat)]      }]...[/CONTRAST...]
                    {REPEATED               }
                    {POLYNOMIAL [({1,2,3,...})]}
                    {            {metric   }  }
                    {[BASIS] SPECIAL(matrix) }
[/CRITERIA=[CONVERGE({0.001**})]] [ITERATE({20**})] [DELTA({0.5**})]
           {eps   }              {n   }           {d   }
            [DEFAULT]]
[/DESIGN=effect effect... effect BY effect...] [/DESIGN...]
```

** Default if the subcommand is omitted.

Contents

32.1	OVERVIEW
32.2	OPERATION
32.3	LOGLINEAR Specification
32.4	Logit Model
32.5	Specifying Cell Covariates
32.6	DESIGN Subcommand
32.7	Specifying Main Effects Models
32.8	Specifying Interactions
32.9	Specifying Cell Covariates
32.10	Single-Degree-of-Freedom Partitions
32.11	CWEIGHT Subcommand
32.12	GRESID Subcommand
32.13	PRINT and NOPRINT Subcommands
32.14	PLOT Subcommand
32.15	CONTRAST Subcommand
32.16	Contrasts for a Multinomial Logit Model
32.17	Contrasts for a Linear Logit Model
32.18	Contrasts for a Logistic Regression Model
32.19	CRITERIA Subcommand
32.20	WIDTH Subcommand
32.21	MISSING Subcommand
32.22	LOGLINEAR EXAMPLES
32.23	Example 1: A General Log-linear Model
32.24	Example 2: A Multinomial Logit Model
32.25	Example 3: Frequency Table Models
32.26	Example 4: A Linear Logit Model
32.27	Example 5: Logistic Regression On Category Variables
32.28	Example 6: Multinomial Response Models
32.29	Example 7: A Distance Model

32

Chapter 32   LOGLINEAR

The LOGLINEAR procedure is a general procedure that does model fitting, hypothesis testing, and parameter estimation for any model that has categorical variables as its major components. As such, LOGLINEAR subsumes a variety of related techniques, including general models of multi-way contingency tables, logit models, logistic regression on category variables, quasi-independence models, and so on.

32.1
OVERVIEW

LOGLINEAR models cell frequencies using the multinomial response model and produces maximum likelihood estimates of parameters by means of the Newton-Raphson algorithm. Output includes observed and expected cell frequencies and percentages; residuals, standardized residuals, and adjusted residuals; and the Pearson and likelihood-ratio chi-square statistics. For models with dependent variables, LOGLINEAR prints an analysis of dispersion, along with two measures of association. You can request printing of the design matrix; parameter estimates, standard errors, standardized values, and confidence intervals; and the correlation matrix of parameter estimates. You can produce plots of the adjusted residuals against observed and expected counts, as well as normal and detrended normal plots of the adjusted residuals. Examples of models that can be tested with LOGLINEAR and the display produced begin with Section 32.22.

LOGLINEAR is a subcommand-driven procedure. At a minimum, specify the variables you wish to analyze. (See Sections 32.3 through 32.5.) Optionally, specify subcommands in the following contexts.

Specifying the Model. Use the DESIGN subcommand to specify the model or models to be fit. (See Section 32.6.)

Cell Weights and Structural Zeros. Use the CWEIGHT subcommand to specify cell weights, such as structural zeros, for the model. (See Section 32.11.)

Optional Printed Output. Use the PRINT and NOPRINT subcommands to control the types of display output. (See Section 32.13.)

Optional Plots. Use the PLOT subcommand to produce optional plots of adjusted residuals against observed and expected counts, and normal and detrended normal plots. (See Section 32.14.)

Linear Combinations. Use the GRESID subcommand to calculate linear combinations of observed cell frequencies, expected cell frequencies, and adjusted residuals. (See Section 32.12.)

Contrasts. Use the CONTRAST subcommand to indicate the type of contrast desired for a factor. (See Section 32.15.)

Criteria for Algorithm. Use the CRITERIA subcommand to control the values of algorithm tuning parameters. (See Section 32.19.)

Formatting Options. Use the WIDTH subcommand to control the width of the display output. (See Section 32.20.)

Missing Values. Use the MISSING subcommand to include cases with user-missing values in the analysis. (See Section 32.21.)

32.2 OPERATION

To perform the LOGLINEAR procedure, you must name the variables being analyzed and indicate the dependent variable and any cell covariates. The variables specification must come first. The DESIGN subcommand specifies the model to be fit. (See Section 32.6.) One model is produced for each DESIGN subcommand. All subcommands can be used more than once and, with the exception of the DESIGN subcommand, are carried from model to model unless explicitly overridden. The subcommands that affect a DESIGN subcommand should be placed before the DESIGN subcommand. If subcommands are placed after the last DESIGN subcommand, LOGLINEAR generates the saturated model.

All subcommands begin with the subcommand keyword followed by an optional equals sign and specifications. Subcommands are preceded with a slash. Subcommand keywords can be abbreviated to the first three characters.

32.3 LOGLINEAR Specification

The only required specification for LOGLINEAR is the set of variables used in the models. LOGLINEAR analyzes two classes of variables: categorical and continuous. *Categorical variables* are used to define the cells of the table. *Continuous variables* can be used as cell covariates.

Categorical variables must be numeric and integer. Specify a range in parentheses indicating the minimum and maximum values. For example,

```
LOGLINEAR  DPREF(2,3) RACE(1,2)
```

builds a 2 × 2 frequency table for analysis. Cases with values outside the range are excluded from the analysis and noninteger values within the range are truncated for purposes of building the table. In general, the value range specified should match the values in the data. That is, if the range specified for a variable is 1 and 4, there should be cases for values 1, 2, 3, and 4. Empty categories waste workspace and can cause computational problems.

If several variables have the same range, you can specify the range following the last variable in the list, as in:

```
LOGLINEAR  DPREF(2,3) RACE CAMP(1,2)
```

This is a general log-linear model since no BY keyword appears. The design defaults to a saturated model in which all main effects and interaction effects are fitted. Figure 32.3 shows the default display output for this LOGLINEAR command.

Figure 32.3   Default LOGLINEAR display

```
Correspondence Between Effects and Columns of Design/Model 1

Starting  Ending
Column    Column    Effect Name

   1         1      DPREF
   2         2      RACE
   3         3      CAMP
   4         4      DPREF BY RACE
   5         5      DPREF BY CAMP
   6         6      RACE BY CAMP
   7         7      DPREF BY RACE BY CAMP

- - - - - - - - - - - - - - - - - - - - - - - - - - - - - - - - - - - - - - - - -

*** ML converged at iteration  3. The converge criterion =   .00000

- - - - - - - - - - - - - - - - - - - - - - - - - - - - - - - - - - - - - - - - -


Observed, Expected Frequencies and Residuals

     Factor          Code        OBS. count & PCT.   EXP. count & PCT.   Residual   Std. Resid.   Adj. Resid.


DPREF            NORTH
  RACE             BLACK
    CAMP             NORTH        770.50 ( 9.58)      770.50 ( 9.58)       .0000       .0000         .0000
    CAMP             SOUTH       1257.50 (15.64)     1257.50 (15.64)       .0000       .0000         .0000
  RACE             WHITE
    CAMP             NORTH       1059.50 (13.18)     1059.50 (13.18)       .0000       .0000         .0000
    CAMP             SOUTH        965.50 (12.01)      965.50 (12.01)       .0000       .0000         .0000

DPREF            SOUTH
  RACE             BLACK
    CAMP             NORTH        306.50 ( 3.81)      306.50 ( 3.81)       .0000       .0000         .0000
    CAMP             SOUTH       1962.50 (24.41)     1962.50 (24.41)       .0000       .0000         .0000
  RACE             WHITE
    CAMP             NORTH        338.50 ( 4.21)      338.50 ( 4.21)       .0000       .0000         .0000
    CAMP             SOUTH       1380.50 (17.17)     1380.50 (17.17)       .0000       .0000         .0000

- - - - - - - - - - - - - - - - - - - - - - - - - - - - - - - - - - - - - - - - -


Goodness-of-Fit test statistics

    Likelihood Ratio Chi Square =      .00000    DF = 0   P = 1.000
              Pearson Chi Square =      .00000    DF = 0   P = 1.000


- - - - - - - - - - - - - - - - - - - - - - - - - - - - - - - - - - - - - - - - -


Estimates for Parameters
DPREF

  Parameter       Coeff.        Std. Err.      Z-Value     Lower 95 CI    Upper 95 CI

      1         .1575252134       .01342      11.73948        .13123         .18383

RACE

  Parameter       Coeff.        Std. Err.      Z-Value     Lower 95 CI    Upper 95 CI

      2         .0247736448       .01342       1.84624       -.00153         .05107

CAMP

  Parameter       Coeff.        Std. Err.      Z-Value     Lower 95 CI    Upper 95 CI

      3        -.4574210756       .01342     -34.08906       -.48372        -.43112

DPREF BY RACE

  Parameter       Coeff.        Std. Err.      Z-Value     Lower 95 CI    Upper 95 CI

      4        -.0383431255       .01342      -2.85750       -.06464        -.01204

DPREF BY CAMP

  Parameter       Coeff.        Std. Err.      Z-Value     Lower 95 CI    Upper 95 CI

      5         .3581873327       .01342      26.69372        .33189         .38449

RACE BY CAMP

  Parameter       Coeff.        Std. Err.      Z-Value     Lower 95 CI    Upper 95 CI

      6        -.1292284098       .01342      -9.63068       -.15553        -.10293

DPREF BY RACE BY CAMP

  Parameter       Coeff.        Std. Err.      Z-Value     Lower 95 CI    Upper 95 CI

      7        -.0164584710       .01342      -1.22656       -.04276         .00984
```

Figure 32.3 contains three major sets of information. The first set of information consists of the observed frequencies, the expected frequencies, and three types of residuals. The column labeled CODE contains value labels identifying the cells. If none are defined, it uses the observed value. Note that the table prints only the first eight characters of the value label. Since this is a saturated model, all residuals are zero with the exception of rounding error. Similarly, the goodness-of-fit statistics, which constitute the second set of information, are also zero. The third set of information concerns the parameter estimates; it is composed of the value of the coefficient, the standard error of the coefficient, the standardized value (labeled Z-VALUE) of the coefficient, and the 95% confidence interval for the coefficient. The standardized value is distributed approximately as a standard normal variate. Thus, only the main effect for RACE and the interaction effect for DPREF by RACE by CAMP are not significant at the .05 level.

32.4
Logit Model

Use the BY keyword to segregate the independent variables from the dependent variables in a logit model, as in:

```
LOGLINEAR  DPREF(2,3) BY RACE CAMP(1,2)
```

Categorical variables preceding the keyword BY are the dependent variables; categorical variables following the keyword BY are the independent variables. Up to nine variables can be included as independent variables following the keyword BY. Usually you also specify a DESIGN subcommand to request the desired logit model (see Section 32.6 and the annotated example).

LOGLINEAR prints an analysis of dispersion and two measures of association: entropy and concentration. These measures are discussed in Haberman (1982) and can be used to quantify the magnitude of association among the variables. Both are proportional reduction in error measures. The entropy statistic is analogous to Theil's entropy measure (1970) while the concentration statistic is analogous to Goodman and Kruskal's tau-b. Both statistics measure the strength of association between the dependent variable and the predictor variable set. Figure 32.4 is the display of these measures produced by the above LOGLINEAR command.

Figure 32.4   Measures of association for the logit model

```
Analysis of Dispersion

                                  Dispersion
    Source of Variation      Entropy  Concentration     DF

        Due to Model         412.935      399.496
        Due to Residual     5160.398     3620.741
        Total               5573.334     4020.237      8040

* * * * * * * * * * * * * * * * * * * *  L O G   L I N E A R   A N A L Y S I S  * * * * * * * * * * * * * * * * * * * * * * * *

Measures of Association

        Entropy  =    .074091
    Concentration =   .099371
```

32.5
Specifying Cell Covariates

Cell covariates are specified at the end of the variables specification following the keyword WITH, as in:

```
LOGLINEAR DPREF(2,3) RACE CAMP(1,2) WITH CONSTANT
```

Cell covariates are continuous variables and do not need a value range specification. You cannot name a variable as both a categorical variable and a cell covariate. To enter cell covariates into a model, you must specify them on the DESIGN subcommand (see Section 32.6). Cell covariates are not applied on a case-by-case basis. The mean covariate value for a cell in the contingency table is applied to that cell.

32

32.6
DESIGN Subcommand

The DESIGN subcommand specifies the model or models to be fit. The default model, requiring no specification, is the saturated model. All main effects and all interaction effects are fit in the saturated model. If you are using the keyword BY on the variables specification to define a logit model, the completely saturated model contains redundant effects. These are ignored for the analysis.

You can use one or more DESIGN subcommands on a LOGLINEAR command. Each DESIGN subcommand specifies one model. Specify simple effects by naming variables listed on the variables specification. Specify interactions using the keyword BY. Specify single-degree-of-freedom partitions in parentheses following the variable name. The degrees of freedom are calculated from the number of nonzero fitted cells minus the number of parameter estimates.

32.7
Specifying Main Effects Models

To fit the A main effect only on a simple crosstabulation between A and B, specify:

```
LOGLINEAR A(1,4) B(1,5)/
  DESIGN=A/
```

This model tests the homogeneity of B-category probabilities; it fits the marginal frequencies on A, but assumes that membership in any of the categories of B is equiprobable.

To fit the A and B main effects, specify:

```
LOGLINEAR A(1,4) B(1,5)/
  DESIGN=A,B/
```

This model tests the independence of A and B. It fits the marginals on both A and B and is formally identical to the standard chi-square test of independence in contingency tables.

32.8
Specifying Interactions

Use the BY keyword to specify interaction terms. To fit the saturated model, which consists of the A main effect, the B main effect, and the interaction of A and B, specify:

```
LOGLINEAR A(1,4)B(1,5)/
  DESIGN=A,B,A BY B/
```

For the general log-linear model, this DESIGN specification is the same as the default model. That is, the following specification is equivalent to the above:

```
LOGLINEAR A(1,4)B(1,5)/
  DESIGN/
```

32.9
Specifying Cell Covariates

To include cell covariates, you must first identify them on the variables list by naming them after the keyword WITH. Then, simply specify the variable name(s) on the DESIGN subcommand, as in:

```
LOGLINEAR HUSED WIFED(1,4) WITH DISTANCE/
  DESIGN=HUSED WIFED DISTANCE/
```

You can specify an interaction of a cell covariate and an independent variable. However, interactions between cell covariates are not allowed. Instead, use COMPUTE to create interaction variables. Example 7 (see Section 32.29) uses a cell covariate to specify a distance function.

To specify an *equiprobability model,* use a cell covariate that is actually a constant of 1 on the DESIGN subcommand, as in:

```
COMPUTE  X=1
LOGLINEAR  MONTH(1,18) WITH X/
  DESIGN=X
```

This model tests whether the frequencies in the 18-cell table are equal. Example 3 (Section 32.25) uses a covariate to obtain the equiprobability model.

ANNOTATED EXAMPLE OF A LOGIT MODEL

The logit model is a special case of the general log-linear model in which one or more variables are treated as dependent, and the rest are used as independent variables. Typically, logit models use dichotomous variables but can be used for polytomous variables. This example uses dichotomous variables to analyze data from *The American Soldier* by Stouffer et al. (1948). The researchers interviewed soldiers in training camps. The variables used in this example are

- PREF—preference for training camps, where 1=stay in the same camp, 2=move to a northern camp, 3=move to a southern camp, 4=move—but undecided about location, and 5=undecided.

- RACE—race of soldier, where 1=black and 2=white.

- ORIGIN, CAMP—geographic origin and geographic location of camp, where 1=north and 2=south.

- FREQ—actual cell count obtained from the published table.

In this example, we transform the preference variable into the dichotomy north vs. south. Typically, the first step in fitting a logit model is to use a saturated model and remove nonsignificant effects. This example fits only the significant effects in the interest of parsimony. The SPSS-X commands are

```
TITLE 'Stouffer''s American Soldier'
DATA LIST LIST / RACE  ORIGIN  CAMP  PREF  FREQ
WEIGHT BY FREQ
VARIABLE LABELS RACE 'RACE OF RESPONDENT'
 ORIGIN 'GEOGRAPHICAL ORIGIN'
 CAMP 'PRESENT CAMP'
 PREF 'PREFENCE FOR LOCATION'
VALUE LABELS RACE 1 'BLACK' 2 'WHITE'
 /ORIGIN 1 'NORTH' 2 'SOUTH'
 /CAMP 1 'NORTH' 2 'SOUTH'
 /PREF 1 'STAY' 2 'GO NORTH' 3 'GO SOUTH'
  4 'MOVE UNDECIDED' 5 'UNDECIDED'

COMMENT COLLAPSE CATEGORIES INTO A DICHOTOMY
DO IF (CAMP EQ 1)
+   RECODE PREF(1=2)(3=3)(ELSE=0) INTO DPREF
+   ELSE
+   RECODE PREF(1=3)(2=2)(ELSE=0) INTO DPREF
END IF

VARIABLE LABELS DPREF 'PREFERENCE FOR LOCATION'
VALUE LABELS DPREF 2 'NORTH' 3 'SOUTH'

LOGLINEAR DPREF(2,3) BY RACE ORIGIN CAMP(1,2)
    /PRINT=DEFAULT ESTIM
    /DESIGN=DPREF, DPREF BY RACE, DPREF BY ORIGIN, DPREF BY CAMP,
     DPREF BY ORIGIN BY CAMP
BEGIN DATA
1 1 1 1 196
1 1 1 2 191
1 1 1 3  36
1 1 1 4  41
1 1 1 5  52
2 2 2 1 481
...
2 2 2 2  91
2 2 2 3 389
2 2 2 4  91
2 2 2 5  91
END DATA
```

- The DATA LIST command reads the data with a LIST format. The LIST format is a freefield format with each case beginning on a new record (see Chapter 5).

- Variable FREQ is the actual cell count obtained from the published table. The WEIGHT command weights each case (which represents a cell) back to the sample size (see Chapter 11).

- The transformations inside the DO IF—END IF structure transform the five category preference variables into a dichotomy (see Chapters 7 and 9).

- The LOGLINEAR command specifies one design. The DESIGN subcommand specifies the dependent variable, as well as interactions involving the dependent variable. Note that this design is not the saturated model. When you specify a logit model with the keyword BY and do not use a DESIGN subcommand, LOGLINEAR implicitly includes all the effects and interactions of independent factors (see Section 32.6). See Haberman (1979) for more details.

- The PRINT subcommand prints the frequencies and residuals table as well as the estimates for the parameters (see Section 32.13).

Figures A and B contain portions of the display for this job. Figure A shows the final model fit. The chi-square statistics show a good fit, and all of the adjusted residuals are less than 1.

Figure B shows the parameter estimates for the final model. To obtain regression-like coefficients multiply the estimates by 2 (see Haberman, 1978, p. 294). Use these coefficients to obtain log-odds coefficients; use their anti-log to translate the model into odds rather than log odds. Table A shows the model coefficients.

Model coefficients

Effect	Coefficient	Coefficient*2	Antilog
DPREF	0.135	0.270	1.311
DPREF BY RACE	1.450		
DPREF BY ORIGIN	1.239	3.452	
DPREF BY CAMP	2.136		
DPREF BY ORIGIN BY CAMP	-.074	-.149	0.862

The regression-like model implied by the coefficients is

$$\ln(F_{ijk1}/F_{ijk2}) = B + B(A)_i + B(B)_j + B(C)_k + B(BC)_{jk}$$

where F is an expected frequency, and

B equals	0.270
$B(A)_i$ equals	0.371 for i =1
	−0.371 for i =2
$B(B)_j$ equals	1.239 for j =1
	−1.239 for j =2
$B(C)_k$ equals	0.759 for k =1
	−0.759 for k =2
$B(BC)_{jk}$ equals	−0.149 for j =k
	0.149 for j ne k.

To evaluate the model in terms of odds rather than log odds, use an analogous multiplicative model, with the antilogs shown in Table A as coefficients. That is,

$$(F_{ijk}1/F_{ijk2}) = T * T(A)_i * T(B)_j * T(C)_k * T(BC)_{jk}$$

where

T equals	1.311
$T(A)_i$ equals	1.450 for i =1
	1/1.450 for i =2
$T(B)_j$ equals	3.452 for j =1
	1/3.452 for j =2
$T(C)_k$ equals	2.136 for k =1
	1/2.136 for k =2
$T(BC)_{jk}$ equals	0.862 for j =k
	1/.862 for j ne k.

Annotated Example of a Logit Model *continued*

For example, consider someone whose race is black, who is originally from the north, and who is presently located in a northern camp. For this individual, $i=j=k=1$ because of the coding of the variable indicated at the beginning of this example. This person's observed odds of preferring northern versus southern camp location is 10.75 (91.49/8.51) from Figure A. The expected odds given the model is 12.072 (92.35/7.65) from Figure A. The model decomposes these expected odds into components

$$12.072=(1.311)(1.450)(3.452)(2.136)(0.862)$$

where the effects are interpretable.

- 1.311 is the mean or overall effect.
- 1.450 is the race effect indicating the net effect of being black versus white on preference of camp location. Other things equal, blacks prefer northern camp locations by 1.450 to 1.
- 3.452 is the net effect of region of origin on present preference. Other things equal, someone originally from the north prefers a northern camp location by 3.452 to 1.
- 2.136 is the net effect of present location on camp preference. Other things equal, someone presently located in the north states a northern preference over twice as often as they state a southern preference.
- 0.862 is the interaction effect between region of origin and present camp location. The effect is negative; this means that the effect of being a northerner in a northern camp is less positive than is indicated by combining the main effect of being a northerner with the main effect of being in a northern camp.

A Model fit

```
Observed, Expected Frequencies and Residuals

     Factor           Code        OBS. count & PCT.    EXP. count & PCT.    Residual    Std. Resid.    Adj. Resid.


DPREF            NORTH
 RACE            BLACK
  ORIGIN          NORTH
   CAMP            NORTH         387.00 (91.49)        390.64 (92.35)        -3.6431        -.1843        -.7714
   CAMP            SOUTH         876.00 (77.80)        879.35 (78.09)        -3.3479        -.1129        -.4178
  ORIGIN          SOUTH
   CAMP            NORTH         383.00 (58.65)        376.80 (57.70)         6.2000         .3194         .9994
   CAMP            SOUTH         381.00 (18.20)        380.21 (18.17)          .7909         .0406         .1131
 RACE            WHITE
  ORIGIN          NORTH
   CAMP            NORTH         955.00 (85.50)        951.36 (85.17)         3.6431         .1181         .7714
   CAMP            SOUTH         874.00 (63.15)        870.65 (62.91)         3.3479         .1135         .4178
  ORIGIN          SOUTH
   CAMP            NORTH         104.00 (37.14)        110.20 (39.36)        -6.2000        -.5906        -.9994
   CAMP            SOUTH          91.00 ( 9.47)         91.79 ( 9.55)         -.7909        -.0825        -.1131

DPREF            SOUTH
 RACE            BLACK
  ORIGIN          NORTH
   CAMP            NORTH          36.00 ( 8.51)         32.36 ( 7.65)         3.6431         .6405         .7714
   CAMP            SOUTH         250.00 (22.20)        246.65 (21.91)         3.3479         .2132         .4178
  ORIGIN          SOUTH
   CAMP            NORTH         270.00 (41.35)        276.20 (42.30)        -6.2000        -.3731        -.9994
   CAMP            SOUTH        1712.00 (81.80)       1712.79 (81.83)         -.7909        -.0191        -.1131
 RACE            WHITE
  ORIGIN          NORTH
   CAMP            NORTH         162.00 (14.50)        165.64 (14.83)        -3.6431        -.2831        -.7714
   CAMP            SOUTH         510.00 (36.85)        513.35 (37.09)        -3.3479        -.1478        -.4178
  ORIGIN          SOUTH
   CAMP            NORTH         176.00 (62.86)        169.80 (60.64)         6.2000         .4758         .9994
   CAMP            SOUTH         870.00 (90.53)        869.21 (90.45)          .7909         .0268         .1131
-----------------------------------------------------------------------------------------------------------------

Goodness-of-Fit test statistics

   Likelihood Ratio Chi Square =    1.44756    DF = 3   P =   .694
           Pearson Chi Square =    1.45707    DF = 3   P =   .692
```

B Parameter estimates

```
Estimates for Parameters
DPREF
```

Parameter	Coeff.	Std. Err.	Z–Value	Lower 95 CI	Upper 95 CI
1	.1352217166	.01518	8.90608	.10546	.16498

```
DPREF BY RACE
```

Parameter	Coeff.	Std. Err.	Z–Value	Lower 95 CI	Upper 95 CI
2	.1857281674	.01557	11.93145	.15522	.21624

```
DPREF BY ORIGIN
```

Parameter	Coeff.	Std. Err.	Z–Value	Lower 95 CI	Upper 95 CI
3	.6195921388	.01687	36.72886	.58653	.65266

```
DPREF BY CAMP
```

Parameter	Coeff.	Std. Err.	Z–Value	Lower 95 CI	Upper 95 CI
4	.3794390119	.01534	24.73658	.34937	.40950

```
DPREF BY ORIGIN BY CAMP
```

Parameter	Coeff.	Std. Err.	Z–Value	Lower 95 CI	Upper 95 CI
5	−.0744977447	.01521	−4.89942	−.10430	−.04470

32.10
Single-Degree-of-Freedom Partitions

A factor name followed by an integer in parentheses refers to a single-degree-of-freedom partition of a specified contrast. For example, you can specify a simultaneous linear logit model, as in:

```
LOGLINEAR A(1,4) BY B(1,5)/
  CONTRAST(B)=POLYNOMIAL/
  DESIGN=A,A BY B(1)/
```

B(1) refers to the first partition of B, which is the linear effect of B; this follows from the contrast specified. Examples 4 (Section 32.26) and 5 (Section 32.27) use single-degree-of-freedom partitions.

32.11
CWEIGHT Subcommand

Use the CWEIGHT subcommand to specify cell weights, such as structural zeros, for a model. By default, all cell weights are equal to 1.

You can specify a numeric variable on the CWEIGHT subcommand, as in:

```
LOGLINEAR  HUSED WIFED(1,4) WITH DISTANCE/
  CWEIGHT=CWT/
```

Name only one SPSS-X variable as a cell-weight variable on a LOGLINEAR command.

An alternative is to specify a matrix of weights enclosed in parentheses on the CWEIGHT subcommand. The matrix must contain the same number of elements as the product of the levels of the categorical variables. If you specify weights for a multiple-factor model, the index value of the rightmost factor increments most rapidly. For example, the CWEIGHT subcommand

```
LOGLINEAR A(1,2) BY B(1,3) C(1,2)
  /CWEIGHT=(0 1 1 1 0 1 1 1 0 1 1 1)
```

assigns cell weights as follows:

```
A B C WEIGHT
1 1 1   0
1 1 2   1
1 2 1   1
1 2 2   1
1 3 1   0
1 3 2   1
2 1 1   1
2 1 2   1
2 2 1   0
2 2 2   1
2 3 1   1
2 3 2   1
```

You can use an asterisk to signify repetitions of the same value, as in

```
LOGLINEAR A(1,2) BY B(1,3) C(1,2)
  /CWEIGHT=(0 3*1 0 3*1 0 3*1)
```

which specifies the same matrix of weights as above. If you use a matrix of weights on the CWEIGHT subcommand, you can specify more than one CWEIGHT subcommand, as in:

```
LOGLINEAR  A B (1,4)/
  CWEIGHT=(0,4*1,0,4*1,0,4*1,0)/
  DESIGN=A,B/
  CWEIGHT=(16*1)/
  DESIGN=A,B
```

The CWEIGHT specification remains in effect until explicitly overridden with another CWEIGHT subcommand. The previous example uses a second CWEIGHT subcommand to return to the default cell weights.

You can use the CWEIGHT subcommand to impose structural, or *a priori*, zeros on the model. This feature is useful in the analysis of symmetric tables. For example, to impose structural zeros on the diagonal of a symmetric crosstabulation table, specify:

```
COMPUTE  CWT=1
IF (HUSED EQ WIFED) CWT=0
LOGLINEAR  HUSED WIFED(1,4) WITH DISTANCE
  /CWEIGHT=CWT
```

CWT equals 0 when HUSED equals WIFED. Alternatively, you can specify the CWEIGHT matrix, as in:

```
/CWEIGHT = (0, 4*1, 0, 4*1, 0, 4*1, 0)
```

Example 7 (see Section 32.29) uses the CWEIGHT subcommand.

32.12
GRESID Subcommand

The GRESID subcommand calculates linear combinations of observed cell frequencies, expected cell frequencies, and adjusted residuals. Specify a variable or variables, or a matrix whose contents are coefficients of the desired linear combinations. The rules of the matrix specification are identical to the rules for CWEIGHT (see Section 32.11). You can specify multiple GRESID subcommands, but only one GRESID subcommand can invoke an SPSS-X variable. If you use a matrix, it must contain as many elements as the number of cells implied by the variables specification, as in:

```
LOGLINEAR  MONTH(1,18) WITH Z/
  GRESID=(6*1,12*0)/
  GRESID=(6*0,6*1,6*0)/
  GRESID=(12*0,6*1)/
  DESIGN=Z
```

The first GRESID subcommand combines the first six months into an "early" effect, the second GRESID subcommand combines the second six months into a "middle" effect, and the third GRESID subcommand combines the last six observations into a "late" effect. For each effect, LOGLINEAR prints out the observed and expected count, the residual, the standardized residual, and the adjusted residual. Example 3 (see Section 32.25) shows the display output for this analysis of a frequency table containing data on 18 consecutive months.

32.13
PRINT and NOPRINT Subcommands

Use the PRINT subcommand to request statistics and display not produced by default. Or use the NOPRINT subcommand to suppress the printing of results. You can use the following keywords on both the PRINT and NOPRINT subcommands.

FREQ   *Observed and expected cell frequencies and percentages.* This is displayed by default.

RESID   *Raw, standardized, and adjusted residuals.* This is displayed by default.

DESIGN   *The design matrix of the model, showing the contrasts used.*

ESTIM   *The parameter estimates of the model.* If you do not specify a design on the DESIGN subcommand, LOGLINEAR generates a saturated model and prints the parameter estimates for the saturated model. LOGLINEAR does not print parameter estimates or correlation matrices of parameter estimates if any sampling zero cells exist in the expected table after DELTA is added. Parameter estimates and a correlation matrix are printed when structural zeros are present.

COR   *The correlation matrix of the parameter estimates.*

ALL   *All available output.*

DEFAULT   *FREQ and RESID.* ESTIM is also printed by default if the DESIGN subcommand is not used.

NONE   *The design information and goodness-of-fit statistics only.* This option overrides all other specifications on the PRINT subcommand. The NONE option applies only to the PRINT subcommand.

By default, LOGLINEAR prints the frequency table and residuals. You can use the PRINT subcommand to request additional items and you can use the NOPRINT subcommand to turn off defaults. You can specify multiple PRINT and NOPRINT subcommands. The specifications are cumulative, as in:

```
LOGLINEAR A(1,2) B(1,2)
  /PRINT=ESTIM
  /NOPRINT=DEFAULT
  /DESIGN=A,B,A BY B
  /PRINT=ALL
  /DESIGN=A,B
```

This LOGLINEAR command specifies two designs. The first design is the saturated model. Since it fits the data exactly, you do not want to see the frequencies and residuals. Rather, you want to see parameter estimates. To print the parameter estimates, specify PRINT=ESTIM, and to suppress the frequencies and residuals output, specify NOPRINT=DEFAULT. The second design is the main effects model, which implicitly tests the hypothesis of no association. The PRINT subcommand prints all available display output for this model.

32.14
PLOT Subcommand

The PLOT subcommand produces optional plots. None are printed by default. The following keywords are available:

RESID *Plots of adjusted residuals against observed and expected counts.*

NORMPROB *Normal and detrended normal plots of the adjusted residuals.*

NONE *No plots.*

DEFAULT *RESID and NORMPROB.*

If you specify a PLOT subcommand with no keywords, no plots are printed. You can use multiple PLOT subcommands on one LOGLINEAR command. The specifications are cumulative. For example,

```
LOGLINEAR  RESPONSE(1,2) BY TIME(1,4)
  /CONTRAST(TIME) = SPECIAL(4*1, 7 14 27 51, 8*1)
  /PLOT=DEFAULT
  /DESIGN=RESPONSE TIME(1) BY RESPONSE
  /PLOT=NONE
  /DESIGN
```

prints RESID and NORMPROB plots for the first design. No plots are printed for the second design. Figure 32.27d is an example of the plots produced by LOGLINEAR.

32.15
CONTRAST Subcommand

The CONTRAST subcommand indicates the type of contrast desired for a *factor*. A factor is a categorical dependent or independent variable. Specify the variable name in parentheses and the contrast chosen, as in

```
LOGLINEAR  MENTHLTH(1,4) BY PARENTSE(1,6)
  /CONTRAST(MENTHLTH)=POLYNOMIAL
```

which applies a polynomial contrast to MENTHLTH.

Contrasts in LOGLINEAR are more general than contrasts in MANOVA. In LOGLINEAR, contrasts do not have to sum to 0 or be orthogonal. The following contrasts are available:

DEVIATION(refcat) *Deviations from the overall effect.* DEVIATION is the default contrast if you do not use the CONTRAST subcommand. Refcat is the category for which parameter estimates are not displayed (they must be obtained as the negative of the sum of the others). By default, refcat is the last category of the variable.

DIFFERENCE

Levels of a factor with the average effect of previous levels of a factor. Also known as *reverse Helmert* contrasts.

HELMERT

Levels of a factor with the average effect of subsequent levels of a factor.

SIMPLE(refcat)

Each level of a factor to the last level. By default, LOG-LINEAR uses the last category of the factor variable as the reference category. Optionally, you can specify the value that you want used as the reference category enclosed in parentheses after the keyword SIMPLE.

REPEATED

Adjacent comparisons across levels of a factor.

POLYNOMIAL(metric)

Orthogonal polynomial contrasts. The default is equal spacing. Optionally, you can specify the coefficients of the linear polynomial in parentheses, indicating the spacing between levels of the treatment measured by the given factor.

[BASIS]SPECIAL(matrix)

User-defined contrast. You must specify as many elements as the number of categories squared. If BASIS is specified before SPECIAL, a basis matrix is generated for the special contrast, which makes the coefficient of the contrast equal to the special matrix. Otherwise, the matrix specified is the basis matrix.

Only one contrast is in effect for each factor for a DESIGN subcommand. If you do not use the CONTRAST subcommand, the default contrast is DEVIATION for each factor. Use separate CONTRAST subcommands for each factor for which you specify contrasts. A contrast specification remains in effect for subsequent designs until explicitly overridden with another CONTRAST subcommand, as in:

```
LOGLINEAR  A(1,4) BY B(1,4)
  /CONTRAST(B)=POLYNOMIAL
  /DESIGN=A A BY B(1)
  /CONTRAST(B)=SIMPLE
  /DESIGN=A A BY B(1)
```

The first CONTRAST subcommand requests polynomial contrasts of B for the first design. The second CONTRAST subcommand requests the default contrast of B, with the last category (value 4) used as the reference category for the second DESIGN subcommand.

You can print the design matrix used for the contrasts by specifying the DESIGN keyword on the PRINT subcommand (see Section 32.13).

32.16
Contrasts for a Multinomial Logit Model

Contrasts are frequently used for a multinomial logit model, in which the dependent variable has more than two categories. The following example builds special contrasts among the five categories of the dependent variable. The variable PREF measures preference for training camps among Army recruits. For PREF, 1=stay, 2=move to north, 3=move to south, 4=move to unnamed camp, and 5=undecided.

```
LOGLINEAR  PREF(1,5) BY RACE ORIGIN CAMP(1,2)
  /CONTRAST(PREF)=SPECIAL(5*1, 1 1 1 1 -4, 3 -1 -1 -1 0, 0 1 1 -2 0,
  0 1 -1 0 0)
```

The four contrasts are (1) move or stay vs. undecided; (2) stay vs. move; (3) named camp vs. unnamed; and (4) northern vs. southern camp. Because these contrasts are orthogonal, SPECIAL and BASIS SPECIAL produce equivalent results. Use BASIS SPECIAL when you wish to obtain parameter estimates for nonorthogonal comparisons.

32.17
Contrasts for a Linear Logit Model

One use of the CONTRAST subcommand is for fitting linear logit models. Example 4 (see Section 32.26) uses education to predict response on an attitude item. The form of the CONTRAST subcommand in Example 4 is as follows:

```
LOGLINEAR RESPONSE(1,2) BY YEAR(0,20)
  /PRINT=DEFAULT ESTIM
  /CONTRAST(YEAR)=SPECIAL(21*1, -10, -9, -8, -7, -6, -5, -4,
                              -3, -2, -1, 0, 1, 2, 3, 4, 5, 6, 7,
                              8, 9, 10, 399*1)
  /DESIGN=RESPONSE RESPONSE BY YEAR(1)
```

YEAR measures years of education and ranges from 0 to 20. Therefore, allowing for the constant effect, YEAR has 20 estimable parameters associated with it. The SPECIAL contrast specifies the constant—that is, 21*1—and the linear effect of YEAR—that is, −10 to 10. The other 399 *1*s fill out the 21*21 matrix. Do not use BASIS SPECIAL for such contrasts.

32.18
Contrasts for a Logistic Regression Model

In Example 5 (Section 32.27), the following CONTRAST is used to transform the independent variable into a metric variable.

```
LOGLINEAR RESPONSE(1,2) BY TIME(1,4)
  /CONTRAST(TIME) = SPECIAL(4*1, 7 14 27 51, 8*1)
  /PRINT=ALL/PLOT=DEFAULT
  /DESIGN=RESPONSE, TIME(1) BY RESPONSE
```

TIME represents elapsed time in days. Therefore, the weights in the contrast represent the metric of the passage of time. Do not use BASIS SPECIAL for such contrasts.

32.19
CRITERIA Subcommand

The CRITERIA subcommand specifies the values of some constants in the Newton-Raphson algorithm, the estimation algorithm in LOGLINEAR. The following keywords are available:

CONVERGE(eps)   *Convergence criterion.* Specify a value for the convergence criterion. The default is .001.

ITERATION(n)   *Maximum number of iterations.* Specify the maximum number of iterations for the algorithm. The default number is 20.

DELTA(d)   *Cell delta value.* The value of delta is added to each cell frequency for the first iteration. For saturated models, it remains in the cell. The default value is .5. LOGLINEAR does not print parameter estimates or correlation matrices of parameter estimates if any sampling zero cells exist in the expected table after DELTA is added. Parameter estimates and correlation matrices are printed in the presence of structural zeros.

DEFAULT   *Default values are used.* You can use DEFAULT to reset the parameters to the default.

For example, to increase the maximum number of iterations to 50, specify:

```
LOGLINEAR  DPREF(2,3) BY RACE ORIGIN CAMP(1,2)
  /CRITERIA=ITERATION(50)
```

Defaults or specifications remain in effect until overriden with another CRITERIA subcommand.

32.20
WIDTH Subcommand

The default display uses the width specified on SET. Use the WIDTH subcommand to specify a different display width. For example, you can specify a width of 72 to avoid wrapping on short-carriage terminals. Only one width can be in effect at a time and it controls all display. The WIDTH subcommand can be placed anywhere after the variables specification. Figure 32.20 is an example of the frequencies and residuals display with WIDTH=72 in effect. This figure uses the same data as Figure 32.3.

```
LOGLINEAR  DPREF(2,3) RACE CAMP(1,2)
  /WIDTH=72
```

Figure 32.20   Narrow display

```
Observed, Expected Frequencies and Residuals
      Factor              Code        OBS count  EXP count  Residual Adj Resid

DD               NORTH
  RACE             BLACK
    CAMP             NORTH           770.50     770.50      .000     .000
    CAMP             SOUTH          1257.50    1257.50      .000     .000
  RACE             WHITE
    CAMP             NORTH          1059.50    1059.50      .000     .000
    CAMP             SOUTH           965.50     965.50      .000     .000

DD               SOUTH
  RACE             BLACK
    CAMP             NORTH           306.50     306.50      .000     .000
    CAMP             SOUTH          1962.50    1962.50      .000     .000
  RACE             WHITE
    CAMP             NORTH           338.50     338.50      .000     .000
    CAMP             SOUTH          1380.50    1380.50      .000     .000
```

Note, however, that the frequencies table displays fewer statistics and has fewer decimal places when narrow format is in effect. Observed and expected percentages are omitted.

32.21
MISSING Subcommand

The MISSING subcommand controls missing values. Its default keyword is LISTWISE, which deletes cases with missing values on any variable listed on the variables specification. Optionally, you may include user-missing values in the analysis with keyword INCLUDE. If you specify INCLUDE, you must also include the missing values in the value range specification.

LISTWISE   *Delete cases with missing values listwise.* This is the default; you can make it explicit by specifying the keyword DEFAULT.

INCLUDE   *Include user-missing values as valid.*

32.22
LOGLINEAR EXAMPLES

You can use LOGLINEAR to analyze many types of designs for categorical variables. Combinations of variables specifications, CWEIGHT, CONTRAST, GRESID, and DESIGN subcommands can produce general log-linear models, logit models, quasi-independence models, logistic regressions on category variables, and others. The following examples and the annotated example, although not exhaustive, demonstrate many of the types of models you can analyze. Most of these examples have been obtained from books and articles on the analysis of categorical data. The examples use the WEIGHT command (Chapter 11) to replicate the published tables.

32.23
Example 1: A General Log-linear Model

The general log-linear model has all dependent variables. This example uses the same data analyzed as a logit model in the annotated example. The general log-linear model treats all variables as jointly dependent. The following LOG-LINEAR command is used to request this model:

```
LOGLINEAR DPREF(2,3) RACE ORIGIN CAMP(1,2)
  /PRINT=DEFAULT ESTIM
  /DESIGN=DPREF, RACE, ORIGIN, CAMP,
    DPREF BY RACE, DPREF BY ORIGIN, DPREF BY CAMP,
    RACE BY CAMP, RACE BY ORIGIN, ORIGIN BY CAMP,
    RACE BY ORIGIN BY CAMP,
    DPREF BY ORIGIN BY CAMP
```

The LOGLINEAR command for the general log-linear model does not use the keyword BY. The DESIGN subcommand uses all the variables as main effects or as part of an interaction term. Compare this with the logit model shown in the annotated example, which uses the dependent variable and interactions involving the dependent variable.

Figures 32.23a and 32.23b are the display produced by this example. Figure 32.23a shows that expected frequencies are identical to the logit model in the annotated example (Figure A). However, observed and expected cell percentages differ. In the logit model, cell percentages sum to 100 across categories of the dependent variable within each combination of independent variable values. In other words, cell percentages in the logit model are comparable to row or column percentages in crosstabulation. In the general model, they sum to 100 across all categories and are comparable to total percentages in a crosstabulation.

Compare Figure 32.23b with Figure B in the annotated example. Note that identical results are produced for effects in common in the two models.

Figure 32.23a   Log-linear model fit for Example 1

```
Observed, Expected Frequencies and Residuals

      Factor          Code         OBS. count & PCT.    EXP. count & PCT.     Residual   Std. Resid.   Adj. Resid.

DPREF            NORTH
 RACE            BLACK
  ORIGIN          NORTH
   CAMP            NORTH        387.00 ( 4.82)      390.64 ( 4.86)       -3.6431      -.1843        -.7714
   CAMP            SOUTH        876.00 (10.90)      879.35 (10.94)       -3.3479      -.1129        -.4178
  ORIGIN          SOUTH
   CAMP            NORTH        383.00 ( 4.77)      376.80 ( 4.69)        6.2000       .3194         .9994
   CAMP            SOUTH        381.00 ( 4.74)      380.21 ( 4.73)         .7909       .0406         .1131
 RACE            WHITE
  ORIGIN          NORTH
   CAMP            NORTH        955.00 (11.88)      951.36 (11.84)        3.6431       .1181         .7714
   CAMP            SOUTH        874.00 (10.87)      870.65 (10.83)        3.3479       .1135         .4178
  ORIGIN          SOUTH
   CAMP            NORTH        104.00 ( 1.29)      110.20 ( 1.37)       -6.2000      -.5906        -.9994
   CAMP            SOUTH         91.00 ( 1.13)       91.79 ( 1.14)        -.7909      -.0825        -.1131

DPREF            SOUTH
 RACE            BLACK
  ORIGIN          NORTH
   CAMP            NORTH         36.00 (  .45)       32.36 (  .40)        3.6431       .6405         .7714
   CAMP            SOUTH        250.00 ( 3.11)      246.65 ( 3.07)        3.3479       .2132         .4178
  ORIGIN          SOUTH
   CAMP            NORTH        270.00 ( 3.36)      276.20 ( 3.44)       -6.2000      -.3731        -.9994
   CAMP            SOUTH       1712.00 (21.30)     1712.79 (21.31)        -.7909      -.0191        -.1131
 RACE            WHITE
  ORIGIN          NORTH
   CAMP            NORTH        162.00 ( 2.02)      165.64 ( 2.06)       -3.6431      -.2831        -.7714
   CAMP            SOUTH        510.00 ( 6.35)      513.35 ( 6.39)       -3.3479      -.1478        -.4178
  ORIGIN          SOUTH
   CAMP            NORTH        176.00 ( 2.19)      169.80 ( 2.11)        6.2000       .4758         .9994
   CAMP            SOUTH        870.00 (10.82)      869.21 (10.82)         .7909       .0268         .1131


Goodness-of-Fit test statistics

     Likelihood Ratio Chi Square =    1.44756    DF = 3   P =  .694
                Pearson Chi Square =    1.45707    DF = 3   P =  .692
```

Figure 32.23b   Parameter estimates for Example 1

```
Estimates for Parameters
DPREF

  Parameter         Coeff.      Std. Err.      Z-Value    Lower 95 CI    Upper 95 CI
      1          .1352217166      .01518       8.90608       .10546         .16498

RACE

  Parameter         Coeff.      Std. Err.      Z-Value    Lower 95 CI    Upper 95 CI
      2          .0355803941      .01363       2.61113       .00887         .06229

ORIGIN

  Parameter         Coeff.      Std. Err.      Z-Value    Lower 95 CI    Upper 95 CI
      3          .0403904261      .01614       2.50201       .00875         .07203

CAMP

  Parameter         Coeff.      Std. Err.      Z-Value    Lower 95 CI    Upper 95 CI
      4         -.4480592813      .01614     -27.76919      -.47968        -.41643

DPREF BY RACE

  Parameter         Coeff.      Std. Err.      Z-Value    Lower 95 CI    Upper 95 CI
      5          .1857281674      .01557      11.93145       .15522         .21624

DPREF BY ORIGIN

  Parameter         Coeff.      Std. Err.      Z-Value    Lower 95 CI    Upper 95 CI
      6          .6195921388      .01687      36.72886       .58653         .65266

DPREF BY CAMP

  Parameter         Coeff.      Std. Err.      Z-Value    Lower 95 CI    Upper 95 CI
      7          .3794390119      .01534      24.73658       .34937         .40950

RACE BY CAMP

  Parameter         Coeff.      Std. Err.      Z-Value    Lower 95 CI    Upper 95 CI
      8         -.1364780340      .01413      -9.65595      -.16418        -.10878

RACE BY ORIGIN

  Parameter         Coeff.      Std. Err.      Z-Value    Lower 95 CI    Upper 95 CI
      9         -.4413477997      .01591     -27.73754      -.47253        -.41016

ORIGIN BY CAMP

  Parameter         Coeff.      Std. Err.      Z-Value    Lower 95 CI    Upper 95 CI
     10         -.0375668525      .01632      -2.30190      -.06955        -.00558

RACE BY ORIGIN BY CAMP

  Parameter         Coeff.      Std. Err.      Z-Value    Lower 95 CI    Upper 95 CI
     11         -.0885302170      .01359      -6.51497      -.11516        -.06190

DPREF BY ORIGIN BY CAMP

  Parameter         Coeff.      Std. Err.      Z-Value    Lower 95 CI    Upper 95 CI
     12         -.0744977447      .01521      -4.89942      -.10430        -.04470
```

32.24
Example 2: A Multinomial Logit Model

The annotated example and Example 1 (see Section 32.23) analyze Stouffer's data with "preference for location" transformed into a dichotomy. Example 2 uses the original five-category preference variable to demonstrate the multinomial logit model. This example uses orthogonal special contrasts to make desired comparisons among the categories of the dependent variable. The LOGLINEAR command is as follows:

```
LOGLINEAR PREF(1,5) BY RACE ORIGIN CAMP(1,2)
  /PRINT=DEFAULT ESTIM
  /CONTRAST(PREF)=SPECIAL(5*1,1 1 1 1 -4,3 -1 -1 -1 0,
    0 1 1 -2 0,0 1 -1 0 0)
  /DESIGN=PREF, PREF BY RACE, PREF BY ORIGIN, PREF BY CAMP,
    PREF BY RACE BY ORIGIN, PREF BY RACE BY CAMP,
    PREF BY ORIGIN BY CAMP, PREF BY RACE BY ORIGIN BY CAMP
```

Figure 32.24 is the display of the parameter estimates for Example 2. This example fits the saturated model. If no DESIGN subcommand had been specified, the saturated model would have also included effects that are redundant when a logit model is specified. Parameter estimates for a multinomial model can be more interpretable when you specify special contrasts as in this example. The CONTRAST subcommand contrasts the movers and stayers vs. the undecided, the movers vs. the stayers, the decided vs. the undecided, and northern vs. southern camps.

Figure 32.24 Parameter estimates for Example 2

Estimates for Parameters

PREF

Parameter	Coeff.	Std. Err.	Z-Value	Lower 95 CI	Upper 95 CI
1	.1234825883	.00807	15.29520	.10766	.13931
2	.0724662120	.00826	8.77654	.05628	.08865
3	.2043174993	.01408	14.51506	.17673	.23191
4	.1282571558	.02068	6.20092	.08772	.16880

PREF BY RACE

Parameter	Coeff.	Std. Err.	Z-Value	Lower 95 CI	Upper 95 CI
5	-.0051416644	.00807	-.63687	-.02097	.01068
6	-.0063669961	.00826	-.77112	-.02255	.00982
7	.0062485789	.01408	.44391	-.02134	.03384
8	.0960361288	.02068	4.64311	.05550	.13658

PREF BY ORIGIN

Parameter	Coeff.	Std. Err.	Z-Value	Lower 95 CI	Upper 95 CI
9	-.0021584482	.00807	-.26736	-.01798	.01367
10	-.0586990400	.00826	-7.10917	-.07488	-.04252
11	-.0025353715	.01408	-.18012	-.03012	.02505
12	.6555140380	.02068	31.69248	.61497	.69605

PREF BY CAMP

Parameter	Coeff.	Std. Err.	Z-Value	Lower 95 CI	Upper 95 CI
13	-.0191848042	.00807	-2.37633	-.03501	-.00336
14	.0320805342	.00826	3.88534	.01590	.04826
15	.0038808442	.01408	.27570	-.02371	.03147
16	-.0156364228	.02068	-.75598	-.05618	.02490

PREF BY RACE BY ORIGIN

Parameter	Coeff.	Std. Err.	Z-Value	Lower 95 CI	Upper 95 CI
17	-.0033156723	.00807	-.41070	-.01914	.01251
18	-.0237329647	.00826	-2.87435	-.03992	-.00755
19	.0611636379	.01408	4.34517	.03357	.08875
20	-.0516750973	.02068	-2.49836	-.09221	-.01114

PREF BY RACE BY CAMP

Parameter	Coeff.	Std. Err.	Z-Value	Lower 95 CI	Upper 95 CI
21	.0030208725	.00807	.37418	-.01280	.01884
22	.1027873616	.00826	12.44880	.08660	.11897
23	-.0189810333	.01408	-1.34845	-.04657	.00861
24	.0076967580	.02068	.37212	-.03284	.04824

PREF BY ORIGIN BY CAMP

Parameter	Coeff.	Std. Err.	Z-Value	Lower 95 CI	Upper 95 CI
25	.0049220965	.00807	.60968	-.01090	.02075
26	.1316990028	.00826	15.95036	.11552	.14788
27	-.0090552616	.01408	-.64330	-.03664	.01853
28	-.0320161528	.02068	-1.54790	-.07256	.00852

PREF BY RACE BY ORIGIN BY CAMP

Parameter	Coeff.	Std. Err.	Z-Value	Lower 95 CI	Upper 95 CI
29	-.0008598058	.00807	-.10650	-.01668	.01496
30	.0217737066	.00826	2.63706	.00559	.03796
31	-.0115700249	.01408	-.82195	-.03916	.01602
32	.0406113662	.02068	1.96346	.00007	.08115

32.25
**Example 3: Frequency
Table Models**

You can use LOGLINEAR to analyze one-dimensional frequency tables by means of chi-square-based analysis. Example 3 uses data on the recall of stressful events over time (Haberman, 1978). Each case in the published table is one recall of a stressful event, and the measure is the length of time since the event occurred in months. The example tests two separate models: the equiprobability model and the log-linear time-trend model. The following SPSS-X commands are used:

```
DATA LIST LIST / MONTH  WT
COMPUTE X=1
COMPUTE Z=MONTH
WEIGHT BY WT
LOGLINEAR MONTH(1,18) WITH X Z
 /PRINT = ALL
 /*USE GRESID TO TEST COMBINATIONS OF THE OBSERVED FREQUENCIES
 /*NOTE:   THE THREE EFFECTS ARE EARLY, MIDDLE, AND LATE
 /GRESID =(6*1,12*0)
 /GRESID=(6*0,6*1,6*0)
 /GRESID=(12*0,6*1)
 /*MODEL 1:   THE EQUIPROBABILITY MODEL
 DESIGN = X/
 /*MODEL 2:   THE LOG-LINEAR TIME-TREND MODEL
 DESIGN = Z/
BEGIN DATA
 1 15  1 0
 2 11  1 0
 3 14  1 0
   ...
16   1  0 1
17   1  0 1
18   4  0 1
END DATA
```

- The DATA LIST command reads two variables: MONTH, scaled from 1 to 18; and WT, which contains the frequencies. It uses the LIST format.
- COMPUTE X=1 computes a vector of 1s.
- The second COMPUTE computes an index vector ranging from 1 to 18.
- The WEIGHT command is used to replicate the original file.
- The LOGLINEAR command names MONTH as the dependent variable and the two index variables as covariates.
- The GRESID subcommands request three linear combinations of the data: the first six, the middle six, and the last six observations, respectively, are combined. Generalized residual contrasts produce some of the statistics already seen: the observed count, the expected count, the residual, the standardized residual, and the adjusted residual.
- DESIGN=X tests the equiprobability model. This model assumes that the probability of dating an event in a particular past month is constant for all months. The covariate is a constant for this type of model.
- DESIGN=Z fits a log-linear time-trend model. The log of the cell probabilities is a linear function of the time before the interview. The index variable reflects the time period being studied for this type of model.

Figure 32.25a shows the frequencies and residuals for the equiprobability model. The expected counts and expected percentages are constant across all cells in the equiprobability model.

Figure 32.25b is the display produced by the GRESID subcommands for the equiprobability model. The model systematically underpredicts the early scores and overpredicts the late scores in a way which cannot be ignored: the adjusted residuals are greater than 4 in magnitude in these two instances.

Figure 32.25c shows the fit under the time-trend model. The expected counts come much closer to the observed counts using this model. With the exception of Month 13, the adjusted residuals are all under 2 in magnitude.

Figure 32.25a   The equiprobability model fit for Example 3

```
Observed, Expected Frequencies and Residuals

      Factor          Code        OBS. count & PCT.   EXP. count & PCT.   Residual    Std. Resid.   Adj. Resid.

MONTH                  1          15.00 (10.20)        8.17 ( 5.56)       6.8333        2.3912        2.4605
MONTH                  2          11.00 ( 7.48)        8.17 ( 5.56)       2.8333         .9915        1.0202
MONTH                  3          14.00 ( 9.52)        8.17 ( 5.56)       5.8333        2.0412        2.1004
MONTH                  4          17.00 (11.56)        8.17 ( 5.56)       8.8333        3.0910        3.1806
MONTH                  5           5.00 ( 3.40)        8.17 ( 5.56)      -3.1667       -1.1081       -1.1402
MONTH                  6          11.00 ( 7.48)        8.17 ( 5.56)       2.8333         .9915        1.0202
MONTH                  7          10.00 ( 6.80)        8.17 ( 5.56)       1.8333         .6415         .6601
MONTH                  8           4.00 ( 2.72)        8.17 ( 5.56)      -4.1667       -1.4580       -1.5003
MONTH                  9           8.00 ( 5.44)        8.17 ( 5.56)       -.1667        -.0583        -.0600
MONTH                 10          10.00 ( 6.80)        8.17 ( 5.56)       1.8333         .6415         .6601
MONTH                 11           7.00 ( 4.76)        8.17 ( 5.56)      -1.1667        -.4082        -.4201
MONTH                 12           9.00 ( 6.12)        8.17 ( 5.56)        .8333         .2916         .3001
MONTH                 13          11.00 ( 7.48)        8.17 ( 5.56)       2.8333         .9915        1.0202
MONTH                 14           3.00 ( 2.04)        8.17 ( 5.56)      -5.1667       -1.8080       -1.8604
MONTH                 15           6.00 ( 4.08)        8.17 ( 5.56)      -2.1667        -.7582        -.7802
MONTH                 16           1.00 (  .68)        8.17 ( 5.56)      -7.1667       -2.5078       -2.5805
MONTH                 17           1.00 (  .68)        8.17 ( 5.56)      -7.1667       -2.5078       -2.5805
MONTH                 18           4.00 ( 2.72)        8.17 ( 5.56)      -4.1667       -1.4580       -1.5003

- - - - - - - - - - - - - - - - - - - - - - - - - - - - - - - - - - - - - - - - - - - - - - - - - - - -

Goodness-of-Fit test statistics

    Likelihood Ratio Chi Square =    50.84270    DF = 17   P =   .000
              Pearson Chi Square =    45.36735    DF = 17   P =   .000
```

Figure 32.25b   Generalized residuals for the equiprobability model for Example 3

```
Generalized Residual

    Contrast                            OBS. count   EXP. count    Residual    Std. Resid.   Adj. Resid.

        1                                  73.0         49.00      24.0000       3.4286       4.1991
        2                                  48.0         49.00      -1.0000       -.1429       -.1750
        3                                  26.0         49.00     -23.0000      -3.2857      -4.0242
```

Figure 32.25c   The time-trend model fit for Example 3

```
Observed, Expected Frequencies and Residuals

      Factor          Code        OBS. count & PCT.   EXP. count & PCT.   Residual    Std. Resid.   Adj. Resid.

MONTH                  1          15.00 (10.20)       15.17 (10.32)       -.1711        -.0439        -.0516
MONTH                  2          11.00 ( 7.48)       13.95 ( 9.49)      -2.9520        -.7903        -.8873
MONTH                  3          14.00 ( 9.52)       12.83 ( 8.73)       1.1692         .3264         .3551
MONTH                  4          17.00 (11.56)       11.80 ( 8.03)       5.2002        1.5138        1.6111
MONTH                  5           5.00 ( 3.40)       10.85 ( 7.38)      -5.8516       -1.7763       -1.8625
MONTH                  6          11.00 ( 7.48)        9.98 ( 6.79)       1.0204         .3230         .3355
MONTH                  7          10.00 ( 6.80)        9.18 ( 6.24)        .8223         .2714         .2804
MONTH                  8           4.00 ( 2.72)        8.44 ( 5.74)      -4.4402       -1.5284       -1.5751
MONTH                  9           8.00 ( 5.44)        7.76 ( 5.28)        .2380         .0854         .0881
MONTH                 10          10.00 ( 6.80)        7.14 ( 4.86)       2.8617        1.0711        1.1065
MONTH                 11           7.00 ( 4.76)        6.56 ( 4.47)        .4353         .1699         .1762
MONTH                 12           9.00 ( 6.12)        6.04 ( 4.11)       2.9629        1.2059        1.2560
MONTH                 13          11.00 ( 7.48)        5.55 ( 3.78)       5.4480        2.3121        2.4214
MONTH                 14           3.00 ( 2.04)        5.11 ( 3.47)      -2.1059        -.9320        -.9818
MONTH                 15           6.00 ( 4.08)        4.70 ( 3.19)       1.3044         .6020         .6381
MONTH                 16           1.00 (  .68)        4.32 ( 2.94)      -3.3183       -1.5968       -1.7032
MONTH                 17           1.00 (  .68)        3.97 ( 2.70)      -2.9713       -1.4910       -1.6003
MONTH                 18           4.00 ( 2.72)        3.65 ( 2.48)        .3479         .1820         .1965

- - - - - - - - - - - - - - - - - - - - - - - - - - - - - - - - - - - - - - - - - - - - - - - - - - - -

Goodness-of-Fit test statistics

    Likelihood Ratio Chi Square =    24.57038    DF = 16   P =   .078
              Pearson Chi Square =    22.71450    DF = 16   P =   .122
```

Figure 32.25d shows the output from the GRESID specifications for the time-trend model. In this model, the early, middle, and late contrasts now conform more closely to the observed frequencies than in the equiprobability model.

Figure 32.25d   Generalized residuals for the time-trend model for Example 3

Generalized Residual						
Contrast		OBS. count	EXP. count	Residual	Std. Resid.	Adj. Resid.
1		73.0	49.00	24.0000	3.4286	4.1991
2		48.0	49.00	−1.0000	−.1429	−.1750
3		26.0	49.00	−23.0000	−3.2857	−4.0242

32.26
Example 4: A Linear Logit Model

Example 4 is a linear logit model with one predictor. The level of education in years is used to predict the attitude of men toward women staying at home rather than working (Haberman, 1982). This variable is dichotomous. The SPSS-X commands are as follows:

```
DATA LIST LIST/YEAR RESPONSE WT
WEIGHT BY WT
VALUE LABELS RESPONSE 1 'AGREE' 2 'DISAGREE'
LOGLINEAR RESPONSE(1,2) BY YEAR(0,20)
 /PRINT=DEFAULT ESTIM
 /CONTRAST(YEAR)=SPECIAL(21*1, −10, −9, −8, −7, −6, −5, −4,
                         −3, −2, −1, 0, 1, 2, 3, 4, 5, 6, 7,
                         8, 9, 10, 399*1 )
 /DESIGN=RESPONSE RESPONSE BY YEAR(1)
 /BEGIN DATA
  0 1   4
  0 2   2
   ...
 20 1   3
 20 2  20
 END DATA
```

- The DATA LIST command reads YEAR, RESPONSE, and WT, which is the frequency for each cell.
- The WEIGHT command weights the table to the original sample size.
- The variables specification on the LOGLINEAR command uses the keyword BY to define a logit model.
- The CONTRAST subcommand specifies a special contrast. The full design matrix is a 21*21 matrix. The first effect fit is the constant effect, so the special contrast begins with 21 1s. The second effect is the linear effect, parameterized as years of education minus 10. Higher order effects are not of interest, so 1s are used to fill out the matrix.
- The DESIGN subcommand fits the RESPONSE effect and the RESPONSE by linear-YEAR effect.

Figure 32.26a shows the linear logit fit. The chi-square statistics are all nonsignificant, and the largest adjusted residual is 1.99. Figure 32.26b shows the analysis of dispersion and the two measures of association. The two statistics indicate that there is about a 10% reduction in errors of classification on the response variable with knowledge of years of education. Figure 32.26c is the parameter estimates for the model.

You could get the same results by first calculating a variable equal to YEAR−10 and then specifying this new variable as a covariate on the LOGLINEAR command, as in:

```
COMPUTE X=YEAR−10
LOGLINEAR RESPONSE(1,2) BY YEAR (0,20) WITH X
  /PRINT=DEFAULT ESTIM
  /DESIGN=RESPONSE RESPONSE BY X
```

Using this approach, you do not need to specify the CONTRAST subcommand on the LOGLINEAR command.

Figure 32.26a Linear logit model fit for Example 4

```
Observed, Expected Frequencies and Residuals

     Factor          Code        OBS. count & PCT.   EXP. count & PCT.    Residual   Std. Resid.   Adj. Resid.

RESPONSE         AGREE
   YEAR            0             4.00 (66.67)         5.34 (89.07)        -1.3444      -.5815       -1.7884
   YEAR            1             2.00 (99.99)         1.73 (86.58)          .2684       .2040         .5599
   YEAR            2             4.00 (99.99)         3.34 (83.62)          .6552       .3583         .8948
   YEAR            3             6.00 (66.67)         7.21 (80.16)        -1.2141      -.4520       -1.0385
   YEAR            4             5.00 (50.00)         7.62 (76.17)        -2.6171      -.9483       -1.9887
   YEAR            5            13.00 (65.00)        14.33 (71.67)        -1.3336      -.3523        -.6901
   YEAR            6            25.00 (73.53)        22.67 (66.69)         2.3266       .4886         .8993
   YEAR            7            27.00 (64.29)        25.75 (61.30)         1.2533       .2470         .4212
   YEAR            8            75.00 (60.48)        68.98 (55.63)         6.0243       .7254        1.2564
   YEAR            9            29.00 (50.00)        28.88 (49.80)          .1167       .0217         .0320
   YEAR           10            32.00 (41.56)        33.86 (43.98)        -1.8627      -.3201        -.4469
   YEAR           11            36.00 (37.89)        36.40 (38.32)         -.4014      -.0665        -.0886
   YEAR           12           115.00 (31.94)       118.65 (32.96)        -3.6453      -.3347        -.4957
   YEAR           13            31.00 (30.69)        28.29 (28.01)         2.7138       .5103         .6348
   YEAR           14            28.00 (26.17)        25.19 (23.54)         2.8145       .5608         .6885
   YEAR           15             9.00 (28.13)         6.27 (19.59)         2.7317      1.0911        1.2470
   YEAR           16            15.00 (12.00)        20.20 (16.16)        -5.2023     -1.1574       -1.4309
   YEAR           17             3.00 ( 9.38)         4.24 (13.24)        -1.2355      -.6003        -.6659
   YEAR           18             1.00 ( 3.45)         3.12 (10.77)        -2.1237     -1.2016       -1.3136
   YEAR           19             2.00 (13.33)         1.31 ( 8.72)          .6920       .6051         .6443
   YEAR           20             3.00 (13.04)         1.62 ( 7.03)         1.3835      1.0881        1.1594

RESPONSE         DISAGREE
   YEAR            0             2.00 (33.33)          .66 (10.93)         1.3444      1.6603        1.7884
   YEAR            1              .00 (  .00)          .27 (13.42)         -.2684      -.5181        -.5599
   YEAR            2              .00 (  .00)          .66 (16.38)         -.6552      -.8095        -.8948
   YEAR            3             3.00 (33.33)         1.79 (19.84)         1.2141       .9085        1.0385
   YEAR            4             5.00 (50.00)         2.38 (23.83)         2.6171      1.6954        1.9887
   YEAR            5             7.00 (35.00)         5.67 (28.33)         1.3336       .5603         .6901
   YEAR            6             9.00 (26.47)        11.33 (33.31)        -2.3266      -.6913        -.8993
   YEAR            7            15.00 (35.71)        16.25 (38.70)        -1.2533      -.3109        -.4212
   YEAR            8            49.00 (39.52)        55.02 (44.37)        -6.0243      -.8121       -1.2564
   YEAR            9            29.00 (50.00)        29.12 (50.20)         -.1167      -.0216        -.0320
   YEAR           10            45.00 (58.44)        43.14 (56.02)         1.8627       .2836         .4469
   YEAR           11            59.00 (62.11)        58.60 (61.68)          .4014       .0524         .0886
   YEAR           12           245.00 (68.06)       241.35 (67.04)         3.6453       .2346         .4957
   YEAR           13            70.00 (69.31)        72.71 (71.99)        -2.7138      -.3182        -.6348
   YEAR           14            79.00 (73.83)        81.81 (76.46)        -2.8145      -.3112        -.6885
   YEAR           15            23.00 (71.88)        25.73 (80.41)        -2.7317      -.5385       -1.2470
   YEAR           16           110.00 (88.00)       104.80 (83.84)         5.2023       .5082        1.4309
   YEAR           17            29.00 (90.63)        27.76 (86.76)         1.2355       .2345         .6659
   YEAR           18            28.00 (96.55)        25.88 (89.23)         2.1237       .4175        1.3136
   YEAR           19            13.00 (86.67)        13.69 (91.28)         -.6920      -.1870        -.6443
   YEAR           20            20.00 (86.96)        21.38 (92.97)        -1.3835      -.2992       -1.1594
```

```
Goodness-of-Fit test statistics

   Likelihood Ratio Chi Square =    18.94502    DF = 19   P =   .460
              Pearson Chi Square =    19.40725    DF = 19   P =   .431
```

Figure 32.26b Linear logit model analysis of dispersion for Example 4

```
Analysis of Dispersion

                                      Dispersion
   Source of Variation        Entropy  Concentration    DF

      Due to Model             81.988      72.577
      Due to Residual         767.922     526.044
      Total                   849.911     598.621      1304
```

Figure 32.26c Linear logit model parameter estimates for Example 4

```
Estimates for Parameters

RESPONSE

Parameter         Coeff.        Std. Err.        Z-Value      Lower 95 CI    Upper 95 CI

     1         -.1210376490        .03334        -3.63002        -.18639        -.05568

RESPONSE BY YEAR(1)

Parameter         Coeff.        Std. Err.        Z-Value      Lower 95 CI    Upper 95 CI

     2         -.1170135446        .01009       -11.59226        -.13680        -.09723
```

32.27
Example 5: Logistic Regression On Category Variables

In the logistic regression model, a dichotomous dependent variable is predicted by one or more independent variables. In LOGLINEAR, the independent variables must be categorical, and one must be measured at the interval level of measurement.

Example 5 is a logistic regression in which a contrast is used to transform the categorical independent variable into a metric variable. The data for this example is taken from Dixon (1979). At a specified time, measured in number of days, a number of objects are tested and the number of failures are recorded. In this example, time is a metric variable, not merely an evenly spaced ordinal variable. RESPONSE is the dependent variable, and TIME is the independent variable. WT defines the number of observations in each cell. The following SPSS-X commands are used:

```
TITLE A LOGISTIC REGRESSION EXAMPLE FROM BMDP(1979) P.517.1
DATA LIST LIST/ RESPONSE TIME WT *
VALUE LABELS RESPONSE 1 'SUCCESS' 2 'FAILURE'
IF (WT = 0) WT = .00001
WEIGHT BY WT

LOGLINEAR RESPONSE(1,2) BY TIME(1,4)
        /CONTRAST(TIME) = SPECIAL(4*1, 7 14 27 51, 8*1)
        /PRINT = ALL/PLOT = DEFAULT
        /DESIGN = RESPONSE, TIME(1) BY RESPONSE
/BEGIN DATA
1 1  55
2 1   0
1 2 155
2 2   2
1 3 152
2 3   7
1 4  13
2 4   3
END DATA
```

- Since the log of 0 is undefined, sampling zeros (not structural zeros) should always be changed to some small positive number in log-linear analysis. Many corrections have been suggested, such as adding 0.5 to each cell or using pseudo-Bayes estimates (Bishop, Feinberg, & Holland, 1975; Goodman, 1971). In this example, the IF command changes sampling zeros to .00001.

- The BY keyword in the variables specification on LOGLINEAR indicates a logit model.

- The PRINT subcommand requests all printed materials, and the PLOT subcommand requests the default plots.

- The SPECIAL contrast on the CONTRAST subcommand specifies the metric of time. The constant effect is specified first, followed by the linear effect in the metric of time: 7, 14, 27, 51. Since no higher order effect is of interest, the matrix is filled out with 1s.

- The DESIGN subcommand fits RESPONSE and RESPONSE by linear-TIME.

Figure 32.27a shows the design matrix for the model. Figure 32.27b shows the logistic regression fit. Overall, the fit is good. Both chi-square statistics are nonsignificant, and all adjusted residuals are well under 2 in magnitude. Figure 32.27c shows the estimated parameters and the correlation matrix of parameter estimates. As in logit models, you can multiply the two parameter values by 2 to obtain the constant and the regression coefficient for the logistic model. Finally, Figure 32.27d shows the normal and detrended normal plots of the residuals against their expected values produced by the NORMPROB default keyword. The plots show the characteristic S-curve shape associated with logistic regression.

Figure 32.27a Model design for Example 5

```
Correspondence Between Effects and Columns of Design/Model 1

   Starting  Ending
    Column   Column   Effect Name

      1        1      RESPONSE
      2        2      TIME(1) BY RESPONSE

- - - - - - - - - - - - - - - - - - - - - - - - - - - - - - - - - - - - - - -


   Design Matrix

   1-RESPONSE  2-TIME

   Factor                              Parameter

     1    2                        1          2

     1    1          1.00000    7.00000
     1    2          1.00000   14.00000
     1    3          1.00000   27.00000
     1    4          1.00000   51.00000
     2    1         -1.00000   -7.00000
     2    2         -1.00000  -14.00000
     2    3         -1.00000  -27.00000
     2    4         -1.00000  -51.00000
```

Figure 32.27b Model fit for Example 5

```
Observed, Expected Frequencies and Residuals

     Factor          Code       OBS. count & PCT.    EXP. count & PCT.    Residual   Std. Resid.   Adj. Resid.


RESPONSE    SUCCESS
  TIME                  1        55.00 (100.0)       54.57 (99.22)         .4271       .0578         .7103
  TIME                  2       155.00 (98.73)      154.87 (98.64)         .1322       .0106         .1226
  TIME                  3       152.00 (95.60)      152.99 (96.22)        -.9867      -.0798        -.6085
  TIME                  4        13.00 (81.25)       12.57 (78.58)         .4275       .1206         .6964

RESPONSE    FAILURE
  TIME                  1          .00 (  .00)          .43 (  .78)        -.4271      -.6535        -.7103
  TIME                  2         2.00 ( 1.27)         2.13 ( 1.36)        -.1322      -.0905        -.1226
  TIME                  3         7.00 ( 4.40)         6.01 ( 3.78)         .9867       .4024         .6085
  TIME                  4         3.00 (18.75)         3.43 (21.42)        -.4275      -.2309        -.6964

- - - - - - - - - - - - - - - - - - - - - - - - - - - - - - - - - - - - - - -

Goodness-of-Fit test statistics

   Likelihood Ratio Chi Square =    1.09592   DF = 2   P =  .578
             Pearson Chi Square =     .67485   DF = 2   P =  .714
```

Figure 32.27c Estimated parameters for Example 5

```
Estimates for Parameters

RESPONSE

Parameter        Coeff.        Std. Err.       Z-Value     Lower 95 CI     Upper 95 CI

    1        2.7075864999        .36377         7.44312       1.99460         3.42058

TIME(1) BY RESPONSE

Parameter        Coeff.        Std. Err.       Z-Value     Lower 95 CI     Upper 95 CI

    2        -.0403479334        .01118        -3.60955       -.06226         -.01844

- - - - - - - - - - - - - - - - - - - - - - - - - - - - - - - - - - - - - - -


Covariance(below) and Correlation(above) Matrices of Parameter Estimates

Parameter                           Parameter

              1          2

    1       .13233    -.91014
    2      -.00370     .00012
```

Figure 32.27d   Plot of adjusted residuals for Example 5

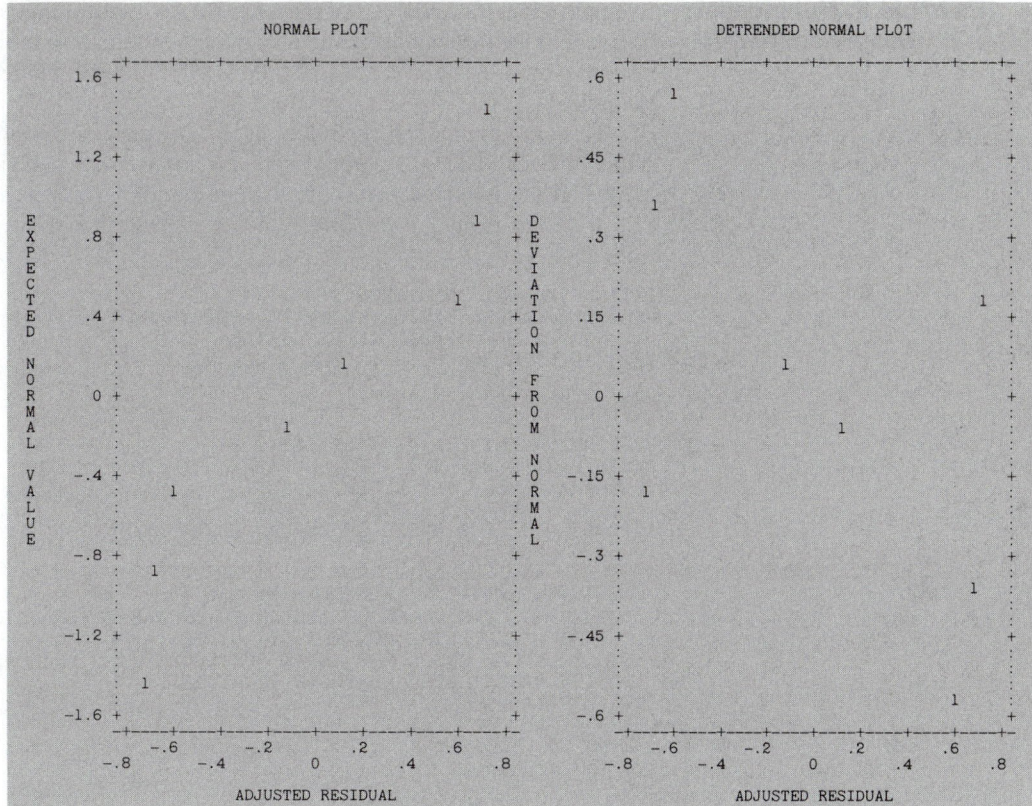

If the metric of the time measure is recorded on your data, you can specify the metric variable as a cell covariate and not specify the CONTRAST subcommand, as in:

```
DATA LIST LIST/RESPONSE TIME X WT
IF (WT = 0) WT = .00001
WEIGHT BY WT
LOGLINEAR RESPONSE (1,2) BY TIME(1,4) WITH X
  /PRINT=ALL/PLOT=DEFAULT
  /DESIGN=RESPONSE, X BY RESPONSE
/BEGIN DATA
1 1 7 55
2 1 7 0
1 2 14 155
2 2 14 2
1 3 27 152
2 3 27 7
1 4 51 13
2 4 51 3
END DATA
```

This approach can easily be extended to two or more independent variables with the metric values of the independent variables recorded in separate variables and specified as covariates on the LOGLINEAR variables specification and DESIGN subcommand.

32.28
Example 6: Multinomial Response Models

Example 6 illustrates the use of the CONTRAST subcommand and single-degree-of-freedom partitions to analyze a 4 × 6 crosstabulation table. The multinomial response models fit are generalizations of the logit model in the annotated example.

This example models the relationship between two variables— mental health status (MENTHLTH) by parental socioeconomic status (SES) (Haberman, 1979). MENTHLTH is scaled from 1 to 4 corresponding to Well and Impaired poles. SES is scaled from 1 to 6 corresponding to High and Low poles. The SPSS-X commands are

```
DATA LIST LIST/ MENTHLTH SES WT *
VARIABLE LABELS MENTHLTH 'MENTAL HEALTH CATEGORY'
            SES 'PARENTAL SE STATUS'
VALUE LABELS MENTHLTH 1 'WELL'  2 'MILD'  3 'MODERATE' 4 'IMPAIRED'
 /SES 1 'A--HIGH' 2 'B' 3 'C' 4 'D' 5 'E' 6 'F--LOW'
WEIGHT BY WT

LOGLINEAR MENTHLTH(1,4) BY SES(1,6)
 /CONTRAST(MENTHLTH) = POLYNOMIAL
 /CONTRAST(SES) = POLYNOMIAL
 /PRINT = DEFAULT ESTIM
 /*MODEL 1:   THE MODEL OF COLUMN HOMOGENEITY
 /DESIGN=MENTHLTH
 /*MODEL 2:   THE SIMULTANEOUS LINEAR LOGIT MODEL
 /DESIGN = MENTHLTH, MENTHLTH BY SES(1)
 /*MODEL 3:   THE MODEL OF LINEAR BY LINEAR INTERACTION
 /DESIGN = MENTHLTH, MENTHLTH(1) BY SES(1)
 /*MODEL 4:   A MODEL FOR KNOWN ROW SCORES AND UNKNOWN COLUMN SCORES
 /DESIGN = MENTHLTH, MENTHLTH(1) BY SES
/BEGIN DATA
1 1  64 7
1 2  57 4
1 3  57 3
1 4  72 8
1 5  36 9
1 6  21 5
...
4 1  46 7
4 2  40 5
4 3  60 6
4 4  94 8
4 5  78 9
4 6  71 9
END DATA
```

• The BY keyword in the variables specification indicates a logit model.

• The CONTRAST subcommands specify polynomial contrasts for MENTHLTH and SES. The polynomial contrast is often useful in the analysis of polytomous variables.

• The PRINT subcommand requests the DEFAULT (keywords FREQ and RESID) and ESTIM display output for all models.

• In Model 1, only the dependent variable appears on the DESIGN subcommand. This model is termed the model for column homogeneity because it fits the same expected cell percentage to all frequencies of a given column. Model 1 fits three parameters associated with the MENTHLTH effect and assumes no association between MENTHLTH and SES.

• Model 2 is termed the simultaneous linear logit model. It fits three parameters for the MENTHLTH effect, plus three parameters for the MENTHLTH by linear-SES interaction. That is, each dependent-variable logit is a linear function of the parents' socioeconomic score.

- Model 3 is the model of the linear-by-linear interaction. It fits four parameters—three for MENTHLTH and one for the linear-by-linear interaction of MENTHLTH and SES. Model 3 is the most parsimonious model accounting for association between MENTHLTH and SES.

- Model 4 is a model for known row scores and unknown column scores. Scores are given for the independent variable categories, but scores for the categories of the dependent variable are unknown. "Unknown" means that no scale for the dependent variable is assumed. The model fits three parameters for the MENTHLTH effect and five for the MENTHLTH-linear by SES interaction. Model 4 stands somewhat apart from Models 2 and 3 but appears here for the sake of completeness.

Figure 32.28a shows the Model 1 fit. The goodness-of-fit statistics show lack of fit of this model.

Figure 32.28b shows the Model 2 fit. The goodness-of-fit statistics indicate good fit, and the adjusted residuals are all less than 2 in magnitude.

Figure 32.28c shows the Model 3 fit. Model 3 fits the data, and since Model 3 is simpler it is preferable to Model 2. Figure 32.28d shows the parameter estimates for Model 3.

Finally, Figure 32.28e shows the Model 4 fit.

Figure 32.28a   Model 1 fit for Example 6

```
Observed, Expected Frequencies and Residuals

        Factor          Code          OBS. count & PCT.    EXP. count & PCT.     Residual    Std. Resid.    Adj. Resid.

MENTHLTH        WELL
   SES          A--HIGH             64.00 (24.43)        48.45 (18.49)        15.5458       2.2333         2.6956
   SES          B                   57.00 (23.27)        45.31 (18.49)        11.6898       1.7366         2.0835
   SES          C                   57.00 (19.86)        53.08 (18.49)         3.9223        .5384          .6557
   SES          D                   72.00 (18.75)        71.02 (18.49)          .9831        .1167          .1474
   SES          E                   36.00 (13.58)        49.01 (18.49)       -13.0090      -1.8583        -2.2453
   SES          F--LOW              21.00 ( 9.68)        40.13 (18.49)       -19.1319      -3.0200        -3.5879

MENTHLTH        MILD
   SES          A--HIGH             94.00 (35.88)        95.01 (36.27)        -1.0145       -.1041         -.1421
   SES          B                   94.00 (38.37)        88.85 (36.27)         5.1506        .5464          .7413
   SES          C                  105.00 (36.59)       104.08 (36.27)          .9193        .0901          .1241
   SES          D                  141.00 (36.72)       139.26 (36.27)         1.7422        .1476          .2109
   SES          E                   97.00 (36.60)        96.10 (36.27)          .8976        .0916          .1251
   SES          F--LOW              71.00 (32.72)        78.70 (36.27)        -7.6952       -.8675        -1.1654

MENTHLTH        MODERATE
   SES          A--HIGH             58.00 (22.14)        57.13 (21.81)          .8651        .1144          .1410
   SES          B                   54.00 (22.04)        53.43 (21.81)          .5723        .0783          .0959
   SES          C                   65.00 (22.65)        62.59 (21.81)         2.4133        .3050          .3793
   SES          D                   77.00 (20.05)        83.74 (21.81)        -6.7398       -.7365         -.9500
   SES          E                   54.00 (20.38)        57.79 (21.81)        -3.7892       -.4984         -.6149
   SES          F--LOW              54.00 (24.88)        47.32 (21.81)         6.6783        .9708         1.1775

MENTHLTH        IMPAIRED
   SES          A--HIGH             46.00 (17.56)        61.40 (23.43)       -15.3964      -1.9649        -2.4470
   SES          B                   40.00 (16.33)        57.41 (23.43)       -17.4127      -2.2981        -2.8446
   SES          C                   60.00 (20.91)        67.25 (23.43)        -7.2548       -.8846        -1.1116
   SES          D                   94.00 (24.48)        89.99 (23.43)         4.0145        .4232          .5516
   SES          E                   78.00 (29.43)        62.10 (23.43)        15.9006       2.0178         2.5155
   SES          F--LOW              71.00 (32.72)        50.85 (23.43)        20.1488       2.8255         3.4634

- - - - - - - - - - - - - - - - - - - - - - - - - - - - - - - - - - - - - - - - - - - - -

Goodness-of-Fit test statistics

    Likelihood Ratio Chi Square =    47.41785    DF = 15   P =  .000
          Pearson Chi Square =    45.98526    DF = 15   P =  .000
```

Figure 32.28b Model 2 fit for Example 6

```
Observed, Expected Frequencies and Residuals

     Factor        Code          OBS. count & PCT.   EXP. count & PCT.   Residual   Std. Resid.   Adj. Resid.

  MENTHLTH       WELL
     SES           A--HIGH          64.00 (24.43)       68.57 (26.17)     -4.5659      -.5514        -.9982
     SES           B                57.00 (23.27)       55.68 (22.73)      1.3160       .1764         .2345
     SES           C                57.00 (19.86)       56.11 (19.55)       .8943       .1194         .1475
     SES           D                72.00 (18.75)       63.94 (16.65)      8.0551      1.0073        1.2970
     SES           E                36.00 (13.58)       37.23 (14.05)     -1.2278      -.2012        -.2600
     SES           F--LOW           21.00 ( 9.68)       25.47 (11.74)     -4.4717      -.8860       -1.2001

  MENTHLTH       MILD
     SES           A--HIGH          94.00 (35.88)       96.92 (36.99)     -2.9192      -.2965        -.5489
     SES           B                94.00 (38.37)       91.00 (37.14)      2.9996       .3144         .4651
     SES           C               105.00 (36.59)      106.01 (36.94)     -1.0063      -.0977        -.1368
     SES           D               141.00 (36.72)      139.68 (36.38)      1.3176       .1115         .1625
     SES           E                97.00 (36.60)       94.02 (35.48)      2.9814       .3075         .4584
     SES           F--LOW           71.00 (32.72)       74.37 (34.27)     -3.3731      -.3911        -.6501

  MENTHLTH       MODERATE
     SES           A--HIGH          58.00 (22.14)       55.70 (21.26)      2.2967       .3077         .5053
     SES           B                54.00 (22.04)       53.27 (21.74)       .7302       .1000         .1327
     SES           C                65.00 (22.65)       63.20 (22.02)      1.7973       .2261         .2847
     SES           D                77.00 (20.05)       84.82 (22.09)     -7.8228      -.8494       -1.1176
     SES           E                54.00 (20.38)       58.15 (21.94)     -4.1502      -.5442        -.7379
     SES           F--LOW           54.00 (24.88)       46.85 (21.59)      7.1489      1.0444        1.5913

  MENTHLTH       IMPAIRED
     SES           A--HIGH          46.00 (17.56)       40.81 (15.58)      5.1885       .8122        1.2173
     SES           B                40.00 (16.33)       45.05 (18.39)     -5.0458      -.7518        -.9794
     SES           C                60.00 (20.91)       61.69 (21.49)     -1.6853      -.2146        -.2711
     SES           D                94.00 (24.48)       95.55 (24.88)     -1.5499      -.1586        -.2115
     SES           E                78.00 (29.43)       75.60 (28.53)      2.3967       .2756         .3903
     SES           F--LOW           71.00 (32.72)       70.30 (32.40)       .6959       .0830         .1421
- - - - - - - - - - - - - - - - - - - - - - - - - - - - - - - - - - - - - - - - - - - - - - - - - - - - - -

Goodness-of-Fit test statistics

     Likelihood Ratio Chi Square =    6.28076    DF = 12   P =  .901
               Pearson Chi Square =    6.28911    DF = 12   P =  .901
```

Figure 32.28c Model 3 fit for Example 6

```
Observed, Expected Frequencies and Residuals

     Factor        Code          OBS. count & PCT.   EXP. count & PCT.   Residual   Std. Resid.   Adj. Resid.

  MENTHLTH       WELL
     SES           A--HIGH          64.00 (24.43)       65.29 (24.92)     -1.2908      -.1598        -.2304
     SES           B                57.00 (23.27)       54.21 (22.13)      2.7865       .3784         .4850
     SES           C                57.00 (19.86)       55.91 (19.48)      1.0917       .1460         .1802
     SES           D                72.00 (18.75)       65.28 (17.00)      6.7234       .8322        1.0473
     SES           E                36.00 (13.58)       38.96 (14.70)     -2.9616      -.4745        -.5793
     SES           F--LOW           21.00 ( 9.68)       27.35 (12.60)     -6.3491     -1.2141       -1.4999

  MENTHLTH       MILD
     SES           A--HIGH          94.00 (35.88)      104.42 (39.86)    -10.4234     -1.0200       -1.4673
     SES           B                94.00 (38.37)       94.94 (38.75)      -.9375      -.0962        -.1350
     SES           C               105.00 (36.59)      107.20 (37.35)     -2.1991      -.2124        -.2967
     SES           D               141.00 (36.72)      137.04 (35.69)      3.9569       .3380         .4807
     SES           E                97.00 (36.60)       89.56 (33.80)      7.4385       .7860        1.0640
     SES           F--LOW           71.00 (32.72)       68.84 (31.72)      2.1645       .2609         .3509

  MENTHLTH       MODERATE
     SES           A--HIGH          58.00 (22.14)       50.15 (19.14)      7.8546      1.1092        1.3647
     SES           B                54.00 (22.04)       49.92 (20.37)      4.0821       .5778         .7022
     SES           C                65.00 (22.65)       61.72 (21.50)      3.2845       .4181         .5185
     SES           D                77.00 (20.05)       86.39 (22.50)     -9.3863     -1.0099       -1.3171
     SES           E                54.00 (20.38)       61.81 (23.33)     -7.8150      -.9940       -1.2521
     SES           F--LOW           54.00 (24.88)       52.02 (23.97)      1.9801       .2745         .3421

  MENTHLTH       IMPAIRED
     SES           A--HIGH          46.00 (17.56)       42.14 (16.08)      3.8597       .5946         .8101
     SES           B                40.00 (16.33)       45.93 (18.75)     -5.9312      -.8752       -1.0996
     SES           C                60.00 (20.91)       62.18 (21.66)     -2.1771      -.2761        -.3454
     SES           D                94.00 (24.48)       95.29 (24.82)     -1.2940      -.1326        -.1766
     SES           E                78.00 (29.43)       74.66 (28.17)      3.3381       .3863         .5292
     SES           F--LOW           71.00 (32.72)       68.80 (31.70)      2.2045       .2658         .3994
- - - - - - - - - - - - - - - - - - - - - - - - - - - - - - - - - - - - - - - - - - - - - - - - - - - - - -

Goodness-of-Fit test statistics

     Likelihood Ratio Chi Square =    9.89512    DF = 14   P =  .770
               Pearson Chi Square =    9.73185    DF = 14   P =  .782
```

Figure 32.28d   Model 3 parameter estimates for Example 6

```
Estimates for Parameters

MENTHLTH

Parameter          Coeff.        Std. Err.      Z-Value      Lower 95 CI      Upper 95 CI

    1          .0492160727        .05392        .91272        -.05647          .15490
    2         -.3217618318        .05109       -6.29802       -.42190         -.22163
    3          .3941588489        .04777       8.25112         .30053          .48779

MENTHLTH(1) BY SES(1)

Parameter          Coeff.        Std. Err.      Z-Value      Lower 95 CI      Upper 95 CI

    4          .8482955490        .14037       6.04331         .57317         1.12342
```

Figure 32.28e   Model 4 fit for Example 6

```
Observed, Expected Frequencies and Residuals
       Factor        Code        OBS. count & PCT.    EXP. count & PCT.    Residual    Std. Resid.    Adj. Resid.

MENTHLTH       WELL
  SES          A--HIGH          64.00 (24.43)        60.15 (22.96)         3.8488       .4963          .8867
  SES          B                57.00 (23.27)        57.26 (23.37)         -.2596      -.0343         -.0613
  SES          C                57.00 (19.86)        56.43 (19.66)         .5650        .0752          .1285
  SES          D                72.00 (18.75)        69.86 (18.19)         2.1389       .2559          .4423
  SES          E                36.00 (13.58)        38.52 (14.53)         -2.5159     -.4054         -.6281
  SES          F--LOW           21.00 ( 9.68)        24.78 (11.42)         -3.7773     -.7588        -1.0953

MENTHLTH       MILD
  SES          A--HIGH          94.00 (35.88)       102.54 (39.14)         -8.5431     -.8437        -1.2335
  SES          B                94.00 (38.37)        96.31 (39.31)         -2.3059     -.2350         -.3410
  SES          C               105.00 (36.59)       107.58 (37.48)         -2.5776     -.2485         -.3684
  SES          D               141.00 (36.72)       140.38 (36.56)         .6185        .0522          .0805
  SES          E                97.00 (36.60)        89.22 (33.67)         7.7829       .8240         1.2233
  SES          F--LOW           71.00 (32.72)        65.97 (30.40)         5.0252       .6187          .9149

MENTHLTH       MODERATE
  SES          A--HIGH          58.00 (22.14)        52.46 (20.02)         5.5397       .7648          .9781
  SES          B                54.00 (22.04)        48.61 (19.84)         5.3907       .7732          .9837
  SES          C                65.00 (22.65)        61.54 (21.44)         3.4601       .4411          .5687
  SES          D                77.00 (20.05)        84.65 (22.05)         -7.6538     -.8319        -1.1133
  SES          E                54.00 (20.38)        62.02 (23.40)         -8.0181    -1.0181        -1.3021
  SES          F--LOW           54.00 (24.88)        52.72 (24.29)         1.2815       .1765          .2213

MENTHLTH       IMPAIRED
  SES          A--HIGH          46.00 (17.56)        46.85 (17.88)         -.8454      -.1235         -.2297
  SES          B                40.00 (16.33)        42.83 (17.48)         -2.8251     -.4317         -.7925
  SES          C                60.00 (20.91)        61.45 (21.41)         -1.4475     -.1847         -.3692
  SES          D                94.00 (24.48)        89.10 (23.20)         4.8964       .5187         1.1104
  SES          E                78.00 (29.43)        75.25 (28.40)         2.7511       .3171          .7058
  SES          F--LOW           71.00 (32.72)        73.53 (33.88)         -2.5294     -.2950         -.7011


- - - - - - - - - - - - - - - - - - - - - - - - - - - - - - - - - - - - - - - - - - - - - - - - - -


Goodness-of-Fit test statistics

  Likelihood Ratio Chi Square =    6.82933    DF = 10    P =   .741
          Pearson Chi Square =    6.78143    DF = 10    P =   .746
```

32.29
Example 7: A Distance Model

Example 7 demonstrates the use of the CWEIGHT subcommand to impose zeros on the diagonal of a symmetric table and the use of a covariate to fit a model with a distance function. Distance models are used for ordered symmetric tables. Example 7 models the relationship between husband's education level (HUSED) and wife's education level (WIFED) (Haberman, 1979). HUSED and WIFED are ordinal variables with four levels. The original table has one empty cell. There is no woman with a graduate degree whose husband has less than a high-school education. To avoid degree-of-freedom problems, this cell is set to a small number in the table. The SPSS-X commands are

```
TITLE 'HABERMAN''S DISTANCE MODEL, PAGE 500'
DATA LIST  LIST/ HUSED WIFED WT *
VARIABLE LABELS  HUSED 'HUSBAND''S EDUCATION'
                 WIFED 'WIFE''S EDUCATION'
VALUE LABELS  HUSED WIFED 1 '< HS' 2 'HS OR JC'
   3 'COLLEGE' 4 'GRAD DEG'
WEIGHT  BY WT
COMPUTE  DISTANCE=ABS(HUSED - WIFED)
COMPUTE  CWT=1
IF (HUSED EQ WIFED) CWT=0

LOGLINEAR  HUSED WIFED(1,4) WITH DISTANCE
  /CWEIGHT=CWT/PRINT DEF ESTIM
  /DESIGN=HUSED WIFED DISTANCE
/BEGIN DATA
1 1 259
1 2 123
1 3   2
1 4   0.1
2 1  82
2 2 370
2 3  30
2 4   7
3 1   5
3 2  59
3 3  34
3 4   4
4 1   2
4 2  41
4 3  29
4 4   8
END DATA
FINISH
```

- The DATA LIST command defines HUSED, WIFED, and WT, which is the frequency count for each cell.
- The WEIGHT command weights the table to the original sample size.
- The first COMPUTE command computes the distance function, which is the absolute distance between husband's and wife's education.
- The second COMPUTE and the IF command create the variable CWT. CWT is set to 0 for the cases in the diagonal cells of the table and to 1 for all other cases.
- The variables specification on the LOGLINEAR command defines a general log-linear model with the distance function as a covariate.
- The CWEIGHT subcommand specifies the variable CWT, which imposes zeros on the diagonal.
- The DESIGN subcommand names the main effects and the covariate. Note that it is not a saturated model.

Figure 32.29 contains the fit and parameter estimates for the model.

Figure 32.29 Display for Example 7

```
Observed, Expected Frequencies and Residuals

    Factor          Code        OBS. count & PCT.   EXP. count & PCT.    Residual    Std. Resid.   Adj. Resid.


 HUSED         | HS
 WIFED         | HS                  .00 (   .00)        .00 (   .00)       .0000        .0000        .0000
 WIFED         HS OR JC          123.00 (32.02)      121.97 (31.76)       1.0255        .0929        .7573
 WIFED         COLLEGE             2.00 (   .52)       2.71 (   .70)      -.7054       -.4289       -.5375
 WIFED         GRAD DEG            .10 (   .03)        .42 (   .11)      -.3201       -.4939       -.5183

 HUSED         HS OR JC
 WIFED         | HS               82.00 (21.35)       83.03 (21.62)      -1.0255      -.1125       -.7573
 WIFED         HS OR JC            .00 (   .00)        .00 (   .00)       .0000        .0000        .0000
 WIFED         COLLEGE            30.00 ( 7.81)       31.14 ( 8.11)      -1.1391      -.2041       -.6068
 WIFED         GRAD DEG            7.00 ( 1.82)        4.84 ( 1.26)       2.1646       .9844       1.4648

 HUSED         COLLEGE
 WIFED         | HS                5.00 ( 1.30)        3.47 (   .90)       1.5295       .8210       1.0818
 WIFED         HS OR JC           59.00 (15.36)       58.68 (15.28)       .3151        .0411        .1594
 WIFED         COLLEGE             .00 (   .00)        .00 (   .00)       .0000        .0000        .0000
 WIFED         GRAD DEG            4.00 ( 1.04)        5.84 ( 1.52)      -1.8445      -.7630      -1.2593

 HUSED         GRAD DEG
 WIFED         | HS                2.00 (   .52)       2.50 (   .65)      -.5040       -.3185       -.3863
 WIFED         HS OR JC           41.00 (10.67)       42.34 (11.02)      -1.3406      -.2060       -.7058
 WIFED         COLLEGE            29.00 ( 7.55)       27.16 ( 7.07)       1.8445       .3540       1.2593
 WIFED         GRAD DEG            .00 (   .00)        .00 (   .00)       .0000        .0000        .0000


Goodness-of-Fit test statistics

   Likelihood Ratio Chi Square =    2.99300   DF = 4   P =  .559
            Pearson Chi Square =    2.98686   DF = 4   P =  .560


Estimates for Parameters

HUSED

Parameter       Coeff.        Std. Err.      Z-Value      Lower 95 CI    Upper 95 CI

      1      -.1633790844       .12325      -1.32561       -.40495         .07819
      2       .5976368139       .16018       3.73106        .28369         .91159
      3      -.8950079354       .12962      -6.90487      -1.14906        -.64095

WIFED

Parameter       Coeff.        Std. Err.      Z-Value      Lower 95 CI    Upper 95 CI

      4       .2489999000       .15437       1.61301       -.05356         .55156
      5      1.3946797275       .14979       9.31103       1.10110        1.68826
      6      -.7316830779       .15862      -4.61287      -1.04257        -.42079

DISTANCE

Parameter       Coeff.        Std. Err.      Z-Value      Lower 95 CI    Upper 95 CI

      7      -1.6821952195       .20332      -8.27375      -2.08070       -1.28369
```

Syntax

MANOVA

```
MANOVA dependent varlist [BY factor list (min,max) [factor list...]
                          [WITH covariate list]]

[/WSFACTORS=name (levels) name...]
[/TRANSFORM [(varlist [/varlist])]=[ORTHONORM] [{CONTRAST}]]
    [{DEVIATIONS (refcat) }]             {BASIS   }
     {DIFFERENCE            }
     {HELMERT               }
     {SIMPLE (refcat)       }
     {REPEATED              }
     {POLYNOMIAL [(metric)] }
     {SPECIAL (matrix)      }
[/WSDESIGN=effect effect...]
[/MEASURE=newname newname...]
[/RENAME={newname} {newname}...]
         {*       } {*      }

[/MISSING=[LISTWISE] [INCLUDE]]
[/{PRINT  }= [CELLINFO ([MEANS] [SSCP] [COV] [COR] [ALL])]]
  {NOPRINT }

     [HOMOGENEITY ([BARTLETT] [COCHRAN] [BOXM] [ALL])]

     [DESIGN ([ONEWAY] [OVERALL] [DECOMP] [BIAS] [SOLUTION]
              [REDUNDANCY] [COLLINEARITY] [ALL])]

     [ERROR ([SSCP] [COV] [COR] [STDDEV] [ALL])]

     [SIGNIF ([MULTIV] [EIGEN] [DIMENR] [UNIV] [HYPOTH]
              [AVERF] [AVONLY] [HF] [GG] [EFSIZE]
              [SINGLEDF] [BRIEF] [STEPDOWN] [ALL] [NONE])]

     [PARAMETERS ([ESTIM] [ORTHO] [COR] [NEGSUM] [ALL])]
                 [EFSIZE] [OPTIMAL])]
[/PLOT=[CELLPLOTS] [STEMLEAF] [ZCORR] [NORMAL] [BOXPLOTS]]
       [ALL]
[/PCOMPS [COR] [NCOMP(n)] [MINEIGEN(eigencut)]
         [COV] [ROTATE(rottype)] [ALL]]
[/DISCRIM [RAW] [STAN] [ESTIM] [COR] [ALL]
          [ROTATE(rottype)] [ALPHA({.25})]]
                                   {a  }
[/OMEANS [VARIABLES(varlist)] [TABLES ({factor name   })]]
                                      {factor BY factor}
                                      {CONSTANT        }
[/PMEANS [VARIABLES(varlist)] [TABLES ({factor name   })]]
                                      {factor BY factor}
                                      {CONSTANT        }
          [PLOT]
[/RESIDUALS [CASEWISE] [PLOT]]
[/METHOD=[MODELTYPE ({MEANS       })]
                    {OBSERVATIONS}
         [ESTIMATION ({QR      } {NOLASTRES} {NOBALANCED} {CONSTANT   })]
                     {CHOLESKY} {LASTRES  } {BALANCED  } {NOCONSTANT}
         [SSTYPE ({UNIQUE    })]]
                 {SEQUENTIAL}
[/MATRIX=[IN({file})]  [OUT({file})]]
             {*   }        {*   }
[/ANALYSIS [({CONDITIONAL  })]=dependent varlist
            {UNCONDITIONAL}    [WITH covariate varlist]
                               [/dependent varlist...]]
[/PARTITION (factorname)[=({1,1...  })]]
                          {df,df...}
                          {DEVIATION [(refcat)]   }
                          {SIMPLE [(refcat)]      }
                          {DIFFERENCE             }
[/CONTRAST (factorname)={HELMERT                 }]
                          {REPEATED               }
                          {POLYNOMIAL[({1,2,3...})]}
                          {           {metric   }  }
                          {SPECIAL (matrix)       }
[/CRITERIA=[ZETA ({1.0E-8})] [EPS ({1.0E-8})]]
                 {zeta  }         {eps   }
           {WITHIN           }         {W }
[/ERROR={RESIDUAL          } or {R }]
           {WITHIN + RESIDUAL}         {WR}
           {n                }
[/POWER=[T({.05})] [F({.05})] [{APPROXIMATE}]]
           {a  }     {a  }     {EXACT      }
[/CINTERVAL=[{INDIVIDUAL}][({.95})]] [UNIVARIATE ({BONFER })]]
            {JOINT     }    {a  }                {SCHEFFE}

                                [MULTIVARIATE ({ROY     })]]
                                              {PILLAI  }
                                              {BONFER  }
                                              {HOTELLING}
                                              {WILKS   }

        [CONSTANT...]                               }
        [effect effect...]                          }
        [CONTIN (varlist)...]                       }
        [effects BY effects...]                     }
[/DESIGN={[effects {WITHIN} effects...]            }]
         {        {W     }                          }
        [effect + effect...]                        }
        [factor (level)... [WITHIN factor (partition)...]]]
        [MUPLUS...]                                 }
        [MWITHIN...]                                }
        [{terms-to-be-tested} {AGAINST} {WITHIN  }  {W }]]
        [{term=n            } {VS     } {RESIDUAL} or {R }]
                                        {WR       }  {RW}
                                        {n        }
```

Contents

33.1	OVERVIEW
33.2	OPERATION
33.3	Variable Specification
33.7	DESIGN Subcommand
33.19	ANALYSIS Subcommand
33.20	Repeated Measures Designs
33.24	MEASURE Subcommand
33.25	TRANSFORM Subcommand
33.30	RENAME Subcommand
33.31	METHOD Subcommand
33.35	PARTITION Subcommand
33.36	CONTRAST Subcommand
33.37	CRITERIA Subcommand
33.38	ERROR Subcommand
33.39	PRINT and NOPRINT Subcommands
33.47	PCOMPS Subcommand
33.48	DISCRIM Subcommand
33.49	OMEANS Subcommand
33.50	PMEANS Subcommand
33.51	PLOT Subcommand
33.52	RESIDUALS Subcommand
33.53	POWER Subcommand
33.54	CINTERVAL Subcommand
33.55	MISSING Subcommand
33.56	MATRIX Subcommand
33.59	EXAMPLES OF COMMON DESIGNS
33.60	Univariate Analysis of Variance
33.66	Randomized Block Designs
33.70	Latin and Other Squares
33.71	Nested Designs
33.72	MANOVA EXAMPLES
33.73	Example 1: Analysis of Covariance Designs
33.74	Example 2: Multivariate One-Way ANOVA
33.75	Example 3: Multivariate Multiple Regression, Canonical Correlation
33.76	Example 4: Repeated Measures
33.77	Example 5: Repeated Measures with a Constant Covariate
33.78	Example 6: Repeated Measures with a Varying Covariate
33.79	Example 7: A Doubly Multivariate Repeated Measures Design
33.80	Example 8: Profile Analysis

33

MANOVA was originally designed and programmed by Philip Burns of Northwestern University.

Chapter 33   MANOVA

SPSS-X MANOVA is a generalized multivariate analysis of variance and covariance program. The procedure performs univariate and multivariate linear estimation and tests of hypotheses for any crossed and/or nested design with or without covariates. You have complete control of the model specification. For example, you can test for effects jointly, or you can specify single-degree-of-freedom partitions. Also, you can specify interaction effects between factors and covariates.

33.1
OVERVIEW

With MANOVA, you can perform analysis of variance and analysis of covariance, and you can analyze designs such as randomized block, split-plot, nested, and repeated measures designs. You can also estimate multivariate regressions and obtain principal components, discriminant function coefficients, canonical correlations, and other statistics for a variety of general linear models. In addition, you can calculate observed power and effect sizes, Scheffé optional contrasts, redundancy checks, and simultaneous univariate or multivariate confidence intervals. Section 33.59 gives some examples of common designs and Section 33.72 through Section 33.81 gives some extended examples with output.

Specifying Within-Subjects Designs, Pooled Results, and VariableTransformations. The WSFACTORS subcommand provides the within-subjects factors for a repeated measures design. (See Section 33.21.) The WSDESIGN subcommand specifies the model for the within-subjects factors. (See Section 33.22.) The MEASURE subcommand specifies names for pooled results in doubly multivariate repeated measures designs. (See Section 33.24.) The TRANSFORM subcommand requests a linear transformation of the dependent variables and covariates. (See Section 33.25.) The RENAME subcommand renames the transformed variables. (See Section 33.30.)

Optional Printed Output. The PRINT, PCOMPS, DISCRIM, OMEANS, PMEANS, and RESIDUALS subcommands specify optional printed output. The PLOT subcommand specifies optional line-printer plots. (See Sections 33.39 through 33.52.)

Computational Options and Model Specifications. The ANALYSIS subcommand subsets and/or reorders the variables named on the MANOVA specification. (See Section 33.19.) The DESIGN subcommand specifies the design model to be analyzed. The DESIGN specification should be the last subcommand of a complete MANOVA specification. (See Section 33.7.) The METHOD subcommand provides several options for parameter estimation. (See Section 33.31.) The PARTITION subcommand subdivides the degrees of freedom of a factor. (See Section 33.35.) The CONTRAST subcommand specifies the type of contrast desired for a factor. (See Section 33.36.) The CRITERIA subcommand sets two algorithm-tuning parameters, which are used throughout the MANOVA procedure. (See Section 33.37.) The ERROR subcommand specifies the error term to be used in the model. (See Section 33.38.) The MISSING subcommand controls missing values. (See Section 33.55.)

Matrix Materials. MANOVA writes a set of matrix materials that it can read in a subsequent analysis. The MATRIX subcommand writes matrices (see Section 33.57) and also reads matrices (see Section 33.58). If you contemplate further analyses, you can save the computational time required to build intermediate matrices by saving these matrix materials and reusing them.

33.2
OPERATION

MANOVA has a large number of subcommands. The variables specification is the only required specification, and it must come first (see Section 33.3).

The MANOVA subcommands fall into four general categories: subcommands that specify the design, subcommands that control the format and amount of output, subcommands that control the reading and writing of matrix materials, and subcommands that specify computational options and model specifications.

The DESIGN subcommand (Section 33.7) specifies the model to be fit. One model is produced for each DESIGN subcommand. All subcommands can be used more than once and, with the exception of the DESIGN subcommand, carry from model to model unless explicitly overridden.

All subcommands begin with the subcommand keyword followed by an optional equals sign and specifications. All subcommands are separated with a slash. Subcommand keywords can be abbreviated to the first three characters.

The following is an example of specifications for MANOVA:

```
MANOVA Y BY A(1,3) B(1,4) WITH X
  /PMEANS
  /METHOD=SSTYPE(SEQUENTIAL)
  /DESIGN=A,B
  /METHOD=SSTYPE(UNIQUE)
  /DESIGN=A,B,A BY B
```

The MANOVA specification specifies an analysis of covariance model with Y as the dependent variable, X as the covariate, and A and B as factor variables with three and four levels respectively. The PMEANS subcommand prints predicted means. The METHOD subcommand indicates sequential sums of squares. These two options apply to the first DESIGN specification, which requests a main effects model. The second METHOD subcommand requests the regression approach for estimating the parameters in the second DESIGN specification (a full factorial model). The PMEANS subcommand also applies to the second DESIGN.

Note that if the last subcommand is not a DESIGN specification, MANOVA generates a full factorial model specification for the problem.

33.3
Variable Specification

The MANOVA specification lists the variables to be used in models. MANOVA uses three types of variables. *Dependent variables* are continuous variables. *Factors* are categorical variables. *Covariates* are continuous variables. You can specify dependent variables, dependent variables and factors, dependent variables and covariates, or all three.

33.4
Dependent Variable List

The *dependent variable list* specifies variables to be used as dependent variables in the analysis. It must be the first list. You can use the TO convention to refer to consecutive variables. For example,

```
MANOVA DRUG1 TO DRUG4
  /WSFACTORS=TRIAL(4)
```

specifies only dependent variables and produces a repeated measures design with no between-subjects factor. By default, MANOVA treats a list of dependent variables as jointly dependent, implying a multivariate design. However, you can change the role of a variable or its inclusion status in the analysis with the ANALYSIS specification (see Section 33.19).

33.5
Factor List

The *factor list* follows the keyword BY and specifies those variables to be used as factors in the analysis. Follow each factor with an integer value range enclosed in parentheses: the first integer denotes the lowest value for a factor and the second integer denotes the highest. For example,

```
MANOVA  Y BY A(1,3)
```

specifies one factor with three levels. Cases with values outside these bounds are excluded from the analysis. If several factors have the same value range, you can specify a list of factors followed by a single value range in parentheses. For example,

```
MANOVA Y BY FACTOR1 FACTOR2 FACTOR3(3,5)
```

excludes all cases in which the values of FACTOR1, FACTOR2, or FACTOR3 lie outside the range 3 through 5 and includes cases with values 3, 4, and 5.

Since MANOVA requires consecutive integer values for factor levels, you should recode noninteger values for factors into consecutive integer values. For example, you could recode the six-value alphanumeric variable RELIGION, with values 'CATH', 'PROT', 'JEW ', 'NONE', 'OTHE', and ' ', into an integer factor, as in

```
RECODE RELIGION('CATH'=1)('PROT'=2)('JEW '=3)('NONE'=4)
  ('OTHE'=5)('       '=99) INTO NRELIG
MISSING VALUES NRELIG(99)
```

The MISSING VALUES command defines category 99 as missing. Therefore, NRELIG is a five-category factor. You can then specify

```
MANOVA ATTIT1 BY NRELIG(1,5)
```

on the MANOVA command.

If you have a wide value range for a factor in which most categories are empty, you must recode the variable to consecutive values. For example, suppose that factor F has three nonempty categories, represented by the numeric codes 1, 3, and 20. To recode F to have consecutive values 1, 2, and 3, specify

```
RECODE F(1=1) (3=2) (20=3)
MANOVA Y BY F(1,3)
```

Certain "one-cell" designs, such as univariate and multivariate regression analysis, canonical correlation, and one-sample Hotelling's T^2, do not require a factor specification. To perform these analyses, omit the keyword BY and the factor list.

33.6
Covariate List

The *covariate list* following the keyword WITH specifies the continuous variable or variables to be used as covariates in the analysis. For example,

```
MANOVA  Y BY A(1,3) WITH X
```

specifies one dependent variable, Y; one factor with three levels, A; and one covariate, X. Omit the keyword WITH and the covariate list if there are no covariates in the model.

33.7
DESIGN Subcommand

The DESIGN subcommand specifies the between-subjects model for the analysis. You can use multiple DESIGN subcommands. The DESIGN subcommand should be the last subcommand for a given model. All the other optional subcommands apply to a subsequent DESIGN subcommand. The default model is a full factorial model. Use the DESIGN subcommand to specify a list of effects for the model. Separate effects by blanks or commas.

The following sections describe design specifications.

33.8
Simple Main Effects

To specify a model that includes only the main effect terms, list the factors on the DESIGN subcommand, as in

```
MANOVA Y BY CAT(1,2) DRUG(1,3)
  /DESIGN= CAT,DRUG
```

33.9
Interaction Terms

The keyword BY indicates an interaction term. The three-way interaction of A, B, and C is written as A BY B BY C. To specify a model containing main effects A, B, and C and the A by B and B by C interactions, specify

```
MANOVA Y BY A B C (1,3)
  /DESIGN= A, B, C, A BY B, B BY C
```

33.10
Partitions of Degrees of Freedom for Effects

Use the PARTITION subcommand (Section 33.35) prior to specifying partitions of degrees of freedom for effects, as in

```
MANOVA Y BY TREATMNT(1,4)
  /CONTRAST(TREATMNT)=SPECIAL(1 1 1 1, 1 -1 0 0, 4 4 -8 0,
                                4 4 1 -9)
  /PARTITION(TREATMNT)
  /DESIGN=TREATMNT(1),TREATMNT(2),TREATMNT(3)
```

To refer to a given subdivision of a factor on the DESIGN subcommand, follow the factor name by the number, in parentheses, of the subdivision. Thus, if AGE has 12 levels and appears in a partition subcommand, as in

```
PARTITION(AGE) = (6,3,2)
/DESIGN = AGE(2) BY TREATMNT
```

AGE(2) refers to the second partition containing three degrees of freedom. This differs from subscripts used with WITHIN and MWITHIN, which refer to factor levels rather than partitions.

33.11
CONTIN Keyword

The keyword CONTIN (alias POOL) pools several continuous variables into a single effect. Continuous variables included in the design cannot be specified in the previous ANALYSIS subcommand as either dependent variables or covariates. The order of variables excluded from an analysis is the same relative order as defined by the original MANOVA variable list. For example, in

```
MANOVA A, B, C BY F(1,2) WITH D, E
 /ANALYSIS = B WITH D
```

the order of the interval variables excluded from the analysis is A, C, and E. To incorporate all interval variables from A to E into a single effect with as many degrees of freedom as variables in the list, specify

```
/DESIGN = CONTIN(A TO E)
```

The following specifications are also valid:

```
/DESIGN = CONTIN(A,B,C TO E,F)
/DESIGN = CONTIN(A)
/DESIGN = A, CONTIN(B), CONTIN(C TO E)
```

B and CONTIN(B) are identical. You cannot use the TO convention outside of parentheses.

The CONTIN keyword allows for unusual covariate analyses. For example,

```
MANOVA A,B,C,D BY F1,F2 (1,2)
 /ANALYSIS = A / METHOD = SSTYPE (SEQ)
 /DESIGN = CONTIN(B, C), F1, D, F2
```

eliminates covariates B and C from both factors F1 and F2 but eliminates covariate D from only factor F2.

If the DESIGN specification above did not include CONTIN, it would generate a covariate analysis with covariates B and C not pooled, with covariate B unadjusted, and with covariate C adjusted for B. The rest of the covariate analysis is the same as the previous one. This example assumes that sequential sums of squares, given by METHOD = SSTYPE (SEQ), are being used.

33.12
Interactions Between Factors and Continuous Variables

You can specify interactions between factors and continuous variables that have been excluded via an ANALYSIS subcommand. However, you cannot specify interactions between or among continuous variables. For example, suppose FAC1 is a factor and COV1 and COV2 are continuous variables. The following are some of the valid interactions you can specify

```
COV1 BY FAC1
CONTIN(COV1, COV2) BY FAC1
FAC1 BY COV2
```

You *cannot* specify covariate-by-covariate interaction terms. Use COMPUTE commands to create interactions between or among interval variables. For example,

```
COMPUTE XX = X * X
COMPUTE XY = X * Y
MANOVA X, Y, XX, XY BY FAC(1,4)
 /ANALYSIS = Y
 /DESIGN = X, XX, XY, FAC
```

computes two interaction terms, XX and XY, to use in the design.

An important use of factor-by-variable interactions is to produce an effect which tests the homogeneity-of-regression hypothesis fundamental to the analysis of covariance. For example, assume an analysis with one dependent variable Y and two covariates, Z1 and Z2, with two factors AGE and TREATMNT. To test the hypothesis of parallel (homogeneous) regressions, use

```
MANOVA Y, Z1,Z2 BY AGE(1,5),TREATMNT(1,3)
 /ANALYSIS = Y
 /DESIGN = CONTIN(Z1 Z2),AGE,TREATMNT, AGE BY TREATMNT,
           CONTIN(Z1,Z2) BY AGE +
           CONTIN(Z1,Z2) BY TREATMNT +
           CONTIN(Z1,Z2) BY AGE BY TREATMNT
```

The last effect, a pooled covariate-by-factor effect, tests the parallelism hypothesis. It is important that the effects of the common regression CONTIN(Z1,Z2) and group mean differences (AGE, TREATMNT, and AGE BY TREATMNT) be removed before testing the effect of separate regressions provided by CONTIN(Z1,Z2) BY AGE + CONTIN(Z1,Z2) BY TREATMNT + CONTIN(Z1,Z2) BY AGE BY TREATMNT.

33.13
Nested Designs

WITHIN, or W, indicates nesting, as in

```
/DESIGN = AGE WITHIN TREATMNT
/DESIGN = TREATMNT, COV1 WITHIN TREATMNT
```

The second design calculates the regression coefficients of the continuous variable COV1 within each cell of the factor TREATMNT. The term to the left of WITHIN is nested in the term to the right of WITHIN, up to the end of the term or a plus sign, as in

```
DESIGN = A WITHIN B BY C BY D
```

This design states that factor A is nested within B by C by D.

33.14
Pooled Effects

A plus sign (+) pools effects. For example,

```
DESIGN=AGE + AGE BY TREATMNT
```

combines the terms AGE and AGE by TREATMNT into a single term. Note that keyword BY is evaluated before the plus sign.

33.15
MUPLUS Keyword

Use MUPLUS to obtain estimates which consist of the sums of the parameter values and the grand means of the dependent variables. For example,

```
DESIGN = MUPLUS AGE
```

adds the means for each dependent variable to the parameters for each level of AGE. This process produces weighted marginals for each of the dependent variables by AGE. Since these means are adjusted for any covariates present, they are also the customary *adjusted means* when covariates are used.

You can obtain unweighted means by specifying the full factorial model, excluding those terms "contained" by an effect, and prefixing the effect whose means are to be found by MUPLUS. For example, to find the unweighted marginal means for AGE in a two-factor design, specify

```
DESIGN = MUPLUS AGE, TREATMNT, AGE BY TREATMNT
```

You can use the OMEANS (Section 33.49) and PMEANS (Section 33.50) subcommands to display marginal and adjusted means. However, only by using the MUPLUS approach can you obtain the standard errors of the marginal means. Specify only one MUPLUS keyword on a given DESIGN subcommand.

33.16
Error Terms

Three of the most frequently used error terms are (1) within-cells, (2) residual, and (3) combined within-cells and residual. These error terms are represented by the following keywords on the DESIGN subcommand:

• WITHIN or W—within-cells error terms.
• RESIDUAL or R—residual error term.
• WR or RW—combined within-cells and residual error terms.

To test a term against one of these error terms, name the term followed by keywords VS or AGAINST and the error term keyword. For example, to test the term AGE by SEX against the residual error term, specify

```
DESIGN=AGE BY SEX AGAINST RESIDUAL
```

For many designs, such as components of variance models, the common error terms are not sufficient. You can create up to 10 user-defined error terms by declaring any term in the design to be an error term. To create an error term, specify

```
term = n
```

where n is an integer from 1 to 10. For example,

```
DESIGN=AGE BY TREATMNT = 1
```

designates the term AGE by TREATMNT as error term 1.

To use a special error term in a test of significance, specify

```
term (VS)   n
     (AGAINST)
```

For example, to define AGE by TREATMNT as special error term 2 and test it against the residual error term, specify

```
DESIGN=AGE BY TREATMNT = 2 VS RESIDUAL
```

You can specify a complete nested design, as in

```
DESIGN=A VS 1,B WITHIN A=1 VS 2,
    C WITHIN B WITHIN A=2 VS WITHIN
```

This design specifies that A be tested against error term 1, which is the effect of B nested within A, and that B be tested against error term 2. Error term 2 is defined as C nested within B nested within A and is tested against the within-cells error term.

Any term present in the design but not given in the DESIGN specification is lumped into the residual error term.

33.17
CONSTANT Keyword

Use the keyword CONSTANT to include the constant term in a model. Generally, MANOVA automatically includes the constant (correction to mean) term in the model. However, if you specify NOCONSTANT in the METHOD subcommand (Section 33.31), MANOVA does not include the constant unless you specifically include it in the DESIGN by using the keyword CONSTANT, as in

```
DESIGN = CONSTANT, AGE
```

You can specify an error term for the constant, as in

```
DESIGN = CONSTANT VS 1
```

If you use the keyword CONSTANT you cannot use CONSTANT as a variable name.

33.18
MWITHIN Keyword

The MWITHIN keyword on the DESIGN or WSDESIGN subcommand suppresses the reparameterization of factors. This allows you to test simple effects for repeated measures designs. Several MWITHIN keywords can appear on a single WSDESIGN subcommand to ease the testing of simple effects in repeated measures designs. Consider the following:

```
MANOVA  Y1 Y2 Y3 BY GROUP(1,2)
    /WSFACTOR=TIME(3)
    /WSDESIGN=MWITHIN TIME(1) MWITHIN TIME(2) MWITHIN TIME(3)
    /DESIGN=GROUP
```

TIME(1) refers to the first level of TIME, not the first partition. The WSDESIGN =MWITHIN specification generates an identity matrix to transform Y1, Y2, and Y3; that is, no transformation is performed. The F statistic corresponding to GROUP by MWITHIN TIME(1) tests the difference in means between Group 1 and Group 2 at the first level of TIME. Similarly, the F value of GROUP by MWITHIN TIME(2) tests the difference between Group 1 and Group 2 at the second level of TIME.

To test the simple effects of TIME within each group of subjects, specify

```
MANOVA  Y1 Y2 Y3 BY GROUP(1,2)
    /WSFACTORS=TIME(3)
    /WSDESIGN=TIME
    /DESIGN=MWITHIN GROUP(1) MWITHIN GROUP(2)
```

33.19
ANALYSIS Subcommand

The ANALYSIS subcommand subsets and reorders the dependent variables and covariates. You can specify only one ANALYSIS subcommand per DESIGN subcommand. You can drop variables from an analysis, change dependent variables to covariates, or change covariates to dependent variables.

The ANALYSIS specification completely overrides the dependent variable list and covariates list in the MANOVA command specification. However, the ANALYSIS specification does not affect factors. Variables not included in the ANALYSIS subcommand may be incorporated into the analysis via the DESIGN subcommand (see Section 33.7). You can name only those variables in the original variable list of the MANOVA command.

You can use the ANALYSIS subcommand with the keyword WITH to redefine dependent variables and covariates. For example,

```
MANOVA A,B,C BY FAC(1,4)
     /ANALYSIS=A,B WITH C
```

changes C from a dependent variable to a covariate, while

```
MANOVA A,B,C BY FAC(1,4) WITH D,E
     /ANALYSIS=A,B,C,D WITH E
```

changes covariate D to a dependent variable.

You can delete dependent or covariate variables from the analysis, as in

```
MANOVA A,B,C BY FAC(1,4) WITH D,E
     /ANALYSIS=A
```

which deletes variables B, C, D, and E from the analysis.

You can use the ANALYSIS subcommand to request separate analyses. The lists must not overlap; that is, they must not name the same variables. For example,

```
MANOVA A,B,C BY FAC(1,4) WITH D,E
     /ANALYSIS = (A,B/ C/ D WITH E)
```

specifies three analyses: the first with A and B as dependent variables, the second with C as a dependent variable, and the third with D as a dependent variable and E a covariate. You can specify the same analysis using three separate ANALYSIS subcommands; however, separate ANALYSIS subcommands require complete re-estimation for all subsequent designs. The single subcommand above is much cheaper to use because it requires reordering only already-computed estimates.

To request three separate analyses and variable F as a global covariate, specify

```
MANOVA A, B, C, D, E, F BY FAC(1,4)
     /ANALYSIS = ( A, B/ C/ D WITH E ) WITH F
```

which is equivalent to

```
MANOVA A, B, C, D, E, F BY FAC(1,4)
 /ANALYSIS = A B WITH F
 /DESIGN
 /ANALYSIS = C WITH F
 /DESIGN
 /ANALYSIS = D WITH E F
```

You can use special keywords CONDITIONAL and UNCONDITIONAL when specifying multiple analyses. UNCONDITIONAL specifies that each list be used "as is," independent of the others. UNCONDITIONAL is the default. CONDITIONAL requests that subsequent lists include as covariates all previous dependent variables on that ANALYSIS subcommand. For example,

```
MANOVA A, B, C, D, E, F BY FAC(1,4)
     /ANALYSIS(CONDITIONAL) = (A B C / D E ) WITH F
```

is equivalent to

```
MANOVA A, B, C, D, E, F BY FAC(1,4)
     /ANALYSIS = A B C WITH F
     /DESIGN
     /ANALYSIS = D E WITH A B C F
```

when applied to the same design. You can specify a final covariate list outside the parentheses. These covariates apply to every list within the parentheses, regardless of whether you specify CONDITIONAL or UNCONDITIONAL. The variables in this global covariate list must not be specified in the individual lists.

33.20
Repeated Measures Designs

When the same experimental unit is measured on several different occasions, it is a *repeated measures* design. There are two ways of setting up data for a repeated measures design, commonly referred to as the univariate and multivariate approaches. While you can use either approach in SPSS-X MANOVA, the multivariate approach will give the univariate approach results in addition to the multivariate results. The multivariate approach is also much simpler to specify (see Figures 33.23a and 33.23b). The univariate approach must be used, however, if there are missing values for some of the repeated measures.

MANOVA has two subcommands for specifying the multivariate approach: WSFACTORS and WSDESIGN. The WSFACTORS subcommand is required for the multivariate approach and assumes you want a full factorial model. By default, it prints averaged F-tests, Greenhouse-Geisser and Huynh-Feldt epsilons, and the Mauchly test.

If you don't want a full factorial model, you add the WSDESIGN subcommand to your specification. The WSDESIGN subcommand is optional in the repeated measures design and can only be used in conjunction with the WSFACTORS subcommand.

33.21
WSFACTORS Subcommand

The WSFACTORS subcommand provides the names and number of levels for within-subjects factors when you use the multivariate data setup. For examples of the use of the WSFACTORS subcommand, see Sections 33.76 through 33.79.

To supply a within-subjects factor name (TRIAL) for DRUG1 to DRUG4, specify

```
MANOVA  DRUG1 TO DRUG4
   /WSFACTORS=TRIAL(4)
```

Each name follows the naming conventions of SPSS-X, and each name must be unique. That is, a within-subjects factor name cannot be the same as that of any dependent variable, between-subjects factor, or covariate on the MANOVA command. The within-subjects factors exist only during the MANOVA analysis.

Specify WSFACTORS once in a given MANOVA command. WSFACTORS must be the first subcommand after the MANOVA specification. Specify no more than 20 within-subjects and grouping factors altogether. To specify a single within-subjects factor with four levels, use

```
MANOVA  DRUG1 TO DRUG4
   /WSFACTORS = TRIAL(4)
```

To specify two within-subjects factors, the first with two levels and the second with three levels, use

```
MANOVA  Y1 TO Y6 BY GROUP(1,2)
   /WSFACTORS = DRUG(2),DOSE(3)
```

The order in which you name dependent variables on the MANOVA specification *must* correspond to the order and levels of named within-subjects factors. Because of this, the number of dependent variables on the MANOVA specification is necessarily an integral multiple of the product of the number of levels of the within-subjects factors.

For example, suppose you measure temperature and weight at two different times (AM and PM) on three successive days in four groups of animals. In this case, you have a repeated measures design with one between-subjects factor (GROUP) and two within-subjects factors (AMPM and DAY). Use the following MANOVA specifications to indicate the experimental structure:

```
MANOVA TEMP1 TO TEMP6,WEIGHT1 TO WEIGHT6 BY GROUP(1,4)
   /WSFACTORS = AMPM(2), DAY(3)
```

The dependent variables, temperature and weight, each have six values across occasions, represented by six variables. The order in which you list variables is *crucial*: it must correspond to the matching levels of the within-subjects factors. For the above example, the correspondence between dependent variables and within-subjects effects is as follows:

Variable	AMPM	DAY
TEMP1, WEIGHT1	1	1
TEMP2, WEIGHT2	1	2
TEMP3, WEIGHT3	1	3
TEMP4, WEIGHT4	2	1
TEMP5, WEIGHT5	2	2
TEMP6, WEIGHT6	2	3

The index value of the rightmost within-subjects factor in the WSFACTORS list, in this case DAY, increments most rapidly.

33.22
WSDESIGN Subcommand

By default, MANOVA assumes a full factorial model for both within-subject and between-subject factors. If you do not want a full factorial model, use the WSDESIGN subcommand to specify a within-subjects model and create a corresponding within-subjects transformation matrix. You can specify the same specifications on the WSDESIGN subcommand as on the DESIGN subcommand (Section 33.7), except for any of the following:

- Error term references and definitions.
- The MUPLUS keyword.
- The CONSTANT keyword.
- Interval-level variables.
- Between-subjects factors.

The first row of the transformation matrix generated from this design is always a row of ones corresponding to the constant term. MANOVA generates successive rows of the transformation matrix in left-to-right order, based on the indicated effects.

Consider the example discussed in Section 33.21. Recall that weight and temperature are measured at two different times (AM and PM) on three successive days in four groups of animals. Assume we want a comparison of the two levels of the AMPM factor and comparisons of the three days in the DAY factor. The following subcommands specify a design of interest:

```
MANOVA TEMP1 TO TEMP6,WEIGHT1 TO WEIGHT6 BY GROUP(1,4)
   /WSFACTORS = AMPM(2), DAYS(3)
   /WSDESIGN = AMPM, DAYS, AMPM BY DAYS
```

33.23
Univariate and Multivariate Approaches

The following example is taken from *SPSS-X Advanced Statistics* and also appears in *SPSS/PC+ Advanced Statistics*.

Bacon (1980) conducted an experiment in which subjects were given a number to memorize. They were then asked if a "probe" digit were included in the memorized number, and told to press a button indicating their choice. Half the 24 right-handed subjects were instructed to respond with their left hand in order to assess the effect of hemisphere dominance. Also, half of the time the probe digit was present, while the other half of the time it was absent. Each subject was tested on 60 memorized numbers, 20 each of two, three, and four digits in random order, and the average latency of response (in milliseconds) was computed for each subject.

The WITHIN-SUBJECT factors in this experiment are DIGIT (two, three, or four digits) and CONDITION (whether the probe digit was present or absent).

The BETWEEN-SUBJECT factor is HAND (which hand the subject was required to use to signal his choice).

The univariate and multivariate approaches are shown below. Note that the data are actually entered differently for the two approaches. In the multivariate approach, each subject is a case, with different variables for response time for each of the WITHIN-SUBJECTS conditions. In the univariate approach, each response is a case (giving 6 cases per subject), and SUBJECT is a variable that is numbered from 1 to 12 within each hand condition.

Univariate approach.

```
DATA LIST FREE/RESPONSE DIGIT COND HAND SUBJECT
VALUE LABELS COND 1 'Present' 2 'Absent'
             /HAND 1 'Right' 2 'Left'
BEGIN DATA
574 2 1 1 1
606 3 1 1 1
619 4 1 1 1
654 2 2 1 1
662 3 2 1 1
690 4 2 1 1
439 2 1 1 2
503 3 1 1 2
547 4 1 1 2
591 2 2 1 2
596 3 2 1 2
626 4 2 1 2
 ...
END DATA
MANOVA RESPONSE BY DIGIT(2,4) COND(1,2) HAND(1,2) SUBJECT(1,12)/
   DESIGN=HAND VS 1,
          SUBJECT W HAND = 1,
          DIGIT VS 2,
          HAND BY DIGIT VS 2,
          DIGIT BY SUBJECT W HAND = 2
          COND VS 3,
          HAND BY COND VS 3,
          COND BY SUBJECT W HAND = 3
          DIGIT BY COND VS 4,
          HAND BY DIGIT BY COND VS 4,
          DIGIT BY COND BY SUBJECT W HAND = 4
```

Multivariate approach.

```
DATA LIST FREE/P2DIGIT P3DIGIT P4DIGIT NP2DIGIT NP3DIGIT NP4DIGIT HAND
VARIABLE LABELS P2DIGIT 'Two digits - present'
                P3DIGIT 'Three digits - present'
                P4DIGIT 'Four digits - present'
                NP2DIGIT 'Two digits - not present'
                NP3DIGIT 'Three digits - not present'
                NP4DIGIT 'Four digits - not present'

BEGIN DATA
574 606 619 654 662 690 1
439 503 547 591 596 626 2
 ...
END DATA
MANOVA P2DIGIT P3DIGIT P4DIGIT NP2DIGIT NP3DIGIT NP4DIGIT BY HAND(1,2)/

   WSFACTOR=COND(2) DIGIT(3)/
   WSDESIGN=DIGIT COND DIGIT BY COND/
   DESIGN=HAND
```

The output for the multivariate run includes Mauchly's test of sphericity, Greenhouse-Geisser, Huynh-Feldt, and a Lower-bound Epsilon, multivariate and the univariate-approach tests for each set of tests involving within-subject factors. The output from the tests involving DIGIT by COND are shown in Figure 33.23.

Figure 33.23   Multivariate-approach output for DIGIT by COND tests

```
Tests involving 'DIGIT BY COND' Within-Subject Effect.

Mauchly sphericity test, W =        .87321
Chi-square approx. =               2.84712 with 2 D. F.
Significance =                      .241

Greenhouse-Geisser Epsilon =        .88748
Huynh-Feldt Epsilon =              1.00000
Lower-bound Epsilon =               .50000

AVERAGED Tests of Significance that follow multivariate tests are equivalent to
univariate or split-plot or mixed-model approach to repeated measures.
Epsilons may be used to adjust d.f. for the AVERAGED results.

_ _ _ _ _ _ _ _ _ _ _ _ _ _ _ _ _ _ _ _ _ _ _ _ _ _ _ _ _ _ _ _ _ _ _ _ _ _ _
EFFECT .. HAND BY DIGIT BY COND
Multivariate Tests of Significance (S = 1, M = 0, N = 9 1/2)

Test Name          Value      Exact F Hypoth. DF   Error DF  Sig. of F

Pillais           .07632      .86760     2.00       21.00      .434
Hotellings        .08263      .86760     2.00       21.00      .434
Wilks             .92368      .86760     2.00       21.00      .434
Roys              .07632
Note.. F statistics are exact.

_ _ _ _ _ _ _ _ _ _ _ _ _ _ _ _ _ _ _ _ _ _ _ _ _ _ _ _ _ _ _ _ _ _ _ _ _ _ _
EFFECT .. DIGIT BY COND
Multivariate Tests of Significance (S = 1, M = 0, N = 9 1/2)

Test Name          Value      Exact F Hypoth. DF   Error DF  Sig. of F

Pillais           .00956      .10138     2.00       21.00      .904
Hotellings        .00965      .10138     2.00       21.00      .904
Wilks             .99044      .10138     2.00       21.00      .904
Roys              .00956
Note.. F statistics are exact.

_ _ _ _ _ _ _ _ _ _ _ _ _ _ _ _ _ _ _ _ _ _ _ _ _ _ _ _ _ _ _ _ _ _ _ _ _ _ _
Tests involving 'DIGIT BY COND' Within-Subject Effect.

AVERAGED Tests of Significance for MEAS.1 using UNIQUE sums of squares
Source of Variation           SS        DF       MS         F  Sig of F

WITHIN CELLS               20138.11     44     457.68
DIGIT BY COND                 88.17      2      44.08      .10     .908
HAND BY DIGIT BY COND        613.39      2     306.69      .67     .517
```

33.24
MEASURE Subcommand

You can use SPSS-X MANOVA to analyze *doubly multivariate* repeated measures designs in which subjects are measured on two or more responses on two or more occasions. SPSS-X prints the pooled or "averaged" results as well as the multivariate results. You can optionally use the MEASURE subcommand to label the measures in the multivariate pooled results, as in

```
MANOVA  TEMP1 TO TEMP6, WEIGHT1 TO WEIGHT6 BY GROUP(1,4)
        /WSFACTOR=AMPM(2), DAYS(3)
        /MEASURE=TEMP WEIGHT
        /WSDESIGN=AMPM DAYS, AMPM BY DAYS
        /PRINT = SIGNIF(AVERF)
        /DESIGN
```

If you specify names on the MEASURE subcommand, SPSS-X uses the indicated names. If you omit the MEASURE subcommand MANOVA prints the results but uses its own labeling. For an example of the use of the MEASURE subcommand, see Section 33.79.

33.25
TRANSFORM Subcommand

The TRANSFORM subcommand specifies linear transformations of the dependent variables and covariates. Specify variable lists in parentheses separated by slashes. Each list must contain the same number of variables. MANOVA applies the indicated transformation to each list. By default, MANOVA transforms all dependent variables and covariates. Variables not included in one of the lists are left untouched. For example,

```
MANOVA  Y1 Y2 Y3 BY A B(1,3) WITH X1 X2 X3
        /TRANSFORM(Y1 Y2 Y3)=REPEATED
```

transforms Y1, Y2, and Y3. Specify any number of TRANSFORM subcommands in a MANOVA job. A TRANSFORM subcommand is in effect until MANOVA encounters another one.

MANOVA generates a set of transformed variables to test the between and within subject effects. MANOVA automatically generates variable names in the form T1, T2, ... Tn for the transformed variables whenever you do not use the RENAME subcommand (Section 33.30) to rename them yourself. The procedure will internally use these new names in subsequent steps, though you can still refer to them by their old names.

Seven types of transformations are available. You can specify keywords CONTRAST, BASIS, or ORTHONORM prior to the type of transformation.

CONTRAST *Generate the transformation matrix directly from the contrast matrix of the given type. CONTRAST is the default.*

BASIS *Generate the transformation matrix from the one-way basis corresponding to the specified CONTRAST.*

ORTHONORM *Orthonormalize the transformation matrix by rows before use. MANOVA zeroes out redundant rows. By default, MANOVA does not orthonormalize rows.*

Use any of the following transformation keywords after the CONTRAST or BASIS keyword (if specified).

DEVIATIONS(refcat) *Compare a dependent variable with the mean of the dependent variables in the list. By default, MANOVA omits the comparison of the last variable to the variable list. However, you can omit a variable other than the last by specifying the number of the omitted variable in parentheses.*

DIFFERENCE *Compare a dependent variable with the mean of the previous dependent variables in the list. Also known as reverse Helmert.*

HELMERT *Compare a dependent variable with the mean of the subsequent dependent variables in the list.*

SIMPLE(refcat) *Compare each dependent variable with the last. However, you can specify a variable other than the last as a reference variable by giving the number of the variable in parentheses.*

REPEATED *Compare contiguous variable pairs, thereby producing difference scores. (See Section 33.26.)*

POLYNOMIAL(metric) *Fit orthogonal polynomials to the variables in the transformation list. The default metric is equal spacing; you can specify your own metric. (See Section 33.27.)*

SPECIAL(matrix) *Your own transformation matrix reflecting combinations of interest. The matrix must be square with the number of rows and columns equal to the number of variables being transformed. (See Section 33.28.)*

Some examples of the use of TRANSFORM follow in Sections 33.26, 33.27, and 33.28.

33.26 REPEATED Keyword

Schematically, the REPEATED keyword produces the following transformation:

```
(VAR1)             (1/p   1/p  1/p  . . .  1/p  1/p)   (VAR1)
(VAR2)             ( 1    −1   0   . . .   0    0 )    (VAR2)
(VAR3)             ( 0     1  −1   . . .   0    0 )    (VAR3)
  .     =          (            . . . )                  .
  .                (            . . . )                  .
  .                (            . . . )                  .
(VARp)             ( 0     0   0   . . .   1   −1 )    (VARp)
(new variables)    (p ×p transformation matrix)    (old variables)
```

where p is the number of variables being transformed. For example, the specification TRANSFORM(A,B,C)=REPEATED results in the following for each case:

- A is replaced by $(A+B+C)/3$
- B is replaced by $(A-B)$
- C is replaced by $(B-C)$

This transformation is useful in profile analysis and repeated measures designs where difference scores are used.

33.27
POLYNOMIAL Keyword

MANOVA fits orthogonal polynomials to the variables in the transformation list. The mean of the variables replaces the first variable, the linear component replaces the second variable, the quadratic component replaces the third variable, and so on.

Supply the metric for the polynomial transformation in parentheses following the POLYNOMIAL keyword. The metric indicates the spacing between the points represented by the values of the variables. For equal spacing, specify a metric consisting of the integers 1 to p, where p is the number of variables transformed, as in

```
TRANSFORM(A,B,C,D) = POLYNOMIAL(1,2,3,4)
```

Since equal spacing is the default, you can specify POLYNOMIAL without indicating the metric. You can also indicate unequal spacing. For example, consider fitting a set of five variables representing five successive measurements of body weight. To explore the significance of any curvilinear trend in the change in body weight with respect to time, you must extract the various polynomial components.

Assume the following scheme:

Variable	Contents
WT1	Body weight on 1st day
WT2	Body weight on 3rd day
WT3	Body weight on 7th day
WT4	Body weight on 12th day
WT5	Body weight on 20th day

The following TRANSFORM subcommand builds the desired polynomial components:

```
TRANSFORM(WT1,WT2,WT3,WT4,WT5)=POLYNOMIAL(1,3,7,12,20)
```

The transformation in matrix terms is

(WT1)	mean	(		)	(WT1)
(WT2)	linear comp.	(	orthogonal polynomial	)	(WT2)
(WT3)	quadratic comp. =	(	coefficients generated	)	(WT3)
(WT4)	cubic comp.	(	from metric	)	(WT4)
(WT5)	quartic comp.	(		)	(WT5)
(new variables)		(	transformation matrix	)	(old variables)

The results of the transformation are

New variable	Original contents for each case replaced by
WT1	(WT1+WT2+WT3+WT4+WT5) / 5
WT2	linear component of polynomial
WT3	quadratic component of polynomial
WT4	cubic component of polynomial
WT5	quartic component of polynomial

33.28
SPECIAL Keyword

The arbitrary transformation matrix is entered rowwise in parentheses following the SPECIAL keyword. The matrix must be square with the number of rows and columns equal to the number of variables being transformed. For example, the transformation

$$(1 \quad 1 \quad -1)$$
$$(2 \quad 0 \quad 1)$$
$$(1 \quad 0 \quad -1)$$

appears as

```
TRANSFORM(VAR1,VAR2,VAR3)=SPECIAL( 1   1  -1,
                                   2   0   1,
                                   1   0  -1 )
```

33.29
Multiple Variable Lists

You can apply the same transformation to subsets of dependent variables. For example, you might want to apply a special transformation to VAR1 to VAR3 and VAR4 to VAR6. In matrix terms, we represent the transformation as follows:

(VAR1)		(1 1 −1 0 0 0)	(VAR1)
(VAR2)		(2 0 1 0 0 0)	(VAR2)
(VAR3)	=	(1 0 −1 0 0 0)	(VAR3)
(VAR4)		(0 0 0 1 1 −1)	(VAR4)
(VAR5)		(0 0 0 2 0 1)	(VAR5)
(VAR6)		(0 0 0 1 0 −1)	(VAR6)

The TRANSFORM specification is as follows:

```
TRANSFORM(VAR1 TO VAR3, VAR4 TO VAR6) =
  SPECIAL(1  1  -1  0  0  0,
          2  0   1  0  0  0,
          1  0  -1  0  0  0,
          0  0   0  1  1 -1,
          0  0   0  2  0  1,
          0  0   0  1  0 -1 )
```

You can abbreviate this specification using multiple variable lists:

```
TRANSFORM(VAR1 TO VAR3/VAR4 TO VAR6) =
  SPECIAL(  1   1  -1
            2   0   1
            1   0  -1 )
```

You can use the RENAME subcommand to give the transformed variables new names which reflect the transformation employed (see Section 33.25). If you use RENAME, MANOVA uses the new names for the duration of the analysis. If you do not use RENAME, MANOVA uses the variable names in the form T1, T2, ... TN.

If you specify the TRANSFORM keyword on the PRINT subcommand when you use the TRANSFORM subcommand, MANOVA prints the transformation matrix (see Section 33.39).

33.30
RENAME Subcommand

Use the RENAME subcommand to rename dependent variables and covariates when you have transformed them using either the TRANSFORM or WSDESIGN subcommand. All dependent variables and covariates must be accounted for in the RENAME specification, even if they are not being renamed. You can use an asterisk (*) in the RENAME subcommand to indicate the variables not to be renamed, as in

```
MANOVA A,B,C,V4,V5 BY TREATMNT(1,3)
 /TRANSFORM(A,B,C)=REPEATED
 /RENAME = MEANABC, AMINUSB, BMINUSC, *, *
```

The results of the TRANSFORM subcommand are

OLD VARIABLE	TRANSFORMED VARIABLE	TRANSFORMED MEANING
A	MEANABC	(A+B+C)/3
B	AMINUSB	A−B
C	BMINUSC	B−C
V4	V4 (unchanged)	V4
V5	V5 (unchanged)	V5

The RENAME subcommand supplies new names to clarify the transformation. Successive output from this MANOVA job prints the transformed variable names, MEANABC, ANIMUSB, and BMINUSC instead of the old variable names, A,B, and C respectively. The following example uses renaming after a polynomial transformation.

```
MANOVA WT1,WT2,WT3,WT4,WT5 BY TREATMNT(1,3)
 /TRANSFORM = POLYNOMIAL (1,2,3,4,5)
 /RENAME = MEAN,LINEAR,QUAD,CUBIC,QUARTIC
```

Successive output from this MANOVA run prints the five polynomial component names instead of the variable names WT1 to WT5.

References to the dependent variables or covariates in specifications following the RENAME subcommand *must* use the new names. MANOVA does not retain the old names.

33.31
METHOD Subcommand

Use the METHOD subcommand to control computational aspects of your MANOVA analysis. Three keywords are available:

MODELTYPE   *The model for parameter estimation.*
ESTIMATION   *How parameters are to be estimated.*
SSTYPE   *The method of partitioning sums of squares.*

Each keyword has several options available. Specify these options in parentheses following the keyword.

33.32
MODELTYPE Keyword

The MODELTYPE keyword specifies the model for parameter estimation. MODELTYPE provides two options:

MEANS. Requests that MANOVA use the cell means model in parameter estimation; this is the default.

OBSERVATIONS. Requests that MANOVA use the observations model in parameter estimation. When you specify continuous variables in the DESIGN subcommand, MANOVA automatically uses the observations model. Computing parameter estimates using the observations model is much costlier than obtaining the same estimates using the means model. Thus, you should use the observations model only when appropriate.

33.33
ESTIMATION Keyword

The ESTIMATION keyword specifies how MANOVA is to estimate parameters. This task is the fundamental numerical process in MANOVA. The ESTIMATION keyword presents four binary choices.

QR or CHOLESKY Keywords. QR, the default, estimates parameters using Householder transformations to effect a QR (orthogonal) decomposition of the design matrix. This method bypasses the normal equations and the inaccuracies that can result from creating the cross-product matrix, and it generally results in extremely accurate estimates of the parameters. A less expensive—and sometimes less accurate procedure—is to solve the normal equations using the Cholesky method. Select this method by specifying the CHOLESKY keyword.

NOBALANCED or BALANCED Keywords. By default, MANOVA assumes that you are analyzing an unbalanced design. However, if your design is balanced and orthogonal, you can request balanced processing by specifying the BALANCED keyword. Balanced processing can result in substantial savings in processing time. Use the BALANCED keyword if your design meets the following requirements:

• All cells are filled.
• The cell-means model applies.
• The cell sizes for all cells are equal.
• The contrast type for each factor is orthogonal.

MANOVA cannot detect a balanced design; you must tell MANOVA to use it. If you request balanced processing but the design does not conform to the above requirements, then MANOVA reverts to the general unbalanced processing using either QR or Cholesky estimation, whichever you specify.

LASTRES or NOLASTRES Keywords. The LASTRES keyword causes MANOVA to compute the last effect in the design by subtracting the among-groups sum of squares and cross-products from the total sum of squares and cross-products. LASTRES can also be valuable in analyses involving missing cells—the labor of determining the confounded effects is saved. NOLASTRES reverses the effect of LASTRES. Note that the last effect with LASTRES specified *must not* contain any interval variables. Also, do not use LASTRES with UNIQUE sum of squares decomposition; the sum of squares will not add up to the total sum of squares unless the design is balanced. Thus, the sum of squares for the last effect cannot be computed by subtraction. NOLASTRES, the default, calculates all terms as specified in the design.

CONSTANT or NOCONSTANT Keywords. CONSTANT requests that the model include a constant (intercept) term, even if you do not explicitly specify one in the DESIGN subcommand. CONSTANT is the default. The sum of squares for the CONSTANT term does not appear on the output. (This is not the same as NOCONSTANT since all effects are still adjusted for the CONSTANT, even though the constant term is not printed.) To request the sum of squares for the CONSTANT, specify the keyword CONSTANT on the DESIGN subcommand, as in

```
MANOVA Y BY A(1,2) B(1,3)
   /DESIGN=CONSTANT A B A BY B
```

NOCONSTANT suppresses the constant term from the model. In this case, MANOVA does not fit the constant unless you explicitly specify it in the DESIGN subcommand.

33.34
SSTYPE Keyword

SPSS-X MANOVA offers two different methods of partitioning the sums of squares.

UNIQUE Keyword. UNIQUE, the default, uses the regression approach in which each term is corrected for every other term in the model. With this approach, sums of squares for various components of the model do not add up to the total sum of squares unless the design is balanced. In designs with no empty cells, UNIQUE is the method of weighted squares of means.

SEQUENTIAL Keyword. SEQUENTIAL requests a hierarchical decomposition of the sums of squares in which each term is adjusted only for the terms which precede it in the DESIGN statement. This is an orthogonal decomposition, and the sums of squares in the model do add up to the total sums of squares. SEQUENTIAL is also termed the method of fitting constants.

SEQUENTIAL prints the model summary, R-Square, and adjusted R-Square statistics at the end of the ANOVA table. These are not printed if you request UNIQUE sums of squares. For balanced designs, specify SEQUENTIAL if you want this additional information in your analysis.

33.35
PARTITION Subcommand

The PARTITION subcommand subdivides the degrees of freedom associated with a factor. Specify the factor name in parentheses following the subcommand keyword. Following an equals sign, specify a parenthetical list of integers to indicate the degrees of freedom for each partition. The number of degrees of freedom associated with a factor is one less than the number of levels for the factor. Each value in the partition list must be greater than zero and less than or equal to the total number of degrees of freedom for the factor. Further, the sum of the partition degrees of freedom must be less than or equal to the total number of degrees of freedom for the factor. The maximum number of partitions allowed for a factor (achieved by specifying all individual degrees of freedom equal to one) is likewise the total number of degrees of freedom for the factor. If the total sum of the degrees of freedom is less than the degrees of freedom for the factor, then MANOVA builds a final partition category containing the remaining degrees of freedom.

For example, consider the factor TREATMNT, which has 12 levels, or 11 degrees of freedom. To partition TREATMNT into single degrees of freedom, specify

```
PARTITION(TREATMNT) = (1,1,1,1,1,1,1,1,1,1,1)
```

or use a repeat factor by specifying an asterisk, as in

```
PARTITION(TREATMNT) = (11*1)
```

A third way to request a single-degree-of-freedom partition is as follows:

```
PARTITION(TREATMNT)
```

The default degrees-of-freedom vector consists of all ones. This is also the initial partition ascribed to any factor.

To partition TREATMNT into three subdivisions, the first containing three degrees of freedom, the second two degrees of freedom, and the third six degrees of freedom, specify

```
PARTITION(TREATMNT) = (3,2,6)
```

You can also effect the same partition by specifying:

```
PARTITION(TREATMNT) = (3,2)
```

MANOVA automatically generates a third partition with 6 ($11-3-2$) degrees of freedom in this case.

33.36
CONTRAST Subcommand

Use the CONTRAST subcommand to specify the contrast desired for a factor:

```
                                DEVIATION  (refcat)
                                DIFFERENCE
                                HELMERT
CONTRAST(factorname) =          SIMPLE   (refcat)
                                /REPEATED
                                POLYNOMIAL  (metric)
                                SPECIAL (matrix)
```

where *factorname* is the factor whose contrast is being selected.

DEVIATION   *The deviations from the grand means.*

In matrix terms, these contrasts have the form

```
mean   (     1/k        1/k       . . .        1/k        1/k)
df(1)  (1 −1/k         −1/k       . . .       −1/k       −1/k)
df(2)  (  −1/k       1 −1/k       . . .       −1/k       −1/k)
 .                              .
 .                              .
 .                              .
```

where k is the number of levels for the factor. For example, the deviation contrasts for a factor with three levels are as follows:

```
(   1/3      1/3      1/3)
(   2/3     −1/3     −1/3)
( −1/3      2/3     −1/3)
```

MANOVA omits the deviation for the last category. However, the deviation effect for this reference category equals the negative sum of the deviations for the other categories since the deviations must sum to zero.

To omit a category other than the last, specify the number of the omitted category in parentheses after the DEVIATION keyword. For example, the subcommand

```
CONTRAST(FACTOR) = DEVIATION(2)
```

where FACTOR has three levels, results in a contrast matrix of the form

```
(   1/3      1/3      1/3)
(   2/3     −1/3     −1/3)
( −1/3     −1/3      2/3)
```

which obtains the deviations for the first and third categories and omits the second.

DIFFERENCE   *Difference or reverse Helmert contrasts.* Compare levels of a factor with the mean of the previous levels of the factor.

The general matrix form is

mean	(	1/k	1/k	1/k	. . . 1/k)
df(1)	(	−1	1	0	. . . 0)
df(2)	(	−1/2	−1/2	1	. . . 0)

.
.
.

df(k −1) (−1/(k −1)   −1/(k −1)   −1/(k −1) . . .   1)

where k is the number of levels of the factor. For example, a factor with four levels has a difference contrast matrix of the following form:

(1/4	1/4	1/4	1/4)
(−1	1	0	0)
(−1/2	−1/2	1	0)
(−1/3	−1/3	−1/3	1)

SIMPLE   *Simple contrasts.* Compare each level of a factor to the last.

The general matrix form is

mean	(1/k	1/k . . . 1/k	1/k)
df(1)	(1	0 . . . 0	−1)
df(2)	(0	1 . . . 0	−1)

.
.
.

df(k-1) (0   0   . . . 1   −1)

where k is the number of levels of the factor.

For example, a factor with four levels has a simple contrast matrix of the following form:

(1/4	1/4	1/4	1/4)
(1	0	0	−1)
(0	1	0	−1)
(0	0	1	−1)

To use another category besides the last as a reference category, specify the level of the reference category in parentheses after the SIMPLE keyword. For example, the request

```
CONTRAST(FACTOR) = SIMPLE(2)
```

where FACTOR has four levels produces a contrast matrix of the form

(1/4	1/4	1/4	1/4)
(1	−1	0	0)
(0	−1	1	0)
(0	−1	0	1)

HELMERT   *Helmert contrasts.* Compare levels of a factor with the mean of the subsequent levels of the factor.

The general matrix form is

mean	(1/k	1/k	...	1/k	1/k)
df(1)	(1	$-1/(k-1)$	...	$-1/(k-1)$	$-1/(k-1)$)
df(2)	(0	1	...	$-1/(k-2)$	$-1/(k-2)$)
.	(		.	.	)
.	(		.	.	)
.	(		.	.	)
df(k-2)	(0	0	1	$-1/2$	$-1/2$)
df(k-1)	(0	0	...	1	-1)

where k is the number of levels of the factor. For example, a factor with four levels has a Helmert contrast matrix of the following form:

$$
\begin{pmatrix}
1/4 & 1/4 & 1/4 & 1/4 \\
1 & -1/3 & -1/3 & -1/3 \\
0 & 1 & -1/2 & -1/2 \\
0 & 0 & 1 & -1
\end{pmatrix}
$$

POLYNOMIAL   *Orthogonal polynomial contrasts.*

You can specify the spacing between levels of the treatment measured by the given factor. You can signify equal spacing by specifying consecutive integers from 1 to k, where k is the number of levels of the factor. Equal spacing is the default if you omit a metric. For example,

    CONTRAST(DRUG) = POLYNOMIAL

is the same as

    CONTRAST(DRUG) = POLYNOMIAL (1,2,3)

Equal spacing is not always necessary, however. For example, suppose factor DRUG represents different dosages of a drug given to three groups. If the dosage administered to the second group is twice that of the first group, and that of the third group is three times that of the first group, then the treatment levels are equally spaced and an appropriate metric for this situation consists of consecutive integers:

    CONTRAST(DRUG)=POLYNOMIAL(1,2,3)

If, however, the dosage administered to the second group is four times the dosage level given the first group, and the dosage given the third group is seven times that of the first, then an appropriate metric is:

    CONTRAST(DRUG)=POLYNOMIAL (1,4,7)

In either case, the result of the contrast specification is that the first degree of freedom for DRUG contains the linear effect of the dosage levels and the second degree of freedom contains the quadratic effect. In general, the first degree of freedom receives the linear effect, the second degree of freedom the quadratic effect, the third degree of freedom the cubic, and so on for the higher order effects. Polynomial contrasts are especially useful in tests of trends and for investigating the nature of response surfaces. You can also use polynomial contrasts to perform nonlinear curve-fitting, such as curvilinear regression.

REPEATED   *Compare adjacent levels of a factor.*

The general matrix form is

```
mean     (1/k    1/k    1/k    . . .   1/k    1/k)
df(1)    ( 1     −1     0      . . .   0      0 )
df(2)    ( 0      1    −1      . . .   0      0 )
  .      (              .                      )
  .      (              .                      )
  .      (              .                      )
df(k −1) ( 0      0     0      . . .   1     −1 )
```

where *k* is the number of levels for the factors.

For example, the repeated contrasts for a factor with four levels areas follows:

```
(1/4    1/4    1/4    1/4)
( 1     −1     0      0 )
( 0      1    −1      0 )
( 0      0     1     −1 )
```

These contrasts are useful in profile analysis and wherever difference scores are needed.

SPECIAL   *A user-defined contrast.*

SPECIAL allows entry of special contrasts in the form of square matrices with as many rows and columns as there are levels of the factor. The first row entered is always the mean, or constant, effect, and represents the set of weights indicating how MANOVA is to average other factors, if any, over the given factor. Generally, this contrast is a vector of ones.

The remaining rows of the matrix contain the special contrasts indicating the desired comparisons between levels of the factor. Usually, orthogonal contrasts are the most useful. Orthogonal contrasts are statistically independent and nonredundant. Contrasts are *orthogonal* if (1) for each row, contrast coefficients sum to zero, and (2) the products of corresponding coefficients for all pairs of disjoint rows also sum to zero.

For example, suppose TREATMNT has four levels and you want to compare the various levels of treatment with each other. An appropriate special contrast is

```
(1    1    1    1)    weights for mean calculation
(3   −1   −1   −1)    compare 1st with 2nd through 4th
(0    2   −1   −1)    compare 2nd with 3rd and 4th
(0    0    1   −1)    compare 3rd with 4th
```

which you specify by means of the following CONTRAST subcommand:

```
CONTRAST(TREATMNT) = SPECIAL(  1    1    1    1
                               3   −1   −1   −1
                               0    2   −1   −1
                               0    0    1   −1 )
```

Each row except the means row sums to zero:

```
Row 2   3 + (−1) + (−1) + (−1) = 3 − 3 = 0
Row 3   2 + (−1) + (−1)        = 2 − 2 = 0
Row 4   1 + (−1)               = 1 − 1 = 0
```

Products of each pair of disjoint rows sum to zero:

```
Rows 2 and 3   3(0) + (−1)(2) + (−1)(−1) + (−1)(−1) = 0
Rows 2 and 4   3(0) + (−1)(0) + (−1)( 1) + (−1)(−1) = 0
Rows 3 and 4   0(0) + ( 2)(0) + (−1)( 1) + (−1)(−1) = 0
```

The special contrasts need not be orthogonal. However, they must not be linear combinations of each other. If they are, MANOVA reports the linear dependency and ceases processing. Difference, Helmert, and polynomial contrasts are orthogonal contrasts.

33.37
CRITERIA Subcommand

The CRITERIA subcommand sets important constants used throughout the MANOVA procedure.

ZETA(zeta)   *Set the absolute value of zero used for printing purposes and when constructing basis matrices for estimation.* The default value of ZETA is 10^{-8}.

EPS(eps)   *Set the relative value of zero used in checking the diagonal elements of matrices when performing the QR reduction or Cholesky decompositions.* The default value of EPS is 10^{-8}.

33.38
ERROR Subcommand

The ERROR subcommand specifies the default error term for each between-subjects effect in subsequent designs.

WITHIN   *Within-cells error term.* Can be abbreviated to W.

RESIDUAL   *Residual error term.* Can be abbreviated to R.

WITHIN+RESIDUAL   *Pooled within-cells and residual error terms.* Can be abbreviated to WR or RW.

n   *Model term.*

MANOVA chooses an error term based on the following criteria:

- MANOVA uses the within-cells error term if it exists.
- If there is no within-cells error, MANOVA uses the residual error.
- For designs processed using the observations model, the pooled within-cells and residual error term is the default.

If you request both the pooled within-cells and residual errors and one of these does not exist, then MANOVA uses the other error term alone.

You can designate a model term as the default error by giving its error term number. You must explicitly define the error term numbers in the DESIGN subcommand. If the specified error term number is not defined for a particular design, then MANOVA does not carry out the significance tests using that error term, although MANOVA presents the parameter estimates and hypothesis sums of squares.

For example, in the command

```
MANOVA DEP BY A(1,2), B(1,4)
 /ERROR = 1
 /DESIGN = A, B, A BY B = 1
 /DESIGN = A, B
```

the default error term, error term 1, applies to the first design since the A by B term is present in the model and is defined as error term 1. However, the A by B term is not present in the second design, and no other term has been defined as error 1 instead. Thus, no significance tests for A and B are printed, although the hypothesis sums of squares are reported.

33.39
PRINT and NOPRINT Subcommands

The PRINT and NOPRINT subcommands control the amount of printed output produced by MANOVA. The syntax for both subcommands is identical. PRINT requests that specified output be produced while NOPRINT suppresses output. PRINT and NOPRINT control several classes of information. Each general specification has several subspecifications. For example,

```
MANOVA  Y BY A(1,3) WITH X
        /PRINT=CELLINFO(MEANS)
```

prints cell means. The following general specifications are available:

CELLINFO   *Cells information.*
HOMOGENEITY   *Homogeneity-of-variance tests.*
DESIGN   *Design information.*
ERROR   *Error matrices.*
SIGNIF   *Significance tests.*
PARAMETERS   *Estimated parameters.*
TRANSFORM   *Transformation matrix.*

33.40
CELLINFO Keyword

Use CELLINFO to request the following statistics:

MEANS   *Cell means, standard deviations, and counts.*
SSCP   *Cell sums of squares and cross-products matrices.*
COV   *Cell variance-covariance matrices.*
COR   *Cell correlation matrices.*
ALL   *MEANS, SSCP, COV, and COR.*

For example,

```
MANOVA  Y BY A(1,3)
        /PRINT=CELLINFO(MEANS)
```

prints the means of Y for each category of A.

33.41
HOMOGENEITY Keyword

Use HOMOGENEITY to request a test for homogeneity of variance:

BARTLETT   *Bartlett-Box F test.*
COCHRAN   *Cochran's C.*
BOXM   *Box's M (multivariate case only).*
ALL   *BARTLETT, COCHRAN, and BOXM.*

Box's *M* is especially useful in the analysis of repeated measures designs when you have used the multivariate setup. See Section 33.76 for an example of this use of Box's *M*. Note that computation of Box's *M* requires the variance-covariance matrices for each cell and thus can be an expensive statistic in terms of computer time and memory.

33.42
DESIGN Keyword

Use DESIGN to request the following:

ONEWAY   *The one-way basis for each factor.*
OVERALL   *The overall reduced-model basis (design matrix).*
DECOMP   *The QR/CHOLESKY decomposition of the design.*
BIAS   *Contamination coefficients displaying the bias present in the design.*
SOLUTION   *Coefficients of the linear combinations of the cell means being tested.*
REDUNDANCY   *Exact linear combinations of parameters which form a redundancy. This keyword only prints a table if QR (the default) is the estimation method.*
COLLINEARITY *Collinearity diagnostics for design matrices. These diagnostics include the singular values of decomposition, condition indices corresponding to each singular value, and the proportion of variance of the corresponding parameter accounted for by each principal component. For greatest accuracy, use the QR method of estimation whenever you request collinearity diagnostics.*
ALL   *All DESIGN options.*

The decomposition of the design (DECOMP) and the bias (BIAS) computed from the decomposition can provide valuable information on the confounding of the effects and the estimability of the chosen contrasts. This is particularly useful in designs with unpatterned empty cells. Likewise, the solution matrix shows the exact linear combinations of cell means used to test effects and can be useful when you are interpreting effects.

33.43
ERROR Keyword

ERROR prints the following statistics:

SSCP   *Error sums of squares and cross-products matrix.*
COV   *Error variance-covariance matrix.*
COR   *Error correlation matrix and standard deviations.*
STDV   *Error standard deviations (univariate case).*
ALL   *SSCP, COV, COR, and STDV.*

When you specify ERROR(COR) in the multivariate case, MANOVA routinely prints the determinant and Bartlett's test of sphericity, which is a test of whether the error correlation matrix is the identity matrix. The test of sphericity is especially useful when the dependent variables are transformed variables in a repeated measures analysis. See the examples in Sections 33.72 through 33.80.

33.44
SIGNIF Keyword

SIGNIF prints the following statistics:

MULTIV   *Multivariate F tests for group differences (default display).*
EIGEN   *Eigenvalues of $S_h S_e^{-1}$.*
DIMENR   *A dimension-reduction analysis.*
UNIV   *Univariate F tests (default display except for repeated measures designs).*
HYPOTH   *The hypothesis SSCP matrix.*
STEPDOWN   *Roy-Bargmann step-down F tests.*
AVERF   *An averaged F test, for repeated measures (default for repeated measures designs).*
BRIEF   *A shortened multivariate output. BRIEF overrides all the above.*
AVONLY   *Averaged results only. Use with repeated measures.*
SINGLEDF   *Single-degree-of-freedom listings of effects.*
HF   *The Huynh-Feldt corrected significance values for averaged univariate F-tests (use with repeated measures designs).*
GG   *The Greenhouse-Geisser corrected significance values for averaged univariate F tests (use with repeated measures designs).*
EFSIZE   *The effect size for the univariate F and T tests.*
ALL   *All SIGNIF statistics listed above.*
NONE   *No statistics.*

The output with BRIEF specified consists of a table similar in appearance to a univariate ANOVA table but with the generalized *F* and Wilks' lambda replacing the univariate *F*.

33.45
PARAMETERS Keyword

PARAMETERS prints output relating to the estimated parameters.

ESTIM   *The estimates themselves, along with their standard errors, t tests, and confidence intervals.*
ORTHO   *The orthogonal estimates of parameters used to produce the sums of squares.*
COR   *Correlations among the parameters.*
NEGSUM   *For main effects, the negative sum of the other parameters (representing the parameter for the omitted category).*

EFSIZE *The effect size values.*
OPTIMAL *Optimal Scheffé contrast coefficients.*
ALL *ESTIM, ORTHO, COR, NEGSUM, EFSIZE, and OPTIMAL.*

33.46
TRANSFORM Keyword

The transformation matrix shows how MANOVA is transforming the variables in the analysis when you use the multivariate setup in repeated measures and specify a WSFACTORS command. To display this matrix, specify

```
PRINT = TRANSFORM
```

To override this, specify NOPRINT=TRANSFORM later on the MANOVA command.

33.47
PCOMPS Subcommand

The PCOMPS subcommand requests a principal components analysis of each error SSCP in a multivariate design. COR prints principal components of the error correlation matrix; COV prints principal components of the error variance-covariance matrix. Factors extracted from these matrices are corrected for group differences and covariates. Such factors tend to be more useful than factors extracted from an uncorrected matrix when significant group differences are present or when a significant amount of error variance is accounted for by the covariates.

The PCOMPS subcommand has the following keywords:

COR *Principal components analysis of the error correlation matrix.*
COV *Principal components analysis of the error variance-covariance matrix.*
ROTATE(rottype) *Rotation of the principal component loadings.* For rottype, substitute VARIMAX, EQUAMAX, QUARTIMAX, or NOROTATE.
NCOMP(n) *The number of principal components to be rotated.* Specify n, or let n default to all components extracted.
MINEIGEN(eigcut) *The eigenvalue cutoff value for principal component extraction.*
ALL *COR, COV, NCOMP, and MINEIGEN.*

The ROTATE(rottyp) keyword specifies a rotation technique for the principal component loadings. Rotation can aid interpretation of the principal components. You can choose from three rotation algorithms—VARIMAX, EQUAMAX, and QUARTIMAX. Use NOROTATE to inhibit rotation. If you do not specify ROTATE, no rotation is done. Because MANOVA does not specify a default algorithm for ROTATE, no rotation is done when you specify ALL.

When ROTATE is in effect, MANOVA rotates *all* components. To rotate fewer components, specify the number in parentheses after the NCOMP keyword or specify the cutoff value for eigenvalues on the MINEIGEN keyword. For example,

```
PCOMPS=COR ROTATE(VARIMAX) NCOMP(3)
```

rotates the first three components, while

```
PCOMPS=COR ROTATE(VARIMAX) MINEIGEN(1.5)
```

rotates those components with eigenvalues greater than 1.5.

If you specify an *n* greater than the number of components, MANOVA simply rotates all components. If you specify an *n* less than two, MANOVA rotates at least two components. However, if fewer than two eigenvalues are greater than *eigcut*, no rotation is performed.

A principal components analysis requires the extraction of eigenvalues and eigenvectors. This is an expensive process if there is a large dependent variable list.

33.48
DISCRIM Subcommand

The DISCRIM subcommand requests a canonical analysis of dependent and independent variable sets in multivariate analyses. If the predictor set of variables is continuous, MANOVA prints a canonical correlation analysis. If the predictor set of variables is categorical, MANOVA prints a canonical discriminant analysis. For covariates, DISCRIM produces a canonical analysis. See Section 33.75 for an example of both canonical discriminant and canonical correlation analyses in MANOVA.

The DISCRIM subcommand has the following keywords:

RAW   *Raw discriminant function coefficients.*

STAN   *Standardized discriminant function coefficients.*

ESTIM   *Effect estimates in discriminant function space.*

COR   *Correlations between the dependent and canonical variables defined by the discriminant functions.*

ROTATE(rottyp) *Rotation of the matrix of correlations between dependent and canonical variates. Specify VARIMAX, EQUAMAX, or QUARTIMAX.*

ALPHA(alpha)   *The significance level of the canonical variate. The default is .25.*

ALL   *RAW, STAN, ESTIM, COR, ROTATE and ALPHA.*

The ROTATE keyword provides rotation of the correlations between the dependent and canonical variates obtained for each effect. MANOVA does this in the case of canonical discriminant analysis but not in the case of multivariate regression.

MANOVA does not perform rotation unless there are at least two significant canonical variates. The number of significant canonical variates depends on the rank of $S_h S_e^{-1}$ for a given effect and also on the significance level chosen. This significance level is .25 by default, but you can change the test significance level by using the ALPHA(alpha) keyword. The alpha value specified with ALPHA indicates the cutoff value for the significance of the discriminant functions in multivariate analysis; alpha must be a decimal number from 0 to 1. MANOVA reports discriminant analysis results only for those functions with a significance level less than alpha. The default value of alpha is .25. Setting alpha=1.0 results in the printing of all discriminant functions. Specifying alpha to be negative or greater than 1 results in alpha being set to the default of .25.

```
DISCRIM=RAW ALPHA(0.0) /      reports no functions
DISCRIM=RAW ALPHA(1.0) /      reports all functions
DISCRIM=RAW ALPHA(.05) /      reports functions significant
                                  at .05 level or better
```

33.49
OMEANS Subcommand

The OMEANS (observed means) subcommand prints tables of the means of continuous variables for levels or combinations of levels of the factors. You can use the OMEANS subcommand by itself, or with a keyword specification. If you don't specify a keyword, the OMEANS subcommand displays the same output as PRINT=CELLINFO(MEANS).

Since output from OMEANS is displayed once before the analysis of any particular design, you should specify the OMEANS subcommand only once per MANOVA command. OMEANS displays confidence intervals for the cell means if you have SET WIDTH=132.

The OMEANS subcommand has the following keywords:

VARIABLES *Continuous variables for which you want means.* Specify the variables in parentheses after the VARIABLES keyword. You can request means for the dependent variable or any covariates. If you omit the VARIABLES keyword, MANOVA displays observed means for all dependent variables and all covariates.

TABLES *Factors for which you want the observed means displayed.* List the factors, or combinations of factors separated with BY, in parentheses. MANOVA displays observed means of the factors named. It displays both weighted means (based on all cases) and unweighted means (where all cells are weighted equally, regardless of the number of cases they contain). If you enter the keyword CONSTANT, MANOVA displays the grand mean.

Consider a two-way analysis of covariance for the data displayed in Table 33.49, with Y as the response variable and X as the covariate.

Table 33.49 Data for the Two-Way Ancova

		A 1		A 2		A 3		A 4	
		Y	X	Y	X	Y	X	Y	X
B	1	8	2	8	7	10	5	6	3
		7	5	9	9			4	5
	2	6	4	8	3	6	2	9	3
		7	5	6	2	8	5		

The weighted mean for a particular treatment is obtained by summing the scores of all subjects receiving that treatment and dividing by the total number of subjects included in the sum. For example, the weighted mean of Y for the first level of factor B (B_1) is

$$(8+7+8+9+10+6+4)/7 = 7.429$$

The unweighted treatment mean is obtained by averaging the cell means receiving that treatment. Thus the unweighted mean of Y for B_1 is

$$(7.5+8.5+10+5)/4 = 7.75$$

You can print tables of observed means with the keyword TABLE. For the above example,

```
OMEANS=TABLES(A B, A BY B)
```

prints the treatment means (weighted and unweighted) of Y and X for factors A, B, and A by B in the following tables:

A (collapsing over B)
B (collapsing over A)
A BY B (the observed cell means themselves)

For example,

```
OMEANS=VARIABLE(Y),TABLES(A,B)
```

requests the treatment means of Y for factors A and B. The combined observed means are given in Figure 33.49.

Use the keyword CONSTANT to obtain grand means. For example,

```
OMEANS=VARIABLES(Y) TABLES(CONSTANT)
```

prints only the grand mean for variable Y.

Figure 33.49   Observed means of Y for factors A and B

```
Combined Observed Means for A
Variable .. Y
            A
            1          WGT.     7.00000
                       UNWGT.   7.00000
            2          WGT.     7.75000
                       UNWGT.   7.75000
            3          WGT.     8.00000
                       UNWGT.   8.50000
            4          WGT.     6.33333
                       UNWGT.   7.00000

- - - - - - - - - - - - - - - -
Combined Observed Means for B
Variable .. Y
            B
            1          WGT.     7.42857
                       UNWGT.   7.75000
            2          WGT.     7.14286
                       UNWGT.   7.37500
```

33.50
PMEANS Subcommand

The PMEANS (predicted means) subcommand prints a table of the predicted cell means of the dependent variable, both adjusted and unadjusted for the effect of covariates in the cell. PMEANS prints means for each cell, predicted from the factor. Covariates are not predicted. For comparison, PMEANS also prints the observed cell means. Note that this is an expensive set of statistics to produce.

You can specify the PMEANS subcommand by itself or with keywords. If you specify PMEANS by itself, with no keyword, it prints a table showing for each cell the observed mean of the dependent variable, the predicted mean adjusted for the effect of covariates in that cell, the predicted mean unadjusted for covariates, and the raw and standardized residuals from the estimated means.

The PMEANS subcommand has the following keywords:

VARIABLES   *Dependent variables for which you want tables of predicted means.* Used in multivariate MANOVA.

TABLES   *Additional tables showing adjusted predicted means for specified factors or combinations of factors.* Enter the names of factors or combinations of factors in parentheses after this keyword. For each factor or combination, MANOVA displays the predicted means (adjusted for covariates) collapsed over all other factors.

PLOT   *A plot of predicted means for each cell.*

The format of the variable list and the table requests for the PMEANS subcommand is the same as for the OMEANS subcommand. For example,

```
MANOVA  Y BY A(1,4) B(1,2) WITH X
        /PMEANS=TABLES(A)
```

prints the predicted means for variable Y for the A table. If no covariates are present in the model, the adjusted mean (labeled **ADJ. MEAN** in the output) and the predicted mean (labeled **EST. MEAN** in the output) are the same and are equal to the predicted cell mean (Finn, 1974, p. 376).

To obtain tables of combined (adjusted) predicted means, specify

```
PMEANS=TABLES(A,B)
```

which produces a table of the adjusted and predicted means of Y for each cell and the marginal predicted means for factors A and B (see Figures 33.50a and 33.50b). Note that if the variable and factor lists are not both given in the PMEANS subcommand, only the output shown in Figure 33.50b is printed.

Cells from PMEANS output are numbered so that the levels on the factor named last in the MANOVA variables specification are incremented first (as in output for PRINT=CELLINFO). A table showing the levels of each factor corresponding to each cell number is displayed at the beginning of the MANOVA output.

Figure 33.50a   Adjusted means of Y for factors A and B

```
Combined Adjusted Means for A
Variable .. Y
            A
            1        UNWGT.      7.03571
            2        UNWGT.      7.60714
            3        UNWGT.      8.50000
            4        UNWGT.      7.10714
- - - - - - - - - - - - - - - - - - - - -
Combined Adjusted Means for B
Variable .. Y
            B
            1        UNWGT.      7.62500
            2        UNWGT.      7.50000
```

Figure 33.50b   Adjusted and estimated means for Y

```
Adjusted and Estimated Means
Variable .. Y
      Factor        Code        Obs. Mean    Adj. Mean    Est. Mean    Raw Resid.    Std. Resid.

A                    1
   B                 1           7.50000      7.60714      7.50000       .00000         .00000
   B                 2           6.50000      6.46429      6.50000       .00000         .00000

A                    2
   B                 1           8.50000      7.96429      8.50000       .00000         .00000
   B                 2           7.00000      7.25000      7.00000       .00000         .00000

A                    3
   B                 1          10.00000      9.89286     10.00000       .00000         .00000
   B                 2           7.00000      7.10714      7.00000       .00000         .00000

A                    4
   B                 1           5.00000      5.03571      5.00000       .00000         .00000
   B                 2           9.00000      9.17857      9.00000       .00000         .00000
```

In designs with covariates and multiple error terms, use the ERROR subcommand to designate which error terms's regression coefficients are to be used in calculating the predicted means. For example,

```
MANOVA DEP BY A B C(1,3)
    /PMEANS
    /ERROR=1
    /DESIGN A, B WITHIN A = 1, C VS W
```

uses error term 1 to standardize residuals. Predicted means are suppressed if the last term is being calculated by subtraction (METHOD = ESTIM(LASTRES)) or the design contains the MUPLUS keyword (see Section 33.7).

If you use the WSFACTORS and WSDESIGN subcommands to do a repeated measures design, PMEANS prints the means of the orthonormalized variables. For non-repeated measures designs, if you use the TRANSFORM subcommand, PMEANS uses the scale of the transformed variables.

33.51
PLOT Subcommand

The PLOT subcommand requests exploratory and diagnostic line-printer plots. The following plots are available:

CELLPLOTS   *Plot cell statistics, including a plot of cell means vs. cell variances, a plot of cell means vs. cell standard deviations, and a histogram of cell means, for each interval variable (response variables and covariates) defined in the MANOVA specification.* The first two plots aid in detecting heteroscedasticity (nonhomogeneous variances) and in determining an appropriate transformation of the data (if one is needed). The third plot gives distributional information for the cell means.

BOXPLOTS   *Plot a boxplot for each interval variable (Tukey, 1977).* Boxplots provide a simple graphic means of comparing the cells in terms of mean location and spread. Note that the data must be stored in memory for these plots as well. Again, if there is not enough memory, boxplots are not produced.

Figure 33.51a   Cell plots

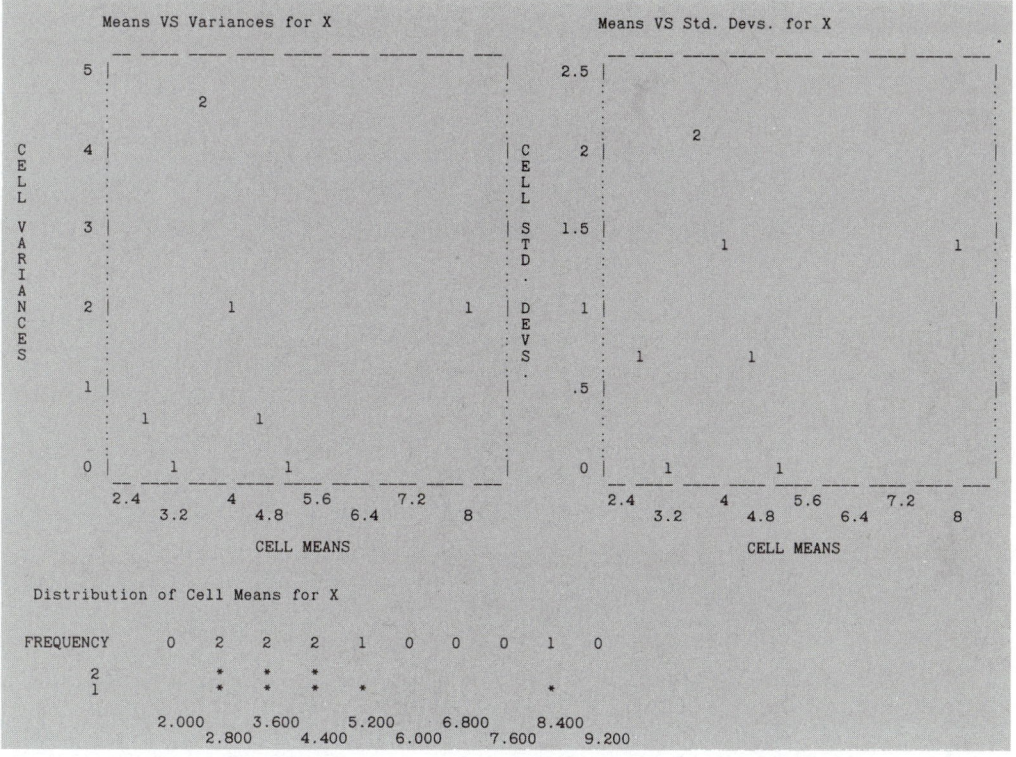

Figure 33.51b   Boxplot

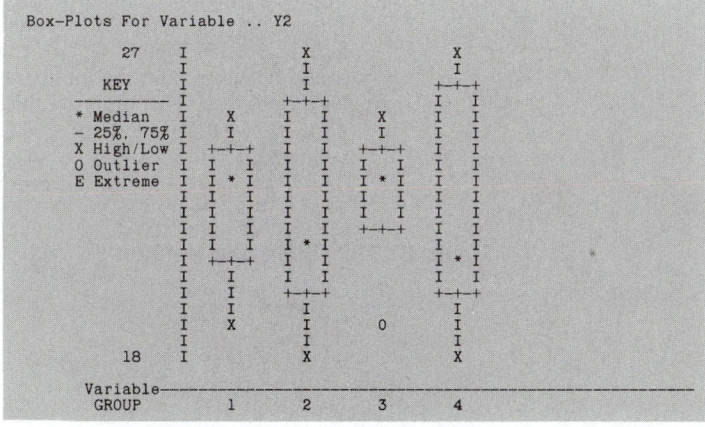

NORMAL   *Plot a normal plot and a detrended normal plot for each continuous variable.* MANOVA ranks the scores on each variable and plots the ranks against the expected normal deviate or detrended expected normal deviate for that rank. These plots aid in detecting non-normality and outlying observations. Note that these plots are expensive in terms of memory, because all data must be stored in order to compute ranks. Should there not be enough memory to store the data, SPSS-X MANOVA prints a warning and skips these plots.

Figure 33.51c Normal plots

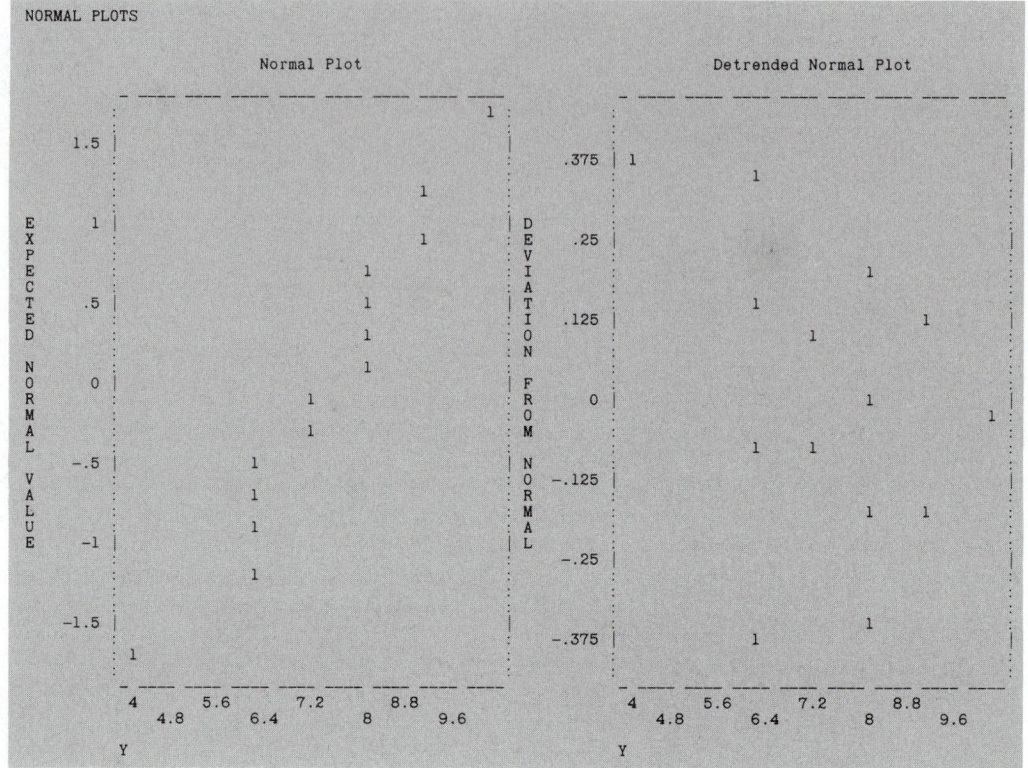

STEMLEAF   *Plot a stem-and-leaf display for each interval variable (Tukey, 1977).* This displays a condensed frequency distribution, which preserves the data scores. In Figure 33.51d, the numbers to the left of the dots are called the stem, and the numbers to the right of the dot are called the leaf. Each leaf represents a value. For example, in the first line of the plot, 10.156, 10 is the stem, .156 is the leaf, and 10.156 represents three values 10.1, 10.5, and 10.6. Again, these plots require storage of all data in memory and are not produced if the data do not fit.

Figure 33.51d Stem-and-leaf plot

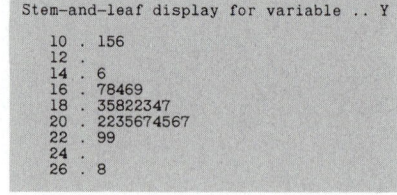

ZCORR   *Plot a half-normal plot of the within-cells correlations among the dependent variables in a multivariate analysis.* MANOVA first transforms the correlations using Fisher's Z transformation. A straight line indicates that no significant correlations exist among the dependent variables.

Figure 33.51e   Half-normal plot of partial correlations

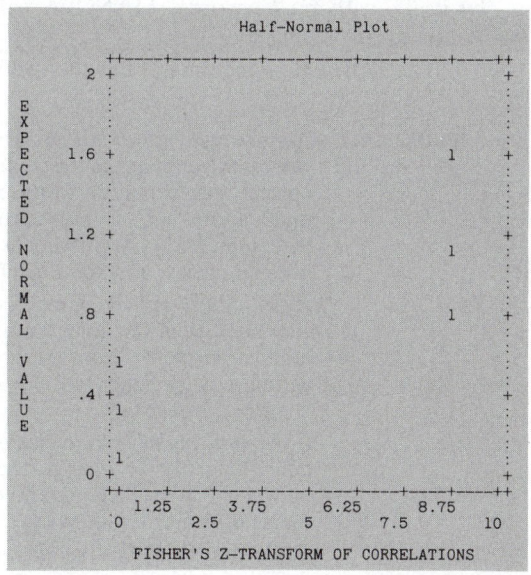

33.52
RESIDUALS Subcommand

The RESIDUALS subcommand displays and plots casewise values and residuals for your models. The RESIDUALS subcommand has the following keywords:

CASEWISE *A case-by-case listing of the observed, predicted, residual, and standard- ized residual values for each dependent variable.*

PLOT *A plot of observed values, predicted values, and case numbers vs. the standardized residuals, plus normal and detrended normal probability plots for the standardized residuals (5 plots in all).*

To print predicted values and residuals without plotting them, specify CASE-WISE. To plot the values without printing them, specify PLOT. To both print and plot these values, specify

```
RESIDUALS=CASEWISE PLOT
```

Use the ERROR subcommand to specify the error term to be used to standardize the residuals if one other than the default error term is produced.

If a designated error term does not exist for a given design, no predicted values or residuals are calculated. If you specify RESIDUALS without any specifications, CASEWISE output is displayed.

33.53
POWER Subcommand

The POWER subcommand requests observed power values based on fixed-effect assumptions for all univariate and multivariate F and T tests. Both approximate and exact power values can be computed, though exact multivariate power is printed only when there is one hypothesis degree of freedom.

To request power values, specify the appropriate keywords after the POWER subcommand, along with the type of test (either F or T), and the significance level at which the power is to be calculated. If you specify the POWER subcommand by itself, with no keywords, MANOVA calculates the observed power of all F-tests at .05 significance level.

The POWER subcommand has the following keywords:

APPROXIMATE   *Approximate power values.* This is the default. Approximate power values for univariate tests are derived from an Edgeworth-type normal approximation to the non-central beta distribution, and for multivariate tests, from procedures presented by Muller and Peterson (1983). Approximate values are normally accurate to three decimal places, and are much cheaper to compute than exact values.

EXACT   *Exact power values.* Exact power values for univariate tests are computed from the non-central incomplete beta distribution, and for multivariate tests, from the non-central F distribution. Exact multivariate power values will be printed only if there is one hypothesis degree of freedom.

F(a)   *F test and alpha level at which the power is to be calculated.* The default is .05. To change the default, specify a decimal number between 0 and 1 in parentheses after F. The numbers 0 and 1 themselves are not allowed.

T(a)   *T test and the alpha level at which the power is to be calculated.* The default is .05. To change the default, specify a decimal number between 0 and 1 in parentheses after T. The numbers 0 and 1 themselves are not allowed.

In addition, for univariate F and t tests, MANOVA computes a measure of the effect size based on partial eta-squared:

```
partial eta-squared=dfh*F/(dfh*F+dfe)
```

which is an overestimate of the actual effect size. However, it is a consistent measure of effect size and is applicable to all F and t tests. For a discussion of effect size measures see Cohen (1977) or Hays (1981).

Exact multivariate power is only available when there is one hypothesis degree of freedom. In this case all the multivariate criteria have identical power which can be found from the non-central F distribution. For all other cases, approximate power values for Pillai's Trace, Hotelling's Trace, and Wilks' Lambda are obtained using the methods given by Muller and Peterson(1983). These approximate power estimates have been found to be accurate to about two digits (Muller & Peterson, 1983). For information on the multivariate generalizations of power and effect size, see Muller & Peterson (1983), Green (1978), Huberty(1972) and Kennedy (1970).

Example. The following command reproduces the example from Figure 33.23b, with the power and effect sizes added.

```
MANOVA P2DIGIT P3DIGIT P4DIGIT NP2DIGIT NP3DIGIT NP4DIGIT BY HAND(1,2)
   /WSFACTOR=COND(2) DIGIT(3)
   /WSDESIGN=DIGIT COND DIGIT BY COND
   /PRINT=SIGNIF(EFSIZE)
   /POWER
   /DESIGN=HAND
```

Figure 33.53 shows the results. Note that the power of the multivariate HAND BY DIGIT BY COND test (.18) is greater than the power of the the univariate (AVERF) test (.155) in this example.

Figure 33.53 Power and effect sizes

```
Tests involving 'DIGIT BY COND' Within-Subject Effect.


Mauchly sphericity test, W =        .87321
Chi-square approx. =                2.84712 with 2 D. F.
Significance =                       .241

Greenhouse-Geisser Epsilon =         .88748
Huynh-Feldt Epsilon =               1.00000
Lower-bound Epsilon =                .50000

AVERAGED Tests of Significance that follow multivariate tests are equivalent to
univariate or split-plot or mixed-model approach to repeated measures.
Epsilons may be used to adjust d.f. for the AVERAGED results.
- - - - - - - - - - - - - - - - - - - - - - - - - - - - - - - - - - -
EFFECT .. HAND BY DIGIT BY COND
Multivariate Tests of Significance (S = 1, M = 0, N = 9 1/2)

Test Name        Value      Exact F Hypoth. DF   Error DF  Sig. of F

Pillais         .07632      .86760        2.00      21.00      .434
Hotellings      .08263      .86760        2.00      21.00      .434
Wilks           .92368      .86760        2.00      21.00      .434
Roys            .07632
Note.. F statistics are exact.

- - - - - - - - - - - - - - - - - - - - - - - - - - - - - - - - - - -
Multivariate Effect Size and Observed Power at .0500 Level

TEST NAME    Effect Size   Noncent.       Power

 (All)           .076       1.735          .18

- - - - - - - - - - - - - - - - - - - - - - - - - - - - - - - - - - -
EFFECT .. DIGIT BY COND
Multivariate Tests of Significance (S = 1, M = 0, N = 9 1/2)

Test Name        Value      Exact F Hypoth. DF   Error DF  Sig. of F

Pillais         .00956      .10138        2.00      21.00      .904
Hotellings      .00965      .10138        2.00      21.00      .904
Wilks           .99044      .10138        2.00      21.00      .904
Roys            .00956
Note.. F statistics are exact.

- - - - - - - - - - - - - - - - - - - - - - - - - - - - - - - - - - -
Multivariate Effect Size and Observed Power at .0500 Level

TEST NAME    Effect Size   Noncent.       Power

 (All)           .010        .203          .06

- - - - - - - - - - - - - - - - - - - - - - - - - - - - - - - - - - -
Tests involving 'DIGIT BY COND' Within-Subject Effect.

AVERAGED Tests of Significance for MEAS.1 using UNIQUE sums of squares
Source of Variation          SS      DF        MS        F  Sig of F

WITHIN CELLS            20138.11      44    457.68
DIGIT BY COND              88.17       2     44.08      .10     .908
HAND BY DIGIT BY COND     613.39       2    306.69      .67     .517

- - - - - - - - - - - - - - - - - - - - - - - - - - - - - - - - - - -
Effect Size Measures and Observed Power at the .0500 Level
                                  Partial Noncen-
Source of Variation      ETA Sqd   trality     Power

DIGIT BY COND               .004     .193       .064
HAND BY DIGIT BY COND       .030    1.340       .155
```

33.54
CINTERVAL Subcommand

The CINTERVAL subcommand requests simultaneous confidence intervals for each parameter estimate and regression coefficient. Both univariate (Scheffé and Bonferroni) and multivariate (Roy, Pillai, Bonferroni, Hotelling, and Wilks) confidence intervals are available. You can request either joint or individual univariate and multivariate confidence intervals, and also vary the confidence level. You can request only one type of confidence interval per design.

To request confidence intervals, specify the CINTERVAL subcommand followed by the appropriate keywords. Without any specifications, CINTERVAL will automatically print individual univariate confidence intervals at the .95 level.

The CINTERVAL subcommand has the following keywords:

INDIVIDUAL(a)
    Individual confidence intervals, and the confidence level desired. The default is .95. To change the default, specify any decimal number between 0 and 1 in parentheses after INDIVIDUAL. When individual intervals are requested, BONFER and SCHEFFE will have no effect.

JOINT(a)
    Joint confidence intervals, and the confidence level desired. The default is .95. To change the default, specify any decimal number between 0 and 1 in parentheses after JOINT.

UNIVARIATE(type)
    Univariate confidence interval, and its type. Specify either SCHEFFE for Scheffé intervals or BONFER for Bonferroni intervals in parentheses after UNIVARIATE. The default specification is SCHEFFE.

MULTIVARIATE(type)
    Multivariate confidence interval, and its type. Specify either ROY for Roy's largest root, PILLAI for Pillai's trace, BONFER for Bonferroni intervals, HOTELLING for Hotelling's trace, or WILKS for Wilks' Lambda in parentheses after MULTIVARIATE. The default specification is ROY.

MANOVA provides either individual or joint confidence intervals at any desired confidence level. You can compute joint confidence intervals using either Scheffé or Bonferroni intervals. Scheffé intervals are based on all possible contrasts, while Bonferroni intervals are based on the number of contrasts actually made. For a large number of contrasts, Bonferroni intervals will be larger than Scheffé. Timm (1975) provides a good discussion of which intervals are best for certain situations. Both Scheffé and Bonferroni intervals are computed separately for each term in the design.

You can also compute multivariate confidence intervals. The Wilks, Pillai and Hotelling intervals are computed by approximating the percentage points with percentage points of the F distribution. These approximate confidence intervals are thought to match exact intervals well across a wide range of alpha levels especially for large sample sizes (Burns, 1984). Use of these intervals, however, has not been widely investigated. For Roy intervals, an approximation given by Pillai (1967) is used. This approximation is accurate for upper percentage points, (.95 to 1) but not as good for lower percentage points. Thus, the user is restricted to the range .95 to 1 for Roy intervals. Bonferroni intervals, based on the Student's t distribution, are also available.

If you want joint intervals within each dependent variable, rather than across all dependent variables, request univariate Scheffé or Bonferroni intervals. If you want multivariate intervals separately for each parameter, choose individual multivariate intervals. For individual multivariate confidence intervals the hypothesis degrees of freedom is set to 1, in which case Hotelling, Pillai, Wilks and Roy intervals will be identical and equivalent to that those computed from percentage points of Hotellings T-squared distribution. Individual Bonferroni intervals will differ, and for a small number of dependent variables, will generally be shorter.

Example. The following example is from Winer (1971). This is an analysis-of-covariance example where three groups of students were assigned to one of three different teaching methods. An aptitude test was given before training, and each student took an achievement test on the material presented after the teaching period. Winer shows that there is a significant effect of treatment after adjusting for the linear trend of aptitude. Perhaps the first treatment was actually the present teaching method, and the experimenter was interested in how methods 2 and 3 compare to method 1. In that case, since there are only two contrasts of interest, Bonferroni intervals would be appropriate. The following command is used for the analysis:

```
MANOVA ACH BY METHOD(1,3) WITH APT
  /CINTERVAL=UNIV(BON) JOINT(.99)
  /CONTRAST=SPECIAL(1  1  1
                    1 -1  0
                    1  0 -1)
  /DESIGN
```

Figure 33.54 shows joint 99% Bonferroni intervals for the two contrasts of interest. These contrasts are performed on the adjusted means of the three treatments. The mean adjusted achievement tests were higher for students being taught by methods 2 or 3 than that for method 1 (as seen by the negative coefficents for the two contrasts). Since neither interval around these contrasts includes 0, both methods are significantly better than the method 1.

Figure 33.54   99% Bonferroni confidence intervals

```
Estimates for ACH adjusted for 1 covariate
--- Joint univariate .9900 BONFERRONI confidence intervals
METHOD

Parameter    Coeff.   Std. Err.    t-Value    Sig. t  Lower -99%  CL-  Upper
        2  -2.1877551    .45446    -4.81395    .00016   -3.79789    -  .57762
        3  -1.8612245    .42396    -4.39013    .00040   -3.36328    -  .35917
```

33.55
MISSING Subcommand

By default, cases with missing values on any of the variables named in the MANOVA specification are not included in the analysis. Use the MISSING subcommand to control missing values. The minimum specification is a single keyword. The default keywords are EXCLUDE and LISTWISE.

LISTWISE   *Exclude missing values listwise.* Cases with missing values for any variable named on the MANOVA variable list are excluded from the analysis. This is the default.

INCLUDE   *Include user-defined missing values.* User-missing values are treated as valid. For factors, you must include the missing-value codes within the range specified on the MANOVA variable list. It may be necessary to recode these values so they will be adjacent to the other factor values. You must also include the missing values within the range for categorical variables to enter the cases into the analysis. System-missing values cannot be included in the analysis.

EXCLUDE   *Exclude both user-missing and system-missing values.*

The INCLUDE and EXCLUDE keywords are mutually exclusive; however, each can be specified with LISTWISE. For example, to include user-missing values in an analysis that excludes system missing values listwise, specify

```
MANOVA Y BY CAT(1,2) DRUG (1,3)/ DESIGN=CAT,DRUG
       /MISSING=INCLUDE LISTWISE
```

33.56
MATRIX Subcommand

MANOVA can write matrix materials built from the raw data it reads. It can also read matrix materials written by previous MANOVA procedures. To read and write matrices in MANOVA, you use the MATRIX subcommand.

The MATRIX subcommand has two keywords, IN and OUT, which you use to specify the matrix file in parentheses. When you use both IN and OUT on the same MANOVA procedure you can specify each on a separate MATRIX subcommand, or both on the same subcommand. For example,

```
MANOVA MATRIX=IN(FILEONE)
         /MATRIX=OUT(FILETWO)
```

is the same as

```
MANOVA MATRIX=IN(FILEONE) OUT(FILETWO)
```

33.57
OUT Keyword

The OUT keyword on MATRIX specifies the file to which the matrix is written. There are two options:

(file) *Write the correlation matrix to a system file.* MANOVA creates a system file containing the matrix materials. The name of the file is specified in parentheses. The system file is stored on disk and can be retrieved at any time.

(*) *Replace the active file with the correlation matrix.* The matrix materials replace the active file. The correlation matrix is *not* stored on disk. It is resident in the active file. For this specification, you can use an empty set of parentheses () in place of the asterisk in parentheses (*).

The matrix materials include the N, mean, and standard deviation. Documents from the original file will not be included in the matrix file and will not be present if the matrix file becomes the active file. (For a discussion on documents, see Chapter 6.)

In the following example, MANOVA reads data from Fisher's iris data (used in Example 2 at the end of this chapter) and writes one set of matrix materials to the file named MANDATA:

```
GET FILE IRIS
MANOVA SEPALLEN SEPALWID PETALLEN PETALWID BY TYPE(1,3)
         /MATRIX=OUT(MANDATA)
```

The active file is still the file named IRIS. Subsequent commands are executed on file IRIS.

To write the same matrix to the active file so that it is available to subsequent commands, specify the following:

```
GET FILE IRIS
MANOVA SEPALLEN SEPALWID PETALLEN PETALWID BY TYPE(1,3)
         /MATRIX=OUT(*)
LIST
```

The active file is replaced with the matrix materials. The LIST command is executed on the matrix file, not on the file named IRIS.

Format of the Matrix System File. Figure 33.57 shows the matrix system file produced by the above commands. The file has two special variables created by SPSS-X: ROWTYPE_ and VARNAME_. Variable ROWTYPE_ is a short string variable having values N, MEAN, CORR (for Pearson correlation coefficient) and STDDEV. The next variable, VARNAME_, is a short string variable whose values are the names of the variables and covariates used to form the correlation matrix. When ROWTYPE_ is CORR, VARNAME_ gives the variable associated with that row of the correlation matrix. Between ROWTYPE_ and VARNAME_ in Figure 33.57 is the factor variable TYPE defined in the BY portion of the MANOVA variable list. (Factor variables receive the system missing value on vectors that represent pooled values.) The remaining variables are the variables used to form the correlation matrix. (See Chapter 13 for more information on matrix system files.)

Variable Order. When split-file processing is in effect, the first variables in the matrix system file will be the split variables, followed by ROWTYPE_, the factor variable(s), VARNAME_, then the variables used to form the correlation matrix. A full set of matrix materials is written for each subgroup defined by the split variable(s). A split variable cannot have the same variable name as any other variable written to the matrix system file. If a split file is in effect when a matrix is written, the same split file must be in effect when that matrix is read into another procedure.

Additional Statistics. In addition to the CORR values, MANOVA always includes with the matrix materials:

• The total weighted number of cases used to compute each correlation coefficient.

• A vector of N's for each cell in the data.

• A vector of MEAN's for each cell in the data.

• A vector of pooled standard deviations STDDEV. This is the square root of the within cells mean square error for each variable.

This information appears in the order shown in Figure 33.57.

Figure 33.57   A matrix system file

```
FILE:       MATRIX FILE

ROWTYPE. TYPE VARNAME.   SEPALLEN    SEPALWID    PETALLEN    PETALWID

N            .          150.000000  150.000000  150.000000  150.000000
MEAN         1           50.0600000  34.2800000  14.6200000   2.4600000
N            1           50.0000000  50.0000000  50.0000000  50.0000000
MEAN         2           59.3600000  27.7000000  42.6000000  13.2600000
N            2           50.0000000  50.0000000  50.0000000  50.0000000
MEAN         3           65.8800000  29.7400000  55.5200000  20.2600000
N            3           50.0000000  50.0000000  50.0000000  50.0000000
CORR         .  SEPALLEN  1.0000000    .5302358    .7561642    .3645064
CORR         .  SEPALWID   .5302358   1.0000000    .3779162    .4705346
CORR         .  PETALLEN   .7561642    .3779162   1.0000000    .4844589
CORR         .  PETALWID   .3645064    .4705346    .4844589   1.0000000
STDDEV       .           5.1478944   3.3968773   4.3033447   2.0465002
```

NUMBER OF CASES READ =   12   NUMBER OF CASES LISTED =   12

**33.58
IN Keyword**   The IN keyword on MATRIX specifies the file from which the matrix is read. There are two options:

(file)   *Read the correlation matrix from a matrix system file.*

(*)   *Read the correlation matrix from the active file.* The active file must be an appropriate matrix system file. For this specification, you can use an empty set of parentheses () in place of the asterisk in parentheses (*).

MATRIX=IN cannot be used in place of GET or DATA LIST to begin a new SPSS-X command file. MATRIX is a subcommand on MANOVA and MANOVA cannot run before an active file is defined.

   In the following example, one set of matrix materials is read from the file named MANDATA. This specification assumes the current active file is not the file MANDATA:

```
MANOVA SEPALLEN SEPALWID PETALLEN PETALWID BY TYPE(1,3)
     /MATRIX=IN(MANDATA)
```

SPSS-X reads variable names, variable and value labels, and print and write formats from the dictionary of the matrix system file named MANDATA.

   Records in the matrix system file MANOVA reads can be in any order, with the following exceptions:

• The order of split file groups cannot be violated.

• All CORR vectors must appear contiguously within each split file group.
  When MANOVA reads matrix materials, it ignores the record containing the total number of cases. In addition, it skips unrecognized records. (MANOVA does not issue a warning when it skips records.)

   To begin a new command file and immediately read a matrix, first GET the matrix file, then specify IN(*) on MATRIX, as in

```
GET FILE=MANDATA
MANOVA SEPALLEN SEPALWID PETALLEN PETALWID BY TYPE(1,3)
     /MATRIX=IN(*)
```

ANNOTATED EXAMPLE FOR MANOVA (REPEATED MEASURES)

MANOVA provides extensive facilities for repeated measures analysis. This example is, to a great degree, a simple generalization of the paired *t* test situation. Instead of measurements on two occasions, however, there are measurements on four occasions. The same subjects are measured on each occasion, so a simple one-way analysis of variance is inappropriate. This analysis takes advantage of the *multivariate setup*, in which all of a subject's scores across occasions reside in the same SPSS-X case. That is, the data have the following structure:

Case	Subject	Score 1	Score 2	Score 3	Score 4
1	1	30	28	16	34
2	2	14	18	10	22

This is in contrast to the *univariate setup*, in which a subject's scores across occasions spill down the cases, as in

Case	Subject	Score
1	1	30
2	1	28
3	1	16
4	1	34
5	2	14
6	2	18
7	2	10
8	2	22

On balance, we recommend the multivariate setup because the univariate setup has certain drawbacks. First, the univariate setup forces you to spread your data over many more cases, and you pay for processing time by the case. Second, analysis of the univariate setup implies that you are using a mixed-model analysis of variance approach to the data. That is, *subject* is a random effect nested under between-subjects factors, when the latter are present. In this approach, certain *symmetry conditions* must be met (Huynh & Mandevill, 1979), and in practice these conditions are quite restrictive. Third, specification of the DESIGN subcommand in the univariate mixed model can be very complicated. Fourth, the univariate setup is computationally inefficient, in the sense that it can take much more memory and processing time than the equivalent multivariate setup. Fifth, in most cases, the univariate results are fully retrievable from a MANOVA job that uses the multivariate setup.

You should note that while all repeated measures examples shown in this document use the multivariate setup for the data, you will see references to statistics produced using the multivariate approach and statistics produced using the univariate approach. The latter set of statistics are produced using a multivariate setup, but they are the same statistics that MANOVA would produce if the univariate approach had been used. These univariate statistics are printed by default and are labeled AVERAGED TESTS OF SIGNIFICANCE.

There are a few situations where you might turn to the univariate setup. When assumptions are met, the univariate approach has greater power. Under certain data configurations, the univariate mixed model makes fuller use of the data, such as in the following situations: too small a number of subjects in the model, too many empty cells in the repeated measures model, or the imposition of certain designs on the repeated measures, such as latin square order.

The data used for this example is an experiment which studies the effects of four drugs upon reaction time to a series of tasks (Winer, 1971). The subjects are trained in the tasks prior to the experiment, so that the learning of the tasks does not confound the analysis. There are five subjects in the analysis. The experimenter observes each subject under each drug, and the order of administration of drugs is randomized. The SPSS-X commands are

```
TITLE A BASIC REPEATED MEASURES EXAMPLE
COMMENT THE DATA REPRESENT 4 MEASURES ON 5 INDIVIDUALS.
 THIS IS A SIMPLE REPEATED MEASURES DESIGN.
 THE DATA COME FROM WINER, PAGE 268.
DATA LIST / DRUG1 DRUG2 DRUG3 DRUG4 (4F3.0)
MANOVA DRUG1 TO DRUG4/
 WSFACTORS=TRIAL(4)/
 CONTRAST(TRIAL)=SPECIAL(4*1, 1,-1,0,0,
                        1,1,0,-2, 1,1,-3,1)/
 WSDESIGN=TRIAL/
 PRINT=CELLINFO(MEANS)
  TRANSFORM
  ERROR(COR)
  SIGNIF(UNIV)/
 DESIGN/
BEGIN DATA
 30 28 16 34
 14 18 10 22
 24 20 18 30
 38 34 20 44
 26 28 14 30
END DATA
```

- The TITLE command prints a title at the top of each page of display output, and the COMMENT command inserts comments that print back with the commands on the display (see Chapter 4).

- The DATA LIST command defines four variables from the data in the command file (see Chapter 5).

- The MANOVA specification names DRUG1 to DRUG4 as four joint dependent variables. There are no between-subjects factors or covariates in the analysis.

- The WSFACTORS subcommand defines TRIAL as a within-subjects factor. A *4* is placed in parentheses after the factor name since there are four drugs. MANOVA builds the indicated orthonormal transformation matrix and uses this matrix to transform the original response variables. MANOVA then cycles through the within-subjects effects defined by the WSDESIGN subcommand and represented by sets of the transformed variables (see Section 33.21).

- The CONTRAST subcommand specifies a special set of contrasts for comparisons of the means across scores. The within-subjects factor requires *orthogonal* contrasts, so you could specify difference, helmert, or polynomial contrasts. The example uses SPECIAL, supplying contrasts among the means. If you do not specify orthogonal contrasts for the within-subjects factor, MANOVA takes your specified contrasts and orthonormalizes them. The first row of the special matrix is always the contrast for the overall mean and is typically a set of 1s. The remaining rows of the matrix contain the special contrasts signifying the desired comparisons between levels of the factor. From an inspection of the four means, we decide on the following comparisons: (1) the mean of DRUG1 versus the mean of DRUG2; (2) the means of DRUG1 and DRUG2 versus the mean of DRUG4; and (3) the means of DRUG1, DRUG2, and DRUG4 versus DRUG3 (see Section 33.36).

- The WSDESIGN subcommand specifies TRIAL, the one within-subjects factor (see Section 33.22).

- The PRINT subcommand has four specifications. CELLINFO prints the means (see Figure A). TRANSFORM prints the orthonormalized transformation matrix, which directly reflects the contrasts on the within-subjects factor (see Figure B). ERROR(COR) prints the error correlation matrix along with some ancillary statistics. Assessment of the statistics tells whether or not it is appropriate to work with the univariate approach statistics (see Figure F). SIGNIF(UNIV) prints the univariate statistics (i.e. single degree of freedom contrasts). (see Figure H).

- Finally, the DESIGN subcommand specifies the model for the between-subjects factor. Since there is no between-subjects factor in this model, the DESIGN subcommand simply triggers the analysis (see Section 33.7).

Annotated Example for MANOVA *continued*

Portions of the display output are shown in Figures A through H.

- Figure A shows the cell means and standard deviations. Inspection of the cell means provides a rationale for the special contrast used in the analysis. Notice that the means for DRUG1 and DRUG2 have the smallest difference. Then, the mean for DRUG4 has a smaller difference from these two than does the mean for DRUG3. Finally, the mean for DRUG3 is most different from the others.

- Figure B shows the orthonormalized transformation matrix with contrasts on the means. The original contrasts on the CONTRAST subcommand are orthogonal. MANOVA normalizes the contrasts so that the sum of squares of any column of the matrix is 1.

- Figure C shows the beginning of the default display of the multivariate repeated measures analysis. MANOVA tells you that it is using transformed variables in the analysis; this is signified in the Note.

- Figure D shows the test of significance for the between-subjects effect, which in this example is just the overall constant.

- Figure E shows the next cycle of the analysis, which is the test for the TRIAL within-subjects effect. MANOVA jointly tests the three transformed variables, making this a multivariate test.

- Figure F shows the results from specifying ERROR(COR). Mauchly's test of sphericity tests whether the covariance matrix of the transformed variables has a constant variance on the diagonal and zeroes off the diagonal. The observed significance level of the test, .470, does not reject the null hypothesis of sphericity, so, we assume that the variances of the transformed variables are equal. If the observed significance level is small, and the sphericity assumption appears to be violated, an adjustment to the numerator and denominator degrees of freedom can be made. Two estimates of this adjustment, called Huynh-Feldt and Greenhouse-Geisser epsilon, are available in MANOVA. To obtain this adjustment, specify PRINT=SIGNIF(HF) for the Huynh-Feldt epsilon, or PRINT=SIGNIF(GG) for the Greenhouse-Geisser epsilon. The Greenhouse-Geisser epsilon tends to be more conservative than the Huynh-Feldt epsilon especially for small sample sizes. The lowest value possible for epsilon is also printed. When the Huynh-Feldt epsilon exceeds the value of one, MANOVA prints a value of one. To use either of these adjustments, multiply degrees of freedom in both the numerator and the denominator of the F-ratio by epsilon, and then evaluate the significance of the F-ratio with the new degrees of freedom. Given that there is no between-subjects factor, these data satisfy the *symmetry conditions* that must be met if you wish to apply the univariate-approach statistical results. For more on the symmetry conditions, see Example 4 in Section 33.76.

- Figure G shows the multivariate tests of significance of the trial within-subjects effect. The multivariate tests are significant at the .05 level.

- Figure H shows the univariate tests of significance where variable T2 represents the second contrast specified with the contrast subcommand, comparing trials one and two (1,-1,0 0). Similarly, variables T3 and T4 represent the third and fourth contrasts specified by the contrast subcommand, comparing trial 4 to trials 1 and 2 (1,1,0 2) and comparing trial 3 to trials 1, 2,and 4 respectively.

- Finally, Figure I shows the averaged test of significance for the drug effect; these are the *univariate approach* statistics. There are 12 error degrees of freedom for this test, while there are two error degrees of freedom for the multivariate tests. Given the error correlation results above, the averaged test is appropriate. The observed level of significance of this test is less than .0005, so the averaged *F* test corroborates the multivariate test results.

A Cell means and standard deviations

```
Cell Means and Standard Deviations
Variable .. DRUG1
                                      Mean   Std. Dev.      N   95 percent Conf. Interval

For entire sample                    26.400    8.764        5     15.519      37.281

- - - - - - - - - - - - - - - - - - - - - - - - - - - - - - - - - - - - - - - - - - -
Variable .. DRUG2
                                      Mean   Std. Dev.      N   95 percent Conf. Interval

For entire sample                    25.600    6.542        5     17.477      33.723

- - - - - - - - - - - - - - - - - - - - - - - - - - - - - - - - - - - - - - - - - - -
Variable .. DRUG3
                                      Mean   Std. Dev.      N   95 percent Conf. Interval

For entire sample                    15.600    3.847        5     10.823      20.377

- - - - - - - - - - - - - - - - - - - - - - - - - - - - - - - - - - - - - - - - - - -
Variable .. DRUG4
                                      Mean   Std. Dev.      N   95 percent Conf. Interval

For entire sample                    32.000    8.000        5     22.067      41.933
```

B Orthonormalized transformation matrix

```
Orthonormalized Transformation Matrix (Transposed)

              T1            T2            T3            T4

DRUG1       .50000        .70711        .40825        .28868
DRUG2       .50000       -.70711        .40825        .28868
DRUG3       .50000        .00000        .00000       -.86603
DRUG4       .50000        .00000       -.81650        .28868
```

C Transformed variables for between-subject effect

```
Order of Variables for Analysis

  Variates     Covariates

    T1

    1 Dependent Variable
    0 Covariates

- - - - - - - - - - - - - - - - - - - - - - - - - - -
Note..   TRANSFORMED variables are in the variates column.
         These TRANSFORMED variables correspond to the
         Between-subject effects.
```

D Analysis of variance for CONSTANT

```
Tests of Between-Subjects Effects.

Tests of Significance for T1 using UNIQUE sums of squares
Source of Variation        SS        DF        MS         F    Sig of F

WITHIN CELLS             680.80       4      170.20
CONSTANT              12400.20        1    12400.20      72.86    .001
```

E Transformed variables for the within-subject effect

```
Order of Variables for Analysis

  Variates     Covariates

    T2
    T3
    T4

    3 Dependent Variables
    0 Covariates

- - - - - - - - - - - - - - - - - - - - - - - - - - -
Note..   TRANSFORMED variables are in the variates column.
         These TRANSFORMED variables correspond to the
         'TRIAL' WITHIN-SUBJECT effect.
```

**Annotated Example for
MANOVA** *continued*

F Correlation and sphericity statistics

```
WITHIN CELLS Correlations with Std. Devs. on Diagonal
```

	T2	T3	T4
T2	2.56905		
T3	-.64875	1.73205	
T4	.29109	.14199	4.31277

```
- - - - - - - - - - - - - - - - - - - - - - - - - - - - - - -
Tests involving 'TRIAL' Within-Subject Effect.


Mauchly sphericity test, W =        .18650
Chi-square approx. =            4.57156 with 5 D. F.
Significance =                      .470

Greenhouse-Geisser Epsilon =        .60487
Huynh-Feldt Epsilon =              1.00000
Lower-bound Epsilon =               .33333

AVERAGED Tests of Significance that follow multivariate tests are equivalent to
univariate or split-plot or mixed-model approach to repeated measures.
Epsilons may be used to adjust d.f. for the AVERAGED results.
```

G Multivariate tests of significance

```
EFFECT .. TRIAL
Multivariate Tests of Significance (S = 1, M = 1/2, N = 0)
```

Test Name	Value	Exact F	Hypoth. DF	Error DF	Sig. of F
Pillais	.97707	28.41231	3.00	2.00	.034
Hotellings	42.61846	28.41231	3.00	2.00	.034
Wilks	.02293	28.41231	3.00	2.00	.034
Roys	.97707				

```
Note.. F statistics are exact.
```

H Univariate tests of specified contrasts

```
EFFECT .. TRIAL (CONT.)
Univariate F-tests with (1,4) D. F.
```

Variable	Hypoth. SS	Error SS	Hypoth. MS	Error MS	F	Sig. of F
T2	1.60000	26.40000	1.60000	6.60000	.24242	.648
T3	120.00000	12.00000	120.00000	3.00000	40.00000	.003
T4	576.60000	74.40000	576.60000	18.60000	31.00000	.005

I Averaged test of significance

```
Tests involving 'TRIAL' Within-Subject Effect.

AVERAGED Tests of Significance for DRUG using UNIQUE sums of squares
```

Source of Variation	SS	DF	MS	F	Sig of F
WITHIN CELLS	112.80	12	9.40		
TRIAL	698.20	3	232.73	24.76	.000

33.59
EXAMPLES OF
COMMON DESIGNS

Sections 33.60 through 33.71 describe some of the more commonly used designs which can be analyzed with MANOVA. These sections include sample MANOVA command setups to produce these designs. Sections 33.72 through 33.80 also provide examples with annotated output.

33.60
Univariate Analysis of Variance

The basic features of MANOVA useful for univariate analysis of variance are illustrated in the following example taken from Winer (1971, p. 436). An experiment was conducted to evaluate the relative effectiveness of three drugs (factor DRUG) in bringing about behavioral changes in two categories of patients (factor CAT). Three patients in each category were assigned at random to one of three drugs, and criterion ratings (Y) were made for each patient.

The MANOVA specification defines Y as the dependent variable and CAT and DRUG as the factor variables with two and three levels, respectively. Since only one dependent variable (Y) is indicated, a univariate analysis of variance is requested.

```
MANOVA  Y BY CAT(1,2) DRUG(1,3)
```

The default model generated from the MANOVA specification is a full factorial model.

Additional printed output can be obtained by using the PRINT subcommand. For instance, tests of homogeneity of within-cells variance are produced by specifying:

```
MANOVA Y BY CAT(1,2) DRUG(1,3)
/PRINT=HOMOGENEITY(BARTLETT,COCHRAN)
```

The cell statistics, including the mean, standard deviation, number of observations, and the 95% confidence intervals for the population means can be obtained using:

```
MANOVA Y BY CAT(1,2) DRUG(1,3)
/PRINT=CELLINFO(MEANS)
```

33.61
Specifying a Model with the DESIGN Subcommand

If the desired model is not full factorial, the model must be specified using the DESIGN subcommand. To specify a model that includes only the main effect terms, use

```
MANOVA Y BY CAT(1,2) DRUG(1,3)
   /DESIGN= CAT,DRUG
```

33.62
Specifying the ERROR Term

Unless otherwise requested, the within-cells mean square is used as the denominator for all the F values. If there is no within-cells error, the residual error is used. The residual mean square is the mean square for all terms not specified in the DESIGN subcommand. For example, if the model containing only main effects for DRUG and CAT is requested using

```
DESIGN= CAT,DRUG
```

the residual error term is the mean square for the CAT by DRUG interaction. See Section 33.38 for rules governing the use of the ERROR subcommand. Use the DESIGN subcommand to indicate whether different error terms are to be used for the various terms in the design specification. See Section 33.7 for further details.

33.63
Using DESIGN and ERROR

The following specification requests a main effects model. The pooled interaction term (denoted as *R* for residual) and the within-cells error (denoted as *W*) are used as the error.

```
MANOVA   Y BY CAT(1,2) DRUG(1,3)
         /ERROR=W+R
         /DESIGN=CAT,DRUG
```

The ERROR subcommand must precede the design specification to which it applies.

The following produces the same results:

```
MANOVA Y BY CAT(1,2) DRUG(1,3)
       /DESIGN = CAT VS W+R, DRUG VS W+R
```

33.64
Partitioning the Sum of Squares

Often it is desirable to partition the sum of squares associated with the various effects into a number of components that are more relevant to the individual questions of interest (see Cochran & Cox, 1957). In MANOVA, partitions are controlled by the keyword PARTITION followed by the name of the factor and the degrees of freedom associated with each component. To partition the sum of squares for factor DRUG into two components with one degree of freedom each, specify

```
MANOVA   Y BY CAT(1,2) DRUG(1,3)
         /PARTITION(DRUG)=(1,1)
         /DESIGN=CAT,DRUG(1),DRUG(2),CAT BY DRUG
```

The first component is denoted by DRUG(1), and the second by DRUG(2).

The default contrasts used for partitioning are deviation contrasts (see Section 33.36). In this example, the deviation contrasts are not orthogonal, so the two contrasts for DRUG(1) and DRUG(2) are not independent.

33.65
Contrasts

MANOVA allows specification of six different contrast types: deviation, difference, Helmert, simple, repeated, and polynomial. You can also specify any other contrast matrix via the SPECIAL keyword.

For example, to specify user-supplied orthogonal contrasts for the DRUG factor, use the following:

```
MANOVA   Y BY CAT(1,2) DRUG(1,3)
         /CONTRAST(DRUG)=SPECIAL(1 1 1 -1 2 -1 1 0 -1)
         /PARTITION(DRUG)=(1,1)
         /DESIGN=CAT,DRUG(1),DRUG(2),CAT BY DRUG(1),CAT BY DRUG(2)
```

The first set of coefficients (1 1 1) is always the weights for obtaining the constant term. Following the weights vector are the contrasts. The number of contrasts should be equal to the degrees of freedom for the factor. The first contrast (−1 2 −1) defines a contrast between level 2 and the combination of levels 1 and 3 for factor DRUG. The second contrast (1 0 −1) requests a comparison between levels 1 and 3 of DRUG. For most applications, you should be sure that each set of contrast coefficients sum to zero.

Since the inner product of the two contrasts is 0 and the sample sizes in all cells are equal, i.e., $(-1)(1) + 2(0) + (-1)(-1) = 0$, the two contrasts are independent. In this example, the DRUG(1) partition can be used to test the hypothesis $\beta_2 = (\beta_1 + \beta_3)/2$ while the second contrast tests $\beta_1 = \beta_3$.

33.66
Randomized Block Designs

In randomized block designs, the experimental unit is divided into groups (blocks). The main object is to keep the experimental errors within each group as small as possible. The accuracy of the experiment is increased by making comparisons within the resulting relatively homogeneous experimental units.

33.67
Complete Randomized Block Designs

A randomized block design is called complete if each block contains every level of the treatment. Table 33.67 is an example of a complete randomized block design with four treatments, A, B, C, and D, and three blocks.

Table 33.67   Complete randomized block design

Block

1	2	3
A	D	A
B	B	C
C	A	B
D	C	D

Let Y, TRT, and BLK be the response, treatment, and block variables, respectively. The MANOVA specifications needed to perform the analysis of this design are as follows:

```
MANOVA    Y BY BLK(1,3) TRT(1,4)
    /DESIGN=BLK,TRT
```

In most applications the significance of the block differences is assumed, and treatment effects are corrected for the block effects. Although it does not make any difference here since the design is balanced and complete, in general the treatment effects should be adjusted.

33.68
Balanced Incomplete (Randomized) Block Designs (BIB)

In some randomized block designs it may not be possible to apply all treatments in every block. If the block size is less than the number of treatments, the design is called incomplete. An incomplete block design is called balanced if

• Each block contains exactly k treatments.

• Each treatment appears in r blocks.

• Any pair of treatments appears together l times.

Thus a BIB can be described in terms of the parameters t (number of treatments), b (number of blocks), k, r, and l.

The following example is taken from Cochran and Cox (1957, p. 443). It is a BIB design with $t=6$, $b=15$, $k=2$, $r=5$, and $l=1$. The blocks are grouped into 5 replications.

The MANOVA specification for this analysis is as follows:

```
MANOVA   DEP BY REPLICS(1,5) TREATMNT(1,6) BLOCKS(1,3)
    /DESIGN=REPLICS TREATMNT BLOCKS W REPLICS
    /DESIGN=REPLICS BLOCKS W REPLICS TREATMNT
```

The first design specification requests the blocks within replications adjusted for treatment effects. The second specification asks for the treatment effects adjusted for the blocks.

33.69
Partially Balanced Incomplete Block Designs (PBIB)

Because balanced incomplete block designs often require a large number of blocks, it may not be possible to find a design that fits the size of the experiment. A general class of BIB designs that do not have the uniform variances for treatment contrasts but still permit the estimation of treatment differences are the partially balanced incomplete block designs.

PBIB designs represent a large class of designs, many of which can be found in Cochran and Cox (1957). An example with $t=15$, $b=15$, $k=4$, and $r=4$ is given on page 456 of that text. The MANOVA specifications are as follows:

```
MANOVA  DEP BY BLOCKS(1,15) TREATMNT(1,15)
   /DESIGN=BLOCKS TREATMNT
```

33.70
Latin and Other Squares

A Latin square is a design in which each treatment appears exactly once in each row and column. The main interest is still on the estimation of treatment differences, but there are two restrictions on the randomization of the treatment assignment.

The following MANOVA specifications can be used to analyze a 4×4 Latin square:

```
MANOVA Y BY ROW(1,4),COL(1,4),TRT(1,4)
   /DESIGN=ROW,COL,TRT
```

If another restriction on the randomization is placed on a Latin square, a Graeco-Latin square results. The analysis of variance for a Graeco-Latin square is very similar to that for a Latin square. Use GREEK to denote the third restriction factor on a 4×4 Graeco-Latin square. The MANOVA specification would be as follows:

```
MANOVA Y BY ROW(1,4), COL(1,4), GREEK(1,4), TRT(1,4)
   /DESIGN=ROW,COL,GREEK,TRT
```

Note that a small Graeco-Latin square design may not be very practical, since very few degrees of freedom are left for the residual.

33.71
Nested Designs

A nested design arranges the experimental units hierarchically. For example, consider an experiment to compare the yield of wheat per acre for different areas in a given state. Five counties are selected at random, and then three townships are randomly selected from each county. From each township two farms are selected and the yield of wheat per acre is obtained. The resulting experiment produces 30 ($5 \times 3 \times 2$) experimental units. The factors in this experiment are county and township, and the township effects are *nested* under the county factor, since a given township appears only under one of the five counties. In other words, the county factor is not *crossed* with township factor and so the interaction between county and township is not estimable.

The model for this two-factor nested design is

$$Y_{ijk} = \mu + \alpha_i + \beta_{j(i)} + \epsilon_{ijk}$$

where α_i is the county effect and $\beta_{j(i)}$ is the township effect nested under the county effect.

Since α_i should be tested against variation within α_i, i.e., $\beta_{j(i)}$, the following MANOVA specfications can be used:

```
MANOVA Y BY COUNTY(1,5),TOWN(1,3)
   /DESIGN=COUNTY VS 1, TOWN WITHIN COUNTY=1 VS WITHIN
```

The first keyword WITHIN (or just W) indicates nesting. The DESIGN specification requests that COUNTY be tested against error term 1 which is the effect of TOWN (nested within COUNTY), and that the within-cells error term (the second WITHIN) be used for testing the TOWN effect.

When crossing and nesting are both used in the design, attention must be paid to the choice of appropriate error terms for testing the various effects. Consider a three-factor example, with factors A, B, and C. If C is nested within B and B is nested within A, the DESIGN specification is

```
DESIGN=A VS 1,.B W A=1 VS 2, C W B W A=2 VS WITHIN
```

If C is nested within B and B is crossed with A, the DESIGN specification is

```
DESIGN=A VS 2, B VS 1, C W B=1 VS WITHIN,
       A BY B VS 2, A BY C W B=2 VS WITHIN
```

An experiment was conducted to compare a new gun-loading method with the existing one (Hicks, 1973, p. 195). Three teams were chosen randomly from each of three groups. Each team used the two methods of gun loading in random order. The MANOVA specifications are as follows:

```
MANOVA RESP BY METHOD(1,2) GROUP TEAM(1,3)
    DESIGN=METHOD VS 1, GROUP VS 2,
    METHOD BY GROUP VS 1, TEAM W GROUP=2,
    METHOD BY TEAM W GROUP=1
```

33.72
MANOVA EXAMPLES

MANOVA can be used to analyze many different types of designs. The following examples, although not exhaustive, demonstrate some of the more commonly used models. Most of these examples have been obtained from books and articles.

33.73
Example 1: Analysis of Covariance Designs

An analysis of covariance design is a specialized analysis of variance which allows you to parcel out the effect of a covariate. In this example, from Winer (1971), there is one factor, A, which represents three methods of training and one covariate, X, which is an aptitude test score. The dependent variable, Y, is the score on an achievement test administered after the training program. Thus, this design allows you to determine the effect of a factor (training method), on achievement, controlling for the effect of a covariate (aptitude). The SPSS-X commands are

```
COMMENT THE DATA COME FROM WINER'S STATISTICAL PRINCIPLES
 IN EXPERIMENTAL DESIGN, PAGE 776.
 Y IS A DEPENDENT VARIABLE.
 X IS A COVARIATE.
 A IS A FACTOR.
DATA LIST / A 1 X Y 2-5
COMMENT I.   THE FIRST MANOVA PORTION DOES A ONEWAY ANALYSIS OF VARIANCE.
MANOVA Y BY A(1,3)/
 DESIGN/
BEGIN DATA
data lines
END DATA
COMMENT II.   THE SECOND MANOVA PORTION
 DOES A DEFAULT ANALYSIS OF COVARIANCE.
 NOTE:   THE DEFAULT ASSUMES HOMOGENEOUS SLOPES.
MANOVA Y BY A(1,3) WITH X/
 PMEANS/
 DESIGN/
 /* III.   THE THIRD MANOVA PORTION TESTS THE FACTOR BY COVARIATE
 /* INTERACTION TERM.   THIS TESTS WHETHER THE PARALLEL SLOPES
 /* ASSUMPTION IS WARRANTED.
 ANALYSIS=Y/
 DESIGN= X, A, A BY X/
 /* IV.   THE FOURTH MANOVA PORTION SHOWS HOW TO FIT SEPARATE
 /* SLOPES.   YOU WOULD DO THIS IF THE FACTOR BY COVARIATE
 /* INTERACTION TERM IS SIGNIFICANT.
 DESIGN= X WITHIN A, A
```

- The DATA LIST command reads the three variables, A, X, and Y, from the data included in the command file (see Chapter 5).
- The first MANOVA command specifies a one-way analysis of variance using the default DESIGN subcommand (see Section 33.7).
- The second MANOVA command specifies the second through fourth models. The second model is a default analysis of covariance using the default DESIGN subcommand. The default analysis fits covariates, factors, and factor-by-factor interactions if you specify more than one factor, and assumes homogeneous slopes.
- The PMEANS subcommand prints predicted means for the second through fourth models (see Section 33.39).
- The third analysis shows how to test the assumption of homogeneous slopes. The ANALYSIS subcommand indicates the dependent variable (see Section 33.19). The DESIGN subcommand indicates effects, including the factor-by-covariate interaction.
- The fourth analysis shows how MANOVA can be used to analyze nested designs. The WITHIN keyword on the DESIGN subcommand fits separate regression models within each of the three groups of factor A.

Portions of the display output are shown in Figures 33.73a through 33.73e.

- Figure 33.73a shows the default display for the first analysis. The display includes an analysis of variance table.
- Figure 33.73b shows the default display for the second analysis, which includes the covariate X. MANOVA prints the analysis of variance table and regression statistics associated with X.

Figure 33.73a   Example 1: Results for first analysis

```
Tests of Significance for Y using UNIQUE sums of squares
Source of Variation            SS        DF        MS          F  Sig of F

WITHIN CELLS                 26.86       18       1.49
A                            36.95        2      18.48      12.38     .000
```

Figure 33.73b   Example 1: Results for second analysis

```
Tests of Significance for Y using UNIQUE sums of squares
Source of Variation            SS        DF        MS        F  Sig of F

WITHIN CELLS                 10.30       17        .61
REGRESSION                   16.56        1      16.56    27.32     .000
A                            16.93        2       8.47    13.97     .000
- - - - - - - - - - - - - - - - - - - - - - - - - - - - - - - - - - - - - - - - - - - - - - - - - -
Correlations between Covariates and Predicted Dependent Variable
        COVARIATE

VARIABLE        X

Y             1.00000

- - - - - - - - - - - - - - - - - - - - - - - - - - - - - - - - - - - - - - - - - - - - - - - - - - -
Averaged Squared Correlations between Covariates and Predicted Dependent Variable

VARIABLE       AVER. R-SQ

X             1.00000
Regression analysis for WITHIN CELLS error term
--- Individual Univariate .9500 confidence intervals
Dependent variable .. Y

COVARIATE            B         Beta     Std. Err.     t-Value    Sig. of t    Lower -95%    CL- Upper

X         .7428571429   .7851199742      .14213       5.22671       .000       .44300       1.04272
```

33

- Figure 33.73c shows the table of actual and predicted means for the second analysis requested with the PMEANS subcommand. MANOVA prints the observed means, the adjusted means, which are adjusted for the covariate, and the estimated means, which are the cell means estimated with knowledge of A.

- Figure 33.73d shows the analysis of variance table for the third analysis. Since the A by X interaction is not significant (significance of F = .605), we do not reject the hypothesis of parallel slopes. That is, we can assume that the effect of change in the covariate X on the dependent variable Y is the same across all three levels of the factor A.

- Finally, Figure 33.73e shows the analysis of variance table for the fourth analysis. The X WITHIN A effect is the joint effect of the separate regressions. Since the third analysis shows the factor-by-covariate interaction to be nonsignificant, the second analysis is the preferred solution.

Figure 33.73c   Example 1: Adjusted means for second analysis

Adjusted and Estimated Means Variable .. Y Factor	Code	Obs. Mean	Adj. Mean	Est. Mean	Raw Resid.	Std. Resid.
A	1	4.42857	4.88844	4.42857	.00000	.00000
A	2	7.57143	7.07619	7.57143	.00000	.00000
A	3	6.71429	6.74966	6.71429	.00000	.00000

Figure 33.73d   Example 1: Analysis of variance table for third analysis

Tests of Significance for Y using UNIQUE sums of squares Source of Variation	SS	DF	MS	F	Sig of F
WITHIN+RESIDUAL	9.63	15	.64		
X	15.67	1	15.67	24.40	.000
A	6.69	2	3.35	5.21	.019
A BY X	.67	2	.33	.52	.605

Figure 33.73e   Example 1: Analysis of variance table for fourth analysis

Tests of Significance for Y using UNIQUE sums of squares Source of Variation	SS	DF	MS	F	Sig of F
WITHIN+RESIDUAL	9.63	15	.64		
X WITHIN A	17.22	3	5.74	8.94	.001
A	6.69	2	3.35	5.21	.019

33.74
Example 2: Multivariate One-Way ANOVA

A multivariate one-way analysis of variance with one three-level factor and four dependent variables was performed. In addition to the standard test for the difference in means, you can obtain a canonical discriminant analysis. When analyzing data structures of this type, you can consider turning the problem around and using the DISCRIMINANT procedure (see Chapter 27).

The data are the iris data from Fisher (1936). Fisher collected four measures on each of three species of irises. The four measures are the four dependent variables and the species is the factor variable. There are 50 observations in each species group. The SPSS-X commands are

```
TITLE IRISDATA - TO DO ANYTHING WITH FISHER'S IRIS DATA
COMMENT FISHER'S IRIS DATA IS THE CLASSICAL DISCRIMINANT
 ANALYSIS EXAMPLE.  WE WILL USE IT TO ILLUSTRATE
 MULTIVARIATE ONEWAY ANALYSIS OF VARIANCE.
DATA LIST / SEPALLEN 1-2 SEPALWID PETALLEN PETALWID 3-11 TYPE 12-13
VARIABLE LABELS SEPALLEN 'SEPAL LENGTH'
   SEPALWID 'SEPAL WIDTH'
   PETALLEN 'PETAL LENGTH'
   PETALWID 'PETAL WIDTH'
   TYPE 'TYPE OF IRIS'
VALUE LABELS TYPE 1 'SETOSA' 2 'VERSICOLOR' 3 'VIRGINICA'
MANOVA SEPALLEN SEPALWID PETALLEN PETALWID BY TYPE(1,3)/
 PRINT=SIGNIF(EIGEN)
       CELLINFO(MEANS)
       HOMOGENEITY(BOXM)
       ERROR(COR)/
 DISCRIM(RAW STAN ESTIM COR)/
 DESIGN/
BEGIN DATA
...
END DATA
```

- The TITLE command prints a title on each page of the display output, and the COMMENT command inserts comments that print back with the commands on the display (see Chapter 4).

- The DATA LIST command reads five variables—SEPALLEN, SEPALWID, PETALLEN, PETALWID, and TYPE—from the data in the command file (see Chapter 5).

- The VARIABLE LABELS and VALUE LABELS commands assign labels that are printed on the display output (see Chapter 5).

- The MANOVA specification lists four dependent variables (SEPALLEN, SEPALWID, PETALLEN, PETALWID) and one factor (TYPE) with three levels.

- The PRINT subcommand requests several types of displays (see Section 33.39).

- SIGNIF(EIGEN) prints the Eigenvalues and canonical correlations.

- CELLINFO(MEANS) prints the group means for each of the dependent variables (see Figure 33.74a).

- HOMOGENEITY(BOXM) prints Box's M statistic, which is a multivariate test for homogeneity of variance (see Figure 33.74b).

- ERROR(COR) prints the error correlation matrix, the standard deviations of the dependent variables, and Bartlett's test of sphericity (see Figure 33.74c).

- The DISCRIM subcommand requests a canonical discriminant analysis relating the four dependent variables to the TYPE factor. RAW prints discriminant function coefficients, STAN prints standardized discriminant function coefficients, ESTIM prints effect estimates in discriminant function space, and COR prints correlations between the dependent variables and the canonical variables defined by the discriminant functions (see Figure 33.74e).

Figures 33.74a through 33.74e show portions of the display.

- Figure 33.74a shows the cell means and standard deviations displayed with CELLINFO(MEANS). There are large differences in both means and standard deviations for the four dependent variables by the type of iris.

- Figure 33.74b shows the tests for homogeneity-of-dispersion matrices displayed with HOMOGENEITY(BOXM). Both the F approximation and the chi-square approximation indicate rejection of the hypothesis of homogeneity.

- Figure 33.74c shows the results of specifying ERROR(COR). The within-cells correlations are the pooled within-groups correlations between the four dependent variables; that is, differences in TYPE are taken into account. MANOVA displays the standard deviations of the four variables on the diagonal. The Bartlett test of sphericity tests whether the within-cells correlation matrix is the identity matrix. Given the low significance level, this assumption is rejected. The F_{max} statistic tests whether the four within-cells variances are equal. A table for the F_{max} distribution is found in Winer (1971).

Figure 33.74a   Example 2: Cell statistics

```
          CELL NUMBER
            1   2   3
Variable
  TYPE          1   2   3

Cell Means and Standard Deviations
Variable .. SEPALLEN      SEPAL LENGTH
     FACTOR          CODE              Mean   Std. Dev.        N   95 percent Conf. Interval

   TYPE          SETOSA               50.060    3.525         50    49.058    51.062
   TYPE          VERSICOL             59.360    5.162         50    57.893    60.827
   TYPE          VIRGINIC             65.880    6.359         50    64.073    67.687
 For entire sample                    58.433    8.281        150    57.097    59.769
 - - - - - - - - - - - - - - - - - - - - - - - - - - - - - - - - - - - - - - - - - - - -
Variable .. SEPALWID      SEPAL WIDTH
     FACTOR          CODE              Mean   Std. Dev.        N   95 percent Conf. Interval

   TYPE          SETOSA               34.280    3.791         50    33.203    35.357
   TYPE          VERSICOL             27.700    3.138         50    26.808    28.592
   TYPE          VIRGINIC             29.740    3.225         50    28.823    30.657
 For entire sample                    30.573    4.359        150    29.870    31.277
 - - - - - - - - - - - - - - - - - - - - - - - - - - - - - - - - - - - - - - - - - - - -
Variable .. PETALLEN      PETAL LENGTH
     FACTOR          CODE              Mean   Std. Dev.        N   95 percent Conf. Interval

   TYPE          SETOSA               14.620    1.737         50    14.126    15.114
   TYPE          VERSICOL             42.600    4.699         50    41.265    43.935
   TYPE          VIRGINIC             55.520    5.519         50    53.952    57.088
 For entire sample                    37.580   17.653        150    34.732    40.428
 - - - - - - - - - - - - - - - - - - - - - - - - - - - - - - - - - - - - - - - - - - - -
Variable .. PETALWID      PETAL WIDTH
     FACTOR          CODE              Mean   Std. Dev.        N   95 percent Conf. Interval

   TYPE          SETOSA                2.460    1.054         50     2.160     2.760
   TYPE          VERSICOL             13.260    1.978         50    12.698    13.822
   TYPE          VIRGINIC             20.260    2.747         50    19.479    21.041
 For entire sample                    11.993    7.622        150    10.764    13.223
```

Figure 33.74b   Example 2: Tests for homogeneity-of-dispersion matrices

```
Multivariate test for Homogeneity of Dispersion matrices

Boxs M =                         146.66325
F WITH (20,77566) DF =             7.04526, P =   .000 (Approx.)
Chi-Square with 20 DF =          140.94305, P =   .000 (Approx.)
```

Figure 33.74c   Example 2: Within-cells correlations results

```
WITHIN CELLS Correlations with Std. Devs. on Diagonal

                   SEPALLEN       SEPALWID        PETALLEN        PETALWID

SEPALLEN            5.14789
SEPALWID             .53024       3.39688
PETALLEN             .75616        .37792        4.30334
PETALWID             .36451        .47053         .48446        2.04650


Statistics for WITHIN CELLS correlations

Log(Determinant) =                -1.61179
Bartlett test of sphericity =    233.44151 with 6 D. F.
Significance =                        .000

F(max) criterion =                6.32755 with (4,147) D. F.
```

- Figure 33.74d shows the default display of multivariate significance for the hypothesis that all group means are equal. All test statistics, Pillais, Hotellings, Wilks, and Roys, indicate rejection of the hypothesis. The S, M, and N in the top righthand corner of the multivariate results are degrees of freedom measures. For more information about these measures, see *SPSS Update 7-9*. The Eigenvalues and Canonical Correlations display shows that the canonical discriminant analysis has two dimensions. This follows the standard criterion, which takes the lesser of the number of dependent variables and number of groups minus one as the maximum dimensionality of a problem. The first of the two dimensions, with an eigenvalue of 32.19, is overwhelmingly predominant. The figure also shows the univariate tests of significance.

- Figure 33.74e shows the results of specifying the DISCRIM subcommand. The correlations between dependent and canonical variables show that the first function is primarily the petal measures, whereas the second function is primarily the width measures.

Figure 33.74d Example 2: Multivariate, canonical, and univariate test results

```
EFFECT .. TYPE
Multivariate Tests of Significance (S = 2, M = 1/2, N = 71 )

Test Name          Value        Approx. F      Hypoth. DF       Error DF        Sig. of F

Pillais           1.19190        53.46649          8.00          290.00           .000
Hotellings       32.47732       580.53210          8.00          286.00           .000
Wilks              .02344       199.14534          8.00          288.00           .000
Roys               .96987
Note.. F statistic for WILK'S Lambda is exact.

- - - - - - - - - - - - - - - - - - - - - - - - - - - - - - - - - - - - - - - - - - - - - - - - - - -

Eigenvalues and Canonical Correlations

Root No.      Eigenvalue         Pct.        Cum. Pct.      Canon Cor.

    1          32.19193        99.12126       99.12126        .98482
    2            .28539          .87874      100.00000        .47120

- - - - - - - - - - - - - - - - - - - - - - - - - - - - - - - - - - - - - - - - - - - - - - - - - - -

EFFECT .. TYPE (CONT.)
Univariate F-tests with (2,147) D. F.

Variable      Hypoth. SS       Error SS       Hypoth. MS       Error MS            F         Sig. of F

SEPALLEN      6321.21333     3895.62000       3160.60667       26.50082      119.26450         .000
SEPALWID      1134.49333     1696.20000        567.24667       11.53878       49.16004         .000
PETALLEN     43710.28000     2722.26000      21855.14000       18.51878     1180.16118         .000
PETALWID      8041.33333      615.66000       4020.66667        4.18816      960.00715         .000
```

Figure 33.74e Example 2: Canonical discriminant results

```
Correlations between DEPENDENT and canonical variables
             Canonical Variable

Variable              1                  2

SEPALLEN          -.22260            -.31081
SEPALWID           .11901            -.86368
PETALLEN          -.70607            -.16770
PETALWID          -.63318            -.73724
```

33.75
Example 3: Multivariate Multiple Regression, Canonical Correlation

MANOVA can be used to do both multivariate multiple regression and canonical correlation analyses. Multivariate multiple regression is a procedure which allows you to predict values of one set of variables given the values of another set of variables. Canonical correlation is a similar procedure which analyzes the relationship between two sets of variables. MANOVA produces multivariate results, individual regression results, and analysis of residuals although residual analysis is not as extensive in MANOVA as in REGRESSION. Since there is no canonical correlation procedure in SPSS-X, use MANOVA to do canonical correlation analysis.

The data for this example come from Finn (1974). The data were obtained from tests administered to 60 eleventh-grade students in a western New York metropolitan school. There are two dependent variables—synthesis and evaluation—which measure achievement. The independent variables are of three types. First, there is *general intelligence*, as measured by a standard test. Second, there are three measures of creativity. *Consequences obvious* "involves the ability of the subject to list direct consequences of a given hypothetical event." *Consequences remote* "involves identifying more remote or original consequences of similar situations." *Possible jobs* "involves the ability to list a quantity of occupations that might be represented by a given emblem or symbol" (p. 11). Third, in his analysis, Finn uses multiplicative interactions of the three creativity measures with intelligence to assess whether creativity has a greater effect on the achievement of individuals having high intelligence than on individuals of low intelligence. Finn uses standard scores for the independent variables. The SPSS-X commands are

```
TITLE FINN'S MULTIVARIATE MULTIPLE REGRESSION
DATA LIST   / SYNTH 1 EVAL 3 CONOBV 5-8(1) CONRMT 9-12(1)
 JOB 14-17(1) INTEL 19-23(1)
MISSING VALUES SYNTH TO INTEL(9.9)
DESCRIPTIVES INTEL CONOBV CONRMT JOB/
   MISSING=LISTWISE/
   SAVE
BEGIN DATA
 ...
END DATA
COMMENT USE COMPUTE TO CREATE INTERACTION TERMS.
COMPUTE CI1=ZCONOBV*ZINTEL
COMPUTE CI2=ZCONRMT*ZINTEL
COMPUTE CI3=ZJOB*ZINTEL
MANOVA  SYNTH EVAL WITH ZINTEL ZCONOBV ZCONRMT ZJOB CI1 CI2 CI3/
 PRINT=
   ERROR(SSCP COV COR)
   SIGNIF(HYPOTH STEPDOWN EIGEN)/
 DISCRIM(RAW,STAN,ESTIM,COR,ALPHA(1.0))/
 RESIDUALS=PLOT/
 DESIGN
```

- The TITLE command prints a title at the top of each page of the display output (see Chapter 4).

- The DATA LIST command defines six variables. SYNTH and EVAL are the dependent variables, and CONOBV, CONRMT, JOB, and INTEL are the independent variables (see Chapter 5).

- The SAVE subcommand on the DESCRIPTIVES procedure computes standardized scores for the intelligence and creativity measures. The new variables—ZINTEL, ZCONOBV, ZCONRMT, and ZJOB—are automatically added to the active file. The MISSING subcommand on DESCRIPTIVES specifies listwise deletion of missing values for the calculation (see Chapter 26).

- The COMPUTE commands compute three interaction variables—CI1, CI2, and CI3—from the standardized variables created with DESCRIPTIVES (see Chapter 7).

- The MANOVA specification names SYNTH and EVAL as joint dependent variables and specifies seven covariates—ZINTEL, ZCONOBV, ZCONRMT, ZJOB, CI1, CI2, and CI3.

- The PRINT subcommand requests several displays (see Section 33.39). The ERROR keyword prints the error sums-of-squares and cross-products matrix, the error variance-covariance matrix, and the error correlation matrix with standard deviations on the diagonal (see Figure 33.75a).

- The SIGNIF keyword has three specifications. HYPOTH prints the hypothesis sums-of-squares and cross-products matrices (see Figure 33.75a). STEPDOWN prints the Roy-Bargmann step-down F tests for the dependent variables (see Figure 33.75b). EIGEN prints the eigenvalues and canonical correlations (see Figure 33.75b).

- The DISCRIM subcommand requests a canonical analysis. The results correspond to canonical correlation analysis since a set of continuous dependent variables is related to a set of continuous independent variables. The RAW keyword prints canonical function coefficients; the STAN keyword prints standardized canonical function coefficients; the ESTIM function produces effect estimates in canonical function space; the COR keyword prints correlations between the original variables and the canonical variables defined by the canonical functions; the ALPHA keyword, which specifies 1, sets a cutoff value of the canonical functions in the analysis to 1. Thus, the discriminant analysis will be printed regardless of the significance of each effect. The maximum possible number of canonical functions in in this analysis is two (see Figures 33.75a and 33.75d).

- The RESIDUALS subcommand produces plots of the observed and predicted values and case number against standardized residuals and normal and detrended normal probability plots for the standardized residuals (see Figures 33.75f through 33.75h).

Portions of the output are shown in Figures 33.75a through 33.75h.

- Figure 33.75a shows within-cells statistical results. The correlation of .37978 is the partial correlation of SYNTH and EVAL, taking into account the independent variable set. The two standard deviations, 1.37049 and 1.51256 are located on the diagonal and are adjusted. Figure 33.75a also shows the adjusted variance-covariance matrix, the error SSCP matrix, and the hypothesis SSCP matrix for the regression effect.

Figure 33.75a   Example 3: Within-cells results and hypothesis SSCP

```
Adjusted WITHIN CELLS Correlations with Std. Devs. on Diagonal

                   SYNTH                EVAL

SYNTH              1.37049
EVAL                .37978             1.51256

 - - - - - - - - - - - - - - - - - - - - - - - - - - - - - - - - - -

Statistics for ADJUSTED WITHIN CELLS correlations

Log(Determinant) =                   -.15575
Bartlett test of sphericity =         7.86554 with 1 D. F.
Significance =                         .005

F(max) criterion =                    1.21806 with (2,52) D. F.

 - - - - - - - - - - - - - - - - - - - - - - - - - - - - - - - - - -

Adjusted WITHIN CELLS Variances and Covariances

                   SYNTH                EVAL

SYNTH              1.87825
EVAL                .78726             2.28783

 - - - - - - - - - - - - - - - - - - - - - - - - - - - - - - - - - -

Adjusted WITHIN CELLS Sum-of-Squares and Cross-Products

                   SYNTH                EVAL

SYNTH             97.66914
EVAL              40.93736           118.96726

 - - - - - - - - - - - - - - - - - - - - - - - - - - - - - - - - - -

Adjusted Hypothesis Sum-of-Squares and Cross-Products

                   SYNTH                EVAL

SYNTH             81.18086
EVAL              69.41264            67.21607
```

- Figure 33.75b shows the default display and the step-down display. Both the multivariate and univariate test results indicate that the predictor set has statistically significant impact on the dependent variables. While two dimensions are fit, it appears that one dimension will suffice. Of the two eigenvalues, the first eigenvalue has most of the variance associated with it, while the second eigenvalue has relatively little variability associated with it. Likewise, the first canonical correlation is moderately sized, while the second canonical correlation is negligible in magnitude. Provided that you accept the ordering of the criterion variables—SYNTH, then EVAL—the step-down F tests show that after taking SYNTH into account EVAL does not contribute to the association with the predictors.

Figure 33.75b   Example 3: Test results and dimensionality statistics

```
Multivariate Tests of Significance (S = 2, M = 2 , N = 24 1/2)

Test Name              Value         Approx. F        Hypoth. DF       Error DF        Sig. of F

Pillais                .55946        2.88501           14.00           104.00           .001
Hotellings            1.05995        3.78553           14.00           100.00           .000
Wilks                  .47077        3.33286           14.00           102.00           .000
Roys                   .49886
Note.. F statistic for WILK'S Lambda is exact.
- - - - - - - - - - - - - - - - - - - - - - - - - - - - - - - - - - - - - - - - - - - - - - - - -
Eigenvalues and Canonical Correlations

Root No.       Eigenvalue          Pct.        Cum. Pct.       Canon Cor.       Sq. Cor

    1            .99544          93.91374       93.91374         .70630          .49886
    2            .06451           6.08626      100.00000         .24617          .06060
- - - - - - - - - - - - - - - - - - - - - - - - - - - - - - - - - - - - - - - - - - - - - - - - -
EFFECT .. WITHIN CELLS Regression (CONT.)
Univariate F-tests with (7,52) D. F.

Variable       Sq. Mul. R        Mul. R     Adj. R-sq.     Hypoth. MS      Error MS            F      Sig. of F

SYNTH.           .45390          .67372       .38039        11.59727       1.87825       6.17450       .000
EVAL             .36102          .60085       .27500         9.60230       2.28783       4.19712       .001
- - - - - - - - - - - - - - - - - - - - - - - - - - - - - - - - - - - - - - - - - - - - - - - - -
Roy-Bargman Stepdown F - tests

Variable       Hypoth. MS        Error MS     StepDown F     Hypoth. DF      Error DF      Sig. of F

SYNTH          11.59727          1.87825       6.17450            7             52          .000
EVAL            2.32700          1.99625       1.16569            7             51          .339
```

- Figure 33.75c shows canonical results for the two dependent variables. Recall that only the first canonical function is statistically significant. Correlations between the dependent variables and the first canonical variable are of similar magnitude. The part of the figure labeled "VARIANCE EXPLAINED BY CANONICAL VARIABLES OF DEPENDENT VARIABLES" provides a *redundancy analysis* (Cooley & Lohnes, 1971).

Figure 33.75c   Example 3: Canonical results for dependent variables

```
Raw canonical coefficients for DEPENDENT variables
        Function No.

Variable                   1                   2

SYNTH                  .40444             -.59708
EVAL                   .22637              .66958
- - - - - - - - - - - - - - - - - - - - - - - - - - - - - - - - - - - - - - - - - - - - -
Standardized canonical coefficients for DEPENDENT variables
        Function No.

Variable                   1                   2

SYNTH                  .70415            -1.03956
EVAL                   .40212             1.18946
- - - - - - - - - - - - - - - - - - - - - - - - - - - - - - - - - - - - - - - - - - - - -
Correlations between DEPENDENT and canonical variables
        Function No.

Variable                   1                   2

SYNTH                  .94733             -.32027
EVAL                   .82794              .56081
- - - - - - - - - - - - - - - - - - - - - - - - - - - - - - - - - - - - - - - - - - - - -
Variance explained by canonical variables of DEPENDENT variables

CAN. VAR.       Pct Var DEP      Cum Pct DEP      Pct Var COV      Cum Pct COV

    1            79.14597         79.14597         39.48249         39.48249
    2            20.85403        100.00000          1.26379         40.74628
```

- Figure 33.75d shows the analogous canonical results for the covariates. The correlations between covariates and the first canonical variable load most heavily on intelligence (ZINTELL).
- Figure 33.75e shows the default display of the regression results for the two dependent variables.

Figure 33.75d   Example 3: Canonical results for the covariates

```
Raw canonical coefficients for COVARIATES
        Function No.

COVARIATE              1              2

ZINTEL              .84825         -.10334
ZCONOBV             .26535          .22951
ZCONRMT             .19301          .47229
ZJOB               -.06403         -.27927
CI1                -.01367         1.03503
CI2                -.07571         -.32373
CI3                 .20707         -.04665

- - - - - - - - - - - - - - - - - - - - - - - - - - - - - - - - -
Standardized canonical coefficients for COVARIATES
        CAN. VAR.

COVARIATE              1              2

ZINTEL              .84825         -.10334
ZCONOBV             .26535          .22951
ZCONRMT             .19301          .47229
ZJOB               -.06403         -.27927
CI1                -.01172          .88718
CI2                -.10086         -.43125
CI3                 .21699         -.04889

- - - - - - - - - - - - - - - - - - - - - - - - - - - - - - - - -
Correlations between COVARIATES and canonical variables
        CAN. VAR.

Covariate              1              2

ZINTEL              .94646         -.09081
ZCONOBV             .30260         -.06104
ZCONRMT             .56188          .41804
ZJOB                .57787         -.12674
CI1                 .17980          .86843
CI2                 .49440         -.01020
CI3                 .44879          .06254

- - - - - - - - - - - - - - - - - - - - - - - - - - - - - - - - -
Variance explained by canonical variables of the COVARIATES

CAN. VAR.    Pct Var DEP    Cum Pct DEP    Pct Var COV    Cum Pct COV

    1          15.07395       15.07395       30.21700       30.21700
    2            .83195       15.90590       13.72818       43.94518
```

Figure 33.75e   Example 3: Regression results

```
Regression analysis for WITHIN CELLS error term
--- Individual Univariate .9500 confidence intervals
Dependent variable .. SYNTH

COVARIATE        B            Beta        Std. Err.    t-Value    Sig. of t    Lower -95%   CL- Upper

ZINTEL     1.0023512430    .5757069427     .21712      4.61656      .000        .56667       1.43804
ZCONOBV     .2776146958    .1594498026     .23559      1.17836      .244       -.19514        .75037
ZCONRMT     .1600206225    .0919088832     .23801       .67232      .504       -.31759        .63763
ZJOB       -.0362511873   -.0208211047     .26665      -.13595      .892       -.57132        .49882
CI1        -.1579989581   -.0777852272     .23587      -.66986      .506       -.63130        .31530
CI2        -.0437613943   -.0334827218     .21472      -.20380      .839       -.47463        .38711
CI3         .2476316265    .1490442859     .25225       .98169      .331       -.25855        .75381

- - - - - - - - - - - - - - - - - - - - - - - - - - - - - - - - - -
Regression analysis for WITHIN CELLS error term   (CONT.)
Dependent variable .. EVAL

COVARIATE        B            Beta        Std. Err.    t-Value    Sig. of t    Lower -95%   CL- Upper

ZINTEL      .8558201889    .4817682025     .23963      3.57146      .001        .37497       1.33667
ZCONOBV     .3319337197    .1868559699     .26002      1.27659      .207       -.18982        .85369
ZCONRMT     .3163316155    .1780730529     .26269      1.20422      .234       -.21079        .84345
ZJOB       -.1350002789   -.0759959190     .29429      -.45873      .648       -.72554        .45554
CI1         .2396401468    .1156316040     .26032       .92057      .362       -.28273        .76201
CI2        -.1580420000   -.1185157835     .23698      -.66690      .508       -.63358        .31749
CI3         .2036655892    .1201436854     .27840       .73156      .468       -.35498        .76231
```

- Figure 33.75f shows two plots. The plot of the observed versus predicted values for SYNTH reflects the multiple R for the model. The plot of the observed values versus the residuals shows the way in which residuals vary in sign and magnitude across values of the dependent variable.

- Figure 33.75g shows two plots: the plot of the residuals versus the predicted values and the plot of case number versus residuals. The latter plot is useful when there is some meaning to the order of cases in your file.

Figure 33.75f   Example 3: Observed values vs. predicted values and residuals

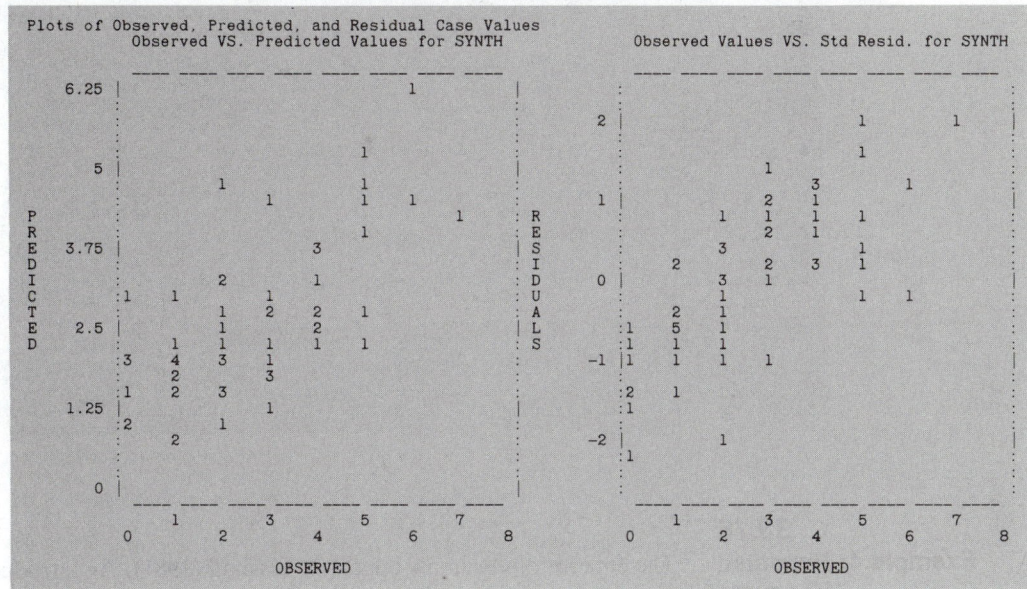

Figure 33.75g   Example 3: Residuals vs. predicted values and order

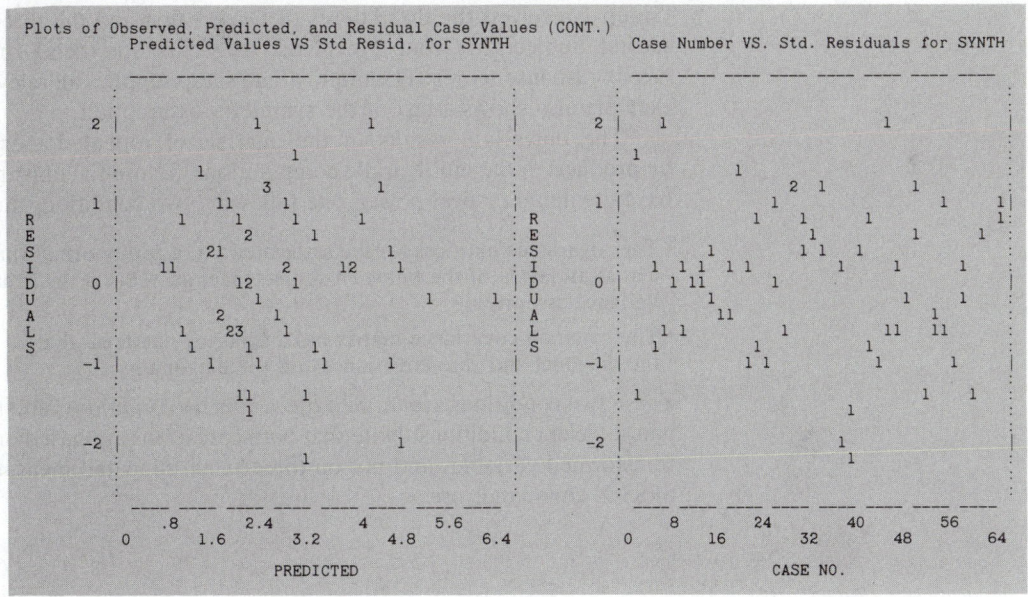

• Finally, Figure 33.75h shows the normal plot of the residuals and the detrended normal plot of the residuals.

Figure 33.75h   Example 3: Normal plot and detrended normal plot

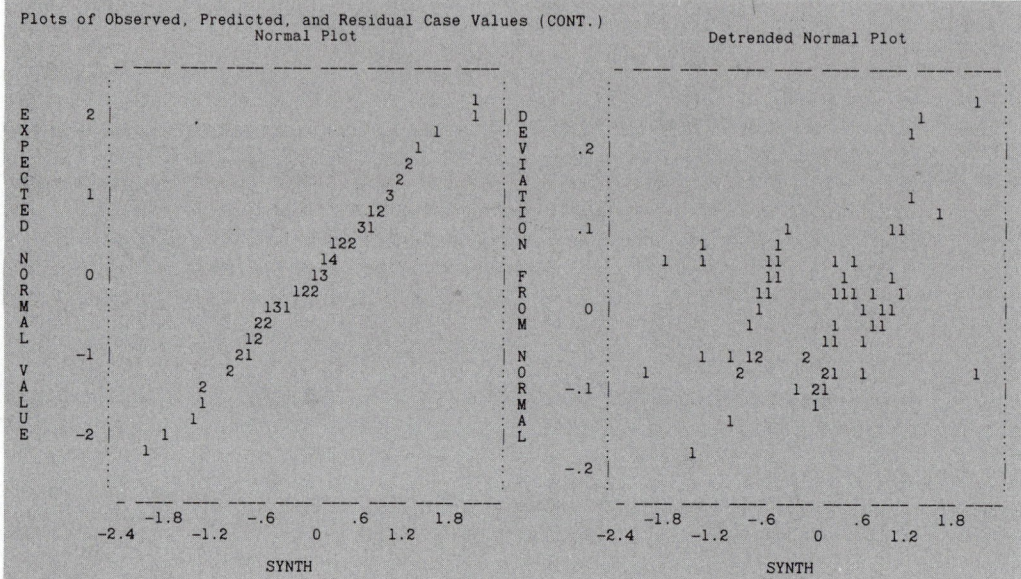

33.76
Example 4: Repeated Measures

The data for this example appear in Elashoff (1981). An introductory discussion is found in the annotated example for MANOVA. There is one between-subjects factor, GROUP, with two levels. There are two within-subjects factors: two types of drugs are administered at each of three doses. This study aims to estimate the relative potency of the two drugs in inhibiting a response to a stimulus. Subjects in Group 1 received the three doses of Drug 1 first and the three doses of Drug 2 second. Subjects in Group 2 received Drug 2 first and then Drug 1. Every subject has six response scores. The multivariate setup supplies all relevant statistics. This example also shows a test of the symmetry assumption.

The univariate results of the analysis of repeated measures designs are by-products of the multivariate computations. To use the univariate results, which have greater statistical power, the following two conditions must be met:

• The covariance matrices for the associated set of orthonormal variables are identical across all levels of the between-subjects factors. This is the usual homogeneity-of-variance assumption.

• The common covariance matrix has a sphericity pattern, that is, equal variances on the diagonal and zero covariances off the diagonal.

These two conditions are termed the *symmetry conditions*, and they are necessary and sufficient conditions. Note that both conditions are based on the orthonormal transformed variables and not on the original repeated measures variables. The SPSS-X commands are

```
TITLE A REPEATED MEASURES DESIGN EXAMPLE
COMMENT THIS EXAMPLE HAS 2 WITHIN-SUBJECTS FACTORS
 AND 1 BETWEEN SUBJECT FACTOR
DATA LIST / Y1 Y2 Y3 Y4 Y5 Y6 1-18 GROUP 20
MANOVA Y1 TO Y6 BY GROUP(1,2)/
 WSFACTOR=DRUG(2) DOSE(3)/
 CONTRAST(DOSE)=POLYNOMIAL(1,2,6)/
 WSDESIGN=DRUG, DOSE,DRUG BY DOSE/
 PRINT=TRANSFORM
  HOMOGENEITY(BOXM)
  ERROR(COR)
  SIGNIF(AVERF)/
 DESIGN/
BEGIN DATA
 19 22 28 16 26 22 1
 11 19 30 12 18 28 1
 20 24 24 24 22 29 1
 21 25 25 15 10 26 1
 18 24 29 19 26 28 1
 17 23 28 15 23 22 1
 20 23 23 26 21 28 1
 14 20 29 25 29 29 1
 16 20 24 30 34 36 2
 26 26 26 24 30 32 2
 22 27 23 33 36 45 2
 16 18 29 27 26 34 2
 19 21 20 22 22 21 2
 20 25 25 29 29 33 2
 21 22 23 27 26 35 2
 17 20 22 23 26 28 2
END DATA
```

- The TITLE command prints a title at the top of each page of display output, and the COMMENT command inserts comments that print back with the commands on the display (see Chapter 4).

- The DATA LIST command defines seven variables from the data in the command file (see Chapter 5).

- The MANOVA specification names six joint dependent variables—Y1 to Y6—and one between-subjects factor—GROUP.

- The WSFACTORS subcommand defines the within-subjects factors, DRUG with 2 levels and DOSE with 3 levels. The order in which you specify the factors is crucial; you *must* specify them in the order corresponding to the dependent variable list. Conversely, name your dependent variables in a known and intended order. Note that the index value of the rightmost within-subjects factor increments most rapidly (see Section 33.21).

- The CONTRAST subcommand specifies a polynomial contrast for DOSE. The spacing 1,2,6 reflects the levels of administered doses in the experiment (see Section 33.36). CONTRAST must be specified before the WSDESIGN subcommand.

- The WSDESIGN subcommand specifies the full factorial model for the within-subjects factors (see Section 33.22). This subcommand is optional because MANOVA assumes a full factorial model by default.

- The PRINT subcommand specifies several useful statistics. TRANSFORM prints the orthonormalized transformation matrix, which shows how MANOVA transforms the dependent variables to build the within-subjects effects (see Figure 33.76b). HOMOGENEITY(BOXM) prints a multivariate test for the homogeneity-of-dispersion matrices. Data for which the homogeneity assumption is not rejected meet the first condition for symmetry indicated above (see Figure 33.76a). ERROR(COR) prints within-cells correlations and standard deviations when more than one transformed variable corresponds to a within-subjects effect (see Figures 33.76e and 33.76i). SIGNIF(AVERF) prints the average F, which is a univariate approach statistic (see Figure 33.76h).

- The DESIGN subcommand specifies the between-subjects design. By default, MANOVA enters the one between-subjects factor (see Section 33.7).

Portions of the display output are shown in Figures 33.76a through 33.76k.

- Figure 33.76a shows the multivariate test for homogeneity-of-dispersion matrices. Given the large significance levels, the test does not reject the hypothesis of homogeneity. The data do not appear to violate the first symmetry condition.

Figure 33.76a   Example 4: Symmetry condition 1

```
                CELL NUMBER
                 1    2
Variable
   GROUP          1    2

Cell Number .. 1

Determinant of Variance-Covariance matrix =        4138.01612
LOG(Determinant) =                                    8.32797

- - - - - - - - -

Cell Number .. 2

Determinant of Variance-Covariance matrix =       23150.55748
LOG(Determinant) =                                   10.04977

- - - - - - - - -

Determinant of pooled Variance-Covariance matrix   329610.63417
LOG(Determinant) =                                   12.70567

- - - - - - - - - - - - - - - - - - - - - - - - - - - - -

Multivariate test for Homogeneity of Dispersion matrices

Boxs M =                          49.23512
F WITH (21,720) DF =               1.21162, P =    .233 (Approx.)
Chi-Square with 21 DF =           26.87836, P =    .175 (Approx.)
```

- Figure 33.76b shows the orthonormalized transformation matrix. Column 1 is the constant effect; column 2 is the drug effect; column 3 is the dose-linear effect; column 4 is the dose-quadratic effect; column 5 is the drug-by-dose-linear interaction; and column 6 is the drug-by-dose-quadratic interaction.
- Figure 33.76c shows the default display of tests of significance for T1, the transformed-Y1, which is the constant within-subjects effect. The constant within-subjects effect tests the between-subjects factor.
- Figure 33.76d shows the default display of tests of significance for T2, the transformed-Y2, which is the drug within-subjects effect. This effect tests drug and group by drug.
- Figure 33.76e shows the within-cells correlations and standard deviations for T3 and T4, the transformed-Y3 and transformed-Y4 variables respectively, which jointly correspond to the dose within-subjects effect. Mauchly's test of sphericity is nonsignificant, so the data do not appear to violate the second symmetry condition

Figure 33.76b   Example 4: Within-subjects design

```
Orthonormalized Transformation Matrix (Transposed)

              T1          T2          T3          T4          T5          T6

Y1          .40825      .40825     -.37796      .43644     -.37796      .43644
Y2          .40825      .40825     -.18898     -.54554     -.18898     -.54554
Y3          .40825      .40825      .56695      .10911      .56695      .10911
Y4          .40825     -.40825     -.37796      .43644      .37796     -.43644
Y5          .40825     -.40825     -.18898     -.54554      .18898      .54554
Y6          .40825     -.40825      .56695      .10911     -.56695     -.10911
```

Figure 33.76c   Example 4: Constant within-subjects effect

```
Tests of Between-Subjects Effects.

Tests of Significance for T1 using UNIQUE sums of squares
Source of Variation         SS       DF       MS         F    Sig of F

WITHIN CELLS             532.98      14      38.07
CONSTANT               55632.51       1   55632.51   1461.32      .000
GROUP                    270.01       1     270.01      7.09      .019
```

for the dose within-subjects effect. Since the first symmetry condition was also met (see Figure 33.76a), you can use *univariate* test results in assessing the dose-related effects.

- Figures 33.76f and 33.76g show the default display of multivariate test results for dose-related effects. Figure 33.76h shows the univariate approach (averaged) test results for the dose-related effects.

Figure 33.76d   Example 4: DRUG within-subjects effect

```
Tests involving 'DRUG' Within-Subject Effect.

Tests of Significance for T2 using UNIQUE sums of squares
Source of Variation        SS      DF      MS         F  Sig of F

WITHIN CELLS            375.65     14    26.83
DRUG                    348.84      1   348.84     13.00    .003
GROUP BY DRUG           326.34      1   326.34     12.16    .004
```

Figure 33.76e   Example 4: Symmetry condition 2 for DOSE effect

```
WITHIN CELLS Correlations with Std. Devs. on Diagonal

                      T3                 T4

T3                 3.75557
T4                 -.10921            2.58427

- - - - - - - - - - - - - - - - - - - - - - - - - - - - - - - - - - - - -

Tests involving 'DOSE' Within-Subject Effect.


  Mauchly sphericity test, W =        .86193
  Chi-square approx. =               1.93158 with 2 D. F.
  Significance =                      .381

  Greenhouse-Geisser Epsilon =        .87868
  Huynh-Feldt Epsilon =              1.00000
  Lower-bound Epsilon =               .50000

AVERAGED Tests of Significance that follow multivariate tests are equivalent to
univariate or split-plot or mixed-model approach to repeated measures.
Epsilons may be used to adjust d.f. for the AVERAGED results.
```

Figure 33.76f   Example 4: GROUP by DOSE multivariate tests

```
EFFECT .. GROUP BY DOSE
Multivariate Tests of Significance (S = 1, M = 0, N = 5 1/2)

Test Name          Value        Exact F     Hypoth. DF     Error DF     Sig. of F

Pillais           .18262       1.45223         2.00         13.00         .270
Hotellings        .22342       1.45223         2.00         13.00         .270
Wilks             .81738       1.45223         2.00         13.00         .270
Roys              .18262
Note.. F statistics are exact.
```

Figure 33.76g   Example 4: DOSE multivariate test results

```
EFFECT .. DOSE
Multivariate Tests of Significance (S = 1, M = 0, N = 5 1/2)

Test Name          Value        Exact F     Hypoth. DF     Error DF     Sig. of F

Pillais           .79534      25.26075         2.00         13.00         .000
Hotellings       3.88627      25.26075         2.00         13.00         .000
Wilks             .20466      25.26075         2.00         13.00         .000
Roys              .79534
Note.. F statistics are exact.
```

Figure 33.76h   Example 4: DOSE and GROUP by DOSE univariate results

```
Tests involving 'DOSE' Within-Subject Effect.

AVERAGED Tests of Significance for Y using UNIQUE sums of squares
Source of Variation        SS      DF      MS         F  Sig of F

WITHIN CELLS            290.96     28    10.39
DOSE                    758.77      2   379.39     36.51    .000
GROUP BY DOSE            42.27      2    21.14      2.03    .150
```

- Figure 33.76i shows the within-cells correlations and related statistics for T5 and T6, the transformed-Y5 and transformed-Y6 variables respectively, which jointly correspond to the drug-by-dose interactions. This time, test statistics lead to rejection of the second symmetry condition. Therefore, you should use the *multivariate* test results in assessing effects.

- Figures 33.76j and 33.76k show the default display of multivariate test results for the drug-by-dose effects. Given the observed levels of significance, no effects are statistically significant.

Figure 33.76i Example 4: Symmetry condition 2 for DRUG by DOSE effect

```
WITHIN CELLS Correlations with Std. Devs. on Diagonal

                        T5                  T6

T5              3.31754
T6               .57501              2.58715

- - - - - - - - - - - - - - - - - - - - - - - - - - - - - - - - - - - -

Tests involving 'DRUG BY DOSE' Within-Subject Effect.


   Mauchly sphericity test, W =          .62962
   Chi-square approx. =                 6.01422 with 2 D. F.
   Significance =                        .049

   Greenhouse-Geisser Epsilon =         .72973
   Huynh-Feldt Epsilon =                .85129
   Lower-bound Epsilon =                .50000

AVERAGED Tests of Significance that follow multivariate tests are equivalent to
univariate or split-plot or mixed-model approach to repeated measures.
Epsilons may be used to adjust d.f. for the AVERAGED results.
```

Figure 33.76j Example 4: GROUP by DRUG by DOSE results

```
EFFECT .. GROUP BY DRUG BY DOSE
Multivariate Tests of Significance (S = 1, M = 0, N = 5 1/2)

Test Name           Value        Exact F      Hypoth. DF        Error DF        Sig. of F

Pillais             .14314       1.08583          2.00            13.00            .366
Hotellings          .16705       1.08583          2.00            13.00            .366
Wilks               .85686       1.08583          2.00            13.00            .366
Roys                .14314
Note.. F statistics are exact.
```

Figure 33.76k Example 4: DRUG by DOSE results

```
EFFECT .. DRUG BY DOSE
Multivariate Tests of Significance (S = 1, M = 0, N = 5 1/2)

Test Name           Value        Exact F      Hypoth. DF        Error DF        Sig. of F

Pillais             .12604        .93739          2.00            13.00            .417
Hotellings          .14421        .93739          2.00            13.00            .417
Wilks               .87396        .93739          2.00            13.00            .417
Roys                .12604
Note.. F statistics are exact.
```

33.77
Example 5: Repeated Measures with a Constant Covariate

This example shows repeated measures analysis with a constant covariate. You must specify as many covariates as dependent variables. If the covariate is constant across the repeated measures factor, use COMPUTE to create as many replicates of the covariate as you need.

The data are obtained from a 2×2 factorial experiment with repeated measures on factor B (Winer, 1971). Variables Y1 and Y2 are scores for the two occasions. Factor A is the between-subjects factor. There are four subjects under each level of factor A. The covariate measure X is obtained before the administration of any of the treatments, and it is therefore constant for both levels of the within-subjects factor B. The SPSS-X commands are

```
TITLE COVARIATE CONSTANT OVER TRIALS:  WINER, PAGE 803
DATA LIST / A, X, Y1, Y2 (4F3.0)
COMPUTE X2 = X
MANOVA Y1, Y2 BY A(1,2) WITH X, X2/
 WSFACTORS = B( 2 )/
 WSDESIGN = B/
 PRINT= TRANSFORM/
 DESIGN = A/
BEGIN DATA
data lines
END DATA
```

- The TITLE command prints a title at the top of each page of display output (see Chapter 4).
- The DATA LIST command defines four variables from the data in the command file (see Chapter 5).
- The COMPUTE command computes X2, which is a copy of the covariate X (see Chapter 7).
- The MANOVA specification specifies Y1 and Y2 as joint dependent variables, A as the between-subjects factor, and X and X2 as covariates. In the general case, the number of covariates *must* be an integer multiple of the number of dependent variables. In this case, the number of variables in the two sets is equal.
- The WSFACTORS subcommand specifies B as the within-subjects factor (see Section 33.21).
- The WSDESIGN subcommand specifies the within-subjects design, which here simply names B (see Section 33.22).
- The PRINT subcommand specifies printing of the orthonormalized transformation matrix (see Sections 33.39 and 33.46 and Figure 33.77a).
- The DESIGN subcommand specifies the between-subjects design (see Section 33.7).

Portions of the display output are shown in Figures 33.77a through 33.77c.

- Figure 33.77a shows the orthonormalized transformation matrix. Note the block diagonal structure of the transformation matrix. MANOVA uses the same transformations on dependent variable–covariate pairs. Column 1 is the transformation producing new Y1; column 2 is the transformation producing new Y2; column 3 is the transformation producing new X; and column 4 is the transformation producing new X2.

Figure 33.77a   Example 5: Orthonormalized transformation matrix

```
Orthonormalized Transformation Matrix (Transposed)

                    T1              T2              T3              T4

Y1              .70711          .70711          .00000          .00000
Y2              .70711         -.70711          .00000          .00000
X               .00000          .00000          .70711          .70711
X2              .00000          .00000          .70711         -.70711
```

- Figure 33.77b shows the default display of the test for the between-subjects effect. MANOVA uses transformed-Y1 and transformed-X in the analysis. The analysis of variance table shows a test of significance for the between-subjects factor, A, adjusted for covariate X. Differences in means on the between-subjects factor are not statistically significant. The second table shows that the correlation between the covariate, X (transformed into T3) and the predicted dependent variable, Y1 (transformed into T1), is 1.00. If there is only one covariate, this correlation will always be 1. If there were multiple covariates, this display would show the relative importance of the covariates in their predicted values. The third table shows that the squared correlation between the variables in the second table, Y1(T1) and X(T3), is also 1.00. Again, this display allows you to evaluate the relative importance of multiple covariates. The fourth table shows that the regression coefficient for X(T3) is 1.022.
- Figure 33.77c shows the default display of the test for the B within-subjects effect. The analysis of variance table contains tests of significance for B and the A by B interaction.

Figure 33.77b   Example 5: Between-subjects effects

```
Tests of Significance for T1 using UNIQUE sums of squares
Source of Variation        SS      DF       MS          F    Sig of F

WITHIN CELLS             61.30      5     12.26
REGRESSION              166.58      1    166.58       13.59     .014
CONSTANT                400.67      1    400.67       32.68     .002
A                        44.49      1     44.49        3.63     .115
- - - - - - - - - - - - - - - - - - - - - - - - - - - - - - - - - - - - - - - -
Correlations between Covariates and Predicted Dependent Variable
          COVARIATE

VARIABLE               T3

T1                  1.00000

- - - - - - - - - - - - - - - - - - - - - - - - - - - - - - - - - - - - - - - -
Averaged Squared Correlations between Covariates and Predicted Dependent Variable

VARIABLE           AVER. R-SQ

T3                  1.00000
Regression analysis for WITHIN CELLS error term
---- Individual Univariate .9500 confidence intervals
Dependent variable .. T1

COVARIATE              B           Beta      Std. Err.     t-Value    Sig. of t    Lower -95%   CL- Upper

T3         1.0219435737    .8549858355       .27724      3.68611        .014        .30927      1.73462
```

Figure 33.77c   Example 5: B Within-subjects effect

```
Tests involving 'B' Within-Subject Effect.

Tests of Significance for T2 using UNIQUE sums of squares
Source of Variation        SS      DF       MS          F    Sig of F

WITHIN CELLS              6.37      6      1.06
B                        85.56      1     85.56       80.53     .000
A BY B                     .56      1       .56         .53     .494
```

33.78
Example 6: Repeated Measures with a Varying Covariate

You can use MANOVA to perform repeated measures analysis with a varying covariate. The model is a 3×2 factorial experiment with repeated measures on factor B (Winer, 1971). There are three subjects in each group. You can obtain regression coefficients for both the between-subjects effect and the within-subjects effect. See Winer for a discussion of a statistic which tests the equality of these two regression coefficients. In this analysis, since there are only two levels of the within-subjects factor, the univariate and multivariate approaches are identical. However, for a model which has more than two levels on any of the within-subjects factors with covariates varying over the repeated measures trials, interpret the multivariate results with caution. In certain models, there may be some question concerning the propriety of controlling for all covariates. The SPSS-X commands are

```
TITLE COVARIATE VARYING OVER TRIALS:  WINER, PAGE 806.
DATA LIST / GROUP, B1X, B1Y, B2X, B2Y (5F3.0)
VALUE LABELS GROUP 1 'A1' 2 'A2' 3 'A3'
MANOVA B1Y, B2Y BY GROUP(1,3) WITH B1X, B2X/
  WSFACTOR = B( 2 )/
  WSDESIGN /
  PRINT = TRANSFORM/
  DESIGN/
BEGIN DATA
  1  3  8  4 14
  1  5 11  9 18
  1 11 16 14 22
  2  2  6  1  8
  2  8 12  9 14
  2 10  9  9 10
  3  7 10  4 10
  3  8 14 10 18
  3  9 15 12 22
END DATA
```

- The TITLE command prints a title at the top of each page of display output (see Chapter 4).
- The DATA LIST command defines five variables from the data in the command file, and the VALUE LABELS command assigns labels to the values for variable GROUP (see Chapter 5).
- The MANOVA command specifies B1Y and B2Y as joint dependent variables, GROUP as a three-level between-subjects factor, and B1X and B2X as covariates. The two dependent variables and two covariates contain pairs of scores obtained on two occasions.
- The WSFACTORS subcommand specifies B as the two-level within-subjects factor (see Section 33.21).
- The WSDESIGN subcommand specifies the single within-subjects factor (see Section 33.22).
- The PRINT subcommand prints the orthonormalized transformation matrix (see Sections 33.39, 33.46, and Figure 33.78a).
- The DESIGN subcommand specifies the between-subjects design (see Sections 33.7).

Portions of the display output are shown in Figures 33.78a through 33.78c.

- Figure 33.78a shows the orthonormalized transformation matrix, which is block diagonal. Columns 1 and 2 correspond to transformations of the dependent variables, while columns 3 and 4 correspond to transformations of the covariates.
- Figure 33.78b shows the tests of significance for the between subjects effects. The REGRESSION, and CONSTANT effects are significant whereas GROUP is not significant.
- Figure 33.78c shows the tests of significance for the B within-subjects effect. REGRESSION and the B effects are significant, while the GROUP BY B interaction is not.

Figure 33.78a   Example 6: Orthonormalized transformation matrix

```
Orthonormalized Transformation Matrix (Transposed)

                    T1              T2              T3              T4

    B1Y           .70711          .70711          .00000          .00000
    B2Y           .70711         -.70711          .00000          .00000
    B1X           .00000          .00000          .70711          .70711
    B2X           .00000          .00000          .70711         -.70711
```

Figure 33.78b   Example 6: Constant between-subjects effect

```
Tests of Between-Subjects Effects.

Tests of Significance for T1 using UNIQUE sums of squares
Source of Variation          SS        DF        MS          F    Sig of F

WITHIN CELLS               44.37        5       8.87
REGRESSION                132.63        1     132.63      14.95      .012
CONSTANT                  128.79        1     128.79      14.51      .013
GROUP                      54.26        2      27.13       3.06      .136
```

Figure 33.78c   Example 6: Within-subjects effect

```
Tests involving 'B' Within-Subject Effect.

Tests of Significance for T2 using UNIQUE sums of squares
Source of Variation          SS        DF        MS          F    Sig of F

WITHIN CELLS                3.00        5        .60
REGRESSION                 10.00        1      10.00      16.68      .010
B                          31.55        1      31.55      52.61      .001
GROUP BY B                  2.34        2       1.17       1.95      .236
```

33.79
Example 7: A Doubly Multivariate Repeated Measures Design

This example illustrates how to analyze a doubly multivariate repeated measures design using the multivariate setup. The data consist of 53 subjects with 15 response variables recorded for each subject. Each of five types of tests are administered on three occasions to the subjects. Therefore, time is a within-subjects factor. There are two between-subjects factors: a two-level sex variable and a three-level group variable.

The model is multivariate in two senses. First, when a subject is measured across occasions with respect to a given item, the multivariate setup specifies each of the scores on the same SPSS-X case. Second, each subject is measured with respect to more than one item at each occasion, thereby inducing multivariate considerations. This example illustrates the use of the MEASURE subcommand to label the results of the univariate approach.

Use the following rules when performing this type of analysis with MANOVA:

- Specify variables measuring a given attribute across occasions consecutively and in order.
- The number of dependent variables in the MANOVA specification must be an integer multiple of the number of within-subjects levels.

The SPSS-X commands are

```
TITLE  A MULTIVARIATE REPEATED MEASURES DESIGN.
COMMENT THIS A DOUBLY MULTIVARIATE REPEATED MEASURES DESIGN WITH
 THE DATA AS FOLLOWS:
                                        TIME

          1                   2                   3

          PREDIS              POSTDIS             FOLODIS
          PREPROB             POSTPROB            FOLOPROB
          PRESELF             POSTSELF            FOLOSELF
          PRENEG              POSTNEG             FOLONEG
          PRETHER             POSTTHER            FOLOTHER

DATA LIST / GROUP, SEX, PREDIS, PREPROB, PRESELF, PRENEG,
 PRETHER, POSTDIS, POSTPROB, POSTSELF, POSTNEG, POSTTHER,
 FOLODIS, FOLOPROB, FOLOSELF, FOLONEG, FOLOTHER
 (2F1.0,4X,2F6.3,3F3.0,2F6.3,3F3.0,2F6.3,3F3.0)
MANOVA PREDIS POSTDIS FOLODIS PREPROB POSTPROB FOLOPROB
 PRESELF POSTSELF FOLOSELF PRENEG POSTNEG FOLONEG
 PRETHER POSTTHER FOLOTHER BY SEX(1,2), GROUP(1,3)/
 WSFACTOR = TIME( 3 )/
 MEASURE = DIS PROB SELF NEG THER/
 CONTRAST(TIME) = POLYNOMIAL(1 2 3)/
 WSDESIGN = TIME /
 PRINT = SIGNIF(HYPOTH)/
 DESIGN/
BEGIN DATA
...
END DATA
```

- The TITLE command prints a title at the top of each page of display output, and the COMMENT command inserts comments that print back with the commands on the display (see Chapter 4).
- The DATA LIST command defines 17 variables from the data in the command file (see Chapter 5).
- The MANOVA command specifies the 15 dependent variables and the two between-subjects factors. The prefixes PRE, POST, and FOLO indicate the three occasions. The root names DIS, PROB, SELF, NEG, and THER indicate the five types of measures. Notice the order of the variables. All DIS variables appear first, then all PROB variables, and so on. Within each group of three variables, the order of time is the same.
- The WSFACTORS subcommand specifies TIME as a within-subjects factor. The number of dependent variables in the MANOVA specification is an integer multiple of the number of levels of the within-subjects factor (see Section 33.21).

- The MEASURE subcommand lists five names, which MANOVA uses for labeling univariate results (see Section 33.24).
- The CONTRAST subcommand specifies a polynomial contrast for TIME (see Section 33.36).
- The WSDESIGN subcommand specifies the within-subjects factor, TIME. This command specification is optional because MANOVA assumes a full factorial model by default (see Section 33.22).
- The PRINT subcommand prints the hypothesis SSCP matrices (Figure 33.79d) and the averaged statistics corresponding to the univariate approach (Figure 33.79f). AVERF does not need to be specified as the averaged f statistics will be printed as the default for all repeated measures designs.
- The DESIGN subcommand specifies the between-subjects design (see Sections 33.7).

Portions of the display output are shown in Figures 33.79a through 33.79g.

- Figures 33.79a, 33.79b, 33.79c show the multivariate tests of significance for the SEX by GROUP interaction, the GROUP effect, and the SEX effect respectively.

Figure 33.79a Example 7: SEX by GROUP effect

```
EFFECT .. SEX BY GROUP
AVERAGED Multivariate Tests of Significance (S = 2, M = 1 , N = 20 1/2)

Test Name              Value        Approx. F      Hypoth. DF         Error DF        Sig. of F

Pillais                .14819         .70421          10.00             88.00            .718
Hotellings             .16349         .68665          10.00             84.00            .734
Wilks                  .85594         .69560          10.00             86.00            .726
Roys                   .11102
Note.. F statistic for WILK'S Lambda is exact.
```

Figure 33.79b Example 7: GROUP effect

```
EFFECT .. GROUP
AVERAGED Multivariate Tests of Significance (S = 2, M = 1 , N = 20 1/2)

Test Name              Value        Approx. F      Hypoth. DF         Error DF        Sig. of F

Pillais                .21069        1.03618          10.00             88.00            .420
Hotellings             .24626        1.03428          10.00             84.00            .422
Wilks                  .79657        1.03574          10.00             86.00            .421
Roys                   .16727
Note.. F statistic for WILK'S Lambda is exact.
```

Figure 33.79c Example 7: SEX effect

```
EFFECT .. SEX
AVERAGED Multivariate Tests of Significance (S = 1, M = 1 1/2, N = 20 1/2)

Test Name              Value         Exact F       Hypoth. DF         Error DF        Sig. of F

Pillais                .20556        2.22525           5.00             43.00            .069
Hotellings             .25875        2.22525           5.00             43.00            .069
Wilks                  .79444        2.22525           5.00             43.00            .069
Roys                   .20556
Note.. F statistics are exact.
```

- Figure 33.79d shows the adjusted hypothesis SSCP matrix for the SEX by GROUP by TIME effect, and Figure 33.79e shows the default multivariate-approach test statistics for the SEX by GROUP by TIME effect.
- Figure 33.79f shows the "averaged" adjusted hypothesis SSCP matrix for the SEX by GROUP by TIME effect. This matrix results from the univariate approach to the data. MANOVA uses the names supplied on the MEASURES subcommand to label the pooled effects. Compare this matrix with the one in Figure 33.79d. In the averaged hypothesis SSCP matrix, for example, the DIS sum of squares is .49423. This number is the trace of the submatrix in Figure 33.79d formed by all DIS effects, that is, POSTDIS and FOLODIS. In other words, .49423 is the sum of .16123 and .33300. MANOVA similarly combines submatrix trace elements of the multivariate-

approach adjusted hypothesis SSCP matrix to compute the rest of the elements of the univariate-approach adjusted hypothesis SSCP matrix. Although not shown, the averaged error SSCP matrix is similarly computed.

• Finally, Figure 33.79g shows the univariate-approach test statistics for the SEX by GROUP by TIME effect. Compare this with Figure 33.79e.

Figure 33.79d   Example 7: Hypothesis SSCP matrix for SEX by GROUP by TIME effect

```
EFFECT .. SEX BY GROUP BY TIME
Adjusted Hypothesis Sum-of-Squares and Cross-Products
                    T2            T3            T5            T6            T8            T9           T11

T2             .16123
T3            -.19762        .33300
T5             .14595       -.04226        .33777
T6            -.13805        .13589       -.17512        .13043
T8             .15726       -.92824       -.96459        .13527       6.11199
T9            -.28690        .89645        .56024        .04571      -4.69360       3.77997
T11           3.86160      -6.37783       1.02034      -2.70282      17.09124     -16.74162     122.28503
T12          -1.13667       1.42390       -.98278        .96199      -1.35733       2.20682     -27.78012
T14           3.35852      -7.96836      -2.75699      -1.46204      34.48205     -29.09195     150.22274
T15           1.97603       -.26219       5.03949      -2.48460     -15.57064       9.44523       8.19825

                   T12           T14           T15

T12           8.02386
T14         -24.97956     233.39190
T15         -13.20086     -50.47842      75.60308
```

Figure 33.79e   Example 7: Multivariate approach for SEX by GROUP by TIME effect

```
EFFECT .. SEX BY GROUP BY TIME
Multivariate Tests of Significance (S = 2, M = 3 1/2, N = 18 )

Test Name          Value        Approx. F      Hypoth. DF       Error DF      Sig. of F

Pillais           .47001        1.19806          20.00           78.00          .279
Hotellings        .63755        1.17947          20.00           74.00          .296
Wilks             .58008        1.18930          20.00           76.00          .287
Roys              .30669
Note.. F statistic for WILK'S Lambda is exact.
```

Figure 33.79f   Example 7: Averaged hypothesis SSCP matrix

```
EFFECT .. SEX BY GROUP BY TIME
Adjusted Hypothesis Sum-of-Squares and Cross-Products
                    DIS           PROB          SELF           NEG          THER

DIS             .49423
PROB            .28184        .46820
SELF           1.05372       -.91888       9.89196
NEG            5.28550       1.98233      19.29806     130.30889
THER           3.09633      -5.24159      43.92728     137.02188     308.99498
```

Figure 33.79g   Example 7: Univariate approach for SEX by GROUP by TIME effect

```
EFFECT .. SEX BY GROUP BY TIME
AVERAGED Multivariate Tests of Significance (S = 4, M = 0, N = 44 )

Test Name          Value        Approx. F      Hypoth. DF       Error DF      Sig. of F

Pillais           .23198        1.14512          20.00          372.00          .301
Hotellings        .25801        1.14172          20.00          354.00          .305
Wilks             .78311        1.14534          20.00          299.45          .302
Roys              .12791
```

33.80
Example 8: Profile Analysis

In the previous repeated measures examples, we imposed a design on the dependent variables using an implicit orthonormal transformation of the dependent variables. The distinct dependent variables were really measures of the same items across occasions. However, not all analyses require a formal treatment structure on the dependent variables; instead, you may simply be interested in making specific kinds of comparisons among nonrepeated dependent variables. Such analyses are termed *profile analyses*.

Data in profile analysis consist of *p* commensurable responses that have been collected from independent sampling units grouped according to *k* treatments or experimental conditions. In profile analysis, there are three questions of interest:

- *Parallelism of profiles.* Are the population-mean profiles similar, in the sense that the line segments of adjacent tests are parallel?
- *Equal treatment levels.* Assuming parallelism, are the treatment levels equal?
- *Equal response means.* Assuming parallelism, are the response means equal?

The analysis proceeds very much along the same lines as that for repeated measures data. That is, you transform the data to new variables which incorporate the effects of interest. The difference from repeated measures analysis lies in the nature of the data themselves: profile analysis does not assume any correspondence between treatment interventions and dependent variables. Also, the pooled results are generally not of interest. You should *not* request orthonormalization of the new variables in profile analysis. This example appears in Morrison (1976, p. 210). Three scales—A, B, and C—measuring certain maternal attitudes are administered to 21 mothers participating in a study of child development. As part of the study, each mother has been assigned to one of four socioeconomic status (SES) groups. Thus, there are three responses, four treatment levels, and 21 subjects. The three hypotheses to be tested are

- Are the scale profiles in the four SES groups parallel?
- Given 1, are class effects equal over all responses?
- Given 1, are response means equal?

To conduct the tests, first transform the observations to the differences of scales A and B and scales B and C. The SPSS-X commands are

```
TITLE PROFILE ANALYSIS
COMMENT THIS EXAMPLE IS FROM MORRISON, P.209.
DATA LIST / SOCLASS 1 A 3-4 B 6-7 C 9-10
REPORT VARS=A B C/
 BREAK=SOCLASS/
 SUM=MEAN/
BEGIN DATA
1 19 20 18
1 20 21 19
1 19 22 22
1 18 19 21
1 16 18 20
1 17 22 19
1 20 19 20
1 15 19 19
2 12 14 12
2 15 15 17
2 15 17 15
2 13 14 14
2 14 16 13
3 15 14 17
3 13 14 15
3 12 15 15
3 12 13 13
4  8  9 10
4 10 10 12
4 11 10 10
4 11  7 12
END DATA
MANOVA A,B,C BY SOCLASS(1,4)/
 TRANSFORM= REPEATED/
 RENAME= AVERAGE,AMINUSB,BMINUSC /
 PRINT=TRANSFORM/
 ANALYSIS =(AMINUSB, BMINUSC/AVERAGE)/
 DESIGN/
```

- The TITLE command prints a title at the top of each page of display output, and the COMMENT command inserts comments that print back with the commands on the display (see Chapter 4).

- The DATA LIST command defines four variables from the data in the command file (see Chapter 5).

- REPORT displays the means on the three response variables within each of the four SES groups (see Figure 33.80a and Chapter 47).

- The MANOVA command names A, B, and C as three response variables and SOCLASS as a four-level factor.

- TRANSFORM creates three transformed variables: an average effect and two adjacent differences, A-B and B-C (see Section 33.25).

- The RENAME subcommand names the transformed variables for use on the display output (see Section 33.30).

- The PRINT subcommand prints the transformation matrix (see Figure 33.80b).

- The ANALYSIS subcommand specifies two analyses. In the first analysis, AMINUSB and BMINUSC are joint dependent variables, and in the second analysis, AVERAGE is the dependent variable. The first analysis tests Hypotheses 1 and 3 stated above; the second analysis tests Hypothesis 2 (see Section 33.19).

- The DESIGN subcommand indicates the default design, which enters the SOCLASS effect (see Section 33.7).

Portions of the display output are shown in Figures 33.80a through 33.80e.

- Figure 33.80a shows the output from REPORT. The rows of means are the four "profiles" corresponding to the four levels of SES.

- Figure 33.80b shows the transposed transformation matrix. Column 1 is the average effect; column 2 is the A-B difference; and column 3 is the B-C difference.

Figure 33.80a   Example 8: REPORT output showing mean profiles

```
PROFILE ANALYSIS                                                                    PAGE    1
    SOCLASS         A           B           C
        1
      Mean         18          20          20
        2
      Mean         14          15          14
        3
      Mean         13          14          15
        4
      Mean         10           9          11
```

Figure 33.80b   Example 8: Transformation matrix

```
Transformation Matrix (Transposed)
                  AVERAGE        AMINUSB        BMINUSC
  A               .33333        1.00000         .00000
  B               .33333       -1.00000        1.00000
  C               .33333         .00000       -1.00000
```

- Figure 33.80c shows the variables used for the first analysis. Transformed and renamed variables AMINUSB and BMINUSC are joint dependent variables in the first analysis.

- The first portion of figure 33.80d shows the tests of significance of the SOCLASS effect on the joint dependent variables. This portion of the output shows a test for Hypothesis 1—the test of parallelism. The second portion shows nonsignificant test statistics which indicate that AMINUSB and BMINUSC are the same across SES levels, in which case you can assume that the profiles are parallel. In the output, the significance levels of the test statistics are indeed large enough to assume parallelism.

- Figure 33.80e shows the results for the second analysis specified on the ANALYSIS subcommand. The dependent variable is AVERAGE. If there are no significant differences in the means of AVERAGE across the four levels of SOCLASS, then we do not reject Hypothesis 2—the test of equal class effects. However, the highly significant F statistic for SOCLASS leads to rejection of the hypothesis of equal means. The SOCLASS parameter estimates, while not exhausting the comparisons that can be made, show that the mean of level 1 differs significantly from the means of the other levels.

Figure 33.80c   Example 8: Model 1 variables

```
Order of Variables for Analysis

   Variates      Covariates

   AMINUSB
   BMINUSC

   2 Dependent Variables
   0 Covariates

- - - - - - - - - - - - - - - - - - - - - - - - - - - - -
Note..  TRANSFORMED variables are in the variates column.
```

Figure 33.80d   Example 8: Test of parallelism

```
EFFECT .. SOCLASS
Multivariate Tests of Significance (S = 2, M = 0, N = 7 )

Test Name          Value        Approx. F    Hypoth. DF     Error DF      Sig. of F

Pillais            .48726        1.82526        6.00          34.00          .123
Hotellings         .68534        1.71336        6.00          30.00          .152
Wilks              .56333        1.77253        6.00          32.00          .136
Roys               .33724
Note.. F statistic for WILK'S Lambda is exact.

- - - - - - - - - - - - - - - - - - - - - - - - - - - - - - - - - - - - - - - - - - -
EFFECT .. SOCLASS (CONT.)
Univariate F-tests with (3,17) D. F.

Variable      Hypoth. SS     Error SS     Hypoth. MS     Error MS          F          Sig. of F

AMINUSB        24.60952      51.20000      8.20317        3.01176       2.72371         .077
BMINUSC        24.30952      61.50000      8.10317        3.61765       2.23990         .121
```

Figure 33.80e   Example 8: Test of equality of class effects

```
Order of Variables for Analysis

   Variates      Covariates

   AVERAGE

   1 Dependent Variable
   0 Covariates

- - - - - - - - - - - - - - - - - - - - - - - - - - - - -
Note..  TRANSFORMED variables are in the variates column.
- - - - - - - - - - - - - - - - - - - - - - - - - - - - -
Tests of Significance for AVERAGE using UNIQUE sums of squares
Source of Variation        SS      DF      MS        F    Sig of F

WITHIN CELLS             19.81     17     1.17
SOCLASS                 247.97      3    82.66    70.93     .000
```

Syntax

MEANS

General mode:

```
MEANS [TABLES=]varlist BY varlist [BY...] [/varlist...]
    [/MISSING={TABLE**  }]
             {INCLUDE  }
             {DEPENDENT}
    [/FORMAT={LABELS** }  {NAMES**}   {VALUES**}  {TABLE**}]
             {NOLABELS }  {NONAMES}   {NOVALUES}  {TREE   }
             {NOCATLABS}
    [/CELLS=[DEFAULT**]  [MEAN**   ]   [ALL]]
            [COUNT**  ]  [STDDEV** ]
            [SUM      ]  [VARIANCE]
    [/STATISTICS=[ANOVA] [LINEARITY] [ALL] [NONE] ]
```

Integer mode:

```
MEANS VARIABLES=varlist({min,max         }) [varlist...]
                       {LOWEST,HIGHEST}
    /{TABLES    }=varlist BY varlist [BY...] [/varlist...]
     {CROSSBREAK}
    [/MISSING={TABLE**  }]
             {INCLUDE  }
             {DEPENDENT}
    [/FORMAT={LABELS** }  {NAMES**}   {VALUES**}]
             {NOLABELS }  {NONAMES}   {NOVALUES}
             {NOCATLABS}
    [/CELLS=[DEFAULT**]  [MEAN**   ]   [ALL]]
            [COUNT**  ]  [STDDEV** ]
            [SUM      ]  [VARIANCE]·
    [/STATISTICS=[ANOVA] [LINEARITY] [ALL] [NONE] ]
```

**Default if the subcommand is omitted.

Contents

34.1   OVERVIEW

34.2   OPERATION

34.3   TABLES Subcommand

34.4   General Mode

34.5   Integer Mode

34.6   VARIABLES Subcommand

34.7   CROSSBREAK Subcommand

34.8   CELLS Subcommand

34.9   STATISTICS Subcommand

34.10   MISSING Subcommand

34.11   FORMAT Subcommand

34.12   Narrow Output

34.13   LIMITATIONS

34

Chapter 34   MEANS

MEANS (alias BREAKDOWN) calculates means and variances for a criterion or dependent variable over subgroups of cases defined by independent or control variables. This operation is similar to crosstabulation, where each mean and standard deviation summarize the distribution of a complete row or column of a contingency table.

34.1
OVERVIEW

In MEANS, you can operate in either general or integer mode, modify cell information, request additional statistics, control the handling of user-missing values, and obtain crosstabular and tree formats.

Methods for Building Tables. MEANS operates in two different modes: general and integer. *General mode* operates via the TABLES subcommand and requires fewer specifications. (See Section 34.4.) It also offers an optional tree format for the output. *Integer mode* operates via the TABLES and VARIABLES subcommands and requires that you specify the minimum and maximum values for the variables. This mode builds tables more efficiently. (See Section 34.5.)

Cell Information. By default, MEANS displays means, standard deviations, and cell counts for a dependent variable across groups defined by one or more independent variables. Optionally, you can also display sums and variances. (See Section 34.8.)

Additional Statistics. In addition to the statistics displayed for groups, you can obtain a one-way analysis of variance and test of linearity. (See Section 34.9.)

Missing Values. By default, MEANS excludes cases with missing values on a tablewide basis. You can request that user-missing values be included or that cases missing only on the dependent variable be deleted. (See Section 34.10.)

Formatting Options. You can request a tree format with general mode and suppress labels and values in either mode. (See Section 34.11.) With integer mode you can obtain a crosstabular format (See Section 34.7.)

34.2
OPERATION

Procedure MEANS operates via subcommands and associated keywords. The specifications for these subcommands depend on whether you want to use the *general mode* or the *integer mode* to build tables, and whether you request CROSSBREAK tables. Each of the three methods has advantages and disadvantages in computational efficiency, statistics, and additional options.

• General mode permits alphanumeric or noninteger control variables with no range specifications. (See Section 34.4.) It also provides the optional tree format.

• Integer mode builds breakdown tables more quickly. However, it requires more space if the matrix of control variables has many empty cells. By specifying the appropriate bounds, you can eliminate outliers for the criterion variable or select a subset of the values of the control variables. (See Section 34.5.)

• The CROSSBREAK subcommand prints tables of two or more control variables in a crosstabular format and displays statistics for each of two variables controlling for the other. The optional analysis of variance table and test of linearity are not available for CROSSBREAK. (See Section 34.7.)

Sections 34.8 through 34.11 outline the optional subcommands available for MEANS. To specify an optional subcommand, use the appropriate subcommand followed by an optional equals sign and the desired keyword. The CELLS and STATISTICS subcommands can be used without keywords. Separate multiple keywords on a single subcommand with at least one space or comma. Separate subcommands with slashes. For example, to include user-defined missing values in an analysis, specify

```
MEANS TABLES=PCTRAISE BY LOCATN81 BY GRADE81S
     /MISSING=INCLUDE
```

You can specify the subcommands in MEANS in any order, provided the VARIABLES subcommand precedes the TABLES or CROSSBREAK subcommands in integer mode. Unless otherwise indicated, all subcommand keywords apply to general and integer mode and to the table and CROSSBREAK formats.

34.3
TABLES Subcommand

Use the TABLES subcommand with MEANS in both general and integer modes.

34.4
General Mode

To run MEANS in general mode, use the TABLES subcommand followed by one or more dependent variables, the keyword BY, and one or more independent variables. For example, the command

```
MEANS  TABLES=PCTRAISE BY GRADE81
```

produces one table displayed in Figure 34.4a. PCTRAISE is the *criterion* variable, the variable to be summarized. This is the dependent variable and must be numeric. The values of GRADE81, the independent variable, define the groups. Independent variables can be numeric or string; long strings are truncated to short strings, however, for purposes of defining categories. Use the REPORT procedure to break down variables by long strings. (See Chapter 47.)

Figure 34.4a A one-way MEANS table

```
             D E S C R I P T I O N   O F   S U B P O P U L A T I O N S

Criterion Variable      PCTRAISE
      Broken Down by    GRADE81      JOB GRADE IN 1981


Variable       Value  Label                          Mean     Std Dev    Cases

For Entire Population                                 .1257     .1034      159

GRADE81           2                                   .0079     .0111        2
GRADE81           3                                   .0872     .0536       23
GRADE81           4                                   .0851     .1077       26
GRADE81           5                                   .1219     .0648       15
GRADE81           6                                   .1505     .0742       24
GRADE81           7                                   .1291     .0518        8
GRADE81           8                                   .1917     .1253       11
GRADE81           9                                   .1087     .0205        3
GRADE81          10                                   .1372     .1184       20
GRADE81          11                                   .1985     .1771       12
GRADE81          12                                   .0975     .0602        6
GRADE81          13                                   .1610     .1454        5
GRADE81          14                                   .0835     .0522        3
GRADE81          15                                   .0811     .0000        1

 Total Cases = 275
Missing Cases = 116 or  42.2 Pct
```

The actual command keyword TABLES is not required to operate MEANS in general mode. For example, the following commands produce identical displays:

```
MEANS  TABLES=SALARY82 BY YRHIRED

MEANS  SALARY82 BY YRHIRED
```

If you use the keyword TABLES for general mode, as shown in the examples in this section, you must also include the equals sign.

A maximum of six dimensions can be specified on an analysis list: one dependent variable and up to five independent variables separated by the keyword BY. For example,

```
MEANS  TABLES=RAISE81 BY DEPT81 BY GRADE81S
```

breaks down RAISE81 by DEPT81 and by GRADE81S within DEPT81. Figure 34.4b shows the output from this command. The first variable always becomes the dependent or criterion variable. The independent variables are entered into the table in the order in which they appear following the TABLES subcommand, proceeding from left to right. The values of the last variable change most quickly.

Although the MEANS tables list is the same as the CROSSTABS tables list (see Chapter 25), in CROSSTABS the values of the last variable change most slowly. MEANS prints subpopulation statistics for each category of the first independent variable. However, for subsequent variables, it prints statistics only for each category of the variable within a category of the preceding independent variable. For example, Figure 34.4b shows means for RAISE81 for categories of DEPT81 but shows means for GRADE81S only within categories of DEPT81, not for each grade. You can specify the order of controlling variables to obtain the most useful intermediate subpopulation statistics or use the CROSSBREAK format to display subpopulation statistics for two independent variables (see Section 34.7).

Figure 34.4b   A two-way MEANS table

```
            D E S C R I P T I O N   O F   S U B P O P U L A T I O N S

Criterion Variable      RAISE81      INCREASE IN SALARY OVER 1980
    Broken Down by      DEPT81       DEPARTMENT CODE IN 1981
               by       GRADE81S


Variable        Value  Label                     Mean      Std Dev    Cases

For Entire Population                         1628.1384   1429.2467     159

DEPT81              1  ADMIN                   1472.1316   1113.9585      38
  GRADE81S       1.00                           716.4167    286.2629      12
  GRADE81S       2.00                          1210.6000    495.5833      15
  GRADE81S       3.00                          2653.1818   1354.6461      11

DEPT81              2  PROJECT DIRECTORS       1811.5357   2368.0374      28
  GRADE81S       1.00                           517.5625    857.3076      16
  GRADE81S       2.00                           910.0000    343.9477       3
  GRADE81S       3.00                          4412.4444   2500.8318       9

DEPT81              3  CHICAGO OPERATIONS      1484.9194   1072.1964      62
  GRADE81S       1.00                           988.4375    954.6331      16
  GRADE81S       2.00                          1368.1250    389.3723      16
  GRADE81S       3.00                          1812.0000   1270.4910      30

DEPT81              4  ST LOUIS OPERATIONS     1940.1613   1280.0114      31
  GRADE81S       1.00                           791.1429    339.8639       7
  GRADE81S       2.00                          1928.0769    868.5525      13
  GRADE81S       3.00                          2685.6364   1550.8244      11

   Total Cases = 275
Missing Cases = 116 or  42.2 Pct
```

You can specify more than one dependent variable and more than one independent variable in each dimension. Use the keyword TO to name a set of adjacent variables in the active file, as in:

```
MEANS  TABLES=RAISE79 TO RAISE81 BY DEPT TO AGE
```

This command will produce MEANS tables for all the variables between and including RAISE79 and RAISE81 by all the variables between and including DEPT and AGE. You can also use variable lists to request higher-order breakdowns. The variables to the right of the last BY change most quickly. Within lists separated with a BY, variables rotate from left to right. For example,

```
MEANS  TABLES=VAR1 TO VAR3 BY VAR4 VAR5 BY VAR6 TO VAR8
```

produces 18 tables. The first table is VAR1 by VAR4 by VAR6 and the second is VAR1 by VAR4 by VAR7. The combinations of VAR1 and VAR5 follow the combinations of VAR1 and VAR4. The last table produced is VAR3 by VAR5 by VAR8.

You can specify up to 30 tables lists on one MEANS command and up to 250 tables over all the lists together. A maximum of 200 variables can be named or implied by all the tables lists. Use multiple TABLES subcommands, or a slash, to separate tables lists on one TABLES subcommand. For example,

```
MEANS  TABLES=RAISE82 BY GRADE/SALARY BY DEPT
```

specifies two tables, RAISE82 by GRADE and SALARY by DEPT. If you omit a slash between tables lists, MEANS includes the variables as if one analysis list had been supplied. If the preceding command had no slash, as in

```
MEANS  TABLES=RAISE82 BY GRADE SALARY BY DEPT
```

it would produce two tables, RAISE82 by GRADE by DEPT and RAISE82 by SALARY by DEPT.

34.5
Integer Mode

To run MEANS in integer mode, the values of all the independent variables must be integers. Two subcommands are required. The VARIABLES subcommand (see Section 34.6) specifies all the variables to be used in the MEANS procedure and the minimum and maximum values for building tables. The TABLES subcommand specifies the tables lists. In integer mode, the equals sign following the VARIABLES and TABLES subcommands is optional. Repeated VARIABLES and TABLES subcommands are allowed.

In integer mode, the TABLES subcommand names the tables list and has the same syntax as the TABLES subcommand in general mode. You can use multiple TABLES subcommands or name multiple tables lists separated by slashes on one TABLES subcommand. Like general mode, integer mode can process up to 30 tables lists. However, you cannot specify more than 100 tables over all the lists, and you cannot name or imply more than 100 variables on all the tables lists. Variables named on the TABLES subcommand must have been previously named or implied on the VARIABLES subcommand.

There is one important difference between the tables request in integer mode and the tables request in general mode. In integer mode, the order of variables implied on the TABLES subcommand is established by the order variables are named or implied on the VARIABLES subcommand. In general mode, the order of variables implied on the tables lists is established by their order in the active file.

Integer mode can produce more tables in a given amount of core storage space than general mode, and the processing is faster. In integer mode, you define the dimensions of the table with the independent variables, rather than having SPSS-X calculate the dimensions based on values encountered in your data. In addition, integer mode has an alternate CROSSBREAK display format (see Section 34.7).

34.6
VARIABLES Subcommand

The VARIABLES subcommand is followed by a list of variables. This list identifies variables to be included on the TABLES subcommand. Specify the lowest and highest values in parentheses after each variable. These values must be integers. You can *not* use LOWEST, LO, HIGHEST, HI with independent variables. For example, the command

```
MEANS   VARIABLES=DEPT81(1,4) EEO81(1,9) RAISE81(LO,HI)/
     TABLES=RAISE81 BY DEPT81 BY EEO81
```

produces the table in Figure 34.6 where RAISE81 has a range from the lowest to the highest value, DEPT81 has a range from 1 to 4, and EEO81 has a range from 1 to 9. The final variable or set of variables and their range must be followed by a slash. A maximum of 100 variables can be named or implied by the VARIABLES subcommand.

Figure 34.6   A two-way breakdown using integer mode

```
            D E S C R I P T I O N   O F   S U B P O P U L A T I O N S

Criterion Variable      RAISE81     INCREASE IN SALARY OVER 1980
       Broken Down by   DEPT81      DEPARTMENT CODE IN 1981
                  by    EEO81       E.E.O. CLASSIFICATION IN 1981


Variable          Value  Label                   Mean      Std Dev    Cases

For Entire Population                          1628.1384  1429.2467     159

DEPT81              1    ADMIN                  1472.1316  1113.9585      38
  EEO81             1    OFF-MGR                2684.5000  1413.1278      10
  EEO81             2    PROF                   2470.0000      .0000       1
  EEO81             3    TECH                   1592.6667   622.8975       3
  EEO81             5    CLERICAL                937.6000   467.2766      15
  EEO81             7    OPERTIVS               1690.0000      .0000       1
  EEO81             9    SERVICE                 761.7500     2.1213       8

DEPT81              2    PROJECT DIRECTORS      1811.5357  2368.0374      28
  EEO81             2    PROF                   4875.0000  2567.7152       7
  EEO81             3    TECH                   4160.0000      .0000       1
  EEO81             5    CLERICAL                621.9000   805.6582      20

DEPT81              3    CHICAGO OPERATIONS     1484.9194  1072.1964      62
  EEO81             1    OFF-MGR                1561.5833   870.6716      12
  EEO81             2    PROF                   2719.3333  1190.4942       3
  EEO81             3    TECH                   1959.7500  1326.5256       4
  EEO81             5    CLERICAL               1333.2326  1059.4303      43

DEPT81              4    ST LOUIS OPERATIONS    1940.1613  1280.0114      31
  EEO81             1    OFF-MGR                3176.8750  1547.3501       8
  EEO81             3    TECH                   1625.0000    91.9239       2
  EEO81             5    CLERICAL               1499.0476   890.6131      21

   Total Cases = 275
Missing Cases = 116 or  42.2 Pct
```

You do not have to specify an explicit range for dependent variables because they are usually continuous and are not assumed to be integers. However, you must provide bounds. Use keywords LOWEST (or LO) and HIGHEST (or HI) for criterion variables. You can also use explicit bounds to eliminate outliers from the calculation of the summary statistics. Explicit numeric bounds must be specified as integers. For example, (0,HI) excludes nonnegative values.

You must specify a range for each variable to be used in the MEANS procedure and several variables can have the same range. For example,

```
MEANS   VARIABLES=DEPT80 DEPT81 DEPT82 (1,3) GRADE81S (1,4)
     SALARY82 (LO,HI)/
     TABLES=SALARY82 BY DEPT80 TO DEPT82 BY GRADE81S
```

defines 1 as the lowest value and 3 as the highest value for DEPT80, DEPT81, and DEPT82. Variables may appear in any order. However, the order in which you place them on the VARIABLES subcommand affects their implied order on the TABLES subcommand as described in Section 34.2.

MEANS uses the bounds you specify to allocate tables. One cell is allocated for each possible combination of values of the control variables for a requested table before the data are read. Therefore, if you specify more generous bounds than the control variables actually have, you are wasting some space. If the table is sparse because the control variables do not have values falling throughout the range specified, you might consider using the general mode or recoding the control variables. If, on the other hand, values of control variables fall outside the range you specify, cases with these values are considered missing and are not used in the computation of the table.

34.7
CROSSBREAK
Subcommand

To print tables in a crosstabular form when using integer mode, use the CROSSBREAK subcommand in place of the TABLES subcommand. It has exactly the same specification field as the TABLES subcommand. The equals sign following the CROSSBREAK subcommand is optional. As with the TABLES subcommand, repeated CROSSBREAK subcommands are allowed. However, you cannot mix CROSSBREAK and TABLES subcommands.

The following command produces the crossbreak table displayed in Figure 34.7:

```
MEANS  VARIABLES=RAISE81(LO,HI) DEPT81(1,4) EEO81(1,9)/
     CROSSBREAK=RAISE81 BY DEPT81 BY EEO81
```

Tables printed in crossbreak form resemble CROSSTABS tables, but their contents are considerably different. The cells contain means, counts, and standard deviations for the dependent variable. The first independent variable defines the rows and the second independent variable defines the columns. The CROSS-BREAK format is especially suited to breakdowns with two control variables. The CROSSBREAK subcommand prints separate subtables for each combination of values when you specify three or more dimensions. Note that the crossbreak table in Figure 34.7 displays overall means for each value of EEO81 in the column margins and overall means for each value of DEPT81 in the row margins.

Figure 34.7   A table in CROSSBREAK format

```
                                    C R O S S - B R E A K D O W N

      Criterion Variable    RAISE81
         Broken Down by      DEPT81
                   by        EEO81
                             EEO81
                    Mean I
                   Count I                                                                          Row
                  Std Dev I                                                                        Total
                         I      1  I      2  I      3  I      5  I      7  I      9  I
      DEPT81      --------+---------+---------+---------+---------+---------+---------+
                1  I  2684.50 I  2470.00 I  1592.67 I   937.60 I  1690.00 I   761.75 I  1472.13
                   I     10  I      1  I      3  I     15  I      1  I      8  I      38
                   I  1413.13 I         I   622.90 I   467.28 I         I     2.12 I  1113.96
                   +---------+---------+---------+---------+---------+---------+
                2  I         I  4875.00 I  4160.00 I   621.90 I         I         I  1811.54
                   I         I      7  I      1  I     20  I         I         I      28
                   I         I  2567.72 I         I   805.66 I         I         I  2368.04
                   +---------+---------+---------+---------+---------+---------+
                3  I  1561.58 I  2719.33 I  1959.75 I  1333.23 I         I         I  1484.92
                   I     12  I      3  I      4  I     43  I         I         I      62
                   I   870.67 I  1190.49 I  1326.53 I  1059.43 I         I         I  1072.20
                   +---------+---------+---------+---------+---------+---------+
                4  I  3176.88 I         I  1625.00 I  1499.05 I         I         I  1940.16
                   I      8  I         I      2  I     21  I         I         I      31
                   I  1547.35 I         I    91.92 I   890.61 I         I         I  1280.01
                   +---------+---------+---------+---------+---------+---------+
      Column Total    2366.63    4068.45    2002.70    1164.76    1690.00     761.75    1628.14
                          30         11         10         99          1          8        159
                        1403.33    2344.41    1131.10     950.99                  2.12    1429.25

      116 Missing Observations
```

34.8
CELLS Subcommand

By default, MEANS prints the means, standard deviations, and cell counts in each cell. Use the CELLS subcommand to modify cell information.

You can specify the CELLS subcommand by itself, or with a keyword or keywords. If you specify the CELLS subcommand by itself, with no keywords, MEANS prints ALL cell information (defined below). If you specify a keyword or keywords, MEANS prints only the information you request.

The following keywords can be specified on the CELLS subcommand:

DEFAULT   *Print the means, standard deviations, and cell counts in each cell.* This is the default if you omit the CELL subcommand.

MEAN   *Print cell means.*

STDDEV   *Print cell standard deviations.*

COUNT   *Print cell frequencies.*

SUM   *Print cell sums.*

VARIANCE   *Print variances.*

ALL   *Print the means, counts, standard deviations, sums, and variances in each cell.* This is the default if you specify the CELLS subcommand by itself, with no keyword(s).

34.9
STATISTICS Subcommand

MEANS automatically computes means, standard deviations, and counts for subpopulations. Optionally, you can obtain a one-way analysis of variance for each table as well as a test of linearity. The STATISTICS subcommand computes additional statistics. Statistics you request on the STATISTICS subcommand are computed *in addition to* the default statistics or those you request on the CELLS subcommand.

You can use the STATISTICS subcommand by itself or with a keyword or keywords. If you use the STATISTICS subcommand by itself, with no keyword, MEANS computes ANOVA (defined below). If you specify a keyword, MEANS computes the additional statistics you request.

The following keywords can be specified on the STATISTICS subcommand:

ANOVA   *Analysis of variance.* Prints a standard analysis of variance table and calculates *ETA* and *ETA²*. This is the default if you specify the STATISTICS subcommand by itself, with no keyword.

LINEARITY   *Test of linearity.* Calculates the sums of squares, degrees of freedom, and mean square associated with linear and nonlinear components, as well as the *F* ratio, Pearson's *r*, and *r²*. ANOVA *must* be requested to obtain LINEARITY. LINEARITY is ignored if the control variable is a short string.

ALL   *Both ANOVA and LINEARITY.*

NONE   *No additional statistics.* This is the default if you omit the STATISTICS subcommand.

If you specify a two-way or higher-order breakdown, the second and subsequent dimensions are ignored in the analysis of variance table. For example,

```
MEANS TABLES=INCOME BY SEX BY RACE
     /STATISTICS=ANOVA
```

produces a breakdown of INCOME by RACE within SEX but computes an analysis of variance only for INCOME by SEX. To obtain a two-way and higher analysis of variance, use procedure ANOVA (Chapter 20) or MANOVA (Chapter 33). Procedure ONEWAY (Chapter 39) calculates a one-way analysis of variance with multiple comparison tests. The STATISTICS subcommand is not available if you use the CROSSBREAK subcommand.

The following commands modify the table shown in Figure 34.4a so that it displays the optional statistics available on MEANS (see Figure 34.9):

```
MEANS TABLES=PCTRAISE BY GRADE81
    /STATISTICS=ALL
```

Figure 34.9   Optional statistics

```
                       Sum of                    Mean
Source                 Squares        D.F.       Square          F        Sig.

Between Groups          .2532         13.         .0195        1.9682     .0273

  Linearity             .0749          1           .0749       7.5663     .0067
  Dev. from Linearity   .1783         12           .0149       1.5017     .1297

              R =  .2106        R Squared =   .0444

Within Groups          1.4348        145          .0099

              Eta =  .3873      Eta Squared =   .1500


                    A N A L Y S I S   O F   V A R I A N C E

Criterion Variable      PCTRAISE
   Broken Down by       GRADE81     JOB GRADE IN 1981


   Value  Label                     Sum        Mean      Std Dev   Sum of Sq   Cases

     2                              .02        .0079       .0111      .0001        2
     3                             2.00        .0536       .0633      .0633       23
     4                             2.21        .0851       .1077      .2900       26
     5                             1.83        .1219       .0648      .0588       15
     6                             3.61        .1505       .0742      .1265       24
     7                             1.03        .1291       .0518      .0188        8
     8                             2.11        .1917       .1253      .1570       11
     9                              .33        .1087       .0205      .0008        3
    10                             2.74        .1372       .1184      .2664       20
    11                             2.38        .1985       .1771      .3449       12
    12                              .58        .0975       .0602      .0181        6
    13                              .80        .1610       .1454      .0846        5
    14                              .25        .0835       .0522      .0055        3
    15                              .08        .0811       .0000      .0000        1

Within Groups Total              19.99        .1257       .0995     1.4348      159
```

34.10
MISSING Subcommand

By default, MEANS deletes cases with missing values on a tablewide basis. A case missing on any of the variables specified for a table is not used. Every case contained in a table will have a complete set of nonmissing values for all variables in that table. When you separate tables requests with a slash, missing values are handled separately for each list.

The MISSING subcommand controls missing values, and the following keywords can be specified on it:

TABLE *Delete cases with missing values on a tablewide basis.* This is the default if you omit the MISSING subcommand.

INCLUDE *Include user-defined missing values.* Handles user-defined missing values as if they were not missing.

DEPENDENT *Exclude cases with missing values for the dependent variable only.* A case is included if it has a valid value for the dependent variable, although it may have missing values for the independent variables. Missing values are ignored for control variables.

34.11
FORMAT Subcommand

By default, MEANS prints variable and value labels and the names and values of independent variables. All tables print in report format.

The FORMAT subcommand controls table formats, and the following keywords can be specified on it:

LABELS *Print both variable and value labels for each table.* This is the default if you omit the FORMAT subcommand.

NOLABELS *Suppress variable and value labels.*

NOCATLABS *Suppress value (category) labels.*

NAMES *Print the names of independent variables.* This is the default if you omit the FORMAT subcommand.

NONAMES *Suppress names of independent variables.*

VALUES *Print the values of independent variables.* This is the default if you omit the FORMAT subcommand.

NOVALUES *Suppress values of independent variables.* This is useful when there are category labels.

TABLE *Print each table in report format.* This is the default if you omit the FORMAT subcommand.

TREE *Print each table in tree format.* This option is available for general mode only (see below).

TREE Keyword. You can request a tree format for a MEANS table in general mode with the FORMAT=TREE specification. The individual cells of the MEANS table are printed as blocks. Figure 34.11 shows the tree format produced by the following commands:

```
MEANS  TABLES=PCTRAISE BY LOCATN81 BY GRADE81S
      /FORMAT=TREE
```

The first column of blocks contains the statistics for PCTRAISE by the first independent variable, LOCATN81. The second column shows the breakdown for PCTRAISE by GRADE81S within LOCATN81.

Figure 34.11 A tree-format MEANS table

```
      D E S C R I P T I O N   O F   S U B P O P U L A T I O N S

Criterion Variable    PCTRAISE
    Broken Down by    LOCATN81
                by    GRADE81S

For Entire Population
Mean            .1257
Std Dev         .1034
N               (159)

Variable   LOCATN81      Variable   GRADE81S

Code              1      Code           1.00
CHICAGO
Mean          .1200      Mean          .0817
Std Dev       .1094      Std Dev       .0910
N             (128)      N              (44)

                         Code           2.00

                         Mean          .1188
                         Std Dev       .0529
                         N              (34)

                         Code           3.00

                         Mean          .1545
                         Std Dev       .1391
                         N              (50)

Code              5      Code           1.00
ST. LOUIS
Mean          .1495      Mean          .0914
Std Dev       .0697      Std Dev       .0380
N              (31)      N               (7)

                         Code           2.00

                         Mean          .1874
                         Std Dev       .0794
                         N              (13)

                         Code           3.00

                         Mean          .1416
                         Std Dev       .0428
                         N              (11)

  Total Cases = 275
Missing Cases = 116 or   42.2 Pct
```

ANNOTATED EXAMPLE FOR MEANS

This example analyzes personnel data from Hubbard Consultants Inc., a small industrial consulting firm with headquarters in Chicago and a branch office in St. Louis. MEANS is used to examine salaries in 1981 by sex within department and job grade. The SPSS-X commands are

```
GET  FILE=HUB
RECODE  GRADE81 (1 THRU 4=1) (5 THRU 7=2) (8 THRU 15=3) (ELSE=COPY)
    INTO GRADE81S/
VALUE LABELS  GRADE81S  (1) GRADES 1-4 (2) GRADES 5-7 (3) GRADES 8-15
MISSING VALUES  GRADE81S(0)
MEANS  SALARY81 BY DEPT81 BY GRADE81S BY SEX
FINISH
```

- The GET command defines the data to SPSS-X and selects the variables needed for analysis (see Chapter 6).

- The RECODE command collapses the fifteen values of GRADE81 into three values and contains them in variable GRADE81S (see Chapter 7).

- The VALUE LABELS command assigns labels to the new variable GRADE81S (see Chapter 5).

- The MISSING VALUES command defines 0 as the missing value for GRADE81S (see Chapter 5).

- The MEANS command specifies a three-way breakdown of salaries in general mode. SALARY81 is the dependent variable (see Section 34.4).

- Since no missing-value option is specified, MEANS deletes cases with missing values on a tablewide basis.

Output from MEANS

```
               D E S C R I P T I O N   O F   S U B P O P U L A T I O N S

Criterion Variable   SALARY81     YEARLY SALARY IN 1981
     Broken Down by  DEPT81       DEPARTMENT CODE IN 1981
                by   GRADE81S
                by   SEX          EMPLOYEE'S SEX


Variable          Value  Label                  Mean     Std Dev   Cases

For Entire Population                         15096.2125  8074.3872    160

DEPT81              1    ADMIN                15537.8421  9810.5522     38
   GRADE81S      1.00    GRADES 1-4           10076.8333  1685.2658     12
      SEX           1    MALE                 10106.5455  1764.2221     11
      SEX           2    FEMALE                9750.0000     .0000      1

   GRADE81S      2.00    GRADES 5-7           11952.7333  2019.7453     15
      SEX           1    MALE                 13910.0000     .0000      1
      SEX           2    FEMALE               11812.9286  2019.2662     14

   GRADE81S      3.00    GRADES 8-15          26384.0909 12759.5664     11
      SEX           1    MALE                 34125.0000 15498.1047      5
      SEX           2    FEMALE               19933.3333  4858.3605      6

DEPT81              2    PROJECT DIRECTORS    15314.4286  8146.9522     28
   GRADE81S      1.00    GRADES 1-4           11340.5625  1999.6042     16
      SEX           1    MALE                 10583.9000  1143.2161     10
      SEX           2    FEMALE               12601.6667  2566.9469      6

   GRADE81S      2.00    GRADES 5-7           12826.6667  2015.3494      3
      SEX           2    FEMALE               12826.6667  2015.3494      3

   GRADE81S      3.00    GRADES 8-15          23208.3333 10558.8272      9
      SEX           1    MALE                 28613.0000 11587.9159      5
      SEX           2    FEMALE               16452.5000  2953.7674      4

DEPT81              3    CHICAGO OPERATIONS   14925.3016  7705.3167     63
   GRADE81S      1.00    GRADES 1-4            9922.1765  1536.2349     17
      SEX           1    MALE                 10458.5000   836.5073      2
      SEX           2    FEMALE                9850.6667  1612.6409     15

   GRADE81S      2.00    GRADES 5-7           12334.7500  2190.5735     16
      SEX           1    MALE                 13641.3333  3333.0827      3
      SEX           2    FEMALE               12033.2308  1903.0008     13

   GRADE81S      3.00    GRADES 8-15          19142.0333  9294.0232     30
      SEX           1    MALE                 28418.0000 15680.5949      5
      SEX           2    FEMALE               17286.8400  6471.7384     25

DEPT81              4    ST LOUIS OPERATIONS  14705.0968  6624.5319     31
   GRADE81S      1.00    GRADES 1-4            9445.4286   680.5620      7
      SEX           1    MALE                  9197.5000   873.2769      2
      SEX           2    FEMALE                9544.6000   679.0183      5

   GRADE81S      2.00    GRADES 5-7           12340.0000  1925.6254     13
      SEX           1    MALE                 11700.0000  1357.2398      3
      SEX           2    FEMALE               12532.0000  2087.3897     10

   GRADE81S      3.00    GRADES 8-15          20847.2727  7667.4707     11
      SEX           1    MALE                 21775.0000     .0000      1
      SEX           2    FEMALE               20754.5000  8075.7134     10

   Total Cases = 275
Missing Cases = 115 or  41.8 Pct
```

34.12
Narrow Output

If you set the width to 80 columns and the tables you request require more room, a fatal error occurs. (See Chapter 4 for a more complete discussion of SET WIDTH.) The exception is the CROSSBREAK format, where tables will wrap if they don't fit in the specified width.

If you specify a width of 80 columns, you can specify:

- All but two numeric columns.
- All but value labels.
- All but name and value (the categories are identified by the value labels only), and one numeric column.
- Up to 3 variables in tree format. If you request more and they cannot fit in 80 columns, a fatal error occurs.

If you want to print sums and variances, you should use the default width of 132 columns or set the width to 96 columns or more.

34.13
LIMITATIONS

The following limitations apply to MEANS in general mode:

- A maximum of 200 variables total per MEANS command.
- A maximum of 250 tables.
- A maximum of 6 dimensions per table.
- A maximum of 30 tables lists per MEANS command.
- A maximum of 200 value labels printed on any single table.

The following limitations apply to MEANS in integer mode:

- A maximum of 100 variables named or implied on the VARIABLES subcommand.
- A maximum of 100 variables named or implied on the TABLES subcommand.
- A maximum of 100 tables.
- A maximum of 6 dimensions per table.
- A maximum of 30 tables lists per MEANS command.
- A maximum of 200 nonempty rows and columns in a CROSSBREAK table.

Syntax

MULT RESPONSE

```
MULT RESPONSE GROUPS=groupname['label'](itemlist ({value1,value2}))...
                                              {value      }
                      [groupname...]
 /VARIABLES=itemlist(min,max) [itemlist...]
 /FREQUENCIES=itemlist
 /TABLES=itemlist BY itemlist... [BY itemlist] [(PAIRED)]
        [/itemlist BY...]
 [/MISSING=[{TABLE**}] [INCLUDE]]
            {MDGROUP}
            {MRGROUP}
 [/FORMAT={LABELS**}  {TABLE**  }]
          {NOLABELS}  {CONDENSE}
                      {ONEPAGE }
 [/BASE={CASES**   }]
        {RESPONSES}
 [/CELLS=[COUNT**] [ROW    ] [ALL]]
                   [COLUMN]
                   [TOTAL ]
```

**Default if the subcommand is omitted.

Contents

35.1   INTRODUCTION TO MULTIPLE RESPONSE ITEMS

35.2   Constructing Group Variables

35.3   Crosstabulations

35.4   OVERVIEW

35.5   OPERATION

35.6   GROUPS Subcommand

35.7   VARIABLES Subcommand

35.8   FREQUENCIES Subcommand

35.9   TABLES Subcommand

35.10 CELLS Subcommand

35.11 BASE Subcommand

35.12 MISSING Subcommand

35.13 FORMAT Subcommand

35.14 Stub and Banner Tables with the COUNT Command

35.15 LIMITATIONS

35

Chapter 35   MULT RESPONSE

Procedure MULT RESPONSE displays multiple response items in univariate tables and multivariate crosstabulations. *Multiple response items* are questions that can have more than one value for an individual case. For example, survey questions often ask respondents to indicate which magazines they read or to rank in importance a list of political issues. Variables that record these responses cannot be handled directly by procedures like FREQUENCIES and CROSS-TABS but are conveniently displayed in MULT RESPONSE tables.

35.1 INTRODUCTION TO MULTIPLE RESPONSE ITEMS

The example in this section illustrates the use of multiple response items in a marketing research survey. The data in these tables are fictitious and should not be interpreted as real.

An airline might survey passengers flying a particular route to evaluate competing carriers. In this example, American Airlines wants to know about its passengers' use of other airlines on the Chicago–New York route and the relative importance of schedule and service in selecting an airline. The flight attendant hands each passenger a brief questionnaire upon boarding which looks like Figure 35.1. The first question is a multiple response question because the passenger can circle more than one airline. However, this question cannot be coded directly because an SPSS-X variable can have only one value for each case. You must use several variables to map the responses to this question. There are two ways to do this. One is to define a variable corresponding to each of the choices (i.e., AMERICAN, UNITED, TWA, EASTERN, OTHER). If the passenger circles United, the UNITED variable is assigned a code of 1, otherwise 0. This is the *multiple dichotomy method* of mapping variables.

Figure 35.1   An in-flight questionnaire

Circle *all* airlines that you have flown at least one time
in the last six months on this route:

  American   United   TWA   Eastern Other:_____

Which is more important in selecting a flight?

  Schedule   Service

(Circle only one.)

Thank you for your cooperation.

The other way to map the responses is the *multiple response method*, in which you estimate the maximum number of possible responses to the question and set up the same number of variables, with codes used to specify the airline flown. By perusing a sample of the questionnaires, you might discover that no user has flown more than three different airlines on this route in the last six months. Further, you find that, due to the deregulation of airlines, 10 other airlines are named in the OTHER category. Using the multiple response method, you would define three variables, coded as 1=American, 2=United, 3=TWA, 4=Eastern, 5=Republic, 6=USAir, and so on. If a given passenger circles TWA and American, the first variable has a code of 1, the second has a code of 3, and the third variable has some missing-value code. Another passenger might have circled American and entered USAir. Thus, the first variable has a code of 1, the second a code of 6, and the third a missing-value code. If you use the multiple dichotomy method, you end up with 14 separate variables to map no more than three responses per passenger. Although either method of mapping multiple answers is feasible for this survey, the method you choose depends upon the distribution of responses.

35.2
Constructing Group Variables

Each variable created from the survey question about airlines is an *elementary variable*. To analyze a multiple response item, you must combine the elementary variables into *groups*. The specific technique for grouping variables depends on whether you have defined multiple dichotomy variables or multiple response variables. For example, if the airline survey asks only about three airlines (American, United, TWA) and you use multiple dichotomies to account for multiple responses, the separate frequency tables would resemble Table 35.2a. When you create a multiple dichotomy group, each of the three variables becomes a category of the group variable. The tabulated values represent the "Have flown" category of each elementary variable. Table 35.2b shows the frequencies for this multiple dichotomy group. The 75 people using American Airlines are the 75 cases with code 1 for the variable representing American Airlines in Table 35.2a. Because some people circled more than one response, 120 responses are recorded for 100 respondents.

Table 35.2a Dichotomies tabulated separately

American

Category Label	Code	Frequency	Relative Frequency
Have flown	1	75	75.0
Have not flown	0	25	25.0
	Total	100	100.0

United

Category Label	Code	Frequency	Relative Frequency
Have flown	1	30	30.0
Have not flown	0	70	70.0
	Total	100	100.0

TWA

Category Label	Code	Frequency	Relative Frequency
Have flown	1	15	15.0
Have not flown	0	85	85.0
	Total	100	100.0

Table 35.2b   Multiple dichotomies tabulated as a group

Airlines
(Tabulating 1)

Variable	Frequency	Relative Frequency
American	75	62.5
United	30	25.0
TWA	15	12.5
Total	120	100.0

If you discover that no respondent mentioned more than two airlines, you could create two multiple response variables, each having three codes, one for each airline. The frequency tables for these elementary variables would resemble Table 35.2c. When you create a multiple response group, the values are tabulated by adding the same codes in the elementary variables together. The resulting set of values is the same as those for each of the elementary variables. Table 35.2d shows the frequencies for this multiple response group. For example, the 30 responses for United are the sum of the 25 United responses for the multiple response item Airline 1 and the five United responses for Airline 2.

Table 35.2c   Multiple response items tabulated separately

Airline 1

Category Label	Code	Frequency	Relative Frequency
American	1	75	75.0
United	2	25	25.0
Total		100	100.0

Airline 2

Category Label	Code	Frequency	Relative Frequency
United	2	5	5.0
TWA	3	15	15.0
Missing	99	80	80.0
Total		100	100.0

Table 35.2d   Multiple response items tabulated as a group

Airlines

Category Label	Code	Frequency	Relative Frequency
American	1	75	62.5
United	2	30	25.0
TWA	3	15	12.5
Total		120	100.0

35.3
Crosstabulations

Both multiple dichotomy and multiple response groups can be crosstabulated with other variables in MULT RESPONSE. In the airline passenger survey, the airline choices can be crosstabulated with the question asking why people choose different airlines. If you have organized the first question into dichotomies as in Table 35.2a, the three crosstabulations of the dichotomy variables with the schedule/service question would resemble Table 35.3a. If you had chosen the multiple response group method and created two multiple response variables, the two crosstabulations would resemble Table 35.3b. With either method, the crosstabulation of the elementary variable and the group variable would resemble Table 35.3c. Each row in Table 35.3c is the "Have flown" row for the three dichotomy variables. Like codes are added together for the multiple response group. For example, 21 respondents have flown United and think schedule is most important in selecting a flight. The 21 cases are a combination of 20 people who flew United as Airline 1 and circled Schedule plus one person who flew United as Airline 2 and circled Schedule.

Table 35.3a   Dichotomies crosstabulated separately

American

		Schedule	Service	Row Total
Have flown		41	34	75
Have not flown		20	5	25
	Column Total	61	39	100

United

		Schedule	Service	Row Total
Have flown		21	9	30
Have not flown		40	30	70
	Column Total	61	39	100

TWA

		Schedule	Service	Row Total
Have flown		8	7	15
Have not flown		53	32	85
	Column Total	61	39	100

Table 35.3b   Multiple response variables crosstabulated separately

Airline 1

		Schedule	Service	Row Total
American		41	34	75
United		20	5	25
	Column Total	61	39	100

Airline 2

		Schedule	Service	Row Total
United		1	4	5
TWA		8	7	15
Missing		52	28	80
	Column Total	61	39	100

Table 35.3c   A group crosstabulated

Airlines

	Schedule	Service	Row Total
American	41	34	75
United	21	9	30
TWA	8	7	15
Column Total	61	39	100

35.4 OVERVIEW

MULT RESPONSE combines elementary variables into multiple dichotomy groups and multiple response groups to produce univariate tables and multivariate crosstabulations for these groups and elementary SPSS-X variables. In addition to the tables, you can specify percentaging, formatting, and missing-value options and create stub and banner tables.

Cell Counts and Percentages. By default, crosstabulations do not include any percentages. You can request row, column, and total table percentages. Optionally, you can also base percentages on responses instead of respondents. (See Section 35.10.)

Missing Values. By default, MULT RESPONSE excludes cases with missing values on a table-by-table basis. Optionally, you can request that user-missing values be handled as if they were not missing or that cases be deleted listwise from the tabulation of group variables. (See Section 35.12.)

Formatting Options. You can suppress the printing of value labels, print tables on an 8½-by-11-inch page, and request condensed-format frequency tables. (See Section 35.13.)

Stub and Banner Tables. With appropriate data transformations, you can create tables with more than one variable in each dimension. You can do this with the COUNT command. (See Section 35.14.)

35.5 OPERATION

Procedure MULT RESPONSE operates via "major" and optional subcommands. The major subcommands (GROUPS, VARIABLES, FREQUENCIES, and TABLES) define the groups and variables that will be included in your analysis and determine the type of table display used for the tabulation. They are discussed in Sections 35.6 through 35.9.

You must use at least two of the four major subcommands: either the GROUPS subcommand to define one or more groups or the VARIABLES subcommand to define elementary variables, and either the FREQUENCIES or TABLES subcommand to request tables. You must specify those major subcommands you use in the following order: GROUPS, VARIABLES, FREQUENCIES, TABLES.

You can also use three or all four major subcommands. However, you can only specify each major subcommand once per MULT RESPONSE command.

To specify a major subcommand, use the appropriate subcommand followed by an optional equals sign and the desired group name or item list. Separate subcommands with slashes.

• The GROUPS subcommand names groups of multiple response items to be analyzed and determines how the variables will be combined. (See Section 35.6.)

• The VARIABLES subcommand identifies all elementary variables to be analyzed. (See Section 35.7.)

• The FREQUENCIES subcommand requests frequency tables for items identified by the GROUPS and VARIABLES subcommands. (See Section 35.8.)

• The TABLES subcommand requests the crosstabulation of items identified by the GROUPS and VARIABLES subcommands. (See Section 35.9.)

MULT RESPONSE has four optional subcommands:

• CELLS prints cell counts and percentages. (See Section 35.10.)
• BASE bases cell percentages on respondents. (See Section 35.11.)
• MISSING controls missing values. (See Section 35.12.)
• FORMAT controls formatting options. (See Section multhd18..)

All major subcommands must precede all optional subcommands. You can specify the optional subcommands in any order.

To specify an optional subcommand, use the appropriate subcommand followed by an optional equals sign and the desired keyword. Separate multiple keywords on a single subcommand with at least one space or comma. Separate subcommands with slashes. For example, to include user-defined missing values in an analysis, specify

```
MULT RESPONSE  GROUPS=MAGS 'MAGAZINES READ' (TIME TO STONE (2))
   /FREQUENCIES=MAGS
   /MISSING=INCLUDE
```

35.6
GROUPS Subcommand

The GROUPS subcommand defines both *multiple dichotomy* and *multiple response* groups. You must specify a name for the group, with an optional label, followed by a list of the elementary variables in the group and the value(s) to be used in the tabulation. Enclose the variable list in parentheses and enclose the values in an inner set of parentheses following the last variable in the list. The elementary variables must have integer values. You can specify up to 20 groups. You can name or imply up to 100 elementary variables on the GROUPS and VARIABLES subcommands together.

For example, assume that you have data from a survey on magazine readership. Since a respondent may read several different magazines, readership is a multiple response question. This question can be coded as a series of dichotomies about specific magazines. Alternatively, you may give the respondent a list of magazines and ask which ones are read. If the magazines are coded as a series of dichotomies, you can use the elementary variables as controls in crosstabulation or as selection variables. On the other hand, if the list is lengthy (for example, 100 magazines plus open-ended items) and the average number of magazines read is moderate, you may choose the multiple response coding scheme. If the most well-read respondent reads five different magazines, then the coding scheme must allow for five variables representing magazines read. In the following command, the GROUPS subcommand creates MAGS, a *multiple dichotomy group*:

```
MULT RESPONSE  GROUPS=MAGS 'MAGAZINES READ' (TIME TO STONE (2))
   /FREQUENCIES=MAGS
```

The group label, 'MAGAZINES READ', is optional and can be up to 40 characters in length, including imbedded blanks. For compatibility with other types of SPSS-X labels, apostrophes are used to delimit the label, but they are not required. The group MAGS is tabulated from all the variables between and including TIME and STONE. Use the keyword TO to name an adjacent set of variables in the active file. To define a multiple dichotomy group, specify only one tabulating value following the variable list. Each elementary variable becomes a value of the group variable and the number of cases that have the tabulating value becomes the frequency. However, if no case has the tabulating value for a given component variable, that variable does not appear in the tabulation.

A *multiple response group* requires minimum and maximum values to define the inclusive range for the elementary variables in the group. In this case the group variable takes on the same range of values as the elementary variables. The frequencies for these values are tabulated across all the elementary variables in the list. For example, the command

```
MULT RESPONSE   GROUPS=PROBS 'PERCEIVED NATIONAL PROBLEMS'
   (PROB1 TO PROB3 (1,9))
   /FREQUENCIES=PROBS
```

defines the multiple response group PROBS using the elementary variables between and including PROB1 and PROB3. Values from 1 to 9 are used to tabulate the group variable. Totally empty categories are not printed in either frequency or crosstabular tables.

MULT RESPONSE builds tables in the same manner as the integer mode in procedures FREQUENCIES (Chapter 29) and CROSSTABS (Chapter 25). Therefore, if you define a multiple response group with a very wide range, the tables require substantial amounts of workspace. If the component variables are sparsely distributed, you might consider recoding them to minimize the workspace required.

You can use any valid SPSS-X variable name for the group. The group name should be unique; however, you may reuse an existing variable name, provided both the elementary variable and group variable are not specified in the same MULT RESPONSE command. The group names and labels exist only during the execution of MULT RESPONSE and disappear once MULT RESPONSE has been executed. Reference to the group names in other procedures results in errors.

35.7
VARIABLES Subcommand

The VARIABLES subcommand names elementary variables used in frequencies tables and crosstabulations. The VARIABLES subcommand follows the GROUPS subcommand. The following example uses the VARIABLES subcommand to name variables SEX and EDUC so they can be used in a frequencies table:

```
MULT RESPONSE  GROUPS=MAGS 'MAGAZINES READ' (TIME TO STONE (2))
   /VARIABLES SEX(1,2) EDUC(1,3)
   /FREQUENCIES=MAGS SEX EDUC
```

The VARIABLES subcommand has the same specification field in MULT RESPONSE as in FREQUENCIES (Chapter 29), CROSSTABS (Chapter 25), and MEANS (Chapter 34). Each variable is followed by a minimum and maximum value in parentheses. To provide the same minimums and maximums for a set of variables, specify a variable list followed by a range specification. You can also use the keyword TO to name a set of adjacent variables on the active file. The minimums and maximums allocate cells for tables that use the elementary variables named on the VARIABLES subcommand. You can specify any numeric variables with the VARIABLES subcommand, but nonintegers are truncated.

The items named by the GROUPS subcommand can be used in frequencies tables and crosstabulations, but you must name them again with the VARIABLES subcommand, along with a range for the values. For example, to use the variable TIME as an item in a group and also use it in a table, specify:

```
MULT RESPONSE  GROUPS=MAGS 'MAGAZINES READ' (TIME TO STONE (2))
   /VARIABLES=EDUC (1,3) TIME (1,2)
   /TABLES=MAGS BY EDUC TIME
```

You do not have to respecify the items in the groups if they will not be used in any tables.

You may wish to use MULT RESPONSE only to produce crosstabulations of elementary variables in order to take advantage of its special formatting options. In that case, the GROUPS subcommand is not required and the VARIABLES subcommand becomes the first subcommand.

ANNOTATED EXAMPLE FOR MULT RESPONSE

This example analyzes a 465-case sample from a survey about magazine readership and organizational memberships. The variables are

- TIME, NEWSWEEK, U.S.NEWS, STONE, REPUBLIC—dichotomous variables which show whether the respondent regularly read *Time*, *Newsweek*, *U.S. News and World Report*, *Rolling Stone*, or *New Republic* magazines.
- PROB1, PROB2, PROB3—elementary variables created from a multiple response item asking the respondent to name three national problems from a list of nine problems.
- EDUC—the respondent's education, coded in three categories.
- SEX—the respondent's sex, coded 1=male, 2=female.

This example examines the distribution of magazine readership and national problems by education and sex. The SPSS-X commands are

```
GET  FILE=MRESFILE
MULT RESPONSE  GROUPS=MAGS 'MAGAZINES READ' (TIME TO REPUBLIC (2))
   PROBS 'NATIONAL PROBLEMS MENTIONED' (PROB1 TO PROB3 (1,9))
   /VARIABLES=EDUC (1,3) SEX (1,2)
   /TABLES=EDUC SEX BY MAGS PROBS
   /CELLS=COLUMN
FINISH
```

- The GET command defines the data to SPSS-X and selects the variables needed for analysis (see Chapter 6).
- The MULT RESPONSE command creates a multiple dichotomy group, MAGS, from the elementary variables between and including TIME and REPUBLIC, and creates a multiple response group, PROBS, from the elementary variables between and including PROB1 and PROB3. Two other elementary variables, EDUC and SEX, are referenced on the VARIABLES subcommand. The TABLES subcommand requests four crosstabulations: EDUC by MAGS, EDUC by PROBS, SEX by MAGS, and SEX by PROBS.
- The CELLS subcommand requests column percentages in the tables.

A Output from the MULT RESPONSE command

```
                    * * *  C R O S S T A B U L A T I O N  * * *
        EDUC      HIGHEST EDUCATIONAL ATTAINMENT OF RESP
     BY MAGS      (TABULATING    2) MAGAZINES READ

                  MAGS
                  COUNT  IREADS TI READS NE READS U. READS RO READS RE
                  COL PCT IME REGUL WSWEEK R S. NEWS  LLING ST PUBLIC R  ROW
                         IARLY     EGUL    & WO      ONE      EGUL     TOTAL
                         ITIME    INEWSWEEKIU.S.NEWSISTONE    IREPUBLICI
     EDUC         -------+--------+--------+--------+--------+--------+
                     1  I     23 I     23 I      0 I      0 I      0 I    46
     GRADE SCHOOL     I   13.0 I   12.0 I    0.0 I    0.0 I    0.0 I  12.4
                    -------+--------+--------+--------+--------+--------+
                     2  I     46 I     60 I     37 I    115 I     30 I   145
     HIGH SCHOOL      I   26.0 I   31.4 I   20.4 I  100.0 I   32.3 I  39.1
                    -------+--------+--------+--------+--------+--------+
                     3  I    108 I    108 I    144 I      0 I     63 I   180
     COLLEGE          I   61.0 I   56.5 I   79.6 I    0.0 I   67.7 I  48.5
                    -------+--------+--------+--------+--------+--------+
                  COLUMN     177      191      181      115       93      371
                   TOTAL    47.7     51.5     48.8     31.0     25.1    100.0

     PERCENTS AND TOTALS BASED ON RESPONDENTS

        371 VALID CASES        94 MISSING CASES
```

```
          * * *  C R O S S T A B U L A T I O N  * * *

   EDUC     HIGHEST EDUCATIONAL ATTAINMENT OF RESP
   BY PROBS (GROUP) NATIONAL PROBLEMS MENTIONED
```

		RECESSIO N	INFLATIO N	LACK OF RELIGION	WATERGAT E	RACIAL C ONFLICT	UNIONS T OO STRON G	BIG BUSI NESS	COMMUNIS T AGGRES SION	WEATHER	ROW TOTAL
COUNT COL PCT		1	2	3	4	5	6	7	8	9	
EDUC GRADE SCHOOL	1	32	0	23	0	69	0	32	0	39	124
		26.9	0.0	15.3	0.0	75.0	0.0	22.7	0.0	59.1	27.6
HIGH SCHOOL	2	60	108	37	30	23	0	55	30	0	145
		50.4	75.0	24.7	23.3	25.0	0.0	39.0	21.7	0.0	32.3
COLLEGE	3	27	36	90	99	0	9	54	108	27	180
		22.7	25.0	60.0	76.7	0.0	100.0	38.3	78.3	40.9	40.1
COLUMN TOTAL		119 26.5	144 32.1	150 33.4	129 28.7	92 20.5	9 2.0	141 31.4	138 30.7	66 14.7	449 100.0

```
PERCENTS AND TOTALS BASED ON RESPONDENTS

   449 VALID CASES          16 MISSING CASES
```

```
          * * *  C R O S S T A B U L A T I O N  * * *

   SEX      OBSERVED SEX OF RESPONDENT
   BY MAGS  (TABULATING   2) MAGAZINES READ
```

		READS TI ME REGUL IARLY ITIME	READS NE WSWEEK R EGUL INEWSWEEK	READS U. S. NEWS & WO IU.S.NEWS	READS RO LLING ST ONE ISTONE	READS RE PUBLIC R EGUL IREPUBLIC	ROW TOTAL
COUNT COL PCT		1	2	3	4	5	
SEX MALE	1	82	119	64	92	66	208
		46.3	62.3	35.4	70.2	71.0	53.7
FEMALE	2	95	72	117	39	27	179
		53.7	37.7	64.6	29.8	29.0	46.3
COLUMN TOTAL		177 45.7	191 49.4	181 46.8	131 33.9	93 24.0	387 100.0

```
PERCENTS AND TOTALS BASED ON RESPONDENTS

   387 VALID CASES          78 MISSING CASES
```

```
          * * *  C R O S S T A B U L A T I O N  * * *

   SEX      OBSERVED SEX OF RESPONDENT
   BY PROBS (GROUP) NATIONAL PROBLEMS MENTIONED
```

		RECESSIO N	INFLATIO N	LACK OF RELIGION	WATERGAT E	RACIAL C ONFLICT	UNIONS T OO STRON G	BIG BUSI NESS	COMMUNIS T AGGRES SION	WEATHER	ROW TOTAL
COUNT COL PCT		1	2	3	4	5	6	7	8	9	
SEX MALE	1	37	78	87	84	62	9	93	66	39	231
		31.1	54.2	58.0	65.1	67.4	100.0	66.0	47.8	59.1	51.4
FEMALE	2	82	66	63	45	30	0	48	72	27	218
		68.9	45.8	42.0	34.9	32.6	0.0	34.0	52.2	40.9	48.6
COLUMN TOTAL		119 26.5	144 32.1	150 33.4	129 28.7	92 20.5	9 2.0	141 31.4	138 30.7	66 14.7	449 100.0

```
PERCENTS AND TOTALS BASED ON RESPONDENTS

   449 VALID CASES          16 MISSING CASES
```

35.8
FREQUENCIES
Subcommand

The FREQUENCIES subcommand requests frequency tables for groups and elementary variables. All groups must be created by the GROUPS subcommand and all elementary variables must be named on the VARIABLES subcommand. The following commands produce a frequency table for a multiple dichotomy group:

```
MULT RESPONSE  GROUPS=MAGS 'MAGAZINES READ' (TIME TO STONE (2))
   /FREQUENCIES=MAGS
```

Figure 35.8a shows the frequencies for the "2" or "Yes" responses to the four dichotomy variables comprising the multiple dichotomy group MAGS. The category labels come from the variable labels defined for the four elementary variables. The NAME column gives the names of variables in the group. The first column of percentages is based on the number of responses and always sums to 100. The second column of percentages is based on the number of respondents or valid cases. These percentages may sum to as high as $n \times 100$, where n is the number of elementary variables comprising the group, since each case can contribute n times to the frequencies. If you want the percentage of cases based upon the survey sample size, include a category to account for cases missing on all dichotomy variables. If an individual reads none of the four magazines, the case is missing for the group.

Figure 35.8a A multiple dichotomy frequency table

```
GROUP MAGS       MAGAZINES READ
     (VALUE TABULATED =     2)

                                                      PCT OF  PCT OF
DICHOTOMY LABEL                       NAME     COUNT  RESPONSES  CASES

READS TIME REGULARLY                  TIME      177    26.0    45.7

READS NEWSWEEK REGULARLY              NEWSWEEK  191    28.1    49.4

READS U.S. NEWS & WORLD REPORT REGULARLY  U.S.NEWS  181    26.6    46.8

READS ROLLING STONE REGULARLY         STONE     131    19.3    33.9
                                                     -----  -----  -----
                            TOTAL RESPONSES    680   100.0   175.7

     78 MISSING CASES         387 VALID CASES
```

These commands produce a frequency table for a multiple response group:

```
MULT RESPONSE  GROUPS=PROBS 'NATIONAL PROBLEMS MENTIONED' (PROB1 TO
   PROB3 (1,9))/ FREQUENCIES=PROBS
```

The frequencies in Figure 35.8b are summed for each value across the component variables in the PROBS multiple response group. The category labels come from the value labels attached to the *first* variable in the group. If categories are missing for the first variable but are present for other variables in the group, define a value label for the missing categories. Percentages based on responses and respondents are printed. A case is missing for the group if it is missing for *all* the component variables in the group.

You can use the keyword TO only to imply a set of adjacent items *of the same type* whose order is determined by the order in which they were named on either the GROUPS or VARIABLES subcommands. For example, the command

```
MULT RESPONSE
   GROUPS=MAGS 'MAGAZINES READ' (TIME TO STONE (2))
          PROBS 'PERCEIVED NATIONAL PROBLEMS' (PROB1 TO PROB3 (1,9))
          MEMS 'SOCIAL ORGANIZATION MEMBERSHIPS' (VFW AMLEG ELKS (1))
   /VARIABLES SEX(1,2) EDUC(1,3)
   /FREQUENCIES=MAGS TO MEMS SEX EDUC
```

specifies frequency tables for MAGS, PROBS, MEMS, SEX, and EDUC. You cannot specify MAGS TO EDUC because SEX and EDUC are elementary variables, while MAGS, PROBS, and MEMS are group variables.

Figure 35.8b   A multiple response frequency table

```
GROUP PROBS      NATIONAL PROBLEMS MENTIONED

                                                    PCT OF   PCT OF
CATEGORY LABEL                          CODE  COUNT  RESPONSES  CASES

RECESSION                                 1    119   12.0     26.5

INFLATION                                 2    144   14.6     32.1

LACK OF RELIGION                          3    150   15.2     33.4

WATERGATE                                 4    129   13.1     28.7

RACIAL CONFLICT                           5     92    9.3     20.5

UNIONS TOO STRONG                         6      9    0.9      2.0

BIG BUSINESS                              7    141   14.3     31.4

COMMUNIST AGGRESSION                      8    138   14.0     30.7

WEATHER                                   9     66    6.7     14.7
                                              ----   -----    -----
                           TOTAL RESPONSES     988  100.0    220.0

       16 MISSING CASES        449 VALID CASES
```

35.9
TABLES Subcommand

The TABLES subcommand names the crosstabulations to be produced by MULT RESPONSE and follows the FREQUENCIES subcommand (when used). The TABLES subcommand specification field is exactly the same as the TABLES subcommands for CROSSTABS (Chapter 25) and MEANS (Chapter 34). Both elementary and group items can be tabulated together. You can specify up to five dimensions for a table. Use the keyword BY to separate the dimensions. The first item list defines the rows of the tables; the next item list defines the columns of the tables. Subsequent item lists define controls producing subtables.

The following commands produce a crosstabulation of an elementary variable by a multiple dichotomy group:

```
MULT RESPONSE  GROUPS=MAGS 'MAGAZINES READ' (TIME TO STONE (2))
   /VARIABLES=EDUC (1,3)/TABLES=EDUC BY MAGS
   /CELLS=ALL
```

The CELLS subcommand (Section 35.10) requests row, column, and two-way table total percentages.

In Figure 35.9a, the rows correspond to categories of the variable EDUC and the columns correspond to the components of the multiple dichotomy group MAGS. The labels for the group variable include the elementary variable name and its variable label. The value labels for the columns print on three lines with eight characters per line. To avoid splitting words, you can reverse the row and column variables or redefine the variable labels. Although Figure 35.9a appears to be a standard crosstabulation, the relationship between cells and marginals is less straightforward. Row and column marginals are *respondents,* but cell frequencies are *responses.* Because MAGS is a group variable, a case may appear in more than one cell within a row. In this example the row frequencies for people with a high-school education sum to 258 (46+60+37+115). However, only 145 respondents have a high-school education (as indicated by the row marginal). Therefore, the average high-school graduate must read more than one of the four magazines. Note also that the column marginals sum to more than 371. Because EDUC is an elementary variable, column frequencies sum to the column total. By default, MULT RESPONSE bases percentages on respondents (cases). Thus, some of the row percentages also sum to over 100. You may choose to base percentages on responses (see Section 35.10).

Figure 35.9a   A dichotomy group tabulated with a simple variable

```
           * * *  C R O S S T A B U L A T I O N  * * *

   EDUC        HIGHEST EDUCATIONAL ATTAINMENT OF RESP
BY MAGS        (TABULATING    2) MAGAZINES READ


               MAGS

            COUNT   IREADS TI READS NE READS U. READS RO
            ROW PCT IME REGUL WSWEEK R S. NEWS LLING ST   ROW
            COL PCT IARLY     EGUL     & WO     ONE       TOTAL
            TAB PCT ITIME    INEWSWEEKIU.S.NEWSISTONE   I
EDUC                --------+--------+--------+--------+
               1  I    23  I    23  I     0  I     0  I     46
  GRADE SCHOOL    I  50.0  I  50.0  I   0.0  I   0.0  I   12.4
                  I  13.0  I  12.0  I   0.0  I   0.0  I
                  I   6.2  I   6.2  I   0.0  I   0.0  I
                  +--------+--------+--------+--------+
               2  I    46  I    60  I    37  I   115  I    145
  HIGH SCHOOL     I  31.7  I  41.4  I  25.5  I  79.3  I   39.1
                  I  26.0  I  31.4  I  20.4  I 100.0  I
                  I  12.4  I  16.2  I  10.0  I  31.0  I
                  +--------+--------+--------+--------+
               3  I   108  I   108  I   144  I     0  I    180
  COLLEGE         I  60.0  I  60.0  I  80.0  I   0.0  I   48.5
                  I  61.0  I  56.5  I  79.6  I   0.0  I
                  I  29.1  I  29.1  I  38.8  I   0.0  I
                  +--------+--------+--------+--------+
              COLUMN   177      191      181      115      371
              TOTAL   47.7     51.5     48.8     31.0    100.0

PERCENTS AND TOTALS BASED ON RESPONDENTS

   371 VALID CASES           94 MISSING CASES
```

The following commands tabulate a multiple dichotomy group with a multiple response group, shown in Figure 35.9b:

```
MULT RESPONSE  GROUPS=MAGS 'MAGAZINES READ' (TIME TO STONE (2))
   PROBS 'NATIONAL PROBLEMS MENTIONED' (PROB1 TO PROB3 (1,9))
   /TABLES=MAGS BY PROBS
   /CELLS=ALL
```

Because both the row and column variables are groups, neither row nor column totals sum to the sample size, and percentages exceed 100. This table also includes table percentages within the cells.

Each cell in a MULT RESPONSE crosstabulation is created by adding together the individual cells of a number of component crosstabulations. Cells corresponding to the tabulated values are combined to build the printed table. Multiple response groups are formed by adding the cells for like values. Thus, when a multiple response group is crosstabulated, MULT RESPONSE adds together the cells from the components to produce the printed table containing multiple response groups. For example, in Figure 35.9b, the cell in the upper-left corner of the crosstabulation has 23 cases. This is the number of respondents who read *Time* regularly and named "Recession" as PROB1, PROB2, or PROB3.

Figure 35.9b Two groups tabulated together

```
            * * * C R O S S T A B U L A T I O N * * *

   MAGS      (TABULATING     2) MAGAZINES READ
BY PROBS      (GROUP) NATIONAL PROBLEMS MENTIONED


               PROBS
          COUNT IRECESSIO INFLATIO LACK OF  WATERGAT RACIAL C UNIONS T BIG BUSI COMMUNIS WEATHER
          ROW PCT IN       N        RELIGION E        ONFLICT  OO STRON NESS     T AGGRES          ROW
          COL PCT I                                            G                 SION             TOTAL
          TAB PCT I    1 I    2 I    3 I    4 I    5 I    6 I    7 I    8 I    9 I
MAGS          +--------+--------+--------+--------+--------+--------+--------+--------+--------+
        TIME  I    23 I   55 I   72 I  102 I    0 I    9 I   43 I   84 I   27 I    177
READS TIME REGULARLY I 13.0 I 31.1 I 40.7 I 57.6 I  0.0 I  5.1 I 24.3 I 47.5 I 15.3 I   47.7
              I 20.9 I 38.2 I 56.7 I 79.1 I  0.0 I100.0 I 39.4 I 60.9 I 54.0 I
              I  6.2 I 14.8 I 19.4 I 27.5 I  0.0 I  2.4 I 11.6 I 22.6 I  7.3 I
              +--------+--------+--------+--------+--------+--------+--------+--------+--------+
      NEWSWEEK I   37 I   32 I  109 I   72 I   23 I    9 I   27 I   54 I   50 I    191
READS NEWSWEEK REGUL I 19.4 I 16.8 I 57.1 I 37.7 I 12.0 I  4.7 I 14.1 I 28.3 I 26.2 I   51.5
              I 33.6 I 22.2 I 85.8 I 55.8 I100.0 I100.0 I 24.8 I 39.1 I100.0 I
              I 10.0 I  8.6 I 29.4 I 19.4 I  6.2 I  2.4 I  7.3 I 14.6 I 13.5 I
              +--------+--------+--------+--------+--------+--------+--------+--------+--------+
      U.S.NEWS I   64 I   27 I  100 I   72 I    0 I    0 I   27 I   99 I   27 I    181
READS U.S. NEWS & WO I 35.4 I 14.9 I 55.2 I 39.8 I  0.0 I  0.0 I 14.9 I 54.7 I 14.9 I   48.8
              I 58.2 I 18.8 I 78.7 I 55.8 I  0.0 I  0.0 I 24.8 I 71.7 I 54.0 I
              I 17.3 I  7.3 I 27.0 I 19.4 I  0.0 I  0.0 I  7.3 I 26.7 I  7.3 I
              +--------+--------+--------+--------+--------+--------+--------+--------+--------+
        STONE I   60 I   78 I   37 I    0 I   23 I    0 I   55 I    0 I    0 I    115
READS ROLLING STONE I 52.2 I 67.8 I 32.2 I  0.0 I 20.0 I  0.0 I 47.8 I  0.0 I  0.0 I   31.0
              I 54.5 I 54.2 I 29.1 I  0.0 I100.0 I  0.0 I 50.5 I  0.0 I  0.0 I
              I 16.2 I 21.0 I 10.0 I  0.0 I  6.2 I  0.0 I 14.8 I  0.0 I  0.0 I
              +--------+--------+--------+--------+--------+--------+--------+--------+--------+
        COLUMN     110     144     127     129     23      9     109     138     50     371
        TOTAL     29.6    38.8    34.2    34.8    6.2    2.4    29.4    37.2   13.5   100.0

PERCENTS AND TOTALS BASED ON RESPONDENTS

   371 VALID CASES         94 MISSING CASES
```

If you crosstabulate two groups, MULT RESPONSE tabulates all components of the first group with all components of the second group, pooling the responses. Alternatively, you can pair the first variable in the first group with the first variable in the second group, the second variable in the first group with the second variable in the second group, and so on.

To produce more than one table, name one or more items for each dimension of the tables. Use the keyword TO to imply a set of adjacent variables of the same type, as described for the FREQUENCIES subcommand. The following example specifies two crosstabulations:

```
MULT RESPONSE  GROUPS=MAGS 'MAGAZINES READ' (TIME TO STONE (2))
    MEMS 'SOCIAL ORGANIZATION MEMBERSHIPS' (VFW AMLEG ELKS (1))
    /VARIABLES EDUC (1,3)/TABLES=MEMS MAGS BY EDUC
```

You can specify up to 10 tables lists on one MULT RESPONSE command. By using both the FREQUENCIES subcommand and all the tables lists on the TABLES subcommand, you can name or imply a maximum of 100 groups and elementary variables. Use a slash to separate each tables list, as in

```
MULT RESPONSE  GROUPS=MAGS 'MAGAZINES READ' (TIME TO STONE (2))
    /VARIABLES SEX (1,2) EDUC (1,3)
    /TABLES=MAGS BY EDUC SEX/EDUC BY SEX
```

which produces two tables from the first tables list and one table from the second tables list.

PAIRED Keyword. By default, when MULT RESPONSE tabulates one multiple response group with another, it tabulates each variable in the first group with each variable in the second group and sums the counts for each cell. In the example above about magazine readership, this kind of tabulation gives useful cell frequencies. However, other types of problems may require a more selective crosstabulation. For example, a file about pregnancies, where each case is a mother, contains information for up to three pregnancies. P1SEX, P2SEX, and P3SEX are variables for the sex of each child born to the mother. P1AGE,

P2AGE, and P3AGE are variables for the age of the mother at the onset of each pregnancy, recoded into four categories. The following MULT RESPONSE command defines two multiple response groups, PSEX and PAGE:

```
MULT RESPONSE  GROUPS=PSEX 'SEX OF CHILD' (P1SEX P2SEX P3SEX (1,2))
    PAGE 'AGE OF ONSET OF PREGNANCY' (P1AGE P2AGE P3AGE (1,4))
    /TABLES=PSEX BY PAGE
```

If you tabulate PSEX with PAGE, a case with information on three pregnancies would occur in nine component tables,

> P1SEX BY P1AGE
> P1SEX BY P2AGE
> P1SEX BY P3AGE
> .
> .
> .
> P3SEX BY P3AGE

and would produce the crosstabulation in Figure 35.9c. If a mother had two boys and two pregnancies between ages 20 and 24, she would appear four times in the summed table. This may not be the information you desire. Rather, you might be interested in the number of male births occurring for pregnancies beginning between ages 20 and 24. In effect, this table is the sum of three tables:

> P1SEX BY P1AGE
> P2SEX BY P2AGE
> P3SEX BY P3AGE

To produce this type of table for two multiple response groups, use the special keyword PAIRED in parentheses on the TABLES subcommand following the last variable named for a specific tables list. The command

```
MULT RESPONSE  GROUPS=PSEX 'SEX OF CHILD' (P1SEX P2SEX P3SEX (1,2))
    /PAGE 'AGE OF ONSET OF PREGNANCY' (P1AGE P2AGE P3AGE (1,4))
    /TABLES=PSEX BY PAGE (PAIRED)
```

produces a paired crosstabulation of PSEX by PAGE, shown in Figure 35.9d.

Figure 35.9c A crosstabulation of two groups

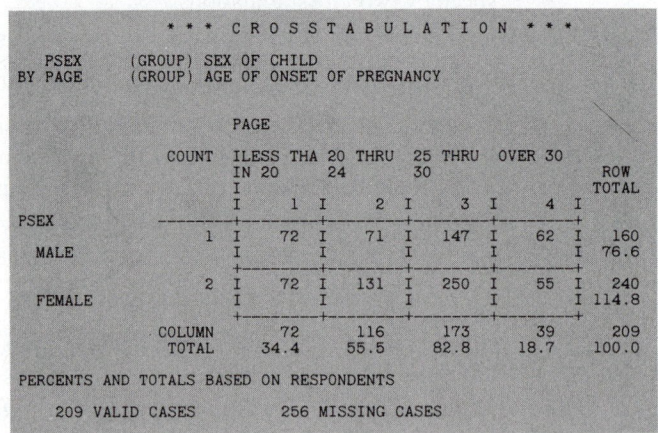

When you request paired crosstabulations, the order of the elementary variables on the GROUPS subcommand determines the construction of the table. For example, the group PSEX could legitimately be defined with the elementary variables P1SEX and P2SEX reversed on the GROUPS subcommand, as in:

```
MULT RESPONSE  GROUPS=PSEX 'SEX OF CHILD' (P2SEX P1SEX P3SEX (1,2))
    /PAGE 'AGE OF ONSET OF PREGNANCY' (P1AGE P2AGE P3AGE (1,4))
    /TABLES=PSEX BY PAGE (PAIRED)
```

However, pairing PSEX with PAGE would then result in a table where the cells were based on the frequencies for P2SEX paired with P1AGE and P1SEX paired with P2AGE.

A paired table request can also contain elementary variables and multiple dichotomy groups. However, only items within multiple response groups are paired. For example, the following command, in which EDUC is a simple variable, pairs only PSEX with PAGE:

```
MULT RESPONSE  GROUPS=PSEX 'SEX OF CHILD' (P1SEX P2SEX P3SEX (1,2))
   PAGE 'AGE OF ONSET OF PREGNANCY' (P1AGE P2AGE P3AGE (1,4))
   /VARIABLES=EDUC (1,3)
   /TABLES=PSEX BY PAGE BY EDUC (PAIRED)
```

Figure 35.9d   A crosstabulation of two paired groups

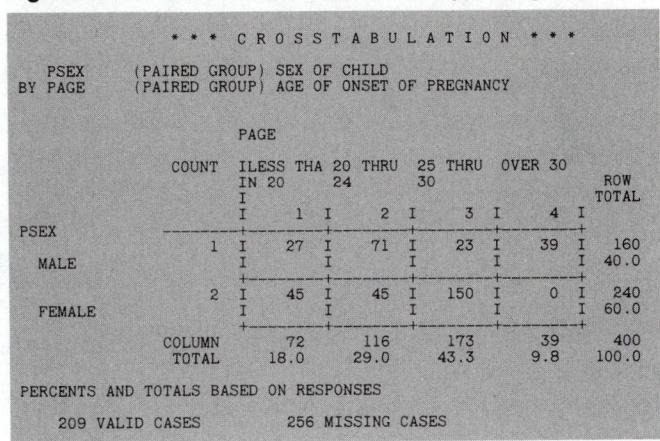

The paired option also applies to a multiple response group used as a controlling variable in a three-way or higher order table.

Paired tables are identified in the output by the adjective PAIRED GROUP in the table header. Percentages in paired tables are always based upon responses rather than respondents.

35.10
CELLS Subcommand

By default, MULT RESPONSE prints cell counts but no cell percentages. Use the CELLS subcommand to request percentages for crosstabulations. You can specify CELLS by itself or with a keyword(s). CELLS by itself, with no further specifications, requests ALL available cell percentages. If you specify a keyword(s) on CELLS, MULT RESPONSE prints cell counts plus the percentage(s) you request. The count cannot be eliminated from the table cells.

COUNT   *Print cell counts. This is the default if you omit the CELL subcommand.*

ROW   *Print row percentages.*

COLUMN   *Print column percentages.*

TOTAL   *Print two-way table total percentages.*

ALL   *Print cell counts, row percentages, column percentages, and two-way table total percentages. This is the default if you specify the CELLS subcommand by itself, with no keywords.*

Figures 35.9a and 35.9b display tables with all of these statistics. The cell percentages are based on respondents.

35.11
BASE Subcommand

Use the BASE subcommand to obtain cell percentages based on responses rather than respondents. Specify only one of the BASE subcommand's two keywords:

CASES   *Base cell percentages on respondents.* This is the default if you omit the BASE subcommand. You cannot use this specification for paired tables.

RESPONSES   *Base cell percentages on responses.* This is the default if you request paired tables and it cannot be overridden.

The following commands use the BASE subcommand to produce table marginals based on responses, as shown in Figure 35.11.

```
MULT RESPONSE  GROUPS=PROBS 'NATIONAL PROBLEMS MENTIONED'
   (PROB1 TO PROB3 (1,9))/VARIABLES=EDUC (1,3)
   /TABLES=EDUC BY PROBS
   /CELLS=ROW COLUMN
   /BASE=RESPONSES
```

Figure 35.11   A table with cell percentages based on responses

```
               * * * C R O S S T A B U L A T I O N * * *
   EDUC     HIGHEST EDUCATIONAL ATTAINMENT OF RESP
 BY PROBS   (GROUP) NATIONAL PROBLEMS MENTIONED

            PROBS

      COUNT IRECESSIO INFLATIO LACK OF  WATERGAT RACIAL C UNIONS T BIG BUSI COMMUNIS WEATHER
    ROW PCT IN        N        RELIGION E         ONFLICT  OO STRON NESS     T AGGRES          ROW
    COL PCT I                                             G                  SION              TOTAL
            I     1 I     2 I     3 I     4 I     5 I     6 I     7 I     8 I     9 I
 EDUC       --------+--------+--------+--------+--------+--------+--------+--------+--------+
          1 I    32 I     0 I    23 I     0 I    69 I     0 I    32 I     0 I    39 I    195
 GRADE SCHOOL I 16.4 I   0.0 I  11.8 I   0.0 I  35.4 I   0.0 I  16.4 I   0.0 I  20.0 I   19.7
            I  26.9 I   0.0 I  15.3 I   0.0 I  75.0 I   0.0 I  22.7 I   0.0 I  59.1 I
            --------+--------+--------+--------+--------+--------+--------+--------+--------+
          2 I    60 I   108 I    37 I    30 I    23 I     0 I    55 I    30 I     0 I    343
 HIGH SCHOOL I 17.5 I  31.5 I  10.8 I   8.7 I   6.7 I   0.0 I  16.0 I   8.7 I   0.0 I   34.7
            I  50.4 I  75.0 I  24.7 I  23.3 I  25.0 I   0.0 I  39.0 I  21.7 I   0.0 I
            --------+--------+--------+--------+--------+--------+--------+--------+--------+
          3 I    27 I    36 I    90 I    99 I     0 I     9 I    54 I   108 I    27 I    450
 COLLEGE    I   6.0 I   8.0 I  20.0 I  22.0 I   0.0 I   2.0 I  12.0 I  24.0 I   6.0 I   45.5
            I  22.7 I  25.0 I  60.0 I  76.7 I   0.0 I 100.0 I  38.3 I  78.3 I  40.9 I
            --------+--------+--------+--------+--------+--------+--------+--------+--------+
     COLUMN    119      144      150      129       92        9      141      138       66     988
     TOTAL    12.0     14.6     15.2     13.1      9.3      0.9     14.3     14.0      6.7   100.0

 PERCENTS AND TOTALS BASED ON RESPONSES

   449 VALID CASES        16 MISSING CASES
```

35.12
MISSING Subcommand

By default, MULT RESPONSE deletes cases with missing values on a table-by-table basis for both elementary variables and groups. Also, values falling outside the specified range are not tabulated and are included in the missing category. Therefore, specifying a range that excludes missing values is equivalent to the default treatment of missing values.

The MISSING subcommand controls missing values. Its minimum specification is a single keyword. The default keyword is TABLE.

By default, a case is considered missing for a multiple dichotomy group if none of its component variables contain the tabulating value. For example, if the multiple dichotomy group consists of three elementary variables with the tabulating value of 1, at least one of the three variables must have the value 1 for a given case to be tabulated. Keyword MDGROUP overrides the default and specifies listwise deletion for multiple dichotomy groups.

By default, a case is considered missing for a multiple response group if none of its components have valid values falling within the tabulating range. Thus cases with missing or excluded values on some but not all of the components of a group are included in tabulations of the group variable. Keyword MRGROUP overrides the default and specifies listwise deletion for multiple response groups.

When you exclude missing values listwise for either multiple dichotomy groups or multiple response groups, you can INCLUDE user-missing values in the analysis.

The MISSING subcommand has the following keywords:

TABLE   *Exclude missing values.* Missing values are excluded on a table-by-table basis for both elementary variables and groups. This is the default if you omit the MISSING subcommand.

INCLUDE   *Include user-defined missing values.* User-defined missing values are included in tables if they are encompassed by the range specification on the GROUPS or VARIABLES subcommands.

MDGROUP   *Exclude missing values listwise for multiple dichotomy groups.* Cases missing on any elementary dichotomy variable are excluded from the tabulation of the multiple dichotomy group.

MRGROUP   *Exclude missing values listwise for multiple response groups.* Cases missing on any elementary variable are excluded from the tabulation of the multiple response group.

35.13
FORMAT Subcommand

By default, MULT RESPONSE prints the value labels defined for variables in frequency and crosstabulation tables. It prints the crosstab tables with up to 10 column categories across a page. For frequencies tables, MULT RESPONSE uses more than one page to print frequencies with more than 20 categories.

The FORMAT subcommand controls table formats. Its minimum specification is a single keyword. The FORMAT subcommand has the following keywords:

LABELS   *Print value labels in frequency and crosstabulation tables.* This is the default if you omit the FORMAT subcommand.

NOLABELS   *Suppress value labels in frequency and crosstabulation tables.* You cannot suppress the printing of variable labels used as value labels for multiple dichotomy groups.

TABLE   *Print crosstab tables* with up to 10 column categories across a page. This is the default if you omit the FORMAT subcommand.

CONDENSE   *Print a condensed-format frequency table.* Prints frequency tables in a three-up condensed format for all multiple response groups and elementary variables. This option does not apply to multiple dichotomy groups.

ONEPAGE   *Print a conditional condensed-format frequency table.* Frequency tables print in a three-up condensed format if the multiple response group or elementary variable has more than 20 categories. Items with fewer categories print in the default format. This option does not apply to multiple dichotomy groups.

35.14
Stub and Banner Tables with the COUNT Command

Although the method of combining variables within MULT RESPONSE is probably indicated by the coding scheme used, you may want to group together in a table a series of items that do not have parallel codes. Since MULT RESPONSE combines elementary variables on one dimension of a table, with appropriate data transformations, you can create tables with more than one variable across the top and more than one variable down the side. Such tables are commonly called *stub and banner* tables. The following commands produce a stub and banner table:

```
COUNT  MALE=SEX(1)/FEMALE=SEX(2)/HIGHSCH=EDUC(1,2)/COLLEGE=EDUC(3)
MULT RESPONSE   GROUPS=VITAMINS 'USE NUTRITIONAL SUPPLEMENTS'
  (C TO NONE(1)) DEMOGRAP 'DEMOGRAPHICS' (MALE FEMALE HIGHSCH
  COLLEGE(1))
  /TABLES=VITAMINS BY DEMOGRAP
  /CELLS=COLUMN
```

Figure 35.14 displays this crosstabulation of two dichotomy groups, VITAMINS and DEMOGRAP. VITAMINS is a standard dichotomy group based on series of questions about nutritional supplements. DEMOGRAP places together two very different types of variables, sex and educational level. Because a multiple dichotomy only tabulates one value for a variable, transformations are used to map all the categories for one variable into several variables. Although this can be done in a variety of ways, this computation uses the COUNT command. To keep the table relatively simple, people with grade-school educations were combined with people with high-school educations.

The elementary variable NONE is included in the tabulation to account for cases missing on all the other dichotomy variables and to obtain correct percentaging. The row total shows the higher number of cases for the two original variables, SEX and EDUC, used to create the elementary variables for the group DEMOGRAP. For example, the row labeled "MULTI" in Figure 35.14 shows 40 males and 33 females, or a total of 73 cases, and 40 people with high school and 27 people with college, or a total of 67 cases. The row total is 73, reflecting the higher number of cases over the two variables.

Figure 35.14   A MULT RESPONSE stub and banner table

```
              * * *  C R O S S T A B U L A T I O N  * * *
   VITAMINS (TABULATING    1) USE NUTRITIONAL SUPPLEMENTS
 BY DEMOGRAP (TABULATING    1) DEMOGRAPHICS

                      DEMOGRAP
              COUNT  I
              COL PCT I                                          ROW
                     I                                          TOTAL
                     IMALE    IFEMALE  IHIGHSCH ICOLLEGE I
 VITAMINS      ------+--------+--------+--------+--------+
               C     I    22 I    16 I    26 I    10 I     38
                     I   8.9 I   7.3 I   9.7 I   5.6 I    8.2
                     +--------+--------+--------+--------+
               E     I     5 I     8 I     7 I     6 I     13
                     I   2.0 I   3.7 I   2.6 I   3.3 I    2.8
                     +--------+--------+--------+--------+
               MULTI I    40 I    33 I    40 I    27 I     73
                     I  16.2 I  15.1 I  14.9 I  15.0 I   15.7
                     +--------+--------+--------+--------+
               MULTIRON I 23 I    14 I    28 I     8 I     37
                     I   9.3 I   6.4 I  10.4 I   4.4 I    8.0
                     +--------+--------+--------+--------+
               MULTZINC I 14 I    18 I    16 I    15 I     32
                     I   5.7 I   8.3 I   5.9 I   8.3 I    6.9
                     +--------+--------+--------+--------+
               A     I    17 I    19 I    18 I    15 I     36
                     I   6.9 I   8.7 I   6.7 I   8.3 I    7.7
                     +--------+--------+--------+--------+
               NONE  I   168 I   154 I   184 I   130 I    322
                     I  68.0 I  70.6 I  68.4 I  72.2 I   69.2
                     +--------+--------+--------+--------+
              COLUMN     247     218     269     180      465
               TOTAL    53.1    46.9    57.8    38.7    100.0

 PERCENTS AND TOTALS BASED ON RESPONDENTS

    465 VALID CASES          0 MISSING CASES
```

35.15
LIMITATIONS

The following limitations apply to MULT RESPONSE:

- One set of subcommands per MULT RESPONSE command.
- A maximum of 100 elementary variables named or implied by the GROUPS and VARIABLES subcommands together.
- A maximum of 20 groups defined on the GROUPS subcommand.
- A maximum of 32,767 categories for a multiple response group or an elementary variable.
- A maximum of 10 tables lists on the TABLES subcommand.
- A maximum of 5 dimensions per table.
- A maximum of 100 groups and elementary variables named or implied on the FREQUENCIES and TABLES subcommands together.
- A maximum of 200 nonempty rows in a single table.
- A maximum of 200 nonempty columns in a single table.
- MULT RESPONSE stores category labels in WORKSPACE. If there is insufficient space to store the labels after the tables are built, the labels are not printed.

Syntax

Nonlinear Regression

```
MODEL PROGRAM varname=value [varname=value ...
transformation commands
[DERIVATIVES PROGRAM
 transformation commands]
```

Procedure CNLR (Constrained NonLinear Regression):

```
[CONSTRAINED FUNCTIONS
 transformation commands]

CNLR depvar WITH varlist

 [/FILE=file]    [/OUTFILE=file]

 [/PRED=varname]

 [/SAVE [PRED] [RESID[(varname)]] [DERIVATIVES] [LOSS]]

 [/CRITERIA=[ITER n] [MITER n] [CKDER {0.5**}]
                                      {n   }

        [ISTEP {1E+20**}] [FPR n] [LFTOL n]
               {n      }

        [LSTOL n] [STEP {2**}] [NFTOL n]
                        {n  }

        [FTOL n] [OPTOL n] [CRSHTOL {.01**}]]
                                    {n    }

 [/BOUNDS=expression, expression, ...]

 [/LOSS=varname]

 [/BOOTSTRAP [=n]]
```

Procedure NLR (NonLinear Regression):

```
NLR depvar WITH varlist

 [/FILE=file]    [/OUTFILE=file]

 [/PRED=varname]

 [/SAVE [PRED] [RESID [(varname)] [DERIVATIVES]]

 [/CRITERIA=[ITER {100**}] [CKDER {0.5**}]
                  {n    }         {n   }

   [SSCON {1E-8**}]  [PCON {1E-8**}]  [RCON {1E-8**}]]
          {n     }         {n     }         {n     }
```

**Default if subcommand is omitted.

Contents

36.1   OVERVIEW

36.2   OPERATION: CNLR AND NLR
36.3   The Model Program
36.4   Initial Values
36.5   Derivatives Program
36.6   Constrained Functions Program
36.7   CNLR/NLR Subcommands
36.8   The Regression Variables
36.9   FILE Subcommand
36.10   OUTFILE Subcommand
36.11   PRED Subcommand
36.12   SAVE Subcommand
36.13   CRITERIA Subcommand
36.14   CNLR Subcommands
36.15   BOUNDS Subcommand
36.16   LOSS Subcommand
36.17   BOOTSTRAP Subcommand
36.18   Weighting Cases
36.19   Missing Values
36.20   Underflows, Overflows, and Values out of Range
36.21   Common Convergence Problems

36.22 EXAMPLES
36.23   Regression with Restrictions
36.24   Grafted Polynomials: A Segmented Model
36.25   Linearizing a Problem for Good Initial Values
36.26   Logistic Regression on Disaggregated Data
36.27   Minimizing an Analytic Function
36.28   Using CNLR to Solve Linear Programming
           Problems
36.29   Robust Regression via Iteratively Reweighted
           Least Squares

Chapter 36 Nonlinear Regression: CNLR and NLR

Nonlinear regression is used to estimate parameter values and regression statistics for models that are not linear in their parameters. SPSS-X has two procedures for estimating nonlinear equations. CNLR (Constrained NonLinear Regression) uses a sequential quadratic programming algorithm and can be used for both constrained and unconstrained problems. The NLR (NonLinear Regression) procedure uses a Levenberg-Marquardt algorithm and can only be used for unconstrained problems.

The CNLR procedure is more general. It allows linear and nonlinear constraints on any combination of parameters. It will estimate parameters by minimizing any smooth loss function (objective function), and can optionally compute bootstrap estimates of parameter standard errors and correlations. The individual bootstrap parameter estimates can optionally be saved on a separate system file.

Both programs estimate the values of the parameters for the model and, optionally, compute and save predicted values, residuals, and derivatives. Final parameter estimates can be saved on a system file and used in subsequent analyses.

36.1
OVERVIEW

CNLR and NLR use much of the same syntax. Sections 36.3 through 36.13 discuss features common to both procedures. In these sections, the notation [C]NLR means that either the CNLR or NLR procedure can be specified. Sections 36.14 through 36.17 document additional features used only by CNLR.

Nonlinear regression commands fall into three categories:

- Model specification. The required MODEL PROGRAM command followed by transformation commands specifies the model to be fit and initial parameter estimates.
- Derivatives specification. The optional DERIVATIVES command followed by transformation commands specifies the derivatives. If you do not supply derivatives, they will be calculated numerically by the program. If derivatives are provided by the user, computational time is reduced.
- Regression specification. The required CNLR or NLR command specifies the dependent and independent variables for the nonlinear regression, iteration criteria and other solution controls, as well as optional output to be printed and/or saved.

36.2
OPERATION: CNLR
AND NLR

To run either procedure, you must first use the MODEL PROGRAM command to provide the initial parameter estimates and a transformation statement to define the model. You must also include either the CNLR or the NLR command to provide the regression specifications.

For example, to estimate the parameters of the logistic model

$$Y = c/(a + e^{(a+b\,x)})$$ **Equation 36.2**

with starting values of a=4, b=−.4, and c=200, specify

```
MODEL PROGRAM A=4 B=-.4 C=200
COMPUTE pred=C/(A + EXP (A + B * X))
[C]NLR Y with X
```

- The MODEL PROGRAM command assigns starting values to the three parameters (A, B, C) that are to be estimated (see Section 36.3).
- The COMPUTE command gives the nonlinear function that is to be fit (see Section 36.3).
- The CNLR or NLR command specifies Y as the dependent variable and X as the independent variable (see Section 36.7). Both X and Y are on the active file. By default, the procedure assumes that the variable name assigned to the model to be estimated is PRED. If you use a different name you will have to indicate this on the [C]NLR command (see Section 36.11). The procedure also specifies the default nonlinear regression statistics (see Section 36.6).

36.3
The Model Program

The first step in estimating a nonlinear regression model is to determine the model you want to fit. There is no "default" model; you must specify the equation that best describes your data. The equation is specified in the model program.

The MODEL PROGRAM command assigns variable names and initial values to the parameters and signifies the beginning of the model program. The statements immediately following the MODEL PROGRAM command are SPSS-X transformation commands that specify the nonlinear equation.

For example, consider the following equation, which is the sum of two exponentials:

$$Y = Ae^{Bx} + Ce^{Dx}$$

Equation 36.3

The equation has four parameters (A, B, C, and D), which must be estimated from the data. The data in this case consist of values for the independent variable X and the dependent variable Y. To estimate the model using [C]NLR you must first assign variable names and starting values to each of the parameters. Any acceptable SPSS-X variable name can be used for a parameter. To assign the variable names A, B, C, and D to the parameters and starting values of 10, 0, 5, and 0, specify

```
MODEL PROGRAM  A=10 B=0 C=5 D=0
```

You must specify each parameter individually on the MODEL PROGRAM command; you cannot use the TO keyword. The command MODEL PROGRAM must begin in column 1.

The equation specification can contain any kind of computational command (such as COMPUTE, IF, DO IF, LOOP, END LOOP, END IF, RECODE, or COUNT) in the transformation language. It can also contain output commands (WRITE, PRINT, or XSAVE). It cannot contain input commands (like DATA LIST, GET, MATCH FILES, or ADD FILES).

Your specified equation is used to calculate predicted values for the dependent variable, based on the parameter estimates and the values of the independent variables. By default, the program assumes that the variable name PRED is assigned to the result of the transformation. If you want to use a different variable name, supply the name on the [C]NLR command (see Section 36.7).

For example, you can use the following model program to assign starting values and names to the four parameters A, B, C, and D and to define the model to be fit as the sum of two exponentials:

```
MODEL PROGRAM A=10 B=0 C=5 D=0
COMPUTE PRED= A*exp(B*X) + C*exp(D*X)
```

36.4
Initial Values

You must specify initial values for all parameters. Good initial values are important to the procedure and may provide a better solution in fewer iterations. In addition, computational difficulties can sometimes be avoided by a good choice of initial values. Poor initial values can result in no solution, a local rather than global solution, or a physically impossible solution.

There are a number of ways to determine initial values for nonlinear models. Milliken (1987) and Draper and Smith (1981) describe several approaches, which are summarized below. Especially for the CNLR procedure, zero should be avoided as an initial value, since it provides no information on the scale of the parameter.

Linearize the Model. If you ignore the error term, quite often a linear form of the model can be derived. You can then use regression to estimate the coefficients in the linear model, and transform back to the nonlinear equation, if necessary.

Consider the model $y = e^{(a+b\,x)} + \epsilon$. If we ignore the additive error term (ϵ) we can take natural logs of both sides and estimate the linear model:

```
COMPUTE LNY=LN(Y)
REGRESSION VARS=LNY X /DEP=LNY/ENTER X
```

Then we can use the REGRESSION parameter estimate of the CONSTANT for a and the parameter estimate of X for b as initial values.

Use Properties of the Nonlinear Model. Quite often, the parameters have certain interpretations in the nonlinear model. Examining the behavior of the equation at its minimum and maximum, as well as the behavior when all the X's approach zero and infinity will quite often give good insight for initial values. For example, if you know that a process should be close to 2 at X=0 for the model $y = e^{(a+b\,x)}$, an appropriate starting value for a will be the natural log of 2.

Solve a System of Equations. By taking as many data points as you have parameters, you can simultaneously solve the resulting system of equations. The model $y = e^{(a+b\,x)}$ involves two parameters, a and b. Take two cases, (y_1, x_1) and (y_2, x_2), and solve the system of equations:

$$\ln(y_1) = a + bx_1$$
$$\ln(y_2) = a + bx_2$$

Then

$$\ln(y_1) - \ln(y_2) = bx_1 - bx_2$$

$$b = \frac{\ln(y_1) - \ln(y_2)}{x_1 - x_2}$$

and

$$a = \ln(y_1) - bx_1$$

Combination of the Above. Generally, a combination of the above techniques will be easiest to use. For the above example, suppose we already guess by properties of the model that a is 10. Then we need only one case to estimate b. (See Sections 36.24 and 36.25.)

36.5
Derivatives Program

Nonlinear estimation is iterative and requires determination of direction and step size at each iteration based on the values of the derivatives of the model with respect to each of the parameters. You can supply some or all of the derivatives using the derivatives program, or you can allow the program to analytically estimate the derivatives. If you supply the derivatives, computational time is reduced. In some situations, if you supply derivatives the solution may actually be better.

The derivatives program consists of the DERIVATIVES command, followed by transformation statements for each of the derivatives. This set of statements can contain any kind of computational command (such as COMPUTE, IF, DO IF, LOOP, END LOOP, END IF, RECODE, or COUNT) in the transformation language. It can also contain output commands (WRITE, PRINT, or XSAVE). It cannot contain input commands (like DATA LIST, GET, MATCH FILES, or ADD FILES).

The DERIVATIVES command must follow the model program. To name the derivatives, specify the prefix "D." before each parameter name. For example, the derivative name for the parameter named PARM1 must be D.PARM1.

The following derivatives program can be used to specify derivatives for the sum of two exponentials model described in Section 36.3:

```
DERIVATIVES
COMPUTE D.A = exp (B * X)
COMPUTE D.B = A * exp (B * X) * X
COMPUTE D.C = exp (D * X)
COMPUTE D.D = C * exp (D * X) * X
```

The previous program can also be written as:

```
DERIVATIVES
COMPUTE D.A = exp (B * X)
COMPUTE D.B = A * X * D.A
COMPUTE D.C = exp (D * X)
COMPUTE D.D = C* X * D.C
```

You do not need to supply all of the derivatives. Those that are not supplied will be estimated by the program. During the first iteration of the nonlinear estimation procedure, derivatives calculated in the derivatives program are compared with numerically calculated derivatives. This serves as a check on the values you supply (see Section 36.13).

36.6
Constrained Functions Program

The optional CONSTRAINED FUNCTION command followed by transformation commands specifies nonlinear constraints and is discussed in Section 36.15. CONSTRAINED FUNCTION is specified after the model program and the derivatives program (when used). It can only be used with, and must precede, the CNLR command.

36.7
CNLR/NLR Subcommands

Once the model, and optionally the derivatives and nonlinear constrained functions, have been specified, use either the CNLR or NLR command to provide information about the dependent and independent variables to be used in the regression. The [C]NLR command must follow the last statement of the model, derivatives, or constrained functions program.

For example, to obtain default output for the sum of two exponentials model specify:

```
[C]NLR Y WITH X
```

In this example the observed dependent variable is Y, and the independent variable, which must follow keyword WITH, is X.

The following is the complete SPSS-X job for the sum of two exponentials example (Section 36.3):

```
DATA LIST FREE/ Y X
BEGIN DATA
 . . .
END DATA
MODEL PROGRAM A=10 B=0 C=5 D=0
COMPUTE PRED= A*exp(B*X) + C*exp(D*X)
DERIVATIVES
COMPUTE D.A = exp (B * X)
COMPUTE D.B = A * exp (B * X) * X
COMPUTE D.C = exp (D * X)
COMPUTE D.D = C * exp (D * X) * X
[C]NLR Y WITH X
FINISH
```

36.8
The Regression Variables

After the command [C]NLR, specify the name of the observed dependent variable, the keyword WITH, and all of the independent variables. Also specify any variables on your *active* file that you used in the model, derivatives, and constrained functions programs to create the temporary variables. Do not list the variables you created in these programs. In the example in Section 36.7, the only variable from the active file used in the model and derivatives programs is X. All of the other variables are temporary variables created for the nonlinear task.

The example in Sections 36.9 through 36.12 uses a data set for a study of stopping distance for cars traveling at different speeds given in Hald (1952). While Hald tries to fit different linear regression functions to the data, Draper and Smith (1981) suggest a nonlinear model of the form

$$Y = AX^B + \epsilon$$ **Equation 36.8a**

If we ignore the error term, this model can be linearized as

$$\ln(Y) = \ln(A) + B*\ln(X)$$ **Equation 36.8b**

to get starting values for the nonlinear model. REGRESSION can then be used to estimate the initial values. The commands for the job are:

```
TITLE Nonlinear Regression
SUBTITLE Stopping Distance Example
DATA LIST FREE/ SPEED STOP
BEGIN DATA
 . . .
END DATA
COMPUTE LNSTOP=LN(STOP)
COMPUTE LNSPEED=LN(SPEED)
REGRESSION DEP=LNSTOP/ENTER LNSPEED
```

The output for the regression is given in Figure 36.8a. The parameter estimate for LNSPEED, 1.6, will be the starting value for B. The CONSTANT parameter estimate is actually the ln(A) parameter in the linearized formula (equation 36.8a). Thus, the starting value for A will be exp(−.729669), or .5.

Figure 36.8a   Regression output for linear equation

Variable	B	SE B	Beta	T	Sig T
LNSPEED	1.602391	.139538	.856239	11.484	.0000
(Constant)	−.729669	.375846		−1.941	.0581

Using this information, the [C]NLR command is:

```
MODEL PROGRAM A=.5 B=1.6
COMPUTE PRED=A*SPEED**B
[C]NLR STOP WITH SPEED
```

Figure 36.8b shows the output from CNLR. Output from the NLR procedure would be similar.

Figure 36.8b   Output from CNLR for stopping distance example

```
There are 50 cases.  There is enough memory for them all.

 Iteration Residual SS              A            B

    0.1    10928.76115   .500000000   1.60000000
    1.1    10923.60069   .500280429   1.60039093
    2.1    10920.27500   .511540819   1.59278646
    3.1    10896.62041   .529804334   1.58496143
    4.1    10892.35245   .549645962   1.57258345
    5.1    10889.76984   .578451776   1.55500522
    6.1    10889.06690   .582544633   1.55331893
    7.1    10888.96771   .588587450   1.54987710
    8.1    10888.96431   .589578394   1.54934314

Run stopped after 8 major iterations.
Optimal solution found.


Nonlinear Regression Summary Statistics       Dependent Variable STOP

 Source              DF   Sum of Squares   Mean Square

 Regression           2    114014.03569    57007.01784
 Residual            48     10888.96431      226.85342
 Uncorrected Total   50    124903.00000

 (Corrected Total)   49     32538.98000

 R squared = 1 - Residual SS / Corrected SS =     .66536

                                       Asymptotic 95 %
                          Asymptotic   Confidence Interval
 Parameter   Estimate     Std. Error   Lower        Upper

 A           .589578394   .335620490   -.085231828  1.264388616
 B          1.549343143   .192032948   1.163235024  1.935451263

Asymptotic Correlation Matrix of the Parameter Estimates

                 A          B

 A           1.0000     -.9969
 B           -.9969     1.0000
```

36.9
FILE Subcommand

[C]NLR can read starting values from two sources: from the MODEL PROGRAM command, as shown in Section 36.3, or from a system file created by a previous [C]NLR procedure. Section 36.10 explains how to write the model program's final parameter values to a system file. The system file stores the values as a single case for each split-file group.

Use the FILE subcommand to read parameter values from a system file. The only specification on FILE is a file reference to identify the system file. When starting values are read from a file, they do not need to be specified on the MODEL PROGRAM command. The MODEL PROGRAM command simply names the parameter variables that correspond to the variables in the system file. For example, in the commands

```
MODEL PROGRAM A B
COMPUTE PRED=A*SPEED**B
[C]NLR STOP WITH SPEED /FILE=PARAM
```

the FILE subcommand reads values from the system file PARAM. The MODEL PROGRAM command names the system file variables. You do not need to name the variables in the order they occur in the system file, and you do not need to name all the variables contained in the file.

If split-file processing is in effect, the starting values for the first subfile are taken from the first case of the parameter system file. Subfiles are matched with cases in order until the starting value file runs out of cases; all subsequent subfiles use the starting values for the last case.

If you want to add new parameters to your model, you can read values for existing parameters from a system file and specify values for the new parameters on the MODEL PROGRAM command. For example, the commands

```
MODEL PROGRAM A B C=1 D=3
COMPUTE PRED=A*SPEED**B + C*SPEED**D
[C]NLR Y WITH X /FILE=IN
```

add parameters C and D to the model. Starting values for parameters A and B are read from the system file. Starting values for C and D are specified on the MODEL PROGRAM command.

To read starting values from a system file and then replace those system file values with the final results from [C]NLR, specify the same file on the FILE and OUTFILE subcommands (see Section 36.10). The input file is read completely before anything is written on the output file. For example, the following commands read starting values from the file PARAM and then write the final parameter values to the same file:

```
MODEL PROGRAM A B
COMPUTE PRED=A*SPEED**B
[C]NLR STOP WITH SPEED /FILE=PARAM /OUTFILE=PARAM
```

The output file writes over the input file. If in addition to the final estimates you want to save the starting values you used for the analysis, specify different files on the FILE and OUTFILE subcommands.

36.10
OUTFILE Subcommand

To store final parameter estimates for use in a subsequent job, use the OUTFILE subcommand. The only specification on OUTFILE is a file, as in

```
MODEL PROGRAM A=.5 B=1.6
COMPUTE PRED=A*SPEED**B
[C]NLR STOP WITH SPEED
     /OUTFILE=PARAM
```

Figure 36.10 shows the system file generated by the OUTFILE subcommand. You can read the values from the system file into subsequent [C]NLR procedures by using the FILE subcommand (Section 36.9).

Figure 36.10   System file with parameter values

A	B	SSE	NCASES
.59	1.55	10888.9643	50

NUMBER OF CASES READ =   1   NUMBER OF CASES LISTED =   1

The system file created by the OUTFILE subcommand stores the following variables:

- All the split-file variables (OUTFILE writes one case of values for each split-file group in the active file).
- All the parameter variables named on the MODEL PROGRAM command.
- The sum of squared residuals (named SSE).
- The number of cases on which the analysis was based (named NCASES).

The labels, formats, and missing values of the split-file variables and the parameter variables are those defined for them previous to their use in the [C]NLR procedure. The SSE and NCASES variables have no labels or missing values. The print and write format for SSE is F10.8. The print and write format for NCASES is F8.0.

36.11
PRED Subcommand

The PRED subcommand identifies the predicted values variable for [C]NLR. Its only specification is a variable name, which must be identical to the variable name you use to calculate predicted values in the model program. For example, in the commands

```
MODEL PROGRAM A=.5 B=1.6
COMPUTE PSTOP=A*SPEED**B
[C]NLR STOP WITH SPEED
    /PRED=PSTOP
```

the COMPUTE command creates a variable named PSTOP to temporarily store the predicted values for the dependent variable STOP. The PRED subcommand on [C]NLR identifies PSTOP for the [C]NLR procedure.

If the transformation statement names the predicted values variable PRED, you can omit the PRED subcommand on [C]NLR. If the transformation statement uses any other name for the predicted values variable, the PRED subcommand is required.

You can assign variable labels to the predicted values variable and change its print and write formats in the model program. You should not specify missing values. Like the parameter variables, the predicted variable is not saved on the active file unless you specify it on the SAVE subcommand (see Section 36.12).

36.12
SAVE Subcommand

By default, the predicted values, residuals, and derivatives are created as temporary variables by the model and derivatives programs and are not saved permanently. To save these statistics, you must use the SAVE subcommand.

The minimum specification on SAVE is a single keyword. The following keywords are available and can be used in any combination. SAVE appends the specified variables to the active file in the following order: the predicted variable, the residuals variable, the derivative variables, and the loss variable.

PRED
Save the predicted values. The variable's name, label, and formats are those you specify for it (or allow [C]NLR to assign by default) in the model program.

RESID [(varname)]
Save the residuals variable. By default, the name of the variable is the keyword name RESID. You can substitute for RESID any keyword that begins with RES. For example, to name the residuals variable RESIDUAL, specify SAVE=RESIDUAL. Optionally, you can specify a name for the variable in parentheses. For example, to name the residuals variable RCOUNT, specify SAVE= RESID(RCOUNT).

The residuals variable has the same print and write format as the predicted variable created in the model program. It has no variable label and no values defined as missing. It is system-missing for any case in which either the dependent variable is missing or the predicted value cannot be computed.

DERIVATIVES
Save the derivative variables. The derivative variable names are created by adding the prefix D. to to the parameter names. For example, the derivative variable for parameter A is named D.A. Derivative variables use the print and write formats of the predicted variable and have no value labels or defined missing values. Derivative variables are saved in the same order as the parameters named on the MODEL PROGRAM command. Derivatives are saved for all parameters, whether or not the derivative was supplied in the derivatives program.

LOSS
Save the user-specified loss function variable. This specification is available only if the LOSS subcommand has also been specified (see Section 36.16). LOSS is only available with CNLR.

The following commands save three types of variables on the active file:

```
MODEL PROGRAM A=.5  B=1.6
COMPUTE PSTOP=A*SPEED**B
[C]NLR STOP WITH SPEED /PRED=PSTOP
   /SAVE=PRED RES(RSTOP) DER
LIST
```

The PRED subcommand is required in this example because the predicted variable in the model program is named PSTOP. However, the variable is still identified by the keyword PRED on the SAVE subcommand. Figure 36.12 shows the first few cases in the output generated by the LIST command.

Figure 36.12   Active file when [C]NLR saves statistics

SPEED	STOP	PSTOP	RSTOP	D.A	D.B
4.00	2.00	5.05	-3.05	8.57	7.00
4.00	10.00	5.05	4.95	8.57	7.00
7.00	4.00	12.02	-8.02	20.39	23.39
7.00	22.00	12.02	9.98	20.39	23.39

The names of the saved variables cannot already exist on the active file, except as temporary variable names (names of variables created after the TEMPORARY or MODEL PROGRAM commands). If a naming conflict exists, the variables are not created.

Asymptotic standard errors of predicted values and residuals, and special residuals used for outlier detection and influential case analysis are not provided by the [C]NLR procedure. However, the asymptomatically correct values for all these statistics can be calculated using the REGRESSION procedure. To do so, use the [C]NLR residuals as dependent variable and the derivatives as independent variables, as in

```
MODEL PROGRAM A=.5 B=1.6
COMPUTE PSTOP=A*SPEED**B
[C]NLR STOP WITH SPEED /PRED=PSTOP /SAVE=PRED RES(RSTOP) DER

REGRESSION VARIABLES=RSTOP D.A D.B
           /DEP=RSTOP /ENTER
           /CASEWISE /SAVE SEPRED
```

The casewise plots and the saved standard errors of prediction are valid for the nonlinear equation. In the same way, you can produce partial regression plots and other diagnostics of the regression.

36.13
CRITERIA Subcommand

The optional CRITERIA subcommand controls the criteria [C]NLR uses in its algorithm. CRITERIA keywords can be specified in any order. The minimum specification is a criteria keyword and a specified value. The default criterion is in effect for any keyword you omit from the CRITERIA specification.

Keywords available for the CRITERIA subcommand differ between CNLR and NLR. The following sections discuss the keywords available for each separately.

Iteration Criteria for CNLR. The CNLR procedure uses Gill, Murray, Saunders, and Wright's NPSOL (Version 4.03) Fortran Package for Nonlinear Programming. The CRITERIA subcommand of CNLR gives the control features of NPSOL. Full documentation for the NPSOL package is given in Gill, Murray, Saunders, and Wright (1986). The following section summarizes the NPSOL documentation.

CNLR uses a sequential quadratic programming algorithm, with a quadratic programming subproblem to determine the search direction. If constraints or bounds are specified, the first step is to find a point that is feasible with respect to those constraints. Each major iteration sets up a quadratic program to find the search direction, p. Minor iterations are used to solve this subprogram. Then, the major iteration determines a steplength α by a linesearch, and the function is evaluated at the new point. An optimal solution is found when the optimality tolerance criterion is met.

The CRITERIA subcommand has the following keywords when used with CNLR:

ITER n

Maximum number of major iterations. Specify any positive integer for n. The default is $\max(50,3(p+m_L)+10m_N)$, where *p* is the number of parameters, m_L is the number of linear constraints, and m_N is the number of nonlinear constraints. If the search for a solution stops because this limit is exceeded, CNLR issues a warning message.

MINORITERATION n

Maximum number of minor iterations. Specify any positive integer. This is the number of minor iterations allowed within each major iteration. The default is $\max(50,3(n+m_L+m_N))$.

CKDER n

Critical value for derivative checking. Specify a number between 0 and 1 for n. The default is .5. Specify 0 to disable this criterion.

On the first iteration, CNLR always checks any derivatives calculated on the derivatives program by comparing them with numerically calculated derivatives. For each comparison, it computes an agreement score. A score of 1 indicates agreement to machine precision; a score of 0 indicates definite disagreement. If a score is less than 1, either an incorrect derivative was supplied or there are numerical problems in estimating the derivative. The lower the score, the more likely it is that the supplied derivatives are incorrect. Highly correlated parameters may cause disagreement even when a correct derivative is supplied. Be sure to check the derivatives if the agreement score is not 1.

During the first iteration, CNLR checks each derivative score. If any score is below 1, it begins printing a table to show the worst (lowest) score for each derivative. If any score is below the critical value, the program stops.

CRSHTOL n

Crash tolerance. Used to determine if initial values are within their specified bounds. A constraint of the form $a'X \geq L$ is considered a valid part of the working set if $|a'X - L| \leq$ CRSHTOL $(1+|L|)$. Specify any value between 0 and 1. The default value is .01.

STEPLIMIT n

Step limit. The step limit can prevent very early steps from going too far from good initial estimates. This bound prevents CNLR from making a change in the length of the parameter vector of more than a factor of STEPLIMIT in the CNLR algorithm. Specify any positive value. The default value is 2.

FTOLERANCE n

Feasibility tolerance. This is the maximum absolute difference allowed for both linear and nonlinear constraints for a solution to be considered "feasible." Specify any value greater than 0. The default value is the square root of your machine's epsilon.

LFTOLERANCE n

Linear feasibility tolerance. If specified, this overrides FTOLERANCE for linear constraints and bounds. Specify any value greater than 0. The default value is the square root of your machine's epsilon.

NFTOLERANCE n

Nonlinear feasible tolerance. If specified, this overrides FTOLERANCE for nonlinear constraints. Specify any value greater than 0. The default value is the square root of your machine's epsilon.

LSTOLERANCE n

Line search tolerance. This value must be between 0 and 1 (but not including 1), and controls the accuracy required of the line search that forms the innermost search loop. The default value, .9, specifies an inaccurate search. This is appropriate for many problems, particularly if nonlinear constraints are involved.

A smaller positive value, corresponding to a more accurate line search, may give better performance if there are no nonlinear constraints, all (or most) derivatives are supplied in the derivatives program, and the data fit in memory.

OPTOLERANCE n *Optimality tolerance.* If an iteration point is a feasible point, and the next step will not produce a relative change in either the parameter vector or the objective function of more than the square root of OPTOLERANCE, an optimal solution has been found. OPTOLERANCE can also be thought of as the number of significant digits in the objective function at the solution. For example, if OPTOLERANCE=10^{-6}, the objective function should have approximately 6 significant digits accuracy. Specify any number between the FPRECISION value and 1. The default value is your machine's epsilon **0.8.

FPRECISION n *Function precision.* This is a measure of the accuracy with which the objective function can be measured. It acts as a relative precision when the function is large, and an absolute precision when the function is small. For example, if the objective function is larger than 1 and 6 significant digits are desired, FPRECISION should be 1E−6. If, however, the objective function is of the order .001, FPRECISION should be 1E−9 to get six digits of accuracy. Specify any number between 0 and 1.

The choice of FPRECISION can be very complicated for a badly scaled problem. Chapter 8 of Gill, Murray, and Wright (1981) gives some scaling suggestions. The default value is your machine's epsilon **0.8.

ISTEP n *Infinite step size.* This value is the magnitude of the change in parameters that is defined as infinite. That is, if the change in the parameters at a step is greater than ISTEP, the problem is considered unbounded, and estimation stops. Specify any positive number. The default value is 1E+20.

Iteration Criteria for NLR. The NLR procedure uses an adaptation of subroutine LMSTR from the MINPACK package by Burton S. Garbow, Dudley V. Goetschel, Kenneth E. Hillstrom, and Jorge J. More. Since the NLR algorithm differs substantially from CNLR, the CRITERIA subcommand for NLR has a different set of keywords.

The NLR procedure uses the Levenberg-Marquardt method for computing parameter estimates. At each iteration, NLR evaluates the estimates against a set of control criteria. The iterative calculations continue until one of five cutoff points is met, at which point the iterations stop and the reason for stopping is printed.

The CRITERIA subcommand has the following keywords when used with NLR:

ITER n *Maximum number of iterations allowed.* Specify any positive integer for n. The default is 100 iterations per parameter. If the search for a solution stops because this limit is exceeded, NLR issues a warning message.

SSCON n *Convergence criterion for the sum of squares.* Specify any non-negative number for n. The default is 1E−8. If successive iterations fail to reduce the sum of squares by this proportion, the procedure stops. Specify 0 to disable this criterion.

PCON n *Convergence criterion for the parameter values.* Specify any non-negative number for n. The default is 1E−8. If successive iterations fail to change any of the parameter values by this proportion, the procedure stops. Specify 0 to disable this criterion.

RCON n *Convergence criterion for the correlation between the residuals and the derivatives.* Specify any non-negative number for n. The default is 1E−8. If the largest value for the correlation between the residuals and the derivatives becomes this small, the procedure stops because it lacks the information it needs to estimate a direction for its next move. This criterion is often referred to as a gradient convergence criterion. Specify 0 to disable this criterion.

CKDER n *Critical value for derivative checking.* Specify a number between 0 and 1 for n; the default is .5. Specify 0 to disable this criterion.

On the first iteration, NLR always checks any derivatives calculated on the derivatives program and compares them with numerically calculated derivatives. For each comparison, it computes an agreement score. A score of 1 indicates agreement to machine precision; a score of 0 indicates definite disagreement. If a score is less than 1, either an incorrect derivative was supplied or there are numerical problems in estimating the derivative. The smaller the score the more likely it is that the derivative (or the model) is incorrectly computed. Highly correlated parameters may cause disagreement even when a correct derivative is supplied. Be sure to check the derivatives if the agreement score is not 1.

During the first iteration, NLR checks each derivative score. If any score is below 1, it prints a table to show the worst (lowest) score for each derivative. If any score falls below the CKDER value, the procedure stops.

The following specification changes the default settings for the keywords ITER, SSCON, and CKDER:

```
MODEL PROGRAM A=.5 B=1.6
COMPUTE PRED=A*SPEED**B
NLR STOP WITH SPEED
   /CRITERIA=ITER(80) SSCON=.000001
```

Because no specification is made for PCON, RCON, or CKDER, their default settings are in effect. You can specify each keyword's value in parentheses, after an equals sign, or after a space or comma.

36.14
CNLR Subcommands

The BOUNDS, LOSS, and BOOTSTRAPS subcommands are available only for use with CNLR. They cannot be used with NLR.

36.15
BOUNDS Subcommand

The BOUNDS subcommand can be used to specify both linear and nonlinear constraints.

Simple Bounds and Linear Constraints. The BOUNDS subcommand can be used to impose bounds on parameter values. These bounds can involve either single parameters or a linear combination of parameters and can be either equalities or inequalities. All bounds are specified on the same BOUNDS subcommand and are separated by semicolons, as in

```
/BOUNDS 5 > A;
       B > 9;
     .01 < 2*A + C < 1;
       D + 2*E = 10
```

The only variables allowed on the BOUNDS subcommand are parameter variables (those that were specified in the model program). When a parameter is multiplied by a constant, the constant must be specified first. Only multiplication, addition, and subtraction can be used. All the relational operators can be used, and they can be specified as either a symbol or the two-letter abbreviation (see Chapter 9). When two relational operators are used (as in the third bound above) they must both be in the same direction.

Nonlinear Constraints. Nonlinear constraints on the parameters can also be specified. The constrained function must be calculated and stored in a variable by a CONSTRAINED FUNCTION program, directly before the CNLR command. The constraint is then specified on the BOUNDS subcommand as bounds on that variable.

```
MODEL PROGRAM A=5 B=.3
COMPUTE PRED = ...
CONSTRAINED FUNCTION
COMPUTE DIFF=A-10**B
CNLR Y WITH X, Z
  /BOUNDS DIFF > 0
```

In general, nonlinear bounds will not be obeyed until an optimal solution has been found. This is different than simple and linear bounds, which are satisfied at each iteration. The constrained functions must be smooth near the solution.

36.16
LOSS Subcommand

By default, CNLR minimizes the sum of squared residuals. You can specify a different loss function for CNLR to minimize. You must first compute the loss function in the model program and then use the LOSS subcommand in CNLR to specify the name of the computed variable, as in:

```
MODEL PROGRAM  A=1 B=1
COMPUTE PRED=EXP(A+B*T)/(1+EXP(A+B*T))
COMPUTE LOSS=-W*(Y*LN(PRED)+(1-Y)*LN(1-PRED))
CNLR Y WITH T W/LOSS=LOSS
```

The minimizing algorithm may fail if it is given a loss function that is not smooth, such as the absolute value of residuals. If you supply derivatives, you must supply the derivative of each parameter with respect to the loss function, rather than the predicted value. The easiest way to do this is in two steps: first compute derivatives of the model, and then compute derivatives of the loss function with respect to the model and multiply by the model derivatives. For the above example, the derivatives program would look like this:

```
DERIVATIVES
COMPUTE D.A=PRED/(1+EXP(A+B*T))
COMPUTE D.B=T*PRED/(1+EXP(A+B*T))
COMPUTE D.A=(-W*(Y/PRED - (1-Y)/(1-PRED)) * D.A)
COMPUTE D.B=(-W*(Y/PRED - (1-Y)/(1-PRED)) * D.B)
```

When LOSS is used, the usual summary statistics are not computed. Standard errors, confidence intervals, and correlations of the parameters are available only if the BOOTSTRAP subcommand is specified (see Section 36.17).

36.17
BOOTSTRAP Subcommand

Bootstrapping is a way of estimating the standard error of a statistic using repeated samples from your original data set. This is done by sampling with replacement to get many samples of the same size as the original data set.

The BOOTSTRAP subcommand with CNLR provides bootstrap estimates of the parameter standard errors, confidence intervals, and correlations. First, the nonlinear equation is estimated for each sample. The standard error of each parameter estimate is then calculated as the standard deviation of the boot-strapped estimates. Parameter values from the original data are used as starting values for each bootstrap sample. Even so, bootstrapping is computationally expensive.

By default, the BOOTSTRAP subcommand generates bootstrap results based on $10*p*(p+1)/2$ samples, where p is the number of parameters. That is, 10 samples are drawn for each statistic (standard error or correlation) to be calculated. You can specify a number on the BOOTSTRAP subcommand to take a different number of samples.

If the OUTFILE subcommand is specified, a case is written to the output file for each bootstrap sample. The first case in the file will be the actual parameter estimates, followed by the bootstrap samples. After eliminating the first case (using SELECT IF), you can use other SPSS-X procedures (such as FREQUEN-CIES) to examine the bootstrap distribution.

The following commands will produce bootstrap standard errors for the stopping distance example:

```
MODEL PROGRAM A=.5 B=1.6
COMPUTE PSTOP=A*SPEED**B
CNLR STOP WITH SPEED /BOOTSTRAP /OUTFILE=PARAM /PRED=PSTOP
GET FILE=PARAM
LIST
SELECT IF ($CASENUM > 1)
FREQUENCIES A B /FORMAT=NOTABLE/HISTOGRAM
```

Figure 36.17a shows the bootstrap standard errors, confidence intervals, and parameter correlation matrix. The bootstrap estimates are saved in the file PARAM. After the PARAM file is retrieved, the LIST command shows the 30 different sample estimates, along with the original estimate (Figure 36.17b). The NCASES here refers to the number of distinct cases in the sample, since cases are duplicated in each bootstrap sample. Finally, Figure 36.17c shows the histograms from FREQUENCIES of the bootstrapped parameter estimates.

Figure 36.17a   Bootstrap standard errors

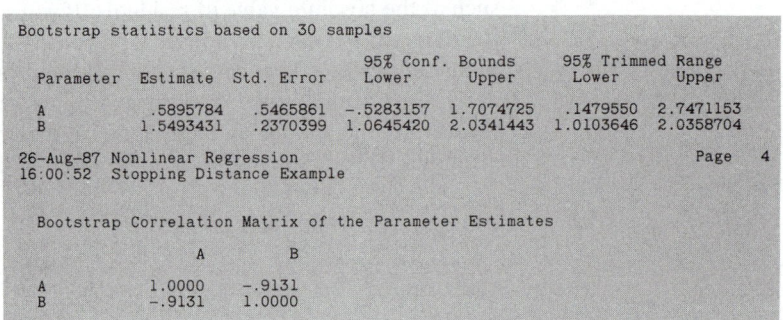

```
Bootstrap statistics based on 30 samples

                                    95% Conf. Bounds      95% Trimmed Range
   Parameter  Estimate  Std. Error  Lower      Upper      Lower      Upper

   A          .5895784  .5465861   -.5283157  1.7074725   .1479550  2.7471153
   B         1.5493431  .2370399   1.0645420  2.0341443  1.0103646  2.0358704

26-Aug-87 Nonlinear Regression                                    Page    4
16:00:52  Stopping Distance Example


Bootstrap Correlation Matrix of the Parameter Estimates

                  A         B

   A          1.0000    -.9131
   B          -.9131    1.0000
```

Figure 36.17b   The PARAM system file

```
     A        B         SSE      NCASES  SAMPLE

    .59     1.55  10888.9643        50      1
    .42     1.67  11152.3800        30      2
    .98     1.37   8409.17812       38      3
    .23     1.88  11539.4885        32      4
    .74     1.50   9913.33882       31      5
    .36     1.72  15829.0708        30      6
   1.80     1.17  13580.2475        33      7
    .46     1.64   8717.68195       34      8
    .24     1.87  13864.6946        27      9
    .54     1.58   9259.85855       33     10
    .54     1.58  11354.4104        30     11
    .18     1.95   8281.47928       30     12
    .29     1.77   7339.76973       32     13
   1.13     1.35  13591.6116        37     14
    .28     1.80  10416.4579        34     15
    .85     1.43  14449.7892        30     16
    .91     1.42  12527.9529        32     17
   1.40     1.24   7295.56894       31     18
    .77     1.48   9994.10521       33     19
   1.24     1.31   9531.98053       34     20
    .15     2.04   8647.15736       30     21
    .57     1.56   7819.84055       34     22
    .67     1.52  10313.9450        33     23
   1.00     1.35  11484.6662        30     24
   2.75     1.01  12142.2984        29     25
    .62     1.53   8719.81935       30     26
    .31     1.77  12288.8269        32     27
    .59     1.56   8798.50742       31     28
    .34     1.74   8393.37457       29     29
   1.02     1.38  11001.3134        31     30
    .66     1.50   6609.76805       34     31

NUMBER OF CASES READ =      31    NUMBER OF CASES LISTED =      31
```

Figure 36.17c   Histograms of the bootstrapped parameter estimates

```
26-Aug-87 Nonlinear Regression                                              Page    8
16:48:20  Stopping Distance Example


A

     COUNT   MIDPOINT   ONE SYMBOL EQUALS APPROXIMATELY   .20 OCCURRENCES

         0     -.05
         1      .10   *****
         6      .25   ******************************
         4      .40   *******************
         5      .55   **************************
         4      .70   ********************
         2      .85   **********
         3     1.00   ***************
         1     1.15   *****
         1     1.30   *****
         1     1.45   *****
         0     1.60
         1     1.75   *****
         0     1.90
         0     2.05
         0     2.20
         0     2.35
         0     2.50
         0     2.65
         1     2.80   *****
         0     2.95
                       I....+....I....+....I....+....I....+....I....+....I
                       0         2         4         6         8        10
                                        HISTOGRAM FREQUENCY

VALID CASES     30      MISSING CASES       0

26-Aug-87 Nonlinear Regression                                              Page    9
16:48:20  Stopping Distance Example


B

     COUNT   MIDPOINT   ONE SYMBOL EQUALS APPROXIMATELY   .10 OCCURRENCES

         1     1.02   **********
         0     1.07
         0     1.12
         1     1.17   **********
         1     1.22   **********
         0     1.27
         1     1.32   **********
         4     1.37   ******************************************
         2     1.42   ********************
         1     1.47   **********
         4     1.52   ******************************************
         4     1.57   ******************************************
         1     1.62   **********
         1     1.67   **********
         2     1.72   ********************
         2     1.77   ********************
         1     1.82   **********
         2     1.87   ********************
         0     1.92
         1     1.97   **********
         1     2.02   **********
                       I....+....I....+....I....+....I....+....I....+....I
                       0         1         2         3         4         5
                                        HISTOGRAM FREQUENCY

VALID CASES     30      MISSING CASES       0
```

36.18
Weighting Cases

If case weighting is in effect, [C]NLR uses case weights when calculating the residual sum of squares and derivative matrices. The degrees of freedom in the ANOVA table are based on unweighted cases.

When the model program is first invoked for each case, the weight variable's value is set equal to its value in the active file. The model program may recalculate that value. For example, to effect a robust estimation, the model program may recalculate the weight variable value as an inverse function of the residual magnitude. Be aware that [C]NLR uses the weight variable's value *after* the model program executes.

[C]NLR ignores cases that have missing, negative, or zero weights.

ANNOTATED EXAMPLE FOR CNLR/NLR

Draper and Smith (1981) pose the following exercise. Under adiabatic conditions, the wind speed Y is given by the nonlinear model:

$$Y = a*\ln(b*X + c) + e$$

where

X = the nominal height of the anemometer
a = friction velocity
b = 1 + (zero point displacement)/(roughness length)
c = 1/(roughness length)

The data are as follows:

```
  X     Y

 40 490.2
 80 585.3
160 673.7
320 759.2
640 837.5
```

To arrive at good initial values, consider the model without the error term:

$$Y = a*\ln(b*X + c)$$

Simple algebraic manipulation transforms the model into linear form. First, divide both sides by *a*:

$$Y/a = \ln(b*X + c)$$

Then, use the EXP function, which is the inverse of the natural logarithm:

$$\exp(Y/a) = b*X + c$$

The model is now in linear form. The dependent variable, exp(Y/a) should be regressed on X to obtain estimates of *b* and *c*. To determine the value to use for *a*, you need to consider the magnitudes of the Y values. Recall that the transcendental number *e* is 2.7183 to four decimal places. Thus *e* raised to the Y power, represented as exp(Y), will be outside the bounds of machine storage if Y is at all large, as is the case here. Considering the scale of the Y variable, we decide to set *a* equal to 100 initially. If you choose naive initial values for *a*, *b*, and *c*, chances are you will get CNLR off to a bad start. Having gone through the above exercise, however, we can confidently supply initial values to CNLR.

The following SPSS-X commands show how to arrive at initial estimates for CNLR:

```
TITLE NLRDS7--EXAMPLE G
SET WIDTH=80
DATA LIST / X 1-3 Y 5-9(1)
PLOT PLOT=Y WITH X
BEGIN DATA
 40 490.2
 80 585.3
160 673.7
320 759.2
640 837.5
END DATA

* LET A=100 SO THAT EXP DOESN'T PRODUCE TOO LARGE NUMBERS
COMPUTE EY=EXP(Y/100)
REGRESSION VAR=EY,X/DEP=EY/ENTER
```

Figure A shows the plot of the Y versus X association. The relationship is nonlinear.

A The functional form

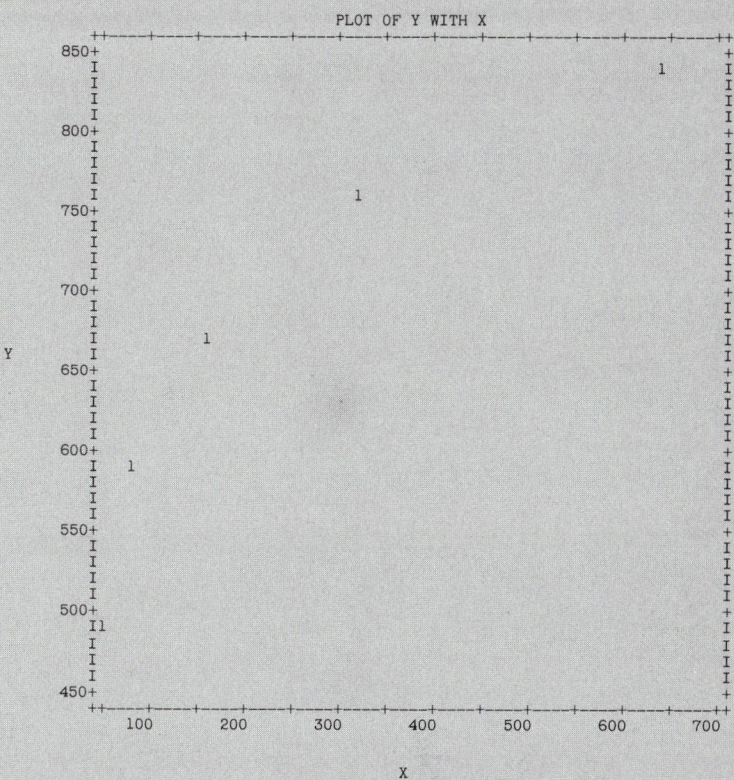

Figure B shows the regression used to get initial values for *b* and *c*.

B Regression results

```
Multiple R            .99940
R Square              .99879
Adjusted R Square     .99839
Standard Error      69.22830

Analysis of Variance
                  DF    Sum of Squares        Mean Square
Regression         1    11886580.22650     11886580.22650
Residual           3       14377.67112         4792.55704

F =    2480.21675     Signif F =  .0000

------------------- Variables in the Equation -------------------

Variable              B        SE B       Beta         T   Sig T

X              7.065892     .141880    .999396    49.802   .0000
(Constant)  -223.259958   46.867778              -4.764   .0176
```

Recall that we set *a* to 100. The initial values for *b* and *c* are 7.06 and -223, respectively. The following commands show how to use CNLR to estimate the model. Because this is an unconstrained model, you can also use NLR to estimate the model parameters.

```
MODEL PROGRAM
 A=100 B=7.06 C=-223.26
COMPUTE PRED=A*LN(B*X+C)
CNLR Y WITH X/PRED=PRED/SAVE PRED
PLOT
  FORMAT=OVERLAY
 /PLOT=PRED WITH X;Y WITH X
```

Figure C shows the iteration history from CNLR. CNLR takes some time to get to a final solution, but an inspection of values as they change across iterations reveals that nothing is awry.

C Iteration history

```
Iteration Residual SS          A           B           C
    0.1   6822.703884   100.000000   7.06000000  -223.26000
    1.1   6118.219759   100.003582   7.12842901  -223.25826
    2.1   5980.044858    99.3079691   7.18318715  -223.18102
    3.1   2189.215593    99.8751558   7.25081504  -203.17519
    4.1    969.0682157    99.8829723   7.03269110  -178.53483
    5.1    346.3380776    99.9820119   6.63396701  -146.30177
    6.1    241.2809321   100.221852    6.34390202  -126.98157
    7.1    233.1632074   100.394696    6.22140934  -120.56186
    8.1    228.9660802   100.567447    6.12718119  -116.91714
    9.1    210.6108403   101.510838    5.64880982  -100.76343
   10.1    191.6216324   103.042276    4.94957998   -79.980740
   11.1    153.9276211   103.806125    4.71805881   -76.312618
   12.1    112.9684153   106.405708    3.96720857   -64.516989
   13.1    101.8552912   106.152748    4.11125134   -69.138780
   14.1     85.09714967   106.154607    4.07803645   -64.325743
   15.1     70.26699518   106.994246    3.85660498   -58.647174
   16.1     54.07086976   108.832385    3.36853918   -46.433765
   17.1     39.48809011   109.300201    3.30711370   -45.456518
   18.1     27.88877849   110.894789    2.96953110   -37.284674
   19.1     17.59942496   111.803782    2.81864042   -33.199641
   20.1     13.63701498   112.864153    2.63353107   -29.260726
   21.1     10.60925934   113.656352    2.54067173   -28.092029
   22.1      8.256672638   114.694027    2.36235821   -23.152804
   23.1      8.072032652   114.278682    2.43409724   -24.442493
   24.1      7.315334149   114.556909    2.39300009   -23.887380
   25.1      7.154980179   114.885783    2.34353251   -22.746051
   26.1      7.060824167   114.965846    2.33415995   -22.554616
   27.1      7.014235706   115.119098    2.31424523   -22.106372
   28.1      7.013278395   115.143743    2.31105767   -22.038259
   29.1      7.013265870   115.146801    2.31065500   -22.028887
   30.1      7.013265849   115.146881    2.31064486   -22.028764
```

Run stopped after 30 major iterations.
Optimal solution found.

Figure D shows the remaining CNLR results. The ANOVA for the regression shows that the fit of the final solution is very good. As in the example in Section 36.25, using 5 data points to estimate a 3-parameter model is a highly parameterized situation. This is reflected in the high correlations of the estimates. The standard error of the *c* coefficient is relatively large. This dovetails with the iteration history shown in Figure C, wherein CNLR began with an initial value of -223 and ended up with a final value of -22.

D CNLR results

```
Nonlinear Regression Summary Statistics      Dependent Variable Y

    Source          DF  Sum of Squares  Mean Square

    Regression       3  2314527.69673  771509.23224
    Residual         2        7.01327       3.50663
    Uncorrected Total 5 2314534.71000

   (Corrected Total) 4    75525.34800


R squared = 1 - Residual SS / Corrected SS =     .99991

                                Asymptotic 95 %
                     Asymptotic  Confidence Interval
    Parameter  Estimate  Std. Error   Lower         Upper

    A         115.14688147  2.040557217  106.36707239  123.92669055
    B           2.310644855   .280311478    1.104561908    3.516727803
    C         -22.02876418  6.409410588  -49.60623215    5.548703779

Asymptotic Correlation Matrix of the Parameter Estimates

             A         B         C

    A      1.0000   -.9963     .9666
    B      -.9963    1.0000    -.9802
    C       .9666   -.9802    1.0000
```

Figure E shows a plot of PRED versus X superimposed on a value of Y versus X. The fit is very good.

E The fitted function

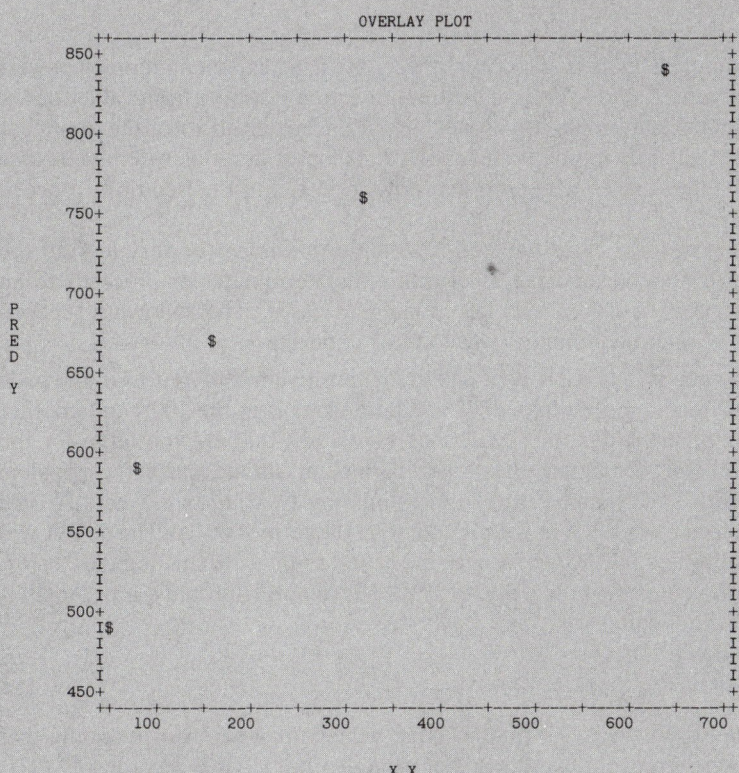

```
                              OVERLAY PLOT
        ++----+----+----+----+----+----+----+----+----+----+----++
   850+                                          $           +
      I                                                      I
      I                                                      I
      I                                                      I
   800+                                                      +I
      I                                                      I
      I                                                      I
      I                                                      I
      I                       $                              I
   750+                                                      +I
      I                                                      I
      I                                                      I
      I                                                      I
   700+                                                      +
      I                                                      I
P     I                                                      I
R     I          $                                           I
E  650+                                                      +
D     I                                                      I
Y     I                                                      I
      I                                                      I
   600+                                                      +
      I    $                                                 I
      I                                                      I
      I                                                      I
   550+                                                      +
      I                                                      I
      I                                                      I
      I                                                      I
   500+                                                      +
      I$                                                     I
      I                                                      I
      I                                                      I
   450+                                                      +
        ++----+----+----+----+----+----+----+----+----+----+----++
          100   200   300   400   500   600   700

                              X X

1:PRED WITH X   2:Y WITH X   $:Multiple occurrence
   5 cases        5 cases
```

36.19
Missing Values

Cases with missing values for any of the dependent or independent variables named on the [C]NLR command are excluded. Predicted values, but not residuals, can be calculated for cases with missing values on the dependent variable.

36.20
Underflows, Overflows, and Values out of Range

For many nonlinear models, especially those involving exponentiation or powers of large data values, underflows, overflows, or errors resulting from values out of range can occur. The program may "fix" itself and go on to solve the nonlinear problem if not all of the points were involved. The next iteration will then be able to step back into an area where no overflows occur, and the iterations proceed normally.

However, in some cases the step is so large that none (or very few) of the cases can be evaluated, and the algorithm either terminates or proceeds to an incorrect solution based on the few remaining cases. The following sections discuss ways to avoid continuing overflows or underflows.

Rescale Parameters. The CNLR procedure is sensitive to differences in the scale of the parameters being estimated. If one parameter is in the 100's and another parameter is of the order .1, CNLR may take steps that are too large for the smaller parameter. Rescaling the larger parameter should make the problem better behaved. For example, instead of estimating A, you can estimate A/1000 and then replace the term A in your model with the term 1000*A. The new A will simply be multiplied by 1000 to recover the actual term, as will its standard error.

For example, for the model $y = e^{(a+b\,x)}$, if a is of order 100 and b is of order .1, use the following model:

```
MODEL PROGRAM A=.1 B=.1
COMPUTE PRED=EXP(1000*A+B*X)
```

Rescale Data. If all the cases contain large values for a variable, rescaling that variable may help prevent overflows. For example, if YEAR is recorded as 1971, 1972, etc., you can subtract 1970 to get values 1, 2, 3, etc. In other situations, you may want to divide by 1000, 10000, or some other number that will put the variable on a more reasonable scale. However, rescaling should not be done without examining the nonlinear function to determine if the change in scale may alter the parameters being estimated. Many nonlinear models are not scale invariant.

Adjust BOUNDS. When a model includes parameters as exponents, large values of those parameters may cause overflows. The most straightfoward way to deal with this problem is to limit the size of those parameters by using the BOUNDS subcommand in CNLR.

Generally, both parameters and data values are involved in the expression that becomes too large. However, only constants and parameters can be specified on the BOUNDS subcommand. If the model is $y = e^{(a+b\,x)}$, you cannot put a bound on A+B*X since X is not a parameter. Instead, pick the largest and smallest value of X in your data set (or perhaps the largest and smallest possible values of X) and use these values in the BOUNDS statement.

For example, if X ranges from 0 to 100, the BOUNDS would be:

```
/BOUNDS A < 50; A+100*B < 50
```

This assures that the combination A+B*X will never exceed 50.

Adjust STEPLIMIT. By adjusting the maximum length of a step in CNLR, you may be able to avoid under and overflows. However, if the step limit is too small, the algorithms may not converge at all. The STEPLIMIT is a bound on the relative change in the norm of the parameter space. Thus, it is advisable to rescale the parameters before adjusting STEPLIMIT.

36.21
Common Convergence Problems

There are many problems that can occur when fitting a nonlinear equation. One of them is failure of the algorithm to converge. That is, changes between successive iterations are not small enough to satisfy the termination criteria. In this case the program issues a message and stops.

When CNLR or NLR does not converge, the first step is try the other procedure. The algorithms are very different and will in general not get "stuck" at the same place. You can also try a different set of starting values. If you have not already supplied derivatives, try to add them. In the presence of ill conditioning, numerically estimating derivatives can cause problems.

When the NLR procedure has trouble with overflow, underflow, or values out of range, as discussed in Section 36.20, it will either terminate abnormally or give a message telling why it stops. You can change the criteria involved to make NRL converge based on a different criterion.

The CNLR procedure is less straightforward. If at termination you get a message other than "Optimal Solution Found," you will need to try some of the hints discussed below. In addition, even when the optimal solution has been found, you should check that the loss function and parameter estimates are reasonable and have not changed much from the previous iteration. It is always a good idea to try the other procedure whenever possible to verify the solution.

The following are some common situations that may occur in CNLR.

Algorithm accepts initial point as final solution. If CNLR stops without moving from the initial point, try altering the initial point slightly and decrease or increase the STEPLIMIT. If underflows, overflows, or values out of range occur, they should be resolved first, using the techniques outlined in Section 36.20.

Cannot improve on current point. This message occurs when a steplength α that will decrease the loss function cannot be found, yet the optimality tolerance has not been satisfied. This can happen for a variety of reasons. One approach is to try increasing the OPTOL criteria. If the values of the loss function are large, a second approach is to try either or both of the following:

- Increase STEPLIMIT. A value of 50, 100 or even higher might help. The large value of the loss function may be because the parameters are still a long way from the optimal values.
- Rescale the loss function. When the loss function is extremely large, it is hard to satisfy the OPTOL criteria.

For example:

```
MODEL PROGRAM ...
COMPUTE PRED=...
COMPUTE L=(Y-PRED)**2 / 1000000
CNLR Y WITH X /LOSS=L /CRITERIA STEPLIMIT=100
```

A third possibility is that the point actually is an optimal solution or else very close to being optimal. You can try to input these estimates as initial values and use a very small STEPLIMIT. If the model can be run in NLR, you can also verify that the solution is optimal by using the NLR procedure.

36.22
EXAMPLES

The following examples show how to use CNLR and NLR to do nonlinear estimation in a variety of settings. A theme running through the examples is showing how to get good initial estimates for CNLR and NLR.

36.23
Regression with Restrictions

You can use CNLR (and NLR) to estimate regressions in which you wish to impose *a priori* restrictions on the parameters. The following simple example, taken from Fuller's *Introduction to Statistical Time Series* (1976), illustrates this.

Consider a linear regression with one dependent variable and two predictor variables. Ordinarily, the form of your model would be:

$$Y = B0 + B1*X1 + B2*X2 + e$$

and you would use a regression program to estimate B0, B1, and B2. Suppose that you wish to fit a model in which the coefficient for X2 is the square of the coefficient of X1. Your model is:

$$Y = B0 + B1*X1 + (B1**2)*X2 + e$$

There is no way to obtain this special treatment of the parameter estimates in REGRESSION. However, this problem is easily done in CNLR (or NLR).

The following SPSS-X commands show how use REGRESSION to get starting values for CNLR.

```
TITLE NLRFUL1--REGRESSION WITH RESTRICTIONS
SET WIDTH=80
* THIS EXAMPLE IS FROM PAGE 218 AND FOLLOWING OF FULLER
*   "INTRODUCTION TO STATISTICAL TIME SERIES"
DATA LIST / Y 1-2 X1 4 X2 6
BEGIN DATA
 9 2 4
19 7 8
11 1 9
14 3 7
 9 7 0
 3 0 2
END DATA

SUBTITLE RUN OLS REGRESSION
REGRESSION VAR=Y,X1,X2/DEP=Y/ENTER X1 X2
```

The coefficients printed by REGRESSION are optimal coefficients when no restrictions are placed on the estimation. The coefficients can be used directly as initial values for B0 and B1. Figure 36.23a shows the results.

Figure 36.23a   Regression results

```
Multiple R            .98112
R Square              .96260
Adjusted R Square     .93767
Standard Error       1.34366

Analysis of Variance
                    DF      Sum of Squares      Mean Square
Regression           2          139.41709         69.70855
Residual             3            5.41624          1.80541

F =      38.61085       Signif F =   .0072


---------------------- Variables in the Equation -----------------

Variable            B          SE B        Beta         T    Sig T

X2           1.149604      .169009     .764195      6.802   .0065
X1           1.262448      .200812     .706298      6.287   .0081
(Constant)    .877152     1.260588                   .696   .5366
```

With no restrictions, the estimated equation is:

predicted Y = .877 + 1.262*X1 + 1.150*X2

The R-squared for the model is .9626.

The following SPSS-X commands run CNLR on Fuller's problem:

```
SUBTITLE RUN CNLR
MODEL PROGRAM
 B0=0.877 B1=1.262
COMPUTE PRED=B0 + B1*X1 + B1*B1*X2
CNLR Y WITH X1 X2/PRED=PRED
```

- The MODEL PROGRAM command specifies initial values for the parameters to be estimated and signals the beginning of a block of statements culminating in a nonlinear least-squares regression.
- The COMPUTE statement specifies the model.
- Note that the coefficient of X2 is literally B1 squared.
- The CNLR command specifies the nonlinear least-squares regression of Y on X1 and X2. The PRED subcommand indicates that the model predicted values are found in variable PRED.

The iteration history shown in Figure 36.23b indicates that CNLR uses the supplied initial values. In 6 iterations, CNLR obtains a solution.

Figure 36.23b   Iteration history

```
Iteration  Residual SS          B0            B1

    0.1    47.37971704   .877000000   1.26200000
    1.1    12.62397643   .872603400   1.16905280
    2.1     7.214250937  .872384139   1.11940823
    3.1     6.990845762  1.27748749   1.09500424
    4.1     6.938820409  1.23248517   1.09126633
    5.1     6.938336260  1.24125323   1.09128025
    6.1     6.938336252  1.24133040   1.09127598

Run stopped after 6 major iterations.
Optimal solution found.
```

Figure 36.23c shows the nonlinear regression results. With the imposed restriction on the estimation of the X2 coefficient, the estimated model is

predicted Y = 1.241 + 1.091*X1 + 1.191*X2

where the X2 coefficient is obtained by literally squaring the X1 coefficient. The R-squared value for the estimated model is .9521. CNLR also prints the ANOVA table for the regression, estimated asymptotic standard errors and 95% confidence limits for the parameter estimates, and the correlations of the estimates.

Figure 36.23c   CNLR results

```
Nonlinear Regression Summary Statistics      Dependent Variable Y

  Source                 DF  Sum of Squares  Mean Square

  Regression              2     842.06166     421.03083
  Residual                4       6.93834       1.73458
  Uncorrected Total       6     849.00000

  (Corrected Total)       5     144.83333

  R squared = 1 - Residual SS / Corrected SS =      .95209

                                          Asymptotic 95 %
                            Asymptotic   Confidence Interval
  Parameter    Estimate     Std. Error    Lower         Upper

  B0         1.241330402  1.172858977  -2.015048163   4.497708967
  B1         1.091275979   .073167674    .888129949   1.294422010

  Asymptotic Correlation Matrix of the Parameter Estimates

                    B0         B1

  B0            1.0000     -.8887
  B1            -.8887      1.0000
```

**36.24
Grafted Polynomials: A
Segmented Model**

In this example, we look at a time series consisting of United States wheat yields from 1908 to 1971. The example comes from Fuller's *Introduction to Statistical Time Series* (1976).

Figure 36.24a is a plot of the data. The plot shows that wheat yields were more or less level for the first 20 to 30 years and then increased over the rest of the span. It is not at all clear what functional form would describe the behavior of the plot in its entirety. One approach is to use SPSS-X Trends procedures such as CURVEFIT or EXSMOOTH to model the series. The approach used here is to model pieces or segments of the series using low-order functional forms, such as linear functions and quadratic functions.

Figure 36.24a   Plot of wheat yields

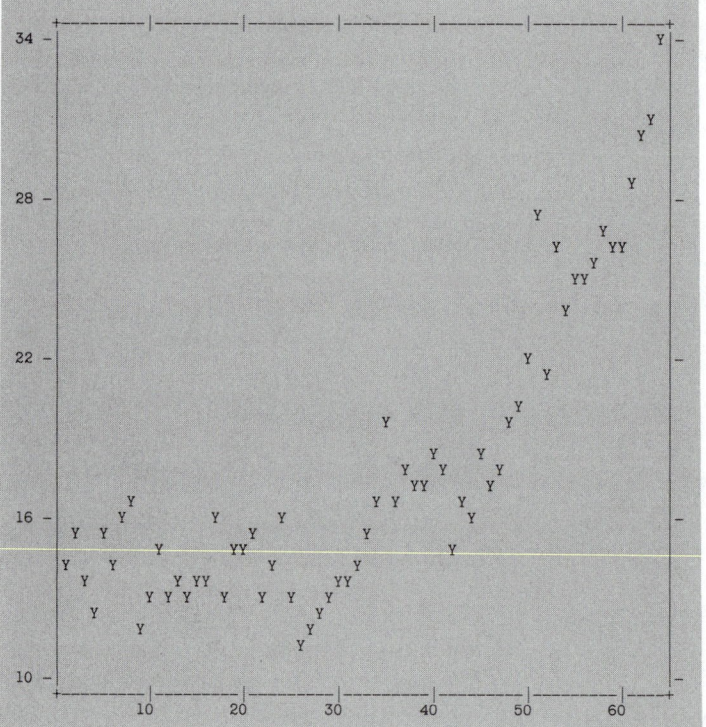

Following Fuller, the use of grafted polynomials assumes that "the time series may be divided into periods of length A such that the mean function in each period is adequately approximated by a quadratic in time. Furthermore the mean function possesses a continuous first derivative" (p. 394). To approximate the trend line of wheat yields, we fit a function that is constant for the first 25 years, increases at a quadratic rate until 1961, and is linear for the last 10 years. In general, an examination of the plot of the series should suggest the number of pieces, the join points, and the functional forms in the pieces. In this example, we are fixing the join points. Subsequently, we will show how to estimate them.

The following SPSS-X commands fit grafted polynomials to the U.S. wheat yield series:

```
TITLE NLRFUL2A--GRAFTED POLYNOMIALS WITH FIXED JOIN POINTS
SET WIDTH=80
* THIS EXAMPLE COMES FROM PAGE 396 AND FOLLOWING OF FULLER,
*  "INTRODUCTION TO STATISTICAL TIME SERIES"
*   DATA ARE UNITED STATES WHEAT YIELDS--1908 TO 1971
DATA LIST FREE / Y
COMPUTE Y=Y/10

COMPUTE T=$CASENUM

BEGIN DATA
                                      143 155 137
124 151 144 161 167 119 132 148 129 135
127 138 133 160 128 147 147 154 130 142
163 131 112 121 122 128 136 133 141 153
168 195 164 177 170 172 182 179 145 165
160 184 173 181 198 202 218 275 216 261
239 250 252 258 265 263 259 284 306 310
339
END DATA
TSPLOT VAR=Y
TEMPORARY
SELECT IF T <= 25
DESCRIPTIVES Y

MODEL PROGRAM
 B0=14 B1=0.01
DO IF T <= 25
COMPUTE PRED=B0
ELSE IF T > 25 AND T <= 54
COMPUTE PRED=B0+B1*(T-25)*(T-25)
ELSE IF T > 54
COMPUTE PRED=B0+B1*((54-25)*(54-25)+54*(T-54))
END IF

CNLR Y WITH T/SAVE PRED
TSPLOT VAR=PRED,Y
```

- The variable T is simply "time" expressed by sequential integers. We need variable T in order to do trend regression.

- TSPLOT, a procedure available with SPSS-X Trends, produces a horizontal sequential plot of the wheat yield series.

- The block of commands TEMPORARY, SELECT IF, and DESCRIPTIVES is used to obtain an initial estimate for the level at the beginning of the series.

- The MODEL PROGRAM command specifies the initial values for the parameters to be estimated and signals the beginning of a block of commands culminating in a nonlinear regression.

- The DO IF/END IF structure specifies the segmented model. Years 25 and 54 are the join points. For T less than or equal to 25, the model is a level regression with parameter B0. For T between 25 and 54, the model is a quadratic in time with parameters B0 and B1. For T greater than 54, the model is a linear function of time with parameters B0 and B1. As you might guess, there is an art to specifying statements of this sort. Notice that at the first join point, T=25, the model statements for the level segment and the quadratic segment produce the same predicted value, and at the second join point, T=54, the model statements for the quadratic segment and the linear segment produce the same predicted value.

- The CNLR command specifies Y as the dependent variable and T as the independent variable. It also uses SAVE to save predicted values.

- The final TSPLOT command produces a plot in which the fitted trend is superimposed on the observed series.

Figure 36.24b shows the resulting CNLR output. CNLR converges quickly. This is because we have used CNLR to solve a problem that can be done using ordinary regression. To see this, you might build an independent variable X as follows:

$$X = \begin{cases} 0, & 1<=t<=25 \\ (t-25)^{**}2, & 25<=t<=54 \\ 841+54*(t-54), & 54<=t<=64 \end{cases}$$

where t=1 for 1908. Then, use REGRESSION and regress Y on X including an intercept term. The equation for the estimated trend line is

predicted Y = 13.97 + .0123*X

just as we obtained here. Figure 36.24c shows the fitted trend line.

Figure 36.24b   CNLR results

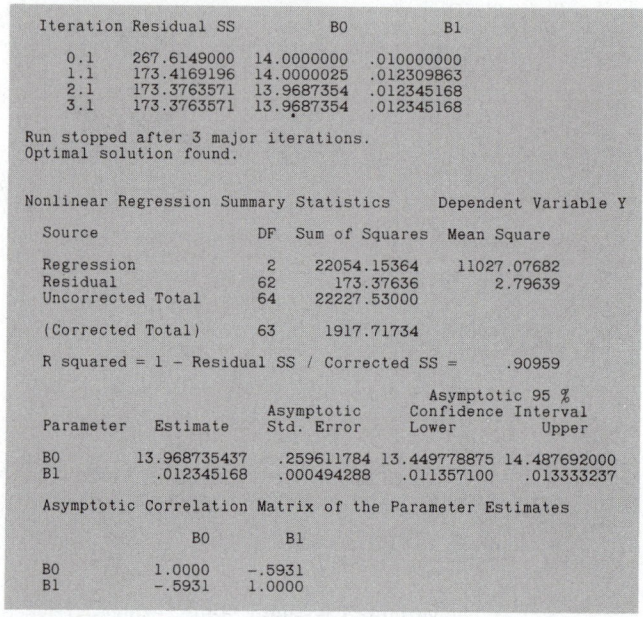

Figure 36.24c   Plot of fitted function

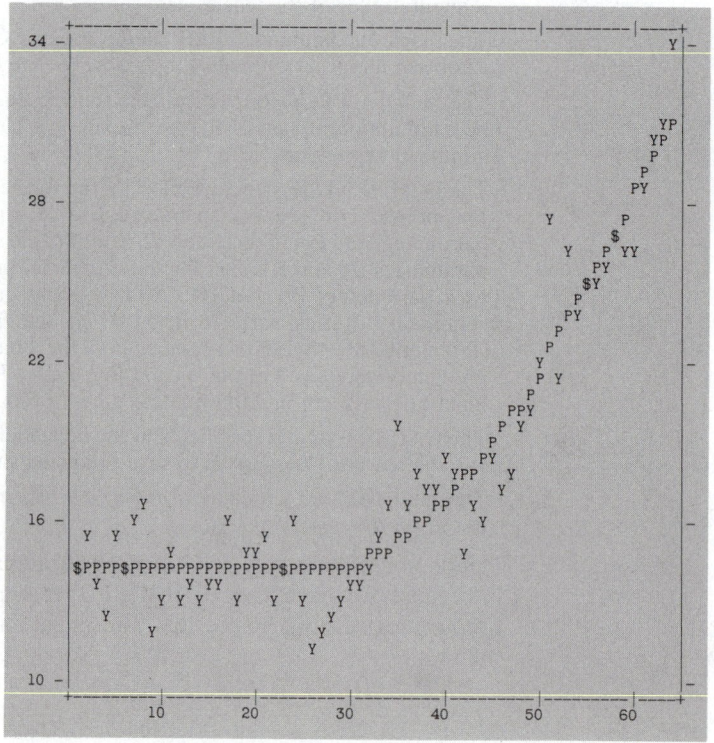

If the above example can be done in REGRESSION, why use CNLR? In this example, we assumed that we know the join points. If you want to use the data to estimate the join points, then the problem is indeed a nonlinear regression problem. It turns out that the above setup is easily modified to solve the more difficult problem of estimating the join points. The model program is:

```
MODEL PROGRAM
 B0=13.97 B1=0.0123 K1=25 K2=54
DO IF T <= K1
COMPUTE PRED=B0
ELSE IF T > K1 AND T <= K2
COMPUTE PRED=B0+B1*(T-K1)*(T-K1)
ELSE IF T > K2
COMPUTE PRED=B0+B1*((K2-K1)*(K2-K1)+K2*(T-K2))
END IF

CNLR Y WITH T/PRED=PRED
```

The rest of the job is as before. Note that there are two additional parameters—$K1$ and $K2$—representing the join points. The MODEL PROGRAM statement specifies parameter estimates from the previous run as initial values for $B0$ and $B1$, and our guesses of 25 and 54 as initial values for the join points.

Figure 36.24d shows the CNLR output produced by the above specification. The resulting solution has a slightly smaller residual sum of squares. The parameter estimates $B0$ and $B1$ have not changed much. The initial guesses of 25 and 54 turn out to have been good ones.

Figure 36.24d   Iteration history

Iteration	Residual SS	B0	B1	K1	K2
0.1	173.4102016	13.9700000	.012300000	25.0000000	54.0000000
1.1	173.3764235	13.9700000	.012343743	25.0000000	54.0000000
2.1	173.2412076	13.9458767	.012547336	25.2460283	54.0288124
3.1	173.0434791	14.0180805	.012727706	25.6113083	54.0716663
4.1	173.0417917	14.0198918	.012733675	25.6117603	54.0849659
5.1	173.0415989	14.0199757	.012734547	25.6130378	54.1000283
6.1	173.0409950	14.0201634	.012730088	25.6117569	54.1732263
7.1	173.0404710	14.0202932	.012718133	25.6048813	54.2664188
8.1	173.0401890	14.0203104	.012704466	25.5958103	54.3374559
9.1	173.0401448	14.0202566	.012699988	25.5923167	54.3471836
10.1	173.0401424	14.0202330	.012699809	25.5919958	54.3430999
11.1	173.0401424	14.0202308	.012699918	25.5920510	54.3420942

```
Run stopped after 11 major iterations.
Optimal solution found.
```

Nonlinear Regression Summary Statistics   Dependent Variable Y

Source	DF	Sum of Squares	Mean Square
Regression	4	22054.48986	5513.62246
Residual	60	173.04014	2.88400
Uncorrected Total	64	22227.53000	
(Corrected Total)	63	1917.71734	

R squared = 1 − Residual SS / Corrected SS =   .90977

Parameter	Estimate	Asymptotic Std. Error	Asymptotic 95 % Confidence Interval Lower	Upper
B0	14.020230799	.318564556	13.383006812	14.657454785
B1	.012699918	.003615380	.005468081	.019931755
K1	25.592051014	3.449934328	18.691154892	32.492947136
K2	54.342094246	17.231712420	19.873537422	88.810651070

36.25
Linearizing a Problem for Good Initial Values

You must supply CNLR (and NLR) with initial values of all parameters. Specifying bad initial values can lead to bad consequences: the procedure may not converge to a solution; or the procedure may converge to a solution that does not provide the true minimum value of the residual sum of squares; or the solution may have parameter values that are physically impossible given the phenomenon at hand. On the other hand, good initial values will often enable the procedure to converge to a solution—hopefully the right solution—and converge much faster than otherwise.

One of the best ways to arrive at good initial values is to attempt to linearize the problem and obtain estimates via REGRESSION. This is illustrated in the following example.

Draper and Smith (1981) pose this problem as an exercise. The relationship between the yield of a crop, Y, and the amount of fertilizer, X, applied to that crop has been formulated to be

$$Y = a - bp^x + e$$

where a, b, and p are parameters to be estimated, and p is bounded by 0 and 1. The values of X and Y are as follows:

```
X      Y

0    44.4
1    54.6
2    63.8
3    65.7
4    68.9
```

The basic strategy for coming up with good initial values is to try to get the model into a form where you can usefully take logarithms, since logging "transforms" exponentiation into multiplication and multiplication into addition. Thus, a term involving multiplication and exponentiation is linearized.

Consider the model omitting the error term:

$$Y = a - bp^x$$

Subtract a from both sides:

$$Y - a = -bp^x$$

Take negatives of both sides (because you cannot take a logarithm of a negative number):

$$a - Y = bp^x$$

Take logs of both sides:

$$\begin{aligned} \ln(a - Y) &= \ln(bp^x) \\ &= \ln(b) + \ln(p^x) \\ &= \ln(b) + X*\ln(p) \end{aligned}$$

At this point you have the desired linear form:

$$\ln(a - Y) = \ln(b) + \ln(p)*X$$

Choose a so that $(a - Y)$ is positive, and then regress $\ln(a - Y)$ on X. Antilogs of the resulting regression coefficients will supply initial values for b and p.

The following SPSS-X commands show how to estimate initial values using REGRESSION for use in CNLR:

```
TITLE NLRDS5--EXERCISE D FROM DRAPER AND SMITH CH 10
* RELATIONSHIP BETWEEN CROP YIELD AND AMOUNT OF FERTILIZER
SET WIDTH=80
DATA LIST / X 1 Y 3-6(1)
BEGIN DATA
0 44.4
1 54.6
2 63.8
3 65.7
4 68.9
END DATA
PLOT PLOT=Y WITH X

* ESTIMATE A BY YMAX PLUS SOMETHING--LET A=70
COMPUTE DEPVAR=LN(70-Y)
REGRESSION VAR=DEPVAR,X/DEP=DEPVAR/ENTER
* REGRESSION GIVES INT=3.88 SLOPE=-.76;
*   ANTILOGS ARE 29 AND .47
```

- The PLOT command produces a plot showing the form of the Y versus X association. An examination of the plot will help you determine the functional form of the relationship, as well as plausible and implausible values of the parameters.

- DEPVAR is the transformed dependent variable needed for regression. Our guess for the value of a is 70, which is larger than any Y value, thereby ensuring that the value evaluated by the LN function is positive.

- The REGRESSION command regresses DEPVAR on X. The intercept and slope estimates from this regression are used to obtain initial values for b and p.

Figure 36.25a shows the plot of Y versus X. The nonlinear association of Y and X is evident.

Figure 36.25a   The functional form

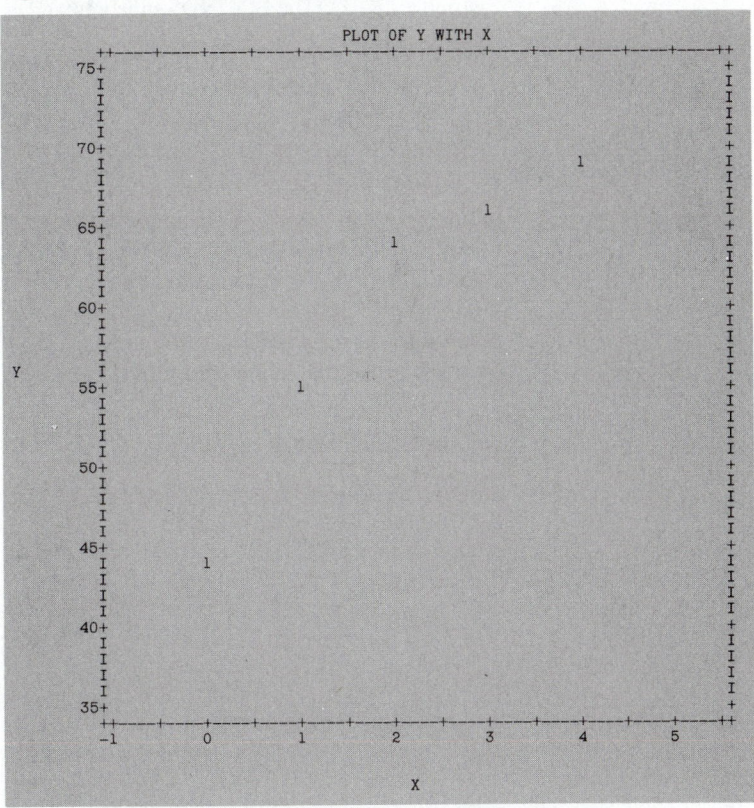

Figure 36.25b shows the output from REGRESSION. The antilog of 3.38 is 29.52. This becomes the initial value for b. The antilog of $-.75$ is .469. This becomes the initial value for p.

Figure 36.25b   Regression results

```
Multiple R              .98126
R Square                .96287
Adjusted R Square       .95049
Standard Error          .27141

Analysis of Variance
                    DF      Sum of Squares      Mean Square
Regression           1            5.73097          5.73097
Residual             3             .22099           .07366

F =     77.79854      Signif F =   .0031


------------------ Variables in the Equation ------------------

Variable              B          SE B        Beta         T    Sig T

X               -.757032       .085828    -.981260    -8.820   .0031
(Constant)      3.385150       .210234                16.102   .0005
```

The following SPSS-X commands run the nonlinear regression in CNLR:

```
MODEL PROGRAM
 A=70 B=29 P=.47
COMPUTE PRED=A-B*P**X
CNLR Y WITH X/PRED=PRED
 /BOUNDS 0 < P < 1/SAVE PRED
PLOT
 FORMAT=OVERLAY
 /PLOT=Y WITH X;PRED WITH X
```

- The MODEL PROGRAM command specifies initial values for the parameters and signals the beginning of a block of commands culminating in CNLR.
- The COMPUTE command specifies the model.
- CNLR specifies the regression of Y on X. The PREDICTED subcommand names variable PRED. The BOUNDS subcommand constrains the parameter estimate of p to lie within the interval (0,1). The SAVE subcommand saves the predicted values from the regression. Since BOUNDS is specified, you must use CNLR. If the problem were unconstrained, you could use NLR.
- The PLOT command produces an overlay plot showing Y versus X and PRED versus X. This shows how well the estimated model fits the observed values.

Figure 36.25c shows the output from CNLR. The iteration history shows that the initial values are good. CNLR converges quickly to a solution in the neighborhood of the initial values. CNLR prints the parameter estimates and their standard errors. Note the broad 95% confidence limits. We are estimating a model on five data points, so we should not expect much precision. With five data points and three parameters, the model is also highly parameterized, so the high correlations of the estimates are not surprising.

Figure 36.25c   CNLR results

```
 Iteration Residual SS           A             B             P

   0.2      16.49653383    70.0000000    29.0000000    .470000000
   1.1      10.74575450    70.1922983    28.4434176    .529112127
   2.2       4.480015479   70.5431977    26.5334335    .542658747
   3.1       4.172684227   71.6954703    27.3110889    .593210526
   4.1       3.720234102   71.5964337    27.4434258    .577965876
   5.1       3.616030024   71.9414089    27.8200371    .584801598
   6.1       3.570464383   72.3415954    28.1778166    .594667097
   7.1       3.568824817   72.4230603    28.2430745    .596594769
   8.1       3.568804824   72.4323386    28.2515272    .596784828
   9.1       3.568804798   72.4326326    28.2518771    .596790136

Run stopped after 9 major iterations.
Optimal solution found.


Nonlinear Regression Summary Statistics       Dependent Variable Y

  Source                 DF  Sum of Squares  Mean Square

  Regression              3    18083.09120    6027.69707
  Residual                2        3.56880       1.78440
  Uncorrected Total       5    18086.66000

  (Corrected Total)       4      397.30800

  R squared = 1 - Residual SS / Corrected SS =       .99102

                                            Asymptotic 95 %
                            Asymptotic     Confidence Interval
  Parameter   Estimate      Std. Error     Lower         Upper

  A         72.432632595   3.186401989   58.722651381  86.142613810
  B         28.251877129   3.102811346   14.901557422  41.602196836
  P           .596790136    .080996274     .248201295    .945288977

Asymptotic Correlation Matrix of the Parameter Estimates

                   A           B           P

  A             1.0000       .9131       .9434
  B              .9131      1.0000       .7901
  P              .9434       .7901      1.0000
```

Figure 36.25d is the plot of PRED versus X superimposed on the plot of Y versus X. The predicted points fit the observed points very well.

Figure 36.25d   The fitted function

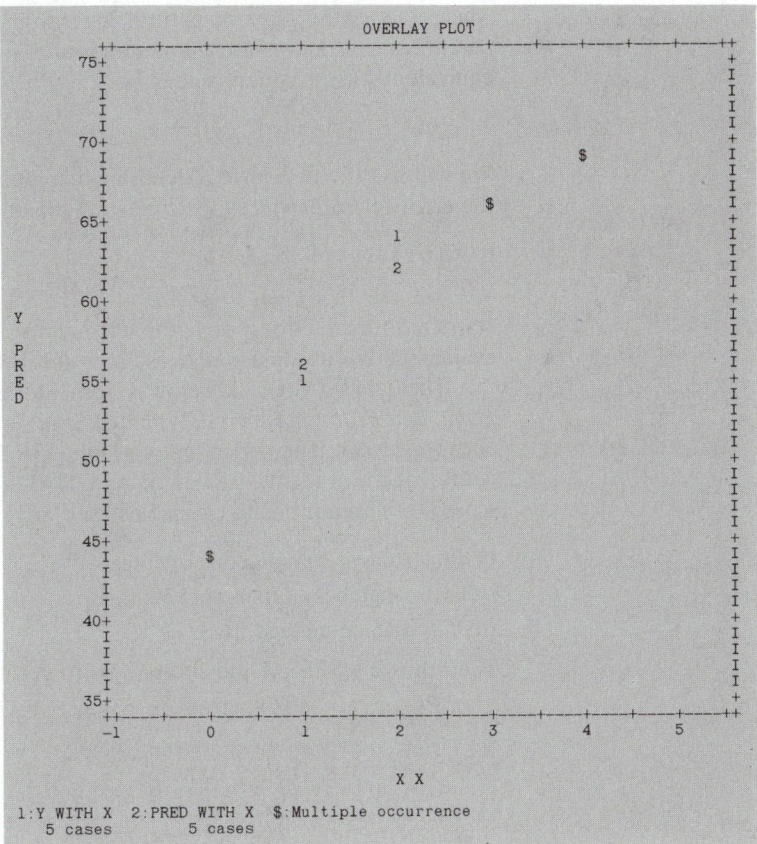

36.26
Logistic Regression on Disaggregated Data

Using the LOSS subcommand, you can program CNLR to do maximum likelihood estimation. If you know the likelihood function or the log-likelihood function for a particular problem, you can specify its negative on the LOSS subcommand, since minimizing the negative of the log-likelihood is equivalent to maximizing the likelihood. This example illustrates this by performing logistic regression in CNLR.

Suppose you have a single dichotomous dependent variable Y scored 0 or 1 and a single continuous independent variable X. A naive regression of Y on X has a number of problems. In particular

• The predicted values from the linear regression are not bounded to the interval (0,1).

• The errors from the linear regression are heteroscedastic.

A consequence of heteroscedasticity is a loss of efficiency in estimation, which manifests itself in larger standard errors than would otherwise be the case. One remedy for this is the weighted least square, which can be done with REGRES-

SION using the /REGWGT subcommand. An alternative approach is to use logistic regression. The logistic transformation remedies both problems.

The logistic regression model is expressed as:

$$Y = \exp(a + b*X)/(1 + \exp(a + b*X)) + e$$

where *exp* is the base of natural logarithms raised to the power indicated in parentheses, *a* and *b* are parameters, and *e* is an error term. An algebraically equivalent form frequently seen is:

$$Y = 1/(1 + \exp(-(a+b*X))) + e$$

We will use the first form. Algebraic manipulation of the logistic form (ignoring the error term) produces the following linearized form:

$$\ln(Y/(1-Y))=a+b*X$$

We will use this form to arrive at initial values for CNLR. Note that if Y is restricted to values of 0 or 1, the left-hand side of the linearized form cannot be evaluated. We use linear regression to substitute usable values for Y.

The data set analyzed below is from Aldrich and Nelson's *Linear Probability, Logit, and Probit Models* (1984) in the Sage series *Quantitative Applications in the Social Sciences*. The dependent variable, GRADE, is a student's final grade in a course. If the student receives an A, GRADE is scored 1, otherwise GRADE is scored 0. Three predictor variables used are

- GPA—student's grade point average.
- TUCE—number of right answers in a pre-test.
- PSI—teaching method used.

The following SPSS-X job shows how to get initial estimates for CNLR:

```
TITLE LOGISTIC REGRESSION ON DISAGGREGATED DATA
SET WIDTH=80
SUBTITLE LOGISTIC REGRESSION IN CNLR
DATA LIST FILE='LOGIS DATA'
 / GPA 1-4(2) TUCE 6-7 PSI 9 GRADE 11
VARIABLES LABELS
 GPA 'ENTERING GRADE POINT AVERAGE'
 TUCE 'PRETEST SCORE'
 PSI 'TEACHING METHOD'
 GRADE 'FINAL GRADE'
VALUE LABELS PSI 1 'PSI USED' 0 'OTHER   METHOD'/
 GRADE 1 'A' 0 'B OR C'
FORMATS PSI(F2.0)
LIST /FORMAT=NUM

SUBTITLE USE TWO REGRESSIONS TO ESTIMATE STARTING VALUES
REGRESSION VAR=GRADE,GPA,TUCE,PSI/DEP=GRADE/ENT/
 SAVE=PRED(PREDREG)
IF (PREDREG GE .999) PREDREG=.999
IF (PREDREG LE .001) PREDREG=.001
COMPUTE LOGIT=LN(PREDREG/(1-PREDREG))
REGRESSION VAR=LOGIT,GPA,TUCE,PSI/DEP=LOGIT/ENT
```

- The LIST command lists the data.

- The first REGRESSION regresses GRADE on the three predictor variables and saves the predicted values in PREDREG.

- Since the predicted values from ordinary regression are not guaranteed to lie within the interval (0, 1), we use IF statements to reset any extreme value to a value within the desired interval.

- The variable LOGIT contains the desired dependent variable for arriving at initial estimates for CNLR. Using ln(GRADE/(1-GRADE)) as the dependent variable is not appropriate, since the GRADE scores 0 and 1 produce an expression which cannot be evaluated. Using PREDREG in place of GRADE eliminates this problem.

36

• The second REGRESSION produces the coefficients that we will use as initial estimates in CNLR.

Figure 36.26a shows a listing of the data. Figure 36.26b shows the results from the first regression. Regressing GRADE directly on the predictors gives rise to the linear probability model. If we interpret the results, we find that GPA is the most important predictor, followed by PSI, and TUCE is unimportant. An interesting result is that even though objections to the linear probability model can be raised (as we did above), in practice you can often use it. For guidelines, see Leo Goodman's article *A Comparison of the Usual and Modified Multiple Regression Approaches* (1975) or Aldrich and Nelson.

Figure 36.26a   The data

```
        GPA TUCE PSI GRADE

     1  2.66  20   0    0
     2  2.89  22   0    0
     3  3.28  24   0    0
     4  2.92  12   0    0
     5  4.00  21   0    1
     6  2.86  17   0    0
     7  2.76  17   0    0
     8  2.87  21   0    0
     9  3.03  25   0    0
    10  3.92  29   0    1
    11  2.63  20   0    0
    12  3.32  23   0    0
    13  3.57  23   0    0
    14  3.26  25   0    1
    15  3.53  26   0    0
    16  2.74  19   0    0
    17  2.75  25   0    0
    18  2.83  19   0    0
    19  3.12  23   1    0
    20  3.16  25   1    1
    21  2.06  22   1    0
    22  3.62  28   1    1
    23  2.89  14   1    0
    24  3.51  26   1    0
    25  3.54  24   1    1
    26  2.83  27   1    1
    27  3.39  17   1    1
    28  2.67  24   1    0
    29  3.65  21   1    1
    30  4.00  23   1    1
    31  3.10  21   1    0
    32  2.39  19   1    1

NUMBER OF CASES READ =      32    NUMBER OF CASES LISTED =      32
```

Figure 36.26b   The linear probability model

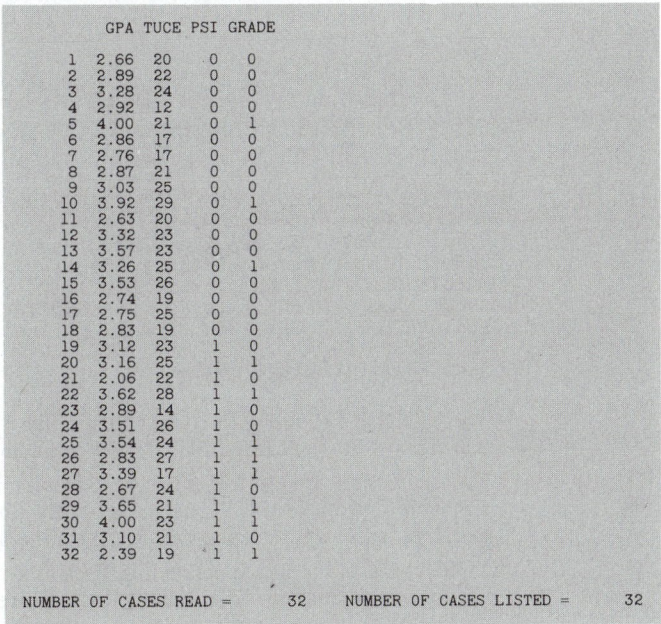

```
Multiple R               .64490
R Square                 .41590
Adjusted R Square        .35332
Standard Error           .38806

Analysis of Variance
                    DF      Sum of Squares      Mean Square
Regression           3             3.00228          1.00076
Residual            28             4.21647           .15059

F =      6.64566       Signif F =  .0016


------------------ Variables in the Equation ------------------

Variable            B          SE B        Beta         T    Sig T

PSI            .378555      .139173     .395388     2.720   .0111
GPA            .463852      .161956     .448620     2.864   .0078
TUCE           .010495      .019483     .084854      .539   .5944
(Constant)   -1.498017      .523889                -2.859   .0079
```

Figure 36.26c shows the results of the second regression. The regression coefficients from this regression are the desired starting values.

Figure 36.26c   Regression for initial estimates

```
Multiple R              .93089
R Square                .86656
Adjusted R Square       .85226
Standard Error         1.11834

Analysis of Variance
                        DF      Sum of Squares      Mean Square
Regression               3          227.41554          75.80518
Residual                28           35.01946           1.25070

F =        60.61044        Signif F =  .0000


————————————— Variables in the Equation ——————————

Variable            B           SE B        Beta          T     Sig T

PSI          3.235026       .401083      .560392      8.066     .0000
GPA          3.350037       .466743      .537365      7.177     .0000
TUCE          .215265       .056148      .288653      3.834     .0007
(Constant) -18.179207      1.509799                 -12.041     .0000
```

The following SPSS-X commands show how to set up logistic regression using CNLR. Because the LOSS subcommand is needed, this analysis cannot be done in NLR.

```
SUBTITLE SUPPLY LOSS FUNCTION TO GET ML SOLUTION
MODEL PROGRAM
 B0=-18.18 B1=3.35 B2=.215 B3=3.235
COMPUTE LIN=B0+B1*GPA+B2*TUCE+B3*PSI
COMPUTE PRED=EXP(LIN)/(1+EXP(LIN))
COMPUTE LOSS=-GRADE*LN(PRED)-(1-GRADE)*LN(1-PRED)
CNLR GRADE WITH GPA,TUCE,PSI
 /LOSS=LOSS
 /CRITERIA STEPLIMIT .01
```

• The MODEL PROGRAM command specifies the initial values for the parameters and signals the beginning of a block of commands culminating in CNLR.

• The expression for the logistic regression functional form is a lengthy one, so we specify it in two COMPUTE statements. LIN is a linear combination of the predictor variables with an intercept term. PRED is the logistic regression function.

• LOSS contains the loss function appropriate for maximum likelihood estimation of the logistic regression. The default least-squares solution is not equivalent to the maximum likelihood solution. This is different from ordinary least-squares regression where, with suitable assumptions satisfied, the least-squares solution is also maximum likelihood.

• The CNLR command specifies the dependent and independent variables. The PRED subcommand indicates which transformation statement contains the functional form for the predicted values. The LOSS subcommand indicates which transformation statement contains the loss function. The CRITERIA subcommand sets STEPLIMIT to a value smaller than the default.

The results of running the above commands are shown in Figure 36.26d. CNLR finds the optimal solution in 15 iterations. CNLR prints no other output because we use a loss function that is not least squares to estimate the model. To see standard errors, use the subcommand

```
/BOOTSTRAP
```

to calculate bootstrap estimates of the parameter standard errors. (Be aware that this can be computationally expensive.) Figure 36.26e shows the output from CNLR when bootstrapping is specified.

Figure 36.26d   Iteration history

Iteration	Loss funct	B0	B1	B2	B3
0.1	13.53319134	−18.180000	3.35000000	.215000000	3.23500000
1.1	13.49246235	−18.179623	3.35113685	.221235300	3.23499319
2.1	13.38982742	−18.112974	3.50910209	.198796914	3.13918479
3.1	13.32425424	−17.995858	3.61946078	.181205227	3.02663493
4.1	13.28408263	−17.836484	3.68617398	.167336853	2.93502582
5.1	13.25585602	−17.657348	3.71690357	.157070938	2.86656085
6.1	13.23209377	−17.472247	3.72495769	.149323446	2.81411031
7.1	13.13551804	−16.356723	3.69196153	.112501462	2.56009100
8.1	13.06931850	−15.299721	3.56679325	.088873055	2.39241293
9.1	12.99936646	−14.311099	3.36459321	.077069525	2.29889303
10.1	12.92820623	−13.398257	3.09266157	.076575936	2.27401401
11.1	12.91403010	−13.264041	3.02871749	.079416558	2.28822768
12.1	12.89909254	−13.144473	2.94732941	.084934311	2.31894216
13.1	12.89033733	−13.037611	2.85600851	.092127541	2.36026942
14.1	12.88963508	−13.014935	2.82479687	.095078005	2.37814655
15.1	12.88963425	−13.020157	2.82591093	.095137826	2.37855112

Run stopped after 15 major iterations.
Optimal solution found.

Figure 36.26e   CNLR with bootstrapped standard errors

Loss function value 12.8896342

Parameter	Estimate	Std. Error	95% Conf. Bounds Lower	Upper	95% Trimmed Range Lower	Upper
B0	−13.020281	16.7220357	−46.200427	20.1598660	−73.968886	−7.1651168
B1	2.8259254	3.5332948	−4.1848980	9.8367488	.6831617	14.8482310
B2	.0951409	.3011101	−.5023268	.6926087	.0000000	.7920758
B3	2.3785656	3.8228445	−5.2067874	9.9639185	.3892628	14.5916878

Bootstrap Correlation Matrix of the Parameter Estimates

	B0	B1	B2	B3
B0	1.0000	−.9078	−.6801	−.5298
B1	−.9078	1.0000	.3411	.4126
B2	−.6801	.3411	1.0000	.2851
B3	−.5298	.4126	.2851	1.0000

With four parameters in the model, CNLR did $10*4*(4+1)/2$, or 100, bootstrap samples by default. The estimation took roughly 90 CPU seconds on an IBM 4381. The estimated standard errors are disconcertingly large. This is in part due to the fact that the sample size is 32. With more data, the estimated standard errors ought to become smaller. Raising the number of bootstrap samples will not necessarily improve the bootstrap standard errors.

As an exercise, you might run the above data example in PROBIT. To do so, specify the following commands:

```
COMPUTE ONE=1
PROBIT GRADE OF ONE WITH GPA,TUCE,PSI
 /MODEL=LOGIT
 /LOG=NONE
```

To make CNLR calculate the same model as PROBIT, use the following expression for LIN in the model program:

```
COMPUTE LIN=-10+2*(B0+B1*GPA+B2*TUCE+B3*PSI)
```

In other words, PROBIT scales the parameters relative to the logistic function form indicated above. The reason for this is to make the parameter estimates from PROBIT's logistic regression comparable in scale to the parameter estimates from PROBIT's probit regression.

One virtue of running logistic regression in CNLR is that you can save the predicted values and the residuals. You can then use the predicted values to assess how well the logistic regression model fits the data. One way to do this is as follows:

```
CNLR GRADE WITH GPA,TUCE,PSI
 /LOSS=LOSS
 /CRITERIA STEPLIMIT .01
 /SAVE PRED

SUBTITLE DIAGNOSTICS
IF PRED >= 0.5 PROB1=1
IF PRED <  0.5 PROB1=0
FORMATS PRED(F6.3)/PROB1(F1)
CROSSTABS GRADE BY PROB1
 /STATISTICS ALL
```

The SAVE subcommand saves the predicted values in variable PRED because PRED is the name of the predicted value variable. The crosstabulation of GRADE against PROB1 shows correct and incorrect predictions.

36.27
Minimizing an Analytic Function

You can use CNLR to find the minimum of an analytic function. In this example, we use Rosenbrock's function:

$$F(x1,x2) = 100(x1^2 - x2)^2 + (1 - x1)^2$$

This function has a slowly descending valley with steep sides, the bottom of which curves in the shape of a parabola. The minimum is known to occur at $x1=1$, $x2=1$.

The following SPSS-X commands show how to find the minimum of Rosenbrock's function using CNLR:

```
TITLE NLRROSEN--TRICKING CNLR INTO MINIMIZING AN ANALYTIC FUNCTION
* THE LOSS FUNCTION EXPRESSES ROSENBROCK'S FUNCTION
*  THE KNOWN MINIMUM IS X1=1, X2=1
SET WIDTH=80
DATA LIST FREE / Y X                      /* "DUMMY" VARIABLES
BEGIN DATA
0 0
0 0
END DATA

MODEL PROGRAM
 X1=-1.2 X2=1
COMPUTE PRED=0
COMPUTE LOSS=100*(X1**2 - X2)**2 + (1 - X1)**2
CNLR Y WITH X/PRED=PRED/LOSS=LOSS
```

- The DATA LIST command reads in variables X and Y, both of which are irrelevant to solving the problem at hand. They are read in to establish an active file and to supply two names for the CNLR command.
- The MODEL PROGRAM command specifies the initial values for the parameters and signals the beginning of a block of commands culminating in CNLR. Initial values will affect the number of iterations in which CNLR converges.
- PRED is set equal to 0. PRED is not actually used at all, but CNLR expects to find this variable name.
- Variable LOSS contains the analytic function to be minimized.
- Variables Y and X specified on CNRL are not directly relevant to the analysis.

Figure 36.27 shows the output. Within tuning parameter precision, CNLR has found the minimum of Rosenbrock's function.

Figure 36.27   Minimizing the Rosenbrock function

```
Iteration  Loss funct            X1            X2

     0.1   48.40000000   -1.2000000    1.00000000
     1.1   19.18196298   -1.1214613    1.03205662
     2.1   18.44856601   -1.1507685    1.10982757
     3.1    8.638738655   -1.0650819    1.15781017
     4.1    8.107707859   -1.0132343    1.02392009
     5.1    7.614803234    -.90837598    .784464885
     6.1    7.269011230    -.86154526    .701131784
     7.1    5.768387740    -.67808968    .433688790
     8.1    4.914426597    -.53884166    .260487371
     9.1    3.682205647    -.32659668    .135168738
    10.1    3.033319415    -.14849061   -.02240603
    11.1    2.859662618    -.19446876    .032272211
    12.1    2.603711212    -.13567325    .007406379
    13.1    2.291088511    -.00111052   -.03785666
    14.1    2.018604166    .019260642   -.02141260
    15.1    1.596980563    .197654014   -.00026878
    16.1    1.213494696    .221346182    .051105010
    17.1     .9141239640   .360353005    .107965089
    18.1     .7724232626   .413128821    .150231878
    19.1     .5812508025   .490232218    .257866786
    20.1     .3292577616   .613031127    .363607174
    21.1     .2910925140   .646921627    .404057014
    22.1     .1263841103   .750323548    .560063570
    23.1     .1041949411   .795261483    .622351420
    24.1     .0574767782   .848152885    .711826180
    25.1     .0282354390   .881695209    .778489601
    26.1     .0132905945   .931018062    .862450913
    27.1     .0069733795   .951001172    .901108074
    28.1     .0018131718   .970682053    .942909534
    29.1     .0003298250   .990890709    .980959227
    30.1     .0000638563   .995956126    .991533951
    31.1     .0000011347   .999269285    .998520831
    32.1    4.9338E-08    1.00007511    1.00013643
    33.1    2.0671E-09     .999992960    .999989058
    34.1    4.5479E-11     .999995236    .999990451

Run stopped after 34 major iterations.
Optimal solution found.
```

36.28
Using CNLR to Solve Linear Programming Problems

Although CNLR is not explicitly designed to do so, you can use CNLR to solve linear programming problems. Linear programming is a special form of optimizing under constraints. If you do a lot of this sort of work, or if your problems are very large, you should acquire special-purpose software which will probably work more efficiently than CNLR. Nevertheless, we will show how to use CNLR to solve a type of problem known as a "transportation problem".

This example is found in Bruce Feiring's *Linear Programming: An Introduction* (1986) in the Sage Series *Quantitative Applications in the Social Sciences*.

A plastics manufacturer has two plants, one located in Salt Lake City and one in Denver. There are three distribution warehouses, in Los Angeles, Chicago, and New York. The Salt Lake City plant can supply 120 tons per week and the Denver plant can supply 140 tons per week. The Los Angeles warehouse needs at least 100 tons each week to meet demands, Chicago needs at least 60 tons weekly, and New York needs at least 80 tons per week. Shipping costs in dollars per ton are as follows:

	To: Los Angeles	Chicago	New York
From:			
Salt Lake City	5	7	9
Denver	6	7	10

The question is: How many tons of plastics should be shipped from each plant to each warehouse to minimize the total shipping cost while meeting demands and not exceeding supplies? To answer this, following Feiring, use the following variables:

- X11, the number of tons shipped from Salt Lake City to Los Angeles.
- X12, the number of tons shipped from Salt Lake City to Chicago.
- X13, the number of tons shipped from Salt Lake City to New York.
- X21, the number of tons shipped from Denver to Los Angeles.
- X22, the number of tons shipped from Denver to Chicago.
- X23, the number of tons shipped from Denver to New York.

This problem contains a set of supply-and-demand constraints that can be specified on the BOUNDS subcommand. The costs to be minimized are specified on the loss function. The following SPSS-X job commands show how to do this:

```
TITLE NLRLP3--CNLR SOLVES LINEAR PROGRAMMING PROBLEM
SET WIDTH 80
* EXAMPLE FROM PAGE 18 AND FF. OF FEIRING'S
*  "LINEAR PROGRAMMING:  AN INTRODUCTION"
DATA LIST FREE / Y X                       /* "DUMMY" VARIABLES
BEGIN DATA
0 0
END DATA

MODEL PROGRAM
 X11=1 X12=1 X13=1 X21=1 X22=1 X23=1
COMPUTE PRED=0
COMPUTE LOSS=5*X11+7*X12+9*X13+6*X21+7*X22+10*X23

CNLR Y WITH X
 /PRED=PRED
 /LOSS=LOSS
 /BOUNDS
  X11+X12+X13 <= 120;
  X21+X22+X23 <= 140;
  100 <= X11+X21;
   60 <= X12+X22;
   80 <= X13+X23;
    0 <= X11;
    0 <= X12;
    0 <= X13;
    0 <= X21;
    0 <= X22;
    0 <= X23;
```

As in the example in Section 36.27, there are no relevant data to be read. Instead, we read in "dummy" data so that SPSS-X has an active file.

- The MODEL PROGRAM command specifies initial values for the parameters and signals the beginning of a block of commands culminating in the CNLR command. You cannot use NLR to solve this problem since NLR works only for unconstrained minimization problems and does not work for loss functions other than least squares.

- The first COMPUTE command creates a variable PRED that is always 0. This is needed because CNLR expects a PRED variable. PRED is not actually used, however, since the LOSS function is only a function of X.

- The second COMPUTE creates variable LOSS, which contains the cost function to be minimized.

- The CNLR command specifies X and Y as variables, even through they aren't really used. The BOUNDS subcommand specifies the supply and demand constraints. In addition, simple non-negativity constraints are imposed.

CNLR produces the output shown in Figure 36.28. The display includes the iteration number, the value of the loss function, the values of the X variables, and the values of the linear constraints. Given supply-and-demand constraints and the cost function, the optimal solution is to ship 100 tons from Salt Lake City to Los Angeles; 20 tons from Salt Lake City to New York; 60 tons from Denver to Chicago; and ship 60 tons from Denver to New York.

Figure 36.28   Linear programming solution

```
Iteration  Loss funct        X11         X12         X13         X21
                             X22         X23    Lin Con  1  Lin Con  2
                        Lin Con  3  Lin Con  4  Lin Con  5

   0.1     1720.000000   99.0000000  20.0000000   1.00000000   1.00000000
                         40.0000000  79.0000000  120.000000  120.000000
                        100.000000   60.0000000   80.0000000
   1.3     1718.000004   99.9999981  18.0000038   1.99999811   .000001892
                         41.9999962  78.0000019  120.000000  120.000000
                        100.000000   60.0000000   80.0000000
   2.3     1717.000001  100.000000   17.0000006   2.99999924   .000000000
                         42.9999994  77.0000008  120.000000  120.000000
                        100.000000   60.0000000   80.0000000
   3.1     1700.000000   99.9999917    .000000000  20.0000083   .000008340
                         60.0000000  59.9999917  120.000000  120.000000
                        100.000000   60.0000000   80.0000000
   4.1     1700.000000   99.9999470    .000000000  20.0000530   .000053001
                         60.0000000  59.9999470  120.000000  120.000000
                        100.000000   60.0000000   80.0000000

Run stopped after 4 major iterations.
Optimal solution found.
```

This approach an also be used to solve nonlinear problems with general forms for the cost function and the constraints. Use the CONSTRAINED FUNCTION command and the BOUNDS subcommand to specify the nonlinear programming model in question.

36.29
Robust Regression via Iteratively Reweighted Least Squares

When you use ordinary least-squares regression, the estimated parameters for the regression can be affected by influential points. The REGRESSION procedure provides some ways to detect influential points, but finding influential points and outliers is not necessarily completely straightforward. Moreover, the question becomes what to do about influential points and outliers. You might consider deleting an influential point and re-running the regression. As an alternative, you might differentially weight the points in such a way that points with large residuals have less impact on the parameter estimates than in the ordinary least-squares solution. Statisticians have proposed different weights to use in this situation. Using CNLR or NLR, it is not difficult to perform robust regression via iterative estimation. For a good discussion of this topic, see relevant portions of Hoaglin, Mosteller, and Tukey's *Understanding Robust and Exploratory Data Analysis* (1983).

The example we look at comes from Montgomery and Peck's *Introduction to Linear Regression Analysis* (1982). The dependent variable, Y, is the amount of time required by a route driver to service the soft-drink machines in a given location. The independent variables are X1, the number of cases of the product stocked, and X2, the distance walked by the route driver. There are 25 observations on delivery time.

We begin by fitting a linear model using ordinary regression:

```
TITLE SOFT DRINK DELIVERY TIME
* EXAMPLE FROM MONTGOMERY AND PECK
*   RAMSAY'S E FUNCTION WITH A=0.3
DATA LIST LIST / Y X1 X2
VARIABLE LABELS
 Y 'DELIVERY TIME IN MINUTES'
 X1 'NUMBER OF CASES'
 X2 'DISTANCE IN FEET'

SUBTITLE RUN ORDINARY LEAST SQUARES REGRESSION
REGRESSION VAR=Y,X1,X2/DEP=Y/ENTER/
 CASE=ALL DEFAULT ZRESID SRESID SDRESID LEV COOK/
 SCAT=(*RESID,*PRED)(*RESID,X1)(*RESID,X2)/
 SAVE=RESID(RESIDREG)
BEGIN DATA
16.68  7  560
11.50  3  220
12.03  3  340
14.88  4   80
13.75  6  150
18.11  7  330
 8.00  2  110
17.83  7  210
79.24 30 1460
21.50  5  605
40.33 16  688
21.00 10  215
13.50  4  255
19.75  6  462
24.00  9  448
29.00 10  776
15.35  6  200
19.00  7  132
 9.50  3   36
35.10 17  770
17.90 10  140
52.32 26  810
18.75  9  450
19.83  8  635
10.75  4  150
END DATA
```

- The minimum required syntax for REGRESSION consists of the VARIABLES subcommand, the DEPENDENT subcommand, and a method.
- The CASEWISE subcommand prints casewise results for the DEFAULT variables (the dependent variable, the predicted values, and residuals), plus the standardized residuals, the studentized residuals, the studentized deleted residuals, the leverage, and Cook's d.
- The SCATTERPLOT subcommand prints scatterplots of the specified variables. The most important diagnostic plots are the plot of the residuals versus the fitted values, along with plots of the residuals versus each of the independent variables.
- The SAVE subcommand saves the residuals in the variable named RESIDREG.

Figure 36.29a shows the ordinary least-squares regression results. The prediction equation resulting from regression is:

predicted Y = 2.341 + 1.616*X1 + .014*X2

Residual analysis shows whether the assumptions of the regression model have been met and whether there are any influential points in the analysis (an influential point being a point whose presence or absence makes a difference in the parameter estimates). Figure 36.29b shows the casewise results from regression.

The largest residual is 7.4197, associated with case 9. Since residuals are not scale-free, it is difficult to know how large that value is. Moreover, if a point is influential, it pulls the fit toward it, so that the magnitude of the residual is not as large as it would be otherwise. The standardized residual for point 9 is greater

Figure 36.29a   Ordinary least-squares regression

			Analysis of Variance			
Multiple R	.97959			DF	Sum of Squares	Mean Square
R Square	.95959		Regression	2	5550.81092	2775.40546
Adjusted R Square	.95592		Residual	22	233.73168	10.62417
Standard Error	3.25947					

F =   261.23511   Signif F =   .0000

------------------- Variables in the Equation -------------------

Variable	B	SE B	Beta	T	Sig T
X2	.014385	.003613	.301308	3.981	.0006
X1	1.615907	.170735	.716272	9.464	.0000
(Constant)	2.341231	1.096730		2.135	.0442

Figure 36.29b   Residual analysis: casewise results

```
Casewise Plot of Standardized Residual

*: Selected   M: Missing
```

Case #	Y	*PRED	*RESID	*ZRESID	*SRESID	*SDRESID	*LEVER	*COOK D
1	16.68	21.7081	-5.0281	-1.5426	-1.6277	-1.6956	.0618	.1001
2	11.50	10.3536	1.1464	.3517	.3648	.3575	.0307	.0034
3	12.03	12.0798	-.0498	-.0153	-.0161	-.0157	.0587	.0000
4	14.88	9.9556	4.9244	1.5108	1.5797	1.6392	.0454	.0776
5	13.75	14.1944	-.4444	-.1363	-.1418	-.1386	.0350	.0005
6	18.11	18.3996	-.2896	-.0888	-.0908	-.0887	.0029	.0001
7	8.00	7.1554	.8446	.2591	.2704	.2646	.0418	.0022
8	17.83	16.6734	1.1566	.3548	.3667	.3594	.0237	.0031
9	79.24	71.8203	7.4197	2.2764	3.2138	4.3108	.4583	3.4193
10	21.50	19.1236	2.3764	.7291	.8133	.8068	.1563	.0538
11	40.33	38.0925	2.2375	.6865	.7181	.7099	.0461	.0162
12	21.00	21.5930	-.5930	-.1819	-.1933	-.1890	.0737	.0016
13	13.50	12.4730	1.0270	.3151	.3252	.3185	.0211	.0023
14	19.75	18.6825	1.0675	.3275	.3411	.3342	.0382	.0033
15	24.00	23.3288	.6712	.2059	.2103	.2057	.0011	.0006
16	29.00	29.6629	-.6629	-.2034	-.2227	-.2178	.1259	.0033
17	15.35	14.9136	.4364	.1339	.1380	.1349	.0194	.0004
18	19.00	15.5514	3.4486	1.0580	1.1130	1.1193	.0563	.0440
19	9.50	7.7068	1.7932	.5501	.5788	.5698	.0564	.0119
20	35.10	40.8880	-5.7880	-1.7757	-1.8735	-1.9967	.0617	.1324
21	17.90	20.5142	-2.6142	-.8020	-.8778	-.8731	.1253	.0509
22	52.32	56.0065	-3.6865	-1.1310	-1.4500	-1.4896	.3516	.4510
23	18.75	23.3576	-4.6076	-1.4136	-1.4437	-1.4825	.0013	.0299
24	19.83	24.4029	-4.5729	-1.4029	-1.4961	-1.5422	.0806	.1023
25	10.75	10.9626	-.2126	-.0652	-.0675	-.0660	.0266	.0001

than 2. The Studentized residual for point 9 is greater than 3. Taken together, these two statistics indicate that point 9 is relatively poorly fit. The Studentized deleted residual for point 9 is greater than 4. Points 9 and 22 have the largest values of leverage and Cook's d. These statistics indicate that the presence or absence of point 9 in particular makes a difference in the values of the parameter estimates.

Figure 36.29c shows scatterplots of the residuals versus the predicted values and the independent variables. Point 9 is in the border of each plot near the upper right-hand corner. It appears that point 9 is influential, since if we disregard it, there is evidence of downward slope among the rest of the points in each scatterplot.

Ordinary least squares minimizes the sum of squared residuals. Robust regression minimizes some function of the residuals in such a way as to dampen the effect of observations that would be very influential if least squares were used. Rather than work with the residuals directly, it is useful to scale the residuals to come up with scale-invariant estimates. To scale the residuals, we must calculate s, a robust estimate of scale. A common way to do this is to use this formula:

$$s = (\text{MEDIAN} (\text{ABS}(e - \text{MEDIAN}(e))))/0.6745$$

where e indicates the residuals from OLS regression.

Figure 36.29c   Residual analysis: scatterplot

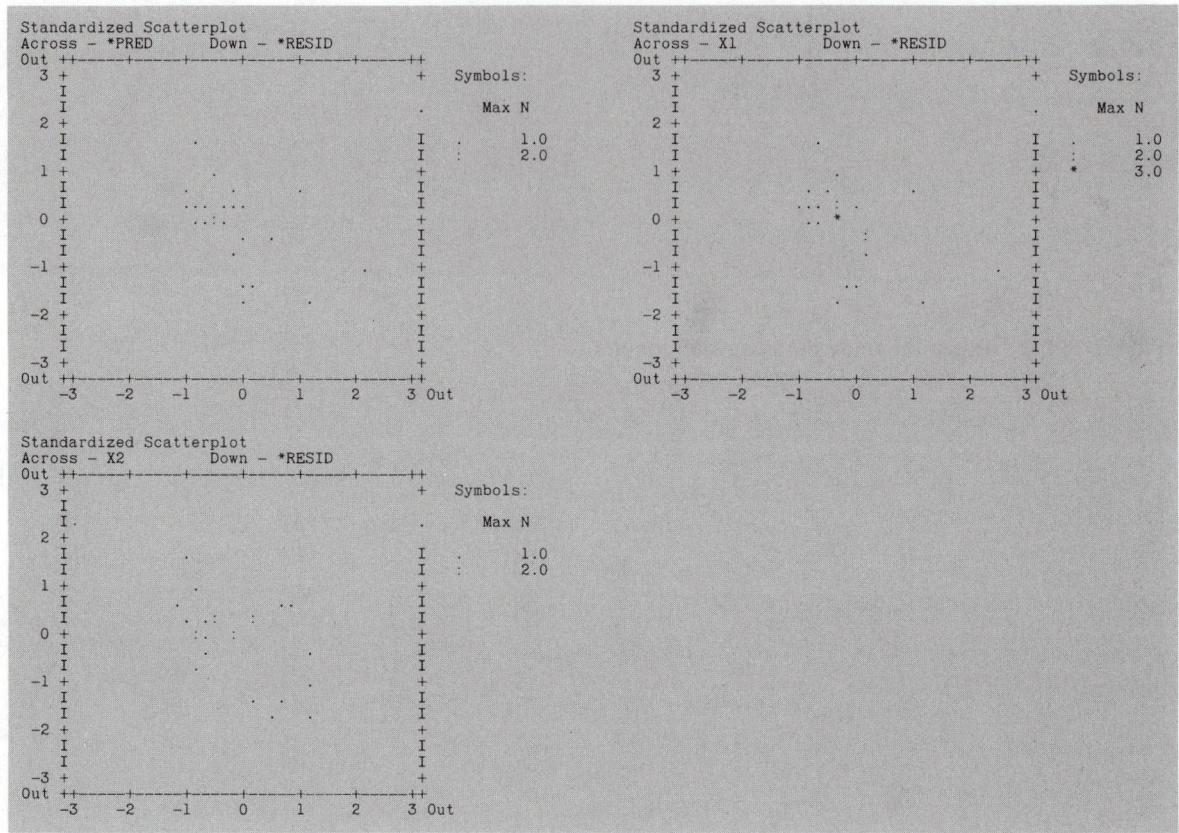

Figure 36.29d   Frequency distribution of residuals

RESIDREG Residual					
VALUE LABEL	VALUE	FREQUENCY	PERCENT	VALID PERCENT	CUM PERCENT
	-5.78797	1	4.0	4.0	4.0
	-5.02808	1	4.0	4.0	8.0
	-4.60757	1	4.0	4.0	12.0
	-4.57285	1	4.0	4.0	16.0
	-3.68653	1	4.0	4.0	20.0
	-2.61418	1	4.0	4.0	24.0
	-.66293	1	4.0	4.0	28.0
	-.59304	1	4.0	4.0	32.0
	-.44440	1	4.0	4.0	36.0
	-.28957	1	4.0	4.0	40.0
	-.21258	1	4.0	4.0	44.0
	-.04979	1	4.0	4.0	48.0
	.43636	1	4.0	4.0	52.0
	.67120	1	4.0	4.0	56.0
	.84462	1	4.0	4.0	60.0
	1.02701	1	4.0	4.0	64.0
	1.06754	1	4.0	4.0	68.0
	1.14639	1	4.0	4.0	72.0
	1.15660	1	4.0	4.0	76.0
	1.79319	1	4.0	4.0	80.0
	2.23749	1	4.0	4.0	84.0
	2.37641	1	4.0	4.0	88.0
	3.44862	1	4.0	4.0	92.0
	4.92435	1	4.0	4.0	96.0
	7.41971	1	4.0	4.0	100.0
	TOTAL	25	100.0	100.0	

MEDIAN   .436

VALID CASES   25   MISSING CASES   0

The following SPSS-X commands show how to obtain the robust estimate of scale for the residuals:

```
SET WIDTH=80
SUBTITLE FIND ROBUST ESTIMATE OF RESIDUAL SCALE
FREQUENCIES VAR=RESIDREG /STATISTICS=MEDIAN
```

RESIDREG contains the residuals from the OLS regression. FREQUENCIES finds the median residual value. Figure 36.29d shows the frequency table for RESIDREG. The median is .43636. For larger samples, you can suppress the frequency table and print just statistics using the STATISTICS subcommand.

Having determined the median residual, we use SNUM to calculate the absolute values of the median deviation scores. The second FREQUENCIES command is used to find the median of these scores:

```
COMPUTE SNUM=ABS(RESIDREG-0.43636)
FORMATS SNUM(F8.5)
FREQUENCIES VAR=SNUM  /STATISTICS=MEDIAN
```

The median is 1.09929. Again, for larger files you can suppress the frequency table and just print statistics.

Figure 36.29e   Frequency distribution of SNUM

```
SNUM
                                                      VALID      CUM
       VALUE LABEL             VALUE  FREQUENCY  PERCENT  PERCENT  PERCENT

                                .00000      1       4.0      4.0      4.0
                                .23484      1       4.0      4.0      8.0
                                .40826      1       4.0      4.0     12.0
                                .48615      1       4.0      4.0     16.0
                                .59065      1       4.0      4.0     20.0
                                .63118      1       4.0      4.0     24.0
                                .64894      1       4.0      4.0     28.0
                                .71003      1       4.0      4.0     32.0
                                .72024      1       4.0      4.0     36.0
                                .72593      1       4.0      4.0     40.0
                                .88076      1       4.0      4.0     44.0
                               1.02940      1       4.0      4.0     48.0
                               1.09929      1       4.0      4.0     52.0
                               1.35683      1       4.0      4.0     56.0
                               1.80113      1       4.0      4.0     60.0
                               1.94005      1       4.0      4.0     64.0
                               3.01226      1       4.0      4.0     68.0
                               3.05054      1       4.0      4.0     72.0
                               4.12289      1       4.0      4.0     76.0
                               4.48799      1       4.0      4.0     80.0
                               5.00921      1       4.0      4.0     84.0
                               5.04393      1       4.0      4.0     88.0
                               5.46444      1       4.0      4.0     92.0
                               6.22433      1       4.0      4.0     96.0
                               6.98335      1       4.0      4.0    100.0
                                          -----   -----    -----
                               TOTAL       25     100.0    100.0

MEDIAN       1.099

VALID CASES    25    MISSING CASES    0
```

The robust estimate of scale is given by

1.09929/0.6745 = 1.62978.

Having estimated s, we can now set up the robust regression:

```
SUBTITLE FIND IRLS SOLUTION
COMPUTE WT=1
WEIGHT BY WT
MODEL PROGRAM
 B0=2.341 B1=1.616 B2=.014
COMPUTE PREDNLR=B0+B1*X1+B2*X2
COMPUTE Z=(Y-PREDNLR)/1.62978
* LET A=0.3 IN RAMSAY'S FUNCTION
COMPUTE WT=EXP(-0.3*ABS(Z))
NLR Y WITH X1,X2/PRED=PREDNLR/SAVE PRED RESID(RESIDNLR)
```

- The weight variable, WT, is set to 1 for all cases initially.
- The WEIGHT command weights by WT.
- The MODEL PROGRAM command specifies the initial values for the parameters and signals the beginning of a block of commands culminating in a nonlinear least-squares regression. The initial values are the parameter estimates from OLS regression.
- The first COMPUTE command creates PREDNLR, which contains the predicted values. Notice that the form of the model is linear.
- The second COMPUTE command creates Z, which contains the scaled residuals. The numerator in the expression computes the residuals, and the denominator is the scaling factor determined above.
- WT is computed from the scaled residuals. The particular weighting scheme specified is known as Ramsay's Ea function. Sources such as Montgomery and Peck (1982) or Hoaglin, Mosteller, and Tukey (1983) have a detailed discussion of some of the weights available.
- The NLR command specifies the regression. The PRED subcommand names PREDNLR as the predicted values. The SAVE subcommand saves the predicted values (variable PREDNLR) and the residuals (variable RESIDNLR). NLR updates the predicted values and the weights at each iteration until convergence occurs.

Figure 36.29f shows the NLR results (the iteration history is omitted from the figure).

Figure 36.29f   NLR results

```
Nonlinear Regression Summary Statistics      Dependent Variable Y

  Source             DF      Weighted SS    Weighted MS

  Regression          3      9370.22450     3123.40817
  Residual           22        83.33028        3.78774
  Uncorrected Total  25      9453.55478

  (Corrected Total)  24      2287.70519

  R squared = 1 - Residual SS / Corrected SS =      .96357

                                          Asymptotic 95 %
                         Asymptotic     Confidence Interval
  Parameter   Estimate   Std. Error    Lower        Upper

  B0        3.767420263  .820798330  2.065188711  5.469651814
  B1        1.483133509  .118097144  1.238215022  1.728051996
  B2         .013057843  .002669447   .007521749   .018593937

Asymptotic Correlation Matrix of the Parameter Estimates

                  B0        B1        B2

  B0          1.0000    -.2719    -.3378
  B1          -.2719    1.0000    -.7305
  B2          -.3378    -.7305    1.0000
```

From NLR, the robust regression model is:

predicted Y = 3.767 + 1.483*X1 + .013*X2

Note the change in the values of the coefficients when we move from OLS regression to robust regression.

Finally, we display the robust regression predicted values, residuals, and weights:

```
SUBTITLE COMPUTE AND DISPLAY FINAL CASE WEIGHTS
COMPUTE Z=RESIDNLR/1.62978
COMPUTE WT=EXP(-0.3*ABS(Z))
FORMATS WT(F8.6)
LIST VAR=Y,PREDNLR,RESIDNLR,WT/FORMAT=NUMBERED
```

The iterated weights computed in the model program are stored in temporary form. To see them you must compute them outside the model program. Figure 36.29g shows the listing.

Figure 36.29g   Listing

	Y	PREDNLR	RESIDNLR	WT
1	16.68	21.46	−4.78	.414702
2	11.50	11.09	.41	.927230
3	12.03	12.66	−.63	.891081
4	14.88	10.74	4.14	.467095
5	13.75	14.62	−.87	.851253
6	18.11	18.46	−.35	.937874
7	8.00	8.17	−.17	.969183
8	17.83	16.89	.94	.841345
9	79.24	67.33	11.91	.111573
10	21.50	19.08	2.42	.640894
11	40.33	36.48	3.85	.492414
12	21.00	21.41	−.41	.927958
13	13.50	13.03	.47	.917072
14	19.75	18.70	1.05	.824093
15	24.00	22.97	1.03	.826614
16	29.00	28.73	.27	.951802
17	15.35	15.28	.07	.986796
18	19.00	15.87	3.13	.562367
19	9.50	8.69	.81	.860992
20	35.10	39.04	−3.94	.484628
21	17.90	20.43	−2.53	.628055
22	52.32	52.91	−.59	.897789
23	18.75	22.99	−4.24	.458050
24	19.83	23.92	−4.09	.470651
25	10.75	11.66	−.91	.845984

Note the differential weighting of the data points accomplished through the use of robust regression with Ramsay's function as the criterion. In particular, point 9 is downweighted much more than any of the other points.

Syntax

NONPAR CORR

```
NONPAR CORR [VARIABLES=] varlist [WITH varlist] [/varlist...]

  [/MISSING={PAIRWISE**}]
            {INCLUDE   }
            {LISTWISE  }

  [/PRINT={ONETAIL**}  {SIG**}  {SPEARMAN**}]
          {TWOTAIL  }  {NOSIG}  {KENDALL   }
                                {BOTH      }

  [/FORMAT={MATRIX**}]
           {SERIAL  }

  [/MATRIX=OUT({*   })]
               {file}

  [/SAMPLE]
```

**Default if the subcommand is omitted.

Contents

37.1 OVERVIEW

37.2 OPERATION

37.3 VARIABLES Subcommand

37.4 PRINT Subcommand

37.5 SAMPLE Subcommand

37.6 MISSING Subcommand

37.7 FORMAT Subcommand

37.8 MATRIX Subcommand

37.9 LIMITATIONS

37

Chapter 37 NONPAR CORR

NONPAR CORR computes two rank-order correlation coefficients, Spearman's rho and Kendall's tau-*b*, with their significance levels. You can obtain either or both coefficients. When you use NONPAR CORR, SPSS-X automatically computes the ranks and stores the cases in memory. Therefore, memory required is directly proportional to the number of cases being analyzed.

37.1
OVERVIEW

NONPAR CORR produces one or more matrices of correlation coefficients. For each coefficient, NONPAR CORR prints the number of cases used and the significance level. You can specify methods of handling missing data, optional formats, and random sampling of cases. NONPAR CORR also writes matrix materials that can be used by other procedures.

Coefficients and Significance Levels. By default, NONPAR CORR computes Spearman coefficients. Below each coefficient it prints both the number of cases and the one-tailed significance level. Optionally, you can request a two-tailed test, suppress the number of cases and significance level for each coefficient, compute only the Kendell coefficients, or compute both Spearman and Kendall coefficients. (See Section 37.4.)

Random Sampling. NONPAR CORR must store cases in memory for ranking. You can request a random sample of cases when there is not enough space to store all the cases. (See Section 37.5.)

Missing Values. By default, NONPAR CORR excludes cases with missing values on a pair-by-pair basis. Optionally, you can request that user-missing values be handled as if they were valid or that cases with missing values be deleted listwise. (See Section 37.6.)

Formatting Options. By default, NONPAR CORR prints correlations in matrix format. You can also print them in serial format. (See Section 37.7.)

Matrix Output. NONPAR CORR allows you to write matrix materials to a system file. The matrix materials include the number of cases used to compute each coefficient and either the Spearman or Kendall coefficients for each variable, whichever you specify. These materials can be read by other SPSS-X procedures. (See Section 37.8.)

Statistics. There are no optional statistics for NONPAR CORR. All statistics available for the requested coefficients are printed by default.

37.2
OPERATION

The only required subcommand on NONPAR CORR is the VARIABLES subcommand, which specifies the list of variables to be analyzed (see Section 37.3). The actual keyword VARIABLES can be omitted.

Sections 37.4 through 37.8 describe the optional subcommands. You can specify these subcommands in any order, separated by slashes. However, you must first specify the variables to be used in the analysis before you can specify any of the optional subcommands. For example, to include user-defined missing values in an analysis, specify

```
NONPAR CORR VARIABLES=SPPRES PAPRES16 PRESTIGE SATHOBBY SATFA
    /MISSING=INCLUDE
```

37.3
VARIABLES Subcommand

The VARIABLES subcommand names the variable list. The actual keyword VARIABLES is optional. If you explicitly specify keyword VARIABLES, an equals sign must precede the variable list. You can use keyword TO in the list to refer to consecutive variables in the active file. The variables must be numeric.

Depending on how you specify the variable list, NONPAR CORR prints either a lower-triangular or a rectangular matrix. If you provide a simple list of variables, NONPAR CORR prints the correlations of each variable with every other variable in the list in a lower-triangular matrix. For example, the command

```
NONPAR CORR VARIABLES=PRESTIGE SPPRES PAPRES16 DEGREE PADEG MADEG
```

produces the triangular matrix in Figure 37.3a. The correlation of a variable with itself (the diagonal) and redundant coefficients are not printed. Specify a simple variable list when you want to write the correlation matrix to a matrix system file (see Section 37.8). As indicated in the banner in Figure 37.3a, the default coefficients produced by NONPAR CORR are Spearman correlations. The

Figure 37.3a   A lower-triangular default matrix

```
-------------- S P E A R M A N   C O R R E L A T I O N   C O E F F I C I E N T S --------------


SPPRES          .3608
              N(  258)
              SIG .000


PAPRES16        .2934         .2021
              N(  382)    N(  235)
              SIG .000     SIG .001


DEGREE          .5262         .3864         .3438
              N(  461)    N(  277)    N(  412)
              SIG .000     SIG .000     SIG .000


PADEG           .2397         .1306         .3908         .3820
              N(  352)    N(  219)    N(  376)    N(  377)
              SIG .000     SIG .027     SIG .000     SIG .000


MADEG           .1781         .1323         .2593         .3829         .5965
              N(  406)    N(  244)    N(  372)    N(  442)    N(  356)
              SIG .000     SIG .019     SIG .000     SIG .000     SIG .000


              PRESTIGE       SPPRES      PAPRES16       DEGREE        PADEG

" . " IS PRINTED IF A COEFFICIENT CANNOT BE COMPUTED.
```

number of cases upon which the correlations are based and the one-tailed significance level are printed for each correlation. To obtain Kendall coefficients, you must use the PRINT subcommand (see Section 37.4).

To obtain the rectangular matrix, specify two variable lists separated by keyword WITH. NONPAR CORR then prints a rectangular matrix of variables in the first list correlated with variables in the second list. For example,

```
NONPAR CORR VARS=PRESTIGE SPPRES PAPRES16 WITH DEGREE PADEG MADEG
```

produces the nine correlations shown in Figure 37.3b. The variables listed before keyword WITH define the rows of the matrix, and those listed after keyword WITH define the columns. Unless a variable is in both lists, there are no identity coefficients in the matrix. If you want to write the correlation matrix for use with another procedure or program, do not use keyword WITH (see Section 37.8).

Figure 37.3b   A matrix from a variable list using WITH

```
-------------- S P E A R M A N   C O R R E L A T I O N   C O E F F I C I E N T S --------------

                 DEGREE        PADEG         MADEG

PRESTIGE         .5262         .2397         .1781
               N(  461)      N(  352)      N(  406)
               SIG .000      SIG .000      SIG .000


SPPRES           .3864         .1306         .1323
               N(  277)      N(  219)      N(  244)
               SIG .000      SIG .027      SIG .019


PAPRES16         .3438         .3908         .2593
               N(  412)      N(  376)      N(  372)
               SIG .000      SIG .000      SIG .000

" . " IS PRINTED IF A COEFFICIENT CANNOT BE COMPUTED.
```

You can request more than one matrix on a NONPAR CORR command. Use a slash to separate the specifications for each of the requested matrices. For example,

```
NONPAR CORR VARIABLES=SPPRES PAPRES16 PRESTIGE/
                SATCITY WITH SATHOBBY SATFAM
```

produces two correlation matrices. The first matrix contains three coefficients in triangular form. The second matrix is rectangular and contains two coefficients. You can specify up to 25 variable lists with one NONPAR CORR command and name (or imply) up to 100 variables on all lists.

If all cases have a missing value for a given pair of variables, or if they all have the same value for a variable, the coefficient cannot be computed. Because Spearman's rho and Kendall's tau-*b* coefficients always have a value in the range −1.00 to +1.00, NONPAR CORR prints a decimal point if a correlation cannot be computed.

ANNOTATED EXAMPLE FOR NONPAR CORR

This example analyzes a 500-case sample from the 1980 General Social Survey. The variables are

- PRESTIGE—the respondent's occupational prestige scale score.
- SPPRES—the spouse's occupational prestige scale score.
- PAPRES16—the father's occupational prestige scale score when the respondent was growing up.
- DEGREE, PADEG, MADEG—the highest educational degree earned by the respondent, the father, and the mother, respectively. Each of these variables has four categories to code high school, junior college, college, and graduate degrees.

This example determines the degree to which variation in three measures of occupational prestige and three measures of educational attainment are related. NONPAR CORR computes nonparametric correlation coefficients for the ranked data. The SPSS-X commands are

```
GET  FILE GSS80/KEEP PRESTIGE SPPRES PAPRES16 DEGREE PADEG MADEG
NONPAR CORR VARIABLES=PRESTIGE TO MADEG/
   MISSING=LISTWISE/
   FORMAT=SERIAL/
   PRINT=BOTH
FINISH
```

- The GET command defines the data to SPSS-X and selects the variables needed for the analysis (see Chapter 6).
- The NONPAR CORR command requests correlation coefficients for one simple variable list. This form of the NONPAR CORR command produces a lower-triangular matrix (see Section 37.3).
- The MISSING subcommand excludes missing values listwise. Cases missing on any of the six variables are not used in the calculation of any coefficients (see Section 37.6).
- The FORMAT subcommand prints each lower-triangular matrix in serial format (see Section 37.7).
- The PRINT subcommand requests both Kendall and Spearman correlation matrices (see Section 37.4).

Output from the NONPAR CORR command

```
- - - - - - - - - - - - - - K E N D A L L   C O R R E L A T I O N   C O E F F I C I E N T S - - - - - - - - - - - - - -

VARIABLE          VARIABLE          VARIABLE          VARIABLE          VARIABLE          VARIABLE
PAIR              PAIR              PAIR              PAIR              PAIR              PAIR
--------          --------          --------          --------          --------          --------


PRESTIGE   .2354  PRESTIGE   .1970  PRESTIGE   .4564  PRESTIGE   .1618  PRESTIGE   .1987  SPPRES     .1386
WITH     N( 192)  WITH     N( 192)  WITH     N( 192)  WITH     N( 192)  WITH     N( 192)  WITH     N( 192)
SPPRES   SIG .000  PAPRES16 SIG .000  DEGREE   SIG .000  PADEG    SIG .003  MADEG    SIG .000  PAPRES16 SIG .003


SPPRES     .2875  SPPRES     .0975  SPPRES     .0707  PAPRES16   .2642  PAPRES16   .2875  PAPRES16   .1949
WITH     N( 192)  WITH     N( 192)  WITH     N( 192)  WITH     N( 192)  WITH     N( 192)  WITH     N( 192)
DEGREE   SIG .000  PADEG    SIG .047  MADEG    SIG .116  DEGREE   SIG .000  PADEG    SIG .000  MADEG    SIG .001


DEGREE     .3434  DEGREE     .3141  PADEG      .5545
WITH     N( 192)  WITH     N( 192)  WITH     N( 192)
PADEG    SIG .000  MADEG    SIG .000  MADEG    SIG .000
```

" . " IS PRINTED IF A COEFFICIENT CANNOT BE COMPUTED.

```
- - - - - - - - - - - - - - S P E A R M A N   C O R R E L A T I O N   C O E F F I C I E N T S - - - - - - - - - - - - - -

VARIABLE          VARIABLE          VARIABLE          VARIABLE          VARIABLE          VARIABLE
PAIR              PAIR              PAIR              PAIR              PAIR              PAIR
--------          --------          --------          --------          --------          --------


PRESTIGE   .3374  PRESTIGE   .2694  PRESTIGE   .5547  PRESTIGE   .1996  PRESTIGE   .2435  SPPRES     .1971
WITH     N( 192)  WITH     N( 192)  WITH     N( 192)  WITH     N( 192)  WITH     N( 192)  WITH     N( 192)
SPPRES   SIG .000  PAPRES16 SIG .000  DEGREE   SIG .000  PADEG    SIG .003  MADEG    SIG .000  PAPRES16 SIG .003


SPPRES     .3613  SPPRES     .1175  SPPRES     .0851  PAPRES16   .3332  PAPRES16   .3440  PAPRES16   .2368
WITH     N( 192)  WITH     N( 192)  WITH     N( 192)  WITH     N( 192)  WITH     N( 192)  WITH     N( 192)
DEGREE   SIG .000  PADEG    SIG .052  MADEG    SIG .120  DEGREE   SIG .000  PADEG    SIG .000  MADEG    SIG .000


DEGREE     .3710  DEGREE     .3387  PADEG      .5774
WITH     N( 192)  WITH     N( 192)  WITH     N( 192)
PADEG    SIG .000  MADEG    SIG .000  MADEG    SIG .000
```

" . " IS PRINTED IF A COEFFICIENT CANNOT BE COMPUTED.

37.4
PRINT Subcommand

By default, NONPAR CORR prints Spearman correlation coefficients. Below each coefficient it prints the number of cases and the significance level. The significance level is based on a one-tailed test.

Use the PRINT subcommand to request the Kendall correlation coefficient or both Spearman and Kendall coefficients. Both coefficients are based on ranks. You can also use PRINT to switch to a two-tailed test and to suppress the display of the number of cases and significance level.

The following keywords are available on PRINT:

SPEARMAN *Spearman's rho.* Only Spearman coefficients are displayed. This is the default if you omit the PRINT subcommand.

KENDALL *Kendall's tau-b.* Only Kendall coefficients are displayed.

BOTH *Kendall and Spearman coefficients.* Both coefficients are displayed. If you use the MATRIX subcommand (Section 37.8) to write the correlation matrix to a system file, only Spearman's coefficient will be written with the matrix materials.

SIG *Print the number of cases and significance level.* This is the default.

NOSIG *Suppress the printing of the number of cases and significance level.* An asterisk (*) following a coefficient indicates significance at the .01 level or less. Two asterisks (**) following a coefficient indicate significance at the .001 level or less.

ONETAIL *One-tailed test of significance.* This test is appropriate when the direction of the relationship between a pair of variables can be specified in advance of the analysis. This is the default.

TWOTAIL *Two-tailed test of significance.* This test is appropriate when the direction of the relationship cannot be determined in advance, as is often the case in exploratory data analysis.

Figure 37.4 shows a triangular matrix with the number of cases and significance level suppressed. The matrix was produced by the following commands:

```
NONPAR CORR VARIABLES=PRESTIGE SPPRES PAPRES16 DEGREE PADEG MADEG
   /PRINT=NOSIG
```

If you use keyword WITH in a variable list, the display will be a rectangular matrix similar to Figure 37.3b, with the number of cases suppressed and asterisks indicating significance levels.

Figure 37.4 Correlation matrix with PRINT=NOSIG

```
- - - - - - - - - - SPEARMAN CORRELATION COEFFICIENTS - - - - - - - - - - -


SPPRES         .3608**
PAPRES16       .2934**    .2021**
DEGREE         .5262**    .3864**    .3438**
PADEG          .2397**    .1306      .3908**    .3820**
MADEG          .1781**    .1323      .2593**    .3829**    .5965**

               PRESTIGE   SPPRES     PAPRES16   DEGREE     PADEG


* - SIGNIF. LE .01      ** - SIGNIF. LE .001        " . " IS PRINTED IF A COEFFICIENT CANNOT BE COMPUTED.
```

If you specify both FORMAT=SERIAL (Section 37.7) and PRINT=NOSIG, as in

```
NONPAR CORR VARIABLES=PRESTIGE SPPRES PAPRES16 DEGREE PADEG MADEG/
   FORMAT=SERIAL/
   PRINT=NOSIG
```

only FORMAT=SERIAL will be in effect.

37.5
SAMPLE Subcommand

NONPAR CORR must store cases in memory to build matrices. You may not have sufficient computer resources to store all the cases to produce the coefficients requested. The SAMPLE subcommand allows you to select a random sample of cases when there is not enough space to store all the cases. To request a random sample, simply specify the subcommand, as in:

```
NONPAR CORR VARIABLES=PRESTIGE SPPRES PAPRES16 DEGREE PADEG MADEG/
    SAMPLE
```

The SAMPLE subcommand has no additional specifications.

37.6
MISSING Subcommand

By default, NONPAR CORR deletes cases with missing values on a pair-by-pair basis. A case missing on one or both of the pair of variables for a specific correlation coefficient is not used for that coefficient. Because each coefficient is based on all cases that have valid codes on that particular pair of variables, the maximum information available is used in every calculation. This also results in a set of coefficients based on a varying number of cases.

Use the MISSING subcommand to specify alternative missing-value treatments. The following keywords are available:

PAIRWISE   *Exclude missing values pairwise.* Cases missing for one or both of a pair of variables for a specific correlation coefficient are excluded from the analysis. This is the default.

LISTWISE   *Exclude missing values listwise.* Cases missing on any variable named in a list are excluded from all analyses. Each variable list on a command is evaluated separately. If you specify multiple variable lists, a case missing for one matrix might be used in another matrix. This option decreases the amount of memory required and significantly decreases computational time.

INCLUDE   *Include user-defined missing values.* User-missing values are treated as if they are not missing.

Only one of these keywords can be specified on MISSING.

37.7
FORMAT Subcommand

The FORMAT subcommand controls the format of the correlation matrix. The following keywords are available:

MATRIX   *Print correlations in matrix format.* This is the default if you omit the FORMAT subcommand.

SERIAL   *Print correlations in serial string format.* Coefficients from the first row of the matrix are printed first, followed by coefficients from the second row, and so on for all of the rows in the matrix. Each coefficient is identified with the name of the variables for which it was calculated. The number of cases and significance level are printed below the correlation, just as they are in matrix format.

Figure 37.7 shows the output from the following example with FORMAT= SERIAL in effect:

```
NONPAR CORR VARIABLES=PRESTIGE SPPRES PAPRES16 WITH DEGREE PADEG MADEG/
    FORMAT=SERIAL
```

Figure 37.7   Correlation matrix with FORMAT=SERIAL

```
 - - - - - - - - - - - - S P E A R M A N   C O R R E L A T I O N   C O E F F I C I E N T S - - - - - - - - - - - -

 VARIABLE              VARIABLE              VARIABLE              VARIABLE              VARIABLE              VARIABLE
 PAIR                  PAIR                  PAIR                  PAIR                  PAIR                  PAIR
 ─────                 ─────                 ─────                 ─────                 ─────                 ─────

 PRESTIGE    .5262     PRESTIGE    .2397     PRESTIGE    .1781     SPPRES      .3864     SPPRES      .1306     SPPRES      .1323
 WITH     N(  461)     WITH     N(  352)     WITH     N(  406)     WITH     N(  277)     WITH     N(  219)     WITH     N(  244)
 DEGREE   SIG .000     PADEG    SIG .000     MADEG    SIG .000     DEGREE   SIG .000     PADEG    SIG .027     MADEG    SIG .019


 PAPRES16    .3438     PAPRES16    .3908     PAPRES16    .2593
 WITH     N(  412)     WITH     N(  376)     WITH     N(  372)
 DEGREE   SIG .000     PADEG    SIG .000     MADEG    SIG .000

 " . " IS PRINTED IF A COEFFICIENT CANNOT BE COMPUTED.
```

37.8
MATRIX Subcommand

Use the MATRIX subcommand to write matrix materials to a system file. The matrix materials always include the number of cases used to compute each coefficient, and either the Spearman (RHO) or the Kendall (TAUB) correlation coefficient for each variable, whichever you specify. If you want to use the RHO or TAUB matrix as a correlation matrix for another procedure, you must first use the RECODE command to change the ROWTYPE_ value RHO or TAUB to CORR.

You cannot write both Spearman's and Kendall's coefficients to the same matrix system file. If you want a matrix of both Spearman's and Kendall's coefficients, specify separate NONPAR CORR commands for each coefficient and define different matrix system outfiles for each command. If you specify BOTH on the PRINT subcommand, NONPAR CORR prints a matrix in the listing file for both coefficients, but it writes only the Spearman coefficients to the matrix system file.

NONPAR CORR can write matrix materials for a simple variable list but not for variable lists containing the keyword WITH. If you specify more than one variable list on NONPAR CORR, only the last variable list that does not use keyword WITH is written to the matrix system file. For example,

```
NONPAR CORR VARIABLES=PRESTIGE SPPRES PAPRES16 DEGREE PADEG MADEG/
    PRESTIGE TO DEGREE/PRESTIGE WITH DEGREE/
  MATRIX OUT(NPMAT)
```

writes only the matrix for PRESTIGE TO DEGREE to the matrix system file, which is named NPMAT.

OUT Keyword. The OUT keyword on MATRIX specifies the file to which the matrix is written. There are two options:

(file) *Write the correlation matrix to a system file.* NONPAR CORR creates a system file containing the matrix materials. The name of the file is specified in parentheses. The system file is stored on disk and can be retrieved at any time.

(*) *Replace the active file with the correlation matrix system file.* The matrix materials replace the active file. The correlation matrix is *not* stored on disk. It is resident in the active file.

Documents from the original file will not be included in the matrix file and will not be present if the matrix file becomes the active file. (For a discussion of documents, see Chapter 6.)

In the following example, one set of matrix materials is written to the file named NPMAT:

```
GET FILE GSS80/KEEP PRESTIGE SPPRES PAPRES16 DEGREE PADEG MADEG
NONPAR CORR VARIABLES=PRESTIGE TO MADEG/
  MATRIX OUT(NPMAT)
```

The active file is still the file named GSS80. Subsequent commands are executed on file GSS80.

To write the same matrix to the active file so that it is available to subsequent commands, specify the following:

```
GET FILE GSS80/KEEP PRESTIGE SPPRES PAPRES16 DEGREE PADEG MADEG
NONPAR CORR VARIABLES=PRESTIGE TO MADEG/
  MATRIX OUT(*)
LIST
DISPLAY DICTIONARY
```

The original active file is replaced by the matrix system file. The LIST and DISPLAY commands are executed on the matrix file, not on the file named GSS80.

Format of the Matrix System File. Figure 37.8 shows the matrix system file produced by the above commands. The file includes two special variables created by SPSS-X: ROWTYPE_ and VARNAME_. Variable ROWTYPE_ is a short string variable with values N and RHO (for Spearman's correlation coefficient). If you specify Kendall's coefficient, the values are N and TAUB. The next variable, VARNAME_, is a short string variable whose values are the names of the variables used to form the correlation matrix. When ROWTYPE_ is RHO (or TAUB), VARNAME_ gives the variable associated with that row of the correlation matrix. The remaining variables in the file are the variables used to form the correlation matrix.

Figure 37.8   A matrix system file

```
FILE:      CORRELATION MATRIX FILE

ROWTYPE_ VARNAME_   PRESTIGE      SPPRES     PAPRES16      DEGREE       PADEG       MADEG

N          PRESTIGE 461.000000  258.000000  382.000000  461.000000  352.000000  406.000000
N          SPPRES   258.000000  277.000000  235.000000  277.000000  219.000000  244.000000
N          PAPRES16 382.000000  235.000000  412.000000  412.000000  376.000000  372.000000
N          DEGREE   461.000000  277.000000  412.000000  500.000000  377.000000  442.000000
N          PADEG    352.000000  219.000000  376.000000  377.000000  377.000000  356.000000
N          MADEG    406.000000  244.000000  372.000000  442.000000  356.000000  442.000000
RHO        PRESTIGE 1.0000000     .3607682    .2933617    .5261820    .2396762    .1780776
RHO        SPPRES    .3607682   1.0000000     .2021454    .3863999    .1305904    .1323265
RHO        PAPRES16  .2933617    .2021454   1.0000000     .3438384    .3908421    .2592909
RHO        DEGREE    .5261820    .3863999    .3438384   1.0000000     .3820381    .3828630
RHO        PADEG     .2396762    .1305904    .3908421    .3820381   1.0000000     .5964534
RHO        MADEG     .1780776    .1323265    .2592909    .3828630    .5964534   1.0000000


NUMBER OF CASES READ =       12    NUMBER OF CASES LISTED =       12
```

When split-file processing is in effect (see Chapter 15), the first variables in the matrix system file will be the split variables, followed by ROWTYPE_, VARNAME_, and the variables used to form the correlation matrix. A full set of matrix materials is written for each split-file group defined by the split variable(s). A split variable cannot have the same variable name as any other variable written to the matrix system file. If split-file processing is in effect when a matrix is written, the same split file must be in effect when that matrix is read by any procedure. (See Chapter 13 for more information on matrix system files.)

Additional Statistics. NONPAR CORR always includes with the matrix materials the number of cases used to compute each coefficient, as shown in Figure 37.8. This information immediately precedes the correlation matrix in your output file.

Missing Values. With PAIRWISE treatment of missing values (the default), the matrix of N's used to compute each coefficient is included with the matrix materials. With LISTWISE or INCLUDE treatments, a single N used to calculate all coefficients is included with the matrix materials.

37.9
LIMITATIONS

The following limitations apply to NONPAR CORR:

• A maximum of 25 variable lists.
• A maximum of 100 variables total per NONPAR CORR command.

Syntax

NPAR TESTS

```
NPAR TESTS [CHISQUARE=varlist[(lo,hi)]/] [/EXPECTED={EQUAL      }]
                                                     {f1,f2,...fn}

[/K-S({UNIFORM[,lo,hi]})=varlist]
      {NORMAL[,m,sd] }
      {POISSON[,m]   }
[/RUNS({MEAN  })=varlist]
       {MEDIAN}
       {MODE  }
       {value }
[/BINOMIAL[(p)]=varlist[({v1,v2})]]]
                        {value }
[/MCNEMAR=varlist [WITH varlist [(PAIRED)]]]
[/SIGN=varlist [WITH varlist [(PAIRED)]]]
[/WILCOXON=varlist [WITH varlist [(PAIRED)]]]
[/COCHRAN=varlist]
[/FRIEDMAN=varlist]
[/KENDALL=varlist]
[/MEDIAN[(value)]=varlist BY var (v1,v2)]
[/M-W=varlist BY var (v1,v2)]
[/K-S=varlist BY var (v1,v2)]
[/W-W=varlist BY var (v1,v2)]
[/MOSES[(n)]=varlist BY var (v1,v2)]
[/K-W=varlist BY var (v1,v2)]
[/MISSING={ANALYSIS**}  [INCLUDE]]
          {LISTWISE }
[/SAMPLE]
[/STATISTICS=[DESCRIPTIVES]  [QUARTILES] [ALL]]
```

**Default if the subcommand is omitted.

Contents

38.1 INTRODUCTION TO NONPARAMETRIC TESTS

38.2 OVERVIEW

38.3 OPERATION

38.4 One-Sample Tests

38.5 CHISQUARE Subcommand

38.6 K-S Subcommand (One-Sample Test)

38.7 RUNS Subcommand

38.8 BINOMIAL Subcommand

38.9 Tests for Two Related Samples

38.10 MCNEMAR Subcommand

38.11 SIGN Subcommand

38.12 WILCOXON Subcommand

38.13 Tests for *k* Related Samples

38.14 COCHRAN Subcommand

38.15 FRIEDMAN Subcommand

38.16 KENDALL Subcommand

38.17 Tests for Two Independent Samples

38.18 MEDIAN Subcommand (Two-Sample Test)

38.19 M-W Subcommand

38.20 K-S Subcommand (Two-Sample Test)

38.21 W-W Subcommand

38.22 MOSES Subcommand

38.23 Tests for *k* Independent Samples

38.24 MEDIAN Subcommand (*k*-Sample Test)

38.25 K-W Subcommand

38.26 STATISTICS Subcommand

38.27 MISSING Subcommand

38.28 SAMPLE Subcommand

38.29 LIMITATIONS

38

Chapter 38   NPAR TESTS

Procedure NPAR TESTS is a collection of nonparametric tests that make minimal assumptions about the underlying distributions of data. Many of these tests are based upon ranks, so this procedure must store cases in memory. The amount of memory required is directly proportional to the number of cases being analyzed. In addition to the nonparametric tests available in NPAR TESTS, the k-sample chi-square and Fisher's exact test are available in procedure CROSSTABS (see Chapter 25).

38.1 INTRODUCTION TO NONPARAMETRIC TESTS

A wide variety of nonparametric tests are available in NPAR TESTS. Table 38.1 summarizes the tests available. All of these tests are described in Siegel (1956). The tests differ in their assumptions about the level of measurement, the hypotheses being tested, and the organization of data. One-sample tests analyze one variable, tests for two related samples compare one variable with another, tests for k related samples compare several variables, and independent-samples tests analyze one variable grouped by categories of another variable.

Table 38.1   Nonparametric tests available in NPAR TESTS

Data organization	Nominal scale	Ordinal scale
One sample	Chi-square Runs Binomial	Kolmogorov-Smirnov
Two related samples	McNemar	Sign Wilcoxon Kendall coefficient of concordance
k related samples	Cochran Q	Friedman two-way Anova Kendall coefficient of concordance
Two independent samples		Median Mann-Whitney Kolmogorov-Smirnov Wald-Wolfowitz Moses
k independent samples		Median Kruskal-Wallis

38.2 OVERVIEW

NPAR TESTS produces one or more nonparametric tests. In addition to the test statistics, you can specify optional statistics, methods of handling missing data, and random sampling. You can also request special pairing with tests for two related samples. Most of the examples used in this chapter are taken from Siegel (1956). You should consult Siegel for interpretations of the results.

Selecting Nonparametric Tests. The nonparametric tests available with NPAR TESTS require specific types of data organization. NPAR TESTS include one-sample tests (Sections 38.5 through 38.8), tests for two related samples (Sections 38.10 through 38.12), tests for *k* related samples (Sections 38.14 through 38.16), tests for two independent samples (Sections 38.18 through 38.22), and tests for *k* independent samples (Sections 38.24 and 38.25).

Special Pairing for Two Related Samples. If you specify tests for two related samples, a simple variable list produces all possible pairs of variables. Two variable lists separated by the keyword WITH pair all variables in the first list with all variables in the second list. Optionally, you can request sequential pairing. (See Section 38.9.)

Optional Statistics. In addition to the statistics associated with each test, you can obtain the mean, minimum, maximum, and standard deviation for each variable named on all the subcommands, as well as medians and quartiles. (See Section 38.26.)

Missing Values. By default, NPAR TESTS excludes cases with missing values on a test-by-test basis. Optionally, you can request that user-missing values be handled as if they were valid or that cases with missing values be deleted listwise. (See Section 38.27.)

Random Sampling. NPAR TESTS must store cases in memory for tests that use ranks. You can request a random sample of cases when there is not enough space to store all the cases. (See Section 38.28.)

38.3
OPERATION

The general form of the NPAR TESTS command is

NPAR TESTS *testname* [(*parameters*)] = *varlist*

where *testname* is one of the available subcommands, *parameters* are any additional specifications for that subcommand, and *varlist* is the list of variables to be tested. The form of the variable list depends on the data organization required for the test. You can use keyword TO in variable lists to refer to consecutive variables in the active file.

You can request any or all of the available tests on one NPAR TESTS command. Subcommands are separated by slashes. The equals sign is optional in all subcommands.

38.4
One-Sample Tests

A one-sample test uses the entire set of observations for the variable being tested. One-sample tests have the following general form:

NPAR TESTS *testname* [(*parameters*)] = *varlist*

You must specify the name of the test and one or more variables to be tested. Each variable in the list produces one test. For example, the command

```
NPAR TESTS  CHISQUARE = GRADE EVAL1 TO EVAL5
```

specifies one-sample chi-square tests for GRADE and all the variables between and including EVAL1 and EVAL5.

The following one-sample tests are available:

CHISQUARE   *Chi-square one-sample test.* This is a goodness-of-fit test. For data that fall into categories, it tests whether a significant difference exists between the observed number of cases in each category and the expected number specified (see Section 38.5).

K-S   *Kolmogorov-Smirnov one-sample test.* This is a goodness-of-fit test. For interval-level data, K-S tests whether the observations could reasonably have come from a particular distribution where you specify uniform, normal, or Poisson distributions (see Section 38.6).

RUNS *Runs test.* This is a test of randomness for dichotomous variables to determine whether the order or sequence in which observations are obtained is random (see Section 38.7).

BINOMIAL *Binomial test.* This is a test for goodness of fit for dichotomous variables. It tests whether or not a significant difference exists between the observed number in each category and the expected number under a specified binomial distribution (see Section 38.8).

**38.5
CHISQUARE Subcommand**

Subcommand CHISQUARE (alias CHI-SQUARE) performs the one-sample chi-square test. CHISQUARE tabulates a variable into categories and computes a chi-square statistic based on the differences between observed and expected frequencies. By default, the CHISQUARE test assumes equal expected frequencies. To specify expected frequencies, use the associated EXPECTED subcommand.

The two subcommands have the following general form:

NPAR TESTS CHISQUARE = *varlist* [(lo,hi)]
         /EXPECTED = *f1, f2, ... fn*

The range following the variable list is optional. If you do not specify a range, each distinct value encountered is defined as a category. For example, the command

NPAR TESTS **CHISQUARE = RANK**

computes a chi-square test using every value encountered for the variable RANK. If you do specify a range, integer-valued categories are established for each value within the inclusive range. Noninteger values are truncated, and cases with values outside the bounds are excluded. For example,

NPAR TESTS CHISQUARE = RANK **(1,4)**

uses only the values 1 through 4 for the chi-square test of the variable RANK.

EXPECTED Subcommand. To specify expected frequencies, percentages, or proportions, use a value list on the EXPECTED subcommand. You must specify a value greater than zero for each observed category of the data. The values listed after the EXPECTED subcommand are summed. Each value is then divided by this sum to calculate the proportion of cases expected in the corresponding category. For example,

NPAR TESTS CHISQUARE = RANK (1,4)/**EXPECTED** = 3 4 5 4

specifies values for four categories of variable RANK. The value list is interpreted as proportions, not absolute values. The command above specifies that the expected proportions are 3/16, 4/16, 5/16, and 4/16 for categories 1, 2, 3, and 4, respectively. You can specify the same expected proportion for two or more consecutive categories with an asterisk (*), as in:

NPAR TESTS CHISQUARE = A (1,5)/ EXPECTED = 12, **3*16**, 18

This command tests the observed frequencies for variable A against the hypothetical distribution of 12/78 occurrences of category 1; 16/78 occurrences each of categories 2, 3, and 4; and 18/78 occurrences of category 5.

You can use the keyword EQUAL to specify equal expected proportions, as in:

NPAR TESTS CHISQUARE = RANK/ EXPECTED = **EQUAL**

This command produces the same results as the CHISQUARE subcommand alone.

The EXPECTED subcommand applies to all variables named on the preceding CHISQUARE subcommand. If you want to specify different expected proportions for each variable, use multiple combinations of the CHISQUARE and EXPECTED subcommands. If you want to test the same variable against different proportions, you can also use multiple combinations.

Example. The following example requests two chi-square tests. First, the frequencies for all categories of POSTPOS are compared against equal expected frequencies. The second CHISQUARE subcommand specifies eight expected proportions.

```
TITLE  'NPAR TESTS'
SUBTITLE  'CHISQUARE TEST, SIEGEL, P. 45'
DATA LIST  /POSTPOS 1-2 NWINS 4-5
VAR LABELS  POSTPOS 'POST POSITION'/
WEIGHT  BY NWINS
NPAR TESTS  CHISQUARE = POSTPOS/
     CHISQUARE = POSTPOS/EXPECTED=22,20,4*18,16,14
BEGIN DATA
 2 19
 7 15
 4 25
 5 17
 8 11
 3 18
 6 10
 1 29
END DATA
```

This example produces the output in Figure 38.5. For each test, the display shows the number of observed cases and expected cases in each category; the residual (observed minus expected) for each category; and the chi-square statistic, degrees of freedom, and significance of the chi-square.

Figure 38.5   One-sample chi-square test

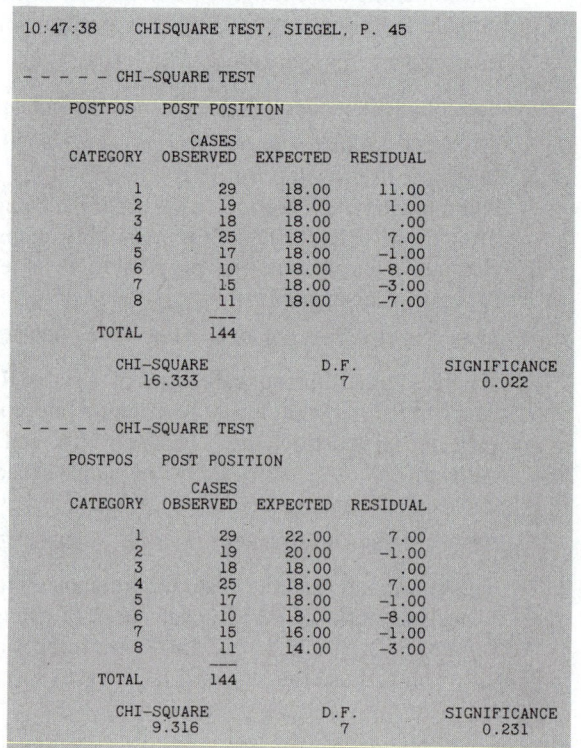

**38.6
K-S Subcommand
(One-Sample Test)**

Subcommand K-S (alias KOLMOGOROV-SMIRNOV) performs a Kolmogorov-Smirnov one-sample test (for a Kolmogorov-Smirnov two-sample test, see Section 38.20). K-S compares the cumulative distribution function for a variable with a specified distribution, which may be uniform, normal, or Poisson. The Kolmogorov-Smirnov Z is computed from the largest difference (in absolute value) between the observed and theoretical distribution functions.

The K-S subcommand for one-sample tests has the general form

NPAR TESTS K-S (*dis* [*parameters*]) = *varlist*

where *dis* is one of the three distributions: UNIFORM, NORMAL, or POISSON. Each of these distributions has optional parameters:

UNIFORM *Uniform distribution.* The optional parameters are the minimum and maximum values (in that order). If you do not specify them, K-S uses the observed minimum and maximum values.

NORMAL *Normal distribution.* The optional parameters are the mean and standard deviation (in that order). If you do not specify them, K-S uses the observed mean and standard deviation.

POISSON *Poisson distribution.* The one optional parameter is the mean. If you do not specify it, K-S uses the observed mean. A word of caution about testing against a Poisson distribution: if the mean of the test distribution is large, evaluating the probabilities is a very time-consuming process. If a mean of 100,000 or larger is used, K-S uses a normal approximation to the Poisson distribution.

For example, the command

NPAR TESTS K-S (UNIFORM) = A

compares the distribution for variable A with a uniform distribution which has the same range as variable A, while the command

NPAR TESTS K-S (NORMAL, 0, 1) = B

compares the distribution for variable B with a normal distribution which has a mean of 0 and standard deviation of 1.

K-S assumes that the test distribution is entirely specified in advance. When parameters of the test distribution are estimated from the sample, the distribution of the test statistic changes. NPAR TESTS does not provide any correction for this.

Example. The following example tests variable X against a uniform distribution with a range of 0 through 1.

```
TITLE    'NPAR TESTS'
SUBTITLE  'KOLMOGOROV–SMIRNOV TEST, CONOVER, P. 296'
DATA LIST   /X 1-3 (3)
NPAR TESTS   K-S (UNIFORM, 0, 1) = X
BEGIN DATA
621
503
203
477
710
581
329
480
554
382
END DATA
```

Figure 38.6 is the output produced by the K-S subcommand. It prints the distribution selected for the test; the most extreme positive, negative, and absolute differences; and the Kolmogorov-Smirnov Z and its significance.

Figure 38.6   Kolmogorov-Smirnov Z (test)

```
10:49:26    KOLMOGOROV-SMIRNOV TEST, CONOVER, P. 296


- - - - - KOLMOGOROV - SMIRNOV GOODNESS OF FIT TEST

      X


      TEST DISTRIBUTION  -  UNIFORM      RANGE:    .000 TO 1.000

            CASES:  10

            MOST EXTREME DIFFERENCES
      ABSOLUTE        POSITIVE        NEGATIVE        K-S Z      2-TAILED P
      0.29000         0.29000         -0.22900        0.917        0.370
```

38.7
RUNS Subcommand

Subcommand RUNS performs the runs test to determine the randomness of observations for dichotomous variables. A run is defined as a sequence of one of the values which is preceded and followed by the other data value (or the end of the series). For example, the following sequence

| 1 1 | 0 0 0 | 1 | 0 0 0 0 | 1 | 0 | 1 |

contains seven runs (vertical bars are used to separate the runs).

The RUNS subcommand has the following general form:

NPAR TESTS RUNS (*cutpoint*) = *varlist*

You must specify a cutting point to dichotomize the variable. You can use either the observed mean, median, or mode or a specified value as a cutting point. Specify one of the following for *cutpoint*:

MEAN *Mean.* All values below the observed mean are one category. All values equal to or greater than the mean are the other category.

MEDIAN *Median.* All values below the observed median are one category; values equal to or greater than the median are the other category.

MODE *Mode.* All values below the observed mode are one category; values equal to or greater than the mode are the other category.

value *Specified value.* All values below the specified value are one category; values equal to or above the specified value are the other category.

Even though the variable may be dichotomized already, you still must specify a cutting point. For example, if the variable has values 0 and 1, you can use 1 as the cutting point.

Example. The following example of the RUNS subcommand also illustrates the use of SPSS-X to analyze several files in one execution. The variable SCORE is defined on the first active file and two runs tests are performed, one with the sample median as the cutting point and the other with the value 24.5 as the cutting point. Then the DATA LIST command defines a new active file containing the variable SEX, for which another runs test is performed.

```
TITLE  'NPAR TESTS'
SUBTITLE  'RUNS TEST, SIEGEL, P. 55'
DATA LIST  /SCORE 1-2
VAR LABELS  SCORE 'AGGRESSION SCORE'
NPAR TESTS  RUNS(MEDIAN) = SCORE/
   RUNS(24.5) = SCORE
BEGIN DATA
31
23
36
 ...
 7
 6
 8
END DATA
SUBTITLE  'RUNS TEST, SIEGEL, P. 57'
DATA LIST  /SEX 1
NPAR TESTS  RUNS (1)=SEX/
BEGIN DATA
1
0
1
 ...
0
1
1
END DATA
```

Figure 38.7 is the output produced by the RUNS subcommand. For each test, the display shows the test value (cutting point), number of runs, number of cases below the cutting point, number of cases equal to or greater than the cutting point, and test statistic Z with its significance level.

Figure 38.7   Runs test

```
10:50:23    RUNS TEST, SIEGEL, P. 55


- - - - - RUNS TEST

     SCORE     AGGRESSION SCORE


         RUNS:  10              TEST VALUE = 25.0 (MEDIAN)

         CASES:  12   LT MEDIAN
                 12   GE MEDIAN           Z = -1.0436
                 --
                 24   TOTAL     2-TAILED P =   .2967


- - - - - RUNS TEST

     SCORE     AGGRESSION SCORE


         RUNS:  10              TEST VALUE = 24.5000

         CASES:  12   LT 24.5000
                 12   GE 24.5000          Z = -1.0436
                 --
                 24   TOTAL     2-TAILED P =   .2967

10:50:25    RUNS TEST, SIEGEL, P. 57


- - - - - RUNS TEST

     SEX


         RUNS:  35          TEST VALUE = 1

         CASES:  20   LT 1
                 30   GE 1            Z =  2.9794
                 --
                 50   TOTAL 2-TAILED P =   .0029
```

38.8
BINOMIAL Subcommand

Subcommand BINOMIAL performs the binomial test. It compares the observed frequency in each category of a dichotomous variable with expected frequencies under a binomial distribution. BINOMIAL tabulates a variable into two categories based on the way you specify a cutting point.

The BINOMIAL subcommand has the general form

NPAR TESTS BINOMIAL[(p)] = *varlist(value or value1,value2)*

where *p* is the proportion of cases expected in the *first* category. The proportion is compared to the test proportion and the significance test is performed. The default test proportion is .5, but you can specify any other proportion. In any case, BINOMIAL computes a two-tailed probability.

else, BINOMIAL computes a one-tailed probability.

If you name one value in parentheses following the variable list, it is used as a cutting point. All cases equal to or less than the cutting point form the first category; all remaining cases form the second category. If you specify two values in parentheses following the variable list, all cases with *value1* are in the first category and all cases with *value2* are in the second category. The frequencies in these categories are compared to the proportion you specify for *p*, or to .5 if you do not specify *p*.

Example. The following example tests the distribution of the variable METHOD against the default proportion of .5. METHOD is a dichotomous variable with two values, 1 and 2.

```
TITLE   'NPAR TESTS'
SUBTITLE  'BINOMIAL TEST, SIEGEL, P. 40'
DATA LIST   /METHOD 1
NPAR TESTS   BINOMIAL=METHOD(1,2)
BEGIN DATA
1
1
1
  ...
1
2
2
END DATA
```

Figure 38.8 is the output produced by the BINOMIAL subcommand. It displays the test proportion of cases, number of cases in each category, and significance level.

Figure 38.8   Binomial test

```
10:52:23    BINOMIAL TEST, SIEGEL, P. 40


- - - - - BINOMIAL TEST
     METHOD


     CASES
        16    = 1              TEST PROB. =    .5000
         2    = 2
        --                     2-TAILED P =    .0013
        18    TOTAL
```

38.9
Tests for Two Related Samples

Tests for two related samples compare pairs of variables and have the following general form:

NPAR TESTS *testname = varlist* [WITH *varlist*]

You must specify the name of the test and two or more variables to be tested.

The following tests are available for two related samples:

MCNEMAR *McNemar test.* This is a test of difference in changes of proportions for dichotomous variables. It is most useful in "before and after" experimental designs to detect any significant changes in proportions of subjects from one category to another (see Section 38.10).

SIGN *Sign test.* This test compares the signs of the differences between pairs of variables for each observation (see Section 38.11).

WILCOXON *Wilcoxon matched-pairs signed-ranks test.* This test analyzes the differences between the paired observations, also taking into account the magnitude of the differences (see Section 38.12).

If you specify a simple variable list, a test is performed for each variable paired with every other variable on the list. For example, the command

```
NPAR TESTS  MCNEMAR = A B C
```

produces McNemar tests for each possible pair of variables: A with B, A with C, and B with C. To obtain tests for specific pairs of variables, use two variable lists separated by keyword WITH. Each variable in the first list will be tested with each variable in the second list. For example,

```
NPAR TESTS  SIGN = A WITH B C
```

produces sign tests for A with B and A with C. No test is performed for B with C.

(PAIRED) Keyword. Keyword (PAIRED) used in conjunction with WITH provides additional control over which variables are paired together. When you specify (PAIRED), the first variable in the first list is paired with the first variable in the second list, the second variable in the first list is paired with the second variable in the second list, and so on. You must name or imply the same number of variables in both lists. For example,

```
NPAR TESTS  MCNEMAR = A B WITH C D (PAIRED)
```

pairs A with C and B with D. You must specify (PAIRED) after the second variable list. You cannot use (PAIRED) if keyword WITH is not specified.

38.10
MCNEMAR Subcommand

Subcommand MCNEMAR performs the McNemar test. It tabulates a 2×2 table for each pair of dichotomous variables. If your data are not dichotomous, you must recode them. The test is not performed for variables with more than two values. A chi-square statistic is computed for cases with different values for the two variables. If fewer than 30 cases change values from the first variable to the second variable, the binomial distribution is used to compute the significance level.

The MCNEMAR subcommand has the following general form:

```
NPAR TESTS  MCNEMAR = varlist
```

Example. The following example performs the McNemar test for variables CONTACT1 with CONTACT2.

```
TITLE   'NPAR TESTS'
SUBTITLE   'MCNEMAR TEST, SIEGEL, P. 65'
DATA LIST   /CONTACT1 CONTACT2 NUMBER 1-6
WEIGHT  BY NUMBER
NPAR TESTS   MCNEMAR = CONTACT1 CONTACT2
BEGIN DATA
 1-114
 1 1 4
-1-1 3
-1 1 4
END DATA
```

Figure 38.10 is the output produced by the MCNEMAR subcommand. It prints the 2 × 2 table, the chi-square statistic, and its significance level.

Figure 38.10   McNemar test

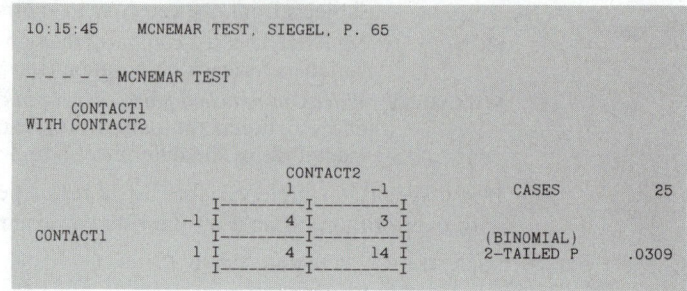

```
10:15:45   MCNEMAR TEST, SIEGEL, P. 65

- - - - - MCNEMAR TEST

      CONTACT1
WITH CONTACT2


                        CONTACT2
                      1        -1              CASES        25
                 I--------I--------I
            -1 I    4 I      3 I
                 I--------I--------I          (BINOMIAL)
    CONTACT1                                  2-TAILED P   .0309
             1 I    4 I     14 I
                 I--------I--------I
```

**38.11
SIGN Subcommand**

Subcommand SIGN performs the sign test. It counts the positive and negative differences between each pair of variables and ignores zero differences. Under the null hypothesis for large sample sizes, the test statistic Z is approximately normally distributed with mean 0 and variance 1. The binomial distribution is used to compute an exact significance level if 25 or fewer differences are observed.

The SIGN subcommand has the following general form:

NPAR TESTS SIGN = *varlist*

Example. In the following example, the SIGN subcommand is used first to test MOTHER with FATHER, and then to test BEFORE with AFTER.

```
TITLE  'NPAR TESTS'
SUBTITLE  'SIGN TEST, SIEGEL, P. 70'
DATA LIST  /MOTHER FATHER 1-2
VAR LABELS  MOTHER 'MOTHER''S INSIGHT RATED'/
            FATHER 'FATHER''S INSIGHT RATED'
NPAR TESTS  SIGN = FATHER WITH MOTHER
BEGIN DATA
42
43
53
...
55
53
51
END DATA
SUBTITLE  'SIGN TEST, SIEGEL, P. 73'
DATA LIST  /BEFORE AFTER 1-2 COUNT 3-4
WEIGHT  BY COUNT
RECODE  BEFORE AFTER (0 = -1)
NPAR TESTS  SIGN = BEFORE WITH AFTER
BEGIN DATA
1059
11 7
00 8
0126
END DATA
```

This example produces the output in Figure 38.11. For each test, the display shows the number of positive and negative differences. The first sign test uses the significance level from the binomial distribution because only 17 differences are observed. The second sign test uses the significance level from the Z statistic because more than 25 differences are observed.

Figure 38.11   Sign test

```
10:53:48    SIGN TEST, SIEGEL, P. 70


- - - - - SIGN TEST

        FATHER      FATHER'S INSIGHT RATED
WITH MOTHER    MOTHER'S INSIGHT RATED


            CASES

            3   - DIFFS (MOTHER LT FATHER)
           11   + DIFFS (MOTHER GT FATHER)     (BINOMIAL)
            3     TIES                         2-TAILED P =        .0574
           --
           17     TOTAL

10:53:50    SIGN TEST, SIEGEL, P. 73


- - - - - SIGN TEST

      BEFORE
WITH AFTER


            CASES

           59   - DIFFS (AFTER LT BEFORE)            Z =       3.4709
           26   + DIFFS (AFTER GT BEFORE)
           15     TIES                         2-TAILED P =       .0005
          ---
          100     TOTAL
```

**38.12
WILCOXON Subcommand**

Subcommand WILCOXON performs the Wilcoxon matched-pairs signed-ranks test. WILCOXON computes the differences between the pair of variables, ranks the absolute differences, sums the positive and negative ranks, and computes the test statistic Z from the positive and negative rank sums. Under the null hypothesis, Z is approximately normally distributed with mean 0 and variance 1 for large sample sizes.

The WILCOXON subcommand has the following general form:

NPAR TESTS WILCOXON = *varlist*

Example. The following example performs two Wilcoxon tests. The first example matches SCHOOL with HOME. The second example computes DUM as a constant with value 0 and matches it with D.

```
TITLE  'NPAR TESTS'
SUBTITLE  'WILCOXON MATCHED PAIRS TEST, SIEGEL, P. 79'
DATA LIST  /SCHOOL HOME 1-4
VAR LABELS  SCHOOL 'SOCIAL PERCEPTIVENESS OF SCHOOL TWIN'/
            HOME 'SOCIAL PERCEPTIVENESS OF HOME TWIN'
NPAR TESTS  WILCOXON = ALL
BEGIN DATA
8263
6942
7374
4337
5851
5643
7680
8582
END DATA
SUBTITLE 'WILCOXON MATCHED PAIRS, SIEGEL, P. 82'
DATA LIST /D 1-2
COMPUTE  DUM=0
VAR LABELS  D 'DECISION LATENCY TIME'/
NPAR TESTS  WILCOXON = D WITH DUM
BEGIN DATA
-2
0
0
  ...
2
3
-1
END DATA
```

Figure 38.12 is the output produced by these two WILCOXON tests. For each test, the display shows the mean positive and negative ranks for each variable; the number of positive, negative, and tied ranks; and the test statistic Z and its significance level.

Figure 38.12 The Wilcoxon matched-pairs signed-ranks test

```
11:11:31    WILCOXON MATCHED PAIRS TEST, SIEGEL, P. 79

- - - - - WILCOXON MATCHED-PAIRS SIGNED-RANKS TEST
    SCHOOL      SOCIAL PERCEPTIVENESS OF SCHOOL TWIN
WITH HOME       SOCIAL PERCEPTIVENESS OF HOME TWIN

   MEAN RANK    CASES

       5.33         6   - RANKS (HOME LT SCHOOL)
       2.00         2   + RANKS (HOME GT SCHOOL)
                    0     TIES  (HOME EQ SCHOOL)
                    -
                    8     TOTAL

        Z =  -1.9604              2-TAILED P =  .0500

11:11:33    WILCOXON MATCHED PAIRS, SIEGEL, P. 82

- - - - - WILCOXON MATCHED-PAIRS SIGNED-RANKS TEST
    D           DECISION LATENCY TIME
WITH DUM

   MEAN RANK    CASES

      14.90        20   - RANKS (DUM LT D)
       8.83         6   + RANKS (DUM GT D)
                    4     TIES  (DUM EQ D)
                   --
                   30     TOTAL

        Z =  -3.1113              2-TAILED P =  .0019
```

38.13
Tests for *k* Related Samples

Tests for k related samples compare sets of variables and have the following general form:

NPAR TESTS *testname = varlist*

You must specify the name of the test and two or more variables to be tested. The k variables in the list produce one test for k related samples.

The following tests are available for k related samples:

COCHRAN *Cochran's Q test.* This is a test of difference of proportions. It tests whether the proportions in the categories are the same over all variables (see Section 38.14).

FRIEDMAN *Friedman test.* FRIEDMAN tests the null hypothesis that the k samples have been drawn from the same population (see Section 38.15).

KENDALL *Kendall's W coefficient of concordance.* Kendall's W is a measure of agreement among raters or judges. Each case is one judge's rating of several entities (variables) (see Section 38.16).

38.14
COCHRAN Subcommand

Subcommand COCHRAN performs the Cochran Q test. It tabulates a $2 \times k$ contingency table (category vs. variable) for dichotomous variables and computes the proportions for each variable. If your data are not dichotomous, you must recode them. Cochran's Q statistic has approximately a chi-square distribution.

The COCHRAN subcommand has the following general form:

NPAR TESTS COCHRAN = *varlist*

Example. The following example tests variables R1, R2, and R3; each variable has a value of 0 or 1.

```
TITLE   'NPAR TESTS'
SUBTITLE   'COCHRAN Q TEST, SIEGEL, P. 164'
DATA LIST   /R1 TO R3 1-3
VAR LABELS  R1 'RESPONSE TO NICE INTERVIEW'/
            R2 'RESPONSE TO RESERVED INTERVIEW'/
            R3 'RESPONSE TO HARSH INTERVIEW'
NPAR TESTS  COCHRAN = R1 TO R3
BEGIN DATA
111
111
110
 ...
010
100
000
END DATA
```

Figure 38.14 is the output produced by the COCHRAN subcommand. It displays the number of cases in each category for each variable, Cochran's Q with its degrees of freedom, and the significance level for Q.

Figure 38.14 Cochran Q test

```
10:55:55    COCHRAN Q TEST, SIEGEL, P. 164


- - - - - COCHRAN Q TEST


  CASES

  = 1  = 0   VARIABLE

   13    5   R1            RESPONSE TO NICE INTERVIEW
   13    5   R2            RESPONSE TO RESERVED INTERVIEW
    3   15   R3            RESPONSE TO HARSH INTERVIEW

            CASES         COCHRAN Q        D.F.   SIGNIFICANCE
             18           16.6667            2          .0002
```

38.15
FRIEDMAN Subcommand

Subcommand FRIEDMAN peforms the Friedman test. It ranks k variables from 1 to k for each case, calculates the mean rank for each variable over all the cases, and then calculates a test statistic with approximately a chi-square distribution.

The FRIEDMAN subcommand has the following general form:

NPAR TESTS FRIEDMAN = *varlist*

Example. The following example analyzes variables RR, RU, and UR.

```
TITLE   'NPAR TESTS'
SUBTITLE   'FRIEDMAN TWO-WAY TEST, SIEGEL, P. 171'
DATA LIST   /RR RU UR 1-3
VAR LABELS  RR 'TOTAL REINFORCEMENT'/
            RU 'PARTIAL WITH REINFORCED TRIAL'/
            UR 'PARTIAL WITH UNREINFORCED TRIAL'
NPAR TESTS  FRIEDMAN = RR RU UR
BEGIN DATA
264
462
396
 ...
321
642
231
END DATA
```

Figure 38.15 is the output produced by the FRIEDMAN subcommand. It displays the mean rank for each variable, the chi-square statistic with its degrees of freedom, and the significance level for the chi-square.

Figure 38.15 Friedman test

```
10:56:33    FRIEDMAN TWO-WAY TEST, SIEGEL, P. 171

- - - - - FRIEDMAN TWO-WAY ANOVA

   MEAN RANK    VARIABLE

       2.19    RR          TOTAL REINFORCEMENT
       2.36    RU          PARTIAL WITH REINFORCED TRIAL
       1.44    UR          PARTIAL WITH UNREINFORCED TRIAL

       CASES          CHI-SQUARE        D.F.    SIGNIFICANCE
         18             8.5833            2          .0137
```

38.16
KENDALL Subcommand

Subcommand KENDALL calculates Kendall's W (coefficient of concordance). It ranks k variables from 1 to k for each case, calculates the mean rank for each variable over all the cases, and then calculates Kendall's W and a corresponding chi-square statistic, correcting for ties. W ranges between 0 and 1, with 0 signifying no agreement and 1 signifying complete agreement.

The KENDALL subcommand has the following general form:

NPAR TESTS KENDALL = *varlist*

This test assumes that each case is a judge or rater. If you want to perform this test with variables as judges and cases as entities, you must first transpose your data matrix.

Example. The following example uses 3 judges and 10 entities:

```
TITLE   'NPAR TESTS'
SUBTITLE  'KENDALL W, SIEGEL, P. 234'
DATA LIST  /A B C D E F G H I J 1-40(1)
NPAR TESTS  KENDALL = ALL
BEGIN DATA
 1.0 4.5 2.0 4.5 3.0 7.5 6.0 9.0 7.5 10.
 2.5 1.0 2.5 4.5 4.5 8.0 9.0 6.5 10. 6.5
 2.0 1.0 4.5 4.5 4.5 4.5 8.0 8.0 8.0 10.
END DATA
```

Figure 38.16 is the output produced by the KENDALL subcommand. It displays the number of cases, Kendall's W, the chi-square statistic with its degrees of freedom, and the test of significance for the chi-square. A small probability indicates a high degree of concordance.

Figure 38.16 Kendall coefficient of concordance

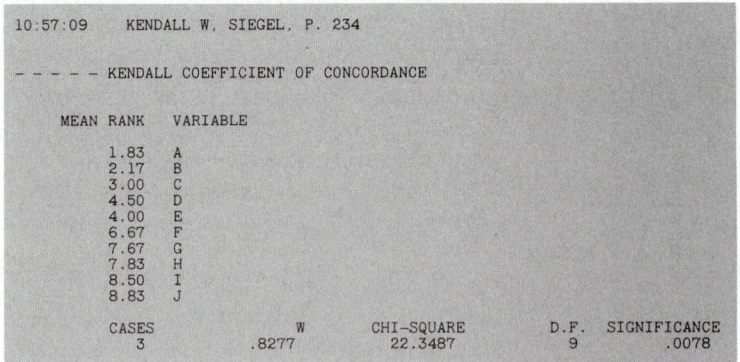

```
10:57:09    KENDALL W, SIEGEL, P. 234

- - - - - KENDALL COEFFICIENT OF CONCORDANCE

   MEAN RANK    VARIABLE

       1.83    A
       2.17    B
       3.00    C
       4.50    D
       4.00    E
       6.67    F
       7.67    G
       7.83    H
       8.50    I
       8.83    J

       CASES              W        CHI-SQUARE      D.F.    SIGNIFICANCE
         3              .8277       22.3487          9          .0078
```

38.17
Tests for Two Independent Samples

Tests for two independent samples compare two groups of cases on one variable. These tests have the following general form:

NPAR TESTS *testname* = *varlist* BY *var*(*value1*,*value2*)

You must specify the name of the test and one or more variables to be tested. Each variable in the list produces one test. The variable following the keyword BY splits the file into two groups or samples. All cases with *value1* are in the first group, and all cases with *value2* are in the second group.

The following tests are available for two independent samples:

MEDIAN *Two-sample median test.* This test determines whether the two groups are drawn from populations with the same median (see Section 38.18).

M-W *Mann-Whitney* U *test.* Like the median test, M-W tests whether the two groups are drawn from the same population. It is more powerful than the median test because it uses the rank of each case, not just its location relative to the median (see Section 38.19).

K-S *Kolmogorov-Smirnov two-sample test.* This is a test of homogeneity of distribution. It is sensitive to any difference between the two distributions, including the median, dispersion, skewness, and so on (see Section 38.20).

W-W *Wald-Wolfowitz runs test.* This is also a test of homogeneity of distributions (see Section 38.21).

MOSES *Moses test of extreme reactions.* This is a test of difference in range. It treats the first group as the control group and the second as the experimental group (see Section 38.22).

38.18
MEDIAN Subcommand (Two-Sample Test)

Subcommand MEDIAN performs the two-sample median test. MEDIAN tabulates a 2×2 contingency table with counts of the number of cases greater than the median and less than or equal to the median for the two groups. You can specify a value as a cutting point or use the median calculated from the data. If the total number of cases is greater than 30, a chi-square statistic is computed. Fisher's exact procedure (one-tailed) is used to compute the significance level for 30 or fewer cases.

The MEDIAN subcommand has the following general form:

NPAR TESTS MEDIAN [(*value*)] = *varlist* BY *var*(*value1*,*value2*)

The value in parentheses following the MEDIAN subcommand is the test median. If the test median is not specified, the calculated median is used.

The MEDIAN subcommand performs either a two-sample or a *k*-sample test, depending on how the cutting point for the variable that groups the cases is specified. For a two-sample test, the cutting point can be specified using one of two methods. With the first method, *value2* must equal *value1* + 1. With the second method, *value1* must be larger than *value2*. If you use a variable that has more than two values and *value1* is smaller than *value2*, a *k*-sample median test is performed (see Section 38.24).

Example. The following example performs two tests on the variable ANXIETY grouped by the variable EXPLAIN. The first test specifies a median of 10.5; the second test uses the sample median.

```
TITLE   'NPAR TESTS'
SUBTITLE  'MEDIAN TEST, SIGEL P. 114'
DATA LIST   /EXPLAIN 1 ANXIETY 3-4
VAR LABELS   EXPLAIN 'ORAL EXPLANATION OF ILLNESS CODE'/
             ANXIETY 'ORAL SOCIALIZATION ANXIETY'/
VALUE LABELS   EXPLAIN 1 'ABSENT' 2 'PRESENT'/
NPAR TESTS   MEDIAN (10.5) = ANXIETY BY EXPLAIN (1,2)/
   MEDIAN = ANXIETY BY EXPLAIN (1,2)
BEGIN DATA
2 10
2 10
2 10
  ...
1 7
1 7
1 6
END DATA
```

Figure 38.18 is the output produced by the MEDIAN subcommand. For each test, the display shows the 2 × 2 table of cases above the median and cases equal to or below the median, the chi-square statistic, and its significance level.

Figure 38.18 Two-sample median test

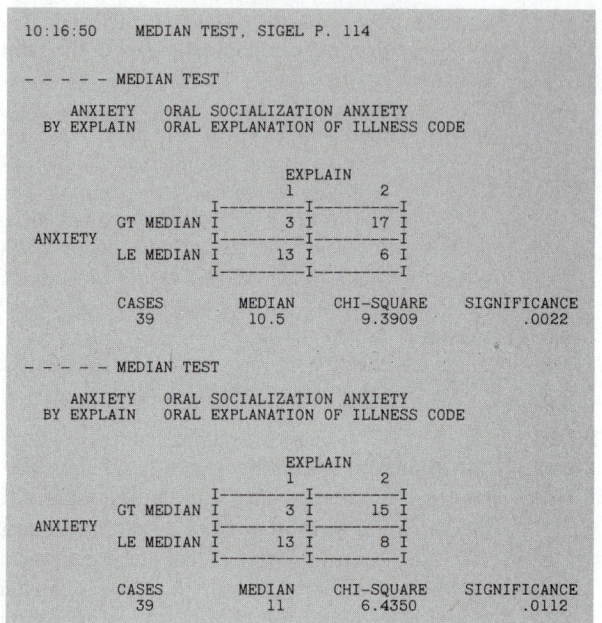

```
10:16:50    MEDIAN TEST, SIGEL P. 114


- - - - - MEDIAN TEST

         ANXIETY    ORAL SOCIALIZATION ANXIETY
       BY EXPLAIN   ORAL EXPLANATION OF ILLNESS CODE


                              EXPLAIN
                              1         2
                      I----------I----------I
             GT MEDIAN I    3 I      17 I
                      I----------I----------I
    ANXIETY           I----------I----------I
             LE MEDIAN I   13 I       6 I
                      I----------I----------I

            CASES         MEDIAN      CHI-SQUARE    SIGNIFICANCE
             39           10.5         9.3909          .0022

- - - - - MEDIAN TEST

         ANXIETY    ORAL SOCIALIZATION ANXIETY
       BY EXPLAIN   ORAL EXPLANATION OF ILLNESS CODE


                              EXPLAIN
                              1         2
                      I----------I----------I
             GT MEDIAN I    3 I      15 I
                      I----------I----------I
    ANXIETY           I----------I----------I
             LE MEDIAN I   13 I       8 I
                      I----------I----------I

            CASES         MEDIAN      CHI-SQUARE    SIGNIFICANCE
             39            11          6.4350          .0112
```

38.19
M-W Subcommand

Subcommand M-W (alias MANN-WHITNEY) performs the Mann-Whitney U test. It ranks all the cases in order of increasing size and computes the test statistic U, the number of times a score from Group 1 precedes a score from Group 2. If the samples are from the same population, the distribution of scores from the two groups in the ranked list should be random; an extreme value of U indicates a nonrandom pattern. For samples with fewer than 30 cases, the exact significance level for U is computed using the algorithm of Dineen and Blakesly (1973). For larger samples, U is transformed into a normally distributed Z statistic.

The M-W subcommand has the following general form:

NPAR TESTS M-W = *varlist* BY *var(value1,value2)*

Example. The following example tests TRIALS by GROUP:

```
TITLE   'NPAR TESTS'
SUBTITLE  'MANN-WHITNEY TEST, SIEGEL, P. 119'
DATA LIST   /GROUP 1 TRIALS 3-5
NPAR TESTS   M-W = TRIALS BY GROUP (0,1)
BEGIN DATA
0 78
0 64
0 75
0 45
0 82
1 110
1 70
1 53
1 51
END DATA
```

Figure 38.19 is the output produced by the M-W subcommand. It prints the mean rank for each group, the Mann-Whitney U statistic, the Wilcoxon W (the rank sum of the smaller group), the exact significance level of U (or W), and the Z statistic and its probability level corrected for ties.

Figure 38.19   Mann-Whitney *U* test

```
10:58:29     MANN-WHITNEY TEST, SIEGEL, P. 119


- - - - - MANN-WHITNEY U - WILCOXON RANK SUM W TEST


     TRIALS
   BY GROUP


  MEAN RANK      CASES

       5.20        5   GROUP = 0
       4.75        4   GROUP = 1
                    -
                    9   TOTAL

                                         EXACT            CORRECTED FOR TIES
       U            W              2-TAILED P           Z       2-TAILED P
       9.0         19.0              0.9048         -0.2449       0.8065
```

38.20
K-S Subcommand
(Two-Sample Test)

Subcommand K-S (alias KOLMOGOROV-SMIRNOV) performs the Kolmogorov-Smirnov two-sample test (for a Kolmogorov-Smirnov one-sample test, see Section 38.6). K-S computes the observed cumulative distributions for both groups and the maximum positive, negative, and absolute differences. The Kolmogorov-Smirnov Z is then computed along with the two-tailed probability level based on the Smirnov (1948) formula. The one-tailed test can be used to determine whether the values of one group are generally larger than the values of the other group.

The K-S subcommand for two-sample tests has the following general form:

NPAR TESTS K-S = *varlist* BY *var(value1,value2)*

Example. The following example performs two separate K-S tests. First PCTERR by GRADE is analyzed, and then IDENTED by GROUP is analyzed.

```
TITLE   'NPAR TESTS'
SUBTITLE  'K-S TWO-SAMPLE TEST, SIEGEL, P. 130'
DATA LIST   /PCTERR 1-4(1) GRADE 6-7
VAR LABELS   PCTERR 'PERCENTAGE OF ERRORS'/
             GRADE 'GRADE IN SCHOOL'
NPAR TESTS   K-S = PCTERR BY GRADE (7,11)
BEGIN DATA
39.1 7
41.2 7
45.2 7
  ...
24.3 11
32.4 11
32.6 11
END DATA
SUBTITLE  'K-S TWO-SAMPLE TEST, SIEGEL, P. 133'
DATA LIST   /IDENTED 1-2  GROUP 4 NUMBER 6-7
VAR LABELS   IDENTED 'PHOTOS ''IDENTIFIED'''/
WEIGHT  BY NUMBER
NPAR TESTS   K-S = IDENTED BY GROUP (1,2)
BEGIN DATA
 1 1 11
 1 2  1
 4 1  7
  ...
19 1  5
19 2  6
END DATA
```

Figure 38.20 is the output produced by the K-S subcommand. For each test, the display shows the number of cases in each group; the most extreme positive, negative, and absolute differences; and the Kolmogorov-Smirnov Z and its significance.

Figure 38.20   Kolmogorov-Smirnov two-sample test

```
10:59:10    K-S TWO-SAMPLE TEST, SIEGEL, P. 130


- - - - - KOLMOGOROV - SMIRNOV 2-SAMPLE TEST

     PCTERR      PERCENTAGE OF ERRORS
    BY GRADE     GRADE IN SCHOOL


         CASES

        10    GRADE = 7
        10    GRADE = 11
        --
        20    TOTAL

WARNING - DUE TO SMALL SAMPLE SIZE, PROBABILITY TABLES SHOULD BE CONSULTED.

             MOST EXTREME DIFFERENCES
        ABSOLUTE      POSITIVE      NEGATIVE      K-S Z      2-TAILED P
        0.70000       0.0          -0.70000      1.565        0.015

10:59:12    K-S TWO-SAMPLE TEST, SIEGEL, P. 133


- - - - - KOLMOGOROV - SMIRNOV 2-SAMPLE TEST

     IDENTED     PHOTOS 'IDENTIFIED'
    BY GROUP


         CASES

        44    GROUP = 1
        54    GROUP = 2
        --
        98    TOTAL

WARNING - DUE TO SMALL SAMPLE SIZE, PROBABILITY TABLES SHOULD BE CONSULTED.

             MOST EXTREME DIFFERENCES
        ABSOLUTE      POSITIVE      NEGATIVE      K-S Z      2-TAILED P
        0.40572       0.00253      -0.40572      1.998        0.001
```

38.21
W-W Subcommand

Subcommand W-W (alias WALD-WOLFOWITZ) performs the Wald-Wolfowitz runs test. W-W combines observations from both groups and ranks them from lowest to highest. If the samples are from the same population, the two groups should be randomly scattered throughout the ranking. A runs test is performed using group membership as the criterion. If there are ties involving observations from both groups, both the minimum and maximum number of runs possible are calculated. If the total sample size is 30 cases or fewer, the exact one-tailed significance level is calculated. Otherwise, the normal approximation is used.

The W-W subcommand has the following general form:

NPAR TESTS W-W = *varlist* BY *var(value1,value2)*

Example. The following example performs two tests. The test is first performed on SCORE by SEX, and then on TRIALS by TYPE.

```
TITLE  'NPAR TESTS'
SUBTITLE  'WALD-WOLFOWITZ TEST, SIEGEL, P. 139'
DATA LIST  /SEX 1 SCORE 3-5
VAR LABELS  SCORE 'AGGRESSION SCORE'
NPAR TESTS  W-W = SCORE BY SEX (1,2)
BEGIN DATA
1  86
1  69
   ...
2  20
2  15
END DATA
SUBTITLE  'WALD-WOLFOWITZ, SIEGEL, P. 142'
DATA LIST  /TYPE 1 TRIALS 3-4
VAR LABELS  TRIALS 'RELEARNING TRIALS REQUIRED'
NPAR TESTS  W-W = TRIALS BY TYPE (0,1)
BEGIN DATA
0 20
0 55
   ...
1 15
1 14
END DATA
```

Figure 38.21 is the output produced by the W-W subcommand. The display shows the number of cases in each group, the exact number of runs for the first example (since there are no ties), and the test statistic Z with its significance level. The second example contains ties so both the maximum and minimum possible number of runs are displayed along with their test statistic and significance level.

Figure 38.21   Wald-Wolfowitz runs test

```
11:01:12    WALD-WOLFOWITZ TEST, SIEGEL, P. 139

- - - - - WALD-WOLFOWITZ RUNS TEST
      SCORE      AGGRESSION SCORE
   BY SEX


        CASES

          12   SEX = 1
          12   SEX = 2
          --
          24   TOTAL
                                                    EXACT
                             RUNS          Z      1-TAILED P
EXACT NUMBER OF RUNS:         4         -3.5481      .0001
                 NO INTER-GROUP TIES ENCOUNTERED.



11:01:14    WALD-WOLFOWITZ, SIEGEL, P. 142

- - - - - WALD-WOLFOWITZ RUNS TEST
     TRIALS      RELEARNING TRIALS REQUIRED
   BY TYPE


        CASES

           8   TYPE = 0
          21   TYPE = 1
          --
          29   TOTAL
                                                    EXACT
                             RUNS          Z      1-TAILED P
      MINIMUM POSSIBLE:        4         -3.8635      .0001
      MAXIMUM POSSIBLE:        6         -2.9079      .0023

      WARNING -- THERE ARE   1 INTER-GROUP TIES INVOLVING   3 CASES.
```

**38.22
MOSES Subcommand**

Subcommand MOSES performs the Moses test of extreme reactions. This test arranges the scores from the groups in a single ascending sequence. The span of the control group is computed as the number of cases in the sequence containing the lowest and highest control score. The exact significance level can be computed for the span. Chance outliers can easily distort the range of the span. To minimize this problem, you can specify that a certain number of outliers be trimmed from each end of the span. No adjustments are made for tied observations.

The MOSES subcommand has the following general form:

NPAR TESTS MOSES [(n)] = *varlist* BY *var(value1,value2)*

The value *n* in parentheses is the number of cases trimmed from each end. If you do not specify *n*, MOSES automatically trims 5% of the cases from each end. *Value1* corresponds to the control group.

Example. The following example tests SCORE by SECTION. The first test uses SECTION=1 as the control group. The second uses SECTION=2 as the control group.

```
TITLE  'NPAR TESTS'
SUBTITLE  'MOSES TEST, EXTREME REACTION, SIEGEL, P. 149'
DATA LIST   /SCORE 1-2 SECTION 4
VAR LABELS   SCORE 'ATTRIBUTION OF AGGRESSION'
NPAR TESTS   MOSES = SCORE BY SECTION (1,2)/
   MOSES = SCORE BY SECTION (2,1)
BEGIN DATA
25 2
 5 2
14 2
  ...
10 1
10 1
11 1
END DATA
```

Figure 38.22 is the output produced by the MOSES subcommand. For each test, the display shows the number of cases in each group, the span of the control group and its significance level for the full set of cases, and the span of the control group after outliers are removed.

Figure 38.22   Moses test of extreme reaction

```
11:02:11    MOSES TEST, EXTREME REACTION, SIEGEL, P. 149


- - - - - MOSES TEST OF EXTREME REACTIONS

    SCORE     ATTRIBUTION OF AGGRESSION
 BY SECTION


            CASES

    (CONTROL)   9  SECTION = 1
 (EXPERIMENTAL) 9  SECTION = 2
                --
                18  TOTAL

1-TAILED P    SPAN OF CONTROL GROUP
  .1471          14   OBSERVED
  .0767           9   AFTER REMOVING 1 OUTLIER(S) FROM EACH END

- - - - - MOSES TEST OF EXTREME REACTIONS

    SCORE     ATTRIBUTION OF AGGRESSION
 BY SECTION


            CASES

    (CONTROL)   9  SECTION = 2
 (EXPERIMENTAL) 9  SECTION = 1
                --
                18  TOTAL

1-TAILED P    SPAN OF CONTROL GROUP
  1.0000         18   OBSERVED
   .9588         15   AFTER REMOVING 1 OUTLIER(S) FROM EACH END
```

38.23
Tests for *k* Independent Samples

Tests for *k* independent samples compare *k* groups of cases on one variable. These tests have the following general form:

NPAR TESTS *testname* = *varlist* BY *var(value1,value2)*

You must specify the name of the test and one or more variables to be tested. Each variable in the list produces one test. The variable following the keyword BY splits the file into *k* groups. *Value1* and *value2* specify minimum and maximum values for the grouping variable. For example,

NPAR TESTS K-W = SCORE BY CLASS (1,5)

specifies five samples or groups. This syntax resembles that used for the two-independent-sample tests. However, for *k*-sample tests, *value1* and *value2* are interpreted as a range of categories, whereas for two-sample tests, they are interpreted as the two categories.

The following tests are available for *k* independent samples:

MEDIAN *k-sample median test.* This is an extension of the two-sample median test and determines whether *k* groups are drawn from populations with the same median (see Section 38.24).

K-W *Kruskal-Wallis one-way analysis of variance test.* K-W tests whether all *k* samples are from the same population (see Section 38.25).

38.24
MEDIAN Subcommand
(*k*-Sample Test)

Subcommand MEDIAN performs the *k*-sample median test, an extension of the two-sample median test. MEDIAN tabulates a $2 \times k$ contingency table with counts of the number of cases greater than the median and less than or equal to the median for the *k* groups. You can specify a value as a cutting point or use the median calculated from the data. A chi-square statistic for the table is computed.

The MEDIAN subcommand has the following general form:

NPAR TESTS MEDIAN [(value)] = *varlist* BY *var(value1,value2)*

The value in parentheses following the MEDIAN subcommand is the test median. If the test median is not specified, the calculated median is used. The values specified for the variable that groups the cases determines whether a two-sample or *k*-sample test is performed. If you use a variable that has more than two values and *value1* is smaller than *value2*, a *k*-sample median test is performed. For example, in

```
NPAR TESTS  MEDIAN = A BY B (1,3)/MEDIAN = A BY B (3,1)
```

the first test is a *k*-sample median test with three groups, while the second is a two-sample median test for Groups 1 and 3 (see Section 38.18 for a discussion of the two-sample median test).

Example. The following example produces a median test for six groups, then recodes the grouping variable, VISITS, and produces the same test for four groups.

```
TITLE  'NPAR TESTS'
SUBTITLE  'K-SAMPLE MEDIAN TEST, SIEGEL, P.182'
DATA LIST  /VISITS 1 EDUC 3
VAR LABELS  VISITS 'VISITS TO SCHOOL'/
           EDUC 'LEVEL OF EDUCATION'
NPAR TESTS  MEDIAN = VISITS BY EDUC (1,6)
BEGIN DATA
4 1
3 1
0 1
 ...
2 5
2 6
6 6
END DATA
RECODE  EDUC (4 THRU 6=4)
NPAR TESTS  MEDIAN = VISITS BY EDUC (1,4)
```

Figure 38.24 is the output produced by the MEDIAN subcommand. For each test, the display shows the $2 \times k$ table, the chi-square statistic, the degrees of freedom, and the significance level for the chi-square.

Figure 38.24   A _k_-sample median test

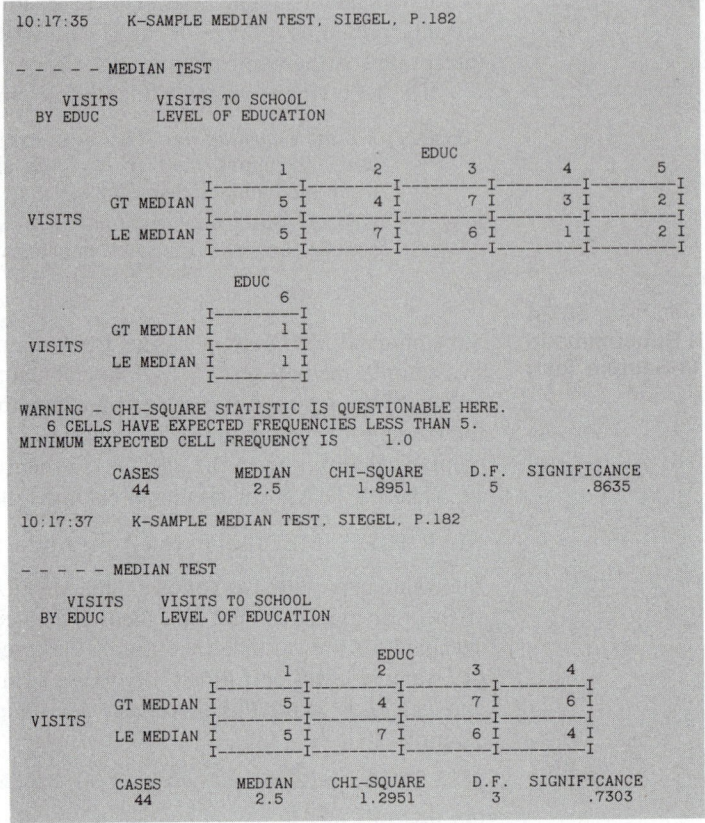

```
10:17:35    K-SAMPLE MEDIAN TEST, SIEGEL, P.182


- - - - - MEDIAN TEST

     VISITS    VISITS TO SCHOOL
   BY EDUC     LEVEL OF EDUCATION

                                           EDUC
                          1         2         3         4         5
                     I---------I---------I---------I---------I---------I
            GT MEDIAN I    5  I    4  I    7  I    3  I    2  I
   VISITS            I---------I---------I---------I---------I---------I
            LE MEDIAN I    5  I    7  I    6  I    1  I    2  I
                     I---------I---------I---------I---------I---------I

                           EDUC
                          6
                     I---------I
            GT MEDIAN I    1  I
   VISITS            I---------I
            LE MEDIAN I    1  I
                     I---------I

WARNING - CHI-SQUARE STATISTIC IS QUESTIONABLE HERE.
   6 CELLS HAVE EXPECTED FREQUENCIES LESS THAN 5.
MINIMUM EXPECTED CELL FREQUENCY IS       1.0

         CASES      MEDIAN    CHI-SQUARE    D.F.   SIGNIFICANCE
          44          2.5      1.8951        5        .8635

10:17:37    K-SAMPLE MEDIAN TEST, SIEGEL, P.182


- - - - - MEDIAN TEST

     VISITS    VISITS TO SCHOOL
   BY EDUC     LEVEL OF EDUCATION

                                   EDUC
                          1         2         3         4
                     I---------I---------I---------I---------I
            GT MEDIAN I    5  I    4  I    7  I    6  I
   VISITS            I---------I---------I---------I---------I
            LE MEDIAN I    5  I    7  I    6  I    4  I
                     I---------I---------I---------I---------I

         CASES      MEDIAN    CHI-SQUARE    D.F.   SIGNIFICANCE
          44          2.5      1.2951        3        .7303
```

Figure 38.25   Kruskal-Wallis one-way analysis of variance

```
- - - - - KRUSKAL-WALLIS 1-WAY ANOVA

     WEIGHT    BIRTH WEIGHT
   BY LITTER

   MEAN RANK     CASES

       31.70        10     LITTER = 1
       27.06         8     LITTER = 2
       41.40        10     LITTER = 3
       34.69         8     LITTER = 4
       17.58         6     LITTER = 5
       30.50         4     LITTER = 6
       11.92         6     LITTER = 7
       18.00         4     LITTER = 8

                   --

                   56     TOTAL

                                           CORRECTED FOR TIES
         CASES   CHI-SQUARE  SIGNIFICANCE  CHI-SQUARE  SIGNIFICANCE
          56       18.4639     0.0100        18.5654     0.0097

11:03:57    KRUSKAL-WALLIS, SIEGEL, P. 187


- - - - - KRUSKAL-WALLIS 1-WAY ANOVA

     AUTSCORE   AUTHORITARIANISM SCORE
   BY GROUP

   MEAN RANK     CASES

        4.40         5     GROUP = 1
        7.40         5     GROUP = 2
       11.50         4     GROUP = 3

                   --

                   14     TOTAL

                                           CORRECTED FOR TIES
         CASES   CHI-SQUARE  SIGNIFICANCE  CHI-SQUARE  SIGNIFICANCE
          14        6.4057     0.0406         6.4057     0.0406

11:03:59    KRUSKAL-WALLIS, SIEGEL, P. 190
```

38.25
K-W Subcommand

Subcommand K-W (alias KRUSKAL-WALLIS) performs the Kruskal-Wallis one-way analysis of variance test. It ranks all cases from the *k* groups in a single series, computes the rank sum for each group, and computes the Kruskal-Wallis *H* statistic, which has approximately a chi-square distribution.

The K-W subcommand has the following general form:

NPAR TESTS K-W = *varlist* BY *var(value1,value2)*

Every value in the range *value1* to *value2* forms a group.

Example. The following example first analyzes AUTSCORE by GROUP and then analyzes WEIGHT by LITTER.

```
TITLE  'NPAR TESTS'
SUBTITLE  'KRUSKAL—WALLIS, SIEGEL, P. 187'
DATA LIST  /AUTSCORE 1-3 GROUP 5
VAR LABELS  AUTSCORE 'AUTHORITARIANISM SCORE'
NPAR TESTS  K-W = AUTSCORE BY GROUP (1,3)
BEGIN DATA
 96 1
128 1
 83 1
 61 1
101 1
 82 2
124 2
132 2
135 2
109 2
115 3
149 3
166 3
147 3
END DATA
SUBTITLE  'KRUSKAL—WALLIS, SIEGEL, P. 190'
DATA LIST  /WEIGHT 1-3(1) LITTER 5
VAR LABELS  WEIGHT 'BIRTH WEIGHT'
NPAR TESTS  K-W = WEIGHT BY LITTER (1 8)
BEGIN DATA
2.0 1
2.8 1
3.3 1
 ...
2.4 8
3.0 8
1.5 8
END DATA
```

Figure 38.25 is the output produced by the K-W subcommand. For each test, the display shows the mean rank for each group, the number of cases in each group, the chi-square statistic and its significance level uncorrected for ties, and the chi-square statistic and its significance level corrected for ties.

38.26
STATISTICS Subcommand

In addition to the statistics provided for each test, you can also obtain two types of summary statistics for variables named on each of the subcommands. Use the STATISTICS subcommand to request the following statistics for NPAR TESTS:

DESCRIPTIVES *Univariate statistics.* Prints the mean, maximum, minimum, standard deviation, and number of nonmissing cases for each variable named on the combined subcommands.

QUARTILES *Quartiles and number of cases.* Prints values corresponding to the 25th, 50th, and 75th percentiles for each variable named on the combined subcommands.

ALL *All statistics available on NPAR TESTS.*

The following example produces the Kruskal-Wallis test shown in the lower half of Figure 38.25 and requests both statistics available with the STATIS-TICS subcommand:

```
SUBTITLE   'KRUSKAL—WALLIS, SIEGEL, P. 190'
DATA LIST   /WEIGHT 1–3(1) LITTER 5
VAR LABELS   WEIGHT 'BIRTH WEIGHT'
NPAR TESTS   K-W = WEIGHT BY LITTER (1 8)/
     STATISTICS = ALL
BEGIN DATA
2.0 1
2.8 1
3.3 1
  ...
2.4 8
3.0 8
1.5 8
END DATA
```

Figure 38.26 displays these statistics.

Figure 38.26   Statistics available in NPAR TESTS

```
11:05:54    KRUSKAL—WALLIS, SIEGEL, P. 190


                  N       MEAN     STD DEV  MINIMUM  MAXIMUM   LABEL

WEIGHT           56      2.7214     .6695      1.1      4.4     BIRTH WEIGHT
LITTER           56      3.8571    2.2192      1.0      8.0


                                  (MEDIAN)
                         25TH       50TH       75TH
                 N     PERCENTILE PERCENTILE PERCENTILE   LABEL

WEIGHT          56       2.325      2.800      3.200     BIRTH WEIGHT
LITTER          56       2.000      3.500      5.750
```

38.27
MISSING Subcommand

By default, NPAR TESTS deletes cases with missing values on a test-by-test basis. For subcommands where you can specify several tests, it evaluates each test separately for missing values. For example,

```
NPAR TESTS  MEDIAN = A B BY GROUP (1,5)
```

specifies two tests, A by GROUP and B by GROUP. A case missing for GROUP is excluded from both tests, but a case missing for A is not excluded for the test for B if it is not missing for B.

Use the MISSING subcommand to specify alternative missing-value treatments. The following keywords can be specified:

ANALYSIS   *Exclude missing values on a test-by-test basis.* This is the default if you omit the MISSING subcommand.

LISTWISE   *Exclude missing values listwise.* Cases missing on any variable named on any subcommand are excluded from all analyses.

INCLUDE   *Include user-missing values.* User-defined missing values are treated as if they were not missing.

The ANALYSIS and LISTWISE keywords are mutually exclusive; however, each can be specified with INCLUDE. For example, to include user-missing values in an analysis that excludes system-missing values listwise, specify

```
NPAR TESTS  MEDIAN = A B BY GROUP (1,5)
     MISSING=INCLUDE LISTWISE
```

38.28
SAMPLE Subcommand

NPAR TESTS must store cases in memory. You may not have sufficient computer resources to store all the cases to produce the tests requested. The SAMPLE subcommand allows you to select a random sample of cases when there is not enough space to store all the cases. The SAMPLE subcommand has no additional specifications.

38

Because sampling would invalidate a runs test, this option is ignored when you use the RUNS subcommand.

38.29
LIMITATIONS

The following limitations apply to NPAR TESTS:

- A maximum of 100 subcommands.
- A maximum of 500 variables total per NPAR TESTS command.
- A maximum of 200 values for subcommand CHISQUARE.

Syntax

ONEWAY

```
ONEWAY  varlist BY varname(min,max)
[/POLYNOMIAL=n] [/CONTRAST=coefficient list] [/CONSTRAST=...]
[/RANGES={LSD          }({0.05 }) ] [/RANGES=...]
         {DUNCAN       } {alpha}
         {SNK          }
         {TUKEYB       }
         {TUKEY        }
         {LSDMOD       }
         {SCHEFFE      }
         {ranges values}
[/MISSING={ANALYSIS**}  [{EXCLUDE**}]]
          {LISTWISE  }   {INCLUDE  }
[/HARMONIC={NONE** or PAIR}]
           {ALL          }
[/FORMAT={NOLABELS**}]
         {LABELS    }
[/MATRIX =[NONE**] [IN({*    })] [OUT({*    })]]
                      {file}        {file}
[/STATISTICS=[NONE        **]]
             [DESCRIPTIVES]
             [EFFECTS     ]
             [HOMOGENEITY ]
             [ALL         ]
```

**Default if the subcommand is omitted.

Contents

39.1   OVERVIEW

39.2   OPERATION

39.3   Specifying the Design

39.4   POLYNOMIAL Subcommand

39.5   CONTRAST Subcommand

39.6   RANGES Subcommand
39.7   User-Specified Ranges

39.8   HARMONIC Subcommand

39.9   STATISTICS Subcommand

39.10 MISSING Subcommand

39.11 FORMAT Subcommand

39.12 MATRIX Subcommand

39.13 OUT Keyword
39.14 IN Keyword

39.15 LIMITATIONS

39

Chapter 39   ONEWAY

Procedure ONEWAY produces a one-way analysis of variance for an interval-level variable by one independent variable. Although procedures ANOVA (Chapter 20) and MANOVA (Chapter 33) can also produce a one-way analysis of variance, ONEWAY performs several optional tests not available in those procedures. You can test for trends across categories, specify contrasts, and use a variety of range tests.

39.1
OVERVIEW

ONEWAY can analyze several dependent variables by one independent variable with one specification of the procedure. By default, ONEWAY produces a standard analysis of variance table for each dependent variable. In addition to the analysis of variance table, you can specify optional statistical tests, formats, and methods of handling missing data. ONEWAY also reads and writes matrix materials.

Tests for Trends. The POLYNOMIAL subcommand partitions the between-groups sum of squares into linear, quadratic, cubic, and higher-order trend components. (See Section 39.4.)

A Priori Contrasts. The CONTRAST subcommand requests contrasts tested by the t statistic. You can specify up to ten different contrast vectors. (See Section 39.5.)

Range Tests. The RANGE subcommand requests any of seven different range tests for comparisons of all possible pairs of group means. (See Section 39.6.)

Optional Statistics. In addition to the default display, you can obtain means, standard deviations, and other descriptive information about each group. Both fixed- and random-effects measures as well as several tests for homogeneity of variance are available through the STATISTICS subcommand. (See Section 39.9.)

Missing Values. By default, ONEWAY excludes cases with missing values on a pair-by-pair basis. Optionally, the MISSING subcommand can request that user-missing values be handled as if they were valid or that cases with missing values be deleted listwise. (See Section 39.10.)

Formatting Options. The FORMAT subcommand can obtain group labels derived from value labels. (See Section 39.11.)

Matrix Input and Output. The MATRIX subcommand writes means, standard deviations, and category frequencies to a system file that can be used in subsequent ONEWAY jobs. It also reads matrix materials consisting of means, category frequencies, pooled variance, and degrees of freedom for the pooled variance. (See Section 39.12.)

39.2
OPERATION

Procedure ONEWAY requires a dependent variable list and the independent variable with its range of integer values. All ONEWAY subcommands are optional and may be entered in any order, provided they appear after the variable list.

39.3
Specifying the Design

A ONEWAY analysis list contains a dependent variable list and one independent (grouping) variable with its minimum and maximum values. Use only one analysis list per ONEWAY command. For example, the command

```
ONEWAY  WELL BY EDUC6 (1,6)
```

specifies a one-way analysis of variance of WELL, the dependent variable, by EDUC6, the independent variable with minimum and maximum values of 1 and 6. Figure 39.3 shows the output from this command.

You can name up to 100 dependent variables but only one independent variable per analysis list. Dependent variables must be numeric. The independent variable follows the keyword BY, and you must include a value range specifying the highest and lowest values to be used in the analysis. These values are separated by a comma and enclosed in parentheses.

While you can specify any number of categories for the independent variable, contrasts and multiple comparison tests are not available for more than 50 groups. ONEWAY deletes empty groups for the analysis of variance and range tests. The independent variable must have integer values. Noninteger values encountered in the independent variable are truncated.

Figure 39.3 Analysis of variance table from ONEWAY

```
- - - - - - - - - - - - - - - - - - - - - - - - - O N E W A Y - - - - - - - - - - - - - - - - - - - - - - - - - - - - - - -

        Variable   WELL      SENSE OF WELL-BEING SCALE
        By Variable  EDUC6    EDUCATION IN 6 CATEGORIES

                            ANALYSIS OF VARIANCE

                                  SUM OF        MEAN        F       F
            SOURCE          D.F.  SQUARES       SQUARES     RATIO   PROB.

BETWEEN GROUPS               5    361.3217      72.2643    11.5255  .0000

WITHIN GROUPS              494   3097.3463       6.2699

TOTAL                      499   3458.6680
```

39.4
POLYNOMIAL Subcommand

The POLYNOMIAL subcommand partitions the between-groups sum of squares into linear, quadratic, cubic, or higher-order trend components. Specify this subcommand after the analysis specification, as in:

```
ONEWAY  WELL BY EDUC6 (1,6)
   /POLYNOMIAL = 2
```

The value specified in the POLYNOMIAL subcommand denotes the highest degree polynomial to be used. This value must be a positive integer less than or equal to 5 and less than the number of groups. Use only one POLYNOMIAL subcommand per ONEWAY command. If you specify more than one, SPSS-X uses only the last one named.

When you use the POLYNOMIAL subcommand with balanced designs, ONEWAY computes the sum of squares for each order polynomial from weighted polynomial contrasts, using the group code as the metric. These contrasts are orthogonal; hence the sum of squares for each order polynomial is statistically independent. If the design is unbalanced and there is equal spacing between groups, ONEWAY also computes sums of squares using the unweighted polynomial contrasts. These contrasts are not orthogonal. The deviation sums of squares are always calculated from the weighted sums of squares (Speed, 1976).

Figure 39.4 is the analysis of variance table with second-order (quadratic) polynomial contrasts specified for an unbalanced design.

Figure 39.4   Polynomial contrasts

```
- - - - - - - - - - - - - - - - - - - - - - - - - O N E W A Y - - - - - - - - - - - - - - - - - - - - - - - - -

        Variable   WELL      SENSE OF WELL-BEING SCALE
        By Variable  EDUC6    EDUCATION IN 6 CATEGORIES

                              ANALYSIS OF VARIANCE

                                    SUM OF         MEAN          F      F
          SOURCE            D.F.    SQUARES       SQUARES      RATIO   PROB.

  BETWEEN GROUPS             5      361.3217      72.2643     11.5255  .0000

    UNWEIGHTED  LINEAR TERM  1      257.3422      257.3422    41.0439  .0000
    WEIGHTED   LINEAR TERM   1      307.2051      307.2051    48.9966  .0000
    DEVIATION FROM  LINEAR   4       54.1166       13.5291     2.1578  .0727

    UNWEIGHTED  QUAD. TERM   1        6.6073        6.6073     1.0538  .3051
    WEIGHTED   QUAD. TERM    1       16.6406       16.6406     2.6540  .1039
    DEVIATION FROM   QUAD.   3       37.4759       12.4920     1.9924  .1142

  WITHIN GROUPS            494     3097.3463        6.2699

  TOTAL                    499     3458.6680
```

39.5
CONTRAST Subcommand

The CONTRAST subcommand specifies a priori contrasts to be tested by the t statistic. The specification for the CONTRAST subcommand is a vector of coefficients, with each coefficient corresponding to a category of the grouping variable. For example, the command

```
ONEWAY  WELL BY EDUC6(1,6)
   /CONTRAST = -1 -1 -1 -1 2 2
```

contrasts the combination of the first four groups with the combination of the last two groups. On the other hand, the command

```
ONEWAY  WELL BY EDUC6(1,6)
   /CONTRAST = -1 0 0 0 0 1
```

contrasts the first group with the last group. You can also specify fractional weights, as in:

```
/CONTRAST = -1 0 0 0 .5 .5
```

This subcommand contrasts Group 1 and the combination of Groups 5 and 6.

For most applications, the coefficients should sum to zero. Those sets that do not sum to zero are used, but a warning message is printed. In addition, you can use the repeat notation $n * c$ to specify the same coefficient for a consecutive set of means. For example,

```
/CONTRAST = 1 4*0 -1
```

specifies a contrast coefficient of 1 for Group 1, 0 for Groups 2 through 5, and −1 for Group 6. You must specify a contrast for every group implied by the range specification in the analysis list, even if a group is empty. However, you do not have to specify trailing zeros. For example,

```
/CONTRAST = -1 2*0 1 2*0
```

```
/CONTRAST = -1 0 0 1 0 0
```

```
/CONTRAST = -1 2*0 1
```

all specify the same set of contrast coefficients for a six-group analysis.

You can specify only one set of contrast coefficients per CONTRAST subcommand and no more than 50 coefficients per set. SPSS-X ignores the CONTRAST subcommand if the range of values for the group variable exceeds 50. The maximum number of CONTRAST subcommands per ONEWAY procedure is 10. For example,

```
ONEWAY  WELL BY EDUC6 (1,6)
    /CONTRAST = 2*-1, 2*1
    /CONTRAST = 2*0, 2*-1, 2*1
    /CONTRAST = 2*-1, 2*0, 2*1
```

specifies three different contrasts for the one-way analysis of variance model. Figure 39.5 shows the output produced by these CONTRAST subcommands. Output for each contrast list includes the value of the contrast, the standard error of the contrast, the t statistic, the degrees of freedom for t, and the two-tailed probability of t. Both pooled- and separate-variance estimates are printed.

Figure 39.5   Contrasts

```
- - - - - - - - - - - - - - - -  - - - - - - - - - O N E W A Y - - - - - - - - - - - - - - - - - - - - - - - -


            Variable  WELL         SENSE OF WELL-BEING SCALE
          By Variable EDUC6         EDUCATION IN 6 CATEGORIES


    CONTRAST COEFFICIENT MATRIX

                Grp 1      Grp 3      Grp 5
                    Grp 2      Grp 4      Grp 6
    CONTRAST 1  -1.0  -1.0   1.0   1.0   0.0   0.0

    CONTRAST 2   0.0   0.0  -1.0  -1.0   1.0   1.0

    CONTRAST 3  -1.0  -1.0   0.0   0.0   1.0   1.0
```

			POOLED VARIANCE ESTIMATE			SEPARATE VARIANCE ESTIMATE			
	VALUE	S. ERROR	T VALUE	D.F.	T PROB.	S. ERROR	T VALUE	D.F.	T PROB.
CONTRAST 1	3.3207	0.5230	6.349	494.0	0.000	0.5401	6.148	252.5	0.000
CONTRAST 2	1.1517	0.6613	1.742	494.0	0.082	0.6108	1.886	123.2	0.062
CONTRAST 3	4.4724	0.6990	6.398	494.0	0.000	0.6984	6.404	172.7	0.000

39.6
RANGES Subcommand

The RANGES subcommand specifies any of seven different tests appropriate for multiple comparisons between means. Each RANGES subcommand specifies one test. For example,

```
ONEWAY  WELL BY EDUC6 (1,6)
    /POLYNOMIAL = 2
    /CONTRAST = 2*-1,2*1
    /CONTRAST = 2*0, 2*-1, 2*1
    /CONTRAST = 2*-1,2*0,2*1
    /RANGES = SNK
    /RANGES = SCHEFFE (.01)
    /HARMONIC=ALL
```

produces two different range tests. Figure 39.6a shows the output produced by this example. ONEWAY does not calculate the range tests if more than 50 groups are encountered in the data. A maximum of 10 RANGES subcommands are permitted, and they cannot be separated by CONTRAST or POLYNOMIAL subcommands.

Figure 39.6a   Multiple group comparisons

```
- - - - - - - - - - - - - - - - - - - - - - - - - - - O N E W A Y - - - - - - - - - - - - - - - - - - - - - - - - -

         Variable   WELL       SENSE OF WELL-BEING SCALE
         By Variable EDUC6      EDUCATION IN 6 CATEGORIES


MULTIPLE RANGE TEST


SCHEFFE PROCEDURE
RANGES FOR THE 0.010 LEVEL -

         5.53    5.53    5.53    5.53    5.53

THE RANGES ABOVE ARE TABLE RANGES.
THE VALUE ACTUALLY COMPARED WITH MEAN(J)-MEAN(I) IS..
      1.7706 * RANGE * DSQRT(1/N(I) + 1/N(J))

   (*) DENOTES PAIRS OF GROUPS SIGNIFICANTLY DIFFERENT AT THE 0.010 LEVEL


                             G G G G G G
                             r r r r r r
                             p p p p p p

         Mean      Group      1 2 3 4 5 6

         2.6462    Grp 1
         2.7737    Grp 2
```

Figure 39.6b   Homogeneous subsets

```
- - - - - - - - - - - - - - - - - - - - - - - - - - - O N E W A Y - - - - - - - - - - - - - - - - - - - - - - - - -

         Variable   WELL       SENSE OF WELL-BEING SCALE
         By Variable EDUC6      EDUCATION IN 6 CATEGORIES


MULTIPLE RANGE TEST


STUDENT-NEWMAN-KEULS PROCEDURE
RANGES FOR THE 0.050 LEVEL -

         2.81    3.34    3.65    3.88    4.05

HARMONIC MEAN CELL SIZE =      62.7235
THE ACTUAL RANGE USED IS THE LISTED RANGE *       0.3162

   (*) DENOTES PAIRS OF GROUPS SIGNIFICANTLY DIFFERENT AT THE 0.050 LEVEL


                             G G G G G G
                             r r r r r r
                             p p p p p p

         Mean      Group      1 2 3 4 5 6

         2.6462    Grp 1
         2.7737    Grp 2
         4.1796    Grp 3      * *
         4.5610    Grp 4      * *
         4.6625    Grp 5      * *
         5.2297    Grp 6      * *


   HOMOGENEOUS SUBSETS    (SUBSETS OF GROUPS, WHOSE HIGHEST AND LOWEST MEANS
                           DO NOT DIFFER BY MORE THAN THE SHORTEST
                           SIGNIFICANT RANGE FOR A SUBSET OF THAT SIZE)


SUBSET  1

GROUP       Grp 1      Grp 2
MEAN        2.6462     2.7737
- - - - - - - - - - - - - - - - - - - - - - - - - - -

SUBSET  2

GROUP       Grp 3      Grp 4      Grp 5      Grp 6
MEAN        4.1796     4.5610     4.6625     5.2297
- - - - - - - - - - - - - - - - - - - - - - - - - - -
```

The following tests can be specified with the RANGES subcommand:

LSD   *Least-significant difference.* Any alpha between 0 and 1 can be specified. The default alpha is .05.

DUNCAN   *Duncan's multiple range test.* The default alpha is .05. Only .01, .05, and .10 are used. DUNCAN uses an alpha value of .01 if the alpha specified is less than .05; .05 if the alpha specified is greater than or equal to .05 but less than .10; and .10 if the alpha specified is greater than or equal to .10.

SNK   *Student-Newman-Keuls.* Only .05 is available as the alpha value.

TUKEYB   *Tukey's alternate procedure.* Only .05 is available as the alpha value.

TUKEY   *Honestly significant difference.* Only .05 is available as the alpha value.

LSDMOD   *Modified LSD.* Any alpha between 0 and 1 can be specified. The default alpha is .05.

SCHEFFE *Scheffe's test.* Any alpha between 0 and 1 can be specified. The default alpha is .05.

Range tests produce two types of output, depending on the design and the procedure used to calculate the range tests. First, range tests always produce multiple comparisons between all groups (see Figure 39.6a). In this type of output, nonempty group means are sorted in ascending order. Asterisks in the matrix indicate significantly different group means. For example, the asterisks in Figure 39.6a indicate that the means for Groups 3 through 6 are significantly different from the means for Groups 1 and 2.

In addition to this output, homogeneous subsets are calculated for balanced designs and for all designs when HARMONIC=ALL is used. (See Section 39.8.) Figure 39.6b shows this type of output. In this example, two subsets are produced. The first subset includes Groups 1 and 2, and the second includes Groups 3 through 6. The means of the groups included within a subset are *not* significantly different.

39.7
User-Specified Ranges

You can specify any other type of range by coding specific range values. You can specify up to $k - 1$ range values in ascending order, where k is the number of groups and where the range value times the standard error of the combined subset is the critical value. For example,

```
ONEWAY  WELL BY EDUC6(1,6)
   /RANGES=2.81, 3.34, 3.65, 3.88, 4.05
```

produces the same results as in the SNK test displayed in Figure 39.6b. If less than $k - 1$ values are specified, the last value specified is used for the remaining ones. You can also specify *n* repetitions of the same value with the form $n * r$. To use a single critical value for all subsets, specify one range value, as in:

```
ONEWAY  WELL BY EDUC6(1,6)
   /RANGES=5.53
```

This specification produces the same results as the Scheffe test displayed in Figure 39.6a.

39.8
HARMONIC Subcommand

The HARMONIC subcommand determines the sample size estimate to be used when the N's are not equal in all groups. Either only the sample sizes in the two groups being compared are used, or an average sample size of all groups is used.

The default keyword for HARMONIC is NONE, which uses the harmonic mean of the sizes of just the two groups being compared. To use the harmonic mean of *all* group sizes, specify keyword ALL. If ALL is used, ONEWAY calculates homogeneous subsets for SCHEFFE, TUKEY, TUKEYB, and LSDMOD tests on unbalanced designs. Specify only one keyword on the HARMONIC subcommand.

39

NONE   *Harmonic mean of the sizes of the two groups being compared.* You may also use keyword PAIR as an alias for NONE.

ALL   *Harmonic mean of group sizes as sample sizes for range tests.* If the harmonic mean is used for unbalanced designs, ONEWAY determines homogeneous subsets for all range tests.

39.9
STATISTICS Subcommand

By default ONEWAY calculates the analysis of variance table. It also calculates any statistics specified by the CONTRASTS and RANGES subcommands.

Use the STATISTICS subcommand to request additional statistics. The default keyword for STATISTICS is NONE, for no additional statistics. Available statistics through the STATISTICS subcommand include DESCRIPTIVE statistics, fixed and random EFFECTS statistics, and HOMOGENEITY of variance tests. You can specify any one or all of these statistics on the STATISTICS subcommand.

NONE   *No optional statistics.* This is the default.

DESCRIPTIVES   *Group descriptive statistics.* Prints the number of cases, mean, standard deviation, standard error, minimum, maximum, and 95% confidence interval for each dependent variable for each group.

EFFECTS   *Fixed- and random-effects statistics.* Prints the standard deviation, standard error, and 95% confidence interval for the fixed-effects model, and the standard error, 95% confidence interval, and estimate of between-component variance for the random-effects model.

HOMOGENEITY   *Homogeneity-of-variance tests.* Prints Cochran's *C*, the Bartlett-Box *F*, and Hartley's *F* max.

ALL   *All statistics available for ONEWAY.*

The following command generates the statistics shown in Figure 39.9:

```
ONEWAY   WELL BY EDUC6 (1,6)
        /STATISTICS=ALL
```

Figure 39.9   Statistics available with ONEWAY

GROUP	COUNT	MEAN	STANDARD DEVIATION	STANDARD ERROR	MINIMUM	MAXIMUM	95 PCT CONF INT FOR MEAN	
Grp 1	65	2.6462	2.7539	.3416	-4.0000	8.5000	1.9638 TO	3.3285
Grp 2	95	2.7737	2.8674	.2942	-5.0000	8.5000	2.1896 TO	3.3578
Grp 3	181	4.1796	2.4220	.1800	-4.0000	9.0000	3.8243 TO	4.5348
Grp 4	82	4.5610	2.1450	.2369	-.5000	9.0000	4.0897 TO	5.0323
Grp 5	40	4.6625	2.3490	.3714	-1.0000	8.0000	3.9113 TO	5.4137
Grp 6	37	5.2297	2.3291	.3829	-1.5000	9.0000	4.4532 TO	6.0063
TOTAL	500	3.8920	2.6327	.1177	-5.0000	9.0000	3.6607 TO	4.1233
FIXED EFFECTS MODEL			2.5040	.1120			3.6720 TO	4.1120
RANDOM EFFECTS MODEL				.4492			2.7374 TO	5.0466

```
RANDOM EFFECTS MODEL - ESTIMATE OF BETWEEN COMPONENT VARIANCE      0.8491


Tests for Homogeneity of Variances

    Cochrans C = Max. Variance/Sum(Variances) =   .2209, P =   .093 (Approx.)
    Bartlett-Box F =                             1.905 , P =   .090
    Maximum Variance / Minimum Variance          1.787
```

39.10
MISSING Subcommand

The MISSING subcommand controls missing values. Its default keywords are ANALYSIS and EXCLUDE. ANALYSIS excludes cases with missing values on an analysis-by-analysis basis. Use keyword LISTWISE to delete cases on a variable-by-variable basis. EXCLUDE determines that user-missing values are not used in the analysis. Use keyword INCLUDE to treat user-missing values as valid.

ANALYSIS   *Exclude missing values on a pair-by-pair basis.* A case missing on either the dependent variable or grouping variable for a given analysis is not used for that analysis. Also, a case outside the range specified for the grouping variable is not used. This is the default.

LISTWISE   *Exclude missing values listwise.* Cases missing on any variable named are excluded from all analyses.

EXCLUDE   *Exclude user-missing values.* This is the default.

INCLUDE   *Include user-missing values.* User-defined missing values are included in the analysis.

You can specify up to two keywords on the MISSING subcommand. Keywords ANALYSIS and LISTWISE are mutually exclusive. Each can be used with either INCLUDE or EXCLUDE. To include user-missing values in the analysis, you must explicitly specify INCLUDE. EXCLUDE is in effect whenever INCLUDE is not specified.

39.11
FORMAT Subcommand

By default, ONEWAY identifies groups as GRP1, GRP2, GRP3, etc. Use the FORMAT subcommand to identify the groups by their value labels. The FORMAT subcommand has only two keywords, NOLABELS and LABELS. NOLABELS is the default.

NOLABELS   *Suppress value labels.* This is the default.

LABELS   *Use the first eight characters from value labels for group labels.* The value labels are those defined for the independent variable.

Figure 39.11 shows the output from the following example of range tests specified with FORMAT=LABELS:

```
ONEWAY  WELL BY EDUC6(1,6) /RANGES=TUKEY
        /FORMAT=LABELS
```

Figure 39.11 Output with FORMAT=LABELS

```
- - - - - - - - - - - - - - - - - - - - - - - - O N E W A Y - - - - - - - - - - - - - - - - - - - - - - - - - -

         Variable  WELL       SENSE OF WELL-BEING SCALE
      By Variable  EDUC6      EDUCATION IN 6 CATEGORIES


   MULTIPLE RANGE TEST


   TUKEY-HSD PROCEDURE
   RANGES FOR THE 0.050 LEVEL -

        4.05    4.05    4.05    4.05    4.05

   THE RANGES ABOVE ARE TABLE RANGES.
   THE VALUE ACTUALLY COMPARED WITH MEAN(J)-MEAN(I) IS..
           1.7706 * RANGE * DSQRT(1/N(I) + 1/N(J))

     (*) DENOTES PAIRS OF GROUPS SIGNIFICANTLY DIFFERENT AT THE 0.050 LEVEL


                             G S H S C G
                             R O I O O R
                             A M G M L A
                             D E H E L D
                             E       E
                               H S C G S
                               S I C O E C
        Mean      Group       C G H L   H

        2.6462    GRADE SC
        2.7737    SOME HIG
        4.1796    HIGH SCH    * *
        4.5610    SOME COL    * *
        4.6625    COLLEGE     * *
        5.2297    GRAD SCH    * *
```

ANNOTATED EXAMPLE FOR ONEWAY

This example analyzes a 500-case sample from the 1980 General Social Survey. The variables are

- WELL—the respondent's score on a scale measuring sense of well-being. WELL is the dependent variable, computed from measures of happiness, health, life, helpfulness of others, trust of others, and satisfaction with city, hobbies, family life and friendships.
- EDUC—the respondent's education in six categories, where the original codes are years of education completed.

In this example we determine the degree to which sense of well-being differs across educational levels. The SPSS-X commands are

```
GET FILE GSS80/KEEP EDUC HAPPY HEALTH LIFE HELPFUL TRUST
                    SATCITY SATHOBBY SATFAM SATFRND
COUNT  X1=HAPPY HEALTH LIFE HELPFUL TRUST SATCITY SATHOBBY
          SATFAM SATFRND(1)
COUNT  X2=HAPPY HEALTH SATCITY SATHOBBY SATFAM SATFRND(2)
COUNT  X3=HEALTH HELPFUL TRUST (3)
COUNT  X4=SATCITY SATHOBBY SATFAM SATFRND(6)
COUNT  X5=HAPPY LIFE (3)
COUNT  X6=SATCITY SATHOBBY SATFAM SATFRND(7)
COMPUTE WELL=X1 + X2*.5 - X3*.5 - X4*.5 - X5 - X6
VAR LABELS  WELL 'SENSE OF WELL-BEING SCALE'
RECODE  EDUC (0 THRU 8=1)(9,10,11=2)(12=3)(13,14,15=4)
             (16=5)(17,18,19,20=6) INTO EDUC6
VAR LABELS  EDUC6 'EDUCATION IN 6 CATEGORIES'
VALUE LABELS  EDUC6 1 'GRADE SCHOOL OR LESS' 2 'SOME HIGH SCHOOL'
                    3 'HIGH SCH GRAD' 4 'SOME COLLEGE' 5 'COLLEGE GRAD'
                    6 'GRAD SCH'
ONEWAY  WELL BY EDUC6(1,6)
    /POLYNOMIAL = 2
    /CONTRAST = 2*-1, 2*1
    /CONTRAST = 2*0, 2*-1, 2*1
    /CONTRAST = 2*-1, 2*0, 2*1
    /RANGES = SNK
    /RANGES = SCHEFFE (.01)
    /STATISTICS  ALL
FINISH
```

- The GET command defines the data to SPSS-X and selects the variables needed for analysis (see Chapter 6).
- The COUNT and COMPUTE commands create variable WELL by counting the number of "satisfied" responses for each variable on the scale and computing a weighted sum of these responses (see Chapter 7).
- The RECODE command creates the variable EDUC6 which contains the recoded six categories of education (see Chapter 7).
- The VAR LABELS and VALUE LABELS commands assign labels to the new variables, WELL and EDUC6 (see Chapter 5).
- The ONEWAY command names WELL as the dependent variable and EDUC6 as the independent variable. The minimum and maximum values for EDUC6 are 1 and 6 (see Figure 39.3).
- The POLYNOMIAL subcommand specifies second-order polynomial contrasts. The sum of squares using the unweighted polynomial contrasts is calculated because the analysis design is unbalanced (see Figure 39.4).
- The CONTRAST subcommands request three different contrasts (see Figure 39.5).
- The RANGES subcommands calculate multiple comparisons between means using the Student-Newman-Keuls and Scheffe tests (see Figures 39.6a and 39.6b).
- The STATISTICS subcommand requests all the optional statistics (see Figure 39.9).

39.12
MATRIX Subcommand

ONEWAY can both read and write matrix materials. It writes means, standard deviations, and frequencies to a matrix system file that can be used by subsequent ONEWAY procedures. In addition, it reads means, frequencies, pooled variance, and degrees of freedom for the pooled variance.

Use the MATRIX subcommand to read and write matrix materials to a system file. The MATRIX subcommand has two keywords, IN and OUT, which you use to specify the matrix file in parentheses. When you use both IN and OUT on the same ONEWAY procedure you can specify each on a separate MATRIX subcommand, or both on the same subcommand. For example,

```
ONEWAY MATRIX IN(FILEONE)
       /MATRIX OUT(FILETWO)
```

is the same as

```
ONEWAY MATRIX IN(FILEONE) OUT(FILETWO)
```

If you specify IN and OUT on separate MATRIX subcommands, ONEWAY issues a warning to inform you that, should a conflict arise in the specifications, only the last MATRIX subcommand will be executed.

The MATRIX subcommand also recognizes keyword NONE (the default). Use MATRIX=NONE to explicitly indicate the data are not matrix materials.

39.13
OUT Keyword

The OUT keyword on MATRIX specifies the file to which the matrix is written. There are two options:

(file) *Write the matrix to a system file.* ONEWAY creates a system file containing the matrix materials. The name of the file is specified in parentheses. The system file is stored on disk and can be retrieved at any time.

(*) *Replace the active file with the matrix system file.* The matrix materials replace the active file. The matrix is *not* stored on disk. It is resident in the active file.

ONEWAY includes the mean, standard deviation, and number of cases with the matrix materials. Documents from the original file will not be included in the matrix file and will not be present if the matrix file becomes the active file. (For a discussion on documents, see Chapter 6.)

In the following example one set of matrix materials is written to the file named ONEDATA:

```
GET FILE=GSS80
ONEWAY  WELL BY EDUC6(1,6)
            /MATRIX=OUT (ONEDATA)
```

The active file is still the file named GSS80. Subsequent commands are executed on file GSS80.

To write the same matrix, but have it available to subsequent commands, specify the following:

```
GET FILE=GSS80
ONEWAY  WELL BY EDUC6(1,6)
            /MATRIX=OUT (*)
LIST
```

The active file is replaced with the matrix system file. The LIST command is executed on the matrix file, not on the file named GSS80.

Format of the Matrix System File. Figure 39.13 shows the matrix system file produced by the above commands. The file includes two special variables created by SPSS-X: ROWTYPE_ and VARNAME_. Variable ROWTYPE_ is a short string variable having values MEAN, STDDEV, N. The next variable in the file is the independent variable, in this instance variable EDUC6. VARNAME_ is a short string variable that never has values for procedure ONEWAY. VARNAME₋ is included with the matrix materials so ONEWAY's matrix output can be read by procedures that expect to read a VARNAME₋ variable and generate an error message if they don't find it in the data. The remaining variable(s) in the matrix file is the dependent variable(s), in this instance the single variable WELL.

Figure 39.13   A matrix system file

```
FILE:       MATRIX FILE

ROWTYPE_    EDUC6 VARNAME_        WELL

MEAN         1.00                2.64615
STDDEV       1.00                2.75387
N            1.00               65.00000
MEAN         2.00                2.77368
STDDEV       2.00                2.86743
N            2.00               95.00000
MEAN         3.00                4.17956
STDDEV       3.00                2.42202
N            3.00              181.00000
MEAN         4.00                4.56098
STDDEV       4.00                2.14503
N            4.00               82.00000
MEAN         5.00                4.66250
STDDEV       5.00                2.34900
N            5.00               40.00000
MEAN         6.00                5.22973
STDDEV       6.00                2.32915
N            6.00               37.00000

NUMBER OF CASES READ =      18    NUMBER OF CASES LISTED =      18
```

When split-file processing is in effect (see Chapter 15), the first variables in the matrix system file will be the split variables, followed by ROWTYPE₋, the independent variable, VARNAME₋, and the dependent variable(s). A full set of matrix materials is written for each splitfile group defined by the split variable(s). A split variable cannot have the same variable name as any other variable written to the matrix system file. If split-file processing is in effect when a matrix is written, the same split file must be in effect when that matrix is read by any procedure. (See Chapter 13 for more information on matrix system files.)

Additional Statistics. ONEWAY writes only one type of matrix: a matrix with the mean, standard deviation, and number of cases for each factor level. ONEWAY can read the matrices it writes, and it can also read matrix materials that include the means, category frequencies, pooled variance, and degrees of freedom for the pooled variance. The pooled variance has a ROWTYPE₋ value MSE, and its degrees of freedom have the ROWTYPE₋ value DFE. Section 39.14 shows this type of matrix input for procedure ONEWAY.

Missing Values. Missing value treatment affects the values written to a matrix system file. When reading a matrix system file, be sure to specify a missing value treatment on ONEWAY that is compatible with the treatment used to generate the matrix materials.

39.14
IN Keyword   Procedure ONEWAY reads two types of matrices. The first type includes:

• A vector of frequencies for each factor level.
• A vector of means for each factor level.
• A vector of standard deviations.

The second type includes:

• A vector of frequencies for each factor level.
• A vector of means for each factor level.

• A record containing the pooled variance (within-group mean square error).

• The degrees of freedom for the MSE.

The IN keyword on MATRIX specifies the file from which the matrix is read. There are two options: Keyword IN provides the following options:

(file)   *Read the matrix materials from a matrix system file.*

(*)   *Read the matrix materials from the active file.* The active file must be an appropriate matrix system file.

MATRIX=IN cannot be used in place of GET or DATA LIST to begin a new SPSS-X command file. MATRIX is a subcommand on ONEWAY and ONEWAY cannot run before an active file is defined.

In the following example, one set of matrix materials is read from the file named ONEMAT. This specification assumes the current active file is not the file ONEWAY:

```
ONEWAY  WELL BY EDUC6(1,6)
        /MATRIX=IN(ONEDATA)
```

SPSS-X reads variable names, variable and value labels, and print and write formats from the dictionary of the matrix system file named ONEDATA. The dependent variables named on ONEWAY may be a subset of the dependent variables in the matrix system file.

Variable Order. Generally, matrix rows, independent variables, and dependent variables can be in any order in the matrix system file read by keyword IN. However, all split file variables must precede variable ROWTYPE_, and all split group rows must be contiguous. ONEWAY ignores unrecognized ROWTYPE_ values.

To begin a new command file and immediately read a matrix, first GET the matrix file, then specify IN(*) on MATRIX. Alternatively, ONEWAY can read a matrix written to the active file by another procedure. In the following annotated example, ONEWAY uses matrix input from the MATRIX DATA command.

```
MATRIX DATA VARIABLES=EDUC ROWTYPE_ WELL /FACTOR=EDUC
BEGIN DATA
1 N 65
2 N 95
3 N 181
4 N 82
5 N 40
6 N 37
1 MEAN 2.6462
2 MEAN 2.7737
3 MEAN 4.1796
4 MEAN 4.5610
5 MEAN 4.6625
6 MEAN 5.2297
. MSE 6.2699
. DFE 494
END DATA
LIST
ONEWAY WELL BY EDUC(1,6) /MATRIX=IN(*) /RANGES=DUNCAN
```

• The MATRIX DATA command reads raw matrix data and creates an active file that, for each factor in the data, contains a vector of frequencies and a vector of means. The active file also includes one record each for the pooled variance and the degrees of freedom for the MSE.

• The LIST command displays the matrix materials in the active file, as shown in Figure 39.14.

• Procedure ONEWAY reads the data matrix. An asterisk (*) is specified as the IN file on the MATRIX subcommand because the data are in the active file. A Duncan Multiple Range test is then performed. Figure 39.14 shows the results of the ONEWAY analysis.

Figure 39.14   MATRIX DATA with procedure ONEWAY

```
ROWTYPE_ EDUC VARNAME_      WELL

N            1         65.0000
MEAN         1          2.6462
N            2         95.0000
MEAN         2          2.7737
N            3        181.0000
MEAN         3          4.1796
N            4         82.0000
MEAN         4          4.5610
N            5         40.0000
MEAN         5          4.6625
N            6         37.0000
MEAN         6          5.2297
MSE          .          6.2699
DFE          .        494.0000


NUMBER OF CASES READ =      14    NUMBER OF CASES LISTED =      14


- - - - - - - - - - - - - - - - -  - - - - - - - - - O N E W A Y - - - - - - - - - - - - - - - - - - - - - - - - - - - - -


        Variable  WELL
     By Variable  EDUC


Group       Grp 1        Grp 2        Grp 3        Grp 4        Grp 5        Grp 6

COUNT         65.          95.         181.          82.          40.          37.
MEAN        2.6462       2.7737       4.1796       4.5610       4.6625       5.2297


                         ANALYSIS OF VARIANCE

                                    SUM OF        MEAN          F       F
             SOURCE        D.F.     SQUARES      SQUARES      RATIO   PROB.

BETWEEN GROUPS              5       361.3150     72.2630     11.5254   .0000

WITHIN GROUPS             494      3097.3306      6.2699

TOTAL                     499      3458.6456

- - - - - - - - - - - - - - - - -  - - - - - - - - - O N E W A Y - - - - - - - - - - - - - - - - - - - - - - - - - - - - -


        Variable  WELL
     By Variable  EDUC


MULTIPLE RANGE TEST


DUNCAN PROCEDURE
RANGES FOR THE 0.050 LEVEL -

        2.78    2.93    3.02    3.09    3.15

THE RANGES ABOVE ARE TABLE RANGES.
THE VALUE ACTUALLY COMPARED WITH MEAN(J)-MEAN(I) IS..
     1.7706 * RANGE * DSQRT(1/N(I) + 1/N(J))

  (*) DENOTES PAIRS OF GROUPS SIGNIFICANTLY DIFFERENT AT THE 0.050 LEVEL


                         G G G G G
                         r r r r r
                         p p p p p
     Mean      Group     1 2 3 4 5 6

     2.6462    Grp 1
     2.7737    Grp 2
     4.1796    Grp 3     * *
     4.5610    Grp 4     * *
     4.6625    Grp 5     * *
     5.2297    Grp 6     * * *
```

39.15
LIMITATIONS

The following limitations apply to procedure ONEWAY.

- A maximum of 100 dependent variables and 1 independent variable.
- An unlimited number of categories for the independent variable. However, contrasts and range tests are not performed if the actual number of nonempty categories exceeds 50.
- Only 1 POLYNOMIAL subcommand.
- A maximum of 10 CONTRAST subcommands and 10 RANGES subcommands.
- Any alpha values between 0 and 1 are permitted for the LSD, LSDMOD, and SCHEFFE range tests. SNK, TUKEY, and TUKEYB use an alpha value of .05, regardless of what is specified. DUNCAN uses an alpha value of .01 if the alpha specified is less than .05; .05 if the alpha specified is greater than or equal to .05 but less than .10; .10 if the alpha specified is greater than or equal to .10; or .05 if no alpha is specified.

Syntax

PARTIAL CORR

```
PARTIAL CORR [VARIABLES=] varlist [WITH varlist]
                          BY control list (levels)
[/MISSING={LISTWISE**}  [{EXCLUDE**}]]
          {ANALYSIS }   {INCLUDE  }
[/SIGNIFICANCE={ONETAIL**}]
              {TWOTAIL }
[/FORMAT={MATRIX** }]
         {SERIAL   }
         {CONDENSED}
[/MATRIX=[NONE**] [IN({*    })] [OUT({*    })]]
                     {file}        {file}
[/STATISTICS=[NONE**] [CORR] [DESCRIPTIVES] [BADCORR] [ALL]]
```

**Default if the subcommand is omitted.

Contents

40.1   OVERVIEW

40.2   OPERATION
40.3   VARIABLES Subcommand
40.4   Correlation List
40.5   Control List and Order Values
40.6   Specifying Multiple Analyses
40.7   SIGNIFICANCE Subcommand
40.8   STATISTICS Subcommand
40.9   MISSING Subcommand
40.10   FORMAT Subcommand
40.11   MATRIX Subcommand
40.12   OUT Keyword
40.13   IN Keyword

40.14 LIMITATIONS

40

Chapter 40   PARTIAL CORR

Procedure PARTIAL CORR produces partial correlation coefficients that describe the relationship between two variables while adjusting for the effects of one or more additional variables. PARTIAL CORR first calculates a matrix of Pearson product-moment correlations. Alternatively, it can read the zero-order correlation matrix as input. Other procedures that produce zero-order correlation matrices that can be read by PARTIAL CORR include CORRELATIONS (Chapter 24), REGRESSION (Chapter 45), DISCRIMINANT (Chapter 27), and FACTOR (Chapter 28).

40.1 OVERVIEW

PARTIAL CORR produces one matrix of partial correlation coefficients for each of up to five order values. For each coefficient, PARTIAL CORR prints the degrees of freedom and the significance level. You can specify optional statistics, formats, and methods of handling missing data. PARTIAL CORR also reads and writes matrix materials that can be used by other procedures.

Significance Levels. By default, the significance level for each partial correlation coefficient is based on a one-tailed test. Optionally, you can request that the significance level be calculated using a two-tailed test. (See Section 40.7.)

Optional Statistics. In addition to the partial correlation coefficient, degrees of freedom, and significance level, you can obtain the mean, standard deviation, and number of nonmissing cases for each variable, and zero-order correlation coefficients for each pair of variables. (See Section 40.8.)

Missing Values. By default, PARTIAL CORR excludes cases with missing values on a listwise basis. Optionally, you can request that missing values be handled as if they were valid or that cases with missing values be deleted on an analysis-by-analysis basis. (See Section 40.9.)

Formatting Options. You can print more rows and columns of coefficients than the default allows and suppress the degrees of freedom and significance level for each coefficient. You can also print only the nonredundant coefficients. (See Section 40.10.)

Matrix Input and Output. PARTIAL CORR can read and write zero-order correlation matrices. (See Section 40.11.)

40.2
OPERATION

To use PARTIAL CORR, you must specify a VARIABLES subcommand that supplies a variable list to be correlated, one or more control variables following the keyword BY, and a list of order values in parentheses that define the level of control. (See Sections 40.3 through 40.5.) If VARIABLES is the first subcommand used on PARTIAL CORR, the VARIABLES keyword itself may be omitted. Sections 40.7 through 40.13 describe the optional subcommands available for PARTIAL CORR.

40.3
VARIABLES Subcommand

The VARIABLES subcommand requires three types of information:

• A *correlation list* of one or more pairs of variables for which partial correlations are desired. This list does *not* include the control variables.
• A *control list* of one or more variables that will be used as controls for the variables in the correlation list.
• One or more *order values* indicating the order of partials desired from the correlation and control list.

For example, the command

```
PARTIAL CORR VARIABLES=PUBTRANS MECHANIC BUSDRVER BY NETPURSE (1)
```

produces a square matrix containing three unique first-order partial correlations: PUBTRANS correlated with MECHANIC, controlling for NETPURSE; PUBTRANS with BUSDRVER, controlling for NETPURSE; and MECHANIC with BUSDRVER, controlling for NETPURSE. The *1* in parentheses indicates a first-order partial correlation. Figure 40.3 shows this partial correlation matrix.

Figure 40.3   First-order partial correlations

```
- - - - - - - - - - - - -  P A R T I A L   C O R R E L A T I O N   C O E F F I C I E N T S  - - - - - - - - - - - - - -

CONTROLLING FOR..    NETPURSE


              PUBTRANS   MECHANIC   BUSDRVER

PUBTRANS       1.0000      .4545      .5430
              (    0)     (   40)    (   40)
              P= .       P= .001    P= .000

MECHANIC        .4545     1.0000      .6122
              (   40)     (    0)    (   40)
              P= .001    P= .       P= .000

BUSDRVER        .5430      .6122     1.0000
              (   40)     (   40)    (    0)
              P= .000    P= .000    P= .

 (COEFFICIENT / (D.F.) / SIGNIFICANCE)        (" . " IS PRINTED IF A COEFFICIENT CANNOT BE COMPUTED)
```

If VARIABLES is the first subcommand used on PARTIAL CORR, the subcommand name VARIABLES may be omitted. For example, the above command can also be specified as follows:

```
PARTIAL CORR  PUBTRANS MECHANIC BUSDRVER BY NETPURSE (1)
```

If VARIABLES is not the first subcommand specified on PARTIAL CORR, the equals sign is required.

40.4
Correlation List

The correlation list specifies pairs of variables to be correlated while controlling for the variable(s) in the control list. The correlation list can take one of two forms. Both forms of the specification permit the use of the keyword TO to reference consecutive variables. If you provide a simple list of variables, PARTIAL CORR computes the partial correlation of each variable with every other variable in the list, producing a square or lower-triangular matrix (see the example above and Figure 40.3). The partial correlation of a variable with itself is always 1.0000 and appears on the diagonal of the matrix. Each pair of variables appears twice in the matrix (for example, PUBTRANS with MECHANIC, and MECHANIC with PUBTRANS). Since the partial correlation coefficient is a symmetrical measure, these two values are identical, and the upper and lower triangles of the matrix are mirror images of each other.

Alternatively, you can request specific variable pairs by using the keyword WITH. One variable list followed by the keyword WITH and a second variable list produces a rectangular matrix of partial correlation coefficients. The first variable list defines the rows of the matrix and the second list defines the columns. For example,

```
PARTIAL CORR  RENT FOOD PUBTRANS WITH TEACHER MANAGER BY NETSALRY(1)
```

produces the matrix in Figure 40.4.

Figure 40.4 A matrix using the keyword WITH

```
- - - - - - - - - - - - - PARTIAL  CORRELATION  COEFFICIENTS - - - - - - - - - - - - - -

CONTROLLING FOR..    NETSALRY


               TEACHER    MANAGER

RENT            -.3577      .1479
              (    40)    (    40)
              P= .010    P= .175

FOOD             .1104      .0724
              (    40)    (    40)
              P= .243    P= .324

PUBTRANS         .1721     -.1475
              (    40)    (    40)
              P= .138    P= .176


(COEFFICIENT / (D.F.) / SIGNIFICANCE)      (" . " IS PRINTED IF A COEFFICIENT CANNOT BE COMPUTED)
```

40.5
Control List and Order Values

The control list names the variables to be used as controls for each pair of variables specified by the correlation list. You can specify up to 100 control variables. The control list precedes the order values that specify the exact partials to be computed. You can specify up to 5 order values. The order values must be integers between 1 and the number of control variables.

The correlation between a pair of variables is referred to as a zero-order correlation, controlling for one variable produces a first-order partial correlation, controlling for two variables produces a second-order partial, and so on. The number of control variables determines the orders that can be requested, while the order value or values indicate the partial correlation matrix or matrices to be printed.

One partial will be produced for every unique combination of control variables which add up to the order value. For example,

```
PARTIAL CORR  RENT WITH TEACHER BY NETSALRY, NETPRICE (1)
```

produces two first-order partials: RENT with TEACHER, controlling for NET-SALRY; and RENT with TEACHER, controlling for NETPRICE. The command

```
PARTIAL CORR  RENT WITH TEACHER BY NETSALRY, NETPRICE (2)
```

produces one second-order partial of RENT with TEACHER, controlling simultaneously for NETSALRY and NETPRICE. You can specify both sets of partials with one PARTIAL CORR command, as in:

```
PARTIAL CORR  RENT WITH TEACHER BY NETSALRY, NETPRICE (1,2)
```

You must use the order value even if you specify only one control variable. The following command produces both first-order and third-order partial correlations:

```
PARTIAL CORR   RENT FOOD PUBTRANS BY NETSALRY NETPURSE NETPRICE (1,3)
```

Figure 40.5 displays the four matrices produced by this command.

40.6
Specifying Multiple Analyses

You can specify up to 25 partial correlation analyses on one PARTIAL CORR command, and you can name or imply up to 400 variables total. To specify multiple analyses, use multiple VARIABLES subcommands, or a slash (/) to separate each set of specifications on one VARIABLES subcommand. For example,

```
PARTIAL CORR   RENT FOOD WITH TEACHER BY NETSALRY NETPRICE (1,2)
  /WCLOTHES MCLOTHES BY NETPRICE (1)
```

produces three matrices for the first correlation list, control list, and order values. The second correlation list, control list, and order value produce one matrix.

PARTIAL CORR computes the zero-order correlation matrix for each analysis list separately. Depending upon the distribution of missing values in the variables, different sets of cases may be used for different analysis lists despite variables common to them (see Section 40.9).

40.7
SIGNIFICANCE Subcommand

The SIGNIFICANCE subcommand determines whether the significance level is based on a one-tailed or two-tailed test. By default, the significance level (which prints below the partial correlation coefficient) is based on a one-tailed test. This is appropriate when the direction of the relationship between a pair of variables can be specified in advance of the analysis. When the direction of the relationship cannot be determined in advance, a two-tailed test is appropriate. Keyword TWOTAIL requests a two-tailed test.

ONETAIL   *One-tailed test of significance.*
TWOTAIL   *Two-tailed test of significance.*

Figure 40.5   Multiple order values

```
- - - - - - - - - - - - - - P A R T I A L   C O R R E L A T I O N   C O E F F I C I E N T S - - - - - - - - - - - - - - -

CONTROLLING FOR..    NETSALRY

                  RENT       FOOD     PUBTRANS
RENT            1.0000       .1921      -.2136
               (    0)      (   41)    (   41)
                P= .        P= .109    P= .084

FOOD             .1921      1.0000       .2558
               (   41)      (    0)    (   41)
                P= .109     P= .       P= .049

PUBTRANS        -.2136       .2558      1.0000
               (   41)      (   41)    (    0)
                P= .084     P= .049    P= .

(COEFFICIENT / (D.F.) / SIGNIFICANCE)        (" . " IS PRINTED IF A COEFFICIENT CANNOT BE COMPUTED)


- - - - - - - - - - - - - - P A R T I A L   C O R R E L A T I O N   C O E F F I C I E N T S - - - - - - - - - - - - - - -

CONTROLLING FOR..    NETPURSE

                  RENT       FOOD     PUBTRANS
RENT            1.0000       .2970       .0590
               (    0)      (   41)    (   41)
                P= .        P= .027    P= .354

FOOD             .2970      1.0000       .5085
               (   41)      (    0)    (   41)
                P= .027     P= .       P= .000

PUBTRANS         .0590       .5085      1.0000
               (   41)      (   41)    (    0)
                P= .354     P= .000    P= .

(COEFFICIENT / (D.F.) / SIGNIFICANCE)        (" . " IS PRINTED IF A COEFFICIENT CANNOT BE COMPUTED)


- - - - - - - - - - - - - - P A R T I A L   C O R R E L A T I O N   C O E F F I C I E N T S - - - - - - - - - - - - - - -

CONTROLLING FOR..    NETPRICE

                  RENT       FOOD     PUBTRANS
RENT            1.0000      -.6933      -.5690
               (    0)      (   41)    (   41)
                P= .        P= .000    P= .000

FOOD            -.6933      1.0000       .4382
               (   41)      (    0)    (   41)
                P= .000     P= .       P= .002

PUBTRANS        -.5690       .4382      1.0000
               (   41)      (   41)    (    0)
                P= .000     P= .002    P= .

(COEFFICIENT / (D.F.) / SIGNIFICANCE)        (" . " IS PRINTED IF A COEFFICIENT CANNOT BE COMPUTED)


- - - - - - - - - - - - - - P A R T I A L   C O R R E L A T I O N   C O E F F I C I E N T S - - - - - - - - - - - - - - -

CONTROLLING FOR..    NETSALRY NETPURSE NETPRICE

                  RENT       FOOD     PUBTRANS
RENT            1.0000      -.6104      -.4580
               (    0)      (   39)    (   39)
                P= .        P= .000    P= .001

FOOD            -.6104      1.0000       .2583
               (   39)      (    0)    (   39)
                P= .000     P= .       P= .052

PUBTRANS        -.4580       .2583      1.0000
               (   39)      (   39)    (    0)
                P= .001     P= .052    P= .

(COEFFICIENT / (D.F.) / SIGNIFICANCE)        (" . " IS PRINTED IF A COEFFICIENT CANNOT BE COMPUTED)
```

40.8
STATISTICS Subcommand

The partial correlation coefficient, degrees of freedom, and significance level are automatically printed on PARTIAL CORR. You can obtain additional statistics with the STATISTICS subcommand.

When omitted, the STATISTICS subcommand defaults to NONE, for no additional statistics. When used, STATISTICS calculates only the additional statistics you request.

NONE *No additional statistics. This is the default if you omit the STATISTICS subcommand.*

CORR *Zero-order correlations with degrees of freedom and significance level.*

DESCRIPTIVES *Mean, standard deviation, and number of nonmissing cases. Descriptive statistics are not available with matrix input.*

BADCORR *Zero-order correlation coefficients if and only if any of the zero-order correlations are noncomputable. Noncomputable coefficients are printed as a period (.).*

ALL *All additional statistics available with PARTIAL CORR.*

If both statistics CORR and BADCORR are requested, CORR takes precedence over BADCORR and the zero-order correlations are printed. The commands

```
PARTIAL CORR VARIABLES=BUS WCLOTHES RENT FOOD BY NTCPRI, NTCPUR (1)
            /MISSING=ANALYSIS
            /STATISTICS=CORR DESCRIPTIVES
```

produce the display in Figure 40.8.

Figure 40.8   Statistics available with PARTIAL CORR

```
VARIABLE          MEAN      STANDARD DEV    CASES

BUS             42.9535      27.3652          43
WCLOTHES        80.7111      30.1945          45
RENT           120.0889      94.2250          45
FOOD            70.4667      18.7442          45
NTCPRI          81.3778      20.2376          45
NTCPUR          58.7045      28.8062          44



- - - - - - - - - - - - - - P A R T I A L   C O R R E L A T I O N   C O E F F I C I E N T S - - - - - - - - - - - - - - - - -

ZERO ORDER PARTIALS


              BUS      WCLOTHES      RENT        FOOD       NTCPRI      NTCPUR

BUS         1.0000       .4547      -.0466       .5612       .3973       .8759
          (    0)     (   41)     (   41)     (   41)     (   41)     (   41)
          P= .        P= .001     P= .383     P= .000     P= .004     P= .000

WCLOTHES     .4547      1.0000       .5461       .4082       .7040       .3058
          (   41)     (    0)     (   43)     (   43)     (   43)     (   42)
          P= .001     P= .        P= .000     P= .003     P= .000     P= .022

RENT        -.0466       .5461      1.0000       .2598       .7640      -.1288
          (   41)     (   43)     (    0)     (   43)     (   43)     (   42)
          P= .383     P= .000     P= .        P= .042     P= .000     P= .202

FOOD         .5612       .4082       .2598      1.0000       .7344       .2952
          (   41)     (   43)     (   43)     (    0)     (   43)     (   42)
          P= .000     P= .003     P= .042     P= .        P= .000     P= .026

NTCPRI       .3973       .7040       .7640       .7344      1.0000       .0976
          (   41)     (   43)     (   43)     (   43)     (    0)     (   42)
          P= .004     P= .000     P= .000     P= .000     P= .        P= .264

NTCPUR       .8759       .3058      -.1288       .2952       .0976      1.0000
          (   41)     (   42)     (   42)     (   42)     (   42)     (    0)
          P= .000     P= .022     P= .202     P= .026     P= .264     P= .


(COEFFICIENT / (D.F.) / SIGNIFICANCE)        (" . " IS PRINTED IF A COEFFICIENT CANNOT BE COMPUTED)
```

40.9
MISSING Subcommand

The MISSING subcommand controls missing values. By default, MISSING deletes cases with missing values on a LISTWISE basis. A case missing on any of the variables listed, including the set of control variables, is not used. Listwise deletion ensures that the partial correlations are computed from the same population. When you specify multiple analysis lists, missing values are handled separately for each analysis list.

Keyword ANALYSIS on the MISSING subcommand excludes cases on a pair-by-pair basis when the zero-order correlation matrix is calculated. A case missing on one or both of a pair of variables is not used. Pairwise deletion has the advantage of using as much of the data as possible. However, there are two problems in using pairwise deletion. First, the number of cases differ across coefficients; second, the coefficients represent different populations since they are based on different cases (with some overlap). When pairwise deletion is in effect, the degrees of freedom for a particular partial coefficient is based on the smallest number of cases used in the calculation of any of the simple correlations.

With either LISTWISE or ANALYSIS treatment of missing values, you can INCLUDE user-defined missing values as if they were not missing, or EXCLUDE user-defined missing values. By default, user-missing values are excluded.

LISTWISE *Exclude missing values listwise.* Cases missing on any of the variables listed, including the set of control variables, are not used in the calculation of zero-order correlation coefficients. This is the default.

ANALYSIS *Exclude missing values on a pair-by-pair basis.* Cases missing on one or both of a pair of variables are not used in the calculation of zero-order correlation coefficients.

EXCLUDE *Exclude user-missing values.* User-defined missing values are excluded from the analysis. This is the default.

INCLUDE *Include user-missing values.* User-defined missing values are included in the analysis.

40.10
FORMAT Subcommand

The FORMAT subcommand determines page format. Its default keyword is MATRIX, which requires four print lines per matrix row and displays the degrees of freedom and the significance level. Keyword CONDENSED requires only one print line per matrix row and suppresses the degrees of freedom and significance. A single star (*) following a coefficient indicates significance at the .01 level or less. Two stars (**) following a coefficient indicate significance at the .001 level or less. The commands

```
PARTIAL CORR VARIABLES=BUS WCLOTHES RENT FOOD BY NTCPRI (1)
          /FORMAT=CONDENSED
```

produce the matrix in Figure 40.10a.

The default output also prints redundant coefficients. Keyword SERIAL prints only the nonredundant coefficients. They are displayed in serial string format with the coefficients from the first row of the matrix printed first, followed by all the unique coefficients from the second row and so on for all the rows of the matrix. Six coefficients are printed across the page and each is identified with the names of the variables for which it was calculated. The degrees of freedom and significance level are printed below the partial just as they are in the matrix form of the output. Figure 40.10b is the output from the following example with keyword SERIAL in effect.

```
PARTIAL CORR VARIABLES=BUSDRVER MECHANIC ENGINEER TEACHER COOK BY NET-
SALRY (1)
          /FORMAT=SERIAL
```

Figure 40.10a Modifying the default output with condensed format

```
- - - - - - - - - - - - - - P A R T I A L   C O R R E L A T I O N   C O E F F I C I E N T S - - - - - - - - - - - - - - -

CONTROLLING FOR..    NTCPRI

                BUS    WCLOTHES       RENT       FOOD

BUS          1.0000        .2889     -.4875**     .4337*
WCLOTHES      .2889       1.0000      -.0668      -.1637
RENT         -.4875**      -.0668     1.0000      -.6628**
FOOD          .4337*       -.1637     -.6628**    1.0000

  * - SIGNIF. LE .01      ** - SIGNIF. LE .001      (" . " IS PRINTED IF A COEFFICIENT CANNOT BE COMPUTED)
```

Figure 40.10b Modifying the default output with serial format

```
- - - - - - - - - - - - - - P A R T I A L   C O R R E L A T I O N   C O E F F I C I E N T S - - - - - - - - - - - - - - -

CONTROLLING FOR..    NETSALRY

VARIABLE            VARIABLE            VARIABLE            VARIABLE            VARIABLE            VARIABLE
PAIR                PAIR                PAIR                PAIR                PAIR                PAIR
--------            --------            --------            --------            --------            --------


BUSDRVER    .3713   BUSDRVER   -.1947   BUSDRVER    .4669   BUSDRVER   -.1246   MECHANIC   -.1480   MECHANIC    .4075
WITH    DF =  39    WITH    DF =  39    WITH    DF =  39    WITH    DF =  39    WITH    DF =  39    WITH    DF =  39
MECHANIC SIG .008   ENGINEER SIG .111   TEACHER SIG .001    COOK     SIG .219   ENGINEER SIG .178   TEACHER SIG .004

MECHANIC    .2598   ENGINEER   -.5198   ENGINEER    .3208   TEACHER    -.1422
WITH    DF =  39    WITH    DF =  39    WITH    DF =  39    WITH    DF =  39
COOK     SIG .050   TEACHER SIG .000    COOK     SIG .020   COOK     SIG .188

  " . " IS PRINTED IF A COEFFICIENT CANNOT BE COMPUTED.
```

If you specify both CONDENSED and SERIAL, only SERIAL will be in effect.

MATRIX *Print the degrees of freedom and significance level in matrix format. This is the default.*

CONDENSED *Suppress the printing of the degrees of freedom and significance level.*

SERIAL *Print only the nonredundant coefficients in serial string format.*

40.11
MATRIX Subcommand

Use the MATRIX subcommand to write matrix materials to a system file, or to read matrix materials into PARTIAL CORR. The matrix materials PARTIAL CORR writes can be used by subsequent PARTIAL CORR procedures, or by other SPSS-X procedures that read correlation type matrices (see Chapter 13, Table 13.1). In addition to the Pearson correlation coefficients, the matrix materials PARTIAL CORR writes include the mean, standard deviation, and number of cases used to compute each coefficient. However, if PARTIAL CORR reads matrix data for its input, then writes matrix materials based on that data, the outfile matrix will not include means and standard deviations with the matrix materials.

The MATRIX subcommand has two keywords, IN and OUT, which you use to specify the matrix file in parentheses. When you use both IN and OUT on the same PARTIAL CORR procedure you can specify each on a separate MATRIX subcommand, or both on the same subcommand. For example,

```
PARTIAL CORR VARIABLES=varlist
             /MATRIX IN(FILEONE)
             /MATRIX OUT(FILETWO)
```

is the same as

```
PARTIAL CORR VARIABLES=varlist
             /MATRIX IN(FILEONE) OUT(FILETWO)
```

40.12
OUT Keyword

The OUT keyword on MATRIX specifies the file to which the matrix is written. There are two options:

(file) *Write the (zero order) correlation matrix to a system file.* PARTIAL CORR creates a system file containing the matrix materials. The name of the file is specified in parentheses. The system file is stored on disk and can be retrieved at any time.

(*) *Replace the active file with the correlation matrix system file.* The matrix materials replace the active file. The correlation matrix is *not* stored on disk. It is resident in the active file.

PARTIAL CORR writes a full square matrix for the analysis specified on the first VARIABLES subcommand (or first variable list if you omit the keyword VARIABLES). The matrix materials include all the variables specified on the first VARIABLES subcommand, including those specified after keywords WITH (when used) and BY. Documents from the original file will not be included in the matrix file and will not be present if the matrix file becomes the active file. (For a discussion of documents, see Chapter 6.)

In the following example, one set of matrix materials is written to the file named PTMAT:

```
GET FILE=CITY
PARTIAL CORR VARIABLES=BUSDRVER MECHANIC ENGINEER TEACHER COOK
BY NET-SALRY(1)
          /MATRIX=OUT (PTMAT)
```

The active file is still the file named CITY. Subsequent commands are executed on file CITY.

To write the same matrix to the active file so that it is available to subsequent commands, specify the following:

```
GET FILE=CITY
PARTIAL CORR VARIABLES=BUSDRVER MECHANIC ENGINEER TEACHER COOK
BY NET- SALRY(1)
          /MATRIX=OUT (*)
LIST
```

The original active file is replaced by the matrix system file. The LIST command is executed on the matrix file, not on the file named CITY.

Format of the Matrix System File. Figure 40.12 shows the matrix system file produced by the above commands. The file includes two special variables created by SPSS-X: ROWTYPE_ and VARNAME_. Variable ROWTYPE_ is a short string variable with values N, MEAN, STDDEV, and CORR (for Pearson's correlation coefficient). The next variable, VARNAME_, is a short string variable whose values are the names of the variables used to form the correlation matrix. When ROWTYPE_ is CORR, VARNAME_ gives the variable associated with that row of the correlation matrix. The remaining variables in the file are the variables used to form the correlation matrix.

Figure 40.12   A matrix system file

```
FILE:     MATRIX FILE

ROWTYPE_ VARNAME_   BUSDRVER   MECHANIC   ENGINEER   TEACHER      COOK    NETSALRY

N                  42.0000000 42.0000000 42.0000000 42.0000000 42.0000000 42.0000000
MEAN               43.1904762 50.8571429 60.1428571 38.2619048 64.8333333 50.1190476
STDDEV             27.6522289 31.3575536 26.8005928 25.7871773 30.9183951 24.7949664
CORR     BUSDRVER  1.0000000   .9176343   .7922298   .9139388   .6798282   .9493783
CORR     MECHANIC   .9176343  1.0000000   .7660355   .8925314   .7514616   .9177745
CORR     ENGINEER   .7922298   .7660355  1.0000000   .6574572   .7514890   .8666183
CORR     TEACHER    .9139388   .8925314   .6574572  1.0000000   .6214841   .8932145
CORR     COOK       .6798282   .7514616   .7514890   .6214841  1.0000000   .7436449
CORR     NETSALRY   .9493783   .9177745   .8666183   .8932145   .7436449  1.0000000


NUMBER OF CASES READ =        9   NUMBER OF CASES LISTED =        9
```

When split-file processing is in effect (see Chapter 15), the first variables in the matrix system file will be the split variables, followed by ROWTYPE_, VARNAME_, and the variables used to form the correlation matrix. A full set of matrix materials is written for each split-file group defined by the split variable(s). A split variable cannot have the same variable name as any other variable written to the matrix system file. If split-file processing is in effect when a matrix is written, the same split file must be in effect when that matrix is read by any procedure. (See Chapter 13 for more information on matrix system files.)

Additional Statistics. PARTIAL CORR always includes with the matrix materials the mean, standard deviation, and number of cases used to compute each coefficient, as shown in Figure 40.12. This information immediately precedes the correlation matrix in your output file.

Missing Values. With pairwise treatment of missing values (the treatment of the default keyword ANALYSIS), the matrix of N's used to compute each coefficient is included with the matrix materials. With LISTWISE treatment, a single N used to calculate all coefficients is included with the matrix materials. When reading a matrix system file, be sure to specify a missing value treatment on PARTIAL CORR that is compatible with the treatment used to generate the matrix materials. For example, if user-missing values were included in the analysis that generated the matrix, be sure to specify MISSING=INCLUDE on the PARTIAL CORR procedure that reads the matrix.

**40.13
IN Keyword**

The IN keyword on MATRIX specifies the file from which the matrix is read. When the matrix materials are read from a file other than the active file, both the active file and the matrix system file specified by the keyword IN on PARTIAL CORR must contain all the variables referenced by the VARIABLES subcommand(s) on PARTIAL CORR. Keyword IN has two options:

(file) *Read the correlation matrix from a matrix system file.* Both the active file and the matrix file must contain all the variables referenced by the VARIABLES subcommand(s) on PARTIAL CORR.

(*) *Read the correlation matrix from the active file.* The active file must be an appropriate matrix system file.

MATRIX=IN cannot be used in place of GET or DATA LIST to begin a new SPSS-X command file. MATRIX is a subcommand on PARTIAL CORR and PARTIAL CORR cannot run before an active file is defined.

In the following example, one set of correlation matrix materials is read from the file named CORMTX. This specification assumes the current active file is not the file CORMTX:

```
PARTIAL CORR VARIABLES=BUSDRVER MECHANIC ENGINEER TEACHER COOK
    BY NETSALRY(1)
  /MATRIX=IN(CORMTX)
```

SPSS-X reads variable names, variable and value labels, and print and write formats from the dictionary of the matrix system file named CORMTX. Both the active file and the CORMTX file must contain all the variables referenced by the VARIABLES subcommand(s) on PARTIAL CORR.

To begin a new command file and immediately read a matrix, first GET the matrix file, then specify IN(*) on MATRIX. Alternatively, PARTIAL CORR can read a matrix written to the active file by another procedure. In the following annotated example, PARTIAL CORR uses matrix input from the REGRESSION procedure.

```
GET FILE=CITY
REGRESSION MATRIX=OUT(*) /VARIABLES=NETPURSE PUBTRANS MECHANIC BUSDRVER
          /DEPENDENT=NETPURSE /ENTER
PARTIAL CORR  PUBTRANS MECHANIC BUSDRVER BY NETPURSE(1) /MATRIX=IN(*)
```

- The GET command defines the data to SPSS-X and selects the variables needed for the analysis.
- The REGRESSION command computes correlations among the specified variables. The MATRIX=OUT(*) specification writes a matrix system file and replaces the active file with the matrix system file.
- The MATRIX=IN(*) specification on PARTIAL CORR reads the matrix materials REGRESSION has written to the active file.

40.14 LIMITATIONS

The limitations in effect for PARTIAL CORR are

- A maximum of 25 requests on a single PARTIAL CORR command. Each request must contain a correlation list, a control list and order values.
- A maximum of 400 variables total can be named or implied per PARTIAL CORR command.
- A maximum of 100 control variables.
- A maximum of 5 different order values per single list. The largest order value that can appear is 100.

ANNOTATED EXAMPLE FOR PARTIAL CORR

This example analyzes 1979 prices and earnings in 45 cities around the world, compiled by the Union Bank of Switzerland. The variables are

- RENT—the average gross monthly rent in the city, expressed as a percentage above or below that of Zurich, where Zurich equals 100%.

- FOOD—the average net cost of 39 different food and beverage items in the city, expressed as a percentage above or below that of Zurich, where Zurich equals 100%.

- PUBTRANS—the average cost of a three-mile taxi ride within city limits, expressed as a percentage above or below that of Zurich, where Zurich equals 100%.

- NETPRICE—the city's net price level, based on more than 100 goods and services weighted by consumer habits. NETPRICE is expressed as a percentage above or below that of Zurich, where Zurich equals 100%.

- NETPURSE—the city's net purchasing power level, calculated as the ratio of labor expended (measured in number of working hours) to the cost of more than 100 goods and services weighted by consumer habits. NETPURSE is expressed as a percentage above or below that of Zurich, where Zurich equals 100%.

- NETSALRY—the city's net salary level, calculated from net average hourly earnings in 12 occupations. NETSALRY is expressed as a percentage above or below that of Zurich, where Zurich equals 100%.

In this example we determine the degree to which the costs of rent, food, and public transportation are related to each other, while adjusting for the effects of prices, purchasing power, and salary levels. We use PARTIAL CORR to first compute the zero-order correlations between all six variables and then compute three matrices of first-order partials that remove the effects of NETPRICE, NETPURSE, and NETSALRY, respectively. The SPSS-X commands are

```
GET   FILE=CITY/
      RENAME (NTCPRI NTCPUR NTCSAL = NETPRICE NETPURSE NETSALRY)
      /KEEP RENT FOOD PUBTRANS NETPRICE NETPURSE NETSALRY
PARTIAL CORR VARIABLES=RENT TO PUBTRANS BY NETPRICE TO NETSALRY(1)
             /STATISTICS=CORR DESCRIPTIVES
             /FORMAT=CONDENSED
FINISH
```

- The GET command defines the data to SPSS-X, renames three variables, and selects the variables needed for analysis (see Chapter 6).

- The PARTIAL CORR command requests three sets of first-order partial correlations for all pairs of variables implied by RENT, FOOD, and PUBTRANS. The first set of partials controls for NETPRICE, the second set controls for NETPURSE, and the third set controls for NETSALRY (see Section 40.2).

- The STATISTICS subcommand on PARTIAL CORR requests the mean, standard deviation, and number of nonmissing cases for each variable and the zero-order correlation coefficients for each pair of variables implied by the correlation list and the control list (see Section 40.8).

- The FORMAT subcommand on PARTIAL CORR suppresses the printing of the degrees of freedom and significance levels in the zero-order correlation matrix and the first-order partial correlation matrices (see Section 40.10).

- Since no missing-value option is specified, listwise deletion of missing cases is in effect (see Section 40.9).

Output from PARTIAL CORR

```
VARIABLE          MEAN        STANDARD DEV     CASES

RENT           121.7500         94.6455          44
FOOD            71.0000         18.6123          44
PUBTRANS        48.8182         24.6381          44
NETPRICE        82.1591         19.7731          44
NETPURSE        58.7045         28.8062          44
NETSALRY        50.3409         24.2946          44
```

```
- - - - - - - - - - - - - P A R T I A L   C O R R E L A T I O N   C O E F F I C I E N T S - - - - - - - - - - - - - -
ZERO ORDER PARTIALS


             RENT       FOOD      PUBTRANS    NETPRICE    NETPURSE     NETSALRY

RENT        1.0000      .2434      -.0346      .7646**    -.1288        .1531
FOOD         .2434     1.0000       .5639**    .7224**     .2952        .5800**
PUBTRANS    -.0346      .5639**    1.0000      .3953*      .6234**      .7247**
NETPRICE     .7646**    .7224**     .3953*    1.0000       .0976        .4824**
NETPURSE    -.1288      .2952       .6234**    .0976      1.0000        .9012**
NETSALRY     .1531      .5800**     .7247**    .4824**     .9012**     1.0000


  * - SIGNIF. LE .01      ** - SIGNIF. LE .001          (" . " IS PRINTED IF A COEFFICIENT CANNOT BE COMPUTED)
```

```
- - - - - - - - - - - - - P A R T I A L   C O R R E L A T I O N   C O E F F I C I E N T S - - - - - - - - - - - - - -
CONTROLLING FOR..    NETPRICE


             RENT       FOOD      PUBTRANS

RENT        1.0000     -.6933**    -.5690**
FOOD        -.6933**   1.0000       .4382*
PUBTRANS    -.5690**    .4382*     1.0000


  * - SIGNIF. LE .01      ** - SIGNIF. LE .001          (" . " IS PRINTED IF A COEFFICIENT CANNOT BE COMPUTED)
```

```
- - - - - - - - - - - - - P A R T I A L   C O R R E L A T I O N   C O E F F I C I E N T S - - - - - - - - - - - - - -
CONTROLLING FOR..    NETPURSE


             RENT       FOOD      PUBTRANS

RENT        1.0000      .2970       .0590
FOOD         .2970     1.0000       .5085**
PUBTRANS     .0590      .5085**    1.0000


  * - SIGNIF. LE .01      ** - SIGNIF. LE .001          (" . " IS PRINTED IF A COEFFICIENT CANNOT BE COMPUTED)
```

```
- - - - - - - - - - - - - P A R T I A L   C O R R E L A T I O N   C O E F F I C I E N T S - - - - - - - - - - - - - -
CONTROLLING FOR..    NETSALRY


             RENT       FOOD      PUBTRANS

RENT        1.0000      .1921      -.2136
FOOD         .1921     1.0000       .2558
PUBTRANS    -.2136      .2558      1.0000


  * - SIGNIF. LE .01      ** - SIGNIF. LE .001          (" . " IS PRINTED IF A COEFFICIENT CANNOT BE COMPUTED)
```

Syntax

PLOT

```
PLOT [HSIZE = {80**}] [/VSIZE = {40**}]
              {n  }               {n  }
     [/CUTPOINT = {EVERY({1**})}]
                  {      { n  } }
                  {value list   }
     [/SYMBOLS = {ALPHANUMERIC**                      }]
                 {NUMERIC                             }
                 {'symbols'[,'overplot symbols']      }
                 {X'hexsymbs'[,'overplot hexsymbs']   }
                 {DEFAULT                             }
     [/MISSING = [{PLOTWISE**}] [INCLUDE]]
                  {LISTWISE  }
     [/FORMAT = {DEFAULT**        }]
                {CONTOUR[({10})]}
                {        { n }  }
                {OVERLAY          }
                {REGRESSION       }
     [/TITLE = 'title']
     [/HORIZONTAL = ['title'] [STANDARDIZE] [REFERENCE(value list)]
                    [MIN(min)] [MAX(max)] [UNIFORM]]
     [/VERTICAL = ['title'] [STANDARDIZE] [REFERENCE(value list)]
                  [MIN(min)] [MAX(max)] [UNIFORM]]
     /PLOT = varlist WITH varlist [(PAIR)] [BY varname] [;varlist...]
     [/PLOT=...]
```

** Default if the subcommand is omitted.

Contents

41.1   OVERVIEW

41.2   OPERATION

41.3   PLOT Subcommand
41.4   Control and Contour Variables
41.5   TITLE Subcommand
41.6   VERTICAL and HORIZONTAL Subcommands
41.7   FORMAT Subcommand
41.8   Bivariate Scatterplots
41.9   Contour Plots
41.10   Overlay Plots
41.11   Regression Plots

41.12   HSIZE and VSIZE Subcommands
41.13   HSIZE and VSIZE with HORIZONTAL and VERTICAL

41.14   Controlling Plot Symbols
41.15   SYMBOLS Subcommand
41.16   CUTPOINT Subcommand

41.17   MISSING Subcommand

41.18   LIMITATIONS

41

788

Chapter 41 PLOT

Procedure PLOT produces two-dimensional line-printer plots. You can request simple scatterplots, scatterplots with a control variable and/or regression statistics, contour plots, and overlay plots. You can choose from a variety of options for plot symbols, and you can add reference lines. You have control over size, labeling, and scaling of each axis, and for a series of plots, you can constrain the axes to be uniform.

41.1 OVERVIEW

PLOT produces line-printer plots for variables named on the required PLOT subcommand. Additional subcommands control custom labels, axis values, plot area and symbols, and reference lines.

Plot Types. By default, PLOT produces a bivariate scatterplot. Use the FORMAT subcommand to request regression, overlay, or contour plots. (See Section 41.7.)

Axes and Titles. The PLOT subcommand specification is the default plot title. To specify a different title, use the TITLE subcommand. (See Section 41.5.) By default, PLOT uses variable labels or variable names for axis labels, and the minimum and maximum values of the data determine axis values. To specify other formatting parameters for the axes, you can use the HORIZONTAL and VERTICAL subcommands. (See Section 41.6.) For each axis, you can request a title, the minimum and maximum values, reference lines at specified locations, and standardization of variables.

Plot Symbols. By default, procedure PLOT uses 1 through 9, A through Z, and an asterisk to plot points. Each symbol represents the number of cases at a plot position, with 1 indicating 1 case, A indicating 10 cases, and the asterisk indicating 36 or more cases. You can use the SYMBOLS subcommand to specify custom plotting symbols and overprint symbols. (See Section 41.15.) You can use the CUTPOINT subcommand to specify each symbol's frequency category. (See Section 41.16.)

Plot Area. PLOT uses default vertical and horizontal dimensions for the area that a plot covers on the page. To specify different dimensions for all plots requested on a PLOT command, use the VSIZE and HSIZE subcommands. (See Section 41.12.)

Missing Values. By default, procedure PLOT excludes from each plot those cases that have missing values on any of the variables for that plot. Use the MISSING subcommand to include user-defined missing values or to delete cases with missing values from all the plots specified on a PLOT command. (See Section 41.17.)

41.2
OPERATION

The only required subcommand on PLOT is the PLOT subcommand. There are two types of optional subcommands: global subcommands (HSIZE, VSIZE, CUTPOINT, SYMBOLS, and MISSING) and local subcommands (FORMAT, TITLE, HORIZONTAL, and VERTICAL).

You can specify each of the global subcommands only once, and each must be prior to the first occurrence of the PLOT subcommand. You can use the PLOT subcommand and accompanying local subcommands more than once within a PLOT command. However, local subcommands apply only to the *immediately following* PLOT subcommand. A PLOT subcommand must be the last subcommand you specify. You must use a slash to separate every subcommand from the next.

41.3
PLOT Subcommand

Use the PLOT subcommand to specify the variables to plot. Specify the variables for the vertical (Y) axis, then the keyword WITH, then the variables for the horizontal (X) axis.

By default, PLOT creates separate plots for all combinations formed by each variable on the left side of the WITH keyword with each variable on the right. However, you can choose to plot only corresponding pairs of variables by using the keyword PAIR in parentheses. In the following,

```
PLOT = Y1 Y2  WITH  X1 X2/

PLOT = Y1 Y2  WITH  X1 X2 (PAIR) /
```

the first PLOT subcommand specifies four plots, showing Y1 with X1, Y1 with X2, Y2 with X1, and Y2 with X2. The second PLOT subcommand specifies only two plots, showing Y1 with X1 and Y2 with X2.

Use semicolons to separate multiple plot lists. For example,

```
PLOT = BONUS WITH TENURE SALNOW;SALNOW WITH SALBEG
```

requests three scatterplots. The first request produces plots of BONUS with TENURE and BONUS with SALNOW. The second request produces the plot of SALNOW with SALBEG (see Figure 41.3b).

In the output, an information table precedes the plots you request on a PLOT subcommand (see Figure 41.3a). This table shows the number of cases used, the size of the plot, and a list of symbols and frequencies. The default size of plots is 80 print positions wide and 40 print lines high. The default symbols are 1–9, A–Z, and an asterisk (*), and each symbol corresponds to a particular frequency of cases. Thus, the G in the lower left-hand corner of Figure 41.3b (where beginning salary is 4,000 and current salary is 6,000) represents 16 cases with those salary values.

Figure 41.3a Data information table

```
Data    Information

         474 unweighted cases accepted.

Size of the plots

   Horizontal size is 80
     Vertical size is 40

Frequencies and symbols used (not applicable for control or overlay plots)

          1 - 1      11 - B     21 - L     31 - V
          2 - 2      12 - C     22 - M     32 - W
          3 - 3      13 - D     23 - N     33 - X
          4 - 4      14 - E     24 - O     34 - Y
          5 - 5      15 - F     25 - P     35 - Z
          6 - 6      16 - G     26 - Q     36 - *
          7 - 7      17 - H     27 - R
          8 - 8      18 - I     28 - S
          9 - 9      19 - J     29 - T
         10 - A      20 - K     30 - U
```

In the default plot shown in Figure 41.3b, the values along the axes are scaled according to the minimum and maximum observed values for each variable. The default plot title gives the names of the variables plotted. The vertical and horizontal axis titles are variable labels for SALNOW and SALBEG. PLOT would have used variable names if no labels had been provided.

There are no limits to the number of PLOT subcommands or to the number of variables on the PLOT command.

Figure 41.3b   A default plot

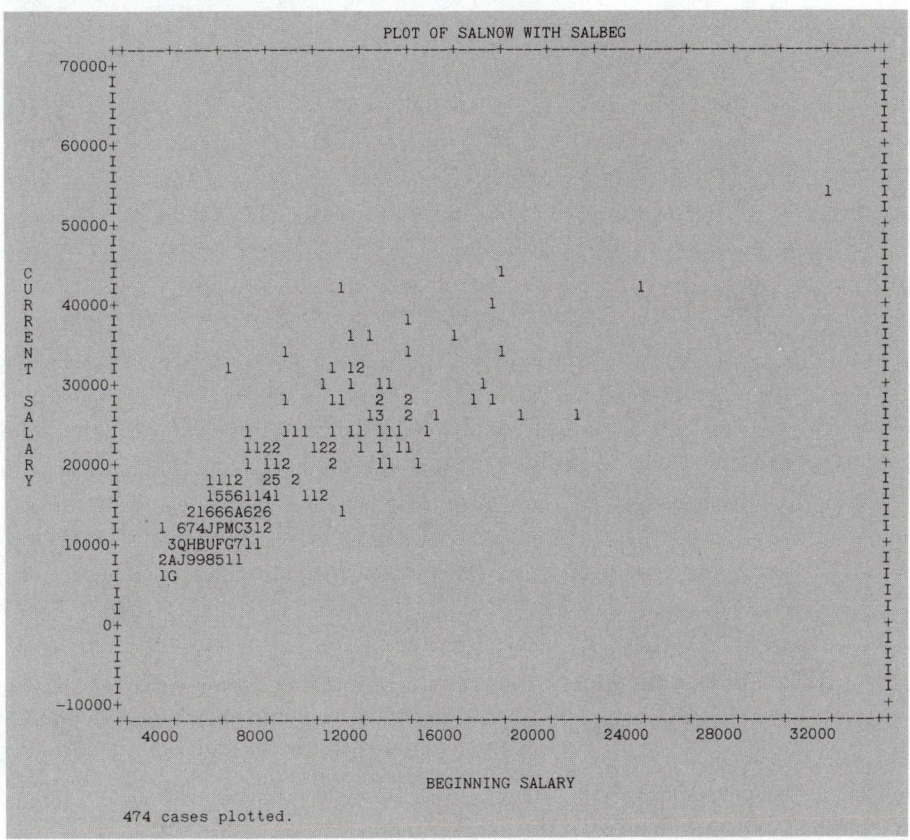

41.4
Control and Contour
Variables

Use the BY keyword on a PLOT subcommand's variable list to specify a control variable or a contour variable for a set of plots. You can specify only one such variable on any plot list. Producing a contour plot requires the FORMAT subcommand (see Section 41.9). The commands

```
VALUE LABELS SEX 1 'MALE' 2 'FEMALE'
PLOT PLOT=SALNOW WITH SALBEG BY SEX
```

produce the control plot shown in Figure 41.4. The symbol at each position indicates the value(s) of the control variable for the case(s) at that position. PLOT uses the first character of the control variable's value label as the plot symbol. If no value labels are supplied, PLOT uses the first character of the actual value. For the numeric value 28, the symbol would be 2; for the string value MALE, the symbol would be M. PLOT does not check uniqueness of symbols, but you can use the VALUE LABELS command to create appropriate value labels that prevent ambiguity. In Figure 41.4, the symbol M represents male employees, and the symbol F represents female employees. The symbol $ at a print position indicates that more than one control value occurs for the two or more cases at that position.

Figure 41.4 Default plot with a control variable

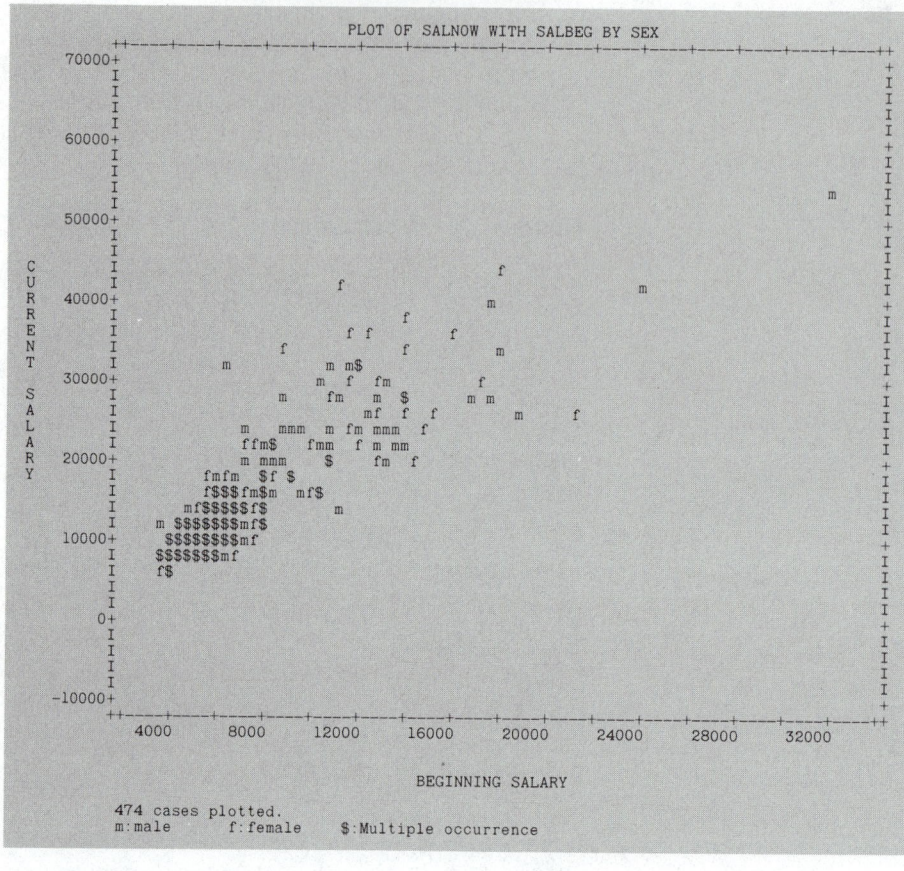

41.5
TITLE Subcommand

You can provide a title for a plot with the TITLE subcommand. Enclose your own descriptive title for a plot in apostrophes on the TITLE subcommand. The default title of a plot uses either the names of the variables for a bivariate plot or the type of plot requested on the FORMAT subcommand (see Section 41.7). The command

```
PLOT TITLE='Plot of Beginning Salary on Current Salary'
 /PLOT=SALNOW WITH SALBEG
```

requests a title that overrides the default.

A title can contain up to 60 characters. A title longer than the horizontal width specified on the HSIZE subcommand (see Section 41.12) will be truncated.

41.6
VERTICAL and
HORIZONTAL
Subcommands

You can specify axis labels with the HORIZONTAL and VERTICAL subcommands. These two subcommands also control minimum and maximum values plotted, standardization of axes, provisions for reference lines, and whether the axes have uniform scales on different plots. Adjusting minimum and maximum values is especially useful when you want to focus on a subset of a larger plot. The minimum and maximum value specifications function like a TEMPORARY SELECT IF transformation (see Chapter 11). PLOT excludes values outside the specified range from the immediately following PLOT subcommand. PLOT scales the axes to include the specified values. However, to ensure that integers or simple decimals are on the axes, PLOT may extend the scales slightly beyond the specified minimum and maximum.

You can also use the VERTICAL or HORIZONTAL subcommand to designate a label for each axis, to choose the positions of reference lines, and to specify standardization of values.

41

The VERTICAL and HORIZONTAL subcommands have the same keyword specifications:

'label'
: *Label of axis.* You can specify a label of up to 40 characters. The default is the variable label for the variable on the axis. If there is no variable label, PLOT uses the variable name. If you specify a label longer or wider than the plot frame size (see Section 41.12), the label will be truncated.

MIN(min)
: *Minimum value included on axis.* The default is the minimum observed value. With the MIN option, only data values greater than or equal to *min* are plotted. The axis scale includes this value.

MAX(max)
: *Maximum value included on axis.* The default is the maximum observed value. With the MAX option, only data values less than or equal to *max* are plotted. The axis scale includes this value.

UNIFORM
: *Uniform values on axis.* This option specifies that all plots will have scales with the same values on the (vertical or horizontal) axis. Uniform scales also result if you specify both MIN and MAX. If you specify UNIFORM but not MIN and MAX, PLOT determines the minimum and maximum across all variables for the axis.

REFERENCE(value list)
: *Reference lines for axis.* For either axis, this option specifies values at which to draw reference lines perpendicular to the axis (see Figure 41.10). You can specify up to 10 reference lines for each axis.

STANDARDIZE
: *Standardize variables on axis.* With this option, PLOT standardizes variables to have a mean of 0 and a standard deviation of 1. This option is useful if you want to overlay plots of variables that otherwise would have different scales.

The command

```
PLOT TITLE='Annual Salary by Age, XYZ Corporation  1983'
    /VERTICAL='Annual salary before taxes' MIN (500) MAX (75000)
        REFERENCE(25000,50000)
    /HORIZONTAL='Age of employee' MIN (18) MAX (65)
        REFERENCE (33,48)
         /PLOT=INCOME WITH AGE
```

produces a bivariate scatterplot with labeled axes that include values of INCOME between 500 and 75,000 and values of AGE between 18 and 65. The keyword REFERENCE requests reference lines at 25,000 and 50,000 on the vertical axis and at 33 and 48 on the horizontal axis.

41.7
FORMAT Subcommand

Procedure PLOT produces four main types of plots: scatterplots, contour plots, overlay plots, and regression plots. The FORMAT subcommand specifies the plot type for the immediately following PLOT subcommand.

41.8
Bivariate Scatterplots

The default plot is a bivariate scatterplot (see Section 41.3b). To obtain a bivariate scatterplot, you can omit the FORMAT subcommand or specify FORMAT= DEFAULT.

41.9
Contour Plots

A contour plot is similar to a control plot in that symbols on either plot indicate values of the control variable for the cases represented at the positions of the symbols. However, the control variable for a contour plot is a continuous variable. You specify a contour variable after the BY keyword on the PLOT subcommand (see Section 41.4).

The CONTOUR keyword on the FORMAT subcommand requests a recoding of the control variable into *n* equal-width intervals corresponding to *n* plotting symbols. When more than one contour level occurs at a print position,

PLOT prints the symbol for the highest level. You can specify a maximum of 35 contour levels for each contour plot. If you do not specify the number of levels the number defaults to 10.

The command

```
PLOT FORMAT=CONTOUR(10)
 /TITLE 'SOLUBILITY OF AMMONIA IN WATER'
 /HORIZONTAL='ATMOSPHERIC PRESSURE'
 /VERTICAL='TEMPERATURE'
 /PLOT=TEMP WITH PRESSURE BY CONCENT
```

requests a contour plot with ten levels of the variables named on the PLOT subcommand. Labels are specified for the HORIZONTAL and VERTICAL axes. The resulting plot appears in Figure 41.9. The minimum data value is shown on each axis. To ensure equal-width scale categories, PLOT extends the axis values beyond the maximum values obtained from the data. The boundary values of each level of the control variable appear below the plot.

Figure 41.9   A contour plot

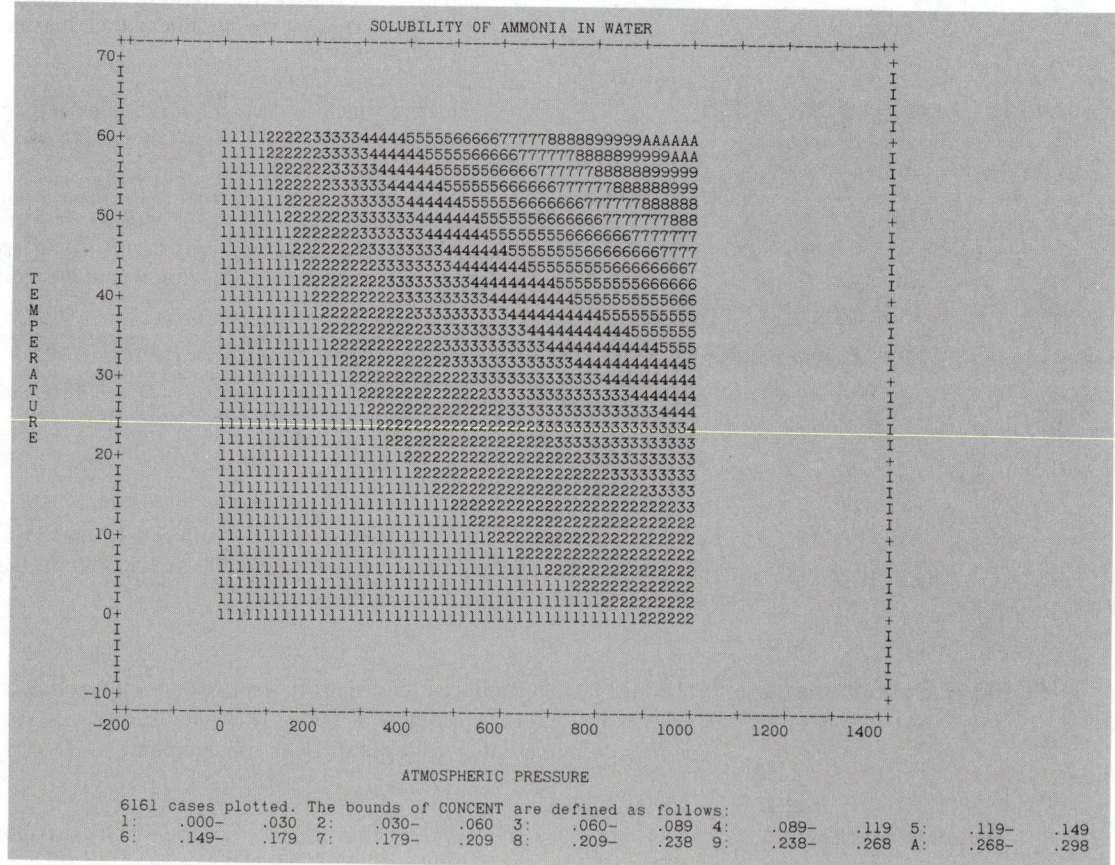

41.10
Overlay Plots

The OVERLAY keyword on the FORMAT subcommand tells SPSS-X to put all plots specified on the following PLOT subcommand in one frame. You can overlay only bivariate plots (simple scatterplots and regression plots), not control or contour plots. You can overlay up to 20 plots in one plot frame. PLOT selects a unique symbol for each plot to be overlaid, plus a symbol to represent multiple plots in one print position.

You can overlay plots by specifying groups of variables on either side of the keyword WITH. The command

```
PLOT FORMAT=OVERLAY
 /TITLE 'MARRIAGE AND DIVORCE RATES  1900-1983'
 /VERTICAL='RATES PER 1000 POPULATION'
 /HORIZONTAL='YEAR' REFERENCE (1918,1945) MIN (1900) MAX (1983)
 /PLOT=MARRATE DIVRATE WITH YEAR
```

requests two plots to be overlaid in one frame. The TITLE specification provides a title for the plot. The VERTICAL subcommand provides a label for the vertical axis. The HORIZONTAL subcommand provides a label, specifies that reference lines be drawn perpendicular to points 1918 and 1945, and specifies 1900 and 1983 as minimum and maximum data values to plot. The PLOT subcommand specifies the variables for the overlay. Figure 41.10 shows the result.

Figure 41.10   An overlay plot

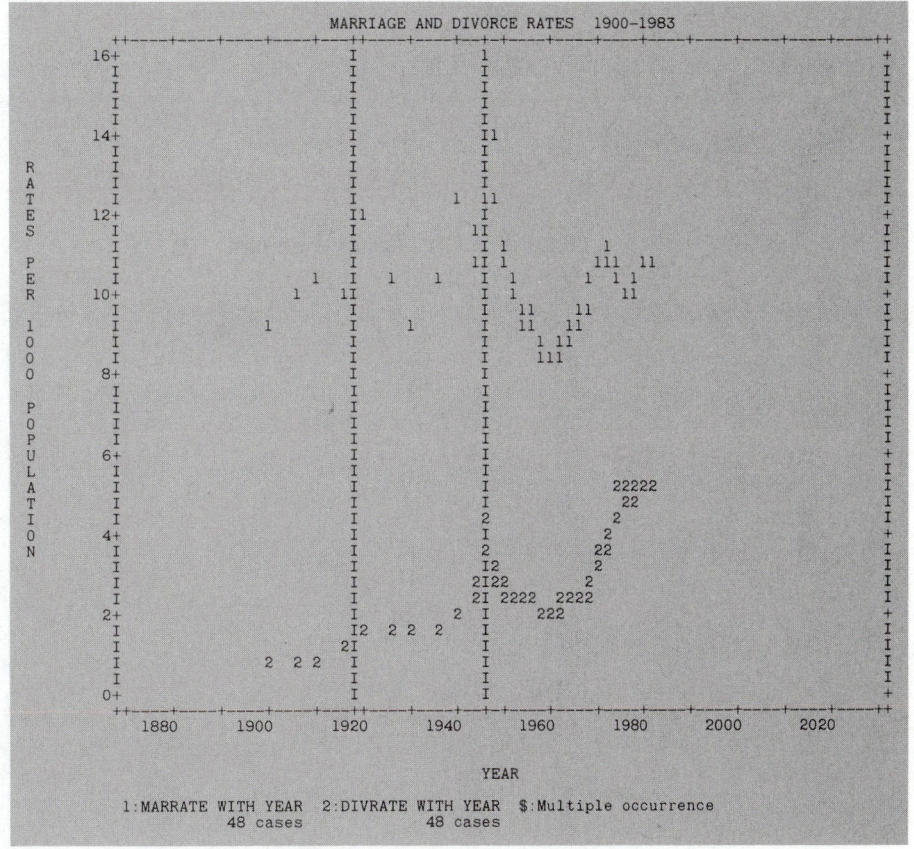

41.11
Regression Plots

With the REGRESSION keyword, PLOT calculates and prints statistics for the regression of the vertical-axis variable on the horizontal-axis variable. PLOT produces a scatterplot and marks regression-line intercepts with the letter R. For example, the command

```
PLOT TITLE='SALARY REGRESSION'
 /VERTICAL='CURRENT ANNUAL SALARY'
 /HORIZONTAL= 'ANNUAL STARTING SALARY'
 /FORMAT=REGRESSION
 /PLOT=SALNOW WITH SALBEG
```

requests a fully labeled regression plot of SALNOW with SALBEG. Figures 41.11a and 41.11b show the resulting data table and plot. Figure 41.11b includes the regression statistics after the plot and shows the Rs on the upper horizontal and lower vertical lines. You can connect the Rs to draw the regression line.

You can also request regression plots with control variables. For example, the command

```
PLOT FORMAT=REGRESSION
 /PLOT=A B C WITH D; Y WITH X BY Z
```

requests regression statistics for three bivariate plots and one control plot. In a control plot, you do not get separate regression statistics for each control category. Instead, regression statistics are pooled over all categories.

Figure 41.11a   Regression plot data information

```
Data    Information

        474 unweighted cases accepted.

Size of the plots

   Horizontal size is 80
    Vertical size is 40

Frequencies and symbols used (not applicable for control or overlay plots)

       1 - 1     11 - B     21 - L     31 - V
       2 - 2     12 - C     22 - M     32 - W
       3 - 3     13 - D     23 - N     33 - X
       4 - 4     14 - E     24 - O     34 - Y
       5 - 5     15 - F     25 - P     35 - Z
       6 - 6     16 - G     26 - Q     36 - *
       7 - 7     17 - H     27 - R
       8 - 8     18 - I     28 - S
       9 - 9     19 - J     29 - T
      10 - A     20 - K     30 - U
```

Figure 41.11b   Regression plot

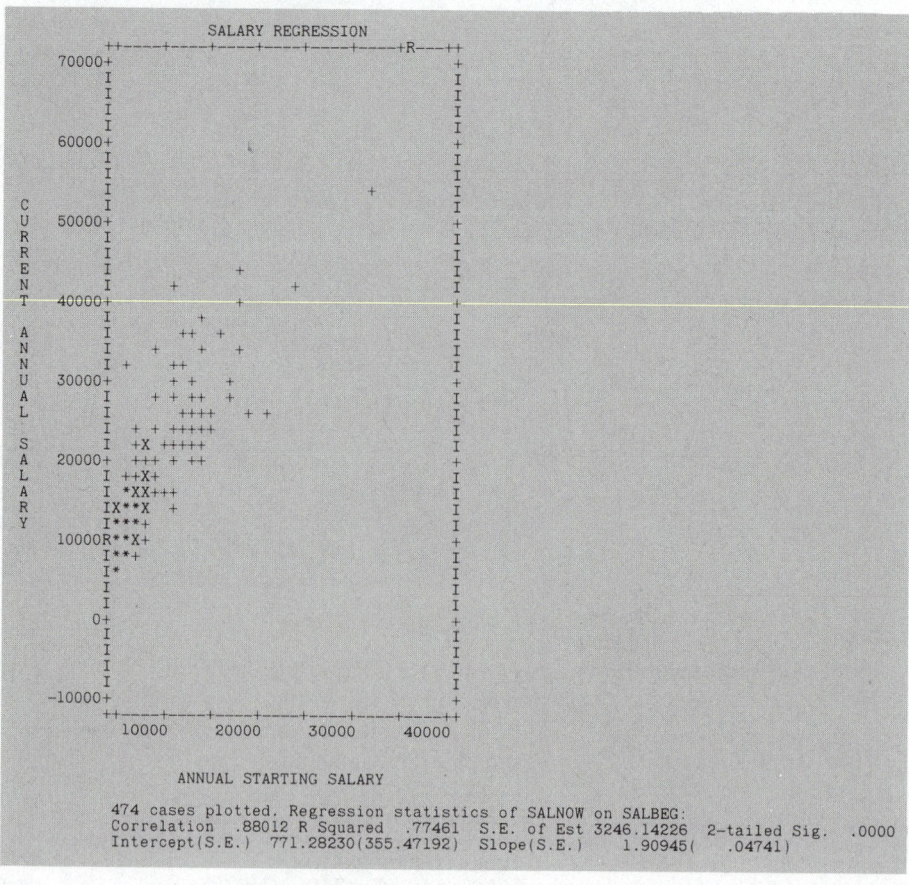

41.12
HSIZE and VSIZE Subcommands

Use the HSIZE and VSIZE subcommands to specify dimensions for your plots. The HSIZE and VSIZE subcommands must precede all PLOT subcommands and can be specified only once. All plots requested on one PLOT command are drawn to the same specified size.

41

The default size of your plot depends on current page size. With a typical computer page width of 132 horizontal print positions and a typical page length (vertically) of 59 lines, the default width is 80 positions and the default length is 40 lines. You can override the defaults by using the VSIZE and HSIZE subcommands. The VSIZE subcommand specifies the vertical frame size (length) of the plot, and the HSIZE subcommand specifies the horizontal frame size (width). For example,

```
PLOT VSIZE=30/HSIZE=70
 /PLOT= Y WITH X
```

requests a length of 30 print lines and a width of 70 print positions. The specified size does *not* include print lines for the plot frames or for auxiliary information such as titles, axis scale numbers, regression statistics, or the symbol table.

The size specified on HSIZE must be at least 15 positions less than the size specified on the SET WIDTH command (or its default). Thus, if you specify SET WIDTH=80, the largest horizontal size you can request (and the default) is 65. If you specify a VSIZE greater than the length specified on SET LENGTH, VSIZE will override the length, but the symbol table and other information normally printed below a plot will appear on the following page. To ensure that this information will print on the same page, the length on SET LENGTH should be at least 20 lines longer than VSIZE. To see the current setting of WIDTH and LENGTH on your system, use the SHOW command. To change these parameters, use the SET command (see Chapter 4).

41.13
HSIZE and VSIZE with
HORIZONTAL and VERTICAL

When you specify HSIZE or VSIZE in conjunction with a HORIZONTAL or VERTICAL minimum value, PLOT uses the minimum value as the starting point of the axis. To provide equal-interval, integer scale values, PLOT may extend an axis beyond the minimum and maximum values specified on the HORIZONTAL or VERTICAL subcommand. For example, the command

```
PLOT VSIZE=30 /HSIZE=70
 /FORMAT=OVERLAY
 /TITLE 'MARRIAGE AND DIVORCE RATES  1900-1983'
 /VERTICAL='RATES PER 1000 POPULATION'
 /HORIZONTAL='YEAR' REFERENCE (1918,1945) MIN (1900) MAX (1983)
 /PLOT=MARRATE DIVRATE WITH YEAR
```

Figure 41.13 Control plot with axis size defined

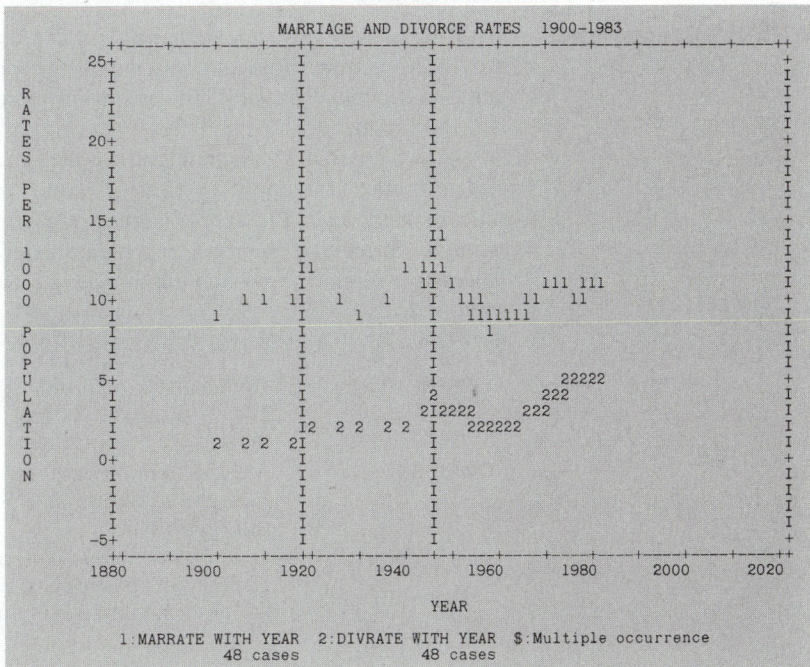

produces the plot shown in Figure 41.13. The plot area is 30 lines by 70 characters. The values on the horizontal axis starts at 1900, and the maximum value on the horizontal axis is slightly greater than 1983. With the VSIZE and HSIZE subcommands deleted, the preceding command produces the plot shown in Figure 41.10, which is larger and has different values on the scales.

41.14
Controlling Plot Symbols

Two subcommands, CUTPOINT and SYMBOLS, control the frequencies that plotted symbols represent and the characters for the symbols in plots.

Use the CUTPOINT subcommand to adjust the frequencies represented by each plot symbol in bivariate plots (simple scatterplots and regression plots). The SYMBOLS subcommand lets you specify which characters represent a given frequency value in bivariate scatter and regression plots, overlay, and contour plots. In addition, the SYMBOLS subcommand lets you specify overprint characters to add intensity to plots or to extend the character set. Both CUTPOINT and SYMBOLS must precede the first PLOT subcommand and can be specified only once on a PLOT command. All requested plots use the same cutpoint values and symbols.

You cannot use SYMBOLS specifications for scatterplots with control variables or for regression plots with control variables. For these plots, procedure PLOT assigns the symbols. However, you can determine what the symbols will be by giving the control variables appropriate names or value labels (see Section 41.4). Table 41.14 summarizes the subcommands affecting plot symbols.

Table 41.14 Subcommands for symbol control

Plot type	Meaning of each symbol	Subcommand(s) for controlling symbols
Bivariate scatter or regression	Frequency of cases	CUTPOINT SYMBOLS
Control	Value of control variable	None (see Section 41.4)
Overlay	Identity of overlaid plot	SYMBOLS
Contour	Level of contour variable	SYMBOLS FORMAT (for number of levels)

41.15
SYMBOLS Subcommand

With the SYMBOLS subcommand, you can use the default plotting symbols or provide your own. You can even define overprinted combinations of characters and hexadecimal characters, thus allowing you to plot characters not available on your keyboard.

The SYMBOLS subcommand applies to bivariate, overlay, and contour plots. It does not apply to control plots. You can use only one SYMBOL subcommand on a PLOT command, and you can specify a maximum of 36 symbols. Successive symbols represent increasing frequencies in scatterplots, successive subplots in overlay plots, and successive contour-variable intervals in contour plots.

The available keywords for the SYMBOLS subcommand are:

ALPHANUMERIC   *Alphanumeric plotting symbols.* PLOT uses the characters 1–9, A–Z, and * as plot symbols. Thus, * represents 36 or more cases at a print position. This is the default symbol set.

NUMERIC   *Numeric plotting symbols.* PLOT uses the characters 1–9 and * as plot symbols. Thus, * represents 10 or more cases at a print position.

'symbols'[,'ovprnt']   *List of plot symbols.* You can provide your own list of symbols enclosed in apostrophes. Optionally, you can specify a second list of overprinting symbols separated from the first list by a comma or space. The overprinting symbols can be either hexadecimal representations (preceded by an X) or keyboard characters.

X'hexsym'[,'ovprnt']   *List of hexadecimal plot symbols.* Indicate hexadecimal symbols by specifying X before the hexadecimal representation list enclosed in apostrophes. Optionally, you can specify a second list of overprinting symbols separated from the first list by a comma or space. The overprinting symbols can be either hexadecimal representations or keyboard characters.

If you want to overprint only some symbols, use a combination of blanks and symbols in the second list, as in

```
PLOT SYMBOLS = '.+O',' X'
/PLOT = Y BY X
```

The first specified symbol is a period, the second is a plus, and the third is X printed over O. Although the symbols in the second list overlie those in the first, the first two "symbols" in the second list are blanks, leaving only the X as an actual overprinting character.

The following command specifies a set of symbols with overprint symbols to obtain the contour plot shown in Figure 41.15. The plot uses successive symbols to represent lowest to highest levels of the control variable.

```
PLOT FORMAT=CONTOUR (10)
 /HSIZE=50/VSIZE=30
 /SYMBOLS='.-=*+OXOXM',' -OW'
 /TITLE 'SOLUBILITY OF AMMONIA IN WATER'
 /HORIZONTAL='ATMOSPHERIC PRESSURE'
 /VERTICAL='TEMPERATURE'
 /PLOT=TEMP WITH PRESSURE BY CONCENT
```

Figure 41.15   Contour plot with overprint symbols

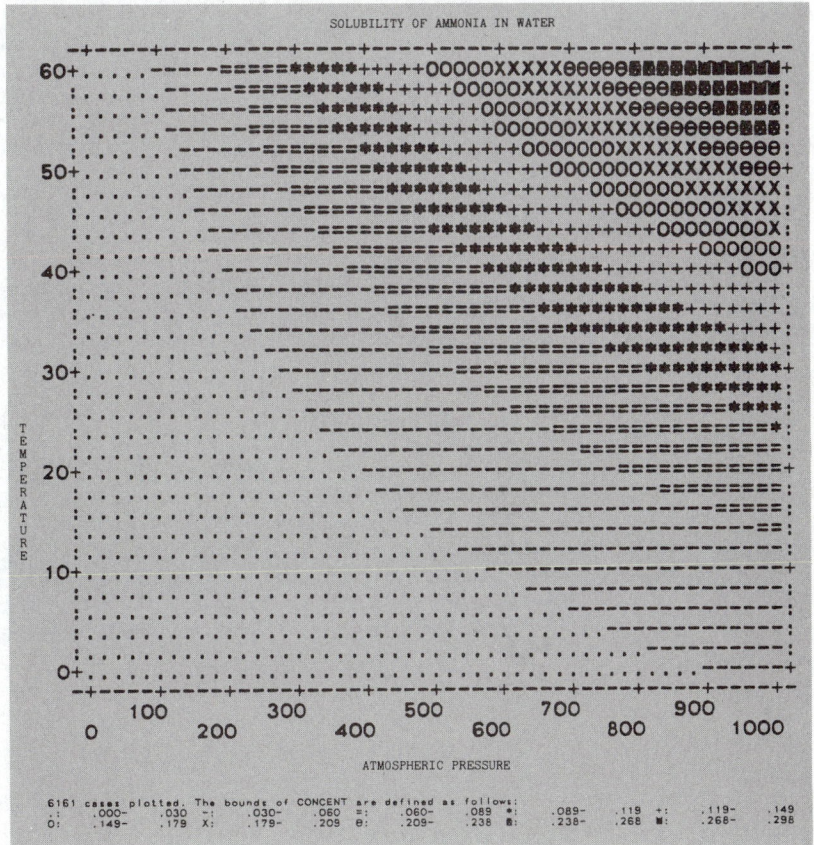

ANNOTATED EXAMPLE FOR PLOT

This example plots the values from a derived formula for the relationship of age, weight, and systolic blood pressure. The variables are

• AGE—age in years.

• WEIGHT—weight in pounds.

• PRESSURE—systolic blood pressure.

The SPSS-X commands are

```
INPUT PROGRAM
+ LOOP #I=15 TO 85 BY 1
+  LOOP #J=100 TO 350 BY 10
+   COMPUTE AGE=#I
+   COMPUTE WEIGHT=#J
+   COMPUTE PRESSURE=59.4+0.909*AGE
    -0.0005*AGE*AGE+0.1*WEIGHT+.00085*WEIGHT*WEIGHT-.0004*AGE*WEIGHT
+  END CASE
+  END LOOP
+ END LOOP
+END FILE
END INPUT PROGRAM
VARIABLE LABELS PRESSURE 'SYSTOLIC BLOOD PRESSURE'
PLOT HSIZE = 38
     /VSIZE = 25
     /SYMBOLS = '.-+oxOXNPX '          0#'
     /TITLE='PRESSURE WITH WEIGHT'
     /HORIZONTAL='WEIGHT IN POUNDS'
     /PLOT = PRESSURE WITH WEIGHT
     /FORMAT = CONTOUR
     /TITLE='WEIGHT WITH AGE BY PRESSURE'
     /HORIZONTAL='YEARS OF AGE' MIN(15) MAX(85)
     /PLOT = WEIGHT WITH AGE BY PRESSURE
```

• The commands between INPUT PROGRAM and END INPUT PROGRAM create the data to plot.

• The VARIABLE LABELS command assigns a label to PRESSURE.

• The PLOT command requests two separate 25×38 plots. Each plot uses 10 symbols, two of which are overprinted (see Figure A).

• The first TITLE and HORIZONTAL subcommands label the plot and one axis.

• The first PLOT subcommand specifies plotting variables PRESSURE and WEIGHT. In the absence of a FORMAT specification, a bivariate scatterplot is produced (see Figure B).

• The FORMAT subcommand specifies that the next plot is a contour plot (see Figure C).

• The second TITLE subcommand produces a title different from that in the first.

• The second HORIZONTAL subcommand specifies a horizontal axis label and minimum and maximum values to include on the axis. To produce equal-interval scale values, the scale may extend beyond these values.

A Data information

```
Data    Information
        1846 unweighted cases accepted.

Size of the plots

    Horizontal size is 38
       Vertical size is 25

Frequencies and symbols used (not applicable for control or overlay plots)

          1 - .
          2 - -
          3 - +
          4 - o
          5 - x
          6 - O
          7 - X
          8 - N
          9 - P
         10 - #
```

B Bivariate scatterplot

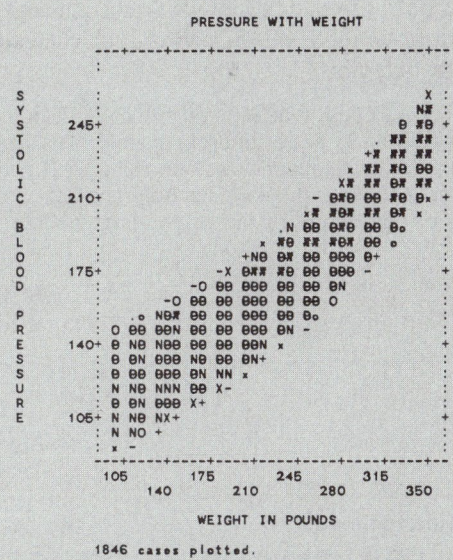

PRESSURE WITH WEIGHT

1846 cases plotted.

C Contour plot

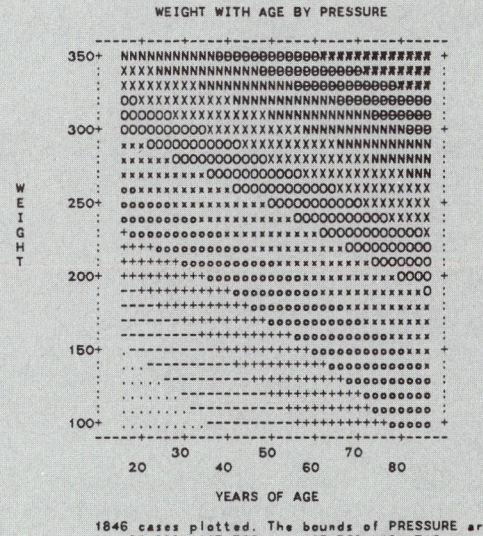

WEIGHT WITH AGE BY PRESSURE

1846 cases plotted. The bounds of PRESSURE are defined as follows:
.: 90.822- 107.768   -: 107.768- 124.713   +: 124.713- 141.659   o: 141.659- 158.604   x: 158.604- 175.550
O: 175.550- 192.495   X: 192.495- 209.441   N: 209.441- 226.386   θ: 226.386- 243.332   ☀: 243.332- 260.277

41.16
CUTPOINT Subcommand

By default, frequency plots use successive symbols in print positions corresponding to 1, 2, 3... cases, respectively (see Figure 41.3a). To define your own set of frequency values for the successive symbols, use the CUTPOINT subcommand. You can specify the desired interval width on the EVERY keyword, or you can use a value list in parentheses to specify cutpoints:

EVERY(n) *Frequency intervals of width* n. The default is an interval size of 1, meaning that each individual frequency up to 35 has a different symbol. The last default frequency interval includes all frequencies greater than 35. If you specify SYMBOLS as well as EVERY, the last symbol specified will represent all frequencies greater than those for the next-to-last symbol.

(value list) *Cutpoints at the values specified.*

You can request up to 35 cutpoints. You can specify only one CUTPOINT subcommand on a PLOT command, and it applies only to bivariate plots, not to control, overlay, or contour plots. If you specify

```
PLOT  CUTPOINT=EVERY(4)
/PLOT = Y WITH X
```

Figure 41.16 Regression plot with cutpoints defined

```
Data    Information

        474 unweighted cases accepted.

Size of the plots

    Horizontal size is 35
    Vertical size is 40

Frequencies and symbols used (not applicable for control or overlay plots)

            4 - +
            8 - X
           12 - *

                        SALARY REGRESSION
              ---+----+----+----+----+----+----+--R-+----
        54000+                                    ++
C
        48000+                                     +
C
U
R
R       42000+        +                +           +
E
N
T                             +       +
                                    +
A       36000+              ++                     +
N
N                    +    +
U                 +    +
U       30000+        +  ++   +                    +
A                     +    +
L               +  + ++   +
                      +++  +   +   +
S                       + ++
A       24000+       ++ ++++                       +
L               +++ +++ +
A               +++ ++ ++
R               ++  + + +
Y                + +     +
        18000+   + +++
                ++ + +
                XX++++
                +X*++   +
                X*X+
        12000+ +XX**+                             +
                ****+
                ***++
                +**X+
                +*
         6000+  X                                 +
              -R-+----+----+----+----+----+----+----
              4250   12750  21250  29750
                 8500   17000   25500

                     ANNUAL STARTING SALARY

        474 cases plotted. Regression statistics of SALNOW on SALBEG:
        Correlation  .88012 R Squared  .77461  S.E. of Est 3246.14226  2-tailed Sig.  .0000
        Intercept(S.E.)  771.28230(355.47192)  Slope(S.E.)   1.90945(  .04741)
```

1 will represent 1 to 4 cases at a print position, 2 will represent 5 to 8 cases, and so forth. If you specify

```
PLOT  CUTPOINT= (4, 10, 25)
 /PLOT = Y WITH X
```

1 will represent 1 to 4 cases at a print position, 2 will represent 5 to 10 cases, 3 will represent 11 to 25 cases, and 4 will represent 26 or more cases.

The command

```
PLOT HSIZE=35
 /CUTPOINT=EVERY(4)
 /SYMBOLS='+X*'
 /TITLE='SALARY REGRESSION'
 /VERTICAL='CURRENT ANNUAL SALARY'
 /HORIZONTAL= 'ANNUAL STARTING SALARY'
 /FORMAT=REGRESSION
 /PLOT=SALNOW WITH SALBEG
```

produces the plot shown in Figure 41.16. The data information shows the size of the plot as well the frequency values and symbols. Frequencies of 1–4 appear as +, frequencies of 5–8 appear as X, and frequencies of 9 or more appear as *.

41.17
MISSING Subcommand

Use the MISSING subcommand to change or make explicit the treatment of cases with missing values. You can use only one MISSING subcommand on a PLOT command. Three specifications are available:

PLOTWISE *Exclude cases with missing values plotwise.* For each plot within a single frame, cases are deleted that have missing values on any variable for that plot. This is the default.

LISTWISE *Exclude cases with missing values listwise.* Cases with missing values on any variable named on any PLOT subcommand are deleted from all plots specified on the PLOT command.

INCLUDE *Include user-defined missing values as valid.*

If you specify

```
PLOT MISSING = LISTWISE
 /FORMAT=REGRESSION
 /PLOT = Y WITH A; Z WITH B
```

PLOT excludes cases with missing values on any of the variables Y, A, Z, and B.

For overlay plots, plotwise deletion applies to each subplot requested, not to the full list specified on the PLOT subcommand. With the command

```
PLOT FORMAT=OVERLAY
 /PLOT = INCOME82 TAXES82 WITH YEAR82
```

cases with missing values on INCOME82 or YEAR82 will be deleted from that subplot only, and cases with missing values on TAXES82 or YEAR82 will be deleted from the other subplot. The complete overlay plot may have a different number of cases for each subplot that is overlaid. The number of cases plotted in each subplot is stated below the plot frame.

41.18
LIMITATIONS

There are no limitations on the number of plots requested or on the number of variables specified on a PLOT command. The following limitations apply to the optional subcommands:

- A maximum of 60 characters for a title specified on the TITLE subcommand.
- A maximum of 36 symbols per SYMBOLS subcommand.
- A maximum of 35 cutpoints per CUTPOINT subcommand.
- A maximum of 10 reference points on each HORIZONTAL or VERTICAL subcommand.
- A maximum of 40 characters per label on each HORIZONTAL or VERTICAL subcommand.

Syntax

PROBIT

```
PROBIT response count varname OF observation count varname
       [WITH varlist] [BY varname(min,max)]
  [/MISSING={LISTWISE**}] [/MODEL={PROBIT**}] [/LOG[={10**  }]]
           {INCLUDE  }          {LOGIT  }        {2.718*}
           {DEFAULT  }          {BOTH   }        {base  }
                                                 {NONE  }
  [/PRINT=[ALL] [CI**] [FREQ**] [RMP**] [PARALL] [NONE] [DEFAULT]]
  [/CRITERIA=[CONVERGE({0.001**})] [ITERATE({20**})] [P({0.15**})]]
                      {eps   }             {n  }      {p    }
  [/NATRES[=c]]
```

**Default if the subcommand is omitted.
* Default if the subcommand is included and the specification omitted.

Contents

42.1   OVERVIEW

42.2   OPERATION

42.3   Variable Specification

42.4   MODEL Subcommand

42.5   LOG Subcommand

42.6   CRITERIA Subcommand

42.7   NATRES Subcommand

42.8   PRINT Subcommand

42.9   Using Data in Case-by-Case Form

42.10   MISSING Subcommand

42.11 LIMITATIONS

42

Chapter 42   PROBIT

The PROBIT procedure can be used to estimate the effects of one or more independent variables on a dichotomous dependent variable (such as dead or alive, employed or unemployed, product purchased or not). The program is optimized for dose-response analyses and related models, but PROBIT can also estimate logistic regression models. The models estimated by PROBIT have a variety of applications. For example, you can model responses of subjects to varying doses of several drug preparations; analyze mortality rates of weeds treated with varying levels of different herbicide solutions; relate purchase rates of a product to tested sale prices; and predict labor force participation from a set of demographic variables.

42.1 OVERVIEW

PROBIT calculates maximum likelihood estimates for the parameters of the requested response model. The procedure automatically prints estimates of the regression coefficient and intercept terms, their standard errors, a covariance matrix of parameter estimates, and a Pearson chi-square goodness-of-fit test of the model.

Specifying the Model. You can specify either or both a PROBIT or LOGIT response model for the observed response proportions (See Section 42.4.)

Transform Predictors. You can specify the base of the log transformation applying to all predictors. You can also request no log transformation of the predictors. (See Section 42.5.)

Natural Response Rates. With the NATRES subcommand, you can instruct PROBIT to estimate the natural response rate (threshold) of the model, or you can supply a known natural response rate as a constraint on the model solution. (See Section 42.7.)

Algorithm Control Parameters. You can specify values of algorithm control parameters such as the limit on iterations. (See Section 42.6.)

Missing Values. By default, PROBIT excludes all cases with missing values, though you can instruct PROBIT to include cases with user-missing values. (See Section 42.10.)

42.2
OPERATION

The PROBIT procedure operates via a variable list and subcommands. The variable list is the only required specification. The variables must include a response count, an observation count, and at least one predictor. A categorical grouping variable is optional.

All PROBIT subcommands are also optional. Each begins with a subcommand keyword followed by an optional equals sign and subcommand specifications. Subcommands can be named in any order and are separated from each other by a slash. Each subcommand can appear only once.

For procedure PROBIT, generally you should not enter data for individual observations. PROBIT expects predictor values, response counts, and total number of observations as the input case. If the data are available only in case-by-case form, first use AGGREGATE, if possible, to compute the required response and observation counts (see Section 42.9). If you enter individual cases, PROBIT skips the plot of transformed response proportions and predictor values, and it reports an incorrect chi-square goodness-of-fit test. You can still use PROBIT for models with individual observations, however, because parameter estimates and their standard errors will be accurate.

42.3
Variable Specification

The PROBIT variable specification identifies the variables for response count, observation count, groups, and predictors. The variable specification is required.

The variable specification must appear immediately after the command keyword PROBIT. The specification shows the response count variable, then the keyword OF, then the observation count variable, as in

```
PROBIT R OF N
```

which indicates that the number of observations having the measured response appears in variable R, and the total number of observations is in N. (OF is not a reserved word and can be used as a variable name.) If the value of the response count variable exceeds that of the observation count variable, a procedure error will occur and halt PROBIT execution.

You can specify one or more continuous predictors following the keyword WITH. The number of predictors is limited only by available workspace.

You can specify one categorical grouping variable. To do so, put the variable name after the keyword BY. This variable must be numeric and must contain only integers. Specify a range in parentheses to indicate the minimum and maximum values. Each integer value in the range defines a group. Cases having values for the grouping variable outside this range are excluded from the analysis.

The BY and WITH keyword clauses can appear in either order but must follow the response and observation count variables. Thus, the command

```
PROBIT  R OF N BY ROOT(1,2) WITH X
```

is equivalent to

```
PROBIT  R OF N WITH X BY ROOT(1,2)
```

Each command specifies X as a continuous variable and ROOT as a categorical grouping variable used to predict response rates. Groups are identified by the levels of variable ROOT, which may be 1 or 2. For each combination of predictor and grouping variables, the variable R contains the number of observations with the response of interest, and N contains the total number of observations. Figure 42.3 shows the case and model information that PROBIT displays for a program including either of the above commands.

Figure 42.3 Case and model information

```
DATA  Information

        9 unweighted cases accepted.
        0 cases rejected because of out-of-range group values.
        0 cases rejected because of missing data.
        1 Cases rejected because of LOG-transform can't be done.


GROUP Information

       ROOT      Level  N of Cases    Label
                     1           4        1
                     2           5        2


MODEL Information

       ONLY Normal Sigmoid is requested.
```

42.4
MODEL Subcommand

The MODEL subcommand specifies the form of the dichotomous response model. The keywords are:

PROBIT *Probit response model.* This is the default.

LOGIT *Logit response model.*

BOTH *Both probit and logit response models.* PROBIT prints all the output for the logit model followed by the output for the probit model.

For example,

```
PROBIT  R OF N BY ROOT(1,2) WITH X
 /MODEL = BOTH
```

specifies that both the probit and logit response models be applied to the response frequency R, given N total observations.

The response models can be thought of as transformations (T) of response rates, which are proportions or probabilities (p). For the probit response model, the program uses

$$T(p) = PROBIT(p) + 5$$

A probit is the inverse of the cumulative standard normal distribution function. Thus, for any proportion, the probit transformation returns the value below which that proportion of standard normal deviates is found. Hence:

$$T(0.025) = PROBIT(0.025) + 5 = -1.96 + 5 = 3.04$$
$$T(0.400) = PROBIT(0.400) + 5 = -0.25 + 5 = 4.75$$
$$T(0.500) = PROBIT(0.500) + 5 = 0.00 + 5 = 5.00$$
$$T(0.950) = PROBIT(0.950) + 5 = 1.64 + 5 = 6.64$$

A logit is simply the natural log of the odds ratio, $p/(1 - p)$. In the PROBIT procedure, the response function is given as

$$T(p) = \log_e(p/(1 - p))/2 + 5$$

The simple logit is scaled by 2 to produce values similar to those derived from the probit transformation. Hence:

$$T(0.025) = LOGIT(0.025)/2 + 5 = -1.83 + 5 = 3.17$$
$$T(0.400) = LOGIT(0.400)/2 + 5 = -0.20 + 5 = 4.80$$
$$T(0.500) = LOGIT(0.500)/2 + 5 = 0.00 + 5 = 5.00$$
$$T(0.950) = LOGIT(0.950)/2 + 5 = 1.47 + 5 = 6.47$$

The transformations, whether logit or probit, add 5 to make the new values uniformly positive (or nearly so), as in Finney (1971).

The transformed response variable is predicted as a linear function of other variables. In the simple case of one predictor and no subgroups, the PROBIT procedure estimates maximum likelihood values for the intercept (a) and slope (b) of the regression equation

$$T(p) = a + bx$$

where T is one of the response functions discussed above and the x's are predictor values after any requested transformation. In terms of the original variables, for the probit model,

$$Y = (a - 5) + bx$$

and for the logit model,

$$Y = ((a - 5) + bx) \times 2$$

where a and b are the parameters that are printed. If you define subgroups and multiple predictor variables, PROBIT estimates a separate intercept (a_i) for each subgroup and a regression coefficient (b_j) for each predictor (see Figure 42.4).

Figure 42.4   Default PROBIT statistics

```
ML converged at iteration  6.  The converge criterion =    .00003

Parameter Estimates (PROBIT model:  (PROBIT(p) + 5) = Intercept + BX ):
                     Note 5 added to intercept.

                Regression Coeff.   Standard Error    Coeff./S.E.
        X            2.40277            .13559          17.72046


                Intercept   Standard Error   Intercept/S.E.   ROOT
                 2.32297        .20659          11.24437        1
                 2.96230        .16399          18.06439        2

Pearson  Goodness-of-Fit  Chi Square =       7.632    DF = 6   P =  .266

Since Goodness-of-Fit Chi square is NOT significant, no heterogeneity
factor is used in the calculation of confidence limits.
```

42.5
LOG Subcommand

The LOG subcommand specifies the base of the logarithmic transformation of the predictor variables if such a transformation is desired. The subcommand applies to *all* predictors. The specifications are:

10 *Logarithm base of 10.* This is the default if you do not specify a LOG subcommand.

2.718 *The natural logarithmic base, e.* This is the default if you specify the LOG subcommand without an explicit base.

base *Logarithm base other than defaults.* To specify any other base, indicate its numeric value following the equals sign on the LOG subcommand.

NONE *No transformation of the predictors.*

For example, for a base 2 logarithmic transformation, specify:

```
/LOG = 2
```

The LOG subcommand applies to all predictors. If you want to transform only selected predictors, use COMPUTE commands before the PROBIT procedure. Then specify NONE on the LOG subcommand.

42.6
CRITERIA Subcommand

Use the CRITERIA subcommand to specify the values of PROBIT algorithm-control parameters. CRITERIA has three keywords:

CONVERGE(eps) *Convergence criterion.* Specify the cutoff value of the convergence criterion for the iterative estimation algorithm. The default value is .001.

ITERATE(n) *Iteration limit.* Specify the maximum number of iterations. The default is 20.

P(p) *Heterogeneity criterion probability.* Specify the cutoff value for the significance of the goodness-of-fit test. The default is .15. The cutoff value determines whether a heterogeneity factor is included in calculations of confidence levels for effective levels of a predictor (see Section 42.8). If the chi-square is not significant, the heterogeneity factor is not included.

42.7
NATRES Subcommand

You can use the NATRES subcommand two ways. You can instruct the program to estimate the natural (or threshold) response rate of the model. Alternatively, you can supply a known natural response rate as a constraint on the solution.

You must provide a control level to use NATRES to estimate the natural response rate of the model. Indicate the control level by giving a 0 value to any of the predictor variables. For example,

```
DATA LIST FREE / SOLUTION DOSE NOBSN NRESP
PROBIT NRESP OF NOBSN BY SOLUTION(1,4) WITH DOSE
 /NATRES
BEGIN DATA
1   5 100 20
1 10  80 30
1   0 100 10
  ...
END DATA
```

reads four variables and requests a default analysis with an estimate of the natural response rate. The predictor variable, DOSE, has a value of 0 for the third case. The response count (10) and the observation count (100) for this case establish the control level for the analysis.

If you already know the natural response rate and wish to use it in the model, specify a constant on the NATRES subcommand, as in

```
 /NATRES = c
```

where c is the known natural response rate. The value of c must lie between 0 and 1 but cannot be equal to 0 or 1. For example,

```
DATA LIST FREE / SOLUTION DOSE NOBSN NRESP
PROBIT NRESP OF NOBSN BY SOLUTION(1,4) WITH DOSE
 /NATRES = 0.10
BEGIN DATA
1   5 100 20
1 10  80 30
  ...
END DATA
```

reads four variables and requests an analysis in which the natural response rate is set to .10. No control level is included in the data.

42.8
PRINT Subcommand

Use the PRINT subcommand to produce statistics and displays not produced by default or to document the default output explicitly. The available keywords are:

DEFAULT *FREQ, CI, and RMP.* This is the default output if the subcommand is omitted.

ALL *All available output.* This is the same as requesting FREQ, CI, RMP, and PARALL.

FREQ *Frequencies.* Display a table of observed and predicted frequencies with their residual values (see Figure E in Annotated Examples). If you enter observations on a case-by-case basis, this listing can be quite lengthy.

CI *Fiducial confidence intervals.* Print Finney's (1971) fiducial confidence intervals for the levels of the predictor needed to produce each proportion of responses (see Figures G and H in Annotated Examples). PROBIT displays this default output only for single-predictor models. If you specify a categorical grouping variable, PROBIT produces a table of confidence intervals for each group. If the Pearson chi-square goodness-of-fit test is significant, PROBIT uses a heterogeneity factor to calculate the limits.

RMP *Relative median potency.* Display the relative median potency (RMP) of each pair of groups defined by the grouping variable (see Figure I in Annotated Examples). PROBIT prints this default output only for single-predictor models. For any pair of groups, the RMP is the ratio of the *stimulus tolerances* in those groups. Stimulus tolerance is the value of the predictor necessary to produce a 50% response rate. If the derived model for one predictor and two groups estimates that a predictor value of 21 produces a 50% response rate in the first group, and a predictor value of 15 produces a 50% response rate in the second group, the relative median potency would be   21/15 = 1.40. In biological assay analyses, RMP measures the comparative strength of preparations.

PARALL   *Parallelism test.* Produce a test of the parallelism of regression lines for different levels of the grouping variable (see Figure C in Annotated Examples). This test prints a chi-square value with one degree of freedom and its associated probability. It requires an additional pass through the data and thus additional processing time.

NONE   *No conditional printed output.* You can use this option to override any other specification on the PRINT subcommand for PROBIT. If you specify NONE, only the unconditional output is printed: the PROBIT case and model information (see Figure A in Annotated Examples), the PROBIT plot (for a single-predictor model) (see Figure F), and the parameter estimates and covariances for the PROBIT model (see Figure C).

42.9
Using Data in
Case-by-Case Form

PROBIT expects response counts and observation counts as input. In general, you should not enter data for individual observations. If there is only one observation per case, the procedure issues a warning, skips the plot, and reports an incorrect chi-square goodness-of-fit statistic. The test is incorrect because of the incorrect number of degrees of freedom. Parameter estimates and their standard errors, however, are still accurate.

The following dose-response model (from Finney, 1971) illustrates case-by-case analysis. A researcher tests four different preparations at varying doses and observes whether each subject responds. The data are individually recorded for each subject, with 1 indicating a response and 0 indicating no response. The number of observations is always 1 and is stored in variable SUBJECT. The SPSS-X commands used are:

```
DATA LIST FREE / PREPARTN DOSE RESPONSE
COMPUTE SUBJECT = 1
PROBIT RESPONSE OF SUBJECT BY PREPARTN(1,4) WITH DOSE
BEGIN DATA
1 1.5 0
   ...
4 20.0 1
END DATA
```

Figure 42.9a shows the information PROBIT provides on the model it estimates. PROBIT warns that the data are in case-by-case form and gives the consequences of this condition.

Figure 42.9a   Case and model information for case-by-case analysis

```
DATA  Information

      1231 unweighted cases accepted.
          0 cases rejected because of out-of-range group values.
          0 cases rejected because of missing data.
          0 Cases rejected because of LOG-transform can't be done.

Group Information

      PREPARTN  Level  N of Cases   Label
                  1        346        1
                  2        270        2
                  3        260        3
                  4        355        4


MODEL Information

      ONLY Normal Sigmoid is requested.

- - - - - - - - - - - - - - - - - - - - - - - - - - - - - - - - - - - - - - - - - - - - - - -

>Warning # 13520
>Data are not in collapsed form as required by PROBIT.  The plot is skipped.
```

Figure 42.9b shows the parameter estimates and covariances. Parameter estimates and their standard errors are accurate, even though the goodness-of-fit test is wrong. PROBIT prints predicted and observed frequencies for all 1,231 individual input cases unless this output is suppressed. A portion of this output is shown in Figure 42.9c. The expected response is the probability times the number of cases, and since the number of cases is 1 in this example, the expected responses and the probability are identical.

Figure 42.9b Parameter estimates from case-by-case analysis

```
ML converged at iteration  6.  The converge criterion =   .00008

Parameter Estimates (PROBIT model:  (PROBIT(p) + 5) = Intercept + BX ):
                 Note 5 added to intercept.

             Regression Coeff.  Standard Error    Coeff./S.E.
   DOSE              2.46849          .17261        14.30061


             Intercept  Standard Error  Intercept/S.E.  PREPARTN
              3.62073        .11422        31.70031         1
              3.85861        .12019        32.10350         2
              4.98028        .08823        56.44885         3
              2.44082        .18942        12.88596         4

Pearson  Goodness-of-Fit  Chi Square =   1229.088    DF = 1226   P =  .470

Since Goodness-of-Fit Chi square is NOT significant, no heterogeneity
factor is used in the calculation of confidence limits.
```

Figure 42.9c Predicted and observed frequencies from case-by-case analysis

```
Observed and Expected Frequencies

                     Number of   Observed   Expected
   PREPARTN   DOSE    Subjects   Responses  Responses   Residual    Prob
       1       .18       1.0        .0         .172      -.172     .17244
       1       .18       1.0        .0         .172      -.172     .17244
       1       .18       1.0        .0         .172      -.172     .17244
       1       .18       1.0        .0         .172      -.172     .17244
       1       .18       1.0        .0         .172      -.172     .17244
     ...
       4      1.30       1.0       1.0         .743       .257     .74293
       4      1.30       1.0       1.0         .743       .257     .74293
       4      1.30       1.0       1.0         .743       .257     .74293
       4      1.30       1.0       1.0         .743       .257     .74293
       4      1.30       1.0       1.0         .743       .257     .74293
```

To produce collapsed input cases for problems having a predictor and a grouping variable or for problems having more than one predictor, you can use procedure AGGREGATE. For the dose-response model just analyzed, the data recorded for each subject can be collapsed into cases representing all subjects who received the same preparation at the same dose. SPSS-X commands for analyzing the data in this way are:

```
DATA LIST FREE/PREPARTN DOSE RESPONSE
AGGREGATE OUTFILE=*
 /BREAK=PREPARTN DOSE
 /SUBJECTS=N(RESPONSE)
 /NRESP=SUM(RESPONSE)
BEGIN DATA
    1.00     1.50      .00
    ...
    4.00    20.00     1.00
END DATA
PROBIT NRESP OF SUBJECTS BY PREPARTN(1,4) WITH DOSE
```

Here, procedure AGGREGATE computes collapsed cases for observations having the same values for the group and predictor variables, PREPARTN and DOSE. The number of cases having a nonmissing response is recorded in the aggregated variable SUBJECTS. Because RESPONSE is coded as 0 for no response and 1 for a response, the SUM of the values gives the number of observations with a response (see Chapter 18). The PROBIT specification in this example then requests a default analysis.

Figure 42.9d shows the case and model information. Unlike the previous analysis, now there are only 14 aggregated cases instead of the 1,231 individual cases.

Figure 42.9d   Case and model information for analysis of collapsed cases

```
DATA  Information

       14 unweighted cases accepted.
        0 cases rejected because of out-of-range group values.
        0 cases rejected because of missing data.
        0 Cases rejected because of LOG-transform can't be done.


Group Information

     PREPARTN  Level  N of Cases    Label
                 1         3          1
                 2         3          2
                 3         3          3
                 4         5          4


MODEL Information

     ONLY Normal Sigmoid is requested.
```

The parameter estimates shown in Figure 42.9e are the same as those shown for individual cases in Figure 42.9b. The chi-square test, however, is correct and indicates an excellent fit to the data.

Figure 42.9e   Parameter estimates from analysis of collapsed cases

```
ML converged at iteration  4.  The converge criterion =   .00001

Parameter Estimates (PROBIT model:  (PROBIT(p) + 5) = Intercept + BX ):
              Note 5 added to intercept.

            Regression Coeff.  Standard Error    Coeff./S.E.
 DOSE            2.46849            .17261         14.30061


            Intercept  Standard Error  Intercept/S.E.  PREPARTN
             3.62073       .11422        31.70031         1
             3.85861       .12019        32.10349         2
             4.98029       .08823        56.44885         3
             2.44082       .18942        12.88596         4

 Pearson  Goodness-of-Fit  Chi Square =      3.863    DF = 9   P =  .920

 Since Goodness-of-Fit Chi square is NOT significant, no heterogeneity
 factor is used in the calculation of confidence limits.
```

Figure 42.9f shows the observed and expected frequencies. With only 14 combinations of values, the observed and predicted frequencies become meaningful.

Figure 42.9f   Observed and expected frequencies from analysis of collapsed cases

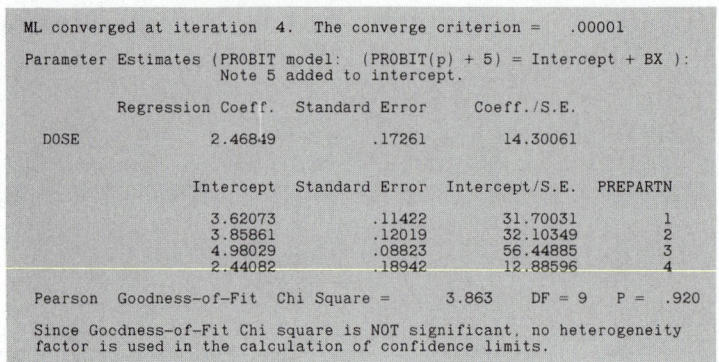

```
Observed and Expected Frequencies

                         Number of   Observed   Expected
     PREPARTN    DOSE    Subjects    Responses  Responses   Residual    Prob
         1        .18      103.0       19.0       17.761      1.239     .17243
         1        .48      120.0       53.0       50.419      2.581     .42015
         1        .78      123.0       83.0       86.832     -3.832     .70595

         2        .18       60.0       14.0       14.392      -.392     .23987
         2        .48      110.0       54.0       56.596     -2.596     .51451
         2        .78      100.0       81.0       78.215      2.785     .78215

         3       -.12       90.0       31.0       33.427     -2.427     .37141
         3        .18       80.0       54.0       52.873      1.127     .66092
         3        .48       90.0       80.0       78.892      1.108     .87658

         4        .70       60.0       13.0       12.132       .868     .20220
         4        .88       85.0       27.0       29.317     -2.317     .34491
         4       1.00       60.0       32.0       27.832      4.168     .46387
         4       1.18       90.0       55.0       57.112     -2.112     .63457
         4       1.30       60.0       44.0       44.576      -.576     .74293
```

42.10
MISSING Subcommand

The MISSING subcommand specifies the missing-value treatment. The available keywords are shown below. Cases containing system-missing values for any variable in the analysis are always deleted.

LISTWISE   *Delete cases with missing values listwise.* PROBIT deletes cases having a missing value for any variable. This is the default, and you can make it explicit by using the keyword DEFAULT.

INCLUDE   *Include user-missing values.* PROBIT treats user-missing values as valid.

PROBIT tells you how many cases it rejected because of missing data (see Figure 42.3).

42.11
LIMITATIONS

The following limitations apply to PROBIT:

• Only one prediction model can be tested in a single PROBIT procedure, although both probit and logit response models can be requested for that prediction.

• Confidence limits, the plot of transformed response proportions and predictor values, and computation of relative median potency are necessarily limited to single-predictor models.

ANNOTATED EXAMPLES FOR PROBIT

You can use PROBIT for a variety of dichotomous response models. The examples shown here illustrate two of the most common applications: dose-response models and logistic regression models.

Example 1

The following (based on a dose-response model) shows the use of the PROBIT procedure to analyze an example from Finney (1971).

```
SET WIDTH = 80
TITLE    PROBIT ANALYSIS. DATA FROM 'PROBIT' BY FINNEY P.132
DATA LIST / ROOT 1 X 3-7 N 9-11 R 13-15
PROBIT  R OF N BY ROOT(1,2) WITH X
 /MODEL = BOTH
 /NATRES
 /PRINT = ALL
BEGIN DATA
1 148.0 142 142
1 100.0 127 126
1  48.0 128 115
1  12.0 126  58
2  62.0 125 125
2  46.0 117 115
2  31.0 127 114
2  14.8  51  40
2   3.8 132  37
2   0.0 129  21
END DATA
```

- The SET command restricts the output to 80 columns (see Chapter 4).
- The TITLE command sets up a title for the run (see Chapter 4).
- The DATA LIST command reads the variables ROOT, X, N, and R from the data included in the command file (see Chapter 5).
- The PROBIT command specifies that the number of responses is in variable R and the number of observations is in N. The response rate will be predicted from variable X. Two groups are defined by variable ROOT (see Section 42.3).
- The MODEL subcommand specifies both probit and logit response models. (see Section 42.4).
- The NATRES subcommand requests an estimate of the natural response rate (or threshold) for each model. This specification requires that a control level be entered with the data (see Section 42.7).
- The PRINT subcommand requests all available output (see Section 42.8).
- The first data case shows 142 responses for the 142 observations with an X of 148.0 in the first group. The second-to-last case shows 37 responses for the 132 observations with an X of 3.8 in the second group. The last case has a value of 0.0 for predictor X, so the response rate used as the control level is 21 out of 129.

Figure A shows the case and model information displayed by PROBIT. When both models are estimated, all output for the logit model is printed before that for the probit model. Selected output from the logit model and all the output from the probit model are shown in Figures A through I.

A PROBIT case and model information

```
DATA  Information

          9 unweighted cases accepted.
          0 cases rejected because of out-of-range group values.
          0 cases rejected because of missing data.
          0 Cases rejected because of LOG-transform can't be done.


GROUP Information

     ROOT      Level  N of Cases    Label
                 1         4          1
                 2         5          2


MODEL Information

       BOTH Probit and Logit models are requested.


Natural Response rate to be estimated

       The number of  subjects in the CONTROL group    129.0
       The number of responses in the CONTROL group     21.0
```

Figure B shows the parameter estimates from the logit model. Figure C shows these estimates from the probit model. The number of iterations required to reach the convergence criterion and the final value for the criterion are printed first. The default cutoff values for these terms are 20 iterations and a convergence criterion of .001. If the convergence criterion had failed to reach the cutoff value in the allotted iterations, PROBIT would have printed an appropriate message and the estimates from the iterations that were completed.

B Parameter estimates and covariances for logit model

```
ML converged at iteration  6.  The converge criterion =   .00095

Parameter Estimates (LOGIT model:  (LOG(p/(1-p))/2 + 5) = Intercept + BX ):
                Note 5 added to intercept and logit divided by 2.

          Regression Coeff.  Standard Error     Coeff./S.E.

    X           2.45569           .19850          12.37135


          Intercept  Standard Error  Intercept/S.E.  ROOT

             2.02382       .30064        6.73182        1
             2.59473       .28483        9.10988        2

Estimate of Natural Response Rate = .172976  with  S.E. =    .03147

Pearson  Goodness-of-Fit  Chi Square =      8.966   DF = 6   P =  .176
         Parallelism Test Chi Square =       .048   DF = 1   P =  .826

Since Goodness-of-Fit Chi square is NOT significant, no heterogeneity
factor is used in the calculation of confidence limits.
- - - - - - - - - - - - - - - - - - - - - - - - - - - - - - - - - - - -

Covariance(below) and Correlation(above) Matrices of Parameter Estimates

                 X    NAT RESP

X            .03940     .42344
NAT RESP     .00264     .00099
```

C Parameter estimates and covariances for probit model

```
ML converged at iteration  6.  The converge criterion =   .00063

Parameter Estimates (PROBIT model:  (PROBIT(p) + 5) = Intercept + BX ):
                Note 5 added to intercept.

          Regression Coeff.  Standard Error     Coeff./S.E.

    X           2.78382           .20654          13.47809


          Intercept  Standard Error  Intercept/S.E.  ROOT

             1.59842       .33212        4.81282        1
             2.26158       .30366        7.44765        2

Estimate of Natural Response Rate = .168731  with  S.E. =    .03177

Pearson  Goodness-of-Fit  Chi Square =      5.933   DF = 6   P =  .431
         Parallelism Test Chi Square =       .050   DF = 1   P =  .823

Since Goodness-of-Fit Chi square is NOT significant, no heterogeneity
factor is used in the calculation of confidence limits.
- - - - - - - - - - - - - - - - - - - - - - - - - - - - - - - - - - - -

Covariance(below) and Correlation(above) Matrices of Parameter Estimates

                 X    NAT RESP

X            .04266     .46719
NAT RESP     .00307     .00101
```

Next, PROBIT prints parameter estimates with their standard errors (see Figures B and C). Three kinds of parameters are estimated: a regression coefficient, group intercepts, and a natural response rate. Probit and logit models produced similar estimates. The regression coefficient for X is positive and large relative to its standard error. PROBIT produces separate intercept estimates for each group. Because no value labels are defined for ROOT, the actual values of the variable are used to label the subgroup intercepts. The second group has the greater response rate. Finally, PROBIT produces the estimate of the threshold or natural response rate.

Annotated Examples for PROBIT *continued*

Following the parameter estimates, PROBIT reports two chi-square statistics and their associated probabilities. The goodness-of-fit test prints by default. It tests whether residuals are distributed homogeneously about the regression line. If this test is significant, PROBIT uses a heterogeneity factor to calculate confidence limits. A large chi-square can indicate that a different response model or predictor transformation is required. In this example, the probit model has the better fit. The PRINT subcommand requests all output, which includes the parallelism chi-square. This test indicates whether regression slopes differ between subgroups. Since the test is not significant, the regression slopes are treated as equivalent.

PROBIT estimated more than one parameter (excluding intercepts), so it automatically prints their covariance/correlation matrix. The diagonal entries (variances) simply equal the squares of the standard errors. The off-diagonal correlation and covariance terms indicate how much the estimate of the natural response rate depends on the estimate of the coefficient for X, and vice versa. Here, the two estimates are moderately correlated. In multiple predictor models, this matrix is useful for examining multicollinearity.

Figures D and E show the observed and predicted frequencies from logit and probit models. PROBIT prints one row for each input case. The first column labels each case with the value of the grouping variable, ROOT. The second column shows the values for the predictor, X. PROBIT can display values for no more than six predictors when WIDTH is set to 132 columns, even though all predictors are used in the calculations. The procedure prints the number of observations and the number of responses in the next two columns. The following two columns contain the number of responses predicted by the response model ("Expected Responses") and the differences between the observed number of responses and those predicted ("Residual"). The probit response model in this example has smaller residual values than the logit, indicating a better fit to the data. The final column ("Prob") contains the predicted probability (or proportion) of responses for the predictor and group values in each row.

D Observed and predicted frequencies for logit model

Observed and Expected Frequencies

ROOT	X	Number of Subjects	Observed Responses	Expected Responses	Residual	Prob
1	2.17	142.0	142.0	140.728	1.272	.99105
1	2.00	127.0	126.0	124.406	1.594	.97958
1	1.68	128.0	115.0	116.388	-1.388	.90928
1	1.08	126.0	58.0	43.158	14.842	.34252
2	1.79	125.0	125.0	122.735	2.265	.98188
2	1.66	117.0	115.0	113.057	1.943	.96630
2	1.49	127.0	114.0	117.491	-3.491	.92512
2	1.17	51.0	40.0	36.644	3.356	.71850
2	.58	132.0	37.0	16.255	20.745	.12314

E Observed and predicted frequencies for probit model

```
Observed and Expected Frequencies

                     Number of   Observed    Expected
ROOT           X     Subjects    Responses   Responses    Residual    Prob
      1      2.17      142.0       142.0      141.411        .589     .99586
      1      2.00      127.0       126.0      125.075        .925     .98485
      1      1.68      128.0       115.0      115.136       -.136     .89950
      1      1.08      126.0        58.0       43.540      14.460     .34556

      2      1.79      125.0       125.0      123.477       1.523     .98782
      2      1.66      117.0       115.0      113.566       1.434     .97065
      2      1.49      127.0       114.0      116.994      -2.994     .92121
      2      1.17       51.0        40.0       35.611       4.389     .69825
      2       .58      132.0        37.0       17.215      19.785     .13042
```

Figure F displays the plot of probit-transformed response proportions against log-transformed values of the predictor, X. The plotting character (1 or 2) is the number of the group in which the observation appears. Because output width is restricted to 80, the plot appears in compact form. In this plot, the relation of the variables appears linear, and the response rate appears greater in the second group.

F PROBIT plot for single-predictor probit model

```
* * * * * * * * * * * * P R O B I T   A N A L Y S I S * * * * * * * * * * * *
                      LOG(X) VS. PROBIT
```

Annotated Examples for
PROBIT *continued*

Figures G and H present the confidence intervals for estimated effects of the predictor, X. For each group, PROBIT prints a table of estimated values for X to produce selected response rates from .01 to .99. Ninety-five percent fiducial confidence intervals are provided for these estimates (Finney, 1971). If the chi-square test had been significant, PROBIT would have used a heterogeneity factor to calculate the limits. The stimulus tolerance (the predictor estimate for a response rate of .50) is 16.66914 in the first group and 9.63145 in the second. If an output width of 132 is in effect, PROBIT also prints effective levels and confidence limits for the log-transformed predictor.

G Confidence intervals for effects by group in probit model

```
Confidence Limits for Effective X


ROOT        1           1

                        95% Confidence Limits
Prob            X           Lower           Upper

.01         2.43358     1.49073         3.54171
.02         3.04907     1.93470         4.32588
.03         3.51801     2.28205         4.91252
.04         3.91772     2.58346         5.40658
.05         4.27613     2.85742         5.84556
.06         4.60690     3.11310         6.24774
.07         4.91792     3.35578         6.62356
.08         5.21417     3.58886         6.97966
.09         5.49906     3.81465         7.32052
.10         5.77505     4.03482         7.64936
.15         7.07305     5.08714         9.18084
.20         8.30973     6.11123         10.62212
.25         9.54165     7.14783         12.04574
.30         10.80286    8.22256         13.49459
.35         12.11989    9.35637         15.00163
.40         13.51780    10.56970        16.59764
.45         15.02357    11.88506        18.31571
.50         16.66914    13.32937        20.19508
.55         18.49495    14.93677        22.28584
.60         20.55513    16.75274        24.65562
.65         22.92596    18.84086        27.40085
.70         25.72099    21.29482        30.66690
.75         29.12076    24.26177        34.68812
.80         33.43794    27.99319        39.87663
.85         39.28435    32.97398        47.05259
.90         48.11391    40.33717        58.20446
.91         50.52864    42.31936        61.31620
.92         53.28947    44.57021        64.90462
.93         56.49958    47.16756        69.11658
.94         60.31387    50.22763        74.17417
.95         64.97941    53.93463        80.43461
.96         70.92390    58.60507        88.52214
.97         78.98231    64.85143        99.66931
.98         91.12938    74.10608        116.83386
.99         114.17768   91.23083        150.43803
```

H Confidence intervals for effects by group in probit model

```
Confidence Limits for Effective X

ROOT        2         2

                         95% Confidence Limits
Prob          X        Lower        Upper
.01       1.40612      .83171      2.10009
.02       1.76176     1.07972      2.56433
.03       2.03271     1.27386      2.91142
.04       2.26367     1.44239      3.20359
.05       2.47075     1.59564      3.46308
.06       2.66188     1.73871      3.70072
.07       2.84158     1.87455      3.92270
.08       3.01275     2.00506      4.13295
.09       3.17737     2.13153      4.33413
.10       3.33683     2.25489      4.52814
.15       4.08682     2.84506      5.43077
.20       4.80137     3.42031      6.27872
.25       5.51318     4.00355      7.11474
.30       6.24190     4.60933      7.96390
.35       7.00289     5.24966      8.84530
.40       7.81060     5.93636      9.77656
.45       8.68064     6.68260     10.77649
.50       9.63145     7.50419     11.86722
.55      10.68641     8.42131     13.07685
.60      11.87678     9.46096     14.44321
.65      13.24665    10.66101     16.02005
.70      14.86163    12.07738     17.88828
.75      16.82601    13.79805     20.17822
.80      19.32048    15.97345     23.11903
.85      22.69855    18.89332     27.16715
.90      27.80029    23.23349     33.43063
.91      29.19552    24.40515     35.17469
.92      30.79073    25.73677     37.18463
.93      32.64554    27.27463     39.54249
.94      34.84944    29.08777     42.37234
.95      37.54519    31.28554     45.87376
.96      40.97993    34.05583     50.39565
.97      45.63609    37.76202     56.62695
.98      52.65468    43.25367     66.22119
.99      65.97202    53.41327     85.00558
```

You can compute the relative median potency (RMP) as the ratio of the stimulus tolerances in the two groups. The tolerances (from Figures G and H, for Prob = .50) are 16.66914 and 9.63145, which have a ratio of 1.73070. The RMP and its confidence limits appear in Figure I. The confidence limits do not include 1, so the difference is significant.

I Estimates of relative median potency (RMP) from probit model

```
Estimates of Relative Median Potency

                         95% Confidence Limits
ROOT       Estimate     Lower        Upper

1 VS.  2    1.7307     1.34843      2.30803
```

Annotated Examples for
PROBIT *continued*

Example 2   You can use PROBIT to perform logistic regression by specifying the LOGIT
response model with no log transformation of the predictors. Because the data are
likely to be in uncollapsed form, you must compute an observation count variable
whose value is equal to 1 for every case. You can avoid printing a case listing of
observed and predicted frequencies by using the PRINT subcommand.

The General Social Survey for 1982 provides data for predicting whether a
person feels safe and secure at home. The data can be analyzed by the following
SPSS-X commands:

```
GET FILE=GSS82 / KEEP = PRESTIGE AGE EDUC SEX INCOME82 FEARHOME
                       BURGLR ROBBRY OWNGUN NEWS TVHOURS
RECODE OWNGUN FEARHOME (0=9) (1=1) (2,3=0)
RECODE INCOME82 (18=SYSMIS)
COMPUTE ONECASE = 1
MISSING VALUES OWNGUN FEARHOME (8,9)
PROBIT FEARHOME OF ONECASE WITH AGE SEX EDUC PRESTIGE INCOME82
        OWNGUN BURGLR ROBBRY NEWS TVHOURS
 /MODEL = LOGIT
 /LOG = NONE
 /PRINT = NONE
```

• The GET command accesses the file and keeps only those variables that will be used
  in this job (see Chapter 6).

• The first RECODE command changes FEARHOME so that 1 represents the
  response of feeling safe and secure in one's home, and 0 represents fear and
  insecurity. RECODE also changes OWNGUN to 1 for gun owners and 0 otherwise
  (see Chapter 7).

• COMPUTE produces an observation count variable, ONECASE, which indicates
  there is only one observation per case (see Chapter 7).

• The MISSING VALUES command specifies that 0 will be accepted as valid for
  FEARHOME and OWNGUN (see Chapter 5).

• The PROBIT specification identifies FEARHOME (with a value of 0 or 1) as the
  response count and ONECASE (always 1) as the observation count. The PROBIT
  command also specifies 10 predictors, including variables representing age and sex,
  socioeconomic status, gun ownership, recent victimization by crime, and exposure to
  communications media (see Section 42.3).

• The MODEL subcommand requests only the logit response model (see Section
  42.4).

• The LOG subcommand indicates that predictor variables will not be transformed
  logarithmically (see Section 42.5).

• Because PRINT specifies NONE, no optional display output will be produced. Only
  the case and model information and the parameter estimates and covariances will be
  printed (see Section 42.8).

Figure J displays the case and model information that was printed. Only 184 of
1,506 input cases were omitted because of missing values for the response variable
or one of the predictors. The type of model is stated.

J Case and model information for logistic regression

```
DATA  Information

     1322 unweighted cases accepted.
      184 cases rejected because of missing data.

MODEL Information

     ONLY Logistic Model is requested.
```

Figure K presents the parameter estimates for the logistic regression model, their standard errors, and their covariances. The reported goodness-of-fit test is incorrect. For logistic regression, chi-square is not a meaningful measure. Three predictors—SEX, BURGLR, and ROBBRY—had large coefficients relative to their standard errors. These results indicate that persons who are male and were not crime victims in the preceding year are more likely to feel safe and secure in their homes. PROBIT prints the covariance matrix of parameter estimates whenever there is more than one predictor or when NATRES is specified. You can use this matrix to detect problems of collinearity among the predictors.

K Parameter estimates and covariances

```
ML converged at iteration  7.  The converge criterion =    .00000

Parameter Estimates (LOGIT model:  (LOG(p/(1-p))/2 + 5) = Intercept + BX ):
                 Note 5 added to intercept and logit divided by 2.

          Regression Coeff.  Standard Error    Coeff./S.E.

   AGE         -.00086          .00263          -.32695
   SEX         -.35930          .09224         -3.89515
   EDUC         .03351          .01830          1.83053
   PRESTIGE     .00172          .00391           .43997
   INCOME82     .01549          .01053          1.47110
   OWNGUN       .00472          .08803           .05360
   BURGLR       .59751          .11864          5.03634
   ROBBRY       .55632          .20559          2.70599
   NEWS        -.00985          .03730          -.26414
   TVHOURS     -.01676          .01932          -.86778


          Intercept   Standard Error   Intercept/S.E.

           3.78163        .53380          7.08429

Goodness-of-Fit  Chi Square =   1259.523   DF = 1311   P =   .843

Since Goodness-of-Fit Chi square is NOT significant, no heterogeneity
factor is used in the calculation of confidence limits.

- - - - - - - - - - - - - - - - - - - - - - - - - - - - - - - - - - - - - - - -

Covariance(below) and Correlation(above) Matrices of Parameter Estimates
```

	AGE	SEX	EDUC	PRESTIGE	INCOME82	OWNGUN	BURGLR	ROBBRY	NEWS	TVHOURS
AGE	.00001	-.05523	.40984	-.19823	.10917	.03340	-.09191	-.00387	.27129	-.01735
SEX	-.00001	.00851	-.10309	-.00163	.10448	.13886	-.02411	-.05503	.01335	-.02420
EDUC	.00002	-.00017	.00034	-.46592	-.20142	.08113	-.00197	.04466	.17719	.02864
PRESTIGE	.00000	.00000	-.00003	.00002	-.17934	.01144	.01359	-.04624	.01670	.07635
INCOME82	.00000	.00010	-.00004	-.00001	.00011	-.18728	-.01083	-.07506	.12304	.15946
OWNGUN	.00001	.00113	.00013	.00000	-.00017	.00775	-.01696	.00771	-.00129	.00628
BURGLR	-.00003	-.00026	.00000	.00001	-.00001	-.00018	.01408	-.11673	.01536	.06326
ROBBRY	.00000	-.00104	.00017	-.00004	-.00016	.00014	-.00285	.04227	.03882	-.10154
NEWS	.00003	.00005	.00012	.00000	.00005	.00000	.00007	.00030	.00139	.00160
TVHOURS	.00000	-.00004	.00001	.00001	.00003	.00001	.00014	-.00040	.00000	.00037

Syntax

PROXIMITIES

```
PROXIMITIES varlist
[/MISSING={LISTWISE**} ]
             {INCLUDE }
[/STANDARDIZE=[{VARIABLE}] [{NONE   }] ]
               {CASE    }   {Z      }
                            {SD     }
                            {RANGE  }
                            {MAX    }
                            {MEAN   }
                            {RESCALE}


[/VIEW={CASE**   } ]
        {VARIABLE}
[/MEASURE=[{NONE              }] [ABSOLUTE] [REVERSE] [RESCALE]
            {EUCLID**          }
            {SEUCLID           }
            {COSINE            }
            {CORR              }
            {BLOCK             }
            {CHEBYCHEV         }
            {POWER(p,r)        }
            {MINKOWSKI(p)      }
            {CHISQ             }
            {PH2               }
            {RR[(p[,np])]      }
            {SM[(p[,np])]      }
            {JACCARD[(p[,np])] }
            {DICE[(p[,np])]    }
            {SS1[(p[,np])]     }
            {RT[(p[,np])]      }
            {SS2[(p[,np])]     }
            {K1[(p[,np])]      }
            {SS3[(p[,np])]     }
            {K2[(p[,np])]      }
            {SS4[(p[,np])]     }
            {HAMANN[(p[,np])]  }
            {OCHIAI[(p[,np])]  }
            {SS5[(p[,np])]     }
            {PHI[(p[,np])]     }
            {LAMBDA[(p[,np])]  }
            {D[(p[,np])]       }
            {Y[(p[,np])]       }
            {Q[(p[,np])]       }
            {BEUCLID[(p[,np])] }
            {SIZE[(p[,np])]    }
            {PATTERN[(p[,np])] }
            {BSEUCLID[(p[,np])]}
            {BSHAPE[(p[,np])]  }
            {DISPER[(p[,np])]  }
            {VARIANCE[(p[,np])]}
            {BLWMN[(p[,np])]   }
[/ID=varname ]
[/PRINT [={PROXIMITIES**}] ]
          {NONE         }
[/MATRIX=[IN({file}] [OUT({file})]]]
             {*   }        {*   }
```

**Default if the subcommand is omitted.

Contents

43.1   OVERVIEW

43.2   OPERATION

43.3   Variable Specification

43.4   STANDARDIZE Subcommand

43.5   VIEW Subcommand

43.6   MEASURE Subcommand

43.7   Measures for Continuous Data

43.8   Measures for Frequency Count Data

43.9   Measures for Binary Data

43.10   PRINT Subcommand

43.11   ID Subcommand

43.12   MISSING Subcommand

43.13   MATRIX Subcommand

43.14   OUT Keyword

43.15   IN Keyword

43.16   Recoding a PROXIMITIES matrix for procedure FACTOR

43.17   LIMITATIONS

43

Chapter 43 PROXIMITIES

PROXIMITIES computes measures of similarity, dissimilarity, or distance. PROXIMITIES lets you choose among a great variety of different measures. It computes the measures between pairs of cases or pairs of variables for moderate-sized data sets (see Section 43.17). You can use output from PROXIMITIES as input matrices for procedure ALSCAL (Chapter 19), CLUSTER (Chapter 23), or FACTOR (Chapter 28). To learn more about proximity matrices and their uses, consult Anderberg (1973) and Romesburg (1984).

43.1
OVERVIEW

PROXIMITIES can standardize the data, and it can compute a proximity measure that you specify. You can have PROXIMITIES print the results, and you can use subcommands for output (as well as input) of files containing proximity matrices.

Missing Values. PROXIMITIES automatically performs listwise deletion of cases with missing values. (See Section 43.12.) You can choose to include or exclude cases with user-missing values.

Standardizing Data. You can standardize the values for each variable or each case by any of several different methods. (See Section 43.4.)

Proximity Measures. PROXIMITIES can compute many similarity, dissimilarity, and distance measures. (See Section 43.6.) (Similarity measures increase with greater similarity; dissimilarity and distance measures decrease.) PROXIMITIES can compute measures for continuous data, frequency count data, and binary data. You can request only one measure in any one PROXIMITIES procedure.

File Output. You can write a computed distance matrix to an SPSS-X system file. (See Section 43.14.) In this way, you can pass a matrix computed by PROXIMITIES to procedure CLUSTER, ALSCAL, or FACTOR.

File Input. You can read a similarity, dissimilarity, or distance matrix from the matrix input file. This option lets you rescale or transform existing proximity matrices. (See Section 43.15.)

Printed Output. You can have PROXIMITIES print a computed matrix. (See Section 43.10.) By default, PROXIMITIES identifies cases by sequence number. Optionally you can specify a string variable that contains an identifier for each case. (See Section 43.11.)

43.2
OPERATION

The only required specification on the PROXIMITIES command is a variable list (see Section 43.3). The command

```
PROXIMITIES A B C
```

would compute Euclidean distances between cases based on the values of variables A, B, and C. You can specify any of seven optional subcommands in any order following the variable specification. A subcommand must begin with the subcommand keyword and may be followed by an optional equals sign and specifications. Each subcommand must be preceded by a slash and should be specified no more than once.

43.3
Variable Specification

The variable list appears immediately after the PROXIMITIES command. You can use the variable specification in three distinct ways. First, it can identify the variables for computing proximities between cases. Second, it can identify the variables for computing proximities between variables. Third, it can provide labels for the items represented in a proximity matrix read from an input file.

If your data are matrix materials (see Section 43.13), you may omit the variable list. This is true only for matrix input.

43.4
STANDARDIZE Subcommand

Use the STANDARDIZE subcommand to standardize data values for either cases or variables before computing proximities. You can specify one of two options to control the direction of standardization:

VARIABLE *Standardize the values for each variable.* This is the default.

CASE *Standardize the values within each case.*

You can choose among several standardization methods. These allow you to equalize selected properties of the values. You may specify only one standardization method on the STANDARDIZE subcommand, though you may include VARIABLE or CASE, as in

```
/STANDARDIZE=CASE RANGE
```

NONE *Do not standardize.* Compute proximities using the original values. This is the default if you do not use the STANDARDIZE subcommand.

Z *Standardize values to Z scores, having zero mean and unit standard deviation.* PROXIMITIES subtracts the mean from each value for the variable or case being standardized and then divides by the standard deviation of the values. If a standard deviation is zero, PROXIMITIES sets all values for the case or variable to zero. The Z specification is the default on the STANDARDIZE subcommand.

RANGE *Standardize values to unit range.* PROXIMITIES divides each value for the variable or case being standardized by the range of the values. If the range is zero, PROXIMITIES leaves all values unchanged.

RESCALE *Standardize values to a range of zero to one.* From each value for the variable or case being standardized, PROXIMITIES subtracts the minimum value and then divides by the range. If a range is zero, PROXIMITIES sets all values for the case or variable to .50.

MAX *Standardize values to a maximum magnitude of one.* PROXIMITIES divides each value for the variable or case being standardized by the maximum of the values. If the maximum of a set of values is zero, PROXIMITIES uses an alternate process to produce a comparable standardization: it divides by the absolute magnitude of the smallest value and adds one.

MEAN   *Standardize values to unit mean.* PROXIMITIES divides each value for the variable or case being standardized by the mean of the values. If a mean is zero, PROXIMITIES adds one to all values for the case or variable to produce a mean of one.

SD   *Standardize values to unit standard deviation.* PROXIMITIES divides each value for the variable or case being standardized by the standard deviation of the values. PROXIMITIES does not change the values if their standard deviation is zero.

43.5
VIEW Subcommand

Use the VIEW subcommand to indicate whether to compute proximities between cases or between variables.

CASE   *Compute proximity values between cases.* This is the default.

VARIABLE *Compute proximity values between variables.*

43.6
MEASURE Subcommand

You can use the MEASURE subcommand to select the similarity, dissimilarity, or distance measure that PROXIMITIES computes. With any one PROXIMITIES command, you can specify only one measure. However, you can specify a transformation as well as a measure on the MEASURE subcommand, as in

```
PROXIMITIES A B C
  /MEASURE=EUCLID REVERSE
```

where EUCLID indicates the measure, and REVERSE indicates the transformation. Three transformations are available for the values PROXIMITIES computes or reads:

ABSOLUTE *Take the absolute values of the proximities.* Use ABSOLUTE where the sign of the values indicates the direction of the relations (as with correlation coefficients), but only the magnitude of the relations is of interest.

REVERSE   *Transform similarity values into dissimilarities, or vice-versa.* Use this specification to reverse the ordering of the proximities by negating the values.

RESCALE   *Rescale the proximity values to a range of zero to one.* RESCALE standardizes the proximities by first subtracting the value of the smallest and then dividing by the range. You would not usually use RESCALE with measures that are already standardized on meaningful scales, as are correlations, cosines, and many binary coefficients.

If you specify more than one transformation, PROXIMITIES does them in the order listed above: first ABSOLUTE, then REVERSE, then RESCALE.

You have a great many choices for the measure that PROXIMITIES computes between items. You can choose among measures for continuous data, frequency count data, or binary data. In addition, the keyword NONE specifies that no measure is to be computed.

NONE   *Do not compute proximity measures.* Use the NONE specification only if you input an existing proximity matrix using the IN keyword on the MATRIX subcommand. Doing this lets you apply the ABSOLUTE, REVERSE, and/or RESCALE transformations to an existing matrix of proximity values.

Each entry in the proximity matrix that PROXIMITIES computes represents a pair of items. The items can be either cases or variables, as you specify on the VIEW subcommand (see Section 43.5). When the items are cases, the computation for each pair of cases involves pairs of values for specified variables. When the items are variables, the computation for each pair of variables involves pairs of values for the variables across all the cases.

43.7
Measures for Continuous Data

To obtain proximities for continuous data, you can use one of eight specifications on the MEASURE subcommand:

EUCLID
Euclidean distance. This is the default specification for MEASURE. The distance between two items, x and y, is the square root of the sum of the squared differences between the values for the items.

$$EUCLID(x,y) = SQRT(\Sigma_i(x_i - y_i)^2)$$

SEUCLID
Squared Euclidean distance. The distance between two items is the sum of the squared differences between the values for the items.

$$SEUCLID(x,y) = \Sigma_i(x_i - y_i)^2$$

CORRELATION
Correlation between vectors of values. This is a pattern similarity measure.

$$CORRELATION(x,y) = \frac{\Sigma_i(Z_{xi}Z_{yi})}{N}$$

where Z_{xi} is the (standardized) Z-score value of x for the *i*th case or variable, and N is the number of cases or variables.

COSINE
Cosine of vectors of values. This is a pattern similarity measure.

$$COSINE(x,y) = \frac{\Sigma_i(x_iy_i)}{SQRT((\Sigma_ix_i^2)(\Sigma_iy_i^2))}$$

CHEBYCHEV
Chebychev distance metric. The distance between two items is the maximum absolute difference between the values for the items.

$$CHEBYCHEV(x,y) = max_i|x_i - y_i|$$

BLOCK
City-block, or Manhattan, distance. The distance between two items is the sum of the absolute differences between the values for the items.

$$BLOCK(x,y) = \Sigma_i|x_i - y_i|$$

MINKOWSKI(p)
Distance in an absolute Minkowski power metric. The distance between two items is the *p*th root of the sum of the absolute differences to the *p*th power between the values for the items. Appropriate selection of the integer parameter *p* yields Euclidean and many other distance metrics.

$$MINKOWSKI(x,y) = (\Sigma_i|x_i - y_i|^p)^{1/p}$$

POWER(p,r)
Distances in an absolute power metric. The distance between two items is the *r*th root of the sum of the absolute differences to the *p*th power between the values for the items. Appropriate selection of integer parameters *p* and *r* yields Euclidean, squared Euclidean, Minkowski, city-block, and many other distance metrics.

$$POWER(x,y) = (\Sigma_i|x_i - y_i|^p)^{1/r}$$

43.8
Measures for Frequency Count Data

You can use either of two specifications on the MEASURE subcommand to obtain proximities for frequency count data:

CHISQ   *Chi-square test of equality for two sets of frequencies.* The magnitude of this similarity measure depends on the total frequencies of the two cases or variables whose proximity is computed. Expected values are from the model of independence of cases (or variables), x and y.

$$CHISQ(x,y) = SQRT \left(\frac{\Sigma_i(x_i - E(x_i))^2}{E(x_i)} + \frac{\Sigma_i(y_i - E(y_i))^2}{E(y_i)} \right)$$

PH2   *Phi-squared between sets of frequencies.* This is the CHISQ measure normalized by the square root of the combined frequency. Therefore, its value does not depend on the total frequencies of the two cases or variables whose proximity is computed.

$$PH2(x,y) = SQRT \left(\frac{1}{N} \left(\frac{\Sigma_i(x_i - E(x_i))^2}{E(x_i)} + \frac{\Sigma_i(y_i - E(y_i))^2}{E(y_i)} \right) \right)$$

43.9
Measures for Binary Data

Different binary measures emphasize different aspects of the relation between sets of binary values. However, you specify all the measures in the same way. Each has two optional integer-valued parameters, *p* (present) and *np* (not present). If you specify both parameters, PROXIMITIES uses the value of the first as an indicator that a characteristic is present and the value of the second as an indicator that a characteristic is absent. PROXIMITIES skips all other values. For example, the specification

```
/MEASURE=RR(1,2)
```

tells PROXIMITIES to compute Russell and Rao coefficients from data in which 1 indicates the presence of a characteristic and 2 indicates the absence of a characteristic. Other values are ignored. If you specify only the first parameter, PROXIMITIES uses that value to indicate presence and all other values to indicate absence. For example, the specification

```
/MEASURE=SM(2)
```

tells PROXIMITIES to compute simple matching coefficients from data in which 2 indicates presence and all other values indicate absence. If you specify no parameters, PROXIMITIES assumes that 1 indicates presence and 0 indicates absence.

Using the indicators for presence and absence within each item (case or variable), PROXIMITIES constructs a 2×2 contingency table for each pair of items in turn. It uses this table to compute a proximity measure for the pair.

| | Item 2 characteristics | |
	Present	Absent
Item 1 characteristics		
Present	a	b
Absent	c	d

PROXIMITIES computes all binary measures from the values of a, b, c, and d. These values are tallies across variables (when the items are cases) or tallies across cases (when the items are variables). For example, if variables V, W, X, Y, Z have values 0, 1, 1, 0, 1 for case 1 and values 0, 1, 1, 0, 0 for case 2 (where 1 indicates presence and 0 indicates absence), the contingency table is

	Case 2 characteristics	
	Present	Absent
Case 1 characteristics		
Present	2	1
Absent	0	2

The available binary measures include matching coefficients, conditional probabilities, predictability measures, and others.

Matching Coefficients. Table 43.9 shows a classification scheme for the PROXIMITIES matching coefficients. In this scheme, *matches* are joint presences (value a in the contingency table) or joint absences (value d). *Nonmatches* are equal in number to value b plus value c. Matches and nonmatches may be weighted equally or not. The three coefficients JACCARD, DICE, and SS2 are related monotonically; SM, SS1, and RT also are related monotonically. All the coefficients in Table 43.9 are similarity measures, and all except two (K1 and SS3) range from 0 to 1. (K1 and SS3 have a minimum value of 0 and no upper limit.)

Table 43.9 Binary matching coefficients in PROXIMITIES

	Joint absences excluded from numerator	Joint absences included in numerator
All matches included in denominator		
Equal weight for matches and nonmatches	RR	SM
Double weight for matches		SS1
Double weight for nonmatches		RT
Joint absences excluded from denominator		
Equal weight for matches and nonmatches	JACCARD	
Double weight for matches	DICE	
Double weight for nonmatches	SS2	
All matches excluded from denominator		
Equal weight for matches and nonmatches	K1	SS3

RR[(p[,np])] *Russell and Rao similarity measure.* This is the binary dot product.

$$RR(x,y) = \frac{a}{a + b + c + d}$$

SM[(p[,np])] *Simple matching similarity measure.* This is the ratio of the number of matches to the total number of characteristics.

$$SM(x,y) = \frac{a + d}{a + b + c + d}$$

JACCARD[(p[,np])] *Jaccard similarity measure.* This is also known as the *similarity ratio.*

$$JACCARD(x,y) = \frac{a}{a + b + c}$$

DICE[(p[,np])] *Dice (or Czekanowski, or Sorenson) similarity measure.*

$$DICE(x,y) = \frac{2a}{2a + b + c}$$

SS1[(p[,np])] *Sokal and Sneath similarity measure 1.*

$$SS1(x,y) = \frac{2(a + d)}{2(a + d) + b + c}$$

RT[(p[,np])] *Rogers and Tanimoto similarity measure.*

$$RT(x,y) = \frac{a + d}{a + d + 2(b + c)}$$

SS2[(p[,np])] *Sokal and Sneath similarity measure 2.*

$$SS2(x,y) = \frac{a}{a + 2(b + c)}$$

K1[(p[,np])] *Kulczynski similarity measure 1.* This measure has a minimum value of 0 and no upper limit. It is undefined when there are no nonmatches (b=0 and c=0). Therefore, PROXIMITIES assigns an artificial upper limit of 9999.999 to K1 when it is undefined or exceeds this value.

$$K1(x,y) = \frac{a}{b + c}$$

SS3[(p[,np])] *Sokal and Sneath similarity measure 3.* This measure also has a minimum value of 0, has no upper limit, and is undefined when there are no nonmatches (b=0 and c=0). As with K1, PROXI-MITIES assigns an artificial upper limit of 9999.999 to SS3 when it is undefined or exceeds this value.

$$SS3(x,y) = \frac{a + d}{b + c}$$

Conditional Probabilities. The following three binary measures yield values that you can interpret in terms of conditional probability. All three are similarity measures.

K2[(p[,np])] *Kulczynski similarity measure 2.* This yields the average conditional probability that a characteristic is present in one item given that the characteristic is present in the other item. The measure is an average over both items acting as predictors. It has a range of 0 to 1.

$$K2(x,y) = \frac{a/(a + b) + a/(a + c)}{2}$$

SS4[(p[,np])] *Sokal and Sneath similarity measure 4.* This yields the conditional probability that a characteristic of one item is in the same state (presence or absence) as the characteristic of the other item. The measure is an average over both items acting as predictors. It has a range of 0 to 1.

$$SS4(x,y) = \frac{a/(a + b) + a/(a + c) + d/(b + d) + d/(c + d)}{4}$$

HAMANN[(p[,np])] *Hamann similarity measure.* This measure gives the probability that a characteristic has the same state in both items (present in both or absent from both) minus the probability that a characteristic has different states in the two items (present in one and absent from the other). HAMANN has a range of −1 to +1 and is monotonically related to SM, SS1, and RT.

$$HAMANN(x,y) = \frac{(a + d) - (b + c)}{a + b + c + d}$$

Predictability Measures. The following four binary measures assess the association between items as the predictability of one given the other. All four measures yield similarities.

LAMBDA[(p[,np])] *Goodman and Kruskal lambda (similarity).* This coefficient assesses the predictability of the state of a characteristic on one item (presence or absence) given the state on the other item. Specifically, lambda measures the proportional reduction in error using one item to predict the other, when the directions of prediction are of equal importance. Lambda has a range of 0 to 1.

$$Lambda(x,y) = \frac{\max(a,b) + \max(c,d) + \max(a,c) + \max(b,d) - \max(a + c, b+d) - \max(a +b, c + d)}{2(a + b + c + d)}$$

D[(p[,np])] *Anderberg's D (similarity).* This coefficient assesses the predictability of the state of a characteristic on one item (presence or absence) given the state on the other. D measures the actual reduction in the error probability when one item is used to predict the other. The range of D is 0 to 1.

$$D(x,y) = \frac{\max(a,b) + \max(c,d) + \max(a,c) + \max(b,d) + \max(a + c, b+d) + \max(a +b, c + d)}{2(a + b + c + d)}$$

Y[(p[,np])]   *Yule's Y coefficient of colligation (similarity).* This is a function of the cross ratio for a 2×2 table. It has a range of -1 to $+1$.

$$Y(x,y) = \frac{SQRT(ad) - SQRT(bc)}{SQRT(ad) + SQRT(bc)}$$

Q[(p[,np])]   *Yule's Q (similarity).* This is the 2×2 version of Goodman and Kruskal's ordinal measure *gamma.* Like Yule's Y, Q is a function of the cross ratio for a 2×2 table and has a range of -1 to $+1$.

$$Q(x,y) = \frac{ad - bc}{ad + bc}$$

Other Binary Measures. The remaining binary measures available in PROXIMITIES are either binary equivalents of association measures for continuous variables or measures of special properties of the relation between items.

OCHIAI[(p[,np])]   *Ochiai similarity measure.* This is the binary form of the cosine. It has a range of 0 to 1 and is a similarity measure.

$$OCHAIA(x,y) = SQRT(\frac{a}{a + b} \cdot \frac{a}{a + c})$$

SS5[(p[,np])]   *Sokal and Sneath similarity measure 5.* This is a similarity measure. Its range is 0 to 1.

$$SS5(x,y) = \frac{ad}{SQRT((a + b)(a + c)(b + d)(c + d))}$$

PHI[(p[,np])]   *Fourfold point correlation (similarity).* This is the binary form of the Pearson product-moment correlation coefficient. Phi is a similarity measure, and its range is 0 to 1.

$$PHI(x,y) = \frac{ad - bc}{SQRT ((a + b)(a + c)(b + d)(c + d))}$$

BEUCLID[(p[,np])]   *Binary Euclidean distance.* This is a distance measure. Its minimum value is 0, and it has no upper limit.

$$BEUCLID(x,y) = SQRT(b + c)$$

BSEUCLID[(p[,np])]   *Binary squared Euclidean distance.* This is also a distance measure. Its minimum value is 0, and it has no upper limit.

$$BSEUCLID(x,y) = b + c$$

SIZE[(p[,np])]   *Size difference.* This is a dissimilarity measure with a minimum value of 0 and no upper limit.

$$SIZE(x,y) = \frac{(b - c)^2}{(a + b + c + d)^2}$$

PATTERN[(p[,np])] *Pattern difference.* This is also a dissimilarity measure. Its range is 0 to 1.

$$\text{PATTERN}(x,y) = \frac{bc}{(a + b + c + d)^2}$$

BSHAPE[(p[,np])] *Binary shape difference.* This dissimilarity measure has no upper or lower limit.

$$\text{BSHAPE}(x,y) = \frac{(a + b + c + d)(b + c) - (b - c)^2}{(a + b + c + d)^2}$$

DISPER[(p[,np])] *Dispersion similarity measure.* This similarity measure has a range of -1 to $+1$.

$$\text{DISPER}(x,y) = \frac{ad - bc}{(a + b + c + d)^2}$$

VARIANCE[(p[,np])] *Variance dissimilarity measure.* This dissimilarity measure has a minimum value of 0 and no upper limit.

$$\text{VARIANCE}(x,y) = \frac{b + c}{4(a + b + c + d)}$$

BLWMN[(p[,np])] *Binary Lance-and-Williams nonmetric dissimilarity measure.* Also known as the Bray-Curtis nonmetric coefficient, this dissimilarity measure has a range of 0 to 1.

$$\text{BLWMN}(x,y) = \frac{b + c}{2a + b + c}$$

43.10
PRINT Subcommand

PROXIMITIES always prints the name of the measure it computes and the number of cases (see Figure 43.10a). In addition, you can use either of the following keywords with the PRINT subcommand to specify printing of the proximity matrix.

PROXIMITIES *Print the matrix of the proximities between items.* This is the default. The matrix may have been either read or computed. When the number of cases or variables is large, this specification produces a large volume of output and uses significant CPU time (see Figure 43.10b).

NONE *Do not print the matrix of proximities.*

Figure 43.10a Printed output of number of cases and name of measure

```
* * * * * * * * * * * * P R O X I M I T I E S * * * * * * * * * * * * * * * *

Data Information

        22 unweighted cases accepted.
         3 cases rejected because of missing value.

Squared Euclidean dissimilarity measure used.
```

Figure 43.10b   A computed dissimilarity matrix

```
Squared Euclidean Dissimilarity Coefficient Matrix

    Case          1            2            3            4            5

     2     1497.8076
     3      106.4896     806.6370
     4      335.7888    3247.8643     818.6799
     5     2899.5271    8561.8047    4114.5469    1263.0967
     6      971.9021    4882.5898    1720.5356     169.0064     517.7527
     7      661.9050    4148.7891    1297.6436      55.2272     790.8511
     8     2612.0105    8062.2539    3770.6606    1075.8445       7.5130
     9     4369.8633     751.3770    3114.3811    7123.4063   14385.6445
    10     1585.8032    6162.3203    2512.0203     462.7227     196.9034
    11     3386.4690    9387.1992    4691.0781    1592.7651      20.3022
    12      489.0835    3695.4839    1050.4954      14.4792    1007.4626
    13       78.1740     893.4807       3.0674     734.4531    3923.8147
    14     1160.9475      21.6380     565.4277    2742.9023    7728.3945
    15      900.9116      75.5702     389.0139    2332.9182    7029.1875
    16        5.6559    1327.9541      65.5000     422.3618    3146.1370
    17     1730.7749    6446.7813    2693.7422     543.2170     150.0680
    18      346.4128    3282.3088     835.3687        .2926    1242.0027
    19      151.5801    2600.2307     511.3428      36.2283    1725.7593
    20     2855.5576    8486.1328    4061.9136    1234.1841        .2136
    21     2557.8745    7967.6563    3705.2314    1041.7258      10.9920
    22     1697.4617    6383.0547    2652.5327     525.0669     160.3241


    Case          6            7            8            9           10

     7       31.9175
     8      401.0542     644.2974
     9     9462.6953    8431.0820   13735.8594
    10       78.6624     198.8349     127.4958   11216.9570
    11      731.3577    1054.9946      51.7585   15449.4609     339.7014
    12       85.3059      13.2709     841.0171    7779.2383     313.6716
    13     1600.1609    1191.8367    3588.0313    3283.2922    2362.9480
    14     4256.9219    3574.9521    7254.1523    1026.0676    5458.5625
    15     3744.2676    3104.9795    6577.2266    1303.2310    4873.4375
    16     1119.2764     782.4729    2846.2532    4076.8240    1769.0891
    17      110.8200     252.2044      90.5409   11599.5625       3.6735
    18      160.1253      50.7028    1056.4441    7174.3242     450.2390
    19      357.9990     180.2515    1505.6096    6146.6406     757.0076
    20      499.1614     767.9177       5.5111   14287.5781     185.7171
    21      379.0364     617.5984       .6568   13612.3359     116.4006
    22      102.0117     239.8557      98.5876   11513.7617       2.6734


    Case         11           12           13           14           15

    12     1303.9492
    13     4489.2305     954.8120
    14     8512.6953    3155.2236     638.7573
    15     7779.2422    2714.4280     449.4502      16.8432
    16     3654.3708     592.9253      42.9101    1012.6299     770.0967
    17      275.6973     380.5256    2540.4861    5726.0313    5126.9727
    18     1568.0229      12.4786     751.0337    2774.3025    2362.2834
    19     2106.9380      96.1329     445.3198    2150.1948    1789.4778
    20       23.7824     981.7180    3872.7488    7656.5430    6960.7383
    21       58.5794     810.9810    3525.2979    7164.2617    6492.0781
    22      289.0537     365.2937    2500.5396    5665.6680    5070.1250


    Case         16           17           18           19           20

    17     1923.0654
    18      434.9402     529.0437
    19      211.7656     858.6499      39.9257
    20     3100.4265     140.1453    1213.1941    1691.9805
    21     2790.3809      80.5574    1022.1165    1465.0322       8.3184
    22     1888.3218        .2612     511.0376     835.3984     150.1256


    Case         21

    22       88.1643
```

43.11
ID Subcommand

Use the ID subcommand to specify an identifying string variable for cases. You can name any string variable on your file as the identifier. PROXIMITIES uses the values of this variable to identify cases in procedure output. By default, it identifies cases by case number alone. The form of the subcommand is

```
/ID=varname
```

43.1
ANNOTATED
EXAMPLE FOR
PROXIMITIES

This example shows how PROXIMITIES can produce matrix materials for input to CLUSTER. Data are in-line for this example:

```
SET WIDTH=80

TITLE Crime Rates for Selected Cities 1979
SUBTITLE Data from  Uniform Crime Reports for the United States

DATA LIST / CITY 1-17(A) MURDER 18-21 RAPE 23-25 ROBBERY 27-30
            ASSAULT 32-34 BURGLARY 36-39 LARCENY 41-44
            MOTOR 46-49

VARIABLE LABELS MURDER   'Murders per 100,000 People'
                RAPE     'Forcible Rapes per 100,000 People'
                ROBBERY  'Robberies per 100,000 People'
                ASSAULT  'Aggravated Assaults per 100,000 People'
                BURGLARY 'Burglaries, B & E per 100,000 People'
                LARCENY  'Larceny, thefts per 100,000 People'
                MOTOR    'Motor Thefts per 100,000 People'

BEGIN DATA
San Francisco     17.0 101 1016 542 2618 5149 1290
Dallas            34.8 111  505 647 2997 5443  890
Baltimore         31.0  71 1072 788 2139 4367  856
Los Angeles       27.4  88  714 685 2596 3549 1373
Detroit           35.9 109  907 619 2598 2820 1708
Houston           40.4  91  575 171 3022 3335 1517
New York          24.4  55 1161 622 2506 3106 1262
San Diego         11.6  40  348 256 2406 4730  902
Cleveland         45.6 102  958 514 2412 2364 2251
Washington, D.C.  27.4  75 1055 452 2051 4393  550
Indianapolis      17.9  85  400 310 1664 3683  672
San Antonio       20.6  44  204 224 1990 3588  560
Chicago           28.0  54  473 354 1091 3074 1027
Milwaukee          9.8  44  247 171 1325 3498  655
Philadelphia      21.9  48  503 255 1193 1927  752
END DATA

PROXIMITIES MURDER TO MOTOR
  /VIEW=VARIABLE
  /MATRIX=OUT(*)

CLUSTER
  /MATRIX=IN(*)
  /PRINT=DISTANCE SCHEDULE
```

- The PROXIMITIES command specifies the variables MURDER through MOTOR for computing the data matrix.
- The VIEW subcommand indicates that proximities are to be computed between variables, not cases.
- The MATRIX subcommand writes the computed matrix to the active file for CLUSTER to read. Since the MEASURE subcommand does not appear, the computed matrix will consist of Euclidean distances between cases.
- The CLUSTER command omits the variable list. All variables from the input matrix are therefore used in the cluster analysis.
- The MATRIX subcommand indicates that matrix data are in the active file.
- The PRINT subcommand requests the cluster agglomeration schedule as well as the computed distances between cases.

The computed dissimilarity matrix for variables

```
* * * * * * * * * * * * * * P R O X I M I T I E S * * * * * * * * * * * * * * *


Data Information

        15 unweighted cases accepted.
         0 cases rejected because of missing value.

Euclidean measure used.
- - - - - - - - - - - - - - - - - - - - - - - - - - - - - - - - - - - - - - - -

Euclidean Dissimilarity Coefficient Matrix

Variable        MURDER          RAPE          ROBBERY        ASSAULT        BURGLARY

RAPE           202.0030
ROBBERY       2788.8428      2610.9871
ASSAULT       1772.7927      1590.8474      1233.7617
BURGLARY      8627.9258      8436.2539      6185.6484      7027.9414
LARCENY      14588.4023     14400.4453     12220.1641     13007.3242     6743.8477
MOTOR         4466.1953      4283.5117      2283.2639      3020.9238     4708.1719

Variable        LARCENY

MOTOR        11043.0586

- - - - - - - - - - - - - - - - - - - - - - - - - - - - - - - - - - - - - - - -
```

43.12
MISSING Subcommand

You can use the MISSING subcommand to change or to make explicit the treatment of cases with missing values. You can specify MISSING=LISTWISE or MISSING=INCLUDE.

LISTWISE   *Delete cases with missing values listwise.* This is the default.

INCLUDE   *Include user-missing values as valid.* This option deletes listwise only those cases with system-missing values.

43.13
MATRIX Subcommand

PROXIMITIES can both read and write matrix materials. It writes proximity type matrices that can be used by PROXIMITIES or other procedures (see Chapter 13, Table 13.1). Procedures CLUSTER and ALSCAL can read a proximity matrix directly. Procedure FACTOR can read a correlation matrix written by PROXIMITIES, but you must first use RECODE to change the ROWTYPE_ value PROX to a ROWTYPE_ value CORR (see Section 43.16). Also, if using a proximity matrix in FACTOR, you may *not* use the ID subcommand in PROXIMITIES.

Use the MATRIX subcommand to read and write matrix materials. The MATRIX subcommand has two keywords, IN and OUT, which you use to specify the matrix file in parentheses. When you use both IN and OUT on the same PROXIMITIES procedure you can specify each on a separate MATRIX subcommand, or both on the same subcommand. For example,

```
PROXIMITIES varlist
  /MATRIX IN(FILEONE)
  /MATRIX OUT(FILETWO)
```

is the same as

```
PROXIMITIES varlist
  /MATRIX IN(FILEONE) OUT(FILETWO)
```

43.14
OUT Keyword

The OUT keyword on MATRIX specifies the file to which the matrix is written. There are two options:

(file)   *Write the matrix to a system file.* PROXIMITIES creates a system file containing the matrix materials. The output file is specified in parentheses. The system file is stored on disk and can be retrieved at any time.

(*)   *Replace the active file with the matrix system file.* The matrix materials replace the active file. The matrix is *not* stored on disk. It is resident in the active file.

If VIEW=VARIABLE, the variables on the new file will have the names and labels of the original variables. If VIEW=CASE (the default), the names of the variables on the new file will be CASE1, CASE2...CASEn, where *n* is the number of cases in the file or in the largest split-file group. The new file will preserve the names and values of any split-file variables in effect. For example,

```
PROXIMITIES  VAR1 TO VAR20
  /MATRIX=OUT(DISTOUT)
```

produces a default Euclidean distance matrix for cases by using variables VAR1 through VAR20 and saves the matrix on the SPSS-X file DISTOUT. The names of the variables on this file will be CASE1, CASE2...CASEn. Documents from the original file will not be included in the matrix file and will not be present if the matrix file becomes the active file. (For a discussion on documents, see Chapter 6.)

In the following example one set of matrix materials is written to file PROXMTX:

```
GET FILE=CRIME
PROXIMITIES MURDER TO MOTOR
   /ID=CITY
   /MEASURE=EUCLID
   /MATRIX=OUT(PROXMTX)
```

The active file is still the file defined by the handle CRIME. Subsequent commands are executed on CRIME.

To write the same matrix, but have it available to subsequent commands, specify the following:

```
GET FILE=CRIME
PROXIMITIES MURDER TO MOTOR
   /ID=CITY
   /MEASURE=EUCLID
   /MATRIX=OUT(*)
LIST
DISPLAY DICTIONARY
```

The active file is still the file CRIME. Subsequent commands are executed on CRIME.

Format of the Matrix System File. Figure 43.14 shows the matrix system file produced by the above commands (results of the DISPLAY command are shown only for variable ROWTYPE_). The file includes two special variables created by SPSS-X: ROWTYPE_ and VARNAME_. Variable ROWTYPE_ is a short string variable having values PROX, for proximity measure. PROX is assigned value labels containing the distance measure used to create the matrix. It is also assigned a similarity/dissimilarity keyword. In this example, the distance measure is *EUCLID* and the similarity/dissimilarity keyword is *DISSIMILARITY*, as shown in Figure 43.14. Variable CITY is the identifying string variable named on the ID subcommand. It is used to identify cases (see Section 43.11). Up to 20 characters can be displayed for the identifying variable; id variables longer than 20 characters are truncated. The identifying variable is present only when VIEW= CASE (the default; see Section 43.5) and the ID subcommand is used. The next variable in the matrix file, variable VARNAME_, is a short string variable whose values are the case numbers of the ID variable. The remaining variables in the matrix file are the distance variables used to form the matrix.

Figure 43.14   A matrix system file

```
FILE:      MATRIX FILE

ROWTYPE_ CITY              VARNAME_      CASE1       CASE2      CASE3      CASE4      CASE5      CASE6      CASE7      CASE8

PROX      San Francisco    CASE1         .0000     814.0269  1045.9773  1636.8577  2370.1467  1959.1096  2053.4780   950.1677
PROX      Dallas           CASE2       814.0269      .0000   1496.0215  2006.7471  2805.5029  2251.5161  2505.0427  1020.2466
PROX      Baltimore        CASE3      1045.9773  1496.0215      .0000   1133.2859  1840.3933  1705.8193  1387.5959  1006.8323
PROX      Los Angeles      CASE4      1636.8577  2006.7471  1133.2859      .0000    828.1233   729.1794   649.2656  1404.7251
PROX      Detroit          CASE5      2370.1467  2805.5029  1840.3933   828.1233      .0000    890.3674   597.2847  2187.2817
PROX      Houston          CASE6      1959.1096  2251.5161  1705.8193   729.1794   890.3674      .0000    965.4382  1663.0964
PROX      New York         CASE7      2053.4780  2505.0427  1387.5959   649.2656   597.2847   965.4382      .0000   1890.0500
PROX      San Diego        CASE8       950.1677  1020.2466  1006.8323  1404.7251  2187.2817  1663.0964  1890.0500      .0000


NUMBER OF CASES READ =      8     NUMBER OF CASES LISTED =      8

FILE:      MATRIX FILE

           LIST OF VARIABLES ON THE ACTIVE FILE

NAME                                                          POSITION

ROWTYPE_                                                          1
                  PRINT FORMAT: A8
                  WRITE FORMAT: A8

         VALUE       LABEL
           PROX      DISSIMILARITY      EUCLID
```

To assure the display file would not be forced to wrap, only 8 cases were included in the analysis that generated Figure 43.14. With a large number of variables, the display file wraps and the matrix format is less readable. Nonetheless, the matrix values are equally as accurate and just as useful when used as matrix input values.

When split-file processing is in effect (see Chapter 15), the first variables in the matrix system file will be the split variables, followed by ROWTYPE_, the case identifier variable (if VIEW=CASE and the ID subcommand is used), VARNAME_, and the distance variable(s). A full set of matrix materials is written for each splitfile group defined by the split variable(s). A split variable cannot have the same variable name as any other variable written to the matrix system file. If split-file processing is in effect when a matrix is written, the same split file must be in effect when that matrix is read by any procedure. (See Chapter 13 for more information on matrix system files.)

Additional Statistics. PROXIMITIES writes a variety of proximity type matrices. Each has ROWTYPE_ values of PROX. PROXIMITIES neither reads nor writes additional statistics with its matrix materials.

Missing Values. Missing value treatment affects the values written to a matrix system file. When reading a matrix system file, be sure to specify a missing value treatment on PROXIMITIES that is compatible with the treatment used to generate the matrix materials.

43.15
IN Keyword

The IN keyword on MATRIX specifies the file from which the matrix is read. There are two options:

(file)   *Read the matrix materials from a matrix system file.*

(*)   *Read the matrix materials from the active file.* The active file must be an appropriate matrix system file.

MATRIX=IN cannot be used in place of GET or DATA LIST to begin a new SPSS-X command file. MATRIX is a subcommand on PROXIMITIES and PROXIMITIES cannot run before an active file is defined.

In the following example, one set of matrix materials is read from the file named PROXMTX. This specification assumes the current active file is not the file PROXMTX:

```
PROXIMITIES CASE1 TO CASE8
  /ID=CITY
  /MATRIX=IN(PROXMTX)
```

SPSS-X reads variable names, variable and value labels, and print and write formats from the dictionary of file PROXMTX. You may omit the variable list on PROXIMITIES when reading matrix input. By default, all variables in the matrix system file are used in the analysis. When you specify a variable list, the variables you specify may be a subset of the variables resident in the matrix file.

The order among rows and variables in the input matrix file is unimportant, so long as values for split file variables precede values for ROWTYPE_. PROXIMITIES ignores unrecognized ROWTYPE_ values. In addition, it ignores variables present in the matrix file that are not specified (or used by default) on the PROXIMITIES variable list.

To begin a new command file and immediately read a matrix, first GET the matrix file, then specify IN(*) on MATRIX. Alternatively, PROXIMITIES can read a matrix written to the active file by a previous PROXIMITIES procedure.

```
GET FILE=CRIME
PROXIMITIES MURDER TO MOTOR
  /ID=CITY
  /MATRIX=OUT(*)
PROXIMITIES
  /MATRIX=IN(*)
  /STANDARDIZE
```

- The GET command defines the data to SPSS-X.
- The first PROXIMITIES command specifies variables for the analysis and reads the raw data from file CRIME. The ID subcommand specifies CITY as the case identifying variable. The MATRIX subcommand determines that the resulting matrix is written to the active file.
- The variable list is omitted on the second PROXIMITIES command. This is permitted because the presence of the MATRIX subcommand indicates data are matrix materials. The specification on MATRIX indicates that data are resident in the active file. The slash preceding the MATRIX subcommand is required because there is an implied variable list present. Without the slash, PROXIMITIES would attempt to interpret MATRIX as a variable name rather than a subcommand name.

43.16
Recoding a PROXIMITIES Matrix for Procedure FACTOR

In this example, PROXIMITIES and FACTOR are used for a Q factor analysis, in which factors account for variance shared among observations rather than among variables. Procedure FACTOR does not perform Q factor analysis without some preliminary transformation such as that provided by PROXIMITIES. Because the number of cases exceeds the number of variables, the model is not of full rank and FACTOR will print a warning. This is a common occurrence when inputting case by case matrices from PROXIMITIES to FACTOR.

Before you can use the PROXIMITIES matrix for FACTOR, you must RECODE the ROWTYPE_ values, changing them from PROX to CORR:

```
GET FILE=CRIME
PROXIMITIES    MURDER TO MOTOR
  /MEASURE=CORR
  /MATRIX=OUT(*)

RECODE ROWTYPE_ ('PROX' = 'CORR')

FACTOR MATRIX IN(COR=*)
```

- The GET command defines the data to SPSS-X.
- The PROXIMITIES command specifies variables for the analysis. Because the matrix materials will be used in procedure FACTOR, the ID subcommand is *not* specified.
- The MEASURE subcommand selects correlation as the similarity measure for computing proximities.
- The MATRIX subcommand on PROXIMITIES writes the correlation matrix materials to the active file.
- The RECODE command recodes ROWTYPE_ values from PROX to CORR so procedure FACTOR can read the matrix.
- When FACTOR reads matrix materials, it reads all the variables in the file. The MATRIX subcommand on FACTOR indicates that the matrix is a correlation matrix, and data are in the active file.

43.17
LIMITATIONS

The following limitations apply to PROXIMITIES:

- Storage requirements increase rapidly with the number of cases and the number of items (cases or variables) for which PROXIMITIES computes coefficients. PROXIMITIES keeps the raw data for the current split-file group in memory. You may not be able to compute a proximity matrix for more than 150 cases and a small number of variables in an 80K-byte workspace.
- PROXIMITIES ignores case weights when computing coefficients.

Syntax

QUICK CLUSTER

```
QUICK CLUSTER varlist
[/MISSING=[{LISTWISE**}] [INCLUDE]]
          {PAIRWISE }
          {DEFAULT  }
[/FILE=file]
[/INITIAL=(value list)]
[/CRITERIA=[CLUSTER({2**})] [NOINITIAL] [NOUPDATE]]
                    {k  }
[/PRINT=[INITIAL**] [CLUSTER] [ID(varname)] [DISTANCE] [ANOVA]
        [NONE]]
[/OUTFILE=file]
[/SAVE=[CLUSTER(varname)] [DISTANCE(varname)]]
```

** Default if the subcommand is omitted.

Contents

44.1   OVERVIEW

44.2   OPERATION

44.3   Variable Specification

44.4   Standardization

44.5   CRITERIA Subcommand

44.6   Initial Cluster Centers

44.7   INITIAL Subcommand

44.8   FILE Subcommand

44.9   PRINT Subcommand

44.10 Saving Results

44.11 OUTFILE Subcommand

44.12 SAVE Subcommand

44.13 Extremely Large Numbers of Cases

44.14 MISSING Subcommand

44

Chapter 44 QUICK CLUSTER

You can use QUICK CLUSTER for efficient clustering of a large number of cases into a requested number of groups. The QUICK CLUSTER algorithm produces clusters by finding cluster centers based on the values of the cluster variables and by assigning cases to the centers that are nearest. You can specify a simplified version of the algorithm to facilitate clustering when the number of cases is extremely large. (For other clustering methods, see Chapter 23.)

After clustering your cases, QUICK CLUSTER prints the final cluster centers and the number of cases in each cluster. QUICK CLUSTER also can display the cluster membership of each case. For subsequent analyses or reports, you can save the final cluster centers, the classification of each case, and the distance from each case to its interim (classification) cluster center.

OVERVIEW The QUICK CLUSTER algorithm has three steps. The first step selects *initial* cluster centers. A center is an estimate of the average value of each clustering variable for the cases in a cluster. (A center includes one value for each variable.) You can choose the way QUICK CLUSTER selects the initial centers, or you can provide initial centers yourself. By default, QUICK CLUSTER selects k cases with well-separated, nonmissing values as initial centers, where k is the number of clusters you request. This selection provides a good starting point for the next two steps of the algorithm. If you specify NOINITIAL on the CRITERIA subcommand (see Section 44.5), QUICK CLUSTER selects the first k cases without missing values as initial cluster centers. The NOINITIAL option followed by the remaining steps of the default QUICK CLUSTER algorithm makes QUICK CLUSTER equivalent to McQueen's k-means clustering method.

The second step of the algorithm updates the values of the initial cluster centers to derive the *classification* cluster centers. (You can eliminate this step to cluster a very large number of cases; see Section 44.13.) QUICK CLUSTER assigns each case in turn to the nearest cluster center (measuring by squared Euclidean distance). When a case is assigned, the procedure updates the center to a mean for the cases that are thus far in the cluster. As cases are processed, the centers migrate to concentrations of observations.

The final step of the algorithm reassigns each case to the nearest of the updated (classification) cluster centers, yielding the final clusters. The *final* cluster centers result from the variable means for the cases in the final clusters.

The cluster solution depends on the order of cases in the file: if the order changes, the cluster solution changes. To minimize the discrepancy, run QUICK CLUSTER until the solution stabilizes. This might require multiple runs. Use the OUTFILE subcommand to save final centers on one run, and the FILE subcommand on the next run to use those final centers as initial centers.

Algorithm Specifications. You can specify what the number of clusters will be, how to select initial cluster centers, and whether to update the centers (see Section 44.5).

Initial Cluster Centers. By default, QUICK CLUSTER chooses the initial cluster centers, but it can read initial cluster centers from a system file instead (see Section 44.8). Alternatively, you can provide initial centers within the program itself (see Section 44.7).

Optional Printed Output. You can print the cluster membership of each case with the distance of each case from its classification cluster center (see Section 44.9). You can also choose to print the distances between the final cluster centers as well as a univariate analysis of variance between clusters for each clustering variable.

Saving Results. You can write the final cluster centers to a system file (see Section 44.11). You can save the cluster membership of each case on the SPSS-X active file (see Section 44.12). You can also save on the active file the distance from each case to its classification cluster center.

Missing Values. By default, QUICK CLUSTER performs listwise deletion of cases with missing values. You can choose pairwise deletion instead (using only nonmissing values to determine distances between a case and a cluster center), and you can accept user-missing values as valid (see Section 44.14).

44.2
OPERATION

A variable list is the only required specification on a QUICK CLUSTER command. For example, the command

```
QUICK CLUSTER  A B C D
```

produces a default two-group clustering of cases based on the values of variables A, B, C, and D. Otherwise, QUICK CLUSTER is subcommand driven. Following the variable specification, you can specify any of seven optional subcommands in any order.

44.3
Variable Specification

A variable list must appear immediately after the QUICK CLUSTER command. This specification identifies the variables used to cluster the cases.

44.4
Standardization

The QUICK CLUSTER procedure uses squared Euclidean distance, which equally weights all clustering variables. If the variables are measured in units that are not comparable, the procedure gives more weight to variables with large variances. However, you can standardize the variables before clustering by using procedure DESCRIPTIVES (see Chapter 26).

44.5
CRITERIA Subcommand

You can use the CRITERIA subcommand to specify the desired number of clusters and options for the QUICK CLUSTER algorithm. You can use any of three keywords on the CRITERIA subcommand:

CLUSTER(k)   *Number of clusters.* QUICK CLUSTER assigns cases to *k* clusters. The default is two clusters.

NOINITIAL   *No initial cluster center selection.* This keyword specifies that as initial centers, QUICK CLUSTER uses the first *k* cases without missing values, where *k* is the number of clusters specified on the CLUSTER keyword. If you do not use NOINITIAL, QUICK CLUSTER selects as initial centers *k* cases without missing values, and—at the expense of greater processing time—the selection process guarantees that the cases are well separated.

NOUPDATE   *No updating of cluster centers.* This option produces a very quick clustering, but the results are not as good as those from the default procedure. You should choose this option when you use QUICK CLUSTER to classify cases on the basis of a previous clustering.

44.6
Initial Cluster Centers

You can set initial cluster centers either by entering them in your procedure specifications (see Section 44.7) or by reading them from a system file (see Section 44.8).

44.7
INITIAL Subcommand

You can use the INITIAL subcommand to set the initial cluster centers in your program. You must include a value for each clustering variable for as many clusters as you request. If you specify 4 clustering variables and request 3 clusters, you must supply 12 values, as in

```
QUICK CLUSTER   A B C D
 /CRITERIA = CLUSTER(3)
 /INITIAL = (13 24  1  8
              7 12  5  9
             10 18 17 16)
```

In this example, the initial center of the first cluster has a value of 13 for variable A, 24 for variable B, 1 for C, and 8 for D.

44.8
FILE Subcommand

You can use the FILE subcommand to obtain initial cluster centers from a system file. Use the following commands to read initial cluster centers from a system file:

```
QUICK CLUSTER   A B C D
 /FILE=INIT
 /CRITERIA = CLUSTER(3)
```

In this example, the initial cluster centers are read from file INIT. The four clustering variables are A, B, C, and D. QUICK CLUSTER assigns the cases to three clusters.

44.9
PRINT Subcommand

QUICK CLUSTER always prints the classification and final cluster centers and the number of cases in each cluster. You can also use the PRINT subcommand with any of the following specifications for printed output:

INITIAL *Initial cluster centers.* The initial cluster centers print by default, whether they are read from a file, specified in the program, or selected from input cases in the first phase of the clustering process. When SPLIT FILES is in effect, the initial cluster center for each split file is printed, followed by the cluster results for each subfile.

ID(varname) *Identifying variable for cases.* You can name any variable on your file as the identifier. QUICK CLUSTER uses the values of this variable to identify cases in procedure output. By default, QUICK CLUSTER identifies cases by case number.

CLUSTER *Cluster membership.* QUICK CLUSTER prints an identifying label for each case, a value indicating the cluster to which each case belongs, and the distance between each case and its classification cluster center. If you cluster a very large number of cases, this option produces a large volume of output.

DISTANCE *Distances between final cluster centers.* You can use this option to determine how well separated are the individual pairs of clusters. When you request a very large number of clusters, this option can be computationally expensive.

ANOVA *Univariate F tests for each clustering variable.* For each clustering variable, this option prints a univariate F test for the derived clusters. The F tests are only descriptive. You should *not* interpret the resulting probabilities to test the null hypothesis of no differences among clusters. Cases are systematically assigned to clusters to maximize differences on the clustering variables. Statistics after clustering are also available through procedure DISCRIMINANT (see Chapter 27) or MANOVA (see Chapter 33).

NONE *Unconditional output.* You can use the keyword NONE on the PRINT subcommand for QUICK CLUSTER to print only the unconditional output: classification and final cluster centers and the number of cases in each cluster. NONE also overrides any other specification you use on the PRINT subcommand. If you use other specifications with NONE on the PRINT subcommand, the others will be ignored.

44.10
Saving Results

You can save different clustering results on a system file (see Section 44.11) or on the active file (see Section 44.12).

44.11
OUTFILE Subcommand

Use the OUTFILE subcommand to save the final cluster centers on a system file. You can later use these final cluster centers as initial cluster centers for a different sample of cases that use the same variables. You can also cluster the final cluster centers themselves to obtain clusters of clusters. For example, the command

```
QUICK CLUSTER A B C D
 /CRITERIA = CLUSTER(3)
 /OUTFILE = QC1
```

writes the cluster centers to file QC1.

44.12
SAVE Subcommand

Use the SAVE subcommand to save the cluster membership of cases and to save the distances from the classification cluster centers as new variables on the SPSS-X active file.

CLUSTER(varname)   *Cluster membership.* The saved variable has integer values indicating the cluster to which each case belongs. The values range from 1 to the number of clusters.

DISTANCE(varname)   *Distance from nearest classification cluster center.*

44.13
Extremely Large Numbers of Cases

When you have a great many cases, directly clustering them all may be impractical. Instead, you can cluster a sample of the cases and then use the cluster solution for the sample to classify the very large group of cases. This requires two uses of QUICK CLUSTER (see Annotated Example 2). The first involves all three steps of the QUICK CLUSTER algorithm (see Section 44.1) and thus three passes through the data for the selected sample; the second involves only the third step and thus only one pass through the very large data set.

The first QUICK CLUSTER obtains a cluster solution for a sample of the cases and uses the OUTFILE subcommand to save the final cluster centers to a system file. The second QUICK CLUSTER uses the FILE subcommand to define the final cluster centers from the first analysis as the initial cluster centers for the second analysis. You can specify NOUPDATE on the CRITERIA subcommand so QUICK CLUSTER will directly assign each case to the cluster with the nearest center.

44.14
MISSING Subcommand

You can use the MISSING subcommand to change or make explicit the treatment of cases with missing values. You can use any of four keywords with the MISSING subcommand.

LISTWISE   *Perform listwise deletion of cases with missing values.* A case with missing values on any of the clustering variables is deleted. You can make this default treatment explicit by specifying either LISTWISE or DEFAULT.

PAIRWISE   *Perform pairwise deletion for missing values.* QUICK CLUSTER computes squared Euclidean distance between cases and cluster centers by using all nonmissing pairs of values. Cluster centers have no missing values. However, when a case has missing values for some clustering variables and the PAIRWISE option is in effect, the case is assigned to the cluster that is nearest on the nonmissing values.

INCLUDE   *Treat user-missing values as valid.* QUICK CLUSTER uses cases having values that you declared as missing.

ANNOTATED EXAMPLES FOR QUICK CLUSTER

These examples show how an analysis with QUICK CLUSTER compares with a known classification and how QUICK CLUSTER can be used with an extremely large number of cases.

Example 1

The following job uses Fisher's classic data on irises to group the irises into clusters. The clusters are then compared with the actual botanical classification.

```
TITLE   CLUSTERING  FISHER'S IRIS DATA WITH QUICK CLUSTER

COMMENT       FISHER'S IRIS DATA PROVIDE THE CLASSIC EXAMPLE
              OF CLASSIFICATION. THIS PROGRAM USES THE DATA
              TO ILLUSTRATE SPSS-X QUICK CLUSTER.

DATA LIST / SEP.LEN 1-2 SEP.WID PET.LEN PET.WID 3-11 IRISTYPE 13
VARIABLE LABELS   SEP.LEN  'SEPAL LENGTH'
                  SEP.WID  'SEPAL WIDTH'
                  PET.LEN  'PETAL LENGTH'
                  PET.WID  'PETAL WIDTH'
                  IRISTYPE 'TYPE OF IRIS'
VALUE LABELS    IRISTYPE (1) SETOSA (2) VERSICOLOR (3) VIRGINICA

SUBTITLE CLUSTERING IRISES BY DEFAULT METHOD
COMMENT       DO A DEFAULT QUICK CLUSTER ANALYSIS AND SAVE THE CLUSTER
              MEMBERSHIP AS A VARIABLE, CLUSTMEM, ON THE ACTIVE FILE.
QUICK CLUSTER   SEP.LEN TO PET.WID
 /CRITERIA = CLUSTER(3)
 /PRINT = INITIAL  ANOVA
 /SAVE = CLUSTER(CLUSTMEM)

BEGIN DATA
50 33 14 02 1
   . . .
53 37 15 02 1
END DATA

VARIABLE LABELS CLUSTMEM 'CLUSTERS FROM DEFAULT METHOD'

SUBTITLE VALIDITY OF CLUSTERS OBTAINED BY DEFAULT METHOD
COMMENT     COMPARE DERIVED CLUSTERS WITH ACTUAL IRIS TYPES.
CROSSTABS VARIABLES = IRISTYPE CLUSTMEM (1,3)
 /TABLES = IRISTYPE BY CLUSTMEM
 /STATISTICS = CHISQ LAMBDA UC
```

- The DATA LIST command defines five variables, and the VARIABLE LABELS command labels them.
- The VALUE LABELS command assigns labels to the three values of variable IRISTYPE—three actual types of irises.
- The QUICK CLUSTER command specifies clustering based on the values of four variables: SEP.LEN, SEP.WID, PET.LEN, and PET.WID.
- The CRITERIA subcommand specifies three clusters.
- The PRINT subcommand specifies initial cluster centers and an analysis of variance table describing differences between clusters for each of the four clustering variables.
- The SAVE subcommand saves the cluster membership of each case in a new variable, CLUSTMEM, on the SPSS-X active file.
- The CROSSTABS command crosstabulates the cluster membership variable with variable IRISTYPE, which identifies the actual type of iris.
- The STATISTICS subcommand requests a chi-square test of significance plus two measures of the predictability of iris types from the cluster types.

The output from QUICK CLUSTER appears in Figure A. The classification and final cluster centers and the number of cases in each cluster always print.

Annotated Examples for
QUICK CLUSTER
continued

A The QUICK CLUSTER output for the iris data

```
Initial Cluster Centers.

Cluster      SEP.LEN       SEP.WID       PET.LEN       PET.WID

    1        58.0000       40.0000       12.0000        2.0000
    2        77.0000       38.0000       67.0000       22.0000
    3        49.0000       25.0000       45.0000       17.0000
```

```
Classification Cluster Centers.

Cluster      SEP.LEN       SEP.WID       PET.LEN       PET.WID

    1        51.0091       35.5029       13.5981        2.3147
    2        72.7018       34.1981       63.3840       21.8201
    3        59.9192       27.5660       47.4896       16.9838
```

```
Final Cluster Centers.

Cluster      SEP.LEN       SEP.WID       PET.LEN       PET.WID

    1        50.0600       34.2800       14.6200        2.4600
    2        70.8696       31.2609       60.1304       21.4348
    3        60.1558       27.9610       45.7532       15.3636
```

```
Analysis of Variance.

Variable     Cluster MS   DF      Error MS     DF          F      Prob

SEP.LEN      3645.6374    2       19.9018      147.0   183.1817   .000
SEP.WID       611.6477    2       10.9347      147.0    55.9365   .000
PET.LEN     21598.9198    2       22.0048      147.0   981.5565   .000
PET.WID      3734.5515    2        8.0809      147.0   462.1462   .000
```

```
Number of Cases in each Cluster.

Cluster      unweighted cases    weighted cases

    1             50.0                50.0
    2             23.0                23.0
    3             77.0                77.0

Missing            0
Total            150.0               150.0
```

B Comparing clusters to the actual botanical classifications

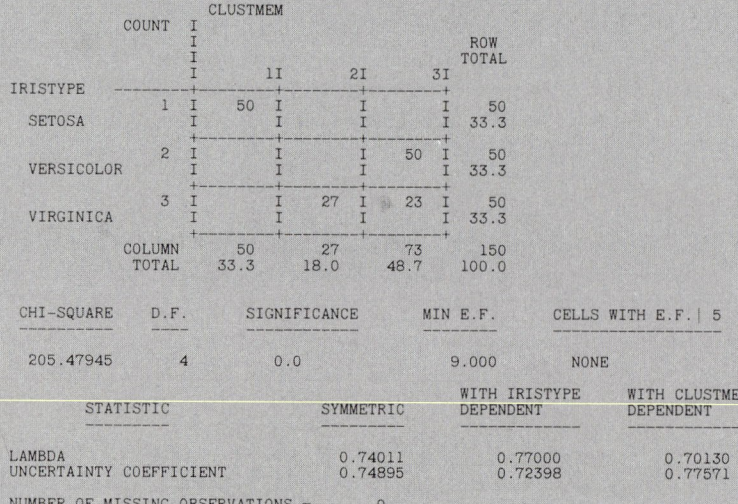

```
                   CLUSTMEM
          COUNT  I
                 I
                 I
                 I       1I       2I       3I     ROW
                                                  TOTAL
IRISTYPE  -------+--------+--------+--------+
            1  I    50  I        I        I    50
  SETOSA    I        I        I        I    33.3
          -------+--------+--------+--------+
            2  I        I        I    50  I    50
VERSICOLOR  I        I        I        I    33.3
          -------+--------+--------+--------+
            3  I        I    27  I    23  I    50
 VIRGINICA  I        I        I        I    33.3
          -------+--------+--------+--------+
          COLUMN      50       27       73     150
          TOTAL     33.3     18.0     48.7    100.0
```

```
CHI-SQUARE    D.F.    SIGNIFICANCE      MIN E.F.      CELLS WITH E.F. | 5
---------     ----    ------------      --------      -----------------

205.47945      4          0.0            9.000             NONE
```

```
                                        WITH IRISTYPE    WITH CLUSTMEM
    STATISTIC              SYMMETRIC     DEPENDENT        DEPENDENT
    ---------              ---------     -------------    -------------

LAMBDA                      0.74011       0.77000          0.70130
UNCERTAINTY COEFFICIENT     0.74895       0.72398          0.77571

NUMBER OF MISSING OBSERVATIONS =       0
```

Figure B presents output from the CROSSTABS procedure. The SAVE subcommand of QUICK CLUSTER added variable CLUSTMEM to the SPSS-X file. CLUSTMEM indicates the cluster membership of each case. IRISTYPE contains the actual botanical classification of each case. (Usually the actual classifications are unknown. Classifying the cases is the purpose of clustering.) The CROSSTABS output shows that the clusters are strongly associated with the actual classifications.

Example 2   The following program produces a clustering based on a sample of cases:

```
TITLE CLUSTERING CASES

GET FILE=CLUSDATA
COMPUTE SAMPFLAG = UNIFORM(1)

TEMPORARY
SELECT IF  SAMPFLAG < 0.10
QUICK CLUSTER  A B C D E F G H
 /CRITERIA = CLUSTER(5)
 /OUTFILE = CLUSCENT

QUICK CLUSTER  A B C D E F G H
 /FILE = CLUSCENT
 /CRITERIA = CLUSTER(5) NOUPDATE
 /SAVE = CLUSTER(CLUSTMEM)

SAVE FILE = CLUSMEMS
```

- The data are from SPSS-X file CLUSDATA.
- The TEMPORARY and SELECT IF commands select cases based on the value of variable SAMPFLAG, which is generated from a pseudo-uniform distribution. (This avoids the potential biases of sampling, say, a set of cases that happen to be first in the large group.) Approximately 10% of the cases are included.
- The first QUICK CLUSTER command clusters the sampled cases based on the values of eight variables, A through H.
- The CRITERIA subcommand specifies five clusters.
- The OUTFILE subcommand saves the final cluster centers on the file CLUSCENT.
- The second QUICK CLUSTER command reads inital cluster centers from the file CLUSCENT. These are the final cluster centers from the preceding analysis on a sample of the cases.
- The CRITERIA subcommand specifies five clusters and skips the cluster-center update phase of the clustering procedure.
- The program produces only default output. No PRINT subcommand is included.
- The program saves the cluster membership of each case in a new variable, CLUSTMEM, on the SPSS-X active file.
- The SAVE command saves the data, including the new variable, on the SPSS-X system file CLUSMEMS.

Syntax

REGRESSION

```
REGRESSION [MATRIX=[IN({file})] [OUT({file})]]
                       {*   }         {*   }

[/WIDTH={132**}]
        {n   }

[/SELECT={varname relation value}

[/MISSING={LISTWISE**     }] [INCLUDE]]
          {PAIRWISE       }
          {MEANSUBSTITUTION}

[/DESCRIPTIVES=[DEFAULTS] [MEAN] [STDDEV] [CORR] [COV]
               [VARIANCE] [XPROD] [SIG] [N] [BADCORR]
               [ALL] [NONE**]]

[/VARIABLES={varlist    }]
            {(COLLECT)**}
            {ALL        }

[/CRITERIA=[DEFAULTS**] [TOLERANCE({0.0001**}.)] [MAXSTEPS(n)]
                                  {value   }

           [PIN({0.05**})] [POUT({0.10**})]
                {value }         {value }

           [FIN({3.84 })] [FOUT({2.71 })]]
                {value}          {value}

[/STATISTICS=[DEFAULTS**] [R**] [COEFF**] [ANOVA**] [OUTS**]
             [ZPP] [LABEL] [CHA] [CI] [F] [BCOV] [SES] [LINE]
             [HISTORY] [XTX] [COND] [END] [TOL] [ALL]]

[/{NOORIGIN**}]
  {ORIGIN   }

[/REGWGT=varname]

/DEPENDENT=varlist

[/METHOD=]{STEPWISE [varlist]   } [...] [/...]
          {FORWARD [varlist]    }
          {BACKWARD [varlist]   }
          {ENTER [varlist]      }
          {REMOVE varlist       }
          {TEST(varlist)(varlist)...}

[/RESIDUALS=[DEFAULTS] [ID(varname)] [DURBIN] [{SEPARATE}]
                                              {POOLED  }
            [HISTOGRAM({ZRESID     })] [OUTLIERS({ZRESID     })]
                       {tempvarlist}            {tempvarlist}
            [NORMPROB({ZRESID     })] [SIZE({LARGE})]]
                      {tempvarlist}         {SMALL}

[/CASEWISE=[DEFAULTS] [{OUTLIERS({ 3   })}]
                       {         {value} }
                       {ALL             }

            [PLOT({ZRESID })] [{DEPENDENT PRED RESID}]]
                  {tempvar}    {tempvarlist         }

[/SCATTERPLOT=[SIZE({SMALL})] (varname,varname)...]
                    {LARGE}

[/PARTIALPLOT=[{ALL    }] [SIZE({SMALL})]]
               {varlist}         {LARGE}

[/SAVE=tempvar(newname) tempvar(newname)...]
```

Temporary variables for residuals analysis are: PRED, ADJPRED, SRESID, MAHAL, RESID, ZPRED, SDRESID, COOK, DRESID, ZRESID, SEPRED, LEVER.
**Default if the subcommand is omitted.

Contents

45.1 OVERVIEW

45.2 OPERATION

45.3 DEPENDENT Subcommand

45.4 METHOD Subcommand

45.5 VARIABLES Subcommand

45.6 REGWGT Subcommand

45.7 Equation-Control Subcommands

45.8 CRITERIA Subcommand

45.9 STATISTICS Subcommand

45.10 ORIGIN and NOORIGIN Subcommands

45.11 Analysis of Residuals

45.12 Temporary Variables

45.13 RESIDUALS Subcommand

45.14 CASEWISE Subcommand

45.15 WIDTH Subcommand

45.16 SCATTERPLOT Subcommand

45.17 PARTIALPLOT Subcommand

45.18 SAVE Subcommand

45.19 MISSING Subcommand

45.20 SELECT Subcommand

45.21 DESCRIPTIVES Subcommand

45.22 MATRIX Subcommand

45.23 OUT Keyword

45.24 IN Keyword

45

Chapter 45   REGRESSION

Procedure REGRESSION calculates multiple regression equations (weighted or unweighted) and associated statistics and plots. Several methods of selecting variables for the equations are available, as are statistics for analyzing residuals and influential observations. Several types of plots, including partial regression plots, can be displayed.

45.1
OVERVIEW

To use REGRESSION, you must name a variable list for which a correlation matrix is computed (Section 45.5), a dependent variable for a regression equation (Section 45.3), and a method of selecting blocks of independent variables (Section 45.4). For each block of variables selected, REGRESSION presents statistics for the resulting equation (including R^2 and analysis of variance), regression coefficients and associated statistics for the independent variables in the equation, and statistics for variables being considered that are not in the equation.

The options for procedure REGRESSION fall into four main groups: options for control of individual equations (Sections 45.7 through 45.10), for analysis of residuals (Sections 45.11 through 45.18), for missing values and selection of cases (Sections 45.19 through 45.20), and for reading and writing matrices (Sections 45.22 through 45.25).

Equation-Control Subcommands. With these optional subcommands, you can control the calculation and display of each equation. You can specify the statistics displayed as the equations are built (Section 45.9), the criteria used by the variable selection method (Section 45.8), and whether or not regression is through the origin (Section 45.10).

Analysis of Residuals. REGRESSION can compute 12 temporary variables for analyzing residuals. For these variables, you can control the display of the residuals summary statistics (Section 45.13) and the display of casewise residuals and related statistics (Section 45.14). You can request standardized scatterplots (Section 45.16) and partial regression plots (Section 45.17). You can also save the temporary variables to the active file (Section 45.18).

Missing Values and Selection of Cases. You can specify the treatment of cases with missing values (Section 45.19), and you can select a subset of cases for estimating the model (Section 45.20). These subcommands can be used only once.

Reading and Writing Matrices. Procedure REGRESSION can read and write matrix materials (Sections 45.23 and 45.24). The matrix materials may have been written by previous REGRESSION procedures or by other SPSS-X procedures such as CORRELATIONS or PARTIAL CORR.

45.2
OPERATION

Two subcommands are required on REGRESSION: DEPENDENT, which initiates the equation(s) and defines at least one dependent variable (see Section 45.3); and METHOD, which specifies the method to be used in selecting independent variables (see Section 45.4). All other subcommands are optional or have default values.

A Note on Defaults. There are two types of defaults. *Passive defaults* occur with no explicit effort on your part. You do not need to specify the subcommand keyword for a passive default. *Active defaults* result when you specify subcommand keywords. For example, the following three specifications are equivalent:

```
/DESCRIPTIVES
/DESCRIPTIVES=DEFAULTS
/DESCRIPTIVES=MEAN STDDEV CORR
```

The default descriptive statistics can be produced by specifying only the DESCRIPTIVES subcommand, by specifying the DEFAULTS keyword on the DESCRIPTIVES subcommand, or by explicitly stating the three default statistics (the means, standard deviations, and the correlation matrix). In this chapter, two asterisks (**) following a keyword signify a passive default and one asterisk (*) signifies an active default.

45.3
DEPENDENT
Subcommand

The DEPENDENT subcommand specifies a list of dependent variables and requests that an equation be built for each. The minimum specification is a single variable. If you name more than one dependent variable, REGRESSION uses the same independent variables and methods for each one. All methods are executed for the first dependent variable, then the second, and so on. No variable named on the DEPENDENT subcommand is treated as an independent variable in any model associated with that DEPENDENT subcommand. Each DEPENDENT subcommand initiates a new regression model, and you can specify more than one DEPENDENT subcommand for the same VARIABLES subcommand.

There are two ways to specify multiple dependent variables on the same REGRESSION command. First, you can name more than one variable on a DEPENDENT subcommand:

```
REGRESSION     VARIABLES=IQ TO ACHIEVE
               /DEPENDENT=ACHIEVE IQREPORT/STEPWISE
```

In this example, REGRESSION first uses ACHIEVE as the dependent variable, then IQREPORT as the dependent variable in a new regression model. IQREPORT is not used as an independent variable when ACHIEVE is the dependent variable, and ACHIEVE is not used as an independent variable when IQREPORT is the dependent variable.

The second way to specify multiple dependent variables on the same REGRESSION command is to use multiple DEPENDENT subcommands:

```
REGRESSION     VARIABLES=IQ TO ACHIEVE
               /DEPENDENT=ACHIEVE/STEPWISE
               /DEPENDENT=IQREPORT/ENTER ACHIEVE,SES,IQ
```

In this example, unlike the previous example, IQREPORT is an independent variable in the first model, and ACHIEVE is an independent variable in the second model. Multiple DEPENDENT subcommands are useful when you wish to specify different criteria or statistics for separate equations (see Section 45.7).

45.4
METHOD Subcommand

The METHOD subcommand specifies a variable selection method and a block of variables to be evaluated using the method. You can omit the keyword METHOD itself. You must include a variable list on the METHOD subcommand if you specify REMOVE or TEST as the method for building the regression equation or if VARIABLES=(COLLECT). Otherwise, the variable list is optional, and all variables that pass the tolerance criteria are candidates for entry into the equation (see Section 45.8).

The following are the specifications available for the METHOD subcommand:

FORWARD *Forward entry.* Variables in the block are added to the equation one at a time. At each step, the variable with the smallest probability-of-F value is entered if the value is smaller than the entry criterion, PIN, and if the variable passes the tolerance tests (see Section 45.8).

BACKWARD *Backward elimination.* Variables in the block are considered for removal. At each step, the variable with the largest probability-of-F value is removed if this value is larger than POUT (see Section 45.8). If no variables are in the equation when BACKWARD is specified, all independent variables passing the tolerance criteria are entered at that point.

STEPWISE *Stepwise selection.* If independent variables are already in the equation, the variable with the largest probability of F is removed if this value is larger than POUT (see Section 45.8). The equation is then recomputed without the removed variable, and the evaluation process is repeated until no more independent variables can be removed. Then, the independent variable that has the smallest probability of F and is not in the equation is entered if the probability value is smaller than PIN and if the variable passes the tolerance tests. Next, all variables are again examined for removal. This process continues until no variables in the equation need to be removed and no variables not in the equation are eligible for entry, or until the maximum number of steps has been reached.

ENTER *Forced entry.* Variables in a block are entered one at a time in order of decreasing tolerance but are treated as a single block for statistics computed for changes in the equation. If you want to specify an order of entry regardless of tolerance, use multiple ENTER subcommands. Specification of ENTER without a variable list enters *all* independent variables that pass the tolerance criteria.

REMOVE *Forced removal.* All named variables are removed from the equation as a single block. REMOVE requires a variable list.

TEST *Test of subsets of independent variables.* This option computes R^2 change and its test of significance for the exclusion of each specified subset from a complete model. The complete model includes all the variables named on TEST, and the subsets are removed separately. You must specify each subset in its own parentheses following the TEST keyword. A variable can be in more than one subset, and each subset can include any number of variables. All variables used in the subsets must have been previously named on the VARIABLES subcommand.

Multiple METHOD Subcommands. You can specify multiple METHOD subcommands for the same equation. For example, you may want to see how the independent variables would enter in stepwise fashion, but you may want all the variables ultimately in the equation, as in:

```
REGRESSION VARIABLES=SAVINGS TO GROWTH
     /DEPENDENT=SAVINGS/STEPWISE/ENTER
```

You can also use multiple METHOD subcommands to specify a subset of variables and their order of entry into the equation. For example, the command

```
REGRESSION VARIABLES=SAVINGS TO GROWTH
          /DEPENDENT=SAVINGS
          /ENTER POP15/ENTER POP75/ENTER INCOME/ENTER GROWTH
          /DEPENDENT=SAVINGS
          /ENTER INCOME/FORWARD
          /DEPENDENT=SAVINGS
          /FORWARD POP15 POP75 INCOME
```

produces three separate equations, each using SAVINGS as the dependent variable. Variables enter the first equation in the order POP15, POP75, INCOME, and GROWTH. In the second equation, INCOME enters first, followed by all other variables. In the third equation, only POP15, POP75, and INCOME are candidates for entry.

The following annotated example illustrates how TEST and ENTER function together. The output is shown in Figure 45.4.

```
REGRESSION DEPENDENT=SAVINGS
            /TEST(POP15,POP75)(POP15,INCOME)
            /ENTER GROWTH
```

- REGRESSION first builds the full equation of all the variables named on the first METHOD subcommand: SAVINGS regressed on POP15, POP75 and INCOME. For each set of test variables, the hypothesis degrees of freedom, sum of squares, R^2 change, F statistic, significance level of F, and the source variables being tested
- The second METHOD subcommand adds GROWTH to the equation. Variables POP15, POP75, and INCOME are already in the equation at this point.

Figure 45.4 Output for TEST and ENTER used together

```
                         * * * *   M U L T I P L E   R E G R E S S I O N   * * * *

Listwise Deletion of Missing Data

Equation Number 1    Dependent Variable..   SAVINGS   AVG AGG PERSONAL SAVINGS R

Beginning Block Number  1.  Method: Test      POP15     POP75     INCOME


Variable(s) Entered on Step Number   1..   INCOME   AVG LEVEL REAL PER-CAP DISPOSABLE INC
                                     2..   POP15    AVG % POP UNDER 15 YEARS OLD
                                     3..   POP75    AVG % POP OVER 75 YEARS OLD

Hypothesis Tests

            Sum of
     DF     Squares   Rsq Chg         F   Sig F    Source

      2    222.11012   .22581   7.15718   .0020    POP15     POP75
      2    171.31962   .17417   5.52053   .0071    POP15     INCOME

      3    269.86502            5.79734   .0019    Regression
     46    713.76323                               Residual
     49    983.62825                               Total


_____


Multiple R            .52379    Analysis of Variance
R Square              .27436                           DF    Sum of Squares    Mean Square
Adjusted R Square     .22703    Regression              3        269.86502       89.95501
Standard Error       3.93911    Residual               46        713.76323       15.51659

                                F =      5.79734     Signif F =   .0019

------------------ Variables in the Equation ------------------        ------------- Variables not in the Equation -------------

Variable          B         SE B       Beta       T   Sig T     Variable   Beta In   Partial  Min Toler      T  Sig T

INCOME    -8.33765E-04   9.3250E-04  -.184389   -.894  .3759     GROWTH     .262420  .297217   .150851    2.088  .0425
POP15        -.492143     .149043  -1.005257  -3.302  .0019
POP75       -1.567627    1.120794   -.451621  -1.399  .1686
(Constant)  31.457463    7.482163              4.204  .0001

End Block Number    1


Equation Number 1    Dependent Variable..   SAVINGS   AVG AGG PERSONAL SAVINGS R

Beginning Block Number  2.  Method: Enter      GROWTH


Variable(s) Entered on Step Number   4..   GROWTH    AVG % GROWTH RATE OF DPI

Multiple R            .58177    Analysis of Variance
R Square              .33846                           DF    Sum of Squares    Mean Square
Adjusted R Square     .27965    Regression              4        332.91725       83.22931
Standard Error       3.80266    Residual               45        650.71100       14.46024

                                F =      5.75573     Signif F =   .0008

------------------ Variables in the Equation ------------------

Variable          B         SE B       Beta       T   Sig T

INCOME    -3.37075E-04   9.3109E-04  -.074545   -.362  .7190
POP15        -.461197     .144642   -.942046  -3.189  .0026
POP75       -1.691425    1.083593   -.487287  -1.561  .1255
GROWTH        .409687     .196196    .262420   2.088  .0425
(Constant)  28.566291    7.354492              3.884  .0003

End Block Number    2   All requested variables entered.
```

45

45.5
VARIABLES Subcommand

The VARIABLES subcommand is optional and, if omitted, defaults to (COLLECT). When used, it must precede the DEPENDENT and METHOD subcommands. Only one VARIABLES subcommand is allowed.

When used, the VARIABLES subcommand specifies the variables for the analyses. Its minimum specification is a list of two variables or the keyword ALL or (COLLECT).

ALL
: *Include all user-defined variables that are on the active file.* The keyword ALL is not recommended unless you are using all of your variables in subsequent DEPENDENT and METHOD subcommands. If you specify VARIABLES=ALL, REGRESSION computes correlations for all of your variables, whether you use them in subsequent steps or not. The computation may require substantially more memory than you need to use.

(COLLECT)**
: *Include all variables named on the DEPENDENT and METHOD* subcommands. If (COLLECT) is used, the METHOD subcommand(s) must have variable lists. This is the default if the VARIABLES subcommand is omitted.

In the following example, the VARIABLES subcommand is omitted and therefore defaults to (COLLECT). (COLLECT) indicates that the program should assemble all variables named on the DEPENDENT and METHOD subcommands. These are SAVINGS, POP15, POP75, INCOME, and GROWTH.

```
REGRESSION    DEPENDENT=SAVINGS
              /METHOD=ENTER POP15 POP75 INCOME GROWTH
```

45.6
REGWGT Subcommand

The REGWGT subcommand specifies a variable for estimating weighted least-squares models. The only specification on REGWGT is the name of the variable containing the weights, as in

```
REGRESSION VARIABLES=IQ TO ACHIEVE/ REGWGT=WGT_1
           /DEPENDENT=VARY/ METHOD=ENTER/ SAVE=PRED(P) RESID(R)
```

The weights of the named variable must correspond in number and order to the cases to which they apply. Only one weight variable can be specified per REGWGT subcommand. In the above example, cases are weighted using the values of WGT_1, a variable generated by Trends procedure WLS. The predicted values and residual values are added to the active file as variables P and R.

The default display with REGWGT is the usual REGRESSION display, which includes statistics on the equation (including R^2 and analysis of variance), on variables in the equation (including regression coefficients), and on variables being considered that are not in the equation. By default, a constant is included in the equation.

REGWGT must follow the VARIABLES subcommand and precede the DEPENDENT subcommand. REGWGT can be used with any other REGRESSION subcommand except MATRIX with the IN specification (Section 45.24). REGWGT can be used with MATRIX OUT. If more than one REGWGT subcommand is specified on a REGRESSION subcommand, only the last one is executed.

Residuals. Residuals saved from equations using the REGWGT subcommand are not weighted. To compute weighted residuals for diagnostic purposes, specify

```
COMPUTE WRES = RESID * SQRT(WGT)
```

where RESID is the name of the variable containing regression residuals and WGT is the name of the weight variable specified on the REGWGT subcommand.

REGWGT is in effect for all equations and determines how the correlation matrix is built. Thus, if you specify REGWGT on a REGRESSION procedure that writes matrix materials to a system file (see Section 45.24), subsequent REGRESSION procedures using that file will also be weighted. For example, in the commands

```
REGRESSION MATRIX=OUT(*)/ REGWGT=WGT_1
            /DEPENDENT=VARY/ METHOD=ENTER

REGRESSION MATRIX=IN(*)/ DEPENDENT=VARY/ METHOD=FORWARD
```

the second REGRESSION command does *not* use the REGWGT subcommand but still performs WLS since the file it reads was created when REGWGT was in effect.

45.7
Equation-Control Subcommands

You can place three optional subcommands between the VARIABLES subcommand and the DEPENDENT subcommand: CRITERIA, STATISTICS, and ORIGIN. Use the CRITERIA subcommand to change the entry and removal criteria REGRESSION uses in developing an equation. Use the STATISTICS subcommand to control the statistics displayed. Use the ORIGIN subcommand to request regression through the origin. All equation-control subcommands are in effect for subsequent equations unless the subcommands are later specified differently.

45.8
CRITERIA Subcommand

The CRITERIA subcommand controls the statistical criteria used in building regression equations. The minimum specification is a criterion keyword and its arguments, if any. A CRITERIA subcommand must appear before the DEPENDENT subcommand that initiates an equation and after the VARIABLES subcommand. If the CRITERIA subcommand is omitted or included with no specifications, the default criteria are in effect.

Tolerance and Minimum Tolerance Criteria. Variables must pass both tolerance and minimum tolerance tests to enter and remain in a regression equation. Tolerance is the proportion of a variable's variance not accounted for by other independent variables in the equation. The minimum tolerance associated with a given variable not in the equation is the smallest tolerance any variable already in the equation would have if the given variable were included.

Testing Independent Variables. If a variable passes the tolerance criteria, it is tested further if you are using the FORWARD, BACKWARD, or STEPWISE method.

• FORWARD selects variables according to the probability of *F*-to-enter (keyword PIN). Specify FIN to use *F*-to-enter instead.

• BACKWARD selects variables according to the probability of *F*-to-remove (keyword POUT). Specify FOUT to use *F*-to-remove instead.

• STEPWISE uses both PIN and POUT. If the criterion for entry (PIN, or FIN if specified) is less stringent than the criterion for removal (POUT, or FOUT if specified), the STEPWISE method can cause the same variable to cycle in and out, over and over, until the maximum number of steps is reached. If you specify a PIN value that is larger than POUT, or a FIN value that is smaller than FOUT, REGRESSION issues a warning message and adjusts the POUT or FOUT values.

The criteria keywords are:

DEFAULTS**   *PIN(0.05), POUT(0.1), and TOLERANCE(0.0001)*. If you do not specify a CRITERIA subcommand, these are the defaults. If you have changed the criteria for an equation, use the keyword DEFAULTS to restore these defaults.

PIN(value)   *Probability of* F-*to-enter*. The default value is 0.05.

POUT(value)	*Probability of* F-*to-remove*. The default value is 0.10.
FIN(value)	F-*to-enter*. If no value is specified, the default is 3.84.
FOUT(value)	F-*to-remove*. If no value is specified, the default is 2.71.
TOLERANCE(value)	*Tolerance*. The default value is 0.0001. The default or specified value applies to both tolerance tests.
MAXSTEPS(n)	*Maximum number of steps*. For the STEPWISE method, the default is twice the number of independent variables. For the FORWARD and BACKWARD methods, the default maximum is the number of variables meeting the PIN and POUT or FIN and FOUT criteria. The MAXSTEPS value applies to the total model. The default value for the total model is the sum of the maximum number of steps over each method in the model.

REGRESSION uses the last criterion that it encounters in the subcommand. For example,

```
CRITERIA=PIN(.03) FIN(2.0)
```

first sets the criterion to a probability of *F*-to-enter of 0.03. This is overriden by the FIN specification, which sets the criterion to an *F* value of 2.0.

The following example demonstrates how the CRITERIA subcommand can be used to test independent variables in REGRESSION:

```
REGRESSION      VARS=SALARY TO VERBAL
                /CRITERIA=PIN(.1) TOL(.0001)
                /DEP=VERBAL/FORWARD
                /CRITERIA=DEFAULTS
                /DEP=VERBAL/FORWARD
```

The CRITERIA subcommand for the first equation relaxes the default criteria for entry, and the CRITERIA subcommand for the second equation reestablishes the defaults.

45.9
STATISTICS Subcommand

The STATISTICS subcommand controls the display of statistics for an equation and for the independent variables. The STATISTICS subcommand must appear before the DEPENDENT subcommand. It remains in effect for all new equations until overridden by another STATISTICS subcommand.

There are four types of STATISTICS keywords: global specifications, specifications of summary statistics for the equation, of statistics for the independent variables, and of step summary statistics.

The global specifications are:

DEFAULTS[**]	*R, ANOVA, COEFF, and OUTS*. In the absence of any STATISTICS subcommand, these are the default statistics displayed.
ALL	*Print all summary statistics except LABEL,* F, *LINE, and END*.

The keywords for specifying summary statistics for the equations are:

R[**]	*Multiple* R. Print the multiple R, R^2, adjusted R^2, and standard error of the estimate.
ANOVA[**]	*Analysis of variance table*. Print the analysis of variance table for the model, F value for multiple R, and significance level of F.
CHA	*Change in* R^2. Print the change in R^2 between steps, F value for change in R^2, and significance level of F.
BCOV	*Variance-covariance matrix for unstandardized regression coefficients*. Print a matrix with the following elements: variances of the regression estimates on the diagonal, the covariances of the regression estimates below the diagonal, and correlations of the regression estimates above the diagonal.
XTX	*Sweep matrix*. Print the current status of the sweep matrix.
COND	*Condition number bounds*. Print the lower and upper bounds for the condition number of the submatrix of the sweep matrix which contains independent variables already entered. (See Berk, 1977.)

The keywords for specifying statistics for the independent variables are:

COEFF**   *Regression coefficients.* Print the unstandardized regression coefficient (*B*), the standard error of *B*, standardized regression coefficient (beta), *t* value for *B*, and two-tailed significance level of *t* for each variable in the equation.

OUTS**   *Coefficients and statistics for variables not yet in the equation.* Print the standardized regression coefficient (beta) if the variable were to enter the equation at the next step, *t* value for *B*, significance level of *t*, partial correlation with the dependent variable controlling for all variables in the equation, and minimum tolerance.

ZPP   *Correlation, part, and partial correlation.* Print the zero-order correlation of each independent variable in the equation with the dependent variable, the part correlation for each independent variable, and the partial correlation with the dependent variable controlling for the other independent variables in the equation.

CI   *95% confidence interval for the unstandardized regression coefficient.*

SES   *Approximate standard error of beta.* (See Meyer & Younger, 1976.)

TOL   *Tolerance and minimum tolerance.*

LABEL   *Variable labels.*

F   F *value for* B *and its significance level.* Displayed instead of the *t* value. Significance of *t* is the same as the significance of *F* in this case.

The keywords for specifying step summary statistics are:

LINE   *Print a single summary line of output for each step performed. Print full output on completion of each method.* This option differs from END, which prints the full output only on completion of the model.

HISTORY *Print a final summary report.* The contents are the summary statistics computed at each step.

END   *Print one line per step (for methods STEPWISE, FORWARD, or BACKWARD) or one line per block (ENTER, REMOVE). Print full output only on completion of the model.* This option differs from LINE, which prints the full output on completion of each method block.

Figure 45.9 shows a display produced by specifying ALL on the STATISTICS subcommand.

45.10
ORIGIN and NOORIGIN Subcommands

The ORIGIN and NOORIGIN subcommands control whether or not the constant in a regression equation is suppressed. ORIGIN requests regression through the origin and suppresses the constant term. Once specified, ORIGIN remains in effect until NOORIGIN is requested. If neither subcommand is specified, NOORIGIN is the default and all equations include a constant term (intercept).

The subcommands are simply ORIGIN or NOORIGIN, without additional specifications. ORIGIN or NOORIGIN must be specified before the DEPENDENT and METHOD subcommands they modify, as in

```
REGRESSION    VARIABLES=GNP TO M1
              /ORIGIN
              /DEPENDENT=GNP/FORWARD
```

If you request regression through the origin, all sums of squares are uncorrected and R^2 statistics are not directly interpretable (see Montgomery & Peck, 1982).

When you specify the MATRIX subcommand (see Section 45.22) you cannot use both ORIGIN and NOORIGIN on the same REGRESSION procedure. If you want to use matrices for building multiple regression models, some passing through the origin and others not, specify separate REGRESSION commands for those with ORIGIN and those with NOORIGIN.

ORIGIN/NOORIGIN determines the way the correlation matrix is built. These keywords *cannot* be used to reverse their effect if reading matrix materials. In fact, whichever is specified on the REGRESSION command that writes matrix

Figure 45.9   Output for STATISTICS=ALL

```
* * * *   M U L T I P L E   R E G R E S S I O N   * * * *

Listwise Deletion of Missing Data

Equation Number 1   Dependent Variable..   SAVINGS   AVG AGG PERSONAL SAVINGS R

Beginning Block Number  1.  Method:  Enter

Variable(s) Entered on Step Number  1..    GROWTH   AVG % GROWTH RATE OF DPI
                                    2..    POP75    AVG % POP OVER 75 YEARS OLD
                                    3..    INCOME   AVG LEVEL REAL PER-CAP DISPOSABLE INC
                                    4..    POP15    AVG % POP UNDER 15 YEARS OLD

                                                          Analysis of Variance
Multiple R            .58177                                             DF    Sum of Squares    Mean Square
R Square              .33846     R Square Change    .33846   Regression    4      332.91725        83.22931
Adjusted R Square     .27965     F Change          5.75573   Residual     45      650.71100        14.46024
Standard Error       3.80266     Signif F Change    .0008
                                                             F =     5.75573    Signif F =   .0008

Condition number bounds:     6.629,      66.101

Var-Covar Matrix of Regression Coefficients (B)
Below Diagonal: Covariance   Above: Correlation

              GROWTH       POP75      INCOME       POP15

GROWTH        .03849     -.05471      .25546      .10246
POP75        -.01163     1.17417     -.36704      .76537
INCOME     4.667E-05  -3.703E-04   8.669E-07      .17989
POP15         .00291      .11996   2.423E-05      .02092

XTX Matrix

              GROWTH       POP75      INCOME       POP15   I   SAVINGS
                                                          I
GROWTH       1.07430     -.14601      .44968      .25877   I   -.26242
POP75        -.14601     6.62906    -1.60490     4.80179   I    .48729
INCOME        .44968    -1.60490     2.88418      .74443   I    .07454
POP15         .25877     4.80179      .74443     5.93762   I    .94205
-----------------------------------------------------------+
SAVINGS       .26242     -.48729     -.07454     -.94205   I    .66154



Equation Number 1   Dependent Variable..   SAVINGS   AVG AGG PERSONAL SAVINGS R


--------------------------------- Variables in the Equation ---------------------------------

Variable           B         SE B     95% Confdnce Intrvl B      Beta    SE Beta  Correl  Part Cor  Partial  Tolerance      T

GROWTH        .409687      .196196      .014529     .804845    .262420   .125671  .304787  .253183  .297217   .930841    2.088
POP75       -1.691425     1.083593    -3.873892     .491041   -.487287   .312175  .316521 -.189260 -.226637   .150851   -1.561
INCOME   -3.37075E-04  9.3109E-04     -.002212     .001538   -.074545   .205913  .220340 -.043894 -.053889   .346719    -.362
POP15        -.461197      .144642     -.752520    -.169875   -.942046   .295446 -.455538 -.386604 -.429294   .168418   -3.189
(Constant)  28.566291     7.354492    13.753602   43.378980                                                              3.884

-------- in --------

Variable   Sig T

GROWTH     .0425
POP75      .1255
INCOME     .7190
POP15      .0026
(Constant) .0003


End Block Number  1   All requested variables entered.


* * * * * * * * * * * * * * * * * * * * * * * * * * * * * * * *

                        Summary table
                        -------------

Step  MultR   Rsq   AdjRsq  F(Eqn)  SigF  RsqCh    FCh SigCh        Variable  BetaIn  Correl
 1                                                         In:  GROWTH    .3048   .3048   AVG % GROWTH RATE OF DPI
 2                                                         In:  POP75     .3090   .3165   AVG % POP OVER 75 YEARS OLD
 3                                                         In:  INCOME    .0436   .2203   AVG LEVEL REAL PER-CAP DISPOS
 4   .5818  .3385  .2797   5.756   .001  .3385   5.756  .001  In:  POP15    -.9420  -.4555  AVG % POP UNDER 15 YEARS OLD
```

materials to a system file must also be used on any subsequent procedure that reads that matrix file. For example, in the commands

```
REGRESSION MATRIX=OUT(*)/ VARIABLES=GNP TO M1
                /ORIGIN
                /DEPENDENT=GNP/FORWARD

REGRESSION MATRIX=IN(*)/ VARIABLES=GNP TO M1
                /ORIGIN
                /DEPENDENT=GNP/ ENTER
```

the second REGRESSION procedure *must* specify ORIGIN because ORIGIN was specified on the REGRESSION command the wrote the matrix materials.

45.11
Analysis of Residuals

Use the following subcommands for analysis of residuals: RESIDUALS, CASE-WISE, SCATTERPLOT, PARTIALPLOT, and SAVE. Any or all of these can be specified in any order. None of them can be specified if you are reading matrix materials from the active file. If you are reading a matrix from an outside file, residuals can be requested if the active file contains the actual data. For each analysis, REGRESSION can calculate up to 12 temporary variables. These variables contain several types of residuals, predicted values, and related measures. Optionally, these variables can be added to the active file for analysis with other SPSS-X procedures.

45.12
Temporary Variables

The following temporary variables are available for the analysis of residuals:

PRED   *Unstandardized predicted values.*

RESID   *Unstandardized residuals.*

DRESID   *Deleted residuals.*

ADJPRED   *Adjusted predicted values.*

ZPRED   *Standardized predicted values.*

ZRESID   *Standardized residuals.*

SRESID   *Studentized residuals.*

SDRESID   *Studentized deleted residuals. (See Hoaglin & Welsch, 1978.)*

SEPRED   *Standard errors of the predicted values.*

MAHAL   *Mahalanobis' distances.*

COOK   *Cook's distances. (See Cook, 1977.)*

LEVER   *Leverage values. (See Velleman & Welsch, 1981.)*

If you use the RESIDUALS or CASEWISE subcommands, REGRESSION computes the four temporary variables PRED, RESID, ZPRED, and ZRESID by default. Other residuals are expensive to calculate for large numbers of cases and/or variables, and you must specifically request them, as in

```
RESIDUALS=DEFAULTS NORMPROB(DRESID)
```

The residual summary statistics table in the printed output contains 4 or 12 entries, depending on whether you request an optional residuals statistic. Casewise plots are performed only for default residuals and those you specifically request.

45.13
RESIDUALS Subcommand

The RESIDUALS subcommand controls the display and labeling of summary information on outliers as well as the display of the Durbin-Watson statistic and of histograms and normal probability plots for the temporary variables. If you use the RESIDUALS subcommand, it must follow the last method keyword for an equation. All calculations and plots requested on the subcommand are based on the regression equation produced as a result of the last method specified. Specifications for the RESIDUALS subcommand are:

DEFAULTS*	*SIZE(LARGE), DURBIN, NORMPROB(ZRESID), HISTO-GRAM(ZRESID), and OUTLIERS(ZRESID).*
SIZE(plotsize)	*Plot size.* The size can be SMALL or LARGE. The default is LARGE. Four small histograms or normal probability plots can be displayed on a single page if the page width is at least 120 (see Section 45.15) and the page length is at least 58 (see Chapter 4).
HISTOGRAM(varlist)	*A histogram of the temporary variable or variables named.* The default variable is ZRESID. Other variables that can be plotted include ZPRED, ADJPRED, SRESID, and SDRESID.
NORMPROB(varlist)	*A normal probability (P-P) plot of standardized values.* The default variable is ZRESID. Other variables that can be plotted are PRED, RESID, ZPRED, DRESID, ADJPRED, SRESID, and SDRESID.
OUTLIERS(varlist)	*The 10 worst outliers based on values of the variables specified.* The default variable is ZRESID. Other variables that can be used include RESID, SRESID, SDRESID, DRESID, MAHAL, and COOK.
DURBIN	*Durbin-Watson test statistic.*
ID(varname)	*Use the values from this variable to label casewise or outlier plots.* Any variable in your file can be named. If ID(varname) is not specified, cases are identified by case number. ID also labels the list of cases obtained from the CASEWISE subcommand (see Section 45.14).
POOLED	*Display pooled plots and statistics for selected and unselected cases.* The default is SEPARATE, so that if SELECT is in effect, separate copies of the summary statistics and all plots are produced for selected and unselected cases.

For example,

```
RESID=DEFAULT SIZE(SMALL) ID(COUNTRY)
```

requests residuals statistics and plots. DEFAULT implies a normal probability plot of standardized residuals, a histogram of standardized residuals, a table showing the 10 worst outliers based on the values of the standardized residuals, the Durbin-Watson statistic, and the large plot size. SIZE(SMALL) overrides the large size. ID(COUNTRY) names COUNTRY as a variable to identify the cases on outlier plots.

45.14
CASEWISE Subcommand

The CASEWISE subcommand identifies a variable for casewise plotting, specifies variables for casewise printed output, and controls selection of the cases. Variables that can be included in the display are the 12 temporary variables and the dependent variable. All candidate variables cannot be displayed in one analysis. The widest page (see Section 45.15) allows a maximum of eight variables in a display. However, you can save all the temporary variables (see Section 45.18) and use them in subsequent procedures such as LIST, REPORT, or PLOT.

The CASEWISE subcommand has the following specifications:

DEFAULTS*	*OUTLIERS(3), PLOT(ZRESID), DEPENDENT, PRED, and RESID.*
OUTLIERS(value)	*Limit plot to outliers defined by this value.* The plot contains those cases whose absolute value is at least as large as the value you specify. The default value is 3. The alternative to a casewise plot of outliers is a plot of all cases (keyword ALL). This is not recommended for large files because it results in a line being printed for each case.
ALL	*Include all cases in the casewise plot.* Alternative to the OUTLIERS keyword.

PLOT(varname)   *Plot the values of this temporary variable in the casewise plot.* The default variable is ZRESID. You can also specify RESID and DRESID, both of which will be standardized for the plot, or the already standardized SRESID and SDRESID.

varlist   *Display the values of the specified variables.* You can specify a subset of the 12 temporary variables, but not all 12. The defaults are DEPENDENT (the dependent variable), PRED, and RESID.

For example, the subcommand

```
CASEWISE=DEFAULTS ALL MAHAL COOK SRESID SDRESID
```

plots the standardized residuals in the casewise plot and displays the dependent variable SAVINGS and the six temporary variables PRED, RESID, SRESID, SDRESID, MAHAL, and COOK for all cases. Figure 45.14 shows the output from this subcommand. The variable COUNTRY was declared as the ID variable on the RESIDUALS subcommand.

Figure 45.14 Casewise plot for 50 nations

```
                          * * * *   M U L T I P L E   R E G R E S S I O N   * * * *

Equation Number 1    Dependent Variable..    SAVINGS   AVG AGG PERSONAL SAVINGS R


Casewise Plot of Standardized Residual

*: Selected   M: Missing

                 -3.0      0.0      3.0
Case # COUNTRY    0:..............:0    SAVINGS    *PRED    *RESID    *SRESID    *SDRESID    *MAHAL    *COOK D
   1 Australi    .       .  *   .        11.43    10.5663    .8637     .2352      .2328     2.3379    .0008
   2 Austria     .       * .   .         12.07    11.4538    .6162     .1728      .1709     4.9187    .0008
   3 Belgium     .       . *   .         13.17    10.9511   2.2189     .6108      .6065     3.3066    .0072
   4 Bolivia     .      *. .   .          5.75     6.4484   -.6984    -.1925     -.1904     3.4041    .0007
   5 Brazil      .       .* .  .         12.88     9.3271   3.5529     .9686      .9679     2.4283    .0140
   6 Canada      .       .*    .          8.79     9.1066   -.3166    -.0908     -.0898     6.7815    .0003
   7 Chile       . *     .     .           .60     8.8422  -8.2422   -2.2091    -2.3134      .8476    .0378
   8 Colombia    .      *. .   .          4.98     6.4317  -1.4517    -.3932     -.3895     1.8278    .0019
   9 Costa Ri    .       .  *  .         10.78     5.6549   5.1251    1.4017     1.4173     2.7179    .0321
  10 Denmark     .       .  *  .         16.85    11.4497   5.4003    1.4669     1.4865     2.0932    .0288
  11 Ecuador     .      *. .   .          3.59     5.9957  -2.4057    -.6538     -.6496     2.1426    .0058
  12 Finland     .      *. .   .         11.24    12.9210  -1.6810    -.4639     -.4598     3.5301    .0044
  13 France      .       . *   .         12.64    10.1646   2.4754     .7004      .6964     5.6940    .0155
  14 Germany     .       *. .  .         12.55    12.7306   -.1806    -.0497     -.0492     3.3005    .0000
  15 Greece      .      *. .   .         10.67    13.7863  -3.1163    -.8622     -.8597     3.7544    .0159
  16 Guatemal    .      *  .   .          3.01     6.3653  -3.3553    -.9103     -.9086     1.9841    .0107
  17 Honduras    .       .* .  .          7.70     6.9900    .7100     .1926      .1905     1.9639    .0005
  18 Iceland     .    * . .    .          1.27     7.4805  -6.2105   -1.6940    -1.7312     2.4743    .0435
  19 India       .       .* .  .          9.00     8.4914    .5086     .1388      .1373     2.5212    .0003
  20 Ireland     .       . *   .         11.34     7.9490   3.3910    1.0047     1.0048     9.4195    .0544
  21 Italy       .       . *   .         14.28    12.3533   1.9267     .5244      .5201     2.2790    .0039
  22 Jamaica     .      *. .   .          7.72    10.7385  -3.0185    -.8564     -.8538     5.9172    .0240
  23 Japan       .       .  *  .         21.10    15.8185   5.2815    1.5760     1.6032     9.9621    .1428
  24 Korea       .    * . .    .          3.98    10.0870  -6.1070   -1.6571    -1.6910     1.9992    .0356
  25 Libya       .      *. .   .          8.89    11.7195  -2.8295   -1.0871    -1.0893     1.3687    .2681
  26 Luxembou    .      *. .   .         10.35    12.0208  -1.6708    -.4556     -.4556     3.2511    .0040
  27 Malaysia    .      *. .   .          4.71     7.6805  -2.9705    -.8080     -.8048     2.2178    .0091
  28 Malta       .       . *   .         15.48    12.5052   2.9748     .8153      .8123     2.9108    .0115
  29 Netherla    .       . *   .         14.65    14.2244    .4256     .1174      .1161     3.4601    .0003
  30 New Zeal    .       .* .  .         10.67     8.3845   2.2855     .6180      .6137     1.6767    .0044
  31 Nicaragu    .       .* .  .          7.30     6.6536    .6464     .1744      .1725     1.4872    .0003
  32 Norway      .       *. .  .         10.25    11.1217   -.8717    -.2349     -.2325     1.3687    .0006
  33 Panama      .     * . .   .          4.44     7.7342  -3.2942    -.8837     -.8815      .9297    .0063
  34 Paraguay    .     * . .   .          2.02     8.1458  -6.1258   -1.6699    -1.7049     2.4193    .0416
  35 Peru        .       . . * .         12.70     6.1606   6.5394    1.7785     1.8239     2.2074    .0440
  36 Philippi    .       . . * .         12.78     6.1050   6.6750    1.8146     1.8638     2.1685    .0452
  37 Portugal    .       *. .  .         12.49    13.2586   -.7686    -.2127     -.2104     3.7803    .0010
  38 South Af    .       .* .  .         11.14    10.6569    .4831     .1314      .1299     2.2101    .0002
  39 South Rh    .       . *   .         13.30    12.0087   1.2913     .3707      .3671     6.8996    .0053
  40 Spain       .       *. .  .         11.77    12.4413   -.6713    -.1838     -.1818     2.8091    .0006
  41 Sweden      .     * . .   .          6.86    11.1201  -4.2601   -1.1970    -1.2029     5.0955    .0406
  42 Switzerl    .       . *   .         14.13    11.6431   2.4869     .6795      .6754     2.6262    .0073
  43 Taiwan      .       . *   .         11.90     9.3639   2.5361     .6945      .6905     2.8399    .0082
  44 Tunisia     .      *. .   .          2.81     5.6280  -2.8180    -.7703     -.7668     2.6738    .0096
  45 Turkey      .      *. .   .          5.13     7.7957  -2.6657    -.7153     -.7114      .9625    .0042
  46 U.K.        .      *. .   .          7.81    10.5025  -2.6925    -.7533     -.7496     4.7290    .0150
  47 U.S.        .       *. .  .          7.56     8.6712  -1.1112    -.3580     -.3545    15.3703    .0128
  48 Uruguay     .      *. .   .          9.24    11.5040  -2.2640    -.6269     -.6226     3.8193    .0085
  49 Venezuel    .     * . .   .          9.22     5.5874   3.6326     .9994      .9993     3.2478    .0189
  50 Zambia      .       . .  *.         18.56     8.8091   9.7509    2.6509     2.8536     2.1722    .0966
Case # COUNTRY    0:..............:0    SAVINGS    *PRED    *RESID    *SRESID    *SDRESID    *MAHAL    *COOK D
                 -3.0      0.0      3.0
```

**45.15
WIDTH Subcommand**   You can control the width of output from REGRESSION by using the WIDTH subcommand. The width you choose affects the volume of regression statistics displayed and the amount of information displayed in a casewise plot. This is especially so when the width is quite narrow.

The default width is 132 characters, but you can specify any width from 72 to 132, as in:

```
REGRESSION     WIDTH=120
               /VARIABLES=Y TO X10
               /DEPENDENT=Y
               /ENTER
```

The WIDTH subcommand can appear anywhere in a REGRESSION program. If you have more than one WIDTH subcommand, REGRESSION uses the width from the last specification. If you include both the WIDTH subcommand and SET WIDTH, (see Chapter 4), the narrower of the two widths will be in effect.

45.16
SCATTERPLOT Subcommand

The SCATTERPLOT subcommand names pairs of variables for scatterplots and controls the size of plots. The minimum specification is a pair of variables in parentheses. The first variable named is plotted along the vertical axis, and the second variable is plotted along the horizontal axis. Different symbols represent single and multiple points at individual print positions.

The SCATTERPLOT subcommand has the following specifications:

SIZE(plotsize)   *Set the size of the plots.* The default is SMALL. The LARGE size requires substantially more computer memory and should be used only when detailed plots are necessary. Four small scatterplots can fit on a single page if the page width is at least 121 (see Section 45.15) and the page length is at least 58 (see Chapter 4).

(varname,varname)   *Plot the variables specified.* Specify as many pairs, each within parentheses, as you want plots. You can plot any variable named on the VARIABLES subcommand as well as most of the temporary variables. For the SCATTERPLOT subcommand, the keyword for each of the eligible temporary variables must be preceded by an asterisk: *PRED, *RESID, *ZPRED, *ZRESID, *DRESID, *ADJPRED, *SRESID, and *SDRESID. You can also save any of the 12 temporary variables—including SEPRED, MAHAL, COOK, and LEVER—on the active file (see Section 45.18) and plot them later by using the PLOT procedure.

All scatterplots are standardized. That is, specifying *RESID is the same as specifying *ZRESID, and *PRED is the same as *ZPRED. To obtain unstandardized scatterplots, save temporary variables on the active file for subsequent processing with procedure PLOT.

The following subcommand specifies two scatterplots: residuals against predicted values and residuals against a dependent variable.

```
SCATTERPLOT (*RES,*PRE)(*RES,SAVINGS)
```

45.17
PARTIALPLOT Subcommand

Use the PARTIALPLOT subcommand to request partial regression plots and to control the size of these plots. Partial regression plots are scatterplots of the residuals of the dependent variable against the residuals of a specified independent variable when both of these variables are regressed on the other independent variables. At least two independent variables must be in the equation if partial plots are to be produced.

All plots are standardized and are displayed in descending order of the standard error in *B*. The PARTIALPLOT subcommand has the following specifications:

SIZE(plotsize)   *Set the size of the plots.* The default is SMALL, and the alternative is LARGE. Four small partial plots can fit on a single page if the page width is at least 121 (see Section 45.15), and the page length is at least 58 (see Chapter 4).

varlist   *List of variables to be plotted.* You can specify any of the variables entered into the equation. The default is all the independent variables, and you can make it explicit with the keyword ALL.

Figure 45.17 displays the partial regression plots produced by the following command:

```
REGRESSION VARIABLES=SAVINGS TO GROWTH
    /DEP=SAVINGS/ENTER
    /RESIDUALS=DEFAULTS/PARTIALPLOT
```

Figure 45.17   Partial regression plots

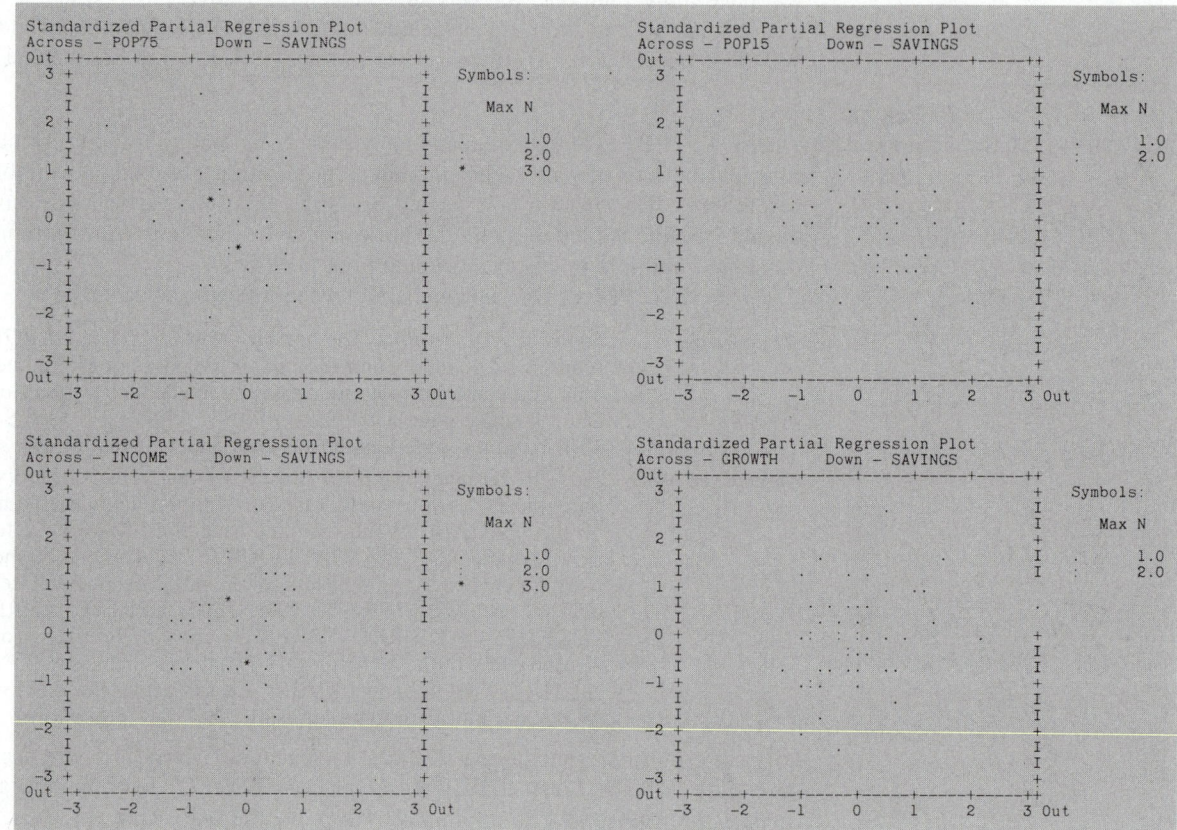

45.18
SAVE Subcommand

Use the SAVE subcommand to save any or all of the 12 temporary variables. The general form of the SAVE subcommand is:

SAVE tempvar(newname), tempvar(newname),.../

where *tempvar* is a temporary variable, and *newname* is a name that conforms to all SPSS-X conventions for naming variables. The name you supply for *newname* must be unique to all variables on the active file.

For example,

```
REGRESSION      VARIABLES=SAVINGS TO GROWTH
    /DEPENDENT=SAVINGS/ENTER
    /SAVE PRED(PREDSR)
/PLOT PLOT PREDSR WITH SAVINGS
```

saves the predicted values on the variable named PREDSR. Then the PLOT procedure plots the predicted values against the values of the dependent variable SAVINGS. Figure 45.18 shows a portion of the output from these commands.

When replacing the active file with matrix materials (see Section 45.24), you cannot use the SAVE subcommand.

Figure 45.18   A plot using a saved temporary variable

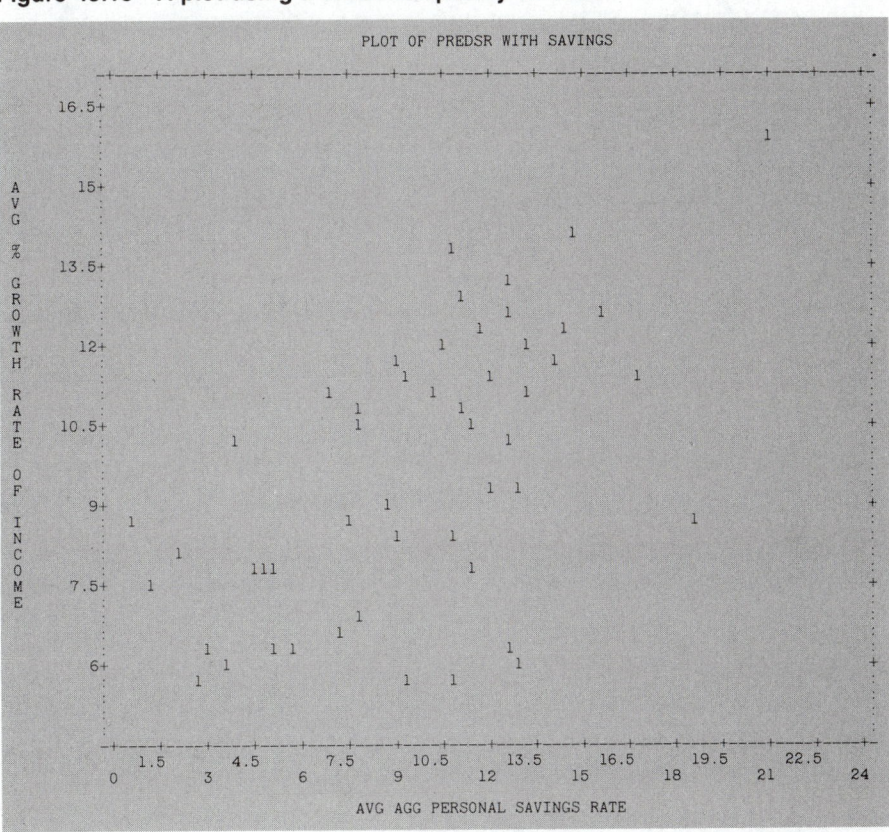

45.19
MISSING Subcommand

Use the MISSING subcommand and the following keywords to specify alternative missing-value treatments. The MISSING subcommand controls what part of the data is used to create the correlation matrix.

LISTWISE**   *Delete cases with missing values listwise.* This is the default. REGRESSION uses only those cases that have valid values for all variables named on the VARIABLES subcommand.

PAIRWISE   *Delete cases with missing values pairwise.* REGRESSION computes each correlation coefficient by using cases with complete data for the pair of variables correlated.

MEANSUBSTITUTION   *Replace missing values with the variable mean.* All cases are used in the analyses. The substitutions are treated as valid observations.

INCLUDE   *Include cases with user-missing values.* You can use this option with one of the other MISSING specifications. If you specify INCLUDE, REGRESSION treats all user-missing values (but not system-missing values) as valid, cases are not excluded because of user-missing values, and with MEAN-SUBSTITUTION, user-missing values are included in the computation of means.

When residuals and predicted values are requested (see Sections 45.11–45.18), they are created missing or valid based on whether any values they require are missing or not. Predicted values are valid if all values of the independent variables entered in the equation are valid. Residual values are valid if all values of the independent variables entered in the equation are valid and if the values of the dependent variable are valid.

ANNOTATED EXAMPLE FOR REGRESSION

The task is to predict the average aggregate personal savings rate of a country as a function of the age distribution of the population, the average level of real per capita disposable income, and the average percentage growth rate of real per capita disposable income. The data are 50 cases taken from an example in Belsley, Kuh, and Welsch (1980).

The variables are

- SAVINGS—the average aggregate personal savings rate in a country during the period 1960–1970.
- POP15—the average percentage of the population under 15 years of age during the period 1960–1970.
- POP75—the average percentage of the population over 75 years of age during the period 1960–1970.
- INCOME—the average level of real per capita disposable income during the period 1960–1970, measured in United States dollars.
- GROWTH—the average percentage growth rate of INCOME during the period 1960–1970.

The SPSS-X commands are

```
DATA LIST FILE=COUNTRY/COUNTRY 1-8(A) SAVINGS POP15 POP75
               INCOME GROWTH 11-60
VAR LABELS     SAVINGS 'Avg Agg Personal Savings Rate'
               POP15 'Avg % Pop under 15 years old'
               POP75 'Avg % Pop over 75 years old'
               INCOME 'Avg level real per-cap disposable inc'
               GROWTH 'Avg % growth rate of dpi'
PRINT FORMATS  SAVINGS TO GROWTH(F7.2)
REGRESSION  VARS=SAVINGS TO GROWTH/DEP=SAVINGS/ENTER
    /RESID=DEFAULT SIZE(SMALL) ID(COUNTRY)
    /CASEWISE=DEFAULT ALL MAHAL COOK SRESID SDRESID LEVER
    /SCATTERPLOT (*RES,*PRE)/PARTIALPLOT
```

- The DATA LIST command defines the variables in file handle COUNTRY. The VAR LABELS command assigns labels to the variables. The PRINT FORMATS command assigns a print format to the variables.
- The REGRESSION command requests a direct-entry regression analysis with variable SAVINGS as the dependent variable.
- The RESIDUALS subcommand requests the default residuals results. In addition, the SIZE(SMALL) keyword overrides the default plot sizes so that small plots are displayed. The ID(COUNTRY) keyword specifies that the values for variable COUNTRY are to be used to label outlier plots. Figure A shows the residuals statistics and outlier plots. Figure B displays the histogram of the standardized residuals and the normal probability plot.
- The CASEWISE subcommand requests a casewise plot of the standardized residuals for all cases. The dependent variable and the temporary variables PRED, RESID, MAHAL, COOK, SRESID, and SDRESID are also listed for all cases. Because of the page width limitation, the specified variable LEVER is not displayed. The output is shown in Figure 45.14.
- The SCATTERPLOT subcommand requests a plot of the residuals against the predicted values. Since *RES is specified first, it is plotted along the vertical axis. Figure C shows the plot.
- The PARTIALPLOT subcommand requests separate partial regression plots of the residuals of the dependent variable SAVINGS against the residuals of each independent variable when both variables are regressed on the rest of the independent variables. The output is shown in Figure 45.17.

A Residuals statistics and outliers

```
Residuals Statistics:

                  Min         Max     Mean   Std Dev    N

*PRED          5.5874     15.8185   9.6710   2.6066    50
*ZPRED        -1.5666      2.3584    .0000   1.0000    50
*SEPRED         .7344      2.7722   1.1481    .3612    50
*ADJPRED       5.2366     14.9290   9.7052   2.6865    50
*RESID        -8.2422      9.7509    .0000   3.6441    50
*ZRESID       -2.1675      2.5642    .0000    .9583    50
*SRESID       -2.2091      2.6509   -.0031   1.0053    50
*DRESID       -8.5616     10.4213   -.0342   4.0378    50
*SDRESID      -2.3134      2.8536    .0000   1.0293    50
*MAHAL          .8476     25.0613   3.9200   3.9842    50
*COOK D         .0000       .2681    .0229    .0440    50
*LEVER          .0173       .5115    .0800    .0813    50

Total Cases =       50


Durbin-Watson Test =    1.68579


Outliers - Standardized Residual

  Case #   COUNTRY      *ZRESID

     50    Zambia      2.56423
      7    Chile      -2.16749
     36    Philippi    1.75534
     35    Peru        1.71969
     18    Iceland    -1.63321
     34    Paraguay   -1.61093
     24    Korea      -1.60598
     10    Denmark     1.42014
     23    Japan       1.38890
      9    Costa Ri    1.34776
```

B Histogram and normal probability plot

```
Histogram - Standardized Residual

NExp N      (* = 1 Cases,    . : = Normal Curve)
0  .04   Out
0  .08   3.00
1  .20   2.67 *
0  .45   2.33
0  .91   2.00 .
2 1.67   1.67 *:.
3 2.74   1.33 **:
3 4.03   1.00 ***.
7 5.31    .67 ****:.**
4 6.26    .33 ****.
6 6.62    .00 ******.
8 6.26   -.33 *****:.**
9 5.31   -.67 ****:.****
3 4.03  -1.00 ***.
0 2.74  -1.33    .
3 1.67  -1.67 *:.*
0  .91  -2.00 .
1  .45  -2.33 *
0  .20  -2.67
0  .08  -3.00
0  .04   Out
```

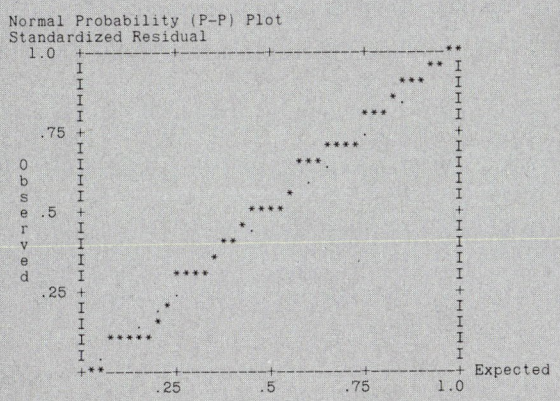

```
Normal Probability (P-P) Plot
Standardized Residual
```

C Residuals against predicted values

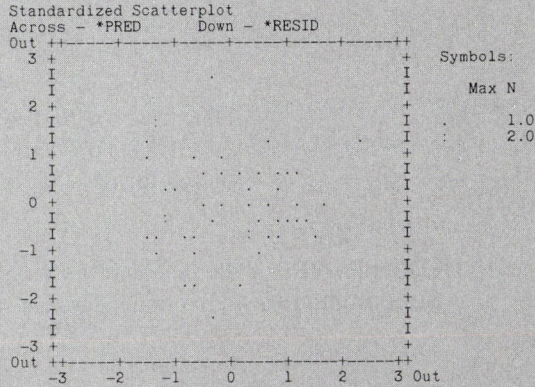

45.20
SELECT Subcommand

By default, REGRESSION considers all cases on the active file for inclusion in the analysis. Use the SELECT subcommand to select a subset of your cases for computing the regression equation. Only cases for which the logical expression on SELECT is true are included in the calculation of the correlation matrix and regression statistics. All other cases, including those with missing values for the variable named on SELECT, are not selected. By default, residuals and predicted values are calculated and reported for both selected and unselected cases (see Section 45.11).

The general form of the SELECT subcommand is as follows:

SELECT= varname relation value/

where *relation* can be EQ, NE, LT, LE, GT, or GE.

Do not use a variable from a temporary transformation as a selection variable. If you use a variable created from a temporary transformation (with IF and COMPUTE statements), the variable will disappear when the data are read a second time. The file will be read more than once if you request residuals processing. If the selection variable is the result of a temporary recode specification, the value of the variable will change when the file is read a second time.

The SELECT subcommand does not override SELECT IF and SAMPLE commands placed before the REGRESSION command in your SPSS-X job. No residuals or predictors are generated for cases deleted from the active file with SELECT IF or SAMPLE commands.

The following example demonstrates the use of the SELECT subcommand:

```
REGRESSION  SELECT SEX EQ 'BOYS'
            /VARIABLES=IQ TO ACHIEVE
            /DEPENDENT=ACHIEVE
            /METHOD=STEP
            /RESIDUALS=NORMPROB
```

Only cases with the value BOYS for the variable SEX are included in the REGRESSION correlation matrix. Separate normal probability plots are displayed for boys and girls.

45.21
DESCRIPTIVES Subcommand

By default, REGRESSION does not display descriptive statistics. However, you can obtain descriptive statistics by using the DESCRIPTIVES subcommand. DESCRIPTIVES provides univariate statistics (such as the mean and standard deviation) as well as bivariate statistic (such as the correlation coefficient).

You can use the following keyword specifications on DESCRIPTIVES to display statistics for all variables on the VARIABLES subcommand:

NONE**	*Do not display descriptive statistics.* This is the default if the subcommand is omitted.
DEFAULTS*	*MEAN, STDDEV, and CORR.* These are the defaults if the subcommand is included.
ALL	*MEAN, STDDEV, VARIANCE, and CORR.*
MEAN	*Variable means.*
STDDEV	*Variable standard deviations.*
VARIANCE	*Variable variances.*
COV	*Covariance matrix.*
XPROD	*Cross-product deviations from the mean.*
CORR	*Correlation matrix.*
SIG	*One-tailed significance levels for the correlation coefficients.*
BADCORR	*Display the correlation matrix only if some coefficients cannot be computed.*
N	*Numbers of cases used to compute correlation coefficients.* Use this option with PAIRWISE or MEANSUBSTITUTION treatments of missing values (see Section 45.19).

The following example produces the output displayed in Figure 45.21:

```
REGRESSION VARS=SAVINGS TO GROWTH
           /DESCRIPTIVES=DEFAULTS VARIANCE SIG COV XPROD
           /DEP=SAVINGS/ENTER
```

Figure 45.21   Example of DESCRIPTIVES subcommand output

```
                  * * * *   M U L T I P L E   R E G R E S S I O N   * * * *

Listwise Deletion of Missing Data

              Mean    Std Dev    Variance    Label

SAVINGS      9.671      4.480      20.074    AVG AGG PERSONAL SAVINGS RATE
POP15       35.090      9.152      83.754    AVG % POP UNDER 15 YEARS OLD
POP75        2.293      1.291       1.666    AVG % POP OVER 75 YEARS OLD
INCOME    1106.778    990.851  981785.907    AVG LEVEL REAL PER-CAP DISPOSABLE INC
GROWTH       3.758      2.870       8.236    AVG % GROWTH RATE OF DPI

N of Cases =    50

Correlation, Covariance, 1-tailed Sig, Cross-Product:

              SAVINGS        POP15        POP75         INCOME        GROWTH

SAVINGS         1.000        -.456         .317           .220          .305
               20.074     -18.679        1.830        978.181         3.919
                 .999         .000         .013           .062          .016
              983.628     -915.253      89.694      47930.881       192.032

POP15           -.456        1.000        -.908          -.756         -.048
              -18.679       83.754     -10.732       -6856.989        -1.256
                 .000         .999         .000           .000          .371
             -915.253     4103.951     -525.852     -335992.453       -61.549

POP75            .317        -.908        1.000           .787          .025
                1.830      -10.732        1.666        1006.527          .094
                 .013         .000         .999           .000          .431
               89.694     -525.852       81.638      49319.844         4.596

INCOME           .220        -.756         .787          1.000         -.129
              978.181    -6856.989     1006.527      981785.907      -368.187
                 .062         .000         .000           .999          .185
            47930.881  -335992.453    49319.844    48107509.444    -18041.139

GROWTH           .305        -.048         .025          -.129         1.000
                3.919       -1.256         .094        -368.187         8.236
                 .016         .371         .431           .185          .999
              192.032      -61.549        4.596      -18041.139       403.572
```

REGRESSION first displays the requested univariate statistics—in this example, the variable means, standard deviations, and variances. Next, bivariate statistics are displayed in square format with a title indicating the order of display in each cell. In this example, first the correlation coefficient is printed, then the sample covariance, then the significance level of the correlation coefficient, and finally the cross-product deviations from the mean.

45.22
MATRIX Subcommand

REGRESSION can write matrix materials built from the raw data it reads. It can read matrix materials written by previous REGRESSION runs or by other SPSS-X procedures such as CORRELATIONS (see Chapter 13, Table 13.1). However, a REGRESSION procedure that performs residual analysis cannot read matrix materials from the active file, nor can it replace the active file with the matrix system file.

To read and write matrices in REGRESSION, you use the MATRIX subcommand. When used, the MATRIX subcommand must be the first subcommand you specify on REGRESSION.

The MATRIX subcommand has two keywords, IN and OUT, which you use to specify the matrix file in parentheses. When you use both IN and OUT on the same REGRESSION procedure you can specify each on a separate MATRIX subcommand, or both on the same subcommand. For example,

```
REGRESSION MATRIX IN(FILEONE)
           /MATRIX OUT(FILETWO)
```

is the same as

```
REGRESSION MATRIX IN(FILEONE) OUT(FILETWO)
```

When you specify the MATRIX subcommand, you cannot use both ORIGIN and NOORIGIN on the same REGRESSION procedure. If you want to use matrices for building multiple regression models, some passing through the origin and others not, specify separate REGRESSION commands for those with ORIGIN and those with NOORIGIN. In addition, you cannot use the REGWGT subcommand if you use the keyword IN on the MATRIX subcommand (Section 45.6). However, REGWGT is in effect if it was specified when writing the matrix. You cannot change the way REGRESSION deals with REGWGT, ORIGIN/ NOORIGIN, or missing values if reading a matrix. The way these issues were specified when creating the matrix remain in effect.

45.23
OUT Keyword

You can use REGRESSION to write matrix materials to a system file. The matrix materials include the mean, standard deviation, number of cases used to compute each coefficient, and Pearson correlation coefficient for each variable.

To write matrix materials, you use the MATRIX OUT specification. You have two options with MATRIX OUT: you can write the matrix file to a system file, or you can replace the active file with the matrix system file. Documents from the original file will not be included in the matrix file and will not be present if the matrix file becomes the active file. (For a discussion on documents, see Chapter 6.)

MATRIX OUT, therefore, provides two options:

(file) *Write the correlation matrix to a system file.* REGRESSION creates a system file containing the matrix materials. The system file is stored on disk and can be retrieved at any time.

(*) *Replace the active file with the correlation matrix system file.* The matrix materials replace the active file. The correlation matrix is NOT stored on disk. It is resident in the active file. You cannot use this specification if you intend to perform residual analysis (that is, if you use the RESIDUALS, CASEWISE, SCATTERPLOT, PARTIALPLOT, or SAVE subcommands).

In the following example one set of matrix materials is written to the file named REGDATA:

```
GET FILE COUNTRY/KEEP SAVINGS POP15 POP75 INCOME GROWTH
REGRESSION      MATRIX OUT(REGDATA)
                /VARS=SAVINGS TO GROWTH
                /MISS=PAIRWISE
                /DEP=SAVINGS/ENTER
```

The active file is still the file named COUNTRY. Subsequent commands are executed on file COUNTRY.

To write the same matrix, but have it available to subsequent commands, specify the following:

```
GET FILE COUNTRY/KEEP SAVINGS POP15 POP75 INCOME GROWTH
REGRESSION      MATRIX OUT(*)
                /VARS=SAVINGS TO GROWTH
                /MISS=PAIRWISE
                /DEP=SAVINGS/ENTER
LIST
DISPLAY DICTIONARY
```

The active file is replaced with the correlation matrix. The LIST and DISPLAY commands are executed on the matrix file, not on the file named COUNTRY.

Format of the Matrix System File. Figure 45.23 shows the matrix system file produced by the above commands. The file has two special variables created by SPSS-X: ROWTYPE_ and VARNAME_. Variable ROWTYPE_ is a short string variable having values MEAN, STDDEV, N, and CORR (for Pearson correlation coefficient). The next variable, VARNAME_, is a short string variable whose values are the names of the variables used to form the correlation matrix. When ROWTYPE_ is CORR, VARNAME_ gives the variable associated with that row of the correlation matrix. The remaining variables in the file are the variables used to form the correlation matrix.

If you use the ORIGIN subcommand (Section 45.10) in the analysis, to suppress the constant term, value OCORR is written to the matrix system file rather than value CORR. OCORR indicates that the regression passes through the origin.

Figure 45.23   A matrix system file

```
FILE:      MATRIX FILE

ROWTYPE_ VARNAME_     SAVINGS       POP15        POP75      INCOME       GROWTH

MEAN                 9.6710000  35.0896000    2.2930000 1106.77840    3.7576000
STDDEV               4.4804069   9.1517272    1.2907714  990.851102    2.8698706
N         SAVINGS   50.0000000  50.0000000   50.0000000   50.0000000  50.0000000
N         POP15     50.0000000  50.0000000   50.0000000   50.0000000  50.0000000
N         POP75     50.0000000  50.0000000   50.0000000   50.0000000  50.0000000
N         INCOME    50.0000000  50.0000000   50.0000000   50.0000000  50.0000000
N         GROWTH    50.0000000  50.0000000   50.0000000   50.0000000  50.0000000
CORR      SAVINGS    1.0000000   -.4555381     .3165211    .2203401     .3047872
CORR      POP15      -.4555381   1.0000000    -.9084787   -.7561744    -.0478257
CORR      POP75       .3165211   -.9084787    1.0000000    .7869876     .0253214
CORR      INCOME      .2203401   -.7561744     .7869876   1.0000000    -.1294784
CORR      GROWTH      .3047872   -.0478257     .0253214   -.1294784    1.0000000

NUMBER OF CASES READ =      12    NUMBER OF CASES LISTED =       12
```

No split variables (see Chapter 15) are present in Figure 45.23. When split variables are present in a matrix system file they occur first in the file, followed by ROWTYPE_, VARNAME_, and the variables used to form the correlation matrix. A full set of matrix materials is written for each subgroup defined by the split variable(s). A split variable cannot have the same variable name as any other variable written to the matrix system file. If a split file is in effect when a matrix is written, the same split file must be in effect when that matrix is read by any procedure. (See Chapter 13 for more information on matrix system files.)

Additional Statistics. REGRESSION always includes with the matrix materials the mean, standard deviation, and number of cases used to compute each coefficient, as shown in Figure 45.23. This information immediately precedes the correlation matrix in the output file.

Missing Values. With PAIRWISE treatment of missing values (see Section 45.19), the matrix of N's used to compute each coefficient is included with the matrix materials. With LISTWISE treatment (the default) or MEANSUBSTITUTION, a single N used to calculate all coefficients is included with the matrix materials.

45.24
IN Keyword

The MATRIX IN specification reads a correlation matrix. There are two specifications you can make with MATRIX IN:

(file)   *Read the correlation matrix from a matrix system file.*

(*)   *Read the correlation matrix from the active file.* The active file must be an appropriate matrix system file. You cannot read a matrix from the active file if you intend to perform residual analysis (that is, if you use the RESIDUALS, CASEWISE, SCATTERPLOT, PARTIALPLOT, or SAVE subcommands).

MATRIX=IN cannot be used in place of GET or DATA LIST to begin a new SPSS-X command file. MATRIX is a subcommand on REGRESSION and REGRESSION cannot run before an active file is defined.

In the following example, one set of matrix materials is read from the file named REGMAT. This specification assumes the current active file is not the file REGMAT:

```
REGRESSION MATRIX IN(REGMAT)
           /VARIABLES=X1 TO X10
           /DEPENDENT=X3
           /METHOD=STEPWISE X5 X2 X9 X7
```

SPSS-X reads variable names, variable and value labels, and print and write formats from the dictionary of the matrix system file named REGMAT. Variables on the VARIABLES, DEPENDENT, and METHOD subcommands need not be in the same order as the variables in the matrix system file.

To begin a new command file and immediately read a matrix, first GET the matrix file, then specify IN(*) on MATRIX. Alternatively, REGRESSION can read a matrix written to the active file by another procedure. In the following annotated example, REGRESSION uses matrix input from the CORRELA-TIONS procedure. Because CORRELATIONS uses pairwise deletion to handle missing data, you must specify MISSING=PAIRWISE to read the matrix into REGRESSION.

```
GET FILE=RAWDATA/KEEP VAR1 TO VAR7
CORRELATIONS VAR1 TO VAR7
    /MATRIX OUT(*)
REGRESSION MATRIX IN(*)
            /VARIABLES=VAR1 TO VAR7
            /MISSING=PAIRWISE
            /DEPENDENT=VAR1
            /ENTER VAR2 TO VAR7
```

- The GET command defines the data to SPSS-X and selects the variables needed for the analysis.
- The CORRELATIONS command computes correlations among seven variables. The MATRIX subcommand writes a matrix system file. The OUT(*) specification replaces the active file with the matrix system file.
- The MATRIX IN subcommand on REGRESSION reads the matrix materials CORRELATIONS has written into the active file.
- The VARIABLES subcommand names the variables to be used in the regression analysis.
- The MISSING subcommand specifies pairwise deletion of missing values.
- The DEPENDENT subcommand specifies VAR1 as the dependent variable.
- The METHOD subcommand enters VAR2 to VAR7 with the ENTER method.

Syntax

RELIABILITY

```
RELIABILITY VARIABLES=varlist
 [/SCALE(scalename)=varlist [/SCALE... ]]
 [/MODEL={ALPHA          }] [/VARIABLES...]
         {SPLIT[(n)]     }
         {GUTTMAN        }
         {PARALLEL       }
         {STRICTPARALLEL }
 [/MISSING={EXCLUDE**} ]
           {INCLUDE  }
 [/FORMAT={LABELS**} ]
          {NOLABELS}
 [/MATRIX =[IN({*    })] [OUT({*    })] [NOPRINT]]
              {file}         {file}
 [/METHOD=COV]
 [/STATISTICS=[DESCRIPTIVE] [SCALE    ] [{ANOVA   }] [ALL]]
              [COV        ] [TUKEY    ] [{FRIEDMAN}]
              [CORR       ] [HOTELLING] [{COCHRAN }]
 [/SUMMARY=[MEANS   ]  [COV ]  [TOTAL]]
           [VARIANCE]  [CORR]  [ALL  ]
```

**Default if the subcommand is omitted.

Contents

46.1   INTRODUCTION TO RELIABILITY MODELS

46.2   OVERVIEW

46.3   OPERATION

46.4   VARIABLES Subcommand

46.5   SCALE Subcommand

46.6   MODEL Subcommand

46.7   SUMMARY Subcommand

46.8   STATISTICS Subcommand

46.9   Analysis of Variance

46.10 Tests for the Violation of Assumptions

46.11 Friedman's Analysis of Variance for Ranked Data

46.12 Analysis of Variance of Dichotomous Data

46.13 METHOD Subcommand

46.14 MISSING Subcommand

46.15 FORMAT Subcommand

46.16 MATRIX Subcommand

46.17 OUT Keyword

46.18 IN Keyword

46.19 LIMITATIONS

RELIABILITY was written by Dr. David A. Specht, Monsanto Agricultural Products, with the assistance of Thomas A. Bubolz, Iowa State University. Support was provided by the Department of Sociology and Computer Center of Iowa State University. Dr. William J. Kennedy and the staff of the Statistical Programming and Numerical Analysis Section of the Iowa State University Statistical Laboratory provided valuable assistance.

46

Chapter 46   RELIABILITY

Procedure RELIABILITY performs an item analysis on the components of additive scales by computing commonly used coefficients of reliability. RELIA-BILITY also prints basic summary statistics including item means, standard deviations, inter-item covariance and correlation matrices, scale means, and item-to-item correlations. You can also use RELIABILITY to perform a repeated measures design analysis of variance, a two-way factorial analysis of variance with one observation per cell, Tukey's test for additivity, Hotelling's T^2 test for equality of means in repeated measures designs, and Friedman's two-way analysis of variance on ranks. For more complex repeated measures designs, see MANOVA (Chapter 33).

RELIABILITY accepts data in the form of cases or correlation matrices. In addition, RELIABILITY can write correlation-type matrix materials to a system file.

46.1
INTRODUCTION TO RELIABILITY MODELS

Procedure RELIABILITY provides a number of reliability coefficients for multiple-item scales, using a number of different approaches to reliability definition and estimation. The choice of approach depends upon the assumptions. In general, the computations performed are designed for those situations where the goal is to assess the reliability of a sum or weighted sum across variables as an estimate of a case's true score.

RELIABILITY does not actually compute composite or scale scores. However, once you have analyzed a set of items, you can construct scores using the transformations available with SPSS-X (see Chapter 7).

Five different models are available in procedure RELIABILITY. (For a discussion of their use and the underlying assumptions, see Cronbach, 1951; Guttman, 1945; and Kristof, 1963.)

Alpha Model. The ALPHA model computes Cronbach's α and standardized item α (Cronbach, 1951). If the data are in dichotomous form, α is equivalent to reliability coefficient KR-20 (Kuder-Richardson-20). Coefficient α is the maximum likelihood estimate of the reliability coefficient if the parallel model is assumed to be true. If only two items are used, α is also equal to Guttman's split-half coefficient. This is the default model in procedure RELIABILITY.

Split Model. The SPLIT model partitions the variables in the scale into two subsets. The sum is computed for each subset and the reliability calculations make use of only the information contained in the two sums for each case. RELIABILI-TY calculates the correlation between the two sums, the Spearman-Brown split-half coefficient, the unequal length Spearman-Brown coefficient, and the Guttman split-half coefficient. In addition, it also calculates coefficient α for each part.

Guttman Model. The GUTTMAN model computes the six coefficients proposed by Guttman (1945).

Parallel Model. The PARALLEL model computes a correction for the bias of α using the correction proposed by Kristof (1963). In addition, RELIABILITY prints the estimated true score variance of an individual item, the estimated error variance of an individual item, and the reliability of an individual item.

Strictly Parallel Model. The STRICTPARALLEL model computes the same measures of reliability as for the parallel model with the additional assumptions that items have the same means, the same true score variances over a set of objects being measured, and the same error variance over replications (Kristof, 1963).

46.2 OVERVIEW

To use RELIABILITY, you need only specify a set of variables from which an intermediate matrix is computed. A scale that references variables in the matrix (ALL) and a model (ALPHA) are supplied by default. You can override the default scale and model with the SCALE and MODEL subcommands. In addition, you can specify multiple sets of variables, multiple scales, and multiple models.

Specifying the Variable List. The VARIABLES subcommand is required and is used to specify all variables from which one or more scales are evaluated. Use multiple VARIABLES subcommands to specify multiple intermediate matrices. (See Section 46.4.)

Forming the Scale. The optional SCALE subcommand specifies the set of variables forming the scale and defaults to ALL. You can specify multiple SCALE subcommands. (See Section 46.5.)

Specifying the Model. The optional MODEL subcommand specifies the model being tested and defaults to ALPHA. (See Section 46.6.)

Specifying Item Statistics. The optional SUMMARY subcommand specifies item statistics (see Section 46.7).

Specifying Other Statistics and Analysis of Variance. The optional STATISTICS subcommand specifies item and scale statistics. Statistics include the item means and standard deviations. (See Section 46.8.) Several analysis of variance models can also be requested, including a repeated measures model with no between-subjects factors, a factorial design with one observation per cell, a two-way randomized block design, an analysis of variance upon ranks (see Section 46.11) and an analysis of variance upon dichotomous data (see Section 46.12).

Reading and Writing Matrix Materials. The optional MATRIX subcommand can read and write correlation matrix materials. (See Section 46.16.)

Printing Labels. The optional FORMAT subcommand determines whether variable labels print with the output. The default is to print the labels. (See Section 46.15.)

Obtaining Coefficients. The optional METHOD subcommand provides a way to force RELIABILITY to use a covariance matrix in calculations. (See Section 46.13.)

Handling Missing Values. By default, RELIABILITY excludes cases with missing values listwise from the construction of the matrix. Optionally, you can request that missing values be handled as if they were valid. (See Section 46.14.)

46.3
OPERATION

The VARIABLES subcommand on RELIABILITY is required. All other subcommands are optional. Each subcommand begins with a subcommand keyword followed by an equals sign. Subcommand specifications are separated by slashes.

46.4
VARIABLES Subcommand

The VARIABLES subcommand specifies all the variables to be named on one or more SCALE subcommands. If the SCALE subcommand is omitted, all the variables named on VARIABLES are tested. Each VARIABLES subcommand builds a covariance matrix and vector of means. The variable list on the VARIABLES subcommand follows the usual SPSS-X conventions for variable lists. For example,

```
RELIABILITY  VARIABLES=ITEM1 ITEM2 ITEM3 ITEM4 ITEM5
```

computes one matrix to be used for the scale. All five variables specified are used in the scale. The keyword TO can be used to name a contiguous set of variables. Only numeric variables can be used, and cases with missing values are deleted from the computation of the matrix. A case missing from one or more variables named on the VARIABLES subcommand is not used in the computation of the intermediate matrix.

46.5
SCALE Subcommand

The SCALE subcommand specifies the scale to be tested. The SCALE subcommand has an arbitrary scale name in parentheses followed by the set of variables composing the scale, as in:

```
RELIABILITY  VARIABLES=ITEM1 ITEM2 ITEM3 ITEM4 ITEM5
  /SCALE(RATING)=ITEM1 TO ITEM5
```

The scale name identifies the particular analysis in the display. It can be a maximum of eight characters and must be composed of the letters A to Z and digits 0 to 9. All variables named on the SCALE subcommand must be named on the preceding VARIABLES subcommand. You can use the keyword TO on the SCALE subcommand only to imply a set of adjacent variables whose order is determined by the order in which they were named on the VARIABLES subcommand. If you omit the SCALE subcommand, the default is ALL.

ALL   *Reference all variables named on the VARIABLES subcommand.* This is the default.

The following example produces the default display shown in Figure 46.5:

```
SET WIDTH 132
DATA LIST   /ITEM1 TO ITEM5 1-10
RELIABILITY  VARIABLES=ITEM1 TO ITEM5
  /SCALE (TESTSCOR) = ITEM1 TO ITEM5
BEGIN DATA
 1 1 1 1 1
 1 1 1 1 0
 1 1 1 0 1
 1 1 0 1 0
 1 1 1 0 0
 1 1 0 0 1
 1 1 0 0 0
 0 1 1 0 0
 1 0 1 0 0
 1 0 0 0 0
END DATA
FINISH
```

With no other specifications, this display lists the variables in the scale and their associated labels (if defined) and prints the number of valid cases, number of items, and Cronbach's α. The SCALE subcommand in the above command is optional, since it references all the variables on the VARIABLES subcommand.

Figure 46.5   RELIABILITY default display

```
                                R E L I A B I L I T Y   A N A L Y S I S   -   S C A L E   (T E S T S C O R)
    1.        ITEM1
    2.        ITEM2
    3.        ITEM3
    4.        ITEM4
    5.        ITEM5


RELIABILITY COEFFICIENTS

N OF CASES =      10.0                        N OF ITEMS =  5

ALPHA =    0.3682
```

You can specify several SCALE subcommands following one VARIABLES subcommand, as in

```
RELIABILITY  VARIABLES=ITEM1 TO ITEM10
   /SCALE(VERBAL)=ITEM1 ITEM3 ITEM5 ITEM7 ITEM9
   /SCALE(MATH)=ITEM2 ITEM4 ITEM6 ITEM8 ITEM10
```

which specifies two analyses using the matrix computed from the VARIABLES subcommand. If missing data are present, specifying the analyses in this manner can produce different results than using two VARIABLES subcommands. For example,

```
RELIABILITY  VARIABLES=ITEM1 ITEM3 ITEM5 ITEM7 ITEM9
   /SCALE(VERBAL)=ITEM1 TO ITEM9
   /VARIABLES=ITEM2 ITEM4 ITEM6 ITEM8 ITEM10
   /SCALE(MATH)=ITEM2 TO ITEM10
```

deletes missing values listwise on the first VARIABLES subcommand only for ITEM1, ITEM3, ITEM5, ITEM7, and ITEM9 (see Section 46.14). The covariance matrix is not affected by missing values on the other variables. The second VARIABLES subcommand creates a new matrix that uses only ITEM2, ITEM4, ITEM6, ITEM8, and ITEM10.

46.6
MODEL Subcommand

By default, RELIABILITY uses model ALPHA, which computes Cronbach's α and standardized item α. The MODEL subcommand specifies the type of reliability analysis and follows the SCALE subcommand to which it applies. Specify the keyword MODEL, an equals sign, and one of the keywords listed below. For example, the command

```
RELIABILITY  VARIABLES=ITEM1 ITEM2 ITEM3 ITEM4 ITEM5
   /MODEL=SPLIT
```

results in a split-half coefficient analysis. The following types of reliability analyses are available in procedure RELIABILITY:

ALPHA   *Cronbach's α and standardized item α.* Standardized item α is computed if RELIABILITY uses solution method COV (see Section 46.13). By default with ALPHA in effect, RELIABILITY does *not* use method COV.

SPLIT(n)   *Split-half coefficients.* If you specify SPLIT with no specification for *n*, the items are split into the two halves by their order on the

SCALE subcommand, with the first $n/2$ items named in the first part and the remaining items in the second. If the scale is composed of an odd number of variables, the first part contains the additional variable. For example, if the scale specifies five variables, the first part contains the first three named and the second part the remaining two variables.

If you want the variables to be split into unequal parts, specify the number of variables to be contained in the second part in parentheses following the keyword SPLIT. For example, MODEL=SPLIT(3) uses the last three variables named (or used by default) by the SCALE subcommand for the second part and uses all the other variables for the first part.

GUTTMAN   *Guttman's lower bounds for true reliability.*

PARALLEL   *Maximum likelihood reliability estimate under parallel assumptions.*

STRICTPARALLEL   *Maximum likelihood reliability estimate under strictly parallel assumptions.*

The MODEL subcommand follows the SCALE subcommand and applies only to the immediately preceding SCALE subcommand. RELIABILITY uses the default of ALPHA if a SCALE subcommand is not followed by a MODEL subcommand.

46.7
SUMMARY Subcommand

The SUMMARY subcommand prints summary statistics for the scale. There are no default summary statistics.

MEANS   *Summary statistics or item means.* The average item mean over the number of items, the variance of the item means, the largest item mean, the smallest, the range of the item means, and the ratio of the largest to the smallest.

VARIANCE   *Summary statistics for item variances.* The display VARIANCE statistic is identical to MEAN but is based upon item variances rather than item means.

COV   *Summary statistics for inter-item covariances.* The output from COV is identical to MEANS and VARIANCE but is based upon covariances.

CORR   *Summary statistics for inter-item correlations.* The output from CORR is identical to MEANS, VARIANCE, and COV but is based upon correlations.

TOTAL   *Item total statistics.* The display from TOTAL includes five statistics dealing with the relationship between the individual items and the items as a set. For each item the following are calculated:

Scale mean if item deleted. This is the mean the scale scores would have if the particular item were deleted from the scale.

Scale variance if item deleted. This is the variance the scale scores would have if the particular item were deleted from the scale.

Corrected item total correlations. This is the correlation between that item's score and the scale scores computed from the other items in the set.

Squared multiple correlations. Each item is regressed upon the remaining items in the set making up the scale and the squared multiple correlation coefficient is computed. (This is only computed if method COV is used. See Section 46.13.)

Alpha if item deleted. For each item, Cronbach's α is computed from the other items in the scale.

Figure 46.7 shows the summary statistics for the following example:

```
RELIABILITY  VARIABLES=ITEM1 TO ITEM5
   /SUMMARY=MEANS VARIANCE COVARIANCE CORR TOTAL
```

Figure 46.7 Summary statistics

```
                        R E L I A B I L I T Y   A N A L Y S I S  -  S C A L E   (T E S T S C O R)
      1.      ITEM1
      2.      ITEM2
      3.      ITEM3
      4.      ITEM4
      5.      ITEM5

          # OF CASES =      10.0

ITEM MEANS          MEAN     MINIMUM    MAXIMUM      RANGE    MAX/MIN    VARIANCE
                   .5800      .3000      .9000      .6000     3.0000      .0770

ITEM VARIANCES      MEAN     MINIMUM    MAXIMUM      RANGE    MAX/MIN    VARIANCE
                   .2022      .1000      .2667      .1667     2.6667      .0043

INTER-ITEM
COVARIANCES         MEAN     MINIMUM    MAXIMUM      RANGE    MAX/MIN    VARIANCE
                   .0211     -.0444      .0667      .1111    -1.5000      .0011

INTER-ITEM
CORRELATIONS        MEAN     MINIMUM    MAXIMUM      RANGE    MAX/MIN    VARIANCE
                   .0980     -.2722      .3273      .5995    -1.2027      .0362

ITEM-TOTAL STATISTICS

                  SCALE        SCALE      CORRECTED
                  MEAN       VARIANCE       ITEM-         SQUARED        ALPHA
                 IF ITEM     IF ITEM        TOTAL        MULTIPLE       IF ITEM
                 DELETED     DELETED     CORRELATION    CORRELATION     DELETED

ITEM1            2.0000      1.3333        .0000         .2929          .4222
ITEM2            2.1000       .9889        .3180         .3092          .2097
ITEM3            2.3000      1.1222        .0406         .1250          .4488
ITEM4            2.6000       .9333        .2857         .2308          .2222
ITEM5            2.6000       .9333        .2857         .2308          .2222


RELIABILITY COEFFICIENTS     5 ITEMS

ALPHA =   .3682          STANDARDIZED ITEM ALPHA =    .3520
```

46.8
STATISTICS Subcommand

The STATISTICS subcommand computes descriptive statistics for variables forming the scale.

DESCRIPTIVE *Item means and standard deviations.*

COV *Inter-item variance-covariance matrix.*

CORR *Inter-item correlations.*

SCALE *Scale means and scale variances.*

ANOVA *Analysis of variance table. See Section 46.9 for more information.*

TUKEY *Tukey test for additivity. See Section 46.10 for more information.*

HOTELLING *Hotelling's T^2. See Section 46.10 for more information.*

FRIEDMAN *Friedman's chi-square and Kendall's coefficient of concordance. See Section 46.11 for more information.*

COCHRAN *Cochran's Q. See Section 46.12 for more information.*

Figure 46.8 shows the statistics for the following example:

```
RELIABILITY  VARIABLES=ITEM1 TO ITEM5
   /STATISTICS=DESC COV CORR SCALE
```

Figure 46.8   Scale and item statistics

```
                              R E L I A B I L I T Y   A N A L Y S I S   -   S C A L E   (T E S T S C O R)
     1.    ITEM1
     2.    ITEM2
     3.    ITEM3
     4.    ITEM4
     5.    ITEM5

                         MEAN          STD DEV        CASES
     1.    ITEM1         .9000          .3162          10.0
     2.    ITEM2         .8000          .4216          10.0
     3.    ITEM3         .6000          .5164          10.0
     4.    ITEM4         .3000          .4830          10.0
     5.    ITEM5         .3000          .4830          10.0


                 COVARIANCE MATRIX

                 ITEM1         ITEM2         ITEM3         ITEM4         ITEM5

     ITEM1        .1000
     ITEM2       -.0222         .1778
     ITEM3       -.0444         .0222         .2667
     ITEM4        .0333         .0667         .0222         .2333
     ITEM5        .0333         .0667         .0222         .0111         .2333



                 CORRELATION MATRIX

                 ITEM1         ITEM2         ITEM3         ITEM4         ITEM5

     ITEM1       1.0000
     ITEM2       -.1667        1.0000
     ITEM3       -.2722         .1021        1.0000
     ITEM4        .2182         .3273         .0891        1.0000
     ITEM5        .2182         .3273         .0891         .0476        1.0000



                              R E L I A B I L I T Y   A N A L Y S I S   -   S C A L E   (T E S T S C O R)
     # OF CASES =        10.0

                                                        # OF
     STATISTICS FOR      MEAN      VARIANCE    STD DEV  VARIABLES
          SCALE         2.9000      1.4333     1.1972      5


     RELIABILITY COEFFICIENTS       5 ITEMS

     ALPHA =   .3682              STANDARDIZED ITEM ALPHA =    .3520
```

46.9
Analysis of Variance

You can use procedure RELIABILITY to perform a single-factor repeated measures design analysis of variance, a two-way factorial design with one observation per cell, a complete randomized block design analysis of variance, and Friedman's analysis of variance on ranks. Table 46.9 gives the basic relationship between the organization of data within SPSS-X and the terminology usually used by statistical texts discussing these procedures. If your data are organized according to Table 46.9, the ANOVA keyword on the STATISTICS subcommand produces the analysis of variance table and labels it with repeated measures design terminology.

ANOVA   *Analysis of variance table.*

Table 46.9   Data organization for analysis of variance

SPSS-X processing	Repeated measures	Two-way factorial	Randomized blocks
case(row)	person(object)	treatment A	block
variable(column)	measure(judge)	treatment B	treatment

The following commands produce an analysis of variance for a repeated measures design involving the effects of four successive drug treatments:

```
TITLE  'WINER, PAGE 268'
DATA LIST /DRUG1 TO DRUG4 1-12
RELIABILITY  VARIABLES=DRUG1 TO DRUG4
   /STATISTICS=ANOVA
BEGIN DATA
 30 28 16 34
 14 18 10 22
 24 20 18 30
 38 34 20 44
 26 28 14 30
END DATA
```

Figure 46.9 A repeated measures design

```
                              R E L I A B I L I T Y   A N A L Y S I S   -   S C A L E   (R E A C T I O N)
    1.     DRUG1
    2.     DRUG2
    3.     DRUG3
    4.     DRUG4



                        ANALYSIS OF VARIANCE

SOURCE OF VARIATION      SUM OF SQ.      DF      MEAN SQUARE      F        PROB.

BETWEEN PEOPLE             680.8000       4        170.2000
WITHIN PEOPLE              811.0000      15         54.0667
  BETWEEN MEASURES         698.2000       3        232.7333    24.7589    .0000
  RESIDUAL                 112.8000      12          9.4000
TOTAL                     1491.8000      19         78.5158

    GRAND MEAN =            24.9000
```

See Figure 46.9 for the output from these commands.

46.10
Tests for the Violation of Assumptions

RELIABILITY optionally provides a test for the violation of the assumption of additivity and a test for the equality of multivariate means.

Tukey's test for additivity is used to detect the presence of interaction effects. The underlying model for analysis of variance designs within RELIABILITY does not contain a term for interaction. Tukey's test provides a test to decide if a transformation is necessary to achieve additivity and suggests a suitable transformation. To obtain Tukey's test, specify TUKEY on the STATISTICS subcommand.

Hotelling's T^2 tests the assumption of the equality of means for repeated measures designs involving more than two variables. To obtain Hotelling's T^2 test, specify HOTELLING on the STATISTICS subcommand. This statistic uses a great deal of extra computation time because it requires an inversion of the matrix of order $k-1$, where k is the number of variables in the scale.

TUKEY   *Tukey test for additivity.*
HOTELLING *Hotelling's* T^2.

The following commands produce an analysis of variance table, Tukey's test, and Hotelling's T^2 for a repeated measures design:

```
RELIABILITY  VARIABLES=DRUG1 TO DRUG4
   /STATISTICS=ANOVA TUKEY HOTELLING
```

The analysis of variance table appears in Figure 46.9. Figure 46.10 shows Tukey's test and Hotelling's T^2.

46

Figure 46.10   Tests for the violation of assumptions

```
TUKEY ESTIMATE OF POWER TO WHICH OBSERVATIONS
MUST BE RAISED TO ACHIEVE ADDITIVITY           =      -0.1691


HOTELLINGS T-SQUARED =     170.4739       F =     28.4123      PROB. =   .0342
     DEGREES OF FREEDOM:               NUMERATOR =      3     DENOMINATOR =     2
```

**46.11
Friedman's Analysis of
Variance for Ranked Data**

If you have a repeated measures design in which the data are already in the form of ranks, you can obtain Friedman's chi-square statistic for the analysis of variance rather than the usual *F* statistic, and Kendall's coefficient of concordance. To obtain the coefficient specify FRIEDMAN and ANOVA on the STATISTICS subcommand. The data must be in the form of ranks. When data are entered in the form of ranks, the determinant of the covariance matrix is zero and many of the reliability coefficients are not computable.

FRIEDMAN   *Friedman's chi-square and Kendall's coefficient of concordance.* This option affects only the analysis of variance table produced by keyword ANOVA on the STATISTICS subcommand. Data must be in the form of ranks. If both FRIEDMAN and COCHRAN are specified on STATISTICS, COCHRAN is used (see Section 46.12).

Figure 46.11 is an example of the use of keyword FRIEDMAN in conjunction with keyword ANOVA on the STATISTICS subcommand. The following commands produce this output:

```
TITLE 'WINER, PAGE 301'
DATA LIST    /METHOD1 TO METHOD4 1-8
RELIABILITY  VARIABLES = METHOD1 TO METHOD4
  /STATISTICS=FRIEDMAN ANOVA
BEGIN DATA
 3 2 1 4
 4 3 1 2
 2 4 1 3
 1 3 2 4
 2 3 1 4
 1 4 2 3
 2 3 1 4
 1 4 2 3
END DATA
```

Friedman's chi-square statistic and Kendall's coefficient are also available in procedure NPAR TESTS (see Chapter 38). NPAR TESTS does not require that the data be in the form of ranks, but the number of cases which can be analyzed is limited by the available workspace.

Figure 46.11   Analysis of variance on ranks

```
                       R E L I A B I L I T Y   A N A L Y S I S   -   S C A L E   (R A N K S)
   1.      METHOD1
   2.      METHOD2
   3.      METHOD3
   4.      METHOD4

   # OF CASES =       8.0


                 ANALYSIS OF VARIANCE
SOURCE OF VARIATION    SUM OF SQ.      DF    MEAN SQUARE    CHI-SQUARE PROB.

BETWEEN PEOPLE      7.7715612E-16       7       .0000
WITHIN PEOPLE           40.0000        24      1.6667
   BETWEEN MEASURES     22.7500         3      7.5833       13.6500     .0034
   RESIDUAL             17.2500        21       .8214
TOTAL                   40.0000        31      1.2903

GRAND MEAN =        2.5000

COEFFICIENT OF CONCORDANCE W =     0.5688
```

ANNOTATED EXAMPLE FOR RELIABILITY

The following example demonstrates the use of RELIABILITY to analyze an attitude scale of confidence in institutions in the United States. The data come from a 500-case sample of the 1980 General Social Survey. Respondents were asked how much confidence they have in the people running the following institutions: banks and financial institutions, major companies, organized religion, education, the executive branch of the federal government, organized labor, the press, medicine, television, the United States Supreme Court, the scientific community, Congress, and the military. The SPSS-X commands are

```
GET  FILE=GSS80/KEEP CONFINAN TO CONARMY
RELIABILITY  VARIABLES=ALL
  /MODEL=STRICTPARALLEL
  /SUMMARY=TOTAL
  /STATISTICS=ANOVA TUKEY HOTELLING
FINISH
```

- The GET command defines the data to SPSS-X and selects the variables needed for analysis (see Chapter 6).

- The RELIABILITY command analyzes the scale formed from the 13 confidence variables and uses the STRICTPARALLEL model (see Sections 46.4, 46.5, and 46.6).

- The SUMMARY subcommand produces item-total statistics (see Section 46.7).

- The STATISTICS subcommand produces the analysis of variance table, the Tukey test for additivity, and Hotelling's T^2 (see Sections 46.8, 46.9, and 46.10).

RELIABILITY display

```
* * * * * * * * * R E L I A B I L I T Y   A N A L Y S I S   F O R   S C A L E   (C O N F I N D   ) * * * * * * * * * *

           1.     CONFINAN         BANKS & FINANCIAL INSTITUTIONS
           2.     CONBUS           MAJOR COMPANIES
           3.     CONCLERG         ORGANIZED RELIGION
           4.     CONEDUC          EDUCATION
           5.     CONFED           EXECUTIVE BRANCH OF FEDERAL  GOVERNMENT
           6.     CONLABOR         ORGANIZED LABOR
           7.     CONPRESS         PRESS
           8.     CONMEDIC         MEDICINE
           9.     CONTV            TELEVISION
          10.     CONJUDGE         U.S.   SUPREME COURT
          11.     CONSCI           SCIENTIFIC COMMUNITY
          12.     CONLEGIS         CONGRESS
          13.     CONARMY          MILITARY
```

   # OF CASES =   415.0

ITEM-TOTAL STATISTICS	SCALE MEAN IF ITEM DELETED	SCALE VARIANCE IF ITEM DELETED	CORRECTED ITEM- TOTAL CORRELATION	SQUARED MULTIPLE CORRELATION	ALPHA IF ITEM DELETED
CONFINAN	22.83614	17.89579	.45504	.29889	.78312
CONBUS	22.84096	18.63165	.35560	.24236	.79177
CONCLERG	22.85542	18.31721	.36933	.16713	.79118
CONEDUC	22.84578	18.06795	.46520	.23213	.78232
CONFED	22.45783	18.04592	.46921	.29611	.78197
CONLABOR	22.51807	18.42419	.37634	.21017	.79017
CONPRESS	22.71084	18.81474	.32146	.22199	.79465
CONMEDIC	23.10361	18.01581	.49617	.27397	.77984
CONTV	22.55181	18.59091	.36696	.19377	.79077
CONJUDGE	22.74458	17.57711	.50607	.31250	.77826
CONSCI	23.10361	18.66315	.39099	.21854	.78865
CONLEGIS	22.41446	18.07902	.52769	.34814	.77793
CONARMY	22.79518	17.73814	.49305	.29034	.77959

                    ANALYSIS OF VARIANCE

SOURCE OF VARIATION	SS	DF	MEAN SQUARE	F	PROBABILITY
BETWEEN PEOPLE	669.74124	414	1.61773		
WITHIN PEOPLE	1858.92308	4980	0.37328		
BETWEEN MEASURES	240.96311	12	20.08026	61.65711	0.0
RESIDUAL	1617.95996	4968	0.32568		
NONADDITIVITY	0.00408	1	0.00408	0.01253	0.91086
BALANCE	1617.95588	4967	0.32574		
TOTAL	2528.66432	5394	0.46879		

   GRAND MEAN =   1.89601

   TUKEY ESTIMATE OF POWER TO WHICH OBSERVATIONS MUST BE RAISED TO ACHIEVE ADDITIVITY =   0.9778486


```
* * * * * * * * * R E L I A B I L I T Y   A N A L Y S I S   F O R   S C A L E   (C O N F I N D   ) * * * * * * * * * *
```

       HOTELLINGS T-SQUARED =   694.59442   F =   56.34492
       DEGREES OF FREEDOM * * NUMERATOR =   12   DENOMINATOR=   403   PROBABILITY = 0.00000

   TEST FOR GOODNESS OF FIT OF MODEL STRICTLYPARALLEL

   CHI SQUARE =   965.61859   DEGREES OF FREEDOM =   101
       LOG OF DETERMINANT OF UNCONSTRAINED MATRIX =   -13.6742999
       LOG OF DETERMINANT OF CONSTRAINED MATRIX =   -11.3189635
       PROBABILITY =   .00000

       PARAMETER ESTIMATES

       ESTIMATED COMMON MEAN=   1.89601
       ESTIMATED COMMON VARIANCE =   0.4697294
          ERROR VARIANCE =   0.3732777
           TRUE VARIANCE =   0.0964517
       ESTIMATED COMMON INTERITEM CORRELATION =   0.2036639

       ESTIMATED RELIABILITY OF SCALE =   .7687736
       UNBIASED ESTIMATE OF RELIABILITY =   .7704451

46.12
Analysis of Variance of Dichotomous Data

If the data in an analysis of variance model are in the form of dichotomies (having only two possible values), RELIABILITY can be used to obtain Cochran's Q. Cochran's Q tests the hypothesis of no change in the proportion of successful outcomes over time. To obtain Cochran's Q in place of the usual F test, specify COCHRAN and ANOVA on the STATISTICS subcommand.

COCHRAN   *Cochran's Q.*

Figure 46.12 is an example of analysis of variance of dichotomous data. The following commands produce this display:

```
TITLE  'WINER, Page 304'
DATA LIST   /TIME1 TO TIME5 1-10
RELIABILITY  VARIABLES=TIME1 TO TIME5
 /STATISTICS=COCHRAN ANOVA
BEGIN DATA
 0 0 0 0 0
 0 0 1 1 0
 0 0 1 1 1
 0 1 1 1 1
 0 0 0 0 1
 0 1 0 1 1
 0 0 1 1 1
 1 0 0 1 1
 1 1 1 1 1
 1 1 1 1 1
END DATA
```

Figure 46.12   Analysis of variance on dichotomous data

```
                R E L I A B I L I T Y   A N A L Y S I S   -   S C A L E   (O V E R T I M E)
     1.      TIME1
     2.      TIME2
     3.      TIME3
     4.      TIME4
     5.      TIME5


             ANALYSIS OF VARIANCE

SOURCE OF VARIATION      SUM OF SQ.        DF       MEAN SQUARE      Q          PROB.

BETWEEN PEOPLE             4.5800           9           .5089
WITHIN PEOPLE              7.6000          40           .1900
   BETWEEN MEASURES        2.0800           4           .5200      10.9474     .0272
   RESIDUAL                5.5200          36           .1533
TOTAL                     12.1800          49           .2486

     GRAND MEAN =          0.5800
```

46.13
METHOD Subcommand

RELIABILITY uses one of two different computing methods, depending upon the model specified and the subcommands used. You can use the METHOD subcommand to specify keyword COV, which forces RELIABILITY to use a covariance matrix in calculations. The METHOD subcommand has only the single keyword, COV.

By default, RELIABILITY tries *not* to compute a covariance matrix. It attempts to use a faster method than COV that, for large problems, requires less workspace. However, the method RELIABILITY tries to use can only compute coefficients for models ALPHA and SPLIT, and does not compute a number of optional statistics or read and write matrix materials. RELIABILITY uses a covariance matrix in calculations only when it cannot avoid doing so, or when you specify METHOD=COV.

Method COV computes a covariance matrix for each VARIABLES subcommand. You can obtain all the optional statistics, and use any model with COV.

The alternative method RELIABILITY prefers to use continues processing a scale containing zero variance and leaves the item in the scale. Method COV deletes items with zero variance and continues processing. If you want method

COV and do not request any of the models or statistics which force it, specify COV on the METHOD subcommand.

COV   *Use a covariance matrix.* This method should be specified if you want any of the following:

Deletion of items with zero variance from the scales in which they occur. The treatment used affects coefficient α, the TUKEY test (Section 46.10), and the analysis of variance (Section 46.9).

Squared multiple correlations. These are included in the item total statistics (Section 46.7) when Method COV is used, but not when the alternative method is used.

Standardized item α.

To summarize, RELIABILITY does *not* use a covariance matrix in calculations if you specify

- Only ALPHA or SPLIT models.
- Only MISSING=INCLUDE, FORMAT=NOLABELS, and STATISTICS= COCHRAN.
- Only STATISTICS=DESCRIPTIVE SCALE ANOVA TUKEY and SUMMARY= TOTAL.

METHOD=COV is automatically used if you specify

- A model other than ALPHA or SPLIT.
- MATRIX=OUT(file), or METHOD=COV, or STATISTICS=FRIEDMAN.
- COV, CORR, or HOTELLING on the STATISTICS subcommand, or MEANS, VARIANCE, COV, or CORR on the SUMMARY subcommand.

46.14
MISSING Subcommand

The MISSING subcommand controls missing values. Its default keyword is EXCLUDE, which deletes cases with missing values on a listwise basis. To include cases with user-missing values, specify keyword INCLUDE.

EXCLUDE   *Delete missing values listwise.* A case missing on any of the variables listed on the VARIABLES subcommand is not used. Each VARIABLES subcommand is evaluated independently for missing values. This is the default.

INCLUDE   *Include user-missing values.* User-defined missing values are treated as valid values.

46.15
FORMAT Subcommand

By default, the FORMAT subcommand prints the variable label associated with each variable at the beginning of the display. To suppress the printing of variable labels, specify keyword NOLABELS.

LABELS   *Print variable labels.* This is the default.

NOLABELS   *Suppress variable labels.*

46.16
MATRIX Subcommand

RELIABILITY can both read and write matrix materials. It writes correlation type matrices and includes the N's, means, and standard deviations with the matrix materials. These matrix materials can be used by RELIABILITY or other procedures (see Chapter 13, Table 13.1).

Use the MATRIX subcommand to read and write matrix materials. The MATRIX subcommand has two keywords, IN and OUT, which you use to specify the matrix file in parentheses. When you use both IN and OUT on the same RELIABILITY procedure you can specify each on a separate MATRIX subcommand, or both on the same subcommand. For example,

```
RELIABILITY VARIABLES=varlist
  /MATRIX IN(FILEONE)
  /MATRIX OUT(FILETWO)
```

is the same as

```
RELIABILITY VARIABLES=varlist
  /MATRIX IN(FILEONE) OUT(FILETWO)
```

If both IN and OUT are used on the same RELIABILITY command and there are one or more grouping variables, these variables are treated as if they were split variables. Values of the grouping variables are passed on to the output matrix.

46.17
OUT Keyword

The OUT keyword on MATRIX specifies the file to which the matrix is written. There are two options:

(file) *Write the matrix to a system file.* RELIABILITY creates a system file containing the matrix materials. The output file is specified in parentheses. The system file is stored on disk and can be retrieved at any time.

(*) *Replace the active file with the matrix system file.* The matrix materials replace the active file. The matrix is *not* stored on disk. It is resident in the active file.

RELIABILITY writes only correlation type matrices and includes the number of cases, mean, and standard deviation with the matrix materials. Documents from the original file will not be included in the matrix file and will not be present if the matrix file becomes the active file. (For a discussion on documents, see Chapter 6.)

RELIABILITY prints the scale analyses when it writes matrix materials. If you don't want the scale analyses to print, specify keyword NOPRINT on MATRIX, as in

```
RELIABILITY  VARIABLES=TIME1 TO TIME5
  /MATRIX=OUT(*) NOPRINT
```

NOPRINT *Do not print the scale analyses with matrix output.*

In the following example one set of matrix materials is written to file **RELMTX**:

```
DATA LIST   /TIME1 TO TIME5 1-10
RELIABILITY  VARIABLES=TIME1 TO TIME5
  /MATRIX=OUT(RELMTX)
BEGIN DATA
 0 0 0 0 0
 0 0 1 1 0
 0 0 1 1 1
 0 1 1 1 1
 0 0 0 0 1
 0 1 0 1 1
 0 0 1 1 1
 1 0 0 1 1
 1 1 1 1 1
 1 1 1 1 1
END DATA
LIST
```

The active file is still the file defined by DATA LIST. Subsequent commands are executed on the file defined by DATA LIST.

To write the same matrix, but have it available to subsequent commands, specify the following:

```
DATA LIST   /TIME1 TO TIME5 1-10
RELIABILITY  VARIABLES=TIME1 TO TIME5
  /MATRIX=OUT(*)
BEGIN DATA
 0 0 0 0 0
 0 0 1 1 0
 0 0 1 1 1
 0 1 1 1 1
 0 0 0 0 1
 0 1 0 1 1
 0 0 1 1 1
 1 0 0 1 1
 1 1 1 1 1
 1 1 1 1 1
END DATA
LIST
```

The active file is replaced with the matrix system file. The LIST command is executed on the matrix file, not on the file defined by DATA LIST.

Format of the Matrix System File. Figure 46.17 shows the matrix system file produced by the above commands. The file includes two special variables created by SPSS-X: ROWTYPE_ and VARNAME_. Variable ROWTYPE_ is a short string variable having values N, MEAN, STDDEV, and CORR. The next variable in the file variable VARNAME_, is a short string variable whose values are the names of the variables used to form the correlation matrix. When ROWTYPE_ is CORR, VARNAME_ gives the variable associated with that row of the correlation matrix. The remaining variables in the matrix file are the variables used to form the correlation matrix.

Figure 46.17 A matrix system file

```
FILE:      MATRIX FILE

ROWTYPE_ VARNAME_      TIME1      TIME2      TIME3      TIME4      TIME5

N                  10.0000000 10.0000000 10.0000000 10.0000000 10.0000000
MEAN                 .3000000   .4000000   .6000000   .8000000   .8000000
STDDEV               .4830459   .5163978   .5163978   .4216370   .4216370
CORR     TIME1     1.0000000   .3563483   .0890871   .3273268   .3273268
CORR     TIME2      .3563483  1.0000000   .2500000   .4082483   .4082483
CORR     TIME3      .0890871   .2500000  1.0000000   .6123724   .1020621
CORR     TIME4      .3273268   .4082483   .6123724  1.0000000   .3750000
CORR     TIME5      .3273268   .4082483   .1020621   .3750000  1.0000000


NUMBER OF CASES READ =        8    NUMBER OF CASES LISTED =        8
```

When split-file processing is in effect (see Chapter 15), the first variables in the matrix system file will be the split variables, followed by ROWTYPE_, VARNAME_, and the dependent variable(s). A full set of matrix materials is written for each splitfile group defined by the split variable(s). A split variable cannot have the same variable name as any other variable written to the matrix system file. If split-file processing is in effect when a matrix is written, the same split file must be in effect when that matrix is read by any procedure. (See Chapter 13 for more information on matrix system files.)

If grouping variables are in the matrix input file (for example, if you are reading matrix materials written by such procedures as ONEWAY or DISCRIMINANT) their values print between ROWTYPE_ and VARNAME_. However, though grouping variables are displayed among the matrix variables, they are treated like split-file variables and do not affect computations.

Additional Statistics. RELIABILITY writes only correlation type matrices that include the number of cases, mean, and standard deviation for each split-file group. An input matrix must have all these records in order for RELIABILITY to read the matrix materials.

Missing Values. Missing value treatment affects the values written to a matrix system file. When reading a matrix system file, be sure to specify a missing value treatment on RELIABILITY that is compatible with the treatment used to generate the matrix materials.

46.18
IN Keyword

The IN keyword on MATRIX specifies the file from which the matrix is read. There are two options:

(file)   *Read the matrix materials from a matrix system file.*

(*)   *Read the matrix materials from the active file.* The active file must be an appropriate matrix system file.

MATRIX=IN cannot be used in place of GET or DATA LIST to begin a new SPSS-X command file. MATRIX is a subcommand on RELIABILITY and RELIABILITY cannot run before an active file is defined.

In the following example, one set of matrix materials is read from the file named RELMTX. This specification assumes the current active file is not the file RELMTX:

```
RELIABILITY VARIABLES=ALL
  /MATRIX=IN (RELMTX)
```

SPSS-X reads variable names, variable and value labels, and print and write formats from the dictionary of the file RELMTX. RELMTX must have records of type N, MEAN, STDDEV, and CORR for each split file group.

To begin a new command file and immediately read a matrix, first GET the matrix file, then specify IN(*) on MATRIX. Alternatively, RELIABILITY can read a matrix written to the active file by another procedure. In the following example, RELIABILITY uses matrix input from procedure CORRELATIONS:

```
GET FILE=RAWDATA
CORRELATIONS VARIABLES=VAR1 TO VAR5
  /MATRIX=OUT(*)
RELIABILITY VARIABLES=VAR1 TO VAR5
  /MATRIX=IN(*)
```

46.19
LIMITATIONS

The following limitations apply to procedure RELIABILITY:

- A maximum of 10 VARIABLES subcommands.
- A maximum of 50 SCALE subcommands.
- A maximum of 500 variables referenced on the combined VARIABLES subcommands. Each mention of a variable counts one toward this limit.
- A maximum of 500 variables referenced on one SCALE subcommand.
- A maximum of 1,000 variables referenced on the combined SCALE subcommands. Each mention of a variable counts one toward this limit.
- If insufficient workspace is available to handle multiple VARIABLES subcommands, RELIABILITY deletes them in the reverse order they were specified until the allocated workspace is sufficient.

Syntax

REPORT

```
REPORT
 [/FORMAT=[{MANUAL  }] [{NOLIST   }] [ALIGN({LEFT  })]
          {AUTOMATIC}   {LIST[(n)]}       {CENTER}
                                          {RIGHT }

          [TSPACE({1})] [CHDSPACE({1})] [FTSPACE({1 })]
                  {n}            {n}             {n}
          [SUMSPACE({1})] [COLSPACE({4})] [BRKSPACE({ 1  })]
                    {n}             {n}             {  n }
                                                    {-1†}
          [LENGTH({1,length})] [MARGINS({1,width})]
                  {n,n    }             {n,n    }
                  {*,*    }             {*,*    }
          [CHALIGN({TOP    })] [UNDERSCORE({OFF})]
                   {BOTTOM†}               {ON†}
          [PAGE1({1})] [MISSING {'.'}]]
                 {n}            {'s'}
 [/OUTFILE=file]
 [/STRING=stringname (varname[(width)]) [(BLANK)] ['literal...'] )
 /VARIABLES=varname ({VALUE}) [+ varname({VALUE})] ['col head']
                     {LABEL}              {LABEL}
                     {DUMMY}              {DUMMY}
 [(option list)]
where option list can contain any of the following:
      width  OFFSET({0     })  {LEFT  }
                    {n     }   {CENTER}
                    {CENTER†}  {RIGHT }
 [/MISSING={VAR            }]
           {NONE           }
           {LIST(varlist{1})}
                        {n}
 [   /TITLE='line1' 'line2'...]  [   /FOOTNOTE='line1' 'line2'...]
         or                            or
 [/TITLE=LEFT 'line1' 'line2'...] [/FOOTNOTE=LEFT 'line1' 'line2'...]
 [      CENTER 'line1' 'line2'...] [       CENTER 'line1' 'line2'...]
 [      RIGHT 'line1' 'line2'...]  [       RIGHT 'line1' 'line2'...]
 [/BREAK=varlist [(TOTAL)] ['col head'] [(option list)]]

where option list can contain any of the following:
      width  {VALUE }  {NOTOTAL}  SKIP({1})  PAGE[(RESET)]
             {LABEL†}  {TOTAL  }       {n}
      OFFSET({0     })  UNDERSCORE[(varlist)]  {LEFT  }  {NONAME}
             {n     }                          {CENTER}  {NAME  }
             {CENTER†}                         {RIGHT }
 [/SUMMARY=function...['summary title'][(break col #1)]
          [SKIP({0})]]
                {n}
or
 [/SUMMARY=PREVIOUS[({1})]]
                    {n}
where function is
  aggregate [(varname[({PLAIN })][(d)][varname...]))]
                      {DOLLAR}
                      {COMMA }
or
  composite(agg(varname)...)[(report col[({PLAIN })][(d)])]]
                                         {DOLLAR}
                                         {COMMA }
```

†Default if FORMAT=AUTOMATIC.

Aggregate functions:

VALIDN	VARIANCE	PCLT(n)
SUM	KURTOSIS	PCIN(min,max)
MIN	SKEWNESS	FREQUENCY(min,max)
MAX	MEDIAN(min,max)	PERCENT(min,max)
MEAN	MODE(min,max)	
STDDEV	PCGT(n)	

Composite functions:

DIVIDE(agg(varname) agg(varname)[factor]
PCT(agg(varname) agg(varname)
SUBTRACT(agg(varname) agg(varname)
ADD(agg(varname) agg(varname)...)[factor]
GREAT(agg(varname) agg(varname)...)
LEAST(agg(varname) agg(varname)...)
AVERAGE(agg(varname) agg(varname)...)
MULTIPLY(agg(varname) agg(varname)...)[factor]

Contents

47.1	OVERVIEW
47.2	OPERATION
47.3	Report Organization
47.4	Basic Subcommands
47.5	Basic Reports
47.6	Preparing Data for REPORT
47.7	Trial Runs
47.8	Creating a Separate Listing File
47.9	BASIC REPORTS WITH AUTOMATIC FORMAT
47.10	Summary and Listing Reports
47.11	Specifying Report Variables
47.12	Defining Break Groups
47.13	Requesting Summary Statistics
47.14	Reports with Multiple Statistics
47.15	Column Headings
47.16	REPORT LAYOUT CRITERIA
47.17	Margins and Report Alignment
47.18	Column Widths
47.19	Report Contents
47.20	Justifying and Centering Contents in Columns
47.21	ADDITIONAL REPORT FEATURES
47.22	Reports with Multiple Break Levels
47.23	Generating Summary Statistics
47.24	Summary Titles
47.25	Reports with Totals
47.26	Using Composite Functions
47.27	Nested Composite Functions
47.28	Print Formats for Summaries
47.29	Adding Titles and Footnotes
47.30	Stacking Report Variables in a Column
47.31	Combining Break Groups in a Column
47.32	Repeating Summary Specifications
47.33	Creating Temporary String Variables
47.34	STRING Display
47.35	An Application Using STRING
47.36	Handling Missing Values
47.37	Changing the Missing-Value Indicator
47.38	OVERRIDING REPORT'S DEFAULT LAYOUT
47.39	Automatic versus Manual Format
47.40	Formatting Keywords and their Defaults
47.41	Overriding the Column Settings
47.42	Aligning the Report
47.43	Adjusting Margins
47.44	Adjusting Column Widths
47.45	Changing Column Headings
47.46	Positioning Column Headings
47.47	Heading Underscores
47.48	Underscores Between Listings and Summaries
47.49	Moving Summary Titles
47.50	Aligning Report Contents
47.51	Changing Column Contents
47.52	Adjusting Intercolumn Spacing
47.53	Overriding the Row Settings
47.54	The Report Page Layout
47.55	Adjusting Space Between Rows
47.56	Specifying Page Lengths
47.57	Alternative Page Numbers
47.58	Listing Reports with Totals
47.59	Displaying Multiple Statistics on One Line
47.60	LIMITATIONS
47.61	REPORT COMPARED WITH OTHER PROCEDURES
47.62	Producing CROSSBREAK-like Tables
47.63	Producing CROSSTABS-like Tables
47.64	REPORT and Other SPSS-X Commands
47.65	Split-File Processing

47

Chapter 47   REPORT

Case listings and descriptive statistics are basic tools for studying and presenting data. You can obtain case listings with LIST, frequency counts and descriptive statistics with FREQUENCIES and DESCRIPTIVES, and subpopulation statistics with MEANS. Each of these procedures uses a format designed to make the information clear; but if that format isn't what you need for presentation, you have limited control. REPORT gives you that control.

REPORT is a formatting tool. It allows you to present case listings and summary statistics (including frequencies) in report format. Your report can be one page long, or it can be hundreds of pages long. (If it is one page, you might consider using TABLES, whose specialty is formatting data for a one-page presentation.) With REPORT's subcommands and keywords you can specify the variables you want to summarize or list, and organize them into subgroups. You can calculate summary statistics on the report variables, and also calculate cross-variable statistics that are unavailable in other procedures, such as the ratio of two means.

In addition, REPORT provides a keyword AUTOMATIC to facilitate report design. This keyword automatically implements a set of the basic REPORT design features you are likely to want on most reports.

47.1
OVERVIEW

An SPSS-X report is made up of columns and rows. Columns arrange the variable information you want to see listed or summarized. Rows list the cases or groups you want to evaluate.

Summary reports display summary statistics for groups of cases. The summary information consists of the statistic or statistics you request for the report variables. Each statistic prints in a separate row on the report, referred to as a *summary line*.

Listing reports list individual cases. The case listings comprise the values and/or labels recorded for each of the report variables. In addition to listing cases, a listing report can display summary statistics.

In general, you should run summary reports when you have many cases and aren't interested in the specific value of each case. You should run listing reports when you have a relatively small number of cases and it's important to see the values or labels of each.

47.2
OPERATION

The VARIABLES subcommand is required on every REPORT command. The BREAK and SUMMARY subcommands are required on all *summary reports*. The FORMAT subcommand with keyword LIST is required on all *listing reports*.

The BREAK and SUMMARY subcommands are associated. You cannot use a SUMMARY subcommand without an associated BREAK subcommand. You can use multiple BREAK subcommands, and you can specify multiple SUMMARY subcommands for each BREAK.

Though VARIABLES is the only subcommand required on every REPORT, the following order must be observed among subcommands when they are used:

- The FORMAT subcommand must precede all other subcommands.
- The VARIABLES subcommand must precede the BREAK subcommand.
- The OUTFILE subcommand must precede the BREAK subcommand.
- The SUMMARY subcommand must immediately follow its associated BREAK subcommand. Multiple SUMMARIES associated with the same BREAK must be specified consecutively.
- The STRING subcommand must precede the VARIABLES subcommand.
- The TITLE and FOOTNOTE subcommands can appear anywhere after FORMAT, except between the BREAK and SUMMARY subcommands.
- The MISSING subcommand must follow the VARIABLES subcommand and precede the first BREAK subcommand.

47.3
Report Organization

To set up any SPSS-X report, you must consider:

- Whether you want case listings, summary statistics, or both. These will define the order of your report down the page. They will reflect the order of cases in your active file.
- Which variables you want to include on the report and in which order you want them to appear across the report.

Figure 47.3a is a summary report presenting summary statistics organized by division. Figure 47.3b presents a similar report for the same company with case listings included. (Only data for Carpeting and Appliances are shown in Figure 47.3b.)

Figure 47.3a   Summary personnel report

```
Personnel Data                                                              PAGE    1

                        Tenure      Tenure
                          in          in
Division        Age     Company     Grade     Salary--Annual
-----------     -----   -------     ------    --------------

Carpeting
Mean            30.75    4.04        3.31        $11,754
Appliances
Mean            31.11    3.81        3.54        $12,508
Furniture
Mean            36.87    4.79        4.08        $13,255
Hardware
Mean            36.20    4.60        4.57        $17,580
TOTAL
Mean            33.73    4.34        3.79        $13,179
```

This second report—a listing report—includes variables that identify a branch and employee last name, in addition to division. The last names are alphabetized within each branch store, and each branch store is identified within each division. *Division* defines the primary order of the rows. *Branch store* defines their secondary order. Alphabetizing the last names provides a convenient order for reading and identifying individual listings. The last row within each division is a summary line that displays the mean for the numeric report variables age, tenure, etc., for that division.

Figure 47.3b   Personnel report with case listings

```
Personnel Data                                                                    PAGE     1

                                        Tenure    Tenure
                  Branch                   in        in
Division          Store     Last Name    Age      Company   Grade    Salary——Annual
----------        ------    ----------   ---      -------   -----    -------------

Carpeting         Suburban  Cochran      22.00     3.92     3.08     $10,900
                            Ford         27.00     3.67     2.17      $9,200
                            Hoawinski    23.00     3.92     3.08     $10,900
                            Tygielski    35.00     6.00     5.33     $19,500

                  Downtown  Dan          36.00     3.83     3.25     $10,000
                            Gates        24.00     4.00     3.25     $10,000
                            Jones        44.00     4.83     4.33     $15,690
                            Katz         33.00     3.75     3.25     $10,000
                            Lavelle      27.00     4.33     3.17     $10,000
                            Mahr         33.00     2.67     2.67      $9,335
                            McAndrews    35.00     3.50     3.00     $15,520
                            Mulvihill    30.00     4.08     3.08     $10,000

Mean                                     30.75     4.04     3.31     $11,754

Appliances        Suburban  Johnson      42.00     6.50     6.50     $18,000
                            Martin       26.00     2.92     2.08      $8,000
                            Parris       24.00     3.17     3.17      $8,975
                            Powell       21.00     2.67     2.67      $8,700
                            Sanders      38.00     5.00     4.42     $28,300

                  Downtown  Provenza     33.00     3.42     2.92      $8,900
                            Sedowski     30.00     2.67     2.67      $7,500
                            Shavilje     32.00     2.92     2.92      $8,900
                            Snolik       34.00     5.08     4.50     $15,300

Mean                                     31.11     3.81     3.54     $12,508
```

47.4
Basic Subcommands

Four basic subcommands determine the appearance of the reports in Figures 47.3a and 47.3b:

FORMAT   Determines the report's general page layout and whether cases are listed. Precedes all other subcommands on any REPORT command.

VARIABLES   Specifies the variables that determine the report's columns. The order you list these *report variables* on the VARIABLES subcommand determines the order columns appear on the report. The VARIABLES subcommand is required.

BREAK   Specifies the variable(s) that break the report rows into subgroups. Break variables always print on the left side of the report, to the right of all the report variables.

SUMMARY   Names a statistic or set of statistics to calculate. Optionally controls summary line titles and print formats for summary cells.

REPORT has other subcommands, but the four above are the ones you'll use most often.

47.5
Basic Reports

Sections 47.9 through 47.15 demonstrate basic report concepts using employee information from a personnel department. The following commands define the records from that personnel department:

```
TITLE   Personnel Data
DATA LIST /S1 1-3 S2 4-5 S3 6-9
          LNAME 10-21(A) NAME 22-33(A)
          SEX 34 GRADE 35 (A) STORE 36 SALARY 37-41
          DIVISION 42 SHIFT 43 BDAY BMONTH BYEAR 44-49
          CMONTH CYEAR JMONTH JYEAR 50-57 MGRNM 58-67(A)
COMPUTE   AGE=87-BYEAR
COMPUTE   TENURE=(12-CMONTH +(12*(87-CYEAR)))/12
COMPUTE   JTENURE=(12-JMONTH +(12*(87-JYEAR)))/12
FORMATS   AGE (F5.2) TENURE JTENURE (F4.2) SALARY (DOLLAR7)
RECODE    GRADE('C'=4)('X'=1)('S'=2)('M'=3) INTO JOBGRADE
VARIABLE LABELS JOBGRADE 'Job Grade'
          STORE 'Branch Store'
          DIVISION 'Division'
          LNAME 'Last Name'
          NAME 'First Name'
          MGRNM "Manager's Name"
          SALARY 'Salary--Annual'
          AGE 'Age'
          SEX 'Sex'
          SHIFT 'Shift'
          TENURE 'Tenure in Company'
          JTENURE 'Tenure in Grade'
VALUE LABELS JOBGRADE 1 'Sales Staff' 2 'Supervisory Staff'
          3 'Managerial Staff' 4 'Support Staff'/
          SEX 1 'Female' 2 'Male'/
          STORE 1 'Suburban' 2 'Downtown'/
          DIVISION 1 'Carpeting' 2 'Appliances' 3 'Furniture'
          4 'Hardware'/
          SHIFT 1 'First' 2' Second' 3 'Weekend'
BEGIN DATA
388551234Ford         Harriet L.    1C1 920011201155 479108001iver Nelson
625144710Cochran      Sandra L.     1X1109001123 960 179117901iver Nelson
700155726Hoawinski    Pamela S.     1X1109001123 959 179117901iver Nelson
              .
              .
              .
492554519Carlyle      Theresa S.    1X21905043 8 94212761276Sheila Potts
701 02337Syms         Ellis E.      2C12250042281150 878 878Sheila Potts
278878955Jacobesen    Hans B.       2C2220004217 238 678 678Sheila Potts
END DATA
```

- The TITLE command provides a title for the job.

- The DATA LIST command identifies the variables and their location in the inline data contained within the BEGIN DATA and END DATA commands.

- The COMPUTE commands transform recorded data information on each employee into age, tenure, and tenure within a job grade.

- The FORMATS command provides printing instructions for the computed variables. A variable's format affects REPORT's ability to properly align data within the report columns.

- The RECODE command creates numeric versions of alphabetic data.

- The VARIABLE LABELS command provides descriptive labels for the variables. REPORT uses these labels as default column headings. Labels are assigned to SEX, DIVISION, and SHIFT to get upper and lower case.

- The VALUE LABELS command provides descriptive labels for the values recorded for the specified variables.

Once you've defined the active file you can run procedure REPORT. If you wanted to run a report that shows the division averages for employee age, length of employment, time in current position, and salary, you would use the following commands:

```
SORT CASES BY DIVISION
REPORT FORMAT=AUTOMATIC
      /VARIABLES=AGE TENURE JTENURE SALARY
      /BREAK=DIVISION
      /SUMMARY=MEAN
```

- The SORT CASES command ensures that cases (employees) from the same division reside together in the file.

- The REPORT command specifies the report procedure.

• The FORMAT subcommand sets up the way the report will be presented on the page. The keyword AUTOMATIC facilitates report design by automatically implementing the basic REPORT features you are most likely to use. AUTOMATIC features are used only if you specify FORMAT = AUTOMATIC.

• The VARIABLES subcommand determines the report columns and their order.

• The BREAK subcommand specifies the variable that breaks the report rows into subgroups.

• The SUMMARY subcommand names the mean as the statistic to calculate.

These report commands use one break variable, DIVISION, to split the personnel file into separate divisions. Figure 47.5 shows the report. REPORT calculates the means for age, salary, tenure within company, and tenure within job grade for each division of the company.

Figure 47.5 Personnel report with AUTOMATIC format

```
Personnel Data                                                                    PAGE    1

                       Tenure      Tenure
                         in          in
Division      Age     Company      Grade    Salary--Annual
---------    -----    -------     -------    --------------

Carpeting
Mean         30.75     4.04         3.31        $11,754
Appliances
Mean         31.11     3.81         3.54        $12,508
Furniture
Mean         36.87     4.79         4.08        $13,255
Hardware
Mean         36.20     4.60         4.57        $17,580
```

Many of REPORT's features depend on how the data are organized in the file. For example, the SORT command plays an important part in the REPORT display. The next section discusses data considerations.

47.6
Preparing Data for
REPORT

The BREAK and SUMMARY subcommands are closely associated. As you can see in Figures 47.3a and 47.3b, when REPORT calculates a statistic, it calculates it for each sub-group defined by the variable you name on the BREAK subcommand. When the value of the break variable changes, REPORT calculates and prints the statistics you requested on the SUMMARY subcommand. It then prints the next value of the break variable and resumes reading cases until the value of the break variable changes again. It prints the requested summary statistics every time it reads a change in the value for the break variable.

However, REPORT does not organize the data as it reads the cases and computes the summaries. Instead it reads cases in the order they reside in the file, listing them (if you request a listing) while keeping track of information you requested for summaries.

Before you run REPORT, therefore, you must organize data in the file so all cases with the same value for the break variable reside together. It doesn't matter if the values are in ascending, descending, or some other order—only that all the cases in the same group are together.

To organize data in the file, you use the SORT CASES command immediately before the REPORT command. For example

SORT CASES BY DIVISION

organizes the data in Figure 47.5 by the subgroups Carpeting, Appliances, Furniture, and Hardware. If you wanted to further subdivide these divisions according to the subgroupings of other variables, you would name additional variables on the SORT CASES command. For example

```
SORT CASES BY DIVISION STORE
```

groups the data in Figure 47.6 into the divisions of Carpeting, Appliances, Furniture, and Hardware, then organizes the data within each division according to the subgroups of variable STORE, which are Suburban and Downtown.

Specify the variables on the SORT CASES command in the order you intend to use them in successive BREAK subcommands within REPORT. The following commands produce the report in Figure 47.6:

```
SORT CASES BY DIVISION STORE LNAME
REPORT FORMAT=AUTOMATIC LIST
       /VARS=LNAME AGE TENURE JTENURE SALARY
       /BREAK=DIVISION
       /SUMMARY=MEAN
       /BREAK=STORE
```

Notice the specification of LNAME on the SORT CASES command. Alphabetizing the last names provides a convenient order for reading and identifying individual employees within each store. However, those names do not define subgroups on the report. LNAME is not a break variable; it's a report variable defined on the VARIABLES subcommand. You can list report variables on the SORT CASES command as long as you list them *after* all of your break variables.

Figure 47.6   Personnel report with case listings

```
Personnel Data                                                                                  PAGE   1

                                             Tenure    Tenure
                     Branch                     in        in
Division             Store    Last Name    Age  Company   Grade    Salary—Annual
--------             -----    ---------    ---  -------   -----    -------------

Carpeting   Suburban   Cochran      22.00    3.92     3.08      $10,900
                       Ford         27.00    3.67     2.17       $9,200
                       Hoawinski    23.00    3.92     3.08      $10,900
                       Tygielski    35.00    6.00     5.33      $19,500

            Downtown   Dan          36.00    3.83     3.25      $10,000
                       Gates        24.00    4.00     3.25      $10,000
                       Jones        44.00    4.83     4.33      $15,690
                       Katz         33.00    3.75     3.25      $10,000
                       Lavelle      27.00    4.33     3.17      $10,000
                       Mahr         33.00    2.67     2.67       $9,335
                       McAndrews    35.00    3.50     3.00      $15,520
                       Mulvihill    30.00    4.08     3.08      $10,000

Mean                                30.75    4.04     3.31      $11,754

Appliances  Suburban   Johnson      42.00    6.50     6.50      $18,000
                       Martin       26.00    2.92     2.08       $8,000
                       Parris       24.00    3.17     3.17       $8,975
                       Powell       21.00    2.67     2.67       $8,700
                       Sanders      38.00    5.00     4.42      $28,300

            Downtown   Provenza     33.00    3.42     2.92       $8,900
                       Sedowski     30.00    2.67     2.67       $7,500
                       Shavilje     32.00    2.92     2.92       $8,900
                       Snolik       34.00    5.08     4.50      $15,300

Mean                                31.11    3.81     3.54      $12,508
```

47.7
Trial Runs

Because REPORT is so flexible and the output has so many components, you may decide you want to override some of the AUTOMATIC format decisions. To refine a report with a minimal cost in computer resources, you can run several reports with different specifications using a small file until you obtain your intended format. Obviously, the larger the file, the more important it is to access a small subset of that file in trying out various REPORT specifications. To process a subset of the file as inexpensively as possible, use one of the following techniques:

- You can use the N OF CASES command when reading raw data or when accessing a system file to limit the number of cases read (see Chapter 11). SPSS-X does not attempt to read more cases than the number specified on the N OF CASES command. For example, assume the file contains 10,000 cases. If you specify 10 on the N OF CASES command, REPORT only reads the first 10 cases.

- If the REPORT contains breaks, and the labeling and spacing of breaks are important considerations, you can obtain a subset of the entire file containing cases from several breaks by using the SAMPLE command (see Chapter 11).

47.8
Creating a Separate Listing File

By default, REPORT directs its output to the same listing file as the rest of the output in your job. You can use the OUTFILE subcommand to send a report to a separate listing file. You must specify the OUTFILE subcommand after the FORMAT subcommand but before the BREAK subcommand. The commands

```
SORT CASES BY DIVISION
REPORT FORMAT=AUTOMATIC
      /OUTFILE=RPTLST
      /VARS=AGE TENURE JTENURE SALARY
      /BREAK=DIVISION
      /SUMMARY=MEAN
```

send the report to file RPTLST. The separate listing file receives only the report, without command printback or system messages. To append other reports to the same listing file, name the file on the OUTFILE subcommand of subsequent REPORT procedures.

47.9
BASIC REPORTS WITH AUTOMATIC FORMAT

REPORT's most comprehensive format specification is FORMAT= AUTOMATIC. By specifying the keyword AUTOMATIC, you instruct REPORT to center column headings and data when appropriate, bottom align and underscore all column headings, print labels rather than values for all break variables, include variable labels among the factors it evaluates when determining column widths, and shrink the report if it's too wide for its margins.

To specify an SPSS-X report with automatic format, you combine the SORT CASES and REPORT commands with the FORMAT subcommand and the keyword AUTOMATIC. The following commands generate the summary report in Figure 47.9:

```
SORT CASES BY DIVISION
REPORT FORMAT=AUTOMATIC
      /VARIABLES=AGE TENURE JTENURE SALARY
      /BREAK=DIVISION
      /SUMMARY=MEAN
```

Figure 47.9   Personnel report with AUTOMATIC format

```
Personnel Data                                                              PAGE    1

                          Tenure      Tenure
                            in          in
Division        Age      Company      Grade    Salary--Annual
----------     -----     -------     ------    --------------

Carpeting
Mean           30.75      4.04        3.31        $11,754
Appliances
Mean           31.11      3.81        3.54        $12,508
Furniture
Mean           36.87      4.79        4.08        $13,255
Hardware
Mean           36.20      4.60        4.57        $17,580
```

The keyword AUTOMATIC instructs REPORT to do the following for the report in Figure 47.9:

- Align the bottom lines of all column headings.
- Underline all the column headings.
- Print the labels Carpeting, Appliances, Furniture, and Hardware instead of the values 1, 2, 3, and 4 for the break variable DIVISION.
- Left-justify the column heading for DIVISION and the divisions and summary titles within the column.
- Center the column headings for variables AGE, TENURE, JTENURE, and SALARY.
- Center the numeric data within their columns. (If data on your reports do not appear centered, refer to Section 47.20 for a possible explanation.)

Sections 47.16 through 47.20 outline in more detail the criteria AUTOMATIC uses to accomplish these and other tasks. Sections 47.38 through 47.59 explain how you can override each setting that does not meet your presentation needs.

47.10
Summary and Listing Reports

The FORMAT subcommand determines whether a report is a summary or a listing report. By default, the FORMAT subcommand does not list cases. If you want case listings, you must request them with the keyword LIST.

Summary Report. A summary report displays summary statistics but does not list cases. To run a summary report, specify:

```
REPORT FORMAT=AUTOMATIC
       /VARIABLES=varlist
       /BREAK=variable
       /SUMMARY=function
```

In addition to the VARIABLES subcommand, at least one BREAK and one SUMMARY subcommand are required for every summary report. You do not complete the specification for a summary report until you use the SUMMARY subcommand to name the statistic you want calculated.

   The commands that generate the report in Figure 47.9 provide a good example of a summary report:

```
SORT CASES BY DIVISION
REPORT FORMAT=AUTOMATIC
       /VARIABLES=AGE TENURE JTENURE SALARY
       /BREAK=DIVISION
       /SUMMARY=MEAN
```

The BREAK subcommand specifies that the report be ordered by DIVISION, and the SUMMARY subcommand stipulates that the mean AGE, TENURE, JTENURE, and SALARY be calculated for each subgroup of DIVISION.

Listing Reports. A listing report displays individual case listings and can also display summary statistics. The keyword LIST on the FORMAT subcommand requests a listing report:

```
REPORT FORMAT=AUTOMATIC LIST
```

The keyword LIST applies to all variables named on the VARIABLES subcommand. You cannot selectively specify variables to list. Only two subcommands are required for a listing report: the FORMAT subcommand and the VARIABLES subcommand.

   For example, to run a report that provides an alphabetical list of employees and shows their age, tenure in the company, and tenure within a job grade, you would specify:

```
SORT CASES BY LNAME
REPORT FORMAT=AUTOMATIC LIST
       /VARS=LNAME AGE TENURE JTENURE
```

Figure 47.10a shows the listing report.

Figure 47.10a   Listing report

```
Personnel Data                                                          PAGE    1

                          Tenure       Tenure
                          in           in
Last Name        Age      Company      Grade
-------------    -----    -------      -------

Baker            42.00    5.25         3.75
Blount           41.00    5.25         3.75
Carlyle          40.00    6.00         6.00
Cochran          22.00    3.92         3.08
Cochran          39.00    5.50         5.50
Dan              36.00    3.83         3.25
Farkas           37.00    4.42         3.67
Ford             27.00    3.67         2.17
Ford             36.00    4.50         3.67
Gates            24.00    4.00         3.25
Golden           42.00    4.50         3.67
Gonzales         42.00    4.75         4.75
Hoawinski        23.00    3.92         3.08
Jacobesen        44.00    4.50         4.50
Johnson          42.00    6.50         6.50
Jones            44.00    4.83         4.33
Katz             33.00    3.75         3.25
Lavelle          27.00    4.33         3.17
Logan            43.00    4.50         3.67
Mahr             33.00    2.67         2.67
Martin           26.00    2.92         2.08
McAndrews        35.00    3.50         3.00
Michel           39.00    5.25         5.25
Miles            33.00    6.83         5.33
Mulvihill        30.00    4.08         3.08
Parris           24.00    3.17         3.17
Powell           21.00    2.67         2.67
Provenza         33.00    3.42         2.92
Pruitt           38.00    6.25         6.25
Rosen            26.00    2.67         2.50
Sanders          38.00    5.00         4.42
Sedowski         30.00    2.67         2.67
Shavilje         32.00    2.92         2.92
Snolik           34.00    5.08         4.50
Syms             32.00    4.33         4.33
Totman           41.00    4.50         3.50
Tygielski        35.00    6.00         5.33
Wajda            26.00    3.17         3.17
Washington       32.00    4.42         3.67
White            25.00    3.92         3.33
Wilson           36.00    4.42         3.75
```

The keyword LIST has an optional argument (n) that controls the spacing of cases. By default, LIST inserts no blank lines between cases. An integer value in parentheses specifies a blank line after every *n* cases. For example, LIST(1) produces a double-spaced listing and LIST(3) lists cases in sets of three. The spacing option (n) makes it easier to read reports with many cases. The following commands generate the report shown in Figure 47.10b (only part of the report is shown):

```
SORT CASES BY LNAME
REPORT FORMAT=AUTOMATIC LIST(3)
       /VARS=LNAME AGE TENURE JTENURE
```

Figure 47.10b   Personnel report with optional spacing

```
Personnel Data                                                          PAGE    1

                          Tenure       Tenure
                          in           in
Last Name        Age      Company      Grade
-------------    -----    -------      -------

Baker            42.00    5.25         3.75
Blount           41.00    5.25         3.75
Carlyle          40.00    6.00         6.00

Cochran          22.00    3.92         3.08
Cochran          39.00    5.50         5.50
Dan              36.00    3.83         3.25

Farkas           37.00    4.42         3.67
Ford             27.00    3.67         2.17
Ford             36.00    4.50         3.67
```

47.11
Specifying Report Variables

The VARIABLES subcommand determines the report columns and their order on the report. The minimum VARIABLES specification is a list of variables, as in

```
VARIABLES=LNAME AGE TENURE JTENURE
```

which instructs REPORT to list or summarize data for variables LNAME, AGE, TENURE, and JTENURE. You can use the keyword TO to imply variables on the VARIABLES subcommand.

Figure 47.10b shows that, by default, REPORT displays values for the variables specified on the VARIABLES subcommand. Frequently when you run a listing report you want to see value labels for the report variables rather than the values themselves. For example, if you want to run a personnel report that includes an employee's sex, you would prefer to see the labels Female and Male rather than the values 1 and 2 on the report. By specifying the keyword (LABEL) after the variable name on the VARIABLES subcommand, you instruct RE-PORT to print labels rather than values for that variable.

For example, to produce a listing report that shows the sex, age, job grade, and work shift for each employee, you would use the following commands:

```
SORT CASES BY LNAME
REPORT FORMAT=AUTOMATIC LIST
     /VARS=LNAME SEX (LABEL) AGE JOBGRADE (LABEL) SHIFT (LABEL)
```

The keyword (LABEL) generates a descriptive report, as you can see in Figure 47.11 (only part of the report is shown).

Figure 47.11   Personnel report with keyword (LABEL)

```
Personnel Data
                                                                        PAGE   1
Last Name       Sex       Age    Job Grade          Shift
-----------     ------    -----  ----------------   -------

Baker           Male      42.00  Sales Staff        Weekend
Blount          Male      41.00  Sales Staff        Weekend
Carlyle         Female    40.00  Sales Staff        Weekend
Cochran         Female    22.00  Sales Staff        First
Cochran         Male      39.00  Sales Staff        Second
Dan             Male      36.00  Sales Staff        Weekend
Farkas          Male      37.00  Sales Staff        First
Ford            Female    27.00  Support Staff      First
Ford            Female    36.00  Sales Staff        Weekend
Gates           Female    24.00  Sales Staff        Second
Golden          Female    42.00  Sales Staff        First
Gonzales        Female    42.00  Support Staff      First
Hoawinski       Female    23.00  Sales Staff        First
Jacobesen       Male      44.00  Supervisory Staff  Second
Johnson         Female    42.00  Sales Staff        Second
```

If the variable list contains a set of inclusive variables implied by the keyword TO, (LABEL) applies to the entire set of variables in the list. However, (LABEL) cannot be implied for a set of variables named individually. For example, in

```
/VARIABLES=V1 TO V5 (LABEL)
```

(LABEL) applies to all variables implied by V1 TO V5. But in

```
/VARIABLES=V1 V2 V3 V4 V5 (LABEL)
```

(LABEL) applies only to V5.

47.12
Defining Break Groups

The BREAK subcommand specifies the variable that breaks the report rows into subgroups. Because the REPORT command does not organize data, you must first use the SORT command to organize cases into the break groups you intend to specify on the BREAK subcommand. The commands

```
SORT CASES BY DIVISION
REPORT FORMAT=AUTOMATIC LIST
        /VARS=AGE TENURE JTENURE SALARY
        /BREAK=DIVISION
        /SUMMARY=MEAN
```

generate the report shown in Figure 47.12. The BREAK=DIVISION subcommand specifies a row for each different value of DIVISION, whose labels are Carpeting, Appliances, Furniture, and Hardware. Notice it isn't necessary to specify (LABEL) on the BREAK subcommand. With FORMAT= AUTOMATIC, (LABEL) is the default for break variables. If the variable has no labels, REPORT prints the values. If the variable has labels but you prefer to see values, specify (VALUE) after the variable name, as in

```
/BREAK=DIVISION(VALUE)
```

Figure 47.12 Personnel report with one break variable

```
Personnel Data                                                          PAGE    1

                       Tenure     Tenure
                         in         in
Division       Age     Company     Grade    Salary--Annual
--------       ---     -------     -----    --------------

Carpeting     27.00     3.67        2.17      $9,200
              22.00     3.92        3.08     $10,900
              23.00     3.92        3.08     $10,900
              24.00     4.00        3.25     $10,000
              30.00     4.08        3.08     $10,000
              27.00     4.33        3.17     $10,000
              33.00     2.67        2.67      $9,335
              33.00     3.75        3.25     $10,000
              44.00     4.83        4.33     $15,690
              36.00     3.83        3.25     $10,000
              35.00     3.50        3.00     $15,520
              35.00     6.00        5.33     $19,500

Mean          30.75     4.04        3.31     $11,754

Appliances    21.00     2.67        2.67      $8,700
              26.00     2.92        2.08      $8,000
              32.00     2.92        2.92      $8,900
              33.00     3.42        2.92      $8,900
              34.00     5.08        4.50     $15,300
              24.00     3.17        3.17      $8,975
              42.00     6.50        6.50     $18,000
              30.00     2.67        2.67      $7,500
              38.00     5.00        4.42     $28,300

Mean          31.11     3.81        3.54     $12,508
```

Break variables print on the left side of the report. When FORMAT = AUTOMATIC, labels from the break variables print on the same line as the values from the report variables. For example, in Figure 47.12, the label Carpeting prints on the same line as the values for the first employee.

The BREAK subcommand is required for all summary reports; it is optional for listing reports. If you do not want to break a listing report into subgroups, omit the BREAK subcommand.

47.13
Requesting Summary Statistics

To request statistics on either a summary or listing report, specify the statistic on a SUMMARY subcommand immediately after the BREAK subcommand (you cannot use a SUMMARY subcommand without a corresponding BREAK subcommand; the BREAK subcommand must precede its associated SUMMARY subcommands).

For example, the commands

```
SORT CASES BY DIVISION
REPORT FORMAT=AUTOMATIC
        /VARS=AGE TENURE SALARY
        /BREAK=DIVISION
        /SUMMARY=MAX
```

request the display of the maximum values recorded for AGE, TENURE, and SALARY at each break level of the variable DIVISION. Figure 47.13 shows the report.

Figure 47.13 Personnel report with one statistic

```
Personnel Data                                                          PAGE    1

                      Tenure
                        in
   Division     Age   Company   Salary--Annual
   --------     ---   -------   -------------

   Carpeting

   Maximum     44.00    6.00      $19,500

   Appliances

   Maximum     42.00    6.50      $28,300

   Furniture

   Maximum     43.00    6.83      $17,050

   Hardware

   Maximum     44.00    6.00      $22,500
```

The following is a partial list of the simple summaries available in REPORT:

VALIDN	*Valid number of cases.* VALIDN is the only function available for string variables.
VARIANCE	*Variance.*
SUM	*Sum of values.*
MEAN	*Mean.*
SD	*Standard deviation.*
MIN	*Minimum value encountered.*
MAX	*Maximum value encountered.*

REPORT can calculate many summary statistics. More complete lists are provided in Section 47.23 on summary aggregate statistics and Section 47.26 on composite functions.

47.14
Reports with Multiple Statistics

Frequently you'll want more than one statistic for each report variable. In the example in Section 47.13 you might want to see the minimum and mean, as well as the maximum for each variable. Adding statistics is simply a matter of including more than one SUMMARY subcommand following the BREAK subcommand. Each SUMMARY subcommand adds another line of summary statistics. The following specifications produce the report in Figure 47.14:

```
SORT CASES BY DIVISION
REPORT FORMAT=AUTOMATIC
        /VARS=AGE TENURE SALARY
        /BREAK=DIVISION
        /SUMMARY=MIN
        /SUMMARY=MEAN
        /SUMMARY=MAX
```

Figure 47.14 Personnel report with multiple statistics

```
Personnel Data                                                              PAGE    1

                        Tenure
                          in
    Division      Age   Company   Salary--Annual
    --------      ---   -------   --------------

    Carpeting

    Minimum      22.00    2.67        $9,200
    Mean         30.75    4.04       $11,754
    Maximum      44.00    6.00       $19,500

    Appliances

    Minimum      21.00    2.67        $7,500
    Mean         31.11    3.81       $12,508
    Maximum      42.00    6.50       $28,300

    Furniture

    Minimum      25.00    3.17        $8,975
    Mean         36.87    4.79       $13,255
    Maximum      43.00    6.83       $17,050

    Hardware

    Minimum      26.00    2.67        $7,450
    Mean         36.20    4.60       $17,580
    Maximum      44.00    6.00       $22,500
```

47.15
Column Headings

Each break and report column has a column heading. By default, REPORT uses the variable label for the heading, which it can print on the report in mixed case. If there is no label, REPORT uses the variable name, which it can print in upper case only.

REPORT wraps default column headings within their column widths, using as many lines as necessary and attempting to split lines meaningfully at spaces. With automatic format, REPORT centers each column heading within the width of its column. However, when value labels or string values exceed the width of the longest word in the heading, REPORT left-justifies the heading.

To specify a column heading, enclose the heading in apostrophes or quotation marks following the variable name on either the VARIABLES or BREAK subcommands. With automatic format, REPORT does not wrap a heading you specify; it prints the heading exactly as you arrange it in your specification. To print the heading on multiple lines, enclose each line within its own set of apostrophes or quotation marks. To include an apostrophe in the heading, use quotation marks around the heading. For example,

```
SORT CASES BY DIVISION
REPORT FORMAT=AUTOMATIC LIST
        /VARIABLES=LNAME 'Employee'
                   AGE "Employee's Age" TENURE JTENURE
        /BREAK=DIVISION 'Company' 'Division'
        /SUMMARY=MEAN
```

produces the report in Figure 47.15 (only the first few lines of the report are shown). Each heading is centered, except for Company Division and Employee. Because DIVISION and LNAME are string variables with values wider than the longest word in the column heading, the column headings are left-justified.

Figure 47.15 Column headings

```
Personnel Data                                                                    PAGE   1

Company                                      Tenure       Tenure
Division        Employee     Employee's Age   in           in
                                             Company      Grade
---------       --------     -------------   -------      -------

Carpeting       Ford            27.00          3.67         2.17
                Cochran         22.00          3.92         3.08
                Hoawinski       23.00          3.92         3.08
                Gates           24.00          4.00         3.25
                Mulvihill       30.00          4.08         3.08
                Lavelle         27.00          4.33         3.17
                Mahr            33.00          2.67         2.67
```

The column heading Employee's Age is considerably wider than any data entered for AGE. Nevertheless, REPORT widens the column to accommodate the specified heading. Though REPORT=AUTOMATIC wraps default headings, it does not wrap headings you specify. If you want Employee's Age to appear on two lines, put separate quotes or apostrophes around each word, as was done for 'Company' 'Division'.

To obtain a column with no heading, specify a blank within apostrophes.

47.16
REPORT LAYOUT CRITERIA

Sections 47.17 through 47.20 outline the criteria REPORT evaluates and implements to format a report. Some specifications it uses are determined by the keyword AUTOMATIC. Others are determined by REPORT's default settings that are in effect whether or not you specify AUTOMATIC.

Sections 47.17 through 47.20 focus primarily on FORMAT=AUTOMATIC. Sections 47.39 and 47.40 discuss the distinctions between FORMAT= AUTOMATIC and FORMAT=MANUAL. Sections 47.41 through 47.59 explain how you can override each of REPORT's automatic and default settings.

47.17
Margins and Report Alignment

Report margins determine the maximum permissible width for any given report. The maximum permissible width is not always the finished report's actual width. For example, a report's margins may allow for a report up to 80 characters wide. The finished report, however, may be only 50 characters wide.

Report alignment refers to a report's position relative to its defined margins. For example, report margins of (1,80) allow for an 80-character report. If the finished report is only 50 characters wide, the report's alignment refers to whether the report is left-justified against column 1 of the margins, right-justified against column 80, or centered between columns 1 and 80.

Margins. REPORT uses a default left margin of 1 and a default right margin equal to your system's default width. Default values differ among installations, but most systems use either 80 or 132 characters as a default right margin.

If you use the SET WIDTH command (Chapter 4) to specify a job width, the SET WIDTH command overrides the system default width and determines REPORT'S default right margin. For example, the commands

```
GET FILE=PERSONNEL
SET WIDTH 90
     .
     .
     .
SORT CASES BY DIVISION
REPORT FORMAT=AUTOMATIC
      /VARS=AGE TENURE JTENURE SALARY
      /BREAK=DIVISION
      /SUMMARY=MEAN
```

set a width of 90 that overrides the system's default width. The specified value 90 becomes REPORT'S default right margin.

Report Alignment. When the actual width of a report is less than the maximum allowed by its margins, its data columns are left-justified within the report margins. Titles and footnotes you specify with the CENTER, LEFT, or RIGHT keywords are also centered, left-justified, or right-justified relative to the report margins.

47.18
Column Widths

When you don't specify a column width for a variable, REPORT determines a default width, using the *maximum* of the following for each variable:

- The widest print format in the column, whether it is a variable print format or a summary print format.
- The width of any temporary variable you define with REPORT's STRING subcommand.
- If you assign a column heading, the length of the longest title line in that heading. For example, VARS = TENURE 'Tenure in Company' 'Measured' 'in Months' specifies 'Tenure in Company' as the longest line in a three-line heading.
- When no column heading is specified, the length of the longest word in the variable label, or the length of the variable name. (If FORMAT=MANUAL, variable labels are not evaluated.)
- If you specify (LABEL), the length of the variable's longest value label. (With FORMAT=AUTOMATIC, (LABEL) is the default for break variables.) REPORT reads value labels from the dictionary, so it's possible for you to exclude a value from your report, yet still have that value's label determine the width of a column. (If FORMAT=MANUAL, REPORT uses the length of the variable's longest value label, up to 20 characters; 20 is the largest value it uses for this criterion with MANUAL format.)

The above are default criteria for all reports, with the exceptions noted in parentheses on the last two items.

The following commands generate the report in Figure 47.18:

```
SORT CASES BY DIVISION LNAME
REPORT FORMAT=AUTOMATIC LIST
      /STRING=SOCSEC(S1 '-' S2 '-' S3)
      /VARS=LNAME '*2' ' ' ' ' 'Last Name'
           SOCSEC '*3' 'Social' 'Security' 'Number'
           TENURE '*4' 'Tenure in Company' 'Measured' 'in Months'
           SALARY '*5' ' ' ' ' 'Salary'
      /BREAK=DIVISION '   *1' ' ' ' ' 'Division'
      /SUMMARY=SUM(SALARY)
```

Only one division from the report is shown. The report's footnotes indicate the criteria that determine each column's width.

Figure 47.18   Column widths

```
    *1            *2            *3              *4               *5
                                Social       Tenure in Company
                                Security        Measured
    Division      Last Name     Number          in Months      Salary
    --------      ---------     ------          ---------      ------

    Appliances    Johnson       412-51-0041        6.50        $18,000
                  Martin        422-48-7446        2.92         $8,000
                  Parris        380-33-4438        3.17         $8,975
                  Powell        522-72-2535        2.67         $8,700
                  Provenza      622-38-7646        3.42         $8,900
                  Sanders       255-83-5836        5.00        $28,300
                  Sedowski      653-88-3365        2.67         $7,500
                  Shavilje      600-36-5625        2.92         $8,900
                  Snolik        955-11-8119        5.08        $15,300

    Sum                                                       $112,575


    Column Widths Determined by:

       *1 Variable's longest label
       *2 Variable print format
       *3 Width of variable created by STRING subcommand
       *4 Width of longest title line in the column heading
       *5 Width of summary print format
```

Intercolumn Spacing. REPORT subtracts the combined column widths of the break and report variables from the REPORT margins. It then divides the result by the number of columns minus 1. It uses this value or 4, whichever is less, as the space between each column.

Automatic Fit. When the above criteria result in a report that is too wide for the report margins, FORMAT=AUTOMATIC shrinks the report. AUTOMATIC performs the following two steps sequentially, stopping as soon as the report fits within the margins:

1 FORMAT=AUTOMATIC reduces intercolumn spacing incrementally until it reaches a minimum intercolumn space of 1. It will never reduce it to 0.

2 As a last resort, AUTOMATIC shortens strings. It begins with the longest string from a string variable at least 15 characters wide. It shortens the string as much as needed, up to 40% of its length. If necessary it repeats the step, using different string variables. It will not shorten the same string twice.

REPORT does not implement the *automatic fit* criteria unless FORMAT = AUTOMATIC.

47.19
Report Contents

By default, FORMAT=AUTOMATIC displays value labels (if assigned) for break variables and values for report variables. (FORMAT=MANUAL displays values for both break and report variables.) You can override the defaults by using the keyword (LABEL) after the variable name to specify labels, and (VALUE) to specify values. Section 47.20 discusses how REPORT aligns values and labels within their columns.

On summary lines REPORT displays the values it calculates for specified statistics.

The following commands generate the report in Figure 47.19 (only one division is shown):

```
SORT CASES BY DIVISION JOBGRADE
REPORT FORMAT=AUTOMATIC LIST
    /VARS=JOBGRADE(LABEL) TENURE SALARY
    /BREAK=DIVISION
    /SUMMARY=MEAN(TENURE SALARY)
```

Because FORMAT=AUTOMATIC, the break variable DIVISION automatically displays its assigned value label. (LABEL) is specified for report variable JOBGRADE to make the column contents more descriptive. TENURE and SALARY display values. The summary line in the report displays a mean for TENURE and SALARY.

Figure 47.19   Report contents

47.20
Justifying and Centering Contents in Columns

Before REPORT positions data in a column, it first determines whether the data are from string or numeric variables. It considers temporary variables you create with REPORT's STRING subcommand (Section 47.33) to be string variables, even if you use numeric variables to create them.

String Variables. FORMAT=AUTOMATIC centers string variables (or numeric variables with LABEL) within their column, based on the length of the longest string (or label) in the data. REPORT reads value labels from the dictionary, so it's possible for you to exclude a value from your report, yet still have that value's label determine the center position for the data. REPORT does not center data unless FORMAT=AUTOMATIC.

If you specify a column width (or with FORMAT=MANUAL, if the maximum default width of 20 is used), values or labels too wide for the assigned width wrap to ensure the entire string is displayed in the column. This applies to both report and break variables. If possible, REPORT breaks strings at a space. Otherwise it displays as many characters as will fit on one line, then wraps the remaining characters to the next line. The lines from a single case all print on the same page. All column data are top-aligned.

Numeric Variables. If you specify (LABEL), FORMAT=AUTOMATIC displays the labels as discussed above for string variables. Without (LABEL), FORMAT=AUTOMATIC centers numeric values, based on the width of the widest variable or summary format in the column. For example, if the widest format is 5 spaces wide and the column is 10 spaces wide, REPORT leaves the two right spaces blank and prints the rightmost digit of all numbers in the third space from the right. REPORT does not center data unless FORMAT=AUTOMATIC.

Sometimes data centered by REPORT appears to be right-justified or off-center. For example, the variables AGE, TENURE, and JTENURE used throughout this chapter are variables computed through the following commands:

```
DATA LIST    /1 S1 1-3 S2 4-5 S3 6-9
                LNAME 10-21(A) NAME 22-41(A)
                SEX 42 GRADE 43 (A) STORE 44 SALARY 45-49
                DIVISION 50 SHIFT 51 BDAY BMONTH BYEAR 52-57
                CMONTH CYEAR JMONTH JYEAR 58-65
COMPUTE      AGE=87-BYEAR
COMPUTE      TENURE=(12-CMONTH +(12*(87-CYEAR)))/12
COMPUTE      JTENURE=(12-JMONTH +(12*(87-JYEAR)))/12
VARIABLE LABELS AGE 'Age' TENURE 'Tenure in Company'
                JTENURE 'Tenure in Grade'
```

Because they are computed variables they default to (F8.2) formats. Figure 47.20a shows how a report would look if you used these computed variables in a report.

Figure 47.20a   Column contents that appear right-justified

```
Personnel Data                                                                PAGE    1

                   Tenure
                     in       Tenure
Division     Age   Company    in Grade   Salary--Annual
--------     ---   -------    --------    --------------

Carpeting   27.00    3.67       2.17        $9,200
            22.00    3.92       3.08       $10,900
            23.00    3.92       3.08       $10,900
            24.00    4.00       3.25       $10,000
            30.00    4.08       3.08       $10,000
            27.00    4.33       3.17       $10,000
            33.00    2.67       2.67        $9,335
            33.00    3.75       3.25       $10,000
            44.00    4.83       4.33       $15,690
            36.00    3.83       3.25       $10,000
            35.00    3.50       3.00       $15,520
            35.00    6.00       5.33       $19,500

Mean        30.75    4.04       3.31       $11,754
```

Data in the columns for AGE, TENURE, and JTENURE appear to be right-justified, when in fact they are centered, *based upon the (F8.2) format*. This happens because the (F8.2) format requires REPORT to reserve enough characters for an 8-digit number—whether or not such a number actually exists in the data. Because no number computed for AGE, TENURE, or JTENURE is greater than five characters, their data appear right-justified. Reducing their formats with the FORMATS command allows REPORT to shift the data to the middle of the column. For example, the commands

```
DATA LIST   /1 S1 1-3 S2 4-5 S3 6-9
              LNAME 10-21(A) NAME 22-41(A)
              SEX 42 GRADE 43 (A) STORE 44 SALARY 45-49
              DIVISION 50 SHIFT 51 BDAY BMONTH BYEAR 52-57
              CMONTH CYEAR JMONTH JYEAR 58-65
COMPUTE   AGE=87-BYEAR
COMPUTE   TENURE=(12-CMONTH +(12*(87-CYEAR)))/12
COMPUTE   JTENURE=(12-JMONTH +(12*(87-JYEAR)))/12
```

FORMATS AGE (F5.2) TENURE JTENURE (F4.2)

```
VARIABLE LABELS AGE 'Age' TENURE 'Tenure in Company'
                JTENURE 'Tenure in Grade'
SORT CASES BY DIVISION
REPORT FORMAT=AUTOMATIC
      /VARIABLES=AGE TENURE JTENURE SALARY
      /BREAK=DIVISION
      /SUMMARY=MEAN
```

generate the report in Figure 47.20b. These commands are identical to those used to generate Figure 47.20a, except for the addition of the FORMATS command to override the default formats for the computed variables AGE, TENURE, and JTENURE.

Figure 47.20b   Column alignment after FORMATS command

```
Personnel Data                                                    PAGE    1

                  Tenure    Tenure
                    in        in
Division    Age   Company   Grade    Salary--Annual
----------  ----  -------   ------   --------------

Carpeting

Mean        30.75   4.04     3.31       $11,754

Appliances

Mean        31.11   3.81     3.54       $12,508

Furniture

Mean        36.87   4.79     4.08       $13,255

Hardware

Mean        36.20   4.60     4.57       $17,580
```

47.21
ADDITIONAL REPORT FEATURES

Once you've mastered the basic report, you may want to implement some of REPORT's additional features. REPORT allows you to

- Specify multiple break levels.
- Generate complex statistics.
- Specify totals.
- Add titles and footnotes.
- Stack variables in a column.
- Create temporary variables.
- Control missing values.

47.22
Reports with Multiple Break Levels

In addition to breaking the personnel data into subgroups organized by division, you might want to further subdivide it. For example, you might want to know the average age, tenure, and salary of employees within each branch store as well as within each division. In addition, you might want to know how many employees work in each division. To find out, you would specify multiple BREAK subcommands to produce a report with multiple break levels, adding columns on the left side of the report.

To specify a report with multiple break levels, first use SORT CASES to specify the break variables in the order you intend to use them. Then invoke successive BREAK subcommands:

```
SORT CASES BY DIVISION STORE
REPORT FORMAT=AUTOMATIC
        /VARS=AGE TENURE SALARY
        /BREAK=DIVISION
        /SUMMARY=MEAN
        /SUMMARY=VALIDN
        /BREAK=STORE
        /SUMMARY=MEAN
```

Means and number of valid cases are requested for each break level of DIVISION. (see Figure 47.22). Only the means are requested for each break level of STORE.

Figure 47.22 Personnel report with multiple breaks

```
Personnel Data                                                                    PAGE     1

                        Tenure
              Branch      in
Division      Store      Age   Company   Salary--Annual
--------      ------     ----  -------   --------------

Carpeting     Suburban

              Mean       26.75   4.37       $12,625

              Downtown

              Mean       32.75   3.87       $11,318
Mean                     30.75   4.04       $11,754
N                           12     12            12
```

Specify BREAK and SUMMARY subcommands in sets. If you don't want any summary statistics at a given break level, omit the SUMMARY subcommand at that level. When you specify a SUMMARY subcommand, REPORT calculates the statistic you request for the specified break level, only. If you want the same statistic for multiple break levels, you must request it at each desired level.

47.23
Generating Summary Statistics

The minimum SUMMARY specification is the name of the aggregate function you want calculated over cases with the same break value. For example, in the command

```
SORT CASES BY DIVISION
REPORT FORMAT=AUTOMATIC
        /VARIABLES=AGE TENURE JTENURE SALARY
        /BREAK=DIVISION
        /SUMMARY=MEAN
```

the SUMMARY subcommand requests the mean of each numeric report variable (AGE, TENURE, JTENURE, and SALARY) for each break group of DIVISION.

If you want to perform the aggregate function only for selected report variables, name the variables in parentheses on the SUMMARY subcommand, as in

```
SORT CASES BY DIVISION
REPORT FORMAT=AUTOMATIC LIST
     /VARIABLES=LNAME AGE TENURE JTENURE SALARY
     /BREAK=DIVISION
     /SUMMARY=MEAN(JTENURE, SALARY)
```

You cannot use the TO keyword on SUMMARY to imply a set of variables.

The following is a complete list of the aggregate functions available in REPORT:

VALIDN	*Valid number of cases.* VALIDN is the only function available for string variables.
VARIANCE	*Variance.*
SUM	*Sum of values.*
MEAN	*Mean.*
STDDEV	*Standard deviation.*
MIN	*Minimum value encountered.*
MAX	*Maximum value encountered.*
SKEWNESS	*Skewness.*
KURTOSIS	*Kurtosis.*
PGT(n)	*Percentage of cases with values greater than the specified value.*
PLT(n)	*Percentage of cases with values less than the specified value.*
PIN(n1,n2)	*Percentage of cases with values between specified values, including those with the specified values.*
FREQUENCY(min,max)	*Frequency counts for all nonmissing values within the range.*
PERCENT(min,max)	*Percentages for all nonmissing values within the range.*
MEDIAN(min,max)	*Median value for all nonmissing values within the range.*
MODE(min,max)	*Modal value for all nonmissing values within the range.*

FREQUENCY, PERCENT, MEDIAN, and MODE are computed using the same algorithms used by procedure FREQUENCIES in *integer* mode. Consequently, noninteger values are truncated in computing these statistics.

For the aggregate functions that include arguments, such as PIN(n1,n2) and FREQUENCY(min,max), specify in parentheses the value or values that define the range you want REPORT to consider in its calculations. Commas between multiple arguments are required. For example, the commands

```
SORT CASES BY DIVISION
REPORT FORMAT=AUTOMATIC LIST
     /VARS=AGE TENURE JTENURE SALARY
     /BREAK=DIVISION
     /SUMMARY=PIN(5,10)
     /SUMMARY=FREQUENCY(8000,10000)
```

determine what percentage of cases have values between 5 and 10, and what values fall between 8,000 and 10,000 and how many of each value there are. It isn't necessary to specify variables for the summaries.

As shown in Figure 47.23, the PIN(5,10) specification reveals in 8.3% of the employees in Carpeting have been with the company for 5–10 years (only one division is shown in Figure 47.23). If you look at the data, you can see that 8.3% is equivalent to one employee, who has been in Carpeting for 6.00 years.

The FREQUENCY(8000,10000) specification produces one Total line and a set of lines that identifies case values. In Figure 47.23, the Total line shows that seven salaries fall within the $8,000 to $10,000 range. The next three lines show the exact salaries that are recorded within the range and the number of employees who receive each salary amount. No values fall between 8,000 and 10,000 for the other three variables, so the frequencies are listed as missing.

Figure 47.23   Aggregate functions with arguments

```
Personnel Data                                                                          PAGE     1

                            Tenure      Tenure
                               in          in
 Division        Age       Company      Grade      Salary--Annual
 ----------      ---       -------      ------     -------------

 Carpeting      27.00        3.67        2.17           $9,200
                22.00        3.92        3.08          $10,900
                23.00        3.92        3.08          $10,900
                24.00        4.00        3.25          $10,000
                30.00        4.08        3.08          $10,000
                27.00        4.33        3.17          $10,000
                33.00        2.67        2.67           $9,335
                33.00        3.75        3.25          $10,000
                44.00        4.83        4.33          $15,690
                36.00        3.83        3.25          $10,000
                35.00        3.50        3.00          $15,520
                35.00        6.00        5.33          $19,500

 In 5.000 t      0.0         8.3%        8.3%             0.0
 Total            .            .           .               7
  9200            .            .           .               1
  9335            .            .           .               1
  10000           .            .           .               5
```

47.24
Summary Titles

By default, REPORT uses summary titles on a report to identify each statistic you request on the SUMMARY subcommand. It displays the summary title in the column corresponding to the break being summarized, aligning the titles with the labels or values in the column. The title prints in mixed case or upper case, depending upon your system's default specifications. For example, the subcommands

```
/BREAK=DIVISION
/SUMMARY=MAX
/SUMMARY=MEAN
```

print the titles *Maximum* and *Mean* in the break column for variable DIVISION.

REPORT's default summary titles are:

Keyword	Title
VALIDN	N
VARIANCE	Variance
SUM	Sum
MEAN	Mean
STDDEV	StdDev
MIN	Minimum
MAX	Maximum
SKEWNESS	Skewness
KURTOSIS	Kurtosis
PGT(n)	>n
PLT(n)	<n
PIN(n1,n2)	In n1 to n2
FREQUENCY(min,max)	Total
PERCENT(min,max)	Total
MEDIAN(min,max)	Median
MODE(min,max)	Mode

You can change the default summary title by enclosing a one-line title in apostrophes or quotation marks, as in

```
/SUMMARY=STDDEV 'Standard Deviation'
```

Use leading blanks to indent summary titles within the break column.

If you specify a summary title wider than its break column, the title extends into the next break column to its right. If the width of the available break columns is insufficient to display the full summary title, the title is truncated, as shown in Figure 47.23.

REPORT allows you to move summary titles between break columns. To do so, specify in parentheses the number of the break column in which you want the summary title to appear.

In the following example, the summary title Mean for the Store: would, by default, print in the second break column because it is defined at the second break level. The (1) after the title specification moves it to the first break column. Figure 47.24 shows the report (only one division is shown):

```
SORT CASES BY DIVISION STORE
REPORT FORMAT=AUTOMATIC
       /VARIABLES=AGE TENURE SALARY
       /BREAK=DIVISION
       /SUMMARY=MEAN 'Mean for the Division:'
       /SUMMARY=VALIDN(AGE) 'Employees in Division:'
       /BREAK=STORE
       /SUMMARY=MEAN '    Mean for the Store:' (1)
```

Figure 47.24 Summary titles

```
Personnel Data                                                          PAGE    1

                     Tenure
            Branch     in
Division    Store     Age    Company   Salary--Annual
--------    ------    ---    -------   -------------

Carpeting   Suburban

   Mean for the Store:   26.75   4.37      $12,625

            Downtown

   Mean for the Store:   32.75   3.87      $11,318

Mean for the Division:   30.75   4.04      $11,754
Employees in Division:      12
```

The specified summary titles Mean for the Division: and Employees in Division: print at each primary break level. The specified summary title Mean for the Store: prints at each secondary break level. It is indented three spaces because three blanks were specified in the title.

All three summary titles begin in the first break column and extend into the second break column. None of them is truncated because none is wider than the combined width of the two break columns.

Although summary titles can only be one line long, when you use multiple SUMMARY subcommands, you can continue a summary title from one summary line to another. For example,

```
/SUMMARY=SUM 'Sums and Averages'
/SUMMARY=MEAN 'Based on 1986 5% Sample'
```

produces a two-line summary with a title continuing from the first to the second line. You can also specify a blank title for any summary line.

**47.25
Reports with Totals**

The keyword (TOTAL) on the BREAK subcommand calculates summary statistics for all the cases in the report. These totals print at the end of the report. You can specify (TOTAL) for both listing and summary reports.

To generate a report that has break-level statistics plus total statistics, specify (TOTAL) after the variable named on any BREAK subcommand, as in:

```
SORT CASES BY STORE DIVISION
REPORT FORMAT=AUTOMATIC
       /VARIABLES=AGE TENURE JTENURE SALARY
       /BREAK=STORE (TOTAL)
       /SUMMARY=VALIDN (AGE) 'Employees:'
       /BREAK=DIVISION
       /SUMMARY=MEAN
```

In this example, REPORT calculates the number of employees who work at each branch store and the total number of employees who work for the company. It prints the summary title Employees for each VALIDN calculation. Figure 47.25a shows that 17 employees work at the suburban store, 24 employees work downtown, and a total of 41 employees work in the company. REPORT calculates a mean for each division but does not calculate a mean for the entire company because (TOTAL) is not specified at the same break level as MEAN.

Figure 47.25a Summary report with totals

```
Personnel Data                                                           PAGE    1

                                  Tenure     Tenure
Branch                              in          in
Store       Division     Age     Company      Grade     Salary--Annual
----------  ----------   ----    -------     -------    --------------

Suburban    Carpeting
            Mean        26.75      4.37        3.42        $12,625
            Appliances
            Mean        30.20      4.05        3.77        $14,395
            Furniture
            Mean        35.29      4.71        4.32        $12,975
            Hardware
            Mean        32.00      4.33        4.33        $22,500
Employees:               17
Downtown    Carpeting
            Mean        32.75      3.87        3.25        $11,318
            Appliances
            Mean        32.25      3.52        3.25        $10,150
            Furniture
            Mean        38.25      4.86        3.86        $13,500
            Hardware
            Mean        37.25      4.67        4.62        $16,350
Employees:               24
TOTAL
Employees:               41
```

When you want REPORT to calculate statistics at the total level that differ from those it calculates at the various break levels, specify (TOTAL) on the first BREAK subcommand and do not name a variable. Use as many SUMMARY subcommands as you need to specify the total statistics you want REPORT to calculate, and then specify your break-level statistics on the SUMMARY subcommands associated with subsequent break levels. For example, when you specify

```
SORT CASES BY DIVISION
REPORT FORMAT=AUTOMATIC
       /VARIABLES=AGE TENURE JTENURE SALARY
       /BREAK= (TOTAL)
       /SUMMARY=VALIDN (AGE) 'Employees:'
       /BREAK=DIVISION
       /SUMMARY=MEAN
```

REPORT calculates the total number of employees in the company but does not calculate the number of employees within each division. It calculates a mean for each division but does not calculate a mean for the entire company. Figure 47.25b shows the report.

Figure 47.25b   Totals that differ from break level summaries

```
Personnel Data                                                          PAGE    1

                          Tenure      Tenure
                            in          in
Division          Age     Company     Grade     Salary--Annual
------------      ---     -------     ------     --------------

Carpeting

Mean             30.75     4.04        3.31        $11,754

Appliances

Mean             31.11     3.81        3.54        $12,508

Furniture

Mean             36.87     4.79        4.08        $13,255

Hardware

Mean             36.20     4.60        4.57        $17,580


Employees:        41
```

Similarly, to generate a listing report that has no break levels but calculates totals, specify (TOTAL) on a BREAK subcommand that does not name a variable. Use as many SUMMARY subcommands as you need to specify the totals you want REPORT to calculate, as in:

```
SORT CASES BY LNAME
REPORT FORMAT=AUTOMATIC LIST
     /VARIABLES=LNAME AGE TENURE JTENURE SALARY
     /BREAK=(TOTAL)
     /SUMMARY=MEAN
     /SUMMARY=VALIDN (JTENURE) 'Total number of employees in the firm:'
```

The BREAK subcommand does not organize the report into subgroups. It requests that each statistic specified on a SUMMARY subcommand be calculated for all the cases on the report. Though the file is sorted by LNAME to alphabetize the listing, SORT CASES is optional since the report has no break variables.

Figure 47.25c   Listing report with totals

```
Personnel Data                                                          PAGE    1

                          Tenure      Tenure
                            in          in
Last Name         Age     Company     Grade     Salary--Annual
------------      ---     -------     ------     --------------

   .
   .
   .
Sedowski         30.00     2.67        2.67        $7,500
Shavilje         32.00     2.92        2.92        $8,900
Snolik           34.00     5.08        4.50       $15,300
Syms             32.00     4.33        4.33       $22,500
Totman           41.00     4.50        3.50       $13,300
Tygielski        35.00     6.00        5.33       $19,500
Wajda            26.00     3.17        3.17        $8,975
Washington       32.00     4.42        3.67       $14,400
White            25.00     3.92        3.33       $11,000
Wilson           36.00     4.42        3.75       $14,000

Mean             33.73     4.34        3.79       $13,179

Total number of employees in the firm:  41
```

Figure 47.25c shows the last lines of the report. The mean values are those for the entire 41 employees. Though there are no break columns on the report, the summary titles Mean and Total number of employees in the firm: begin in the left-most column and are left-justified. The values for each statistic print one row beneath its title, allowing you to specify a summary title that spans as far as the right margin of the report.

47.26
Using Composite
Functions

Although the syntax for composite functions is similar to the syntax required for simple functions, the specifications are used in different ways. The general syntax for specifying a composite function is

composite(agg) ['title'] [(col #)] [(varname [(format)] [(d)])]

where *composite* is the composite function and *agg* is the aggregate statistic used as its argument. The optional specifications in brackets are:

'title'	*Specified summary title.*
(col #)	*Number of the break column to which you want to move the summary title.*
(varname)	*Name of the report variable whose column will display the result of the composite function calculation.*
(format)	*Format for the summary.* Valid formats are PLAIN, DOLLAR, and COMMA. PLAIN is the default.
(d)	*Number of decimal places displayed for the result of the composite function calculation.*

The following is a list of the compsite functions available in REPORT:

DIVIDE(agg() agg() [factor])	*Divide the first argument by the second and multiply by the optional factor.*
MULTIPLY (agg() ... agg() [factor])	*Multiply the arguments.*
PCT(agg() agg())	*Percentage of the first argument over the second.*
SUBTRACT(agg()agg())	*Subtract the second argument from the first argument.*
ADD(agg() ... agg() [factor])	*Add the arguments.*
GREAT(agg() ... agg())	*Give the maximum of the arguments.*
LEAST(agg() ... agg())	*Give the minimum of the arguments.*
AVERAGE(agg() ... agg())	*Give the average of the arguments.*

You can use any numeric SPSS-X variables, not just REPORT variables, as arguments to composite functions. You do not have to name a variable on the VARIABLES subcommand to use it in a composite function.

You cannot use a composite function as an argument to a composite function. You can only use simple functions, variables, and constants. Section 47.27 discusses nested composites using AGGREGATE and MATCH FILES.

There are three basic reasons for using composite functions:

• To place a summary statistic in a column other than the one for which it is calculated. For example, the sum of VARA is printed in the column corresponding to VARA. It can be placed in any other column with a composite such as

```
/SUMMARY=ADD(SUM(VARA)) (VARB)
```

which adds VARA to nothing and places it in VARB's column. The SUBTRACT, GREAT, LEAST, and AVERAGE composite functions can achieve the same result. Section 47.52 explains how to create a blank or *dummy* variable as a space holder for printing a composite summary statistic.

• To manipulate statistics and change the unit of analysis. Certain arithmetic operations between variables produce the same result at either the case level or the subpopulation level. You can subtract the sum of variable A from the sum of variable B and obtain the same answer as subtracting A from B for each case and summing the result. However, dividing the sum of A by the sum of B is not the same as dividing A by B for each case and averaging the results.

• To manipulate variables not defined on the VARIABLES subcommand. For example, you might want to adjust dollar figures by some index when printing means without allocating a column for the index by naming it on the VARIABLES subcommand.

Suppose you want to run a listing report that shows the average age, tenure, and salary of employees, and also reflects what the average salary will be when next year's 7% across-the-board salary increase takes effect. The following commands produce such a report:

```
SORT CASES BY DIVISION LNAME
REPORT FORMAT=AUTOMATIC LIST
       /VARS=LNAME AGE TENURE SALARY
       /BREAK=DIVISION
       /SUMMARY=MEAN
       /SUMMARY=MULTIPLY(MEAN(SALARY)1.07) '7% Raise'
             (SALARY(DOLLAR)(0))
```

Figure 47.26 shows one division from the report. Note that the composite function computes only one result.

Figure 47.26   Report with composite function

```
Personnel Data

                                        Tenure
                                          in
Division      Last Name        Age      Company    Salary——Annual
--------      ---------        ---      -------    -------------

Carpeting     Cochran          22.00     3.92        $10,900
              Dan              36.00     3.83        $10,000
              Ford             27.00     3.67         $9,200
              Gates            24.00     4.00        $10,000
              Hoawinski        23.00     3.92        $10,900
              Jones            44.00     4.83        $15,690
              Katz             33.00     3.75        $10,000
              Lavelle          27.00     4.33        $10,000
              Mahr             33.00     2.67         $9,335
              McAndrews        35.00     3.50        $15,520
              Mulvihill        30.00     4.08        $10,000
              Tygielski        35.00     6.00        $19,500

Mean                           30.75     4.04        $11,754
7% Raise                                             $12,577
```

By default, REPORT prints the result of the composite function calculation in the column defined by the first variable in the function that is also named on the VARIABLES subcommand. To move the result to another variable's column, specify that variable's name in parentheses after you completely define the composite function's argument, as in

```
/SUMMARY=MULTIPLY(MEAN(SALARY)1.07) (LNAME)
```

which places the result in the column defined by LNAME. Unlike simple functions, the composite function result can be placed in any report column including those defined by dummy variables (see Section 47.52) or string variables (see Section 47.33).

To specify a summary title for the composite function, place the title specification after the final parentheses enclosing the arguments. Do not separate the function name from its arguments.

Specify print formats for composites within parentheses. Place the specification after the name of the variable in whose column the result is to be printed. You can specify both the format and number of decimal digits you want printed, as in

```
/SUMMARY=MULTIPLY(MEAN(SALARY)1.07)  '7% Raise'
        (SALARY(DOLLAR)(0))
```

which prints the increased average salary in DOLLAR format with no decimal places.

47.27
Nested Composite Functions

If your report requires a nested composite function, use AGGREGATE (Chapter 18) to compute the required information and then match it back to the active file with the MATCH FILES command (see Chapter 16). For example, assume you want to print the result of the arithmetic expression

```
(A/B)/(C/D)
```

for each break group. The sequence of commands is as follows:

```
GET FILE=SYSFILE
AGGREGATE  OUTFILE=*/BREAK=GROUP
        /SUMA SUMB SUMC SUMD = SUM(A B C D)
COMPUTE  NEWVAR=(SUMA/SUMB)/(SUMC/SUMD)
MATCH FILES FILE=SYSFILE/TABLE=*/BY GROUP
REPORT  VARIABLES= A B C D
       /BREAK=GROUP
       /SUMMARY=MEAN/SUMMARY=ADD(MAX(NEWVAR)) (A(2))
```

AGGREGATE is used to sum A, B, C, and D for the break groups. This becomes the active file, so the COMPUTE command can be used to perform the transformation. MATCH FILES combines these results with the original file and REPORT simply moves the results into the appropriate column.

AGGREGATE and MATCH FILES are also required to carry information across breaks or perform pretotaling operations. See Section 47.62 for an example of pretotaling.

47.28
Print Formats for Summaries

Every summary function has a default display format. For example, the SUM function uses the variable's dictionary display width + 2. Table 47.28 shows the default display formats for each function. The following key should help you understand the table:

Function	Syntax for the summary function
Alias	Alternative syntax
Type	Type of print format
Width	Width of print format
Decimals	Number of decimal places in the print format
F	Standard numeric format
PCT	Percent format
d	Dictionary format definition for the variable

Table 47.28   Default summary formats

Function	Alias	Type	Width	Decimals
VALIDN	N	F	5	0
SUM		d	d+2	d
MEAN		d	d	d
STDDEV	SD or STDEV	d	d	d
VARIANCE		d	d	d
MIN	MINIMUM	d	d	d
MAX	MAXIMUM	d	d	d
SKEWNESS		F	5	2
KURTOSIS		F	5	2
PGT	PCGT	PCT	6	1
PLT	PCLT	PCT	6	1
PIN	PCIN	PCT	6	1
MEDIAN		d	d	d
MODE		d	d	d
PERCENT	RELFREQ	F	6	1
FREQUENCY	ABFREQ	F	5	0
DIVIDE		F	d	0
PCT		PCT	6	2
SUBTRACT		F	d	0
ADD		F	d	0
GREAT		F	d	0
LEAST		F	d	0
AVERAGE		F	d	0
MULTIPLY		F	d	0

To override the default format, specify a format in parentheses after the variable name on the SUMMARY subcommand. You can specify COMMA and DOLLAR formats when they are not the default, or PLAIN to override those formats when they are the default. You can also specify an alternative number of decimal digits by enclosing the desired number in a separate set of parentheses. For example, in the subcommand

```
/SUMMARY=MEAN(AGE SALARY(COMMA)(2) TENURE(0) JTENURE)
```

SUMMARY displays the mean of SALARY in COMMA format with 2 decimal places, and it displays the mean of TENURE in its default format type but with 0 decimal places. The format specification modifies only the variable immediately preceding it; AGE and JTENURE above are unaffected.

For composite functions, the format specifications go within the parentheses that specify the display column for the function, not within the arguments to the function. For example, in the commands

```
/SUMMARY=MULTIPLY(MEAN(SALARY)1.07) (SALARY(2))
```

(SALARY(2)) displayed the increased average salary with 2 decimal places in the SALARY column (see Section 47.26).

If the column is not wide enough to display the specified decimal digits for a given function, REPORT displays fewer decimals. REPORT uses scientific notation or displays asterisks if the column is not wide enough to display the integer portion of the number. Exactly zero is displayed with one zero digit to the left of the decimal point and as many zero digits to the right as specified by the display format. A very small number displays without a zero digit to the left of the decimal point (except for DOLLAR and COMMA).

ANNOTATED EXAMPLE OF REPORT USING SUMMARIES

This example produces a report that summarizes information from a retail company's personnel file. It reports summary statistics for employees in each division of the company within each store. The SPSS-X commands are

```
GET FILE=CHIGDATA
SET CASE=UPLOW

PRINT FORMATS SALARY(DOLLAR7.0)

SORT CASES  BY STORE DIVISION
REPORT FORMAT=AUTOMATIC MARGINS(1,72) LENGTH(1,24) BRKSPACE(-1)
 /VARIABLES=AGE TENURE JTENURE SPACE(DUMMY)' '(4) SALARY
 /TITLE='Chicago Home Furnishing'
 /FOOTNOTE=LEFT 'Tenure measured in months'
 /BREAK=STORE
   /SUMMARY=MEAN 'Average:'
   /SUMMARY=VALIDN '  Count:'(AGE)
 /BREAK=DIVISION 'Product' 'Division' (SKIP(0))
   /SUMMARY=MEAN
```

- The GET command retrieves the system file containing information on the employees in the company (see Chapter 6).

- The SET command ensures that any variable or value labels that were defined in upper and lower case are printed in upper and lower case in the display file (see Chapter 4).

- The PRINT FORMATS command ensures that summaries on variable SALARY are printed with the dollar format (see Chapter 10).

- The SORT CASES command sorts the file into the order required for REPORT (see Chapter 15 and Section 47.6).

- The FORMAT subcommand specifies a summary report (see Section 47.10). The AUTOMATIC keyword implements REPORT's automatic format settings (see Section 47.9). The MARGINS keyword sets the left margin at column 1 and right margin at column 72. The LENGTH keyword sets the top of the report on the first line and the last line of the page on line 24. The BRKSPACE keyword places the summary for each break of DIVISION on the same line as each label of DIVISION (see Section 47.55).

- The VARIABLES subcommand defines four columns in the body of the report. AGE, TENURE, and JTENURE and SALARY are SPSS-X variables. SPACE defines a dummy column for spacing purposes.

- The TITLE subcommand defines a one-line centered title (see Section 47.29).

- The FOOTNOTE subcommand defines a one-line left-justified footnote (see Section 47.29).

- The first BREAK subcommand defines the major break in this two-break report. Variable STORE breaks the file into two categories: the downtown store and the suburban store. Value labels for STORE are printed in the break column (see Section 47.12).

- The first two SUMMARY subcommands print two lines of summary statistics for each store. The first SUMMARY subcommand computes means for AGE, TENURE, JTENURE and SALARY. The second SUMMARY subcommand computes the number of employees in each store (see Section 47.23). Summary titles are assigned to each summary function (see Section 47.24).

- The second BREAK subcommand breaks the file into divisions within each store. The SKIP specification suppresses blank lines between the summary for each division. A column heading is defined for DIVISION (see Section 47.15).

- The last SUMMARY subcommand computes means for AGE, TENURE, JTENURE, and SALARY for each division.

Summary report

Chicago Home Furnishing

Branch Store	Product Division	Age	Tenure in Company	Tenure in Grade	Salary—Annual
Suburban	Carpeting	26.75	4.37	3.42	$12,625
	Appliances	30.20	4.05	3.77	$14,395
	Furniture	35.29	4.71	4.32	$12,975
	Hardware	32.00	4.33	4.33	$22,500
Average:		31.59	4.42	3.95	$13,871
Count:		17			
Downtown	Carpeting	32.75	3.87	3.25	$11,318
	Appliances	32.25	3.52	3.25	$10,150
	Furniture	38.25	4.86	3.86	$13,500
	Hardware	37.25	4.67	4.62	$16,350
Average:		35.25	4.28	3.68	$12,689
Count:		24			

Tenure measured in months

ANNOTATED EXAMPLE OF A LISTING REPORT

This example produces a report using data from the October 1980 issue of *Runner's World* magazine. It lists the top-rated shoes in the survey organized by manufacturer. Measures used by the raters to determine an overall evaluation for each shoe are reported. The SPSS-X commands used to produce this report are

```
TITLE           'RUNNER''S WORLD 1980 SHOE SURVEY'
DATA LIST       FIXED /1 TYPE 1 MAKER 2-3 QUALITY 5-9
                REARIMP FOREIMP FLEX SOLEWEAR 10-29
                REARCONT SOLETRAC 31-40 WEIGHT 42-46 LASTYEAR 48
                PREFER 50-53 STARS 55 NAME 57-72 (A)
VARIABLE LABELS TYPE 'Type' MAKER 'Manufacturer' QUALITY 'Quality'
                REARIMP 'Rearfoot Impact' FOREIMP 'Forefoot Impact'
                FLEX 'Flexibility' SOLEWEAR 'Sole Wear'
                REARCONT 'Rearfoot Control' SOLETRAC 'Sole Traction'
                WEIGHT 'Weight' LASTYEAR '1979 Stars'
                PREFER 'Reader Preference' STARS 'Rating' NAME 'Shoe'
VALUE LABLES    MAKER (1)Adidas (2)Autry (3)Brookfield (4)Brooks
                (5)Converse (6)Reebok (7)New Balance (8)Puma (9)Osaga
                (10)Pony (11)Etonic (12)Nike (13)Saucony
                (14)Wilson-Bata (15)Vol Shoe Corp
                (16)Specs International (17)Power Sport
                (18)Thom McAn Jox (19)Regal Shoes (20)Shoe Corp
                (21)Asics (22)Intl Footwear (23)Eb Sport Intl
                (24)Van Doren/
                TYPE(1)Male (2)Female/
                STARS(6)****** (5)*****/
PRINT FORMATS   QUALITY (F5.3)/REARIMP FOREIMP SOLEWEAR (F4.1)/
                FLEX SOLETRAC (F4.2)/REARCONT WEIGHT (F5.1)/
                PREFER (F4.3)
SELECT IF       STARS GE 5
BEGIN DATA
1 4 3.965  8.3 11.0 1.33 10.0 -13.6  .55 232.4 5 .531 6 Vantage
1 4 3.965  8.5 10.9 1.31 10.0 -16.5  .58 239.1 5      6 Vantage Supreme
. . .
217 3.692 12.9 18.6 2.90  3.5   0.9  .68 280.6 0        LDT 138
221 4.920 13.2 17.6 2.34  2.1   8.6  .63 244.0 0 .026   Tigress 80
END DATA

SORT CASES BY MAKER STARS(D)
REPORT FORMAT=AUTOMATIC MISSING ' ' LIST(4) TSPACE(3)
      /VARS =TYPE(LABEL) NAME STARS(LABEL) REARIMP
              FOREIMP FLEX 'Flexi-' 'bility'
              SOLEWEAR REARCONT SOLETRAC
              WEIGHT LASTYEAR(LABEL) PREFER(LABEL)
        /TITLE='Ratings of Training Shoes'
              'Runner''s World Magazine - October, 1980'
     /FOOTNOTE=LEFT '****** Highly recommended'
                    '***** Recommended'
              RIGHT ' ' 'Page )PAGE'
        /BREAK=MAKER
```

- The TITLE command supplies a title for the job (see Chapter 4).

- The DATA LIST command defines the variables to be used in the report. The data are inline (see Chapter 5).

- The VARIABLE LABELS command supplies variable labels for all the variables (see Chapter 5). These labels are used as default column headings in the report.

- The VALUE LABELS command supplies value labels for the manufacturer, type of shoe, and rating (see Chapter 5). These labels are used in the report columns.

- The PRINT FORMATS command overrides the default print formats (see Chapter 10).

- The SELECT IF command selects shoes with the top two ratings (see Chapter 11).

- The BEGIN DATA command signals the beginning of the inline data and the END DATA command signals the end of the data (see Chapter 5).

- The SORT CASES command sorts cases in descending order of ranking for each manufacturer. They are sorted by manufacturer since the report groups them by manufacturer. They are sorted by descending order of ranking so that the top-rated shoes for the manufacturer are listed first (see Chapter 15).

- The FORMAT subcommand specifies a case listing that displays cases in groups of four. The AUTOMATIC keyword implements REPORT's automatic format settings (see Section 47.9). The MISSING keyword prints a blank in place of the period for variables with missing values (see Section 47.36). The TSPACE keyword inserts three blank lines between the report title and the column headings (see Section 47.55).

- The VARIABLES subcommand names all the SPSS-X variables being listed. Value labels are printed in place of values for variables TYPE and STARS (see Section 47.11).

- The TITLE subcommand prints a two-line centered title (see Section 47.29).

- The FOOTNOTE subcommand prints a two-line left-justified footnote and a two-line right-justified footnote. The first line of the right-justified footnote is blank; the second line uses the special keyword)PAGE to print page numbers (see Section 47.29).

- The BREAK subcommand groups the shoes by manufacturer and prints the manufacturers' names (which were supplied on the VALUE LABELS command).

Report on running-shoe data

Ratings of Training Shoes
Runner's World Magazine — October, 1980

Manufacturer	Type	Shoe	Rating	Rearfoot Impact	Forefoot Impact	Flexi-bility	Sole Wear	Rearfoot Control	Sole Traction	Weight	1979 Stars	Reader Preference
Saucony	Male	TC84	******	9.3	15.1	1.56	6.5	5.2	.85	278.0	0	.028
	Male	Hornet 84	******	9.9	13.1	2.65	7.6	3.0	.68	265.0	4	.097
	Female	MS Trainer	******	10.2	13.3	1.58	6.4	22.4	.86	237.7	5	.053
	Male	Jazz	*****	8.9	12.7	2.04	7.6	-7.0	.64	270.8	0	
	Male	Trainer 80	*****	10.5	14.5	2.18	4.1	11.5	.82	307.6	5	.232
	Female	Jazz	*****	9.0	12.2	1.86	6.1	-7.5	.63	223.0	0	.013
	Female	TC 84	*****	9.3	14.6	1.46	7.5	1.3	.77	231.1	0	
	Female	MS Hornet	*****	9.8	13.2	2.59	6.4	6.5	.67	224.0	4	.046
Nike	Male	Daygreak	******	10.8	15.4	2.17	3.7	7.8	.54	304.2	5	.602
	Male	Yankee	*****	10.9	13.7	1.93	2.0	9.8	.66	276.6	0	
	Female	Liberator	*****	10.6	14.7	2.20	5.8	6.5	.52	254.2	5	.503
Etonic	Male	Eclipse Trainer	******	10.0	12.9	1.65	10.0	-2.6	.51	237.4	0	
	Female	Eclipse Trainer	******	9.6	12.8	1.78	10.0	1.4	.57	204.1	0	
	Male	Stabilizer	*****	10.3	15.5	2.25	1.2	-.6	.53	283.1	4	.232
	Male	Streetfighter	*****	10.8	15.5	2.28	1.4	-.4	.61	266.1	4	.222
	Female	Streetfighter	*****	10.7	15.5	1.66	.7	-7.7	.70	214.1	4	.344
	Female	Stabilizer	*****	10.8	14.4	2.09	2.6	-6.9	.67	235.3	4	.298
Pony	Male	Targa Flex	******	9.6	14.3	1.32	2.5	-22.7	.86	253.0	3	
	Male	Shadow	*****	9.9	13.8	1.53	2.5	-17.9	.77	270.2	0	
	Female	Lady Shadow	*****	10.6	17.4	.91	3.0	-7.1	.90	211.8	0	
Osaga	Male	Fast Rider	*****	10.5	14.0	2.48	4.9	1.9	.66	296.7	5	.025
	Female	KT-26	*****	10.7	17.3	1.66	5.5	8.1	.60	223.1	2	
New Balance	Male	420	*****	9.8	14.8	2.09	1.8	-17.7	.46	267.9	0	.516
	Male	620	*****	12.0	14.6	2.73	1.1	-3.5	.41	242.0	5	.475
	Female	420	*****	9.9	13.9	1.94	1.6	-.7	.46	219.3	0	.411
Reebok	Male	Aztec	******	10.9	12.6	2.07	2.5	3.7	.65	260.8	5	.065
	Male	Shadow I	*****	10.7	13.1	1.79	1.9	-8.7	.63	253.0	0	
	Female	Shadow III	*****	10.2	12.9	1.63	2.4	-24.6	.66	212.8	0	
	Female	Aztec Princess	*****	10.2	12.8	2.18	5.9	-20.3	.70	221.3	5	.033
Converse	Male	Arizona 84	*****	10.1	13.6	1.90	6.6	-5.1	.55	302.9	4	.006
	Female	World Class 84	*****	9.4	14.0	2.19	4.3	-.3	.65	234.7	3	.020
Brooks	Male	Vantage	******	8.3	11.0	1.33	10.0	-13.6	.55	232.4	5	.531
	Male	Vantage Supreme	******	8.5	10.9	1.31	10.0	-16.5	.58	239.1	5	
	Male	Hugger GT	******	8.5	11.2	1.32	9.4	-11.7	.60	234.5	5	.488
	Male	Nighthawk	******	8.7	13.5	1.57	3.1	-8.6	.45	216.7	0	
	Male	Super Villanova	******	10.0	14.1	1.07	10.0	14.4	.61	238.7	5	.155
	Female	Vantage	******	8.1	11.0	1.27	10.0	-13.1	.58	199.9	5	.563

****** Highly recommended
***** Recommended

Ratings of Training Shoes
Runner's World Magazine — October, 1980

Manufacturer	Type	Shoe	Rating	Rearfoot Impact	Forefoot Impact	Flexi-bility	Sole Wear	Rearfoot Control	Sole Traction	Weight	1979 Stars	Reader Preference
Brooks	Female	Hugger GT	******	8.2	11.1	1.28	10.0	-12.7	.60	203.8	0	.126
	Female	Vantage Supreme	******	8.2	11.1	1.34	10.0	.6	.62	201.4	3	.205
	Female	Super Villanova	******	9.0	13.4	1.01	10.0	11.9	.62	195.1	5	.298
	Female	Nighthawk	*****	8.6	13.1	1.54	2.4	-9.3	.45	189.0	0	
Brookfield	Male	Colt	*****	12.4	17.4	2.31	3.5	21.5	1.13	289.3	4	
Autry	Male	Mach III	*****	8.7	13.0	2.13	3.0	-37.6	.66	250.2	4	
	Male	New Jet	*****	9.1	14.5	1.88	4.0	-37.9	.69	242.4	4	
	Male	Concorde	*****	9.2	13.2	2.41	2.0	-33.9	.61	261.7	5	.023
	Female	Cloud 9	*****	9.4	17.6	1.79	2.3	-27.3	.63	198.6	3	
Adidas	Male	TRX Trainer	*****	10.5	16.8	2.07	2.1	-.6	.72	309.0	5	.143
	Male	Marathon Trainer	*****	13.0	17.2	2.75	10.0	14.5	.63	302.3	5	.315
	Female	Marathon Trainer	*****	11.7	16.5	2.14	10.0	17.5	.58	243.6	5	.298

****** Highly recommended
***** Recommended

47.29
Adding Titles and
Footnotes

The TITLE and FOOTNOTE subcommands in REPORT enable you to place titles and footnotes on the left, in the center, and on the right of each page of a report. You can specify as many title and footnote lines as you need by enclosing each line in apostrophes or quotes, separating them by a space or comma. To include an apostrophe in a title, either enclose the string in quotation marks or use double apostrophes not separated by a space. For example,

```
SORT CASES BY DIVISION
REPORT FORMAT=AUTOMATIC LIST
      /VARS=LNAME AGE TENURE SALARY
      /BREAK=DIVISION
      /SUMMARY=MEAN
      /TITLE= 'Personnel Report' "Employees' Profile"
```

specifies a two-line title. Personnel Report prints on the first title line, and Employee's Profile prints beneath it on the second title line. The quotation marks enclosing the second title line assure the apostrophe will print in the title.

To specify the left, right, or center positions for either titles or footnotes, use the following conventions:

```
/TITLE=
    LEFT    'Left-justified title'
    RIGHT   'Right-justified title'
    CENTER 'Centered title'

/FOOTNOTE=
    LEFT    'Left-justified note'
    RIGHT   'Right-justified note'
    CENTER 'Centered note'
```

To specify multiple title and footnote lines in any given positon, don't repeat the positional keywords. For example,

```
/TITLE=LEFT  'Personnel Report' 'As of January 1, 1987'
       RIGHT 'ACME Products' '2201 LaSalle Park'
             'Chicago, Illinois 60611'
```

specifies two left-justified title lines and three right-justified title lines. Repetition of a keyword produces an error. Notice that LEFT, RIGHT, and CENTER are keywords and therefore are not separated by slashes.

If you specify TITLE or FOOTNOTE without any position keywords, the title or footnote is centered. However, if you specify a left or right position on the same subcommand, you must use the keyword CENTER to specify the center position.

If you specify a title or footnote that is wider than the report width, REPORT generates an error message. To specify a blank title, type a space between apostrophes.

Titles and footnotes are optional. You can place them anywhere after the FORMAT subcommand, except between BREAK and SUMMARY. There is no fixed limit to the number of title or footnote lines you can define on a report.

Titles and footnotes print on each page of a multiple-page report. The LEFT, RIGHT, and CENTER alignments are relative to the report's margins (see Section 47.17).

If you don't specify a title, SPSS-X uses its system title as a default when the REPORT width is greater than or equal to the system title's width plus 12. If you use the TITLE command (Chapter 4), REPORT substitutes the title you specify on the TITLE command for the default title. There is no default footnote.

Three special arguments are available in titles and footnotes:

)PAGE   *Print the page number right-justified in a five-character field.*

)DATE   *Print the current date in the form* dd-mmm-yy *right-adjusted in a nine-character field.*

)variable   *Print this variable's value label in this relative position.* You cannot specify a scratch or system variable for)variable, nor can you specify a variable you create with the STRING subcommand (Section 47.33). If you specify a variable that has no value label, the value itself will print, formatted according to its print format.

You can use all three arguments in as many titles and footnotes as you like on a single report. For example, the following are typical uses of these arguments:

```
/TITLE=LEFT  'Personnel Report' 'Prepared on )DATE'
       RIGHT 'Page )PAGE'
/FOOTNOTE=RIGHT 'Regional Manager: )MGRNM'
```

The left title includes the date, and the right title includes a page number. The footnote uses the the)variable specification to print the value label for MGRNM.

One label or value from each variable specified in a)variable argument prints on every page of the report. The label REPORT prints varies from page to page and is chosen from cases determined as follows:

- If a new page starts with a case listing, REPORT takes the labeled value from the first case listed.
- If a new page starts with a BREAK line, REPORT takes the labeled value from the first case of the new break group.
- If a new page starts with a summary line, REPORT takes the labeled value from the last case of the break group being summarized.

You cannot use variables named DATE or PAGE in the)variable argument because they will only print the current date or a page number. If you want to use a variable named DATE or PAGE, change the variable's name with the RENAME VARIABLES command before you use it in the)variable argument.

Each variable you specify with)variable must be defined on the active file, although it does not need to be a variable you've included as a column in your report. For example, in the commands

```
SORT CASES BY STORE DIVISION JOBGRADE LNAME
REPORT FORMAT=AUTOMATIC LIST LENGTH(1,27)
      /VARS=LNAME TENURE JTENURE
      /BREAK=DIVISION (PAGE)
      /SUMMARY=MEAN
      /BREAK=JOBGRADE
      /SUMMARY=MEAN '   Division Average:' (1)
      /TITLE=LEFT 'Personnel Resources'
                  ' '
                  'Branch: )STORE'
      /FOOTNOTE=LEFT 'Regional Manager: )MGRNM'
```

neither STORE nor MGRNM, the variables named on the)variable arguments, are included as columns on the report. Each, however, is defined in the active file.

Figure 47.29 shows a portion of the report. The argument)STORE prints one label from variable STORE, whose value labels are Suburban and Downtown. Specifying STORE as the first variable on SORT CASES assures that all the pages for the Suburban office print before all the pages for the Downtown office.

The PAGE keyword (Section 47.56) on BREAK calls for a new page every time the value of DIVISION changes. The variable MGRNM has no value labels. REPORT therefore prints values (the regional manager's name) for)MGRNM in a left footnote. The LENGTH keyword (Section 47.56) on FORMAT shortens the report page so the footnote prints near the body of the report.

Figure 47.29   Personnel report with title information

```
Personnel Resources
Branch: Suburban

                                           Tenure    Tenure
                                             in        in
Division       Job Grade        Last Name  Company   Grade
----------     ----------       ---------  -------   -------

Appliances     Sales Staff      Johnson      6.50      6.50
                                Martin       2.92      2.08
                                Parris       3.17      3.17

   Division Average:                         4.19      3.92

               Managerial Staff  Sanders     5.00      4.42

   Division Average:                         5.00      4.42

               Support Staff     Powell      2.67      2.67

   Division Average:                         2.67      2.67
Mean                                         4.05      3.77


Regional Manager: Paul Winfeld
```

47.30
Stacking Report Variables in a Column

When FORMAT=LIST, REPORT permits you to stack report variables together in a single column by linking them with plus signs on the VARIABLES subcommand. When you stack variables, specify a column heading that will accurately identify the information in the column. For example,

```
SORT CASES BY DIVISION LNAME
REPORT FORMAT=AUTOMATIC LIST(1)
      /VARS=LNAME
            TENURE + STORE(LABEL) 'Tenure' 'and' 'Location'
            AGE SALARY
      /BREAK=DIVISION
      /SUMMARY=MEAN
```

stacks the variables TENURE and STORE in a single column, as shown in Figure 47.30 (only one division is shown). LNAME, AGE, and SALARY are unaffected. The stacked variables each start a new line on the report and are displayed according to the order you define on the VARIABLES subcommand. REPORT always prints the lines from a single case on the same page.

The column heading Tenure and Location gives the column a descriptive heading. If you don't specify a heading for the stacked column, REPORT uses the default heading from the first variable on the stacked list. In this example, the column heading would have been Tenure in Company, which is inadequate to describe the data in the column. The optional argument (1) after the LIST keyword causes REPORT to insert one blank line between cases, which makes the report easier to read.

Though REPORT reads values from all the stacked variables when it determines column widths, it uses only values from the first variable on the stacked list to calculate summaries. In Figure 47.30, SUMMARY uses all the valid values from TENURE to calculate the mean for the column titled Tenure and Location but ignores all the values for STORE.

Figure 47.30   Report with stacked report variables

```
Personnel Data                                                                    PAGE    1

                       Tenure
                        and
Division    Last Name   Location    Age    Salary--Annual
                        ────────   ────    ──────────────
────────    ─────────

Carpeting   Cochran        3.92   22.00       $10,900
                        Suburban

            Dan            3.83   36.00       $10,000
                        Downtown

            Ford           3.67   27.00        $9,200
                        Suburban

            Gates          4.00   24.00       $10,000
                        Downtown

            Hoawinski      3.92   23.00       $10,900
                        Suburban

            Jones          4.83   44.00       $15,690
                        Downtown

            Katz           3.75   33.00       $10,000
                        Downtown

            Lavelle        4.33   27.00       $10,000
                        Downtown

            Mahr           2.67   33.00        $9,335
                        Downtown

            McAndrews      3.50   35.00       $15,520
                        Downtown

            Mulvihill      4.08   30.00       $10,000
                        Downtown

            Tygielski      6.00   35.00       $19,500
                        Suburban
Mean                       4.04   30.75       $11,754
```

47.31
Combining Break Groups in a Column

To combine break groups in a single column, list multiple variables on the same BREAK subcommand. Be sure to specify a column heading that will accurately identify the information in the column. For example, the commands

```
SORT CASES BY DIVISION SHIFT
REPORT FORMAT=AUTOMATIC
       /VARS=AGE TENURE SALARY
       /BREAK=DIVISION SHIFT 'Division' 'and' 'Shift'
       /SUMMARY=MEAN
```

combine break variables DIVISION and SHIFT in the same column. The column heading Division and Shift gives the column a descriptive heading. If you don't specify a heading for the column, REPORT uses the default heading from the first variable on the BREAK subcommand.

Figure 47.31 shows that REPORT displays the value labels of both break variables in the same column and calculates the mean for AGE, TENURE, and SALARY any time the value of either DIVISION or SHIFT changes. (Only two divisions are shown in the figure.)

You can use keyword TO to imply a list of variables on the BREAK subcommand. REPORT reads the variable order from the dictionary.

Figure 47.31   Report with stacked break variables

```
Personnel Data                                                              PAGE    1

Division
and                    Tenure
                          in
Shift        Age      Company    Salary--Annual
---------             -------
Carpeting
First

Mean        30.57      3.80        $11,649

Carpeting
Second

Mean        24.00      4.00        $10,000

Carpeting
Weekend

Mean        32.75      4.48        $12,375

Appliances
First

Mean        31.17      3.75        $13,062

Appliances
Second

Mean        42.00      6.50        $18,000

Appliances
Weekend

Mean        25.50      2.67         $8,100
```

47.32
Repeating Summary Specifications

If you do not specify one or more SUMMARY subcommands following a BREAK subcommand, no summary statistics are printed for that break level. The special keyword PREVIOUS references a set of SUMMARY subcommands defined for a previous BREAK subcommand. For example,

```
REPORT FORMAT=LIST
       /VARIABLES=NAME AGE TENURE
       /BREAK=DIVISION
       /SUMMARY=MEAN
       /SUMMARY=VALIDN(AGE)
       /BREAK=STORE
       /SUMMARY=PREVIOUS
```

prints means and the valid number of cases for AGE for each STORE within the DIVISION.

PREVIOUS accepts an optional argument in parentheses to point to the particular set of summaries to be copied. For example, PREVIOUS(1) copies all the SUMMARY subcommands applying to the first BREAK subcommand, and PREVIOUS(2) copies summary specifications for the second BREAK subcommand. No other specification can be used on a SUMMARY subcommand using PREVIOUS.

47.33
Creating Temporary String Variables

The STRING subcommand enables you to link together SPSS-X variables and constants to create new temporary variables you can use in REPORT. You can link together both alphanumeric and numeric variables and also intermix them. The STRING subcommand must precede the VARIABLES subcommand.

New STRING variables are temporary and available only to the REPORT procedure. The name you assign them must be unique and must follow SPSS-X variable-naming conventions.

For example, the subcommand

```
/STRING= PHONE (AREA '/' EXCH '-' NUM)
```

creates a string variable named PHONE, which comprises three variables and two constants. You cannot use the keyword TO to create a list of variables on the STRING subcommand.

You can use STRING variables on both the VARIABLES and BREAK subcommands, specifying column headings for them as you do for any other variables. If you don't specify a heading, the default column heading is the name you assign to the STRING variable, and the default column width is the sum of the widths of the linked variables plus the width of additional characters you include in the string.

For example, the command

```
REPORT FORMAT=AUTOMATIC LIST
    /STRING=PHONE (AREA '/' EXCH '-' NUM)
    /VARS=LNAME PHONE 'Telephone Number' AGE TENURE
```

creates STRING variable PHONE and then uses it on the VARIABLES subcommand. Its column heading on the report is Telephone Number, and its column width is the character sum of AREA, EXCH, and NUM, plus 2 to accommodate the slash and the hyphen.

Each variable you link within a string retains the width it was originally assigned on the DATA LIST command (Chapter 5) or FORMATS command (Chapter 10). You can specify an alternative width for each variable by enclosing the width in parentheses immediately after the variable name, as in

```
/STRING=SSN (S1(3) '-' S2(2) '-' S3(4))
```

The maximum width you can specify for any numeric variable is 16 characters. The maximum width for a string variable is the system page width.

47.34
STRING Display

If the width you assign a variable on the STRING subcommand is insufficient to display all its values, REPORT adjusts the STRING display. It prints asterisks on the report in place of numeric values that exceed the width, and right truncates string values that exceed the width. If the values are shorter then the variable's width, REPORT left-fills the column with zeros for numeric values and right-fills the column with blanks for string values. For variables with DOLLAR and COMMA formats, it left-fills the column with blanks. The keyword BLANK indicates the numeric values should be filled with blanks instead of zeros.

For example, assume VARA is a string variable with an A4 format. VARB is a compute variable with a default F8.2 format. The specification

```
/STRING=JOB1 (VARA VARB)
        JOB2 (VARA(2) VARB(3))
        JOB3 (VARA(2) VARB(BLANK)(4))
```

displays the following for a case in which VARA=KJ and VARB=241:

- JOB1 displays KJ 00241.00
- JOB2 displays KJ241
- JOB3 displays KJ 241

47.35
An Application Using
STRING

You can use the STRING subcommand to separate report columns with a column of special characters, such as asterisks or vertical bars. For example,

```
REPORT FORMAT=AUTOMATIC LIST
    /STRING=FILL ('*')
    /VARS=LNAME AGE TENURE FILL(1) ' ' SALARY
```

defines a string variable FILL with the value * for each case. Naming FILL between TENURE and SALARY on the VARIABLES subcommand prints a vertical column of asterisks between those two columns on a listing report. The (1) after FILL on VARIABLES specifies a column width; the space between apostrophes specifies a blank column heading. Figure 47.35 shows the first few lines of the report.

Figure 47.35 Column of special characters

```
Personnel Data                                                                          PAGE    1

                            Tenure
                              in
        Last Name      Age   Company      Salary--Annual

        Ford          27.00   3.67    *        $9,200
        Cochran       22.00   3.92    *       $10,900
        Hoawinski     23.00   3.92    *       $10,900
        Gates         24.00   4.00    *       $10,000
        Mulvihill     30.00   4.08    *       $10,000
        Lavelle       27.00   4.33    *       $10,000
        Mahr          33.00   2.67    *        $9,335
        Katz          33.00   3.75    *       $10,000
        Jones         44.00   4.83    *       $15,690
          .
          .
          .
```

47.36
Handling Missing Values

The MISSING subcommand within REPORT controls the treatment of missing values. You can specify one MISSING subcommand per REPORT command. It must follow the VARIABLES subcommand and precede BREAK.

The MISSING subcommand has three options. MISSING=VAR is the default.

VAR — *Treat missing values separately for each variable named on the VARIABLES subcommand.* Missing values are indicated in case listings but are not included in calculating summary statistics.

LIST(varlist n) — *Eliminate any case with missing values on n or more of the variables named on the variable list.* If a case is missing on fewer than *n* of the variables listed, it is deleted from summaries for those variables for which it is missing but is not deleted from case listings. The default n is 1.

NONE — *Handle all user-defined missing values as though they were not missing.* The keyword NONE applies to the entire set of variables named on the VARIABLES subcommand. It cannot be used to ignore missing-data indicators for some variables selectively.

For example, the subcommand

```
/MISSING=LIST (AGE TENURE SALARY 2)
```

deletes any case with missing values on two or more of the variables AGE, TENURE, and SALARY from case listings and from summaries.

MISSING specifications apply to REPORT-generated strings, as well as to other variables. If one variable in a REPORT-generated string is missing, the string is missing.

Only variables named on the VARIABLES and SUMMARY subcommands are checked for missing values. You must use a SELECT IF command to eliminate cases missing on break variables.

47.37
Changing the Missing-Value Indicator

REPORT uses a period to indicate missing values in case listings, break values, and summary statistics. The MISSING keyword on the FORMAT subcommand enables you to change the default missing-value indicator to any other character, including a blank. To do so, specify any one-character symbol, including a blank, in apostrophes, as in

```
REPORT FORMAT=AUTOMATIC LIST MISSING 'm'
```

47.38
OVERRIDING
REPORT'S DEFAULT
LAYOUT

Once you've run a report using FORMAT=AUTOMATIC, you might decide you want to change one or a number of the format decisions AUTOMATIC has made for you. For instance, you might want more space between the report title and the column headings. Or you might want to adjust the margins of the report.

Though you could specify FORMAT=MANUAL and set all your own specifications, the easiest method is to run a report with AUTOMATIC, determine which specific changes you want to make, leave FORMAT=AUTOMATIC, and make the desired changes by adding keywords to one or more of REPORT's four basic subcommands: FORMAT, VARIABLES, BREAK, and SUMMARY.

47.39
Automatic versus Manual
Format

The FORMAT subcommand's principal keywords are AUTOMATIC and MAN-UAL. The major features of each are described below.

Automatic. FORMAT=AUTOMATIC facilitates report design. It

- Displays labels for break variables.
- Centers string or value labels, based upon the longest string in the data (see Section 47.20); centers numeric data, based upon the widest format in the data or summary (see Section 47.20); and centers column headings. However, it left-justifies column headings if string values or value labels exceed the width of the longest word in the heading (see Section 47.15).
- Bottom aligns and underscores all column headings.
- Extends column widths to accommodate the longest word in a variable label (assuming the label is used for a column heading and no other criteria extend the column width; see Section 47.18).
- Extends column widths to accommodate the variable's longest value label (assuming no other criteria extend the column width; see Section 47.18).
- Shrinks a report if it is too wide for its margins (see Section 47.18).

Manual. FORMAT=MANUAL permits the user to make the major format decisions: It

- Displays values for break variables.
- Right-justifies numeric data and their column headings, and left-justifies string and value labels and their column headings.
- Top aligns and does not underscore column headings.
- Does not extend column widths to accommodate the longest word in a variable label that is used for a column heading.
- Extends column widths to accommodate the variable's longest value label, up to a width of 20. However, the column width can extend beyond 20 if one of the other column width criteria is greater than 20 (see Section 47.18).
- Generates an error message when a report is too wide for its margins.

REPORT's default setting is FORMAT=MANUAL. For example, if you specify

```
REPORT FORMAT=LIST
       /VARS=varlist
```

REPORT generates a listing report with FORMAT=MANUAL. In addition, if you omit the FORMAT subcommand from your REPORT specifications, REPORT generates a summary report with FORMAT=MANUAL. For example, the commands

```
SORT CASES BY DIVISION
REPORT VARIABLES=AGE TENURE JTENURE SALARY
      /BREAK=DIVISION
      /SUMMARY=MEAN
```

generate the report shown in Figure 47.39. Values print for the break variable DIVISION, column headings are not underscored, and data and column headings are not centered. REPORT does not extend the column width for SALARY to accommodate its default column heading Salary—Annual. Instead, it wraps the column heading.

Figure 47.39 Report with omitted FORMAT subcommand

```
Personnel Data                                                          PAGE    1

Division        Age      Tenure     Tenure   Salary—
                            in      in Grade   Annual
                         Company

        1
     Mean      30.75       4.04       3.31    $11,754

        2
     Mean      31.11       3.81       3.54    $12,508

        3
     Mean      36.87       4.79       4.08    $13,255

        4
     Mean      36.20       4.60       4.57    $17,580
```

47.40
Formatting Keywords and their Defaults

In addition to AUTOMATIC and MANUAL, REPORT provides a full range of keywords that allow you to control the format and layout of a report. Not all of them are on the FORMAT subcommand. Each of REPORT's major subcommands has its own keywords, and you can specify the keywords on each subcommand in any order.

Some of the keyword default settings depend upon whether you specify FORMAT=AUTOMATIC or FORMAT=MANUAL. For example, the BREAK subcommand defaults to (LABEL) when FORMAT=AUTOMATIC and (VALUE) when FORMAT=MANUAL.

Table 47.40 provides a list of REPORT's major keywords (each will be discussed in detail in the sections that follow). The default settings of each are shown for both FORMAT=AUTOMATIC and FORMAT=MANUAL.

When you specify a keyword option on the VARIABLES and BREAK subcommands, you must enclose it in parentheses in order to distinguish it from a variable name. The FORMAT subcommand does not require parentheses around the keywords.

For example, in the subcommand

```
/BREAK=DIVISION (PAGE)
```

the parentheses identify (PAGE) as a keyword rather than a variable name.

When you list two or more keyword options for a single variable on either the VARIABLES or BREAK subcommands, you can enclose them all within a single set of parentheses. For example, in the commands

```
SORT CASES BY DIVISION
REPORT FORMAT=AUTOMATIC LIST
      /VARS=LNAME SHIFT(LABEL) TENURE SALARY
      /BREAK=DIVISION (UNDERSCORE PAGE)
      /SUMMARY=MEAN
```

the keywords UNDERSCORE and PAGE are enclosed within a single set of parentheses.

Table 47.40   Default settings for keywords

Subcommand	Keyword	Default for AUTOMATIC	Default for MANUAL
FORMAT	ALIGN	left	left
	BRKSPACE		
	summary report	1	1
	listing report	−1	1
	CHALIGN	bottom	top
	CHDSPACE	1	1
	COLSPACE	4	4
	FTSPACE	1	1
	LENGTH	1,system length	1,system length
	LIST|NOLIST	NOLIST	NOLIST
	MARGINS	1,system length	1,system length
	MISSING	.	.
	PAGE1	1	1
	SUMSPACE	1	1
	TSPACE	1	1
	UNDERSCORE	on	off
VARIABLES	LABEL|VALUE|DUMMY	VALUE	VALUE
	LEFT|CENTER|RIGHT	CENTER	RIGHT for numbers LEFT for strings
	OFFSET	CENTER	0
BREAK	LABEL|VALUE	LABEL	VALUE
	LEFT|CENTER|RIGHT	CENTER	RIGHT for numbers LEFT for strings
	NAME|NONAME	NONAME	NONAME
	OFFSET	CENTER	0
	PAGE	off	off
	SKIP	1	1
	TOTAL|NOTOTAL	NOTOTAL	NOTOTAL
	UNDERSCORE	off	off
SUMMARY	PREVIOUS	1	1
	SKIP	0	0

You cannot enclose any keyword option in the same parentheses as the (VALUE\|LABEL\|DUMMY) specification on the VARIABLES subcommand, or the (TOTAL) specification on a listing report that has no break levels yet still calculates totals.

47.41
Overriding the Column Settings

Sections 47.42 through 47.52 discuss the keywords used to adjust REPORT's columns. See Sections 47.53 through 47.59 for information on adjusting rows.

47.42
Aligning the Report

By default, REPORT left-justifies a report within its margins. For example, if the report margins are (1,80) and the full width of the finished report is 50 columns, the report prints in columns 1 through 50. You can override REPORT's default alignment using the ALIGN on keyword on the FORMAT subcommand.

ALIGN *The report's alignment relative to its margins.* The specification on ALIGN is either LEFT, CENTER, or RIGHT, specified in parentheses. LEFT is the default.

For example,

```
REPORT FORMAT=AUTOMATIC ALIGN(CENTER)
```

centers the report within its margins. For example, if the report margins are (1,80) and the width of the finished report is 50 columns, (CENTER) prints the report in columns 15 through 65. If you specify (RIGHT), the report is right-justified against column 80.

47.43
Adjusting Margins

REPORT's default left margin is 1. Its default right margin is set by the SET command (Chapter 4). If you did not specify SET, the default is your system's right margin. You can override REPORT's default margins by using the MARGINS keyword on the FORMAT subcommand.

MARGINS(l,r) *The left and right margins of the report.* Specify the left and right margins in parentheses.

For example,

```
SORT CASES BY DIVISION
REPORT FORMAT=AUTOMATIC LIST MARGINS(1,70)
     /VARS=LNAME AGE TENURE
     /BREAK=DIVISION
     /SUMMARY=MEAN
```

specifies margins at column 1 on the left and column 70 on the right.

You can specify a single number in parentheses on the MARGINS keyword to indicate the left margin. REPORT will use the default value for the right margin. For example, MARGINS(8) specifies 8 for a left margin and the default value for the right margin.

You can use an asterisk to indicate default values. For example, MARGINS(*,66) specifies the default value for the left margin and 66 for the right. With FORMAT=AUTOMATIC, as you specify narrower margins REPORT squeezes out blanks between columns and then implements the rest of the *automatic fit* procedures (see Section 47.18).

You can extend the right margin beyond your system's default right margin, up to a maximum of 255.

47.44
Adjusting Column Widths

REPORT's default criteria for determining column widths are outlined in Section 47.18. You can change the column width for any variable named on the VARIABLES, BREAK, or STRING subcommand by specifying a width in parentheses after any variable name.

(n) *Set the variable's column width the* n. You can specify (n) after variables named on the VARIABLES, BREAK, or STRING subcommand.

For example,

```
REPORT FORMAT=AUTOMATIC LIST
     /VARIABLES=LNAME AGE(5) TENURE SALARY
```

sets a column width of 5 for the variable AGE. The width cannot be 0.

47.45
Changing Column Headings

To override the default column heading, specify a heading in apostrophes or quotes after any variable named on the VARIABLES, BREAK, or STRING subcommand. REPORT wraps default headings so they fit within the column width. If FORMAT=MANUAL, REPORT also wraps specified headings. If FORMAT=AUTOMATIC, REPORT does not wrap specified headings; instead it widens the column to accommodate the heading.

'heading' *Defined column heading.* You can define a column heading after any variable specified on the VARIABLES, BREAK, or STRING subcommand.

If you want multiple lines in a specified heading, use multiple sets of apostrophes, as in

```
'Break' 'Into Three' 'Lines'
```

which specifies a three-line column heading with the top and bottom lines containing one word and the middle line containing two words.

47.46
Positioning Column Headings

REPORT allows you to center, left-justify, or right-justify headings, top or bottom align them, and adjust the space between the column headings and the report title.

With FORMAT=AUTOMATIC, column headings are centered within their columns. If string values or value labels exceed the width of the longest word in the heading, the heading is left-justified. With FORMAT=MANUAL, column headings are left-justfied for string values or value labels and right-justified for numeric values.

You can override these defaults by specifying one of the following keywords in parentheses after the variable name on the VARIABLES or BREAK subcommand:

(CENTER)   *Center the heading within the column.*
(LEFT)   *Left-justify the heading within the column.*
(RIGHT)   *Right-justify the heading within the column.*

For example,

```
REPORT FORMAT=AUTOMATIC
      /VARIABLES=LNAME AGE(LEFT) TENURE
```

left-justifies the column heading for variable AGE.

The top and bottom alignment of column headings, as well as the spacing between the heading and report, are controlled by the following keywords on the FORMAT subcommand:

CHALIGN   *Top or bottom align the column headings.* The specification after CHALIGN is either TOP or BOTTOM in parentheses. When FORMAT= AUTOMATIC, column headings are bottom aligned by default. When FORMAT=MANUAL, column headings are top aligned by default.

TSPACE(n)   *The number of blank lines between the report title and the column headings.* The default is 1. Specify the number of blank lines you want in parentheses after the keyword TSPACE.

47.47
Heading Underscores

REPORT's heading underscores are either on or off for all columns. You cannot specify underscores for individual variables. REPORT underscores the bottom line of each column heading with an underscore that spans the column's full width. REPORT does not underscore blank or null labels.

Use the UNDERSCORE keyword on the FORMAT subcommand to turn underscores on or off.

UNDERSCORE   *Heading underscores.* The specification on UNDERSCORE is either ON or OFF in parentheses. ON is the default for FORMAT= AUTOMATIC. OFF is the default for FORMAT=MANUAL.

47.48
Underscores Between Listings and Summaries

By default, REPORT does not use an underscore to separate case listings from summary statistics. To request an underscore at any break level, specify (UNDERSCORE) on the BREAK subcommand at that level.

(UNDERSCORE)   *Use an underscore to separate case listings from summary statistics.* Specify (UNDERSCORE) on the BREAK subcommand. At the specified break level, REPORT prints the underscore at the end of the case listings *in preparation for a summary.*

You can specify (UNDERSCORE) once per break level. If you specify (UNDERSCORE) at a break level that has no SUMMARY subcommand, REPORT ignores the underscore request at that level. It also ignores the underscore request if you do not specify a listing report.

You can underscore specific columns by naming their variables in parentheses after the UNDERSCORE keyword. You can name variables individually or use the TO keyword to imply variables in the order they are listed on the VARIA-BLES subcommand. For example, in the commands

```
SORT CASES BY DIVISION LNAME
REPORT FORMAT=AUTOMATIC LIST
        /VARS=LNAME AGE TENURE JTENURE SALARY
        /BREAK=DIVISION (UNDERSCORE(TENURE TO SALARY))
        /SUMMARY=MEAN(TENURE JTENURE SALARY)
```

only the listings for variables TENURE, JTENURE, and SALARY are underscored. Figure 47.48 shows the report (only one division is shown).

Figure 47.48   Underscores that separate listings from summaries

```
Personnel Data                                                                              PAGE    1

                                        Tenure     Tenure
                                          in         in
Division      Last Name       Age       Company     Grade    Salary—Annual
----------    ---------       -----     -------     ------    -------------

Carpeting     Cochran         22.00      3.92        3.08       $10,900
              Dan             36.00      3.83        3.25       $10,000
              Ford            27.00      3.67        2.17        $9,200
              Gates           24.00      4.00        3.25       $10,000
              Hoawinski       23.00      3.92        3.08       $10,900
              Jones           44.00      4.83        4.33       $15,690
              Katz            33.00      3.75        3.25       $10,000
              Lavelle         27.00      4.33        3.17       $10,000
              Mahr            33.00      2.67        2.67        $9,335
              McAndrews       35.00      3.50        3.00       $15,520
              Mulvihill       30.00      4.08        3.08       $10,000
              Tygielski       35.00      6.00        5.33       $19,500
                                        ------      ------     -------

Mean                                     4.04        3.31       $11,754
```

47.49
Moving Summary Titles

By default, summary titles are displayed in the column corresponding to the level of break being summarized. You can move the summary title to any *break column* on the report. Specify the alternative column number in parentheses on the SUMMARY subcommand. For example,

```
/SUMMARY=MEAN(2)
```

displays the summary title Mean in the second break column. You cannot move the summary title into a report variables column.

47.50
Aligning Column Contents

The (OFFSET) keyword moves case listings, computed summaries, break values, and summary titles within their columns. If FORMAT=AUTOMATIC, OFFSET can be used to turn off data centering. You can specify (OFFSET) after variables on the VARIABLES or BREAK subcommand.

(OFFSET)   *Adjust the position of column contents.* The specification on OFFSET is either (*n*) or (CENTER). An (*n*) specification indicates a number of spaces to offset. Right-justified values are offset from the right; left-justified values are offset from the left. (CENTER) centers values within their columns based on their print format.

When you determine the *n* to specify, assume that numeric values are right-justified, and string values and value labels are left-justified. Begin counting spaces from the justified position. Do not count spaces from the value's centered position. For example, in the commands

```
SORT CASES BY DIVISION
REPORT FORMAT=AUTOMATIC LIST
        /VARS=LNAME SHIFT(LABEL)
              TENURE(LEFT) (OFFSET(4))
              SALARY(OFFSET(6))
        /BREAK=DIVISION
        /SUMMARY=MEAN(TENURE SALARY)
```

the OFFSET specifications assume both TENURE and SALARY are right-justified before they are offset. Figure 47.50 shows the report (only one division is shown). The values and summary statistics for the two numeric variables TENURE and SALARY are offset so they appear left-justified. The column heading for TENURE is aligned with the data in the column by left-justifying it with keyword (LEFT). The mean is calculated for TENURE and SALARY, only.

Figure 47.50 Offsetting cells

```
Report Data                                                                          ⌐   PAGE    1


                                        Tenure
                                        in
Division       Last Name      Shift     Company     Salary--Annual
-----------    ----------     -----     -------     --------------

Carpeting      Ford           First     3.7            $9,200
               Cochran        First     3.9           $10,900
               Hoawinski      First     3.9           $10,900
               Gates          Second    4.0           $10,000
               Mulvihill      First     4.1           $10,000
               Lavelle        Weekend   4.3           $10,000
               Mahr           First     2.7            $9,335
               Katz           Weekend   3.8           $10,000
               Jones          First     4.8           $15,690
               Dan            Weekend   3.8           $10,000
               McAndrews      First     3.5           $15,520
               Tygielski      Weekend   6.0           $19,500

Mean                                    4.0           $11,754
```

47.51
Changing Column Contents

The FORMAT, VARIABLES, BREAK, and SUMMARY subcommands each have keywords you can use to change a column's contents.

FORMAT Keywords. The following keywords can be specified on the FORMAT subcommand:

LIST|NOLIST   *Case listings.* If you specify LIST on the FORMAT subcommand, REPORT prints case listings in the body of the report. If you omit the keyword LIST, or specify NOLIST, report does not print listings. If you don't specify case listings on FORMAT, you must use BREAK and SUMMARY subcommands. A report with no case listings and no summaries contains no information.

MISSING 'x'   *Missing-value indicator.* By default, REPORT uses a period to indicate missing values in case listings, break values, and summary statistics. Use the MISSING keyword to change the indicator to any other one-character symbol, including a blank.

For example, to change the missing-value indicator to an m, specify:

```
FORMAT=AUTOMATIC LIST MISSING 'm'
```

BREAK Keywords. The following keywords can be specified after variables named on the BREAK subcommand:

(NAME|NONAME)   *Print the name of the break variable as a prefix to each value or label in the break column.*

For example, if the variable name is STORE and one of its labels is Suburban, BREAK=STORE(NAME) prints STORE: Surburban in the column. When FORMAT=MANUAL, you can use (NAME) with (LABEL). For example, if the variable name is SALARY and one of the value labels is OVER $25,000, BREAK=SALARY(NAME)(LABEL) prints SALARY: OVER $25,000 in the break column. REPORT accounts for the width of the (NAME) prefix in calculating a default column width. If you specify a width and it is insufficient to display the prefix, REPORT ignores (NAME).

BREAK and VARIABLES Keywords. When FORMAT=AUTOMATIC, REPORT prints labels for break variables and values for report variables. When FORMAT =MANUAL, REPORT prints values for both break and report variables. Use the following keywords after any variables named on the BREAK or VARIABLES subcommand to change these defaults:

(VALUE) *Display values rather than labels for that variable.*

(LABEL) *Display labels rather than values for that variable.*

**47.52
Adjusting Intercolumn
Spacing**

By default, REPORT determines column width as follows: it subtracts the combined column widths of the break and report variables from the REPORT margins. It then divides the result by the number of columns minus 1. It uses this value or 4, whichever is least, as the space between each column.

You can use the following keyword on FORMAT to adjust intercolumn spacing:

COLSPACE (n) *The space between all columns. n is the number of spaces you want between each column on the report.* Though REPORT would never choose 0 as a default width between columns, you can specify COLSPACE(0) if you want the minimum space possible between columns. When necessary, FORMAT=AUTOMATIC will override the intercolumn spacing you specify in order to fit a report within the report margins.

Alternatively, you can create a blank dummy variable on the VARIABLES subcommand to insert space between two report columns.

(DUMMY) *Create a blank dummy variable and insert it in the report.* Use the keyword (DUMMY) after a non-existent variable name on the VARIABLES subcommand to create a blank variable. For example, XX(DUMMY) creates a blank variable named XX. You can optionally specify a width (number of blank spaces) after the (DUMMY) keyword. A dummy variable cannot have an existing SPSS-X variable name.

The contents of a dummy column are blank and serve to control spacing between columns or to reserve space for composite statistics computed on other variables (see Section 47.26). For example, the commands

```
SORT CASES BY DIVISION
REPORT FORMAT=AUTOMATIC
        /VARS=AGE TENURE XX(DUMMY)(7)' ' SALARY
        /BREAK=DIVISION
        /SUMMARY=MEAN
```

place a seven-column space holder in Figure 47.52a separating TENURE and SALARY. A blank title is assigned within single quotes to override REPORT's default use of the variable name XX. You can specify more than one dummy variable per report.

Figure 47.52a   Using dummy variables to add space between columns

```
Personnel Data                                                        PAGE    1

                   Tenure
                     in
Division      Age  Company         Salary—Annual
--------      ---  -------         -------------

Carpeting
Mean        30.75    4.04            $11,754
Appliances
Mean        31.11    3.81            $12,508
Furniture
Mean        36.87    4.79            $13,255
Hardware
Mean        36.20    4.60            $17,580
```

To use a dummy column as a space holder for printing a composite summary statistic, specify the dummy variable as the variable whose column will display the result of the composite function calculation, as in

```
SORT CASES BY DIVISION
REPORT FORMAT=AUTOMATIC
        /VARS=AGE TENURE XX(DUMMY) 'Projected' 'Salary'
              SALARY 'Current' 'Salary'
        /BREAK=DIVISION
        /SUMMARY=MEAN
        /SUMMARY=MULTIPLY(MEAN(SALARY)1.07) '7% Raise'
                  (XX(DOLLAR)(0))
```

which specifies variable XX as the variable whose column will display the composite summary. As shown in Figure 47.52b, the summary prints in DOLLAR format with no decimal places.

Figure 47.52b   Dummy variables as space holders for composite summaries

```
Personnel Data                                                              PAGE    1

                      Tenure
                         in     Projected   Current
Division       Age    Company    Salary     Salary

Carpeting

Mean          30.75    4.04                 $11,754
7% Raise                         $12,577

Appliances

Mean          31.11    3.81                 $12,508
7% Raise                         $13,384

Furniture

Mean          36.87    4.79                 $13,255
7% Raise                         $14,183

Hardware

Mean          36.20    4.60                 $17,580
7% Raise                         $18,811
```

47.53
Overriding the Row Settings

REPORT allows you to change the spacing between rows on the report, specify page lengths, and implement alternative page numbering schemes for the report pages.

Each of these tasks is accomplished through keyword specifications. The relationship between the keywords is shown in the page layout in Section 47.54. The rules governing keyword syntax are discussed in Section 47.40.

47.54
The Report Page Layout

Figure 47.54 is a page layout guide to help you visualize the changes you can make in the spacing of SPSS-X report rows. The following alphabetized list of keywords should help you interpret the guide:

BRKSPACE   The number of blank lines between the break value (or label) and the listings.

CHDSPACE   The number of blank lines between the column headings and the listings.

FTSPACE   The minimum number of blank lines between the last listing in the report and the first footnote.

LENGTH   The length of the report page.

LIST   The spacing of case listings.

SKIP   The number of blank lines between a) the break value (or label) and the listings if you specify (SKIP) on the BREAK subcommand, and b) the specified summary line and preceding summary lines at the same break level if you specify SKIP on the SUMMARY subcommand.

SUMSPACE The number of blank lines between the last listing within a break level and the first summary line for that level. Also refers to the number of blank lines between summaries calculated for different break levels.

TSPACE The number of blank lines between the report title and the column headings.

By default, the top of the REPORT page begins at line 1 and ends at the bottom of the page whose length you specify with the SET command (see Chapter 4). If you don't use the SET command, REPORT's default page length is your system's length.

Figure 47.54 The report page layout

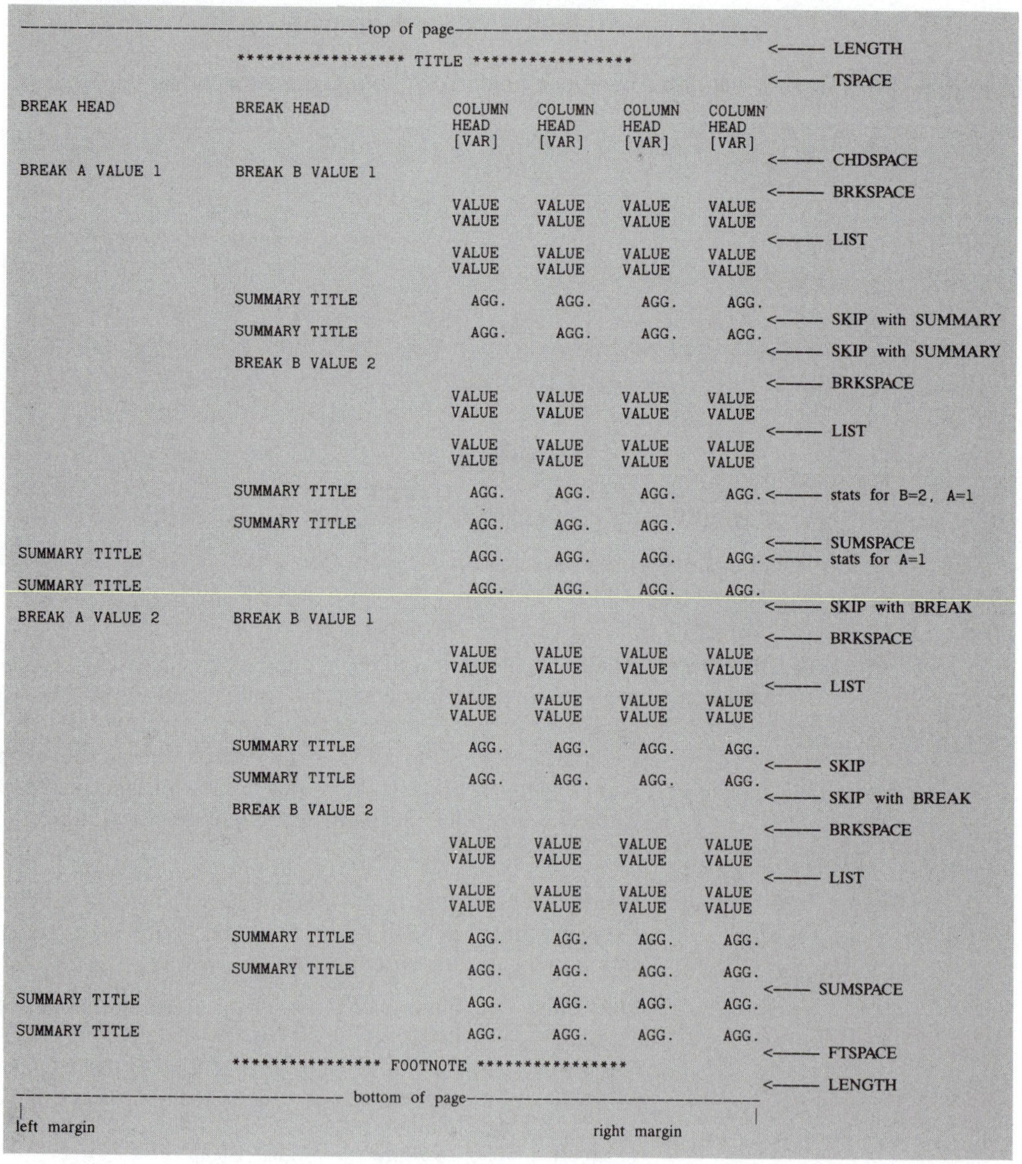

47.55
Adjusting Space Between Rows

Each of REPORT's four major subcommands, FORMAT, VARIABLES, BREAK, and SUMMARY, has keywords that allow you to control row spacing. You can adjust the space between titles and column headings, between headings and listings, between individual rows within the body of the report, and between the body of the report and footnotes.

FORMAT Keywords. The following keywords can be specified on FORMAT to control row spacing:

TSPACE(n)   *The number of blank lines between the report title and the column headings.* The default is 1. Specify the number of blank lines you want in parentheses.

CHDSPACE(n)   *The number of blank lines between the column headings and the first value line.* The default is 1. Specify the number of blank lines you want in parentheses.

LIST(n)   *Spacing of cases.* By default, the keyword LIST inserts no blank lines between cases. An integer value in parentheses specifies a blank line after every *n* cases. For example, LIST(1) produces a double-spaced listing and LIST(3) lists cases in sets of three.

The LIST(n) option makes it easier to read reports with many cases. The following commands generate Figure 47.55a (only the first nine cases are shown):

```
SORT CASES BY DIVISION LNAME
REPORT FORMAT=AUTOMATIC LIST(3)
        /VARS=LNAME AGE TENURE JTENURE
        /BREAK=DIVISION
```

Figure 47.55a   Personnel report with optional spacing

```
Personnel Data                                                                                    PAGE    1

                                  Tenure    Tenure
                                    in        in
Division     Last Name     Age    Company    Grade
----------   ----------   -----   -------   -------

Carpeting    Cochran      22.00    3.92      3.08
             Dan          36.00    3.83      3.25
             Ford         27.00    3.67      2.17

             Gates        24.00    4.00      3.25
             Hoawinski    23.00    3.92      3.08
             Jones        44.00    4.83      4.33

             Katz         33.00    3.75      3.25
             Lavelle      27.00    4.33      3.17
             Mahr         33.00    2.67      2.67
```

BRKSPACE(n)   *The number of blank lines between the break value (or label) and the first case listing or summary line for that break category.* Specify the number of blank lines you want in parentheses. If FORMAT= AUTOMATIC, the default is (1) for summary reports and (−1) for listing reports. If FORMAT=MANUAL, the default is (1) for both summary and listing reports. (For reports with totals but no break variables, see Section 47.58.)

• BRKSPACE(−1) for listing reports moves case listings up two rows, so that the first listing prints in the same row as the BREAK value. This is the default when FORMAT=AUTOMATIC. For example, in Figure 47.55a the case listing for Cochran prints in the same row as the BREAK value Carpeting.

• BRKSPACE(0) on a listing report prints the break value in a row by itself and the first case listing one row below it.

• BRKSPACE(1) prints the BREAK value (or label) in a row by itself and the first summary line or case listing two rows below it. BRKSPACE(1) is the default for all summary reports for listing reports when FORMAT = MANUAL.

For summary reports, if you want the summary or listing values to print on the same line as the break values, specify BRKSPACE(−1) on the FORMAT subcommand, as in:

```
SORT CASES BY DIVISION
REPORT FORMAT=AUTOMATIC BRKSPACE(-1)
        /VARIABLES=AGE TENURE JTENURE SALARY
        /BREAK=DIVISION
        /SUMMARY=MEAN
```

Figure 47.55b shows the report. Notice the summary title Mean does not print on the report. When you specify BRKSPACE(−1) for a summary report, you eliminate the row REPORT uses to display summary titles.

Figure 47.55b   Summary personnel report with BRKSPACE(-1)

```
Personnel Data                                                                  PAGE    1

                     Tenure     Tenure
                       in         in
Division      Age    Company     Grade    Salary--Annual
---------     ---    -------     -----    --------------

Carpeting    30.75    4.04       3.31        $11,754

Appliances   31.11    3.81       3.54        $12,508

Furniture    36.87    4.79       4.08        $13,255

Hardware     36.20    4.60       4.57        $17,580
```

SUMSPACE(n)   *The number of blank lines between the last listing within a break level and the first summary line for that level.* This is also the number of blank lines between summaries calculated for different break levels. The default in each instance is 1.

When you request a summary for a listing report, SUMSPACE controls the spacing between the last case on the report and the first summary line. By default, REPORT inserts a blank line between case listings and the first summary line. SUMSPACE(0) eliminates that blank line, as in:

```
SORT CASES BY DIVISION
REPORT FORMAT=AUTOMATIC LIST SUMSPACE(0)
       /VARS=AGE TENURE SALARY
       /BREAK=DIVISION
       /SUMMARY=MEAN
```

Figure 47.55c shows the report.

Figure 47.55c   Personnel report with SUMSPACE(0)

```
Personnel Data                                                                  PAGE    1

                     Tenure
                       in
Division      Age    Company     Salary--Annual
---------     ---    -------     --------------

Carpeting    27.00    3.67           $9,200
             22.00    3.92          $10,900
             23.00    3.92          $10,900
             24.00    4.00          $10,000
             30.00    4.08          $10,000
             27.00    4.33          $10,000
             33.00    2.67           $9,335
             33.00    3.75          $10,000
             44.00    4.83          $15,690
             36.00    3.83          $10,000
             35.00    3.50          $15,520
             35.00    6.00          $19,500
Mean         30.75    4.04          $11,754
```

When you have a two-break report in which you request statistics for both breaks, SUMSPACE also controls the number of blank lines between the summaries computed for different break levels. For example,

```
SORT CASES BY DIVISION STORE SHIFT
REPORT FORMAT=AUTOMATIC LIST SUMSPACE(0)
       /VARS=AGE TENURE SALARY
       /BREAK=DIVISION
       /SUMMARY=MEAN
       /BREAK=STORE
       /SUMMARY=MEAN
```

eliminates the blank line following the last case in each break group and the summary line for the mean. It also eliminates the blank line between the mean for the downtown store and the mean for the division. Figure 47.55d shows the results (only one division is shown).

Figure 47.55d   Report with two break levels and SUMSPACE(0)

```
Personnel Data                                                                        PAGE    1

                          Tenure
               Branch       in
Division       Store    Age  Company  Salary—Annual
————————       ——————   ———  ————————  —————————————

Carpeting      Suburban 27.00   3.67        $9,200
                        22.00   3.92       $10,900
                        23.00   3.92       $10,900
                        35.00   6.00       $19,500
               Mean     26.75   4.37       $12,625

               Downtown 30.00   4.08       $10,000
                        33.00   2.67        $9,335
                        44.00   4.83       $15,690
                        35.00   3.50       $15,520
                        24.00   4.00       $10,000
                        27.00   4.33       $10,000
                        33.00   3.75       $10,000
                        36.00   3.83       $10,000
               Mean     32.75   3.87       $11,318
Mean                    30.75   4.04       $11,754
```

FTSPACE(n)   *The minimum number of blank lines between the last value line on the page and the first footnote.* The default is 1. Specify the number of blank lines you want in parentheses.

VARIABLES Keywords.   The following keyword can be specified on VARIABLES to control row spacing:

(DUMMY)   *Insert a blank line between stacked variables.* Specify (DUMMY) after a non-existent variable name on the VARIABLES subcommand to insert a blank line between linked variables.

Be sure to specify a column heading that accurately identifies the data in the column. For example,

```
SORT CASES BY DIVISION LNAME
REPORT FORMAT=AUTOMATIC LIST(1)
      /VARS=LNAME
             NAME + X(DUMMY) + STORE(LABEL)
               + SHIFT(LABEL) 'Name, Store' 'and Shift'
             TENURE AGE
      /BREAK=DIVISION
      /SUMMARY=MEAN
```

inserts a blank, or dummy, row between the stacked variables NAME and STORE. (You can also insert a dummy row by specifying a blank space between two plus signs, as in NAME + + STORE + SHIFT.) Figure 47.55e shows the first three cases of the report generated by the above commands. Specifying (1) on the LIST keyword causes REPORT to insert a blank line between cases, which makes the report easier to read.

Figure 47.55e   Using blank rows among stacked variables

```
Personnel Data                                                                        PAGE    1

                        Name, Store    Tenure
                                         in
Division       Last Name  and Shift    Company    Age
————————       —————————  ———————————  ————————   ———

Carpeting      Cochran   Sandra L.       3.92    22.00

                         Suburban
                         First

               Dan       Edwin M.        3.83    36.00

                         Downtown
                         Weekend

               Ford      Harriet L.      3.67    27.00

                         Suburban
                         First
```

BREAK Keywords. The following keyword can be specified on BREAK to control row spacing. (For reports with totals but no break variables, see Section 47.58.)

(SKIP(n))   *Insert n blank lines between the last summary line for a break and the next break line. The default is 1.* Notice that you need parentheses around the entire argument when you specify SKIP on BREAK.

For example, the commands

```
SORT CASES BY STORE
REPORT FORMAT=AUTOMATIC
      /VARIABLES=AGE TENURE JTENURE SALARY
      /BREAK=STORE(SKIP(3))
      /SUMMARY=MIN
      /SUMMARY=MEAN
      /SUMMARY=MAX
```

insert three blank lines between the summaries for the suburban store and the summaries for the downtown store, as shown in Figure 47.55f.

You cannot use both SKIP and PAGE on the same BREAK subcommand.

Figure 47.55f   BREAK subcommand with (SKIP(3))

```
Personnel Data                                                                      PAGE    1

                    Tenure      Tenure
                      in          in
Branch                Company     Grade
Store       Age     Company     Grade     Salary--Annual
-------     ---     -------     ------    --------------

Suburban

Minimum     21.00    2.67        2.08        $8,000
Mean        31.59    4.42        3.95       $13,871
Maximum     42.00    6.50        6.50       $28,300


Downtown

Minimum     24.00    2.67        2.50        $7,450
Mean        35.25    4.28        3.68       $12,689
Maximum     44.00    6.83        6.00       $22,000
```

SUMMARY Keywords. The following keyword can be specified on SUMMARY to control row spacing:

SKIP(n)   *Skip n blank lines between the specified summary line and preceding summary lines at the same break level. The default is 0.*

For example, the commands

```
SORT CASES BY STORE
REPORT FORMAT=AUTOMATIC
        /VARIABLES=AGE TENURE JTENURE SALARY
        /BREAK=STORE
        /SUMMARY=MIN
        /SUMMARY=MEAN SKIP(3)
        /SUMMARY=MAX
```

insert 3 blank lines between the mean and the minimum values in Figure 47.55f. Spacing between the mean and the maximum values is unaffected.

SKIP(n) on the first SUMMARY subcommand for a BREAK skips the specified lines after skipping the number of lines you specify for BRKSPACE on the FORMAT subcommand (see Figure 47.55d).

**47.56
Specifying Page Lengths**   REPORT allows you to specify a uniform page length for all report pages or to specify a page break each time the value of a BREAK variable changes. By default, the page length is set between line 1 and the maximum page length established by the SET command (Chapter 4). If you don't use the SET command, the default setting is LENGTH(1,59).

The following keyword can be specified on FORMAT to control the length of the page:

LENGTH(1,n)   *The page length.* Specify the top and bottom page lines in parentheses. You cannot specify a page length that is longer than the system page length.

You can specify a single number in parentheses on the LENGTH keyword to indicate the top line. REPORT will use the default length for the bottom line. For example, LENGTH(8) specifies 8 for the top line and the system default for the bottom line. In addition, you can use an asterisk to indicate the default value for either the top or bottom line. LENGTH(*,38) specifies the default value for the top line and 38 for the bottom line. (For reports with totals but no break variables, see Section 47.58.)

(PAGE)   *The break level that controls paging.* When you specify (PAGE) after a variable name on any BREAK subcommand, REPORT begins a new page each time the break value changes for the specified variable. The break heading, including all current break values, is repeated on each new page. The page counter increments page numbers by one from Page 1 to the end of the report.

You cannot use both SKIP and PAGE on the same BREAK subcommand.

47.57
Alternative Page Numbers

REPORT's default page number for the first page of every report is 1. To change the beginning page number of any report, specify the following keyword on FORMAT:

PAGE1 (n) *Page number for the first page of the report.* Specify 0 or any positive number for n. For example, FORMAT=PAGE1(3) numbers the first report page Page 3 and increments page numbers from there.

You can also specify the following after a variable name on the BREAK subcommand to reset the page number:

(PAGE(RESET))   *Reset the PAGE1 setting to 1 every time the break value changes for the specified variable.*

47.58
Listing Reports with Totals

To generate a listing report that has no break levels but still calculates totals (Section 47.25), you specify (TOTAL) on a BREAK subcommand that does not name a variable, as in:

```
REPORT FORMAT=AUTOMATIC LIST
       /VARIABLES=varlist
       /BREAK=(TOTAL)
       /SUMMARY=function
```

This special application of the BREAK subcommand modifies REPORT's treatment of break levels and alters the effects of the BRKSPACE, PAGE, and SKIP keywords. The modifications are as follows:

BRKSPACE(n)   *Controls spacing between the summary title and the calculated totals.* The default is BRKSPACE(0). BRKSPACE(−1) has no effect.

The following commands insert two blank lines between the summary title Mean and the mean values, as shown in Figure 47.58a (only the last few cases are shown):

```
REPORT FORMAT=AUTOMATIC LIST BRKSPACE(2)
       /VARIABLES=LNAME AGE TENURE SALARY
       /BREAK=(TOTAL)
       /SUMMARY=MEAN
```

Figure 47.58a   Totals with BRKSPACE(n)

```
Personnel Data                                                                        PAGE    1

                           Tenure
                             in
Last Name         Age      Company     Salary--Annual
_____      ____     _____     _____


   .
   .
Cochran          39.00      5.50        $16,900
Carlyle          40.00      6.00        $19,050
Syms             32.00      4.33        $22,500
Jacobesen        44.00      4.50        $22,000

Mean

                 33.73      4.34        $13,179
```

(SKIP(n))   *Controls spacing between summary lines when specified on the BREAK subcommand.* The default is (SKIP(1)). You cannot specify SKIP(n) on the SUMMARY subcommand for listing reports with totals.

The following commands insert two blank lines between each of the specified total lines, as shown in Figure 47.58b (only the last few cases are shown):

```
REPORT FORMAT=AUTOMATIC LIST
       /VARIABLES=LNAME AGE TENURE SALARY
       /BREAK=(TOTAL) (SKIP(2))
       /SUMMARY=MIN
       /SUMMARY=MEAN
       /SUMMARY=MAX
```

Figure 47.58b   Totals with (SKIP(n))

```
Personnel Data                                                                        PAGE    1

                           Tenure
                             in
Last Name         Age      Company     Salary--Annual
_____      ____     _____     _____


   .
   .
Rosen            26.00      2.67         $7,450
Cochran          39.00      5.50        $16,900
Carlyle          40.00      6.00        $19,050
Syms             32.00      4.33        $22,500
Jacobesen        44.00      4.50        $22,000

Minimum
                 21.00      2.67         $7,450


Mean
                 33.73      4.34        $13,179


Maximum
                 44.00      6.83        $28,300
```

(PAGE)   *Causes a page break after each total line.* The page counter increments page numbers by 1, starting from Page 1, to the end of the report. You cannot specify (PAGE(RESET)).

The following commands cause REPORT to start a new page after it prints each total line:

```
REPORT FORMAT=AUTOMATIC LIST
       /VARIABLES=LNAME AGE TENURE SALARY
       /BREAK=(TOTAL) (PAGE)
       /SUMMARY=MIN
       /SUMMARY=MEAN
       /SUMMARY=MAX
```

REPORT allows you to specify several functions on one SUMMARY subcommand and print the results on the same summary line, as long as you don't try to print more than one statistic in any one column on the report. For example, if you specify

```
SORT CASES BY DIVISION
REPORT FORMAT=MANUAL UNDERSCORE(ON) CHALIGN(BOTTOM)
      /VARIABLES=TENURE JTENURE SALARY AGE
      /BREAK=DIVISION(LABEL)(34)
      /SUMMARY=MAX(TENURE JTENURE)
              MEAN(SALARY AGE) 'Max:Company/Grade
   Mean:Salary/Age'
```

REPORT determines a maximum value for TENURE and JTENURE, and a mean for SALARY and AGE. It displays the value for each on the same line, as shown in Figure 47.59a.

Figure 47.59a   Different functions on one summary

```
Personnel Data                                                                       PAGE    1

                                    Tenure
                                      in      Tenure   Salary--
Division                            Company  in Grade   Annual      Age
_____     _____  _____  _____    _____

Carpeting
Max:Company/Grade; Mean:Salary/Age    6.00      5.33    $11,754     30.75
Appliances
Max:Company/Grade; Mean:Salary/Age    6.50      6.50    $12,508     31.11
Furniture
Max:Company/Grade; Mean:Salary/Age    6.83      6.25    $13,255     36.87
Hardware
Max:Company/Grade; Mean:Salary/Age    6.00      6.00    $17,580     36.20
```

Since different statistics are printed on the same line, a descriptive summary title is specified. Otherwise, REPORT would use the default title of the first function named on the SUMMARY subcommand.

A column width of (34) is specified for DIVISION to accommodate the summary title. FORMAT=MANUAL is specified because it left-justifies value labels in a column, whereas FORMAT=AUTOMATIC centers value labels. FORMAT=MANUAL is less likely to truncate a long summary title.

When you name different statistics on the same SUMMARY subcommand, you must specify variables for each. You *cannot* specify

```
/SUMMARY=SUM MEAN    /* error
```

because REPORT would be unable to print both a sum and a mean on the same line for each eligible variable on the VARIABLES subcommand. The above specification is flagged as an error because it calls for overlapping summaries.

Since FREQUENCY and PERCENT print multiple lines in a summary, you cannot specify either of these functions with another function on a single SUMMARY subcommand. However, you can request the FREQUENCY and PERCENT functions for up to 20 variables, as in

```
/SUMMARY=FREQUENCY(1,10) (AGE) (TENURE)
```

which specifies variables AGE and TENURE for the FREQUENCY function.

When using composite functions, you may not have to specify target columns since the composite function has only one default target column. For example, the subcommand

```
/SUMMARY=PCT(SUM(TENURE)SUM(SALARY))
        PCT(SUM(JTENURE)SUM(SALARY))
```

is valid because the first PCT function prints the result in the column defined by TENURE and the second PCT function prints the result in the column defined by JTENURE, assuming both TENURE and JTENURE are specified on the VARIABLES subcommand.

Figure 47.59b is a two-break report in which four different summary statistics are used on the SUMMARY subcommand. The following commands produce the report:

```
GET FILE=PERSONNEL
GET  FILE=NEWDATA
IF (SEX EQ 1) FSALARY=SALARY
IF (SEX EQ 2) MSALARY=SALARY
COMPUTE LOWSAL=SALARY
FORMATS SALARY FSALARY MSALARY LOWSAL (DOLLAR7)

SORT CASES BY STORE DIVISION
REPORT FORMAT=AUTOMATIC TSPACE(3) BRKSPACE(-1) MARGINS(1,90)
     /VARIABLES=SALARY 'Average' 'Salary'
             LOWSAL '% of' 'Salaries' 'Below 10k'
             MAX(DUMMY) 'Maximum' 'Salary'
             MIN(DUMMY) 'Minimum' 'Salary'
             FSALARY 'Average' 'Salary' 'Women'
             MSALARY 'Average' 'Salary' 'Men'
     /BREAK=STORE (TOTAL) (SKIP(2))
     /SUMMARY=MEAN(2) 'For Store:'  (SALARY FSALARY MSALARY)
             PLT(10000)  (LOWSAL(2))
             ADD(MAX(SALARY))  (MAX(0) (DOLLAR))
             ADD(MIN(SALARY))  (MIN(0) (DOLLAR))
     /BREAK=DIVISION
     /SUMMARY=MEAN ' '  (SALARY FSALARY MSALARY)
             PLT(10000)  (LOWSAL(2))
             ADD(MAX(SALARY))  (MAX(0) (DOLLAR))
             ADD(MIN(SALARY))  (MIN(0) (DOLLAR))
     /TITLE='Analysis of Salaries within Store and Division'
```

Each column of the report in Figure 47.59b is used to describe some aspect of the variable SALARY. Composite functions are used to move the minimum and maximum of SALARY into dummy columns. Data transformations are used to split SALARY into two groups (men and women) as described in Section 47.63. Since a composite cannot be used with the PLT summary statistic, an exact copy of SALARY named LOWSAL is created with a COMPUTE command. The summary title for the primary break level is moved to the secondary break level.

Figure 47.59b Manipulating summaries

Branch Store	Division	Average Salary	% of Salaries Below 10k	Maximum Salary	Minimum Salary	Average Salary Women	Average Salary Men
				Analysis of Salaries within Store and Division			
Suburban	Carpeting	$12,625	25.00%	$19,500	$9,200	$10,333	$19,500
	Appliances	$14,395	60.00%	$28,300	$8,000	$10,919	$28,300
	Furniture	$12,975	28.57%	$17,050	$8,975	$9,925	$15,262
	Hardware	$22,500	0.00	$22,500	$22,500	.	$22,500
	For Store:	$13,871	35.29%	$28,300	$8,000	$10,445	$18,764
Downtown	Carpeting	$11,318	12.50%	$15,690	$9,335	$12,109	$10,000
	Appliances	$10,150	75.00%	$15,300	$7,500	$8,900	$10,567
	Furniture	$13,500	0.00	$14,400	$12,000	$13,300	$13,700
	Hardware	$16,350	25.00%	$22,000	$7,450	$13,250	$19,450
	For Store:	$12,689	20.83%	$22,000	$7,450	$12,429	$12,950
	TOTAL	$13,179	26.83%	$28,300	$7,450	$11,527	$15,092

47.60
LIMITATIONS

The following formal limitations apply to the REPORT procedure:

- A maximum of 10 dummy variables per VARIABLES subcommand.
- A maximum of 50 strings per STRING subcommand.
- The maximum width of a printed report is 255 characters.
- A maximum of 20 MODE and MEDIAN requests per SUMMARY subcommand.
- Neither FREQUENCY nor PERCENT can be named with other statistics on a single SUMMARY subcommand. However, for both functions, you can specify up to 20 variables. In addition, neither FREQUENCY nor PERCENT can be named more than once per subcommand.
- A maximum of 20 PGT, PLT, and PIN requests per SUMMARY subcommand.

Workspace is required to store the following: all labeling information; frequency counts (if summaries request FREQUENCY, PERCENT, MEDIAN, or MODE) for all integers specified in the range; strings; and computed summary statistics.

Memory requirements significantly increase if FREQUENCY, PERCENT, MEDIAN, or MODE is requested with variables having a wide range of values. The amount of workspace required can be calculated as follows:

$20 + 8*(max-min+1)$ bytes per variable per function per break

If TOTAL is in effect on a report that has break variables, workspace requirements are almost doubled. If the same range is used for different statistics for the same variable, only one set of cells is collected. For example,

```
FREQUENCY(1,100)(VARA) PERCENT(1,100)(VARA)
```

requires only 820 bytes.

Memory requirements also increase if value labels are printed for variables with many value labels. The amount of workspace required can be calculated as follows:

$4 + 24*nlabel$ per variable

For example, assume that the case listing contains value labels for the variable STATE and there are 51 value labels corresponding to state names and the District of Columbia. The amount of memory required to store the labels is 1228 bytes.

There should be enough workspace in 5000 bytes for a report of moderate size with a few strings, titles, and footnotes; two break levels; and simple descriptive statistics.

47.61
REPORT COMPARED WITH OTHER PROCEDURES

Many of the features of REPORT can be found in part in other procedures in SPSS-X, and you may have to decide which is more appropriate for a particular job. You can obtain case listings using PRINT or LIST; you can obtain means, sum, variances, and standard deviations for subpopulations using MEANS; you can obtain descriptive statistics by using FREQUENCIES and DESCRIPTIVES; and you can produce aggregate files by using AGGREGATE. The principal advantage of REPORT over other procedures producing essentially the same types of statistics is that its output is compact and its formatting and labeling flexible.

There are other advantages in REPORT that are not so obvious:

- It prints frequency counts with decimal digits if you override the default format. Therefore, if a file contains noninteger weights, REPORT prints the actual sum of the weights, rather than rounding them as FREQUENCIES does.

• You can obtain subpopulation medians without having to resort to multiple SELECT IFs, with a considerable savings in both command preparation and computer expense.

• It's a simple matter to compute and print composite functions such as the sum of one variable divided by the sum of another variable.

There are also some REPORT limitations that other procedures producing the same kinds of output do not have:

• Subpopulations can be defined only once on the break variables. In MEANS, they can be defined by several different variables. For example, one MEANS can define subpopulations first by SEX, then by AGE, etc.

• You can analyze only a limited number of variables on one REPORT command. The number of variables permitted is a function of report width and column widths.

• Frequencies, median, and mode are available only for integer variables.

• You must sort the file on the break variable(s).

47.62
Producing
CROSSBREAK-like Tables

Procedure MEANS optionally formats statistics for variables broken down by two or more variables into a tabular format when the keyword CROSSBREAK is used. REPORT can also produce such a table. In the CROSSBREAK format some of the columns in the report correspond to subsets of the file.

Figure 47.62 is a more complicated version of a CROSSBREAK-like report. Variables TIME0, TIME1, TIME2, and TIME3 are created with COMPUTE commands executed conditionally based on TIME to subset AMOUNT. The file is first aggregated with the AGGREGATE command to obtain the TOTAL variable across all the cases (see Chapter 18). This variable is then spread back to the original file with the MATCH FILES command (see Chapter 16).

The following commands produce this report:

```
DO IF    (TIME GE 90)
COMPUTE    TIME3=AMOUNT
ELSE IF  (TIME GT 60)
COMPUTE    TIME2=AMOUNT
ELSE IF  (TIME GT 30)
COMPUTE    TIME1=AMOUNT
ELSE
COMPUTE    TIME0=AMOUNT
END IF
PRINT FORMATS  TIME3 TO TIME0 (DOLLAR10.2)
COMPUTE CONST=1 /* Compute a constant for AGGREGATE*/
AGGREGATE  OUTFILE=HOLD
        /BREAK=CONST
        /TOTAL=SUM(AMOUNT)

MATCH FILES  TABLE=HOLD/FILE=*/BY CONST /* Place TOTAL back on file */

REPORT  FORMAT=BRKSPACE(-1) MARGINS(1,80) MISSING ' '
              CHDSPACE(1)
        /VARIABLES=AMOUNT'Total'
            TIME0 '0-30 Days'
            TIME1 '31-60 Days'
            TIME2 '61-90 Days'
            TIME3 '90+ Days'
        /TITLE='Summary Statement-Accounts Receivable' '(Aged)'
            ' ' 'Apex Metal Fasteners' 'M.I.S. Report 2'
        /BREAK=INVTYPE(TOTAL)
        /SUMMARY=SUM
        /SUMMARY=PCT(SUM(AMOUNT)SUM(AMOUNT))'% of Type'
                PCT(SUM(TIME0)SUM(AMOUNT))
                PCT(SUM(TIME1)SUM(AMOUNT))
                PCT(SUM(TIME2)SUM(AMOUNT))
                PCT(SUM(TIME3)SUM(AMOUNT))
        /SUMMARY=PCT(SUM(AMOUNT)MAX(TOTAL))'% of Total'
                PCT(SUM(TIME0)MAX(TOTAL))
                PCT(SUM(TIME1)MAX(TOTAL))
                PCT(SUM(TIME2)MAX(TOTAL))
                PCT(SUM(TIME3)MAX(TOTAL))
```

Figure 47.62   A CROSSBREAK application with REPORT

```
                      SUMMARY STATEMENT—ACCOUNTS RECEIVABLE
                                     (AGED)

                              APEX METAL FASTENERS
                                M.I.S. REPORT 2

     INVTYPE              TOTAL      0-30 DAYS    31-60 DAYS    61-90 DAYS     90+ DAYS

     Stove Bolts      $2,501.50       $346.11    $1,345.69       $403.86      $405.84
       % OF TYPE         100.00         13.84        53.80         16.14        16.22
       % OF TOTAL         18.06          2.50         9.72          2.92         2.93

     Wood Screws      $3,417.60     $1,181.00    $1,244.58       $390.51      $601.51
       % OF TYPE         100.00         34.56        36.42         11.43        17.60
       % OF TOTAL         24.68          8.53         8.99          2.82         4.34

     Metal Screws     $3,221.51                    $697.41    $1,982.59      $541.51
       % OF TYPE         100.00                      21.65        61.54        16.81
       % OF TOTAL         23.26                       5.04        14.32         3.91

     Spring Washers   $2,429.97       $512.15      $206.81       $393.69    $1,317.32
       % OF TYPE         100.00         21.08         8.51         16.20        54.21
       % OF TOTAL         17.55          3.70         1.49          2.84         9.51

     Other            $2,278.36       $354.77      $897.57       $579.70      $446.32
       % OF TYPE         100.00         15.57        39.40         25.44        19.59
       % OF TOTAL         16.45          2.56         6.48          4.19         3.22

     TOTAL           $13,848.94     $2,394.03    $4,392.06    $3,750.35    $3,312.50
       % OF TYPE         100.00         17.29        31.71         27.08        23.92
       % OF TOTAL         100.00         17.29        31.71         27.08        23.92
```

47.63
Producing
CROSSTABS-like Tables

REPORT can be used to produce CROSSTABS-like tables where columns correspond to the values of one or more variables. Transformations are required to split a variable into several variables, each one corresponding to a category of the original variable. The easiest means of creating such variables is to use the COUNT command (Chapter 7), as in:

```
COUNT MALE=SEX(1)/FEMALE=SEX(2)
```

In this example, all males on the file have a value of 1 for MALE and a value of 2 for FEMALE. Figure 47.63 is one example of such a CROSSTABS-like report.

Figure 47.63   An affirmative action report

```
FORM T                                       AFFIRMATIVE ACTION PROGRAM                              ORGANIZATION UNIT:   ABCD
                                                                                                          LOCATION:    CHICAGO
                                             QUARTERLY STATISTICAL REPORT                            TIME PERIOD: 6/81 TO 9/81
```

JOB CATEGORIES	TOTAL (1)	MALE (2)	FEMALE (3)	MALE NEGRO (4)	MALE ORIENTAL (5)	MALE INDIAN (6)	MALE SPANISH SURNAME (7)	FEMALE NEGRO (8)	FEMALE ORIENTAL (9)	FEMALE INDIAN (10)	FEMALE SPANISH SURNAME (11)
OFFICIALS & MANAGER	48	19	29	7	0	0	0	18	4	0	0
PERCENTAGES		39.58	60.42	14.58	0.0	0.0	0.0	37.50	8.33	0.0	0.0
PROFESSIONALS	62	29	33	4	3	0	0	6	2	0	0
PERCENTAGES		46.77	53.23	6.45	4.84	0.0	0.0	9.68	3.23	0.0	0.0
TECHNICIANS	98	17	81	4	1	0	0	33	1	0	0
PERCENTAGES		17.35	82.65	4.08	1.02	0.0	0.0	33.67	1.02	0.0	0.0
OFFICE AND CLERICAL	67	18	49	3	1	0	0	12	2	0	3
PERCENTAGES		26.87	73.13	4.48	1.49	0.0	0.0	17.91	2.99	0.0	4.48
TOTAL	275	83	192	18	5	0	0	69	9	0	3
PERCENTAGES		30.18	69.82	6.55	1.82	0.0	0.0	25.09	3.27	0.0	1.09

```
DATE OF SURVEY: 01 MAR 82                                                     PERSON PREPARING REPORT:   JANE BILANDIC
```

The complete set of SPSS-X commands required to produce the report in Figure 47.63 is as follows:

```
GET   FILE=HUB
COMMENT   OBTAIN INTERSECTION OF NONMISSING ETHNIC AND SEX
IF (NOT(MISSING(RACE)) AND NOT(MISSING(SEX))) NOFCASES=1
COMMENT   SET UP VARIABLES COLUMNS
COUNT   MALE=SEX(1)/FEMALE=SEX(2)
MISSING VALUES   MALE FEMALE(0)
DO IF (SEX EQ 1)   /* SET UP COLUMNS FOR MALES
DO REPEAT   OUT=MNEGRO MORIENT MINDIAN MLATINO/
              VAL=2 TO 5
IF   (ETHNIC EQ VAL) OUT=1
END REPEAT
ELSE IF (SEX EQ 2) /* SET UP COLUMNS FOR FEMALES
DO REPEAT   OUT=FNEGRO FORIENT FINDIAN FLATINO/
              VAL=2 TO 5
IF   (ETHNIC EQ VAL) OUT=1
END REPEAT
END IF
SORT CASES  BY JOBGRADE
REPORT   FORMAT=TSPACE(3) BRKSPACE (-1) CHDSPACE (0) LENGTH (1,20)
        /VARIABLES=NOFCASES ' ' ' ' 'TOTAL' ' (1)'(5)
            MALE ' ' ' ' 'MALE' ' (2)'(5)
            FEMALE ' ' ' ' 'FEMALE' ' (3)'(6)
            MNEGRO ' ' 'MALE' 'NEGRO' ' (4)'(5)
            MORIENT ' ' 'MALE' 'ORIENTAL' ' (5)'(8)
            MINDIAN ' ' 'MALE' 'INDIAN' ' (6)'(6)
            MLATINO 'MALE   ' 'SPANISH' 'SURNAME' ' (7)'(7)
            FNEGRO ' ' 'FEMALE' 'NEGRO' ' (8)'(6)
            FORIENT ' ' 'FEMALE' 'ORIENTAL' ' (9)'(8)
            FINDIAN ' ' 'FEMALE' 'INDIAN' ' (10)'(6)
            FLATINO 'FEMALE ' 'SPANISH' 'SURNAME' ' (11)'(7)
        /TITLE LEFT='FORM T'
            CENTER='AFFIRMATIVE ACTION PROGRAM' ' '
                   'QUARTERLY STATISTICAL REPORT'
            RIGHT='ORGANIZATION UNIT:   ABCD'
                  'LOCATION:   CHICAGO'
                  'TIME PERIOD: 6/81 TO 9/81'
        /FOOTNOTE LEFT='DATE OF SURVEY: )DATE'
            RIGHT='PERSON PREPARING REPORT:   JANE BILANDIC'
        /BREAK=JOBCAT (LABEL)(TOTAL)
        /SUMMARY=VALIDN (NOFCASES MALE FEMALE MNEGRO
         MORIENT MINDIAN MLATINO FNEGRO FORIENT FINDIAN FLATINO)
        /SUMMARY=PCT (VALIDN (MALE) VALIDN (NOFCASES))'   PERCENTAGES'
         PCT (VALIDN (FEMALE) VALIDN (NOFCASES))
         PCT (VALIDN (MNEGRO) VALIDN (NOFCASES))
         PCT (VALIDN (MORIENT) VALIDN (NOFCASES))
         PCT (VALIDN (MINDIAN) VALIDN (NOFCASES))
         PCT (VALIDN (MLATINO) VALIDN (NOFCASES))
         PCT (VALIDN (FNEGRO) VALIDN (NOFCASES))
         PCT (VALIDN (FORIENT) VALIDN (NOFCASES))
         PCT (VALIDN (FINDIAN) VALIDN (NOFCASES))
         PCT (VALIDN (FLATINO) VALIDN (NOFCASES))
```

In this example, the IF commands required to produce the report are placed inside a DO REPEAT structure and executed conditionally based on the value of SEX.

47.64
REPORT and Other SPSS-X Commands

REPORT interacts with other SPSS-X commands. Data transformations are required for special types of reports described in previous sections. This section describes other commands that affect both the dimensions and the contents of reports.

The dictionary print formats defined by the PRINT FORMATS command for a variable instructs SPSS-X how to print it. If a variable has a print format that includes no decimal places (F2.0 for example), no decimal digits are printed, even though the internal representation is a decimal number. Thus, misspecified print formats can produce misleading column contents in REPORT.

By default, REPORT uses any label assigned on the VARIABLE LABELS command as the column heading for report and break columns. The VARIABLE LABELS command also permits blank and null variable labels. For example,

```
VARIABLE LABELS VARX''
```

specifies a null label for VARX.

The number of cases "reported" is controlled by the number of cases being processed in a run. You can use N OF CASES to limit the number of cases processed (Section 47.7), or you can use SELECT IF and SAMPLE.

REPORT, unlike many other procedures in SPSS-X, actually begins printing your report as it reads through the data. Thus, if REPORT is the very first procedure in the run, warning messages concerning invalid data fields are interspersed with REPORT output. To avoid this possibility, use some other procedure such as SORT CASES or EXECUTE prior to the report when reading data using the DATA LIST command (Chapter 5), or turn off warning messages with the SET command (Chapter 4).

PRINT and WRITE are transformation utilities that you can use to print cases on the display file. Unless you are using the FILE subcommand on these commands to direct the display to an alternative file, do not use them immediately prior to your REPORT command. Otherwise, their results interleave with REPORT's results. If you are using either PRINT or WRITE in the same job with REPORT, you can avoid the interleaving effect by placing some other procedure (or an EXECUTE command) between these commands and the REPORT command.

47.65
Split-File Processing

Using the SPLIT FILE (Chapter 15) with REPORT is equivalent to specifying the variables named on the SPLIT FILE command as the first break level with the BREAK subcommand. Specifying SPLIT FILE variables as the first BREAK instead of using the SPLIT FILE command has three distinct advantages:

- Less CPU time is required, because various arrays do not have to be reinitialized.
- The TOTAL option in the BREAK subcommand provides statistics over the total of split-file groups.
- The report can be more compact because new breaks begin on a new page only if you select the PAGE option.

Syntax

SURVIVAL

```
SURVIVAL TABLES=survival varlist [BY independent varlist (min,max)...]
                [BY control varlist (min,max)...]
  /INTERVALS=THRU n BY a [, THRU m BY b ...]
  /STATUS=status variable({min,max}) FOR {ALL            }
                         {value  }    {survival varlist}
  [/STATUS=...]
  [/PLOTS({ALL**   })={ALL**           } BY {ALL**               }
          {LOGSURV }  {survival varlist}   {independent varlist}
          {SURVIVAL}
          {HAZARD  }  BY {ALL**          }]
          {DENSITY }     {control varlist}
  [/COMPARE={ALL**           } BY {ALL**              }
            {survival varlist}    {independent varlist}
            BY {ALL**          }]
               {control varlist}
  [/MISSING={GROUPWISE**}  [INCLUDE]]
            {LISTWISE  }
  [/PRINT={TABLE** }]
          {NOTABLE }
  [/CALCULATE={EXACT**    }]
              {COMPARE    }
              {CONDITIONAL}
              {APPROXIMATE}
              {PAIRWISE   }
  [/WRITE[={NONE**}]]
          {TABLES}
          {BOTH  }
```

**Default if the subcommand is omitted.

Contents

48.1   OVERVIEW
48.2   OPERATION
48.3   TABLES Subcommand
48.4   INTERVALS Subcommand
48.5   STATUS Subcommand
48.6   Life Table Output
48.7   Survival Functions
48.8   PRINT Subcommand
48.9   PLOTS Subcommand
48.10   COMPARE Subcommand
48.11   CALCULATE Subcommand
48.12   Pairwise Comparisons
48.13   Approximate Comparisons
48.14   Obtaining Comparisons Only
48.15   Entering Aggregated Data
48.16   MISSING Subcommand
48.17   WRITE Subcommand
48.18   Format
48.19   Record Order
48.20   LIMITATIONS

SURVIVAL was originally designed and implemented by Barry Brown, Marcus Schimek, Herman Walker, and Peggy Wright of M.D. Anderson Hospital, the University of Texas at Houston (Brown, et al., 1979). Their work was supported by the National Cancer Institute grants CA11430 and CA16672. A revised version of this procedure is available in the CDC-6000 version of SPSS distributed by Northwestern University. That version was extensively revised by Barry Brown and Herman Walker and by SPSS Inc. for inclusion in Release 8.

48

Chapter 48   SURVIVAL

Procedure SURVIVAL produces life tables, plots of the survival functions, and subgroup comparisons. An output file can be written for use on graphics devices or with other programs. Survival analysis is useful when the dependent variable represents the time interval between an initial event and a termination event. Although this type of analysis is performed most frequently in medical research, where the detection of a disease is the initial event and the patient's death is the termination event (hence the name survival), it can also be used to study other events such as length of time from marriage to the birth of the first child or number of years employed by the same firm.

48.1
OVERVIEW

The only restrictions in survival analysis are that the initial event must occur, the termination event must occur after the initial event, and the termination event may not occur more than once. In addition to the initial and termination events, two other concepts that are central to survival analysis are *censored observations* and *survival scores*.

Censored Observations. If the termination event has not occurred for an observation by the time data are analyzed, its survival time is the length of time between the initial event for that observation and the time of the analysis. Such observations are considered censored because the survival time is not known exactly, but it is known to be of at least a certain duration. Censored observations can occur either because the termination event has not occurred by the time of the analysis or because an observation is withdrawn from the study for other reasons, such as death from other causes or inability to maintain contact. Censored observations cannot be treated as missing data. Eliminating from the analysis all patients who were still alive at the end of the study period, for example, would not yield very useful results. Survival analysis makes use of both censored and uncensored observations in calculating survival times.

Survival Score. A survival score is calculated for each observation by comparing its survival time to that of all other observations. The score starts at zero and is incremented by one for each observation whose survival time is known to be lower and decremented by one for each observation whose survival time is known to be greater. For observations with the same survival time, no change is made. If one of the observations is censored, the censored observation is considered to have a greater survival time since it is known to have survived at least as long as its survival time. Survival scores are used in comparisons to determine whether groups differ significantly in terms of survival.

Statistic D. For use in subgroup comparisons, a statistic D is calculated from the survival scores using the algorithm of Lee and Desu (1972). D is asymptotically distributed as chi-square with $g-1$ degrees of freedom, where g equals the number of groups, under the null hypothesis that the subgroups are samples from the same survival distribution. The larger the D statistic, the more likely that the subgroups come from different survival distributions. The level of significance of D is also printed.

SURVIVAL can analyze several survival variables in the same specification of the procedure. SURVIVAL produces a life table for each variable listed. First- and second-order control variables can be used to produce subgroup comparisons. Optionally, you can obtain plots of the survival functions and request specific subgroup comparisons. The life table can be written out to a file for use with other programs.

Life Tables. The TABLES subcommand lists the variables to be used in the analysis, including any control variables. Separate life tables are produced for each variable. The three survival functions and their standard errors are included in the life table. (See Section 48.3.)

Intervals. SURVIVAL reports on the survival history at various points, beginning with the initial event. The unit of time on which the survival variables are scaled can be grouped into intervals using the INTERVALS subcommand. (See Section 48.4.)

Survival Status. To determine whether the termination event has occurred for a particular observation, SURVIVAL checks the value of a status variable. The STATUS subcommand lists the status variable associated with each survival variable. (See Section 48.5.)

Producing Plots. To obtain plots of the survival functions for all cases or separately for various subgroups, use the PLOTS subcommand. (See Section 48.9.)

Comparisons. When control variables are listed on the TABLES subcommand, you can request subgroup comparisons using the COMPARE subcommand. Both overall and pairwise comparisons are available. For aggregated data, approximate comparisons can be specified. (See Section 48.10.)

Missing Values. By default, the MISSING subcommand handles missing values on a groupwise basis. Cases with a missing value on a variable are excluded from any calculation that involves that variable. Alternative missing-value treatments are listwise deletion and missing-value inclusion. Negative values on the survival variables are automatically treated as missing. (See Section 48.16.)

Writing Out a File. The WRITE subcommand writes the contents of the life tables, including the labeling information, to a file for use with other programs or with a graphics device that produces high-quality graphics. (See Section 48.17.)

48.2
OPERATION

SURVIVAL requires a TABLES subcommand for naming a survival variable (Section 48.3), an INTERVALS subcommand for setting the period to be examined (Section 48.4), and a STATUS subcommand for identifying the variable that indicates the survival status (Section 48.5). The remaining subcommands are optional and can appear in any order but must be placed after the required subcommands. If you need to calculate the survival variables using information on individual starting dates and the study termination date, use the YRMODA function to take the difference between two dates (see Chapter 7).

48.3
TABLES Subcommand

Use the TABLES subcommand to list the survival variables and control variables that you want to include in the analysis. To request a survival analysis on the variables ONSSURV and RECSURV with no controls, specify:

```
SURVIVAL   TABLES=ONSSURV, RECSURV
           /INTERVALS = THRU 100 BY 10
           /STATUS = OUTCOME (3,4)
```

This form of the TABLES subcommand, combined with appropriate INTER-VALS and STATUS subcommands (Sections 48.4 and 48.5), produces a life table for the variable ONSSURV and a life table for the variable RECSURV. Use the BY keyword to separate the survival variables from the first-order control variables. Use a second BY keyword to separate the first- and second-order control variable lists. Each control variable must be followed by a value range in parentheses. These values must be integers separated by a comma or a blank. Noninteger values in the data are truncated and the case is assigned to a subgroup based on the integer portion of its value on the variable. To specify only one value for a control variable, use the same value for the minimum and maximum, as in TREATMNT(3,3). To request a survival analysis for ONSSURV and RECSURV with TREATMNT as a first-order control and SEX as a second-order control, specify

```
SURVIVAL   TABLES=ONSSURV, RECSURV BY TREATMNT (1,3) BY SEX (1,2)
```

Each combination of TREATMNT and SEX produces a separate life table for each survival variable, for a total of 12 in this example.

48.4
INTERVALS Subcommand

The survival variables are measured in units of time such as days, weeks, months, or years. The INTERVALS subcommand determines the period of time to be examined and how the time will be grouped for the analysis. For a 20-year period measured in months, the subcommand

```
SURVIVAL   TABLES = ONSSURV, RECSURV BY TREATMNT (1,3)
           /INTERVALS = THRU 240 BY 12
           /STATUS = OUTCOME (3,4)
```

analyzes the entire 20-year period and groups the data into 1-year intervals. The first interval is 0–12 months, the second interval 12–24 months and so on.

The first interval always begins at zero. The final interval, in the above example 240+, is created automatically and includes any observations that exceed the specified range. The grouping increment, which follows the BY keyword, is relative to the units in which the survival variable is measured. If in the example above the variable were measured in weeks instead of months, the INTERVALS subcommand would group the data into 12-week intervals and cover a period of 240 weeks.

The period to be examined can be divided into intervals of varying lengths by repeating the THRU and BY keywords, as in

```
SURVIVAL   ONSSURV, RECSURV BY TREATMNT (1,3)
           /INTERVALS = THRU 60 BY 6 THRU 240 BY 12
           /STATUS = OUTCOME (3,4)
```

If the data are recorded in months, this specification groups the first 5 years (60 months) into 6-month intervals and the remaining 15 years into yearly intervals.

The period must be divided in ascending order with no overlap of the values following multiple THRU keywords. If the value following the BY keyword does not divide evenly into the period to which it applies, the endpoint of the period is adjusted upward to the next even multiple of the BY value. For example, the subcommand

```
INTERVALS = THRU 50 BY 6
```

results in a period of 54 with 9 intervals of 6 units each. When the period is divided into intervals of varying lengths by repeating the THRU and BY specifications, the adjustment of one period to produce even intervals changes the starting point of subsequent periods. For example,

```
INTERVALS = THRU 50 BY 6 THRU 100 BY 10 THRU 200 BY 20
```

is automatically readjusted to result in a first period through 54 by 6, a second period through 104 by 10, and a third period through 204 by 20. If the upward adjustment of one period completely overlaps the next period, no adjustment is made and the procedure terminates with an error.

Only one INTERVALS subcommand can be used in a SURVIVAL command. The interval specifications apply to all the survival variables listed on the TABLES subcommand.

48.5
STATUS Subcommand

For each survival variable listed on the TABLES subcommand, you must provide a variable that indicates the survival status of each case. The codes on these status variables distinguish between cases for which the terminal event has occurred and those that either "survived" to the end of the study or were dropped for some reason.

On the STATUS subcommand, specify a status variable with a value range enclosed in parentheses followed by the keyword FOR and the name of one or more of the survival variables. The value range identifies the codes that indicate the terminal event has taken place. For example,

```
SURVIVAL  ONSSURV BY TREATMNT (1,3)
          /INTERVALS = THRU 50 BY 5, THRU 100 BY 10
          /STATUS = OUTCOME (3,4) FOR ONSSURV
```

specifies that a code of 3 or 4 on OUTCOME means the terminal event for the survival variable ONSSURV occurred. If the codes for OUTCOME are (1) alive, (2) dropped from study, (3) dead from unrelated causes, and (4) dead due to illness, all patients who died, regardless of the cause, are considered to have reached the terminal event. To indicate that only those deaths caused by the disease be treated as terminal events, specify

```
/STATUS = OUTCOME (4) FOR ONSSURV
```

All observations that do not have a code in the value range are classified as censored cases. Only one status variable can be listed on a STATUS subcommand. Use separate STATUS subcommands for each of the survival variables or, if appropriate, list more than one survival variable after the FOR keyword. If the FOR keyword is not specified, the status variable specification applies to any of the survival variables not named on another STATUS subcommand.

48.6
Life Table Output

The TABLES, INTERVALS, and STATUS subcommands print one or more life tables depending on the number of survival and control variables specified. The command

```
SURVIVAL  TABLES = ONSSURV BY TREATMNT (1,3)
          /INTERVALS = THRU 50 BY 5 THRU 100 BY 10
          /STATUS = OUTCOME (3,4) FOR ONSSURV
```

produces the life table in Figure 48.6. The 13 columns in the life table contain the following information: the start time of the interval; the number of cases entering the interval; the number withdrawing during the interval (the censored cases); the number exposed to risk (the number entering minus one-half the number withdrawing); the number of terminal events; the proportion of terminal events; the proportion surviving; and the three survival functions and their respective standard errors. Below the table is the median survival time for all cases.

Figure 48.6 Life table

```
LIFE TABLE
      SURVIVAL VARIABLE   ONSSURV   MONTHS FROM ONSET TO DEATH
                     FOR   TREATMNT   PATIENT TREATMENT                       =      1   TREATMENT A

          NUMBER   NUMBER   NUMBER   NUMBER                      CUMUL
          ENTRNG   WDRAWN   EXPOSD    OF             PROPN       PROPN   PROBA-            SE OF    SE OF    SE OF
  INTVL    THIS    DURING     TO     TERMNL   PROPN   SURVI-     SURV    BILITY   HAZARD   CUMUL    PROB-   HAZRD
  START                                      TERMI-                                        SURV-    ABILTY
  TIME    INTVL    INTVL    RISK    EVENTS   NATING   VING    AT END   DENSTY    RATE    IVING     DENS     RATE

   0.0    501.0     0.0    501.0      3.0   0.0060   0.9940   0.9940   0.0012   0.0012   0.003   0.001   0.001
   5.0    498.0     1.0    497.5     16.0   0.0322   0.9678   0.9620   0.0064   0.0065   0.009   0.002   0.002
  10.0    481.0     1.0    480.5     26.0   0.0541   0.9459   0.9100   0.0104   0.0111   0.013   0.002   0.002
  15.0    454.0     0.0    454.0     17.0   0.0374   0.9626   0.8759   0.0068   0.0076   0.015   0.002   0.002
  20.0    437.0     0.0    437.0     23.0   0.0526   0.9474   0.8298   0.0092   0.0108   0.017   0.002   0.002
  25.0    414.0     1.0    413.5     25.0   0.0605   0.9395   0.7796   0.0100   0.0125   0.019   0.002   0.002
  30.0    388.0     1.0    387.5     22.0   0.0568   0.9432   0.7354   0.0089   0.0117   0.020   0.002   0.002
  35.0    365.0     1.0    364.5     24.0   0.0658   0.9342   0.6870   0.0097   0.0136   0.021   0.002   0.003
  40.0    340.0     0.0    340.0     24.0   0.0706   0.9294   0.6385   0.0097   0.0146   0.022   0.002   0.003
  45.0    316.0     1.0    315.5     14.0   0.0444   0.9556   0.6101   0.0057   0.0091   0.022   0.001   0.002
  50.0    301.0     1.0    300.5     34.0   0.1131   0.8869   0.5411   0.0069   0.0120   0.022   0.001   0.002
  60.0    266.0     0.0    266.0     22.0   0.0827   0.9173   0.4963   0.0045   0.0086   0.022   0.001   0.002
  70.0    244.0     2.0    243.0     15.0   0.0617   0.9383   0.4657   0.0031   0.0064   0.022   0.001   0.002
  80.0    227.0     3.0    225.5     24.0   0.1064   0.8936   0.4161   0.0050   0.0112   0.022   0.001   0.002
  90.0    200.0     2.0    199.0     18.0   0.0905   0.9095   0.3785   0.0038   0.0095   0.022   0.001   0.002
 100.0+   180.0   104.0    128.0     76.0   0.5938   0.4063   0.1538     **       **     0.019     **       **

**      THESE CALCULATIONS FOR THE LAST INTERVAL ARE MEANINGLESS.

THE MEDIAN SURVIVAL TIME FOR THESE DATA IS   69.18
```

48.7
Survival Functions

Three survival functions are automatically calculated and included in the life table along with their standard errors. The computation of the survival functions is based on the actuarial method described by Berkson and Gage (1950).

Cumulative Proportion Surviving at End. This is the cumulative survival rate at the end of an interval. It is calculated by multiplying the probabilities of survival up to and including the current interval.

Probability Density. The probability density is the estimated probability per unit time of the terminal event occurring in the interval.

Hazard Rate. The hazard rate is an estimate of the probability per unit time that cases entering the interval will experience the terminal event in the interval.

48.8
PRINT Subcommand

By default, SURVIVAL prints life tables with its output. If you are interested only in the plots and subgroup comparisons available in SURVIVAL, use the PRINT subcommand to suppress the printing of the life tables.

TABLE *Print the life tables.* This is the default.

NOTABLE *Suppress the printing of the life tables.* Only plots and comparisons are printed. The WRITE subcommand, used to write the life tables to a file, can be used when NOTABLES is in effect (see Section 48.17).

48.9
PLOTS Subcommand

In addition to the life tables, SURVIVAL produces plots of the three survival functions. Use the PLOTS subcommand followed by one of the five available keywords to request the plots you want.

ALL *Produce all available function plots.* ALL is the default and is used if PLOTS is specified without any keyword following.

LOGSURV *Produce a plot of the cumulative survival distribution on a logarithmic scale.*

SURVIVAL *Plot the cumulative survival distribution on a linear scale.*

HAZARD *Plot the hazard function.*

DENSITY *Plot the density function.*

You can list multiple keywords in parentheses following the PLOTS subcommand, as in

/**PLOTS** (SURVIVAL, HAZARD)

By default, each function requested is plotted for each survival variable. Individual values of the first-order control variables are represented by their codes in the plots. If second-order controls are used, a separate plot is generated for every value of the second-order control variables. The following specification produces the plot in Figure 48.9 as well as the life table in Figure 48.6:

```
SURVIVAL  TABLES = ONSSURV BY TREATMNT (1,3)
          /INTERVALS = THRU 50 BY 5 THRU 100 BY 10
          /STATUS = OUTCOME (3,4) FOR ONSSURV
          /PLOTS (SURVIVAL)
```

The three treatment groups are represented by the values 1, 2, and 3 in the plot.

Figure 48.9 Plot output for survival function

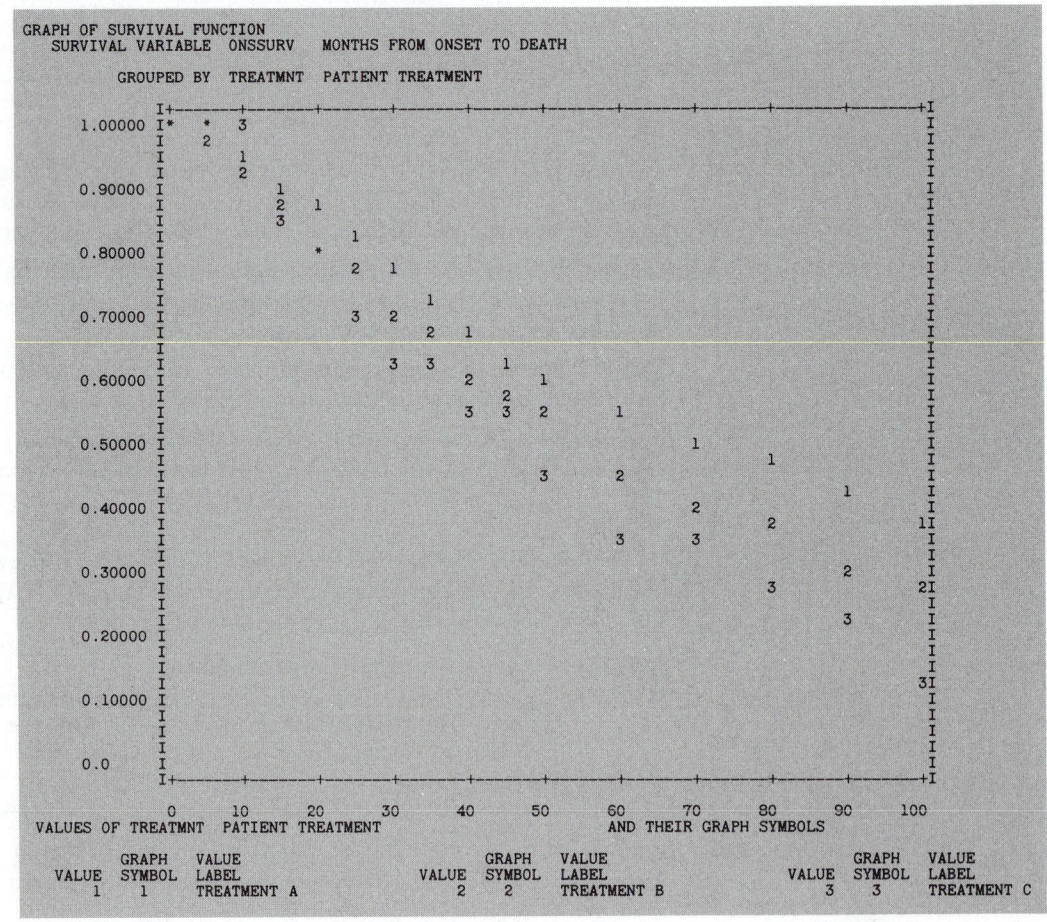

The available plots are defined by the specifications on the TABLES subcommand. To determine the default number of plots produced by SURVIVAL, multiply the number of functions requested by the number of survival variables times the number of first-order controls times the number of distinct values represented in all of the second-order controls. To reduce the number of plots that would be generated by default, use variable lists on the PLOTS subcommand.

The syntax for specifying the survival and control variables is the same as for the TABLES subcommand, except that you do not need to specify value ranges. Only variables that appear on the TABLES subcommand can be listed and their role as survival, first-order, and second-order control variables cannot be altered. You can use the TO keyword to refer to a group of variables and the keyword ALL to refer to an entire set of survival or control variables. Listing some of the variables from a given set (for instance the set of survival variables) automatically eliminates plots for those not listed. For example,

```
SURVIVAL   TABLES = ONSSURV, RECSURV BY TREATMNT (1,3) SEX (1,2)
           /INTERVALS = THRU 50 BY 5, THRU 100 BY 10
           /STATUS = OUTCOME (3,4)
           /PLOTS (ALL) = ONSSURV BY ALL BY ALL
```

eliminates the plots associated with the variable RECSURV.

Since the default for any one of the three possible variable lists is ALL, the above PLOTS subcommand could have been abbreviated to:

```
/PLOTS (ALL) = ONSSURV
```

In addition, since (ALL) after PLOTS is the default,

```
PLOTS = ONSSURV
```

would also result in the same plot.

The variable list on the PLOTS subcommand cannot be used to plot functions both with and without control variables. To accomplish this, create a variable that has the same value for all cases using the COMPUTE command (see Chapter 7). By using this variable as a first- or second-order control (or both), you can produce plots for the entire set of cases.

48.10
COMPARE Subcommand

To compare the survival of subgroups defined by the control variables, use the COMPARE subcommand. COMPARE with no variable list produces a default set of comparisons using the TABLES variable list. At least one survival and one first-order control variable must be specified to make comparisons possible. For example,

```
SURVIVAL   TABLES = ONSSURV BY TREATMNT (1,3)
           /INTERVALS = THRU 50 BY 5, THRU 100 BY 10
           /STATUS = OUTCOME (3,4) FOR ONSSURV
           /COMPARE
```

produces the comparison in Figure 48.10.

Figure 48.10   Subgroup comparisons

```
COMPARISON OF SURVIVAL EXPERIENCE USING THE LEE-DESU STATISTIC
    SURVIVAL VARIABLE  ONSSURV    MONTHS FROM ONSET TO DEATH
           GROUPED BY   TREATMNT  PATIENT TREATMENT

OVERALL COMPARISON    STATISTIC      9.001  D.F.    2   PROB.  0.0111

GROUP  LABEL                   TOTAL N   UNCEN    CEN  PCT CEN  MEAN SCORE

    1  TREATMENT A                 501     383    118    23.55     20.042
    2  TREATMENT B                  97      82     15    15.46    -67.412
    3  TREATMENT C                  26      24      2     7.69   -134.69
```

48.11
CALCULATE
Subcommand

The CALCULATE subcommand calculates comparison of survival for subgroups of cases. Its only specification is a single keyword. Its default keyword is EXACT, for exact comparisons. Optionally, you may obtain pairwise comparisons (see Section 48.12) or approximate comparisons (see Section 48.13). You may also produce only comparisons with no life tables or plots (see Section 48.14).

EXACT	*Calculate exact comparisons*. This is the default.
PAIRWISE	*Perform pairwise comparisons*. (See Section 48.12).
CONDITIONAL	*Calculate approximate comparisons if memory is insufficient.* (See Section 48.13).
APPROXIMATE	*Calculate approximate comparisons only.* (See Section 48.13).
COMPARE	*Produce comparisons only.* Survival tables specified on the TABLES subcommand are not computed and requests for plots are ignored. This allows all available workspace to be used for comparisons. (See Section 48.14). You cannot use the WRITE subcommand (Section 48.17) when this specification is in effect.

48.12
Pairwise Comparisons

You can obtain pairwise comparisons of survival for subgroups of cases using keyword PAIRWISE on the CALCULATE subcommand. Comparisons of each possible pair of values of every first-order control variable are produced along with the overall comparison. Figure 48.12 is the output produced with CALCULATE=PAIRWISE.

```
SURVIVAL   TABLES= ONSSURV BY TREATMNT (1,3)
           /INTERVALS = THRU 50 BY 5, THRU 100 BY 10
           /STATUS = OUTCOME (3,4) FOR ONSSURV
           /COMPARE
           /CALCULATE=PAIRWISE
```

Figure 48.12   Pairwise comparisons

```
COMPARISON OF SURVIVAL EXPERIENCE USING THE LEE-DESU STATISTIC
  SURVIVAL VARIABLE  ONSSURV    MONTHS FROM ONSET TO DEATH
         GROUPED BY  TREATMNT  PATIENT TREATMENT

OVERALL COMPARISON    STATISTIC      9.001  D.F.     2    PROB.   0.0111

GROUP  LABEL                 TOTAL N    UNCEN     CEN   PCT CEN   MEAN SCORE

    1  TREATMENT A              501      383      118    23.55       20.042
    2  TREATMENT B               97       82       15    15.46      -67.412
    3  TREATMENT C               26       24        2     7.69     -134.69

PAIRWISE COMPARISON   STATISTIC      5.042  D.F.     1    PROB.   0.0247

GROUP  LABEL                 TOTAL N    UNCEN     CEN   PCT CEN   MEAN SCORE

    1  TREATMENT A              501      383      118    23.55       13.603
    2  TREATMENT B               97       82       15    15.46      -70.258

PAIRWISE COMPARISON   STATISTIC      4.768  D.F.     1    PROB.   0.0290

GROUP  LABEL                 TOTAL N    UNCEN     CEN   PCT CEN   MEAN SCORE

    1  TREATMENT A              501      383      118    23.55        6.4391
    3  TREATMENT C               26       24        2     7.69     -124.08

PAIRWISE COMPARISON   STATISTIC      0.766  D.F.     1    PROB.   0.3814

GROUP  LABEL                 TOTAL N    UNCEN     CEN   PCT CEN   MEAN SCORE

    2  TREATMENT B               97       82       15    15.46        2.8454
    3  TREATMENT C               26       24        2     7.69      -10.615
```

48.13
Approximate Comparisons

Data can be entered into SURVIVAL on either an individual or an interval-level basis. Whether individual or aggregated data are used affects the outcome of SURVIVAL comparisons. With individual data, you can obtain exact comparisons. For exact comparisons, survival scores are calculated on the basis of the survival experience of each observation. While this method is the most accurate, it requires that all of the data be in memory simultaneously. Thus, exact comparisons may be impractical for large samples. There are also situations in which individual data are not available and data aggregated by interval must be used. See Section 48.15 for a discussion of entering aggregated data.

Keyword APPROXIMATE on the CALCULATE subcommand requests approximate comparisons. Keyword CONDITIONAL produces approximate comparisons only if there is insufficient memory available for exact comparisons. The approximate comparison approach assumes that all events—termination, withdrawal, and so forth—occur at the midpoint of the interval. Under EXACT comparisons, some of these midpoint ties can be resolved. However, if interval widths are not too great, the difference between EXACT and approximate comparisons should be small.

48.14
Obtaining Comparisons Only

To produce only comparisons and no life tables or plots, use keyword COMPARE on the CALCULATE subcommand. The WRITE subcommand, used to write survival tables to a procedure file (see Section 48.17), cannot be used when keyword COMPARE is in effect. If the WRITE subcommand is specified, nothing is written to the output file.

48.15
Entering Aggregated Data

When data are recorded for the entire sample at set points in time instead of on an individual basis, it is necessary to enter aggregated data into SURVIVAL. When aggregated data are used, two records are entered for each interval, one for censored cases and one for uncensored cases. The number of cases included on each record is used as the weight factor (see Chapter 11 for a discussion of the WEIGHT command). If control variables are used, there must be a pair of records (one for censored and one for uncensored cases) for each value of the control variable in each interval. These records must contain the value of the control variable and the number of cases that belong in the particular category as well as values for survival time and status. For example, the commands

```
DATA LIST   / SURVEVAR 1-2 STATVAR 4 SEX 6 COUNT 8
VALUE LABELS   STATVAR 1 'DECEASED' 2 'ALIVE'
               /SEX 1 'FEMALE' 2 'MALE'
WEIGHT   COUNT
SURVIVAL   TABLES = SURVEVAR BY SEX (1,2)
           /INTERVALS = THRU 10 BY 1
           /STATUS = STATVAR (1)
BEGIN DATA
 1 1 1 0
 1 1 1 1
 1 2 2 2
 1 1 2 1
 2 2 1 1
 2 1 1 2
 2 2 2 1
 2 1 2 3
   ...
END DATA
```

read in aggregated data and perform a SURVIVAL analysis when a control variable with two values is used. The first data record has a code of 1 on the status variable, STATVAR, indicating it is an uncensored case and a code of 1 on SEX, the control variable. The number of cases for this subset is 0, the value of the variable COUNT. COUNT is not used in SURVIVAL but is the weight variable. In this example, each interval requires four records to provide all the data for each SURVEVAR interval.

48.16
MISSING Subcommand

The MISSING subcommand controls missing value treatments. The default keyword on MISSING is GROUPWISE, which excludes cases with missing values on a variable from any calculation involving that variable. The MISSING subcommand can also exclude cases listwise. With either groupwise or listwise treatment of system-missing values, you can include user-missing values in the analysis.

With any missing value treatment, negative values on the survival variables are automatically treated as missing data. In addition, cases outside the value range on a control variable are excluded.

GROUPWISE *Exclude missing values groupwise.* Cases with missing values on a variable are excluded from any calculation involving that variable. This is the default.

LISTWISE *Exclude missing values listwise.* Cases missing on any variables named are excluded from the analysis.

INCLUDE *Include missing values.* User-defined missing values are included in the analysis.

48.17
WRITE Subcommand

The optional WRITE subcommand writes data in the survival tables to a procedure file. This file can be used for further analyses or to produce graphics displays. The only specification on the WRITE subcommand is a single keyword. The default keyword when you omit the WRITE subcommand is NONE, which does not produce a procedure file. The WRITE subcommand by itself with no keyword, or the WRITE subcommand with keyword TABLES, writes table data to the procedure file. Keyword BOTH on the WRITE subcommand writes both table data and label records to the file.

NONE *Do not produce a procedure file.* This is the default when you omit the WRITE subcommand.

TABLES *Write out survival table data records.* All survival table statistics are written to a file. This is the default when you specify the WRITE subcommand with no further specification.

BOTH *Write out survival table data and label records.* Variable names, variable labels, and value labels are written out along with the survival table statistics.

When you specify the WRITE subcommand with SURVIVAL, you must use a PROCEDURE OUTPUT command before the SURVIVAL command to specify the procedure file. The OUTFILE subcommand on PROCEDURE OUTPUT names the file, as in

```
PROCEDURE OUTPUT OUTFILE=SURVTBL
SURVIVAL        TABLES=ONSSURV,RECSURV BY TREATMNT(1,3)
                /STATUS = RECURSIT(1,9) FOR RECSURV
                /STATUS = STATUS(3,4) FOR ONSSURV
                /INTERVAL=THRU 50 BY 5 THRU 100 BY 10/PLOTS/COMPARE
                /CALCULATE=CONDITIONAL PAIRWISE
                /WRITE=TABLES
```

which writes the survival table data to a file named SURVTBL.

**ANNOTATED
EXAMPLE FOR
SURVIVAL**

The data in this example are from a study of 647 cancer patients. The variables are

- TREATMNT—the type of treatment received.
- ONSETMO, ONSETYR—month and year cancer was discovered.
- RECURSIT—indicates whether a recurrence took place.
- RECURMO, RECURYR—month and year of recurrence.
- OUTCOME—status of patient at end of study, alive or dead.
- DEATHMO, DEATHYR—month and year of death, or, for those who survived, the date the study ended.

Using these date variables and the YRMODA function, the number of months from onset to recurrence and from onset to death or survival are calculated. These new variables become the survival variables with TREATMNT as the single control variable. The SPSS-X commands are

```
SET WIDTH=132
DATA LIST   FILE = SURVDATA/ 1 TREATMNT 15 ONSETMO 19-20
            ONSETYR 21-22 RECURSIT 48 RECURMO 49-50 RECURYR 51-52
            OUTCOME 56 DEATHMO 57-58 DEATHYR 59-60
COMMENT    TRANSFORM ALL DATES TO RUNNING CALENDAR DAYS
COMPUTE    ONSDATE=YRMODA(ONSETYR,ONSETMO,15)
COMPUTE    RECDATE=YRMODA(RECURYR,RECURMO,15)
COMPUTE    DEATHDT=YRMODA(DEATHYR,DEATHMO,15)

COMMENT    NOW COMPUTE SURVIVAL VARIABLES
COMPUTE    ONSSURV = (DEATHDT-ONSDATE)/30
IF    RECURSIT EQ 0 RECSURV = ONSSURV
IF    RECURSIT NE 0 RECSURV = (RECDATE-ONSDATE)/30

VARIABLE LABELS   TREATMNT 'PATIENT TREATMENT'
                  ONSSURV 'MONTHS FROM ONSET TO DEATH'
                  RECSURV 'MONTHS FROM ONSET TO RECURRENCE'
VALUE LABELS   TREATMNT 1 'TREATMENT A' 2 'TREATMENT B'
               3 'TREATMENT C'
SURVIVAL   TABLES = ONSSURV,RECSURV BY TREATMNT(1,3)
           /STATUS = RECURSIT(1,9) FOR RECSURV
           /STATUS = OUTCOME(3,4) FOR ONSSURV
           /INTERVALS = THRU 50 BY 5 THRU 100 BY 10
           /PLOTS/ COMPARE/ CALCULATE=CONDITIONAL PAIRWISE
```

- The SET command sets the page width to 132 (see Chapter 4).
- The onset, recurrence, and death dates are transformed to running days using the YRMODA function in the COMPUTE command (see Chapter 7). The constant 15 is used as the day argument for YRMODA since only month and year were recorded, not the actual day.
- ONSSURV, the first survival variable, is calculated by taking the difference between the date of death (or survival) and the date the cancer was discovered (ONSDATE). The difference is divided by 30 to convert it from days to months.
- RECSURV, the second survival variable, is calculated conditionally using the IF command (see Chapter 9). For cases with RECURSIT values of 0, indicating no recurrence took place, RECSURV is set equal to ONSSURV.
- The TABLES subcommand in SURVIVAL specifies two survival variables, ONSSURV and RECSURV, and one control variable, TREATMNT (see Section 48.3). The life table for ONSSURV is shown in Figure 48.6.
- The status variable for RECSURV is RECURSIT with codes 1–9, indicating that the termination event, recurrence, took place. OUTCOME is the status variable for ONSSURV with codes 3 and 4 signaling the terminal event, death (see Section 48.5).
- The INTERVALS subcommand groups the first 50 months into 5-month intervals and the remaining 50 months into 10-month intervals (see Section 48.4).
- The default plots are requested using PLOTS (see Section 48.9). Figure 48.9 contains the plot of the survival function for ONSSURV.
- COMPARE with no specifications requests all comparisons (see Section 48.10). The subgroup comparisons for ONSSURV are shown in Figure 48.10.
- Keyword CONDITIONAL on the CALCULATE subcommand requests approximate comparisons if memory is insufficient for exact comparisons (see Section 48.13). Keyword PAIRWISE (see Section 48.12) requests the pairwise output (see Figure 48.12).

48.18
Format
The WRITE subcommand writes five types of records to a procedure file. Keyword TABLES writes record types 30, 31, and 40. Keyword BOTH writes record types 10, 20, 30, 31, and 40. Record type 10, produced only by keyword BOTH, is formatted as follows:

Columns	Content	Format
1–2	Record type (10)	F2.0
3–7	Table number	F5.0
8–15	Name of survival variable	A8
15–55	Variable label of survival variable	A40
56	Number of BY's (0, 1, or 2)	F1.0
57–60	Number of rows in current survival table	F4.0

The number (0, 1, or 2) in column 56 specifies the number of orders of control variables (none, first-order, or first- and second-order controls) that have been applied to the life table. Columns 57–60 specify the number of rows in the life table. This number is the number of intervals in the analysis that show subjects entering; intervals in which no subjects enter are not noted in the life tables. One type 10 record is produced for each life table.

Record type 20, also produced by keyword BOTH, is formatted as follows:

Columns	Content	Format
1–2	Record type (20)	F2.0
3–7	Table number	F5.0
8–15	Name of control variable	A8
16–55	Variable label of control variable	A40
56–60	Value of control variable	F5.0
61–80	Value label for this value	A20

One type 20 record is produced for each control variable on each life table. If only first-order controls have been placed on the survival analysis, one type 20 record will be produced for each table; if second-order controls have also been applied, two type 20 records will be produced per table.

Record type 30, and its continuation 31, produced by both keywords TABLES and BOTH, are formatted as follows:

Columns	Content	Format
1–2	Record type (30)	F2.0
3–7	Table number	F5.0
8–13	Beginning of interval	F6.2
14–21	Number entering interval	F8.2
22–29	Number withdrawn in interval	F8.2
30–37	Number exposed to risk	F8.2
38–45	Number of terminal events	F8.2

Columns	Content	Format
1–2	Record type (31)	F2.0
3–7	Table number	F5.0
8–15	Proportion terminating	F8.6
16–33	Proportion surviving	F8.6
24–31	Cumulative proportion surviving	F8.6
32–38	Probability density	F8.6
40–47	Hazard rate	F8.6
48–54	S.E. of cumulative proportion surviving	F7.4
55–61	S.E. of probability density	F7.4
62–68	S.E. of hazard rate	F7.4

Each pair of type 30 and 31 records contains the information from one line of the life table. As many type 30 and 31 record pairs are output for a table as it has lines (this number is noted in columns 57–60 of the type 10 record for the table).

Record type 40, produced by both keywords TABLES and BOTH, is formatted as follows:

Columns	Content	Format
1–2	Record type (40)	F2.0

Type 40 records indicate the completion of the series of records for one life table.

48.19
Record Order

The SURVIVAL output file contains records for each of the life tables specified on the TABLES subcommand. All records for a given table are produced together in sequence.

The records for the life tables are produced in the same order as the tables themselves. All life tables for the first survival variable are written first. The values of the first- and second-order control variables rotate, with the values of the first-order controls changing most rapidly.

48.20
LIMITATIONS

The following limitations apply to procedure SURVIVAL:

- A maximum of 20 survival variables.
- A maximum of 100 control variables on the first- and second-order control variable lists combined.
- A maximum of 20 THRU . . . BY . . . specifications on the INTERVALS subcommand.
- A maximum of 35 values can appear on a plot.

Syntax

T-TEST

Independent samples:

```
T-TEST GROUPS=varname ({1,2**      }) /VARIABLES=varlist
                       {value      }
                       {value,value}
   [/MISSING={ANALYSIS**}  [INCLUDE]]
            {LISTWISE }
   [/FORMAT={LABELS**}]
           {NOLABELS}
```

Paired samples:

```
T-TEST PAIRS=varlist [WITH varlist [(PAIRED)]] [/varlist ...]
   [/MISSING={ANALYSIS**}  [INCLUDE]]
            {LISTWISE }
   [/FORMAT={LABELS**}]
           {NOLABELS}
```

**Default if the subcommand is omitted.

Contents

49.1   OVERVIEW

49.2   OPERATION
49.3   Independent Samples
49.4   Independent and Paired Designs
49.5   One-Tailed Significance Levels
49.6   GROUPS Subcommand
49.7   VARIABLES Subcommand
49.8   PAIRS Subcommand
49.9   MISSING Subcommand
49.10 FORMAT Subcommand

49.11 LIMITATIONS

49

Chapter 49   T-TEST

T-TEST compares sample means by calculating Student's t and tests the significance of the difference between the means. It tests either independent samples (different groups of cases) or paired samples (different variables). Other procedures that compare group means are ANOVA (Chapter 20), ONEWAY (Chapter 39), and MANOVA (Chapter 33).

49.1 OVERVIEW

T-TEST produces Student's t, degrees of freedom, and two-tailed probability for a comparison of two means. In addition, the mean, standard deviation, and standard error are displayed for each variable.

Independent-Samples Test. The GROUPS and VARIABLES subcommands divide the cases into two groups for a comparison of sample means. Both pooled- and separate-variance estimates are calculated, along with the F value used to test homogeneity of variances and its significance level. (See Section 49.3.)

Paired-Samples Test. The PAIRS subcommand compares means for variables and also reports the difference between means and the correlation coefficient. (See Section 49.8.)

Two-Tailed Significance Levels. T-TEST calculates the probability of the t value based on a two-tailed test of significance.

Missing Values. By default, T-TEST excludes cases with missing values on an analysis-by-analysis basis. The MISSING subcommand handles user-missing values as if they were valid or deletes cases with missing values listwise. (See Section 49.9.)

Formatting Options. The FORMAT subcommand suppresses the printing of variable labels. You can use the SET WIDTH command to restrict the output to an 80-character width. (See Section 49.10.)

Statistics. There are no optional statistics for T-TEST. All statistics available are printed by default.

49.2 OPERATION

The T-TEST command operates by means of subcommands and associated keywords, and you can use the subcommands in any order. (See Sections 49.6 through 49.8.) You can request tests of independent samples and one or more paired samples.

49.3 Independent Samples

An independent-samples test divides the cases into two groups and compares the group means on a single variable. This test requires the GROUPS and VARIABLES subcommands, which must be separated by a slash. You can specify only one independent-samples test per T-TEST command.

49.4
Independent and Paired Designs

You can request both independent- and paired-samples tests on a single T-TEST command. To do so, specify the GROUPS, VARIABLES, and PAIRS subcommands.

```
T-TEST   GROUPS= WORLD(1,3)/VARIABLES=NTCPRI NTCSAL NTCPUR/
         PAIRS=WCLOTHES MCLOTHES
```

49.5
One-Tailed Significance Levels

By default, the probability is based on the two-tailed test. This is appropriate when significant differences in either direction are of interest. When theoretical considerations predict that the difference will be in a given direction (such as the Group 1 mean will be higher than the Group 2 mean), a one-tailed test is appropriate. To calculate the one-tailed probability, divide the two-tailed probability by 2.

49.6
GROUPS Subcommand

The GROUPS subcommand names the variable and the criterion for dividing the cases into two groups. You can name only one variable, which can be either numeric or string. You cannot use long string variables to define the categories. You can use any one of three different methods to define the two groups.

In the first method, a single value in parentheses groups all cases with a code equal to or greater than the value into one group, and the remaining cases into the other group. For example, the command

```
T-TEST GROUPS=WORLD(2)/VARIABLES=NTCPUR
```

groups together all cases with the value of WORLD greater than or equal to 2. The remaining cases go into the other group. See Figure 49.6 for the output from this command.

Figure 49.6   Independent-samples T-TEST

					POOLED VARIANCE ESTIMATE			SEPARATE VARIANCE ESTIMATE		
VARIABLE	NUMBER OF CASES	MEAN	STANDARD DEVIATION	STANDARD ERROR	F VALUE	2-TAIL PROB.	T VALUE	DEGREES OF FREEDOM	2-TAIL PROB.	T VALUE	DEGREES OF FREEDOM	2-TAIL PROB.

GROUP 1 – WORLD   GE   2.
GROUP 2 – WORLD   LT   2.

NTCPUR   NET PURCHASING LEVEL
GROUP 1   19   34.9474   17.831   4.091
                                              1.45   0.420   -6.87   42   0.000   -7.05   41.63   0.000
GROUP 2   25   76.7600   21.491   4.298

Alternatively, if you specify two values in parentheses, one group includes cases with the first value on the grouping variable, and the other includes cases with the second value, as in

```
T-TEST  GROUPS=WORLD(1,3)/VARIABLES=NTCPUR
```

In this example, cases with values other than 1 or 3 for variable WORLD are not used.

If the grouping variable has only two values, coded 1 and 2, respectively, you do not have to specify a value list. For example, the command

```
T-TEST  GROUPS=SEX/VARIABLES=GRADES
```

groups all cases having the value 1 for SEX into one group and cases having the value 2 for SEX into the other group. All other cases are not used.

49.7
VARIABLES Subcommand

The VARIABLES subcommand names the variables being analyzed. You can use only numeric variables. The specifications for the variable list follow the usual SPSS-X conventions (see Chapter 2). For example,

```
T-TEST  GROUPS=WORLD(1,3)/VARIABLES=NTCPRI NTCSAL NTCPUR
```

compares the means of the two groups defined by WORLD for the variables NTCPRI, NTCSAL, and NTCPUR, while

T-TEST GROUPS=WORLD(1,3)/VARIABLES=NTCPRI TO MCLOTHES

compares the means of the groups defined by WORLD for all variables between and including NTCPRI and MCLOTHES.

49.8
PAIRS Subcommand

A paired-samples test compares two variables with each other. A typical application of a paired-samples test is the comparison of pre- and post-course test scores for students in a class. To obtain a paired-samples *t* test, use the PAIRS subcommand.

The PAIRS subcommand names the variables being compared. You can use only numeric variables. The following command produces a comparison of two variables:

T-TEST PAIRS=WCLOTHES MCLOTHES

Figure 49.8 shows the output produced by the PAIRS subcommand.

Figure 49.8   Paired-samples T-TEST

VARIABLE	NUMBER OF CASES	MEAN	STANDARD DEVIATION	STANDARD ERROR	* *	(DIFFERENCE) MEAN	STANDARD DEVIATION	STANDARD ERROR	* *	2-TAIL CORR. PROB.	* *	T VALUE	DEGREES OF FREEDOM	2-TAIL PROB.
WCLOTHES	MEDIUM-PRICED WOMEN'S CLOTHES	80.7111	30.195	4.501	*				*		*			
	45				*	-6.3333	17.916	2.671	* 0.807	0.000	*	-2.37	44	0.022
MCLOTHES	MEDIUM-PRICED MEN'S CLOTHES	87.0444	26.192	3.905	*				*		*			

If you specify a list of variables, each variable is compared with every other variable. For example, the command

T-TEST **PAIRS=TEACHER CONSTRUC MANAGER**

compares TEACHER with CONSTRUC, TEACHER with MANAGER, and CONSTRUC with MANAGER.

You can use the keyword WITH to request a test comparing every variable to the left of the keyword with every variable to the right of the keyword. For example,

T-TEST PAIRS=TEACHER MANAGER **WITH** CONSTRUC ENGINEER

compares TEACHER with CONSTRUC, TEACHER with ENGINEER, MANAGER with CONSTRUC, and MANAGER with ENGINEER. TEACHER is not compared with MANAGER, and CONSTRUC is not compared with ENGINEER.

You can use the slash to separate analysis lists, as in

T-TEST PAIRS=WCLOTHES MCLOTHES/NTCPRI WITH NTCPUR NTCSAL

which specifies two analysis lists.

(PAIRED) Keyword. Use the keyword (PAIRED) for testing paired samples. If you specify the keyword (PAIRED) in addition to the keyword WITH on the PAIRS subcommand, as in

T-TEST PAIRS=TEACHER MANAGER **WITH** CONSTRUC ENGINEER **(PAIRED)**

TEACHER is paired with CONSTRUC and MANAGER is paired with ENGINEER. You must name or imply the same number of variables on each side of the keyword WITH. If the number of variables is not equal, SPSS-X will generate as many T-TESTS as it can and will issue the following warning:

```
>WARNING 11810  LINE   5, (END OF COMMAND)
>The left and right lists are different lengths.  Some variables will be
>omitted.
```

ANNOTATED EXAMPLE FOR T-TEST

The example illustrating T-TEST analyzes 1979 prices and earnings in 45 cities around the world, compiled by the Union Bank of Switzerland. The variables are

- WORLD—the economic class of the country in which the city is located. The 45 cities are divided into three groups: cities in economically developed nations such as the United States and most European nations; cities in nations that are members of the Organization for Petroleum Exporting Countries (OPEC); and cities in underdeveloped countries. These groups are coded from 1 to 3 and are labeled 1ST WORLD, PETRO WORLD, and 3RD WORLD, respectively.

- NTCPRI—the city's net price level, based on more than 100 goods and services weighted by consumer habits. NTCPRI is expressed as the percentage above or below that of Zurich, where Zurich equals 100%.

- NTCSAL—the city's net salary level, calculated from average net hourly earnings in 12 occupations. NTCSAL is expressed as a percentage above or below that of Zurich, where Zurich equals 100%.

- NTCPUR—the city's net purchasing power level, calculated as the ratio of labor expended (measured in number of working hours) to the cost of more than 100 goods and services, weighted by consumer habits. NTCPUR is expressed as a percentage above or below that of Zurich, where Zurich equals 100%.

- WCLOTHES—the cost of medium-priced women's clothes, expressed as the percentage above or below that of Zurich, where Zurich equals 100%.

- MCLOTHES—the cost of medium-priced men's clothes, expressed as the percentage above or below that of Zurich, where Zurich equals 100%.

In this example we compare mean price, salary and purchasing power for cities grouped by economic class. We also compare the mean costs of women's and men's clothes. The SPSS-X commands are:

```
GET FILE=CITY/KEEP=NTCPRI, NTCSAL, NTCPUR, WCLOTHES, MCLOTHES, WORLD
VAR LABELS  WCLOTHES, MEDIUM-PRICED WOMEN'S CLOTHES/
            MCLOTHES, MEDIUM-PRICED MEN'S CLOTHES/
T-TEST  GROUPS=WORLD (1,3)/VARIABLES=NTCPRI NTCSAL NTCPUR/
    PAIRS=WCLOTHES MCLOTHES/NTCPRI WITH NTCPUR NTCSAL
FINISH
```

- The GET command defines the data to SPSS-X and selects the variables needed for analysis (see Chapter 6).

- The VAR LABELS commands assign new labels to the variables WCLOTHES and MCLOTHES (see Chapter 5).

- The T-TEST command requests an independent-samples test and a paired-samples test. For the independent-samples test, the variable WORLD specifies a grouping criterion that compares cities in first-world countries to cities in third-world countries. Cities in petro-world countries are not included.

Output from T-TEST command

```
- - - - - - - - - - - - - - - - - - - - - - - - - T - T E S T - - - - - - - - - - - - - - - - - - - - - - - - - - - - - -

GROUP 1 - WORLD     EQ      1.
GROUP 2 - WORLD     EQ      3.
```

VARIABLE	NUMBER OF CASES	MEAN	STANDARD DEVIATION	STANDARD ERROR	*	F VALUE	2-TAIL PROB.	*	POOLED VARIANCE ESTIMATE			*	SEPARATE VARIANCE ESTIMATE		
								*	T VALUE	DEGREES OF FREEDOM	2-TAIL PROB.	*	T VALUE	DEGREES OF FREEDOM	2-TAIL PROB.
NTCPRI NET PRICE LEVEL					*			*				*			
GROUP 1	25	83.8400	13.309	2.662	*	1.23	0.637	*	3.50	36	0.001	*	3.38	22.28	0.003
GROUP 2	13	67.3077	14.773	4.097	*			*				*			
NTCSAL NET SALARY LEVEL					*			*				*			
GROUP 1	25	64.4000	19.026	3.805	*	2.06	0.210	*	6.33	35	0.000	*	7.18	30.07	0.000
GROUP 2	12	25.6667	13.241	3.822	*			*				*			
NTCPUR NET PURCHASING LEVEL					*			*				*			
GROUP 1	25	76.7600	21.491	4.298	*	1.50	0.493	*	6.28	35	0.000	*	6.74	26.26	0.000
GROUP 2	12	31.9167	17.573	5.073	*			*				*			

```
- - - - - - - - - - - - - - - - - - - - - - - - - T - T E S T - - - - - - - - - - - - - - - - - - - - - - - - - - - - - -
```

VARIABLE	NUMBER OF CASES	MEAN	STANDARD DEVIATION	STANDARD ERROR	*	(DIFFERENCE) MEAN	STANDARD DEVIATION	STANDARD ERROR	*	2-TAIL CORR. PROB.	*	T VALUE	DEGREES OF FREEDOM	2-TAIL PROB.
WCLOTHES MEDIUM-PRICED WOMEN'S CLOTHES		80.7111	30.195	4.501	*				*		*			
	45				*	-6.3333	17.916	2.671	*	0.807 0.000	*	-2.37	44	0.022
MCLOTHES MEDIUM-PRICED MEN'S CLOTHES		87.0444	26.192	3.905	*				*		*			
NTCPRI NET PRICE LEVEL		82.1591	19.773	2.981	*				*		*			
	44				*	23.4545	33.310	5.022	*	0.098 0.528	*	4.67	43	0.000
NTCPUR NET PURCHASING LEVEL		58.7045	28.806	4.343	*				*		*			
NTCPRI NET PRICE LEVEL		82.1591	19.773	2.981	*				*		*			
	44				*	31.8182	22.753	3.430	*	0.482 0.001	*	9.28	43	0.000
NTCSAL NET SALARY LEVEL		50.3409	24.295	3.663	*				*		*			

49.9
MISSING Subcommand

By default, T-TEST deletes cases with missing values on an analysis-by-analysis basis. For independent-samples tests, cases missing on either the grouping variable or the analysis variable are excluded from the analysis of that variable. For paired-samples tests, a case missing on either of the variables in a given pair is excluded from the analysis of that pair. The following keyword options are available using the MISSING subcommand:

ANALYSIS   *Delete cases with missing values on an analysis-by-analysis basis.* This is the default if you omit the MISSING subcommand.

LISTWISE   *Exclude missing values listwise.* A case missing for any variable specified on either the GROUPS or the VARIABLES subcommand is excluded from any independent sample analysis. A case missing for any variable specified on the PAIRS subcommand is excluded from any paired sample analysis.

INCLUDE   *Include user-defined missing values.* User-missing values are included in the analysis.

The ANALYSIS and LISTWISE keywords are mutually exclusive; however, each can be specified with INCLUDE. For example, to include user-missing values in an analysis that excludes system missing values listwise, specify

```
T-TEST  PAIRS=WCLOTHES MCLOTHES/
   MISSING=INCLUDE LISTWISE
```

49.10
FORMAT Subcommand

Figures 49.6 and 49.8 illustrate that, by default, T-TEST prints variable labels. You can suppress variable labels by specifying NOLABELS on the FORMAT subcommand:

LABELS   *Print variable labels.* This is the default if you omit the FORMAT subcommand.

NOLABELS   *Suppress variable labels.*

You can further modify the T-TEST output by using the SET WIDTH command (Chapter 4) to restrict output to a width of 80 characters. For example, the commands

```
GET FILE=CITY
SET WIDTH 80
T-TEST    PAIRS=WCLOTHES MCLOTHES/
   FORMAT=NOLABELS
```

produce the output in Figure 49.10. This is the same analysis shown in Figure 49.8, but with variable labels suppressed and the output width limited to 80 characters.

Figure 49.10   T-TEST output with modified format

```
- - - - - - - - - - - - - - - - T - T E S T- - - - - - - - - - - - - - - - -

VARIABLE    NUMBER                  STANDARD    STANDARD
            OF CASES      MEAN      DEVIATION   ERROR

WCLOTHES
              45        80.7111      30.195      4.501
              45        87.0444      26.192      3.905
MCLOTHES


(DIFFERENCE) STANDARD   STANDARD   *      2-TAIL *   T     DEGREES OF  2-TAIL
    MEAN    DEVIATION    ERROR     * CORR. PROB. * VALUE    FREEDOM    PROB.

   -6.3333   17.916      2.671     * 0.807 0.000 * -2.37      44       0.022
```

49.11
LIMITATIONS

The following limitation applies to procedure T-TEST:

A maximum of 1 GROUPS and 1 VARIABLES subcommand per T-TEST command. Otherwise, T-TEST is constrained only by the amount of work space available on your computer.

Appendixes

Syntax

Macro Facility

```
DEFINE macro name ( [{argument name=}      [!NOEXPAND]
                      {!POSITIONAL= }
    [!DEFAULT (default string)]   {!TOKENS (n)                        }
                                  {!CHAREND ('char')                  }
                                  {!ENCLOSE ('startsym', 'endsym')    }
                                  {!CMDEND                            }
    [/{argument name=} ...] ] )
      {!POSITIONAL= }
macro body
!ENDDEFINE
```

SET command controls:

```
PRESERVE
RESTORE
```

Assignment:

```
!LET
```

Conditional processing:

```
!IF (expression) !THEN statements
    [!ELSE statements]
!IFEND
```

Looping constructs:

```
!DO !varname=start !TO finish [BY step]
    statements   [!BREAK]
!DOEND

!DO !varname !IN (list)
    statements   [!BREAK]
!DOEND
```

Macro directives:

```
!OFFEXPAND
!ONEXPAND
```

String manipulation functions:

```
!LENGTH (string)
!CONCAT (string1,string2)
!SUBSTRING (string,from,[length])
!INDEX (string1,string2)
!HEAD (string)
!TAIL (string)
!QUOTE (string)
!UNQUOTE (string)
!UPCASE (string)
!BLANKS (n)
!NULL
!EVAL (string)
```

Contents

A.1 OPERATION

A.2 The Macro Definition

A.3 The Macro Call

A.4 Examples: Macros without Arguments

A.5 Macros with Arguments

A.6 Assigning Tokens to Arguments

A.7 Positional Arguments

A.8 Keyword Arguments

A.9 Defining Defaults

A.10 Controlling Expansion

A.11 Example: Macros with Arguments

A.12 Macro Utilities

A.13 Macro Directives

A.14 String Manipulation Functions

A.15 SET Subcommands for Use with Macro

A.16 Restoring SET Specifications

A.17 Conditional Processing

A.18 Looping Constructs

A.19 Direct Assignment of Macro Variables

A.20 LIMITATIONS

Appendix A The SPSS-X Macro Facility

The macro facility allows you to build your own blocks of SPSS-X syntax elements and to control the execution of those blocks. In effect, it allows you to create your own SPSS-X commands out of existing ones.

A macro can be useful in several different contexts. For example, a macro can be used to

- Issue a series of the same or similar commands repeatedly, using looping constructs rather than redundant specifications.
- Group sets of variables.
- Produce output from several SPSS-X procedures with a single command.
- Create complex input programs, procedure specifications, or whole jobs that can then be executed with simple specifications.

There are two stages to using a macro: the macro definition and the macro call. In the *macro definition* you specify any part of a valid SPSS-X command and give it a name. In the *macro call* you include the name of the macro as part of an SPSS-X job. SPSS-X expands the macro when it encounters the macro name.

For example, you could define a simple macro such as the following

```
DEFINE sesvars ()
    age sex educ religion
!ENDDEFINE
```

and later in the job use the macro name to refer to the variable list, as in

```
FREQUENCIES VARIABLES=sesvars
```

You can also write macros that require *arguments* when called. For example, you might want to develop a customized version of the FREQUENCIES command. The following specification creates a procedure MYFREQ that uses the FREQUENCIES command with the optional specifications for suppressing the table, producing a histogram, and printing a selection of statistics.

```
DEFINE myfreq (vars = !CHAREND(/))
    frequencies variables = !vars
  /format = notable
  /hbar = normal
  /statistics = default skewness kurtosis
!ENDDEFINE
```

Then, when you call MYFREQ in your job, all you need to do is supply the variables after the VARS argument to run your version of FREQUENCIES:

```
MYFREQ VARS = AGE SEX EDUC RELIGION
```

In this command, the four variables are the *argument* to the macro MYFREQ. When SPSS-X expands the MYFREQ macro, it substitutes the argument, AGE, SEX, EDUC, and RELIGION, for !vars, and executes the resulting commands.

A.1 OPERATION

To use the macro facility, you must specify both the macro definition and the macro call. Section A.2 explains how to set up a macro definition. Section A.3 shows how to call the defined macro.

A.2
The Macro Definition

The general syntax of the macro definition is as follows:

```
DEFINE macro name ([macro arguments])
   macro body
!ENDDEFINE
```

Note: in the examples of macro definition throughout this appendix, the macro name, body, and arguments are shown in lower case for readability. However, macro keywords, which are always preceded by an exclamation point, are shown in upper case.

All macros must start with the SPSS-X DEFINE command and end with the macro !ENDDEFINE command. These commands identify the beginning and end of a macro definition and are used to separate the macro definition from the rest of the command stream.

Immediately after the DEFINE statement, specify the macro name. All macros must have a name. This name will be used to refer to the macro in the macro call. Macro names follow the usual SPSS-X naming conventions (see Chapter 2). In addition, macro names can begin with an exclamation point (!). Since macro names are the only SPSS-X names that may start with an !, you can make sure that the names do not conflict with the other text or variables if you start them with an !.

Immediately after the macro name, specify a set of parentheses that optionally enclose argument definitions. This specification indicates the arguments that will be read when the macro is called. If you do not want include arguments, specify just the parentheses.

Next specify the body of the macro. The macro body can include SPSS-X commands, parts of SPSS-X commands, or macro statements (macro directives, string manipulation statements, or conditional processing statements).

At the end of the macro body, specify the !ENDDEFINE command.

A.3
The Macro Call

The second step in using the macro facility is to invoke the macro with a macro call. The general syntax of the macro call is as follows:

```
macro name  [macro arguments]
```

To call a macro, you specify the macro name and any necessary arguments. If there are no arguments, only the macro name is required.

The macro call initiates macro expansion. When a command is expanded, the commands (or parts of commands) that it contains are executed as part of the SPSS-X command stream. Thus, it is the user's responsibility to ensure that what results after expansion—whether the macro is part of a command, a single command, or a series of commands—is valid SPSS-X syntax.

A.4
Examples: Macros without Arguments

The following two examples demonstrate how a simple macro is defined and called. The first example uses a macro to specify a group of variables. Suppose you want to analyze the same set of variables using a number of procedures. For example, you want to calculate mean income by age, sex, education level, and region of the country, as well as frequency counts for these variables for a group of subjects. The SPSS-X commands are:

```
MEANS  INCOME BY AGE SEX EDUC REGION
FREQUENCIES VARIABLES = AGE SEX EDUC REGION
```

Instead of naming these variables explicitly each time, you could define a macro that contains the variable names and then just specify the macro name to refer to that group of variables. The first step is to define the macro:

```
DEFINE sesvars ()
   age sex educ region
!ENDDEFINE
```

The macro name is SESVARS, and it names variables AGE, SEX, EDUCATION and REGION. The empty set of parentheses indicates the macro has no

A

arguments. To call this macro, you simply specify its name:

```
MEANS INCOME BY SESVARS
FREQUENCIES VARIABLES = SESVARS
```

Every time SESVARS is encountered, it is expanded and replaced with the variable sequence AGE, SEX, EDUC, and REGION. The command sequence after expansion is identical to the sequence above in which the variables are named explicitly.

The next example demonstrates how you can use a macro to repeat a sequence of commands. For example, suppose you test two groups, a normal group and a learning-disabled group, on speed and accuracy of word recognition. Before you use MANOVA to test group differences, you want to be sure that the data meet the assumptions of normality, skewness, and linearity, and have no outliers.

One method is to check the assumption of normality from a histogram, skewness with the skewness statistic available with FREQUENCIES, the assumption of linearity with a scatterplot, and whether or not there are univariate outliers by looking at Z-scores for the data. If there are univariate outliers, you could transform the data, using either a square root or a logarithmic transformation. After you transform the data, you could check to be sure that the transformed data met these assumptions.

The following commands show how this job could be written without the macro facility. The command sequence that checks assumptions, SPLIT FILE BY GROUP, FREQUENCIES, DESCRIPTIVES, SPLIT FILE OFF, and RE-GRESSION, is repeated three times (lines 5–15, lines 19–30, and lines 34–47).

```
1  DATA LIST FILE = MAC4D /GROUP 1    REACTIME 3-5 ACCURACY 7-9
2  VALUE LABELS GROUP      1'NORMAL'
3                          2'LEARNING DISABLED'
4  COMMENT initial occurrence of specified command sequence
5  SPLIT FILE BY GROUP
6  FREQUENCIES/ VARIABLES = REACTIME ACCURACY
7               /HISTOGRAM
8               /STATISTICS = SKEWNESS SESKEW
9  DESCRIPTIVES REACTIME ACCURACY
10 LIST
11 SPLIT FILE OFF
12 REGRESSION     VARIABLES = GROUP REACTIME ACCURACY
13          /DEPENDENT = ACCURACY
14          /ENTER
15          /SCATTERPLOT (REACTIME, ACCURACY)
16
17 COMPUTE REACTIME = SQRT (REACTIME)
18 COMPUTE ACCURACY = SQRT (ACCURACY)
19 COMMENT second occurrence of specified command sequence
20 SPLIT FILE BY GROUP
21 FREQUENCIES/ VARIABLES = REACTIME ACCURACY
22         / HISTOGRAM
23         / STATISTICS = SKEWNESS SESKEW
24 DESCRIPTIVES REACTIME ACCURACY
25 LIST
26 SPLIT FILE OFF
27 REGRESSION     VARIABLES = GROUP REACTIME ACCURACY
28          /DEPENDENT = ACCURACY
29          /ENTER
30          /SCATTERPLOT (REACTIME, ACCURACY)
31
32 COMPUTE REACTIME = LG10 (REACTIME * REACTIME)
33 COMPUTE ACCURACY = LG10 (ACCURACY * ACCURACY)
34 COMMENT third occurrence of specified command sequence
35 SPLIT FILE BY GROUP
36 FREQUENCIES/ VARIABLES = REACTIME ACCURACY
37         / HISTOGRAM
38         / STATISTICS = SKEWNESS SESKEW
39 DESCRIPTIVES REACTIME ACCURACY
40
41 LIST
42 SPLIT FILE OFF
43 REGRESSION     VARIABLES = GROUP REACTIME ACCURACY
44          /DEPENDENT = ACCURACY
45          /ENTER
46          /SCATTERPLOT (REACTIME, ACCURACY)
47 SPLIT FILE OFF
```

This example could have been written using the macro facility, as follows:

```
1  DATA LIST FILE = MAC4D /GROUP 1   REACTIME 3-5 ACCURACY 7-9
2  VALUE LABELS GROUP     1'normal'
3                         2'learning disabled'
4  COMMENT macro definition
5  DEFINE check ()
6  split file by group
7  frequencies  variables = reactime accuracy
8             / histogram
9  descriptives reactime accuracy
10 list
11 split file off
12 regression        variables = group reactime accuracy
13            /dependent = accuracy
14            /enter
15            /scatterplot (reactime, accuracy)
16 !ENDDEFINE
17 CHECK
18 COMPUTE REACTIME = SQRT (REACTIME)
19 COMPUTE ACCURACY = SQRT (ACCURACY)
20 COMMENT macro call
21 CHECK
22 COMPUTE REACTIME = lgl0 (REACTIME * REACTIME)
23 COMPUTE ACCURACY = lgl0 (ACCURACY * ACCURACY)
24 COMMENT macro call
25 CHECK
```

• The name of the macro is CHECK. The empty parentheses indicate that there are no arguments to the macro.

• The macro body (lines 6–15) contains the command sequence to be repeated, SPLIT FILE BY GROUP, FREQUENCIES, DESCRIPTIVES, SPLIT FILE OFF, and REGRESSION. !ENDDEFINE indicates the end of the macro definition.

• The macro is called three times, in lines 17, 21 and 25. Every time CHECK is encountered, it is replaced with the command sequence SPLIT FILE, FREQUENCIES, DESCRIPTIVES, LIST, and REGRESSION. The job using the macro facility is identical to the command sequence in which the specified command sequence is explicitly stated three separate times.

A.5
Macros with Arguments

The macro facility allows you to declare and use *arguments* in the macro definition and then assign specific values to these arguments in the macro call. For example, the following macro contains one argument, ARG1:

```
DEFINE macname (arg1 = !TOKENS(1))
      macro body
!ENDDEFINE
```

You can then assign any value to ARG1 in the macro call, as in:

```
MACNAME   ARG1 = VAR1
```

When the macro is expanded, VAR1 is substituted for ARG1 wherever !ARG1 appears in the macro body.

All arguments in MACRO are either positional or keyword. These argument types are mutually exclusive. *Positional arguments* are declared after the keyword !POSITIONAL in the macro definition. In the macro call, they are identified by their position after the macro name. For example, if one positional argument containing four tokens (see Section A.6) is defined in the macro definition, the macro call

```
MACNAME A B C D
```

substitutes A B C D wherever !1 occurs in the macro body. Section A.7 discusses positional arguments.

Keyword arguments are assigned names in the macro definition and are identified in the macro call by name. For example, if two arguments in the macro definition are assigned the names ARG1 and ARG2, the macro call might be as follows:

```
MACNAME ARG1 = A     ARG2 = B
```

Section A.8 discusses keyword arguments.

There is no limit to the number of arguments that can be specified in a macro. All arguments must be separated with slashes. If you specify both keyword and positional arguments in the same definition, the positional arguments must be defined, used in the macro body, and invoked in the macro call before the keyword arguments.

A.6
Assigning Tokens to
Arguments

In addition to argument type, the argument declaration must include a keyword that indicates which tokens following the macro name are associated with each argument. A *token* is a character or a group of characters that has a predefined function in a specified context. For example,

```
DATA LIST FREE/ VAR1
```

contains five tokens. DATA, LIST, FREE, and VAR1 are groups of characters that are evaluated as one token each. The slash (/) is a special character and is its own token. Any character that is used as a delimiter on an SPSS-X command is a valid token. For example, a comma is a valid token.

The following keywords are available:

!TOKENS (n)   *Assign the next n tokens to the argument. n* can be any positive integer.

For example, when the following macro is called

```
DEFINE macname (!POSITIONAL !TOKENS (3))
       macro body
!ENDDEFINE
```

as in

```
MACNAME ABC DEFG HI
```

the three tokens following MACNAME (ABC, DEFG, and HI) are assigned to the positional argument !1 in the macro body.

!CHAREND ('char')   *Assign all tokens up to the specified character to the argument.* The character must be a one-character string specified in apostrophes and enclosed in parentheses.

For example, when the following macro is called

```
DEFINE macname (!POSITIONAL !CHAREND ('/'))
       macro body
!ENDDEFINE
```

as in

```
MACNAME A B C D / E F
```

all tokens up to the slash (A, B, C, and D) are assigned to the positional argument !1. Note that if the ending character were omitted on the macro call, A B C D E F would be assigned to positional argument !1.

!ENCLOSE ('char','char')   *Assign all tokens between the indicated characters to the argument.* The starting and ending characters can be any special one-character strings enclosed in apostrophes. The two strings must also be separated by a comma and the entire specification enclosed in parentheses.

For example, when the following macro is called

```
DEFINE macname (!POSITIONAL !ENCLOSE('(',')'))
       macro body
!ENDDEFINE
```

as in

```
MACNAME (A B C)
```

The three tokens enclosed in parentheses, A, B, and C, are assigned to the positional argument !1 in the macro body. Note that the starting and ending character can differ.

!CMDEND *Assign to the argument all the remaining text on the macro call, up to the start of the next command.*

Since !CMDEND reads up to the next command, only the last argument in the argument list can be specified with the !CMDEND keyword. If you specify a non-final argument with !CMDEND, the arguments following that argument will be read as text. For example, when the following macro is called

```
DEFINE macname (!POSITIONAL !tokens(2)/
                !POSITIONAL !CMDEND)
      macro body
!ENDDEFINE
```

as in

```
MACNAME A B C D E
```

the first two tokens following MACNAME (A and B) are assigned to the positional argument !1. C, D, and E are assigned to the positional argument !2. If the arguments were declared in the reverse order, as in

```
DEFINE macname  (!POSITIONAL !CMDEND/
                 !POSITIONAL !tokens(2))
      macro body
!ENDDEFINE
```

then all five tokens, A, B, C, D, and E, would be assigned to the first positional argument if the same macro call were used.

Each of the above keywords is useful in different situations:

- The !TOKENS keyword allows you to specify exactly how many tokens are desired. This mechanism allows for access to individual tokens or groups of tokens.
- The !ENCLOSE keyword allows you to group multiple tokens within a specified pair of symbols. This is useful when an indeterminable number of tokens are to be assigned to an argument or when the use of an ending character is not directly possible.
- The !CHAREND keyword allows you to specify the character that will end the argument assignment. Use this keyword when the number of tokens that are assigned is arbitrary and most likely not known in advance.
- The !CMDEND keyword is useful if you want to change the defaults on an existing SPSS-X command. In the example below, the macro MYFREQ contains certain options from the FREQUENCIES command:

```
DEFINE myfreq (!POSITIONAL !CMDEND )
frequencies !1 /
    statistics=default skewness
!ENDDEFINE
MYFREQ VAR = A B/ HIST
```

- MYFREQ is expanded into the following:

```
FREQUENCIES VAR = A B/ HIST /
    STATISTICS=DEFAULT SKEWNESS
```

The arguments for a given macro can use a combination of these keywords. In the following example, note how the variables are specified on the macro call:

```
DATA LIST / VARA 1-2 VARB 4-5 VARC 7-8
DEFINE macdef3 (arg1 = !TOKENS(1)/
                arg2 = !ENCLOSE ('(',')')/
                arg3 = !CHAREND('%'))
frequencies variables = !arg1   !arg2 !arg3
!ENDDEFINE
MACDEF3 ARG1 = VARA  ARG2=(VARB)  ARG3=varc%
```

Because ARG1 is declared with the !TOKENS keyword, the value for ARG1 is simply specified as VARA. ARG2 is specified in parentheses, as indicated in the !ENCLOSE declaration. The value for ARG3 is followed by a percent sign, as indicated in the !CHAREND declaration.

A.7
Positional Arguments

Positional arguments must be declared in the order that they will be specified on the macro call. The first positional argument defined in a macro is referred to by !1 in the macro body, the second positional argument defined is referred to by !2, and so on. Similarly, the value of the first argument in the macro call is assigned to !1, the second argument is assigned to !2, and so on.

The following example shows an argument declaration and macro call using positional arguments:

```
DATA LIST FILE = MAC / VAR1 1-2 VAR2 4-5 VAR3 7-8
COMMENT macro definition
DEFINE macdef (!POS !TOKENS(1)/
               !POS !TOKENS(1)/
               !POS !TOKENS(1))
frequencies    variables = !1 !2 !3
!ENDDEFINE
COMMENT macro call
MACDEF  VAR1    VAR2    VAR3
```

In this example, three positional arguments with one token each are defined. The first positional argument is referenced by !1 in the FREQUENCIES command. Similarly, the second and third positional arguments are referenced by !2 and !3. When the macro is expanded, the the first positional argument (!1) is assigned the value VAR1, the second positional argument (!2) is assigned the value VAR2, and the third positional argument (!3) is assigned the value VAR3. If the macro call had been

```
MACDEF  VAR3    VAR1    VAR2
```

the first positional argument would have been assigned the value var3, the second positional argument would have been assigned the value var1, and the third positional argument would have been assigned the value var2.

A shorthand way of defining the above macro is to assign the three tokens to one argument instead of three:

```
DEFINE macdef (!POS !TOKENS(3))
frequencies variables = !1
!ENDDEFINE
```

Another possibility would be to specify three arguments but then join them all together on one FREQUENCIES command using the symbol !*. The definition would then be:

```
DEFINE macdef (!POS !TOKENS(1)/
               !POS !TOKENS(1)/
               !POS !TOKENS(1))
frequencies    variables = !*
```

In all examples, the macro call would be the same. When you use the !* convention to concatenate arguments, the arguments are concatenated separated by blanks.

A.8
Keyword Arguments

Unlike positional arguments, keyword arguments do not depend on the position of the arguments in the macro call. Instead, they are called with user-defined keywords that can be specified in any order.

Keyword argument definitions contain the argument name, an equals sign, and the !TOKENS, !ENCLOSE, !CHAREND, or !CMDEND keyword. For example,

```
arg2 = !TOKENS(1)
```

defines an argument named ARG2 that contains one token.

Argument names are limited to seven characters and cannot match the character portion of a macro keyword. For example, DEFINE is not a valid argument name. The keyword !POSITIONAL cannot be used in keyword argument definitions.

In the macro body, the argument name is preceded by an exclamation point. On the macro, the argument is specified without the exclamation point, as in the following example:

```
COMMENT macro definition
DEFINE macdef2 (arg1 = !TOKENS(1)/
                arg2 = !TOKENS(1)/
                arg3 = !TOKENS(1))
frequencies  variables = !arg1 !arg2 !arg3
!ENDDEFINE
COMMENT macro call
MACDEF2 ARG1=VAR1  ARG2=VAR2  ARG3=VAR3
```

This example defines three arguments, ARG1, ARG2, and ARG3. In the macro call, ARG1 is assigned the value VAR1, ARG2 is assigned the value VAR2, and ARG3 is assigned the value VAR3. With keyword arguments, you do not need to call the arguments in the order they were defined. For example, the following macro call yields the same results as the one in the example above:

```
MACDEF2 ARG3=VAR3  ARG1=VAR1  ARG2=VAR2
```

A.9
Defining Defaults

Use the optional !DEFAULT keyword in your macro definition to establish default settings for arguments.

!DEFAULT *Default argument.* After !DEFAULT, specify the value you want to use as a default for that argument. A default can be specified for each argument. Then, if you neglect to specify the value for an argument, the argument will be set to the value of the default.

For example, in the following macro definition

```
COMMENT macro definition
DEFINE macdef2 (arg1 = !DEFAULT (vara) !TOKENS(1) /
                arg2 = !TOKENS(1)/
                arg3 = !TOKENS(1))
frequencies  variables = !arg1 !arg2 !arg3
!ENDDEFINE
COMMENT macro call
MACDEF2 ARG2=VARB  ARG3=VARC
```

VARA is defined as the default value for argument ARG1. Since ARG1 is not specified on the macro call, it is set to VARA. If !DEFAULT (vara) were not specified, the value of ARG1 would be set to a null string.

A.10
Controlling Expansion

Use the optional !NOEXPAND keyword to indicate that an argument should not be expanded when the macro is called.

!NOEXPAND *Do not expand the specified argument.* !NOEXPAND applies to one individual argument and is useful only when you have imbedded macros (that is, a macro that calls another macro).

A.11
Example: Macros with Arguments

This example shows how to set up a macro that runs a REPORT job three times, each time with a different break variable. Without the macro facility, this job involves a good deal of redundant code:

```
1  COMMENT first occurrence of the command sequence
2  SORT CASES BY SALESMAN
3  REPORT VARIABLES = EARNINGS
4    /BREAK = SALESMAN
5    /SUMMARY = MEAN
6  COMMENT second occurrence of the command sequence
```

```
7   SORT CASES BY REGION
8   REPORT VARIABLES = EARNINGS
9      /BREAK = REGION
10     /SUMMARY = MEAN
11  COMMENT third occurrence of the command sequence
12  SORT CASES BY MONTH
13  REPORT VARIABLES = EARNINGS
14        /BREAK = MONTH
15        /SUMMARY = MEAN
```

The following macro simplifies the job:

```
1   COMMENT macro definition
2   DEFINE earnrep (varrep = !TOKENS (1))
3   sort cases by !varrep
4   report variables = earnings
5     .  /break = !varrep
6          /summary = mean
7   !ENDDEFINE
8   COMMENT call the macro three times
9   EARNREP VARREP= SALESMAN
10  EARNREP VARREP = REGION
11  EARNREP VARREP = MONTH
```

- In this example, the macro name is EARNREP.

- There is one keyword argument, VARREP, which takes one token.

- In the first macro call (line 9), the argument SALESMAN is substituted for !VARREP when the macro is expanded. This is equivalent to lines 2–5 in the original job.

- Similarly, REGION and MONTH are substituted for !VARREP when the macro is expanded in the second and third calls (lines 10 and 11). These lines are equivalent to lines 7–10 and 12–15 in the original job.

A.12
Macro Utilities

You can specify macro directives, string manipulation functions, or conditional processing for MACRO to perform. The macro directives allow you to turn macro expansion on and off. The string manipulation functions allow you to modify strings. The conditional processing contains the IF construct and looping constructs.

Sections A.13 through A.19 describe these macro functions. Like other macro keywords, all of the function keywords begin with an exclamation point.

A.13
Macro Directives

The following directives can be specified:

!OFFEXPAND/   *Turn macro expansion on or off.* !ONEXPAND activates macro
!ONEXPAND   expansion and !OFFEXPAND stops macro expansion. !OFFEXPAND is effective only when SET MEXPAND is ON (the default). Within a macro definition, use !OFFEXPAND/!ONEXPAND to turn off expansion of certain symbols. All symbols between !OFFEXPAND and !ONEXPAND will not be expanded. Use these functions outside macro definition to prevent unwanted macro expansion.

A.14
String Manipulation
Functions

These functions process one or more character strings and produce either a new character string or a character representation of a numeric result. Since the macro processor is a character handling facility, the concept of number does not exist; therefore, any result that is returned is treated as a character string. The arguments to these functions can be strings, variables, or even other macro calls.

!LENGTH (str)   *Return the length of the specified string.* The result is character representation of the string length. The argument string in the function call can also be a macro argument or another function call. If an argument is used in place of a string and it is set to null, this function will return 0.

!CONCAT (str1, str2 . . .)	*Return a string that is the concatenation the strings.* !CON-CAT(abc,def) returns abcdef.
!SUBSTRING (str, from, [length])	*Return a substring of the specified string.* The substring starts at the position marked *from* and continues for the specified length. If length is not specified, substring begins at *from* and ends at the end of the input string. For example, !SUBSTRING (abcdef, 3, 2) returns cd.
!INDEX (str1, str2)	*Return the position of the first occurrence of string2 in string1.* If string2 is not found in string1, the function returns 0. !INDEX (abcdef,def) returns 4.
!HEAD (str)	*Return the first token within a string.* The input string is not changed. !HEAD ('a b c') returns a.
!TAIL (str)	*Return all tokens except the head token.* The input string is not changed. !TAIL('a b c') returns b c.
!QUOTE (str)	*Put apostrophes around the argument.* !QUOTE replicates any imbedded apostrophe. !QUOTE(abc) returns 'abc'. Assuming !1 equals Bill's, !QUOTE(!1) returns 'Bill''s'.
!UNQUOTE (str)	*Remove quotes and apostrophes from the enclosed string.* Assuming that !1 equals 'abc', !UNQUOTE(!1) is abc. Internal paired quotes are unpaired; if !1 equals 'Bill''s', then !UNQUOTE(!1) is Bill's. !UNQUOTE(!QUOTE(anything)) is anything.
!UPCASE	*Convert all lowercase characters in the argument to upper case.* !UPCASE('abc def') returns ABC DEF.
!BLANKS (n)	*Generate a string containing the specified number of blanks.* The *n* specification must be a positive integer. !BLANKS(5) returns a string of 5 blank spaces. Unless the blanks are quoted, they may not be processed, since macro compresses blanks.
!NULL	*Generate a string of length zero.* This can help determine whether an argument was ever assigned a value, as in !IF (!1 !EQ !NULL) !THEN . . . .
!EVAL	*Scan the argument for possible macro calls.* During macro definition, an argument to a function or an operand in an expression is not scanned for possible macro calls unless the !EVAL function is used. It returns a string that is the expansion of its argument. For example, if MAC1 is a macro, then !EVAL(MAC1) returns the expansion of MAC1. If MAC1 is not a macro, !EVAL(MAC1) returns MAC1.

A.15
SET Subcommands for Use with Macro

The SET command allows you to change certain default settings (see Chapter 4). Four SET subcommands were designed for use with the macro facility.

MPRINT	*Controls whether SPSS-X includes in your display file the command list after macro expansion.* The specification for MPRINT is YES or NO (alias ON or OFF). The default at the start of an SPSS-X job is NO. The MPRINT subcommand is independent of the PRINTBACK command.
MEXPAND	*Controls whether macro expansion will occur.* MEXPAND is on, by default, unless it is set off. Specifying SET MEXPAND OFF will prevent macro expansion. Specifying SET MEXPAND ON will reestablish macro expansion. YES and NO may be used in place of ON and OFF.
MNEST	*Controls the normal maximum nesting level for macros.* The default number of levels that can be nested is 50. The maximum number of levels is storage dependent.
MITERATE	*Controls the maximum loop traversals permitted in macro expansions.* The default number of traversals is 1000.

A.16
Restoring SET Specifications

A macro writer may need to restore the user's SET specifications without knowing what those specifications were. The following SPSS-X commands are available generally within SPSS-X but are especially useful for macro writers.

PRESERVE *Store the current SET specifications at this point in the SPSS-X job.*

A

RESTORE   *Restore the SET specifications to what they were when PRESERVE was*
encountered.

PRESERVE...RESTORE sequences can be nested up to five levels.

A.17
Conditional Processing

The !IF construct allows for conditional processing of the format

```
!IF (expression) !THEN statements
                 [!ELSE statements ]
!IFEND
```

!IF, !THEN, and !IFEND are all required. !ELSE is optional. If the result of the
expression is true, the statements following the !THEN statement are executed. If
the result of the expression is false, the statements following !ELSE are executed
(if any were specified). Otherwise, the program continues. !IF, !IFEND, !THEN,
and !ELSE are reserved keywords within the macro processor.

Valid operators for the expressions include !EQ, !NE, !GT, !LT, !GE, and
!LE, or =,¬=, >, <, >=, <=,¬, &, and |. !OR, !NOT, and !AND are also
allowed. Valid conditional processing and looping constructs are interpreted
after parameter substitution and function execution.

!IF statements can be nested whenever necessary. Parentheses are permitted
to specify the order of evaluation of logical expresssions. The default precedence
is the same as in transformations: !NOT has precedence over !AND, which has
precedence over !OR.

A.18
Looping Constructs

Looping constructs allow repetitive tasks to be accomplished. Loops can be
nested to whatever depth is required, but loops cannot be crossed. There are two
looping constructs in the macro facility, the DO loop and the DO IN loop. The
syntax of the DO loop is as follows:

```
!DO !var = start !TO finish [ !BY step ]
    statements
!BREAK
!DOEND
```

!var must be a variable name that begins with an exclamation point. It is used as
an index in the loop. Start, finish, and step must be numbers or expressions that
evaluate to numbers. The loop begins at the value specified for start and continues
until it reaches the value specified for finish (unless a !BREAK statement is
encountered). The step is optional and can be used to specify a subset of the
iterations. If start is set to 1, finish to 10, and by to 3, the DO loop will be executed
four times with the index variable assigned values 1, 4, 7, and 10.

The statements can be any valid SPSS-X statements or macro commands.
!DOEND specifies the end of the loop. !BREAK is an optional specification. It
can be used in conjunction with conditional processing to cause the loop to be
exited, as in:

```
!IF (i = 5) !THEN !BREAK  !IFEND
```

The example in Section A.8 can be rewritten using a DO loop, as in:

```
DEFINE MACDEF (arg1 = !TOKENS(1)/
               arg2 = !TOKENS(1))
!DO !i = !ARG1 !TO !ARG2
frequencies variables = !CONCAT(var,!i)
!DOEND
!ENDDEFINE
MACDEF ARG1 = 1 ARG2 = 3
```

In this example, the variable I is initially assigned the value 1 (ARG1). ARG1 is
incremented until it equals 3, at which point the DO loop ends. The loop
concatenates VAR and I value 1, VAR and I value 2, and finally VAR and I value
3 on its three iterations. The result of this loop is that FREQUENCIES receives
three variables, VAR1, VAR2, and VAR3.

List Processing Loop. The format of the list processing loop is

```
!DO !var !IN (list)
    statements
!BREAK
!DOEND
```

In a list processing loop, you specify a list to the !IN function and the variable !var will be set to each of the members in the list. The !DO and !DOEND statements begin and end the loop, and !BREAK allows you to exit from the loop. The list can be any expression, although it is usually a string. Only one list can be specified in each list processing loop.

For example, the commands in Section A.8 could also have been specified as a list processing loop:

```
DEFINE macdef (!POS !CHAREND('/') )
!DO !i !IN ( !1)
frequencies variables = !i
!DOEND
!ENDDEFINE
MACDEF VAR1 VAR2 VAR3   /
```

The macro call assigns three variables, VAR1, VAR2, and VAR3, to the positional argument !1. Thus, the list processing loop completes three iterations. In the first iteration, I is set to value VAR1. In the second and third iterations, I is set to VAR2 and VAR3, respectively. Thus, FREQUENCIES receives VAR1, VAR2, and VAR3 as variables.

The example in Section A.11 could also have been rewritten using the list processing loop:

```
DEFINE earnrep (!POS !CHAREND('/') )
!DO !i !IN ( !1)
sort cases by !i
report var = earnings
      /break = !i
      /summary = mean
!DOEND
!ENDDEFINE
MACDEF SALESMAN REGION MONTH /
```

In this example, the positional argument !1 is assigned the three variables, salesman, region, and month. When the list processing loop is executed, the index argument I is set to each of the variables in succession. The macro creates three reports.

A.19
Direct Assignment of Macro Variables

The macro command !LET allows you to assign values to macro variables in the form

```
!LET !var = expression
```

in which !var is a macro variable and the expression must either be a single term or be enclosed in parentheses. !var cannot be one of the reserved macro keywords, and it cannot be the name of one of the arguments within the macro definition. Thus you cannot use !LET to change the value of an argument. !var can be a new variable or one previously assigned by a !DO command or another !LET command. The following are valid !LET commands:

```
!LET !A = 1
!LET !B = !CONCAT(ABC,!SUBSTR(!1,3,1),DEF)
!LET !C = (!2 ¬ = !NULL)
```

The last of these examples evaluates as 0 (false) if !2 is a null string or as 1 (true) if !2 is not a null string.

A.20
LIMITATIONS

The BEGIN DATA/END DATA commands are not allowed within a macro. The DEFINE command is not allowed within a macro.

ANNOTATED EXAMPLE

The purpose of this job is to demonstrate how you could use the macro facility to transpose a matrix. The matrix must already be defined as an active file, either via a GET FILE command or via a DATA LIST command:

```
DEFINE  tpose ( vars     =   !CHAREND('/') /
                  decimal =   !CHAREND('/') !DEFAULT(2)/
                  rows    =   !CHAREND('/') /
                  columns =   !CHAREND('/') / )
formats !vars ( !CONCAT(F16.,!DECIMAL) )
write outfile = tempmatx /  !vars
execute
input program
vector #x(!columns)
data list free file = tempmatx/ #x1 to !CONCAT(#x,!COLUMNS)
compute #nrows = #nrows + 1
compute nrows = #nrows
loop I = 1 to !columns
compute var = #x(i)
end case
end loop
end input program
compute nrows = #nrows
list
sort cases by I
list
vector cols(!rows)
compute cols(nrows) = var
list
aggregate outfile=*
  /presorted
  /break=I
  /var1 TO !CONCAT(var,!rows)= max(cols1 to !CONCAT(cols,!rows) )
!ENDDEFINE
SET WIDTH = 80
DATA LIST FREE / x1 x2 x3 x4
BEGIN DATA
11 12 13 14
21 22 23 24
31 32 33 34
END DATA
TPOSE VARS = x1 x2 x3 x4/  ROWS = 3 / COLUMNS = 4
LIST
```

- The DEFINE statement names the macro TPOSE, and defines four keyword arguments, VARS, ROWS, COLUMNS, and DECIMAL. VARS is the variable list, DECIMALS is the number of digits to the right of the decimal point, ROWS is the number of cases in the matrix and COLUMNS is the number of variables in the matrix.

- The FORMATS command prints and writes the variable VARS in the specified format. !concat(F16.,!decimal), joins the strings F16 and !DECIMAL, where !DECIMAL is the keyword argument specified in the macro definition. If a value for DECIMAL is not specified, its value will default to 2.

- The WRITE command writes to the file TEMPMATX just the variables to be transposed.

- EXECUTE is the procedure to execute the WRITE OUTFILE command above.

- The INPUT PROGRAM and END INPUT PROGRAM statements begin and end the block of commands that build cases from the input file. Figure A shows this file listed in its original order. Figure B shows the file sorted by I, which identifies the column each value came from.

- The VECTOR command creates vector #x, which references four scratch variables, #x1, #x2, #x3, and #x4 (where 4 is the number of columns).

- The DATA LIST statement names TEMPMATX as the data file and #x1, #x2, #x3 and #x4 as the variables.

- The COMPUTE #NROW = #NROW + 1 statement increments the #NROW scratch variable by 1. NROW is the number of rows.

- The LOOP statement loops from 1 to 4 (columns). I is the variable that is used in the transpose. Initially, its value is the number of columns. After the transpose is completed, its value changes to the number of rows.

- The COMPUTE NROW = #NROW statement puts the value of the scratch variable #NROW into the variable nrow. This process changes NROW into a permanent variable from a scratch variable, making NROW accessible to a procedure.

- The COMPUTE VAR = #x(I), makes each of the variables in the matrix a separate case. END CASE causes the individual values of NROWS to be processed as separate cases.
- The END LOOP statement ends the loop structure started by the loop command.
- The SORT CASES command puts NROWS in order by case number, variable I.
- The VECTOR COLS(!ROWS) command creates the vector COLS, which references as many variables as there are rows. In this example, there are three rows, so VECTOR creates three variables, #COLS1, #COLS2, and #COLS3.
- The COMPUTE COLS(NROW) = VAR puts each of the var variables into the correct column according to nrow. The matrix is transposed, but each item is in a separate case (see Figure C).
- The OUTFILE=* subcommand on the AGGREGATE command specifies that the output aggregated file will replace the active file.
- The PRESORTED subcommand on AGGREGATE specifies that the unaggregated file is in the desired order.
- The BREAK=I subcommand on the AGGREGATE command names I as the grouping variable. At this point, the variable I represents rows not columns.
- !CONCAT(VAR,!ROWS) joins !ROWS to the end of VAR. MAX(COLS1 TO !CONCAT(COLS,!ROWS)) computes the maximum value within rows. The MAX subcommand allows AGGREGATE to eliminate missing values generated by the transpose. VAR1 TO !CONCAT(VAR,!ROWS) = MAX(COLS1 TO !CONCAT(COLS,!ROWS)) creates new variables VAR1 to VAR3, where 3 is the number of rows.
- The !ENDDEFINE statement finishes the macro definition.
- The SET WIDTH = 80 command sets the maximum display width for the display file at 80 characters.
- The BEGIN DATA and END DATA commands define the data set to be used in this example.
- The TPOSE statement is the macro call. The macro argument VARS is assigned the values x1, x2, x3, and x4. Similarly, the macro arguments rows and columns are assigned the values 3 and 4, respectively. Since DECIMAL is not assigned a value, its value becomes the default, 2.

Figure A shows the input matrix. Figure B shows the matrix after it has been sorted by I, column, and before the transpose has occurred. Figure C shows the matrix after the transpose has been completed, but before the AGGREGATE procedure has been executed. The AGGREGATE procedure uses the MAX subcommand, but since its purpose is to eliminate missing values, MIN could also have been used. COLS1, COLS2, and COLS3 represent the transposed matrix with missing values produced by the transpose. Figure D shows the final transposed matrix. The missing values are eliminated by use of the AGGREGATE command. AGGREGATE compressed the number of cases from 12 to 4 by assigning the values of each of the three rows (COLS1, COLS2, COLS3) to one case (I1, I2, I3, or I4).

A Input matrix

NROWS	I	VAR
1.00	1.00	11.00
1.00	2.00	12.00
1.00	3.00	13.00
1.00	4.00	14.00
2.00	1.00	21.00
2.00	2.00	22.00
2.00	3.00	23.00
2.00	4.00	24.00
3.00	1.00	31.00
3.00	2.00	32.00
3.00	3.00	33.00
3.00	4.00	34.00

NUMBER OF CASES READ =   12   NUMBER OF CASES LISTED =   12

B Sorted matrix

```
MACRO\    SORT CASES BY I

MACRO\    LIST

   NROWS        I       VAR

    1.00      1.00     11.00
    2.00      1.00     21.00
    3.00      1.00     31.00
    1.00      2.00     12.00
    2.00      2.00     22.00
    3.00      2.00     32.00
    1.00      3.00     13.00
    2.00      3.00     23.00
    3.00      3.00     33.00
    1.00      4.00     14.00
    2.00      4.00     24.00
    3.00      4.00     34.00


NUMBER OF CASES READ =      12    NUMBER OF CASES LISTED =      12
```

C Initial transposed matrix

```
MACRO\    VECTOR COLS( 3 )
MACRO\    COMPUTE COLS(NROWS) = VAR
MACRO\    LIST

   NROWS        I       VAR     COLS1     COLS2     COLS3

    1.00      1.00     11.00     11.00         .         .
    2.00      1.00     21.00         .     21.00         .
    3.00      1.00     31.00         .         .     31.00
    1.00      2.00     12.00     12.00         .         .
    2.00      2.00     22.00         .     22.00         .
    3.00      2.00     32.00         .         .     32.00
    1.00      3.00     13.00     13.00         .         .
    2.00      3.00     23.00         .     23.00         .
    3.00      3.00     33.00         .         .     33.00
    1.00      4.00     14.00     14.00         .         .
    2.00      4.00     24.00         .     24.00         .
    3.00      4.00     34.00         .         .     34.00


NUMBER OF CASES READ =      12    NUMBER OF CASES LISTED =      12
```

D Final transposed matrix

```
MACRO\    AGGREGATE OUTFILE=* /PRESORTED /BREAK=I /VAR1 TO VAR3 = MAX(COLS1 TO
MACRO\       COLS3 )

'AGGREGATE' PROBLEM REQUIRES      256 BYTES OF MEMORY.

A NEW (AGGREGATED) ACTIVE FILE HAS REPLACED THE EXISTING ACTIVE FILE.
IT CONTAINS    4 VARIABLES AND      4 CASES.

MACRO\    list
FILE:     AGGREGATED FILE

       I      VAR1      VAR2      VAR3

    1.00     11.00     21.00     31.00
    2.00     12.00     22.00     32.00
    3.00     13.00     23.00     33.00
    4.00     14.00     24.00     34.00


NUMBER OF CASES READ =       4    NUMBER OF CASES LISTED =       4
```

Appendix B Command Order

Command order in SPSS-X is determined only by the system's need to know and do certain things in logical sequence. One overriding rule that occurs throughout the system is that a variable must exist before it can be mentioned for labeling, transformation, analysis, and so forth. Otherwise, command order is a matter of your own style and of your understanding of how SPSS-X works. This appendix describes the program states SPSS-X goes through as it reads your command groups and executes them.

You can use this appendix to construct your SPSS-X command file if you wish, but you will find that putting your commands together in an order that seems logical to you is probably the best method. However, this appendix will help you considerably if you encounter a problem and are trying to determine why SPSS-X doesn't seem to want to accept your command order or seems to be carrying out your instructions incorrectly.

B.1
PROGRAM STATES

You should assemble your commands in groups that define your active file, transform the data, and analyze it. This order conforms very closely to the order of tasks SPSS-X must go through as it processes your commands. Specifically, SPSS-X checks command order according to the *program state* through which it passes. The program state is a characteristic of the program before and after a command is encountered. There are four program states. Each SPSS-X job starts in the *initial state*. The *input program state* enables SPSS-X to read data. The *transformation state* allows data modifications. The *procedure state* enables the program to begin executing a procedure. Figure B.1a shows how SPSS-X moves through these states. SPSS-X determines the current state from the commands that it already has encountered and then identifies which commands are allowed in that state.

Figure B.1a Program states

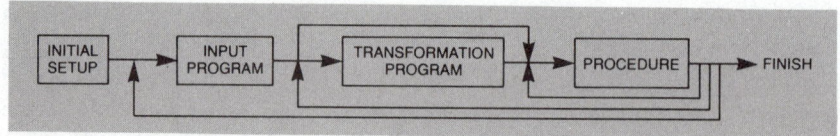

An SPSS-X job must go through initial, input program, and procedure steps to be a complete job. Since all jobs start in the initial state, you need to be concerned primarily with what commands you need to define your active file and to analyze the data. The following commands define a very minimal job:

B

```
GET FILE=DATAIN
FREQUENCIES VARIABLES=ALL
```

The GET command defines the active file and the FREQUENCIES command reads the data file and analyzes it. Thus, SPSS-X goes through the required three states: initial, input, and procedure.

Typically, an SPSS-X job also goes through the transformation state, but it can be skipped as shown in the example above and in the diagram in Figure B.1a. Consider the example SPSS-X job used in Chapter 7 to illustrate the RECODE command (see Figure B.1b). SPSS-X starts in the initial state, where it processes the TITLE command. It then moves into the input state upon encountering the DATA LIST command. SPSS-X can then move into either the transformation or procedure state once the DATA LIST command has been processed.

Figure B.1b   An SPSS-X job

```
TITLE   PILOT FOR COLLEGE SURVEY

DATA LIST   FILE=TESTDATA
  /AGE 1-3 ITEM1 TO ITEM3 5-7

VARIABLE LABELS   ITEM1 'OPINION ON LEVEL OF DEFENSE SPENDING'
  ITEM2 'OPINION ON LEVEL OF WELFARE SPENDING'
  ITEM3 'OPINION ON LEVEL OF HEALTH SPENDING'
VALUE LABELS   ITEM1 TO ITEM3 -1 'DISAGREE' 0 'NO OPINION' 1 'AGREE'
MISSING VALUES   AGE(-99,-98) ITEM1 TO ITEM3 (9)
RECODE   ITEM1 TO ITEM3 (0=1) (1=0) (2=-1) (9=9) (ELSE=SYSMIS)
RECODE   AGE (MISSING=9) (18 THRU HI=1) (LO THRU 18=0) INTO VOTER
PRINT /$CASENUM 1-2 AGE 4-6 VOTER 8-10
VARIABLE LABELS   VOTER 'ELIGIBLE TO VOTE'
VALUE LABELS   VOTER 0 'UNDER 18' 1 '18 OR OVER'
MISSING VALUES   VOTER (9)
PRINT FORMATS   VOTER(F1.0)

FREQUENCIES VARIABLES=VOTER,ITEM1 TO ITEM3
```

In this example, SPSS-X remains in the transformation state after processing each of the commands from VARIABLE LABELS through PRINT FORMATS. SPSS-X then moves into the procedure state to process the FREQUENCIES command. As shown in Figure B.1a, SPSS-X can repeat the procedure state if it encounters a second procedure. SPSS-X can return to the transformation state if it encounters additional transformation commands following the first procedure. Finally, in some jobs SPSS-X can return to the input program state upon encountering commands such as FILE TYPE or MATCH FILES.

B.2 DETERMINING COMMAND ORDER

Table B.2 shows where specific commands can go in the command file in terms of program states and what happens when SPSS-X encounters a command in each of the four program states. If a column contains a dash, the command is accepted in that program state and it leaves the program in that state. If one of the words INPUT, TRANS, or PROC appears in the column, the command is accepted in the program state indicated by the column heading but it moves the program into the state shown in the column. Asterisks in a column indicate errors when SPSS-X encounters the command in that program state. Commands marked with the dagger in the column for the procedure state clear the active file.

The table shows six groups of commands: utility commands (which can go anywhere), file definition commands, input program commands, data transformation commands, restricted transformations, and procedure commands. These groups are discussed in Sections B.3 through B.8.

Table B.2 Commands and program states

	INIT	INPUT	TRANS	PROC
UTILITY COMMANDS				
CLEAR TRANSFORMATIONS	**	PROC	PROC	—
COMMENT	—	—	—	—
DISPLAY	**	—	—	—
DOCUMENT	**	—	—	—
DROP DOCUMENTS	**	—	—	—
EDIT	—	—	—	—
END DATA	—	—	—	—
FILE HANDLE	—	—	—	—
FILE LABEL	—	—	—	—
FINISH	—	—	—	—
HELP	—	—	—	—
INCLUDE	—	—	—	—
INFO	—	—	—	—
MACRO	—	—	—	—
N OF CASES	—	—	—	TRANS
NEW FILE	—	INIT	INIT	INIT†
NUMBERED, UNNUMBERED	—	—	—	—
PROCEDURE OUTPUT	—	—	—	—
SET, SHOW	—	—	—	—
TITLE, SUBTITLE	—	—	—	—
FILE DEFINITION COMMANDS				
ADD FILES	TRANS	**	—	TRANS
DATA LIST	TRANS	—	—	TRANS†
FILE TYPE	INPUT	**	INPUT	INPUT†
GET	TRANS	**	—	TRANS†
GET BMDP	TRANS	**	—	TRANS†
GET OSIRIS	TRANS	**	—	TRANS†
GET SAS	TRANS	**	—	TRANS†
GET SCSS	TRANS	**	—	TRANS†
HOST	—	—	—	—
IMPORT	TRANS	**	—	TRANS†
INPUT PROGRAM	INPUT	**	INPUT	INPUT†
KEYED DATA LIST	TRANS	—	—	TRANS
MATCH FILES	TRANS	**	—	TRANS
MATRIX DATA	TRANS	**	—	TRANS†
RENAME VARIABLES	**	—	—	TRANS
UPDATE	TRANS	**	—	TRANS
INPUT PROGRAM COMMANDS				
END CASE	**	—	**	**
END FILE	**	—	**	**
END FILE TYPE	**	TRANS	**	**
END INPUT PROGRAM	**	TRANS	**	**
POINT	**	—	**	**
RECORD TYPE	**	—	**	**
REPEATING DATA	**	—	**	**
REREAD	**	—	**	**
TRANSFORMATION COMMANDS				
ADD VALUE LABELS	**	—	—	TRANS
COMPUTE	**	—	—	TRANS
CONSTRAINED FUNCTIONS	**	**	—	TRANS
COUNT	**	—	—	TRANS
DERIVATIVES PROGRAM	**	**	—	TRANS
DO IF—END IF	**	—	—	TRANS
DO REPEAT—END REPEAT	**	—	—	TRANS
ELSE	**	—	—	TRANS
ELSE IF	**	—	—	TRANS
FORMATS	**	—	—	TRANS
IF	**	—	—	TRANS
LEAVE	**	—	—	TRANS
LOOP—END LOOP, BREAK	**	—	—	TRANS
MISSING VALUES	**	—	—	TRANS
MODEL PROGRAM	**	**	—	TRANS
NUMERIC	**	—	—	TRANS

PRINT	**	—	—	TRANS
PRINT EJECT	**	—	—	TRANS
PRINT FORMATS	**	—	—	TRANS
PRINT SPACE	**	—	—	TRANS
RECODE	**	—	—	TRANS
SPLIT FILE	**	—	—	TRANS
STRING	**	—	—	TRANS
VALUE LABELS	**	—	—	TRANS
VARIABLE LABELS	**	—	—	TRANS
VECTOR	**	—	—	TRANS
WEIGHT	**	—	—	TRANS
WRITE	**	—	—	TRANS
WRITE FORMATS	**	—	—	TRANS
XSAVE	**	—	—	TRANS

RESTRICTED TRANSFORMATIONS

REFORMAT	**	**	—	TRANS
SAMPLE	**	**	—	TRANS
SELECT IF	**	**	—	TRANS
TEMPORARY	**	**	—	TRANS

PROCEDURES

BEGIN DATA	**	**	PROC	—
EXECUTE	**	**	PROC	—
EXPORT	**	**	PROC	—
LIST	**	**	PROC	—
SAVE	**	**	PROC	—
SAVE SCSS	**	**	PROC	—
SORT CASES	**	**	PROC	—
procedures	**	**	PROC	—

To read the table, first locate the command that concerns you. If you simply want to know where in the SPSS-X command stream it can go, look for columns without asterisks. For example, the COMPUTE command can be used when the program is in the input program state, the transformation state, or the procedure state, but it will cause an error if you try to use it in the initial state. If you want to know what can follow a command, look at each of the four columns next to the command. If the column is dashed, any commands not showing asterisks in the column for that program state can follow the command. If the column contains one of the words INPUT, TRANS, or PROC, any command not showing asterisks in the column for the program state indicated by that word can follow the command. For example, if you are concerned with what commands can follow the INPUT PROGRAM command (Chapter 14), note first that it is allowed only in the initial or procedure states. Then note that INPUT PROGRAM puts SPSS-X into the input program state wherever it occurs legally. This means that commands with dashes or words in the INPUT column can follow the INPUT PROGRAM command. This includes all the utility commands, the DATA LIST command, input program commands, and transformation commands like COMPUTE. Commands that are not allowed after the INPUT PROGRAM command are most of the file definition commands that are their own input program (such as GET), restricted transformations (such as SELECT IF), and procedures.

B.3
Unrestricted Utility Commands

The utility commands can appear in any state. Table B.2 shows this by the absence of asterisks in the columns next to the EDIT through TITLE commands. For example, the EDIT command can appear at any point in the command file.

The dashed lines indicate that after a utility command is processed, the program remains in the same state it was in before the command. The only exception is the N OF CASES command. If SPSS-X is in the procedure state, N OF CASES moves the program to the transformation state. The FINISH command terminates the job wherever it appears. Any commands appearing after FINISH will not be read and therefore will not cause an error.

B.4
File Definition Commands

You can use all the file definition commands in the initial state, the transformation state, and in the procedure state. Most of these commands cause errors if you try to use them in the input program state. You can, however, use DATA LIST, and KEYED DATA LIST in the input program state since there can be and often are multiple DATA LIST or KEYED DATA LIST commands in input programs.

After they are read, the system file commands (ADD FILES, GET, GET SCSS, IMPORT, MATCH FILES, GET ORIRIS, GET SAS, and UPDATE) move SPSS-X directly to the transformation state since these commands are the entire input program. FILE TYPE and INPUT PROGRAM both move SPSS-X into the input program state and require input program commands to complete the input program. Commands in Table B.2 marked with a dagger clear the active file.

B.5
Input Program Commands

The commands associated with the complex file facility (Chapter 12) and commands associated with INPUT PROGRAM (Chapter 14) are allowed only in the input program state.

The RECORD TYPE command for the complex file facility, the POINT command for reading key sequenced data sets, and END CASE, END FILE, REPEATING DATA, and REREAD for specially written input programs leave SPSS-X in the input program state. The two that move SPSS-X on to the transformation state are END FILE TYPE for input programs initiated with FILE TYPE and END INPUT PROGRAM for those initiated with INPUT PROGRAM.

B.6
Transformation Commands

The entire set of transformation commands from ADD VALUE LABELS to XSAVE can appear in the input program state as part of an input program, in the transformation state, or in the procedure state.

When you use transformation commands in the input program state or the transformation state, SPSS-X remains in the same state it was in before the command. When the program is in the procedure state, these commands move SPSS-X back to the transformation state.

B.7
Restricted Transformations

Commands REFORMAT, SAMPLE, SELECT IF, and TEMPORARY are restricted transformation commands because they are allowed in either the transformation state or the procedure state but cannot be used in the input program state.

If you use restricted transformation commands in the transformation state, the program remains in the transformation state. If you use them in the procedure state, they move SPSS-X back to the transformation state.

B.8
Procedures

The procedures and the procedure-like commands (BEGIN DATA, EXECUTE, EXPORT, LIST, SAVE, SAVE SCSS, and SORT CASES) cause the data to be read. These commands, including all procedures, are allowed in either the transformation state or the procedure state.

When the program is in the transformation state, these commands move SPSS-X to the procedure state. When you use these commands in the procedure state, the program remains in that state.

Appendix C IMPORT/EXPORT Character Sets

Communication-formatted portable files do not use positions 1–63 in the following table. Tape-formatted portable files use the complete table. (See Chapter 17 for an explanation of the two types of files.)

POSITION	GRAPHIC	IBM EBCDIC	BURROUGHS EBCDIC	ASCII 7-BIT	ISO 8-BIT	CDC DISPLAY CODE	HIS 6-BIT	ASCII 6-BIT
0	NUL	0		0	0	0		
1	SOH	1		1	1	1		
2	STX	2		2	2	2		
3	ETX	3		3	3	3		
4	SEL	4				156		
5	HT	5		5	9	9		
6	RNL	6				134		
7	DEL	7		7	127	127		
8	GE	8				151		
9	SPS	9				141		
10	RPT	10				142		
11	VT	11		11	11	11		
12	FF	12		12	12	12		
13	CR	13		13	13	13		
14	SO	14		14	14	14		
15	SI	15		15	15	15		
16	DLE	16		16	16	16		
17	DC1	17		17	17	17		
18	DC2	18		18	18	18		
19	DC3	19		19	19	19		
20	DC4	60		60	20	20		
21	NL	21		21		133		
22	BS	22		22	8	8		
23	DOC	23				135		
24	CAN	24		24	24	24		
25	EM	25		25	25	25		
26	UBS	26				146		
27	CU1	27				143		
28	(I)FS[1]	28		28	28	28		
29	(I)GS	29		29	29	29		
30	(I)RS	30		30	30	30		
31	SM,SW	42				138		
32	DS	32				128		
33	SOS	33				129		
34	FS[2]	34				130		
35	WUS	35				131		
36	CSP	43				139		
37	LF	37		37	10	10		
38	ETB	38		38	23	23		
39	ESC	39		39	27	27		
40	(I)US	31		31	31	31		

[1]file separator
[2]field separator

POSITION	GRAPHIC	IBM EBCDIC	BURROUGHS EBCDIC	ASCII 7-BIT	ISO 8-BIT	CDC DISPLAY CODE	HIS 6-BIT	ASCII 6-BIT
41	BYP	36			132			
42	RES	20			157			
43	ENQ	45	45	5	5			
44	ACK	46	46	6	6			
45	BEL	47	47	7	7			
46	SYN	50	50	22	22			
47	IR	51			147			
48	PP	52			148			
49	TRN	53			149			
50	NBS	54			150			
51	EOT	55	55	4	4			
52	SBS	56			152			
53	IT	57			153			
54	RFF	58			154			
55	CU3	59			155			
56	NAK	61	61	21	21			
57	SUB	63	63	26	26			
58	SA	40			136			
59	SFE	41			137			
60	MFA	44			140			
61	reserved							
62	reserved							
63	reserved							
64	0	240	240	48	48	27	0	16
65	1	241	241	49	49	28	1	17
66	2	242	242	50	50	29	2	18
67	3	243	243	51	51	30	3	19
68	4	244	244	52	52	31	4	20
69	5	245	245	53	53	32	5	21
70	6	246	246	54	54	33	6	22
71	7	247	247	55	55	34	7	23
72	8	248	248	56	56	35	8	24
73	9	249	249	57	57	36	9	25
74	A	193	193	65	65	1	17	33
75	B	194	194	66	66	2	18	34
76	C	195	195	67	67	3	19	35
77	D	196	196	68	68	4	20	36
78	E	197	197	69	69	5	21	37
79	F	198	198	70	70	6	22	38
80	G	199	199	71	71	7	23	39
81	H	200	200	72	72	8	24	40
82	I	201	201	73	73	9	25	41
83	J	209	209	74	74	10	33	42
84	K	210	210	75	75	11	34	43
85	L	211	211	76	76	12	35	44
86	M	212	212	77	77	13	36	45
87	N	213	213	78	78	14	37	46
88	O	214	214	79	79	15	38	47
89	P	215	215	80	80	16	39	48
90	Q	216	216	81	81	17	40	49
91	R	217	217	82	82	18	41	50
92	S	226	226	83	83	19	50	51
93	T	227	227	84	84	20	51	52
94	U	228	228	85	85	21	52	53
95	V	229	229	86	86	22	53	54
96	W	230	230	87	87	23	54	55
97	X	231	231	88	88	24	55	56
98	Y	232	232	89	89	25	56	57
99	Z	233	233	90	90	26	57	58
100	a	129	129	97	97			
101	b	130	130	98	98			
102	c	131	131	99	99			
103	d	132	132	100	100			

POSITION	GRAPHIC	IBM EBCDIC	BURROUGHS EBCDIC	ASCII 7-BIT	ISO 8-BIT	CDC DISPLAY CODE	HIS 6-BIT	ASCII 6-BIT
104	e	133	133	101	101			
105	f	134	134	102	102			
106	g	135	135	103	103			
107	h	136	136	104	104			
108	i	137	137	105	105			
109	j	145	145	106	106			
110	k	146	146	107	107			
111	l	147	147	108	108			
112	m	148	148	109	109			
113	n	149	149	110	110			
114	o	150	150	111	111			
115	p	151	151	112	112			
116	q	152	152	113	113			
117	r	153	153	114	114			
118	s	162	162	115	115			
119	t	163	163	116	116			
120	u	164	164	117	117			
121	v	165	165	118	118			
122	w	166	166	119	119			
123	x	167	167	120	120			
124	y	168	168	121	121			
125	z	169	169	122	122			
126	space	64	64	32	32	45	16	0
127	.	75	75	46	46	47	27	14
128	<	76	76	60	60	58	30	28
129	(	77	77	40	40	41	29	8
130	+	78	78	43	43	37	48	11
131	|	79	79					
132	&	80	80	38	38	55	26	6
133	[	173	74	91	91	49	10	59
134	]	189	90	93	93	50	28	61
135	!	90	208	33	33	54	63	61
136	$	91	91	36	36	43	43	4
137	*	92	92	42	42	39	44	10
138	)	93	93	41	41	42	45	9
139	;	94	94	59	59	63	46	27
140	¬ or ^ or ↑	95	95	94	94	62	32	62
141	−	96	96	45	45	38	42	13
142	/	97	97	47	47	40	49	15
143	¦	106		124	124			
144	,	107	107	44	44	46	59	12
145	%	108	108	37	37	51*	60	5
146	_	109	109	95	95	53	58	63
147	>	110	110	62	62	59	14	30
148	?	111	111	63	63	57	15	31
149	`	121		96	96			
150	:	122	122	58	58	0|51	13	26
151	£	123	123	35	35	48	11	3
152	@	124	124	64	64	60	12	32
153	'	125	125	39	39	56	47	7
154	=	126	126	61	61	44	61	29
155	"	127	127	34	34	49	62	2
156	≤	140	140					
157	□	156	156					
158	±	158	158					
159	■	159	159					
160	°		161					
161	†	143						
162	~	161		126	126			
163	−	160	160					
164	⌊	171	171					
165	⌈	172	172					
166	≥	174	174					

POSITION	GRAPHIC	IBM EBCDIC	BURROUGHS EBCDIC	ASCII 7-BIT	ISO 8-BIT	CDC DISPLAY CODE	HIS 6-BIT	ASCII 6-BIT
167	0	176	176					
168	1	177	177					
169	2	178	178					
170	3	179	179					
171	4	180	180					
172	5	181	181					
173	6	182	182					
174	7	183	183					
175	8	184	184					
176	9	185	185					
177	⌐	187	187					
178	¬	188	188					
179	≠	190	190					
180	—	191	191					
181	(	141	141					
182	)	157	157					
183	+	142	192					
184	{	192	139	123	123			
185	}	208	155	125	125			
186	\	224		92	92	61	31	
187	¢	74	224					
188	•	175	175					
189-255	reserved							

C

Appendix D Writing User Programs

The USERPROC facility allows you to add your own procedure or incorporate an existing program into SPSS-X. USERPROC supplies a set of subroutines that read your data, retrieve dictionary information, check for missing values, print headers, and so on. You can read files and transform variables using SPSS-X and then pass them to your USERPROC procedure.

An additional expanded set of facilities, referred to by the term *User Code facility,* increases your ability to incorporate your own analysis programs into SPSS-X. These facilities also let you write interfaces with database management systems so you can extract data for analysis and for display by SPSS-X procedures.

D.1 USER CODE FACILITY

You may want to calculate a statistic or do a type of data analysis that is not available in SPSS-X, access data interactively, extract data from a database management system, or generate random test data. The User Code facility lets you add your own procedure or program to define an active file to SPSS-X. The facility provides for transfer of control to named modules to execute your program. By running your program in this way, you can take advantage of the centralized statistical and reporting tools and the data-handling facilities of SPSS-X. The advantages of this approach include simplified documentation, increased flexibility, uniform command syntax, and simplified command interpretation.

You need to make only minor modifications to run many programs with SPSS-X. With a bit more work, however, you can have your programs use many more SPSS-X features. You can access the variable names and pointers to the variables in the active file, as well as the values of several system variables. You can also use SPSS-X subroutines for accessing labels and other dictionary information, for parsing your specifications on the User Code facility commands, and for handling missing values.

D.2 USER CODE DOCUMENTATION

Documentation for the User Code facility is available in SPSS Inc. *Reports.* The specific report you need depends on the operating system you are using. The report titled *SPSS-X User Code: Adding User Programs to SPSS-X on IBM MVS and CMS Systems* defines the implementation of the User Code facility for these two IBM systems. The report explains in detail how to convert existing programs and create new programs for use with SPSS-X. Several examples show actual code. Example programs are written in FORTRAN and COBOL.

Another report, *SPSS-X User Code: Adding User Programs to SPSS-X on Digital VAX/VMS Systems* defines the User Code facility for VAX/VMS. Programs written for Digital's Common Run-time Language Environment (except in APL) can be included as User Code programs. VAX/VMS User Code facilities are illustrated using FORTRAN-77. The VAX/VMS facilities include those for IBM MVS and CMS and add certain provisions for accessing files and writing aggregation procedures. The VAX/VMS facilities allow you to access files via the SPSS-X FILE HANDLE command and to write very general aggregation procedures that both access an existing SPSS-X active file and create a new active file.

To see if the User Code facilities are available on your version of SPSS-X, print the information available by specifying the OVERVIEW keyword on the INFO command (see Chapter 3). If the facilities are available to you, OVERVIEW will also tell you how to get complete User Code documentation.

D

Appendix E Reading Direct Access and Keyed Files

Syntax

POINT

```
POINT KEY=varname [FILE=file]
```

KEYED DATA LIST

```
KEYED DATA LIST KEY=varname IN=varname
 [FILE=file] [{TABLE  }]
             {NOTABLE}
```

In many instances, a raw data file available to a user of SPSS-X is sequential. That is, the data file is a collection of records that are always processed sequentially from the beginning to the end. Chapters 5 and 12 describe how to read sequential data files. SPSS-X offers a set of facilities for processing files that are not organized sequentially. Thus, you can use SPSS-X to take advantage of the special processing characteristics of nonsequential files directly. You do not need to produce a sequential file from a nonsequential file to input it to SPSS-X. This appendix presents a general discussion of reading nonsequential files and a more complete discussion of reading VSAM files under IBM OS, IBM CMS, and IBM DOS. Consult your local documentation and the INFO file (see Chapter 3) for a more detailed discussion of reading direct access and keyed files under other operating systems.

E.1
OVERVIEW

To read files that are not sequential, there must be a way to indicate which records should be read or where SPSS-X should begin reading records.

Direct Access by Record Number. Some files are organized so that the number of each record is significant. For example, you may have a file of 50 records, each corresponding to one of the United States. If you know the relationship between the states and the record numbers, you can retrieve the data for any specific state. You can use the KEYED DATA LIST command to read specific records from a direct access file (see Sections E.2 through E.8).

Access by Key. Many environments provide a mechanism by which the records in a file can be identified by their contents. For example, a file containing information about a firm's employees may contain each employee's social security number. By taking advantage of the appropriate host system facility, you can use the social security number to identify the records in the file. The social security number would constitute the file's *key*. The KEYED DATA LIST command can also be used to read records in a keyed file (see Sections E.9 through E.12).

Selective Sequential Access by Key. The file organization used for access by a key can also be used to specify a beginning point at which SPSS-X should retrieve records sequentially. You can use the POINT command to specify the key where sequential access is to begin (see Sections E.13 through E.17).

Sequential Access to IBM VSAM Files. Several of the IBM operating systems provide a set of file organizations under an overall facility called the Virtual Storage Access Method (VSAM). In general, SPSS-X permits you to read and write VSAM files in a sequential fashion with SPSS-X commands such as DATA LIST, WRITE, GET, and SAVE (see Sections E.18 through E.23).

E.2
DIRECT ACCESS FILES

There are various types of direct access files. The SPSS-X concept of a direct access file, however, is very specific. The file must be one from which individual records can be selected according to their number. The records in a 100-record direct access file, for example, are numbered from 1 to 100.

Although the concept of record number applies to almost any file, not all files can be treated by SPSS-X as direct access files. In fact, some host environments provide no direct access capabilities at all, and others permit only a narrowly defined subset of all files to be treated as direct access.

Very few files turn out to be good candidates for direct access organization. In the case of an inventory file, for instance, the usual large gaps in the part numbering sequence would result in large amounts of wasted file space. Gaps are not a problem, however, if they are predictable. For instance, if you recognize that telephone Area Codes have first digits of 2 through 9, second digits of 0 or 1, and third digits of 0 through 9, you can transform an Area Code into a record number by using the following COMPUTE statement:

```
COMPUTE RECNUM = 20*(DIGIT1-2) + 10*DIGIT2 + DIGIT3 + 1
```

where DIGIT1, DIGIT2, and DIGIT3 are variables corresponding to the respective digits in the Area Code, and RECNUM is the resulting record number. The record numbers would range from 1, for the nonexistent Area Code 200, through 160, for Area Code 919. The file would then have a manageable number of unused records. Sections E.3 through E.8 describe how to read direct access files.

E.3
The KEYED DATA LIST Command for Direct Access Files

The KEYED DATA LIST command is used to read specific records from direct access files. The variable definition portion of KEYED DATA LIST is the same as that described for DATA LIST (see Chapter 5). The only difference is that no slashes may appear within the definition of the variables (to denote multiple records) since only one record will be read. Four types of subcommands are available for KEYED DATA LIST:

• The FILE subcommand indicates the handle of the file described by the KEYED DATA LIST command (see Section E.4).
• The KEY subcommand specifies the numeric variable whose value will be used to read a record (see Section E.5).
• The IN subcommand creates in the result file a logical variable that flags whether a record was successfully read (see Section E.6).
• The TABLE and NOTABLE subcommands control printing of a summary table that describes the variable definitions (see Section E.7).

The KEYED DATA LIST command may appear in an input program or it may be used as part of the transformation language to change an existing active file. The fact that it may appear in a transformations program sets it apart from all the other SPSS-X input commands, such as GET and DATA LIST, which create new active files when used.

E

**E.4
FILE Subcommand**

Use the FILE subcommand to specify the handle for the data file described by the KEYED DATA LIST command. The file handle must have a corresponding FILE HANDLE command (or, in the case of the IBM OS environment, a corresponding DD statement in the JCL). For example, the specification

```
FILE HANDLE EMPL/ file specifications
KEYED DATA LIST FILE=EMPL KEY=#NXTCASE IN=#FOUND
        /YRHIRED 1-2 SEX 3 JOBCLASS 4
```

indicates that file EMPL is being described. If you omit the FILE subcommand, the KEYED DATA LIST command reads from the last file specified on an SPSS-X input command, such as DATA LIST or REPEATING DATA.

**E.5
KEY Subcommand**

The KEY subcommand is required. It specifies the variable whose value will be used as the direct access key. This variable must already exist as the result of a prior DATA LIST, KEYED DATA LIST, GET, or transformation command. It can be a permanent variable or a scratch variable. For example, the specification

```
FILE HANDLE EMPL/ file specifications
KEYED DATA LIST FILE=EMPL KEY=#NXTCASE IN=#FOUND
        /YRHIRED 1-2 SEX 3 JOBCLASS 4
```

indicates that the value of the existing scratch variable #NXTCASE will be used as the direct access key. The value of this variable must be an integer between 1 and the number of records in the file.

**E.6
IN Subcommand**

The IN subcommand is also required. It specifies a numeric variable whose value is set by the KEYED DATA LIST command according to whether or not the specified record is found. The value of the variable is 1, if the record is successfully read, or 0, if the record is not found. The variable can be a permanent or a scratch variable. For example, the specification

```
FILE HANDLE EMPL/ file specifications
KEYED DATA LIST FILE=EMPL KEY=#NXTCASE IN=#FOUND
        /YRHIRED 1-2 SEX 3 JOBCLASS 4
```

creates the logical scratch variable #FOUND whose value will be 1 if the record indicated by the key value in #NXTCASE is found or 0 if the record does not exist. If the record does not exist, KEYED DATA LIST does no further processing and the values of the variables YRHIRED, SEX, and JOBCLASS do not change. If the record can be read, the values of the variables are updated.

**E.7
TABLE and NOTABLE
Subcommands**

The TABLE and NOTABLE subcommands are optional. These subcommands control whether or not SPSS-X displays a table that summarizes your variable definitions. The TABLE subcommand is the default. To suppress the table, specify NOTABLE, as in

```
FILE HANDLE EMPL/ file specifications
KEYED DATA LIST FILE=EMPL KEY=#NXTCASE IN=#FOUND NOTABLE
        /YRHIRED 1-2 SEX 3 JOBCLASS 4
```

**E.8
Reading Direct Access
Files**

The following example illustrates one application of the KEYED DATA LIST command to read a direct access file. The purpose of this job is to sample 1 out of every 25 records in an employee file. The record numbers are generated by the SPSS-X transformation language; they are not based on data taken from another file. Since the job generates cases, an input program is required. The SPSS-X commands are:

```
FILE HANDLE      EMPL/ file specifications
INPUT PROGRAM
COMPUTE          #INTRVL = TRUNC(UNIF(49))+1    /* Mean interval = 25
COMPUTE          #NXTCASE = #NXTCASE+#INTRVL    /* Next record number
COMPUTE          #EOF = #NXTCASE > 1000         /* End of file check
DO IF            #EOF
+   END FILE
ELSE
+   KEYED DATA LIST  FILE=EMPL, KEY=#NXTCASE, IN=#FOUND, NOTABLE/
                     YRHIRED 1-2 SEX 3 JOBCLASS 4
+   DO IF        #FOUND
+       END CASE                                /* Return a case
+   END IF
END IF
END INPUT PROGRAM
EXECUTE
```

- The FILE HANDLE command (see Chapter 5) defines the handle for the data file to be read by the KEYED DATA LIST command.

- The INPUT PROGRAM and END INPUT PROGRAM commands begin and end the block of commands that build cases from the input file (see Chapter 14).

- The first two COMPUTE statements determine the number of the next record to be selected. This is done in two steps. First, the integer portion is taken from the sum of 1 and a uniform pseudo random number between 1 and 49. The result is a mean interval of 25. Second, the variable #NXTCASE is added to this number to generate the next record number. This record number, #NXTCASE, will be used for the key variable on the KEYED DATA LIST command. The third COMPUTE creates a logical scratch variable, #EOF, that has a value of 0 if the record number is less than or equal to 1000, or 1 if the value of the record number is greater than 1000. (See Chapter 7.)

- The DO IF—END IF structure controls the building of cases. If the record number is out of range, #EOF equals 1, and the END FILE command tells SPSS-X to stop reading data and end the file (see Chapter 14). If the record number is within range, #EOF equals 0, and control passes to the next level of the DO IF—END IF structure. (See Chapter 9.)

- If the record number is within range, the record is read via KEYED DATA LIST using the value of #NXTCASE (see Sections E.4 through E.7). A case is generated if the record exists (#FOUND equals 1).

- The EXECUTE command causes the transformations to be executed (see Chapter 3).

This example illustrates the differences between a DATA LIST command, which always reads the next record in a file, and a KEYED DATA LIST command, which reads a record specified by a unit origin integer. The example also shows that the KEYED DATA LIST command depends on another command to generate the number of the record to be read.

E.9
KEYED FILES

Of the many kinds of keyed files, the ones to which SPSS-X can provide access are generally known as *indexed sequential files*. A file of this kind is basically a sequential file in which the host system maintains an index so that the file may be processed either sequentially or selectively. In effect, such a file consists of an underlying data file that is accessed by way of a file of index entries. The file of index entries may, for example, contain the fact that data record 797 is associated with social security number 476-77-1359. Depending on the implementation, the underlying data may or may not be maintained in sequential order.

The key for each record in the file is generally composed of one or more pieces of information found within the record. An example of a complex key is a customer's last name and house number, plus the consonants in the street name, plus the zip code, plus a uniqueness digit in case there are duplicates. Regardless of the information contained in the key, SPSS-X treats it as a character string.

E

Some implementations have keyed files with more than one key associated with each record. That is, the records in a file can be identified according to different types of information. Although the "primary" key for a file normally must be unique, sometimes the "secondary" keys need not be. Thus, the records in an employee file might be identified by social security number and job classification.

E.10
KEYED DATA LIST
Command for Keyed Files

To read specific records from keyed files, SPSS-X uses a variation of the KEYED DATA LIST command described in Sections E.3 through E.7. The only difference for keyed files is in the use of the KEY subcommand (see Section E.11). The FILE, IN, TABLE and NOTABLE subcommands, and the variable definition portion of the KEYED DATA LIST command operate in the same way as when used to read direct access files. Just as for direct access files, the KEYED DATA LIST command for keyed files can also occur in either an input program or as part of the transformation language.

E.11
KEY Subcommand

As is the case for direct access files, the KEY subcommand is required for keyed files, and it specifies the variable whose values will be used as the keys for the records to be read. This variable must already exist as the result of a prior DATA LIST, KEYED DATA LIST, GET, or transformation command. Unlike the variable for direct access files, the variable for keyed files must be a string variable. The specification

```
FILE HANDLE EMPL/ file specifications
KEYED DATA LIST FILE=EMPL KEY=SSN IN=#OK
      / BIRTH HIRED(2DATE9)
```

indicates that SSN is a string variable whose value will be used to read a record. Where the keys on a file are inherently numbers, such as social security numbers, the STRING function may be used to assign a value to the key variable (see Section E.12).

E.12
Reading Single Records
from Keyed Files

The following example illustrates the use of the KEYED DATA LIST command to read selected records from a keyed file. This example shows how existing cases can be updated on the basis of information read from a keyed file. The SPSS-X commands are:

```
FILE HANDLE STUDENTS/ file specifications
FILE HANDLE COURSES/ file specifications
GET FILE=STUDENTS/KEEP=AGE,SEX,COURSE
STRING #KEY(A4)
COMPUTE #KEY = STRING(COURSE,N4)   /* Create a string key
KEYED DATA LIST FILE=COURSES KEY=#KEY IN=#FOUND NOTABLE
      /PERIOD 13 CREDITS 16
SELECT IF #FOUND
LIST
```

- The first FILE HANDLE command references the SPSS-X system file that contains a course identification for each student. The course identification will be used as the key for selecting one record from a file of courses. The second FILE HANDLE command references the file of courses. (See Chapter 5.)
- The GET command defines the data file to SPSS-X and selects the variables needed for the analysis. (See Chapter 6.)
- The STRING and COMPUTE commands transform the course identification from a numeric value to a string for use as a key. (See Chapter 8.)
- The KEYED DATA LIST command uses the value of the newly created string variable #KEY as the key to search the course file. If a record that matches the value of #KEY is found, #FOUND is set to 1; otherwise it is set to 0. Note that the KEYED DATA LIST appears outside an input program in this example.

- If the course file contains the requested record, #FOUND equals 1, and the case is selected via the SELECT IF command; otherwise, the case will be dropped. (See Chapter 11.)
- The LIST command lists the values of the cases. (See Chapter 31.)

Whether this program represents an efficient solution to the problem at hand depends heavily on the percentage of the records in the course file that need to be accessed. If fewer than 10% of the course file records are read, the use of KEYED DATA LIST probably makes sense. As the percentage of the records that are read increases, a method more likely to be efficient is reading the entire course file and combining it with the student file via the MATCH command. There are no hard and fast rules for determining which method is more economical, but you should be aware that direct retrieval from a keyed file can be costly.

E.13
CONTROLLED SEQUENTIAL ACCESS TO KEYED FILES

Where permitted by the host system, you can use the POINT command to establish a keyed file location at which sequential access is to begin (or resume). In this way, you can read only selected portions of a file rather than read all of it and then use one of the SPSS-X data selection commands to limit the file to the portion you wish to analyze.

E.14
POINT Command

Use the POINT command to read a key-sequenced data set sequentially from a point that a key value controls. The next DATA LIST command executed after the POINT command (for the same file) will read a record whose key value is at least as great as that of the specified key. The POINT command can be used more than once to change the order of retrieval during processing.

POINT must precede the corresponding DATA LIST, and because it must appear in an input program, you cannot use POINT to add cases to an existing file. Two subcommands are available for the POINT command: the FILE subcommand (see Section E.15) and the required KEY subcommand (see Section E.16).

E.15
FILE Subcommand

Use the FILE subcommand to specify the handle for the file to be read by the POINT command. The file handle must have a corresponding FILE HANDLE command (or in the case of the IBM OS environment, a corresponding DD statement in the JCL). For example, the specification

```
FILE HANDLE DRIVERS/ file specifications
POINT FILE=DRIVERS/KEY=#FRSTAGE
```

indicates that file DRIVERS is to be read. If you omit the FILE subcommand, the POINT command will apply to the last file named on an SPSS-X input command, such as DATA LIST.

E.16
KEY Subcommand

The KEY subcommand is required. It specifies the variable whose value will be used as the file key for determining where sequential retrieval (via DATA LIST) will begin or resume. This variable must be a string variable, and it must already exist as the result of a prior DATA LIST, KEYED DATA LIST, GET, or transformation command. It can be a permanent or a scratch variable. For example, the specification

```
FILE HANDLE DRIVERS/ file specifications
POINT FILE=DRIVERS/KEY=#FRSTAGE
```

indicates that the value of the existing scratch variable #FRSTAGE will be used as the file key.

E

If the file contains a record whose key exactly matches the value of the KEY variable, the next DATA LIST command will read that record, the second DATA LIST command will read the next record, and so on. If an exact match is not found, the results depend on the operating system being used. For example, in IBM implementations, reading will begin or resume at the record that has the next higher key. Also in IBM implementations, if the key variable's value is a string that is shorter than the file's key, the key variable's value is logically extended with the lowest character in the collating sequence. For example, if the value of the key variable is the single letter M, retrieval would begin or resume at the first record that had a key (regardless of length) beginning with the letter M or a character higher in the collating sequence.

E.17
Reading Sequential Records from Keyed Files

When using the POINT command, you must realize that the record read with the following DATA LIST command will have a key whose value is equal to or greater than the contents of the variable specified on the KEY subcommand. To prevent an infinite loop, in which the same record is read again and again, either the contents of the key variable must change from case to case or provision must be made to execute the POINT command only once. You should also be aware that the POINT command provides no feedback on whether the file contains a record that exactly matches the specified key. Only by examining the contents of the record read via the subsequent DATA LIST command can a missing-record condition be detected.

The following example illustrates the use of the POINT command to select a subset of records from a keyed file. The example illustrates how to execute the POINT command for only the first case. The file contains information about traffic violations, and it uses the individual's age as the key. Ages between 26 and 30 are selected. The SPSS-X commands are:

```
FILE HANDLE    DRIVERS/ file specifications
INPUT PROGRAM
STRING         #FRSTAGE(A2)
DO IF          #FRSTAGE = ' '       /* First case check
+  COMPUTE     #FRSTAGE = '26'      /* Initial key
+  POINT       FILE=DRIVERS/ KEY=#FRSTAGE
END IF
DATA LIST      FILE=DRIVERS NOTABLE/
               AGE 19-20(A) SEX 21(A) TICKETS 12-13
DO IF          AGE > '30'           /* We want 26 through 30.
+  END FILE
END IF
END INPUT PROGRAM
LIST
```

- The FILE HANDLE command specifies the file handle DRIVERS (see Chapter 5).

- The INPUT PROGRAM and END INPUT PROGRAM commands begin and end the block of commands that build cases (see Chapter 14). The POINT command must appear in an input program.

- The STRING command declares the string variable #FRSTAGE, whose value will be used as the key on the POINT command (see Chapter 8). Since string variables are initialized as blanks, this value can be used as a first case check.

- The first DO IF—END IF structure is only executed if no records have been read, when #FRSTAGE is equal to its initialized value (see Chapter 9). IF the value of #FRSTAGE is equal to a blank, the COMPUTE statement resets #FRSTAGE to the value of the initial key (see Chapter 8). This value is set to 26 because only the ages from 26 to 30 are to be selected.

- The POINT command is executed only during the generation of the first case, and it causes the first execution of the DATA LIST command to read a record whose key is at least 26 (see Sections E.14 though E.16).

- The DATA LIST command reads the variables AGE, SEX, and TICKETS from the file DRIVERS (See Chapter 5).

• The second DO IF—END IF structure executes an END FILE command as soon as a record is read that contains a driver's age greater than 30 (See Chapter 9).

There are three things to notice about this example. First, the POINT command is part of an input program, as is required. Second, the actual reading of data from the keyed file is accomplished via a DATA LIST command rather than via a direct access input command. Third, any feedback about the key of the record read is obtained from the contents of the record.

E.18
IBM VSAM FILES

The Virtual Storage Access Method (VSAM) is an IBM facility for the management of data. This facility exists in parallel with other (older) data management facilities, and its assets are integrity and efficiency. Individual files existing under the general umbrella of VSAM are organized in one of three ways corresponding to sequential, direct, and keyed files: entry sequenced, relative record, and key sequenced data sets. VSAM also permits the establishment and maintenance of multiple keys through an arrangement known as an alternate index.

Entry Sequenced Data Set (ESDS). ESDS files are basically sequential files that are managed through VSAM. Other than requiring somewhat different job control language considerations, an ESDS may be read or written by SPSS-X like any sequential file. An ESDS is referenced by its cluster name.

Relative Record Data Set (RRDS). The RRDS file corresponds to the SPSS-X direct access file. Each record in an RRDS is accessible by its unit origin record number, specified on a KEYED DATA LIST command via a numeric key variable. The entire file may also be read or written sequentially; however, direct update is not supported by SPSS-X. Reference to an RRDS is via the cluster name.

Key Sequenced Data Set (KSDS). The KSDS file corresponds to the SPSS-X notion of a keyed file. Each record in a KSDS is uniquely identified by an alphanumeric key and may be selectively read via a KEYED DATA LIST command that specifies a string key variable. It is also possible to read or write a KSDS sequentially; however, direct update, record deletion, and record insertion are not supported by SPSS-X. Controlled sequential input is facilitated by the POINT command. A KSDS is referenced via its cluster name.

Alternate Index. This is a feature that permits the construction and maintenance of more than a single key structure for one file. It also permits the association of keys with an ESDS. From the point of view of SPSS-X, a data set that is accessed via an alternate index has the same properties as a KSDS and can be selectively read via a KEYED DATA LIST command that specifies a string key variable. It is also possible to read a data set in alternate index sequence and to modify this sequence by use of the POINT command. Access to a file via its alternate index is through a path name. The alternate index itself constitutes a cluster.

E.19
Sequential Access of VSAM Files

In general, SPSS-X can process all three types of VSAM files sequentially. This means that an entire ESDS, KSDS, or RRDS may be read via a DATA LIST command. In addition, a data set may be read sequentially in alternate index sequence. Output to an ESDS is supported for virtually all SPSS-X files except the display file. That is, the OUTFILE parameter for PRINT, WRITE, SAVE, AGGREGATE, and similar commands can reference a file handle associated with an ESDS. A system file saved into an ESDS can subsequently be retrieved via GET, ADD, or MATCH.

It is also possible to write sequentially into a KSDS or an RRDS. However, you must have a significant knowledge of VSAM to grasp what it means to write such a file and to ensure that the record formats, key lengths, and key positions are compatible with the target file. Creating one of these data sets would normally be done via the WRITE command.

E.20
Job Control Language
Considerations

The following discussion offers a simplified overview of the interface between SPSS-X and VSAM via the host system's job control language. It does not mention the steps necessary to define and create VSAM files. Thus, it is oriented solely toward reading existing VSAM files. While the mechanism for communicating the information to the host system differs a bit across systems, basically three pieces of information are required for reading an existing file: its name, the name of its catalog, and its password. In many cases, only the file's name is required.

E.21
Considerations for IBM OS

Under OS, the JCL considerations for reading VSAM files are almost identical to those for reading any sequential disk file. The file must be referenced on a DD statement that will typically contain only a ddname, a dsname, and a disposition. Operands such as volume, unit, space, and DCB are omitted since the associated information is contained in the catalog. Note that the dsname references either a cluster or, in the case of access via an alternate index, a path.

A VSAM data set is always referenced via a catalog. However, the reference is not always via the "master" catalog. When a data set is cataloged in a subsidiary catalog, it is necessary to communicate the name of the subsidiary catalog to the host system via either a JOBCAT DD statement or a STEPCAT DD statement. Since a catalog is itself a VSAM file, these DD statements have the same simple format, that is, a ddname, a dsname, and disposition.

Since VSAM requires dynamic memory at execution time, it is necessary to reserve some space via the EXEC statement PARM operand. As a starting point, you can reserve 64K bytes for VSAM. To give 64K to VSAM, enter PARM= 112K since 48K is the default for host system consumption.

If a VSAM data set has a password, you must communicate that password via a FILE HANDLE command. The FILE HANDLE command must precede the first reference to the file. The FILE HANDLE command consists of the file handle followed by a slash followed by the PASSWORD subcommand. The handle must match both the ddname on the DD statement and the file handle on the DATA LIST, KEYED DATA LIST, or similar command. The password is enclosed in single quotes. For example, the command

```
FILE HANDLE    RAWDATA/ PASSWORD = 'XXYYZ'
```

assumes that a //RAWDATA DD ... statement appears in the JCL and that the password is XXYYZ.

The following illustrates a sample OS job that reads a password-protected ESDS cataloged in a user catalog:

```
//MYJOB     JOB <local accounting information>
//   EXEC SPSSX,PARM=112K
//STEPCAT   DD DSNAME=USERCAT.MINE,DISP=SHR
//RAWDATA   DD DSNAME=MY.RAWDATA,DISP=SHR
//SYSIN     DD *
FILE HANDLE    RAWDATA/ PASSWORD = 'XXYYZ'
DATA LIST      FILE=RAWDATA/ AGE 1-2 SEX 3 RACE 4
LIST
```

As this job shows, reading from a VSAM file differs very little from reading from a sequential disk data set. If MY.RAWDATA were cataloged in the master catalog and did not have a password, the only VSAM-specific consideration would be to increase the memory allocated via the PARM operand on the EXEC statement. That is, the STEPCAT DD statement and the FILE HANDLE command would be unnecessary.

E.22
Considerations for IBM DOS

Reading from a VSAM file is also easy under DOS. Typically, each file requires a simple DLBL JCL statement plus an SPSS-X FILE HANDLE command. The DLBL statement contains the file name, the file label, and the positional parameter VSAM.

If, as is frequently the case, the VSAM file is not cataloged in the "master" catalog, it is necessary to define the user catalog. A user catalog is defined on a DLBL statement with the special file name IJSYSUC.

Under DOS, it is always necessary to enter an SPSS-X FILE HANDLE command for each VSAM file to be accessed. This command must appear among the SPSS-X commands prior to the first reference to the file. The FILE HANDLE command consists of the file handle, a slash, the DTYPE subcommand, a slash, and the optional PASSWORD subcommand. The handle must be the same as the file name on the corresponding DLBL statement and the file handle on the DATA LIST, GET, or similar command. The DTYPE subcommand is required, and it must specify VSAM. The PASSWORD subcommand is optional, and, if present, must specify the file's password enclosed in single quotes. For example, the command

```
FILE HANDLE   RAWDATA/ DTYPE=VSAM/ PASSWORD='XXYYZ'
```

assumes that a // DLBL RAWDATA ... statement appears in the JCL and that the password is XXYYZ.

If any VSAM files are read by an SPSS-X job, provision must be made to reserve sufficient GETVIS space for VSAM itself. This space is reserved via the EXEC statement's SIZE operand.

The following DOS job reads an ESDS as a sequential raw data file:

```
// JOB <local accounting information>
// DLBL       IJSYSUC,'USERCAT.MINE',,VSAM
// DLBL       RAWDATA,'MY.RAWDATA',,VSAM
// EXEC PROC=SPSSX
// EXEC SPSSX,SIZE=500K
FILE HANDLE    RAWDATA/ DTYPE=VSAM/ PASSWORD='XXYYZ'
DATA LIST      FILE=RAWDATA/ AGE 1-2 SEX 3 RACE 4
LIST
```

E.23
Considerations for IBM CMS

Under CMS, there are two mechanisms available for defining files to be used by SPSS-X: a host system FILEDEF command and an SPSS-X FILE HANDLE command. Either mechanism will work when reading VSAM files.

If you choose to use the FILEDEF command, it is necessary to recognize that VSAM files are located on simulated DOS minidisks and must be defined by the DLBL command, which has the same intent as the FILEDEF command has for real or simulated OS commands. If you don't care about OS and DOS, just remember that VSAM files are defined via a DLBL while all other files are defined via a FILEDEF. The following simplified DLBL syntax is sufficient for most SPSS-X applications:

```
DLBL <ddname> <mode> DSN <dsname> ( VSAM )
```

The ddname is restricted to seven or fewer characters and must be the same as the file handle used within the SPSS-X job. The mode is the mode letter at which the minidisk is accessed. The dsname is the full data set name using blanks where the actual data set named uses decimal points. For instance, MY.RAW.DATA would be coded as three separate words: MY RAW DATA. The VSAM option is not always required.

CMS has no inherent knowledge of where the master VSAM catalog is located. At some time during a terminal session, the name of the catalog can be communicated via a DLBL command referencing the special ddname IJSYSCT.

E

Similarly, the name of a user catalog can be communicated via the ddname IJSYSUC.

If you define a password-protected VSAM file via a DLBL command, there are two mechanisms for supplying the password. First, you can simply wait for the file to be opened, at which time the system will prompt you for the password at your terminal. Alternatively, you can include a simple FILE HANDLE command as part of your SPSS-X input. In this case, the FILE HANDLE command consists of the file handle, a slash, and the optional PASSWORD subcommand. The handle is the same as the ddname on the DLBL statement and the file handle on the subsequent DATA LIST, KEYED DATA LIST, or similar command. The password consists of up to eight characters enclosed in single quotes. For example, the command

```
FILE HANDLE    RAWDATA/ PASSWORD = 'XXYYZ'
```

assumes that a DLBL RAWDATA ... statement is issued prior to SPSS-X and that the password is XXYYZ.

The following is an example of CMS and SPSS-X commands used to read a password-protected VSAM file. The CMS commands are:

```
DLBL IJSYSCT D DSN VSAM MASTER CATALOG
DLBL IJSYSUC V DSN USERCAT MINE
DLBL RAWDATA V DSN MY RAWDATA ( VSAM
```

and the SPSS-X commands are:

```
FILE HANDLE    RAWDATA/ PASSWORD = 'XXYYZ'
DATA LIST      FILE=RAWDATA/ AGE 1-2 SEX 3 RACE 4
LIST
```

Notice that the DLBL commands for the master and user catalogs do not include the VSAM option. This option is implied for ddnames IJSYSCT and IJSYSUC.

As an alternative to the use of the host system's DLBL command, the CMS user can define VSAM files completely within the SPSS-X command stream with FILE HANDLE commands. Since most of the information relative to a VSAM file is available from the catalog, the syntax of the FILE HANDLE command is as follows:

```
FILE HANDLE handle/NAME=dsname/FMODE=mode/ACSMETH=VSAM/
[PASSWORD=password]
```

where the handle is restricted to seven or fewer characters and is the name by which the file is referenced by subsequent DATA LIST and similar commands. The NAME subcommand specifies a dsname that is enclosed in quotes and uses decimal points rather than spaces as separators since it is essentially a DOS file name rather than a CMS file name. The dsname does not include the mode letter for its minidisk because the mode letter is supplied via the required FMODE subcommand. The ACSMETH subcommand is required, and it must specify VSAM. The optional PASSWORD subcommand specifies the file's password enclosed in single quotes. The following is an example of an appropriate FILE HANDLE command:

```
FILE HANDLE RAWDATA/NAME='MY.RAWDATA'/FMODE=V/ACSMETH=VSAM
            /PASSWORD='XXYYZ'
```

SPSS-X actually issues a DLBL command when a FILE HANDLE like the one shown above is used. It is possible to take advantage of this fact to incorporate the definitions of the master and user catalogs within the SPSS-X command stream. A FILE HANDLE command for handle IJSYSCT will generate a DLBL for the master catalog, and a FILE HANDLE for handle IJSYSUC will generate a DLBL for a user catalog.

The following set of commands illustrates the reading of a password-protected ESDS that is cataloged in a user catalog:

```
FILE HANDLE    IJSYSCT/NAME='MASTER.CATALOG'/FMODE=D/ACSMETH=VSAM
FILE HANDLE    IJSYSUC/NAME='CATALOG.MINE'/FMODE=V/ACSMETH=VSAM
FILE HANDLE    RAWDATA/NAME='MY.RAWDATA'/FMODE=V/ACSMETH=VSAM/
               PASSWORD='XXYYZ'
DATA LIST      FILE=RAWDATA/ AGE 1-2 SEX 3 RACE 4
LIST
```

The first two FILE HANDLE commands define the master and user catalogs that reside on the D and V disks, respectively. The third FILE HANDLE defines handle RAWDATA as being the user's VSAM file.

E.24
IBM DIRECT ACCESS FILES

Under the IBM OS, DOS, and CMS operating systems, SPSS-X is able to treat a subset of non-VSAM files as direct access. For all three systems, files containing fixed-length unblocked records without keys may be read via the direct access KEYED DATA LIST.

In the case of OS, the files to be read are restricted to those with a direct or sequential organization. Partitioned data sets are not supported.

For DOS, the file must occupy only a single extent. However, the file may reside on either a "count key data" device, such as a 3340, or a "fixed block architecture" device, such as a 3370.

For CMS, there are no restrictions except that the file must contain fixed-length records.

Appendix F   VAX Data Types

Several additional data types are supported in the VAX/VMS environment. Table F.0 defines the formats that support these data types. The table also redefines several SPSS-X formats that differ from the standards given in Chapter 5. For each format, the table below gives:

- The format name.
- The format width (number of digits represented).
- The field width (the physical byte width of the field).
- The number of real or implied decimal places, if applicable.

The table also indicates the default print and write formats assigned to values read on input. The formats are described here in their FORTRAN style, but they can also be used in the column style, as described in Chapter 5.

In the table below, *w* indicates format width and *d* indicates decimal width. Input numeric values beyond the limits of $10E-38$ or $10E+38$ will be transformed to SYSMIS. Numbers that overflow their format will be transformed to SYSMIS on output.

Table F.0   Available data formats

Description	Format	Format width	Field width	Decimal range	Print/Write default
Printable numeric formats					
Standard numeric	Fw.d,Fw	1-31 chars	1-31 bytes	d=max(w)	F
Restricted numeric	Nw	1-31 chars	1-31 bytes	NONE	F
Scientific notation	Ew.d,Ew	1-31 chars	1-31 bytes	d=max(w)	E
Commas in numbers	COMMAw.d, COMMAw	1-31 chars	1-31 bytes	d=max(w)	COMMA
Dollar sign, comma	DOLLARw.d, DOLLARw	1-31 chars	1-31 bytes	d=max(w)	DOLLAR
Hexadecimal of PIB	PIBHEXw	2,4,8,16 chars	1-16 bytes	NONE	F
Octal of PIB	PIBOCTw	1-11 chars	1-11 bytes	NONE	F
Nonprintable numeric formats					
Zoned decimal	Zw.d,Zw	1-31 digits	1-31 bytes	d=max(w)	F
Numeric left separate	LEFTSEPw.d, LEFTSEPw	1-30 digits	1-31 bytes	d=max(w)	F
Numeric left overpunch	LEFTOVRw.d, LEFTOVRw	1-31 digits	1-31 bytes	d=max(w)	F
Numeric right separate	RIGHTSEPw.d, RIGHTSEPw	1-30 digits	1-31 bytes	d=max(w)	F
Numeric right overpunch	RIGHTOVRw.d, RIGHTOVRw	1-31 digits	1-31 bytes	d=max(w)	F
Numeric unsigned	UNSIGNEDw.d, UNSIGNEDw	1-31 digits	1-31 bytes	d=max(w)	F

Table F.0 Available data formats *continued*

Description	Format	Format width	Field width	Decimal range	Print/Write default
Signed integer (Integer binary)	IBw.d, IBw	1,2,4,8,16 bytes	1,2,4,8,16 bytes	d=max(#digits in integer range	E
	BYTE, BYTE.d, BYTEw.d	1 byte	1 byte	d=max(3)	F
	WORD, WORD.d, WORDw.d	2 bytes	2 bytes	d=max(5)	F
	LONG, LONG.d, LONGw.d	4 bytes	4 bytes	d=max(9)	F
	QUAD, QUAD.d, QUADw.d	8 bytes	8 bytes	d=max(20)	F
	OCTA, OCTA.d, OCTAw.d	16 bytes	16 bytes	d=max(31)	E
Unsigned integer (Positive integer binary)	PIBw.d,PIBw	1,2,4,8,16 bytes	1,2,4,8,16 bytes	d=max(#digits in integer range	E
	UBYTE, UBYTE.d UBYTEw.d	1 byte	1 byte	d=max(3)	F
	UWORD, UWORD.d UWORDw.d	2 bytes	2 bytes	d=max(5)	F
	ULONG, ULONG.d ULONGw.d	4 bytes	4 bytes	d=max(9)	F
	UQUAD, UQUAD.d, UQUADw.d	8 bytes	8 bytes	d=max(20)	F
	UOCTA, UOCTA.d UOCTAw.d	16 bytes	16 bytes	d=max(38)	E
Packed decimal	Pw.d, Pw	1-31 digits	1-16 bytes	d=max(w)	F
Floating point (Real binary)	RBw	4,8 bytes	4,8 bytes	NONE	F
	FLOAT	4 bytes	4 bytes	NONE	F
	DFLOAT	8 bytes	8 bytes	NONE	F
	GFLOAT	8 bytes	8 bytes	NONE	F
	HFLOAT	16 bytes	16 bytes	NONE	F
Cobol intermediate	CIT	12 bytes	12 bytes	NONE	F
String formats					
Hexadecimal character	AHEXw	1-255 chars	2-510 bytes	N/A	A
EBCDIC character	EBCDICw	1-255 bytes	1-255 bytes	N/A	A
Varying length character string	VARYING	1-253 chars	2-255 bytes	N/A	A
Date and time formats					
ASCII time	ASCTIME	1-255 chars	1-255 chars	N/A	ASCTIME
ASCII delta time	ASCDELTA	1-255 chars	1-255 chars	N/A	ASCDELTA
Binary time	BINTIME	N/A	N/A	N/A	ASCTIME
Binary delta time	BINDELTA	N/A	N/A	N/A	ASCDELTA
UIC formats					
UIC	UICw	1-255 chars	1-255 chars	N/A	UIC
Rights Identifier	RIGHTSIDw	1-255 chars	1-255 chars	N/A	RIGHTSID

Notes: w=Format width (not necessarily the same as the field width). d=Decimal width. Numbers read that exceed 10E-38 or 10E+38 will be transformed to SYSMIS on input.

F.1
PRINTABLE NUMERICS

Variables with printable numeric formats contain no special characters (for example, linefeeds or carriage returns) and can therefore be read directly when printed or written to a file. For all of these formats, the specified width (w) is the actual physical byte width of the field and, when applicable, the specified decimal value (d) is the number of implied decimal places. The following conventions apply to these format types:

- User-defined missing values are output like any other value (that is, their missing status is ignored).
- Blanks read on input are converted to whatever value is the default for your installation or the value specified on the SET BLANKS command. (The default value is usually SYSMIS. Use the SHOW BLANKS command to display this value.)
- Exponentials (E, +, −) or decimal points embedded in numbers on input override the format specified.
- Numbers which overflow their format width are first condensed by removing punctuation or using scientific notation. If the width is still exceeded, the field is converted to zeros.

Standard Numeric (Fw.d). This format can be used to directly represent:

- Real values between -1E-38 and -1E38.
- The value 0.
- Real values between 1E-38 and 1E38.

Since SPSS-X uses DFLOAT as an internal data type, only 15 digits of precision are available (although numbers with more than 15 digits can be read or written).

Restricted Numeric (Nw). This format can be used to directly represent any integer value between 0 and 1E31. As of Release 3.1, it allows decimals on the VAX. It understands implied decimals (1234 becomes 12.34 when write and print formats are f5.2). The default write and print formats are f.
value 1 when printed or written.

Scientific Notation (Ew.d). This format can be used for any value representable with the standard numeric format. The E format is used primarily for output, although exponentials embedded in numbers are interpreted correctly on input if a printable format with sufficient width to accommodate the entire exponential expression is used.

When listing, printing, or writing variables in E format, a minimum width of 6 is required since this format type will need at least one byte for the value, one byte for the exponential symbol (E), one byte for the sign of the exponent, two bytes for the exponent value (for example, 1E+02), and one byte for the sign (+ or −) of the entire expression. If an E format width less than 6 is used, it will be accepted, but all values will be listed, printed, or written in standard numeric format. Similarly, any value that is listed, printed, or written in E6 format or greater and is less than 6 digits will also be output with standard numeric format.

Commas in Numbers (COMMAw.d). The COMMA format can also be used for any value representable with standard numeric format. When input values contain embedded commas, this format is required and the specified width must be equal to the byte width of the field (including commas). If no commas are in the data, the format treats the values in the same way as standard numeric. On output, this format inserts a comma after every third digit reading from right to left and beginning at the decimal point (for example, the value 1000000 will be converted to 1,000,000 when output with the format COMMA9). Note that the number of commas to be inserted must be accounted for in the width specification; otherwise, standard numeric format will be used.

Dollars in Numbers (DOLLARw.d). This format works identically to the COMMA format except that a dollar sign ($) precedes the number in addition to the embedded commas. This format type is very useful for producing reports that contain dollar amounts.

Hexadecimal of PIB (PIBHEXw) and Octal of PIB (PIBOCTw). These format types can be used to represent any positive integer between 0 and 9E18 (approximately). They can be used to interpret a hexadecimal or octal value on input or to list, print, or write the hexadecimal or octal representation of a positive integer binary value on output. Since these formats are based on the positive integer binary representation of a value, their format widths are governed by the same rules as apply to the PIB format (see Section F.2). The maximum PIB width that can be represented is PIB8 with PIBHEX, PIB4 with PIBOCT.

F.2
NONPRINTABLE
NUMERICS

Variables with nonprintable numeric formats contain special characters (for example, carriage returns, linefeeds). The variables cannot be read directly when printed or written to a file except through the use of a text editor. When values with nonprintable numeric formats are read into SPSS-X, they are automatically assigned default PRINT and WRITE formats that allow you to read them directly. Usually the standard numeric format, F, is assigned. The original formats can be restored by using the PRINT FORMATS, WRITE FORMATS, or FORMATS command.

The width (w) specified for these formats is not always the actual physical byte width of the field. For consistency with the way certain formats are used outside of SPSS-X, the width for the decimal formats Z, LEFTSEP, RIGHTSEP, LEFTOVR, RIGHTOVR, UNSIGNED, and P is the number of digits represented by the data type rather than the physical byte width of the field. Note, however, that when the column style is used for specifying variables on the DATA LIST command, the actual physical location for the decimal value is given. For those format types where the number of digits does not equal the physical byte width of the field (LEFTSEP, RIGHTSEP, and P), the number of columns specified will not equal the actual format width shown in a DISPLAY DICTIONARY or in the DATA LIST table.

The specified decimal width (d) for these formats is a scalar that is used when SPSS-X converts the value to internal form. For example, the signed integer representation of 16.82 is IB2.2, or WORD.2. On output, this value would actually be changed to the WORD representation of 1682 (or 16.82×100). On input, the WORD representation of 1682 would be changed to 16.82 (or 1682/100) when IB2.2 or WORD.2 is used.

The following conventions apply to these format types:

• Missing values are converted to a field of zeros on output.

• Blanks read on input are interpreted as valid values where appropriate. When a blank is not a valid character for the format type, it is converted to whatever value is the default for your installation (usually SYSMIS) or the value specified on the SET BLANKS command.

• Values that overflow their format width will be converted to a field of zeros on output.

Zoned Decimal (Zw.d). This data type overpunches the sign in the rightmost byte. Thus, the format width will be equal to the field width of the variable. All values representable with the standard numeric format can be represented with the zoned format.

Numeric Left Separate (LEFTSEPw.d) and Numeric Right Separate(RIGHTSEPw.d). For both of these data types, one byte is always reserved for the sign (positive or negative); thus, the variable width (the number of digits) will always be one less than the actual physical field width. This difference is important when considering the use of column-style format specifications on the DATA LIST, WRITE, or PRINT command. For example, a variable with the format LEFTSEP7 will require an eight-byte physical field when specifying its column location on input or output. Thus, the following two DATA LIST statements are equivalent:

```
DATA LIST  /VARA VARB (LEFTSEP11,RIGHTSEP2)
DATA LIST  /VARA 1-12 (LEFTSEP) VARB 1-3 (RIGHTSEP2)
```

Numeric Left Overpunch (LEFTOVRw.d) and Numeric Right Overpunch(RIGHTOVRw.d). These decimal data types overpunch the sign in the leftmost and rightmost bytes, respectively. All values representable with the standard numeric format can be represented with the LEFTOVR and RIGHTOVR formats.

Numeric Unsigned (UNSIGNEDw.d). This decimal data type only accepts positive values between 0 and 1E38. Negative values will be converted to SYSMIS.

Signed Integers (IBw.d, BYTE.d, WORD.d, LONG.d, QUAD.d, andOCTA.d). These integer binary data types have a format width equal to the physical byte width of the field. The integer values representable by each data type are the following:

BYTE (IB1)   −128 thru +127
WORD (IB2)   −32768 thru +32767
LONG (IB4)   −2147483648 thru +2147483648
QUAD (IB8)   −3.69E19 thru +3.69E19
OCTA (IB16)   −1.06E37 thru +1.06E37

Unsigned Integers (PIBw.d, UBYTE.d, UWORD.d, ULONG.d, UQUAD.d,and UOCTA.d). These positive integer binary data types have a format width equal to the physical byte width of the field. Only positive integers can be represented with these formats. The values representable by each type are the following:

UBYTE (PIB1)   0 thru +255
UWORD (PIB2)   0 thru +65535
ULONG (PIB4)   0 thru +4294967296
UQUAD (PIB8)   0 thru +7.38E19
UOCTA (PIB16)   0 thru +1.40E38

Packed Decimal (Pw.d). In the case of P, the variable width will always be more than the byte width. The formula

Bytes = (width in digits + 1)/2

represents this relationship. For example, a P10 variable will have a physical byte width (for column-style specifications) of (10 + 1)/2, or 6 (the remainder is rounded up).

Floating Point (RBw, FLOAT, DFLOAT, GFLOAT, HFLOAT). These real binary or floating point data types have format widths equal to their physical byte width. Each data type can represent any floating point value between -1.7E38 and -.29E-38, the value 0, and any value between .29E-38 and 1.7E38. Each type, however, represents a different degree of precision. The precision of each format type is listed below:

FLOAT (RB4)   7 digits
DFLOAT (RB8)   16.5 digits
GFLOAT (8 bytes)   15 digits
HFLOAT (16 bytes)   16.5 digits

Cobol Intermediate Type (CIT). This is a special data type produced and used by COBOL. The format width for this type is always 12, the same as its physical byte width. Values that this type can represent are -10E99 to -10E-99, 0, and 10E-99 to 10E99. This format has 16.5 digits of precision (17 digits outside of SPSS-X) and has its own missing value, known as the COBOL indeterminate value. When missing values are output from SPSS-X using this data type, they are converted to this COBOL indeterminate value.

F.3
STRING FORMATS

The two string formats A and EBCDIC have a one-to-one correspondence between the variable width and physical byte width. The AHEX string format has a variable width equal to the number of characters represented by the hexadecimal string, and it has a physical byte width two times the variable width. Since varying length strings store the length of the string in the first two bytes, the variable width is also expressed in terms of characters represented with an actual physical byte width equal to the number of characters plus two.

F.4
DATE AND TIME FORMATS

The VAX/VMS version of SPSS-X includes four data types specifically for the VAX/VMS binary and ASCII absolute and delta times. The format widths for the binary formats are fixed and cannot be changed. The format widths for ASCII absolute and delta times can range between 1 and 255. The date and time delimiters (− and :) are included when calculating the correct format widths. Other date and time formats are available (see Chapter 5).

F.5
UPIB FORMAT

Unaligned positive integer binary format (UPIB) permits you to read positive integer format (PIB) fields that do not begin and end on byte boundaries. In VAX/VMS bytes, bits are numbered from 0 to 7 with 0 being the least significant. In IBM bytes, bits are numbered from 1 to 8 with 1 being the most significant. Therefore, the valid range of values for the bit specification in UPIB formats is 0 to 7 on the VAX and 1 to 8 on the IBM.

F.6
UIC FORMATS

Two additional data types (formats) have been added to SPSS-X on the VAX: UIC and RIGHTSID. These formats turn an unsigned integer value into an alpha string.

On output, UIC will turn a numeric value (such as those obtained for variable UIC in GET VMS ACCOUNTING) into a string of the form [group,member]. If no equivalent alpha string is found, the numeric form [m,n] will be output. SYSMIS is output as all blanks. On input, UIC will turn an alpha string of one of the forms [group,member], [member], or [m,n] into a numeric value. Strings of the form [member] or [group,member] for which no numeric equivalent is found will be set to SYSMIS.

RIGHTSID behaves in a similar manner except that numeric values are turned into rights identifiers (alpha strings such as DAVIS or SPSSXNET) on output. If no identifier is found, the hexadecimal numeric value is output, and SYSMIS is output as all blanks. Rights identifiers are turned into numeric values on input (if the identifier is not found, the value is set to SYSMIS).

Field widths can be specified on both UIC and RIGHTSID formats. The default field width is 16.

F

Appendix G Portable Files from SAS

TOSPSS

```
PROC TOSPSS* [DATA=ddname.membername]
             [SPSSFILE=file]
             [OUTPUT={SYSTEM  }]
                     {PORTABLE}
             [NOCOMPRESSION];
[VARIABLES varlist;]
[WEIGHT varname;]
```

* A SAS procedure.

TOSPSS is a SAS procedure for converting SAS data sets into SPSS-X system files or portable files. This appendix covers the creation of portable files. (Creation of system files is similar.)

SPSS-X, SPSS/PC+, and SPSS Data Entry II can read portable files. For information about transporting SPSS-X files, see Chapter 17. If you are downloading portable files to be read by SPSS/PC+, see the Command Reference section about IMPORT in the publication *SPSS/PC+*. See the publication *SPSS Data Entry II* for information about using portable files with this SPSS data-entry software.

G.1 FORM OF THE SAS PROCEDURE

To build files, the SAS procedure PROC TOSPSS uses one statement of the form

```
PROC TOSPSS options
```

The following are the available options:

DATA=filename *Input data set name.* This option gives the name of the SAS data set to be converted. If the DATA= option is not used, the SAS default is (_LAST_).

SPSSFILE=filename *Output file name.* If this option is omitted, the name TOSPSS is used.

OUTPUT=form *Form of output.* The specified form can be SYSTEM for an SPSS-X system file or PORTABLE for an SPSS-X portable file. If this option is omitted, an SPSS-X system file is produced.

NOCOMPRESSION *Uncompressed system file.* This option applies only to creating SPSS-X system files. Compression is a technique for reducing the amount of storage that SPSS-X system files need for numeric variables. The NOCOMPRESSION option is used when an uncompressed SPSS-X file is desired. If the option is omitted and OUTPUT=SYSTEM is specified, a compressed system file is produced.

G.2 STATEMENTS USED WITH TOSPSS

By default, TOSPSS copies all variables in the data set to the output file. To reduce the number of variables or to include a weighting variable, the following optional statements are available:

VARIABLES varlist *Variables to be included in the output.* The listed variables are those from the SAS file that are to be included in the portable file. A variable name should not be specified in the list more than once. If no VARIABLES statement is present, all the variables in the SAS data set are included in the portable file.

WEIGHT varname   *A variable designated as a weight variable in the output file.* If a variables statement is given, the weight variable must be mentioned in the list. TOSPSS no longer adds it as the last variable if it is not mentioned. If the WEIGHT statement is omitted, no variable in the output file is used as a weight variable.

G.3
DATA CONVERSION

When you read a file with the IMPORT command, SPSS-X and SPSS/PC+ give you the following information: the file label, the creation date and time, and the case weight variable (if used). The file label is obtained from the data set options used with the SAS DATA statement at the time the file was created. The creation date and time indicate when PROC TOSPSS was run; the date format is dd mm yy, and the time format is hh:mm:ss on a 24-hour clock. The case weight variable is that designated on the WEIGHT statement (see Section H.2).

The following sections describe how conversion of a SAS data set involves transformation of some of the data.

G.4
Variable Types

SAS, SPSS-X, and SPSS/PC+ have two types of variables: numeric and character string. When TOSPSS is used, SAS numeric variables are converted to SPSS-X or SPSS/PC+ numeric variables, and SAS character string variables become character string variables of the same length. A SAS variable with an associated date format is converted to the number of seconds from October 15, 1582, to the current date. A SAS variable with an associated date-time format is converted to the number of seconds from October 15, 1582, to the current date and time.

G.5
Variable Names

SAS, SPSS-X, and SPSS/PC+ use variable names that are up to eight characters long. SAS allows underscores but no other special characters in variable names. During conversion, underscores that are not in the first position usually become dollar signs. For a SAS variable name beginning with an underscore, a unique SPSS-X or SPSS/PC+ name is created that is as much like the SAS name as possible. When the SAS name has less than eight characters, the leading underscore is changed to a U, the symbol # is appended, and other underscores are changed to dollar signs. For other situations, a unique name is created by a more complicated rule. If a SAS variable name is the same as a reserved word in SPSS-X or SPSS/PC+ the # symbol is appended; for example, AND becomes AND#. For each variable name that is changed, a message is printed showing the original name and the converted result.

G.6
Variable Labels

Variables mentioned on a LABEL statement in the SAS DATA step that created the data set are assigned the corresponding labels in SPSS-X or SPSS/PC+.

G.7
Value Labels

Two conditions must be satisfied to obtain value label data from a SAS data set. First, a PROC FORMAT must have been used in the original SAS job with the DDNAME= option, thus saving the SAS-form value labels in the SASLIB library. Second, to associate the format and the value labels with variables in the data set, a FORMAT statement must have been used in the DATA step that created the data set. The corresponding format must be in SASLIB. If it is, the format is read and the table examined to see if there are ranges with the low value equal to the high value. If so, that value can have the associated label, which the table also contains. SPSS-X and SPSS/PC+ value labels assign labels to specific values, not ranges. When TOSPSS is used, SAS value labels with ranges are ignored.

G.8
Print and Write Formats

Format data are present in a SAS data set only if an INFORMAT or a FORMAT statement was used in the DATA step that created the data set. The FORMAT statement gives the format to use on output, so if there is an SPSS-X printable format, it is used as the print format. (SPSS/PC+ attempts to translate formats from SPSS-X that are not available in SPSS/PC+.) If there is no SPSS-X printable format, an attempt to use an INFORMAT is made. For the write format, the INFORMAT, if present, is preferred, but if no INFORMAT is present, an attempt is made to use the format on the FORMAT statement.

If no format information is available, F8.2 is used for numeric variables, and A is used for character string variables. The default for date variables is F14.0, and the default for date-time variables is F16.1.

G.9
Control Characters

When TOSPSS is used, control characters that are in variable labels, value labels, and string values are modified. Each character with a code between decimal 1 and 63 is converted to the character zero.

G.10
Missing Values

SAS has no user-defined missing values. All SAS missing codes are converted to the SPSS-X or SPSS/PC+ system-missing value.

G.11
TOSPSS EXAMPLES

The following examples illustrate the creation of portable files. Using the option OUTPUT=SYSTEM rather than OUTPUT=PORTABLE would result in the production of system files.

G.12
Example 1: Single Data Set Conversion

Suppose an existing SAS data set VOTE.SCORES is to be converted to a portable file. Preceding the PROC TOSPSS statement, the general form of the OS JCL would be:

```
//        JOB  <acct info>
//        EXEC SAS,USERLIB='<library holding TOSPSS >',
//        LIBRARY='<library holding FORMATS for value labels>'
//VOTE DD DSN='<description of data set VOTE>'
//TOSPSS DD <description of target SPSS file>
PROC TOSPSS DATA=VOTE.SCORES OUTPUT=PORTABLE  ;
```

The general form of the CMS statements would be:

```
  SAS
1.MS FILEDEF TOSPSS DISK fn ft fm ;
2.ROC TOSPSS DATA=VOTE.SCORES OUTPUT=PORTABLE ;
3.UN;
4.?/*
```

In this example (with either OS or CMS), all of the variables would be included in the resulting portable file, and no case-weight variable is designated.

G.13
Example 2: Multiple Conversions

Suppose that two SAS data sets, CONGRESS.HOUSE and CONGRESS.SENATE, are to be converted. Prior to the SAS step, the general form of the OS JCL would be:

```
//        EXEC SAS,USERLIB='<library containing TOSPSS>',
//        LIBRARY='<library holding FORMATS for value labels>'
//CONGRESS DD DSN='<description of dataset CONGRESS>'
//HOUSE  DD <description of the SPSS file for CONGRESS.HOUSE>
//SENATE DD <description of the SPSS file for CONGRESS.SENATE>
PROC TOSPSS SPSSFILE=HOUSE DATA=CONGRESS.HOUSE OUTPUT=PORTABLE ;
PROC TOSPSS SPSSFILE=SENATE DATA=CONGRESS.SENATE OUTPUT=PORTABLE ;
```

Under CMS, two filedefs would be required, corresponding to the two dd statements in the OS example.

Suppose there are four variables in the VOTE.SCORES data set, but only the variables PRICE and LOAD are to be included in the portable file. The statements

```
PROC TOSPSS DATA=VOTE.SCORES SPSSFILE=APPLE OUTPUT=PORTABLE ;
VARIABLES PRICE LOAD ;
```

could be used to produce a portable file with the two desired variables. Another statement could be added to designate a case weight variable. The statements

```
PROC TOSPSS DATA=VOTE.SCORES SPSSFILE=APPLE OUTPUT=PORTABLE ;
VARIABLES PRICE LOAD ;
WEIGHT LOAD ;
```

would produce a portable file with the two variables PRICE and LOAD and with LOAD designated as the case weight variable.

Appendix H Help for Old Friends

REFORMAT

```
REFORMAT   {ALPHA  } = varlist [/...]
           {NUMERIC}
```

This chapter summarizes the changes and enhancements made in Releases 2.2 and 3.0 of SPSS-X. Documentation for 2.1 and earlier releases of SPSS-X is provided in the *SPSS-X User's Guide,* 2nd ed.

Throughout this appendix, assume all changes were made in Release 3.0 unless they are specifically identified as 2.2 changes.

H.1
RELEASE 3.0

The following sections describe the new facilities and procedures in SPSS-X.

H.2
New Facilities

currency formats The SET command has 5 new subcommands that enable you to customize currency formats for you own application. (See Chapter 4.)

data formats There are two new formats in SPSS-X: DOTw.d format, where the roles of the comma and dot (period) are reversed, and PCTw.d format, which adds a percent sign (%) to all values. (See Chapter 5.)

interactive-x You can now run SPSS-X in an interactive as well as a batch mode. Using SPSS-X interactively means you can have each command execute immediately, instead of submitting batch command files. (See Chapter 3.)

MATRIX DATA Creates an active file from matrix materials entered in raw data form. Data may be inline or in an external file. (See Chapter 13.)

MCONVERT Converts a correlation matrix and vector of standard deviations to a covariance matrix, or a covariance matrix to a correlation matrix and vector of standard deviations. (See Chapter 13.)

H.3
New Procedures

Release 3.0 introduces two new commands, as well as a full set of add-on procedures for performing time series analysis:

CNLR Uses a sequential quadratic programming algorithm, with a quadratic programming subproblem to perform non-linear regression analysis. (See Chapter 36.)

NLR Uses the Levenberg-Marquardt method to perform non-linear regression analysis. (See Chapter 36.)

TRENDS TRENDS is a new add-on option for SPSS-X. It contains a full set of procedures for performing time series analysis. See the SPSS-X *Trends* User Guide.

H.4
Modified Facilities

The following facilities, available in previous releases, have been modified.

DISPLAY DISPLAY now prints up to 60 characters for variable and value labels.

matrix materials	A new subcommand, the MATRIX subcommand, is used on all procedures that handle matrix materials. In addition, matrices are now stored as system files. OPTIONS commands and READ and WRITE subcommands that handle matrices in earlier releases are not recognized in Release 3.0. (See Chapter 13 for information on matrix materials. Refer to Sections H.12 through H.42 for changes to specific procedures.)
VECTOR	VECTOR now accepts string variables as well as numeric.
FILE HANDLE	The FILE HANDLE command is no longer required to provide file specifications. To refer to a file, you simply specify the file on the appropriate subcommand. Subcommands that refer to files are the FILE, OUTFILE, MATRIX, and WRITE subcommands on various procedures. The FILE HANDLE command is still required for reading column binary sets, and IBM VSAM data sets. (See Chapter 5.)

H.5
Modified Procedures

The following procedures, available in previous versions, have been modified.

BREAKDOWN	BREAKDOWN is now called MEANS. BREAK-DOWN is recognized as an alias.
CONDESCRIPTIVES	CONDESCRIPTIVES is now called DESCRIPTIVES. CONDESCRIPTIVES is recognized as an alias.
OPTIONS and STATISTICS	Procedures that formerly used OPTIONS and STATIS-TICS commands to make specifications now use sub-command and keyword alternatives for the same specifi-cations. Release 3.0 still recognizes the old OPTIONS and STATISTICS commands, except for those OPTION commands that handled matrix materials. However, you cannot use OPTIONS and STATISTICS commands in interactive mode. Refer to Sections H.12 through H.42 for syntax changes made to specific procedures.
PEARSON CORR	PEARSON CORR is now called CORRELATIONS. PEARSON CORR is recognized as an alias.
REPORT	The REPORT procedure has a number of new key-words, all designed to make the procedure easier to use while providing you more control over the report lay-out.

H.6
Interactive X

SPSS-X can now be run in an interactive as well as a batch mode. Using SPSS-X interactively means you can have each command executed immediately, as soon as you've finished entering it, instead of submitting batch command files (see Chapter 3):

- Three new SET subcommands (ENDCMD, NULLINE, HEADER) help you define parameters useful in the interactive environment.

- Commands CLEAR TRANSFORMATIONS, NEW FILE, and HOST enable you to discard previous transformations, discard the active file, or issue commands to your host system during an interactive session without having to end the session.

- A journal file is also created, in addition to the listing file containing your display output. The journal file contains a log of your commands, along with any error or warning messages the commands caused the system to generate.

- On-line HELP is available with interactive mode.

H

H.7
Syntax Differences between Interactive and Batch Modes

The following differences exist between interactive and batch processing.

Command Terminator	Each command you enter in the interactive mode must end with a command terminator.
CMS Line-End Character	For the CMS systems, a special exec is executed when you enter interactive mode. This exec turns off the terminal LINEND character if it is a pound sign (#). This enables you to use scratch variables during the interactive session. Some installations may disable or modify this exec, requiring you to change the line-end character yourself. Check with your system coordinator.
OPTIONS and STATISTICS	You cannot use the OPTIONS and STATISTICS commands in the interactive mode. Instead, you should use the new equivalent subcommands available.

H.8
RELEASE 2.2

Release 2.2 introduced a number of changes that are still available in Release 3.0.

H.9
New Facilities and Procedures

Release 2.2 introduced four new commands to the system.

AUTORECODE	recodes values from one variable into consecutive integers and stores these values in another variable. The original input values automatically are used as value labels.
DROP DOCUMENTS	removes documents from SPSS-X system files.
INCLUDE	processes a file of SPSS-X commands within an SPSS-X job. You supply the file handle of the file containing the commands.
RENAME VARIABLES	changes the names of variables in the active file.
XSORT	The XSORT subcommand on SET specifies which sort program to use in a run. You can see what the default sort program is with SHOW XSORT.

H.10
Modified Facilities

The following facilities, available in previous versions, were modified in Release 2.2.

string values	Both VALUE LABELS and ADD VALUE LABELS have new rules on padding values that are being labeled. There are also new rules for specifying MISSING VALUES for strings.
TEMPORARY	New rules governing reference to scratch variables after the TEMPORARY command.
translator	The jobs XTOPC and PCTOX are no longer available.

H.11
Modified Procedures

The following procedures, available in previous versions, were modified in Release 2.2.

AGGREGATE	no longer stores documents on aggregated output files by default. To save documents on aggregated files, use the new DOCUMENT subcommand.

ALSCAL	now allows you to name a maximum of 100 variables on the VARIABLES subcommand. The old limit was 50 variables.
HILOGLINEAR	contains several changes that affect saturated models.
LOGLINEAR	contains several changes that affect saturated models.
MANOVA	contains several new statistical enhancements. In addition, command syntax and printed output have been simplified.

H.12 PROCEDURE COMMANDS

Procedures in SPSS-X that formerly used OPTIONS and STATISTICS commands to make specifications now use subcommand and keyword alternatives for the same specifications. In addition, those procedures that handle matrix materials now use a MATRIX subcommand to read and write matrix materials. Old syntax for handling matrix materials is not recognized in Release 3.0.

The following sections discuss the specific changes to each procedure. A cross-reference is presented (when applicable) to show the former OPTION or STATISTIC number and the new subcommand or keyword that replaces it.

The following sections also document changes introduced in Release 2.2. Those changes introduced in Release 2.2 are clearly identified as 2.2 changes. Otherwise, the changes were effected in Release 3.0.

H.13 ALSCAL

Generally, "data" read by ALSCAL are already in matrix form. This matrix can be created in either PROXIMITIES or CLUSTER. You do not need to use the MATRIX subcommand to read this file, simply use the VARIABLES subcommand to indicate the variables (or columns) to be used. However, for consistency with other procedures that read matrices, ALSCAL recognized the MATRIX subcommand with one keyword, IN, which you can use for reading matrix materials.

Beginning in Release 2.2, you can name a maximum of 100 variables on the VARIABLES subcommand. The old limit was 50 variables.

H.14 ANOVA

New subcommands and keywords have been added as alternatives to OPTIONS and STATISTICS numbers. The old OPTIONS and STATISTICS numbers are still valid.

New subcommands and keywords and their equivalent OPTIONS and STATISTICS numbers:

OPTION	subcommand:	keyword:
1	MISSING	INCLUDE
2	FORMAT	NOLABELS
3	MAXORDERS	NONE
4,5,6	MAXORDERS	n
7	COVARIATES	WITH
8	COVARIATES	AFTER
9	METHOD	UNIQUE
10	METHOD	HIERARCHICAL

H

STATISTIC	subcommand:	keyword:
1	STATISTICS	MCA
2	STATISTICS	REG
3	STATISTICS	MEAN

H.15
AUTORECODE

The AUTORECODE command (new in Release 2.2) recodes the values of both string and numeric variables to consecutive integers and stores the new values into a different variable. This enhances your ability to recode long string variables into numeric variables that then can be incorporated into the TABLES procedure. It also makes it easier to recode the values of factor variables to consecutive integers, which is the form required by MANOVA, and which reduces the amount of work space needed by other statistical procedures like ANOVA.

H.16
CLUSTER

CLUSTER now uses the MATRIX subcommand with keywords IN and OUT to read and write matrix materials. The READ and WRITE subcommands, along with their keyword specifications, are no longer recognized.

H.17
CORRELATIONS (alias PEARSON CORR)

New subcommands and keywords have been added as alternatives to OPTIONS and STATISTICS numbers. The old OPTIONS and STATISTICS numbers (except those dealing with matrix material) are still valid.

New subcommands and keywords and their equivalent OPTIONS and STATISTICS numbers:

OPTION	subcommand:	keyword:
1	MISSING	INCLUDE
2	MISSING	ANALYSIS
3	PRINT	TWOTAIL
4	MATRIX	OUT
5	PRINT	NOSIG
6	FORMAT	SERIAL
7	(obsolete)	

STATISTIC	subcommand:	keyword:
1	STATISTICS	DESCRIPTIVES
2	STATISTICS	XPROD

- N of cases is printed with keyword SIG and is not printed with NOSIG.
- FORMAT=SERIAL overrides PRINT=NOSIG.

H.18
CROSSTABS

New subcommands and keywords have been added as alternatives to OPTIONS and STATISTICS numbers. The old OPTIONS and STATISTICS numbers are still valid.

New subcommands and keywords and their equivalent OPTIONS and STATISTICS numbers:

OPTION	subcommand:	keyword:
1	MISSING	INCLUDE
2	FORMAT	NOLABELS
3	CELLS	ROW
4	CELLS	COLUMN
5	CELLS	TOTAL
6	FORMAT	NOVALLABS
7	MISSING	REPORT
8	FORMAT	DVALUE
9	FORMAT	INDEX
10	WRITE	CELLS
11	WRITE	ALL
12	FORMAT	NOTABLES
13	CELLS	COUNT
14	CELLS	EXPECTED
15	CELLS	RESIDUALS
16	CELLS	SRESID
17	CELLS	ASRESID
18	CELLS	ALL

STATISTIC	subcommand:	keyword:
1	STATISTICS	CHISQ
2	STATISTICS	PHI
3	STATISTICS	CC
4	STATISTICS	LAMBDA
5	STATISTICS	UC
6	STATISTICS	BTAU
7	STATISTICS	CTAU
8	STATISTICS	GAMMA
9	STATISTICS	D
10	STATISTICS	ETA
11	STATISTICS	CORR

- The COUNT keyword on the CELLS subcommand is the reverse logic from the old syntax: it adds the count rather than removing it.

H.19
DESCRIPTIVES (alias CONDESCRIPTIVES)

New subcommands and keywords have been added as alternatives to OPTIONS and STATISTICS numbers. The old OPTIONS and STATISTICS numbers are still valid.

- The old syntax for specifying znames on the initial varlist is still accepted. Any varname mentioned on the SAVE subcommand without a zname gets a Z-score name assigned. No variable can be mentioned on the SAVE subcommand that is not declared on the initial varlist.
- SKEWNESS and KURTOSIS include the standard errors.
- If you specify /STATISTICS with no keywords, you get the DEFAULT statistics.

H

New subcommands and keywords and their equivalent OPTIONS and STATIS-TICS numbers:

OPTION	subcommand:	keyword:
1	MISSING	INCLUDE
2	FORMAT	NOLABELS
3	SAVE	
4	FORMAT	INDEX
5	MISSING	LISTWISE
6	FORMAT	SERIAL
7	none	

STATISTIC	subcommand:	keyword:
1	STATISTICS	MEAN
2	STATISTICS	SEMEAN
5	STATISTICS	STDDEV
6	STATISTICS	VARIANCE
7	STATISTICS	KURTOSIS
8	STATISTICS	SKEWNESS
9	STATISTICS	RANGE
10	STATISTICS	MINIMUM
11	STATISTICS	MAXIMUM
12	STATISTICS	SUM
13	STATISTICS	DEFAULT

H.20
DISCRIMINANT

New subcommands and keywords have been added as alternatives to OPTIONS and STATISTICS numbers. The old OPTIONS and STATISTICS numbers (except those dealing with matrix materials) are still valid.

The subcommand PRINT has been changed to HISTORY and keywords TABLE and NOTABLE of this subcommand have been changed to END and NOEND.

New subcommands and keywords and their equivalent OPTIONS and STATIS-TICS numbers:

OPTION	subcommand:	keyword:
1	MISSING	INCLUDE
2	MATRIX	OUT
3	MATRIX	IN
4	HISTORY	NOSTEP
5	HISTORY	NOEND
6	ROTATE	COEFF
7	ROTATE	STRUCTURE
8	CLASSIFY	MEANSUB
9	CLASSIFY	UNSELECTED
10	CLASSIFY	UNCLASSIFIED
11	CLASSIFY	SEPARATE

STATISTICS	subcommand:	keyword:
1	STATISTICS	MEAN
2	STATISTICS	STDDEV
3	STATISTICS	COV
4	STATISTICS	CORR
5	STATISTICS	FPAIR
6	STATISTICS	UNIVF
7	STATISTICS	BOXM
8	STATISTICS	GCOV
9	STATISTICS	TCOV
10	PLOT	MAP
11	STATISTICS	RAW
12	STATISTICS	COEFF
13	STATISTICS	TABLE
14	PLOT	CASES
15	PLOT	COMBINED
16	PLOT	SEPARATE

• On the MATRIX subcommand, at least one keyword (OUT or IN) must be specified. Both keywords can be used on the same MATRIX subcommand if you are reading and writing matrices.

H.21
FACTOR

The new MATRIX subcommand has been added to handle matrices. The old READ and WRITE subcommands are no longer recognized. Syntax for the new MATRIX subcommand is:

```
FACTOR VARIABLES=varlist

    [/MATRIX=[IN({COR=*    })]   [OUT({COR=*    })]]]
                 {COR=file}          {COR=file}
                 {FAC=*    }          {FAC=*    }
                 {FAC=file}          {FAC=file}
```

H.22
INPUT MATRIX

The INPUT MATRIX command is obsolete in Release 3.0 and no longer recognized. It was formerly used to specify an input matrix file for procedures that read matrix materials. However, the format of matrix materials has changed in Release 3.0. For more information on the new format for matrix materials, see Chapter 13.

H.23
MANOVA

In Release 3.0. the MATRIX subcommand has been added to handle matrices. The old READ and WRITE subcommands are no longer recognized.

H.24
Overview of Release 2.2 Changes

Both syntax and output for MANOVA were simplified in Release 2.2. In the new syntax, the PRINT and PLOT subcommands were broken down into several smaller, more manageable subcommands. The specifications for repeated-measures were also simplified.

All syntactical changes were implemented so that your existing commands still work as before. In addition, printed output has been revised to remove unnecessary or confusing tables from default output, to improve their appearance, and to enhance interpretability.

Other enhancements included:

• Greenhouse-Geisser and Huynh-Feldt epsilons along with the associated corrected averaged F-tests for repeated measures.

- Replacement of the Bartlett test of sphericity by the more appropriate Mauchly test in repeated-measures designs.
- Collinearity diagnostics for design matrices based on a singular value analysis taken from Belsley, Kuh, and Welsch.
- Exact linear combinations of parameters that form a redundancy.
- Methods for assessing effect size, including measures of univariate and multivariate eta square, univariate R square, and Hay's omega square.
- Observed power for univariate and multivariate significance tests. Both approximate and exact methods are included.
- Simultaneous univariate Scheffe and Bonferroni confidence intervals and simultaneous multivariate confidence intervals for parameter estimates.
- Optimal Scheffe contrast coefficients for each effect.
- Ability to use QR with observations models.

H.25
Changes to
Repeated-Measures Analysis

In the original release of SPSS-X MANOVA, three subcommands (WS-FACTORS, WSDESIGN, and ANALYSIS(REPEATED)) had to be specified for repeated-measures analysis. As of Release 2.2, you only have to specify the WSFACTORS subcommand; the procedure will automatically generate the other two for you.

In addition, default output for repeated-measures analysis has also been changed. Now the procedure only prints multivariate tests, averaged F-tests, Greenhouse-Geisser and Huynh-Feldt epsilons, and Mauchly tests by default. The Mauchly test replaces the Bartlett test of sphericity in repeated-measures designs.

H.26
MEANS (alias
BREAKDOWN)

New subcommands and keywords have been added as alternatives to OPTIONS and STATISTICS numbers. The old OPTIONS and STATISTICS numbers are still valid.

New subcommands and keywords and their equivalent OPTIONS and STATIS-TICS numbers:

OPTION	subcommand:	keyword:
1	MISSING	INCLUDE
2	MISSING	DEPENDENT
3	FORMAT	NOLABELS
4	FORMAT	TREE
5	CELLS	COUNT
6	CELLS	SUM
7	CELLS	STDDEV
8	FORMAT	NOCATLABS
9	FORMAT	NONAMES
10	FORMAT	NOVALUES
11	CELLS	MEAN
12	CELLS	VARIANCE

STATISTIC	subcommand:	keyword:
1	STATISTICS	ANOVA
2	STATISTICS	LINEARITY

- Keyword NOCATLABS for the FORMAT subcommand means no category (value) labels.

• CELLS keywords COUNT, STDDEV, and MEAN reverse the logic of present options. The old OPTIONS 5, 7, and 11 suppressed the information but with the new format, specifying the equivalent keywords causes the information to be reported.

H.27
MULT RESPONSE

New subcommands and keywords have been added as alternatives to OPTIONS and STATISTICS numbers. The old OPTIONS and STATISTICS numbers are still valid.

New subcommands and keywords and their equivalent OPTIONS and STATISTICS numbers:

OPTION	subcommand:	keyword:
1	MISSING	INCLUDE
2	MISSING	MDGROUP
3	MISSING	MRGROUP
4	FORMAT	NOLABELS
5	BASE	RESPONSES
6	none	
7	FORMAT	CONDENSE
8	FORMAT	ONEPAGE

STATISTIC	subcommand:	keyword:
1	CELLS	ROW
2	CELLS	COLUMN
3	CELLS	TOTAL

• Keyword TABLE of the MISSING subcommand excludes user missing values.
• Keyword TABLE of the FORMAT subcommand uses more than one page to print frequencies with more than 20 categories.
• The CASES keyword of the BASE subcommand bases percentages on respondents.

H.28
NONPAR CORR

New subcommands and keywords have been added as alternatives to OPTIONS and STATISTICS numbers. The old OPTIONS and STATISTICS numbers (except those dealing with matrix materials) are still valid.

New subcommands and keywords and their equivalent OPTIONS and STATISTICS numbers:

OPTION	subcommand:	keyword:
1	MISSING	INCLUDE
2	MISSING	LISTWISE
3	PRINT	TWOTAIL
4	MATRIX	OUT
5	PRINT	KENDALL
6	PRINT	SPEARMAN
7	SAMPLE	
8	PRINT	NOSIG
9	FORMAT	SERIAL

• N of cases is printed with SIG and not printed with NOSIG.

- /PRINT keyword BOTH does not cause /MATRIX to write both.
- FORMAT=SERIAL overrides PRINT=NOSIG.

H.29
NPAR TESTS

New subcommands and keywords have been added as alternatives to OPTIONS and STATISTICS numbers. The old OPTIONS and STATISTICS numbers are still valid.

New subcommands and keywords and their equivalent OPTIONS and STATIS-TICS numbers:

OPTION	subcommand:	keyword:
1	MISSING	INCLUDE
2	MISSING	LISTWISE
3	varlist	(PAIR)
4	SAMPLE	

STATISTIC	subcommand:	keyword:
1	STATISTICS	DESCRIPTIVES
2	STATISTICS	QUARTILES

- The (PAIR) keyword is relevant only on a variable list that allows keyword WITH.
- MISSING = ANALYSIS excludes missing cases on an analysis by anslysis basis.

H.30
ONEWAY

New subcommands and keywords have been added as alternatives to OPTIONS and STATISTICS numbers. Most of the old STATISTICS and OPTIONS numbers are still valid. Only those options that dealt with matrix materials are now invalid and require use of the new MATRIX subcommand.

New subcommands and keywords and their equivalent OPTIONS and STATIS-TICS numbers:

OPTION	subcommand:	keyword:
1	MISSING	INCLUDE
2	MISSING	LISTWISE
3	(none)	
4	MATRIX	OUT
6	FORMAT	LABELS
7	MATRIX	IN
8	(none)	
10	HARMONIC	ALL

STATISTIC	subcommand:	keyword:
1	STATISTICS	DESCRIPTIVES
2	STATISTICS	EFFECTS
3	STATISTICS	HOMOGENEITY

- Keywords IN and OUT can both be used on the same MATRIX subcommand.
- Keyword ANALYSIS on subcommand MISSING omits cases with missing values on an analysis-by-analysis (pairwise) basis.

H.31
OPTIONS and STATISTICS

Each procedure in SPSS-X that formerly used OPTIONS and STATISTICS commands to make specifications now uses subcommand and keyword alternatives for the same specification. The old OPTIONS and STATISTICS commands are still recognized by Release 3.0 in batch mode, so you don't have to edit existing jobs. Using the new subcommands instead of the OPTIONS and STATISTICS commands is a requirement only when running SPSS-X interactively. The subcommand and keyword syntax alternatives generate the exact same output as the OPTION or STATISTIC specification they replace.

There is, however, one exception. The MATRIX subcommand reads and writes matrix materials and replaces any OPTIONS specifications that formerly handled matrices. Because the format and handling of matrix materials has changed in Release 3.0, you must edit any existing job that uses an OPTION command to handle a matrix. For example, OPTIONS 4 and 7 are no longer recognized on CORRELATIONS (alias PEARSON CORR) and OPTIONS 2 and 3 are no longer recognized on DISCRIMINANT. For information on the new structure of matrices in Release 3.0, or for information on how to read raw matrix materials into SPSS-X, see Chapter 13.

The following is a list of the procedures affected by these changes. A syntax chart and cross-reference that shows the former OPTIONS and STATISTICS numbers and their current subcommand and keyword alternatives is available in this appendix for each procedure. On the cross-reference, OPTIONS that are no longer recognized by SPSS-X are marked as *obsolete*, whereas OPTIONS that have not been replaced by an alternative subcommand or keyword yet are stilled recognized by SPSS-X have *none* recorded in the column for the new subcommand or keyword name. OPTIONS replaced by the MATRIX subcommand are no longer recognized.

ANOVA	**NONPAR CORR**
CORRELATIONS	**NPAR TESTS**
CROSSTABS	**ONEWAY**
DESCRIPTIVES	**PARTIAL CORR**
DISCRIMINANT	**RELIABILITY**
MEANS	**SURVIVAL**
MULT RESPONSE	**T-TESTS**

OPTIONS that are obsolete on the procedures are:

Command	Obsolete Specification
CORRELATIONS	OPTIONS 4 and 7
DISCRIMINANT	OPTIONS 2 and 3
NONPAR CORR	OPTION 4
ONEWAY	OPTIONS 4, 7, and 8
PARTIAL CORR	OPTIONS 4, 5, and 6
RELIABILITY	OPTIONS 4 through 13, 17

H.32
PARTIAL CORR

New subcommands and keywords have been added as alternatives to OPTIONS and STATISTICS numbers. Most of the old STATISTICS and OPTIONS numbers are still valid. Only those options that dealt with matrix material are now invalid and require use of the new MATRIX subcommand.

H

New subcommands and keywords and their equivalent OPTIONS and STATIS-TICS numbers:

OPTION	subcommand:	keyword:
1	MISSING	INCLUDE
2	MISSING	ANALYSIS
3	SIGNIFICANCE	TWOTAIL
4	MATRIX	IN
5	MATRIX	OUT
6	(obsolete)	
7	FORMAT	CONDENSED
8	FORMAT	SERIAL

STATISTIC	subcommand:	keyword:
1	STATISTICS	CORR
2	STATISTICS	DESCRIPTIVES
3	STATISTICS	BADCORR

- The VARIABLES subcommand can be repeated. The actual keyword VARIABLES is optional.
- OPTION 6 is obsolete and no longer recognized in Release 3.0.

H.33
PROCEDURE OUTPUT

The PROCEDURE OUTPUT command was formerly used by many procedures (for example CLUSTER and DISCRIMINANT) to specify an output file for matrix materials. Because of the changes in the way SPSS-X handles matrix materials, it is no longer used in that context. PROCEDURE OUTPUT in Release 3.0 can only be used to specify output files for cells totals from CROSSTABS, display files from FREQUENCIES, and life table records from SURVIVAL.

H.34
PROXIMITIES

The new MATRIX subcommand has been added to handle matrices. The old READ and WRITE subcommands are no longer recognized.

H.35
QUICK CLUSTER

QUICK CLUSTER now writes final cluster centers to a system file rather than a procedure output file. You use the OUTFILE subcommand to specify the system file; the former WRITE subcommand is no longer recognized. In addition, you no longer need the PROCEDURE OUTPUT command to specify the output file.

To use those final cluster centers as the initial cluster centers in a subsequent QUICK CLUSTER command, you use the FILE subcommand. The former read subcommand is no longer recognized. In addition, you no longer need the INPUT MATRIX command to specify the input file.

H.36
REFORMAT

REFORMAT became available in SPSS-X Release 1.0 to convert SPSS files to files with SPSS-X format. In Release 3.0, it can also be used to convert BMDP files. Instructions from SPSS-X *User's Guide,* 2nd ed., for using REFORMAT with SPSS files are repeated here for your convenience.

In SPSS, all variables were printed as integers unless you used a PRINT FORMATS command to specify that the variable was alphanumeric or to specify the number of decimal places. If you did not use a PRINT FORMATS command when you saved a system file with SPSS, the print formats for alphanumeric and decimal variables are indicated incorrectly on the SPSS system file as integer. When you read an SPSS system file using SPSS-X, these variables have dictionary print and write formats of F8.0. The missing-value specifications are also expressed as integers.

To change the print formats, write formats, and missing-value specifications for variables from alphanumeric to numeric, or from numeric to alphanumeric, use ALPHA and NUMERIC subcommands of the REFORMAT command, as in:

```
REFORMAT ALPHA=NAME1 TO NAME6/ NUMERIC=HOURLY79 TO HOURLY82
```

This command declares NAME1 to NAME6 as alphanumeric variables with dictionary print and write formats of A4. HOURLY79 TO HOURLY82 are declared to be numeric variables with dictionary print and write formats of F8.2 (or the format you specify using the SET command described in Chapter 4). Missing-value specifications for variables named with both the ALPHA and NUMERIC keywords are also changed to conform to the new formats.

After you have reformatted variables from your SPSS system file, you should create an SPSS-X system file by using a SAVE command (or XSAVE). This will save you the time and trouble of having to reformat these variables each time you wish to use them. See Chapter 6 for a discussion of the SAVE and XSAVE commands.

REFORMAT always assigns the print and write format F8.2 (or the format specified using the SET command) to variables specified after the NUMERIC keyword, and A4 to variables specified after the ALPHA keyword. However, you might want to declare a different total length for the variable or a different number of decimal places. For numeric variables, use the PRINT FORMATS, WRITE FORMATS, or FORMATS commands to change the format specifications. See Chapter 10 for a discussion of these commands.

You cannot use the PRINT FORMATS, WRITE FORMATS, or FORMATS commands to change the length of string variables in SPSS-X. To change the length of string variables, you must declare new string variables and use the COMPUTE command to assign the values of the original variable to the new variable. The following commands declare formats of A2 for the variable MMN and A3 for VISDAY:

```
GET FILE R9FILE
STRING XMMN (A2)/XVISDAY (A3)
COMPUTE XMMN=MMN
COMPUTE XVISDAY=VISDAY
SAVE OUTFILE=NEWXFILE/DROP=MMN VISDAY/
     RENAME=(XVISDAY=VISDAY) (XMMN=MMN)
```

The above commands do the following:

- GET accesses the SPSS system file.
- STRING declares XMMN as a string variable with two positions and XVISDAY as a string variable with three positions.
- COMPUTE commands are used to transfer the information from the old system-file variables MMN and VISDAY to the SPSS-X string variables XMMN and XVISDAY.
- The SAVE command saves a new SPSS-X system file. The DROP subcommand drops the SPSS system-file variables with the inappropriate formats. RENAME renames the new SPSS-X string variables to the original names, MMN and VISDAY.

H.37
REGRESSION

The new MATRIX subcommand has been added to handle matrices. The old READ and WRITE subcommands are no longer recognized. If the MATRIX subcommand is used, it must precede all other subcommands.

CRITERIA Subcommand. Keyword TOLERANCE has a new default setting. In previous releases, the default tolerance is .01. In Release 3.0, the default tolerance is .0001.

REGWGT Subcommand. REGWGT is a new REGRESSION subcommand that allows estimation of weighted least-squares models. A variable containing the weights is specified on REGWGT.

H.38
RELIABILITY

New subcommands and keywords have been added as alternatives to OPTIONS and STATISTICS numbers. Most of the old STATISTICS and OPTIONS numbers are still valid. Only those options that dealt with matrix material are now invalid and require use of the new MATRIX subcommand.

The FORMAT subcommand has a new meaning and syntax. It no longer has anything to do with matrix material; instead, it controls the printing of labels in your output. Use the MATRIX subcommand to handle matrix material.

New subcommands and keywords and their equivalent OPTIONS and STATISTICS numbers:

OPTION	**subcommand:**	**keyword:**
1	MISSING	INCLUDE
3	FORMAT	NOLABELS
4	(obsolete)	
5	MATRIX	IN
6	MATRIX	IN
7	MATRIX	IN
8	(obsolete)	
9	(obsolete)	
10	MATRIX	OUT NOPRINT
11	(obsolete)	
12	(obsolete)	
13	(obsolete)	
14	METHOD	COV
15	STATISTICS	FRIEDMAN
16	STATISTICS	COCHRAN
17	(obsolete)	

STATISTIC	**subcommand:**	**keyword:**
1	STATISTICS	DESCRIPTIVES
2	STATISTICS	COV
3	STATISTICS	CORR
4	STATISTICS	SCALE
5	SUMMARY	MEAN
6	SUMMARY	VARIANCE
7	SUMMARY	COV
8	SUMMARY	CORR
9	SUMMARY	TOTAL
10	STATISTICS	ANOVA
11	STATISTICS	TUKEY
12	STATISTICS	HOTELLING

• If there is no SCALE subcommand for a variable list, the default is: SCALE(all) = ALL. (Previously the SCALE subcommand was required.)

H.39
REPORT

The REPORT procedure has a number of new keywords in Release 3.0, all designed to make the procedure easier to use while providing you more control over the report layout.

H.40
Summary of REPORT Changes

The most comprehensive new keyword is the keyword AUTOMATIC on the FORMAT subcommand. By specifying AUTOMATIC, you instruct REPORT to center column headings and data when appropriate, bottom align and underscore all column headings, print labels rather than values for all break variables, include variable labels among the factors it evaluates when determining column widths, and shrink the report if it's too wide for its margins. If you don't want to implement these new features, you can specify the MANUAL format — REPORT's default setting — which presents a report with the same format used by earlier releases of SPSS-X. The following is a summary of the distinctions between AUTOMATIC and MANUAL:

FORMAT AUTOMATIC. Facilitates report design.

1   Displays labels for break variables.
2   Centers string or labelled data, based upon the longest string in the data. Centers numeric data, based upon the widest format in the data or summary. Centers column headings; however, left-justifies column heading if string or labelled data exceed the width of the longest word in the heading.
3   Bottom aligns and underscores all column headings.
4   Extends column widths to accommodate the longest word in a variable label (assuming the label is used for a column heading and no other criteria extend the column width).
5   Extends column widths to accommodate the variable's longest value label (assuming no other criteria extend the column width).
6   Shrinks a report if it is too wide for its margins (called **Automatic Fit).**

FORMAT MANUAL. Permits user to make the major format decisions.

1   Displays values for break variables.
2   Right-justifies numeric data and their column headings; left-justifies string and labelled data and their column headings.
3   Top aligns and does not underscore column headings.
4   Does not extend column widths to accommodate the longest word in a variable label that is used for a column heading.
5   Extends column widths to accommodate the variable's longest value label, up to a width of 20. (However, the column width can extend beyond 20 if one of the other column width criteria is greater than 20.)
6   Generates an error message when a report is too wide for its margins.

The following additional features have been added to REPORT in Release 3.0:

FORMAT Subcommand. In addition to AUTOMATIC and MANUAL, FORMAT has these new keywords and settings:

ALIGN(LEFT|RIGHT|CENTER)	*The report's alignment relative to its margins.* All reports in earlier releases were left aligned relative to the report margins. Left alignment is now the default for all reports in Release 3.0, and ALIGN enables you to center or right-justify a report within the margins.
CHALIGN(TOP|BOTTOM)	*Column heading alignment.* All column headings in earlier releases are top aligned. CHALIGN enables you to bottom align column headings.
UNDERSCORE(ON|OFF)	*Heading underscores.* Column headings in earlier releases cannot be underscored. UNDERSCORE

in Release 3.0 enables you to underscore all column headings.

PAGE1(1|n)   *Page number for the first printed page of a report.* Earlier releases always number the first page of a printed report *Page 1*. PAGE1 in Release 3.0 enables you to specify an alternative number for the first page. For example, if you specify PAGE1(5), the first page of the printed report would be numbered *Page 5*.

VARIABLES Subcommand. The VARIABLES subcommand has two new features:

(OFFSET(0|n|CENTER))   The OFFSET subcommand in previous releases allows you to specify the number of offsetting spaces for data in any of a report's variable columns. In Release 3.0, OFFSET has a new keyword CENTER, which centers data within the column width.

(LEFT|CENTER|RIGHT)   In earlier releases, the only way to move a column heading within the column width is to specify a heading padded with blanks. Keywords LEFT, CENTER, and RIGHT in Release 3.0 enable you to left-justify, center, or right-justify a column heading within the column width. LEFT, RIGHT, and CENTER apply to both a default and a specified heading.

Titles and Footnotes. There is new syntax for specifying titles and footnotes. Earlier releases use 6 positional subcommands: LTITLE, CTITLE, RTITLE, LFOOTNOTE, CFOOTNOTE, and RFOOTNOTE. Release 3.0 uses only 2 subcommands, TITLE and FOOTNOTE, each of which has 3 keywords: LEFT, CENTER, and RIGHT. The old syntax is still recognized.

BREAK Subcommand. In earlier releases, the BREAK subcommand is required on all REPORT commands; if you don't want to break a report into subgroups, you must specify BREAK=(NOBREAK). In Release 3.0, if you don't want to break a report into subgroups, you simply omit the BREAK subcommand.

The following additional new features are available on the BREAK subcommand:

(TOTAL)   In earlier releases, you cannot print totals on a listing report that does not have break variables. TOTAL in release 3.0 gives you that capability.

(PAGE(RESET))   Earlier releases allow you to specify a page break after each break group on the report, but page numbers always continue to increment with each break. In release 3.0, if you specify (PAGE(RESET)), the page counter resets to the PAGE1 setting (on FORMAT) every time the break value changes for the specified break variable.

(OFFSET(0|n|CENTER))   The OFFSET subcommand in previous releases allows you to specify the number of offsetting spaces for data in a break column. In Release 3.0, OFFSET has a new keyword CENTER, which centers data within the column width.

(LEFT|CENTER|RIGHT)   In earlier releases, the only way to move a column heading within the column width is to specify a heading padded with blanks. Keywords LEFT, CENTER, and RIGHT in Release 3.0 enable you to left-justify, center, or right-justify a column heading within the column width. LEFT, RIGHT, and CENTER apply to both a default and a specified heading.

H.41
SURVIVAL

New subcommands and keywords have been added as alternatives to OPTIONS and STATISTICS numbers. The old OPTIONS and STATISTICS numbers are still valid.

New subcommands and keywords and their equivalent OPTIONS and STATIS-TICS numbers:

OPTION	subcommand:	keyword:
1	MISSING	INCLUDE
2	MISSING	LISTWISE
3	CALCULATE	COMPARE
4	PRINT	NOTABLE
5	CALCULATE	CONDITIONAL
6	CALCULATE	APPROXIMATE
7	CALCULATE	PAIRWISE
8	WRITE	TABLES
9	WRITE	BOTH

H.42
T-TEST

New subcommands and keywords have been added as alternatives to OPTIONS and STATISTICS numbers. The old OPTIONS and STATISTICS numbers are still valid.
There are no longer any restrictions on subcommand order.

New subcommands and keywords and their equivalent OPTIONS and STATIS-TICS numbers:

OPTION	subcommand:	keyword:
1	MISSING	INCLUDE
2	MISSING	LISTWISE
3	FORMAT	NOLABELS
4	none	
5	varlist	(PAIRED)

• Keyword (PAIRED) can be used on the PAIRS subcommand to indicate that the lists before and after WITH are to be paired with each other.

References

Aldrich, J. H. and F. D. Nelson. 1984. *Linear probability, logit, and probit Models.* Beverly Hills: Sage.

Anderberg, M. J. 1973. *Cluster analysis for applications.* New York: Academic Press.

Anderson, O. D. 1976. *Time series analysis and forecasting—The Box-Jenkins approach.* Boston: Butterworth.

Andrews, F., J. Morgan, J. Sonquist, and L. Klein. 1973. *Multiple classification analysis.* 2d ed. Ann Arbor: University of Michigan.

Bacon, L. Unpublished data, 1980.

Bancroft, T. A. 1968. *Topics in intermediate statistical methods.* Ames, Iowa: The Iowa State University Press.

Belsley, D. A., E. Kuh, and R. E. Welsch. 1980. *Regression diagnostics.* New York: Wiley and Sons.

Berk, K. N. 1977. Tolerance and condition in regression computation. *Journal of the American Statistical Association* 72:863-66.

Berkson, J., and R. Gage. 1950. Calculation of survival rates for cancer. *Proceedings of the Mayo Clinic* 25:270.

Bishop, Y. M. M., S. E. Fienberg, and P. W. Holland. 1975. *Discrete multivariate analysis.* Cambridge, Mass.: MIT Press.

Bock, R. D. 1975. *Multivariate statistical methods in behavioral research.* New York: McGraw-Hill.

Box, G. E. P., and G. M. Jenkins. 1976. *Time series analysis: Forecasting and control.* San Francisco: Holden-Day.

Brown, B. W., H. Walker, M. Schimeck, and P. R. Wright. 1979. A life table analysis package for SPSS. *American Statistician* 33:225-27.

Burns, P. R. 1984. *SPSS-6000 MANOVA update manual.* Chicago: Vogelback Computing Center.

Carroll, J. D. and J. J. Chang. 1970. Analysis of individual differences in multidimensional scaling via an *n*-way generalization of "Eckart-Young" decomposition. *Psychometrika* 35:238-319.

Carroll, J. D. and J. J. Chang. 1972. *IDIOSCAL (Individual Differences in Orientation Scaling).* Paper presented at the Spring meeting of the Psychometric Society, Princeton, NJ.

Cattell, R. B. 1966. The meaning and strategic use of factor analysis. In *Handbook of multivariate experimental psychology,* ed. R. B. Cattell. Chicago: Rand McNally.

Cochran, W. G., and G. M. Cox. 1957. *Experimental design.* 2d ed. New York: Wiley and Sons.

Cohen, J. 1977. *Statistical power analysis for the behavioral sciences.* New York: Academic Press.

Conover, W. J. 1973. *Practical nonparametric statistics.* New York: Wiley and Sons.

Cook, R. D. 1977. Detection of influential observations in linear regression. *Technometrics* 19:15-18.

Cooley, W. W., and P. R. Lohnes. 1971. *Multivariate data analysis.* New York: Wiley and Sons.

Coombs, C. H. 1964. *A theory of data.* New York: Wiley and Sons.

Cronbach, L. J. 1951. Coefficient alpha and the internal structure of tests. *Psychometrika* 16:297-334.

Davies, O. L. 1954. *Design and analysis of industrial experiments.* New York: Hafner.

Davison, M. L. 1983. *Multidimensional scaling.* New York: Wiley and Sons.

Dineen, L. C., and B. C. Blakesley. 1973. Algorithm AS 62: A generator for the sampling distribution of the Mann-Whitney *U* statistic. *Applied Statistics* 22:269-273.

Dixon, W. J. and M. B. Brown. 1979. *BMDP-79.* Berkeley: University of California Press.

Draper, N. R. and H. Smith. 1981. *Applied Regression Analysis.* New York: Wiley and Sons.

Elashoff, J. D. 1981. Data for the panel session in software for repeated measures analysis of variance. *Proceedings of the Statistical Computing Section.* American Statistical Association.

Everitt, B. S. 1978. *Graphical techniques for multivariate data.* New York: North-Holland.

Feiring, B. R. 1986. *Linear programming: an introduction.* Beverly Hills: Sage.

Finn, J. D. 1974. *A General model for multivariate analysis.* New York: Holt, Rinehart and Winston.

Finney, D. J. 1971. *Probit analysis.* Cambridge: Cambridge University Press.

Fisher, R. A. 1936. The Use of multiple measurements in taxonomic problems. *Annals of Eugenics* 7:179-188.

Fuller, W. A. 1976. *Introduction to statistical time series.* New York: Wiley and Sons.

Gill, P. E., W. Murray, M. A. Saunders, and M. H. Wright. January 1986. *User's guide for NPSOL (version 4.0): A fortran package for nonlinear programming.* Technical Report SOL 86-2, Department of Operations Research, Stanford University.

Gill, P. E., W. Murray, and M. H. Wright. 1981. *Practical Optimization.* London: Academic Press.

Goodman, L. A. 1971. The analysis of multidimensional contingency tables: Stepwise procedures and direct estimation methods for building models for multiple classifications. *Technometrics* 13:33-61.

Goodman, L. A. 1972. Measures of association for cross classifications, IV: Simplification of asymptotic variances. *Journal of the American Statistical Association* 67:415-421.

Goodman, L. A. 1978. *Analyzing qualitative/categorical data.* Cambridge: Abt Books.

Goodman, L. A. 1975. The relationship between modified and usual multiple-regression approaches to the analysis of dichotomous variables. In *Sociological Methodology,* ed. Heise, D. R. San Francisco: Jossey-Bass.

Green, P. 1977. *Analyzing multivariate data.* New York: Wiley.

Guttman, L. 1945. A basis for analyzing test-retest reliability. *Psychometrika* 10:255-282.

Haberman, S. J. 1978. *Analysis of qualitative data,* Vol. 1. New York: Academic Press.

Haberman, S. J. 1979. *Analysis of qualitative data,* Vol. 2. New York: Academic Press.

Haberman, S. J. 1982. Analysis of dispersion of multinomial responses. *Journal of the American Statistical Association* 77:568-80.

Hald, A. 1952. *Statistical Theory with Engineering Applications.* New York: Wiley and Sons.

Harman, H. H. 1967. *Modern factor analysis.* 2d ed. Chicago: University of Chicago Press.

Harman, H. H., and W. H. Jones. 1966. Factor analysis by minimizing residuals (Minres). *Psychometrika* 31:351-368.

Harris, C. W. 1967. On factors and factor scores. *Psychometrika* 32:363-379.

Hays, W. L. 1973. *Statistics for the social sciences.* New York: Holt, Rinehart and Winston, Inc.

Heck, D. L. 1960. Charts of some upper percentage points of the distribution of the largest characteristic root. *Annals of Mathematical Statistics* 31:625-642.

Hicks, C. R. 1973. *Fundamental concepts in the design of experiments.* 2d ed. New York: Holt, Rinehart and Winston.

Hoaglin, D. C. and R. E. Welsch. 1978. The hat matrix in regression and ANOVA. *American Statistician* 32:17-22.

Hoaglin, D. C., F. Mosteller, and J. W. Tukey. 1983. *Understanding robust and exploratory data analysis.* New York: Wiley and Sons.

Huberty, C. J. Multivariate indices of strength of association. *Multivariate Behavioral Research,* 7, (1972), 523-526.

Huynh, H. and G. K. Mandevill. 1979. Validity conditions in repeated measures designs. *Psychological Bulletin* 86:964-973.

Jennrich, R. I. and P. F. Sampson. 1966. Rotation for simple loadings. *Psychometrika* 31:313-323.

Jöreskog, K. G. 1977. Factor analysis by least-squares and maximum likelihood methods. In *Statistical methods for digital computers,* Vol. 3, ed. K. Enslein, A. Ralston, and H. S. Wilf. New York: Wiley and Sons.

Jöreskog, K. G. and D. N. Lawley. 1968. New methods in maximum likelihood factor analysis. *British Journal of Mathematical and Statistical Psychology* 21:85-96.

Kaiser, H. F. 1958. The varimax criterion for analytic rotation in factor analysis. *Psychometrika* 23:187-200.

Kaiser, H. F. 1963. Image analysis. In *Problems in measuring change,* ed. C. W. Harris, 156-66. Madison: University of Wisconsin Press.

Kaiser, H. F. 1970. A second-generation Little Jiffy. *Psychometrika* 35:401-415.

Kaiser, H. F. and J. Caffry. 1965. Alpha factor analysis. *Psychometrika* 30:1-14.

Kristof, W. 1963. The statistical theory of speed-up reliability coefficients when a test has been divided into several equal parts. *Psychometrika* 28:221-238.

Kruskal, J. B. 1964. Nonmetric multidimensional scaling. *Psychometrika* 29:1-27,115-129.

Kruskal, J. B. and M. Wish. 1978. *Multidimensional scaling.* Beverly Hills: Sage Publications, Inc.

Lawley D. N. and A. E. Maxwell. 1971. *Factor analysis as a statistical method.* London: Butterworth.

Lee, E. and M. Desu. 1972. A computer program for comparing k samples with right-censored data. *Computer Programs in Biomedicine* 2:315-21.

Ling, R. F. and H. V. Roberts. 1980. *IDA: A user's guide to the IDA interactive data analysis and forecasting system.* New York: McGraw-Hill.

McGee, V.C. 1968. Multidimensional scaling of n sets of similarity measures: A nonmetric individual differences approach. *Multivariate Behavioral Research* 3:233-248.

Meyer, L. S. and M. S. Younger. 1976. Estimation of standardized coefficients. *Journal of the American Statistical Association* 71:154-57.

Milliken, G. A. July 1987. *A tutorial on nonlinear modeling with an application from pharmacokinetics.* Unpublished manuscript.

Montgomery, D. C. and E. A. Peck. 1982. *Introduction to linear regression analysis.* New York: Wiley and Sons.

Morrison, D. F. 1976. *Multivariate statistical methods.* 2d ed. New York: McGraw-Hill.

Moser, C. A. and G. Kalton. 1972. *Survey methods in social investigation.* 2d ed. New York: Basic Books, Inc.

Mudholkar, G. S., Y. P. Chaubey, & Ching-Choung Lin. Some approximations for the noncentral-F distribution. *Technometrics,* 18, (1976), 351-358.

Muller, K. E. & B. L. Peterson. Practical methods for computing power in testing the multivariate general linear hypothesis. *Computational Statistics & Data Analysis,* 2, (1984), 143-158.

Nelson, C. R. 1973. *Applied time series analysis for managerial forecasting.* San Francisco: Holden-Day.

Norusis, M. J. *SPSS^X advanced statistics guide.* Chicago: SPSS Inc., 1985.

Norusis, M. J. *SPSS/PC+ advanced statistics V2.0.* Chicago: SPSS Inc., 1988.

Pillai, K. C. S. 1967. Upper percentage points of the largest root of a matrix in multivariate analysis. *Biometrika* 54:189-193.

Rao, C. R. 1973. *Linear statistical inference and its applications.* 2d ed. New York: Wiley and Sons.

Romesburg, H. C. 1984. *Cluster analysis for researchers.* Belmont, California: Lifetime Learning Publications.

Roy, J. and R. E. Bargmann. 1958. Tests of multiple independence and the associated confidence bounds. *Annals of Mathematical Statistics* 29:491-503.

Rummel, R. J. 1970. *Applied factor analysis.* Evanston: Northwestern University Press.

Schiffman, S. S., M. L. Reynolds, and F. W. Young. 1981. *Introduction to multidimensional scaling.* New York: Academic Press.

Searle, S. R. 1956. *Linear models.* New York: Wiley and Sons.

Shepard, R. N. 1962. The analysis of proximities: Multidimensional scaling with an unknown distance function. I and II. *Psychometrika* 27:125-140.

Siegel, S. 1956. *Nonparametric statistics for the behavioral sciences.* New York: McGraw-Hill.

Smirnov, N. V. 1948. Table for estimating the goodness of fit of empirical distributions. *Annals of Mathematical Statistics* 19:279-281.

Snedecor, G. W. and W. G. Cochran. 1967. *Statistical methods.* 6th ed. Ames, Iowa: The Iowa State Univeristy Press.

Speed, M. F. 1976. Response curves in the one way classification with unequal numbers of observations per cell. *Procedings of the Statistical Computing Section,* American Statistical Association.

Stouffer, S. A., E. A. Suchman, L. C. Devinney, S. A. Star, and R. M. Williams, Jr. 1949. The American soldier: Adjustments during army life. Vol. 1 of *Studies in social psychology in World War II.* Princeton: Princeton University Press.

Survey Research Center. 1973. *1968 American national election study.* Ann Arbor: Inter-University Consortium for Political Research.

Takane, Y., F. W. Young, and J. de Leeuw. 1977. Nonmetric individual differences multidimensional scaling: An alternating least squares method with optimal scaling features. *Psychometrika* 42:7-67.

Tatsuoka, M. M. 1971. *Multivariate analysis.* New York: Wiley and Sons.

Theil, H. 1970. On the estimation of relationships involving qualitative variables. *American Journal of Sociology* 76:103-154.

Timm, N. H. 1975. *Multivariate analysis with applications in education and psychology.* Monterey, Calif: Brooks/Cole.

Torgerson, W. S. 1952. Multidimensional scaling: I. Theory and method. *Psychometrika* 17:401-419.

Tucker, L. R. 1972. Relations between multidimensional scaling and three-mode factor analysis. *Psychometrika* 37:3-28.

Tukey, J. W. 1977. *Exploratory data analysis.* Reading, Mass.: Addison-Wesley.

Velleman, P. F. and R. E. Welsch. 1981. Efficient computing of regression diagnostics. *American Statistician* 35:234-42.

Weisberg, H. F. and J. G. Rusk. 1970. Dimensions of candidate evaluation. *The American Political Science Review* 64:1167-1185.

Winer, B.J. 1971. *Statistical principles in experimental design.* New York: McGraw-Hill.

Young, F. W. 1972. A model of polynomial conjoint analysis algorithms. In *Multidimensional scaling: Theory and applications in the behavioral sciences,* Vol. 1, ed. R. N. Shepard, A. K. Romney, and S. Nerlove. New York: Academic Press.

Young, F. W. 1975a. Methods for describing ordinal data with ordinal models. *Journal of Mathematical Psychology* 12:416-436.

Young, F. W. 1975b. An asymmetric euclidean model for multiprocess asymmetric data. *Proceedings of the US-Japan Seminar on Multidimensional Scaling.*

Young, F. W. 1978. *Principal directions scaling (note 1): The problem and its solution.* Unpublished note.

Young, F. W. 1979a. *Principal directions scaling (note 2): A new individual differences MDS model.* Unpublished note.

Young, F. W. 1979b. *Principal directions scaling (note 3): Simultaneous analysis of similarity and multivariate data.* Unpublished note.

Young, F.W., D. V. Easterling, and B. H. Forsyth. 1983. The general Euclidean model for scaling three-mode dissimilarities: Theory and applications. In *Research methods for multi-mode data analysis,* ed. H.G. Law, C. W. Synder, J. Hattie, and R. P. McDonald. New York: Praegar Publishers.

Young, F. W., Y. Takane, and R. Lewyckyj. 1978. ALSCAL: A nonmetric multidimensional scaling program with several differences options. *Behavioral Research Methods and Instrumentation* 10:451-453.

Index

A (keyword)
  SORT CASES command, 269
a priori contrasts, 761
ABS (function), 120
ABSOLUTE (keyword)
  PROXIMITIES command, 825
absolute value, 120
ACF (keyword)
  BOX-JENKINS command, 395
active file
  defined, 52, 52-53, 59
  in ADD FILES command, 290
  in AGGREGATE command, 329, 331
  in MATCH FILES command, 279
  in REPORT command, 893-895
  in SAVE SCSS command, 304
  transformations, 139
ACVF (keyword)
  BOX-JENKINS command, 395
ADD (function)
  REPORT command, 915
ADD FILES (command), 290-294
  annotated example, 295
  BY subcommand, 293
  common variables, 291, 294
  concatenating files, 290-293
  dictionary information, 291
  DROP subcommand, 292, 294
  FILE subcommand, 290-291, 293
  FIRST subcommand, 294
  IN subcommand, 292-293, 294
  interleaving files, 293-294
  KEEP subcommand, 292, 294
  key variables, 293
  LAST subcommand, 294
  MAP subcommand, 292, 294
  RENAME subcommand, 291-292, 294
  reordering variables, 292, 294
  with DATA LIST command, 291
  with DROP DOCUMENTS
    command, 290
  with SORT CASES command, 271
ADD VALUE LABELS (command), 71
adding observations
  in ADD FILES command, 290
  in UPDATE (command), 298
adding variables
  in MATCH FILES command, 277-278
  in UPDATE (command), 298
addition, 119
ADJPRED (keyword)
  REGRESSION command, 858

adjusted means
  in MANOVA command, 574
adjusting column widths
  in REPORT command, 934
adjusting margins
  in REPORT command, 934
adjusting space between rows
  in REPORT command, 940-944
AFREQ (keyword)
  FREQUENCIES command, 504
AFTER (keyword)
  ANOVA command, 368
AGGREGATE (command), 329-337
  annotated example, 332-333
  BREAK subcommand, 331
  DOCUMENT subcommand, 334
  functions, 335-336
  missing values, 336-337
  OUTFILE subcommand, 330-331
  PRESORTED subcommand, 334
  variable labels, 334-335
  with MISSING VALUES command,
    337
  with SORT CASES command, 271
  with SPLIT FILE command, 273, 331
aggregate functions, 335-336
  arguments, 336
  defined, 330
  in REPORT command, 909-918
aggregated data
  in SURVIVAL command, 963-964
aggregated file
  defined, 329
AIC (keyword)
  FACTOR command, 485
AINDS (keyword)
  ALSCAL command, 346
ALIGN (keyword)
  REPORT command, 933
aligning columns
  in REPORT command, 933
aligning report cells
  in REPORT command, 907-908,
    936-937
ALL (keyword)
  ANOVA command, 368, 374
  CORRELATIONS command, 422
  CROSSTABS command, 435, 436,
    439
  DESCRIPTIVES command, 450
  DISCRIMINANT command, 465, 470
  MANOVA command, 592-595
  MEANS command, 649

MULT RESPONSE command, 671
  NPAR TESTS command, 756
  ONEWAY command, 765
  PARTIAL CORR command, 780
  RELIABILITY command, 875
ALPHA (keyword)
  FACTOR command, 489
  MANOVA command, 595
  RELIABILITY command, 876
ALPHA (subcommand)
  REFORMAT (command), 1026
alpha factoring, 489
alpha model
  in RELIABILITY command, 873
ALPHANUMERIC (keyword)
  PLOT command, 798
ALSCAL (command), 339-362
  annotated examples, 350-357
  CONDITION subcommand, 343
  CRITERIA subcommand, 347-348
  FILE subcommand, 343-346
  INPUT subcommand, 341
  LEVEL subcommand, 342
  limitations, 362
  matrix input, 341, 360-362
  matrix output, 359-360
  MATRIX subcommand, 360-362
  METHOD subcommand, 346
  MODEL subcommand, 346
  model types, 346
  old friends, 1026
  OUTFILE subcommand, 359-360
  PLOT subcommand, 359
  PRINT subcommand, 358-359
  SHAPE subcommand, 341-342
  variable specification, 341
altering column headings
  in REPORT command, 934-935
alternative page numbers
  in REPORT command, 945
ANALYSIS (keyword)
  NPAR TESTS command, 756
  ONEWAY command, 766
  PARTIAL CORR command, 781
  T-TEST command, 974
ANALYSIS (subcommand)
  DISCRIMINANT command, 460
  FACTOR command, 484-485
  MANOVA command, 575-576
analysis of covariance, 617-619

analysis of variance
  in ANOVA command, 365
  in MANOVA command, 613-614
  in MEANS command, 649
  in ONEWAY command, 759
  in RELIABILITY command, 879-880
AND (keyword)
  logical operator, 164-165
ANOVA (command), 365-377
  annotated example, 372-373
  cell means, 374
  covariates, 367-375
  COVARIATES subcommand, 368
  FORMAT subcommand, 377
  full factorial models, 366-367
  interaction effects, 368-369
  limitations, 377
  MAXORDERS subcommand, 368-369
  METHOD subcommand, 369-370
  MISSING subcommand, 376
  multiple classification analysis,
    375-376
  old friends, 1026
  sums of squares, 369-370
ANOVA (keyword)
  MEANS command, 649
  QUICK CLUSTER command, 843
  REGRESSION command, 855
  RELIABILITY command, 878, 879
ANY (function), 122, 146-147, 150
APPEND (subcommand)
  MCONVERT command, 244
APPROXIMATE (keyword)
  MANOVA command, 602
  SURVIVAL command, 962
AR (keyword)
  FACTOR command, 494
arcsine, 121
arctangent, 121
arguments
  complex, 123
  defined, 120
  in macros, 980-987
  missing values, 130-132
arithmetic operators, 119
ARLAG (subcommand)
  BOX-JENKINS command, 391
ARSIN (function), 121
ARTAN (function), 121
ASCAL (keyword)
  ALSCAL command, 346
ASRESID (keyword)
  CROSSTABS command, 435
assignment expressions
  in IF command, 155
ASSOCIATION (keyword)
  HILOGLINEAR command, 520
asterisk (file name)
  in ADD FILES command, 288, 290,
    291
  in AGGREGATE command, 330-331
  in MATCH FILES command, 279
asterisk (format)
  in DATA LIST command, 64
  in PRINT command, 171-172
  in WRITE command, 177
ASYMMETRIC (keyword)
  ALSCAL command, 341
autocorrelation plots
  in BOX-JENKINS command, 386-387

AUTOMATIC (keyword)
  REPORT command, 904
automatic fit
  in REPORT command, 906
AUTORECODE (command), 379-383
  compared to RECODE, 379
  DESCENDING subcommand, 381
  examples, 381-383
  INTO subcommand, 380-381
  missing values, 381
  old friends, 1026
  PRINT subcommand, 380
  VARIABLES subcommand, 380
AVALUE (keyword)
  CROSSTABS command, 439
AVERAGE (function)
  REPORT command, 915
averaged F test, 593
AVERF (keyword)
  MANOVA command, 593
AVONLY (keyword)
  MANOVA command, 593

backforecasts
  in BOX-JENKINS command, 392
BACKWARD (keyword)
  HILOGLINEAR command, 517-519
  REGRESSION command, 851
BADCORR (keyword)
  PARTIAL CORR command, 780
  REGRESSION command, 866
BALANCED (keyword)
  MANOVA command, 585
bar charts
  in FREQUENCIES command,
    505-508, 508
BART (keyword)
  FACTOR command, 494
BARTLETT (keyword)
  MANOVA command, 592
Bartlett-Box F
  in MANOVA command, 592
  in ONEWAY command, 765
Bartlett's test of sphericity, 485
BASE (subcommand)
  MULT RESPONSE command,
    671-672
basic report
  in REPORT command, 893-895,
    897-904
BASIS (keyword)
  LOGLINEAR command, 549
  MANOVA command, 581
batch processing, 17-18
BAVERAGE (keyword)
  CLUSTER command, 406
BCOV (keyword)
  REGRESSION command, 855
BEGIN DATA (command), 72-73
  in interactive processing, 18
between-subjects factors
  in MANOVA command, 571-575
BEUCLID (keyword)
  PROXIMITIES command, 831
BFR (subcommand)
  BOX-JENKINS command, 392
BIAS (keyword)
  MANOVA command, 592
binary data, 79-80
  in PROXIMITIES, 827-832
BINOMIAL (subcommand)
  NPAR TESTS command, 735, 740

binomial test, 740
BLANK (keyword)
  FACTOR command, 487
  REPORT command, 929
blanks
  delimiters, 13
  reading, 32, 36, 62
BLANKS (subcommand)
  SET command, 32, 36
  SHOW command, 32
!BLANKS (function)
  macro facility, 988
BLKSIZE (subcommand)
  SHOW command, 32
BLOCK (keyword)
  CLUSTER command, 407
  PROXIMITIES command, 826
BLWMN (keyword)
  PROXIMITIES command, 832
BMPD to SPSS-X data conversion
  in GET BMDP (command), 319
BOOTSTRAP (subcommand)
  CNLR command, 689-691
BOTH (keyword)
  NONPAR CORR command, 728
  SURVIVAL command, 964
BOUNDS (subcommand)
  CNLR command, 688-689
BOX (subcommand)
  SET command, 32, 38-39
  SHOW command, 32
BOX-JENKINS (command), 385-395
  annotated example, 396-402
  ARLAG subcommand, 391
  BFR subcommand, 392
  DIFFERENCE subcommand, 388-389
  differencing the series, 388
  ESTIMATE subcommand, 386-387
  estimate subcommands, 391
  final estimates subcommands, 394-395
  fitting parameters, 390-391
  FORECAST subcommand, 386-387
  forecast subcommands, 394
  FPR subcommand, 392-393
  IDENTIFY subcommand, 386-387
  initial estimates subcommands,
    393-394
  ITERATE subcommand, 392
  LAG subcommand, 389-390
  LEAD subcommand, 394
  LOG subcommand, 388
  MALAG subcommand, 391
  ORIGIN subcommand, 394
  P subcommand, 390
  PERIOD subcommand, 389
  perturbation increment
    subcommands, 393
  PLOT subcommand, 395
  POWER subcommand, 388
  PRINT subcommand, 395
  Q subcommand, 390
  SDIFFERENCE subcommand, 389
  SP subcommmand, 390
  SQ subcommand, 390
  steps of analysis, 385
  tolerance subcommands, 393
  transforming the series, 388
  VARIABLE subcommand, 386
Box's M test
  in DISCRIMINANT command, 465
  in MANOVA command, 592

BOXM (keyword)
  DISCRIMINANT command, 465
  MANOVA command, 592
BOXPLOTS (keyword)
  MANOVA command, 598
BREAK (command)
  with DO IF command, 251
  with LOOP command, 251
BREAK (subcommand)
  AGGREGATE command, 331
  REPORT command, 893, 900-903,
    909, 912-915, 927, 934-935,
    935-936, 936-937, 944-945,
    945-946
break cells
  in REPORT command, 906
break groups
  defined, 329-330
  in AGGREGATE command, 331
  in REPORT command, 900-901, 927
break levels
  in REPORT command, 893, 909
break variables
  combining in a column, 927
  in AGGREGATE command, 331
  in REPORT command, 893, 896
!BREAK (command)
  macro facility, 989-990
BREAKDOWN (command), see
    MEANS
BRIEF (keyword)
  MANOVA command, 593
BRKSPACE (keyword)
  REPORT command, 939, 941-942,
    945-946
BSEUCLID (keyword)
  PROXIMITIES command, 831
BSHAPE (keyword)
  PROXIMITIES command, 832
BTAU (keyword)
  CROSSTABS command, 436
BUFFNO (subcommand)
  SHOW command, 32
Burroughs computers, see INFO
    command
BY (keyword)
  BOX-JENKINS command, 389
  CROSSTABS command, 430-432
  LIST command, 533
  LOGLINEAR command, 540-541
  LOOP command, 249
  MANOVA command, 572
  MEANS command, 644-646
  MULT RESPONSE command,
    667-671
  NPAR TESTS command, 746-747,
    752-753
  PARTIAL CORR command, 776
  PLOT command, 791-792
  PROBIT command, 806
  SORT CASES command, 269
  SPLIT FILE command, 272
  SURVIVAL command, 957-958
BY (subcommand)
  ADD FILES command, 293
  MATCH FILES command, 283-284,
    288-289
  UPDATE command, 296-297
!BY (keyword)
  macro facility, 989-990

CALCULATE (subcommand)
  SURVIVAL command, 962-963
canonical correlation analysis, 595,
    622-628
CASE (keyword)
  FILE TYPE NESTED, 207
  PROXIMITIES command, 824-825
CASE (subcommand)
  FILE TYPE GROUPED, 199,
    201-202
  FILE TYPE NESTED, 206, 209
  SET command, 32, 37-38
  SHOW command, 32
$CASENUM (system variable)
  defined, 138
  in LIST command, 534
  in PRINT command, 173
  in PRINT EJECT command, 174-175
  in PRINT SPACE command, 175-176
  with SELECT IF command, 184
cases
  defined, 47
CASES (keyword)
  DISCRIMINANT command, 469, 473
  MULT RESPONSE command, 672
CASES (subcommand)
  LIST command, 532-533
CASEWISE (keyword)
  MANOVA command, 601
CASEWISE (subcommand)
  REGRESSION command, 859-860
casewise plots
  in REGRESSION command, 859-860
CC (keyword)
  CROSSTABS command, 436
CC (subcommand)
  SET command, 32, 39-40
  SHOW command, 32, 39-40
CDC computers, see INFO command
CDFNORM (function), 122
CELLINFO (keyword)
  MANOVA command, 592
CELLPLOTS (keyword)
  MANOVA command, 598
CELLS (keyword)
  CROSSTABS command, 439
CELLS (subcommand)
  CROSSTABS command, 435-436
  MATRIX DATA command, 234
  MEANS command, 649
  MULT RESPONSE command,
    671-672
censored observations
  defined, 955
CENTER (keyword)
  BOX-JENKINS command, 392
  REPORT command, 924-926, 935
CENTROID (keyword)
  CLUSTER command, 406
CFVAR (function), 121
CHA (keyword)
  REGRESSION command, 855
CHALIGN (keyword)
  REPORT command, 935
!CHAREND (keyword)
  macro facility, 983
CHDSPACE (keyword)
  REPORT command, 939, 941
CHEBYCHEV (keyword)
  CLUSTER command, 407
  PROXIMITIES command, 826
chi-square test, 436, 735-736

CHISQ (keyword)
  CROSSTABS command, 436
  PROXIMITIES command, 827
CHISQUARE (subcommand)
  NPAR TESTS command, 734,
    735-736
CHOLESKY (keyword)
  MANOVA command, 585
choosing a sort program
  with SET command, 41
CI (keyword)
  PROBIT command, 809
  REGRESSION command, 856
CIN (keyword)
  BOX-JENKINS command, 395
CINTERVAL (subcommand)
  MANOVA command, 603-605
CKDER (keyword)
  CNLR command, 686
  NLR command, 688
CLASS (keyword)
  DISCRIMINANT command, 475
classification options
  in DISCRIMINANT command, 473
classification plots, 469-472
CLASSIFY (subcommand)
  DISCRIMINANT command, 473
CLEAR TRANSFORMATIONS
    (command), 19
CLUSTER (command), 405-417
  annotated example, 410-411
  ID subcommand, 408
  limitations, 417
  matrix input, 416-417
  matrix output, 414-416
  MATRIX subcommand, 414-417
  MEASURE subcommand, 407
  METHOD subcommand, 406
  MISSING subcommand, 414
  old friends, 1026
  PLOT subcommand, 412-414
  PRINT subcommand, 408-409
  SAVE subcommand, 407-408
  variable specification, 406
CLUSTER (keyword)
  CLUSTER command, 407-408, 408
  QUICK CLUSTER command, 842,
    843-844
!CMDEND (keyword)
  macro facility, 984
CNLR (command), 677-695
  adjust steplimit, 697
  annotated example, 692-695
  BOOTSTRAP subcommand, 689-691
  bounds, 696
  BOUNDS subcommand, 688-689
  CNLR command, 680-682
  CONSTRAINED FUNCTION
    command, 680
  convergence problems, 697
  CRITERIA subcommand, 685-687
  DERIVATIVES command, 680
  examples, 698-692
  FILE subcommand, 682-683
  initial values, 679, 682-683
  iteration criteria, 685-687
  linear constraint, 688
  LOSS subcommand, 689
  missing values, 696
  MODEL PROGRAM command,
    678-679

nonlinear constraint, 688-689
OUTFILE subcommand, 683
overflows, 696-697
PRED subcommand, 684
rescaling data, 696
rescaling parameters, 696
SAVE subcommand, 684-685
saving statistics, 684-685
simple bounds, 688
starting values, 679, 682-683
steplimit, adjust, 697
underflows, 696-697
values out of range, 696-697
weighting cases, 691
with CROSSTABS command, 711-712
with PLOT command, 703-706
with PROBIT command, 711-712
with REGRESSION command, 685,
    698-699, 707-711
writing a system file, 683
COCHRAN (keyword)
    MANOVA command, 592
    RELIABILITY command, 878, 884
COCHRAN (subcommand)
    NPAR TESTS command, 744,
        744-745
Cochran's C
    in MANOVA command, 592
    in ONEWAY command, 765
Cochran's Q
    in NPAR TESTS command, 744-745
    in RELIABILITY command, 884
CODE (subcommand)
    GET BMDP command, 318
COEFF (keyword)
    DISCRIMINANT command, 465
    REGRESSION command, 856
coefficient of variation, 121
COLCONF (keyword)
    ALSCAL command, 345
COLLINEARITY (keyword)
    MANOVA command, 592
COLSPACE (keyword)
    REPORT command, 938
COLUMN (keyword)
    CROSSTABS command, 435
    MULT RESPONSE command, 671
COLUMN (subcommand)
    REREAD command, 264
column binary format
    on DATA LIST command, 84-86
column contents
    in REPORT command, 937-938
column headings
    in REPORT command, 903-904,
        934-935
column widths
    in REPORT command, 905-906, 934
columns
    in REPORT command, 891
COLUMNWISE (keyword)
    AGGREGATE command, 336-337
COMBINED (keyword)
    DISCRIMINANT command, 469
combining break groups
    in REPORT command, 927
combining files, 50
COMM (keyword)
    EXPORT command, 310
    IMPORT command, 312

COMMA (keyword)
    REPORT command, 918
COMMA format, 171, 180
command file
    defined, 52
command terminator
    SET command, 32, 41-42
commands
    case, 9, 106-107
    order, 14
    syntax, 9-13
commas
    delimiters, 13
COMMENT (command), 30
comments, 30
common variables
    in ADD FILES command, 291, 294
    in MATCH FILES command, 280,
        284-285
COMPARE (keyword)
    SURVIVAL command, 962
COMPARE (subcommand)
    SURVIVAL command, 961
COMPLETE (keyword)
    CLUSTER command, 406
complex files
    defined, 49
    with FILE TYPE command, 193-210
    with INPUT PROGRAM command,
        265
composite functions
    in REPORT command, 915-917, 948
COMPRESSED (keyword)
    SAVE command, 97-98
    XSAVE command, 97-98
compression
    scratch files, 41
COMPRESSION (subcommand)
    SET command, 32, 41
    SHOW command, 32
COMPUTE (command)
    annotated examples, 114-115
    missing values, 118, 143
    numeric variables, 117-118
    string variables, 145
    with DO IF command, 156
    with REPORT command, 907-908
CONCAT (function), 147
!CONCAT (function)
    macro facility, 988
concatenating files
    ADD FILES command, 290, 290-293
    raw data files, 262-263
concentration statistic, 540
COND (keyword)
    REGRESSION command, 855
CONDENSE (keyword)
    FREQUENCIES command, 503
    MULT RESPONSE command, 673
CONDENSED (keyword)
    PARTIAL CORR command, 782
CONDESCRIPTIVE, see
        DESCRIPTIVES
CONDITION (subcommand)
    ALSCAL command, 343
CONDITIONAL (keyword)
    MANOVA command, 576
    SURVIVAL command, 962
conditional probabilities
    in PROXIMITIES, 830
conditional processing
    macro facility, 989

confidence intervals
    in REGRESSION command, 856
CONFIG (keyword)
    ALSCAL command, 345
CONSTANT (keyword)
    BOX-JENKINS command, 392
    MANOVA command, 575, 585-586,
        595-596
constants, 119
CONSTRAINED FUNCTION
        (command)
    CNLR command, 680
CONTENT (subcommand)
    GET BMDP command, 318
CONTENTS (subcommand)
    MATRIX DATA command, 235-238
CONTIN (keyword)
    MANOVA command, 572-573
contingency coefficient, 436
CONTINUED (subcommand)
    REPEATING DATA command,
        216-217
contour plots
    PLOT command, 793-794
CONTRAST (keyword)
    MANOVA command, 581
CONTRAST (subcommand)
    LOGLINEAR command, 548-549
    MANOVA command, 587-591
    ONEWAY command, 761-762
CONVERGE (keyword)
    ALSCAL command, 347
    HILOGLINEAR command, 523
    LOGLINEAR command, 550
    PROBIT command, 808
CONVERT (keyword)
    RECODE command, 145, 150
COOK (keyword)
    REGRESSION command, 858
COPY (keyword)
    RECODE command, 117, 144
COR (keyword)
    LOGLINEAR command, 547
    MANOVA command, 592-594
CORR (keyword), see CORRELATION
        keyword
    CROSSTABS command, 436
    DISCRIMINANT command, 465
    MATRIX DATA command, 235
    PARTIAL CORR command, 780
    RELIABILITY command, 877, 878
CORRELATION (keyword)
    FACTOR command, 485
    PROXIMITIES command, 826
    REGRESSION command, 866
CORRELATIONS (command), 419-425
    annotated example, 426-427
    FORMAT subcommand, 423-424
    limitations, 425
    MATRIX subcommand, 424-425
    MISSING subcommand, 423
    old friends, 1026
    PRINT subcommand, 421-422
    significance tests, 421-422
    STATISTICS subcommand, 422-423
COS (function), 121
COSINE (keyword)
    CLUSTER command, 407
    PROXIMITIES command, 826

COUNT (command), 132-133
MISSING keyword, 133
missing values, 133
SYSMIS keyword, 133
with DO IF command, 156
with MULT RESPONSE command,
673-674
COUNT (keyword)
CROSSTABS command, 435
MATRIX DATA command, 235
MEANS command, 649
MULT RESPONSE command, 671
COV (keyword)
DISCRIMINANT command, 465
MANOVA command, 592, 593-594
MATRIX DATA command, 235
REGRESSION command, 866
RELIABILITY command, 877, 878,
885
covariates
defined, 365
in ANOVA command, 367-375
in MANOVA command, 571
COVARIATES (subcommand)
ANOVA command, 368
Cramer's V, 436
criteria
in REPORT command, 904
CRITERIA (subcommand)
ALSCAL command, 347-348
CNLR command, 685-687
FACTOR command, 488-489
HILOGLINEAR command, 523
LOGLINEAR command, 550
MANOVA command, 591
NLR command, 685, 687-688
PROBIT command, 808
QUICK CLUSTER command, 842
REGRESSION command, 854-855
Cronbach's Alpha, 873, 876
CROSSBREAK (subcommand)
MEANS command, 648
CROSSBREAK-like tables
in REPORT command, 950-951
CROSSTABS (command), 429-444
annotated example, 440-441
cell contents, 435-436
cell percentages, 435-436
CELLS subcommand, 435-436
compared to MEANS, 645
expected values, 435-436
FORMAT subcommand, 438-439
general mode, 430-432
indexing tables, 438-439
integer mode, 432-435
limitations, 443-444
MISSING subcommand, 437-438
old friends, 1026
reproducing tables, 443
residuals, 435-436
STATISTICS subcommand, 436-437
TABLES subcommand, 430-432,
434-435
VARIABLES subcommand, 434-435
with CNLR command, 711-712
with PROCEDURE OUTPUT
command, 442-443
with WEIGHT command, 443
WRITE subcommand, 439-443
writing tables, 439-443

CROSSTABS-like tables
in REPORT command, 951-952
crosstabulation
defined, 429
in CROSSTABS command, 429-435
in MEANS command, 648
in MULT RESPONSE command,
659-660
CRSHTOL (keyword)
CNLR command, 686
CTAU (keyword)
CROSSTABS command, 436
CTIME.DAYS (function), 126
CTIME.HOURS (function), 126
CTIME.MINUTES (function), 126
cumulative distribution function, 122
custom currency formats
definition, 179
SET command, 32, 39-40
CUTOFF (keyword)
ALSCAL command, 347
CUTPOINT (subcommand)
PLOT command, 798-803
CWEIGHT (subcommand)
HILOGLINEAR command, 517
LOGLINEAR command, 546-547

D (keyword)
CROSSTABS command, 436
PROXIMITIES command, 830
SORT CASES command, 269-270
d, Somers', 436
DATA (keyword)
ALSCAL command, 358
DATA (option)
TOSPSS procedure, 1023
DATA (subcommand)
GET OSIRIS command, 316
GET SAS command, 313
REPEATING DATA command, 215
data definition, 47, 55-56
annotated example, 74-75
with transformations, 139
data formats
A type, 63
column binary data, 84-86
default, 62
E type, 63
FORTRAN-like, 76-83
in DATA LIST command, 62-63,
76-82
multipunch data, 84-87
N type, 63
table, 77
unaligned postive integer binary data,
86-87
Data General computers, see INFO
command
DATA LIST (command), 57-65, 76-87
annotated example, 74-75
column binary data, 84-86
column locations, 60
data formats, 63, 76-82
decimal places, 62
default data format, 62
dictionary formats, 65
END subcommand, 57, 258-263
FILE subcommand, 58
FIXED keyword, 58
FORTRAN-like formats, 76-83
FREE keyword, 58
LIST keyword, 58

multipunch data, 84-87
naming variables, 60
NOTABLE subcommand, 59
record specification, 59-60, 60-61
RECORDS subcommand, 58
TABLE subcommand, 59
time and date formats, 80-82
unaligned positive integer binary
data, 86-87
with ADD FILES command, 291
with INPUT PROGRAM command,
265-267
with MATCH FILES command, 279
with RECORD TYPE command,
196-197, 200-201
data manipulations
defined, 49-50
data transformations
defined, 49-50
date and time input formats, 80-82
date and time output formats, 178-179
date functions, 123-129
DATE.DMY (function), 124
DATE.MDY (function), 125
DATE.MOYR (function), 125
DATE.QYR (function), 125
DATE.WKYR (function), 125
DATE.YRDAY (function), 125
$DATE (system variable)
defined, 138
DATE) (argument)
REPORT command, 925
dates, 123-129
in REPORT command, 925
DECOMP (keyword)
MANOVA command, 592
DEFAULT (keyword)
DESCRIPTIVES command, 450
LOGLINEAR command, 551
MEANS command, 649
!DEFAULT (keyword)
macro facility, 986
DEFINE (command)
macro facility, 979-993
delimiters, 12-13
DELTA (keyword)
FACTOR command, 488
HILOGLINEAR command, 523
LOGLINEAR command, 550
DENDROGRAM (keyword)
CLUSTER command, 412
DENSITY (keyword)
SURVIVAL command, 960
DEPENDENT (keyword)
MEANS command, 650
DEPENDENT (subcommand)
REGRESSION command, 850
DERIVATIVES (command)
CNLR command, 680
DERIVATIVES (keyword)
CNLR command, 684
DESCENDING (subcommand)
AUTORECODE command, 381
DESCRIPTIVE (keyword)
RELIABILITY command, 878

DESCRIPTIVES (command), 447-452
  annotated example, 452-453
  compared to FREQUENCIES, 447, 450
  FORMAT subcommand, 451-452
  limitations, 452
  MISSING subcommand, 450-451
  old friends, 1026
  SAVE subcommand, 449-450
  STATISTICS subcommand, 450
  variable list, 448
  with SET WIDTH command, 451
  Z scores, 448-450
DESCRIPTIVES (keyword)
  CORRELATIONS command, 422
  NPAR TESTS command, 756
  ONEWAY command, 765
  PARTIAL CORR command, 780
DESCRIPTIVES (subcommand)
  REGRESSION command, 866-867
DESIGN (keyword)
  LOGLINEAR command, 547
  MANOVA command, 592-593
DESIGN (subcommand)
  HILOGLINEAR command, 516-517
  LOGLINEAR command, 541
  MANOVA command, 571-575
DET (keyword)
  FACTOR command, 485
determinant, matrix
  in FACTOR command, 485
DEVIATION (keyword)
  LOGLINEAR command, 548
  MANOVA command, 581, 587
DFE (keyword)
  MATRIX DATA command, 235
DFREQ (keyword)
  FREQUENCIES command, 504
DIAGONAL (keyword)
  MATRIX DATA command, 230
DIAGONAL (subcommand)
  FACTOR command, 487
DICE (keyword)
  PROXIMITIES command, 829
dictionary
  defined, 59, 89
  structure, 106
DICTIONARY (keyword)
  DISPLAY command, 103-104
DICTIONARY (subcommand)
  GET OSIRIS command, 316
dictionary formats
  defined, 49, 178-179
  in AGGREGATE command, 334-335
  in DATA LIST command, 65
  in GET SCSS command, 307
  in PRINT command, 171
  in REPORT command, 952
  in WRITE command, 176
  transformations, 110
DIFFERENCE (keyword)
  LOGLINEAR command, 549
  MANOVA command, 581, 588
DIFFERENCE (subcommand)
  BOX-JENKINS command, 388-389
Digital Equipment Corporation
  computers, see INFO command
DIGITS (subcommand)
  EXPORT command, 311-312
DIMENR (keyword)
  MANOVA command, 593

DIMENS (keyword)
  ALSCAL command, 347
dimension-reduction analysis, 593
DIRECT (keyword)
  DISCRIMINANT command, 460
direct access files, 1005, 1006-1008, 1016
DIRECTIONS (keyword)
  ALSCAL command, 347-348
DISCRIM (subcommand)
  MANOVA command, 595
DISCRIMINANT (command), 455-479
  ANALYSIS subcommand, 460
  annotated example, 466-467
  casewise plots, 473
  classification coefficients, 473-474
  classification plots, 469-472
  classification results table, 468-469
  CLASSIFY subcommand, 473
  classifying cases, 465-474
  direct entry, 460
  discriminant scores, 473
  display options, 465
  FUNCTIONS subcommand, 463-464
  GROUPS subcommand, 457
  HISTORY subcommand, 465
  inclusion levels, 461-462
  limitations, 479
  matrix input, 477-478
  matrix output, 476-478
  MATRIX subcommand, 477-478
  MAXSTEPS subcommand, 463
  METHOD subcommand, 460-461
  MISSING subcommand, 474
  old friends, 1026
  PLOT subcommand, 469-473
  PRIORS subcommand, 468
  ROTATION subcommand, 465
  SAVE subcommand, 474-475
  SELECT subcommand, 459-460
  statistical controls, 463
  STATISTICS subcommand, 464-465, 468-469
  syntax rules, summary, 456-457
  tolerance, 463
  VARIABLES subcommand, 457-458
  with MATRIX DATA command, 229
discriminant analysis
  in DISCRIMINANT command, 455
  in MANOVA command, 595
DISPER (keyword)
  PROXIMITIES command, 832
DISPLAY (command), 103-105
display file
  box characters, 37, 38-39
  defined, 52
  length, 37
  setting case, 37, 37-38
  width, 37,
DISTANCE (keyword)
  CLUSTER command, 408
  QUICK CLUSTER command, 843-844
distance model, 566-567
DIVIDE (function)
  REPORT command, 915
division, 119
DO IF (command), 156-162
  annotated example, 158-159
  missing values, 161
  nested, 161
  with IF command, 156-157

with INPUT PROGRAM command, 266
with PRINT command, 173
with PRINT EJECT command, 174-175
with PRINT SPACE command, 175-176
with SAMPLE command, 190
with SELECT IF command, 190
with XSAVE command, 98-99
DO REPEAT (command), 136-138
!DO (command)
  macro facility, 989-990
DOCUMENT (command), 103
DOCUMENT (subcommand)
  AGGREGATE command, 334
documentation, 21-23
DOCUMENTS (keyword)
  DISPLAY command, 103-104, 104
!DOEND (command)
  macro facility, 989-990
DOLLAR (keyword)
  REPORT command, 918
DOLLAR format, 171, 180
domain errors
  defined, 132
  numeric expressions, 132
DOUBLE (keyword)
  FREQUENCIES command, 503
doubly multivariate repeated measures, 580, 636-638
DOWN (keyword)
  SORT CASES command, 269
DRESID (keyword)
  REGRESSION command, 858
DROP (subcommand)
  ADD FILES command, 292, 294
  EXPORT command, 310
  GET BMDP command, 318-319
  GET command, 92-93
  GET OSIRIS command, 316
  GET SAS command, 314
  IMPORT command, 312
  MATCH FILES command, 281-282
  SAVE command, 96-97
  SAVE SCSS command, 304-305
  UPDATE command, 299
  XSAVE command, 96-97
DROP DOCUMENTS (command), 106, 301
  with ADD FILES command, 290
  with GET command, 106
  with MATCH FILES command, 278
  with UPDATE command, 301
DSER (keyword)
  BOX-JENKINS command, 395
DUMMY (keyword)
  REPORT command, 938-939, 943
DUNCAN (keyword)
  ONEWAY command, 764
Duncan's multiple range test, 764
DUPLICATE (subcommand)
  FILE TYPE GROUPED, 199-200, 202
  FILE TYPE NESTED, 206-207
DURBIN (keyword)
  REGRESSION command, 859
DVALUE (keyword)
  CROSSTABS command, 439
  FREQUENCIES command, 504

ECONVERGE (keyword)
FACTOR command, 488
EDIT (command), 17-18
annotated example, 34-35
EFFECTS (keyword)
ONEWAY command, 765
EFSIZE (keyword)
MANOVA command, 593-594
EIGEN (keyword)
FACTOR command, 486
MANOVA command, 593
element
VECTOR command, 251-252
ELSE (command), 157
ELSE (keyword)
RECODE command, 111, 144
ELSE IF (command), 160-161
!ELSE (keyword)
macro facility, 989
!ENCLOSE (keyword)
macro facility, 983-984
END (keyword)
DISCRIMINANT command, 465
REGRESSION command, 856-857
END (subcommand)
DATA LIST command, 57, 258-263
examples, 258-263
END CASE (command), 254-256, 258
with END FILE command, 257-258
END DATA (command), 72-73
in interactive processing, 18
END FILE (command), 256-258
with END CASE command, 257-258
END FILE TYPE (command), 193-194
END IF (command), 156-162
END INPUT PROGRAM (command),
254-265
with REPEATING DATA command,
212-213
END LOOP (command), 248-251
IF keyword, 250
logical expressions, 250
missing values, 250-251
end of file processing
END subcommand, 258-263
END REPEAT (command), 136-138
PRINT subcommand, 137-138
ENDCMD (subcommand)
SET command, 32, 41-42
SHOW command, 32
!ENDDEFINE (command)
macro facility, 979-993
ENTER (keyword)
REGRESSION command, 851
entropy statistic, 540
EPS (keyword)
MANOVA command, 591
EQ (keyword)
relational operator, 163
EQUAL (keyword)
DISCRIMINANT command, 468
NPAR TESTS command, 735
equals sign
required, 13
EQUAMAX (keyword)
FACTOR command, 494
MANOVA command, 594, 595
equiprobability model, 541, 555-557
ERROR (keyword)
MANOVA command, 592, 593,
597-598

ERROR (subcommand)
MANOVA command, 591
errors
annotated example, 34-35
messages, 26-27
setting maximum, 36
ESTIM (keyword)
HILOGLINEAR command, 520
LOGLINEAR command, 547
MANOVA command, 593, 595
ESTIMATE (subcommand)
BOX-JENKINS command, 386-387
ESTIMATION (keyword)
MANOVA command, 585-586
ETA (keyword)
CROSSTABS command, 436
eta coefficient, 436, 649
EUCLID (keyword)
ALSCAL command, 346
CLUSTER command, 407
PROXIMITIES command, 826
!EVAL (function)
macro facility, 988
EVERY (keyword)
PLOT command, 802
EXACT (keyword)
MANOVA command, 602
SURVIVAL command, 962
EXCLUDE (keyword)
ANOVA command, 376
DISCRIMINANT command, 474
MANOVA command, 605
ONEWAY command, 766
PARTIAL CORR command, 781
RELIABILITY command, 885
EXECUTE (command), 21
EXP (function), 121
EXPECTED (keyword)
CROSSTABS command, 435
EXPECTED (subcommand)
NPAR TESTS command, 735-736
EXPERIMENTAL (keyword)
ANOVA command, 369
exponent function, 121
exponentiation, 119
EXPORT (command), 310-312
DIGITS subcommand, 311-312
DROP subcommand, 310
KEEP subcommand, 310
MAP subcommand, 311
OUTFILE subcommand, 310
RENAME subcommand, 311
TYPE subcommand, 310
EXTRACTION (keyword)
FACTOR command, 485
EXTRACTION (subcommand)
FACTOR command, 489

F (keyword)
MANOVA command, 602
REGRESSION command, 856
FACILITIES (keyword)
INFO command, 22
FACTOR (command), 481-498
alpha factoring, 489
ANALYSIS subcommand, 484-485
annotated example, 490-492
CRITERIA subcommand, 488-489
DIAGONAL subcommand, 487
equamax rotation, 494
EXTRACTION subcommand, 489
factor plots, 486

factor scores, 494-495
FORMAT subcommand, 487-488
generalized least squares, 489
image factoring, 489
limitations, 498
matrix input, 497-498
matrix output, 496-498
MATRIX subcommand, 497-498
maximum likelihood, 489
missing values, 483-484
oblimin rotation, direct, 494
old friends, 1026
PLOT subcommand, 486-487
principal axis factoring, 489
principal components analysis, 489
PRINT subcommand, 485
quartimax rotation, 494
ROTATION subcommand, 494
SAVE subcommand, 494-495
scree plots, 486
statistics, 485
subcommand order, 481-483
syntax summary, 498
unweighted least squares, 489
VARIABLES subcommand, 483
varimax rotation, 494
WIDTH subcommand, 484
with PROXIMITIES command, 839
factor plots
in FACTOR command, 486
factor scores
Anderson-Rubin method, 494
Bartlett method, 494
regression method, 494
factors
defined, 365
FACTORS (keyword)
FACTOR command, 488
FACTORS (subcommand)
MATRIX DATA command, 233-234
FCF (keyword)
BOX-JENKINS command, 395
FCON (subcommand)
BOX-JENKINS command, 394
FGT (function)
AGGREGATE command, 335
FILE (subcommand)
ADD FILES command, 290-291, 293
ALSCAL command, 343-346
CNLR command, 682-683
DATA LIST command, 58
FILE TYPE command, 195
GET BMDP command, 317-318
GET command, 90
INCLUDE command, 20-21
KEYED DATA LIST command, 1007
MATCH FILES command, 278-279,
288-289
MATRIX DATA command, 228
POINT command, 1010
QUICK CLUSTER command, 843
REPEATING DATA command, 215
UPDATE command, 296-297
file definition, 55-57
in DATA LIST command, 57-58
FILE HANDLE (command), 57
MODE subcommand, 57
PASSWORD subcommand, 1014
FILE LABEL (command), 102
file management
defined, 50-51

file specifications, 56-57
FILE TYPE (command)
  CASE subcommand, 199, 206
  DUPLICATE subcommand, 199-200,
    206-207
  FILE subcommand, 195
  GROUPED keyword, 194
  MISSING subcommand, 200, 207-208
  MIXED keyword, 194
  NESTED keyword, 194
  ORDERED subcommand, 200
  RECORD subcommand, 195,
    198-199, 206
  summary table, 210
  WILD subcommand, 195, 199, 206
  with REPEATING DATA command,
    212-213
FILE TYPE GROUPED, 197-198
  CASE subcommand, 199, 201-202
  DUPLICATE subcommand, 199-200,
    202
  MISSING subcommand, 200, 202
  ORDERED subcommand, 200
  OTHER keyword, 201
  RECORD subcommand, 198-199
  SKIP subcommand, 201
  WILD subcommand, 199
  with RECORD TYPE command,
    200-202
FILE TYPE MIXED, 194
  OTHER keyword, 197
  RECORD subcommand, 195
  SKIP subcommand, 197
  WILD subcommand, 195
  with RECORD TYPE command,
    196-197
FILE TYPE NESTED, 202-203
  annotated example, 204-205
  CASE subcommand, 206, 209
  defined, 194
  DUPLICATE subcommand, 206-207
  MISSING subcommand, 207-208
  OTHER keyword, 209
  RECORD subcommand, 206
  SKIP subcommand, 209
  SPREAD subcommand, 209-210
  WILD subcommand, 206
  with RECORD TYPE command,
    208-210
FIN (function)
  AGGREGATE command, 335
FIN (keyword)
  DISCRIMINANT command, 463
  REGRESSION command, 855
FINISH (command), 30-31
  in interactive processing, 18
FIRST (function)
  AGGREGATE command, 336
FIRST (keyword)
  ANOVA command, 368
FIRST (subcommand)
  ADD FILES command, 294
  MATCH FILES command, 289-290
Fisher's exact test, 436
FIXED (keyword)
  DATA LIST command, 58
FLF (keyword)
  BOX-JENKINS command, 395
flow of control
  DO IF command, 162
FLT (function)
  AGGREGATE command, 335

FOOTNOTE (subcommand)
  REPORT command, 924-926
FOR (keyword)
  SURVIVAL command, 958
FORECAST (subcommand)
  BOX-JENKINS command, 386-387
forecast function, 395
FORMAT (subcommand)
  ANOVA command, 377
  CORRELATIONS command, 423-424
  CROSSTABS command, 438-439
  DESCRIPTIVES command, 451-452
  FACTOR command, 487-488
  FREQUENCIES command, 503-505
  LIST command, 533-534
  MATRIX DATA command, 230-231
  MEANS command, 650-651
  MULT RESPONSE command, 673
  NONPAR CORR command, 729
  ONEWAY command, 766
  PARTIAL CORR command, 781-782
  PLOT command, 793-796
  RELIABILITY command, 885
  REPORT command, 893, 930-935,
    937, 938, 940-945
  SET command, 32, 38
  SHOW command, 32
  T-TEST command, 974
formats
  defined, 48
FORMATS (command), 180
  with AGGREGATE command, 335
  with REPORT command, 907-908
FORTRAN-like formats
  in DATA LIST command, 76-83
  in PRINT command, 171
  in WRITE command, 177
FORWARD (keyword)
  REGRESSION command, 851
FOUT (function)
  AGGREGATE command, 335
FOUT (keyword)
  DISCRIMINANT command, 463
  REGRESSION command, 855
FP (subcommand)
  BOX-JENKINS command, 394
FPAIR (keyword)
  DISCRIMINANT command, 465
FPR (subcommand)
  BOX-JENKINS command, 392-393
FPRECISION (keyword)
  CNLR command, 687
FQ (subcommand)
  BOX-JENKINS command, 395
FREE (keyword)
  data formats, 64-65
  DATA LIST command, 58
  MATRIX DATA command, 230
  variable definition, 63-65
FREQ (keyword)
  FREQUENCIES command, 508, 508
  HILOGLINEAR command, 520
  LOGLINEAR command, 547
  PROBIT command, 809
frequencies
  in MULT RESPONSE command,
    658-659
FREQUENCIES (command), 501-512
  annotated example, 510-511
  bar charts, 505-508, 508
  compared to DESCRIPTIVES, 447,
    450

FORMAT subcommand, 503-505
  general mode, 502-503
  histograms, 505-506, 508
  indexing tables, 505
  integer mode, 502-503
  limitations, 512
  missing values, 512
  NTILES subcommand, 509
  PERCENTILES subcommand, 508
  statistics, 509
  VARIABLES subcommand, 502-503
  with NLR command, 718-692
  with PROCEDURE OUTPUT
    command, 505
  writing tables, 505
FREQUENCIES (subcommand)
  MULT RESPONSE command,
    666-667
FREQUENCY (function)
  REPORT command, 910
FRIEDMAN (keyword)
  RELIABILITY command, 878, 881
FRIEDMAN (subcommand)
  NPAR TESTS command, 744, 745
Friedman's analysis of variance
  in NPAR TESTS command, 745
  in RELIABILITY command, 881
FROM (keyword)
  LIST command, 532-533
FSCORE (keyword)
  FACTOR command, 485
FSP (subcommand)
  BOX-JENKINS command, 395
FSQ (subcommand)
  BOX-JENKINS command, 395
FTOLERANCE (keyword)
  CNLR command, 686
FTSPACE (keyword)
  REPORT command, 939, 943
FULL (keyword)
  MATRIX DATA command, 230
functions
  in AGGREGATE command, 334
  in REPORT command, 909-911
  numeric variables, 120-123
  string variables, 147-151
FUNCTIONS (subcommand)
  DISCRIMINANT command, 463-464

gamma, 436
GAMMA (keyword)
  CROSSTABS command, 436
GCOV (keyword)
  DISCRIMINANT command, 465
GE (keyword)
  relational operator, 164
GEMSCAL (keyword)
  ALSCAL command, 346
general linear models, 569-611
general log-linear model, 551-553
general mode
  in CROSSTABS command, 430-432
  in FREQUENCIES command,
    502-503
  in MEANS command, 644-646
GET (command), 90-94
  DROP subcommand, 92-93
  FILE subcommand, 90
  KEEP subcommand, 93-94
  MAP subcommand, 90-91
  RENAME subcommand, 91-92

reordering variables, 93-94
SPSS system files, 1026
VARIABLES subcommand, 104-105
with DROP DOCUMENTS
command, 106
GET BMDP (command), 317-319
case selection, 318
CODE subcommand, 318
CONTENT subcommand, 318
DROP subcommand, 318-319
FILE subcommand, 317-318
formats, 319
identifying information, 318
KEEP subcommand, 318-319
LABEL subcommand, 318
limitations, 319
MAP subcommand, 318-319
missing values, 319
RENAME subcommand, 318-319
SCAN subcommand, 318
subcommand order, 318
variable names, 319
GET OSIRIS (command), 315-317
DATA subcommand, 316
DICTIONARY subcommand, 316
DROP subcommand, 316
KEEP subcommand, 316
MAP subcommand, 316
RENAME subcommand, 316
GET SAS (command), 313-315
DATA subcommand, 313
DROP subcommand, 314
KEEP subcommand, 314
MAP subcommand, 314
RENAME subcommand, 314
SASLIB subcommand, 314
GET SCSS (command), 306-308
$ convention, 308
MASTERFILE subcommand, 307
missing values, 306-307
renaming variables, 308
reserved keywords, 308
VARIABLES subcommand, 308
WORKFILE subcommand, 307
GG (keyword)
MANOVA command, 593
GLS (keyword)
FACTOR command, 489
Graeco-Latin squares
in MANOVA command, 616
GREAT (function)
REPORT command, 915
GRESID (subcommand)
LOGLINEAR command, 547
group variables
in MULT RESPONSE command,
658-660
GROUPED (keyword), see FILE
TYPE GROUPED
grouped files, 197-198
defined, 194
GROUPS (subcommand)
DISCRIMINANT command, 457
MULT RESPONSE command,
662-663
T-TEST command, 970
GROUPWISE (keyword)
SURVIVAL command, 964
GT (keyword)
relational operator, 164
GUTTMAN (keyword)
RELIABILITY command, 877

Guttman model
in RELIABILITY command, 874
Guttman split-half coefficient, 873

H, Kruskal-Wallis, see Kruskal-Wallis H
half-normal plots of partial correlations,
600
HAMANN (keyword)
PROXIMITIES command, 830
HARMONIC (subcommand)
ONEWAY command, 764-765
Harris computers, see INFO command
Hartley's F, 765
HAZARD (keyword)
SURVIVAL command, 960
hazard rate, 959
!HEAD (function)
macro facility, 988
HEADER (keyword)
ALSCAL command, 358
HEADER (subcommand)
SET command, 32, 38
SHOW command, 32
heading underscores
in REPORT command, 935-939
HELMERT (keyword)
LOGLINEAR command, 549
MANOVA command, 581, 588
HELP (command), 23-25
HELP prompt, 23-25
help system, 23-25
example screen, 24
movement within, 24-25
syntax charts, 25
Hewlett-Packard 9000 computers, see
INFO command
HF (keyword)
MANOVA command, 593
HI (keyword), see HIGHEST
HICICLE (keyword)
CLUSTER command, 412
HIERARCHICAL (keyword)
ANOVA command, 369, 370
hierarchical files, see nested files
HIGHEST (keyword)
COUNT command, 132
MISSING VALUES command, 67
RECODE command, 111
HILOGLINEAR (command), 515-528
annotated examples, 524-527
CRITERIA subcommand, 523
CWEIGHT subcommand, 517
DESIGN subcommand, 516-517
limitations, 528
MAXORDER subcommand, 519
METHOD subcommand, 517-519
MISSING subcommand, 528
PLOT subcommand, 522-523
PRINT subcommand, 519-522
structural zeros, 517
variable specification, 516
HISTOGRAM (keyword)
REGRESSION command, 859
histograms
in FREQUENCIES command,
505-506, 508
HISTORY (keyword)
REGRESSION command, 856
HISTORY (subcommand)
DISCRIMINANT command, 465

HOMOGENEITY (keyword)
MANOVA command, 592
ONEWAY command, 765
homogeneity-of-variance tests
in MANOVA command, 592
in ONEWAY command, 765
Honeywell computers, see INFO
command
HORIZONTAL (subcommand)
PLOT command, 792-793
HOST (command), 19
HOTELLING (keyword)
RELIABILITY command, 878, 881
Hotelling's T^2, 881
HSIZE (subcommand)
PLOT command, 796-798
HYPOTH (keyword)
MANOVA command, 593

IBM computers, see INFO command
ICON (subcommand)
BOX-JENKINS command, 393
ID (keyword)
QUICK CLUSTER command, 843
REGRESSION command, 859
ID (subcommand)
CLUSTER command, 408
PROXIMITIES command, 833
REPEATING DATA command, 217
IDENTIFY (subcommand)
BOX-JENKINS command, 386-387
IF (command), 155
annotated example, 158-159
with DO IF command, 156-157
with ELSE command, 157
!IF (command)
macro facility, 989
!IFEND (command)
macro facility, 989
image factoring, 489
IMPORT (command), 312-313
DROP subcommand, 312
KEEP subcommand, 312
MAP subcommand, 313
RENAME subcommand, 312-313
TYPE subcommand, 312
IN (keyword)
ALSCAL command, 360-361
CLUSTER command, 414, 416-417
DISCRIMINANT command, 475-478
FACTOR command, 495-498
MANOVA command, 605-607
ONEWAY command, 768, 769-771
PARTIAL CORR command, 782,
784-785
PROXIMITIES command, 836,
838-839
REGRESSION command, 867-870
RELIABILITY command, 885-886,
888
IN (subcommand)
ADD FILES command, 292-294
KEYED DATA LIST command, 1007
MATCH FILES command, 285
UPDATE command, 299
!IN (keyword)
macro facility, 990
INCLUDE (command), 20-21
FILE subcommand, 20-21

INCLUDE (keyword)
ANOVA command, 376
CLUSTER command, 414
CORRELATIONS command, 423
CROSSTABS command, 437
DESCRIPTIVES command, 451
DISCRIMINANT command, 474
FACTOR command, 484
FREQUENCIES command, 512
HILOGLINEAR command, 528
LOGLINEAR command, 551
MANOVA command, 605
MEANS command, 650
MULT RESPONSE command, 673
NONPAR CORR command, 729
NPAR TESTS command, 756
ONEWAY command, 766
PARTIAL CORR command, 781
PLOT command, 803
PROBIT command, 813
PROXIMITIES command, 836
QUICK CLUSTER command, 844
REGRESSION command, 863
RELIABILITY command, 885
SURVIVAL command, 964
T-TEST command, 974
incomplete randomized block designs
in MANOVA command, 615-616
INCREMENT (keyword)
FREQUENCIES command, 508
increment value
in LOOP command, 249
indentation
commands, 10
continuation, 10
INDEX (function), 147, 149-150, 151
INDEX (keyword)
CROSSTABS command, 439
DESCRIPTIVES command, 451
DISPLAY command, 104
FREQUENCIES command, 505
!INDEX (function)
macro facility, 988
indexing clause
in LOOP command, 248-249
indexing strings, 149-150
indexing variable
in LOOP command, 248-249
INDIVIDUAL (keyword)
MANOVA command, 604
INDSCAL (keyword)
ALSCAL command, 346
INFO (command), 21-23
local documentation, 21
new facilities, 22
new procedures, 22
new releases, 22-23
OUTFILE (subcommand), 23
update documentation, 22
INITIAL (keyword)
FACTOR command, 485
QUICK CLUSTER command, 843
INITIAL (subcommand)
QUICK CLUSTER command, 843
initial state
defined, 994-995
initial value
in LOOP command, 248-249
initial values
CNLR command, 679, 682-683

initialization
LEAVE command, 133
numeric variables, 117-118
scratch variables, 135
string variables, 142
INLINE (keyword)
DATA LIST command, 72
MATRIX DATA command, 228
INPUT (subcommand)
ALSCAL command, 341
input data
file, 52
freefield format, 58
inline, 72-73
INPUT MATRIX (command)
obsolete, 1026
INPUT PROGRAM (command),
254-265
annotated example, 260-261
concatenating raw data files, 262-263
with DATA LIST command, 265-267
with LOOP command, 266-267
with REPEATING DATA command,
212-213
input state, 254
defined, 994-995
integer mode
in CROSSTABS command, 432-435
in FREQUENCIES command,
502-503
in MEANS command, 646-648
interactive mode
SET command, 41-42
interactive processing, 18-20
on an IBM/CMS system, 20
interactive prompts, 18-19
intercolumn spacing
in REPORT command, 906, 938-939
interleaving files
ADD FILES command, 290, 293-294
INTERMED (keyword)
ALSCAL command, 358
INTERVAL (keyword)
ALSCAL command, 342
INTERVALS (subcommand)
SURVIVAL command, 957-958
INTO (keyword)
RECODE command, 116-117,
144-145
INTO (subcommand)
AUTORECODE command, 380-381
INV (keyword)
FACTOR command, 485
inverse, matrix
in FACTOR command, 485
IP (subcommand)
BOX-JENKINS command, 393
IQ (subcommand)
BOX-JENKINS command, 393
ISP (subcommand)
BOX-JENKINS command, 393
ISQ (subcommand)
BOX-JENKINS command, 393
ISTEP (keyword)
CNLR command, 687
item analysis, see RELIABILITY
(command)
ITER (keyword)
ALSCAL command, 347
CNLR command, 686
NLR command, 687

ITERATE (keyword)
FACTOR command, 488
HILOGLINEAR command, 523
PROBIT command, 808
ITERATE (subcommand)
BOX-JENKINS command, 392
ITERATION (keyword)
LOGLINEAR command, 550

JACCARD (keyword)
PROXIMITIES command, 829
$JDATE (system variable)
defined, 138
JOINT (keyword)
MANOVA command, 604
JOURNAL (subcommand)
SET command, 32, 42
SHOW command, 32, 42
journal file, 19-20
defined, 52

K-S (subcommand)
NPAR TESTS command, 734-735,
737-738, 747, 749-750
K-W (subcommand)
NPAR TESTS command, 753, 755
KAISER (keyword)
FACTOR command, 488
Kaiser-Meyer-Olkin test, 485
KEEP (subcommand)
ADD FILES command, 292, 294
EXPORT command, 310
GET BMDP command, 318-319
GET command, 93-94
GET OSIRIS command, 316
GET SAS command, 314
IMPORT command, 312
MATCH FILES command, 281-282
SAVE command, 96-97
SAVE SCSS command, 304-305
UPDATE command, 299
XSAVE command, 96-97
KENDALL (keyword)
NONPAR CORR command, 728
KENDALL (subcommand)
NPAR TESTS command, 744, 746
Kendall's tau-b, 436, 728
Kendall's tau-c, 436
Kendall's W (coefficient of
concordance)
in NPAR TESTS command, 746
in RELIABILITY command, 881
KEY (subcommand)
KEYED DATA LIST command,
1007, 1009
POINT command, 1010-1011
key variables
in ADD FILES command, 293
in MATCH FILES command, 282,
283-284, 288-289
in UPDATE command, 296-297
KEYED DATA LIST (command),
1006-1008, 1009-1010
direct access files, 1006-1008
FILE subcommand, 1007
IN subcommand, 1007
KEY subcommand, 1007, 1009
keyed files, 1009-1010
NOTABLE subcommand, 1007
TABLE subcommand, 1007

keyed files, 1005-1006, 1008-1012
keyword arguments
    macro facility, 985-986
keyword defaults
    in REPORT command, 931-932
keywords
    defined, 9-10, 11-12
    reserved, 11-12
    truncation, 12
KMO (keyword)
    FACTOR command, 485
Kolmogorov-Smirnov Z (test), 737-738,
    749-750
Kruskal-Wallis H (one-way analysis of
    variance), 755
KURTOSIS (function)
    REPORT command, 910
KURTOSIS (keyword)
    DESCRIPTIVES command, 450
    FREQUENCIES command, 509
K1 (keyword)
    PROXIMITIES command, 829
K2 (keyword)
    PROXIMITIES command, 830

LABEL (keyword)
    REGRESSION command, 856
    REPORT command, 900-901, 906,
        937-938
LABEL (subcommand)
    GET BMDP command, 318
labels, see case labels, value labels,
    variable labels
LABELS (keyword)
    ANOVA command, 377
    CROSSTABS command, 439
    DESCRIPTIVES command, 451
    DISPLAY command, 104
    MEANS command, 650
    MULT RESPONSE command, 673
    ONEWAY command, 766
    RELIABILITY command, 885
    T-TEST command, 974
LAG (function), 122, 147, 150
LAG (subcommand)
    BOX-JENKINS command, 389-390
lambda, 436
LAMBDA (keyword)
    CROSSTABS command, 436
    PROXIMITIES command, 830
LAST (function)
    AGGREGATE command, 336
LAST (subcommand)
    ADD FILES command, 294
    MATCH FILES command, 289-290
LASTRES (keyword)
    MANOVA command, 585
Latin squares
    in MANOVA command, 616
LE (keyword)
    relational operator, 164
LEAD (subcommand)
    BOX-JENKINS command, 394
LEAST (function)
    REPORT command, 915
least squares
    in FACTOR command, 489
LEAVE (command), 133-134
    annotated example, 260-261
LEFT (keyword)
    REPORT command, 924-926, 935

LENGTH (function), 147
LENGTH (keyword)
    REPORT command, 925-926, 939,
        945
LENGTH (subcommand)
    REPEATING DATA command, 216
    SET command, 32, 37
    SHOW command, 32
!LENGTH (function)
    macro facility, 987
LENGTH$ (system variable)
    defined, 138
!LET (command)
    macro facility, 990
LEVEL (subcommand)
    ALSCAL command, 342
LEVER (keyword)
    REGRESSION command, 858
LFTOLERANCE (keyword)
    CNLR command, 686
LG10 (function), 121
life tables
    in SURVIVAL command, 958-959
LIMIT (keyword)
    FREQUENCIES command, 504
limitations, see entries under individual
        procedures
    GET OSIRIS (command), 317
LINE (keyword)
    DESCRIPTIVES command, 451
    REGRESSION command, 856
linear logit model, 549-550, 557-558
LINEARITY (keyword)
    MEANS command, 649
LIST (command), 531-535
    $CASENUM system variable, 534
    CASES subcommand, 532-533
    VARIABLES subcommand, 532
    with SELECT IF, 534-535
    with SPLIT FILE command, 533, 534
LIST (keyword)
    data formats, 64-65
    DATA LIST command, 58
    MATRIX DATA command, 230
    REPORT command, 898-899, 930,
        937, 939, 941, 943
    variable definition, 63-65
listing file
    in REPORT command, 897
listing report
    in REPORT command, 891, 898-899
LISTWISE (keyword)
    CLUSTER command, 414
    CORRELATIONS command, 423
    DESCRIPTIVES command, 451
    FACTOR command, 484
    HILOGLINEAR command, 528
    LOGLINEAR command, 551
    MANOVA command, 605
    NONPAR CORR command, 729
    NPAR TESTS command, 756
    ONEWAY command, 766
    PARTIAL CORR command, 781
    PLOT command, 803
    PROBIT command, 813
    PROXIMITIES command, 836
    QUICK CLUSTER command, 844
    REGRESSION command, 863
    SURVIVAL command, 964
    T-TEST command, 974
LN (function), 121

LO (keyword), see LOWEST
local documentation
    INFO command, 21
LOG (subcommand)
    BOX-JENKINS command, 388
    PROBIT command, 808
logarithms, 121
logical expressions, 129-130, 145,
        162-167
    defined, 162
    in COMPUTE, 163
    in DO IF, 156
    in ELSE IF, 160
    in END LOOP, 163, 250
    in IF, 155
    in LOOP, 163, 250
    in SELECT IF, 163, 183-184
    missing values, 166, 184
    order of evaluation, 165
    string variables, 146
logical functions, 122, 122-123
    missing values, 123
logical operators, 164-165
    defined, 164
    missing values, 166-167
logical variables
    defined, 163
logistic regression
    PROBIT (command), 820-821
LOGIT (keyword)
    PROBIT command, 807
logit model, 540, 542-545
    multinomial, 553-554
    simultaneous linear, 546
LOGLINEAR (command), 537-567
    annotated example, 542-545
    cell frequencies, 547
    cell weights, 546-547
    CONTRAST subcommand, 548-549
    covariates, 540, 541
    CRITERIA subcommand, 550
    CWEIGHT subcommand, 546-547
    design matrix, 547
    DESIGN subcommand, 541
    dispersion, analysis of, 540
    distance model, 566-567
    equiprobability model, 541, 555-557
    factor, defined, 548
    frequency table models, 555-557
    general log-linear model, 538-540,
        551-553
    GRESID subcommand, 547
    interactions, 541
    log-linear time-trend model, 555-557
    logistic regression on category
        variables, 550, 559-561
    logit model, 540, 542-545
    logit model, linear, 549-550, 557-558
    logit model, multinomial, 549,
        553-554
    main effects model, 541
    measures of association, 540
    minimum required syntax, 538-540
    MISSING subcommand, 551
    multinomial response models, 562-565
    NOPRINT subcommand, 547-548
    parameter estimates, 547
    PLOT subcommand, 548
    PRINT subcommand, 547-548
    residuals, 547

simultaneous linear logit model, 546
single-degree-of-freedom partitions, 546
statistics, 547-548
structural zeros, 546-547
variable specification, 538-540
WIDTH subcommand, 550-551
LOGSURV (keyword)
    SURVIVAL command, 959
long string, see string variables
LOOP (command), 248-251
    BREAK command, 251
    IF keyword, 250
    indexing clause, 248-249
    logical expressions, 250
    missing values, 250-251
    nested, 251
    with INPUT PROGRAM command, 266-267
    with SET MXLOOPS command, 36-37, 248, 249
    with VECTOR command, 251-252
looping constructs
    macro facility, 989-990
LOSS (keyword)
    CNLR command, 684
LOSS (subcommand)
    CNLR command, 689
LOWER (function), 147, 150
LOWER (keyword)
    MATRIX DATA command, 230
lower case, 106-107
LOWEST (keyword)
    COUNT command, 132
    MISSING VALUES command, 67
    RECODE command, 111
LPAD (function), 147, 148-149
LSD (keyword)
    ONEWAY command, 764
LSDMOD (keyword)
    ONEWAY command, 764
LSTOLERANCE (keyword)
    CNLR command, 686-687
LTRIM (function), 147

M-W (subcommand)
    NPAR TESTS command, 747, 748-749
macro argument terminators, 983-985
macro definition, 980
macro facility, 979-993
    annotated example, 991-993
    !BLANKS (function), 988
    !BREAK (command), 989-990
    !BY (keyword), 989-990
    !CHAREND (keyword), 983
    !CMDEND (keyword), 984
    !CONCAT (function), 988
    conditional processing, 989
    !DEFAULT (keyword), 986
    DEFINE command, 979-993
    !DO (command), 989-990
    !DOEND (command), 989-990
    !ELSE (keyword), 989
    !ENCLOSE (keyword), 983-984
    !ENDDEFINE command, 979-993
    !EVAL (function), 988
    !HEAD (function), 988
    !IF (command), 989
    !IFEND (command), 989
    !IN (keyword), 990
    !INDEX (function), 988

keyword arguments, 985-986
!LENGTH (function), 987
!LET command, 990
looping constructs, 989-990
macro argument terminators, 983-985
macro definition, 980
macro invocation, 980
!NOEXPAND (keyword), 986
!NULL (function), 988
!OFFEXPAND keyword, 987
!ONEXPAND keyword, 987
positional arguments, 985
!POSITIONAL keyword, 982, 985
!QUOTE (function), 988
SET command, 42-43, 988, -989
string manipulation functions, 987-988
!SUBSTRING (function), 988
!TAIL (function), 988
!THEN (keyword), 989
!TO (keyword), 989-990
!TOKENS (keyword), 983
!UNQUOTE (function), 988
!UPCASE (function), 988
macro invocation, 980
MACROS (keyword)
    DISPLAY command, 104
MAHAL (keyword)
    DISCRIMINANT command, 460
    REGRESSION command, 858
main effects model
    in LOGLINEAR, 541
MALAG (subcommand)
    BOX-JENKINS command, 391
Mann-Whitney U test, 748-749
MANOVA (command), 569-641
    analysis of covariance, 617-619
    ANALYSIS subcommand, 575-576
    annotated example, 608-611
    between-subjects factors, 571-575
    boxplots, 598
    canonical correlation analysis, 622-628
    cell statistics, 598
    CINTERVAL subcommand, 603-605
    CONTRAST subcommand, 587-591
    covariate list, 571
    CRITERIA subcommand, 591
    degrees-of-freedom partitions, 586-587
    dependent variable list, 570
    DESIGN subcommand, 571-575
    DISCRIM subcommand, 595
    doubly multivariate repeated measures, 580, 636-638
    ERROR subcommand, 591
    error term, 574-575
    factor list, 571
    Graeco-Latin squares, 616
    half-normal plots of partial correlations, 600
    homogeneity-of-variance tests, 592
    interactions, 572, 573
    Latin squares, 616
    lumped effects, 573-574
    main effects model, 572
    matrix input, 607
    matrix output, 606-607
    MATRIX subcommand, 607
    MEASURE subcommand, 580
    METHOD subcommand, 584-586
    minimum required syntax, 570-571
    MISSING subcommand, 605

multivariate multiple regression, 622-628
multivariate one-way ANOVA, 619-622
multivariate setup, 578-580
nested designs, 573, 616-617
NOPRINT subcommand, 591-594
normal plots, 598-600
observed means, 595-596
old friends, 1026
OMEANS subcommand, 595-596
parameter estimation, 584-586, 593-594
PARTITION subcommand, 572, 586-587
PCOMPS subcommand, 594
plots, 598-600
PMEANS subcommand, 597-598
polynomial transformations, 582-583
POWER subcommand, 601-603
predicted means, 597-598, 601
principal components analysis, 594
PRINT subcommand, 591-594
profile analysis, 638-641
randomized block designs, 615-616
RENAME subcommand, 584
repeated measures analysis, 576-580, 628-635, 608-611
repeated measures, doubly multivariate, 580, 636-638
RESIDUALS subcommand, 601
single-degree-of-freedom partition, 572
statistics, 591-594
stem-and-leaf plots, 600
sums of squares partitions, 586
TRANSFORM subcommand, 580-584
transformation matrix, 594
transformations, 580-584
univariate analysis of variance, 613-614
univariate setup, 578-580
variable specification, 570-571
within-subjects designs, 577-578
WSDESIGN subcommand, 578
WSFACTORS subcommand, 577-578
MAP (keyword)
    DISCRIMINANT command, 469
MAP (subcommand)
    ADD FILES command, 292, 294
    EXPORT command, 311
    GET BMDP command, 318-319
    GET command, 90-91
    GET OSIRIS command, 316
    GET SAS command, 314
    IMPORT command, 313
    MATCH FILES command, 280
    SAVE command, 95
    UPDATE command, 299
    XSAVE command, 95
margins
    in REPORT command, 904-905, 934
MARGINS (keyword)
    REPORT command, 934
master files
    defined, 296-297
MASTERFILE (subcommand)
    GET SCSS command, 307
MAT (keyword)
    MATRIX DATA command, 235

MATCH FILES (command), 277-290
  active file, 279
  annotated example, 286-287
  BY subcommand, 283-284, 288-289
  common variables, 280, 284-285
  dictionary information, 284
  DROP subcommand, 281-282
  FILE subcommand, 278-279, 288-289
  FIRST subcommand, 289-290
  IN subcommand, 285
  KEEP subcommand, 281-282
  key variables, 282, 283-284, 288-289
  LAST subcommand, 289-290
  MAP subcommand, 280
  missing values, 283-284
  nonparallel files, 282-285
  parallel files, 278-279
  RENAME subcommand, 280-281
  reordering variables, 282
  table lookup files, 288-290
  TABLE subcommand, 288-289
  with DATA LIST command, 279
  with DROP DOCUMENTS
      command, 278
  with SORT CASES command, 271,
      284
  with TEMPORARY command, 279
matching coefficients
  in PROXIMITIES, 828-829
matrices
  anti-image covariance, 485
  cell sums of squares and
      cross-products, 592
  correlation, 419-427, 476-478, 485,
      496-498, 592, 606-607, 723-731,
      780, 782«,-785, 868-870
  covariance, 422-423, 592
  factor loading, 496-498
MATRIX (keyword)
  ALSCAL command, 343
  CORRELATIONS command, 423
  NONPAR CORR command, 729
  PARTIAL CORR command, 782
MATRIX (subcommand)
  ALSCAL command, 360-362
  CLUSTER command, 414-417
  CORRELATIONS command, 424-425
  DISCRIMINANT command, 477-478
  FACTOR command, 497-498
  MANOVA command, 607
  MCONVERT command, 243
  NONPAR CORR command, 730-731
  ONEWAY command, 768-771
  PARTIAL CORR command, 782-785
  PROXIMITIES command, 836-839
  REGRESSION command, 869-870
  RELIABILITY command, 885-888
MATRIX DATA (command), 224-241
  active file, 224-225
  CELLS subcommand, 234
  CONTENTS subcommand, 235-238
  data entry format, 230
  entering data, 225-226, 228, 231,
      233-234, 235-236
  FACTORS subcommand, 233-234
  field separators, 226
  FILE subcommand, 228
  FORMAT subcommand, 230-231
  formats, print and write, 231
  matrix shape, 230-231
  N subcommand, 238
  record order, 235-236

ROWTYPE_ and subcommand settings,
    238
ROWTYPE_ variable, 227-228, 233-234,
    236-238, 238
scientific notation, 226
SPLIT subcommand, 231-233
subcommands in relation to
    ROWTYPE_ , 238
VARIABLES subcommand, 227-228
VARNAME_ variable, 227
with DISCRIMINANT command, 229
with ONEWAY command, 239-240,
    770-771
with REGRESSION command,
    240-241
matrix output
  with SPLIT FILE command, 273
matrix system files, 219-224
  format, 221-224
  matrix input, 220-221
  matrix output, 220
  MATRIX subcommand, 220-221
MAX (function), 121, 147, 150
  AGGREGATE command, 335
  REPORT command, 902, 910
MAX (keyword)
  DESCRIPTIVES command, 450
  FREQUENCIES command, 506, 508
  PLOT command, 793
  PROXIMITIES command, 824
MAXIMUM (keyword)
  FREQUENCIES command, 509
maximum function, 121
maximum likelihood
  in FACTOR command, 489
MAXMINF (keyword)
  DISCRIMINANT command, 460
MAXORDER (subcommand)
  HILOGLINEAR command, 519
MAXORDERS (subcommand)
  ANOVA command, 368-369
MAXSTEPS (keyword)
  HILOGLINEAR command, 523
  REGRESSION command, 855
MAXSTEPS (subcommand)
  DISCRIMINANT command, 463
MCA (keyword)
  ANOVA command, 374
McNemar test, 741-742
MCONVERT (command), 241-244
  APPEND subcommand, 244
  general syntax, 242-243
  MATRIX subcommand, 243
  REPLACE subcommand, 243
MDGROUP (keyword)
  MULT RESPONSE command, 673
MEAN (function), 121
  AGGREGATE command, 335
  REPORT command, 902, 910
MEAN (keyword)
  ANOVA command, 374
  DESCRIPTIVES command, 450
  DISCRIMINANT command, 464
  FREQUENCIES command, 509
  MATRIX DATA command, 235
  MEANS command, 649
  NPAR TESTS command, 738
  PROXIMITIES command, 825
  REGRESSION command, 866
MEANS (command), 643-654
  annotated example, 652-653
  CELLS subcommand, 649

compared to CROSSTABS, 645
  CROSSBREAK subcommand, 648
  crosstabulation, 648
  FORMAT subcommand, 650-651
  general mode, 644-646
  integer mode, 646-648
  limitations, 654
  MISSING subcommand, 650
  narrow output, 654
  old friends, 1026
  STATISTICS subcommand, 649-650
  TABLES subcommand, 644-646
  tree format, 651
  VARIABLES subcommand, 647-648
MEANS (keyword)
  MANOVA command, 592
  RELIABILITY command, 877
MEANSUB (keyword)
  FACTOR command, 484
MEANSUBSTITUTION (keyword)
  DISCRIMINANT command, 473
  REGRESSION command, 863
MEASURE (subcommand)
  CLUSTER command, 407
  MANOVA command, 580
  PROXIMITIES command, 825-832
median, 509
MEDIAN (function)
  REPORT command, 910
MEDIAN (keyword)
  CLUSTER command, 406
  FREQUENCIES command, 509
  NPAR TESTS command, 738
MEDIAN (subcommand)
  NPAR TESTS command, 747-748,
    753
median test, 747-748, 753
messages
  errors, notes, warnings, 25-27
METHOD (subcommand)
  ALSCAL command, 346
  ANOVA command, 369-370
  CLUSTER command, 406
  DISCRIMINANT command, 460-461
  HILOGLINEAR command, 517-519
  MANOVA command, 584-586
  REGRESSION command, 850-852
  RELIABILITY command, 884-885
MEXPAND (subcommand)
  SET command, 32, 42-43, 988
  SHOW command, 32
MIN (function), 121, 147, 150
  AGGREGATE command, 335
  REPORT command, 902, 910
MIN (keyword)
  DESCRIPTIVES command, 450
  FREQUENCIES command, 506, 508
  PLOT command, 793
MINEIGEN (keyword)
  FACTOR command, 488
  MANOVA command, 594
MINIMUM (keyword)
  FREQUENCIES command, 509
minimum function, 121
MINKOWSKI (keyword)
  PROXIMITIES command, 826
MINORITERATION (keyword)
  CNLR command, 686

MINRESID (keyword)
  DISCRIMINANT command, 460
MISSING (function), 121
  SELECT IF command, 184
MISSING (keyword)
  COUNT command, 133
  RECODE command, 116, 144
  REPORT command, 930, 937
MISSING (subcommand)
  AGGREGATE command, 336-337
  ANOVA command, 376
  CLUSTER command, 414
  CORRELATIONS command, 423
  CROSSTABS command, 437-438
  DESCRIPTIVES command, 450-451
  DISCRIMINANT command, 474
  FACTOR command, 483-484
  FILE TYPE GROUPED, 200, 202
  FILE TYPE NESTED, 207-208
  FREQUENCIES command, 512
  HILOGLINEAR command, 528
  LOGLINEAR command, 551
  MANOVA command, 605
  MEANS command, 650
  MULT RESPONSE command,
    672-673
  NONPAR CORR command, 729
  NPAR TESTS command, 756
  ONEWAY command, 765-766
  PARTIAL CORR command, 781
  PLOT command, 803
  PROBIT command, 813
  PROXIMITIES command, 836
  QUICK CLUSTER command, 844
  REGRESSION command, 863
  RELIABILITY command, 885
  REPORT command, 930
  SURVIVAL command, 964
  T-TEST command, 974
missing values, see entries under
    individual procedures
  defined, 48, 65-66
  functions, 121
  in arguments, 130-132
  in COMPUTE command, 118
  in COUNT command, 133
  in DO IF command, 161
  in END LOOP command, 250-251
  in logical expressions, 166, 184
  in logical functions, 123
  in LOOP command, 250-251
  in numeric expressions, 130
  in REPORT command, 930
  in SELECT IF command, 184
  in string expressions, 143
  MISSING function, 121
  NMISS function, 121
  suffix, 121
  SYSMIS function, 121
  system-missing, 66
  user-missing, 65-66
  VALUE function, 121
  with logical operators, 166-167
MISSING VALUES (command), 66-68
  redefining missing values, 68
  string variables, 67-68
  value range, 67
  with AGGREGATE command, 337
missing-value indicator
  changing, 930
  in REPORT command, 937

MITERATE (subcommand)
  SET command, 32, 42-43, 988
  SHOW command, 32
MIXED (keyword), see FILE TYPE
    MIXED
mixed files, 194
  defined, 194
ML (keyword)
  FACTOR command, 489
MNEST (subcommand)
  SET command, 32, 42-43, 988
  SHOW command, 32
MOD (function), 121
MODE (function)
  REPORT command, 910
MODE (keyword)
  FREQUENCIES command, 509
  NPAR TESTS command, 738
MODE (subcommand)
  FILE HANDLE command, 57
MODEL (subcommand)
  ALSCAL command, 346
  PROBIT command, 807-808
  RELIABILITY command, 876-877
MODEL PROGRAM (command)
  CNLR/NLR command, 678-679
MODELTYPE (keyword)
  MANOVA command, 584-585
modulo, 121
Moses test of extreme reactions, 747,
  751-752
moving summary titles
  in REPORT command, 936
MPRINT (subcommand)
  SET command, 32, 42-43, 988
  SHOW command, 32
MRGROUP (keyword)
  MULT RESPONSE command, 673
MSE (keyword)
  MATRIX DATA command, 235
MULT RESPONSE (command),
  657-674
  annotated example, 664-665
  BASE subcommand, 671-672
  cell percentages, 671-672
  CELLS subcommand, 671-672
  crosstabulation, 659-660
  FORMAT subcommand, 673
  FREQUENCIES subcommand,
    666-667
  group variables, 658-660
  GROUPS subcommand, 662-663
  limitations, 674
  MISSING subcommand, 672-673
  multiple response items, 657-660
  old friends, 1026
  PAIRED keyword, 669-671
  statistics, 671-672
  stub and banner tables, 673-674
  TABLES subcommand, 667-671
  VARIABLES subcommand, 663
  with COUNT command, 673-674
multidimensional scaling, 339-357
multinomial logit model, 549, 553-554
multinomial response models, 562-565
multiple break levels
  in REPORT command, 909, 948
multiple classification analysis
  in ANOVA command, 375-376
multiple comparisons between means,
  762-764

multiple response items
  defined, 657
  in MULT RESPONSE command,
    657-660
multiple statistics
  in REPORT command, 902-903
multiplication, 119
MULTIPLY (function)
  REPORT command, 915
MULTIPUNCH (keyword)
  FILE HANDLE command, 57
multipunch data, 57
multipunch format
  on DATA LIST command, 84-87
MULTIV (keyword)
  MANOVA command, 593
MULTIVARIATE (keyword)
  MANOVA command, 604-605
multivariate analysis of variance,
  569-611
multivariate F tests, 593
multivariate multiple regression, 622-628
multivariate one-way ANOVA, 619-622
MUPLUS (keyword)
  MANOVA command, 574
MWITHIN (keyword)
  MANOVA command, 575
MXERRS (subcommand)
  SET command, 32, 36
  SHOW command, 32
MXLOOPS (keyword)
  with LOOP command, 249
MXLOOPS (subcommand)
  SET command, 32, 36-37
  SHOW command, 32
  with LOOP command, 248
MXWARNS (subcommand)
  SET command, 33, 36
  SHOW command, 33

N (argument)
  REPORT command, 899
N (function)
  AGGREGATE command, 335
N (keyword)
  ANOVA command, 368
  MATRIX DATA command, 235
  REGRESSION command, 866
N (subcommand)
  MATRIX DATA command, 238
  SHOW command, 33
N OF CASES (command), 186
  with FILE TYPE command, 186
  with REPORT command, 897
N _ MATRIX (keyword)
  MATRIX DATA command, 235
N _ SCALAR (keyword)
  MATRIX DATA command, 235
N _ VECTOR (keyword)
  MATRIX DATA command, 235
NAME (keyword)
  REPORT command, 937
names
  defined, 10-11
NAMES (keyword)
  DISPLAY command, 104
  MEANS command, 651
NATRES (subcommand)
  PROBIT command, 809

NCENTER (keyword)
  BOX-JENKINS command, 392
NCOMP (keyword)
  MANOVA command, 594
NCONSTANT (keyword)
  BOX-JENKINS command, 392
NE (keyword)
  relational operator, 164
NEGATIVE (keyword)
  ALSCAL command, 347
NEGSUM (keyword)
  MANOVA command, 593
NESTED (keyword), see FILE TYPE
  NESTED
nested designs
  in MANOVA command, 573, 616-617
nested files, see FILE TYPE NESTED
NEWPAGE (keyword)
  FREQUENCIES command, 503
Newton-Raphson algorithm, 550
NFTOLERANCE (keyword)
  CNLR command, 686
NLR (command), 677-688
  CRITERIA subcommand, 685,
    687-688
  DERIVATIVES command, 680
  examples, 698-692
  FILE subcommand, 682-683
  initial values, 679, 682-683
  iteration criteria, 685, 687-688
  missing values, 696
  MODEL PROGRAM command,
    678-679
  OUTFILE subcommand, 683
  PRED subcommand, 684
  SAVE subcommand, 684-685
  saving statistics, 684-685
  starting values, 679, 682-683
  weighting cases, 691
  with FREQUENCIES command,
    718-692
  with REGRESSION command, 685
  writing a system file, 683
NMISS (function), 121
  AGGREGATE command, 336
NOBALANCED (keyword)
  MANOVA command, 585
NOBREAK (keyword)
  REPORT command, 901
NOCATLABS (keyword)
  MEANS command, 650
NOCOMPRESSION (option)
  TOSPSS procedure, 1023
NOCONSTANT (keyword)
  MANOVA command, 585-586
NODIAGONAL (keyword)
  MATRIX DATA command, 230
NOEND (keyword)
  DISCRIMINANT command, 465
!NOEXPAND (keyword)
  macro facility, 986
NOINDEX (keyword)
  CROSSTABS command, 439
  DESCRIPTIVES command, 451
NOINITIAL (keyword)
  QUICK CLUSTER command, 842
NOKAISER (keyword)
  FACTOR command, 488
NOLABELS (keyword)
  ANOVA command, 377
  CROSSTABS command, 439

DESCRIPTIVES command, 451
FREQUENCIES command, 503
MEANS command, 650
MULT RESPONSE command, 673
ONEWAY command, 766
RELIABILITY command, 885
T-TEST command, 974
NOLASTRES (keyword)
  MANOVA command, 585
NOLIST (keyword)
  REPORT command, 937
NOMINAL (keyword)
  ALSCAL command, 342
NONAME (keyword)
  REPORT command, 937
NONAMES (keyword)
  MEANS command, 651
NONE (keyword)
  ANOVA command, 368, 374
  CROSSTABS command, 435, 436,
    439
  HILOGLINEAR command, 520
  in REPORT command, 930
  LOGLINEAR command, 547
  MANOVA command, 593
  MEANS command, 649
  ONEWAY command, 765
  PARTIAL CORR command, 780
  SURVIVAL command, 964
NONMISSING (keyword)
  DISCRIMINANT command, 473
NONORMAL (keyword)
  FREQUENCIES command, 508
NONPAR CORR (command), 723-731
  annotated example, 726-727
  FORMAT subcommand, 729
  limitations, 731
  MATRIX subcommand, 730-731
  MISSING subcommand, 729
  old friends, 1026
  PRINT subcommand, 728
  random sampling, 728-729
  SAMPLE subcommand, 728-729
  significance tests, 728
  with WEIGHT command, 187
nonparallel files
  defined, 277
  MATCH FILES command, 282-285
nonparametric tests, see NPAR TESTS
NOORIGIN (keyword)
  REGRESSION command, 868
NOORIGIN (subcommand)
  REGRESSION command, 857-858
NOPRINT (keyword)
  RELIABILITY command, 886
NOPRINT (subcommand)
  LOGLINEAR command, 547-548
  MANOVA command, 591-594
NORD computers, see INFO command
NORMAL (function), 122
NORMAL (keyword)
  FREQUENCIES command, 508
  MANOVA command, 598-600
  NPAR TESTS command, 737
NORMPLOT (keyword)
  HILOGLINEAR command, 522
NORMPROB (keyword)
  LOGLINEAR command, 548
  REGRESSION command, 859
NOROTATE (keyword)
  FACTOR command, 494
  MANOVA command, 594

NOSIG (keyword)
  CORRELATIONS command, 422
  NONPAR CORR command, 728
NOSTEP (keyword)
  DISCRIMINANT command, 465
NOT (keyword)
  logical operator, 165
NOTABLE (keyword)
  FREQUENCIES command, 504
  SURVIVAL command, 959
NOTABLE (subcommand)
  DATA LIST command, 59
  KEYED DATA LIST command, 1007
  PRINT command, 173-174
  REPEATING DATA command, 215
  WRITE command, 177-178
NOTABLES (keyword)
  CROSSTABS command, 439
notes
  display file messages, 25
NOULB (keyword)
  ALSCAL command, 347
NOUPDATE (keyword)
  QUICK CLUSTER command, 842
NOVALLABS (keyword)
  CROSSTABS command, 439
NOVALUES (keyword)
  MEANS command, 651
NOWARN (keyword)
  FILE TYPE GROUPED, 199-202
  FILE TYPE MIXED, 195
  FILE TYPE NESTED, 206-208
NPAR TESTS (command), 733-757
  BINOMIAL subcommand, 735, 740
  CHISQUARE subcommand, 734-736
  COCHRAN subcommand, 744-745
  EXPECTED subcommand, 735-736
  FRIEDMAN subcommand, 744, 745
  K-S subcommand, 734-735, 737-738,
    747, 749-750
  K-W subcommand, 753, 755
  k independent samples, 752-755
  k related samples, 744-746
  KENDALL subcommand, 744, 746
  limitations, 757
  M-W subcommand, 747, 748-749
  MCNEMAR subcommand, 741-742
  MEDIAN subcommand, 747-748, 753
  MISSING subcommand, 756
  MOSES subcommand, 747, 751-752
  old friends, 1026
  random sampling, 756-757
  RUNS subcommand, 735, 738-739
  SAMPLE subcommand, 756-757
  SIGN subcommand, 741, 742
  STATISTICS subcommand, 756
  two independent samples, 746-752
  two related samples, 740-744
  W-W subcommand, 747, 750-751
  WILCOXON subcommand, 741,
    743-744
  with WEIGHT command, 187
NTEST (keyword)
  BOX-JENKINS command, 392
NTILES (subcommand)
  FREQUENCIES command, 509
NU (function)
  AGGREGATE command, 336
!NULL (function)
  macro facility, 988

NULLINE (subcommand)
  SET command, 33, 41-42
  SHOW command, 33
NUMBER (function), 147, 150
NUMBERED (command), 31
NUMBERED (keyword)
  LIST command, 534
NUMBERED (subcommand)
  SHOW command, 33
NUMERIC (command), 136
NUMERIC (keyword)
  PLOT command, 798
NUMERIC (subcommand)
  REFORMAT (command), 1026
numeric expressions, 118-132
  COMPUTE command, 117-118
  defined, 117, 118
  missing values, 130
numeric variables
  defined, 48-49
  in REPORT command, 907-908
  storage, 106, 107
NUMISS (function)
  AGGREGATE command, 336
NVALID (function), 121

OBLIMIN (keyword)
  FACTOR command, 494
OCCURS (subcommand)
  REPEATING DATA command, 214
OCHIAI (keyword)
  PROXIMITIES command, 831
OF (keyword)
  PROBIT command, 806
OFF (keyword)
  SPLIT FILE command, 272
!OFFEXPAND (keyword)
  macro facility, 987
OFFSET (keyword)
  REPORT command, 936-937
OMEANS (subcommand)
  MANOVA command, 595-596
ONEPAGE (keyword)
  FREQUENCIES command, 504
  MULT RESPONSE command, 673
ONETAIL (keyword)
  CORRELATIONS command, 422
  NONPAR CORR command, 728
  PARTIAL CORR command, 778
ONEWAY (command), 759-772
  analysis list, 760
  annotated example, 767
  CONTRAST subcommand, 761-762
  FORMAT subcommand, 766
  HARMONIC subcommand, 764-765
  limitations, 772
  matrix input, 769-771
  matrix output, 768-769
  MATRIX subcommand, 768-771
  MISSING subcommand, 765-766
  old friends, 1026
  POLYNOMIAL subcommand,
    760-761
  RANGES subcommand, 762-764
  ranges, user-specified, 764
  STATISTICS subcommand, 765
  value labels, 766
  with MATRIX DATA command,
    239-240, 770-771
ONEWAY (keyword)
  MANOVA command, 592

!ONEXPAND (keyword)
  macro facility, 987
online assistance, 21
ONLY (keyword)
  GET BMDP command, 318
OPTIMAL (keyword)
  MANOVA command, 594
OPTIONS (command), 20
  old friends, 1026
OPTOLERANCE (keyword)
  CNLR command, 687
OR (keyword)
  logical operator, 164-165
order of commands, 14
  defined, 995-996
  file definition commands, 997
  input programs, 997
  procedure commands, 997
  program states, 995-997
  restricted transformation commands,
    997
  transformation commands, 997
  unrestricted utility commands, 997
order of operations
  numeric expressions, 120
ORDERED (subcommand)
  FILE TYPE GROUPED, 200
ORDINAL (keyword)
  ALSCAL command, 342
ORIGIN (keyword)
  REGRESSION command, 868
ORIGIN (subcommand)
  BOX-JENKINS command, 394
  REGRESSION command, 857-858
ORTHO (keyword)
  MANOVA command, 593
ORTHONORM (keyword)
  MANOVA command, 581
OSIRIS to SPSS-X data conversion
  in GET OSIRIS (command), 316-317
OTHER (keyword)
  FILE TYPE GROUPED, 201
  FILE TYPE MIXED, 197
  FILE TYPE NESTED, 209
OUT (keyword)
  CLUSTER command, 414-415
  CORRELATIONS command, 424-425
  DISCRIMINANT command, 475-476
  FACTOR command, 495-496
  MANOVA command, 605-606
  NONPAR CORR command, 730-731
  ONEWAY command, 768
  PARTIAL CORR command, 782-784
  PROXIMITIES command, 836-837
  REGRESSION command, 867-868
  RELIABILITY command, 885-887
OUTFILE (subcommand)
  AGGREGATE command, 330-331
  ALSCAL command, 359-360
  CNLR command, 683
  EXPORT command, 310
  INFO command, 21-23
  PRINT command, 173-174
  PRINT SPACE command, 175
  QUICK CLUSTER command, 844
  REPORT command, 897
  SAVE command, 95
  SAVE SCSS command, 304
  WRITE command, 177
  XSAVE command, 95
OUTLIERS (keyword)
  REGRESSION command, 859, 859

OUTPUT (option)
  TOSPSS procedure, 1023
output file
  defined, 52
OUTS (keyword)
  REGRESSION command, 856
OVERALL (keyword)
  MANOVA command, 592
overflows
  CNLR command, 696-697
overlay plots
  PLOT command, 794-795
OVERVIEW (keyword)
  INFO command, 25

P (keyword)
  HILOGLINEAR command, 523
  PROBIT command, 808
P (subcommand)
  BOX-JENKINS command, 390
PACF (keyword)
  BOX-JENKINS command, 395
padding strings, 148-149
PAF (keyword)
  FACTOR command, 489
PAGE (keyword)
  REPORT command, 925-926, 945,
    946
page layout
  in REPORT command, 939-940
page lengths
  in REPORT command, 944-945
page numbers
  in REPORT command, 925, 945
page size, see SET command
)PAGE (argument)
  REPORT command, 925
PAGE1 (keyword)
  REPORT command, 945
PAIRED (keyword)
  MULT RESPONSE command,
    669-671
  NPAR TESTS command, 741
  T-TEST command, 971
paired crosstabulations
  in MULT RESPONSE command,
    669-671
PAIRS (subcommand)
  T-TEST command, 971
PAIRWISE (keyword)
  CORRELATIONS command, 423
  FACTOR command, 484
  NONPAR CORR command, 729
  QUICK CLUSTER command, 844
  REGRESSION command, 863
  SURVIVAL command, 962
PARALL (keyword)
  PROBIT command, 810
PARALLEL (keyword)
  RELIABILITY command, 877
parallel files
  defined, 277
  MATCH FILES command, 278-282
parallel model
  in RELIABILITY command, 874
parameter estimates
  in MANOVA command, 593-594
PARAMETERS (keyword)
  MANOVA command, 592, 593-594
PARTIAL CORR (command), 775-785
  annotated example, 786-787
  control variables, 777-778
  correlation list, 777

FORMAT subcommand, 781-782
limitations, 785
matrix input, 784-785
matrix output, 783-784
MATRIX subcommand, 782-785
MISSING subcommand, 781
old friends, 1026
order values, 777-778
SIGNIFICANCE subcommand, 778
STATISTICS subcommand, 780
VARIABLES subcommand, 776
partial correlation coefficient, see
    PARTIAL CORR
partial regression plots
    in REGRESSION command, 861-862
PARTIALPLOT (subcommand)
    REGRESSION command, 861-862
PARTITION (subcommand)
    MANOVA command, 586-587
PASSWORD (subcommand)
    FILE HANDLE command, 1014
PATTERN (keyword)
    PROXIMITIES command, 832
PA1 (keyword)
    FACTOR command, 489
PA2 (keyword)
    FACTOR command, 489
PC (keyword)
    FACTOR command, 489
PCOMPS (subcommand)
    MANOVA command, 594
PCON (keyword)
    NLR command, 687
PCON (subcommand)
    BOX-JENKINS command, 393
PCT (function)
    REPORT command, 915
PEARSON CORR, see
    CORRELATIONS
Pearson correlation coefficient, see also
    CORRELATIONS, 436, 649
PERCENT (function)
    REPORT command, 910
PERCENT (keyword)
    FREQUENCIES command, 507, 508
PERCENTILES (subcommand)
    FREQUENCIES command, 508
PERIOD (subcommand)
    BOX-JENKINS command, 389
period missing value specification
    AGGREGATE command, 337
    suffix, 121
Perkin Elmer computers, see INFO
    command
PGT (function)
    AGGREGATE command, 335
    REPORT command, 910
PHI (keyword)
    CROSSTABS command, 436
    PROXIMITIES command, 831
phi coefficient, 436
PH2 (keyword)
    PROXIMITIES command, 827
PIN (function)
    AGGREGATE command, 335
    REPORT command, 910
PIN (keyword)
    DISCRIMINANT command, 463
    REGRESSION command, 854
PLAIN (keyword)
    REPORT command, 918

PLOT (command), 789-803
    annotated example, 800-801
    contour plots, 793-794
    CUTPOINT subcommand, 798-803
    FORMAT subcommand, 793-796
    HORIZONTAL subcommand,
        792-793
    HSIZE subcommand, 796-798
    limitations, 803-800
    MISSING subcommand, 803
    overlay plots, 794-795
    PLOT subcommand, 790-792
    regression plots, 795-796
    SYMBOLS subcommand, 798-799
    TITLE subcommand, 792
    VERTICAL subcommand, 792-793
    VSIZE subcommand, 796-798
    with CNLR command, 703-706
PLOT (keyword)
    MANOVA command, 597, 601
    REGRESSION command, 860
PLOT (subcommand)
    ALSCAL command, 359
    BOX-JENKINS command, 395
    CLUSTER command, 412-414
    DISCRIMINANT command, 469-473
    FACTOR command, 486-487
    HILOGLINEAR command, 522-523
    LOGLINEAR command, 548
    MANOVA command, 598-600
    PLOT command, 790-792
    SURVIVAL command, 959-961
PLOTWISE (keyword)
    PLOT command, 803
PLT (function)
    AGGREGATE command, 335
    REPORT command, 910
PMEANS (subcommand)
    MANOVA command, 597-598
POINT (command), 1010-1012
    FILE subcommand, 1010
    KEY subcommand, 1010-1011
    keyed files, 1010-1012
POISSON (keyword)
    NPAR TESTS command, 737
POLYNOMIAL (keyword)
    LOGLINEAR command, 549
    MANOVA command, 581, 582-583,
        588
POLYNOMIAL (subcommand)
    ONEWAY (command), 760-761
POOLED (keyword)
    DISCRIMINANT command, 473
    REGRESSION command, 859
portable files
    defined, 52, 308-309
positional arguments
    macro facility, 985
!POSITIONAL (keyword)
    macro facility, 982, 985
POUT (function)
    AGGREGATE command, 335
POUT (keyword)
    DISCRIMINANT command, 463
    REGRESSION command, 855
POWER (keyword)
    CLUSTER command, 407
    PROXIMITIES command, 826
POWER (subcommand)
    BOX-JENKINS command, 388
    MANOVA command, 601-603

PP (subcommand)
    BOX-JENKINS command, 393
PQ (subcommand)
    BOX-JENKINS command, 393
precedence of commands, see order of
    commands
PRED (keyword)
    CNLR command, 684
    REGRESSION command, 858
PRED (subcommand)
    CNLR command, 684
predictability measures
    in PROXIMITIES, 830-831
preparing data
    in REPORT command, 895-896
PRESERVE (command)
    macro facility, 988-989
PRESORTED (subcommand)
    AGGREGATE command, 334
PREVIOUS (keyword)
    REPORT command, 928
PRIME computers, see INFO command
principal axis factoring, 489
principal components analysis, 489, 594
PRINT (command), 170-174
    $CASENUM system variable, 173
    formats, 171
    line specifications, 171-172
    missing values, 174
    NOTABLE subcommand, 173-174
    OUTFILE subcommand, 173-174
    RECORDS subcommand, 173-174
    strings, 172-173
    TABLE subcommand, 173-174
    variable list, 170-171
    with DO IF command, 173
    with REPORT command, 953
    with SORT CASES command, 271
PRINT (subcommand)
    ALSCAL command, 358-359
    AUTORECODE command, 380
    BOX-JENKINS command, 395
    CLUSTER command, 408-409
    CORRELATIONS command, 421-422
    END REPEAT command, 137-138
    FACTOR command, 485
    HILOGLINEAR command, 519-522
    LOGLINEAR command, 547-548
    MANOVA command, 591-594
    NONPAR CORR command, 728
    PROBIT command, 809-810
    PROXIMITIES command, 832-833
    QUICK CLUSTER command, 843
    SURVIVAL command, 959
PRINT EJECT (command), 174-175
    $CASENUM system variable, 174-175
    with DO IF command, 174-175
print formats
    in LIST command, 531
    in PRINT command, 170
    in REPORT command, 917-918
    setting default, 38
PRINT FORMATS (command), 180
    with AGGREGATE command, 335
    with LIST command, 531
    with PRINT command, 170
    with REPORT command, 952
PRINT SPACE (command), 175-176
    $CASENUM system variable, 175-176
    number of lines, 176
    OUTFILE subcommand, 175
    with DO IF command, 175-176

PRINTBACK (subcommand)
  SET command, 33, 38
  SHOW command, 33
PRIORS (subcommand)
  DISCRIMINANT command, 468
PROBIT (command), 805-813
  annotated examples, 814-821
  case-by-case form, 810-812
  CRITERIA subcommand, 808
  limitations, 813
  LOG subcommand, 808
  logistic regression, 820-821
  MISSING subcommand, 813
  MODEL subcommand, 807-808
  NATRES subcommand, 809
  PRINT subcommand, 809-810
  response rate, 809
  variable specification, 806-807
  with CNLR command, 711-712
PROBIT (function), 122
PROBIT (keyword)
  PROBIT command, 807
PROBS (keyword)
  DISCRIMINANT command, 475
PROCEDURE OUTPUT (command)
  old friends, 1026
  with CROSSTABS command, 442-443
  with FREQUENCIES command, 505
  with SURVIVAL command, 964
procedure state
  defined, 994-995
procedures
  update documentation, 22
PROCEDURES (keyword)
  INFO command, 21-23
processing mode, 17-20
profile analysis, 638-641
program states
  defined, 994-995
  order of commands, 995-997
PROX (keyword)
  MATRIX DATA command, 235
PROXIMITIES (command), 824-839
  annotated examples, 834-835
  binary data, 827-832
  continuous data, 826
  frequency count data, 826-827
  ID subcommand, 833
  limitations, 839
  matrix input, 838-839
  matrix output, 836-838
  MATRIX subcommand, 836-839
  MEASURE subcommand, 825-832
  MISSING subcommand, 836
  old friends, 1026
  PRINT subcommand, 832-833
  STANDARDIZE subcommand,
    824-825
  variable specification, 824
  VIEW subcommand, 825
  with FACTOR command, 839
PROXIMITIES (keyword)
  PROXIMITIES command, 832
PSP (subcommand)
  BOX-JENKINS command, 393
PSQ (subcommand)
  BOX-JENKINS command, 393

Q (keyword)
  PROXIMITIES command, 831
Q (subcommand)
  BOX-JENKINS command, 390

Q, Cochran's, 744-745
QR (keyword)
  MANOVA command, 585
quartiles, 756
QUARTILES (keyword)
  NPAR TESTS command, 756
QUARTIMAX (keyword)
  FACTOR command, 494
  MANOVA command, 594, 595
QUICK CLUSTER (command),
    841-844
  annotated examples, 845-847
  CRITERIA subcommand, 842
  FILE subcommand, 843
  INITIAL subcommand, 843
  MISSING subcommand, 844
  old friends, 1026
  OUTFILE subcommand, 844
  PRINT subcommand, 843
  SAVE subcommand, 844
  standardization, 842
  variable specification, 842
  with large number of cases, 844
!QUOTE (function)
  macro facility, 988

r, see Pearson correlation coefficient
R (keyword)
  MANOVA command, 574-575, 591
  REGRESSION command, 855
RACF (keyword)
  BOX-JENKINS command, 395
random numbers
  setting seed, 40
randomized block designs
  in MANOVA command, 615-616
range, see value range
RANGE (function), 122, 146, 148, 150
RANGE (keyword)
  DESCRIPTIVES command, 450
  FREQUENCIES command, 509
  PROXIMITIES command, 824
RANGES (subcommand)
  ONEWAY command, 762-764
rank-order correlation coefficients, see
  NONPAR CORR
RAO (keyword)
  DISCRIMINANT command, 461
RATIO (keyword)
  ALSCAL command, 342
RAW (keyword)
  DISCRIMINANT command, 465
  MANOVA command, 595
RCON (keyword)
  NLR command, 687
RCONVERGE (keyword)
  FACTOR command, 488
reading ASCII/EBCDIC matrix
  materials, 224-238
RECODE (command)
  annotated example, 112-113
  compared to AUTORECODE, 379
  CONVERT keyword, 145
  COPY keyword, 117, 144
  ELSE keyword, 111, 144
  INTO keyword, 116-117, 144-145
  MISSING keyword, 116, 144
  numeric variables, 110-117
  string variables, 143-145
  SYSMIS keyword, 116
  value range, 111, 116
  with DO IF command, 156

RECORD (subcommand)
  FILE TYPE GROUPED, 198-199
  FILE TYPE MIXED, 195
  FILE TYPE NESTED, 206
RECORD TYPE (command)
  CASE subcommand, 201-202, 209
  DUPLICATE subcommand, 202
  MISSING subcommand, 202
  OTHER keyword, 197, 201, 209
  SKIP subcommand, 197, 201, 209
  SPREAD subcommand, 209-210
  with FILE TYPE GROUPED,
    200-202
  with FILE TYPE MIXED, 196-197
  with FILE TYPE NESTED, 208-210
RECORDS (subcommand)
  DATA LIST command, 58
  PRINT command, 173-174
  WRITE command, 177
RECTANGULAR (keyword)
  ALSCAL command, 341
rectangular file
  defined, 47-48
REDUNDANCY (keyword)
  MANOVA command, 592
REFERENCE (keyword)
  PLOT command, 793
REFORMAT (command), 1026
REG (keyword)
  ANOVA command, 374
  FACTOR command, 494
REGRESSION (command), 849-870
  analysis of residuals, 858-863
  annotated example, 864-865
  backward elimination, 851
  CASEWISE subcommand, 859-860
  CRITERIA subcommand, 854-855
  DEPENDENT subcommand, 850
  DESCRIPTIVES subcommand,
    866-867
  display format, 860-861
  equation-control subcommands,
    853-858
  forced entry, 851
  forced removal, 851
  forward entry, 851
  matrix input, 869-870
  matrix output, 868-870
  MATRIX subcommand, 869-870
  METHOD subcommand, 850-852
  minimum required syntax, 850-852
  MISSING subcommand, 863
  missing values, 863
  NOORIGIN subcommand, 857-858
  old friends, 1026
  ORIGIN subcommand, 857-858
  PARTIALPLOT subcommand,
    861-862
  REGWGT subcommand, 853-854
  RESIDUALS subcommand, 858-859
  SAVE subcommand, 862-863
  SCATTERPLOT subcommand, 861
  SELECT subcommand, 866
  STATISTICS subcommand, 855-857
  stepwise selection, 851
  VARIABLES subcommand, 853
  WIDTH subcommand, 860-861
  with CNLR command, 685, 698-699,
    707-711
  with MATRIX DATA command,
    240-241

REGRESSION (keyword)
  PLOT command, 795-796
regression plots
  PLOT command, 795-796
REGWGT (subcommand)
  REGRESSION command, 853-854
relational operators, 163-164
  defined, 163
RELIABILITY (command), 873-888
  alternative computing methods,
    884-885
  analysis of variance, 879-880, 884
  annotated example, 882-883
  FORMAT subcommand, 885
  Friedman's analysis of variance, 881
  limitations, 888
  matrix input, 888
  matrix output, 886-888
  MATRIX subcommand, 885-888
  METHOD subcommand, 884-885
  MISSING subcommand, 885
  MODEL subcommand, 876-877
  old friends, 1026
  repeated measures analysis, 879-880
  scale name, 875
  SCALE subcommand, 875-876
  STATISTICS subcommand, 878-884
  SUMMARY subcommand, 877-878
  tests for violation of assumptions, 881
  variable labels, 885
  VARIABLES subcommand, 875
remainder function, 121
REMOVE (keyword)
  REGRESSION command, 851
RENAME (subcommand)
  ADD FILES command, 291-292, 294
  EXPORT command, 311
  GET BMDP command, 318-319
  GET command, 91-92
  GET OSIRIS command, 316
  GET SAS command, 314
  IMPORT command, 312-313
  MANOVA command, 584
  MATCH FILES command, 280-281
  SAVE command, 95-96
  SAVE SCSS command, 305
  UPDATE command, 298-299
  XSAVE command, 95-96
RENAME VARIABLES (command),
    71-72
reordering variables
  in ADD FILES command, 292, 294
  in GET command, 93-94
  in MATCH FILES command, 282
  in SAVE command, 97
  in UPDDATE (command), 298-299
  in XSAVE command, 97
REPEATED (keyword)
  LOGLINEAR command, 549
  MANOVA command, 581-582, 590
repeated measures analysis, see
    MANOVA command, 879-880
REPEATING DATA (command),
    211-212
  CONTINUED subcommand, 216-217
  DATA subcommand, 215
  FILE subcommand, 215
  ID subcommand, 217
  LENGTH subcommand, 216
  NOTABLE subcommand, 215
  OCCURS subcommand, 214
  STARTS subcommand, 213-214

with DATA LIST command, 212-213
with END INPUT PROGRAM
    command, 212-213
with FILE TYPE command, 212-213
with INPUT PROGRAM command,
    212-213
REPLACE (subcommand)
  MCONVERT command, 243
REPORT (command), 891-953
  aggregate functions, 909-918
  aligning columns, 933
  annotated examples, 919-920, 921-923
  automatic fit, 906
  AUTOMATIC vs MANUAL, 931-932
  basic report, 893-895, 897-904
  basic subcommands, 893
  break cells, 906
  break groups, 900-901
  BREAK subcommand, 893, 900-903,
    909, 912-915, 927, 934-935,
    935-936, 936-937, 944-945,
    945-946
  cell displays, 907-908
  column contents, 937-938
  column headings, 903-904, 934-935
  column widths, 905-906, 934
  columns, 891
  combining break groups, 927
  compared with other procedures,
    949-950
  composite functions, 915-917, 948
  criteria used by
    FORMAT=AUTOMATIC, 904
  CROSSBREAK-like tables, 950-951
  CROSSTABS-like tables, 951-952
  dates, 925
  defaults, 931-932
  FORMAT subcommand, 893,
    930-935, 937, 938, 940-945
  FORMAT=AUTOMATIC, 897-904
  heading underscores, 935
  intercolumn spacing, 906, 938-939
  introduction, 891
  keyword defaults, 931-932
  limitations, 949
  listing reports, 891, 898-899
  margins, 904-905, 934
  MISSING keyword, 930
  MISSING subcommand, 930
  missing values, 930
  missing-value indicator, 930, 937
  multiple break levels, 909, 948
  multiple statistics, 902-903
  old friends, 1026
  OUTFILE subcommand, 897
  overriding automatic column formats,
    931-939
  overriding automatic row formats,
    939-945
  page layout, 939-940
  page length, 944-945
  page numbers, 925, 945
  preparing data, 895-896
  repeating summary specifications, 928
  report alignment, 904-905
  report cells, 906, 936-937
  report contents, 906
  report organization, 892-893
  report variables, 900
  row spacing, 940-944
  rows, 891
  separate listing file, 897
  stacking report variables, 926-927

string and numeric variables, 907-908
STRING subcommand, 928-930, 934
summaries on one line, 947-948
summary cells, 906
summary reports, 891, 898-899
SUMMARY subcommand, 893,
    901-903, 909-918, 936, 941-942,
    944, 945-946, 947-948
summary titles, 911-912, 936
titles and footnotes, 924-926
totals, 912-915, 945-946
underscores, 935-936
using strings, 928-930
VARIABLES subcommand, 893, 900,
    926-927, 934-935, 936-938,
    938-939, 943
with COMPUTE command, 907-908
with FORMATS command, 907-908
with N OF CASES command, 897
with PRINT command, 953
with PRINT FORMATS command,
    952
with SAMPLE command, 897
with SORT CASES, 925-926
with SORT CASES command, 271
with SPLIT FILE command, 953
with VARIABLE LABELS
    command, 953
with WRITE command, 953
REPORT (keyword)
  CROSSTABS command, 437
report alignment
  in REPORT command, 904-905
report cells
  in REPORT command, 906, 936-937
report variables
  in REPORT command, 891, 893, 896,
    900
  stacking, 926-927
REPR (keyword)
  FACTOR command, 485
REREAD (command), 263-264
  COLUMN subcommand, 264
RESCALE (keyword)
  PROXIMITIES command, 824-825
reserved keywords, 11-12
  in GET SCSS command, 308
  in SAVE SCSS command, 304
RESET (keyword)
  REPORT command, 945
RESID (keyword), see RESIDUAL
    keyword
  CNLR command, 684
  CROSSTABS command, 435
  HILOGLINEAR command, 520, 522
RESIDUAL (keyword)
  BOX-JENKINS command, 395
  LOGLINEAR command, 547, 548
  MANOVA command, 574-575, 591
  REGRESSION command, 858
RESIDUALS (subcommand)
  MANOVA command, 601
  REGRESSION command, 858-859
residuals analysis
  in REGRESSION command, 858-863
RESPONSES (keyword)
  MULT RESPONSE command, 672
RESTORE (command)
  macro facility, 988-989
result files
  in ADD FILES command, 290
  in MATCH FILES command, 278

REVERSE (keyword)
  PROXIMITIES command, 825
RIGHT (keyword)
  REPORT command, 924-926, 935
RINDEX (function), 148, 149-150, 151
RMP (keyword)
  PROBIT command, 809-810
RND (function), 120
ROTATE (keyword)
  MANOVA command, 594, 595
ROTATION (keyword)
  FACTOR command, 485, 486
ROTATION (subcommand)
  DISCRIMINANT command, 465
  FACTOR command, 494
rounding function, 120
ROW (keyword)
  ALSCAL command, 343
  CROSSTABS command, 435
  MULT RESPONSE command, 671
row formats
  overriding, 939-945
row spacing
  in REPORT command, 940-944
ROWCONF (keyword)
  ALSCAL command, 345
rows
  in REPORT command, 891
  primary order, 892-893
  secondary order, 892-893
ROWS (keyword)
  ALSCAL command, 341
Roy-Bargmann step-down F test, 593
RPAD (function), 148
RR (keyword)
  PROXIMITIES command, 829
RT (keyword)
  PROXIMITIES command, 829
RTRIM (function), 148, 148-149
RUNS (subcommand)
  NPAR TESTS command, 735,
    738-739
runs test, 738-739
RW (keyword)
  MANOVA command, 574-575, 591

SAMPLE (command), 185-186
  exact-sized sample, 185
  placement, 189
  proportional sample, 185
  with DO IF command, 190
  with other transformations, 189-190
  with REPORT command, 897
  with TEMPORARY command, 189
SAMPLE (subcommand)
  NONPAR CORR command, 728-729
  NPAR TESTS command, 756-757
SAS to SPSS-X data conversion
  in GET SAS (command), 314-315
  TOSPSS procedure, 1024-1025
SASLIB (subcommand)
  GET SAS command, 314
SAVE (command), see also XSAVE
  command, 99-102
  COMPRESSED keyword, 97-98
  DROP subcommand, 96-97
  KEEP subcommand, 96-97
  MAP subcommand, 95
  OUTFILE subcommand, 95
  RENAME subcommand, 95-96
  reordering variables, 97

  UNCOMPRESSED keyword, 97-98
  with TEMPORARY command, 102
SAVE (subcommand)
  CLUSTER command, 407-408
  CNLR command, 684-685
  DESCRIPTIVES command, 449-450
  DISCRIMINANT command, 474-475
  FACTOR command, 494-495
  QUICK CLUSTER command, 844
  REGRESSION command, 862-863
SAVE SCSS (command), 303-306
  DROP subcommand, 304-305
  KEEP subcommand, 304-305
  missing values, 304
  OUTFILE subcommand, 304
  RENAME subcommand, 305
  reserved keywords, 304
SCALE (keyword)
  RELIABILITY command, 878
SCALE (subcommand)
  RELIABILITY command, 875-876
scale analysis, see RELIABILITY
  command
scale name
  in RELIABILITY command, 875
SCAN (subcommand)
  GET BMDP command, 318
SCATTERPLOT (subcommand)
  REGRESSION command, 861
scatterplots, see also PLOT command
  in REGRESSION command, 861
SCHEDULE (keyword)
  CLUSTER command, 408
SCHEFFE (keyword)
  ONEWAY command, 764
Scheffe's test, 764
SCOMPRESSION (subcommand)
  SHOW command, 33
SCORES (keyword)
  DISCRIMINANT command, 475
scratch files
  compression, 41
scratch variables, 10
  defined, 134-135
scree plots
  in FACTOR command, 486
SCSS, see GET SCSS or SAVE SCSS
SD (function), 121
  AGGREGATE command, 335
  REPORT command, 902
SD (keyword)
  MATRIX DATA command, 235
  PROXIMITIES command, 825
SDIFFERENCE (subcommand)
  BOX-JENKINS command, 389
SDRESID (keyword)
  REGRESSION command, 858
SEED (subcommand)
  SET command, 33, 40
  SHOW command, 33
SEKURT (keyword)
  FREQUENCIES command, 509
SELECT (subcommand)
  DISCRIMINANT command, 459-460
  REGRESSION command, 866
SELECT IF (command), 183-185
  annotated example, 188
  MISSING function, 184
  missing values, 184
  placement, 189
  VALUE function, 184
  with $CASENUM, 184

  with DO IF command, 190
  with LIST command, 534-535
  with other transformations, 189-190
  with TEMPORARY command, 189
SEMEAN (keyword)
  DESCRIPTIVES command, 450
  FREQUENCIES command, 509
SEPARATE (keyword)
  DISCRIMINANT command, 470, 473
separate listing file
  in REPORT command, 897
SEPRED (keyword)
  REGRESSION command, 858
SEQUENTIAL (keyword)
  MANOVA command, 586
SER (keyword)
  BOX-JENKINS command, 395
SERIAL (keyword)
  CORRELATIONS command, 423
  DESCRIPTIVES command, 451
  NONPAR CORR command, 729
  PARTIAL CORR command, 782
series plots
  in BOX-JENKINS command, 387
SES (keyword)
  REGRESSION command, 856
SESKEW (keyword)
  FREQUENCIES command, 509
SET (command), 31-44
  annotated example, 34-35
SET WIDTH (command)
  with DESCRIPTIVES command, 451
  with REPORT command, 904-905
  with T-TEST command, 974
SEUCLID (keyword)
  CLUSTER command, 407
  PROXIMITIES command, 826
SHAPE (subcommand)
  ALSCAL command, 341-342
short string, see string variables
SHOW (command), 31-44
  annotated example, 34-35
SIG (keyword)
  CORRELATIONS command, 422
  FACTOR command, 485
  NONPAR CORR command, 728
  REGRESSION command, 866
SIGN (subcommand)
  NPAR TESTS command, 741, 742
sign test, 742
SIGNIF (keyword)
  MANOVA command, 592, 593
SIGNIFICANCE (subcommand)
  PARTIAL CORR command, 778
SIMPLE (keyword)
  LOGLINEAR command, 549
  MANOVA command, 581, 588
SIN (function), 121
SINCE (keyword)
  INFO command, 23
sine, 121
SINGLE (keyword)
  CLUSTER command, 406
  LIST command, 533-534
SINGLEDF (keyword)
  MANOVA command, 593
SIZE (keyword)
  DISCRIMINANT command, 468
  PROXIMITIES command, 831
  REGRESSION command, 859, 861
SKEWNESS (function)
  REPORT command, 910

SKEWNESS (keyword)
DESCRIPTIVES command, 450
FREQUENCIES command, 509
SKIP (keyword)
REPORT command, 939, 944, 946
SKIP (subcommand)
FILE TYPE GROUPED, 201
FILE TYPE MIXED, 197
FILE TYPE NESTED, 209
slash
required, 13
SM (keyword)
PROXIMITIES command, 829
SNK (keyword)
ONEWAY command, 764
SOLUTION (keyword)
MANOVA command, 592
Somers' d, 436
SORT (keyword)
FACTOR command, 487
SORT CASES (command), 269-271
annotated example, 274-275
BY keyword, 269
specifying order, 269-270
string variables, 270-271
with ADD FILES command, 271
with AGGREGATE command, 271
with MATCH FILES command, 271, 284
with PRINT command, 271
with REPORT command, 271, 895-896, 909
with SPLIT FILE command, 272
with UPDATE command, 271, 296-297
SORTED (keyword)
DISPLAY command, 104-105
sorting data
choosing a sort program, 41
source variables
in AGGREGATE command, 334
SP (subcommand)
BOX-JENKINS command, 390
SPEARMAN (keyword)
NONPAR CORR command, 728
Spearman-Brown split-half coefficient, 873
Spearman's rho, 728
SPECIAL (keyword)
LOGLINEAR command, 549
MANOVA command, 581, 583, 590-591
specifying page lengths
in REPORT command, 944-945
SPLIT (keyword)
RELIABILITY command, 876-877
SPLIT (subcommand)
MATRIX DATA command, 231-233
SPLIT FILE (command), 271-273
annotated example, 274-275
with AGGREGATE command, 273, 331
with ALSCAL command, 341
with LIST command, 533, 534
with REPORT command, 953
with SORT CASES command, 272
with TEMPORARY command, 272
split model
in RELIABILITY command, 873

SPREAD (subcommand)
FILE TYPE NESTED, 209-210
SPSSFILE (option)
TOSPSS procedure, 1023
SQ (subcommand)
BOX-JENKINS command, 390
SQRT (function), 121
square root, 121
SRESID (keyword)
CROSSTABS command, 435
REGRESSION command, 858
SSCON (keyword)
NLR command, 687
SSCP (keyword)
MANOVA command, 592-593
SSTYPE (keyword)
MANOVA command, 586
SS1 through SS5 (keywords)
PROXIMITIES command, 829-831
stacking variables
in REPORT command, 926-927
STAN (keyword)
MANOVA command, 595
stand-in variable
DO REPEAT command, 136
standard deviation function, see also SD, STDEV, STDDEV, STDV, 121
STANDARDIZE (keyword)
PLOT command, 793
STANDARDIZE (subcommand)
PROXIMITIES command, 824-825
standardized scores, see Z scores
starting values
CNLR command, 679, 682-683
STARTS (subcommand)
REPEATING DATA command, 213-214
states, see program states
statistic D
defined, 956
STATISTICS (command), 20
old friends, 1026
STATISTICS (subcommand)
CORRELATIONS command, 422-423
CROSSTABS command, 436-437
DISCRIMINANT command, 464-465, 468-469
MEANS command, 649-650
NPAR TESTS command, 756
ONEWAY command, 765
PARTIAL CORR command, 780
REGRESSION command, 855-857
RELIABILITY command, 878-884
STATUS (subcommand)
SURVIVAL command, 958
STDDEV (function)
REPORT command, 910
STDDEV (keyword)
DESCRIPTIVES command, 450
DISCRIMINANT command, 464
FREQUENCIES command, 509
MATRIX DATA command, 235
MEANS command, 649
REGRESSION command, 866
STDV (keyword)
MANOVA command, 593
stem-and-leaf plots, 600
STEMLEAF (keyword)
MANOVA command, 600
STEP (keyword)
DISCRIMINANT command, 465

STEPDOWN (keyword)
MANOVA command, 593
STEPLIMIT (keyword)
CNLR command, 686
STEPWISE (keyword)
REGRESSION command, 851
STIMWGHT (keyword)
ALSCAL command, 345
STRESSMIN (keyword)
ALSCAL command, 347
STRICTPARALLEL (keyword)
RELIABILITY command, 877
strictparallel model
in RELIABILITY command, 874
STRING (command), 141-142
STRING (function), 148, 150
STRING (subcommand)
REPORT command, 928-930, 934
string expressions
defined, 145-146
string functions, 147-151
string manipulation functions
macro facility, 987-988
string variables
defined, 48, 141
in DATA LIST command, 63
in logical expressions, 146
in MISSING VALUES command, 67-68
in REPORT command, 907-908
in SAVE SCSS command, 304
in SORT CASES command, 270-271
missing values, 143
storage, 106, 107
strings
case, 106-107
defined, 12, 142
in COMPUTE command, 142
in PRINT command, 172-173
in RECODE command, 142
in VALUE LABELS command, 68-69
in VARIABLE LABELS command, 68-69
in WRITE command, 177
structural zeros
HILOGLINEAR command, 517
STRUCTURE (keyword)
DISCRIMINANT command, 465
stub and banner tables
in MULT RESPONSE command, 673-674
Student-Newman-Keuls test, 764
Student's t, see T-TEST
subcommands
defined, 9-10
SUBJWGHT (keyword)
ALSCAL command, 345
SUBSTR (function), 148-150
!SUBSTRING (function)
macro facility, 988
substrings, 149-150
SUBTITLE (command), 30
SUBTRACT (function)
REPORT command, 915
subtraction, 119
suffix
missing values, 121, 131
SUM (function), 121
AGGREGATE command, 335
REPORT command, 902, 910

SUM (keyword)
  DESCRIPTIVES command, 450
  FREQUENCIES command, 509
  MEANS command, 649
SUMMARY (subcommand)
  RELIABILITY command, 877-878
  REPORT command, 893, 901-903,
    909-918, 936, 941-942, 944,
    945-946, 947-948
summary cells
  in REPORT command, 906
summary print formats
  in REPORT command, 917-918
summary report
  in REPORT command, 891, 898-899
summary statistics
  in REPORT command, 901-902
summary titles
  alternative break column, 912
  in REPORT command, 936
SUMSPACE (keyword)
  REPORT command, 940, 942-943
SURVIVAL (command), 955-967
  aggregated data, 963-964
  annotated example, 965
  CALCULATE subcommand, 962-963
  COMPARE subcommand, 961
  comparisons, 962-963
  INTERVALS subcommand, 957-958
  life tables, 958-959
  limitations, 967
  MISSING subcommand, 964
  old friends, 1026
  output file, 964-967
  PLOTS subcommand, 959-961
  PRINT subcommand, 959
  STATUS subcommand, 958
  survival functions, 959
  TABLES subcommand, 957
  value range, 958
  with PROCEDURE OUTPUT
    command, 964
  WRITE subcommand, 964-967
SURVIVAL (keyword)
  SURVIVAL command, 960
survival scores
  defined, 955
SYMBOLS (subcommand)
  PLOT command, 798-799
SYMMETRIC (keyword)
  ALSCAL command, 341
syntax, 9-13
  batch mode, 9
  diagrams, 13
  interactive mode, 9
  with EDIT command, 17-18
SYSMIS (function), 121
SYSMIS (keyword)
  COUNT command, 133
  RECODE command, 116
SYSMIS (subcommand)
  SHOW command, 33
$SYSMIS (system variable)
  defined, 138
system files
  annotated example, 100-101
  binary data, 106
  case, 106-107
  compressed, 106
  defined, 51, 52, 89

limitations, 107
structure, 106
system variables, 10, 138
  in SHOW command, 44
system-missing values, 66

T (keyword)
  MANOVA command, 602
T-TEST (command), 969-975
  annotated example, 972-973
  FORMAT subcommand, 974
  GROUPS subcommand, 970
  independent samples, 969-971
  limitations, 975
  MISSING subcommand, 974
  old friends, 1026
  paired samples, 971
  PAIRS subcommand, 971
  significance tests, 970
  VARIABLES subcommand, 970-971
  with SET WIDTH command, 974
t statistic, 761
t test, see T-TEST
TABLE (keyword)
  CROSSTABS command, 437
  DISCRIMINANT command, 465-468
  MEANS command, 650-651
  MULT RESPONSE command, 673,
    673
  SURVIVAL command, 959
TABLE (subcommand)
  DATA LIST command, 59
  KEYED DATA LIST command, 1007
  MATCH FILES command, 288-289
  PRINT command, 173-174
  WRITE command, 177-178
table lookup files
  defined, 277
  MATCH FILES (command), 288-290
TABLES (command)
  SET command, 43-44
TABLES (keyword)
  CROSSTABS command, 439
  MANOVA command, 596, 597
  SURVIVAL command, 964
TABLES (subcommand)
  CROSSTABS command, 430-432,
    434-435
  MEANS command, 644-646
  MULT RESPONSE command,
    667-671
  SURVIVAL command, 957
!TAIL (function)
  macro facility, 988
TAPE (keyword)
  EXPORT command, 310
  IMPORT command, 312
target variables
  in AGGREGATE command, 334
  in COMPUTE command, 117-118,
    146
  in COUNT command, 133
  in RECODE command, 116-117, 144
tau statistics, 436, 728
TBFONTS (subcommand)
  SET command, 33, 43-44
  SHOW command, 33
TB1 (subcommand)
  SET command, 33, 43-44
  SHOW command, 33

TB2 (subcommand)
  SET command, 33, 43-44
  SHOW command, 33
TCON (subcommand)
  BOX-JENKINS command, 393
TCOV (keyword)
  DISCRIMINANT command, 465
TEMPORARY (command), 135-136
  with MATCH FILES command, 279
  with SAVE command, 102
  with SPLIT FILE command, 272
  with XSAVE command, 102
temporary variables, 135
terminal value
  in LOOP command, 248-249
TEST (keyword)
  BOX-JENKINS command, 392
  REGRESSION command, 851
test of linearity, 649
!THEN (keyword)
  macro facility, 989
THRU (keyword)
  BOX-JENKINS command, 388-389
  COUNT command, 132
  MISSING VALUES command, 67
  RECODE command, 111
  SURVIVAL command, 957-958
TIESTORE (keyword)
  ALSCAL command, 348
time and date output formats, 178-179
time functions, 123-129
time input formats, 80-82
time intervals, 123-129
time series analysis, see BOX-JENKINS
    (command)
TIME.DAYS (function), 126
TIME.HMS (function), 125-126
TIME$ (system variable)
  defined, 138
TITLE (command), 29-30
TITLE (subcommand)
  PLOT command, 792
  REPORT command, 924-926
titles
  in REPORT command, 924-926
  SUMMARY subcommand, 936
TO (keyword)
  DATA LIST command, 61
  LIST command, 533
  LOOP command, 248-249
  variable lists, 11
!TO (keyword)
  macro facility, 989-990
tokens
  macro facility, 983
!TOKENS (keyword)
  macro facility, 983
TOL (keyword)
  REGRESSION command, 856
tolerance
  in REGRESSION command, 854
TOLERANCE (keyword)
  DISCRIMINANT command, 463
  REGRESSION command, 855
TOSPSS (procedure), 1023-1026
  DATA option, 1023
  examples, 1025-1026
  NOCOMPRESSION option, 1023
  OUTPUT option, 1023
  SPSSFILE option, 1023
  VARIABLES option, 1023-1024
  WEIGHT option, 1024

TOTAL (keyword)
    CROSSTABS command, 435
    MULT RESPONSE command, 671
    RELIABILITY command, 877
    REPORT command, 912-915, 945-946
totals
    in REPORT command, 912-915,
        945-946
TP (subcommand)
    BOX-JENKINS command, 393
TQ (subcommand)
    BOX-JENKINS command, 393
transaction files
    defined, 296-297
TRANSFORM (keyword)
    MANOVA command, 592, 594
TRANSFORM (subcommand)
    MANOVA command, 580-584
transformation state
    defined, 994-995
transformations
    active file, 139
    execution, 138-139
    in MANOVA command, 580-584
    in PROXIMITIES, 825
    with data definition, 139
treatment effects, defined, 375
TREE (keyword)
    MEANS command, 651
trimming strings, 148-149
TRUNC (function), 120
truncate, 120
truncation of keywords, 12
TSER (keyword)
    BOX-JENKINS command, 395
TSP (subcommand)
    BOX-JENKINS command, 393
TSPACE (keyword)
    REPORT command, 935, 940, 941
TSQ (subcommand)
    BOX-JENKINS command, 393
TUKEY (keyword)
    ONEWAY command, 764
    RELIABILITY command, 878, 881
Tukey's test for additivity, 881
TUKEYB (keyword)
    ONEWAY command, 764
TWOTAIL (keyword)
    CORRELATIONS command, 422
    NONPAR CORR command, 728
    PARTIAL CORR command, 778
TYPE (subcommand)
    EXPORT command, 310
    IMPORT command, 312

U, Mann-Whitney, 748-749
UC (keyword)
    CROSSTABS command, 436
ULS (keyword)
    FACTOR command, 489
unaligned positive integer binary format
    on DATA LIST command, 86-87
uncertainty coefficient, 436
UNCLASSIFIED (keyword)
    DISCRIMINANT command, 473
UNCOMPRESSED (keyword)
    SAVE command, 97-98
    XSAVE command, 97-98
UNCONDITIONAL (keyword)
    ALSCAL command, 343
    MANOVA command, 576

UNDEFINED (subcommand)
    SET command, 33-36
    SHOW command, 33
undefined data values
    with DATA LIST command, 65
underflows
    CNLR command, 696-697
UNDERSCORE (keyword)
    REPORT command, 935-936
underscores
    in REPORT command, 935-936
UNIFORM (function), 122
UNIFORM (keyword)
    NPAR TESTS command, 737
    PLOT command, 793
UNIQUE (keyword)
    ANOVA command, 369-370
    MANOVA command, 586
UNIV (keyword)
    MANOVA command, 593
Univac computers, see INFO command
UNIVARIATE (keyword)
    FACTOR command, 485
    MANOVA command, 604
UNIVF (keyword)
    DISCRIMINANT command, 464
UNNUMBERED (command), 31
UNNUMBERED (keyword)
    LIST command, 533
!UNQUOTE (function)
    macro facility, 988
UNSELECTED (keyword)
    DISCRIMINANT command, 473
UP (keyword)
    SORT CASES command, 269
UPCASE (function), 148-150
!UPCASE (function)
    macro facility, 988
UPDATE (command), 296-299
    adding observations, 298
    adding variables, 298
    annotated example, 300
    BY subcommand, 296-297
    DROP subcommand, 299
    FILE subcommand, 296-297
    IN subcommand, 299
    KEEP subcommand, 299
    key variables, 296-297
    MAP subcommand, 299
    RENAME subcommand, 298-299
    reordering variables, 298-299
    with DROP DOCUMENTS
        command, 301
    with SORT CASES command, 271,
        296-297
update documentation
    INFO command, 22
updating values
    with UPDATE command, 296-297
UPPER (keyword)
    MATRIX DATA command, 230
upper case, 106-107
User Code facility, 1003-1004
user-missing values, 65-66
utilities
    general run control, 29-35
    system files, 102

V, Cramer's, 436
VALIDN (function)
    REPORT command, 902, 910

VALUE (function), 121
    SELECT IF command, 184
VALUE (keyword)
    REPORT command, 906, 938
value labels, 68-71
    case, 37-38
VALUE LABELS (command), 68-69,
    69-71
value range
    RECODE command, 111, 116
VALUES (keyword)
    MEANS command, 651
values out of range
    CNLR command, 696-697
VAR (keyword)
    REPORT command, 930
VARIABLE (keyword)
    DESCRIPTIVES command, 451
    PROXIMITIES command, 824-825
VARIABLE (subcommand)
    BOX-JENKINS command, 386
variable definition, 55-56
    in DATA LIST command, 59
variable labels, 68-69
    case, 37-38
    in AGGREGATE command, 334-335
VARIABLE LABELS (command),
    68-69
    with REPORT command, 953
variable lists
    TO keyword, 11
variable names
    defined, 10-11
    rules for assigning, 60
variable selection methods
    in DISCRIMINANT command,
        460-461
)variable (argument)
    REPORT command, 925-926
variables
    defined, 47
VARIABLES (keyword)
    DISPLAY command, 104
    MANOVA command, 595, 597
VARIABLES (option)
    TOSPSS procedure, 1023-1024
VARIABLES (subcommand)
    ALSCAL command, 341
    AUTORECODE command, 380
    CROSSTABS command, 434-435
    DISCRIMINANT command, 457-458
    FACTOR command, 483
    FREQUENCIES command, 502-503
    GET command, 104-105
    GET SCSS command, 308
    LIST command, 532
    MATRIX DATA command, 227-228
    MEANS command, 647-648
    MULT RESPONSE command, 663
    PARTIAL CORR command, 776
    REGRESSION command, 853
    RELIABILITY command, 875
    REPORT command, 893, 900,
        926-927, 934-935, 936-938,
        938-939, 943
    stacking variables in REPORT,
        926-927
    T-TEST command, 970-971

VARIANCE (function), 121
  REPORT command, 902, 910
VARIANCE (keyword)
  DESCRIPTIVES command, 450
  FREQUENCIES command, 509
  MEANS command, 649
  PROXIMITIES command, 832
  REGRESSION command, 866
  RELIABILITY command, 877
VARIMAX (keyword)
  FACTOR command, 494
  MANOVA command, 594, 595
$VARS (subcommand)
  SHOW command, 33
VECTOR (command), 251-254
  annotated example, 260-261
  short form, 252-253
VERTICAL (subcommand)
  PLOT command, 792-793
VICICLE (keyword)
  CLUSTER command, 412
VIEW (subcommand)
  PROXIMITIES command, 825
VIN (keyword)
  DISCRIMINANT command, 463
VSAM files, 1006, 1012-1016
VSIZE (subcommand)
  PLOT command, 796-798

W (keyword)
  MANOVA command, 574-575, 591
W-W (subcommand)
  NPAR TESTS command, 747,
    750-751
W, Kendall's, see Kendall's W
Wald-Wolfowitz runs test, 750-751
WARD (keyword)
  CLUSTER command, 406
WARN (keyword)
  FILE TYPE GROUPED, 199-202
  FILE TYPE MIXED, 195
  FILE TYPE NESTED, 206-208
warnings
  messages, 26
  setting maximum, 36
  suppressing messages, 36
WAVERAGE (keyword)
  CLUSTER command, 406
WEIGHT (command), 186-189
  annotated example, 188
  BY keyword, 186-187
  changing weights, 187
  OFF keyword, 187
  placement, 189
  with CROSSTABS, 443
  with NONPAR CORR, 187
  with NPAR TESTS, 187
  with TEMPORARY command, 189
WEIGHT (option)
  TOSPSS procedure, 1024
WEIGHT (subcommand)
  SHOW command, 33
weighted marginals
  in MANOVA command, 574

weighting data, 186-189
  changing weights, 187
  effects on tests of significance, 189
  noninteger weights, 187
  turning off weights, 187
WIDTH (subcommand)
  FACTOR command, 484
  LOGLINEAR command, 550-551
  REGRESSION command, 860-861
  SET command, 33, 37
  SHOW command, 33
$WIDTH (system variable)
  defined, 138
WILCOXON (subcommand)
  NPAR TESTS command, 741,
    743-744
Wilcoxon matched-pairs signed-ranks
    test, 743-744
WILD (subcommand)
  FILE TYPE GROUPED, 199
  FILE TYPE MIXED, 195
  FILE TYPE NESTED, 206
WILKS (keyword)
  DISCRIMINANT command, 460
WITH (keyword)
  ANOVA command, 368
  CORRELATIONS command,
    420-421, 424
  LOGLINEAR command, 540-541
  NONPAR CORR command, 725, 730
  NPAR TESTS command, 741
  PARTIAL CORR command, 777
  PLOT command, 790
  PROBIT command, 806
  T-TEST command, 971
WITHIN (keyword)
  MANOVA command, 572-575, 591
within-subjects factors
  in MANOVA command, 577-578
within-subjects transformation matrix
  in MANOVA command, 578
words
  data storage, 106
WORKFILE (subcommand)
  GET SCSS command, 307
WR (keyword)
  MANOVA command, 574-575, 591
WRAP (keyword)
  LIST command, 533
WRITE (command), 176-178
  formats, 177
  NOTABLE subcommand, 177-178
  OUTFILE subcommand, 177
  record specifications, 177
  RECORDS subcommand, 177
  strings, 177
  TABLE subcommand, 177-178
  with REPORT command, 953
WRITE (keyword)
  FREQUENCIES command, 505
WRITE (subcommand)
  CROSSTABS command, 439-443
  SURVIVAL command, 964-967
write formats
  setting default, 38
WRITE FORMATS (command), 180
  with AGGREGATE command, 335

writing user procedures, 1003-1004
WSDESIGN (subcommand)
  MANOVA command, 578
WSFACTORS (subcommand)
  MANOVA command, 577-578

XDATE.DATE (function), 129
XDATE.HOUR (function), 127
XDATE.JDAY (function), 128
XDATE.MDAY (function), 127
XDATE.MINUTE (function), 128
XDATE.MONTH (function), 127
XDATE.QUARTER (function), 128
XDATE.SECOND (function), 128
XDATE.TDAY (function), 128
XDATE.TIME (function), 128-129
XDATE.WEEK (function), 128
XDATE.WKDAY (function), 128
XDATE.YEAR (function), 127
XPROD (keyword)
  CORRELATIONS command, 422
  REGRESSION command, 866
XSAVE (command), 94-99
  annotated example, 100-101
  COMPRESSED keyword, 97-98
  DROP subcommand, 96-97
  KEEP subcommand, 96-97
  MAP subcommand, 95
  OUTFILE subcommand, 95
  RENAME subcommand, 95-96
  reordering variables, 97
  UNCOMPRESSED keyword, 97-98
  with TEMPORARY command, 102
XSORT (subcommand)
  SET command, 33, 41
  SHOW command, 33
XTX (keyword)
  REGRESSION command, 855

Y (keyword)
  PROXIMITIES command, 831
Yates' corrected chi-square test, 436
YES (keyword)
  FILE TYPE GROUPED, 200
  FILE TYPE NESTED, 209-210
  GET BMDP command, 318-319
YRMODA (function), 126-127

Z (keyword)
  PROXIMITIES command, 824
Z scores
  in DESCRIPTIVES command,
    448-450
Z, Kolmogorov-Smirnov, see
    Kolmogorov-Smirnov Z
ZCORR (keyword)
  MANOVA command, 600
ZETA (keyword)
  MANOVA command, 591
ZPP (keyword)
  REGRESSION command, 856
ZPRED (keyword)
  REGRESSION command, 858
ZRESID (keyword)
  REGRESSION command, 858

1   A Sample Job   ■ **Part I   An Introduction to the System**

2   The SPSS-X Language

3   Running the Job

4   Controlling the Environment

                                                       ■ **Part II   Data Definition and Management**
5   Defining Data

6   System Files

7   Numeric Transformations

8   String Transformations

9   Conditional Transformations

10 Printing and Writing Cases

11 Selecting, Sampling, and Weighting Cases

12 Defining Complex File Structures

13 Defining Matrices

14 Input Programs

15 Sorting and Splitting Files

16 Combining System Files

17 File Interfaces

18-   ■ **Part III   Data Analysis and Reporting**
        Procedures
49

A-
        Appendixes
H

REFERENCE CARD

SPSS-X™ User's Guide

3rd Edition

SPSS Inc.
444 North Michigan Avenue
Chicago, Illinois 60611
(312) 329-3500

Copyright © 1988 by SPSS Inc.

All rights reserved. No part of this document may be reproduced in any form by any means without prior written permission of the owners of the copyright.

This card provides a convenient reference to SPSS-X™ Release 3.0. It is arranged by command in alphabetic order. The format diagrams for procedure and nonprocedure commands are constructed according to the following conventions:

Square brackets enclose optional specifications not necessary to the correct completion of the command.

Braces enclose alternative specifications. One of these specifications must be entered in order to complete the specifications correctly. The brackets and braces themselves should not be coded.

Ellipses indicate the possibility of repeating an element in the specifications or the entire cycle of specifications.

Uppercase elements must be entered as they appear in the diagrams.

Lowercase elements describe information to be filled in by the user.

Boldface entries denote defaults. Two asterisks (**) indicate that a specification is a default when its associated subcommand is not specified.

ADD FILES

```
ADD FILES FILE={file}
               {*   }
[/RENAME=(old varlist=new varlist)...]
[/IN=varname]
[/FILE=...]
[/BY varlist]
[/MAP]
[/KEEP={ALL**  }] [/DROP=varlist]
       {varlist}
[/FIRST=varname]   [/LAST=varname]
```
**Default if the subcommand is omitted.

ADD VALUE LABELS

```
ADD VALUE LABELS varlist value 'label' value 'label'...
    [/varlist...]
```

AGGREGATE

```
AGGREGATE OUTFILE={file} [/MISSING=COLUMNWISE] [/DOCUMENT]
                 {*   }
[/PRESORTED] /BREAK=varlist[({A})][varlist...]
                            {D}
 /aggvar['label']aggvar['label']...=function(arguments)
                                    [/aggvar ...]
```

The following functions are available:

SUM	Sum	MEAN	Mean
SD	Standard deviation	MAX	Maximum
MIN	Minimum	PGT	% of cases gt value
PLT	% of cases lt value	PIN	% of cases between values
POUT	% of cases not in range	FGT	Fraction gt value
FLT	Fraction lt value	FIN	Fraction between values
FOUT	Fraction not in range	N	Weighted n
NU	Unweighted n	NMISS	Weighted n of missing
NUMISS	Unweighted n of missing	FIRST	First nonmissing
LAST	Last nonmissing		

ALSCAL

```
ALSCAL  VARIABLES=varlist  [/FILE=file]
      [CONFIG  [({INITIAL})]]
               {FIXED  }
      [ROWCONF [({INITIAL})]]
               {FIXED  }
      [COLCONF [({INITIAL})]]
               {FIXED  }
      [SUBJWGHT[({INITIAL})]]
               {FIXED  }
      [STIMWGHT[({INITIAL})]]
               {FIXED  }
[/INPUT=ROWS ({ALL})]
             { n }
[/SHAPE={SYMMETRIC**}]
        {ASYMMETRIC }
        {RECTANGULAR}
[/LEVEL={ORDINAL**[([UNTIE] [SIMILAR])]}]
        {INTERVAL[({1})]                }
        {         {d}                   }
        {RATIO[({1})]                   }
        {       {d}                     }
        {NOMINAL                        }
[/CONDITION={MATRIX       }]
            {ROW          }
            {UNCONDITIONAL}
[/MODEL  ={EUCLID**}]
  or      {INDSCAL }
 METHOD   {ASCAL   }
          {AINDS   }
          {GEMSCAL }
[/CRITERIA=[NEGATIVE] [CUTOFF({0**})] [CONVERGE({.001})]
                             {c  }             {c   }
           [ITER({30})] [STRESSMIN({.005})] [NOULB]
                 {ni}              {s   }
           [DIMENS({  2**   })] [DIRECTIONS(r)]
                  {min[,max]}
           [CONSTRAIN]          [TIESTORE(n)]]
[/PRINT=[DATA] [HEADER] [INTERMED]]
[/PLOT=[DEFAULT] [ALL]]
[/OUTFILE=file]
[/MATRIX=IN({file})]
           {*   }
```

** Default if the subcommand is omitted.

ANOVA

```
ANOVA [VARIABLES=] varlist BY varlist(min,max)...varlist(min,max)
[WITH varlist]
[/MISSING={EXCLUDE**}]
          {INCLUDE }
[/FORMAT={LABELS**}]
         {NOLABELS}
[/MAXORDERS={ALL** }]
            {n    }
            {NONE }
[/COVARIATES={FIRST**}]
             {WITH  }
             {AFTER }
[/METHOD={EXPERIMENTAL**}]
         {UNIQUE       }
         {HIERARCHICAL }
[/STATISTICS=[MCA] [REG†] [MEAN] [ALL] [NONE]]
```

**Default if the subcommand is omitted.
†REG (table of regression coefficients) is displayed only if the design is relevant.

AUTORECODE

```
AUTORECODE VARIABLES=varlist
 /INTO new varlist
[/DESCENDING]
[/PRINT]
```

BEGIN DATA—END DATA

```
BEGIN DATA
lines of data
END DATA
```

BOX-JENKINS

```
BOX-JENKINS VARIABLE=varlist
  {IDENTIFY}
/ {ESTIMATE}  at least one is required
  {FORECAST}
```

subcommands controlling identification and model specification:

```
   {LOG[={0       }]          }
[/ {     {constant}          }]
   {POWER=(power[,{0       }])}
   {              {constant} }
[/DIFFERENCE=m [THRU n [BY {1}]]]
                          {i}
[/SDIFFERENCE=m [THRU n [BY {1}]] /PERIOD={1}]
                           {i}            {n}
[/LAG={25}]   {P }                    [/{MALAG}=n,n, ...]
      {n }  [/{Q }={0         }]        {ARLAG}
             {SP} {m [THRU n]}
             {SQ}
```

SAVE SCSS

```
SAVE SCSS OUTFILE=file
  [/KEEP={ALL     }] [/DROP=varlist]
         {varlist }
  [/RENAME=(old varlist=new varlist)...]
```

SELECT IF

```
SELECT IF [(]logical expression[)]
```

SET

```
SET [BLANKS={SYSMIS}] [BOX={'-I+[++++++++]'}] [CASE={UPPER}]
           {value }      {X'hexstring '}      {UPLOW}

  [CCA={'-,,,'      }] [CCB={'-,,,'      }] [CCC={'-,,,'      }]
       {'format-spec'}      {'format-spec'}      {'format-spec'}

  [CCD={'-,,,'      }] [CCE={'-,,,'      }]
       {'format-spec'}      {'format-spec'}

  [COMPRESSION={ON }] [ENDCMD={'.'   }] [FORMAT={F8.2}]
              {OFF}          {'string'}        {Fw.d}

  [HEADER={YES}] [JOURNAL=[{ON }] [file]] [LENGTH={59  }]
          {NO }           {OFF}                   {n   }
                                                  {NONE}

  [MEXPAND={ON }] [MITERATE={1000}] [MNEST={50}] [MPRINT={ON }]
          {OFF}            {n   }          {n }          {OFF}

  [MXERRS={40}] [MXLOOPS={40}] [MXWARNS={80}]
         {n }           {n }           {n }

  [NULLINE={YES}]    [PRINTBACK={YES}]
          {NO }                {NO }

  [SCRIPTTAB={'@'      }] [SEED={2000000}]
            {'character'}       {n      }

  [TBFONT={'1234'      }] [TB1={'-I[++++++++'}] [TB2={'          '}]
         {X'hexstring'}       {X'hexstring'}       {X'hexstring'}

  [UNDEFINED={WARN  }] [WIDTH={132}] [XSORT={YES}]
            {NOWARN}           {n }          {OFF}
```

Defaults may differ by installation.

SHOW

```
SHOW [ALL] [BLANKS] [BLKSIZE] [BOX] [BUFNO] [CASE]

     [CCA] [CCB] [CCC] [CCD] [CCE] [COMPRESSION]

     [ENDCMD] [FORMAT] [HEADER] [JOURNAL] [LENGTH]

     [MEXPAND] [MITERATE] [MNEST] [MPRINT]

     [MXERRS] [MXLOOPS] [MXWARNS] [N] [NULLINE]

     [NUMBERED] [PRINTBACK] [SCOMPRESSION] [SCRIPTTAB]

     [SEED] [SYSMIS] [TBFONTS] [TB1] [TB2] [UNDEFINED]

     [WEIGHT] [WIDTH] [XSORT] [$VARS]
```

SORT

```
SORT CASES [BY] varlist[({A})] [varlist...]
                        {D}
```

SPLIT FILE

```
SPLIT FILE {BY varlist}
           {OFF       }
```

STRING

```
STRING varlist (An) [/varlist...]
```

SUBTITLE

```
SUBTITLE [']text[']
```

SURVIVAL

```
SURVIVAL TABLES=survival varlist
                [BY independent varlist (min,max)...]
                [BY control varlist (min,max)...]
  /INTERVALS=THRU n BY a [, THRU m BY b ...]
  /STATUS=status variable({min,max}) FOR {ALL             }
                         {value }        {survival varlist}
  [/STATUS=...]
  [/PLOTS({ALL**    })={ALL**           } BY {ALL**               }
         {LOGSURV  }   {survival varlist}   {independent varlist }
         {SURVIVAL }
         {HAZARD   }   BY {ALL**          }]
         {DENSITY  }      {control varlist}
  [/COMPARE={ALL**           } BY {ALL**               }
            {survival varlist}   {independent varlist }
            BY {ALL**          }]
               {control varlist}
  [/MISSING={GROUPWISE**}    [INCLUDE]]
            {LISTWISE  }
  [/PRINT={TABLE**}]
          {NOTABLE}
  [/CALCULATE={EXACT**    }]
             {COMPARE    }
             {CONDITIONAL}
             {APPROXIMATE}
             {PAIRWISE   }
  [/WRITE[={NONE**}]]
          {TABLES}
          {BOTH  }
```

**Default if the subcommand is omitted.

TEMPORARY

```
TEMPORARY
```

TITLE

```
TITLE [']text[']
```

TOSPSS

```
PROC TOSPSS* [DATA=ddname.membername]
             [SPSSFILE=file]
             [OUTPUT={SYSTEM  }]
                     {PORTABLE}
             [NOCOMPRESSION];
[VARIABLES varlist;]
[WEIGHT varname;]
```

* A SAS procedure.

T-TEST

Independent samples:

```
T-TEST GROUPS=varname ({1,2**     }) /VARIABLES=varlist
                      {value     }
                      {value,value}
  [/MISSING={ANALYSIS**}  [INCLUDE]]
           {LISTWISE  }
  [/FORMAT={LABELS**}]
          {NOLABELS}
```

Paired samples:

```
T-TEST PAIRS=varlist [WITH varlist [(PAIRED)]] [/varlist ...]
  [/MISSING={ANALYSIS**}  [INCLUDE]]
           {LISTWISE  }
  [/FORMAT={LABELS**}]
          {NOLABELS}
```

**Default if the subcommand is omitted.

UPDATE

```
UPDATE FILE={Master File}
           {*          }

  [/RENAME=(old varlist=new varlist)...]
  [/IN=varname]
   /FILE={Transaction File1}
         {*                }
  [/FILE=Transaction File2]
   /BY Key Variables
  [/MAP]
  [/KEEP={ALL**   }] [/DROP=varlist]
         {varlist}
```

**Default if the subcommand is omitted.

VALUE LABELS

```
VALUE LABELS varlist value 'label' value 'label'...
  [/varlist...]
```

VARIABLE LABELS

```
VARIABLE LABELS varname 'label' [/varname...]
```

VECTOR

```
VECTOR {vector name=varlist     } [/vector name...]
       {vector name(n) [format] }
```

WEIGHT

```
WEIGHT {BY varname}
       {OFF       }
```

WRITE

```
WRITE [OUTFILE=file] [RECORDS={1}] [{NOTABLE}]
                              {n}   {TABLE  }
  /{1    } varlist [[col location [(format)]]] [varlist...]
   {rec #}           {(format list)}
                     {*            }

  [/{2    }...]
    {rec #}
```

WRITE FORMATS

```
WRITE FORMATS varlist (format) [varlist...]
```

XSAVE

```
XSAVE OUTFILE=file
  [/KEEP={ALL    }] [/DROP=varlist]
         {varlist}
  [/RENAME=(old varlist=new varlist)...]
  [/MAP] [/{COMPRESSED  }]
           {UNCOMPRESSED}
```

subcommands controlling estimation:

```
[/{CONSTANT }] [/{NCENTER}] [/ITERATE={40}]
  {NCONSTANT}    {CENTER }              {n }
[/FPR={5}] [/BFR={0}] [/{NTEST}]
      {n}        {n}     {TEST }

     {TCON}
[/{PCON}=(n)]   conditional upon CONSTANT
   {ICON}
     {TP }
     {PP }                conditional upon P
     {IP }
     {TQ }
     {PQ }                conditional upon Q
[/{IQ }=(n, ...)]
     {TSP}
     {PSP}                conditional upon SP
     {ISP}
     {TSQ}
     {PSQ}                conditional upon SQ
     {ISQ}
```

subcommands controlling forecasting:

```
[/ORIGIN=m [THRU n]] [/LEAD={12}] [/CIN={95}]
                            {n }         {n }

[/FCON=(n)]              conditional upon CONSTANT
     {FP }              conditional upon P
     {FQ }              conditional upon Q
[/{FSP}=(n, ...)]       conditional upon SP
     {FSQ}              conditional upon SQ
```

subcommands controlling display:

```
[/PRINT=[ACF] [PACF] [ACVF] [SER] [TSER]
        [DSER] [RESID] [RACF]]
[/PLOT=[ACF] [PACF] [SER] [TSER] [FCF] [FLF]
        [CIN] [DSER] [RESID] [RACF]]
```

■ BREAK

```
LOOP ...
DO IF [(] logical expression [)]
BREAK
END IF
END LOOP
```

■ CLEAR TRANSFORMATIONS

```
CLEAR TRANSFORMATIONS
```

■ CLUSTER

```
CLUSTER varlist [/MISSING={LISTWISE**}]
                         {INCLUDE  }
[/MEASURE={SEUCLID** }] [/METHOD={BAVERAGE**}[(rootname)] [,....]]
          {EUCLID    }           {WAVERAGE  }
          {COSINE    }           {SINGLE    }
          {POWER(p,r)}           {COMPLETE  }
          {BLOCK     }           {CENTROID  }
          {CHEBYCHEV }           {MEDIAN    }
          {DEFAULT   }           {WARD      }
[/SAVE=CLUSTER({level   })]  [/ID=varname]
              {min,max }
[/PRINT=[CLUSTER({level   })] [DISTANCE] [SCHEDULE**] [NONE]]
                {min,max }
[/PLOT=[VICICLE**[(min[,max,.inc]])]] [DENDROGRAM] [NONE]]
       [HICICLE[(min[,max,.inc]])]]
[/MATRIX=[IN({file})] [OUT({file})]]
            {*   }        {*   }
```

** Default if the subcommand is omitted.

■ COMMENT

```
COMMENT text
```

■ COMPUTE

```
COMPUTE target variable=expression
```

Arithmetic Operators:

```
+   Addition          -   Subtraction
*   Multiplication    /   Division
**  Exponentiation
```

Arithmetic Functions:

ABS(arg)	Absolute value
RND(arg)	Round
TRUNC(arg)	Truncate
MOD(arg)	Modulus
SQRT(arg)	Square root
EXP(arg)	Exponential
LG10(arg)	Base 10 logarithm
LN(arg)	Natural logarithm
ARSIN(arg)	Arcsin
ARTAN(arg)	Arctangent
SIN(arg)	Sine
COS(arg)	Cosine

Statistical Functions:

SUM[.n](arg list)	Sum of values across argument list
MEAN[.n](arg list)	Mean value across argument list
SD[.n](arg list)	Standard deviation of values across list
VAR[.n](arg list)	Variance of values across list
CFVAR[.n](arg list)	Coefficient of variation of values across list
MIN[.n](arg list)	Minimum value across list
MAX[.n](arg list)	Maximum value across list

Missing Value Functions:

VALUE(varname)	Ignore user-missing
MISSING(varname)	True if missing
SYSMIS(varname)	True if system-missing
NMISS(arg list)	Count number missing values across list
NVALID(arg list)	Number of valid values across list

Cross-case Function:

LAG(varname,n)	Return value of variable n cases before

Logical Functions:

RANGE(varname,range)	True if value of variable is in range
ANY(arg,arg list)	True if value of first arg matches arg list

Other Functions:

UNIFORM(arg)	Uniform pseudo random no. between 0 and n
NORMAL(arg)	Normal pseudo random no. with mean of 0 and std dev of n
CDFNORM(arg)	Return probability random variable falls below n
PROBIT(arg)	Inverse of CDFNORM

The values of "arg" can be numeric values, variables, or expressions.

Date and time aggregation functions:

DATE.DMY(d,m,y)	Read day, month, year and return date
DATE.MDY(m,d,y)	Read month, day, year and return date
DATE.YRDAY(y,d)	Read year, day, number and return date
DATE.QYR(q,y)	Read quarter, year and return quarter start date
DATE.MOYR(m,y)	Read month, year and return month start date
DATE.WKYR(w,y)	Read week, year and return week start date
TIME.HMS(h,m,s)	Read hour, minutes, seconds and return time interval
TIME.DAYS(d)	Read days and return time interval

Date and time conversion functions:

YRMODA(yr,mo,da)	Convert year, month, day to day number
CTIME.DAYS(arg)	Convert time interval to days
CTIME.HOURS(arg)	Convert time interval to hours
CTIME.MINUTES(arg)	Convert time interval to minutes
CTIME.SECONDS(arg)	Convert time interval to seconds

Date and time extraction functions:

XDATE.MDAY(arg)	Return the day of the month
XDATE.MONTH(arg)	Return the month of the year
XDATE.YEAR(arg)	Return the four digit year
XDATE.HOUR(arg)	Return the hour of a day
XDATE.MINUTE(arg)	Return the minute of a hour
XDATE.SECOND(arg)	Return the second of a minute
XDATE.WKDAY(arg)	Return the weekday number
XDATE.JDAY(arg)	Return the day number of a day in a given year
XDATE.QUARTER(arg)	Return the quarter of a date in a given year
XDATE.WEEK(arg)	Return the week number of a date in a given year
XDATE.TDAY(arg)	Return the number of days in a time interval
XDATE.TIME(arg)	Return the time portion of a given date and time
XDATE.DATE(arg)	Return integral portion of date

String Functions:

Function	Definition
ANY(arg,arg list)	Return 1 if value of arg matches value in arg list
CONCAT(arg list)	Join the arguments into a string
INDEX(a1,a2,a3)	Return number indicating position of first occurence of a2 in a1
LAG(arg,n)	Return value of arg n cases before
LENGTH(arg)	Return length of arg
LOWER(arg list)	Convert upper case letters to lower case
LPAD(a1,a2,a3)	Left pad beginning of a1 to length a2 with character a3
LTRIM(a1,a2)	Trim character a2 from beginning of a1
MAX(arg list)	Return maximum value of arg list
MIN(arg list)	Return minimum value of arg list
NUMBER(arg,format)	Convert argument into number using format
RANGE(arg,arg list)	Return 1 if value of arg is in inclusive range of arg list
RINDEX(a1,a2,a3)	Return number indicating rightmost occurence of a2 in a1
RPAD(a1,a2,a3)	Right pad end of a1 to length a2 with character a3
RTRIM(a1,a2)	Trim character a2 from end of a1
STRING(arg,format)	Convert argument into string using format
SUBSTR(a1,a2,a3)	Return substring of a1 beginning with position a2 for length a3
UPCASE(arg list)	Convert lower case letters to upper case

REGRESSION

```
REGRESSION [MATRIX=[IN({file})] [OUT({file})]]
                       {*   }        {*   }

    [/WIDTH={132**}]
            {n   }

    [/SELECT={varname relation value}
    [/MISSING={LISTWISE**      }] [INCLUDE]]
              {PAIRWISE        }
              {MEANSUBSTITUTION}

    [/DESCRIPTIVES=[DEFAULTS] [MEAN] [STDDEV] [CORR] [COV]
                   [VARIANCE] [XPROD] [SIG] [N] [BADCORR]
                   [ALL] [NONE**]]

    [/VARIABLES={varlist     }]
                {(COLLECT)** }
                {ALL         }

    [/CRITERIA=[DEFAULTS**] [TOLERANCE({0.0001**})] [MAXSTEPS(n)]
                                       {value   }

               [PIN({0.05**})] [POUT({0.10**})]
                    {value  }        {value  }

               [FIN({3.84 })] [FOUT({2.71 })]]
                    {value}         {value}

    [/STATISTICS=[DEFAULTS**] [R**] [COEFF**] [ANOVA**] [OUTS**]
                 [ZPP] [LABEL] [CHA] [CI] [F] [BCOV] [SES] [LINE]
                 [HISTORY] [XTX] [COND] [END] [TOL] [ALL]]

    [/{NOORIGIN**}]
      {ORIGIN   }
    [/REGWGT=varname]
    /DEPENDENT=varlist
    [/METHOD=]{STEPWISE [varlist]    }   [...] [/...]
              {FORWARD [varlist]     }
              {BACKWARD [varlist]    }
              {ENTER [varlist]       }
              {REMOVE varlist        }
              {TEST(varlist)(varlist)...}

    [/RESIDUALS=[DEFAULTS] [ID(varname)] [DURBIN]
                [{SEPARATE}] [HISTOGRAM({ZRESID     })]
                [{POOLED }]            {tempvarlist}
                [OUTLIERS({ZRESID     })]
                         {tempvarlist}
                [NORMPROB({ZRESID     })] [SIZE({LARGE})]]
                         {tempvarlist}        {SMALL}

    [/CASEWISE=[DEFAULTS] [{OUTLIERS({  3  })}]
                          {         {value}}
                          {ALL             }
              [PLOT({ZRESID })] [{DEPENDENT PRED RESID}]]
                   {tempvar}     {tempvarlist         }

    [/SCATTERPLOT=[SIZE({SMALL})] (varname,varname)...]
                        {LARGE}

    [/PARTIALPLOT=[{ALL    }] [SIZE({SMALL})]]
                  {varlist}        {LARGE}

    [/SAVE=tempvar(newname) tempvar(newname)...]
```

Temporary variables for residuals analysis are: PRED, ADJPRED, SRESID,
MAHAL, RESID, ZPRED, SDRESID, COOK, DRESID, ZRESID, SEPRED, LEVER.

**Default if the subcommand is omitted.

RELIABILITY

```
RELIABILITY VARIABLES=varlist
    [/SCALE(scalename)=varlist [/SCALE... ]]
    [/MODEL={ALPHA        }] [/VARIABLES...]
            {SPLIT[(n)]   }
            {GUTTMAN      }
            {PARALLEL     }
            {STRICTPARALLEL}
    [/MISSING={EXCLUDE**}]
              {INCLUDE }
    [/FORMAT={LABELS** }]
             {NOLABELS}
    [/MATRIX =[IN({* })] [OUT({* })] [NOPRINT]]
                  {file}       {file}
    [/METHOD=COV]
    [/STATISTICS=[DESCRIPTIVE] [SCALE    ] [{ANOVA   }] [ALL]]
                 [COV        ] [TUKEY    ]  {FRIEDMAN}
                 [CORR       ] [HOTELLING]  {COCHRAN }
    [/SUMMARY=[MEANS   ] [COV ] [TOTAL]]
              [VARIANCE] [CORR] [ALL  ]
```

**Default if the subcommand is omitted.

RENAME VARIABLES

```
RENAME VARIABLES {(varname=varname)  [(varname ...)]}
                 {(varlist=varlist)                 }
```

REPEATING DATA

```
REPEATING DATA [FILE=file] /STARTS=beg pos[-end pos]
    /OCCURS={value  }
            {varname}
    [/LENGTH={value  }] [/CONTINUED[=beg pos[-end pos]]]
             {varname}
    [/ID={col loc}=varname] [/{TABLE  }]
         {format }           {NOTABLE}
    DATA=data list specifications
```

REPORT

```
REPORT
    [/FORMAT=[{MANUAL    }] [{NOLIST }] [ALIGN({LEFT  })]
              {AUTOMATIC}   {LIST[(n)]}        {CENTER}
                                               {RIGHT }

             [TSPACE({1})] [CHDSPACE({1})] [FTSPACE({1 })]
                     {n}             {n}            {n}

             [SUMSPACE({1})] [COLSPACE({4})] [BRKSPACE({ 1 })]
                       {n}             {n}             {n  }
                                                       {-1†}

             [LENGTH({1,length})] [MARGINS({1,width})]
                    {n,n     }            {n,n    }
                    {*,*     }            {*,*    }

             [CHALIGN({TOP    })] [UNDERSCORE({OFF})]
                     {BOTTOM†}               {ON† }

             [PAGE1({1})] [MISSING {'.'}]]
                   {n}             {'s'}
    [/OUTFILE=file]
    [/STRING=stringname (varname[(width)] [(BLANK)] ['literal...'] )
    /VARIABLES=varname ({VALUE}) [+ varname({VALUE})] ['col head']
                       {LABEL }              {LABEL }
                       {DUMMY }              {DUMMY }
        [(option list)]
```

where option list can contain any of the following:
```
        width   OFFSET({0     })   {LEFT  }
                      {n     }   {CENTER}
                      {CENTER†}   {RIGHT }
        [/MISSING={VAR          }]
                  {NONE         }
                  {LIST(varlist{1})}
                              {n}
```

```
[     /TITLE='line1' 'line2'...] [     /FOOTNOTE='line1' 'line2'...]
              or                              or
[/TITLE=LEFT 'line1' 'line2'...] [/FOOTNOTE=LEFT 'line1' 'line2'...]
[      CENTER 'line1' 'line2'...] [        CENTER 'line1' 'line2'...]
[      RIGHT 'line1' 'line2'...]  [        RIGHT 'line1' 'line2'...]
    [/BREAK=varlist [(TOTAL)] ['col head'] [(option list)]]
```

where option list can contain any of the following:
```
        width   {VALUE }  {NOTOTAL} SKIP({1})   PAGE[(RESET)]
                {LABEL†}  {TOTAL  }      {n}
        OFFSET({0     })  UNDERSCORE[(varlist)] {LEFT  } {NONAME}
              {n     }                         {CENTER} {NAME  }
              {CENTER†}                        {RIGHT }
    [/SUMMARY=function...['summary title'][(break col #1)]
             [SKIP({0})]
                  {n}
or
    [/SUMMARY=PREVIOUS[({1})]]
                       {n}
where function is
    aggregate [(varname[({PLAIN })][(d)][varname...]))
                       {DOLLAR}
                       {COMMA }
or
    composite(agg(varname)...)[(report col[({PLAIN })][(d)]))
                                          {DOLLAR}
                                          {COMMA }
```

†Default if FORMAT=AUTOMATIC.

Aggregate functions:

VALIDN	VARIANCE	PCLT(n)
SUM	KURTOSIS	PCIN(min,max)
MIN	SKEWNESS	FREQUENCY(min,max)
MAX	MEDIAN(min,max)	PERCENT(min,max)
MEAN	MODE(min,max)	
STDDEV	PCGT(n)	

Composite functions:

DIVIDE(agg(varname) agg(varname)[factor]
PCT(agg(varname) agg(varname))
SUBTRACT(agg(varname) agg(varname))
ADD(agg(varname) agg(varname)...)[factor]
GREAT(agg(varname) agg(varname)...)
LEAST(agg(varname) agg(varname)...)
AVERAGE(agg(varname) agg(varname)...)
MULTIPLY(agg(varname) agg(varname)...)[factor]

REREAD

```
REREAD [COLUMN=expression]
```

SAMPLE

```
SAMPLE {percentage}
       {n FROM m  }
```

SAVE

```
SAVE OUTFILE=file
    [/KEEP={ALL    }] [/DROP=varlist]
           {varlist}
    [/RENAME=(old varlist=new varlist)...]
    [/MAP] [/{COMPRESSED  }]
             {UNCOMPRESSED}
```

PRINT EJECT

```
PRINT EJECT [OUTFILE=file] [RECORDS={1}] [{NOTABLE }]
                                    {n}   {TABLE   }

 /{1    } varlist [{col location [(format)]}] [varlist...]
  {rec #}          {(format list)          }
                   {*                       }

 [/{2    }...]
   {rec #}
```

PRINT FORMATS

```
PRINT FORMATS varlist(format) [varlist...]
```

PRINT SPACE

```
PRINT SPACE [OUTFILE=file] [numeric expression]
```

PROBIT

```
PROBIT response count varname OF observation count varname
        [WITH varlist] [BY varname(min,max)]
 [/MISSING={LISTWISE**}] [/MODEL={PROBIT**}] [/LOG[={10**  }]]
           {INCLUDE   }          {LOGIT    }          {2.718*}
           {DEFAULT   }          {BOTH     }          {base  }
                                                      {NONE  }
 [/PRINT=[ALL] [CI**] [FREQ**] [RMP**] [PARALL] [NONE] [DEFAULT]]
 [/CRITERIA=[CONVERGE({0.001**})] [ITERATE({20**})] [P({0.15**})]]
                      {eps    }            {n   }      {p       }
 [/NATRES[=c]]
```

**Default if the subcommand is omitted.
* Default if the subcommand is included and the specification omitted.

PROCEDURE OUTPUT

```
PROCEDURE OUTPUT OUTFILE= file
```

PROXIMITIES

```
PROXIMITIES varlist
 [/MISSING={LISTWISE**} ]
           {INCLUDE   }
 [/STANDARDIZE=[{VARIABLE}] [{NONE   }] ]
               [{CASE    }]  {Z      }
                             {SD     }
                             {RANGE  }
                             {MAX    }
                             {MEAN   }
                             {RESCALE}
 [/VIEW={CASE**   } ]
        {VARIABLE }
 [/MEASURE=[{NONE              }] [ABSOLUTE] [REVERSE] [RESCALE]
            {EUCLID**          }
            {SEUCLID           }
            {COSINE            }
            {CORR              }
            {BLOCK             }
            {CHEBYCHEV         }
            {POWER(p,r)        }
            {MINKOWSKI(p)      }
            {CHISQ             }
            {PH2               }
            {RR[(p[,np])]      }
            {SM[(p[,np])]      }
            {JACCARD[(p[,np])] }
            {DICE[(p[,np])]    }
            {SS1[(p[,np])]     }
            {RT[(p[,np])]      }
            {SS2[(p[,np])]     }
            {K1[(p[,np])]      }
            {SS3[(p[,np])]     }
            {K2[(p[,np])]      }
            {SS4[(p[,np])]     }
            {HAMANN[(p[,np])]  }
            {OCHIAI[(p[,np])]  }
            {SS5[(p[,np])]     }
            {PHI[(p[,np])]     }
            {LAMBDA[(p[,np])]  }
            {D[(p[,np])]       }
            {Y[(p[,np])]       }
            {Q[(p[,np])]       }
            {BEUCLID[(p[,np])] }
            {SIZE[(p[,np])]    }
            {PATTERN[(p[,np])] }
            {BSEUCLID[(p[,np])]}
            {BSHAPE[(p[,np])]  }
            {DISPER[(p[,np])]  }
            {VARIANCE[(p[,np])]}
            {BLWMN[(p[,np])]   }
 [/ID=varname ]
 [/PRINT [={PROXIMITIES**}] ]
          {NONE         }
 [/MATRIX=[IN({file})] [OUT({file})]]
             {*   }        {*   }
```

**Default if the subcommand is omitted.

QUICK CLUSTER

```
QUICK CLUSTER varlist
 [/MISSING=[{LISTWISE**}] [INCLUDE]]
            {PAIRWISE  }
            {DEFAULT   }
 [/FILE=file]
 [/INITIAL=(value list)]
 [/CRITERIA=[CLUSTER({2**})] [NOINITIAL] [NOUPDATE]]
                     {k  }
 [/PRINT=[INITIAL**] [CLUSTER] [ID(varname)] [DISTANCE] [ANOVA]
         [NONE]]
 [/OUTFILE=file]
 [/SAVE=[CLUSTER(varname)] [DISTANCE(varname)]]
```

** Default if the subcommand is omitted.

RECODE

For numeric variables:
```
RECODE varlist (value list=value)...(value list=value)
       [INTO varlist]/ [/varlist...]
```

Input Keywords:
LO, LOWEST, HI, HIGHEST, THRU, MISSING, SYSMIS, ELSE

Output Keywords:
COPY, SYSMIS

RECODE

For string variables:
```
RECODE varlist [('string',['string'...]='string')]
       [INTO varlist]/..
```

Input Keywords:
CONVERT, ELSE

Output Keyword:
COPY

RECORD TYPE

For FILE TYPE MIXED
```
RECORD TYPE {value list} [SKIP]
            {OTHER     }
```

For FILE TYPE GROUPED
```
RECORD TYPE {value list} [SKIP] [CASE=col loc]
            {OTHER     }
 [DUPLICATE={WARN  }] [MISSING={WARN  } ]
            {NOWARN}           {NOWARN}
```

For FILE TYPE NESTED
```
RECORD TYPE {value list} [SKIP] [CASE=col loc]
            {OTHER     }
 [SPREAD={YES}] [MISSING={WARN  }]
         {NO }           {NOWARN}
```

REFORMAT

```
REFORMAT {ALPHA  } = varlist [/...]
         {NUMERIC}
```

CORRELATIONS

```
CORRELATIONS [VARIABLES=] varlist [WITH varlist] [/varlist...]
[/MISSING={PAIRWISE**} [INCLUDE]]
          {LISTWISE }

[/PRINT={ONETAIL**} {SIG**} ]
        {TWOTAIL  } {NOSIG}

[/FORMAT={MATRIX**} ]
         {SERIAL  }

[/MATRIX=OUT({*   })]
            {file}

[/STATISTICS=[DESCRIPTIVES] [XPROD] [ALL]]
```

**Default if the subcommand is omitted.

COUNT

```
COUNT varname=varlist(value list) [/varname=...]
```

Numeric value list keywords:
LOWEST LO HIGHEST HI THRU MISSING SYSMIS

CROSSTABS

General mode:

```
CROSSTABS [TABLES=]varlist BY varlist [BY...] [/varlist...]

[/MISSING={TABLE**}]
          {INCLUDE}

[/FORMAT={LABELS** } {AVALUE**} {NOINDEX**} {TABLES**}]
         {NOLABELS } {DVALUE } {INDEX   } {NOTABLES}
         {NOVALLABS}

[/CELLS=[{COUNT**} [ROW   ] [EXPECTED] [SRESID ]]
         {NONE  } [COLUMN] [RESID   ] [ASRESID]
                  [TOTAL ]            [ALL    ]

[/WRITE[={NONE** }]]
         {CELLS }

[/STATISTICS=[CHISQ] [LAMBDA] [BTAU] [GAMMA] [ETA ]
              [PHI ] [UC    ] [CTAU] [D    ] [CORR]
              [CC  ] [NONE  ]                [ALL ]
```

Integer mode:

```
CROSSTABS VARIABLES=varlist(min,max) [varlist...]
/TABLES=varlist BY varlist [BY...] [/varlist...]

[/MISSING={TABLE**}]
          {INCLUDE}
          {REPORT }

[/FORMAT={LABELS** } {AVALUE**} {NOINDEX**} {TABLES**}]
         {NOLABELS } {DVALUE } {INDEX   } {NOTABLES}
         {NOVALLABS}

[/CELLS={COUNT**} [ROW   ] [EXPECTED] [SRESID ]]
        {NONE  } [COLUMN] [RESID   ] [ASRESID]
                 [TOTAL ]            [ALL    ]

[/WRITE[={NONE** }]]
         {CELLS }
         {ALL   }

[/STATISTICS=[CHISQ] [LAMBDA] [BTAU] [GAMMA] [ETA ]
              [PHI ] [UC    ] [CTAU] [D    ] [CORR]
              [CC  ] [NONE  ]                [ALL ]
```

**Default if the subcommand is omitted.

DATA LIST

```
DATA LIST [FILE=file] [{FIXED}] [RECORDS={1}] [{TABLE  }]
                       {FREE }           {n} {NOTABLE}
                       {LIST }
          [END=varname]
/{1    } varlist {col location [(format)]  } [varlist ...]
 {rec #}         {(FORTRAN-like format list)}
[/{2    } ...] [/ ...]
  {rec #}
```

Numeric and string formats:

Format	FORTRAN-like format	Data type
(d)	Fw.d	Numeric (default)
(N)	Nw	Restricted numeric
(E,d)	Ew.d	Scientific notation
(COMMA,d)	COMMAw.d	Numeric with commas
(DOT,d)	DOTw.d	Numeric with dots
(DOLLAR,d)	DOLLARw.d	Numeric with commas and dollar sign
(PCT,d)	PCTw.d	Numeric with percent sign
(Z,d)	Zw.d	Zoned decimal
(A)	Aw	String
(AHEX)	AHEXw	Hexadecimal character
(IB,d)	IBw.d	Integer binary
(P,d)	Pw.d	Packed decimal
(PIB,d)	PIBw.d	Unsigned integer binary
(PIBHEX)	PIBHEXw	Hexadecimal unsigned integer binary
(PK,d)	PKw.d	Unsigned packed decimal
(RB)	RBw	Floating point binary
(RBHEX)	RBHEXw	Hexadecimal floating point binary
	Tn	Tabs to column n
	nX	Skips n columns

Some formats may not be available on all implementations of SPSS^X

Date and time input formats:

Format	FORTRAN-like format	Data input	Type
(DATE)	DATEw	dd/mmm/yyyy	International date
(ADATE)	ADATEw	mmm/dd/yyyy	American date
(JDATE)	JDATEw	yyddd	Julian date
(QYR)	QYRw	qQyyyy	Quarter and year
(MOYR)	MOYRw	mm/yyyy	Month and year
(WKYR)	WKYRw	wkWKyyyy	Week and year
(DATETIME)	DATETIMEw	dd-mmm-yyyy hh:mm:ss.ss	Date and time
(TIME)	TIMEw	hh:mm:ss.ss	Time
(DTIME)	DTIMEw	ddd hh:mm:ss.ss	Days and time
(WKDAY)	WKDAYw	string	Day of the week
(MONTH)	MONTHw	string	Month

*Column binary and unaligned positive integer binary specifications:**

```
startcolumn:startrow [-endrow]
startcolumn:startrow-endcolumn:endrow
startbyte:startbit [-endbit]
startbyte:startbit-endbyte:endbit
```

* Column binary files can be read only if MODE=MULTIPUNCH is specified on the FILE HANDLE command.

DESCRIPTIVES

```
DESCRIPTIVES [VARIABLES=] varname[(zname)] [varname...]

[/MISSING={VARIABLE**} [INCLUDE]]
          {LISTWISE  }

[/FORMAT={LABELS** } {NOINDEX**} {LINE**}]
         {NOLABELS} {INDEX   } {SERIAL}

[/SAVE]

[/STATISTICS=[DEFAULT**] [MEAN**] [MIN**] [SKEWNESS]]
             [STDDEV** ] [SEMEAN] [MAX**] [KURTOSIS]
             [VARIANCE ] [SUM  ] [RANGE] [ALL]
```

**Default if the subcommand is omitted.

DISCRIMINANT

```
DISCRIMINANT GROUPS=varname(min,max) /VARIABLES=varlist
[/SELECT=varname(value)]

[/ANALYSIS=varlist(level) [varlist...]]

[/METHOD={DIRECT**}] [/TOLERANCE={0.001}]
         {WILKS   }              {t    }
         {MAHAL   }
         {MAXMINF }
         {MINRESID}
         {RAO     }

[/MAXSTEPS={2v}]
           {m }

[/FIN={1.0}] [/FOUT={1.0}] [/PIN={1.0**}]
      {fi }         {fo }        {pi  }

[/POUT={1.0**}] [/VIN={0**}]
       {po   }        {vi }

[/FUNCTIONS={g-1,100.0,1.0**}] [/PRIORS={EQUAL     }]
            {nf , cp ,sig  }            {SIZE      }
                                        {value list}

[/SAVE=[CLASS=varname] [PROBS=rootname]
       [SCORES=rootname]]

[/ANALYSIS=...]
[/MISSING={EXCLUDE**}]
          {INCLUDE }

[/MATRIX=[OUT({*   })] [IN({*   })]]
             {file}       {file}

[/HISTORY={STEP**} {END** }]
          {NOSTEP} {NOEND}

[/ROTATE={NONE**   }]
         {COEFF    }
         {STRUCTURE}

[/CLASSIFY={NONMISSING } {POOLED  } [MEANSUB]]
           {UNSELECTED } {SEPARATE}
           {UNCLASSIFIED}

[/STATISTICS=[MEAN  ] [COV ] [FPAIR] [RAW  ] [ALL]]
             [STDDEV] [GCOV] [UNIVF] [COEFF]
             [CORR  ] [TCOV] [BOXM ] [TABLE]

[/PLOT=[MAP] [SEPARATE] [COMBINED] [CASES] [ALL]]
```

**Default if the subcommand is omitted.

DISPLAY

```
DISPLAY [SORTED] [{NAMES**   }] [/VARIABLES=varlist]
                 {INDEX     }
                 {VARIABLES }
                 {LABELS    }
                 {DICTIONARY}

        [MACROS]
        [DOCUMENTS]
```

** Default if the subcommand is omitted.

DOCUMENT

```
DOCUMENT text
```

N OF CASES

```
N OF CASES n
```

Nonlinear Regression

```
MODEL PROGRAM varname=value [varname=value ...
transformation commands
[DERIVATIVES |transformation commands]
```

Procedure CNLR (Constrained NonLinear Regression):

```
[CONSTRAINED FUNCTIONS
 transformation commands]

CNLR depvar WITH varlist

[/FILE=file]    [/OUTFILE=file]

[/PRED=varname]

[/SAVE [PRED] [RESID[(varname)]] [DERIVATIVES] [LOSS]]

[/CRITERIA=[ITER n] [MITER n] [CKDER {0.5**}]
                                     {n    }

         [ISTEP {1E+20**}] [FPR n] [LFTOL n]
                {n     }

         [LSTOL n] [STEP {2**}] [NFTOL n]
                         {n  }

         [FTOL n] [OPTOL n] [CRSHTOL {.01**}]]
                                     {n   }

[/BOUNDS=expression, expression, ...]

[/LOSS=varname]

[/BOOTSTRAP [=n]]
```

Procedure NLR (NonLinear Regression):

```
NLR depvar WITH varlist

[/FILE=file]    [/OUTFILE=file]

[/PRED=varname]

[/SAVE [PRED] [RESID [(varname)]] [DERIVATIVES]]

[/CRITERIA=[ITER {100**}] [CKDER {0.5**}]
                 {n   }          {n   }

   [SSCON {1E-8**}]  [PCON {1E-8**}]  [RCON {1E-8**}]]
          {n    }          {n    }          {n    }
```

**Default if the subcommand is omitted.

NONPAR CORR

```
NONPAR CORR [VARIABLES=] varlist [WITH varlist] [/varlist...]
[/MISSING={PAIRWISE**}]
          {INCLUDE  }
          {LISTWISE }
[/PRINT={ONETAIL**}  {SIG**}  {SPEARMAN**}]
        {TWOTAIL }  {NOSIG}  {KENDALL  }
                             {BOTH     }
[/FORMAT={MATRIX**}]
         {SERIAL  }
[/MATRIX=OUT({*   })]
             {file}
[/SAMPLE]
```

**Default if the subcommand is omitted.

NPAR TESTS

```
NPAR TESTS [CHISQUARE=varlist[(lo,hi)]/]
              [/EXPECTED={EQUAL       }]
                        {f1,f2,...fn}
[/K-S({UNIFORM[,lo,hi]})=varlist]
      {NORMAL[,m,sd]   }
      {POISSON[,m]    }
[/RUNS({MEAN  })=varlist]
       {MEDIAN}
       {MODE  }
       {value }
[/BINOMIAL[(p)]=varlist[({v1,v2})]]
                        {value }
[/MCNEMAR=varlist [WITH varlist [(PAIRED)]]]
[/SIGN=varlist [WITH varlist [(PAIRED)]]]
[/WILCOXON=varlist [WITH varlist [(PAIRED)]]]
[/COCHRAN=varlist]
[/FRIEDMAN=varlist]
[/KENDALL=varlist]
[/MEDIAN[(value)]=varlist BY var (v1,v2)]
[/M-W=varlist BY var (v1,v2)]
[/K-S=varlist BY var (v1,v2)]
[/W-W=varlist BY var (v1,v2)]
[/MOSES[(n)]=varlist BY var (v1,v2)]
[/K-W=varlist BY var (v1,v2)]
[/MISSING={ANALYSIS**}  [INCLUDE]]
          {LISTWISE }
[/SAMPLE]
[/STATISTICS=[DESCRIPTIVES]  [QUARTILES] [ALL]]
```

**Default if the subcommand is omitted.

NUMBERED, UNNUMBERED

```
{NUMBERED  }
{UNNUMBERED}
```

NUMERIC

```
NUMERIC varlist[(format)] [/varlist...]
```

ONEWAY

```
ONEWAY  varlist BY varname(min,max)
[/POLYNOMIAL=n]  [/CONTRAST=coefficient list] [/CONTRAST=... ]
[/RANGES={LSD        }({0.05 }) ] [/RANGES=...]
         {DUNCAN     } {alpha}
         {SNK        }
         {TUKEYB     }
         {TUKEY      }
         {LSDMOD     }
         {SCHEFFE    }
         {ranges values}
[/MISSING={ANALYSIS**}  [{EXCLUDE**}]]
          {LISTWISE }    {INCLUDE }
[/HARMONIC={NONE** or PAIR}]
           {ALL          }
[/FORMAT={NOLABELS**}]
         {LABELS   }
[/MATRIX =[NONE**]  [IN({*   })] [OUT({*   })]]
                       {file}         {file}
[/STATISTICS=[NONE        **]]
             [DESCRIPTIVES]
             [EFFECTS]
             [HOMOGENEITY ]
             [ALL        ]
```

**Default if the subcommand is omitted.

PARTIAL CORR

```
PARTIAL CORR [VARIABLES=] varlist [WITH varlist] BY control
list (levels)
[/MISSING={LISTWISE**}  [{EXCLUDE**}]]
          {ANALYSIS }    {INCLUDE }
[/SIGNIFICANCE={ONETAIL**}]
               {TWOTAIL }
[/FORMAT={MATRIX** }]
         {SERIAL   }
         {CONDENSED}
[/MATRIX=[NONE**]  [IN({*   })] [OUT({*   })]]
                      {file}        {file}
[/STATISTICS=[NONE**]  [CORR] [DESCRIPTIVES] [BADCORR] [ALL]]
```

**Default if the subcommand is omitted.

PLOT

```
PLOT [HSIZE = {80**}]  [/VSIZE = {40**}]
              {n   }             {n   }
[/CUTPOINT = {EVERY({1**})}]
             {      {n  } }
             {value list }
[/SYMBOLS = {ALPHANUMERIC**                       }]
            {NUMERIC                              }
            {'symbols'[,'overplot symbols']       }
            {X'hexsymbs'[,'overplot hexsymbs']    }
            {DEFAULT                              }
[/MISSING = [{PLOTWISE**}] [INCLUDE]]
            {LISTWISE  }
[/FORMAT = {DEFAULT**        }]
           {CONTOUR[({10})]}
           {        {n }   }
           {OVERLAY          }
           {REGRESSION       }
[/TITLE = 'title']
[/HORIZONTAL = ['title'] [STANDARDIZE] [REFERENCE(value list)]
                [MIN(min)] [MAX(max)] [UNIFORM]]
[/VERTICAL = ['title'] [STANDARDIZE] [REFERENCE(value list)]
              [MIN(min)] [MAX(max)] [UNIFORM]]
/PLOT = varlist WITH varlist [(PAIR)] [BY varname]
    [;varlist...]  [/PLOT=...]
```

** Default if the subcommand is omitted.

POINT

```
POINT KEY=varname [FILE=file]
```

PRESERVE

```
PRESERVE
```

PRINT

```
PRINT [OUTFILE=file] [RECORDS={1}] [{NOTABLE}]
                              {n}  {TABLE  }
  /{1    } varlist [{col location [(format)]}] [varlist...]
   {rec #}          {(format list)          }
                    {*                       }

[/{2    }...]
  {rec #}
```

DO IF, ELSE IF, ELSE, END IF

```
DO IF [(]logical expression[)]
  transformations
[ELSE IF [(]logical expression[)]]
  transformations
[ELSE IF [(]logical expression[)]]
    .
    .
    .
[ELSE]
  transformations
END IF
```

DO REPEAT—END REPEAT

```
DO REPEAT stand-in var={varlist    } [/stand-in var=...]
                       {value list}
transformation commands
END REPEAT [PRINT]
```

DROP DOCUMENTS

```
DROP DOCUMENTS
```

EDIT

```
EDIT
```

END CASE

```
END CASE
```

END FILE

```
END FILE
```

EXECUTE

```
EXECUTE
```

EXPORT

```
EXPORT OUTFILE=file
  [/TYPE={COMM**}]
        {TAPE }
  [/KEEP={ALL** }] [/DROP=varlist]
        {varlist}
  [/RENAME=(old varlist=new varlist)...]
  [/MAP]
  [/DIGITS=number]
```

** Default if the subcommand is omitted.

FACTOR

```
FACTOR VARIABLES=varlist† [/MISSING=[{LISTWISE**}] [INCLUDE]]
                                    {PAIRWISE  }
                                    {MEANSUB   }
                                    {DEFAULT   }

  [/WIDTH={132    }]
          {n      }
          {DEFAULT**}
  [/MATRIX=[IN({COR=file})] [OUT({COR=file})]]
              {COR=*   }       {COR=*   }
              {FAC=file}       {FAC=file}
              {FAC=*   }       {FAC=*   }
  [/ANALYSIS=varlist...]
  [/PRINT=[DEFAULT**] [INITIAL**] [EXTRACTION**] [ROTATION**]
          [UNIVARIATE] [CORRELATION] [DET] [INV] [REPR] [AIC]
          [KMO] [FSCORE] [SIG] [ALL]]
  [/PLOT=[EIGEN] [ROTATION (n1,n2)]]
  [/DIAGONAL={value list}]
             {DEFAULT** }
  [/FORMAT=[SORT] [BLANK(n)] [DEFAULT**]]
  [/CRITERIA=[FACTORS(n)] [MINEIGEN({1.0**})] [ITERATE({25**})]
                                    {eig  }            {ni  }
             [RCONVERGE({0.0001**})] [DELTA({0**})] [{KAISER**}]
                        {rl       }          {d  }   {NOKAISER}
             [ECONVERGE({0.001**})]] [DEFAULT**]
                        {el      }
  [/EXTRACTION={PC**  }] [/ROTATION={VARIMAX**}]
               {PAF   }             {EQUAMAX  }
               {ALPHA }             {QUARTIMAX}
               {IMAGE }             {OBLIMIN  }
               {ULS   }             {NOROTATE }

               {GLS     }           {DEFAULT  }
               {ML      }
               {PA1     }
               {PA2     }
               {DEFAULT }
  [/SAVE=[{REG    } ({ALL} rootname)]]
          {BART   }  {n  }
          {AR     }
          {DEFAULT}
  [/ANALYSIS...]
  [/CRITERIA...]       [/EXTRACTION...]
  [/ROTATION...]       [/SAVE...]
```

**Default if the subcommand is omitted.
†Omit VARIABLES with matrix input.

FILE HANDLE

```
FILE HANDLE handle / [MODE=MULTIPUNCH] file specifications
```

Specifications differ by implementation of SPSS-X.

FILE LABEL

```
FILE LABEL label
```

FILE TYPE—END FILE TYPE

For FILE TYPE MIXED

```
FILE TYPE MIXED [FILE=file] RECORD=[varname] col loc
  [WILD={NOWARN}]
        {WARN  }
```

For FILE TYPE GROUPED

```
FILE TYPE GROUPED [FILE=file] RECORD=[varname] col loc
  CASE=[varname] col loc [WILD={WARN  }] [DUPLICATE={WARN  }]
                               {NOWARN}             {NOWARN}

  [MISSING={WARN  }] [ORDERED={YES}]
           {NOWARN}           {NO }
```

For FILE TYPE NESTED

```
FILE TYPE NESTED [FILE=file] RECORD=[varname] col loc
  [CASE=[varname] col loc ] [WILD={NOWARN}] [DUPLICATE={NOWARN}]
                                  {WARN  }             {WARN  }
                                                       {CASE  }

  [MISSING={NOWARN}]
           {WARN  }
END FILE TYPE
```

FINISH

```
FINISH
```

FORMATS

```
FORMATS varlist(format) [varlist...]
```

FREQUENCIES

```
FREQUENCIES VARIABLES=varlist[(min,max)] [varlist...]
  [/FORMAT=[{CONDENSE}] [{NOTABLE }] [NOLABELS] [WRITE]
            {ONEPAGE }   {LIMIT(n)}
           [{DVALUE}] [DOUBLE] [NEWPAGE] [INDEX]]
            {AFREQ }
            {DFREQ }
  [/MISSING=INCLUDE]
  [/BARCHART=[MINIMUM(n)] [MAXIMUM(n)] [{FREQ(n)   }]]
                                       {PERCENT(n)}
  [/HISTOGRAM=[MINIMUM(n)] [MAXIMUM(n)] [{FREQ(n)   }]
                                        {PERCENT(n)}
              [{NONORMAL}] [INCREMENT(n)]]
               {NORMAL  }
  [/HBAR=same as HISTOGRAM]
  [/NTILES=n]
  [/PERCENTILES=value list]
  [/STATISTICS=[DEFAULT] [MEAN] [STDDEV] [MINIMUM] [MAXIMUM]
               [SEMEAN] [VARIANCE] [SKEWNESS] [SESKEW] [RANGE]
               [MODE] [KURTOSIS] [SEKURT] [MEDIAN] [SUM] [ALL]
               [NONE]]
```

GET

```
GET FILE=file
  [/KEEP={ALL    }] [/DROP=varlist]
         {varlist}
  [/RENAME=(old varlist=new varlist)...]
  [/MAP]
```

GET BMDP

```
GET BMDP FILE=file
  [/SCAN={YES }] [/CODE=name]
         {ONLY}
  [/CONTENT=name] [/LABEL=quoted string]
  [/KEEP={ALL** }] [/DROP=varlist]
         {varlist}
  [/RENAME=(old varlist=new varlist)...]
  [/MAP]
```

**Default if the subcommand is omitted.

GET OSIRIS

```
GET OSIRIS DICTIONARY=file1 DATA=file2
  [/RENAME=(old varlist=new varlist)...]
  [/KEEP={ALL** }] [/DROP=varlist]
         {varlist}
  [/MAP]
```

GET SAS

```
GET SAS DATA=ddname.membername [SASLIB=ddname]
  [/KEEP={ALL** }] [/DROP=varlist]
         {varlist}
  [/RENAME=(old varlist=new varlist)...]
  [/MAP]
```

MANOVA

```
MANOVA dependent varlist [BY factor list (min,max) [factor list...]
                         [WITH covariate list]]
   [/WSFACTORS=name (levels) name...]
   [/TRANSFORM [([varlist [/varlist]])]=[ORTHONORM] [{CONTRAST}]]
       [{DEVIATIONS (refcat) }]                      {BASIS   }
       {DIFFERENCE          }
       {HELMERT             }
       {SIMPLE (refcat)     }
       {REPEATED            }
       {POLYNOMIAL [(metric)]}
       {SPECIAL (matrix)    }
   [/WSDESIGN=effect effect...]
   [/MEASURE=newname newname...]
   [/RENAME={newname} {newname}...]
           {*      } {*      }
   [/MISSING=[LISTWISE] [INCLUDE]]
   [/{PRINT  }= [CELLINFO ([MEANS] [SSCP] [COV] [COR] [ALL]))]
     {NOPRINT}

        [HOMOGENEITY ([BARTLETT] [COCHRAN] [BOXM] [ALL])]

        [DESIGN ([ONEWAY] [OVERALL] [DECOMP] [BIAS] [SOLUTION]
                [REDUNDANCY] [COLLINEARITY] [ALL])]

        [ERROR ([SSCP] [COV] [COR] [STDDEV] [ALL])]

        [SIGNIF ([MULTIV] [EIGEN] [DIMENR] [UNIV] [HYPOTH]
                [AVERF] [AVONLY] [HF] [GG] [EFSIZE]
                [SINGLEDF] [BRIEF] [STEPDOWN] [ALL] [NONE])]

        [PARAMETERS ([ESTIM] [ORTHO] [COR] [NEGSUM] [ALL])]
                [EFSIZE] [OPTIMAL])]
   [/PLOT=[CELLPLOTS] [STEMLEAF] [ZCORR] [NORMAL] [BOXPLOTS]]
          [ALL]]
   [/PCOMPS [COR] [NCOMP(n)] [MINEIGEN(eigencut)]
            [COV] [ROTATE(rottype)] [ALL]]
   [/DISCRIM [RAW] [STAN] [ESTIM] [COR] [ALL]
             [ROTATE(rottype)] [ALPHA({.25})]]]
                                      {a  }
   [/OMEANS [VARIABLES(varlist)] [TABLES ({factor name    })]]
                                         {factor BY factor}
                                         {CONSTANT        }
   [/PMEANS [VARIABLES(varlist)] [TABLES ({factor name    })]]
                                         {factor BY factor}
                                         {CONSTANT        }
            [PLOT]]
   [/RESIDUALS [CASEWISE] [PLOT]]
   [/METHOD=[MODELTYPE ({MEANS      })]
                       {OBSERVATIONS}
       [ESTIMATION ({QR      } {NOLASTRES} {NOBALANCED} {CONSTANT  })]
                   {CHOLESKY} {LASTRES  } {BALANCED  } {NOCONSTANT}
       [SSTYPE ({UNIQUE    })]]
               {SEQUENTIAL}
   [/MATRIX=[IN({file})] [OUT({file})]]
              {*   }         {*   }
   [/ANALYSIS ({CONDITIONAL  })=dependent varlist
               {UNCONDITIONAL}  [WITH covariate varlist]
                                [/dependent varlist...]]
   [/PARTITION (factorname)[=({1,1...    })]]
                             {df,df...}
                        {DEVIATION [(refcat)]}
                        {SIMPLE [(refcat)]   }
                        {DIFFERENCE          }
   [/CONTRAST (factorname)={HELMERT             }]
                        {REPEATED            }
                        {POLYNOMIAL[({1,2,3...})]}
                        {           metric    }
                        {SPECIAL (matrix)    }
   [/CRITERIA=[ZETA ({1.0E-8})] [EPS ({1.0E-8})]]
                    {zeta  }          {eps   }
              {WITHIN          }         {W }
   [/ERROR={RESIDUAL        } or {R }]
           {WITHIN + RESIDUAL}    {WR}
           {n               }
   [/POWER=[T({.05})] [F({.05})] [{APPROXIMATE}]]
             {a  }      {a  }    {EXACT      }
   [/CINTERVAL=[{INDIVIDUAL}][({.95}) ]] [UNIVARIATE ({BONFER })]
               {JOINT     }    {a  }                 {SCHEFFE}

              [MULTIVARIATE ({ROY     })]]
                            {PILLAI  }
                            {BONFER  }
                            {HOTELLING}
                            {WILKS   }

           [CONSTANT...]
           [effect effect...]
           [POOL (varlist)...]
           [effects BY effects...]
   [/DESIGN={[effects {WITHIN} effects...]
                      {W     }
           [effect + effect...]
           [factor (level)... [WITHIN factor (partition)...]]
           [MUPLUS...]
           [MWITHIN...]
           {terms-to-be-tested} {AGAINST} {WITHIN  } {W }
           {term=n            } {VS     } {RESIDUAL} or {R }
                                          {WR      }    {RW}
                                          {n       }
```

MATCH FILES

```
MATCH FILES {FILE }={file}
            {TABLE}  {*   }
   [/RENAME=(old varlist=new varlist)...]
   [/IN=varname]
   [/{FILE }=...]
     {TABLE}
   [/BY varlist]
   [/MAP]
   [/KEEP={ALL** }] [/DROP=varlist]
          {varlist}
   [/FIRST=varname] [/LAST=varname]
```
**Default if the subcommand is omitted.

MATRIX DATA

```
MATRIX DATA VARIABLES=varlist    [/FILE= {INLINE**}]
                                        {file   }
   [/SPLIT= varlist]    [/FACTORS= varlist]
   [/CONTENTS= [CORR**] [COV] [MAT] [MSE] [DFE] [MEAN]
               [SD] [PROX] [STDDEV] [N_SCALAR] [N_VECTOR] [N]
               [N_MATRIX] [COUNT]
   [/FORMAT= [{LIST**}] [{LOWER**}] [{DIAGONAL**}]]
             {FREE  }   {UPPER  }   {NODIAGONAL}
                        {FULL   }
   [/CELLS= number of cells]   [/N= sample size]
```
**Default if the subcommand is omitted.

MCONVERT

```
MCONVERT [[/MATRIX=] [IN({*   })] [OUT({*   })]]
                        {file}         {file}
         [{/REPLACE}]
          {/APPEND }
```

MEANS

General mode:
```
MEANS [TABLES=]varlist BY varlist [BY...] [/varlist...]
   [/MISSING={TABLE**  }]
             {INCLUDE  }
             {DEPENDENT}
   [/FORMAT={LABELS** } {NAMES**} {VALUES**} {TABLE**}]
            {NOLABELS} {NONAMES} {NOVALUES} {TREE  }
            {NOCATLABS}
   [/CELLS=[DEFAULT**] [MEAN**  ] [ALL]]
           [COUNT**  ] [STDDEV**]
           [SUM      ] [VARIANCE]
   [/STATISTICS=[ANOVA] [LINEARITY] [ALL] [NONE]]
```

Integer mode:
```
MEANS VARIABLES=varlist({min,max       }) [varlist...]
                       {LOWEST,HIGHEST}
   /{TABLES    }=varlist BY varlist [BY...] [/varlist...]
    {CROSSBREAK}
   [/MISSING={TABLE**  }]
             {INCLUDE  }
             {DEPENDENT}
   [/FORMAT={LABELS** } {NAMES**} {VALUES**}]
            {NOLABELS} {NONAMES} {NOVALUES}
            {NOCATLABS}
   [/CELLS=[DEFAULT**] [MEAN**  ] [ALL]]
           [COUNT**  ] [STDDEV**]
           [SUM      ] [VARIANCE]
   [/STATISTICS=[ANOVA] [LINEARITY] [ALL] [NONE]]
```
**Default if the subcommand is omitted.

MISSING VALUES

```
MISSING VALUES {varlist(value list) [[/]varlist ...]}
               {ALL(value)                          }
```

Keywords for numeric value lists:
LO, LOWEST, HI, HIGHEST, THRU

MULT RESPONSE

```
MULT RESPONSE GROUPS=groupname['label']
                          (itemlist ({value1,value2}))...
                                    {value        }
                          [groupname...]
   /VARIABLES=itemlist(min,max) [itemlist...]
   /FREQUENCIES=itemlist
   /TABLES=itemlist BY itemlist... [BY itemlist] [(PAIRED)]
           [/itemlist BY...]
   [/MISSING=[{TABLE**}] [INCLUDE]]
             {MDGROUP}
             {MRGROUP}
   [/FORMAT={LABELS** } {TABLE** }]
            {NOLABELS} {CONDENSE}
                       {ONEPAGE }
   [/BASE={CASES**   }]
          {RESPONSES}
   [/CELLS=[COUNT**] [ROW   ] [ALL]]
                     [COLUMN]
                     [TOTAL ]
```
**Default if the subcommand is omitted.

GET SCSS

```
GET SCSS MASTERFILE=file [/WORKFILE=file]
                      {ALL**                        }
                      {varlist                      }
        [/VARIABLES={$varlist                       }]
                      {$ALL                          }
                      {(old varlist=new varlist)     }
```

**Default if the subcommand is omitted.

HELP

```
{HELP} [ {topic    [subtopic ] }] [SYNTAX]
{ ?   } {command [subcommand] }
```

HILOGLINEAR

```
HILOGLINEAR varlist (min,max) [varlist (min,max)...]
    [/MISSING = {LISTWISE}] [INCLUDE]
                {DEFAULT }
    [/CWEIGHT = {varname }]
                {(matrix)}
    [/PRINT = [DEFAULT]   [ASSOCIATION]
              [FREQ]      [RESID]
              [ESTIM]     [ALL]
              [NONE]]
    [/PLOT = [DEFAULT]   [RESID]
             [NORMPROB]  [NONE ]]
    [/CRITERIA = [CONVERGE({0.25})] [ITERATE({20})] [P({0.05})]
                           {n   }            {n  }     {prob }
                 [DELTA({0.5})] [MAXSTEPS({10})] [DEFAULT]]
                        {d   }             {n  }
    [/METHOD [= BACKWARD]]
    [/MAXORDER = k]
    [/DESIGN = effectname effectname*effectname ...]
```

HOST

```
HOST [system command]
```

IF

```
IF [()]logical expression[)] target variable=expression
```

The following relational operators can be used in logical expressions:

Symbol	Definition	Symbol	Definition
EQ or =	Equal to	NE or ¬= or <>	Not equal to
LT or <	Less than	LE or <=	Less than or equal to
GT or >	Greater than	GE or >=	Greater than or equal to

The following logical operators can be used in logical expressions:

Symbol	Definition
AND or &	Both relations must be true
OR or |	Either relation can be true
NOT or ¬	Reverses the outcome of an expression

IMPORT

```
IMPORT FILE=file
    [/TYPE={COMM}]
           {TAPE}
    [/KEEP={ALL**  }] [/DROP=varlist]
           {varlist}
    [/RENAME=(old varlist=new varlist)...]
    [/MAP]
    [/DIGITS=number]
```

INCLUDE

```
INCLUDE [FILE**]=file
```

INFO

```
INFO [OUTFILE = file]
     [OVERVIEW]
     [LOCAL]
     [ERRORS]
     [FACILITIES]
     [PROCEDURES]
     [ALL]
     [procedure name] [/procedure name...]
     [SINCE release number]
```

INPUT PROGRAM—END INPUT PROGRAM

```
INPUT PROGRAM
commands to create cases
END INPUT PROGRAM
```

KEYED DATA LIST

```
KEYED DATA LIST KEY=varname IN=varname
    [FILE=file] [ {TABLE  }]
                  {NOTABLE}
```

LEAVE

```
LEAVE varlist
```

LIST

```
LIST [VARIABLES={ALL    }] [/FORMAT=[{WRAP  }] [{UNNUMBERED}]]
                {varlist}             {SINGLE}  {NUMBERED  }
     [/CASES=[FROM {1}] [TO {eof}] [BY {1}]]
                   {n}      {n  }      {n}
```

LOGLINEAR

```
LOGLINEAR varlist(min,max)...[BY] varlist(min,max)
          [WITH covariate varlist]
    [/MISSING={LISTWISE**}] [INCLUDE]
              {DEFAULT   }
    [/WIDTH={132}]
            {72 }
    [/CWEIGHT={varname }] [/CWEIGHT=(matrix)...]
              {(matrix)}
    [/GRESID={varlist }] [/GRESID=...]
             {(matrix)}
    [/PRINT={DEFAULT**}] [/NOPRINT={ESTIM** }]
            {FREQ**   }            {COR**   }
            {RESID**  }            {DESIGN**}
            {DESIGN   }            {RESID   }
            {ESTIM    }            {FREQ    }
            {COR      }            {DEFAULT }
            {ALL      }            {ALL     }
            {NONE     }
    [/PLOT={DEFAULT }
           {RESID   }
           {NORMPROB}
           {NONE**  }
                            {DEVIATION [(refcat)] }
                            {DIFFERENCE           }
                            {HELMERT              }
    [/CONTRAST (varname)={SIMPLE [(refcat)]      }]...[/CONTRAST...
                            {REPEATED             }
                            {POLYNOMIAL [({1,2,3,...})]}
                            {            {metric  } }
                            {[BASIS] SPECIAL(matrix) }
    [/CRITERIA=[CONVERGE({0.001**})] [ITERATE({20**})] [DELTA({0.5**})]
                         {eps    }            {n   }          {d    }
               [DEFAULT]]
    [/DESIGN=effect effect... effect BY effect...] [/DESIGN...]
```

** Default if the subcommand is omitted.

LOOP—END LOOP

```
LOOP [varname=n TO m [BY {1**}]]  [IF [()logical expression[)]]
                         {n  }

transformations
END LOOP [IF [()logical expression[)]]
```

**Default if the subcommand is omitted.

Macro Facility

```
DEFINE macro name ( [{argument name=}     [!NOEXPAND]
                     {!POSITIONAL=  }
     [!DEFAULT (default string)]   {!TOKENS (n)                    }
                                   {!CHAREND ('char')              }
                                   {!ENCLOSE ('startsym', 'endsym')}
                                   {!CMDEND                        }

     [/{argument name=} ...] ] )
       {!POSITIONAL=  }
macro body
!ENDDEFINE
```

SET command controls:

```
PRESERVE
RESTORE
```

Assignment:

```
!LET
```

Conditional processing:

```
!IF (expression) !THEN statements
   [!ELSE statements]
!IFEND
```

Looping constructs:

```
!DO !varname=start !TO finish [BY step]
   statements  [!BREAK]
!DOEND

!DO !varname !IN (list)
   statements  [!BREAK]
!DOEND
```

Macro directives:

```
!OFFEXPAND
!ONEXPAND
```

String manipulation functions:

!LENGTH (string)	!QUOTE (string)
!CONCAT (string1,string2)	!UNQUOTE (string)
!SUBSTRING (string,from,[length])	!UPCASE (string)
!INDEX (string1,string2)	!BLANKS (n)
!HEAD (string)	!NULL
!TAIL (string)	!EVAL (string)